LANDLORD
AND
TENANT LAW

AUSTRALIA AND NEW ZEALAND
The Law Book Company Ltd.
Sydney : Melbourne : Perth

CANADA AND U.S.A.
The Carswell Company Ltd.
Agincourt, Ontario

INDIA
N. M. Tripathi Private Ltd.
Bombay
and
Eastern Law House Private Ltd.
Calcutta and Delhi
M.P.P. House
Bangalore

ISRAEL
Steimatzky's Agency Ltd.
Jerusalem : Tel Aviv : Haifa

MALAYSIA : SINGAPORE : BRUNEI
Malayan Law Journal (Pte.) Ltd.
Singapore and Kuala Lumpur

PAKISTAN
Pakistan Law House
Karachi

LANDLORD
AND
TENANT LAW

by

DAVID YATES, M.A. (Oxon)
Professor of Law,
University of Essex

and

A.J. HAWKINS, LL.M. (Hull)
Solicitor,
Reader in Law,
University of Essex

SECOND EDITION

LONDON
SWEET & MAXWELL
1986

First Edition 1981

Published in 1986 by
Sweet & Maxwell Limited of
11 New Fetter Lane, London.
Computerset by Burgess & Son (Abingdon) Limited.
Printed in Great Britain by
Robert Hartnoll Limited, Bodmin, Cornwall

British Library Cataloguing in Publication Data

Yates, David, 1946—
    Landlord and tenant law.—2nd ed.
    1. Rental housing—Law and legislation
    —England
    I. Title   II. Hawkins, A.J.
    344.2064'344   KD899

ISBN 0–421–35430–5 Pbk

PREFACE

The first edition of this book, although written principally as a student text book, also had the requirements of practitioners in mind. Its pleasing fortune was to be used extensively both for academic purposes, and also by solicitors, barristers, surveyors and property managers. Neither the last edition nor this edition attempts, within the constraints of reasonable length, to be totally exhaustive and comprehensive. There are regularly updated specialist textbooks either in the general fields of landlord and tenant, or on the more special areas of rent reviews, commercial leases, housing etc. Nevertheless, we do hope to set out, in some detail, a discussion of the principles and authorities on currently relevant topics.

Trying to state the law on landlord and tenant is like attempting to hit a moving target, and both are exercises known to cause one to fall into deep and chilly waters. Production of the last edition developed into a race against the passage of the Housing Act 1980 through Parliament. This time, on the statutory front, we have had the consolidation of the Housing Acts, in the shape of the Housing Act 1985, the Housing Associations Act 1985, the Landlord and Tenant Act 1985 and the Housing (Consequential Provisions) Act 1985, all just before our proposed cut off date of January 1, 1986. Fortunately we were also able to include the Agricultural Holdings Act 1986—a well–signalled consolidation.

But statute apart, Her Majesty's judges have made so many note-worthy decisions that many chapters have had to be re-written entirely, and few pages have escaped the ravages of revision.

Perhaps the most significant decision has been *Street* v. *Mountford*. In both residential and commercial areas, it seems that the importance of this case is only just beginning to be fully appreciated. Since the appearance of the last edition the House of Lords has also accepted that, in principle, the contract law doctrine of frustration may apply to leases. The cases on rent review clauses can be regarded as a mine field or a gold field, and there have been significant developments in the area of repairs, on the one hand by landlords seeking to recover the cost of repairs and avoid the troublesome provisions of the Leasehold Property (Repairs) Act 1938 and on the other by tenants seeking to appoint receivers to carry out their landlords' functions. In the field of transfer, *International Drilling Fluids Limited* v. *Louisville Investments (Uxbridge) Limited*, has restated the matters to be considered by a landlord whose consent to assign is sought. The extent to which there remains an inherent equitable jurisdiction to relieve against forfeiture has been much canvassed. In the residential area, apart from the virtual disappearance of licences and the increasing popularity of shortholds, there has, in the public sector, been the introduction of shared ownership leases, a recasting of housing benefits, and substantial alterations to the law affecting housing associations. The "homelessness" legislation has proved to be a growth area all on its own.

In the last two sections, on business tenancies and agricultural tenancies, there have been a number of significant changes. Most cases affecting agricultural tenancies were teasingly altered or reversed by the Agricultural Holdings Act 1984, now part of the consolidation contained in the Agricultural Holdings Act 1986. Policy has changed on the question of succession, and also apparently on the criteria for determining rents.

Professor F.W. Taylor has, as usual, percipiently considered those sections which have been completely recast, and also removed many infelicities that passed unnoticed in the first edition. We are grateful to Mrs. Carol Hobbs for her secretarial help, to Mr. David Johnston for compiling the index, and to our publishers for keeping us speedily supplied with consolidating materials when time was of the essence, and also for coping with a particularly trying production schedule. The law is as stated on January 1, 1986, save that it has also been possible to take account of the consolidations of the Housing Acts and the law relating to agricultural holdings.

Midsummer Day 1986

David Yates and John Hawkins,
School of Law,
University of Essex

ACKNOWLEDGMENTS

The authors and publishers wish to thank the following for permission to reprint material from the reports and periodicals indicated.

Butterworths Law Publishers Ltd.:
The All England Law Reports

The Estates Gazette Ltd:
The Estates Gazette

Incorporated Council of Law Reporting for England and Wales:
Law Reports

CONTENTS

	PAGE
Preface	v
Acknowledgments	vii
Table of Cases	xi
Table of Statutes	lxxxv

PART I. THE GENERAL LAW

1. Landlord and Tenant	1
2. Leases and Licences	9
3. Creation of Leases	49
4. The Lease	101
5. The Operation of the Lease—Rent	151
6. Repair and Maintenance of the Tenanted Property	217
7. Transfer	297
8. Termination	333
9. The Tenanted Property and Third Parties	365

PART II. RESIDENTIAL TENANCIES

10. Establishing the Status for Protection	375
11. Rent Control	413
12. Transfers	433
13. Security of Tenure	447
14. The Framework for Partial Protection	473
15. Long and Shared Ownership Leases	497
16. Council Housing	525
17. Housing Associations	583
18. Financial Assistance with Rented Housing Costs	597
19. Unlawful Eviction, Harassment & Homelessness	607

PART III. BUSINESS TENANCIES

20. The Context of the Business Tenancy Code	637
21. Creation and Management of the Business Tenancy	657

Contents

22. Terminations and Renewals   673
23. Termination on Compulsory Purchase   719
24. Transfer and Protection of Business Goodwill   739

Part IV. Agricultural Tenancies

25. The Statutory Umbrella   755
26. Obligations Imposed During the Tenancy   769
27. Security of Tenure   779
28. Compensation   801

Index   817

TABLE OF CASES

A.B.C. Coupler & Engineering Co. (No. 3), *Re* [1970] 1 W.L.R. 702; 114 S.J. 242;
[1970] 1 All E.R. 650 204
Abbey National Building Society *v.* Maybeech [1985] Ch. 190; [1984] 3 W.L.R. 793;
128 S.J. 721; [1984] 3 All E.R. 262; 271 E.G. 995; 81 L.S.Gaz. 3174 .... 197, 355
Abbeyfield (Harpenden) Society Ltd. *v.* Woods [1968] 1 W.L.R. 374; 111 S.J. 968;
[1968] 1 All E.R. 352n.; 19 P. & C.R. 36, C.A. 10, 17, 20, 28, 29, 31
Abbots Park Estate, *Re*, [1972] 1 W.L.R. 598; 116 S.J. 220; [1972] 2 All E.R. 177; 23
P. & C.R. 180 520
Abernethie *v.* Kleinman Ltd. (A. M. & J.) [1970] 1 Q.B. 10; [1969] 2 W.L.R. 1364;
113 S.J. 307; [1969] 2 All E.R. 790; 20 P. & C.R. 561, C.A. 549, 647
Abingdon R.D.C. *v.* O'Gorman [1968] 2 Q.B. 811; [1968] 3 W.L.R. 240; 112 S.J.
584; [1968] 3 All E.R. 79; 19 P. & C.R. 725, C.A. 201
Abrahams *v.* Wilson [1971] 2 Q.B.; [1971] 2 W.L.R. 923; 115 S.J. 287; [1971] 2 All
E.R. 1114; 22 P. & C.R. 407, C.A. 452
—— *v.* Macfisheries [1925] 2 K.B. 18; 94 L.J.K.B. 562; 133 L.T. 89 .... 300, 306
Abrahart *v.* Webster [1925] 1 K.B. 563; 93 L.J.K.B. 119; 132 L.T. 276; 41 T.L.R. 44;
69 S.J. 141; 22 L.G.R. 754 379
Accountancy Personnel Ltd. *v.* Worshipful Company of Salters (1972) 116 S.J. 240 .. 707
Accuba *v.* Allied Shoe Repairs [1975] 1 W.L.R. 1559; 119 S.J. 775; [1975] 3 All E.R.
782; 30 P. & C.R. 403 .... 179, 181
Ackland *v.* Lutley (1839) 9 Ad. & E. 879; 1 P. & D. 636; 8 L.J.Q.B. 164; 48 R.R.
729 107
Ackroyd *v.* Smith (1850) 10 C.B. 164; 19 L.J.C.P. 315; 15 L.T.(o.s.) 395; 14 Jur.
1047; 138 E.R. 68 51
Adair *v.* Murrell (1982) 263 E.G. 66 .... 428, 436
Adams *v.* Gibney (1830) 6 Bing. 656; 4 Moo. & P. 491; 8 L.J.(o.s.)C.P. 243; 31 R.R.
514 129
—— *v.* Green (1978) 247 E.G. 49, C.A. 710, 715
Addis *v.* Burrows [1948] 1 K.B. 444; [1948] L.J.R. 1033; 64 T.L.R. 169; 92 S.J. 124;
[1948] 1 All E.R. 177, C.A. 109, 347
Addiscombe Garden Estates Ltd. *v.* Crabbe [1958] 1 Q.B. 513; [1957] 3 W.L.R. 980;
101 S.J. 959; [1957] 3 All E.R. 563, C.A.; *affirming* [1957] 2 Q.B. 615; [1957] 2
W.L.R. 964; 101 S.J. 410; [1957] 2 All E.R. 205 .... 5, 15, 16, 17, 33, 102, 647, 653
Adelphi Estates *v.* Christie (1984) 269 E.G. 221, C.A. 171
Adler *v.* Blackman [1953] 1 Q.B. 146; [1952] T.L.R. 809; 96 S.J. 802; [1952] 2 All
E.R. 945, C.A. 345
—— *v.* Upper Grosvenor Street Investments Ltd. [1957] 1 W.L.R. 227; 101 S.J.
132; [1957] 1 All E.R. 229 .... 308, 660
Afan B.C. *v.* Marchant [1980] L.A.G.Bull. 15 622
Afovos Shipping Co. S.A. *v.* Pagnan (R.) and Lli (F.); *Afovos*, The [1983] 1 W.L.R.
195; 127 S.J. 98; [1983] 1 All E.R. 449; [1983] Com.L.R. 83; [1983] 1 Lloyd's
Rep. 335; [1984] 2 L.M.C.L.Q. 189, H.L. 159
Ailion *v.* Spiekerman [1976] Ch. 158; [1976] 2 W.L.R. 556; 120 S.J. 9; [1976] 1 All
E.R. 497; 31 P. & C.R. 369, D.C. 428, 437
Akbarali *v.* Brent L.B.C.; Barnet L.B.C. *v.* Shah [1983] 2 A.C. 309; [1983] 2 W.L.R.
16; 127 S.J. 36; [1983] 1 All E.R. 226; 81 L.G.R. 305; 133 New L.J. 61, H.L. .. 617
Al Saloom *v.* James (Shirley) Travel Services (1981) 125 S.J. 397; 42 P. & C.R. 81,
C.A. 138, 181
Alan Estates Ltd. *v.* W.G. Stores Ltd. [1981] 3 W.L.R. 892; 125 S.J. 567; [1981] 3 All
E.R. 481; [1982] Ch. 511; 43 P. & C.R. 19; 260 E.G. 173, C.A. 89

Albyn Properties *v*. Knox [1977] S.L.T. 41 422
Aldrington Garages Ltd. *v*. Fielder (1978) 247 E.G. 557; 37 P. & C.R. 461,
   C.A. 17, 20, 33
Aldwych Club Ltd. *v*. Copthall Property Co. (1962) 185 E.G. 219 714
Alexander *v*. Mercouris [1979] 1 W.L.R. 1270; 123 S.J. 604; [1979] 3 All E.R. 305;
   252 E.G. 911, C.A. 249
—— *v*. Rayson [1936] 1 K.B. 169; 105 L.J.K.B. 148; 154 L.T. 205; 52 T.L.R. 131; 80
   S.J. 15 81
Alford *v*. Vickery (1842) Car. & M. 280; 56 R.R. 867 349
Ali *v*. Knight (1984) 128 S.J. 64; 81 L.S.Gaz. 198; 272 E.G. 1165, C.A. 706
Allam & Co. Ltd. *v*. Europe Poster Services Ltd. [1968] 1 W.L.R. 638; 112 S.J. 86;
   [1968] 1 All E.R. 826 .... 347, 358
Allan *v*. Liverpool Overseers (1874) L.R. 9 Q.B. 180; 43 L.J.M.C. 69; 30 L.T. 93; 38
   J.P. 261 .... 15, 30
Allen *v*. Jacobs (1949) 100 L.J. 16 449
Allen and Matthews' Arbitration, *Re* [1971] 2 Q.B. 518; [1971] 2 W.L.R. 1249;
   [1971] 2 All E.R. 1259; 22 P. & C.R. 576 781
Alliance Property Co. Ltd. *v*. Shaffer [1949] 1 K.B. 367; [1949] L.J.R. 998; 65 T.L.R.
   111; 93 S.J. 181; [1949] 1 All E.R. 312 401
Allied London Investments Ltd. *v*. Hambro Life Assurance Ltd. (1985) 50 P. & C.R.
   207; 274 E.G. 81; 135 New L.J. 184, C.A. 162, 184, 294, 316, 322
Allnatt London Properties Ltd. *v*. Newton [1984] 1 All E.R. 423; 45 P. & C.R. 94;
   265 E.G. 601, C.A. 308, 338, 656, 675
Alpenstow *v*. Regaliar Properties [1985] 1 W.L.R. 721; 129 S.J. 400; [1985] 2 All
   E.R. 545; 274 E.G. 1141; 135 New L.J. 205; 82 L.S.Gaz. 2241 82
Altmann *v*. Boatman (1963) 186 E.G. 109, C.A. 50
Amalgamated Investment & Property Co. (in liquidation) *v*. Texas Commerce
   International Bank Ltd. [1982] Q.B. 84; [1981] 3 W.L.R. 565; 125 S.J. 623;
   [1981] 3 All E.R. 577; [1981] Com.L.R. 236, C.A. 12
American Cyanamid Co. *v*. Ethicon Ltd. [1975] A.C. 396; [1975] 2 W.L.R. 316;
   119 S.J. 136; [1975] 1 All E.R. 504; [1975] F.S.R. 101; [1975] R.P.C. 513,
   H.L. 631
Amherst *v*. Walker (James) Goldsmith and Silversmith Ltd. (1980) 254 E.G. 123,
   C.A. 181
—— *v*. Walker (James) (Goldsmith & Silversmith) Ltd. (No. 2) [1983] Ch. 305;
   [1983] 3 W.L.R. 334; 127 S.J. 391; [1983] 2 All E.R. 1067; 47 P. & C.R. 85;
   267 E.G. 163, C.A. 180, 182
Amika Motor Ltd. *v*. Colebrook Holdings Ltd. (1981) 259 E.G. 243, C.A. 710
Amoco Australia Pty. Ltd. *v*. Rocco Bros. Motor Engineering Co. Pty. Ltd. [1975]
   A.C. 561; [1975] 2 W.L.R. 779; 119 S.J. 301; [1975] 1 All E.R. 968, D.C. 125
Anderson *v*. Midland Railway (1861) 3 E. & E. 614; 30 L.J.Q.B. 94; 7 Jur.(N.S.) 411;
   3 L.T. 809 44
Andrew *v*. Bridgman [1908] 1 K.B. 596; 77 L.J.K.B. 272; 98 L.T. 656; 52 S.J. 148 307
Angel *v*. Jay [1911] 1 K.B. 666; 80 L.J.K.B. 458; 103 L.T. 809; 55 S.J. 140 148
Angell *v*. Burn (1933) 77 S.J. 337 123
Anglia Building Society *v*. Sheffield C.C. (1983) 266 E.G. 311, C.A. 658
Anglo-Italian Properties *v*. London Rent Assessment Panel [1969] 1 W.L.R. 730;
   113 S.J. 366; [1969] 2 All E.R. 1128; 20 P. & C.R. 567, D.C. 425
Annen *v*. Rattee (1984) 17 H.L.R. 323; 273 E.G. 503, C.A. 11, 360
Anns *v*. Merton L.B.C. [1978] A.C. 728; [1977] 2 W.L.R. 1024; 121 S.J. 377;
   75 L.G.R. 555; [1977] J.P.L. 514; 243 E.G. 523; [1977] L.G.C. 498,
   H.L. 257, 365, 372
Anspach *v*. Charlton Steam Shipping Co. Ltd. [1955] Q.B. 21; [1955] 2 W.L.R. 601;
   99 S.J. 230, C.A. 388
Appah *v*. Parncliffe Investments Ltd. [1964] 1 W.L.R. 1064; 108 S.J. 155; [1964] 1
   All E.R. 838, C.A. 10, 15, 20, 29

Argy Trading Development Co. Ltd. *v.* Lapid Developments Ltd. [1977] 1 W.L.R.
444; [1977] 3 All E.R. 785; [1977] 1 Lloyd's Rep. 67 .... 119, 168
Argyle Motors (Birkenhead) Ltd. *v.* Birkenhead Corp. [1975] A.C. 99; [1974] 2
W.L.R. 71; 118 S.J. 67; [1974] 1 All E.R. 201; 27 P. & C.R. 122; 72 L.G.R.
147, H.L. 733
Arieli *v.* Duke of Westminster (1983) 269 E.G. 535; 24 R.V.R. 45, C.A. 509
Aristocrat Property Investments *v.* Harounoff (1982) 43 P. & C.R. 284; 203 E.G.
352; [1983] H.L.R. 102, C.A. 424
Arlesford Trading Co. Ltd. *v.* Servansingh [1971] 1 W.L.R. 1080; 115 S.J. 507;
[1971] 3 All E.R. 113; 22 P. & C.R. 848, C.A. 325
Armstrong *v.* Sheppard & Short Ltd. [1959] 2 Q.B. 384; [1959] 3 W.L.R. 84; 123 J.P.
401; 103 S.J. 508; [1959] 2 All E.R. 651, C.A. 12
Artemiou *v.* Procopiou [1966] 1 Q.B. 878; [1965] 3 W.L.R. 1011; 109 S.J. 630; [1965]
3 All E.R. 539, C.A. 704
Artillery Mansions *v.* Macartney [1949] 1 K.B. 164; [1949] L.J.R. 405; 64 T.L.R.
576; 92 S.J. 617; [1948] 2 All E.R. 875, C.A. 401, 475
Artisans, Labourers and General Dwellings Co. Ltd. *v.* Whittaker [1919] 2 K.B. 301;
88 L.J.K.B. 859; 121 L.T. 243; 35 T.L.R. 521 44
Artoc Bank Trust *v.* Prudential Assurance Co. [1984] 1 W.L.R. 1181; (1984) 128
S.J. 737; [1984] 3 All E.R. 538; 49 P. & C.R. 65; 271 E.G. 454; 81 L.S.Gaz.
3099 679
Asco Developments *v.* Gordon (1978) 248 E.G. 683 256
Asghar *v.* Ahmed (1984) 17 H.L.R. 25, C.A. 133, 610
Ashby *v.* Wilson [1900] 1 Ch. 66; 69 L.J.Ch. 47; 81 L.T. 480; 48 W.R. 105 127
Aspinall, *Re*, Aspinall *v.* Aspinall [1961] Ch. 526; [1961] 3 W.L.R. 235; 105 S.J. 529;
[1961] 2 All E.R. 751 159
Associated Dairies *v.* Pierce (1983) 265 E.G. 127, C.A. 161, 202
Associated Deliveries Ltd. *v.* Harrison (1984) 49 P. & C.R. 91; 272 E.G. 321,
C.A. 194, 286, 293, 674
Associated London Properties Ltd. *v.* Sheridan (1946) 174 L.T. 103; 62 T.L.R. 80;
[1946] 1 All E.R. 20 138
Associated Provincial Picture Houses *v.* Wednesbury Corp. [1948] 1 K.B. 223;
[1948] L.J.R. 190; 177 L.T. 641; 63 T.L.R. 623; 112 J.P. 55; 92 S.J. 26; [1947]
2 All E.R. 680; 45 L.G.R. 635 .... 558, 630
Atkinson *v.* Bettison [1955] 1 W.L.R. 1127; 99 S.J. 761; [1955] 3 All E.R. 340,
C.A. 698
Attersoll *v.* Stevens (1808) 1 Taunt. 183; 127 E.R. 802 281
Attkins, *Re*, Life *v.* Attkins [1913] 2 Ch. 619; 83 L.J.Ch. 183; 109 L.T. 155; 57 S.J.
785 341
Att.-Gen. *v.* Colchester Corp., *sub nom.* Att.-Gen., *ex rel.* Allen *v.* Colchester B.C.
[1955] 2 Q.B. 207; [1955] 2 W.L.R. 913; 99 S.J. 291; [1955] 2 All E.R. 124; 53
L.G.R. 415 630
—— *v.* Foley (1753) 1 Dick. 363 43
—— *v.* Gayford U.D.C. [1962] Ch. 575; [1962] 2 W.L.R. 998; 126 J.P. 308; 106 S.J.
175; [1962] 2 All E.R. 147; 60 L.G.R. 261; [1962] 1 Lloyd's Rep. 163, C.A. 561
Att.-Gen. (Duchy of Lancaster) *v.* Simcock [1966] Ch. 1; [1965] 2 W.L.R. 1126;
[1965] 2 All E.R. 32 781
Att.-Gen., *ex. rel.* Tilley *v.* Wandsworth L.B.C. [1981] 1 W.L.R. 854; (1981) 125 S.J.
148; [1981] 1 All E.R. 1162; 78 L.G.R.; 11 Fam.Law 119, C.A. 611, 624
Att.-Gen. for Ontario *v.* Canadian Niagara Power Co. [1912] A.C. 852; 82 L.J.P.C.
18; 107 L.T. 629, P.C. 155
Atyeo *v.* Fardoe (1978) 123 S.J. 97; 37 P. & C.R. 494, C.A. 404, 409, 433
Austin *v.* Richards (Dick) Properties Ltd. [1975] 1 W.L.R. 1033; [1975] 2 All E.R.
75; 29 P. & C.R. 377, C.A. 512
Australian Blue Metal Ltd. *v.* Hughes [1963] A.C. 74; [1962] 3 W.L.R. 802; 106 S.J.
628; [1962] 3 All E.R. 335, P.C. 359

Avenue Properties (St. John's Wood) Ltd. *v.* Aisinzon [1977] Q.B. 628; [1976] 2 W.L.R. 740; 120 S.J. 331; [1976] 2 All E.R. 177; 32 P. & C.R. 229, C.A. 378, 424

Avery *v.* Langford (1854) Kay 663; 2 Eq.Rep. 1097; 23 L.J.Ch. 837; 23 L.T.(o.s.) 227; 18 Jur. 905; 2 W.R. 615; 69 E.R. 281 744

Avon County Council *v.* Alliance Property Co. Ltd. (1981) 258 E.G. 1181 187

—— *v.* Clothier (1977) 75 L.G.R. 344; 242 E.G. 1048, C.A. 761

Ayling *v.* Wade [1961] 2 Q.B. 228; [1961] 2 W.L.R. 873; 105 S.J. 365; [1961] 2 All E.R. 399, C.A. 112, 323

Bacon *v.* Grimsby Corp. [1950] 1 K.B. 272; 65 T.L.R. 709; 113 J.P.L. 539; 93 S.J. 742; [1949] 2 All E.R. 875; 48 L.G.R. 42, C.A. 265, 266

Bader Properties *v.* Linley Property Investments (1967) 112 S.J. 71; 19 P. & C.R. 620; [1968] J.P.L. 688; 205 E.G. 655 .... 284, 290

Bagettes *v.* G.P. Estates [1956] Ch. 290; [1956] 2 W.L.R. 773; 100 S.J. 226; [1956] 1 All E.R. 729, C.A. 643

Bahamas International Trust Co. *v.* Threadgold [1974] 1 W.L.R. 1514; 118 S.J. 832; [1974] 3 All E.R. 881, H.L. 761

Bailey *v.* Purser [1967] 2 Q.B. 500; [1967] 2 W.L.R. 1500; 111 S.J. 353, D.C. 457

Bailey (C. H.) *v.* Memorial Enterprises [1974] 1 W.L.R. 728; [1974] 1 All E.R. 1003; 118 S.J. 8; 27 P. & C.R. 188, C.A. 1, 156, 179, 183

Baker *v.* Lewis [1947] K.B. 186; [1947] L.J.R. 468; 175 L.T. 490; 62 T.L.R. 716; [1946] 2 All E.R. 592, C.A. 456

—— *v.* Merckel; Anson (Third Party) [1960] 1 Q.B. 657; [1960] 2 W.L.R. 492; 104 S.J. 231; [1960] 1 All E.R. 668, C.A. 316, 339

Balcomb *v.* Wards Construction (Medway) (1981) 259 E.G. 765 257

Baldock *v.* Murray (1981) 257 E.G. 281, C.A. 474

Bain *v.* Brand (1876) 1 App.Cas. 762 56

—— *v.* Fothergill (1874) L.R. 7 H.L. 158; 43 L.J.Ex. 243 95

Balfour *v.* Barty-King [1957] 1 Q.B. 496; [1957] 2 W.L.R. 84; 101 S.J. 62; [1957] 1 All E.R. 156; [1956] 2 Lloyd's Rep. 646, C.A. 120

—— *v.* Kensington Gardens Mansions Ltd. (1932) 76 S.V. 816; 49 T.L.R. 29 . 310, 661

—— *v.* Weston (1786) 1 T.R. 310 154

Ball *v.* Cullimore (1835) 2 Cr.M. & R. 120; 1 Gale 96; 5 Tyr. 753; 4 L.J.Ex. 137; 150 E.R. 51 16

—— *v.* L.C.C. [1949] 2 K.B. 159; 65 T.L.R. 533; 113 J.P. 315; 93 S.J. 404; [1949] 1 All E.R. 1056; 47 L.G.R 591, C.A. 365

—— *v.* Plummer (1879) 23 S.J. 656 237

Balls Bros. Ltd. *v.* Sinclair [1931] 2 Ch. 325; 100 L.J.Ch. 377; 146 L.T. 300 121

Bandar Property Holdings Ltd. *v.* Darwen (J. S.) (Successors) Ltd. [1968] 2 All E.R. 305; 19 P. & C.R. 785 119

Bangor (Bishop) *v.* Parry [1891] 2 Q.B. 277; 60 L.J.Q.B. 646; 65 L.T. 379; 39 W.R. 541 67

Banham *v.* London Borough of Hackney (1971) 22 P. & C.R. 922 722

Banning *v.* Wright [1972] 1 W.L.R. 972; 116 S.J. 509; [1972] 2 All E.R. 987; 48 T.C. 421; [1972] T.R. 105, H.L. 213

Bannister *v.* Bannister [1948] W.N. 261; 92 S.J. 377; [1948] 2 All E.R. 133, C.A. 12

Barclays Bank Ltd. *v.* Stasek [1957] Ch. 28; [1956] 3 W.L.R. 760; 100 S.J. 800; [1956] 3 All E.R. 439 .... 337, 339

Bardrick *v.* Haydock (1976) 31 P. & C.R. 420, C.A. 396

Barff *v.* Probyn (1895) 64 L.J.Q.B. 557; 73 L.T. 118 [1895–9] All E.R.Rep. 1038 60

Barker *v.* Herbert [1911] 2 K.B. 633; 80 L.J.K.B. 1329; 105 L.T. 349; 75 J.P. 481; 9 L.G.R. 1083; 27 T.L.R. 488 369

Barnard *v.* Towers [1953] 1 W.L.R. 1203; 97 S.J. 607; [1953] 2 All E.R.877, C.A. 451

Barnes *v.* Barratt [1970] 2 Q.B. 657; [1970] 2 W.L.R. 1085; 114 S.J. 265 [1970] 2 All E.R. 483; 21 P. & C.R. 347, C.A. 20, 32, 33, 158, 399, 474

Barnes *v.* City of London Real Property Co. Ltd. [1918] 2 Ch. 18; 87 L.J.Ch. 601; 119
L.T. 293; 34 T.L.R. 361 318
—— *v.* Gorsuch (1982) 43 P. & C.R. 294; (1982) 263 E.G. 253; [1982] M.L.R. 116,
C.A. 396
—— *v.* Ward (1850) 9 C.B. 392; 19 L.J.C.P. 195; 14 Jur. 334; 2 C. & K. 661 369
Baron *v.* Phillips (1978) 38 P. & C.R. 91; 247 E.G. 1079, C.A. 512
Barret *v.* Blagrave (1800) 5 Ves.Jr. 555; 31 E.R. 735; [1775–1802] All E.R.Rep. 118 . 126
Barrett *v.* Hardy Bros. Ltd. [1925] K.B. 220; 94 L.J.K.B. 665; 133 L.T. 249; 41
T.L.R. 426; 69 S.J. 492; 23 L.G.R. 427 381
Barrow *v.* Isaacs & Son [1891] 1 Q.B. 417; 60 L.J.Q.B. 179; 64 L.T. 686; 39 W.R.
338 .... 300, 307
Barrow Green Estate Co. *v.* Walker (Executors of) [1954] 1 W.L.R. 231; 98 S.J. 78;
[1954] 1 All E.R. 204; 52 L.G.R. 130, C.A. 814, 815
Barton *v.* Keeble [1928] Ch. 517; 97 L.J.Ch. 215 123
—— *v.* Reed [1932] 1 Ch. 362; 101 L.J.Ch. 219; 146 L.T. 501 124
Barton (W. J.) *v.* Long Acre Securities (1982) 1 W.L.R. 398 713
Barton Thompson & Co. Ltd. *v.* Stapling Machine Co. Ltd. [1966] Ch. 499; [1966] 2
W.L.R. 1429; 110 S.J. 313; [1966] 2 All E.R. 222 2
Bashir *v.* Commissioner of Lands [1960] A.C. 44; [1959] 3 W.L.R. 996; 103 S.J. 1045;
[1960] 1 All E.R. 117, P.C. 111, 335
Bassett *v.* Whitely (1983) 45 P. & C.R. 87, C.A. 140
Batchelor *v.* Murphy [1926] A.C. 63; 95 L.J.Ch. 89; 134 L.T. 161; 42 T.L.R. 112,
H.L.; *affirming* [1925] Ch. 220, C.A.; *reversing* [1924] 2 Ch. 253 143
Bates *v.* Donaldson [1896] 2 Q.B. 241; 65 L.J.Q.B. 578; 74 L.T. 751; 44 W.R. 659; 60
J.P. 596; [1895–9] All E.R.Rep. 170 .... 306, 308
—— *v.* Pierrepoint (1978) 37 P. & C.R. 420; 251 E.G. 1059, C.A. 510
Bates (Thomas) & Son Ltd. *v.* Wyndham's (Lingerie) Ltd. [1981] 1 W.L.R. 505; 125
S.J. 32; [1981] 1 W.L.R. 505; [1981] 1 All E.R. 1077; 257 E.G. 381; 41 P. &
C.R. 517 .... 140, 150, 158, 178
Bathavon R.D.C. *v.* Carlile [1958] 1 Q.B. 461; [1958] 2 W.L.R. 545; 122 J.P. 240;
102 S.J. 230; [1958] 1 All E.R. 801; 56 L.G.R. 139, C.A. 348, 531
Bathurst (Earl) *v.* Fine [1974] 1 W.L.R. 905; [1974] 2 All E.R. 1160; 28 P. & C.R.
268, C.A. 354
Battlespring *v.* Gates (1983) 268 E.G. 355; 11 H.L.R. 6, C.A. 449
Batty *v.* Metropolitan Property Realisations Ltd. [1978] Q.B. 554; [1978] 2 W.L.R.
500; 122 S.J. 63; [1978] 2 All E.R. 445; 245 E.G. 43; 7 Build.L.R. 1, C.A. 257
Bayley (Keith) Rogers & Co. (A Firm) *v.* Cubes (1975) 21 P. & C.R. 412 139
Baynton *v.* Morgan (1888) 22 Q.B.D. 74; 58 L.J.Q.B. 139; 53 J.P. 166; 37 W.R. 148;
5 T.L.R. 99, C.A. 161, 174, 316, 338
Beacon Carpets Ltd. *v.* Kirby [1985] 2 Q.B. 755; [1984] 3 W.L.R. 489; 128 S.J. 549;
[1984] 2 All E.R. 726; 48 P. & C.R. 445; 81 L.S.Gaz. 1603, C.A. 120, 234
Beauford (Duke) *v.* Patrick. *See* Doe d. Patrick *v.* Beaufort (Duke).
Beard *v.* Beard [1981] 1 W.L.R. 369; [1981] 1 All E.R. 783; 11 Fam.Law 84, C.A. 578
Beardmore Motors *v.* Birch Bros. (Properties) [1959] Ch. 298 [1958] 2 W.L.R. 975;
102 S.J. 419; [1958] 2 All E.R. 311 683
Bebington's Tenancy, *Re*, Bebington *v.* Wildman [1921] 1 Ch. 559; 90 L.J.Ch. 269;
124 L.T. 661; 65 S.J. 343; 37 T.L.R. 409 800
Becker *v.* Partridge [1966] 2 Q.B. 155; [1966] 2 W.L.R. 803; 110 S.J. 187; [1966] 2 All
E.R. 266, C.A. 79
Bedfordshire C.C. *v.* Clarke (1974) 230 E.G. 1587 765
Beebe *v.* Mason (1980) 254 E.G. 987, C.A. 397
Beer *v.* Bowden [1981] 1 W.L.R. 522; [1981] 1 All E.R. 1071; 41 P. & C.R. 317,
C.A. 158, 166, 178, 179, 182, 193
Beesly *v.* Hallwood Estates Ltd. [1961] Ch. 105 .... 89, 145
Beevers *v.* Mason (1978) 37 P. & C.R. 452; 122 S.J. 610; 248 E.G. 781,
C.A. 160, 785

Belcher *v.* Reading Corp. [1950] Ch. 380; 65 T.L.R. 773; 114 J.P. 21; 93 S.J. 742;
    [1949] 2 All E.R. 969; 48 L.G.R. 71 530
Belfour *v.* Weston (1786) 1 Term. 310; 1 R.R. 210 137
Belgravia Insurance Co. Ltd. *v.* Meah [1964] 1 Q.B. 436; [1963] 3 W.L.R. 1033; 107
    S.J. 871; [1963] 3 All E.R. 828, C.A. 197, 198, 356
Bell *v.* Frank & Bartlett Co. [1980] 1 W.L.R. 340; 123 S.J. 804; [1980] 1 All E.R. 356;
    39 P. & C.R. 591; 253 E.G. 903, C.A. 642, 645, 648
Bell London & Provincial Properties Ltd. *v.* Reuben [1947] K.B. 157; [1947] L.J.R.
    251; 176 L.T. 92; 62 T.L.R. 653; 91 S.J. 42; [1946] 2 All E.R. 547, C.A. 468
Bell Street Investments *v.* Wood (1970) 216 E.G. 585 94
Bellaglade, *Re* [1977] 1 All E.R. 319 204
Bendall *v.* McWhirter [1952] 2 Q.B. 466; [1952] 1 T.L.R. 1332; 96 S.J. 344; [1952] 1
    All E.R. 1307; [1952] C.L.Y. 257 197
Bennett *v.* Ireland (1858) E.B. & E. 326; 28 L.J.Q.B. 48; 4 Jur.(N.S.) 1104 234
—— *v.* Ubmack (1828) 3 C.& P. 96; 7 B. & C. 627; 6 L.J.(O.S.)K.B. 175; 1 Man. &
    Ry. 644; 31 R.R. 270 164
Bennett, *Re*, Midland Bank Executor and Trustee Co. Ltd. *v.* Fletcher [1943] 1 All
    E.R. 467; 87 S.J. 102 329
Benninga (Mitcham) Ltd. *v.* Bijistra [1946] K.B. 58; 173 L.T. 298; 61 T.L.R. 519;
    [1945] 2 All E.R. 433 455
Berg *v.* Markhill (1985) 17 H.L.R. 455, C.A. 200, 600
Berkeley *v.* Papadoyannis [1954] 2 Q.B. 149; [1954] 3 W.L.R. 23; 08 S.J. 390; [1954]
    2 All E.R. 409, C.A. 409
Bernays *v.* Prosser [1963] 2 Q.B. 592; [1963] 2 W.L.R. 1255; 107 S.J. 271; [1963] 2 All
    E.R. 321, C.A. 760, 766
Berrey *v.* Lindley (1841) 3 Man. & G. 498; 60 R.R. 558; 4 Scott N.R. 61; 11 L.J.C.P.
    27; 5 Jur. 1061 94
Berry (Herbert) Associates (In Liquidation), *Re* [1977] 1 W.L.R. 1437; 121 S.J. 829;
    [1978] 1 All E.R. 161; [1977] T.R. 247; 52 T.C. 113, H.L. 204
Berry Investments *v.* Attwooll [1964] 1 W.L.R. 693; 108 S.J. 318; [1964] 2 All E.R.
    126; [1964] T.R. 67; 43 A.T.C. 61; 41 T.C. 547 211
Bertie *v.* Beaumont (1812) 16 East. 33 27
Berton *v.* Alliance Economic Investment Co. [1922] 1 K.B. 742; 91 L.J.K.B. 748;
    127 L.T. 422; 66 S.J. 487; 38 T.L.R. 435 124
Betts, *Re*, (1983) 10 H.L.R. 97 617
Betts *v.* Penge U.D.C. [1942] 2 K.B. 154; 111 L.J.K.B. 565; 167 L.T. 205; 58 T.L.R.
    283; 106 J.P. 203; [1942] 2 All E.R. 61 261
Betts (John) & Sons Ltd. *v.* Price (1924) 40 T.L.R. 589 294
Betty's Cafés Ltd. *v.* Phillips Furnishing Stores Ltd. [1959] A.C. 20; [1958] 2 W.L.R.
    513; 102 S.J 263; [1958] 1 All E.R. 607, H.L.; *affirming* [1957] Ch. 67; [1956] 3
    W.L.R. 1134; 100 S.J. 946; [1957] 1 All E.R. 1, C.A.; *reversing* [1956] 1
    W.L.R. 678; 100 S.J. 435; [1956] 2 All E.R. 497 .... 686, 695, 697, 705, 709
Bevington *v.* Crawford (1974) 232 E.G. 191, C.A. 396
Bewlay (Tobacconists) Ltd. *v.* British Bata Shoe Co. Ltd. [1959] 1 W.L.R. 45; 103
    S.J. 33; [1958] 3 All E.R. 652, C.A. 698
Bickel *v.* Courtenay Investments (Nominees) Ltd. [1984] 1 W.L.R. 795; 128 S.J 316;
    [1984] 1 All E.R. 657; 48 P. & C.R. 1; 81 L.S.Gaz. 1291 .... 314, 662
—— *v.* Westminster (Duke of) [1977] Q.B. 517; 34 P. & C.R. 22, C.A. 311, 312
Biggs *v.* Trustees of J.R.S.S.T. Charitable Trust (1965) 109 S.J. 273 648
Biles *v.* Caesar [1957] 1 W.L.R. 156; 101 S.J .108; [1957] 1 All E.R. 151, C.A. 686
Billings (A. C.) & Sons *v.* Riden [1958] A.C. 240; [1957] 3 W.L.R. 496; 101 S.J.
    645; [1957] 3 All E.R. 1, H.L. 257
Binions *v.* Evans [1972] Ch. 359; [1972] 2 W.L.R. 729; 116 S.J. 122; [1972] 2 All E.R.
    70; 23 P. & C.R. 192, C.A. 12, 45
Biondi *v.* Kirklington & Piccadilly Estates Ltd. [1947] L.J.R. 884; 177 L.T. 101; 91
    S.J. 599; [1947] 2 All E.R. 59 139

Birch *v.* Wright (1786) 1 T.R. 378; 1 R.R. 223; [1775–1802] All E.R. Rep. 41 54
Bird *v.* Defonvielle (1846) 2 Car. & K. 415 174
—— *v.* Great Eastern Ry. Co. (1865) 19 C.B.(N.S.) 268; 34 L.J.C.P. 366; 11
    Jur.(N.S.) 782; 13 L.T. 365; 13 W.R. 989 52
—— *v.* Greville (Lord) (1884) Cab. & Ell. 317 240
—— *v.* Hildage [1948] 1 K.B. 91; [1948] L.J.R. 196; 177 L.T. 97; 63 T.L.R. 405; 91
    S.J. 559; [1947] 2 All E.R. 7, C.A. 452
Birmingham Corp. *v.* West Midland Baptist (Trust) Association (Inc.) [1970] A.C.
    874; [1969] 3 W.L.R. 389; 20 P. & C.R. 1052; *sub nom.* Birmingham City
    Corp. *v.* West Midland Baptist (Trust) Association (Inc.) [1969] 3 All E.R.
    172, H.L.; *affirming sub nom.* West Midland Baptist (Trust) Association *v.*
    Birmingham Corp. [1968] 2 Q.B. 188; [1968] 2 W.L.R. 535; [1968] 1 All E.R.
    205; 19 P. & C.R. 9, C.A. 720
Birmingham D.C. *v.* Morris & Jacombs Ltd. (1976) 33 P. & C.R. 27 732
Bishop Auckland Local Board *v.* Bishop Auckland Iron & Steel Co. Ltd. (1882)
    10 Q.B.D. 138; 52 L.J.M.C. 38; 48 L.T. 223; 47 J.P. 389; 31 W.R. 288,
    D.C. 260, 262
Bishopsgate Ltd. *v.* Prudential Assurance Co. Ltd. (1985) 273 E.G. 984,
    C.A. 187, 189
Blackmore *v.* Butler [1954] 2 Q.B. 171; [1954] 3 W.L.R. 62; 98 S.J. 405; [1954] 2 All
    E.R. 403; 52 L.G.R. 345, C.A. 758
Blackstone (David) Ltd. *v.* Burnetts (West End) Ltd. [1973] 1 W.L.R. 1487; 117 S.J.
    894; [1973] 3 All E.R. 782; 27 P. & C.R. 70 195
Blake (Victor) (Menswear) Ltd. *v.* Westminster C.C. (1979) 38 P. & C.R. 448; 249
    E.G. 543 679
Blakesley *v.* Whieldon (1841) 1 Hare 176; 11 L.J.Ch. 164; 6 Jur. 54 97
Blewett *v.* Blewett [1936] 2 All E.R. 188 353
Bloomfield *v.* Ashwright (1983) 47 P. & C.R. 78; 266 E.G. 1095 679
Blore *v.* Giulini [1903] 1 K.B. 356; 72 L.J.K.B. 114; 88 L.T. 235; 51 W.R. 336 139
Blumenthal *v.* Gallery Five Ltd. (1971) 220 E.G. 31 .... 155, 168, 191
Blundell *v.* Obsdale Ltd. (1958) 171 E.G. 491 237
Bocardo S.A. *v.* S. & M. Hotels Ltd. [1980] 1 W.L.R. 17; 123 S.J. 569; [1979] 3 All
    E.R. 737; 39 P. & C.R. 287; 123 E.G. 59, C.A. 187, 308, 338, 660
Boldmark Ltd. *v.* Cohen (1985) 277 E.G. 745, C.A. 134
Bollinger *v.* Costa Brava Wine Co., The (No. 3) [1960] Ch. 262; [1959] 3 W.L.R. 966;
    103 S.J. 1028; [1959] 3 All E.R. 800; [1960] R.P.C. 16 741
Bolsom (Sidney) Investment Trust *v.* Karmios & Co. (London) Ltd. [1956] 1 Q.B.
    529; [1956] 2 W.L.R. 625; 100 S.J. 169; [1956] 1 All E.R. 536, C.A. 691
Bolton Building Society *v.* Cobb [1966] 1 W.L.R. 1; 109 S.J. 852; [1965] 3 All E.R.
    814; [1965] C.L.Y. 2227; 30 Conv. 59 466
Bolton (H. L.) Engineering Co. Ltd. *v.* Graham (T. J.) & Sons Ltd. [1957] 1 Q.B.
    159; [1956] 3 W.L.R. 804; 100 S.J. 816; [1956] 3 All E.R. 624, C.A. 674, 704
Bon-Accord Housing Society Ltd. *v.* Clark [1957] S.L.T. (Sh. Ct.) 24 586
Bonner *v.* Tottenham and Edmonton Permanent Building Society [1899] 1 Q.B. 161;
    68 L.J.Q.B. 114; 79 L.T. 611; 47 W.R. 164 .... 319, 323
Booker *v.* Palmer [1942] 2 All E.R. 674 .... 17, 25, 26, 31
Bookman (Thomas) Ltd. *v.* Nathan [1955] 1 W.L.R. 815; 99 S.J 489; [1955] 2 All
    E.R. 821, C.A. 310, 434
Booth *v.* Thomas [1926] Ch. 397; 95 L.J.Ch. 160; 134 L.T. 464; 70 S.J 365; 42 T.L.R.
    296 151
Boots the Chemist *v.* Street (1983) 268 E.G. 817 150
Borman *v.* Griffith [1930] 1 Ch. 493; 99 L.J.Ch. 295; 142 L.T. 645 104
Borthwick *v.* Evening Post (1888) 37 Ch.D. 449; 57 L.J.Ch. 406; 58 L.T. 252; 36
    W.R. 434; 4 T.L.R. 234, C.A. 741
Borthwick-Norton *v.* Romney Warwick Estates Ltd. [1950] 1 All E.R. 798; 94 S.J.
    281, C.A. 354, 468

Borzak *v.* Ahmed [1965] 2 Q.B. 320; [1965] 2 W.L.R. 1155; 109 S.J .157; [1965] 1 All
E.R. 808 .... 194, 609
Bostock, Chater & Sons Ltd. *v.* Chelmsford Corp. (1973) 26 P. & C.R. 321 735
Boswell *v.* Crucible Steel Co. [1925] 1 K.B. 119; 94 L.J.K.B. 383; 132 L.T. 274 237
Botterill *v.* Bedfordshire C.C. (1985) 273 E.G. 1217, C.A. 698
Bottomley *v.* Bannister [1932] 1 K.B. 458; 101 L.J.K.B. 46; 146 L.T. 68; 48 T.L.R.
39 .... 239, 365
Bourn and Tant *v.* Salmon & Gluckstein Ltd. [1907] 1 Ch. 616; 76 L.J.Ch. 374; 95
L.T. 139; 96 L.T. 629; 70 J.P. 462 117
Bowen *v.* Anderson [1894] 1 Q.B. 164; 42 W.R. 236; 10 R. 47; 58 J.P. 203 42
Bowes-Lyon *v.* Green [1963] A.C. 420; [1961] 3 W.L.R. 1044; 105 S.J. 929; [1961] 3
All E.R. 843, H.L. 53
Bowser *v.* Colby (1841) 1 Hare 109; 11 L.J.Ch. 132; 5 Jur. 1106 [1835–42] All E.R.
Rep. 478 302
Boyd *v.* Wilton [1957] 2 Q.B. 277; [1957] 2 W.L.R. 636; 101 S.J. 301; [1957] 2 All
E.R. 102, C.A. 815, 816
Boyer *v.* Warbey [1953] 1 Q.B 234; [1952] 2 T.L.R. 882; 96 S.J. 802; [1952] 2 All E.R.
976, C.A. 344
Boyer (William) & Sons Ltd. *v.* Adams (1975) 32 B. & C.R. 89 643
Boylan *v.* Mayor of Dublin [1949] I.R. 60 .... 36, 37
Bracey *v.* Read [1963] Ch. 88; [1962] 3 W.L.R. 1194; 106 S.J. 878; [1962] 3 All E.R.
472 .... 52, 642, 654, 758
Bracknell Development Corp. *v.* Greenlees Lennards Ltd. (1981) 260 E.G. 501 191
Bradbury *v.* Wright (1781) 2 Doug. 624 164
Bradford *v.* Chorley B.C. (1985) 83 L.G.R. 623; 17 H.L.R. 305; 275 E.G. 801,
C.A. 223, 245, 251
Bradley *v.* Baylis (1881) 8 Q.B.D. 195; 51 L.J.Q.B. 183; Colt. 163; 46 L.T. 253; 30
W.R. 823; 45 J.P. 847 .... 15, 28
Bradshaw *v.* Baldwin-Wiseman (1985) 49 P. & C.R. 382; 17 H.L.R. 260; 274 E.G.
285, C.A. 459
—— *v.* Pawley [1980] 1 W.L.R. 10; [1979] 3 All E.R. 273; 40 P. & C.R. 496; 253
E.G. 693 .... 89, 108, 157, 184, 498
—— *v.* Smith (1980) 225 E.G. 699 392
Brakspear (W. H.) & Sons Ltd. *v.* Baron [1924] 2 K.B. 88; 93 L.J.K.B. 801; 131 L.T.
538; 68 S.J. 719; 40 T.L.R. 607 107
Bramwell *v.* Bramwell [1942] 1 K.B. 370; 111 L.J.K.B. 430; 58 T.L.R. 1 48; [1942] 1
All E.R. 137 17
Branca *v.* Cobarro [1947] K.B. 854; [1948] L.J.R. 43; 177 L.T. 332; 63 T.L.R. 408;
[1947] 2 All E.R. 101, C.A. 82
Brann *v.* Westminster Anglo-Continental Investment Co. Ltd. (1975) 240 E.G. 927,
C.A. 434, 436
Breams Property Investment Co. Ltd. *v.* Strougler [1948] 2 K.B. 1; [1948] L.J.R.
1515; 64 T.L.R. 292; 92 S.J. 283; [1948] 1 All E.R. 758, C.A. 43, 317
Brendloss *v.* Philips (1602) Cro.Eliz. (1) 895 169
Bresgall & Sons Ltd. *v.* London Borough of Hackney (1976) 32 P. & C.R. 442, Lands
Tribunal 734
Brew Bros. *v.* Snax (Ross) Ltd. [1970] 1 Q.B. 612; [1969] 3 W.L.R. 657; 113 S.J. 795;
[1970] 1 All E.R. 587; 20 P. & C.R. 829, C.A. 222, 231, 249
Brewer *v.* Hill (1794) 2 Anstr. 413; 3 R.R. 596 16
Brewster *v.* Kidgell (or Kitchell or Kitchin) (1697) 1 Salk. 198; 2 *ibid.* 615; 3 *ibid.* 340;
Comb. 424, 426; Carth. 438, 439; 1 Ld.Raym. 317; 5 Mod. 363; 12 Mod. 169;
Holt 175, 669 115
Brighton College *v.* Marriott [1925] 1 K.B. 312; [1926] A.C. 192 664
Brikom Investments Ltd. *v.* Carr [1979] Q.B. 467; [1979] 2 W.L.R. 737; 123 S.J. 182;
[1979] 2 All E.R. 753; 251 E.G. 359; 38 P. & C.R. 326, C.A. 176, 286

Brikom Investments Ltd. *v.* Seaford [1981] 1 W.L.R. 863; 125 S.J. 240; [1981] 2 All
    E.R. 783; 42 P. & C.R. 190; 258 E.G. 750, C.A. 248, 254
Brilliant *v.* Michaels (1945) 114 L.J.Ch. 5; 171 L.T. 361; 88 S.J. 383; [1945] 1 All
    E.R. 121 82
Bristol Cars *v.* R.K.H. (Hotels) (In Liquidation) (1979) 38 P. & C.R. 411; 251 E.G.
    1279, C.A. 690
Bristol C.C. *v.* Rawlins (1977) 34 P. & C.R. 12; 76 L.G.R. 166, C.A. 557
Bristol Corp. *v.* Sinnott [1918] 1 Ch. 62; 87 L.J.Ch. 30; 117 L.T. 644; 82 J.P. 9; 62 S.J.
    53; 15 L.G.R. 871, C.A. 263
—— *v.* Westcott (1879) 12 Ch.D. 461; 41 L.J. 117; 27 W.R. 841 302
Bristol D.C. *v.* Clark [1975] 1 W.L.R. 1443; 119 S.J 659; [1975] 3 All E.R. 976; 30 P.
    & C.R. 441; (1975) 74 L.G.R. 3, C.A. 558, 559
British Anzari (Felixstowe) Ltd. *v.* International Marine Management (U.K.) Ltd.
    [1980] Q.B. 137; [1979] 3 W.L.R. 451; 123 S.J. 64; [1979] 2 All E.R. 1063; 39
    P. & C.R. 189; 250 E.G. 1183 .... 256, 786
British Economical Map Co. Ltd. *v.* Empire Mile End Ltd. [1913] 29 T.L.R. 386 58
British Gas Corp. *v.* Universities Superannuation Scheme [1986] 1 W.L.R. 398; 130
    S.J. 264; [1986] 1 All E.R. 978; 277 E.C. 980; 83 L.S.Gaz. 973; 136 New L.J.
    285 190
British Iron & Steel Corp. Ltd. *v.* Malpern [1946] K.B. 171; 174 L.T. 102; 62 T.L.R.
    149; [1946] 1 All E.R. 408 138
British Petroleum Pension Trust *v.* Behrendt (1985) 276 E.G. 199, C.A. 353
British Railways Board *v.* Bodywright Ltd. (1971) 22 E.G. 651 44
—— *v.* Elgar House (1969) 209 E.G. 1313 167
—— *v.* Herrington [1972] A.C. 877; [1972] 2 W.L.R. 537; 116 S.J. 178; [1972] 1 All
    E.R. 749, H.L. 366
—— *v.* Smith (A. J. A.) Transport Ltd. (1981) 259 E.G. 766 .... 684, 690
British Reinforced Concrete Engineering Co. Ltd. *v.* Schelff [1921] 2 Ch. 563; [1921]
    All E.R. Rep. 202; 91 L.J.Ch. 114; 126 L.T. 230 744
British Salicylates Ltd., *Re* [1919] 2 Ch. 155; 88 L.J.Ch. 258; 121 L.T. 77; [1918–19]
    B. & C.R. 160; 63 S.J. 517 204
Brock *v.* Wollams [1949] 2 K.B. 388; 93 S.J 319; [1949] 1 All E.R. 715, C.A. . 440, 441
Bromley Park Garden Estates *v.* Moss [1982] 1 W.L.R. 1019; 126 S.J. 310; [1982] 2
    All E.R. 890; 44 P. & C.R. 266; 266 E.G., C.A. 308, 309, 311, 660
Broome *v.* Cassell & Co. [1972] A.C. 1027; [1972] 2 W.L.R. 645; 116 S.J. 199;
    [1972] 1 All E.R. 801, H.L. 294
Brough *v.* Nettleton [1921] 2 Ch. 25; 90 L.J.Ch. 373; 124 L.T. 823; 65 S.J. 515 87
Broughton *v.* Snook [1938] Ch. 505; 107 L.J.Ch. 204; 158 L.T. 130; 82 S.J. 112; 54
    T.L.R. 301; [1938] 1 All E.R. 411 87
Brown *v.* Brash [1948] 2 K.B. 247; [1948] L.J.R. 1544; 64 T.L.R. 266; 92 S.J. 376;
    [1948] 1 All E.R. 922, C.A. 409
—— *v.* Draper [1944] K.B. 309; 113 L.J.K.B. 196; 170 L.T. 144; 60 T.L.R. 219;
    [1944] 1 All E.R. 246 444
—— *v.* Gould [1972] Ch. 53; [1971] 3 W.L.R. 334; 115 S.J .406; [1971] 2 All E.R.
    1505; 22 P. & C.R. 871 .... 141, 144, 158, 178, 179
—— *v.* Liverpool Corp. [1969] 3 All E.R. 1345, C.A. 245
—— *v.* Minister of Housing and Local Government [1953] 1 W.L.R. 1370; 118 J.P.
    143; 97 S.J. 797; [1953] 2 All E.R. 1385; 4 P. & C.R. 111 268
—— *v.* Notley (1848) 3 Ex. 219; 18 L.J.Ex. 39; 77 R.R. 698 .... 370, 371
—— *v.* Quilter (1764) Amb. 619; 2 Eden 219 234
—— *v.* Wilson (1949) 93 S.J. 640 764
Brown (John M.) Ltd. *v.* Bestwick [1951] 1 K.B. 21; 66 T.L.R. (Pt. 2) 248; 94 S.J.
    503; [1950] 2 All E.R. 338, C.A. 409
Browne *v.* Flower [1911] 1 Ch. 219; 80 L.J.Ch. 181; 103 L.T. 557; 55 S.J.
    108 .... 130, 131
—— *v.* Powell (1827) 4 Bing. 230; 12 Moore 454; 5 L.J.(o.s.)C.P. 121; 29 R.R. 538 .. 162

Brunner v. Greenslade [1971] Ch. 993; [1970] 3 W.L.R. 891; [1970] 3 All E.R. 833 127
Buchman v. May [1978] 2 All E.R. 993; (1976) 240 E.G. 49, C.A. 21, 403
Buckley v. Lane Herdman & Co. [1977] C.L.Y. 3143 252
Budd v. Marshall (1880) 5 C.P.D. 481; 50 L.J.C.P. 24; 42 L.T. 793; 29 W.R. 148 116
Budd-Scott v. Daniel [1902] 2 K.B. 351; 71 L.J.K.B. 706; 87 L.T. 392; 51 W.R. 134 .. 129
Budget Rent A Car International Inc. v. Mamos (Slough) Ltd. [1977] 121 S.J. 737,
     C.A. 631
Buliver v. Buliver (1819) 2 B. & A. 470 44
Bullock v. Dommitt (1796) 2 Chit. 608; 6 T.R. 650; 3 R.R. 300 234
Burchell v. Hornsby (1808) 1 Camp. 360 281
Burden v. Hannaford [1956] 1 Q.B. 142; [1955] 3 W.L.R. 606; 99 S.J 780; [1955] 3 All
     E.R. 401, C.A. 773, 814
Burgess v. Boetefeur (1844) 7 Man. & G. 481; 8 Scott N.R. 194; 13 L.J.M.C. 122; 8
     Jur. 621 220
Burnett v. Lynch (1826) 5 B. & C. 589; 8 D. & R. 368; 4 L.J.(o.s.)K.B. 274; 29 R.R.
     343; [1924–34] All E.R. Rep. 352 129
Burnett (Marjorie) Ltd. v. Barclay (1980) 125 S.J. 199; 258 E.G. 642 46
Burrowes v. Gradin (1843) 1 Dow. & L. 213; 12 L.J.Q.B. 333; 7 Jur. 942; 67 R.R.
     853 177
Burt v. Haslett (1856) 18 C.B. 162 61
Burton v. Barclay (1831) 7 Bing. 745; 5 M. & P. 785; 9 L.J.(o.s.)C.P. 231; [1824–34]
     All E.R. Rep. 437 338
Bushford v. Falco [1954] 1 W.L.R. 672; 98 S.J. 269; [1954] 1 All E.R. 957, C.A. 410
Buswell v. Goodwin [1971] 1 W.L.R. 92; 115 S.J 77; [1977] 1 All E.R. 418; 22 P. &
     C.R. 162; 69 L.G.R. 201, C.A. 81, 241, 269, 283, 289, 394
Bute (Marquis) v. Thompson (1844) 13 M. & W. 487; 14 L.J.Ex. 95 169
Butler v. Mountview Estates Ltd. [1951] 2 K.B. 563; [1951] 1 T.L.R. 524; [1951] 1 All
     E.R. 693 322
Butler Estates Ltd. v. Bear [1942] 1 K.B. 1; 111 L.J.K.B. 394; 165 L.T. 197; 57
     T.L.R. 666; [1941] 2 All E.R. 794 322
Butt's Case (1600) 7 Co.Rep. 23a; 77 E.R. 445 155
Button's Lease, Re, Inman v. Button [1964] Ch. 263; [1963] 3 W.L.R. 903; 107 S.J.
     830; [1963] 3 All E.R. 708 .... 142, 318
Bwllfa and Merthyr Dare Steam Collieries (1891) Ltd. v. Pontypridd Waterworks
     Co. [1903] A.C. 426; 72 L.J.K.B. 805; 89 L.T. 280; 52 W.R. 193; 19 T.L.R.
     673, H.L. 732
Byrne v. Herbert [1966] 2 Q.B. 121; [1966] 2 W.L.R. 19; 110 S.J .15; [1965] 3 All
     E.R. 705 503

C. & P. Haulage (a firm) v. Middleton [1983] 1 W.L.R. 1461; (1983) 127 S.J. 730;
     [1983] 3 All E.R. 94, C.A. 360
C.B.S. (U.K.) v. London Scottish Properties (1985) 275 E.G. 718 .... 709, 710
Cadbury v. Woodward (1972) 116 S.J. 60; 23 P. & C.R. 281 519
—— v. —— (No. 2) (1972) 146 S.J. 664; 24 P. & C.R. 335 519
Cadle (Percy E.) & Co. Ltd. v. Jacmarch Properties Ltd. [1957] 1 Q.B. 323; [1957] 2
     W.L.R. 80; 101 S.J 62; [1957] 1 All E.R. 148, C.A. 698
Cadogan v. Dimovic [1984] 1 W.L.R. 609; [1984] 2 All E.R. 168; 270 E.G. 37; 48 P.
     & C.R. 288; 81 L.S.Gaz. 663, C.A. 355, 674
Cadogan (Earl) v. Henthorne [1957] 1 W.L.R. 1; 101 S.J. 64; [1956] 3 All E.R.
     851 466
Caerphilly Concrete Products Ltd. v. Owen [1972] 1 W.L.R. 372; [1972] 1 All
     E.R. 248; (1971) 23 P. & C.R. 15, C.A. 141
Cafeteria (Keighley) Ltd. v. Harrison (1956) 168 E.G. 668 642
Cairnplace v. C.B.L. (Property Investment) Co. [1984] 1 W.L.R. 696; 128 S.J.
     281; [1984] 1 All E.R. 315; 47 P. & C.R. 531; 269 E.G. 542; 81 L.S.Gaz.,
     C.A. 90, 147, 717

Calabar Properties Ltd. *v.* Stitcher [1984] 1 W.L.R. 287; (1983) 127 S.J. 785; [1983] 3
All E.R. 759; 268 E.G. 697; 11 H.L.R. 20; 80 L.S.Gaz. 3163, C.A. 251
Calladine *v.* Webster [1951] E.G.D. 300 .... 14, 18, 33
Calthorpe *v.* McOscar [1924] 1 K.B. 716; 93 L.J.K.B. 273; 130 L.T. 691; 68 S.J. 367;
40 T.L.R. 223 .... 220, 222
Cam Gears Ltd. *v.* Cunningham [1981] 1 W.L.R. 1011; 125 S.J. 356; [1981] 2 All
E.R. 560; (1982) 43 P. & C.R. 144; 258 E.G. 749, C.A. 702
Caminer *v.* Northern & London Investment Trust [1951] A.C. 88; 66 T.L.R. (Pt. 2)
184; 114 J.P. 426; 94 S.J. 518; [1950] 2 All E.R. 486; 48 L.G.R. 573, H.L. 369
Campbell *v.* Wenlock (Lord) (1866) 4 F. & F. 716 239
Campden Hill Towers Ltd. *v.* Gardner [1977] Q.B. 823; [1977] 2 W.L.R. 159; (1976)
121 S.J 86; [1977] 1 All E.R. 739; 34 P. & C.R. 175; 13 H.L.R. 64; 242 E.G.
375, C.A. 103, 244, 245, 247
Canadian Pacific Rail Co. *v.* R. [1931] A.C. 414; 100 L.J.P.C. 129; 145 L.T.
129 .... 357, 358, 359
Canas Property Co. Ltd. *v.* K.L. Television Services Ltd. [1970] 2 Q.B. 433; [1970] 2
W.L.R. 1133; 114 S.J. 337; [1970] 2 All E.R. 795; 21 P. & C.R. 601, C.A. 194
Caney *v.* Leith [1937] 2 All E.R. 532; 165 L.T. 483; 53 T.L.R. 596; 81 S.J. 357 82
Cannan *v.* Hartley (1850) 9 C.B. 634; 19 L.J.C.P. 323; 14 Jur. 577; 82 R.R. 478 339
Cannock Chase District Council *v.* Kelly [1978] 1 W.L.R. 1; (1977) 121 S.J 593;
[1978] 1 All E.R. 152; 76 L.G.R. 67; 36 P. & C.R. 219; [1977] J.P.L. 655; 244
E.G. 211, C.A. 558, 559
Cannon Brewery Co. *v.* Nash (1898) 77 L.T. 648; 14 T.L.R. 158 108
Canterbury City Council *v.* Bern (1982) 44 P. & C.R. 178; [1981] J.P.L. 749,
D.C. 276, 277
Capital & Counties Bank Ltd. *v.* Rhodes [1903] 1 Ch. 631; 72 L.J.Ch. 336; 88 L.T.
255; 19 T.L.R. 280; 51 W.R. 470; 47 S.J. 335 340
Capital & National Trust *v.* Golder [1949] W.N. 463; 65 T.L.R. 772; 93 S.J. 755;
[1949] 2 All E.R. 956; [1949] T.R. 395; 31 T.C. 265, C.A. 211
Caplan (I. & H.) Ltd. *v.* Caplan (No. 2) [1963] 1 W.L.R. 1247; 107 S.J 792; [1963] 2
All E.R. 930 .... 647, 675, 693
Cardiff Corp. *v.* Cook [1923] 2 Ch. 115; 92 L.J.Ch. 177; 128 L.T. 530; 87 J.P. 90; 67
S.J. 315; 21 L.G.R 279 721
Cardigan (Earl) *v.* Armitage (1823) 2 B. & C. 197; 3 D. & R. 414; 26 R.R. 313;
[1814–23] All E.R. Rep. 33 .... 105, 106
Cardshops Ltd. *v.* Davies [1971] 1 W.L.R. 591; 115 S.J. 265; [1971] 2 All E.R. 721; 22
P. & C.R. 499, C.A. 715
—— *v.* Lewis (John) Properties Ltd. [1983] Q.B. 161; [1982] 3 W.L.R. 803; 126 S.J.
625; [1982] 3 All E.R. 746; (1983) 45 P. & C.R. 197; 263 E.G. 791, C.A. 751
Carega Properties S.A. *v.* Sharratt (1979) 39 P. & C.R. 76; 252 E.G. 163, H.L.;
sub nom. Joram Developments *v.* Sharratt [1979] 1 W.L.R. 928; 123 S.J. 505 . 441
Carr *v.* I.R.C. [1944] 2 All E.R. 163 664
Carradine Properties Ltd. *v.* Aslam [1976] 1 W.L.R. 442; (1975) 120 S.J. 166; [1976]
1 All E.R. 573; 32 P. & C.R. 12 .... 138, 348
Carshalton Beeches Bowling Club *v.* Cameron (1979) 249 E.G. 1279, C.A. 644, 702
Carter *v.* Cummins (1665) 1 Cas. in Ch. 84; 22 E.R. 706, L.C. 137
—— *v.* Green [1950] 2 K.B. 76; 66 T.L.R. (Pt. 1) 907; 94 S.J. 254; [1950] 1 All E.R.
627, C.A. 464
—— *v.* S.U. Carburettor Co. [1942] 2 K.B. 288; 111 L.J.K.B. 714; 167 L.T. 248; 58
T.L.R. 348; 86 S.J. 252; [1942] 2 All E.R. 228 .... 388, 393
Cartledge *v.* Jopling & Sons Ltd. [1963] A.C. 758; [1963] 2 W.L.R. 210; 107 S.J.
73; [1963] 1 All E.R. 341; [1963] 1 Lloyd's Rep.1, H.L. 372
Castellain *v.* Preston (1883) 1 Q.B.D. 380; 52 L.J.Q.B. 366; 49 L.T. 29; 31 W.R. 557,
C.A. 118
Castle Laundry (London) *v.* Read [1955] 1 Q.B. 586; [1955] 2 W.L.R. 943; 99 S.J.
306; [1955] 2 All E.R. 1543 .... 677, 686

Catling, *Re*, Public Trustee *v*. Catling [1931] 2 Ch. 359; 100 L.J.Ch. 390; 145 L.T.
   613 41
Cavalier *v*. Pope [1906] A.C. 428; 75 L.J.K.B. 609; 95 L.T. 65; 22 T.L.R. 648 37
Celsteel Ltd. *v*. Altan House Holdings Ltd. (No. 2) [1986] 1 All E.R. 598 130
Centaploy Ltd. *v*. Matlodge Ltd. [1974] Ch. 1; [1973] 2 W.L.R. 832; 117 S.J. 394;
   [1973] 2 All E.R. 720; 25 P. & C.R. 317 .... 42, 81, 341
Central & Metropolitan Estates *v*. Compusave (1983) 266 E.G. 900 150
Central Estates (Belgravia) Ltd. *v*. Woolgar (No. 2) [1972] 1 W.L.R. 1048; 116
   S.J. 566; [1972] 3 All E.R. 610, 24 P. & C.R. 103, C.A. 125, 126, 195,
                                              354, 468, 519
Central London Property Trust *v*. High Trees House [1947] K.B. 130; [1956] 1 All
   E.R. 256; [1947] L.J.R. 77; 175 L.T. 333; 62 T.L.R. 557 176
Centrovincial Estates plc *v*. Bulk Storage Ltd. (1983) 127 S.J. 443; 46 P. & C.R. 393;
   268 E.G. 59 .... 162, 184, 294, 316
Chada *v*. Norton Estates Trustees (1985) 276 E.G. 312, Leasehold Valuation
   Tribunal 516
Chalmers *v*. Pardoe [1963] 1 W.L.R. 677; 107 S.J. 435; [1963] 3 All E.R. 552, P.C. 12
Chaloner *v*. Bower (1984) 269 E.G. 725, C.A. 765
Chamberlain *v*. Farr (1942) 112 L.J.K.B. 206; [1942] 2 All E.R. 567 .... 16, 45
Chancellor *v*. Poole (1781) 2 Doug. 764 294
Chandler *v*. Bradley [1897] 1 Ch. 315; 66 L.J.Ch. 214; 75 L.T. 581; 45 W.R. 296 64
—— *v*. Kerley; Horrocks *v*. Forray [1976] 1 W.L.R. 230; (1975) 119 S.J. 866; [1976]
   1 All E.R. 737; 6 Fam.Law 15, C.A. 11
Chandless-Chandless *v*. Nicholson [1942] 2 K.B. 321; 112 L.J.K.B. 19; 167 L.T. 198;
   [1942] 2 All E.R. 315 351
Chaplin *v*. Smith [1926] 1 K.B. 198; 95 L.J.K.B. 449; 134 L.T. 393 306
Chapman *v*. Chapman. *See* McKay (formerly Chapman) *v*. Chapman.
—— *v*. Earl [1968] 1 W.L.R. 1315; 19 P. & C.R. 691, D.C. 420
—— *v*. Freeman [1978] 1 W.L.R. 1298; 122 S.J. 332; [1978] 3 All E.R. 878; 247 E.G.
   295; 36 P. & C.R. 323, C.A. 645
—— *v*. Hughes (1923) 129 L.T. 223; 39 T.L.R. 260; 21 L.G.R. 350; 67 S.J. 518 452
Chappell *v*. Mason (1894) 10 T.L.R. 404 50
Chaproniére *v*. Lambert [1917] 2 Ch. 356; 86 L.J.Ch. 726; 117 L.T. 353; 61 S.J. 592;
   33 T.L.R. 485; [1916–17] All E.R.Rep. 1089 87
Charalambous *v*. Ktori [1972] 3 All E.R. 701 99
Charsley *v*. Jones (1889) 53 J.P. 280; 5 T.L.R. 412 239
Chartered Trust *v*. Maylands Green Estate Co. (1984) 270 E.G. 845 183
Chatham Empire Theatre (1955) Ltd. *v*. Ultrans Ltd. [1961] 1 W.L.R. 817; 105 S.J.
   323; [1961] 2 All E.R. 381 356
Chatsworth Properties Ltd. *v*. Effiam [1971] 1 W.L.R. 144; (1970) 115 S.J. 34; [1971]
   1 All E.R. 604; 22 P. & C.R. 365, C.A. 69
Chatterton *v*. Terrell [1923] A.C. 578; 92 L.J.Ch. 605; 129 L.T. 769; 39 T.L.R. 589 ... 305
Cheapside Land Development Co. *v*. Messels Service Co. (1976) 120 S.J. 554,
   C.A. 179
Chelsea Cloisters (In Liquidation), *Re* (1980) 41 P. & C.R. 98, C.A. 135, 172, 435
Chelsea Estates Ltd *v*. Kadri (1970) 241 E.G. 1356; [1970] E.G.D. 425 195
Cheryl Investments Ltd. *v*. Saldhana [1978] 1 W.L.R. 1329; 122 S.J. 777; [1979] 1 All
   E.R. 5; 37 P. & C.R. 349; 248 E.G. 591, C.A. 549, 646, 647
Chester *v*. Buckingham Travel Ltd. [1981] 1 W.L.R. 96; (1980) 125 S.J. 99; [1981] 1
   All E.R. 386; 42 P. & C.R. 221 .... 98, 302
Chesterfield (Earl) *v*. Bolton (Duke) (1738) Comyns. 627 234
Chez Gerard Ltd. *v*. Greene Ltd. (1983) 268 E.G. 575, C.A. 704
Chipperfield *v*. Shell U.K. Ltd. *See* Warwick & Warwick (Philately) *v*. Shell (U.K.);
   Chipperfield *v*. Shell (U.K.).
Chiswell *v*. Griffon Land and Estates Ltd. [1975] 1 W.L.R. 1181; 119 S.J. 338; [1975]
   2 All E.R. 665; 30 P. & C.R. 211, C.A. 687

Chiverton v. Ede [1921] 2 K.B. 30; 90 L.J.K.B. 491; 124 L.T. 765; 37 T.L.R. 242; 65
 S.J. 260; 19 L.G.R. 217 449
Christina v. Seear (1985) 275 E.G. 898 643
Christophedes v. Cuming (1976) 239 E.G. 275; 120 L.J. 251, C.A. 395
Church v. Brown (1808) 15 Ves.Jr. 258; 10 R.R. 74; [1803–13] All E.R.Rep.
 440 .... 299, 301, 302
Church Commissioners for England v. Ve-ri-best Manufacturing Co. Ltd. [1957] 1
 Q.B. 238; [1956] 3 W.L.R. 990; 100 S.J. 875; [1956] 3 All E.R. 777 355
Church of England Building Society v. Piskor [1954] Ch. 553; [1954] 2 W.L.R. 952;
 98 S.J. 316; [1954] 2 All E.R. 85, C.A. 80
Church of Our Lady of Hal v. Camden L.B.C. (1980) 255 E.G. 991; 40 P & C.R. 472,
 C.A. 270
Churton v. Douglas (1859) Johns. 174; 28 L.J.Ch. 841; 33 L.T.(o.s.) 57; 5 Jur.(N.S.)
 887; 7 W.R. 365; 70 E.R. 385 741
City and Westminster Properties (1934) Ltd. v. Mudd [1959] Ch. 129; [1958] 3
 W.L.R. 312; 102 S.J. 582; [1958] 2 All E.R. 733 .... 148, 150
City Permanent B.S. v. Miller [1952] Ch. 840; [1952] 2 T.L.R. 547; [1952] 2 All E.R.
 621, C.A. 88, 145
Civil Service Co-operative Society Ltd. v. McGrigor's Trustee [1923] 2 Ch. 347; 92
 L.J.Ch. 616; 129 L.T. 789 .... 353, 356
Clare v. Dobson [1911] 1 K.B. 35; 80 L.J.K.B. 158; 103 L.T. 506; 27 T.L.R. 22 323
Clark v. Kirby-Smith [1964] Ch. 506; [1964] 3 W.L.R. 239; 108 S.J. 462; [1964] 2 All
 E.R. 835 751
Clarke v. Glasgow Assurance Co. (1854) 1 Macq. 668 234
—— v. Grant [1950] 1 K.B. 104; [1949] L.J.R. 1450; 65 T.L.R. 241; 93 S.J. 249;
 [1949] 1 All E.R. 768 350
—— v. Hall [1961] 2 Q.B. 331; [1961] 2 W.L.R. 836; 105 S.J. 366; [1961] 2 All E.R.
 365 792
Clarke (Richard) & Co. Ltd. v. Widnall [1976] 1 W.L.R. 845; 120 S.T. 588; [1976] 3
 All E.R. 301, C.A. 357
Clays Lane Housing Co-operative v. Patrick (1985) 49 P. & C.R. 72; (1984) 17
 H.L.R. 188 .... 194, 586, 591
Cleethorpes Borough Council v. Clarkson (1978) 128 New L.J. 680 558
Clegg v. Hands (1890) 44 Ch.D. 503; 59 L.J.Ch. 477; 62 L.T. 502; 38 W.R. 433 317
Clements (Charles) (London) v. Rank City Wall (1978) 246 E.G. 739 714
Cleveland Petroleum Co. Ltd. v. Dartstone Ltd. [1969] 1 W.L.R. 1 16; (1968) 112
 S.J. 962; [1968] 1 All E.R. 201; 20 P. & C.R. 235, C.A. 125, 658
Clifton Securities Ltd. v. Huntley [1948] W.N. 267; 64 T.L.R. 413; 92 S.J. 499; [1948]
 2 All E.R. 283 607
Climie v. Wood (1868) L.R. 3 Ex. 257; affirmed (1869) L.R. 4 Ex. 328; [1861–73] All
 E.R.Rep. 831 56
Clore v. Theatrical Properties Ltd. [1963] 3 All E.R. 483 32
Clydebank Engineering & Shipbuilding Co. v. Yzquierde y Castanedo [1905] A.C.
 6; 74 L.J.P.C. 1; 91 L.T. 666; 21 T.L.R. 58 171
Coates v. Diment [1951] 1 All E.R. 890 .... 784, 791, 802
Coatsworth v. Johnson (1886) 55 L.J.Q.B. 220; 54 L.T. 520; [1886–90] All E.R.Rep.
 547 94
Cobb v. Lane [1952] W.N. 196; [1952] 1 T.L.R. 1037; 96 S.J. 295; [1952] 1 All E.R.
 1199, C.A. 17, 18, 25, 26, 31, 33
—— v. Stokes (1807) 8 Ea. 358; 9 R.R. 464 108
Cobstone Investments Ltd. v. Maxim [1985] Q.B. 140; [1984] 3 W.L.R. 563; (1984)
 128 S.J. 483; [1984] 2 All E.R. 635; (1984) 49 P. & C.R. 173; (1984) 15 H.L.R.
 113; (1984) 272 E.G. 429; (1984) L.S.Gaz. 1683, C.A. 452
Cockburn v. Smith [1924] 2 K.B. 119; 93 L.J.K.B. 764; 131 L.T. 334; 68 S.J. 631; 40
 T.L.R. 476 .... 103, 235, 246

Cocks v. Thanet D.C. [1983] A.C. 286; [1982] 3 W.L.R. 1121; (1982) 126 S.J. 820;
 [1982] 3 All E.R. 1135; (1983) 81 L.G.R. 81; (1984) 24 R.V.R., H.L. . 561, 628,
 629
Coe v. Clay (1829) 5 Bing 440; 7 L.J.(o.s.)C.P. 162; 30 R.R. 699 129
Cohen v. Nessdale [1981] 3 All E.R. 118; [1982] 2 All E.R. 97; 263 E.G. 437 82
—— v. Popular Restaurants [1917] 1 K.B. 480; 86 L.J.K.B. 617; 116 L.T. 477;
 33 T.L.R. 107 .... 307, 318
—— v. Tarnar [1900] 2 Q.B. 609; 69 L.J.Q.B. 904; 83 L.T. 64; 48 W.R. 642 130
Colchester Estates (Cardiff) v. Carlton Industries plc [1984] 3 W.L.R. 693; [1984]
 2 All E.R. 601; 271 E.G. 778; 81 L.S.Gaz. 2699 285
Cole v. Harris [1945] K.B. 474; 114 L.J.K.B. 481; 173 L.T. 50; 61 T.L.R. 440; 89 S.J.
 477; [1945] 2 All E.R. 146 384
—— v. Sury (1627) Lat. 264; Palm. 481; Noy 96 154
Coleman v. Foster (1856) 1 H. & N. 37; 4 W.R. 489 11
Coles v. Trecothick (1804) 9 Ves.Jr. 234; 7 R.R. 167; 1 Smith 233; [1803–1813] All
 E.R.Rep. 14 71
Colley v. Streeton (1823) 2 B. & C. 273; 3 D. & R. 522; 2 L.J.(o.s.)K.B. 25; 26
 R.R. 350 286
Collier v. Hollinshead (1984) 272 E.G. 941 761
—— v. Stoneman [1957] 1 W.L.R. 1108; 101 S.J. 849; [1957] 3 All E.R. 20, C.A. 579
Collin v. Duke of Westminster [1985] Q.B. 581; [1985] 2 W.L.R. 553; (1985) 129 S.J.
 116; [1985] 1 All E.R. 463; 50 P. & C.R. 380; (1984) 17 H.L.R. 246; 273 E.G.
 881; 25 R.V.R. 4; 82 L.S.Gaz. 767, C.A. 518
Collins v. Hopkins [1923] 2 K.B. 617; 92 L.J.K.B. 820; 130 L.T. 21; 21 L.G.R. 773;
 39 T.L.R. 616 .... 240, 543
Combe v. Combe [1951] 2 K.B. 215; [1951] 1 T.L.R. 811; 95 S.J 317; [1951] 1 All
 E.R. 767 177
Comber v. Fleet Electrics Ltd. [1955] 1 W.L.R. 566; 99 S.J. 337; [1955] 2 All E.R.
 161 .... 127, 306
Commissioner for Railways v. Avrom Investments Proprietary Ltd. [1959] 1 W.L.R.
 389; 103 S.J. 293; [1959] 2 All E.R. 63, P.C. 121
Commissioner of Valuation for Northern Ireland v. Fermanagh Protestant Board of
 Education [1969] 1 W.L.R. 1708; 113 S.J. 875; [1969] R.A. 475; *sub nom.*
 Northern Ireland Commissioner of Valuation v. Fermanagh Protestant
 Board of Education 133 J.P. 637; [1969] 3 All E.R. 352, H.L. 28
Compton Group v. Estates Gazette (1978) 36 P. & C.R. 148; (1977) 244 E.G. 799,
 C.A. 167, 187
Concorde Graphics v. Andromeda Investments S.A. (1983) 265 E.G. 386 .... 135, 172,
 219
Congham v. King (1630) Cro.Car. (3) 221; W.Jon. 245 320
Connors Bros. Ltd. v. Connors [1940] 4 All E.R. 179; 57 T.L.R. 76; 85 S.J. 81, P.C. . 745
Constantine v. Imperial Hotels [1944] 1 K.B. 693; [1944] 2 All E.R. 171; 114
 L.J.K.B. 85; 172 L.T. 128; 60 T.L.R. 510 629
Constantine (Joseph) S.S. Line Ltd. v. Imperial Smelting Corp. Ltd. [1942] A.C.
 154; [1941] 2 All E.R. 165; 110 L.J.K.B. 433; 165 L.T. 27; 57 T.L.R. 485; 46
 Com.Cas. 258, H.L. 153, 175
Cook v. Humber (1861) 11 C.B.(N.S.) 33; 31 L.J.C.P. 73; K. & G. 413; 8 Jur.(N.S.)
 698; 5 L.T. 838; 10 W.R. 427 28
—— v. Mott (1961) 178 E.G. 637, C.A. 698
—— v. Shoesmith [1951] 1 K.B. 752; [1951] 1 T.L.R. 194, C.A. 305
Cooke v. Rickman [1911] 2 K.B. 1125; 81 L.J.K.B. 38; 105 L.T. 896; 55 S.J. 668,
 D.C. 165
Cooper v. Blandy (1834) 4 Moo. & S. 562; 3 L.J.C.P. 274; (1834) 1 Bing.N.C. 45; 41
 R.R. 555 165
—— v. Tait (1984) 128 S.J. 416; 48 P. & C.R. 460; 15 H.L.R. 98; [1984] 271 E.G.
 105; 81 L.S.Gaz. 1683, C.A. 396

Cooper's Case (1768) 2 Wils. 375 154
Cooper's Lease, *Re*, Cowan *v*. Beaumont Property Trusts (1968) 19 P. & C.R. 541 ... 306
Cornish *v*. Brook Green Laundry Ltd. [1959] 1 Q.B. 394; [1959] 2 W.L.R. 215;
 [1959] 1 All E.R. 373, C.A. 94
—— *v*. Cleife (1864) 3 H. & C. 446; 34 L.J.Ex. 19; 11 Jur.(N.S.) 181; 11 L.T. 606; 13
 W.R. 389 224
Corporation of the City of London *v*. Cusack-Smith [1955] A.C. 337 167
Corton *v*. Corton [1965] P. 1; [1964] 2 W.L.R. 9; 127 J.P. 46; 106 S.J. 837; [1962] 3
 All E.R. 1025, D.C. 577
Cory (William) & Son Ltd. *v*. Harrison [1906] A.C. 274; 75 L.J.Ch. 714; 93 L.T. 818,
 H.L. 744
Costagliola *v*. Bunting [1958] 1 W.L.R 580; 102 S.J. 364; [1958] 1 All E.R. 846; 56
 L.G.R. 292 792
Cotching *v*. Bassett (1862) 32 Beav. 101; 32 L.J.Ch. 286; 9 Jur.(N.S.) 590; 11
 W.R. 197; 55 E.R. 40 12
Cottage Holiday Associates Ltd. *v*. Customs & Excise Commissioners [1983] Q.B.
 735; [1983] 2 W.L.R. 861; 127 S.J. 69; [1983] S.T.C. 278, V.A.T. Tribunal 40
Cottrill *v*. Steyning and Littlehampton Building Society [1966] 1 W.L.R. 753; (1962)
 106 S.J. 736; [1966] 2 All E.R. 295; 184 E.G. 253; [1962] C.L.Y. 829 142
Countess of Shrewsbury's Case (1600) 5 Co.Rep. 13b; 77 E.R. 68; *sub nom*. Salop
 (Countess) *v*. Crompton Cro.Eliz. 784 281
Cove *v*. Flick [1954] 2 Q.B 326; [1954] 3 W.L.R. 82; 98 S.J. 442; [1954] 2 All E.R.
 441, C.A. 443
Covell Matthews & Partners *v*. French Wools [1978] 1 W.L.R. 1477; (1977) 122 S.J.
 79; [1978] 2 All E.R. 800; 35 P. & C.R. 107; 246 E.G. 1007, C.A. 693
Coventry C.C. *v*. Cartwright [1975] 1 W.L.R. 845; 119 S.J. 235; [1975] 2 All E.R. 99;
 73 L.G.R. 218, D.C. 259, 260
—— *v*. Doyle [1981] 1 W.L.R. 1325; [1981] 2 All E.R. 184; [1981] J.P.L., D.C. 260
Cowper Essex *v*. Acton Local Board (1889) 14 App.Cas. 153; [1886–90] All
 E.R.Rep. 901; 58 L.J.Q.B. 594; 61 L.T. 1; 53 J.P. 756; 38 W.R. 209; 5 T.L.R.
 395, H.L. *reversing* S.C. *sub nom*. R. *v*. Essex (1886) 17 Q.B.D. 447, C.A. 732
Cox *v*. Phillips Industries Ltd. [1976] I.C.R. 138; [1976] 1 W.L.R. 638; (1975) 119 S.J
 760; [1976] 3 All E.R. 161; [1975] I.R.L.R. 334 252
Crabb *v*. Arun D.C. [1976] Ch. 179; [1975] 3 W.L.R. 847; 119 S.J. 711; [1975] 3 All
 E.R. 865; 32 P. & C.R. 70, C.A. 12
Crane *v*. Morris [1965] 1 W.L.R. 1104; 109 S.J. 456; [1965] 3 All E.R. 77,
 C.A. 482, 490
Crate *v*. Miller [1947] K.B. 946; [1947] L.J.R. 1341; 177 L.T. 29; 63 T.L.R. 389; 91
 S.J. 396; [1947] 2 All E.R. 45, C.A. 347
Crawford *v*. Newton (1886) 36 W.R. 54 223
Creery *v*. Summersell and Flowerdew & Co. [1949] Ch. 751; [1979] L.J.R. 1166; 93
 S.J. 357 .... 123, 308
Cresswell *v*. Duke of Westminster (1985) 275 E.G. 461; 25 R.V.R. 144, C.A. 507
—— *v*. Hodgson [1951] 2 K.B. 92; [1951] 1 T.L.R. 414; [1951] 1 All E.R. 710,
 C.A. 449
Cricklewood Property and Investment Trust Ltd. *v*. Leighton's Investment Trust
 Ltd. [1945] A.C. 221; 114 L.J.K.B. 110; 172 L.T. 140; 61 T.L.R. 202; 89
 S.J. 93; *sub nom*. Leighton's Investment Trust *v*. Cricklewood Property
 and Investment Trust [1943] K.B. 493 .... 152, 154
Croft *v*. Blay (William F.) Ltd. [1919] 2 Ch. 343; 88 L.J.Ch. 545; 121 L.T. 18; 63 S.J.
 607; 35 T.L.R. 556 346
Crofton Investment Trust *v*. Greater London Rent Assessment Committee [1967]
 2 Q.B. 955; [1967] 3 W.L.R 256; 111 S.J. 334; [1967] 2 All E.R. 1103,
 D.C. 418, 425
Crossley & Sons Ltd. *v*. Lightowler (1867) 2 Ch.App. 478; 36 L.J.Ch. 584; 16 L.T.
 438; 15 W.R. 801, L.C. 106

Crowhurst *v.* Maidment [1953] 1 Q.B 23; [1952] 2 T.L.R. 723; 96 S.J. 783; [1952] 2
All E.R. 808, C.A. 409
Crowhurst Park, *Re*, Sims-Hilditch *v.* Simmons [1974] 1 W.L.R. 583; (1973) 118
S.J. 331; [1974] 1 All E.R. 991; 28 P. & C.R. 14 .... 326, 701
Crown Estate Commissioners *v.* Wordsworth (1982) 44 P. & C.R. 302; 264 E.G. 439,
C.A. 395
Crown Lands Commissioners *v.* Page [1960] 2 Q.B. 274; [1960] 3 W.L.R. 446; 104
S.J. 642; [1960] 2 All E.R. 726, C.A. 132
Cruise *v.* Tervell [1922] 1 K.B. 664; 91 L.J.K.B. 499; 126 L.T. 750; 20 L.G.R. 418; 66
S.J. 365; 38 T.L.R. 379 .... 133, 405
Cruse *v.* Mount [1933] Ch. 278; 102 L.J.Ch. 74; 148 L.T. 259; 49 T.L.R. 87; 76 S.J.
902 .... 132, 239
Crusoe *d.* Blencowe *v.* Rugby (1770) 2 W.Bl. 766; (1771) 3 Wils. 234; 95 E.R. 1030 ... 303
Cruttwell (or Crutwell) *v.* Lye (1810) 1 Rose 123; 17 Ves.Jr. 335; 17 Ves. 335; 34
E.R. 1929 739
Cuff *v.* Stone (J. & F.) Property Co. Ltd. [1979] A.C. 87; (1978) 38 P. & C.R. 288;
[1978] 3 W.L.R. 241; [1978] 2 All E.R. 833 .... 140, 188
Cumming *v.* Danson (1942) 112 L.J.K.B. 145; 59 T.L.R. 70; 87 S.J. 21; [1942] 2 All
E.R. 653; *sub nom.* Cumming *v.* Dawson, 168 L.T. 35 449
Cunard *v.* Antifyre [1933] 1 K.B. 551; 103 L.J.K.B. 321; 148 L.T. 287; 49 T.L.R.
184 .... 257, 369
Cunliffe *v.* Goodman [1950] 2 K.B. 237; 66 T.L.R. (Pt. 2) 109; 94 S.J. 179; [1950] 1
All E.R. 720, C.A. 704
Curl *v.* Angelo [1948] L.J.R. 1756; 92 S.J. 513; [1948] 2 All E.R. 189, C.A. ... 386, 387
Currie *v.* I.R.C., Durant *v.* I.R.C. [1921] 2 K.B. 332; 90 L.J.K.B. 499; 125 L.T. 33;
37 T.L.R. 371; 12 Tax Cas. 257, 258, C.A. 664
Curteis *v.* Corcoran (1947) 150 E.G. 44 551
Curtin *v.* G.L.C. (1970) 114 S.J. 932; 69 L.G.R. 281, C.A. 510
Curtis *v.* Calgary Investments Ltd. (1983) 47 P. & C.R. 13, C.A. 707
—— *v.* Spitty (1834) 4 Moo. & S. 554; 3 L.J.C.P. 233; 1 Bing.N.C. 15; (1835) 1
Bing.N.C. 756; 1 Scott 737; 1 Hodge 153; 4 L.J.C.P. 236 320
Cutting *v.* Derby (1776) 2 Wm.Bl. 1075 334

D.A.F. Motoring Centre (Gosport) *v.* Hutfield & Wheeler (1982) 263 E.G. 976,
C.A. 705
D.H.N. Food Distributors *v.* Tower Hamlets L.B.C. [1976] 1 W.L.R. 852 17
Daejar Investments *v.* Cornwall Coast Country Club (1985) 50 P. & C.R. 157; (1984)
279 E.G. 1122; 82 L.S.Gaz. 3085 187
Daejan Properties Ltd. *v.* Elliott [1977] L.A.G.Bull. 208 244
Dagg *v.* Lovett (1980) 256 E.G. 491, C.A. 796
Dagger *v.* Shepherd [1946] K.B. 215; 62 T.L.R. 143; [1946] 1 All E.R. 133 .... 41, 347
Daiches *v.* Bluelake Investments [1985] 275 E.G. 462; (1985) 17 H.L.R. 543 258
Daimar Investment Ltd. *v.* Jones (1962) 112 L.J. 424, Cty. Ct. 648
Dakyns *v.* Pace [1958] 1 K.B. 22 385
Dalton *v.* Pickard [1926] 2 K.B. 545n.; 95 L.J.Ch. 1052n.; 136 L.T. 21 336
Daly *v.* Duggan (1839) 11 Eq.R. 311 (Ir.) 155
Dann *v.* Spurrier (1803) 3 Bos. & Pul. 399; 7 R.R. 797; [1803–13] All E.R.Rep. 410 .. 138
Datastream International Ltd. *v.* Oakeep Ltd. [1986] 1 W.L.R. 404; (1985) 130 S.J.
299; [1986] 1 All E.R. 966; (1985) 51 P. & C.R. 218; 277 E.G. 66; (1986) 83
L.S.Gaz. 1399 190
Datnow *v.* Jones (1985) 275 E.G. 145, C.A. 781
Davlia Ltd. *v.* Four Millbank Nominees Ltd. [1978] Ch. 231; [1978] 2 W.L.R. 621;
[1978] 2 All E.R. 557; [1977] 36 P. & C.R. 244; 121 S.J. 851, C.A. 83
Davies *v.* Davies (1888) 38 Ch.D. 499; 57 L.J.Ch. 1093; 58 L.T. 514; 36 W.R. 399 281
—— *v.* Hall [1954] 1 W.L.R. 855; 98 S.J. 370; [1954] 2 All E.R. 330, C.A. 64, 68
—— *v.* Price [1958] 1 W.L.R. 434; 102 S.J. 290; [1958] 1 All E.R. 671, C.A. 782

Davis v. Foots [1940] 1 K.B. 116; 109 L.J.K.B. 385; 56 T.L.R. 54; 83 S.J. 780 239
—— v. Jones (1818) 2 B. & A. 165; 20 R.R. 396 57
—— v. Kingston-upon-Thames Royal London Borough *The Times*, March 27,
   1981 .... 621, 625
—— v. Nisbet (1861) 10 C.B.(N.S.) 752; 31 L.J.C.P. 6; 8 Jur.(N.S.) 9 W.R. 840 661
—— v. Powell [1977] 1 W.L.R. 258; [1976] T.R. 307; [1977] 1 All E.R. 471; [1977]
   S.T.C. 32; (1976) 51 T.C. 492; 242 E.G. 380 .... 808, 813
—— v. Town Properties Investment Corp. Ltd. [1903] 1 Ch. 797; 72 L.J.Ch. 389; 88
   L.T. 665; 51 W.R. 417; *affirming* [1902] 2 Ch. 635 131
Davstone Estates Leases, *Re*, Manprop v. O'Dell [1969] 2 Ch. 378; [1969] 2 W.L.R.
   1287; 113 S.J. 366; [1969] 2 All E.R. 849; 20 P. & C.R. 395 172
Davstone Holdings v. Al-Rifai (1976) 32 P. & C.R. 18 179
Dawson v. Dyer (1883) 5 B. and Ad. 584; 2 N. & M. 559; 39 R.R. 556 130
Day v. Brownrigg (1878) 10 Ch.D. 294; 48 L.J.Ch. 173; 39 L.T. 553; 27 W.R. 217,
   C.A. 741
De Falbe, Ward v. Taylor [1901] 1 Ch. 523, *affirmed sub nom.* Leigh v. Taylor [1902]
   A.C. 157; [1900–3] All E.R.Rep. 520 58
De Falco v. Crawley Borough Council; Silvestri v. Crawley Borough Council [1980]
   Q.B. 460; [1980] 2 W.L.R. 664; (1979) 124 S.J. 82; 78 L.G.R. 180; [1980]
   J.P.L. 392 .... 560, 618, 619, 624, 626, 627, 628, 629, 631, 632
De Jean v. Fletcher [1959] 1 W.L.R. 341; 123 J.P. 244; 103 S.J. 257; [1959] 1 All E.R.
   602, C.A. 479
De Nicolls v. Saunders (1870) L.R. 5 C.P. 589; 39 L.J.C.P. 297; 22 L.T. 661; 18 W.R.
   1106 159
D'Silva v. Lister House Development Ltd. [1971] Ch. 17; [1970] 2 W.L.R. 563;
   [1970] 1 All E.R. 858; 21 P. & C.R. 230 .... 82, 83, 86, 641, 645
Dealex Properties Ltd. v. Brooks [1966] 1 Q.B. 542; [1965] 2 W.L.R. 1241; 109 S.J.
   253; [1965] 1 All E.R. 1080, C.A. 334, 345, 666
Dean and Chapter of Chichester Cathedral v. Lennards Ltd. (1977) 35 P. & C.R.
   309; 244 E.G. 807; 121 S.J. 694, C.A. 180
Deerfield Travel Services Ltd. v. Wardens etc. of the Leathersellers of the City of
   London (1982) 46 P. & C.R. 132, C.A. 666
Defries v. Milne [1913] 1 Ch. 98; 82 L.J.Ch. 1; 107 L.T. 593; 57 S.J. 280
Deith v. Brown [1956] J.P.L. 736; [1956] C.L.Y. 127 758
Delahaye v. Oswestry B.C. *The Times*, July 29, 1980 .... 612, 616, 624
Dellerty v. Pellow [1951] 2 K.B. 858; [1951] 2 T.L.R. 733; 95 S.J. 576; [1951] 2 All
   E.R. 716, C.A. 198, 449
Demuren & Adefope v. Seal Estates Ltd. (1978) 249 E.G. 440; [1979] J.P.L.,
   C.A. 10, 21, 24
Dendy v. Evans [1910] 1 K.B. 263; 79 L.J.K.B. 121; 102 L.T. 4; 54 S.J. 151 351
Denman v. Brise [1949] 1 K.B. 22; [1948] L.J.R. 1388; 64 T.L.R. 335; 92 S.J. 349;
   [1948] 2 All E.R. 141, C.A. 153, 406
Derby & Co. Ltd. v. I.T.C. Pension Trust Ltd. (1977) 245 E.G. 569; [1977] 2 All
   E.R. 890 .... 82, 706
Deering v. Farrington (1674) 1 Mod.Rep. 113; 3 Keb. 304; 86 E.R. 772; *sub nom.*
   Dering v. Farington, Freem.K.B. 368 154
Devonport v. Salford City Council (1983) 8 H.L.R. 54 .... 612, 621, 622, 624
Devonshire (Duke of) v. Brookshaw (1899) 81 L.T. 83; 43 S.J. 675; 63 J.P. 569 658
Dewar v. Goudman [1909] A.C. 72; 78 L.J.K.B. 209; 100 L.T. 2; 25 T.L.R. 137;
   affirming [1908] 1 K.B 94 .... 319, 323
Di Palma v. Victoria Square Properties Co. [1985] 3 W.L.R. 207; 129 S.J. 364; [1985]
   2 All E.R. 676; 50 P. & C.R. 222; 17 H.L.R. 448; 135 New L.J. 462; L.S.Gaz.
   2168, C.A. 197, 198
Dibble v. Bowater (1853) 2 E. & B. 564; 22 L.J.Q.B. 396; 17 Jur. 1054; 1 W.R. 435 ... 159
Dibble (H. E.) Ltd. (trading as Mill Lane Nurseries) v. Moore [1970] 2 Q.B. 181;
   [1969] 3 W.L.R. 748; 20 P. & C.R. 898, C.A. 57

Dickinson v. Boucher (1983) 269 E.G. 1159, C.A. 786
—— v. St. Aubyn [1944] K.B. 454; 113 L.J.K.B 225; 170 L.T. 287; 60 T.L.R. 269;
  [1944] 1 All E.R. 370 139
Diesen v. Samson [1971] S.L.T. 49, Sheriff Ct. 252
Digby v. Atkinson (1815) 4 Camp. 275; 16 R.R. 792 234
Dillwyn v. Llewelyn (1862) 4 De D.G. & J. 517; 31 L.J.Ch. 658; 6 L.T. 878; 8
  Jur.(N.S.) 1068; 10 W.R. 742; 45 E.R. 1285, L.C. 12, 13
Din v. Wandsworth L.B.C. [1983] 1 A.C. 657; [1981] 3 W.L.R. 918; 125 S.J. 828;
  [1981] 3 All E.R. 881; [1982] 1 H.L.R. 73; (1980) L.G.R. 113, H.L. 611, 614,
                                                                                          620, 625
Dinsdale (or Disdale) v. Isles (1673) 2 Lev. 88; 1 Vent. 247; T.Raym. 224; 3 Keb.
  166 43
Diploma Laundry v. Surrey Timber Co. Ltd. [1955] 2 Q.B. 604; [1955] 3 W.L.R. 404;
  99 S.J. 561; [1955] 2 All E.R. 922, C.A. 684
Disdale v. Illes. See Dinsdale v. Isles.
Disraeli Agreement, Re Cleasby v. Park Estate (Hughenden), Re, [1939] Ch. 382;
  108 L.J.Ch. 100; 160 L.T. 156; 82 S.J. 1031; 55 T.L.R. 204; [1938] 4 All
  E.R. 658 .... 791, 808
Distributors and Warehousing Ltd. Re, The Financial Times, November 19,
  1985 .... 316, 330
Dobbs v. Linford [1953] 1 Q.B. 48; [1952] 2 T.L.R. 727; 96 S.J. 763; [1952] 2 All E.R.
  827, C.A. 463
Dobie & Son Ltd. Trade Mark, Re, (1935) 52 R.P.C. 333 740
Dobson v. Jones (1844) 5 Man. & G. 112; 13 L.J.C.P. 126; Bar. & Arn. 243; Cox &
  Atk. 25; 1 Lut.Reg.Cas. 105; Pig & R. 65; 8 Scott N.R. 80; 2 L.T(o.s.)149; 3
  L.T.(o.s.) 77; 8 Jur. 457 27
Dodds v. Walker [1981] 1 W.L.R. 1027; 125 S.J. .463; [1981] 2 All E.R. 609; 42 P. &
  C.R. 131, H.L. 688
Dodson Bull Carpet Co. v. City of London Corporation [1975] 1 W.L.R. 781; (1974)
  119 S.J. 320; [1975] 2 All E.R. 497; (1974) 29 P. & C.R. 311 .... 684. 686
Dodsworth v. Dodsworth (1973) 228 E.G. 1115, C.A. 12
Doe d. Aslin v. Summersett (1830) 1 B. & Ad. 135; 8 L.J.(o.s.)K.B. 369; 35 R.R.
  250 348
—— d. Berkeley (Earl) v. York (Archbishop) (1805) 6 Ea. 86; 102 E.R. 1219;
  [1803–13] All E.R.Rep. 248; sub nom. Doe d. Berkeley (Earl) v. York
  (Archbishop), 2 Smith K.B. 166 339
—— d. Chadborn v. Green (1839) 9 Ad. & E. 658; 8 L.J.Q.B. 100; 1 P. & D. 454; 2
  W.W. & H. 122; 48 R.R. 626 108
—— d. Cheny v. Batten (1775) 9 East 314n.; 1 Cowp. 243; 9 R.R. 570n.; [1775–1802]
  All E.R.Rep. 594 .... 18, 169, 334, 350
—— d. Courtail v. Thomas (1829) 9 B. & C. 288; 4 Can. & Ry. 218; 7 L.J.(o.s.)K.B.
  214; 32 R.R. 680 339
—— d. Darlington (Earl) v. Bond (1826) 5 B. & C. 855; 8 D. & R. 738; 5
  L.J.(o.s.)K.B. 68; 29 R.R. 436 282
—— d. Douglas v. Lock (1835) 2 Ad. & E. 705; 4 L.J.K.B. 113; 113 R.R. 496;
  [1835–42] All E.R.Rep. 13 106
—— d. Edney v. Benham (1845) 7 Q.B. 976; 14 L.J.Q.B. 342; 9 Jur. 662; 68 R.R.
  620 .... 1, 157
—— d. Egremont (Earl) v. Courtenay (1848) 11 Q.B. 702; 17 L.J.Q.B. 151; 75 R.R.
  600; 12 Jur. 454; [1843–60] All E.R.Rep. 685 339
—— d. Goodbehere v. Bevan (1815) 3 M. & S. 353; 2 Rose 456; 16 R.R. 293
  [1814–23] All E.R.Rep. 706 .... 299, 303
—— d. Goody v. Carter (1847) 9 Q.B. 863; 18 L.J.Q.B. 305; 11 Jur. 285 43
—— d. Hughes v. Derry (1840) 9 C. & P. 494 16
—— d. Hull v. Wood (1845) 14 M. & W. 682; 15 L.J.Ex. 41; 9 Jur. 1060 16
—— d. Jackson v. Wilkinson (1824) 3 B. & C. 413; 5 D. & R. 273 165

Doe *d*. Hanley *v*. Wood (1819) 2 B. & Ald. 724; 106 E.R. 529 11
—— *d*. Murrell *v*. Milward (1838) 3 M. & W. 328; 49 R.R. 621; 7 L.J.Ex. 57; 1 H.&
H. 79; 1 Jur. 848 338
—— *d*. Nicholl *v*. McKaeg (1830) 10 B. & C. 721; 5 Man. & Ry. 620; 8
L.J.(o.s.)K.B. 311; 34 R.R. 551 44
—— *d*. Patrick *v*. Beaufort (Duke) (1851) 6 Exch. 498; 20 L.J.Ex. 251; 155 E.R. 640;
sub proceed. sub nom. Beaufort (Duke) *v*. Patrick (1853) 17 Beav. 60 12
—— *d*. Peacock *v*. Raffan (1806) 6 Esp. 4 344
—— *d*. Phillip *v*. Benjamin (1839) 9 A. & E. 644; 1 Per. & Dav. 440; 2 Will.Woll. &
H. 96; 8 L.J.Q.B. 117; 112 E.R. 1356 40
—— *d*. Pitt *v*. Hogg (1824) 4 D. and R. 226; 2 L.J.(o.s.)K.B. 121; 1 C. & P. 160; *sub
nom.* Doe *d*. Pitt *v*. Laming (1824) Ry. & Moo. 36 302
—— *d*. Raines *v*. Kneller (1829) 4 C. & P. 3 152
—— *d*. Shore *v*. Porter (1789) 3 Term. 13; 1 R.R. 626; [1775–1802] All E.R.Rep.
575 .... 344, 345
—— *d*. Stanway *v*. Rock (1842) Car. & M. 549; 4 Man. & G. 30; 11 L.J.C.P. 194;
6 Jur. 266; 61 R.R. 450 43
—— *d*. Tucker *v*. Morse (1830) 1 B. & Ad. 365; 9 L.J.(o.s.)K.B. 77; 39 R.R. 768 157
—— *d*. Warner *v*. Browne (1807) 8 East. 165; 9 R.R. 397 43
—— *d*. Worcester School Trustees *v*. Rowlands (1841) 9 C. & P. 734; 5 Jur. 177; 62
R.R. 766 224
—— *d*. Wyatt *v*. Byron (1845) 1 C.B. 623; 3 D. & L. 31; 14 L.J.C.P. 207; 68 R.R.
786 198
Doherty *v*. Allman (1878) 3 App.Cas. 709; 39 L.T. 129; 26 W.R. 513 282
Dolling *v*. Evans (1867) 36 L.J.Ch. 474; 15 L.T. 604; 15 W.R. 394 83
Dolphin Square Trust Ltd. *v*. Hartman [1967] 1 W.L.R. 586; 111 S.J. 95; [1967] 1 All
E.R. 624, C.A. 586
Dolphin's Conveyance, *Re*, Birmingham Corp. *v*. Boden [1970] 1 Ch. 654; [1970] 3
W.L.R. 31; 114 S.J. 266; [1970] 2 All E.R. 664; 21 P. & C.R. 511 127
Donegal Tweed Co. Ltd. *v*. Stephenson (1929) 98 L.J.K.B. 657; 141 L.T. 262; 45
T.L.R. 503; 73 S.J. 367; 93 J.P. 380 668
Donevan *v*. Read (1832) 3 B. & Ad. 899; 1 L.J.K.B. 269; 37 R.R. 588; [1824–34] All
E.R.Rep. 639 .... 178, 340
Donmar Productions Ltd. *v*. Bart [1967] 1 W.L.R. 740; [1967] 2 All E.R. 803 630
Doran *v*. Carroll (1860) 111 Ch.R. 379 294
Dorling *v*. Honnor Marine Ltd. [1965] Ch. 1; [1964] 2 W.L.R. 195; 107 S.J. 1039;
[1964] 1 All E.R. 241; [1963] 2 Lloyd's Rep. 455; [1964] R.P.C. 160, C.A.;
reversing in part [1964] Ch. 560; [1963] 3 W.L.R. 397; 107 S.J. 738; [1963] 2
All E.R. 495 10
Douglas *v*. Smith [1907] 2 K.B. 568; 76 L.J.K.B. 969; 96 L.T. 826; 71 J.P. 433; 23
T.L.R. 612; 51 S.J. 569; 5 L.G.R. 1004; 2 Smith Reg.Cas. 12 .... 15, 28
Douglas-Scott *v*. Scorgie [1984] 1 W.L.R. 716; (1984) 128 S.J. 264; [1984] 1 All
E.R. 1086; 48 P. & C.R. 109; 13 H.L.R. 97; 269 E.G. 1164; L.S.Gaz. 663,
C.A. 103, 246
Dover *v*. Prosser [1904] 1 K.B. 84; 73 L.J.K.B. 13; 89 L.T. 724; 20 T.L.R. 49; 68 J.P.
37; 48 S.J. 51; 2 L.G.R. 156; 52 W.R. 140; 1 Smith Reg.Cas. 313 28
Dover D.C. *v*. Farrar (1982) 2 H.L.R. 32, D.C. 260, 261
Downer Enterprises, *Re* [1974] 1 W.L.R. 1460; 118 S.J. 829; [1974] 2 All E.R.
1074 204
Dowse *v*. Cale (1690) 2 Vent. 126; *ibid. sub nom.* Douse *v*. Earle, 3 Lev. 264 224
Doyle and O'Hara's Contract, *v*. [1899] 1 I.R. 113 304
Drake & Underwood *v*. L.C.C. (1960) 11 P. & C.R. 427; Lands Tribunal 737
Drane *v*. Evangelou [1978] 1 W.L.R. 455; [1978] 2 All E.R. 437; (1977) 36 P. & C.R.
270; 246 E.G. 137; 121 S.J. 793, C.A. 131, 132, 610
Drebbond Ltd. *v*. Horsham D.C. (1978) 37 P. & C.R. 237; 246 E.G. 1013,
D.C. 181, 182

Drew *v.* Nunn (1879) 4 Q.B.D. 661; 48 L.J.Q.B. 591; 40 L.T. 671; 43 J.P. 541; 27
    W.R. 810, C.A. 162
Druid Development Co. (Bingley) *v.* Kay (1982) 264 E.G. 1080; 44 P. & C.R. 76,
    C.A. 419
Drummond *v.* S. & U. Stores Ltd. (1981) 258 E.G. 1293 287
Drummond (Inspector of Taxes) *v.* Brown (Austin) [1986] Ch. 52; [1984] 3 W.L.R.
    381; (1984) 128 S.J. 532; [1984] 2 All E.R. 699; [1984] S.T.C. 321; 81 L.S.Gaz.
    1844, C.A. 751
Dudley and District Benefit Building Society *v.* Emerson [1949] Ch. 707; [1949]
    L.J.R. 1441; 65 T.L.R. 444; 93 S.J. 512; [1949] 2 All E.R. 252, C.A. 69, 405
Dudlow Estates Ltd. *v.* Sefton Metropolitan Borough Council (1979) 249 E.G. 1271;
    [1979] J.P.L. 385, C.A. 266
Duke of Westminster *v.* Guild [1985] Q.B. 688; [1984] 3 W.L.R. 630; (1984) 128
    S.J. 581; [1984] 3 All E.R. 144; 48 P. & C.R. 42; (1983) 267 E.G. 763,
    C.A. 235, 247, 248, 285
—— *v.* Johnston (1985) 129 S.J. 542; 275 E.G. 241; 25 R.V.R. 108; 17 H.L.R. 550,
    C.A. 511
—— *v.* Oddy (1984) 128 S.J. 316; 15 H.L.R. 80; 270 E.G. 945; 24 R.V.R. 112;
    L.S.Gaz. 1443, C.A. 512
Dumpor's Case (1603) 4 Co.Rep. 1196; 1 Sm.L.C. (13th ed.) 35 298
Dunlop Pneumatic Tyre Co. Ltd. *v.* New Garage & Motor Co. Ltd. [1915] A.C. 79;
    83 L.J.K.B. 1574; 111 L.T. 862; 30 T.L.R. 615 171
Dunraven Securities *v.* Holloway (1982) 264 E.G. 709, C.A. 353
Dunster *v.* Hollis [1918] 2 K.B. 795; 88 L.J.K.B. 331; 120 L.T. 109; 17 L.G.R.
    42 543
Dunthorne & Shore *v.* Wiggins [1943] 113 L.J.Ch. 85; 169 L.T. 381; [1943] 2 All E.R.
    678 44
Duppa *v.* Mayo (1668) 1 Saund. 275; 2 Keb. 576 159
Dutch Oven Ltd. *v.* Egham Estate & Investment Co. Ltd. [1968] 1 W.L.R. 1483; 112
    S.J. 622; [1968] 3 All E.R. 100; 19 P. & C.R. 815 705
Dutton *v.* Bognor Regis U.D.C. [1972] 1 Q.B 373; [1972] 2 W.L.R. 299; (1971)
    116 S.J. 16; 70 L.G.R. 57, *sub nom.* Dutton *v.* Bognor Regis United Building
    Co. [1972] 1 All E.R. 462; [1972] 1 Lloyd's Rep. 227, C.A. 372
Duxbury *v.* Sandiford (1898) 80 L.T. 552; *reversing* 78 L.T. 230 102
Dyson *v.* Kerrier D.C. [1980] 1 W.L.R. 1205; 124 S.J. 497; [1980] 3 All E.R. 313; 78
    L.G.R 603, C.A. 625, 626, 628
Dyson Holdings *v.* Fox [1976] Q.B. 503; [1975] 3 W.L.R. 744; 119 S.J. 744; [1975] 3
    All E.R. 1030; 31 P. & C.R. 229; 239 E.G. 39, C.A. 441, 442

Eagon *v.* Dent [1965] 3 All E.R. 334 142
Eales *v.* Dale [1954] 1 Q.B. 539; [1954] 2 W.L.R. 593; 118 J.P. 255; 98 S.J. 213;
    [1954] 1 All E.R. 717, C.A. 429
Earl of Lonsdale *v.* Att.-Gen. [1982] 1 W.L.R. 887; 126 S.J. 463; [1982] 3 All E.R.
    579; (1983) 45 P. & C.R. 1 .... 169, 649
Earl of Normanton *v.* Giles [1980] 1 W.L.R. 28; [1980] 1 All E.R. 106; (1979) 124 S.J
    47, H.L.; *affirming* (1978) 39 P. & C.R. 478; 248 E.G. 869, C.A. 483
Earthcare Cooperative *v.* Troveworth [1985] C.L.Y.; May 13, 1985, Durham
    County Ct. 342
East Coast Amusement Co. *v.* British Transport Board [1965] A.C. 58; [1963] 2
    W.L.R. 1426; *sub nom.* "Wonderland" Cleethorpes, *Re*, East Coast
    Amusement Co. *v.* British Railways Board 107 S.J. 455; [1963] 2 All E.R.
    775, H.L.; *affirming* [1962] Ch. 696; [1962] 2 W.L.R. 776 .... 669, 712
East End Dwellings Co. Ltd. *v.* Finsbury B.C. [1952] A.C. 109; [1951] 2 T.L.R. 485;
    115 J.P. 477; 95 S.J. 499; [1951] 2 All E.R. 587; 2 P. & C.R. 135, 40 L.G.R.
    669, H.L. 406
Eastern *v.* Islington Corporation (1952) 3 P. & C.R. 145 734

Eastern Telegraph Co. *v.* Dent [1899] 1 Q.B. 835; 68 L.J.Q.B. 564; 78 L.T. 713; 80
    L.T. 459 660
Easthaugh *v.* Macpherson [1954] 1 W.L.R. 1307; 98 S.J. 733; [1954] 3 All E.R. 214,
    C.A. 347
Eastleigh B.C. *v.* Walsh [1985] 1 W.L.R. 525; (1985) 129 S.J. 246; [1985] 2 All E.R.
    112; 83 L.G.R 525; 17 H.L.R 392; 82 L.S.Gaz. 1858, H.L. 16, 21, 547, 612
Ebbetts *v.* Conquest [1896] A.C. 490; *affirming* [1895] 2 Ch. 377; 64 L.J.Ch. 702; 73
    L.T. 69; 44 W.R. 56; 12 R. 430 .... 219, 288, 289
Eccles *v.* Bryant and Pollock [1948] Ch. 93; [1948] L.J.R. 418; 177 L.T. 247; [1947] 2
    All E.R. 865 .... 82, 83
Edge *v.* Boileau (1885) 16 Q.B.D. 117; 55 L.J.Q.B. 90; 53 L.T. 907; 34 W.R.
    103 .... 130, 131
—— *v.* Pemberton (1843) 12 M. & W. 187; 1 Dow. & L. 467; 13 L.J.Ex. 48; 2
    L.T.(o.s.) 152; 152 E.R. 1164 281
Edicron *v.* Whiteley (William) [1984] 1 W.L.R. 59; [1983] 127 S.J. 785; [1984] 1 All
    E.R. 219; 47 P. & C.R. 625; 268 E.G. 1035; 80 L.S.Gaz. 3003, C.A. 750
Edler *v.* Auerbach [1950] 1 K.B. 359; 65 T.L.R. 645; 93 S.J. 727; [1949] 2 All E.R.
    692; 1 P. & C.R. 103 .... 73, 96
Edlingham Ltd. *v.* M.F.I. Furniture Centres Ltd. (1981) 259 E.G. 421 183
Edmunds *v.* Jones [1957] 1 W.L.R. 1118; 101 S.J. 848, C.A. 579
Edwards (J. H.) & Sons *v.* Central London Commercial Estates; Eastern Bazaar *v.*
    Central London Commercial Estates (1984) 271 E.G. 697, C.A. 710
Egerton *v.* Esplanade Hotels, London Ltd. [1947] 2 All E.R. 88 353
—— *v.* Jones [1939] 2 K.B. 702; 161 L.T. 205; 55 T.L.R. 1089; 83 S.J. 688; [1939]
    3 All E.R. 889 .... 354, 355
—— *v.* Sheafe (1606) Lutw. 1151 169
Eichner *v.* Midland Bank Executor and Trustee Co. [1970] 1 W.L.R. 1120; 114
    S.J. 373; [1970] 2 All E.R. 597; 21 P. & C.R. 503, C.A. 695
Eldon (Earl) *v.* Hedley Bros. [1935] 2 K.B. 1; 104 L.J.K.B. 334; 152 L.T. 507; 51
    T.L.R. 313; 79 S.J. 270 772
Elliott *v.* Bishop (1854) 10 Ex. 496; 3 C.L.R. 272; 24 L.J.Ex. 33; 24 L.T.(o.s.) 217; 19
    J.P. 71; 3 W.R. 160; 156 E.R. 534; *sub nom.* Bishop *v.* Elliott, 11 Exch. 113 58
—— *v.* Johnson (1866) L.R. 2 Q.B. 120; 36 L.J.Q.B. 44; 8 B. & S. 38; 15 W.R. 253 .. 313
Ellis *v.* Allen [1914] 1 Ch. 904; 83 L.J.Ch. 590; 110 L.T. 479 307
—— *v.* Torrington (Viscountess) [1920] 1 K.B. 399; 89 L.J.K.B. 369; 122 L.T. 361;
    36 T.L.R. 80 289
Ellis & Sons Amalgamated Properties *v.* Sisman [1948] 1 K.B. 653; [1948] L.J.R.
    929; 64 T.L.R. 11; 91 S.J. 692; [1948] 1 All E.R. 44, C.A. 406
Ellis & Sons Fourth Amalgamated Properties *v.* Southern Rent Assessment Panel
    (1984) 14 H.L.R. 48; 270 E.G. 39 422
Ellis Copp & Co. *v.* Richmond-upon-Thames L.B.C. (1976) 245 E.G. 931; [1978]
    J.P.L. 619, C.A. 265
Elliston *v.* Reacher [1908] 2 Ch. 374; *affirmed* [1908] 2 Ch. 665 127
Elmcroft Developments Ltd. *v.* Tankersley-Sawyer; Same *v.* I.A.B.; Same *v.*
    Rogers (1984) 15 H.L.R. 63; 270 E.G. 140, C.A. 227, 228
Elmdene Estates Ltd. *v.* White [1960] A.C. 528; [1960] 2 W.L.R. 359; 104 S.J. 126;
    [1960] 1 All E.R. 306, H.L. 213, 430, 435
Elphinstone (Lord) *v.* Monkland Iron & Coal (1886) 11 App.Cas. 332 312
Elsden *v.* Pick [1980] 1 W.L.R. 899; 124 S.J. 312; [1980] 3 All E.R. 235; 40 P. & C.R.
    550; 254 E.G. 503, C.A. 779
Elwes *v.* Maw (1802) 3 Ea. 38; 6 R.R. 523; 2 Smith L.C. (13th ed.) 193; [1775–1802]
    All E.R.Rep. 320 60
Embassy Court Residents' Association Ltd. *v.* Lipman (1984) 271 E.G. 545,
    C.A. 172
Enfield L.B.C. *v.* French (1985) 40 P. & C.R. 223; (1984) 83 L.G.R. 750; 17 H.L.R.
    211, C.A. 553, 554

English Exporters (London) Ltd. *v.* Eldonwall Ltd.; Same *v.* Same [1973] Ch. 415;
[1973] 2 W.L.R. 435; (1972) 117 S.J. 224; [1973] 1 All E.R. 726; (1972) 25 P. &
C.R. 379 .... 421, 679, 680, 681, 714
Engvall *v.* Ideal Flats Ltd. [1945] K.B. 205; 114 L.J.K.B. 249; 172 L.T. 134; 61
T.L.R. 210; [1945] 1 All E.R. 230 410
Epps *v.* Rothnie [1945] 2 K.B. 562; 114 L.J.K.B. 511; 173 L.T. 353; 61 T.L.R. 533; 89
S.J. 424; [1946] 1 All E.R. 225 456
Epsom & Ewell B.C. *v.* Bell (C.) (Tadworth) Ltd. [1983] 1 W.L.R. 379; (1983) 127
S.J. 121; [1983] 2 All E.R. 59; 46 P. & C.R. 143; 81 L.G.R. 613; 266 E.G.
808 .... 14, 765
Epsom Grand Stand Association Ltd. *v.* Clarke [1919] W.N. 170; 35 T.L.R. 525; 63
S.J. 642 .... 381, 456
Equity and Law Life Assurance Society *v.* Badfield Ltd. (1985) 276 E.G. 1157 189
Errington *v.* Errington & Woods [1952] 1 K.B. 290; [1952] 1 T.L.R. 231; 96 S.J. 119;
[1952] 1 All E.R. 149, C.A. 10, 15, 16, 17, 18, 21, 25, 26, 31, 448
Erven Warninck Besloten Vennootschap *v.* Townend (J.) & Sons (Hull) [1979] A.C.
731; [1979] 3 W.L.R. 68; 123 S.J. 472; *sub nom.* Erven Warninck B.V. *v.*
Townend (J.) & Sons (Hull) [1979] 2 All E.R. 927; [1979] F.S.R. 397; [1980]
R.P.C. 31, H.L. 741
Esdaile *v.* Lewis [1956] 1 W.L.R. 709; 100 S.J. 433; [1956] 2 All E.R. 357, C.A. 305
Espir *v.* Basil Street Hotel Ltd. [1936] 3 All E.R. 91; 80 S.J. .894, C.A. .. 111, 287, 289
Esso Petroleum Co. Ltd. *v.* Gibbs (Anthony) Financial Services Ltd. (1983) 267
E.G. 351, C.A.; (1982) 262 E.G. 661 182
—— *v.* Harper's Garage (Stourport) Ltd. [1968] A.C. 269; [1967] 2 W.L.R. 871; 111
S.J. 174; [1967] 1 All E.R. 699, H.L. 125
—— *v.* Kingswood Motors (Addlestone) [1974] Q.B. 142; [1973] 3 W.L.R. 780; 117
S.J. 852; [1973] 3 All E.R. 1057; [1973] C.M.L.R. 665 126
—— *v.* Mardon [1976] Q.B 801; [1976] 2 W.L.R. 583; 120 S.J. 131; [1976] 2 All E.R.
5; [1976] 2 Lloyd's Rep. 305, C.A.; *reversing in part* [1975] Q.B. 819; [1975] 2
W.L.R. 147; (1974) 119 S.J. 81; [1975] 1 All E.R. 203 149
Essoldo (Bingo) Ltd.'s Underlease, *Re,* Essoldo *v.* Elcresta (1971) 115 S.J. 967; 23 P.
& C.R. 1 156
Estates Projects *v.* Greenwich B.C. (1979) 251 E.G. 851 .... 179, 189, 669
Etablissement Commercial Kamira *v.* Schiazzano [1985] Q.B 93; [1984] 3 W.L.R.
95; 128 S.J. .432; [1984] 2 All E.R. 465; 48 P. & C.R. 8; 16 H.L.R. 1; 271 E.G.
269; 81 L.S.Gaz. 1684, C.A. 501
Eton College *v.* Bard [1983] Ch. 321; [1983] 3 W.L.R. 231; 127 S.J. 492; [1983] 2 All
E.R. 961; (1984) P. & C.R. 47; (1983) 267 E.G. 442, C.A. 509
Europark (Midlands) *v.* Town Centre Securities (1985) 271 E.G. 289 705
Euston Centre Properties Ltd. *v.* Wilson (H. & J.) Ltd. (1982) 262 E.G.
1079 .... 189, 669, 713
Evans *v.* Collins [1964] 3 W.L.R. 30; 128 J.P. 280; 108 S.J. 542; [1964] 1 All E.R. 808;
62 L.G.R 295, D.C. 530
—— *v.* Jones [1955] 2 Q.B 58; [1955] 2 W.L.R. 936; 99 S.J. 305; [1955] 2 All E.R.
118; 53 L.G.R. 377, C.A. 772, 814
—— *v.* Roper [1960] 1 W.L.R. 814; 124 J.P. 371; 104 S.J. 604; [1960] 2 All E.R. 507,
D.C. 782, 783
Evans (F. R.) (Leeds) Ltd. *v.* English Electric Co. Ltd. (1977) 36 P. & C.R. 185;
(1978) 245 E.G. 657 .... 186, 187
Exhall Coal Mining Co., *Re* (1864) 4 De G.J. & Sm. 377; 4 New Rep. 127; 33 L.J.Ch.
569; 10 Jur.(N.S.) 576; 46 E.R. 964, L.JJ. 204
Expert Clothing Service & Sales *v.* Hillgate House [1985] 3 W.L.R. 359; 129 S.J. 484;
[1985] 2 All E.R. 998; 50 P. & C.R. 317; 275 E.G. 1011; 82 L.S.Gaz. 2010,
C.A. 195, 292, 353
Expresso Coffee Machine Ltd. *v.* Guardian Assurance Co. Ltd. [1959] 1 W.L.R.
250 704

Eyre *v.* Johnson [1946] K.B. 481; [1947] L.J.R. 433; 175 L.T. 132; 62 T.L.R. 400; 90
    S.J. 516; [1946] 1 All E.R. 719 153
—— *v.* Rea [1947] K.B. 567; [1947] L.J.R. 1110; 63 T.L.R. 171; [1947] 1 All E.R.
    415 121

F. & H. Entertainments *v.* Leisure Enterprises; *sub nom.* F. & B. Entertainments *v.*
    Leisure Enterprises (1976) 120 S.J. 331; 240 E.G. 455 149
F.F.F. Estates *v.* London Borough of Hackney [1981] Q.B. 503; [1980] 3 W.L.R.
    909; 124 S.J. 593; [1981] 1 All E.R. 32; (1980) 4 P. & C.R. 54; [1981] J.P.L. 34,
    C.A. 266, 275
F.W.R. Leaseholders *v.* Childs (1962) 106 S.J. 307; 182 E.G. 621, C.A. 394
Facchini *v.* Bryson [1952] 1 T.L.R. 1386; 96 S.J. 395, C.A. 16, 17, 18, 21, 26
Factors (Sundries) Ltd. *v.* Miller [1952] 2 T.L.R. 194; 96 S.J. 546; [1952] 2 All E.R.
    630 .... 354, 355
Fairclough (T. M.) & Sons Ltd. *v.* Berliner [1931] 1 Ch. 60; 100 L.J.Ch. 29; 144
    L.T. 175; 74 S.J. 703; 47 T.L.R. 4 353
Fairview, Church Street, Bromyard, *Re*, [1974] 1 W.L.R. 579; [1974] 1 All E.R.
    1233; 27 P. & C.R. 348 512
Fairweather *v.* St. Marylebone Property Co. Ltd. [1963] A.C. 510; [1962] 2 W.L.R.
    1020; 106 S.J. 368; [1962] 2 All E.R. 288, H.L. 337
Falcon Pipes Ltd. *v.* Stanhope Gate Property Co. Ltd. (1967) 117 New L.J. 1345; 204
    E.G. 1243 684
Family Management *v.* Gray (1979) 253 E.G. 369, C.A. 286, 287, 370
Farimani *v.* Gates (1984) 128 S.J. 615; 271 E.G. 887; 81 L.S.Gaz. 1999,
    C.A. 224, 290, 352
Farlow *v.* Stevenson [1900] 1 Ch. 128; 69 L.J.Ch. 106; 81 L.T. 589; 48 W.R. 213; 15
    T.L.R. 249; 16 T.L.R. 57 116
Farrell *v.* Alexander [1977] A.C. 59; [1976] 3 W.L.R. 145; [1976] 2 All E.R. 721; 32
    P. & C.R. 292, H.L. 378, 428, 435
Farrow's Bank Ltd., *Re* [1921] 2 Ch. 164; 90 L.J.Ch. 465; 125 L.T. 699; 65 S.J. 679;
    37 T.L.R. 847 303
Fawke *v.* Viscount Chelsea [1980] Q.B. 441; [1979] 3 W.L.R. 508; 123 S.J. 387;
    [1979] 3 All E.R. 568; 38 P. & C.R. 504; 250 E.G. 855, C.A. 681, 713
Feather Supplies Ltd. *v.* Ingham [1971] 2 Q.B. 348; [1971] 3 W.L.R. 362; 115 S.J.
    508; [1971] 3 All E.R. 556; 22 P. & C.R. 919, C.A. 388, 404, 414, 470
Featherstone *v.* Staples (1985) 129 S.J. 66; (1985) 49 P. & C.R. 273; (1984) 273 E.G.
    193; (1985) 82 L.S.Gaz. 200 .... 348, 782
Felix *v.* Shiva [1982] Q.B. 82; [1982] 3 W.L.R. 444; 126 S.J. 413; [1982] 3 All E.R.
    263; 264 E.G. 1083, C.A. 197
Fernandes *v.* Parvardin (1982) 264 E.G. 49, C.A. 459
Fernandez *v.* Walding [1968] 2 Q.B. 606; [1968] 2 W.L.R. 583; (1967) 112 S.J. 95;
    [1968] 1 All E.R. 994; 19 P. & C.R. 314, C.A. 698
Feyereisel *v.* Turnidge [1952] 2 Q.B. 29; 96 S.J. 280; *sub nom.* Feyereisel *v.* Parry
    [1952] 1 T.L.R. 700; [1952] 1 All E.R. 728; [1952] C.P.L. 644, C.A. 392
Field *v.* Bankworth (1985) 129 S.J. 891; [1986] 1 All E.R. 362 305
Finbow *v.* Air Ministry [1963] 1 W.L.R. 697; 107 S.J. 535; [1963] 2 All E.R.
    647 .... 14, 18, 762
Finch *v.* Underwood (1876) 2 Ch.D. 310; 45 L.J.Ch. 522; 34 L.T. 779; 24 W.R. 657 ... 140
Finchbourne *v.* Rodrigues [1976] 3 All E.R. 581, C.A. 172, 219, 423
Firstcross Ltd. *v.* Teasdale (1983) 265 E.G. 305 .... 220, 423
Firstcross (formerly Welgelegen N.V.) *v.* East West (Export/Import) (1980) 41 P. &
    C.R. 145; 255 E.G. 355, C.A. 408, 470
Firth *v.* Halloran (1926) 38 C.L.R. 261 (Aus.) 153
Fletcher, *Re*, Reading *v.* Fletcher [1917] 1 Ch. 339; 86 L.J.Ch. 317; 116 L.T. 460; 61
    S.J. 267 341
—— *v.* Davies (1981) 257 E.G. 1149, C.A. 378

Flexman v. Corbett [1930] 1 Ch. 672; 99 L.J.Ch. 370; 143 L.T. 464 98
Florent v. Horez (1983) 48 P. & C.R. 166; 268 E.G. 807; (1984) 12 H.L.R. 1, C.A. 452
Floyd, *Re*, Floyd v. Lyons (J.) & Co. Ltd. [1897] 1 Ch. 633; 66 L.J.Ch. 350; 76 L.T.
      251; 45 W.R. 435 117
Flureau v. Thornhill (1776) 2 W.Bl. 1078; 96 E.R. 635 95
Foley v. Classique Coaches [1934] 2 K.B. 1; [1934] All E.R. 88; 103 L.J.K.B. 550;
      151 L.T. 242, C.A. 158
Ford v. Langford [1949] W.N. 87; [1949] L.J.R. 586; 65 T.L.R. 138; 93 S.J. 102;
      [1949] 1 All E.R. 483, C.A. 28
Foreman v. Beagley [1969] 1 W.L.R. 1387; 113 S.J. 704; [1969] 3 All E.R. 838; 21 P.
      & C.R. 8, C.A. 440
Forster v. Rowland (1861) 7 H. & N. 103; 30 L.J.Ex. 396; 7 Jur.(N.S.) 998 86
Foster v. Day (1968) 208 E.G. 495, C.A. 245, 252
—— v. Robinson [1951] 1 K.B. 149; 66 T.L.R. (Pt. 2) 120; 94 S.J. 474; [1950] 2 All
      E.R. 342, C.A. 17, 339
Fougler v. Arding [1902] 2 K.B. 700; 70 L.J.K.B. 580; 71 L.J.K.B. 499; 84 L.T. 488;
      49 W.R. 442; 50 W.R. 417; 18 T.L.R. 422 .... 114, 115, 116
Fousset v. 27, Welbeck Street (1973) 25 P. & C.R. 277 179
Fowell v. Radford (1969) 114 S.J. 34; (1969) 21 P. & C.R. 99, C.A. 512
Fox v. Dalby (1874) L.R. 10 C.P. 285 28
—— v. Jolly [1916] 1 A.C. 1; 85 L.J.K.B. 1927; 113 L.T. 1025; 59 S.J. 665; 31 T.L.R.
      579 352
Francis v. Cowcliffe (1976) 33 P. & C.R. 368; 239 E.G. 977, D.C. 253
Frankland v. Capstick [1959] 1 W.L.R. 205; 103 S.J. 155; [1959] 1 All E.R. 209,
      C.A. 863
Freehold & Leasehold Shop Properties v. Friends Provident Life Office (1984)
      271 E.G. 451, C.A. 167
Freeman v. Evans [1922] 1 Ch. 36; 91 L.J.Ch. 195; 125 L.T. 195 350
—— v. Wansbeck D.C. (1983) 127 S.J. 550; [1984] 2 All E.R. 746; [1984] L.G.R.
      131; (1983) 80 L.S.Gaz. 2444, C.A. 566
French v. Elliott [1960] 1 W.L.R. 40; 104 S.J. 52; [1959] 3 All E.R. 866 786
—— v. Macale (1842) 2 Dr. & War. 269; 4 Ir.Eq.R. 568; 59 R.R. 675 170
Frigbourg & Treyer v. Northdale Investments (1982) 44 P. & C.R. 284; 126 S.J. 609;
      263 E.G. 660; 79 L.S.Gaz. 1412 .... 693, 710, 749
Frish Ltd. v. Barclays Bank Ltd. [1955] 2 Q.B. 541; [1955] 3 W.L.R. 439; 99 S.J. 561;
      [1955] 3 All E.R. 185, C.A. 644
Fuggle v. Gasden [1948] 2 Q.B. 236; [1948] L.J.R. 1664; 64 T.L.R. 364; 92 S.J. 391;
      [1948] 2 All E.R. 160, C.A. 456
Furness v. Bond (1888) 4 T.L.R. 457 40

G.M.S. Syndicate Ltd. v. Elliott (Gary) Ltd. [1982] Ch. 1; [1981] 2 W.L.R. 478;
      (1980) 124 S.J. 776; [1981] 1 All E.R. 619; (1980) 41 P. & C.R. 124; 258 E.G.
      25 .... 292, 354, 676
G.R.E.A. Real Property Investments v. Williams (1979) 250 E.G. 651 .... 188, 189
Gable Construction Co. Ltd. v. Inland Revenue Comrs. [1970] T.R. 227; 49 A.T.C.
      244; *affirming* [1968] 1 W.L.R. 1426; 112 S.J. 6673; [1968] 2 All E.R.
      968 .... 177, 340
Gaidowski v. Gonville and Caius College, Cambridge [1975] 1 W.L.R. 1066; 119 S.J
      491; [1975] 2 All E.R. 952; 30 P. & E.R. 120, C.A. 507
Gallacher Estates Ltd. v. Walker (1973) 28 P. & C.R. 113, C.A. 515
Gammans v. Ekins [1950] 2 K.B. 328; 66 T.L.R. (Pt. 1) 1139; 94 S.J. 435; [1950] 2 All
      E.R. 140, C.A. 441
Gammon v. Vernon (1687) 2 Lev. 231 T.Jon. 104 320
Gandy v. Jubber (1864–65) 5 B. & S. 78, 485; 9 B. & S. 15; 33 L.J.Q.B. 151; 34
      L.J.Ex. 11; 10 Jur.(N.S.) 652 368
Gardiner v. Deptford Liberal Club [1924] E.G.D. 55 381

Gardner v. Blaxill [1960] 1 W.L.R. 752; 104 S.J. 585; [1960] 2 All E.R. 457 140
—— v. Ingram (1889) 61 L.T. 729 343
—— v. London, Chatham and Dover Rly. Co. (No. 1) Drawbridge v. Same;
    Gardner v. Same (No. 2); Imperial Mercantile Credit Assoc. v. Same (1867)
    L.R. 2 Ch.App. 201; 36 L.J.Ch. 323; 15 L.T. 552; 31 J.P. 87; 15 W.R. 325,
    L.JJ. 258
Gavaghan v. Edwards [1961] 2 Q.B. 220; [1961] 2 W.L.R. 948; 105 S.J. 405; [1961] 2
    All E.R. 477, C.A. 86
Gentle v. Faulkner [1900] 2 Q.B. 267; 69 L.J.K.B. 777; 82 L.T. 708; 16 T.L.R. 397 ... 302
German Securities v. Spiegal (1978) 123 S.J. 164; (1979) 37 P. & C.R. 204; (1978) 250
    E.G. 449, C.A. 685
Gibbs and Houlder Bros. & Co. Ltd.'s Lease, Re [1925] Ch. 575; 94 L.J.Ch. 312; 133
    L.T. 322; 41 T.L.R. 487; 69 S.J. 541, C.A. 310
Gibson v. Hammersmith and City Railway Co. (1863) 32 L.J.Ch. 337 735
—— v. Hammersmith Ry. (1863) 2 Dr. & Sm. 603; 32 L.J.Ch. 337; 9 Jur.(N.S.) 221;
    8 L.T. 43; 11 W.R. 229 59
—— v. Kirk (1841) 1 Q.B. 850; 10 L.J.Q.B. 297; 1 G. & D. 252; 6 Jur. 99 193
—— v. Manchester City Council [1979] 1 W.L.R. 294; 123 S.J. 201; [1979] 1 All
    E.R. 972; 77 L.G.R. 405; [1979] J.P.L. 532, H.L. 574
Gidlaw-Jackson v. Middlegate Properties [1974] 1 Q.B. 361; [1974] 2 W.L.R. 116;
    (1973) 117 S.J. 854; [1974] 1 All E.R. 830; (1973) 27 P. & C.R. 378,
    C.A. 167, 511
Giles v. Hooper (1690) Carth. 135 .... 151, 164
Giles (C. H.) & Co. Ltd. v. Morris [1972] 1 W.L.R. 307; (1971) 116 S.J. 176; [1972] 1
    All E.R. 960 96
Gladstone v. Bower [1960] 2 Q.B. 384; [1960] 3 W.L.R. 575; 104 S.J. 763; [1960] 3
    All E.R. 353; 58 L.G.R. 313, C.A.; *affirming* [1960] 1 Q.B. 70; [1959] 3
    W.L.R. 815; 103 S.J. 835; [1959] 3 All E.R. 475; 58 L.G.R. 75 ...... 649, 766, 793
Glasgow Corp. v. Johnstone [1965] A.C. 609; [1965] 2 W.L.R. 657; 129 J.P. 250; 109
    S.J. 196; [1965] 1 All E.R. 730; 63 L.G.R. 171; [1965] R.V.R. 111; 11 R.R.C.
    127; [1965] R.A. 49 28
Glass v. Kencakes Ltd.; West Layton v. Dean [1966] 1 Q.B. 611; [1965] 2 W.L.R.
    363; 109 S.J. 155; [1964] 3 All E.R. 807 .... 353, 354
Gledhow Autoparts Ltd. v. Delaney [1965] 1 W.L.R. 1366; 109 S.J. 571; [1965] 3 All
    E.R. 288, C.A. 746
Glendyne (Lord) v. Rapley [1978] 1 W.L.R. 601; 122 S.J. 247; [1978] 2 All E.R. 110;
    246 E.G. 573, C.A. 483
Glenwood Lumber Co. v. Phillips [1904] A.C. 405; 73 L.J.P.C. 62; 90 L.T. 741; 20
    T.L.R. 531 (P.C.) 16, 653
Glessing v. Green [1975] 1 W.L.R. 863; 119 S.J. 369; [1975] 2 All E.R. 696; 29 P. &
    C.R. 461, C.A. 89
Gloucester (Bishop of) v. Cunnington [1943] 1 K.B. 101 393
Gluchowska v. Tottenham B.C. [1954] 1 Q.B. 439; [1954] 2 W.L.R. 302; 118 J.P.
    175; 98 S.J. 129; [1954] 1 All E.R. 408; 52 L.G.R. 183, D.C. 414, 477
Godbold v. Martin's Newsagents Ltd. (1983) 268 E.G. 1202 669
Gofor Investments Ltd. v. Roberts (1975) 119 S.J. 320; 29 P. & C.R. 366,
    C.A. 404, 408, 409
Gold v. Brighton Corp. [1956] 1 W.L.R. 1291; 100 S.J. 749; [1956] 3 All E.R. 442,
    C.A. 715
Golden Lion Hotel (Hunstanton) Ltd. v. Carter [1965] 1 W.L.R. 1189; 109 S.J. 648;
    [1965] 3 All E.R. 506 341
Goldfoot v. Welch [1914] 1 Ch. 213; 83 L.J.Ch. 360; 109 L.T. 820 103
Goldsack v. Shore [1950] 1 K.B. 708; 66 T.L.R. (Pt. 1) 636; 94 S.J. 192; [1950] 1 All
    E.R. 276, C.A. 761
Gonin, decd., Re; Gonin v. Garmeson [1979] Ch. 16; [1977] 3 W.L.R. 379; (1977)
    121 S.J. 558; [1977] 2 All E.R. 720 87

Goodman v. Dolphin Square Trust Ltd. (1979) 38 P. & C.R. 257, C.A. ... 583, 585, 591
Goodrich v. Paisner [1957] A.C. 65; [1956] 2 W.L.R. 1053; 100 S.J. 341; [1956] 2 All
    E.R. 176, H.L.; *reversing sub nom.* Paisner v. Goodrich [1955] 2 Q.B. 353;
    [1955] 2 W.L.R. 1071; 99 S.J. 353; [1955] 2 All E.R. 330, C.A. 383, 384
Goodright d. Hall v. Richardson (1789) 3 Term Rep. 462 110
Gordon v. Selico (1985) 129 S.J. 347; 275 E.G. 841; 82 L.S.Gaz. 2087 .... 222, 227
Gorham (Contractors) Ltd. v. Field [1952] C.P.L. 266; 159 E.G. 342, C.A. 18, 25
Gorleston Golf Club Ltd. v. Links Estate (Gorleston) (1959) 109 L.J. 140, Cty. Ct. .. 714
Gorton v. Gregory (1862) 3 B. & S. 90; 31 L.J.Q.B. 302; 6 L.T. 656; 10 W.R. 713 319
Goss v. Nugent (Lord) (1833) 5 B. & Ad. 58; 2 N. & M. 28; L.J.K.B. 127; 39 R.R.
    392 84
Grafton Street, 14, WI, *Re*; De Havilland v. Centrovincial Estates (Mayfair) [1971]
    Ch. 935; [1971] 2 W.L.R. 159 749
Graham v. Peat (1801) 1 EAST 244; 6 R.R. 268 370
—— v. Tate (1813) 1 M. & S. 609; [1803–13] All E.R.Rep.378 117
Granada Theatres v. Freehold Investment (Leytonstone) Ltd. [1959] Ch. 592; [1959]
    1 W.L.R. 570; 103 S.J. 392; [1959] 2 All E.R. 176, C.A.; *varying* [1958] 1
    W.L.R. 845; 102 S.J. 563; [1958] 2 All E.R. 551 .... 218, 237, 252, 285, 294
Grand Junction International Co. v. Bates [1954] 2 Q.B. 160; [1954] 3 W.L.R. 45; 98
    S.J. 405; [1954] 2 All E.R. 385 .... 15, 304, 354
Grant v. Dawkins [1973] 1 W.L.R. 1406; 117 S.J. 665; [1973] 3 All E.R. 897; 27 P. &
    C.R. 158 97
—— v. Gresham (1979) 252 E.G. 55, C.A. 650
Grant & Partners v. Lines and Hallyar (1952) 102 L.J. 416; 160 E.G. 150, Cty. Ct. 381
Gray v. Holmes [1949] T.R. 71; 41 R. & I.T. 117 (1949) 30 T.C. 467 28
Graystone Property Investments v. Margulies (1984) 47 P. & C.R. 472; 296 E.G.
    538, C.A. 103
Grea Real Property Investments v. Williams (1979) 250 E.G. 651 669
Greasley v. Cooke [1980] 1 W.L.R. 1306; 124 S.J. 629; [1980] 3 All E.R. 710,
    C.A. 12
Great Northern Ry. v. Arnold (1916) 33 T.L.R. 114 40
Great Western Ry. v. Bishop (1872) L.R. 7 Q.B. 550; 41 L.J.M.C. 120; 26 L.T. 905;
    37 J.P. 5 *sub nom.* R. v. Glamorgan JJ., Great Western Ry. Co. v. Bishop, 20
    W.R. 969 260
—— v. Smith (1876) 2 Ch.D. 235 336
Greater London Council v. Connolly [1970] 2 Q.B 100; [1970] 2 W.L.R. 658; 114 S.J.
    108; [1970] 1 All E.R. 870, C.A. 158, 558
—— v. Tower Hamlets London Borough (1984) 15 H.L.R. 54, D.C.; (1983) 15
    H.L.R. 57 261
Greater London Properties Ltd.'s Lease, *Re*, Taylor Bros. (Grocers) Ltd. v. Covent
    Garden Properties Co. Ltd. [1959] 1 W.L.R. 503; 103 S.J. 351; [1959] 1 All
    E.R. 728 .... 306, 310
Green v. Ashco Horticulturist Ltd. [1966] 1 W.L.R. 889; 110 S.J. 271; [1966] 2 All
    E.R. 232 104
—— v. Bowes-Lyon [1960] 1 W.L.R. 176; 104 S.J. 189; [1960] 1 All E.R. 301 688
—— v. Eales (1841) 2 Q.B. 225; 11 L.J.K.B. 63; 6 Jur. 436; 1 G. & D. 468; 57 R.R.
    660 .... 237, 251
Greenberg v. Grimsby Corp. (1961) 12 P. & C.R. 212, Lands Tribunal 734
Greene v. Church Commissioners for England [1974] Ch. 467; [1974] 3 W.L.R. 349;
    118 S.J. 700; [1974] 3 All E.R. 609; 29 P. & C.R. 285, C.A. 308, 338
Greenhaven Securities v. Compton (1985) 275 E.G. 628 181
Greenwich L.B.C. v. McGrady (1983) 46 P. & C.R. 233; (1983) 81 L.G.R. 288;
    (1983) 267 E.G. 515, C.A. 348, 529
Greenwoods Tyre Services Ltd. v. Manchester Corp. (1971) 23 P. & C.R. 246, Lands
    Tribunal 727
Gregory v. Mighell (1811) 18 Ves. 328; 11 R.R. 207 282

Gregson v. Lord (Cyril) Ltd. [1963] 1 W.L.R. 41; 106 S.J. 899; [1962] 3 All E.R. 907; [1962] R.V.R. 730, C.A. 705
Gretton v. Mees (1878) 7 Ch.D. 839; 38 L.T. 506; 26 W.R. 607 193
Grey v. Friar (1854) 4 H.L.Cas. 565; 2 C.L.R. 434; 23 L.T.(o.s.) 334; 18 Jur. 1036; 10 E.R. 583, H.L. 139
Grice v. Dudley Corp. [1958] Ch. 329; [1957] 3 W.L.R. 314; 121 J.P. 466; 101 S.J. 591; [1957] 2 All E.R. 673; 55 L.G.R. 493; 9 P. & C.R. 58 .... 720, 721
Griffith v. Hodges (1824) 1 C. &. P. 419 174
—— v. Pelton [1958] Ch. 205; [1957] 3 W.L.R. 522; 101 S.J. 663; [1957] 3 All E.R. 75, C.A. 142, 318
Griffiths v. English (1982) 261 E.G. 257; [1982] H.L.R. 116, C.A. 396
—— v. Pearman [1983] B.T.C. 68 207
—— v. Williams (1977) 248 E.G. 947, C.A. 12
Grigsby v. Melville [1974] 1 W.L.R. 80; 117 S.J. 632; [1973] 3 All E.R. 455; 26 P. & C.R. 182, C.A. 103
Grist v. Bailey [1967] Ch. 532; [1966] 3 W.L.R. 618; 110 S.J. 791; [1966] 2 All E.R. 875 .... 149, 407
Grosvenor (Mayfair) Estates v. Amberton (1983) 265 E.G. 693 387
Grosvenor Hotel Co. v. Hamilton [1894] 2 Q.B. 836; 63 L.J.Q.B. 661; 71 L.T. 362; 42 W.R. 626 .... 129, 131, 132
Grosvenor Settled Estates, Re, Westminster (Duke of) v. McKenna [1932] 1 Ch. 232; 101 L.J.Ch. 145; 146 L.T. 402 336
Groveside Properties v. Westminster Medical School (1984) 47 P. & C.R. 507; (1983) 267 E.G. 593, C.A. 67, 398, 647
Grymes v. Boweren (1830) 6 Bing. 437; 8 L.J.(o.s.)C.P. 140; 4 Moo. & P. 143; 31 R.R. 460 59
Guardian Assurance Co. v. Gants Hill Holdings (1983) 267 E.G. 678 ...... 127, 187, 658
Gudgen v. Besset (1856) 6 E. & B. 986; 26 L.J.Q.B. 36; 3 Jur.(N.s.) 212 193
Gulliver v. Catt [1952] 2 Q.B. 308; [1952] 1 T.L.R. 956; 96 S.J. 245; [1952] 1 All E.R. 929; 50 L.G.R 342, C.A. 808
Guppys (Bridport) Ltd. v. Brookling; Same v. James (1984) 14 H.L.R. 1; (1984) 269 E.G. 846, 942, C.A. 29, 133, 610
—— v. Carpenter [1973] R.V.R. 573 .... 426, 557
—— v. Sandoe (1975) 30 P. & C.R. 69, D.C. 422
Guppys Properties v. Knott (No. 3) (1981) 258 E.G. 1083, D.C. 423
Gutteridge v. Munyard (1834) 7 C. & P. 129; 1 Moo. & R. 334 .... 225, 227
Guys 'n' Dolls Ltd. v. Sade Bros. Catering Ltd. (1984) 269 E.G. 129, C.A. 189
Gwinnell v. Eamer (1875) L.R. 10 C.P. 658; 32 L.T. 835 367
Gwynne v. Manistone (1828) 3 C. & P. 302 40

H.H. Realisations Ltd., Re (1975) 119 S.J. 642; 31 P. & C.R. 249 205
Habib Bank Ltd. v. Habib Bank A.G. Zurich [1981] 1 W.L.R. 1265; (1980) 125 S.J. 512; [1981] 1 All E.R. 650; [1982] R.P.C. 19, C.A. 12
Hagee (London) Ltd. v. Erikson (A.B.) & Larson [1976] Q.B. 209; [1975] 3 W.L.R. 272; 119 S.J. 354; [1975] 3 All E.R. 234; 29 P. & C.R. 512, C.A. 16, 44, 45, 641, 656
Haines v. Herbert [1963] 1 W.L.R. 1401; 107 S.J. 850; [1963] 3 All E.R. 715, C.A. 499
Haldane v. Johnson (1853) 8 Ex. 689; 22 L.J.Ex. 264; 17 Jur. 937 160
Hale, ex p., Re Binns (1875) 1 Ch.D. 285; 45 L.J.Bk. 21; 33 L.T. 706; 24 W.R. 300 203
Hall v. Ball (1841) 3 Man. & G. 242; 10 L.J.C.P. 285; 3 Scott N.R. 577 88
—— v. Burgess (1826) 5 B. & C. 332; 8 D. & R. 67; 4 L.J.(o.s.)K.B. 172 174
—— v. Manchester Corp. (1915) L.J. 84 Ch. 732; 113 L.T. 465; 79 J.P. 385; 31 T.L.R. 416; 13 L.G.R. 1105, H.L. 242
Halliard Property Co. Ltd. v. Nicholas Clarke Investments Ltd. (1984) 269 E.G. 1257 229

Halliard Property Co. Ltd. *v.* Segal (Jack) Ltd. [1978] 1 W.L.R. 377; (1977) 122 S.J. 180; [1978] 1 All E.R. 1219; (1977) 245 E.G. 230; (1978) 36 P. & C.R. 134 .... 335, 353

Hallinan (Lady) *v.* Jones and Jones [1985] C.L.Y. 38 803

Hamilton *v.* Martell Securities Ltd. [1984] Ch. 266; [1984] 2 W.L.R. 699; 128 S.J. 281; [1984] 1 All E.R. 665; 48 P. & C.R. 69; 81 L.S.Gaz. 1211 .... 111, 284, 285, 352

Hammersmith & Fulham L.B. *v.* Harrison [1981] 1 W.L.R. 650; 79 L.G.R. 634; (1982) 44 P. & C.B. 131 623

Hammond *v.* Farrow [1904] 2 K.B. 332; 73 L.J.K.B. 726; 91 L.T. 77; 68 J.P. 352; 20 T.L.R. 497; 2 L.G.R. 817; 1 Konst.Rat.App. 146 .... 113, 164

Hampshire *v.* Wickens (1878) 7 Ch.D. 555; 47 L.J.Ch. 243; 38 L.T. 408; 26 W.R. 491 .... 84, 98, 302

Hampstead and Suburban Properties Ltd. *v.* Diomedons [1969] 1 Ch. 248; [1968] 3 W.L.R. 990; 112 S.J. 656; [1968] 3 All E.R. 545; 19 P. & C.R. 880 .... 125, 126, 658

Hampstead Way Investments *v.* Lewis Weare [1985] 1 W.L.R. 164; 129 S.J. 85; [1985] 1 All E.R. 564; (1985) 274 E.G. 281; 17 H.L.R. 269; 135 New L.J. 127; 82 L.S.Gaz. 847 387

Hanbury *v.* Jenkins [1901] 2 Ch. 401; 70 L.J.Ch. 730; 65 J.P. 631; 49 W.R. 615; 17 T.L.R. 539 51

Hanbury's Settled Estates *v.* Cundy (1887) 58 L.T. 155 170

Hancock & Willis *v.* G.M.S. Syndicate Ltd. (1983) 265 E.G. 473, C.A. 645, 693

Hand *v.* Blow [1901] 2 Ch. 721; 70 L.J.Ch. 687; 85 L.T. 156 W.R. 3 319

Hankey *v.* Clavering [1942] 2 K.B. 326; 111 L.J.K.B. 711; 167 L.T. 193; [1942] 2 All E.R. 311 .... 138, 348

Harrison *v.* Malex (1886) 3 T.L.R. 58 239

Hanson *v.* Church Commissioners for England; R. *v.* London Rent Assessment Committee, *ex p.* Hanson [1978] Q.B. 823; [1977] 2 W.L.R. 848; [1977] 3 All E.R. 404; (1976) 34 P. & C.R. 158 422

—— *v.* Newman [1934] Ch. 298; 103 L.J.Ch. 124; 150 L.T. 345; 50 T.L.R. 191 286

Harbutt's "Plasticine" Ltd. *v.* Wayne Tank & Pump Co. Ltd. [1970] 1 Q.B. 447; [1970] 2 W.L.R. 198; 114 S.J. 29; [1970] 1 All E.R. 225; [1970] 1 Lloyd's Rep. 15, C.A. 251

Harding *v.* Marshall (1983) 267 E.G. 161, C.A. 786

Hardwick *v.* Johnson [1978] 1 W.L.R. 683; (1977) 122 S.J. 162; [1978] 2 All E.R. 935, C.A. 11

Hardy *v.* Fothergill (1888) 13 App.Cas. 351; 58 L.J.Q.B. 44; 59 L.T. 273; 37 W.R. 177; *affirming sub nom.* Morgan *v.* Hardy (1886) 17 Q.B.D. 770; 35 W.R. 254; 56 L.J.Q.B. 363 203

Hare *v.* Burges (1857) 4 K. & J. 45; 27 L.J.Ch. 86 .... 46, 47

—— *v.* Horton (1833) 5 B. & Ad. 715; 2 N. & M. 428; 3 L.J.K.B. 41; 39 R.R. 633 55

Harewood Hotels Ltd. *v.* Harris [1958] 1 W.L.R. 108; 102 S.J. 67; [1958] 1 All E.R. 104, C.A. 711, 713

Harker *v.* Birkbeck (1764) 3 Burr. 1556 370

Harley *v.* King (1835) 2 C.M. & R. 18; 41 R.R. 674; 5 Tyr. 692; 1 Gale 100; 4 L.J.Ex. 144 295

Harmer *v.* Jumbil (Nigeria) Tin Areas Ltd. [1921] 1 Ch. 140; 124 L.T. 418; 65 S.J. 93; 37 T.L.R. 91 132

Harmond Properties Ltd. *v.* Gajdzis [1968] 1 W.L.R. 1858; 112 S.J. 762; [1968] 3 All E.R. 263; 19 P. & C.R. 718, C.A. 349

Harmsworth Pension Fund Trustees *v.* Charrington's Industrial Holdings (1985) 49 P. & C.R. 297; 274 E.G. 588 186

Harnett *v.* Maitland (1847) 16 M. & W. 257; 73 R.R. 490; 4 D. & L. 545; 16 L.J.Ex. 134 281

Harrington *v.* Croydon Corpn. [1968] 1 Q.B. 856; [1968] 2 W.L.R. 67; 111 S.J.
740; [1967] 3 All E.R. 929; 65 L.G.R. 95, C.A. 265
Harris *v.* Birkenhead Corpn. [1976] 1 W.L.R. 279; (1975) 120 S.J. 200; [1976] 1 All
E.R. 341 249
—— *v.* James (1876) 45 L.J.Q.B. 545; 35 L.T. 240 368
—— *v.* Plentex (1980) 40 P. & C.R. 483; 248 E.G. 447 512
—— *v.* Swick Securities [1969] 1 W.L.R. 1604; 113 S.J. 607; [1969] 3 All E.R. 1131;
20 P. & C.R. 965, C.A. 506, 546
Harrison *v.* Hammersmith and Fulham London Borough; Haringay London
Borough *v.* Mosner; Watson *v.* Hackney London Borough [1981] 1 W.L.R.
650; 79 L.G.R. 634; (1982) 44 P. & C.R. 131; *sub nom.* Hammersmith and
Fulham London Borough [1981] 2 All E.R. 588, C.A. 408, 545
—— *v.* Wells [1967] 1 Q.B. 263; [1966] 3 W.L.R. 686; 110 S.J. 619; [1966] 3 All E.R.
524; 119 E.G. 717, C.A. 287
Harrison-Broadley *v.* Smith [1964] 1 W.L.R. 456; 108 S.J. 136; [1964] 1 All E.R. 867,
C.A. 761
Harrogate B.C. *v.* Simpson (1984) 17 H.L.R. 205; (1985) 25 R.V.R. 10,
C.A. 442, 580
Harrowby (Earl) *v.* Snelson [1951] W.N. 11; 95 S.J. 108; [1951] 1 All E.R. 140 349
Hart *v.* Emelkirk; Howroyd *v.* Emelkirk [1983] 1 W.L.R. 1289; (1983) 127 S.J. 156;
[1983] 3 All E.R. 15; (1983) 267 E.G. 946 258
—— *v.* Rogers [1916] 1 K.B. 646; 85 L.J.K.B. 273; 114 L.T. 329; 32 T.L.R. 150 255
—— *v.* Windsor (1844) 12 M. & W. 68; 13 L.J.Ex. 129; 8 Jur. 150 137
Harte *v.* Frampton [1948] 1 K.B. 73; [1948] L.J.R. 1125; 63 T.L.R. 554; 91 S.J. 625;
[1947] 2 All E.R. 604, C.A. 457
Hartley *v.* Minister of Housing and Local Government [1970] 1 Q.B. 413; [1970] 2
W.L.R. 1; 113 S.J. 900; [1969] 3 All E.R. 1658; 21 P. & C.R. 1,
C.A.;*affirming* [1969] 2 Q.B 46; [1969] 2 W.L.R. 137; 133 J.P. 147; 113 S.J.
35; [1969] 1 All E.R. 309; 20 P. & C.R. 166; 67 L.G.R. 332; [1968] C.L.Y.
3810, D.C. 658
Harvard *v.* Shears (1967) 111 S.J. 683; *sub nom.* Havard *v.* Shears 203 E.G. 27,
C.A. 455
Harvey *v.* Crawley Development Corp. [1957] 1 Q.B. 485; [1957] 2 W.L.R. 332; 121
J.P. 166; 101 S.J. 189; [1957] 1 All E.R. 504; 8 P. & C.R. 141; 55 L.G.R. 104,
C.A. 730, 733
—— *v.* Pratt [1965] 1 W.L.R. 1025; 109 S.J. 474; [1965] 2 All E.R. 786, C.A. 40, 82
—— *v.* Stagg (1972) 247 E.G. 463, C.A. 195
Harvey Textiles Ltd. *v.* Hillel (1978) 249 E.G. 1063 703
Haskell *v.* Marlow [1928] 2 K.B. 45; 97 L.J.K.B. 311; 138 L.T. 921; 44 T.L.R. 171 225
Haskins *v.* Lewis [1931] 2 K.B. 1; 100 L.J.K.B. 180; 144 L.T. 378; 47 T.L.R. 195; 95
J.P. 57; 29 L.G.R. 199 409
Hawes *v.* Evenden [1953] 1 W.L.R. 1169; 97 S.J. 587; [1953] 2 All E.R. 737,
C.A. 441
Hawkins *v.* Heath Cole [1976] C.L.Y. 371, C.Ct. 362
—— *v.* Rutt (1793) Peake 248 [186] 161
—— *v.* Price [1947] Ch. 645; [1947] L.J.R. 887; 177 L.T. 108; 91 S.J. 263; [1947] 1
All E.R. 689 .... 83, 84
——, *Re* [1972] Ch. 714; [1972] 3 W.L.R. 265; 116 S.J. 586; [1972] 3 All E.R. 386 159
Hayman *v.* Rowlands [1957] 1 W.L.R. 317; 101 S.J. 170; [1957] 1 All E.R. 321,
C.A. 451
Haytor Granite Co., *Re* (1865) L.R. 1 Ch. 77; 35 L.J.Ch. 154; 12 Jur.(N.S.) 1; 12 L.T.
515; 14 W.R. 186 203
Hayward *v.* Marshall [1952] 2 Q.B. 89; [1952] 1 T.L.R. 779; 96 S.J. 196; [1952] 1 All
E.R. 663, C.A. 385
Haywood *v.* Brunswick Building Society (1881) 8 Q.B.D. 403; 51 L.J.Q.B. 73; 45
L.T. 699; 30 W.R. 299 75

Heap v. Ind, Coope & Allsopp [1940] 2 K.B. 476; 109 L.J.K.B. 724; 163 L.T. 169; 56
  T.L.R. 948; 84 S.J. 536; [1940] 3 All E.R. 634 368
Heath v. Drown [1973] A.C. 498; [1972] 2 W.L.R. 1306; 116 S.J. 414; [1972] 2 All
  E.R. 561; (1971) 23 P. & C.R. 351, H.L. 699, 700
Heathview Tenants Co-operative Ltd., Re, (1980) 258 E.G. 644 423
Hedley Byrne & Co. Ltd. v. Heller & Partners Ltd. [1964] A.C. 465; [1963] 3 W.L.R.
  101; 107 S.J. 464; [1963] 2 All E.R. 575; [1963] 1 Lloyd's Rep. 485, H.L.;
  affirming [1962] 1 Q.B. 396; [1961] 3 W.L.R. 1225; 105 S.J. 910; [1961] 3 All
  E.R. 891, C.A.; *affirming The Times*, December 21, 1960 149
Helby v. Rafferty [1979] 1 W.L.R. 13; (1978) 122 S.J. 418; [1978] 3 All E.R. 1016;
  (1978) 8 Fam.Law. 207; (1978) 247 E.G. 729; (1978) 37 P. & C.R. 376, C.A. ... 441
Hellawell v. Eastwood (1851) 6 Ex. 295; 20 L.J.Ex. 154; 86 R.R. 296 59
Hellier v. Casbard (1665) 1 Lev. 127; 1 Sid. 266; 1 Keb. 679, 791 151
Helman v. Horsham & Worthing Assessment Committee [1949] 2 K.B. 335; [1949]
  L.J.R. 1082; 65 T.L.R. 291; 113 J.P. 236; [1949] 1 All E.R. 776; 42 R. & I.T.
  148, C.A. 15, 28
Hemns v. Wheeler [1948] 2 K.B. 61; [1948] L.J.R. 1024; 64 T.L.R. 236; 92 S.J. 194 ... 406
Henderson v. Arthur [1907] 1 K.B. 10; 76 L.J.K.B. 22; 95 L.T. 772 157
Hennessey's Agreement, Re; Hillman v. Davison [1975] 2 W.L.R. 159; (1974) 118
  S.J. 755; [1975] 1 All E.R. 60; (1974) 29 P. & C.R. 135 498
Henstead's Case (1594) 5 Co.Rep. 10a 43
Herbert v. Byrne [1964] 1 W.L.R. 519, 108 S.J. 196; [1964] 1 All E.R. 882,
  C.A. 498, 499
Heslop v. Burns [1974] 1 W.L.R. 1241; 118 S.J. 581; [1974] 3 All E.R. 406,
  C.A. 17, 25, 26, 44, 45, 158
Hess v. Gitliss [1951] E.G.D. 154, C.A., *affirming* Cty. Ct. 18
Hewitt v. Rowlands (1924) 93 L.J.K.B. 729, 1080; 131 L.T. 757 .... 250, 252
Heywood v. Wellers (A Firm) [1976] Q.B. 446; [1976] 2 W.L.R. 101; (1975) 120 S.J.
  9; [1976] 1 All E.R. 300; [1976] 2 Lloyd's Rep. 88, C.A. 252
Hibernian Property Co. v. Liverpool Corpn. [1973] 1 W.L.R. 751; 117 S.J. 466;
  [1973] 2 All E.R. 1117; 25 P. & C.R. 417; 71 L.G.R. 395 288
Hickman v. Trustees of the Phillimore Kensington Estate (1985) 50 P. & C.R. 476;
  [1985] J.P.L. 565; 274 E.G. 1261, Lands Tribunal 516
Hickmott v. Dorset C.C. (1977) 35 P. & C.R. 195; [1977] J.P.L. 715; 243 E.G. 671,
  C.A. 733
Hickson and Welch v. Cann (Note) (1977) 40 P. & C.R. 218, C.A. 757, 759
High Road (No. 88) Kilburn, Re, [1959] 1 W.L.R. 279; 103 S.J. 221; *sub nom.* High
  Road (No. 88), Kilburn, Re, Meakers v. D.A.W. Consolidated Properties
  [1959] 1 All E.R. 527 .... 679, 708, 715
Highway Properties Ltd. v. Kelley, Douglas & Co. Ltd. (1971) 17 D.L.R. (3d) 626,
  British Columbia, C.A. 153
Hill v. Barclay (1810–11) 16 Ves. 402, 18 Ves. 56; 11 R.R. 147 293
—— v. Harris [1965] 2 Q.B. 601; [1965] 2 W.L.R. 1331; 109 S.J. 333; [1965] 2 All
  E.R. 358, C.A. 77, 658
—— v. Hill [1947] Ch. 231; 176 L.T. 216; 91 S.J. 55; [1947] 1 All E.R. 54,
  C.A. 85, 143
—— v. Rochard [1983] 1 W.L.R. 478; (1983) 127 S.J. 189; [1983] 2 All E.R. 21; 46 P.
  & C.R. 194; 266 E.G. 628, C.A. 450
Hillbank Properties Ltd. v. Hackney L.B.C. [1978] Q.B. 998; [1978] 3 W.L.R. 260;
  (1978) 122 S.J. 401; [1978] 3 All E.R. 343; 37 P. & C.R. 218; 76 L.G.R. 677;
  247 E.G. 807; [1978] J.P.L. 615, C.A. 265, 266, 270, 271
Hiller v. United Dairies [1934] 1 K.B. 57; 103 L.J.K.B. 5; 150 L.T. 74; 50 T.L.R. 20 .. 408
Hillil Property & Investment Co. v. Naraine Pharmacy (1979) 123 S.J. 437; 39 P. &
  C.R. 67; 252 E.G. 1013, C.A. 646, 647
Hillingdon L.B.C. v. Cutler [1968] 1 Q.B. 124; [1967] 3 W.L.R. 246; 65 L.G.R. 535;
  sub nom. Hillingdon Corp. v. Cutler (1967) 111 S.J. 275; *sub nom.* London
  Borough of Hillingdon v. Cutler 131 J.P. 361; [1967] 2 All E.R. 361, C.A. 267

Hills (Patents) Ltd. *v.* Board of Governors of University College Hospital [1956]
    1 Q.B. 90; [1955] 3 W.L.R. 523; 99 S.J. 760; [1955] 3 All E.R. 365,
    C.A. 647, 701
Hilton *v.* Goodhind (1827) 2 C. & P. 591 174
—— *v.* Sutton Steam Laundry [1946] K.B. 65; 115 L.J.K.B. 33; 174 L.T. 31, C.A.;
    [1945] 2 All E.R. 425 326
Hirst *v.* Sargant (1967) 65 L.G.R. 127; 111 S.J. 54; 12 R.R.C. 234; [1966] C.L.Y.
    1255; [1966] R.A. 605, D.C. 28
Hoby *v.* Roebuck & Palmer (1816) 7 Taunt. 157; 2 Marsh. 433; 17 R.R. 477 177
Hodgson *v.* Armstrong [1967] 2 Q.B. 299; [1967] 2 W.L.R. 311; 110 S.J. 907; [1967] 1
    All E.R. 307; [1966] C.L.Y. 6839, C.A. 691
Hoffman *v.* Fineberg [1949] Ch. 245; [1948] L.J.R. 1255; 64 T.L.R. 205; 92 S.J. 245;
    [1948] 1 All E.R. 592 353
Hogg *v.* Brooks (1885) 15 Q.B.D. 256 146
Hogg Bullimore & Co. *v.* Co-operative Insurance Society (1985) 50 P. & C.R. 105 685
Hoggett *v.* Hoggett (1979) 39 P. & C.R. 121, C.A. 409
Holiday Fellowships Ltd. *v.* Hereford (Viscount) [1959] 1 W.L.R. 211; 103 S.J. 156;
    [1959] 1 All E.R. 433, C.A. 237
Holiday Flat Co. *v.* Kuczera [1978] S.L.T. (Sh.Ct.) 47 .... 471, 476
Holland *v.* Hodgson (1872) L.R. 7 C.P. 328; 41 L.J.C.P. 146; 26 L.T. 709; 20 W.R.
    990 (Ex.Ch.) 57, 58
—— *v.* Palser (1817) 2 Stark. 161 159
Holt *v.* Gas Light & Coke Co. (1872) L.R. 7 Q.B. 728; 41 L.J.Q.B. 351; 27 L.T. 442;
    37 J.P. 20 732
Home Counties Dairies *v.* Skilton [1970] 1 W.L.R. 526; 114 S.J. 107; [1970] 1 All
    E.R. 1227; 8 K.I.R. 691, C.A. 746
Honeyman *v.* Marryatt (1855) 6 H.L.C. 112; 26 L.J.Ch. 619; 4 Jur.(N.S.) 17;
    affirming 21 Beav. 14; 3 W.R. 502 84
Hookham *v.* Pottage (1872) 8 Ch.App. 91; *affirming* 26 L.T. 755; 20 W.R. 720 742
Hooper *v.* Clark (1867) L.R. 2 Q.B. 200; 36 L.J.Q.B. 79; 8 B. & S. 150; 16 L.T. 152;
    15 W.R. 347 52
Horn *v.* Sunderland Corp. [1941] 2 K.B. 26; [1941] 1 All E.R. 480; 110 L.J.K.B. 353;
    165 L.T. 298; 105 J.P. 223; 57 T.L.R. 404; 85 S.J. 212; 39 L.G.R. 367 734
Horner *v.* Walker [1923] 2 Ch. 218; 92 L.J.Ch. 573; 129 L.T. 782 86
Hornsby *v.* Maynard [1925] 1 K.B. 514; 94 L.J.K.B. 380; 132 L.T. 575; 41 T.L.R.
    102; 23 L.G.R. 319 .... 33, 158
Horsey Estate Ltd. *v.* Steiger [1899] 2 Q.B. 259; [1899] 2 Q.B. 79; 67 L.J.Q.B. 747;
    68 *ibid.* 743; 79 L.T. 116; 80 *ibid.* 857; 47 W.R. 644; 15 T.L.R. 367 353
Horwitz *v.* Rowson [1960] 1 W.L.R. 803; 124 J.P. 424; 104 S.J. 606; [1960] 2 All E.R.
    881; 11 P. & C.R. 411; 58 L.G.R. 252 123
Hopcutt *v.* Carver (1969) 209 E.G. 1069, C.A. 694
Hopgood *v.* Brown [1955] 1 W.L.R. 213; 99 S.J. 168; [1955] 1 All E.R. 550, C.A. 11
Hopkins Lease, *Re*; Caerphilly Concrete Products *v.* Owen [1972] 1 W.L.R. 372;
    [1972] 1 All E.R. 248; (1971) 23 P. & C.R. 15, C.A. 46
Hopwood *v.* Cannock Chase D.C. (formerly Rugeley Urban D.C.) [1975] 1 W.L.R.
    373; [1975] 1 All E.R. 796; (1974) 29 P. & C.R. 1256; 73 L.G.R. 137, C.A. 245
Horford Investments Ltd. *v.* Lambert [1976] Ch. 39; [1973] 3 W.L.R. 872; 117 S.J.
    814; [1974] 1 All E.R. 131; (1973) 27 P. & C.R. 88, C.A. 20, 392, 409
Horrowitz *v.* Ferrand [1956] 5 C.L. 207 694
Horner *v.* Franklin [1905] 1 K.B. 479; 74 L.J.K.B. 291; 92 L.T. 178; 69 J.P. 117; 21
    T.L.R. 225 113
Houlder Bros. & Co. *v.* Gibbs [1925] Ch. 575; 94 L.J.Ch. 312; 133 L.T. 322; 96 S.J.
    541; 41 T.L.R. 487 (C.A.) 308
Hounslow London Borough *v.* Twickenham Garden Developments Ltd. [1971] Ch.
    233; [1970] 3 W.L.R. 538; 114 S.J. 603; 69 L.G.R. 109; *sub nom.* London
    Borough of Hounslow *v.* Twickenham Garden Developments [1970] 3 All
    E.R. 326 .... 10, 11, 13, 357, 358, 360

House Property and Investment Co., *Re* [1954] Ch. 576; [1953] 3 W.L.R. 1037; 97
S.J. 862; [1953] 2 All E.R. 1525 .... 161, 203, 205
Houseleys Ltd. *v.* Bloomer-Holt Ltd. [1966] 1 W.L.R. 1244; 110 S.J. 387; [1966] 2
All E.R. 966, C.A. 697, 698, 702
Howard *v.* Fanshaw [1895] 2 Ch. 581; 64 L.J.Ch. 666; 73 L.T. 77; 43 W.R. 645; 13 R.
663 197
—— *v.* Shaw (1841) 8 M. & W. 118; 10 L.J.Ex. 334; 58 R.R. 641 .... 44, 193
Howe *v.* Botwood [1913] 2 K.B. 387; 82 L.J.K.B. 569; 108 L.T. 767; 29 T.L.R.
437 113
Howell's Application, *Re* [1972] Ch. 509; [1972] 2 W.L.R. 1346; 116 S.J. 446; [1972]
3 All E.R. 662; (1971) 23 P. & C.R. 266 515
Howkins *v.* Jardine [1951] 1 K.B. 614; [1951] 1 T.L.R. 135; 95 S.J. 75; [1951] 1 All
E.R. 320, C.A. 758, 759
Howson *v.* Buxton (1928) 97 L.J.K.B. 749; 139 L.T. 504 348
Hudson *v.* Cripps [1896] 1 Ch. 265; 65 L.J.Ch. 328; 73 L.T. 741; 44 W.R.
200 .... 127, 130
—— *v.* Osborne (1869) 39 L.J.Ch. 79; 21 L.T. 386 742
—— *v.* Williams (1878) 39 L.T. 632 224
Hughes *v.* Chatham Overseers (1843) 5 Man. & G. 54, 78; 13 L.J.C.P. 44; Bar. &
Arn. 61; Cox & Ack. 14; 1 Lut.Reg.Cas. 51; Pig. & R. 35; 7 Scott N.R. 581; 2
L.T.(o.s.) 149, 189; 8 J.P. 89; 7 Jur. 1136 27
—— *v.* Waite [1957] 1 W.L.R. 713; 101 S.J. 405; [1957] 1 All E.R. 603 69
Humphreys *v.* Miller [1917] 2 K.B. 122; 86 L.J.K.B 1111; 116 L.T. 668; 33 T.L.R.
115 (C.A.) 240
Hunt *v.* Colson (1833) 3 Moo. & S. 790; 38 R.R. 563 28
Hurd *v.* Whaley [1918] 1 K.B. 448; 88 L.J.K.B. 260; 118 L.T. 593; 34 T.L.R. 253 355
Hurst *v.* Hurst (1849) 4 Ex. 571; 19 L.J.Ex. 410; 80 R.R. 698 111
—— *v.* Picture Theatres Ltd. [1915] 1 K.B. 1; 83 L.J.K.B. 1837; 58 S.J. 739; 30
T.L.R. 642 (C.A.) 11, 36, 357, 358
Hussey *v.* Palmer [1972] 1 W.L.R. 1286; 116 S.J. 567; [1972] 3 All E.R. 744, C.A. 12
Hutchinson *v.* Jauncey [1950] 1 K.B. 574; 66 T.L.R. (Pt. 1) 195; 94 S.J. 48; [1950] 1
All E.R. 165, C.A. 408
—— *v.* Lamberth (1983) 270 E.G. 545, C.A. 695
Hyde *v.* Littlefield [1949] E.G.D. 116 19
—— *v.* Pimley [1952] 2 Q.B. 506; [1952] 1 T.L.R. 1561; 96 S.J. 410; [1952] 2 All
E.R. 102, C.A. 312
Hyman *v.* Rose [1912] A.C. 623; 81 L.J.K.B. 1062; L.T. 907; 56 S.J. 535; 28 T.L.R.
432; *reversing sub nom.* Rose *v.* Hyman [1911] 2 K.B. 234; 80 L.J.K.B. 1011;
104 L.T. 619; 55 S.J. 405; 27 T.L.R. 367 .... 292, 354

Ideal Film Renting Co. *v.* Nielsen [1921] 1 Ch. 575; 90 L.J.Ch. 429; 124 L.T. 749; 65
S.J. 379 .... 254, 307
Iggulden *v.* May (1804) 9 Ves.Jr. 325; subsequent proceedings 7 East 237; 3 Smith
K.B. 269; *affirmed* (1807) 2 Bos. & P.N.R. 449 151
Incorporated Council of Law Reporting for England and Wales, *Re* (1888) 22
Q.B.D. 279; 58 L.J.Q.B 90; 60 L.T. 505; *sub nom.* I.R.C. *v.* Incorporated
Council of Law Reporting, 3 T.C. 105 664
Industrial Properties (Barton Mill) Ltd. *v.* Associated Electrical Industries [1977]
Q.B. 580; [1977] 2 W.L.R. 726; (1977) 121 S.J. 155; [1977] 2 All E.R. 293; 242
E.G. 955; 34 P. & C.R. 329, C.A. 79, 286
I.R.C. *v.* Clay; I.R.C. *v.* Buchanan [1914] 3 K.B. 466; [1914–15] All E.R. Rep. 882;
83 L.J.K.B. 1425; 111 L.T. 484; 30 T.L.R. 573; 58 S.J. 610, C.A. 186
—— *v.* Derby (Earl of) [1914] 3 K.B. 1186; 84 L.J.K.B. 248; 109 L.T. 827 94
—— *v.* Maxse [1919] 1 K.B. 647 664
International Drilling Fluids Ltd. *v.* Louisville Investments (Uxbridge) Ltd. [1986] 1
All E.R. 321, C.A.; *affirming* (1985) 129 S.J. 854 .... 308, 309, 660

Table of Cases xliii

International Military Services v. Capital and Counties p.l.c. [1982] 1 W.L.R. 575;
(1982) 126 S.J. 293; [1982] 2 All E.R. 20; 80 L.G.R. 83; 261 E.G. 778 751
International Sales and Agencies Ltd. v. Marcus [1982] 3 All E.R. 551; [1982] 2
C.M.L.R. 46 15
Inwards v. Baker [1965] 2 Q.B 29; [1965] 2 W.L.R. 212; 109 S.J. 75; [1965] 1 All E.R.
446, C.A. 12
Inworth Property Co. v. London Borough of Southwark (1977) 33 P. & C.R. 186;
121 S.J. 16; 76 L.G.R. 263; [1978] J.P.L. 175; (1977) 245 E.G. 935, C.A. 265
Ireland v. Taylor [1949] 1 K.B. 300; [1949] L.J.R. 305; 65 T.L.R. 3; 92 S.J. 408;
[1948] 2 All E.R. 450, C.A. 664
Iron Trades Employers' Insurance Association Ltd. v. Union of Land and House
Investors Ltd. [1937] Ch. 313; 106 L.J.Ch. 206; 156 L.T. 322; 53 T.L.R. 341;
[1937] 1 All E.R. 481; 81 S.J. 159 69
Isaac v. Hotel de Paris Ltd. [1960] 1 W.L.R. 239; 104 S.J. 230; [1960] 1 All E.R. 348,
P.C. 10, 16, 17, 18, 25, 32, 33, 36, 359, 653
Issacs v. Titus [1954] 1 W.L.R. 398; 98 S.J. 143; [1954] 1 All E.R. 470, C.A. 385
Italica Holdings S.A. v. Bayadea (1985) 273 E.G. 888 146
Iveagh (Earl) v. Martin [1961] 1 Q.B. 232; [1960] 3 W.L.R. 210; 104 S.J. 567; [1960] 2
All E.R. 668; 58 L.G.R. 356; [1960] 1 Lloyd's Rep. 692 359
Ives (E. R.) Investment Co. v. High [1967] 2 Q.B. 379; [1967] 2 W.L.R. 789; [1967] 1
All E.R. 504; [1966] C.L.Y. 6674, C.A. 12
Izon v. Gorton (1839) 5 Bing.N.C. 501; 7 Socit 537; 2 Arn. 39; 8 L.J.C.P. 272; 3 Jur.
563; 50 R.R. 772 154

J. W. Capes Ltd. v. Brownlow Trust Ltd. [1950] W.N. 191; 94 S.J. 304; [1950] 1 All
E.R. 894 95
Jackson v. Cator (1800) 5 Ves. 688; 31 E.R. 806, L.C.; [1775–1802] All E.R.Rep.
592 12
—— v. Horizon Holidays Ltd. [1975] 1 W.L.R. 1468; 119 S.J. 759; [1975] 3 All
E.R. 92, C.A. 252
—— v. Simons [1923] 1 Ch. 373; 92 L.J.Ch. 161; 128 L.T. 572; 67 S.J. 262; 39
T.L.R. 147 .... 36, 305
Jackson (Francis) Developments v. Stemp [1943] 2 All E.R. 74; [1951] 2 K.B. 488;
115 J.P. 384; [1951] 2 T.L.R. 97; 95 S.J. 466, C.A. 44, 378
Jacobs v. Chaudhuri [1968] 2 Q.B. 470; [1968] 2 W.L.R. 1098; 112 S.J. 135; [1968] 2
All E.R. 124; 19 P. & C.R. 286, C.A. 644
Jaeger v. Mansions Consolidated Ltd. (1903) 87 L.T. 690; 19 T.L.R. 114; 47 S.J.
147 129
Jacobs v. London C.C. [1950] A.C. 361; 66 T.L.R. (Pt. 1) 659; 114 J.P. 204; 94 S.J.
318; [1950] 1 All E.R. 737; 48 L.G.R. 323, H.L.: affirming [1949] 1 K.B. 685;
93 S.J. 337; [1949] 1 All E.R. 790; 47 L.G.R. 363, C.A. 369
James v. Dean (1804–08) 11 Ves. 383; 15 Ves. 236; 8 R.R. 178 43
—— v. Heim Gallery (London) (1980) 41 P. & C.R. 269; (1980) 256 E.G. 819,
C.A. 182
—— v. Hutton [1950] K.B. 9; 65 T.L.R. 441; 93 S.J. 551; [1949] 2 All E.R. 243,
C.A. 121, 287
Janes (Gowns) v. Harlow Development Corp. (1979) 253 E.G. 799 .... 185, 680
Jarman v. Hale [1899] 1 Q.B. 994; 68 L.J.Q.B. 681 43
Jarvis v. Swan's Tours Ltd. [1973] 1 Q.B. 233; [1972] 3 W.L.R. 954; 116 S.J.
822; [1973] 1 All E.R. 71, C.A. 252
Jeffries v. O'Neill [1983] 46 P. & C.R. 376; (1984) 269 E.G. 131 187
Jelley v. Buckman [1974] Q.B. 488; [1973] 3 W.L.R. 585; [1973] 3 All E.R. 853; 26 P.
& C.R. 215, C.A. 325, 392
Jelson Ltd. v. Blaby D.C. [1977] 1 W.L.R. 1020; 121 S.J. 239; [1978] 1 All E.R. 548;
(1977) 34 P. & C.R. 77; (1977) 75 L.G.R. 624; [1977] J.P.L. 579; 243 E.G. 47,
C.A. 732

Jenkins *v*. Paddington B.C. [1954] J.P.L. 510, D.C. 558
—— *v*. Price [1907] 2 Ch. 229; 76 L.J.Ch. 507; [1908] 1 Ch. 10; 77 L.J.Ch. 41 127
Jervis *v*. Tomkinson (1856) 1 H. & N. 195; 26 L.J.Ex. 41; 4 W.R. 683 169
Jessamine Investment Co. *v*. Schwartz [1977] 2 W.L.R. 145; 120 S.J. 384; [1976] 3 All
    E.R. 521, C.A. 69
Jeune *v*. Queens Cross Properties Ltd. [1974] Ch. 97; [1973] 3 W.L.R. 378; 117 S.J.
    680; [1973] 3 All E.R. 97; 26 P. & C.R. 98 .... 96, 253, 255, 293
Jewel's Case (1588) 5 Co.Rep. 3a; 77 E.R. 51 154
Jinks *v*. Edwards (1856) 11 Ex. 775; 4 W.R. 303 129
Joel *v*. Swaddle [1957] 1 W.L.R. 1094; 101 S.J. 850; [1957] 3 All E.R. 325, C.A. 698
Johnson *v*. Agnew [1980] A.C. 367; [1979] 2 W.L.R. 487; 123 S.J. 217; [1979] 1 All
    E.R. 883; 38 P. & C.R. 424; 251 E.G. 1167, H.L.; *affirming* [1978] Ch. 176;
    [1978] 2 W.L.R. 806; (1977) 122 S.J. 230; [1978] 3 All E.R. 314; (1977) 38 P. &
    C.R. 107, C.A. 97
—— *v*. Leicester Corp. [1934] 1 K.B. 638; [1934] All E.R. 493; 103 L.J.K.B. 541;
    151 L.T. 8; 98 J.P. 165; 50 T.L.R. 214; 78 S.J. 122; 32 L.G.R. 147, C.A. 267
—— *v*. Moreton [1980] A.C. 37; [1978] 3 W.L.R. 538; 122 S.J. 697; [1978] 3 All
    E.R. 37; 37 P. & C.R. 243; 247 E.G. 895, H.L.; *affirming* (1977) 35 P. & C.R.
    378; 241 E.G. 759, C.A. 755, 764, 790, 791
Johnston *v*. Duke of Devonshire (1984) 272 E.G. 661, C.A. 509
Johnstone *v*. Hudlestone (1825) 4 B. & C. 922; 7 D. & R. 411; 4 L.J.(o.s.)K.B. 71; 28
    R.R. 505 342
Jolliffe *v*. Jolliffe [1965] P. 6; [1964] 2 W.L.R. 13; 107 S.J. 78; [1963] 3 All E.R. 295,
    D.C. 577
Jones *v*. Barnett [1984] Ch. 500; [1984] 3 W.L.R. 333; 128 S.J. 517; [1984] 3 All E.R.
    129; 48 P. & C.R. 371; 17 H.L.R. 18; 81 L.S.Gaz. 2299 198
—— *v*. Chappell (1875) L.R. 20 Eq. 539; 44 L.J.Ch. 658 282
—— *v*. Christy (1963) 107 S.J. 374, C.A. 642
—— *v*. Green [1925] 1 K.B. 659 221
—— *v*. Heavens (1877) 4 Ch.D. 636; 25 W.R. 460 170
—— *v*. Herxheimer [1950] 2 K.B. 106; 66 T.L.R. (Pt. 1) 403; 94 S.J. 97; [1950] 1 All
    E.R. 323, C.A. 287
—— *v*. Hill (1817) 7 Taunt. 392; 1 Moore 100; 18 R.R. 508 281
—— *v*. Jenkins (1985) 277 E.G. 644, C.A. 702
—— *v*. Lavington [1903] 1 K.B. 253; 72 L.J.K.B. 98; 88 L.T. 223; 51 W.R. 161; 19
    T.L.R. 77 66
—— *v*. Llanrwst Urban D.C. [1911] 1 Ch. 393; 80 L.J.Ch. 145; 103 L.T. 751; 75 J.P.
    68; 9 L.G.R. 222; 55 S.J. 125; 27 T.L.R. 133 370
—— *v*. Padvatton [1969] 1 W.L.R. 328; 112 S.J. 965; [1969] 2 All E.R. 616, C.A. 81
—— *v*. Phipps (1868) 9 B. & S. 761; L.R. 3 Q.B. 567; 37 L.J.Q.B. 198; 18 L.T. 813;
    16 W.R. 1044 348
—— *v*. Wentworth Securities Ltd. [1980] A.C. 74; (1978) 123 S.J. 34; [1979] 2
    W.L.R. 132; [1979] 1 All E.R. 286; (1978) 38 P. & C.R. 77, H.L. 517
—— *v*. Whitehill [1950] 2 K.B 204; 66 T.L.R. (Pt. 1) 387; 94 S.J. 113; [1950] 1
    All E.R. 71, C.A. 441
Jones (James) & Sons Ltd. *v*. Tankerville (Earl of) [1909] 2 Ch. 440; 78 L.J.Ch. 674;
    101 L.T. 202; 25 T.L.R. 714 11
Joseph *v*. Joseph [1967] Ch. 78; [1966] 3 W.L.R. 631; 110 S.J. 673; [1966] 3 W.L.R.
    486, C.A. 42, 655
—— *v*. L.C.C. (1914) 111 L.T. 276; 30 T.L.R. 508; *sub nom. Re* L.C.C. & Weir's
    Lease, Joseph *v*. L.C.C. 58 S.J. 579 120
Jourdain *v*. Wilson (1821) 4 B. & Ald. 266; 23 R.R. 268 318
Joyce *v*. London Borough of Hackney (1976) L.A.G.Bull. 211 544
Joyner *v*. Weeks [1891] 2 Q.B. 31; 60 L.J.Q.B. 510; 65 L.T. 16; 39 W.R. 583 287
Junction Estates Ltd. *v*. Cope (1974) P. & C.R. 482 .... 161, 677, 678

K., decd., *Re* [1985] 3 W.L.R. 234; 129 S.J. 364; [1985] 2 All E.R. 833; 16 Fam.Law
    19; 135 New L.J. 655; 82 L.S.Gaz. 2242, C.A.; *affirming* [1985] Ch. 85; [1985]
    2 W.L.R. 262; 129 S.J. 132; [1985] 1 All E.R. 403; [1986] 1 F.L.R. 79   5
Kammins Ballrooms Co. Ltd. *v.* Zenith Instruments (Torquay) Ltd. [1971] A.C.
    850; [1970] 3 W.L.R. 287; 114 S.J. 590; [1970] 2 All E.R. 871; 22 P. & C.R. 74,
    H.L.; *affirming* [1970] 1 Q.B. 673; [1969] 3 W.L.R. 799; 113 S.J. 640; [1969] 3
    All E.R. 1268; 20 P. & C.R. 1087, C.A. 691, 706
Kavanagh *v.* Lyroudias (1983) 127 S.J. 595; [1985] 1 All E.R. 560; (1984) 269 E.G.
    629, C.A.   387
Keats *v.* Graham [1960] 1 W.L.R. 30; 104 S.J. 51; [1959] 3 All E.R. 919, C.A.   288
Keen *v.* Holland [1984] 1 W.L.R. 251; (1983) 127 S.J. 764; [1984] 1 All E.R. 75; 47 P.
    & C.R. 639; 269 E.G. 1043; (1983) 80 L.S.Gaz. 3078, C.A. 649, 760
Keeves *v.* Dean; Nunn *v.* Pellegrini [1924] 1 K.B. 685; 93 L.J.K.B. 203; 130 L.T.
    593; 21 L.G.R. 588; 67 S.J. 790; 39 T.L.R. 652   404
Kellett *v.* Alexander; Kellett *v.* Cady (1981) 257 E.G. 494   793
Kelly *v.* Battershell [1949] 2 All E.R. 830, C.A. 127, 132
—— *v.* Rogers [1892] 1 Q.B. 910; 61 L.J.Q.B. 604; 66 L.T. 582; 40 W.R.
    516 .... 130, 323
—— *v.* Woolworth & Co. [1922] 2 I.R. 5   37
Kelsen *v.* Imperial Tobacco Co. (of Great Britain & Ireland) Ltd. [1957] 2 Q.B 334;
    [1957] 2 W.L.R. 1007; 101 S.J. 446; [1957] 2 All E.R. 343   103
Kemble *v.* Farren (1829) 6 Bing. 141; 3 Moo. & P. 425; 7 L.J.(o.s.)C.P. 258; 3 C. &
    P. 623; 31 R.R. 366   170
Kemp *v.* Baerselman [1906] 2 K.B. 604; 75 L.J.K.B. 873; 50 S.J. 615, C.A.   10
—— *v.* Cunningham [1975] L.A.G.Bull. 192   403
—— *v.* Derrett (1814) 3 Camp. 510; 14 R.R. 828 .... 40, 42, 344
Kendall *v.* Baker (1852) 11 C.B. 842; 21 L.J.C.P. 110; 18 L.T.(o.s.) 242; 16 Jur. 479;
    138 E.R. 706   155
Kenilworth Industrial Sites Ltd. *v.* Little (E. C.) & Co. Ltd. [1975] 1 W.L.R. 143; 118
    S.J. 776; [1975] 1 All E.R. 53; (1974) 29 P. & C.R. 141, C.A.; *affirming* [1974]
    1 W.L.R. 1069; 118 S.J. 532; [1974] 2 All E.R. 815; 28 P. & C.R. 263   180
Kenneally *v.* Dunne [1977] Q.B. 837; [1977] 2 W.L.R. 421; [1977] 2 All E.R. 16;
    (1976) 34 P. & C.R. 316; (1976) 242 E.G. 623, C.A. 455, 456
Kenny *v.* Preen [1963] 1 Q.B. 499; [1962] 3 W.L.R. 1233; 106 S.J. 854; [1962] 3 All
    E.R. 814, C.A. 129, 131, 132, 253
—— *v.* Royal Borough of Kingston-upon-Thames (1985) 17 H.L.R. 344; (1985) 274
    E.G. 395, C.A. 266, 271, 272
Kensington and Chelsea B.C. *v.* Haydon (1984) 17 H.L.R. 114, C.A.   612
Kent *v.* Connitt [1953] 1 Q.B. 361; [1953] 2 W.L.R. 41; 97 S.J. 46; [1953] 1 All E.R.
    155; 51 L.G.R. 77, C.A.; *affirming* [1952] W.N. 342; [1952] 2 T.L.R. 209; 50
    L.G.R 641 .... 288, 771, 791, 814
—— *v.* Fittall [1906] 1 K.B. 60; 75 L.J.K.B 310; 94 L.T. 76; J.P. 428; 54 W.R. 225;
    22 T.L.R. 63; 50 S.J. 74; 4 L.G.R. 36; 1 Smith Reg.Cas. 417   16
—— *v.* Millmead Properties (1983) 266 E.G. 899, C.A.   414
Kestell *v.* Langmaid [1950] 1 K.B. 233; 65 T.L.R. 699; 93 S.J. 726; [1949] 2 All E.R.
    749, C.A.   808
Kidder *v.* Birch (1982) 126 S.J. 482; (1983) 46 P. & C.R. 362; (1983) 265 E.G. 773;
    (1982) 79 L.S.Gaz. 988, C.A.   456
Killick *v.* Second Covent Garden Property Co. Ltd. [1973] 1 W.L.R. 658; 117 S.J.
    .417; [1973] 2 All E.R. 337; 25 P. & C.R. 332, C.A.   310
Kimsey *v.* London Borough of Barnet (1976) 3 H.L.R. 45 .... 265, 266
King *v.* Allen (David) & Sons Billposting Ltd. [1916] 2 A.C. 54; 85 L.J.P.C. 229; 114
    L.T. 762, H.L.   357
—— *v.* Cave-Brown-Cave [1960] 2 Q.B 222; [1960] 3 W.L.R. 204; 104 S.J. 567;
    [1960] 2 All E.R. 751; 53 R. & I.T. 373   113
—— *v.* Eversfield [1897] 2 Q.B 475; 66 L.J.Q.B. 809; 77 L.T. 195; 46 W.R. 51   345

King v. King [1981] 41 P. & C.R. 311; (1980) 255 E.G. 1205 .... 140, 158
——, Re, Robinson v. Gray [1963] Ch. 459; [1962] 1 W.L.R. 629; 107 S.J. 134; [1963]
    1 All E.R. 781; [1963] R.V.R. 245, C.A. 118, 224, 234, 290, 317, 325
—— v. Wycombe Ry. (1860) 28 Beav. 104; 29 L.J.Ch. 462; 2 L.T. 107; 24 J.P. 279; 6
    Jur.(N.S.) 239; 54 E.R. 305 721
King's Motors (Oxford) Ltd. v. Lax [1970] 1 W.L.R. 426; 114 S.J. 168; [1969] 3 All
    E.R. 665 .... 140, 158
Kingston v. Ambrian Investment Co. Ltd. [1975] 1 W.L.R. 161; (1974) 119 S.J. 47;
    [1975] 1 All E.R. 120, C.A. 89
Kingswood Estate Co. v. Anderson [1963] 2 Q.B. 169; [1962] 3 W.L.R. 1102; 106
    S.J. 651; [1962] 3 All E.R. 593, C.A. 87, 94, 96
Kirkwood v. Johnson (1979) 38 P. & C.R. 392; (1979) 250 E.G. 239, C.A. 711, 716
Kisch v. Hawes Bros. Ltd. [1935] Ch. 102; 104 L.J.Ch. 86; 152 L.T. 235 64
Kitney v. Greater London Properties (1984) 272 E.G. 786 140
Kling v. Keston Properties (1985) 49 P. & C.R. 212; (1984) 81 L.S.Gaz. 1683 146
Knight, Re, ex p. Voisey (1882) 21 Ch.D. 442; 52 L.J.Ch. 121; 47 L.T. 362; 31 W.R.
    19, C.A. 156
Kovats v. Corporation of Trinity House (1982) 262 E.G. 445 426
Kramer (Michael) & Co. v. Airways Pension Fund Trustees (1976) 246 E.G. 911,
    C.A. 679
Krell v. Henry [1903] 2 K.B. 740; 72 L.J.K.B. 794; 89 L.T. 328; 18 T.L.R. 823; 19
    ibid. 711 153
Kyriacon v. Pandel; February 11, 1980; Shoreditch County Court 607

Labone v. Litherland U.D.C. [1956] 1 W.L.R. 522; 100 S.J. 360; [1956] 2 All E.R.
    215 125
Labouchere v. Dawson (1872) L.R. 13 Eq. 322; 41 L.J.Ch. 427; 25 L.T. 894; 36 J.P.
    404; 20 W.R. 309 742
Lace v. Chantler [1944] K.B. 368; 13 L.J.K.B 282; 170 L.T. 185; 60 T.L.R. 224; 88
    S.J. 135; [1944] 1 All E.R. 305 .... 40, 81, 677
Ladies' Hosiery & Underwear Ltd. v. Parner [1930] 1 Ch. 304; 99 L.J.Ch. 201; 142
    L.T. 299; 46 T.L.R. 171, C.A. 345
Ladup v. Williams & Glyns Bank [1985] 1 W.L.R. 851; 129 S.J. 363; [1985] 2 All
    E.R. 577; 50 P. & C.R. 211; 82 L.S.Gaz. 2249 .... 196, 355
Ladyman v. Wirral Estates [1968] 2 All E.R. 197; 19 P. & C.R. 781 .... 40, 107, 346
Lagan Navigation Co. v. Lambeg Bleaching Co. [1927] A.C. 226; 96 L.J.P.C. 25;
    136 L.T. 417; 91 J.P. 46; 25 L.G.R. 1, H.L. 733
Laing Investment Co. v. Dunn (G. A.) & Co. (1982) 126 S.J. 99; (1981) 262 E.G.
    879 181
Lake v. Bennett [1970] 1 Q.B 663; [1970] 2 W.L.R. 355; 114 S.J. 13; [1970] 1 All E.R.
    457; (1969) 21 P. & C.R. 93, C.A. 505, 506, 512
Lally v. Kensington and Chelsea Royal Borough *The Times*, March 27, 1980 . 612, 613,
    626, 629, 632
Lambe v. Secretary of State for War [1955] 2 Q.B 612; [1955] 2 W.L.R. 1127; 119
    J.P. 415; 99 S.J. 368; [1955] 2 All E.R. 386; 5 P. & C.R. 227; 53 L.G.R. 481,
    C.A. 731
Lambert v. London Borough of Ealing [1982] 1 W.L.R. 550; 126 S.J. 228; [1982] 2
    All E.R. 394; 80 L.G.R. 487, C.A. 624, 625, 629
—— v. Norris (1837) 2 M. & W. 333; 6 L.J.Ex. 109; 46 R.R. 618 177
—— v. Woolworth (F. W.) & Co. Ltd. (No. 2) [1938] Ch. 883; 107 L.J.K.B. 554; 159
    L.T. 317; 54 T.L.R. 806; 82 S.J. 414; [1938] 2 All E.R. 664 .... 121, 662
Lambeth L.B.C. v. Stubbs [1980] J.P.L. 517; 78 L.G.R. 650; 255 E.G. 789, D.C. 260
—— v. Udechuka (1980) 41 P. & C.R. 200, C.A. 398, 476, 533, 560, 593
Lambourn v. McLellan [1903] 2 Ch. 268; 72 L.J.Ch. 617; 88 L.T. 748; 51 W.R. 594;
    19 T.L.R. 529 61
Lampard v. Barker (1984) 272 E.G. 783; 81 L.S.Gaz. 2381, C.A. 765

Land and Premises at Liss, Hants., *Re* [1971] Ch. 986; [1971] 3 W.L.R. 77; 115 S.J.
  446; [1971] 3 All E.R. 380; 22 P. & C.R. 861 36
Land Reclamation Co. Ltd. *v.* Basildon D.C. 302; [1979] 1 W.L.R. 767; 123 S.J.;
  [1979] 2 All E.R. 993; 250 E.G. 549 52,642
Land Securities plc *v.* Receiver for Metropolitan Police District [1983] 1 W.L.R. 439;
  [1983] 2 All E.R. 254; [1983] 46 P. & C.R. 347; 267 E.G. 675 291
Lander & Bagley's Contract, *Re* [1892] 3 Ch. 41; 61 L.J.Ch. 707; 67 L.T. 521 40
Langdon *v.* Horton [1951] 1 K.B. 666; [1951] 1 T.L.R. 238; 95 S.J. 89; [1951] 1 All
  E.R. 60, C.A. 440
Lane *v.* Cox [1897] 1 Q.B. 415; 66 L.J.Q.B. 193; 76 L.T. 135; 45 W.R. 261 239
Langford *v.* Selmes (1857) 3 K. & J. 220; 2 Jur.(M.S) 859 154,303
Langford Property Co. Ltd. *v.* Batten [1951] A.C. 223; 66 T.L.R. (Pt. 2) 958; 94 S.J.
  821; [1950] 2 All E.R. 1079, H.L. 414
—— *v.* Goldrich [1949] 1 K.B. 511; [1949] L.J.R. 663; 93 S.J. 133; [1949] 1 All E.R.
  402, C.A.; *affirming on other grounds* [1948] 2 K.B. 423; [1949] L.J.R. 213; 92
  S.J. 443; [1948] 2 All E.R. 439 379
—— *v.* Tureman [1949] 1 K.B. 29; [1949] L.J.R. 461; 64 T.L.R. 517; 92 S.J. 602
  sub nom. Langford Property Co. *v.* Athanassoglou [1948] 2 All E.R. 722,
  C.A. 386,387
Langton *v.* Henson (1905) 92 L.T. 805 302
Laurence *v.* Lexcourt Holdings Ltd. [1978] 1 W.L.R. 1128; (1977) 122 S.J. 681;
  [1978] 2 All E.R. 810 96,149
Lavender *v.* Betts [1942] 2 All E.R. 72; 167 L.T. 70 131,133,410
Lavery *v.* Pursell (1888) 39 Ch.D. 508; 57 L.J.Ch. 570; 58 L.T. 846; 4 T.L.R. 353; 37
  W.R. 163 83,94
Law *v.* Jones [1974] Ch. 112; [1973] 2 W.L.R. 994; 117 S.J. 305; [1973] 2 All E.R.
  437; 26 P. & C.R. 42, C.A. 86
Law Land Co. Ltd. *v.* Consumers' Association Ltd. (1980) 255 E.G. 617, C.A. 186
Law Shipping Co. Ltd. *v.* I.R.C. [1924] S.C. 74; 12 T.C. 621 208
Lawrance *v.* Hartwell [1946] K.B. 553; 115 L.J.K.B 481; 175 L.T. 150; 62 T.L.R.
  491; 90 S.J. 489; [1946] 2 All E.R. 257 (C.A.) 405
Lawrence Chemical Co. Ltd. *v.* Rubenstein [1982] 1 W.L.R. 284; 126 S.J. 71; [1982]
  1 All E.R. 653, C.A. 200
Lawrence (Frederick) Ltd. *v.* Freeman, Hardy and Willis [1957] Ch. 731; [1959] 3
  W.L.R. 275; 103 S.J. 694; [1959] 3 All E.R. 77, C.A.; *affirming* (1959) 173
  E.G. 441 704
Leakey *v.* National Trust for Places of Historic Interest and Natural Beauty [1980]
  Q.B 485; [1980] 2 W.L.R. 65; (1979) 123 S.J. 606; [1980] 1 All E.R. 17; (1979)
  78 L.G.R. 100, C.A.; *affirming* [1978] 3 All E.R. 234; 76 L.G.R 488 368
Leanse *v.* Egerton (Lord) [1943] K.B. 323; 112 L.J.K.B. 273; 168 L.T. 218; 59
  T.L.R. 191; [1943] 1 All E.R. 489 368
Lear *v.* Blizzard [1983] 3 All E.R. 662; 268 E.G. 1115; 133 New L.J. 893 .... 140, 141,
                                                                                               190, 191
Leather Cloth Co. *v.* Lorsont (1869) L.R. 9, Eq. 345; 39 L.J.Ch. 86; 21 L.T. 661; 34
  J.P. 328; 18 W.R. 572 746
Leatherwoods Ltd. *v.* Total Oil (Great Britain) Ltd. (1984) 270 E.G. 1083 701,702
Lee *v.* Carter (K.) Ltd. [1949] 1 K.B. 85; [1949] L.J.R. 7; 64 T.L.R 536; 92 S.J. 586;
  [1948] 2 All E.R. 690, C.A. 311
—— *v.* Gaskell (1876) 1 Q.B.D. 700; 45 L.J.Q.B 540; 34 L.T. 759; 24 W.R. 824 56
—— *v.* Minister of Transport [1966] 1 Q.B. 111; [1965] 3 W.L.R. 553; 63 L.G.R.
  327; [1965] R.V.R. 427; *sub nom.* Minister of Transport *v.* Lee 129 J.P. 511;
  109 S.J. 494; [1965] 2 All E.R. 986, C.A.; *affirming* (1964) 16 P. & C.R. 62,
  Lands Tribunal 733
—— *v.* Risdon (1816) 7 Taunt. 188; 2 Marsh 495; 17 R.R. 484 59
Lee-Parker *v.* Izzet [1971] 1 W.L.R. 1688; [1971] 3 All E.R. 1099, *sub nom.* Lee-
  Parker *v.* Izzet (Hassan) 115 S.J. 641, 22 P. & C.R. 1098 252,254,255

Lee-Verhulst (Investments) Ltd. *v.* Harwood Trust [1972] 1 Q.B. 204; [1972]
   3 W.L.R. 772; 116 S.J. 801; [1972] 3 All E.R. 619; 24 P. & C.R. 346,
   C.A. 642, 645
Leeds *v.* Cheetham (1827) 1 Sim. 146; 5 L.J.(o.s.)Ch. 105; 27 R.R. 181 .... 119, 234
Leeds & Batley Breweries & Bradbury's Lease, *Re*, Bradbury *v.* Grimble & Co.
   Ltd. [1920] 2 Ch. 548; 89 L.J.Ch. 645; 124 L.T. 189; 65 S.J. 61 143
Leeds Corp. *v.* Jenkinson [1935] 1 K.B. 168; 104 L.J.K.B. 182; 152 L.T. 126; 98 J.P.
   447; 51 T.L.R. 19; 78 S.J. 734; 32 L.G.R. 416, C.A. 531
Leek & Moorlands Building Society *v.* Clark [1952] 2 Q.B 788; [1952] 2 T.L.R. 401;
   96 S.J. 561; [1952] 2 All E.R. 492, C.A. 337, 340, 348
Leeward Securities *v.* Lilyheath Properties (1983) 17 H.L.R. 35; (1984) 271 E.G.
   279, C.A. 310, 311
Legal & General Assurance Society Ltd. *v.* General Metal Agencies Ltd. 113 S.J.
   876; (1969) 20 P. & C.R. 953 .... 195, 334
Legal and General Assurance (Pension Management) Ltd. *v.* Cheshire C.C.
   (1984) 269 E.G. 40, C.A.; *affirming* (1983) 46 P. & C.R. 160; 265 E.G.
   781 .... 138, 181
Lehmann *v.* McArthur (1867–68) L.R. 3 Ch. 496; 37 L.J.Ch. 625; 18 L.T. 806; 16
   W.R. 877; L.R. 3 Eq. 746; 16 L.T. 196; 15 W.R. 551 661
Leicester (Earl of) *v.* Wells-next-the-Sea U.D.C. [1973] Ch. 110; [1972] 3 W.L.R.
   486; 116 S.J. 647; [1972] 3 All E.R. 77; 24 P. & C.R. 72 124
Leigh's Will Trusts, *Re*; Handyside *v.* Durbridge [1970] Ch. 277; [1969] 3 W.L.R.
   649; 113 S.J. 758; [1969] 3 All E.R. 432 5
Leith Properties *v.* Byrne [1983] Q.B 433; [1983] 2 W.L.R. 67; (1982) 126 S.J. 690;
   (1983) 45 P. & C.R. 224; 4 H.L.R. 33, C.A. 62, 454, 466
Leizer *v.* Ostim Properties Ltd. (1965) 109 S.J. .456; 194 E.G. 907, C.A. 715
Lemon *v.* Lardeur [1946] K.B. 613; 115 L.J.K.B. 492; 175 L.T. 121; 62 T.L.R. 600;
   90 S.J. 527; [1946] 2 All E.R. 329 (C.A.) 346, 349
Leppard *v.* Excess Insurance Co. [1979] 1 W.L.R. 512; 122 S.J. 182; [1979] 2 All
   E.R. 668; [1979] 2 Lloyd's Rep. 91; 250 E.G. 751, C.A. 117
Leroux *v.* Brown (1852) 12 C.B. 801; 22 L.J.C.P. 1; 20 L.T.(o.s.); 16 Jur. 1021; 1
   W.R. 22; 138 E.R. 1119 83
Leschallas *v.* Woolf [1908] 1 Ch. 641; 77 L.J.Ch. 345; 98 L.T. 558 61
Lever Finance Ltd. *v.* Needleman's Trustee and Kreutzer [1956] Ch. 375; [1956] 3
   W.L.R. 72; 100 S.J. 400; [1956] 2 All E.R. 378 .... 69, 70
Lewington *v.* Trustees of the Society for the Protection of Ancient Buildings (1983)
   45 P. & C.R. 336; 266 E.G. 997, C.A. 676, 687
Lewis *v.* Barnett (1982) 264 E.G. 1079 180
—— *v.* Campbell (1819) 8 Taunt. 715; *affirmed s.c. sub nom.* Campbell *v.* Lewis
   (1820) 3 B. & Ald. 392; 106 E.R. 706 318
—— *v.* M.T.C. (Cars) Ltd. [1975] 1 W.L.R. 457; 119 S.J. 203; [1975] 1 All E.R. 874;
   29 P. & C.R. 495, C.A.; *affirming* [1974] 1 W.L.R. 1499; 118 S.J. 565; [1974] 3
   All E.R. 423; 28 P. & C.R. 294 .... 334, 345, 686
—— *v.* Weldcrest Ltd. [1978] 1 W.L.R. 1107; 122 S.J. 297; [1978] 3 All E.R. 1226;
   247 E.G. 211; 37 P. & C.R. 331, C.A. 549, 642, 647
Lewis (A.) & Co. (Westminster) *v.* Bell Property Trust [1940] Ch. 345; 109 L.J.Ch.
   132; 163 L.T. 37; 56 T.L.R. 391; 84 S.J. 205; [1940] 1 All E.R. 307 125
Lewis (E. H.) & Son Ltd. *v.* Morelli [1948] W.N. 442; 65 T.L.R. 56; [1948] 2 All E.R.
   1021, C.A. 79
Lewis (Jenkin R.) & Son Ltd. *v.* Kerman [1971] Ch. 477; [1970] 3 W.L.R. 673; 114
   S.J. 769; [1970] 3 All E.R. 414; 21 P. & C.R. 941, C.A. 177, 338, 340
Lewis, *Re* Jennings *v.* Hemsley [1939] Ch. 232; 108 L.J.Ch. 177; 159 L.T. 600; 55
   T.L.R. 53; 82 S.J. 931 329
Lewis and Weksler *v.* Wolking Properties [1978] 1 W.L.R. 403 706
Lewisham Metropolitan Borough *v.* Roberts [1949] 2 K.B. 608; 65 T.L.R. 423; 113
   J.P. 260; [1949] 1 All E.R. 815; 47 L.G.R. 479, C.A. 14

Liddiard v. Waldron [1934] 1 K.B 435; 103 L.J.K.B. 172; 150 L.T. 232; 50 T.L.R.
    172 106
Liford's Case (1614) 11 Co.Rep. 466; 77 E.R. 1206; *sub nom.* Stampe v. Clinton
    (*alias* Liford), 1 Roll.Rep. 95; [1558–1774] All E.R.Rep. 73 .... 58, 105
Lightcliffe & District Cricket and Lawn Tennis Club v. Walton (1977) 245 E.G. 393,
    C.A. 702
Linden v. Sec. of State for Social Services (1986); 130 S.J. 128; [1986] 1 W.L.R. 164 .. 642
Line v. Stephenson (1838) 7 Scott 69; 6 Scott 447; 4 Bing.N.C. 678; 5 *ibid.* 183; 1 Arn.
    385; 7 L.J.C.P. 263 129
Lipmans Wallpapers Ltd. v. Mason & Hodghton Ltd. [1969] 1 Ch. 20; [1968] 2
    W.L.R. 881; (1967) 112 S.J. 152; [1968] 1 All E.R. 1123; 19 P. & C.R. 224 662
Lircata Properties Ltd. v. Jones [1967] 1 W.L.R. 1257; 111 S.J. 542; [1967] 3 All E.R.
    386 196
Lister v. Lane [1893] 2 Q.B 212; 62 L.J.Q.B 583; 69 L.T. 176; 41 W.R. 626; 4 R. 474;
    57 J.P. 725 229
Little Park Service Station Ltd. v. Regent Oil Co. Ltd. [1967] 2 Q.B 655; [1967] 2
    W.L.R. 1036; 111 S.J. 96; [1967] 2 All E.R. 257, C.A. 699
Littlechild v. Holt [1950] 1 K.B 1; [1949] L.J.R. 1299; 65 T.L.R. 270; 93 S.J. 387;
    [1949] 1 All E.R. 933, C.A. 456
Littlewood v. Rolfe [1981] 2 All E.R. 51; (1980) 258 E.G. 168; (1982) 43 P. & C.R.
    262, D.C. 795
Liverpool City Council v. Irwin [1977] A.C. 239; (1976) 238 E.G. 879; (1984) 13
    H.L.R. 38, H.L. 7, 235, 245, 247, 542, 543
Liverpool Corpn. v. Husar [1972] 1 Q.B 48; [1971] 3 W.L.R. 571; [1971] 3 All E.R.
    651; 22 P. & C.R. 994; 70 L.G.R. 117; *sub nom.* Central Estates (Belgravia)
    v. Woolgar 115 S.J. 656; [1971] 3 All E.R. 647; 22 P. & C.R. 988, C.A. 519
Livestock Underwriting Agency v. Corbett & Newton (1955) 165 E.G. 469 697
Lloyd v. Crispe (1813) 5 Taunt. 249; 14 R.R. 744 314
—— v. Sadler [1978] Q.B 774; [1978] 2 W.L.R. 721; 122 S.J. 111; [1978] 2 All E.R.
    529; 35 P. & C.R. 78; 245 E.G. 479, C.A. 406
Lloyd's Bank v. City of London Corpn. [1983] Ch. 192; [1982] 3 W.L.R. 1138; (1982)
    126 S.J. 726; [1983] 1 All E.R. 92; (1983) 45 P. & C.R. 287; (1982) 264 E.G.
    1001, C.A.; *affirming* (1982) 261 E.G. 287 .... 693, 749
—— v. Jones [1955] 2 Q.B. 298; [1955] 3 W.L.R. 5; 99 S.J. 398; 53 L.G.R. 433; *sub*
    nom. Lower Onibury Farm, *Re*; Onibury, Shropshire; Lloyd's Bank v. Jones
    [1955] 2 All E.R. 409, C.A. 123
—— v. Lake [1961] 1 W.L.R. 884; 105 S.J. 467; [1961] 2 All E.R. 30 .... 289, 323
—— v. Marcan [1973] 1 W.L.R. 1387; 117 S.J. 761; [1973] 3 All E.R. 754, C.A.;
    affirming [1973] 1 W.L.R. 339; (1972) 117 S.J. 187; [1973] 2 All E.R. 359; 25
    P. & C.R. 65 68
Lloyd's (Building Investments) Ltd. v. Brown (1949) 153 E.G. 120 33
Lobb (Alex) (Garages) Ltd. v. Total Oil G.B. Ltd. [1985] 1 W.L.R. 173; 129 S.J. 83;
    [1985] 1 All E.R. 303; 273 E.G. 659; 129 S.J. 83; 82 L.S.Gaz. 45, C.A.;
    affirming [1983] 1 W.L.R. 87; (1982) 126 S.J. 768; [1983] 1 All E.R. 944; 133
    New L.J. 401, D.C. 125, 126
Lock v. Pearce [1893] 2 Ch. 328; 61 L.J.Ch. 606; 67 L.T. 164; 40 W.R. 508; [1893] 2
    Ch. 271; 62 L.J.Ch. 582; 68 L.T. 569; 41 W.R. 369; 2 R. 403, C.A. 353
Lockwood v. Lowe [1954] 2 Q.B. 267; [1954] 2 W.L.R. 296; 98 S.J. 127; [1954] 1 All
    E.R. 472, C.A. 384, 385
Loft v. Dennis (1859) 1 E. & E. 474; 28 L.J.Q.B 168; 5 Jur.(N.S.) 727; 7 W.R. 199 234
London and Colonial Co., *Re* (1868) L.R. 5 Eq. 561; 37 L.J.Ch. 393; 18 L.T. 103; 16
    W.R. 577 203
London & County (A. & D.) Ltd. v. Wilfred Sportsman Ltd.; Greenwoods (Hosiers
    & Outfitters) Third Party [1971] Ch. 764; [1970] 3 W.L.R. 418; 114 S.J. 666;
    21 P. & C.R. 788; *sub nom.* London and County (A. & D.) v. Wilfred
    Sportsman (Greenwoods (Hosiers & Outfitters) Third Party) [1970] 2 All
    E.R. 600, C.A. 159, 161, 325

London and Manchester Assurance Co. Ltd. *v.* Dunn (G. A.) & Co. (1983) 265 E.G.
39, 131, C.A.; (1982) 262 E.G. 143, D.C. 181, 182
London and Northern Estates Co. *v.* Schlesigner [1916] 1 K.B 20; 85 L.J.K.B. 369;
114 L.T. 74; 60 S.J. 223; 32 T.L.R. 78 153
London & Provincial Millinery Stores *v.* Barclays Bank Ltd. [1962] 1 W.L.R. 510;
106 S.J. 220; [1962] 2 All E.R. 163, C.A. 709
London and South Western Ry. *v.* Gomm (1882) 209 Ch.D. 562; 51 L.J.Ch. 530; 46
L.T. 449; 30 W.R. 620 (C.A.) 723
London Borough of Hillingdon *v.* Cutler. *See* Hillingdon L.B.C. *v.* Cutler.
London County Council *v.* Hutter [1925] Ch. 626; 95 L.J.Ch. 1; 134 L.T. 56 120
—— *v.* Tobin [1959] 1 W.L.R. 354; 123 J.P. 250; 103 S.J. 272; [1959] 1 All E.R. 649;
57 L.G.R. 649; 57 L.G.R. 113; 10 P. & C.R. 79, C.A.; *affirming sub nom.*
Tobin *v.* London C.C. (1957) 8 P. & C.R. 543 732
London Housing and Commercial Properties *v.* Cowan [1977] Q.B. 148,
D.C. 419, 421
Long (Fred) & Sons Ltd. *v.* Burgess [1959] K.B 115; 65 T.L.R. 606; 93 S.J. 631;
[1949] 2 All E.R. 484, C.A. 326
Long (Nevill) & Co. (Boards) *v.* Firmenich and Co. (1984) 47 P. & C.R. 59,
C.A. 52, 325, 642, 676, 684, 686
Longmuir *v.* Kew [1960] 1 W.L.R. 862; 104 S.J. 665; [1960] 3 All E.R. 26 143
Longrigg, Burrough & Trounson *v.* Smith (1979) 251 E.G. 847, C.A. 19, 345
Lonsdale (Earl) *v.* Att.-Gen. *See* Earl of Lonsdale *v.* Attorney-General.
Lord Strathcona S.S. Co. *v.* Dominion Coal Co. [1926] A.C. 108; [1924] 2 D.L.R.
66; 57 N.S.R. 113 2
Lory *v.* Brent L.B.C. [1971] 1 W.L.R. 823; 115 S.J. 245; 22 P. & C.R. 393; 69 L.G.R.
317; *sub nom.* Lory *v.* London Borough of Brent [1971] 1 All E.R. 1042 765
Lovelock *v.* Margo [1963] 2 Q.B. 786; [1963] 2 W.L.R. 794; 107 S.J. 194; [1963] 2 All
E.R. 13, C.A. 197
Lowe *v.* Adams [1901] 2 Ch. 598; 70 L.J.Ch. 783; 85 L.T. 195; 50 W.R. 37 359
Lowenthal *v.* Vanhoute [1947] K.B. 342; [1947] L.J.R. 421; 177 L.T. 180; 63 T.L.R.
54; [1947] 1 All E.R. 116 350
Lower *v.* Porter [1956] 1 Q.B 325; [1956] 2 W.L.R. 215; 100 S.J. 52; [1956] 1 All E.R.
150, C.A. 429
—— *v.* Sorrell [1963] 1 Q.B 959; [1963] 2 W.L.R. 1; [1962] 3 All E.R. 1074,
C.A. 108, 341, 348, 350
Lowther *v.* Clifford [1927] 1 K.B 130; 95 L.J.K.B 576; 135 L.T. 200; 90 J.P. 113; 24
L.G.R. 231; 70 S.J. 545; 42 T.L.R. 432 114
—— *v.* Heaver (1889) 41 Ch.D. 248; 58 L.J.Ch. 482; 60 L.T. 310; 37 W.R. 465,
C.A. 92
Lovibond & Sons *v.* Vincent [1929] 1 K.B. 687; 98 L.J.K.B. 402; 141 L.T. 116; 45
T.L.R. 383; 93 J.P. 161; 73 S.J. 252; 27 L.G.R. 471 404
Luby *v.* Newcastle-under-Lyme Corp. [1965] 1 Q.B. 214; [1964] 3 W.L.R. 500; 128
J.P. 536; 108 S.J. 541; [1964] 3 All E.R. 169; 62 L.G.R. 622; [1964] R.V.R.
708, C.A.; *affirming* [1964] 2 Q.B 64; [1964] 2 W.L.R. 475; 128 J.P. 138; 107
S.J. 983; [1964] 1 All E.R. 84; 62 L.G.R. 140 .... 530, 531
Luganda *v.* Service Hotels Ltd. [1969] 2 Ch. 209; [1969] 2 W.L.R. 1056; [1969] 2 All
E.R. 692; 20 P. & C.R. 337; *affirming* 113 S.J. 165, C.A. 10, 15, 20, 474,
477, 480
Lumby *v.* Faupel (1904) 90 L.T. 140; 2 L.G.R. 605; 68 J.P. 265; 20 T.L.R. 237 116
Lurcott *v.* Wakely & Wheeler [1911] 1 K.B 905; 80 L.J.K.B. 713; 104 L.T. 290; 55
S.J. 290 .... 228, 230, 231
Luttges *v.* Sherwood (1895) 11 T.L.R 233 161
Luton *v.* Tinsey (1978) 249 E.G. 239, C.A. 766
Luxmore *v.* Robson (1818) 1 B. & Ald. 584; 19 R.R. 396 219
Lynes *v.* Snaith [1899] 1 Q.B 486; 68 L.J.Q.B. 275; 80 L.T. 122; 47 W.R. 411 .... 15, 16

Lyon *v*. Reed (1844) 13 M. & W. 285; 13 L.J.Ex. 377; 3 L.T.O.S. 302; 8 Jur. 762; 153
E.R. 118; [1843–60] All E.R.Rep. 178 339
Lyon & Co. *v*. London City & Midland Bank [1903] 2 K.B. 135; 72 L.J.K.B 465; 88
L.T. 392; 51 W.R. 400; 19 T.L.R. 334; 47 S.J. 386 58
Lyons *v*. Central Commercial Properties London [1958] 1 W.L.R. 869; 102 S.J. 600;
[1958] 2 All E.R. 767, C.A. 694
Lyons & Co. Ltd. *v*. Knowles [1943] K.B. 366; 112 L.J.K.B 449; 168 L.T. 273; 59
T.L.R. 229; 87 S.J. 192; [1943] 1 All E.R. 477 .... 316, 317, 322
Lyttleton Times Co. Ltd. *v*. Warners Ltd. [1907] A.C. 476; 76 L.J.P.C. 100; 97 L.T.
496; 23 T.L.R. 751 131

M.F.I. Properties Ltd. *v*. B.I.C.C. Group Pension Trust Ltd. [1986] 1 All E.R. 974;
277 E.G. 862 190
McCall *v*. Abelesz [1976] Q.B. 585; [1976] 2 W.L.R. 151; (1975) 120 S.J. 81; [1976] 1
All E.R. 727; (1975) 31 P. & C.R. 256; 238 E.G. 335, C.A. 131, 132, 133,
252, 608, 609
McCarrick *v*. Liverpool Corpn. [1947] A.C. 219; [1947] L.J.R. 56; 176 L.T. 11; 62
T.L.R. 730; 111 J.P. 6; 91 S.J. 41; [1946] 2 All E.R. 646, H.L. 235, 241, 250
Maclean *v*. Dunn (1828) 4 Bing. 722; 1 Moo. & P. 761; 6 L.J.(o.s.)C.P. 184; 29 R.R.
714 86
McClinton *v*. McFall (1974) 232 E.G. 707; [1975] C.L.Y. 38, C.A. 758
McCombie *v*. Grand Junction Co. Ltd. [1962] 1 W.L.R. 581; 106 S.J. 389; [1962] 2
All E.R. 65, C.A. 710
McCoy & Co. *v*. Clark (1982) 13 H.L.R. 87, C.A. 251
McCulloch *v*. May (Lewis A.) [1947] W.N. 318; 92 S.J. 54; [1947] 2 All E.R. 845; 65
R.P.C. 58 741
McDonagh *v*. Kent Area Health Authority (1984) 134 New L.J. 567, D.C. 236, 248
MacDonnell *v*. Daly [1969] 1 W.L.R. 1482; 113 S.J. 508; [1969] 3 All E.R. 851; 20 P.
& C.R. 864, C.A. 451, 457
McGreal *v*. Wake (1984) 128 S.J. 116; 13 H.L.R. 107; 269 E.G. 1254; (1984) 81
L.S.Gaz. 739, C.A. 218, 235, 245, 250, 251, 252, 285
McHale *v*. Daneham (1979) 249 E.G. 969; Bloomsbury and Marylebone County
Court 21, 403
McKay (Formerly Chapman) *v*. Chapman [1978] 1 W.L.R. 620; [1978] 2 All
E.R. 548, *sub nom*. Chapman *v*. Chapman (1977) 121 S.J. 849; (1978) 128
N.L.J. 611 28
McKenna *v*. Porter Motors [1956] A.C. 688; [1956] 3 W.L.R. 658; [1956] 3 All E.R.
262, P.C. 702
Mackintosh *v*. Trotter (1838) 3 M. & W. 184; 7 L.J.Ex. 65; 49 R.R. 565 60
Mackworth *v*. Hellard [1921] 2 K.B 755; 90 L.J.K.B. 693; 125 L.T. 451; 37 T.L.R.
469; 85 J.P. 197 399
McMillan *v*. Singh (1984) 17 H.L.R. 120, C.A. 133, 610
McNally *v*. Welltrade International [1978] 1 R.L.R. 490 252
Magdalen College, Oxford *v*. Heritage [1974] 1 W.L.R. 441; 118 S.J. 243; [1974] 1
All E.R. 1065; 27 P. & C.R. 169, C.A.; *affirming* [1973] 1 W.L.R. 1225;
[1973] 3 All E.R. 891; 26 P. & C.R. 226; *sub nom*. President and Scholars of
the College of St. Mary Magdalen in the University of Oxford *v*. Heritage; 117
S.J. 747 .... 781, 786
Maley *v*. Fearn [1946] W.N. 198; [1947] L.J.R. 276; 176 L.T. 203; 62 T.L.R. 693; 91
S.J. 67; [1946] 2 All E.R. 583, C.A. 464
Malhotra *v*. Choudhury [1980] Ch. 52; [1978] 3 W.L.R. 825; (1977) 122 S.J. 681;
[1979] 1 All E.R. 186, C.A. 95, 97
Manchester Bonded Warehouse Co. Ltd. *v*. Carr (1880) 5 C.P.D. 507; 49 L.J.C.P.
809; 43 L.T. 476; 29 W.R. 354 .... 137, 225, 281
Mancetter Developments Ltd. *v*. Garmanson Ltd. and Givertz [1986] 1 All E.R.
449 .... 61, 295

Mandeville *v*. Greater London Council *The Times*, January 28, 1982 530
Manfield & Sons Ltd. *v*. Botchin [1970] 2 Q.B. 612; [1970] 3 W.L.R. 120; 114 S.J.
   338; [1970] 3 All E.R. 143; 21 P. & C.R. 587 .... 16, 44, 641
Mann *v*. Cornella (1980) 254 E.G. 403, C.A. 395, 402
Mann, Crossman & Paulin *v*. Registrar of the Land Registrar [1918] 1 Ch. 202; 87
   L.J.Ch. 81; 117 L.T. 705; 62 S.J. 54; 34 T.L.R. 39 38
Manson *v*. Duke of Westminster [1981] Q.B 323; [1981] 2 W.L.R. 428; (1980) 125
   S.J. 17; [1981] 2 All E.R. 40; (1980) 41 P. & C.R. 159; 259 E.G. 153, C.A. 511
Mapes *v*. Jones (1974) 232 E.G. 717 149
Marchant *v*. Charters [1977] 1 W.L.R. 1181; [1977] 3 All E.R. 918; (1976) 34 P. &
   C.R. 291; 241 E.G. 23, C.A. 10, 17, 20, 29, 402, 477
Marcroft Wagons Ltd. *v*. Smith [1951] 2 K.B 496; 95 S.J. 501; [1951] 2 All E.R.
   271 .... 17, 18, 19, 25, 31, 33, 45, 334, 345, 449
Marela *v*. Machorowski [1953] 1 Q.B 565; [1953] 2 W.L.R. 831; 117 J.P. 220; 97 S.J.
   280; [1953] 1 All E.R. 960, C.A. 394
Markham *v*. Paget [1908] 1 Ch. 697; 77 L.J.Ch. 451; 98 L.T. 605; 24 T.L.R. 426 66
Marks *v*. Warren [1979] 1 All E.R. 29; (1978) 37 P. & C.R. 275; 248 E.G.
   503 .... 302, 304, 660
Marlborough (Duke) *v*. Osborn (1864) 5 B. & S. 67; 33 L.J.Q.B. 148; 10 L.T. 28; 12
   W.R. 418 .... 1, 157
Marsden *v*. Heyes [1927] 2 K.B 1; 96 L.J.K.B. 410; 136 L.T. 593 282
Marsh Ltd. *v*. Coooper [1969] 1 W.L.R. 803; 113 S.J. 324; [1969] 2 All E.R. 498; 20
   P. & C.R. 940, C.A. 476
Marshall *v*. Berridge (1881) 19 Ch.D. 233; 51 L.J.Ch. 329; 45 L.T. 599; 30 W.R.
   93 .... 40, 82, 83
Martin *v*. Smith (1874) L.R. 9 Ex. 50; 43 L.J.Ex. 42; 30 L.T. 268; 22 W.R. 336 40
Martin-Smith *v*. Smale [1954] 1 W.L.R. 247; 98 S.J. 92; [1954] 1 All E.R. 237; 52
   L.G.R 136, C.A. 783
Martyn *v*. Clue (1852) 18 Q.B. 661; 22 L.J.Q.B. 147 317
Marylebone (Stingo Lane) Improvement Act, *ex p*. Edwards, *Re*, (1871) L.R. 12 Eq.
   389; 40 L.J.Ch. 697; 25 L.T. 149; 19 W.R. 1047 721
Mason *v*. Bibby (1864) 2 H. & C. 881; 33 L.J.M.C. 105; 10 Jur.(N.S.) 519; 9 L.T. 692;
   12 W.R. 382 349
—— *v*. Skilling [1974] 1 W.L.R. 1437; (1973) 118 S.J. 810; [1974] 3 All E.R. 977;
   (1973) 29 P. & C.R. 88; *sub nom*. Skilling *v*. Acari's Exrx, (1974) S.L.T. 46,
   H.L. 422, 425
Matania *v*. National Provincial Bank Ltd. (1936) 106 L.J.K.B. 11; 155 L.T. 74; 80
   S.J. 532; [1936] 2 All E.R. 633 131
Matchams Park (Holdings) *v*. Dommett (1984) 272 E.G. 549, C.A. 19, 32
Matthews *v*. Dobbins [1963] 1 W.L.R. 227; 106 S.J. 1052; [1963] 1 All E.R. 417,
   C.A. 161, 196
—— *v*. Smallwood [1910] 1 Ch. 777; 79 L.J.Ch. 322; 102 L.T. 228 .... 195, 355
Matthey *v*. Curling [1922] 2 A.C. 180; 91 L.J.K.B 593; 127 L.T. 247; 66 S.J. 386; 38
   T.L.R. 475 .... 119, 137, 153, 154
Maunsell *v*. Olins [1974] 3 W.L.R. 835; 118 S.J. 882; [1975] 1 All E.R. 16; (1974) 30
   P. & C.R. 1, H.L.; *affirming* [1974] 1 W.L.R. 830; 118 S.J. 278; [1974] 2 All
   E.R. 250; 27 P. & C.R. 460, C.A. 378, 393, 466
Maurice (Lesley) & Co. Ltd. *v*. Willesden Corp. [1953] 2 Q.B 1; [1953] 2 W.L.R.
   892; 117 J.P. 239; 97 S.J. 298; [1953] 1 All E.R. 1014; 51 L.G.R. 334, C.A. 265
Maxted *v*. McAll [1952] C.P.L. 185, C.A. 404, 434
May *v*. Borup [1915] 1 K.B 830; 84 L.J.K.B 823; 113 L.T. 694 347
Mayfield Holdings *v*. Moana Reef [1973] 1 N.Z.L.R. 309, Supreme Court,
   Auckland 13, 357
Mayflower Cambridge *v*. Secretary of State for the Environment (1975) 119 S.J. 590;
   (1975) 30 P. & C.R. 28; 73 L.G.R. 517, D.C. 15
Mayhew *v*. Governors of Harow Road Trust [1985] C.L.Y. 509

Mayhew *v.* Suttle (1854) 4 E. & B. 347; 24 L.J.Q.B 54; 1 Jur.(N.s.) 303 .... 16, 27, 43
Maynard *v.* Maynard [1969] P. 88; [1969] 2 W.L.R. 22; (1968) 112 S.J. 690; [1969] 1
    All E.R. 1; 20 P. & C.R. 52 405
Mayo *v.* Joyce [1920] 1 K.B. 824; 89 L.J.K.B. 561; 122 L.T. 777 110
Meadows *v.* Clerical, Medical and General Life Assurance Society [1981] Ch. 70;
    [1980] 2 W.L.R. 639; (1979) 124 S.J. 257; [1980] 1 All E.R. 454, (1979) 40 P.
    & C.R. 238; 255 E.G. 883 674
Meah *v.* Settor Properties Ltd. [1974] 1 W.L.R. 547; (1973) 118 S.J. 296; [1974] 1 All
    E.R. 1074; (1973) 27 R. & C.R. 148, C.A. 334, 691
Meakers Ltd. *v.* D.A.W. Consolidated Properties Ltd. *See* High Road (No. 88)
    Kilburn, *Re.*
Mecca Leisure Ltd. *v.* Renown Investments (Holdings) Ltd. (1985) 49 P. & C.R. 12;
    (1984) 271 E.G. 989, C.A. 180
Mehmet *v.* Dawson (1983) 270 E.G. 139, C.A. 687
Melces & Co. *v.* Holme [1918] 2 K.B 100; 87 L.J.K.B 942; 119 L.T. 191; 62 S.J. 704 .. 235
Melville *v.* Grapelodge Developments Ltd. (1979) 39 P. & C.R. 179 256
Melwood Units Pty. Ltd. *v.* Commissioner for Main Roads [1979] A.C. 426; (1978)
    38 P. & C.R. 195; [1978] 3 W.L.R. 520; 122 S.J. 434; [1977] 1 All E.R. 161,
    P.C. 732
Mercantile and General Re-insurance Co. *v.* Groves [1974] Q.B 43; [1973] 3 W.L.R.
    248; 117 S.J. 566; [1973] 3 All E.R. 330; 26 P. & C.R. 71; [1973] J.P.L. 427,
    C.A. 788
Meredith *v.* Gilpin (1816) 6 Pr.Exch. 146; 146 E.R. 768 165
Method Developments Ltd. *v.* Jones [1971] 1 W.L.R. 168; (1970) 115 S.J. 13; [1971]
    1 All E.R. 1027; 22 P. & C.R. 141, C.A. 701
Methuen-Campbell *v.* Walters [1979] Q.B 525; [1979] 2 W.L.R. 113; (1978) 122
    S.J. 610; [1979] 1 All E.R. 606; (1978) 38 P. & C.R. 693; 247 E.G. 899,
    C.A. 103, 503, 507
Metrobahn Ltd. *v.* Gehring [1976] 1 W.L.R. 776; 120 S.J. 451; [1976] 3 All E.R. 178;
    32 P. & C.R. 210, C.A. 414, 468
Metrolands Investments *v.* Dewhurst (1986) 277 E.G. 1343, C.A.; [1985] 3 All E.R.
    206; 49 P. & C.R. 334; 274 E.G. 1388; 82 L.S.Gaz. 1415 181
Metropolitan Board of Works *v.* McCarthy [1874] L.R. 7 H.L. 243; 43 L.J.C.P. 385;
    31 L.T. 182; 38 J.P. 820; 23 W.R. 115, H.L.; *affirming* S.C. *sub nom.*
    McCarthy *v.* Metropolitan Board of Works (1872) L.R. 8 C.P. 191, Ex.Ch. ... 733
Metropolitan Properties Ltd. *v.* Jones [1939] 2 All E.R. 202 .... 367, 370
Metropolitan Properties Co. *v.* Noble [1968] 1 W.L.R. 838 423
Metropolitan Properties Co. (F.G.C.) Ltd. *v.* Barder [1968] 1 W.L.R. 286; (1967)
    112 S.J. 15; [1968] 1 All E.R. 536; 19 P. & C.R. 304; 32 Conv. 235, C.A. 392
—— *v.* Cordery (1979) 39 P. & C.R. 10; (1979) 251 E.G. 567, C.A. 464, 470, 661
—— *v.* Cronan (1982) 44 P. & C.R. 1 444
—— *v.* Lannon; R. *v.* London Rent Assessment Panel Committee, *ex p.* Metro-
    politan Properties Co. (F.G.C.) [1969] 1 Q.B 577; [1968] 3 W.L.R. 694; *sub*
    nom. R. *v.* London Rent Assessment Panel Committee, *ex p.* Metropolitan
    Properties Co. (F.G.C.) 112 S.J. 585; *sub nom.* Metropolitan Properties Co.
    (F.G.C) *v.* Lannon [1968] 3 All E.R. 304; 19 P. & C.R. 858, C.A.; *reversing* in
    part [1968] 1 W.L.R. 815; [1968] 1 All E.R. 354; [1968] R.V.R. 236, D.C. 426
Metropolitan Property Holdings Ltd. *v.* Finegold [1975] 1 W.LR.. 349; (1974) 119
    S.J. 151; [1975] 1 All E.R. 389; (1974) 29 P. & C.R. 161, D.C. 424, 425
Meux *v.* Cobley [1892] 2 Ch. 253; 61 L.J.Ch. 449; 66 L.T. 86 282
Mickel *v.* M'Coard, 1913 S.C. 896; 50 S.L.R. 682; 1912 1 S.L.T. 463 283
Middlegate Properties Ltd. *v.* Bilbao, Caroline Construction Co. Ltd. (Third Party)
    (1972) 24 P. & C.R. 329 322
—— *v.* Gidlow-Jackman (1977) 34 P. & C.R. 4, C.A. 284, 290
—— *v.* Messimeris [1973] 1 W.L.R. 168; (1972) 117 S.J. 56; [1973] 1 All E.R. 645; 25
    P. & C.R. 76, C.A. 290, 416

Middleton v. Bull [1951] W.N. 517; (1951) 2 T.L.R. 1010; 95 S.J. 727, C.A. 578
Midland Bank Trust Co. Ltd. v. Green [1980] Ch. 590; [1981] A.C. 513; (1980) 125
    S.J. 33, H.L. 76
—— v. Green (No. 2) [1981] 2 W.L.R. 28; [1981] 1 All E.R. 153; [1981] P. & C.R.
    201, H.L.; *reversing* [1979] 1 W.L.R. 460; (1979) 123 S.J. 142; [1979] 1 All
    E.R. 726 327
—— v. Hett, Stubbs & Kemp (A firm) [1979] Ch. 384; [1978] 3 W.L.R. 167; (1977)
    121 S.J. 830; [1978] 3 All E.R. 571 146
Midland Coal, Coke and Iron Co., *Re* (Craig's Claim) [1895] 1 Ch. 267; 64 L.J.Ch.
    279; 71 L.T. 705; 43 W.R. 680; 12 R. 62; 2 Manson 75 203
Midland Railway Co.'s Agreement, *Re* [1971] Ch. 725; [1971] 2 W.L.R. 625; 115 S.J.
    126; 22 P. & C.R. 360; *sub nom.* Clay (Charles) & Sons v. British Railways
    Board [1971] 1 All E.R. 1007, C.A.; *affirming* [1970] 1 Ch 568; [1970] 2
    W.L.R. 1328; 114 S.J. 473; 21 P. & C.R. 521 .... 42, 43, 81, 341
Midmanbury Properties (Southampton) v. Houghton, T. Clerk & Son (1981) 259
    E.G. 565 423
—— v. Houghton *and* T. Clerk & Son v. Heathfield (No. 2) (1982) 263 E.G. 792 426
Mice End Vestry v. Whitby (1898) 78 L.T. 80 114
Millard v. Wastall [1898] 1 Q.B. 342; 67 L.J.Q.B. 277; 77 L.T. 692; 62 J.P. 135; 46
    W.R. 258; 14 T.L.R. 172; 42 S.J. 215; 18 Cox C.C. 695, D.C. 263
Miller v. Burt (1918) 63 S.J. 117 224
Miller v. Emcer Products Ltd. [1956] Ch. 304; [1956] 2 W.L.R. 267; 100 S.J. 74;
    [1956] 1 All E.R. 237, C.A. 129
Miller v. Wandsworth L.B.C. *The Times*, March 19, 1980 .... 619, 621, 632
Miller and Aldworth Ltd. v. Sharp [1899] 1 Ch. 622; 68 L.J.Ch. 322; 80 L.T. 77; 47
    W.R. 268 87
Millichamp v. Jones [1982] 1 W.L.R. 1422; 126 S.J. 726; [1983] 1 All E.R. 267; 80
    L.S.Gaz. 35; 133 New L.J. 134 2
Millington v. Duffy (1984) 17 H.L.R. 232, C.A. 133, 610
Million Pigs v. Parry (No. 2) (1983) 46 P. & C.R. 333; (1983) 268 E.G. 809 182
Mills v. East London Union Guardians (1872) L.R. 8 C.P. 79; 42 L.J.C.P. 46; 27
    L.T. 557; 21 W.R. 142 286
Mills v. Edwards [1971] 1 Q.B. 379; [1971] 2 W.L.R. 418; (1970) 114 S.J. 973; [1971]
    1 All E.R. 992; 22 P. & C.R. 171, C.A. 779
Milmo v. Carreras [1946] K.B. 306; 174 L.T. 223; [1946] 1 All E.R. 678 ... 39, 303, 315,
    551
Minay v. Sentongo (1982) 126 S.J. 674; (1983) 45 P. & C.R. 190; (1983) 266 E.G.
    433, C.A. 459
Minister of Agriculture and Fisheries v. Huskin [1948] E.G.D. 195 14
—— v. Matthews [1950] 1 K.B 148; *sub nom.* Ministry of Agriculture and Fisheries
    v. Matthews 65 T.L.R. 655; [1949] 2 All E.R. 14, 79
Minister of Aircraft Production v. Hunt [1945] L.J.N. C.C.R. 1 14
Minister of Health v. Bellotti [1944] K.B. 298; 113 L.J.K.B. 436; 170 L.T. 146; 60
    T.L.R. 228; [1944] 1 All E.R. 238 .... 358, 359
Ministry of Agriculture, Fisheries & Foods v. Jenkins [1983] 2 Q.B 317; [1963] 2
    W.L.R. 906; 107 S.J. 234; [1963] 2 All E.R. 147, C.A. 783
Mint v. Good [1951] 1 K.B 517; 94 S.J. 822; [1950] 2 All E.R. 1159; 49 L.G.R. 495,
    C.A. 218, 368, 543
Mitas v. Hyams [1951] 2 T.L.R. 1215, C.A. 177
Mitchell v. London Borough of Ealing [1979] Q.B 1; [1978] 2 W.L.R. 999; 122 S.J.
    213; [1975] 2 All E.R. 779; (1978) 76 L.G.R. 703 350
Mitten v. Fagg (1978) 247 E.G. 901 312
Mitton v. Farrow (1980) 255 E.G. 449, C.A. 761
Moat v. Martin [1950] 1 K.B 175; 65 T.L.R. 660; 93 S.J. 677; [1949] 2 All E.R. 646,
    C.A. 306
Mogridge (W. J.) (Bristol 1937) Ltd. v. Bristol Corpn. [1956] 8 P. & C.R. 78, Lands
    Tribunal 737

Molton Builders *v.* Westminster City Council (1975) 119 S.J. 627; 234 E.G. 115; 30
    P. & C.R. 182, C.A.; *affirming* [1974] J.P.L. 600 187
Monk *v.* Arnold [1902] 1 K.B. 761; 71 L.J.K.B. 441; 86 L.T. 580; 50 W.R. 667 113
—— *v.* Cooper (1727) 2 Str. 763; 1 Ld.Raym. 1477 137
—— *v.* Noyes (1824) 1 C. & P. 265 223
Morphett *v.* Jones (1818) 1 Swans. 172; 1 Wills. Ch. 100; [1814–23] All E.R. Rep.
    612 87
Monro *v.* Burghclere (Lord) [1918] 1 K.B 291; 87 L.J.K.B. 366; 118 L.T. 343; 82 J.P.
    86; 16 L.G.R. 210; 62 S.J. 231; 34 T.L.R. 131 113
Monson (Lord) *v.* Bound [1954] 1 W.L.R. 1321, 98 S.J. 751; [1954] 3 All E.R. 228;
    52 L.G.R. 511 758
Montagu, *Re*, *v.* Browning [1954] 1 W.L.R. 1039; 98 S.J. 492; *sub nom.* Montague *v.*
    Browning [1954] 2 All E.R. 601, C.A. 157, 158
Montague *Re*, *v.* Browning. *See* Montagu, *Re*, *v.* Browning.
Moodie *v.* Hosegood [1952] A.C. 61; [1951] 2 T.L.R. 455; 95 S.J. 499; [1951] 2 All
    E.R. 582, H.L. 439
Moore *v.* Assignment Courier Ltd. [1977] 1 W.L.R. 638; 11 S.J. 155; [1977] 2 All
    E.R. 842; 35 P. & C.R. 400, C.A. 197
Moore and Hulm's Contract, *Re* [1912] 2 Ch. 105; 81 L.J.Ch. 503; 106 L.T. 330; 6
    S.J. 89 54
Moore Properties (Ilford) Ltd. *v.* McKeon [1976] 1 W.L.R. 1278; [1977] 1 All E.R.
    262; (1976) 241 E.G. 387 467
Morar *v.* Chauhan [1985] 1 W.L.R. 1263; [1985] 3 All E.R. 493; 129 S.J. 542; 276
    E.G. 300; 51 P. & C.R. 59; 1365 New L.J. 1010; 82 L.S.Gaz. 3448, C.A. 702
Morford Investments Ltd. *v.* Lambert [1976] Ch. 39 500
Morgan *v.* Davies (1878) 3 C.P.D. 260; 39 L.T. 60; 26 W.R. 816 345
—— *v.* Liverpool Corpn. [1927] 2 K.B 131; 96 L.J.K.B. 234; 136 L.T. 622; 91 J.P.
    26; 25 L.G.R. 79; 71 S.J. 35; 43 T.L.R. 146 .... 235, 242
—— *v.* Murch [1970] 1 W.L.R. 778; 114 S.J. 265; [1970] 2 All E.R. 100, C.A. 440
—— *v.* Taylor (1949) 153 E.G. 3, Cty. Ct. 379
Morleys (Birmingham) Ltd. *v.* Slater [1950] 1 K.B 506; 66 T.L.R. (Pt. 1) 483; 94 S.J.
    146; [1950] 1 All E.R. 331, C.A. 406
Morris *v.* Baron & Co. [1918] A.C. 1; 87 L.J.K.B. 145; 118 L.T. 34 84
—— *v.* Moss (1855) 25 L.J.Ch. 194 740
Morrison *v.* Jacobs [1945] K.B. 577; 173 L.T. 170; 61 T.L.R. 550; [1945] 2 All E.R.
    430 .... 347, 407
Morrison Holdings *v.* Manders Property (Wolverhampton) [1976] 1 W.L.R. 533;
    (1975) 120 S.J. 63; [1976] 2 All E.R. 205; (1975) 32 P. & C.R. 218 .... 646, 675
Morrissey *v.* Galer [1955] 1 W.L.R. 110; 99 S.J. 113; 53 L.G.R. 303; *sub nom.*
    Galer *v.* Morrissey 119 J.P. 165; [1955] 1 All E.R. 380, D.C. 260
Mortimer *v.* Shortall (1842) 2 Dr. & War. 363; 59 R.R. 739; [1835–42] All E.R. Rep.
    229 149
—— *v.* Wilson (1885) 33 W.R. 927 257
Morton *v.* Woods (1869) 9 B. & S. 632; L.R. 4 Q.B. 293; 38 L.J.Q.B. 81; 17 W.R.
    414; *affirming* L.R. 3 Q.B. 658; 37 L.J.Q.B. 242; 18 L.T. 791 43
Moses *v.* Lovegrove [1952] 2 Q.B 533; [1952] 1 T.L.R. 1324; 96 S.J. 344; [1952] 1 All
    E.R. 1279, C.A. 173
Moss (E.) Ltd. *v.* Brown [1946] 2 All E.R. 557, C.A. 31, 33
Moule *v.* Garrett (1870–72) L.R. 5 Ex. 132; L.R. 7 Ex. 101; 41 L.J.Ex. 62; 26
    L.T. 367; 20 W.R. 416 .... 316, 321, 322
Mount *v.* Childs [1948] W.N. 84; (1948) 64 T.L.R. 559; 92 S.J. 498, C.A. 407
Mount Charlotte Investments *v.* Leek & Westbourne Building Society [1976] 1 All
    E.R. 890; (1975) 30 P. & C.R. 410 179
Mountford *v.* Hodkinson [1956] 1 W.L.R. 442; 100 S.J. 301; [1956] 2 All E.R. 17,
    C.A. 779
Mularczyk *v.* Azralnove Investments (1985) 276 E.G. 1064, C.A. 701

Muller v. Trafford [1901] 1 Ch. 54; 70 L.J.Ch. 72; 49 W.R. 132 141
Multiservice Bookbinding v. Marden [1979] Ch. 84; [1978] 2 W.L.R 535; (1977) 122
    S.J. 210; [1978] 2 All E.R. 489; (1977) 35 P. & C.R. 201 191
Mumford Hotels Ltd. v. Wheler [1964] Ch. 117; [1963] 3 W.L.R. 735; 107 S.J. 810;
    [1963] 3 All E.R. 250 .... 118, 119, 168
Murray v. Two Strokes Ltd. [1973] 1 W.L.R. 823; 117 S.J. 447; [1973] 3 All E.R. 357;
    26 P. & C.R. 1 145
Murray Bull & Co. Ltd. v. Murray [1953] 1 Q.B 211; [1952] 2 T.L.R. 1003; 96 S.J.
    852; [1952] 2 All E.R 1079 .... 17, 31, 448
Muskett v. Hill (1839) 5 Bing.N.C. 694; 7 Scott 855; 9 L.J.C.P. 201; 50 R.R. 832 10
Muspratt v. Johnston [1963] 2 Q.B. 383; [1963] 2 W.L.R. 1153; 107 S.J. 252; [1963] 2
    All E.R. 339, C.A. 312, 464
Mykolyshyn v. Noah [1970] 1 W.L.R. 1271; [1971] 1 All E.R. 48; (1970) 21 P. & C.R.
    679; *sub nom.* Noah v. Mykolyshyn (1970) 114 S.J. 684, C.A. 451, 695

Nagel's Lease, *Re*, Allen v. Little Abbey School (Newbury) Ltd. [1974] 1 W.L.R.
    1077; 118 S.J. 532; [1974] 3 All E.R. 34; 28 P. & C.R. 158 143
Naish v. Curzon (1985) 129 S.J. 222; 273 E.G. 1221; (1984) 17 H.L.R. 220; (1985) 82
    L.S.Gaz. 605, C.A. 458
National Car Parks v. Colebrook Estates Ltd. (1982) 266 E.G. 810 714
National Carriers Ltd. v. Panalpine (Northern) Ltd. [1981] A.C. 675; [1981] 2
    W.L.R. 45; (1980) 125 S.J. 46; [1981] 1 All E.R. 161; (1982) 43 P. & C.R. 72,
    H.L. 137, 153, 154, 175, 233
National Coal Board v. Naylor [1972] 1 W.L.R. 908; (1971) 116 S.J. 507; [1972] 1 All
    E.R. 1153; (1971) 23 P. & C.R. 129; 71 L.G.R. 403, D.C. 783
—— v. Neath B.C. [1976] 2 All E.R. 478, D.C. 261, 262
National Electric Theatres v. Hudgell [1939] Ch. 553; 108 L.J.Ch. 249; 160 L.T. 467;
    55 T.L.R. 424; 83 S.J. 257; [1939] 1 All E.R. 567 670
National Provincial Bank Ltd. v. Ainsworth [1965] A.C. 1175; [1965] 3 W.L.R. 1;
    109 S.J. 415; [1965] 2 All E.R. 472, H.L. 11, 12, 442
National Savings Bank Association, *Re, ex p.* Brady (1867) 15 W.R. 753 87
National Westminster Bank plc. v. Arthur Young McCelland Moores & Co. [1985] 1
    W.L.R. 1123; (1985) 129 S.J. 638; [1985] 2 All E.R. 817; 272 E.G. 717, C.A.;
    affirming 273 E.G. 402 189
—— v. B.S.C. Footwear Ltd. (1981) 42 P. & C.R. 90; (1980) 257 E.G. 277,
    C.A. 141, 191
—— v. Hart [1983] Q.B. 773; [1983] 2 W.L.R. 693; [1983] 2 All E.R. 177; (1984) 47
    P. & C.R. 102; (1983) 267 E.G. 252, C.A. 80
Naumann v. Ford (1985) 275 E.G. 542; 82 L.S.Gaz. 1858 324
Neale v. Del Soto [1945] K.B. 144; 114 L.J.K.B. 138; 172 L.T. 65; 61 T.L.R. 145; 89
    S.J. 130; [1945] 1 All E.R. 191 .... 382, 384
New Oriental Bank Corporation (No. 2), *Re* [1895] 1 Ch. 753; 64 L.J.Ch. 439; 72
    L.T. 419; 43 W.R. 523; 2 Manson 301 203
New Zealand Government Property Corpn. v. H.M. & S. [1982] 2 W.L.R. 837;
    [1982] 1 All E.R. 624; [1982] Q.B 1145; 44 P. & C.R. 329; 263 E.G. 765, C.A.;
    affirming [1981] 1 W.L.R. 870 .... 60, 665, 676
Newborough (Lord) v. Jones [1975] Ch. 90; [1974] 3 W.L.R. 52; 118 S.J. 479; [1974]
    3 All E.R. 17; 28 P. & C.R. 215, C.A. 349
Newby v. Sharpe (1877–78) 8 Ch.D. 39; 47 L.J.Ch. 617; 38 L.T. 583; 26 W.R. 685 174
Newham L.B.C. v. Benjamin [1968] 1 W.L.R. 694; 112 S.J. 253; 66 L.G.R. 372; *sub
    nom.* London Borough of Newham v. Benjamin 132 J.P. 220; [1968] 1 All
    E.R. 1195, C.A. 727
—— v. Patel (1984) 13 B.L.R. 77; [1979] J.P.L. 303, C.A. 559
Newfoundland (Government of) v. Newfoundland Railway Co. (1888) 13 A.C.
    199 .... 255, 256
Newman v. Anderton (1806) 2 Bos. & P.N.R. 224 172

Newman *v.* Dorrington Developments Ltd. [1975] 1 W.L.R. 1642; 119 S.J. 611;
[1975] 3 All E.R. 928; 31 P. & C.R. 26 .... 141, 167
—— *v.* Keedwell (1977) 244 E.G. 469; (1978) 35 P. & C.R. 393 782
—— *v.* Real Estate Debenture Corpn. Ltd. (1940) 162 L.T. 183; [1940] 1 All
E.R.131 127
Newton *v.* Osborn (1653) 82 E.R. 800; Style 387 151
Nicoll *v.* First National Developments (1972) 226 E.G. 301, D.C. 425
Nightingale *v.* Courtney [1954] 1 Q.B. 399; [1954] 2 W.L.R. 266; 98 S.J. 110; [1954] 1
All E.R. 362, C.A. 340
Noble *v.* S. Herefordshire D.C. (1984) 17 H.L.R. 80, C.A. 618
Nock *v.* Munk (1982) 263 E.G. 1085 429
Nordenfelt *v.* Maxim Nordenfelt Guns and Ammunition Co. Ltd. [1894] A.C. 535;
[1891–4] All E.R.Rep. 1; 63 L.J.Ch. 908; 71 L.T. 489; 10 T.L.R. 636; 11 R.
1, H.L.; *affirming sub nom.* Maxim Nordenfelt Guns & Ammunition Co. *v.*
Nordenfelt [1893] 1 Ch. 630, C.A. 745, 746, 747
Norfolk Capital Group Ltd. *v.* Kitway Ltd. [1977] Q.B. 506; (1976) 34 P. & C.R. 32,
C.A. 311
Norman *v.* Ricketts (1886) 3 T.L.R. 182 161
Normanton (Earl) *v.* Giles. *See* Earl of Normanton *v.* Giles.
North *v.* Loomes [1919] 1 Ch. 378; 88 L.J.Ch. 217; 120 L.T. 533 .... 84, 86
Northchurch Estates Ltd. *v.* Daniels [1947] Ch. 117; [1947] L.J.R. 6; 176 L.T. 4; 90
S.J. 543; [1946] 2 All E.R. 524 .... 46, 47
Northcote Laundry *v.* Donnelly (Frederick) [1968] 1 W.L.R. 562; 112 S.J. 153;
[1968] 2 All E.R. 50; 19 P. & C.R. 322, C.A. 108, 704
Northern Ireland Commissioner of Valuation *v.* Fermanagh Protestant Board of
Education. *See* Commissioner of Valuation for Northern Ireland *v.* Fer-
managh Protestant Board of Education.
Northern Ireland Trailers Ltd. *v.* Preston Corpn. [1972] 1 W.L.R. 203; (1971) 116
S.J. 100; *sub nom.* Northern Ireland Trailers *v.* County Borough of Preston
[1972] 1 All E.R. 260, D.C. 263
Nottingham City D.C. *v.* Newton; Nottingham Friendship H.A. *v.* Newton [1974] 1
W.L.R. 923; 118 S.J. 462; *sub nom.* Nottingham Corpn. *v.* Newton;
Nottingham Friendship Housing Association *v.* Newton [1974] 2 All E.R.
760; 72 L.G.R. 535, D.C. 262, 263, 544
Nursery *v.* Currie (P.) (Dartford) Ltd. [1959] 1 W.L.R. 273; 103 S.J. 221; [1959] 1 All
E.R. 497, C.A. 702
Nussey *v.* Provincial Bill Posting Co. and Eddison [1909] 1 Ch. 734; 78 L.J.Ch. 539;
100 L.T. 687; 25 T.L.R. 489; 53 S.J. 418, C.A. 658

Oak Pits Colliery Co., *Re* (1882) 21 Ch.D. 322; 51 L.J.Ch. 768; 47 L.T. 7; 30 W.R.
759 204
Oak Property Co. Ltd. *v.* Chapman [1947] K.B. 886; [1947] L.J.R. 1327; 177 L.T.
364; 63 T.L.R. 338; 91 S.J. 324; [1947] 2 All E.R. 1, C.A. 464
Oakacre Ltd. *v.* Claire Cleaners (Holdings) Ltd. [1981] 3 W.L.R. 761; [1981] 3 All
E.R. 667; (1982) 43 P. & C.R. 48; [1982] Ch. 197 97
Oakley *v.* Wilson [1927] 2 K.B 279; 96 L.J.K.B. 783; 137 L.T. 479; 25 L.G.R. 316; 71
S.J. 409; 43 T.L.R. 521 15
Oates *v.* Frith (1615) Hob. 130a 154
O'Brien *v.* Robinson [1973] A.C. 912; [1973] 2 W.L.R. 393; 117 S.J. 187; [1973] 1 All
E.R. 583; 25 P. & C.R. 239, H.L. 235, 244, 250
O'Callaghan *v.* Elliott [1966] 1 Q.B. 601; [1965] 3 W.L.R. 746; 109 S.J. 436; [1965] 3
All E.R. 111, C.A. 105, 169, 649
O'Cedar Ltd. *v.* Slough Trading Co. [1927] 2 K.B. 123; 86 L.J.K.B. 709; 137 L.T.
208; 43 T.L.R. 382 .... 119, 132

Odeon Associated Cinemas Ltd. *v.* Jones [1973] Ch. 288; [1972] 2 W.L.R. 331; (1971) 115 S.J. 850; [1971] T.R. 373; [1972] 1 All E.R. 681; (1971) 48 T.C. 257, C.A.; *affirming* [1971] 1 W.L.R. 442; (1970) 115 S.J. 224; [1971] 2 All E.R. 407; [1970] T.R. 299 209
O'Donoghue *v.* Coalbrook and Broadoak Co. (1872) 26 L.T. 806 164
Official Custodian for Charities *v.* Goldridge (1973) 26 P. & C.R. 191; (1973) 227 E.G. 1467, C.A. 515, 516
—— *v.* Mackey [1985] Ch. 151; [1984] 3 W.L.R. 915; 128 S.J. 751; [1984] 3 All E.R. 689; (1984) 49 P. & C.R. 242; (1984) 81 L.S.Gaz. 3425 355
—— *v.* Mackey (No. 2) [1985] 1 W.L.R. 1308; 129 S.J. 853; [1985] 2 All E.R. 1016; 274 E.G. 398; (1986) 83 L.S.Gaz. 44, 199 355
—— *v.* Parway Estates Developments Ltd. [1985] Ch. 151; [1984] 3 W.L.R. 525; 128 S.J. 549; [1984] 3 All E.R. 679; 48 P. & C.R. 125; (1985) P.C.C. 133; (1984) 270 E.G. 1077; 81 L.S.Gaz. 2382, C.A. 356
Official Trustee of Charity Lands *v.* Ferriman Trust Ltd. [1937] 3 All E.R. 85 320
Ogilvie *v.* Foljambe (1817) 3 Mer. 53; 17 R.R. 13 83
Oland *v.* Burdwick (1595) Cro.Eliz. 460; Moor. 394; Goldsb. 189; 5 Co. 116 44
Old Grovebury Manor Farm Ltd. *v.* Seymour Plant Sales & Hire Ltd. [1979] 1 W.L.R. 263; (1978) 122 S.J. 457; [1979] 1 All E.R. 573; (1978) 37 P. & C.R. 165 .... 174, 193
Old Grovebury Manor Farm Ltd. *v.* Seymour Plant Sales & Hire Ltd. (No. 2) [1979] 1 W.L.R. 1397; 123 S.J. 719; [1979] 3 All E.R. 504; 39 P. & C.R. 99; 252 E.G. 1103, C.A.; *affirming* (1979) 38 P. & C.R. 374 .... 292, 313
Olidowura *v.* Fulmuk [1975] C.L.Y. 1929 405
O'Malley *v.* Seymour (1978) 250 E.G. 1083; [1979] J.P.L. 675, C.A. 22, 33, 35
O'May *v.* City of London Real Property Co. Ltd. [1983] 2 A.C. 726; [1982] 2 W.L.R. 407; [1982] 1 All E.R. 660; (1982) 43 P. & C.R. 351; (1982) 261 E.G. 1185, H.L.; *affirming* [1981] Ch. 216; [1980] 3 W.L.R. 881; (1980) 124 S.J. 847; [1980] 3 All E.R. 466; (1980) 40 P. & C.R. 310; (1980) 255 E.G. 151, C.A. 172, 680, 711, 715, 716
Oppenheimer *v.* British Exchange Bank (1877) 6 Ch.D. 744; 46 L.J.Ch. 882; 37 L.T. 629; 26 W.R. 391 203
—— *v.* Minister of Transport [1942] 1 K.B 242; [1941] 3 All E.R. 485; 111 L.J.K.B 702; 166 L.T. 93; 106 J.P. 46; 58 T.L.R. 86; 40 L.G.R. 23, D.C. 733
O'Reilly *v.* Mackmar; Millbanks *v.* Secretary of State for the Home Department [1983] 2 A.C. 237; [1983] 3 W.L.R. 1096; (1982) 126 S.J. 820; [1982] 3 All E.R. 1124, H.L.; *affirming* O'Reilly *v.* Mackman; Derbyshire *v.* Same; Dougan *v.* Same; Millbanks *v.* Home Office [1982] 3 W.L.R. 604; 126 S.J. 578; [1982] 3 All E.R. 680; 79 L.S.Gaz. 1176, C.A. 561, 628
Orlick (Meat Products) Ltd. *v.* Hastings & Thanet Building Society (1974) 118 S.J. 811; 29 P. & C.R. 126, C.A. 711
Orman Bros. *v.* Greenbaum [1954] 3 All E.R. 731; [1955] 1 All E.R. 610 678
Oscraft *v.* Benabo [1967] 1 W.L.R. 1087; 111 S.J. 520; [1967] 2 All E.R. 548, C.A. 714
O'Toole *v.* Lyons [1948] I.R. 115 312
Ove Arup Inc. *v.* Howland Property Investment Co. (1982) 261 E.G. 149 .... 693, 749
Owen *v.* Gadd [1956] 2 Q.B. 99; [1956] 2 W.L.R. 945; 100 S.J. 301; [1956] 2 All E.R. 28, C.A. 131, 132
Owen Owen Estate Ltd. *v.* Livett [1956] Ch. 1; [1955] 3 W.L.R. 1; 99 S.J. 385; [1955] 2 All E.R. 513 665
Owers, *Re*, Public Trustee *v.* Death and Mount Vernon Hospital [1941] Ch. 389; [1940] 4 All E.R. 225; 110 L.J.Ch. 22; 164 L.T. 337; 57 T.L.R. 80; 84 S.J. 633, C.A. 329
Oxley *v.* Regional Properties Ltd. [1944] 2 All E.R. 510; [1944] 1 K.B. 733; 171 L.T. 129; 60 T.L.R. 519; 88 S.J. 376, C.A.; *reversed* on other grounds [1945] 2 All E.R. 418; [1945] A.C. 347; 114 L.J.K.B 473; 173 L.T. 201; 61 T.L.R. 563, H.L. 410

Pacol Ltd. *v.* Trade Lines Ltd. (1982) 126 S.J. 312; [1982] Com.L.R. 92; [1982] 1
Lloyd's Rep. 456 12
Paddock Investments *v.* Lory (1975) 236 E.G. 803, C.A. 783
Paget *v.* Marshall (1884) 28 Ch.D. 255; 54 L.J.Ch. 575; 51 L.C. 351; 33 W.R. 608 149
Pakwood Transport *v.* 15 Beauchamp Place (1978) 36 P. & C.R. 112 .... 310, 354
Palmer & Harvey Ltd. *v.* Ipswich Corpn. (1953) 4 P. & C.R. 5; Lands Tribunal 732
Palser *v.* Grinling; Property Holding Co. *v.* Mischett [1948] AS.C. 291; [1948] L.J.R.
600; 64 T.L.R. 2; [1948] 1 All E.R. 1 .... 400, 401, 477
Panther Lead Co., *Re* [1896] 1 Ch. 978; 65 L.J.Ch. 499; 44 W.R. 573 ...... 203, 205, 339
Parker *v.* Boggon [1947] K.B. 346; [1947] L.J.R. 509; 63 T.L.R. 4; 91 S.J. 85; [1947] 1
All E.R. 46 .... 309, 310
—— *v.* Briggs (1893) 37 S.J. 452 175
—— *v.* Camden L.B.C.; Newman *v.* Camden L.B.C. [1985] 3 W.L.R. 47; 129 S.J.
417; [1985] 2 All E.R. 141; 17 H.L.R. 380; 82 L.S.Gaz. 2345, C.A. 258
—— *v.* O'Connor [1974] 1 W.L.R. 1160; 118 S.J. 480; [1974] 3 All E.R. 257; 28 P. &
C.R. 355, C.A. 248
—— *v.* Rosenberg [1947] K.B. 371; [1947] L.J.R. 495; 176 L.T. 170; 63 T.L.R. 53;
91 S.J. 116; [1947] 1 All E.R. 87, C.A. 456
—— *v.* Webb (1703) 3 Salk. 5; Holt 75 317
Parker-Knoll *v.* Knoll International [1962] R.P.C. 265, H.L.; *affirming sub nom.*
Parker-Knoll and Parker-Knoll (Textiles) *v.* Knoll International Britain
(Furniture and Textiles) [1961] R.P.C. 346, C.A. 741
Parkus *v.* Greenwood [1950] Ch. 644; 66 T.L.R. (Pt. 1) 496; *sub nom. Re*
Greenwood's Agreement, Parkus *v.* Greenwood [1950] 1 All E.R. 436,
C.A. 46, 141
Paradine *v.* Jane (1647) Aleyn 26; Style 47; [1558–1714] All E.R. Rep. 172; 82 E.R.
897 .... 137, 151, 174
Parmee *v.* Mitchell [1950] 2 K.B. 199; 66 T.L.R. (Pt. 1) 1185; 94 S.J. 302; [1950] 1 All
E.R. 872, C.A. 695
Parmenter *v.* Webber (1818) 8 Taunt. 593; 2 Moore 656; 20 R.R. 575 154
Parrish *v.* Kinsey (1983) 268 E.G. 113, C.A. 786
Parson's *v.* Gage (Viscount) (Trustees of Henry Smith's Charity) [1974] 1 W.L.R.
435; 118 S.J. 463; [1974] 1 All E.R. 1162; 27 P. & C.R. 453, H.L.; *affirming
sub nom.* Parsons *v.* Smith's (Henry) Charity [1973] 1 W.L.R. 845; 117 S.J.
374; [1973] 3 All E.R. 23; 26 P. & C.R. 108, C.A. 507
—— *v.* Parsons [1983] 1 W.L.R. 1390; 127 S.J. 823; (1984) 47 P. & C.R. 494; 269
E.G. 634; 81 L.S.Gaz. 43 348
Parry, decd. *v.* Million Pigs (1981) 260 E.G. 281 .... 791, 802
Pascoe *v.* Turner [1979] 1 W.L.R. 431; (1978) 123 S.J. 164; [1979] 2 All E.R. 945;
(1978) 9 Fam.Law 82, C.A. 12, 13
Patel *v.* Patel [1981] 1 W.L.R. 1342; 121 S.J. 408; [1977] Fam.Law 215 456
Patman *v.* Harland (1881) 17 Ch.D. 353; 50 L.J.Ch. 642; 44 L.T. 728; 29 W.R. 707 77
Patoner *v.* Alexandrakis (1984) 272 E.G. 330, C.A. 464
Paul *v.* Nurse (1828) 8 B. & C. 486; 2 Man. & Ry.K.B. 525; 7 L.J.(o.s.)K.B. 12; 108
E.R. 1123 294
Pawson *v.* Revell [1958] 2 Q.B 360; [1958] 3 W.L.R. 474; 102 S.J. 632; [1958] 3 All
E.R. 233 64
Peabody Donation Fund Governors *v.* Grant (1982) 264 E.G. 925, C.A. 591
—— *v.* Higgins [1983] 1 W.L.R. 1091; 127 S.J. 596; [1983] 3 All E.R. 122,
C.A. 313, 533, 591
—— *v.* Parkinson (Sir Lindsay) & Co. [1985] A.C. 210; [1984] 3 W.L.R. 953; 128
S.J. 753; [1984] 3 All E.R. 529; [1985] L.G.R. 1; (1984) 28 Build.L.R. 1;
[1984] C.I.L.L. 128; 81 L.S.Gaz. 3179, H.L.; *affirming* [1983] 3 W.L.R. 754 .. 372
Peachey Property Corpn. *v.* Robinson [1967] 2 Q.B. 543; [1966] 2 W.L.R. 1386; 110
S.J. 426; [1966] 2 All E.R. 981, C.A. 196, 609
Pearce *v.* Maryon-Wilson [1935] Ch. 188; 104 L.J.Ch. 169; 152 L.T. 443; 78 S.J. 860 . 127

Pearl Assurance *v*. Shaw (1985) 274 E.G. 492 .... 187, 300
Pearlman *v*. Keepers and Governors of Harrow School [1979] Q.B 56; [1978] 3
    W.L.R. 736; [1979] 1 All E.R. 365; (1978) 38 P. & C.R. 136; 247 E.G. 1173;
    [1978] J.P.L. 829, C.A. 237, 508
Peck *v*. Anicar Properties Ltd. [1971] 1 All E.R. 517, C.A. 506
Peffer *v*. Rigg [1977] 1 W.L.R. 285; [1978] 3 All E.R. 745; (1976) 242 E.G. 123 65,
                                                                                                            146
Pellow *v*. Ivey (1933) 49 T.L.R. 422 747
Pelosi *v*. Newcastle Arms Brewery (Nottingham) Ltd. (1981) 125 S.J. 530; 259 E.G.
    247; 43 P. & C.R. 18, C.A. 665
Pembery *v*. Lamdin [1940] 2 All E.R. 434 226
Peninsular Maritime Ltd. *v*. Padseal Ltd. (1981) 259 E.G. 860, C.A. 253, 293
Penn *v*. Dunn [1970] 2 Q.B. 686; [1970] 3 W.L.R. 321; 114 S.J. 532; [1970] 2 All E.R.
    858; 21 P. & C.R. 898, C.A. 444
Pennington *v*. Crossley & Sons (1897) 13 T.L.R. 513 161
Perdana Properties Bhd. *v*. United Orient Leasing Co. Shn. Bhd. [1981] 1 W.L.R.
    1496; 125 S.J. 791, P.C.; [1982] 1 All E.R. 193 200
Perera *v*. Vandiyar [1953] 1 W.L.R. 672; 97 S.J. 332; [1953] 1 All E.R. 1109,
    C.A. 131, 405
Perezic *v*. Bristol Corpn. (1955) 5 P. & C.R. 237; Lands Tribunal 737
Perseus Property Co. *v*. Burberry (1984) 17 H.L.R. 243; (1985) 273 E.G. 405 424
Persey *v*. Bazley (1983) 127 S.J. 579; (1984) 47 P. & C.R. 37; (1983) 267 E.G. 519,
    C.A. 325, 776, 784
Personal Representatives of the Estate of the late Dr. Cotton *v*. Gardiner [1980]
    C.L.Y. 24 775
Petrofina (U.K.) Ltd. *v*. Magnaload Ltd. [1984] 1 Q.B. 127; [1983] 3 W.L.R. 805;
    127 S.J. 729; [1983] 3 All E.R. 33; [1983] 2 Lloyd's Rep. 91; (1984) 25
    Build.L.R. 37; (1983) 80 L.S.Gaz. 2677 117
Peyman *v*. Lanjani [1985] 2 W.L.R. 154; (1984) 128 S.J. 853; [1984] All E.R. 703; 48
    P. & C.R. 398; (1985) 82 L.S.Gaz. 43, C.A. 195
Phené *v*. Popplewell (1862) 12 C.B.(N.S.) 334; 31 L.J.C.P. 235; 8 Jur.(N.S.) 1104; 6
    L.T. 247; 10 W.R. 523 339
Philipson-Stow *v*. Square (Trevor) (1981) 257 E.G. 1262 686
Phillimore *v*. Lane (1925) 133 L.T. 268; 69 S.J. 542; 41 T.L.R. 469 370
Phillips *v*. Lamdin [1949] 2 K.B. 33; [1949] L.J.R. 1293; 93 S.J. 320; [1949] 1 All E.R.
    770 .... 95, 295
—— *v*. Newham L.B.C. (1982) 48 P. & C.R. 54, C.A. 266
—— *v*. Phillips [1973] 1 W.L.R. 615; 117 S.J. 323; [1973] 2 All E.R. 423, C.A. 443
Phipps & Co. (Northampton and Towcester) Breweries Ltd. *v*. Rogers [1925] 1
    K.B. 14; 93 L.J.K.B. 1009; 132 L.T. 240; 89 J.P. 1; 69 S.J. 50; 40 T.L.R.
    849 .... 341, 343, 347
Pickard *v*. Bishop (1975) 119 S.J. 407; 31 P. & C.R. 108; 235 E.G. 133, C.A. 786
Pimms Ltd. *v*. Tallow Chandlers Co. [1964] 2 Q.B 547; [1964] 2 W.L.R. 1129; 108
    S.J. 237; [1964] 2 All E.R. 145, C.A. 308, 309, 311
Pincottt *v*. Moorstons Ltd. (1937) 156 L.T. 139; 81 S.J. 136; [1937] 1 All E.R. 513 302
Pindar *v*. Ainsley and Rutter (1767) 1 T.R. 312; 99 E.R.1113 137
Pinemain *v*. Welbeck International (1985) 129 S.J. 66; (1984) 272 E.G. 1166; 81
    L.S.Gaz. 3426, C.A. 161, 316, 318, 324
Piper *v*. Muggleton [1956] 2 Q.B 569; [1956] 2 W.L.R. 1093; 100 S.J. 360; [1956] 2 All
    E.R. 249, C.A. 683
Pitcher *v*. Tovey (1692) 4 Mod. 71; 1 Salk. 81; 2 Vent. 234; 3 Lev. 295; 1 Show. 340;
    Carth. 177; 12 Mod. 23; Holt 73 .... 1, 157
Pivot Properties *v*. Secretary of State for the Environment (1980) 256 E.G. 1176; 41
    P. & C.R. 248, C.A.; (1979) 39 P. & C.R. 386; 253 E.G. 373 185
Pleasant (Leesee of Hayton) *d*. Hayton *v*. Benson (1811) 14 East 234; 12 R.R. 507 348
Plesser (A.) & Co. *v*. Davis (1983) 267 E.G. 1039 .... 161, 677, 678

Plimmer *v.* Wellington Corp. (1884) 9 App.Cas. 699; 53 L.J.P.C. 105; 51 L.T. 475
(N.Z.) 12, 13
Plinth Property Investments *v.* Mott, May & Anderson (1979) 38 P. & C.R. 361;
(1978) 249 E.G. 1167, C.A.; *affirming* (1977) 38 P. & C.R. 361 .... 185, 186
Plumrose *v.* Real and Leasehold Estate Investment Society [1970] 1 W.L.R. 52; 113
S.J. 1000; [1969] 3 All E.R. 1441; 21 P. & C.R. 52 142
Plymouth Corpn. *v.* Harvey [1971] 1 W.L.R. 549; (1970) 115 S.J. 13; [1971] 1 All
E.R. 623; 22 P. & C.R. 475; 69 L.G.R. 310 .... 335, 357
Pocock *v.* Steel [1985] 1 W.L.R. 229; 129 S.J. 84; [1985] 1 All E.R. 434; 49 P. & C.R.
90; 272 E.G. 1218; (1984) 17 H.L.R. 181, C.A. 458
Pointe Gourde Quarrying and Transport Co. *v.* Sub-Intendant of Crown Lands
[1947] A.C. 565; 63 T.L.R. 486; [1970] R.V.R. 764; 120 S.J. 481, P.C. 732
Poland *v.* Earl Cadogan (1980) 124 S.J. 575; [1980] 3 All E.R. 544; 40 P. & C.R. 321;
250 E.G. 495, C.A. 512, 546
Pole-Carew *v.* Western Counties and General Manure Co. [1920] 2 Ch. 97; 89
L.J.Ch. 559; 123 L.T. 12; 36 T.L.R. 322, C.A. 57
Pole Properties *v.* Feinberg (1981) 259 E.G. 417, C.A.; (1982) 43 P. & C.R.
121 .... 135, 172, 423
Pollock *v.* Brook-Shepherd (1983) 45 P. & C.R. 357, C.A. 509
Pollway Nominees Ltd. *v.* Croydon L.B.C. [1985] 3 W.L.R. 564; (1986) 129 S.J. 590;
[1985] 3 All E.R. 24; 83 L.G.R. 770; 17 H.L.R. 503; 82 L.S.Gaz. 2997, C.A.;
affirming (1984) 128 S.J. 630; 16 H.L.R. 41; [1985] L.G.R. 79; 49 P. & C.R.
97 266
Polyviou *v.* Seeley [1980] 1 W.L.R. 55; (1979) 123 S.J. 586; [1979] 3 All E.R. 853; 39
P. & C.R. 164; 252 E.G. 375, C.A. 676, 688, 691
Ponder *v.* Hillman [1969] 1 W.L.R. 1261; 113 S.J. 605; [1969] 3 All E.R. 694 381
Ponsford *v.* H.M.S. Aerosolo Ltd. [1979] A.C. 63; [1978] 3 W.L.R. 241; 122 S.J.
487; [1978] 2 All E.R. 837; 38 P. & C.R. 270; 247 E.G. 1171, H.L.; *affirming*
[1977] 1 W.L.R. 1029; 121 S.J. 240; [1977] 3 All E.R. 651; 33 P. & C.R. 465,
C.A. 140, 188, 669
Poole *v.* Archer (1684) Skin. 210; 2 Show. 401; 89 E.R. 1007 234
Poppett's (Caterers) Ltd. *v.* Maidenhead B.C. [1971] 1 W.L.R. 69; (1970) 114 S.J.
953; 21 P. & C.R. 851; 68 L.G.R. 701; *sub nom.* Poppet's (Caterers) *v.*
Maidenhead B.C. [1970] 3 All E.R. 289, C.A. 705
Port *v.* Griffith [1938] 1 All E.R. 295; 82 S.J. 154 124
Port Line Steamers *v.* Ben Line Ltd. [1958] 2 Q.B. 146; [1958] 2 W.L.R. 551; 102 S.J.
232; [1958] 1 All E.R. 787; [1958] 1 Lloyd's Rep. 290 2
Portavon Cinema Co. Ltd. *v.* Price and Century Insurance Co. Ltd. [1939] 4 All E.R.
601; 161 L.T. 417; 84 S.J. 152; 45 Com.Cas. 93; 65 Ll.L.Rep. 161 120
Porter *v.* Jones (1942) 112 L.J.K.B 173; [1942] 2 All E.R. 570 .... 251, 252
—— *v.* Swetman (1653) Style 406 151
Post Office *v.* Aquarium Properties (1985) 276 E.G. 923 233
Poster *v.* Slough Estates Ltd. [1969] 1 Ch. 495; [1968] 1 W.L.R. 1515; 112 S.J. 705;
[1968] 3 All E.R. 257; 19 P. & C.R. 841; [1968] J.P.L. 687 678
Potter *v.* I.R.C. (1854) 10 Ex. 147; 23 L.J.Ex. 345; 18 Jur. 778; 2 W.R. 561; 156 E.R.
392; *sub nom.* Re Stamp Duty on Potters' Deed, 2 C.L.R. 1131; *sub nom.*
Att.-Gen. *v.* Potter 23 L.T(o.s.) 269 740
Powell *v.* London & Provincial Bank Ltd. [1893] 2 Ch. 555; 62 L.J.Ch. 795; 69 L.T.
421; 41 W.R. 545; 9 T.L.R. 446; 37 S.J. 476; 2 R. 482, C.A. 71
Powys *v.* Blagrave (1854) 4 De G.M. & G. 448; 24 L.J.Ch. 142 294
Preeper *v.* Preeper (1978) 84 D.L.R. (3d) 74; Nova Scotia Supreme Court 93
Premier Confectionery (London) Co. Ltd. *v.* London Commercial Sale Rooms Ltd.
[1933] Ch. 904; 102 L.J.Ch. 353; 149 L.T. 479; 77 S.J. 523 311
Preston *v.* Norfolk C.C. [1947] .B. 775; [1947] L.J.R. 1301; 177 L.T. 390; 63 T.L.R.
441; [1947] 2 All E.R. 124, C.A.; *affirming* [1946] 2 All E.R. 461 808
Pretty *v.* Bickmore (1873) L.R. 8 C.P. 401; 28 L.T. 704; 21 W.R. 733 .... 367, 368

Price *v.* Dyer (1810) 17 Ves. 356; 11 R.R. 102; [1803–13] All E.R.Rep. 61 138
—— *v.* Esso Petroleum Ltd. (1980) 255 E.G. 243, C.A. 701
—— *v.* Romilly [1960] 1 W.L.R. 1360; 104 S.J. 1060; [1960] 3 All E.R. 429 788
—— *v.* Strange [1978] Ch. 337; [1977] 3 W.L.R. 943; [1978] 36 P. & C.R. 59; (1977)
    121 S.J. 816; [1977] 3 All E.R. 371; 243 E.G. 295, C.A. 96
Printing House Properties Ltd. *v.* Winston (J.) & Co. Ltd. (1982) 263 E.G. 275 182
Pritchard *v.* Briggs [1980] Ch. 338; [1979] 3 W.L.R. 868; (1979) 123 S.J. 705; [1980] 1
    All E.R. 294; (1979) 40 P. & C.R. 1, C.A. 145
Progress Assurance Co., *Re* (1870) L.R. 9 Eq. 370; 39 L.J.Ch. 504; 22 L.T. 707 204
Property and Bloodstock Ltd. *v.* Emmerton; Bush *v.* Property and Bloodstock Ltd.
    [1968] Ch. 94; [1967] 3 W.L.R. 973; [1967] 3 All E.R. 321; *sub nom.* Bush *v.*
    Property and Bloodstock (1967) 111 S.J. 414, C.A.; *affirming* [1967] 2 All
    E.R. 839 308
Property Holding Co. Ltd. *v.* Clark [1948] 1 K.B. 630; [1948] L.J.R. 1066; 64 T.L.R.
    76; [1948] 1 All E.R. 165, C.A. 158, 172, 401
Property Holding & Investment Trust *v.* London Rent Assessment Panel, 113 S.J.
    672; *sub nom.* Property Holding & Investment Trust *v.* Lewis (1969) 20 P. &
    C.R. 808, D.C. 172
Proudfoot *v.* Hart (1890) 25 Q.B.D. 42; 59 L.J.Q.B. 389; 63 L.T. 171; 38 W.R.
    730 .... 219, 220, 221, 222, 223
Provincial Bill-Posting Co. *v.* Low Moor Iron Co. [1909] 2 K.B. 344; 78 L.J.K.B.
    702; 100 L.T. 726; 16 Manson 157, C.A. 200
Public Trustee *v.* Lawrence [1912] 1 Ch. 789; 81 L.J.Ch. 436; 56 S.J. 504 68
Public Trustee *v.* Randag [1966] Ch. 649; [1965] 3 W.L.R. 1156; 109 S.J. 935; [1965] 3
    All E.R. 88 784
Public Trustee *v.* Westbrook [1965] 1 W.L.R. 1160; 109 S.J. 792; [1965] 3 All E.R.
    398, C.A. 333
Puhlohofer *v.* London Borough of Hillingdon [1985] 1 All E.R. 467; [1985] 3 All
    E.R. 734; (1986) 136 N.L.J. 140 .... 611, 613, 614, 619, 621, 629, 632
Pulleng *v.* Curran [1980] 44 P. &C.R. 58, C.A. 549, 646
Purser *v.* Bailey [1967] 2 Q.B. 500; [1967] 2 W.L.R. 1500; 111 S.J. 353; *sub nom.*
    Bailey *v.* Purser [1967] 2 All E.R. 189, C.A.; *affirming* [1967] 1 Q.B 526;
    [1967] 2 All E.R. 146; 110 S.J. 909; *sub nom.* Bailey *v.* Purser [1967] 1 All
    E.R. 188; [1966] C.L.Y. 140, D.C. 783
Punnett, *ex p. Re* Kitchin (1881) 16 Ch.D. 226; 50 L.J.Ch. 226; 50 L.J.Ch. 212; 44
    L.T. 226; 29 W.R. 129, C.A. 740
Pwllbach Colliery Co. Ltd. *v.* Woodman [1915] A.C. 634; *affirming sub nom.*
    Woodman *v.* Pwllbach Colliery Co. Ltd. (1914) 111 L.T. 169, C.A. 105
Pyne *v.* Stallard-Penoyre [1965] Ch. 705; [1965] 2 W.L.R. 120; 108 S.J. 1031; [1965]
    1 All E.R. 487; [1964] T.R. 397; 42 T.C. 183; 43 A.T.C. 373 211

Queen's Club Gardens Estates Ltd. *v.* Bignell [1924] 1 K.B. 117; 93 L.J.K.B. 107;
    130 L.T. 26; 21 L.G.R. 688; 39 T.L.R. 496 346
Queensway Marketing *v.* Associated Restaurants (1984) 271 E.G. 1106 130
Quennel *v.* Maltby [1979] 1 W.L.R. 318; (1978) 122 S.J. .812; [1979] 1 All E.R. 568;
    (1978) 38 P. & C.R. 1; 249 E.G. 1169, C.A. 69, 405
Quick *v.* Taff-Ely B.C. [1985] 3 W.L.R. 981; 129 S.J. 685; [1985] 3 All E.R. 321; 276
    E.G. 452; 135 New L.J. 848, C.A. 229, 240, 245, 247, 543
Quilter *v.* Mapleson (1882) 9 Q.B.D. 672; 52 L.J.Q.B. 44; 47 L.T. 561; 31 W.R. 75 ... 354

R. *v.* Abrol [1972] 116 S.J. 177; [1972] Crim.L.R. 318, C.A. 608
—— *v.* Agricultural Land Tribunal for the South Eastern Area, *ex p.* Bracey [1960]
    1 W.L.R. 911; 104 S.J. 643; [1960] 2 All E.R. 518, D.C. 781
—— *v.* ——, *ex p.* Parslow (1979) 251 E.G. 667, D.C. 781
—— *v.* Barnet etc. Rent Tribunal, *ex p.* Millman [1950] 2 K.B. 506; 66 T.L.R. 1232;
    114 J.P. 390; 94 S.J. 456; [1950] 2 All E.R. 216; 48 L.G.R. 549, D.C. 741

R. *v.* Barnett and Camden Rent Tribunal, *ex p.* Frey Investments [1972] 2 Q.B 342; [1972] 2 W.L.R. 619; (1971) 115 S.J. 967; [1972] 1 All E.R. 1185; 24 P. & C.R. 202 .... 418, 478

—— *v.* Barnett L.B.C., *ex p.* Shah. *See* Akbarali *v.* Brent L.B.C. 617

—— *v.* Basingstoke and Deane B.C., *ex p.* Bassett (1983) 10 H.L.R. 125; (1984) 14 Fam.Law 90 626

—— *v.* Bath City Council, *ex p.* Sangermano (1984) 17 H.L.R. 94 618

—— *v.* Battersea, Wandsworth, Mitcham and Wimbledon Rent Tribunal, *ex p.* Parikh [1957] 1 W.L.R. 410; 121 J.P. 186; 101 S.J. 192; [1957] 1 All E.R. 352; 55 L.G.R. 109, D.C. 474

—— *v.* Beverley B.C., *ex p.* McPhee (1978) 122 S.J. 760; [1979] J.P.L. 94, D.C. 616, 628

—— *v.* Blankley [1979] Crim.L.R. 166, Knightsbridge Crown Court 607

—— *v.* Bloomsbury and Marylebone County Court, *ex p.* Blackburne (1985) 275 E.G. 1273, C.A.; *affirming* (1984) 14 H.L.R. 56 .... 362, 448

—— *v.* Bokhari (1974) 59 Cr.App.R. 303; [1974] Crim.L.R. 559, C.A. 609

—— *v.* Brighton Rent Officers, *ex p.* Elliott (1975) 119 S.J. 370; 29 P. & C.R. 456, D.C. 420

—— *v.* Bristol City Council, *ex p.* Browne [1979] 1 W.L.R. 1437; 123 S.J. 489; [1979] 3 All E.R. 344; 78 L.G.R. 32; [1979] J.P.L. 671, D.C. 614, 615, 617, 632

—— *v.* Bristol Corpn., *ex p.* Hendy [1974] 1 W.L.R. 498; [1974] 1 All E.R. 1047; (1973) 27 P. & C.R. 180; 72 L.G.R. 405, C.A. 527, 632

—— *v.* Cardiff City Council, *ex p.* Cross [1982] R.V.R. 270; (1983) 81 L.G.R. 105; [1983] J.P.L. 245, C.A.; 45 P. & C.R. 156; [1981] J.P.L. 748; (1982) 1 H.L.R. 54 265

—— *v.* Cheshunt (1818) 1 B. & Ald. 473 27

—— *v.* City of Birmingham Corpn. *ex p.* Sale (1983) 9 H.L.R. 35 268

—— *v.* City of London Rent Tribunal, *ex p.* Honig [1951] K.B. 641; [1951] 1 T.L.R. 41; 115 J.P. 42; [1951] 1 All E.R. 195; 49 L.G.R. 252, D.C. 420, 481

—— *v.* City of Westminster, *ex p.* Chambers (1982) 6 H.L.R. 24 621

—— *v.* Croydon and South West London Rent Tribunal, *ex p.* Ryzewska [1977] Q.B. 876; [1977] 2 W.L.R. 389; [1977] 1 All E.R. 312; (1976) 32 P. & C.R. 406; 242 E.G. 879, D.C. 420, 478

—— *v.* Davison-Acres [1980] Crim.L.R. 60 608

—— *v.* Deputy Industrial Injuries Commissioner, *ex p.* Humphreys [1966] 1 Q.B. 1; [1966] 2 W.L.R. 63 460

—— *v.* Dinefwr (Borough of), *ex p.* Marshall (1984) 17 H.L.R. 310 613

—— *v.* Ealing L.B.C., *ex p.* Richardson [1983] J.P.L. 533; (1983) 265 E.G. 691; [1983] M.L.R. 125, C.A. 266

—— *v.* Ealing L.B.C., *ex p.* Sidhu (1982) 80 L.G.R. 534; [1983] H.L.R. 41, 45, D.C. 620, 624

—— *v.* Eastleigh B.C., *ex p.* Evans (1984) 17 H.L.R. 515 .... 621, 624

—— *v.* Epping (Waltham Abbey) JJ., *ex p.* Burlinson [1948] 1 K.B. 79; [1948] L.J.R. 298; 63 T.L.R. 628; 112 J.P. 3; 92 S.J. 27; [1947] 2 All E.R. 537; 46 L.G.R. 6 .... 264, 544

—— *v.* Epsom and Ewell Corp., *ex p.* R.B. Property Investments (Eastern) [1964] 1 W.L.R. 1060; 128 J.P. 478; 108 S.J. 521; [1964] 2 All E.R. 832; 62 L.G.R 498, D.C. 268

—— *v.* Ewing (1976) 65 Cr.App.R. 4; 257 E.G. 55, C.A. 429, 435

—— *v.* Exeter City Council, *ex p.* Gliddon and Draper [1985] 1 All E.R. 493; (1984) 14 H.L.R. 103 .... 613, 623

—— *v.* Fulham, Hammersmith and Kensington Rent Tribunal, *ex p.* Gormly [1952] 1 K.B. 179; [1951] 2 T.L.R. 1037; 116 J.P. 22; 95 S.J. 759; [1951] 2 All E.R. 1030; 50 L.G.R. 238, D.C. 479

R. *v.* Fulham, Hammersmith and Kensington Rent Tribunal, *ex p.* Zerek [1951] 2
K.B. 1; [1951] 1 T.L.R. 423; 115 J.P. 132; 95 S.J. 237; [1951] 1 All E.R. 482;
49 L.G.R. 275, D.C. 420
—— *v.* Greater London Council, *ex p.* Royal Borough of Kensington & Chelsea
The Times, April 7, 1982 530
—— *v.* Guildford Area Tent Tribunal, *ex p.* Grubey [1951] E.G.D. 286 380
—— *v.* Hammersmith & Fulham L.B.C., *ex p.* Duro-Rama (1983) 9 H.L.R. 71; 81
L.G.R. 702 .... 621, 624
—— *v.* Hillingdon L.B., *ex p.* Islam [1983] 1 A.C. 688; (1981) 125 S.J. 809; (1982) 80
L.G.R. 141; 1 H.L. 7107; *sub nom.* Islam *v.* Hillingdon L.B.C. [1981] 3
All E.R. 901, H.L. 614, 620, 621
—— *v.* Hillingdon L.B.C., *ex p.* Streeting [1980] 1 W.L.R. 1430; 124 S.J. 514; [1980]
3 All E.R. 417; 79 L.G.R. 167, C.A.; *affirming* [1981] 1 W.L.R. 1425 . 612, 617,
627
—— *v.* Hillingdon L.B.C., *ex p.* Wilson (1983) 12 H.L.R. 48, 61 .... 621, 624
—— *v.* Hungerford Market Co., *ex p.* Davies (1832) 4 B. & Ad. 327; 1 Nev. &
M.K.B. 112; 110 E.R. 478 721
—— *v.* Kensington and Chelsea L.B.C. Rent Officer, *ex p.* Granatra [1976] Q.B
576 420
—— *v.* Kennedy [1893] 1 Q.B. 533, D.C. 727
—— *v.* Kerrier District Council, *ex p.* Guppy's (Bridport) Ltd. 120 S.J. 646;
[1976] J.P.L. 695, C.A.; *affirming* (1975) 119 S.J. 577; (1976) 32 P. & C.R.
411 264
—— *v.* Lambeth Rent Officer, *ex p.* Fox (1977) 35 P. & C.R. 65; 245 E.G. 569,
D.C. 422
—— *v.* Local Commissioner for Administration for the North and East Area of
England, *ex p.* Bradford Metropolitan Borough Council [1979] Q.B. 287;
[1979] 2 W.L.R. 1; (1978) 122 S.J. 573; [1979] 2 All E.R. 881; (1978) L.G.R.
305; [1978] J.P.L. 767, C.A.; *affirming* [1978] J.P.L. 706 .... 200, 611
—— *v.* L.B. of Hammersmith & Fulham, *ex p.* O'Brian (1985) 17 H.L.R. 471 616
—— *v.* L.B. of Harrow, *ex p.* Holland (1982) 4 H.L.R. 108, C.A. 625
—— *v.* London Rent Assessment Committee, *ex p.* Braq Investments [1969] 1
W.L.R. 970; 113 S.J. .347; [1969] 2 All E.R. 1012; 20 P. & C.R. 606, D.C. 420
—— *v.* London Rent Assessment Committee, *ex p.* St. Georges Court (No. 2)
(1983) 267 E.G. 253 426
—— *v.* London Rent Assessment Panel, *ex p.* Cliftvylle Properties (1983) 266 E.G.
44 423
—— *v.* London and Winchester Properties (1983) 45 P. & C.R. 429 518
—— *v.* Newham JJ., *ex p.* Hunt [1976] 1 W.L.R. 420; 120 S.J. 131; [1976] 1 All E.R.
839; [1976] L.G.R 305, D.C. 264, 544
—— *v.* N. Devon D.C., *ex p.* Lewis [1981] 1 W.L.R. 328; (1980) 124 S.J. 742;
79 L.G.R. 289; *sub nom.* Lewis *v.* North Devon D.C. [1981] 1 All E.R.
27 .... 612, 624
—— *v.* Nottinghamshire Registration Area, *ex p.* Allen (1985) 275 E.G. 251 380
—— *v.* Oxted Justices, *ex p.* Franklin [1976] 1 All E.R. 839 544
—— *v.* Penwith D.C., *ex p.* Hughes [1980] L.A.G.Bull. 188 623
—— *v.* Polycarpou (1983) 9 H.L.R. 129 608
—— *v.* Portsmouth City Council, *ex p.* Knight (1983) 10 H.L.R. 115; [1984] L.G.R.
184; (1984) 14 Fam.Law 304; (1983) 80 L.S.Gaz. 2444 623
—— *v.* Prestel D.C., *ex p.* Fisher (1984) 17 H.L.R. 147 .... 618, 619, 622
—— *v.* Reigate & Banstead B.C., *ex p.* Paris (1984) 15 Fam.Law 28; 17 H.L.R.
103 .... 624, 627
—— *v.* Rent Officer for L.B. of Camden, *ex p.* Ebin [1981] 1 All E.R. 950, D.C. 421
—— *v.* Rent Officer for London Borough of Camden, *ex p.* Plant (1981) 257 E.G.
713 .... 21, 403
—— *v.* Ryedale D.C., *ex p.* Smith (1983) 16 H.L.R. 66 .... 612, 613

R. *v*. Secretary of State for the Environment, *ex p*. Norwich City Council [1982]
Q.B. 808; [1982] 2 W.L.R. 580; 126 S.J. 119; 80 L.G.R. 498; *sub nom*.
Norwich City Council *v*. Secretary of State for the Environment [1982] 1 All
E.R. 737, C.A.; *affirming The Times*, December 19, 1981, D.C. 574, 575, 576
—— *v*. Secretary of State for the Environment and Buckinghamshire C.C., *ex p*.
Powis (A. G.) [1981] 1 All E.R. 788 650
—— *v*. Secretary of State for Health and Social Services, *ex p*. Sheffield C.C. (1985)
18 H.L.R. 6 531
—— *v*. Shipdam (1823) 3 D. & R. 384 27
—— *v*. Slough B.C., *ex p*. Ealing L.B.C. [1981] Q.B. 801; (1980) 125 S.J. 98; [1981]
1 All E.R. 601; (1980) 79 L.G.R. 335 .... 612, 616, 621
—— *v*. South Herefordshire D.C., *ex p*. Miles (1985) 83 L.G.R. 607 .... 619, 626
—— *v*. South Middlesex Rent Tribunal, *ex p*. Beswick (1976) 32 P. & C.R. 67; 239
E.G. 277, D.C. 20, 477
—— *v*. Southampton City Council, *ex p*. Ward (1984) 14 H.L.R. 114 .... 612, 613, 622
—— *v*. Spurrell (1865) L.R. 1 Q.B. 72; 35 L.J.M.C. 74; 13 L.T. 364; 14 W.R.
81 27
—— *v*. Stock (1810) 2 Taunt. 339; 11 R.R. 605 27
—— *v*. Surrey Heath B.C., *ex p*. Li (1984) 16 H.L.R. 79; (1985) 15 Fam.Law 124 623
—— *v*. Swansea City Council, *ex p*. John (1982) 9 H.L.R. 56 .... 612, 622, 624
—— *v*. Swansea City Council, *ex p*. Thomas (1983) 9 H.L.R. 64 624
—— *v*. Thurrock B.C., *ex p*. Williams (1982) 1 H.L.R. 128 612
—— *v*. Tottenham District Rent Tribunal, *ex p*. Fryer Bros. (Properties) [1971] 2
Q.B. 681; [1971] 3 W.L.R. 355; 22 P. & C.R. 911; [1971] 3 All E.R. 563; 115
S.J. 607, C.A. 478
—— *v*. Vale of the White Horse D.C., *ex p*. Smith and Hay (1985) L.G.R. 437;
(1984) 17 H.L.R. 160, D.C. 617
—— *v*. Wandsworth County Court, *ex p*. Wandsworth L.B.C. [1975] 1 W.L.R.
1314; 119 S.J. 529; [1975] 3 All E.R. 390, D.C.; 74 L.G.R. 62 362
—— *v*. Wandsworth L.B., *ex p*. Nimako-Boateng (1984) 14 Fam.Law 117; (1983) 11
H.L.R. 95 .... 624, 627
—— *v*. ——, *ex p*. Rose (1983) 11 H.L.R. 107 624
—— *v*. Waveney D.C., *ex p*. Bowers [1983] Q.B 238; [1982] 3 W.L.R. 661; (1982)
126 S.J. 657; [1982] 3 All E.R. 727; 80 L.G.R. 721, C.A. 618, 620
—— *v*. Wear Valley District Council, *ex p*. Binks [1985] 2 All E.R. 699 360
—— *v*. West Dorset D.C., *ex p*. Phillips (1984) 17 H.L.R. 336 624
—— *v*. Westminster C.C., *ex p*. Ali (1983) 11 H.L.R. 83 622
—— *v*. Westminster City Council, *ex p*. Chambers (1983) 81 L.G.R. 401, D.C. 614
—— *v*. Westminster (City) London Borough Rent Officer, *ex p*. Rendall [1973]
Q.B. 959; [1973] 3 W.L.R. 109; [1973] 3 All E.R. 119; 26 P. & C.R. 83 391
—— *v*. Woodspring D.C., *ex p*. Walters (1984) 16 H.L.R. 73 612
—— *v*. Wyre B.C., *ex p*. Joyce (1983) 11 H.L.R. 73 .... 612, 622
—— *v*. Wyre B.C., *ex p*. Parr [1982] C.L.Y. 1461, C.A. 615
—— *v*. Yuthiwattana (1984) 128 S.J. 661; 80 Cr.App.R. 55; 16 H.L.R. 49; [1984]
Crim.L.R. 562; 81 L.S.Gaz. 2537, C.A. 608
Radaich *v*. Smith (1959) 101 C.L.R. 209 16
Raineri *v*. Miles [1981] A.C. 1050; [1980] 2 W.L.R. 847; 124 S.J. 328; [1980] 2 All
E.R. 145; 41 P. & C.R. 71, H.L.; *affirming* [1980] 2 W.L.R. 189; (1979)
123 S.J. 605; [1979] 3 All E.R. 763; 39 P. & C.R. 129; [1979] 252 E.G. 165,
C.A. 95
Rannie *v*. Irvine (1844) 7 Man. & G. 969; 8 Scott, N.R. 674; 14 L.J.C.P. 10; 4
L.T.(o.s.) 133a; 8 Jur. 1051; 135 E.R. 393 746
Ratners (N. B.) (Jewellers) Ltd. *v*. Lemnoll Ltd. (1980) 255 E.G. 987 .... 680, 681
Ravenseft Properties Application, *Re* [1978] Q.B. 52; [1977] I.C.R. 136; [1977] 2
W.L.R. 432; *sub nom*. Ravenseft Properties *v*. Director-General of Fair
Trading [1977] 1 All E.R. 47 124

Ravenseft Properties Ltd. *v.* Dowstone (Holdings) Ltd. [1980] Q.B. 12; [1979] 2 W.L.R. 898; (1978) 123 S.J. 320; [1979] 1 All E.R. 929; 249 E.G. 51; (1978) 37 P. & C.R. 502, D.C. 222, 228
Rawlance *v.* Croydon Corpn. [1952] Q.B. 803; *sub nom.* Rawlence *v.* Croydon Corp. [1952] 2 T.L.R. 460; 116 J.P. 515; 96 S.J. 530; [1952] 2 All E.R. 535; 50 L.G.R. 576, C.A. 167
Rawlinson *v.* Ames [1925] Ch. 96; 94 L.J.Ch. 113; 132 L.T. 370; 60 S.J. 142 87
Readymix Concrete *v.* Farnborough U.D.C. [1972] C.L.Y. 2020 64
Real & Leasehold Estates Investment Society Ltd. *v.* Medina Shipping Ltd. (1968) 112 S.J. 862; 208 E.G. 733, C.A. 642, 648
Rearden-Smith Line Ltd. *v.* Yngvar Hansen-Tangen [1976] 1 W.L.R. 989; 120 S.J. 719; [1976] 3 All E.R. 570, H.L. 26
Redfern *v.* Reeves (1978) 37 P. & C.R. 364; [1978] 247 E.G. 991, C.A. 700
Redspring Ltd. *v.* Francis [1973] 1 W.L.R. 134; [1973] 1 All E.R. 640; (1972) 25 P. & C.R. 8, C.A. 449, 451, 553
Reed *v.* Cattermole [1937] 1 K.B. 613; 106 L.J.K.B. 407; 156 L.T. 389; 53 T.L.R. 369; 81 S.J. 117; 21 Tax Cas. 35; [1937] 1 All E.R. 541 28
Rees *v.* Marquis of Bute [1916] 2 Ch. 64; 85 L.J.Ch. 421; 114 L.T. 1029; 32 T.L.R. 425; 60 S.J. 528 378
Reeves *v.* Davies [1921] 2 K.B. 486; 90 L.J.K.B. 675; 125 L.T. 354; 37 T.L.R. 431 329
Reddaway (Frank) & Co. Ltd. *v.* Banham [1896] A.C. 199; [1895–99] All E.R.Rep. 313; 65 L.J.Q.B. 381; 74 L.T. 289; 44 W.R. 638; 12 T.L.R. 292; 13 R.P.C. 218, H.L. 741
Regalian Securities *v.* Ramsden [1981] 1 W.L.R. 611; 125 S.J. 324; [1981] 2 All E.R. 65; [1982] H.L.R. 84, H.L. 409, 499
Regalian Securities Ltd. *v.* Scheuer (1982) 32 New L.J. 20; 263 E.G. 973, C.A. 409
Regan *v.* Regan [1977] 1 W.L.R. 84; (1976) 121 S.J. 84; [1977] 1 All E.R. 428; (1977) 75 L.G.R. 257; [1976] Fam.Law 17 577
Regan & Blackburn Ltd. *v.* Rogers [1985] 1 W.L.R. 870; S.J. 449; [1985] 2 All E.R. 180; (1984) 49 P. & C.R. 58; (1985) 82 L.S.Gaz. 2740 250
Regent Oil Co. Ltd. *v.* Gregory (J. A.) (Hatch End) Ltd. [1966] Ch. 402; [1965] 3 W.L.R. 1206; 109 S.J. 833; [1965] 3 All E.R. 673, C.A.; *affirming* [1965] 3 W.L.R. 730; [1965] 2 All E.R. 90 317
Regional Properties Ltd. *v.* City of London Real Property Co. Ltd. (1980) 257 E.G. 64 .... 218, 286, 293
Regional Properties Co. Ltd. *v.* Frankenschwerth [1951] 1 K.B 631; 95 S.J. 106; [1951] 1 All E.R. 178, C.A. 453, 454
Regis Property Co. Ltd. *v.* Dudley [1959] A.C. 370; [1958] 3 W.L.R. 647; 102 S.J. 844; [1958] 3 All E.R. 491, H.L.; *affirming* [1958] 1 Q.B. 346; [1958] 2 W.L.R. 356; 102 S.J. 160; [1958] 1 All E.R. 510, C.A.; *reversing* in part [1957] J.P.L. 817 .... 225, 283
Regis Property Co. *v.* Lewis & Peat [1970] 1 Ch. 695; [1970] 3 W.L.R. 361; 114 S.J. 589; [1970] 3 All E.R. 227; 21 P. & C.R. 761 .... 680, 717
Regor Estates Ltd. *v.* Wright [1951] 1 K.B 689; [1951] 1 T.L.R. 242; 115 J.P. 61; 95 S.J. 106; [1951] 1 All E.R. 219; 49 L.G.R. 241, C.A. 173, 428
Reid *v.* Dawson [1955] 1 Q.B 214; [1954] 3 W.L.R. 810; 98 S.J. 818; [1954] 3 All E.R. 498; 53 L.G.R. 24, C.A. 765
Reindel *v.* Schell (1858) 4 C.B.(N.S.) 97; 27 L.J.C.P. 146; 4 Jur.(N.S.) 310 170
Relvok Properties *v.* Dixon (1973) 25 P. & C.R. 1, C.A. 339
Remnant *v.* L.C.C. (1952) 3 P. & C.R. 185; 160 E.G. 209, Lands Tribunal 736
Remon *v.* City of London Real Property Co. Ltd. [1921] 1 K.B 49; 89 L.J.K.B. 1105; 123 L.T. 617; 18 L.G.R. 691; 36 T.L.R. 869 .... 378, 408
Rendall *v.* Andreae (1892) 61 L.J.Q.B. 630 328
Rendell *v.* Roman (1893) 9 T.L.R. 192 32
René Clare (Haute Couture) *v.* Hallé Concerts Society [1969] 1 W.L.R. 909; 113 S.J. 325; [1969] 2 All E.R. 842; 20 P. & C.R. 378, C.A. 684, 686

Reohorn v. Barry Corp. [1956] 1 W.L.R. 845; 100 S.J. 509; [1956] 2 All E.R. 742,
 C.A. 705, 710
Restormel B.C. v. Buscombe (1982) 12 Fam.Law 207; 14 H.L.R. 91, C.A. 545
Reynolds v. Bannerman [1922] 1 K.B. 719; 91 L.J.K.B. 651; 127 L.T. 300; 20 L.G.R.
 439; 66 S.J. 504; 38 T.L.R. 509 192
Rhodes v. Cornford [1947] 2 All E.R. 601, C.A. 449, 457
——— v. Dalby [1971] 1 W.L.R. 1325; 115 S.J. 623; [1971] 1 All E.R. 1144; (1971) 23
 P. & C.R. 309 .... 68, 305
Rhyl Urban District Council v. Rhyl Amusements Ltd. [1959] 1 W.L.R. 465; 103 S.J.
 327; [1959] 1 All E.R. 257; 57 L.G.R. 19 .... 339, 346
Rice v. Mitchman (1954) 163 E.G. 680 33
Richards v. De Freitas (1974) 29 P. & C.R. 1 .... 159, 161
——— v. Green (1983) 11 H.L.R. 1; 268 E.G. 443, C.A. 409
——— v. Powell (1966) 110 S.J. 330; 198 E.G. 481 81
Richmond v. Savill [1926] 2 K.B. 530; 95 L.J.K.B. 1042; 136 L.T. 15; 70 S.J. 875 335
Richards (C.) & Son v. Karenita (1972) 221 E.G. 25 179
Ricketts v. Enfield Churchwardens [1909] 1 Ch. 544; 78 L.J.Ch. 294; 100 L.T. 362 318
Rider v. Ford [1923] 1 Ch. 541; 129 L.T. 347; 67 S.J. 484 .... 141, 143
Riggs, Re, ex p. Lovell [1901] 2 K.B. 16; 70 L.J.K.B. 541; 84 L.T. 428; 49 W.R. 624; 8
 Manson 233 .... 303, 330
Riley (E. J.) Investments v. Eurostile Holdings [1985] 1 W.L.R. 1139; (1985) 129
 S.J. 523; [1985] 3 All E.R. 181; (1985) 51 P. & C.R. 36; (1985) 135 New L.J.
 887; (1985) 82 L.S.Gaz. 2500, C.A. 688
Rimmer v. Liverpool City Council [1985] Q.B. 1; [1984] 1 All E.R. 930; [1984] 2
 W.L.R. 426; 128 S.J. 225; 47 P. & C.R. 516; 269 E.G. 319; 82 L.G.R. 424; 12
 H.L.R. 23; 81 L.S.Gaz. 664, C.A. 239, 249, 250, 257, 365, 372
Riverlate Properties Ltd. v. Paul [1975] Ch. 133; [1974] 3 W.L.R. 564; [1974] 2 All
 E.R. 656; 28 P. & C.R. 220; sub nom. Riverplate Properties v. Paul 118 S.J.
 644, C.A.; affirming (1973) 227 E.G. 333 149
Roach v. Johannes [1976] C.L.Y. 1549, Lambeth County Court 359
Roberts v. Brett (1865) 11 H.L.C. 337; 34 L.J.Ch. 241; 11 Jur.(N.S.) 377; 12 L.T. 286;
 13 W.R. 587 220
——— v. Church Commissioners for England [1972] 1 Q.B 278; [1971] 3 W.L.R. 566;
 115 S.J. 792; [1971] 3 All E.R. 703, C.A. 108, 498, 510
——— v. Dorset C.C. The Times, August 2, 1976 610
——— v. Rose (1863–64) 3 H. & C. 162; 33 L.J.Ex. 1, 241; 35 ibid. 62; L.T. 1 Ex. 82;
 12 Jur.(N.S.) 78; 13 L.T. 471; 14 W.R. 225 11
Robinson v. Rosher (1841) 1 Y. & C.Ch. 7; 5 Jur. 1006; 62 E.R. 767 319
Rodenhurst Estates Ltd. v. Barnes Ltd. [1936] 2 All E.R. 3; 80 S.J. 405 .... 314, 319
Rodewald v. Rodewald [1977] Fam. 192; [1977] 2 W.L.R. 191; (1976) 121 S.J. 70;
 [1977] 2 All E.R. 609; (1976) 75 L.G.R. 280, C.A. 577
Rodgers v. Nowill (1853) 3 De G.M. & G. 614; 22 L.J.Ch. 404; 20 L.T.(o.s.) 319; 17
 Jur. 171; 1 W.R. 205; 43 E.R. 241, L.JJ. 742
Rodwell v. Gwynne Trusts Ltd. [1970] 1 W.L.R. 327; 114 S.J. 89; [1970] 1 All E.R.
 314; 21 P. & C.R. 113, H.L.; affirming sub nom. Gwynne Trusts v. Rodwell
 [1969] 1 W.L.R. 740; 113 S.J. 285; [1969] 2 All E.R. 435; 20 P. & C.R. 300,
 C.A. 389
Roe v. Russell [1928] 2 K.B. 117; 97 L.J.K.B. 290; 138 L.T. 253; 92 J.P. 81; 26
 L.G.R. 145; 44 T.L.R. 278 463
Roffey v. Henderson (1851) 17 Q.B. 574; 21 L.J.Q.B. 49; 16 Jur. 84 11
Rogers v. Rice [1892] 2 Ch. 170; 61 L.J.Ch. 573; 66 L.T. 640; 40 W.R. 489 198
Roland House Gardens v. Cravitz (1974) 119 S.J. 167; 29 P. & C.R. 432; (1975) 235
 E.G. 683, C.A. 378, 409
Rolls v. Miller (1884) 27 Ch.D. 71; 53 L.J.Ch. 682; 50 L.T. 597; 32 W.R. 806 647
Rookes v. Barnard [1964] A.C. 1129; [1964] 2 W.L.R. 269; 108 S.J. 93; [1964] 1 All
 E.R. 367; [1964] 1 Lloyd's Rep. 28, H.L. 132, 294

Rosenbaum *v.* Belson [1900] 2 Ch. 267; 69 L.J.Ch. 569; 82 L.T. 658; 48 W.R. 522; 44
S.J. 485 86
Ross *v.* Collins [1964] 1 W.L.R. 425; 108 S.J. 117; [1964] 1 All E.R. 861, C.A. 441
Ross Auto Wash *v.* Herbert (1974) 250 E.G. 971 643
Rother *v.* Colchester Corporation [1969] 1 W.L.R. 720; [1969] 2 All E.R. 600; *sub
nom.* Rother *v.* Colchester B.C. (1969) 113 S.J 243 .... 124, 658
Rought (W.) Ltd. *v.* West Suffolk C.C. [1955] 2 Q.B. 338; [1955] 2 W.L.R. 1080; 119
S.J. 433; 99 S.J 354; [1955] 2 All E.R. 337; 48 R. & I.T. 633; 5 P. & C.R. 215,
C.A. 737
Rousou *v.* Photi [1940] 2 K.B. 379; 109 L.J.K.B. 693; 163 L.T. 71; 56 T.L.R. 685; 104
J.P. 300; [1940] 2 All E.R. 528 .... 172, 240
Rowe *v.* Truelove (1976) 241 E.G. 533, C.A. 456
Rowlands (Mark) Ltd. *v.* Berni Inns (1985) 129 S.J. 811; 276 E.G. 191; [1985] 3 All
E.R. 473; [1985] 2 Lloyd's Rep. 437; 135 New L.J. 962; (1986) 83 L.S.Gaz. 35,
C.A.; *affirming* (1984) 134 New L.J. 236 119
Rowley *v.* Adams (1839) 4 Myl. & Cr. 534; 9 L.J.Ch. 34; 2 Jur. 915; 3 Jur. 1069 328
Roy *v.* Westminster City Council (1975) 31 P. & C.R. 458, Lands Tribunal 736
Royal Crown Derby Porcelain Co. Ltd. *v.* Russell [1949] 2 K.B. 417; 93 S.J. 318;
[1949] 1 All E.R. 749, C.A. 455
Royal Life Saving Society *v.* Page. *See* Cheryl Investments *v.* Saldhana.
Royal Philanthropic Society *v.* County (1985) 276 E.G. 1068, C.A. 27
Rubery *v.* Stevens (1832) 4 B. & Ad. 241; 1 N.& M. 182; 2 L.J.K.B. 46; 38 R.R. 242 . 327
Rugby School (Governors) *v.* Tannahill [1935] 1 K.B. 87; 104 L.J.K.B. 159; 152 L.T.
198; 51 T.L.R. 84; 78 S.J. 801 353
Runcorn Association Football Club *v.* Warrington & Runcorn Development Corpn.
(1983) 45 P. & C.R. 183; (1984) 24 R.V.R. 112; [1983] J.P.L. 58; (1982) 264
E.G. 627 724
Russell *v.* Beecham [1924] 1 K.B. 525; 93 L.J.K.B. 441; 130 L.T. 570; 68 S.J. 301;
40 T.L.R. 66 (C.A.) 300, 306
—— *v.* Booker (1982) 263 E.G. 513, C.A. 381, 759
Rutherford *v.* Maurer [1962] 1 Q.B. 16; [1961] 3 W.L.R. 5; 105 S.J. 404; [1961] 2 All
E.R. 775, C.A. 758, 765
Ryall *v.* Kidwell [1914] 3 K.B. 135; 83 L.J.K.B. 1140; 111 L.T. 240; 78 J.P. 377;
12 L.G.R. 997; 30 T.L.R. 503, C.A. 241
Rye *v.* Rye [1962] A.C. 496; [1962] 2 W.L.R. 361; 106 S.J. 94; [1962] 1 All E.R. 146,
H.L.; *affirming* [1961] Ch. 70; [1960] 3 W.L.R. 1052; 104 S.J. 1076; [1960] 3
All E.R. 810, C.A. 65, 340

S.E.D.A.C. Investments *v.* Tanner [1982] 1 W.L.R. 1342; 126 S.J. 609; [1982] 3 All
E.R. 646; 44 P. & C.R. 319; 264 E.G. 615 .... 284, 285, 290, 352
S.I. Pension Trustees Ltd. *v.* Hodson (William) Ltd. (1977) 35 P. & C.R. 54; 121 S.J.
512; 242 E.G. 689 183
Safeway Food Stores Ltd. *v.* Banderway Ltd. (1983) 267 E.G. 850 189
—— *v.* Morris (1980) 254 E.G. 1091 685
St. Catherine's College *v.* Dorling [1980] 1 W.L.R. 66; 123 S.J. 505; [1979] 3 All E.R.
253; [1979] 39 P. & C.R. 110, C.A. 381, 382, 388, 398
St. Edmundsbury and Ipswich Diocesan Board of Finance *v.* Clark (No. 2) [1975] 1
W.L.R. 468; (1974) 119 S.J. 220; [1975] 1 All E.R. 772; 29 P. & C.R. 336,
C.A.; *affirming* on different grounds [1973] 1 W.L.R. 1572 106
St. Pancras B.C. *v.* Frey [1963] 2 Q.B. 586; [1963] 2 W.L.R. 894; 107 S.J. 256; [1963]
2 All E.R. 124; 61 L.G.R. 276, D.C. 557
Salford City Council *v.* McNally [1976] A.C. 379; [1975] 3 W.L.R. 87; 119 S.J.
475; [1975] 2 All E.R. 860; 73 L.G.R. 408, H.L.; *affirming* [1975] 1 W.L.R.
365 .... 261, 262, 263, 264, 280, 544
Salisbury *v.* Gilmore [1942] 2 K.B. 38; [1942] 1 All E.R. 457; 111 L.J.K.B. 593;
166 L.T. 329; *sub nom.* Salisbury *v.* Marcel, 58 T.L.R. 226; 86 S.J. 251, C.A. . 288

Salmon *v.* Seafarer Restaurants Ltd. [1983] 1 W.L.R. 1264; [1983] 3 All E.R. 729;
127 S.J. 581; 80 L.S.Gaz. 2523 366
Salvation Army Trustee Co. Ltd. *v.* West Yorks. M.C.C. (1981) 41 P. & C.R.
179 12
Sampson *v.* Hodson-Pressinger (1981) 125 S.J. 623; [1981] 3 All E.R. 710; 12 H.L.R.
40; 261 E.G. 891, C.A. 130, 367, 368, 369
Samrose Properties Ltd. *v.* Gibbard [1958] 1 W.L.R. 235; 102 S.J. 160; [1958] 1 All
E.R. 502, C.A. 10, 19, 173, 399, 430, 435
Samuel Properties (Developments) *v.* Hayek (1972) 1 W.L..R. 1296; 116 S.J. 764;
[1972] 3 All E.R. 473; 24 P. & C.R. 223, C.A.; *affirming* [1972] 1 W.L.R.
1064 179
Sanderson *v.* Berwick-on-Tweed (Mayor) (1884) 13 Q.B.D. 547; 53 L.J.Q.B. 559;
51 L.T. 495; 33 W.R. 67 131
Sandhil *v.* Franklin (1875) L.R. 10 C.P. 377 40
Saner *v.* Bilton (1878) 7 Ch.D. 815; 47 L.J.Ch. 267; 28 L.T. 281; 26 W.R. 394 175,
218
Sarson *v.* Roberts [1895] 2 Q.B 395; 65 L.J.Q.B. 37; 73 L.T. 174; 43 W.R. 690 240
Saunders *v.* Soper [1975] A.C. 239; [1974] 3 W.L.R. 777; 118 S.J. 863; [1974] 3 All
E.R. 1025, H.L. 432
Sawyer and Withall, *Re* [1919] 2 Ch. 333; 88 L.J.Ch. 474; 63 S.J. 662; 35 T.L.R. 611 .. 167
Saunders-Jacob *v.* Yates [1933] 2 K.B. 240; 102 L.J.K.B. 417; 149 L.T. 209, C.A. 812
Savile Settled Estates, *Re*, Savile *v.* Savile [1931] 2 Ch. 210; 100 L.J.Ch. 274; 145
L.T. 17 339
Scala House and District Property Co. Ltd. *v.* Forbes [1974] A.B. 575; [1973] 3
W.L.R. 14; 117 S.J. 467; [1973] 3 All E.R. 308; 26 P. & C.R. 164, C.A. 353
Scandinavian Trading Tanker Co. A.B. *v.* Flota Petrolera Ecuatoriana, The
Scaptrade [1983] Q.B. 329; [1983] 2 A.C. 694, H.L. 351
Scene Estate *v.* Amos [1957] 2 Q.B. 205; [1957] 2 W.L.R. 1017; 101 S.J. 445; [1957] 2
All E.R. 325; 56 L.G.R. 14, C.A. 765
Schaffer *v.* Griffith (1955) 105 L.J. 188, Cty. Ct. 449
Schalit *v.* Nadler (Joseph) Ltd. [1933] 2 K.B. 79; 102 L.J.K.B. 334; 48 T.L.R. 375 763
Schnabel *v.* Allard [1967] 1 Q.B. 627; [1966] 3 W.L.R. 1295; 110 S.J. 831; [1966] 3 All
E.R. 816; [1966] C.L.Y. 6889, C.A. 343
Schneiders & Sons *v.* Abrahams [1925] 1 K.B. 301; 94 L.J.K.B 408; 132 L.T. 721; 41
T.L.R. 24 452
Scholl Manufacturing Co. Ltd. *v.* Clifton (Slim Line) Ltd. [1967] Ch. 41; [1966] 3
W.L.R. 575; 110 S.J. 687; [1966] 3 All E.R. 16, C.A.; *affirming* [1966] Ch.
298 .... 139, 675, 686
Schroeder (A.) Music Publishing Co. Ltd. *v.* Macaulay [1974] 1 W.L.R. 1308; 118
S.J. 734; [1974] 3 All E.R. 616, H.L.; *affirming sub nom.* Instone *v.* Schroeder
(A.) Music Publishing Co. [1974] 1 All E.R. 171, C.A. 744
Scobie *v.* Collins [1895] 1 Q.B. 375; 64 L.J.Q.B. 10; 71 L.T. 775 43
Scott *v.* Bradley [1971] 1 Ch. 850; [1971] 2 W.L.R. 731; 115 S.J. 172; [1971] 1 All
E.R. 583; 22 P. & C.R. 352 84
Scottish & Newcastle Breweries *v.* Sutton's (Sir Richard) Settled Estates (1985) 276
E.G. 77 186
Scrace *v.* Windust [1955] 1 W.L.R. 475; 99 S.J. 290; [1955] 2 All E.R. 104, C.A. 451
Scrimgeour *v.* Waller (1981) 257 E.G. 61, C.A. 28
Secretary of State for Education and Science *v.* M.B. of Tameside [1977] A.C. 1014;
[1976] 3 W.L.R. 641; 120 S.J. 735; [1976] 3 All E.R. 665, H.L. 574
Secretary of State for Social Services *v.* Rossetti Lodge Investment Co. Ltd. (1975)
119 S.J. 339; [1975] J.P.L. 286; 235 E.G. 501, C.A. 679
Sedleigh-Denfield *v.* O'Callaghan [1940] A.C. 880; 109 L.J.K.B. 893; 164 L.T. 72;
84 S.J. 657; 56 T.L.R. 887; [1940] 3 All E.R. 349 368
Sefton (Earl) *v.* Tophams (No. 2) [1967] 1 A.C. 50; [1966] 2 W.L.R. 814; 110 S.J.
271; [1966] 1 All E.R. 1039, H.L. 124

Segal Securities Ltd. *v.* Thoseby [1963] 1 Q.B. 887; [1963] 2 W.L.R. 403; 106 S.J.
 1053; [1963] 1 All E.R. 500 .... 123, 195
Selby *v.* Selby (1817) 3 Mer. 2; 17 R.R. 1 85
Selim Ltd. *v.* Bickenhall Engineering Ltd. [1981] 3 W.L.R. 1318; [1981] 3 All E.R.
 210; (1982) 43 P. & C.R. 186; (1981) 259 E.G. 1073 .... 250, 290
Selous Street Properties Ltd. *v.* Oroneal Fabrics Ltd. (1984) 270 E.G. 643, 743; 134
 New L.J. 886 .... 162, 184, 294, 316
Selwyn *v.* Hamill (1948) 92 S.J. 71; [1948] 2 All E.R. 70, C.A. 451
Serjeant *v.* Nash, Fiend & Co. [1903] 2 K.B. 304; 72 L.J.K.B. 630; 89 L.T. 112; 19
 T.L.R. 510, C.A.; [1900–03] All E.R. 525 .... 166, 304
Sevenarts Ltd. *v.* Busvine [1968] 1 W.L.R. 1929; 112 S.J. 822; [1969] 1 All E.R. 392;
 20 P. & C.R. 79, C.A. 702
Sevenoaks D.C. *v.* Emmott (1979) 39 P. & C.R. 404; [1980] J.P.L. 517; 78 L.G.R.
 346, C.A. 558
Shackle *v.* Baker (1808) 14 Ves. 468; 33 E.R. 600, L.C. 742
Shanley *v.* Ward (1913) 29 T.L.R. 714, C.A. 309, 311
Sharma *v.* Knight (1986) 136 New L.J. 332 706
Sharneyford Supplies Ltd. *v.* Edge and Barrington Black [1985] 3 W.L.R. 1; [1985] 1
 All E.R. 976; 129 S.J. 316; 50 P. & C.R. 343; 35 New L.J. 288; 82 L.S.Gaz.
 2081 95
Sharpe, *Re* [1980] 1 W.L.R. 219; 124 S.J. 147; 39 P. & C.R. 459; *sub nom.* Sharpe (a
 bankrupt), *Re*, *ex p.* Trustee of the Bankrupt *v.* Sharpe [1980] 1 All E.R.
 198 .... 11, 13
Shaw *v.* Applegate [1977] 1 W.L.R. 970; 121 S.J. 424; [1978] 1 All E.R. 123; 35 P. &
 C.R. 181, C.A. 12
—— *v.* Groom [1970] 2 Q.B 504; [1970] 2 W.L.R. 299; 114 S.J. 14; [1970] 1 All E.R.
 702; 21 P. & C.R. 137, C.A. 163, 432
—— *v.* Kay (1847) 1 Ex. 412; 17 L.J.Ex. 17 108
Sheldon *v.* West Bromwich Corpn. (1973) 117 S.J. 486; (1973) 25 P. & C.R. 360,
 C.A. 235, 244
Shelfer *v.* City of London Electric Lighting Co. [1895] 1 Ch. 287; 64 L.J.Ch. 216; 72
 L.T. 34; 43 W.R. 238; 12 R. 112, C.A. 370
Shell-Mex and B.P. Ltd. *v.* Manchester Garages Ltd. [1971] 1 W.L.R. 612; 115 S.J.
 111; [1971] 1 All E.R. 841, C.A. 5, 10, 16, 17, 19, 32, 36, 357, 641, 653, 654
Shell U.K. Ltd. *v.* Lostock Garage Ltd. [1976] 1 W.L.R. 1187; 120 S.J. 523, C.A. 126
Shelley *v.* L.C.C. [1949] A.C. 56; [1949] L.J.R. 57; 64 T.L.R. 600; 113 J.P. 1; 93 S.J.
 101; [1948] 2 All E.R. 898; 47 L.G.R. 93, H.L.; *affirming sub nom.* L.C.C. *v.*
 Shelley [1948] 1 K.B. 274 .... 558, 561
Shepherd *v.* Lomas [1963] 1 W.L.R. 962; 107 S.J. 435; [1963] 2 All E.R. 902, C.A. 788
Sheridan *v.* Dickson [1970] 1 W.L.R. 1328; 114 S.J. 474; [1970] 3 All E.R. 1049,
 C.A. 411
Sherwood *v.* Moody [1952] 1 T.L.R. 450; 96 S.J. 105; [1952] 1 All E.R. 389; 50
 L.G.R. 180; *sub nom.* Sheerwood *v.* Moody [1952] W.N. 95 .... 393, 799
—— *v.* Tucker [1924] 2 Ch. 440; 94 L.J.Ch. 66; 132 L.T. 86; 68 S.J. 769; 40 T.L.R.
 782 143
Sherwood Close (Barnes) Management Co. Ltd.'s Application, *Re* [1972] Ch. 208;
 [1971] 3 W.L.R. 902; 115 S.J. 740; [1971] 3 All E.R. 1293; *sub nom.* Sherwood
 Close Estate, London, S.W.13, *Re* [1971] 22 P. & C.R. 1031 519
Shiloh Spinners Ltd. *v.* Harding [1973] A.C. 691; [1973] 2 W.L.R. 28; 117 S.J. 34;
 [1973] 1 All E.R. 90; 25 P. & C.R. 48, H.L. 13
Short *v.* Poole Corpn. [1926] Ch. 66; 95 L.J.Ch. 110; [1925] All E.R. 74; 134 L.T.
 110; 90 J.P. 25; 42 T.L.R. 107; 70 S.J. 245; 24 L.G.R. 14, C.A. 558
Short Bros. (Plant) *v.* Edwards (1978) 249 E.G. 539, C.A. 765
Short's Ltd. *v.* Short (1914) 31 R.P.C. 294 741
Siddigui *v.* Rashid [1980] 1 W.L.R. 1018; 124 S.J. 464; [1980] 3 All E.R. 184; 40 P. &
 C.R. 504; 256 E.G. 169, C.A. 451

Sidebotham *v.* Hollond [1895] 1 Q.B 378; 64 L.J.Q.B. 200; 72 L.T. 62; 43 W.R. 228;
  [1891–94] All E.R.Rep. 617 .... 107, 346
Sidnell *v.* Wilson [1966] 2 Q.B. 67; [1966] 2 W.L.R. 560; 110 S.J. 53; [1966] 1 All
  E.R. 681, C.A. 290, 291
Sidney Trading Co. *v.* Finsbury B.C. [1952] 1 T.L.R. 512; 116 J.P. 154; 96 S.J. 182;
  [1952] 1 All E.R. 460; 45 R. & I.T. 134, D.C. 172, 399
Siew Soon Wah *v.* Yong Tong Hong [1973] A.C. 836; [1973] 2 W.L.R. 713; 117 S.J.
  341, D.C. 13
Sills *v.* Watkins [1956] 1 Q.B. 250; [1955] 3 W.L.R. 520; 99 S.J. 761; [1955] 3 All E.R.
  319; 53 L.G.R. 672, C.A. 451
Silsby *v.* Holliman [1955] Ch. 552; [1955] 2 W.L.R. 1090; 99 S.J. 355; [1955] 2 All
  E.R. 373 340
Silvester *v.* Ostrowska [1959] 1 W.L.R. 1060; 108 S.J. 940; [1959] 3 All E.R. 642 352
Simonds (H. & G.) Ltd. *v.* Heywood [1948] 92 S.J. 111; [1948] 1 All E.R.
  260 .... 109, 345
Simons *v.* Associated Furnishers Ltd. [1931] 1 Ch. 379; 10 L.J.Ch. 234; 144 L.T.
  559; 75 S.J. 27; 47 T.L.R. 118 138
Simpson *v.* Eggington (1855) 10 Ex. 845 .... 159, 161
—— *v.* Scottish Union Insurance Co. (1863) 1 H. & M. 618; 32 L.J.Ch. 329 118
Simpson's Motor Sales (London) Ltd. *v.* Hendon Corp. [1964] A.C. 1088; [1963] 2
  W.L.R. 1187; 127 J.P. 418; 107 S.J. 491; [1963] 2 All E.R. 484; 14 P. &
  C.R. 386; 62 L.G.R. 1; [1963] R.V.R. 522, H.L.; *affirming* [1963] Ch. 57,
  C.A. 720, 721
Sims *v.* Wilson [1946] 2 All E.R. 261; 62 T.L.R. 485; 90 S.J. 570, C.A. 456
Singh *v.* Malayan Theatres [1953] A.C. 632; [1963] 3 W.L.R. 491; 97 S.J. 555, P.C. 695
Singh (Gian) & Co. *v.* Nahar [1965] 1 W.L.R. 412; 109 S.J. 74; [1965] 1 All E.R. 768,
  P.C. 302
Sinnott *v.* Bowden [1912] 2 Ch. 414; 81 L.J.Ch. 832; 28 T.L.R. 594 120
Skelton (Wm.) & Son Ltd. *v.* Harrison & Pinder Ltd. [1975] Q.B 361; [1975] 2
  W.L.R. 238; 119 S.J. 98; [1975] 1 All E.R. 182; 29 P. & C.R. 113 .... 53, 325,
  326, 678
Skinner *v.* Cooper [1979] 1 W.L.R. 666; 123 S.J. 302; [1979] 2 All E.R. 836; 39 P. &
  C.R. 319; 250 E.G. 967, C.A. 483, 484
—— *v.* Geary [1931] 2 K.B. 546; 100 L.J.K.B. 718; 145 L.T. 675; 95 J.P. 194; 29
  L.G.R. 599; 47 T.L.R. 597 .... 408, 409
Sky Petroleum Ltd. *v.* V.I.P. Petroleum Ltd. [1974] 1 W.L.R. 576; 118 S.J. 311;
  [1974] 1 All E.R. 954 125
Slater *v.* Worthington's Cash Stores [1941] 1 K.B. 488; 165 L.T. 293, 294; 57 T.L.R.
  468; [1941] 3 All E.R. 28 368
Sleafer *v.* Lambeth B.C. [1960] 1 Q.B. 43; [1959] 3 W.L.R. 485; 103 S.J. 599; [1959] 3
  All E.R. 378; 57 L.G.R. 212, C.A. 543
Slipper *v.* Tottenham and Hampstead Junction Ry. (1867) L.R. 4 Eq. 112; 36
  L.J.Ch. 841; 16 L.T. 446; 15 W.R. 861 303
Smale *v.* Graves (1850) 3 De. G. & Sm. 706; 19 L.J.Ch. 157; 15 L.T.(o.s.) 179; 14
  Jur. 662; 64 E.R. 670 740
—— *v.* Meakers [1957] J.P.L. 415; (1957) 169 E.G. 287; 107 L.J. 268, Cy.C. 687
Smalley *v.* Quarrier [1975] 1 W.L.R. 938; 119 S.J. 440; [1975] 2 All E.R. 688; 30 P. &
  C.R. 419, C.A. 329, 378, 407
Smallwood *v.* Sheppards [1895] 2 Q.B 627; 64 L.J.Q.B. 727; 73 L.T. 219; 44 W.R.
  44 87
Smedley *v.* Chumley & Hawke Ltd. (1981) 125 S.J. 33; 44 P. & C.R. 50; 261 E.G.
  775, C.A. 228, 231, 232
Smiley *v.* Townshend [1950] 2 K.B. 311; 66 T.L.R. (Pt. 1) 546; [1950] 1 All E.R. 530;
  155 E.G. 110, C.A.; *affirming* [1949] 2 All E.R. 817 287
Smith *v.* Anderson (1880) 15 Ch.D. 247 664
—— *v.* Birmingham Corpn. (1974) 29 P. & C.R. 265, Lands Tribunal 734

Smith *v.* Bradford M.C. (1982) 126 S.J. 624; 80 L.G.R. 713; 44 P. & C.R. 171;
  [1983] H.L.R. 86; 79 L.S.Gaz. 1176, C.A. 236, 245, 248, 367
—— *v.* Cardiff Corpn. [1954] 2 Q.B. 210; [1953] 3 W.L.R. 994; 118 J.P. 33; 97
  S.J. 831; [1953] 2 All E.R. 1373; 52 L.G.R. 1, C.A.; *varying* (1953) 162 E.G.
  182 531
—— *v.* —— (No. 2) [1955] Ch. 159; [1955] 2 W.L.R. 126; 119 J.P. 128; 99 S.J. 76;
  [1955] 1 All E.R. 113 .... 530, 531
—— *v.* City Petroleum Co. Ltd. [1940] 1 All E.R. 260 60
—— *v.* Cox [1940] 2 K.B. 558; 109 L.J.K.B. 732; 163 L.T. 330; 56 T.L.R. 899; 84
  S.J. 598; [1940] 3 All E.R. 546 .... 159, 161
—— *v.* Day (1837) 2 M. & W. 684; M. & H. 135; 6 L.J.Ex. 219; 46 R.R. 747;
  [1835–42] All E.R.Rep. 521 54
—— *v.* Gronow [1891] 2 Q.B. 394; 60 L.J.Q.B. 776; 65 L.T. 117; 40 W.R. 46; 7
  T.L.R. 596 329
—— *v.* McGoldrick (1976) 242 E.G. 1047, C.A. 457
—— *v.* Marrable (1843) 11 M. & W. 5; 12 L.J.Ex. 223; 7 Jur. 70; 63 R.R.
  493 .... 239, 543
—— *v.* Metropolitan City Properties (1985) 277 E.G. 753 .... 196, 353
—— *v.* Mills (1899) 16 T.L.R. 59; 44 S.J. 91 224
—— *v.* Morgan [1971] 1 W.L.R. 803; 115 S.J. 288; [1971] 2 All E.R. 1500; 22 P. &
  C.R. 618 144
—— *v.* Nottinghamshire C.C. *The Times*, November 3, 1981, H.L. 9
—— *v.* Poulter [1947] K.B. 339; [1947] L.J.R. 847; 62 T.L.R. 736; 91 S.J. 149;
  [1947] 1 All E.R. 216 467
—— *v.* Raleigh (1814) 3 Camp. 513; 14 R.R. 829 174
—— *v.* St. Michael's, Cambridge, Overseers (1860) 3 E. & E. 383; 3 L.T. 687; 25
  J.P. 133; 7 Jur.(N.S.) 24; 121 E.R. 486; *sub nom.* R. *v.* Smith 30 L.J.M.C.
  74 .... 15, 21
—— *v.* Scott [1973] Ch. 314; [1972] 3 W.L.R. 783; 116 S.J. 785; [1972] 3 All E.R.
  645 367
—— *v.* Seghill Overseers (1875) L.R. 10 Q.B. 422; 44 L.J.M.C. 114; 32 L.T. 859; 23
  W.R. 745 27
—— *v.* Smith (1861) 1 Dr. & Sm. 384; 7 Jur.(N.S.) 652; 4 L.T. 44; 9 W.R.
  406 .... 114, 115
—— *v.* Webster (1876) 3 Ch.D. 49; 45 L.J.Ch. 528; 35 L.T. 44; 24 W.R. 894 86
Smith (A. J.) & Co. *v.* Kirby [1947] 1 All E.R. 459 202
Smith (A. J. A.) Transport Ltd. *v.* British Railways Board (1980) 257 E.G. 1257,
  C.A. 705
Smith (Colin) Music Ltd. *v.* Ridge [1975] 1 W.L.R. 463; 119 S.J. 83; [1975] 1 All E.R.
  290; 29 P. & C.R. 97; 5 Fam.Law 128, C.A. 444
Smith's (Henry) Charity Trustees *v.* A.W.A.D.A. Trading and Promotion Services
  Ltd. (1984) 128 S.J. 130; 47 P. & C.R. 607; 269 E.G. 729; 81 L.S.Gaz. 118,
  C.A. 180
Smith's Lease, *Re*, Smith *v.* Richards [1951] W.N. 51; [1951] 1 T.L.R. 254; [1951] 1
  All E.R. 346 308
Snook *v.* London and West Riding Investments Ltd. [1967] 2 Q.B. 786; [1967] 2
  W.L.R. 1020; 111 S.J. 71; [1967] 1 All E.R. 518, C.A. 21
Solle *v.* Butcher [1950] 1 K.B .671; 66 T.L.R. (Pt. 1) 448; [1949] 2 All E.R. 1107,
  C.A. 81, 149, 407
Soloman, *Re, ex p.* Dressler (1878) 9 Ch.D. 252; 48 L.J.Bcy. 20; 39 L.T. 377; 43 J.P.
  23; 27 W.R. 144; [1874–80] All E.R.Rep. 1194, C.A. 331
Solomon *v.* Orwell [1954] 1 W.L.R. 629; 98 S.J. 248; [1954] 1 All E.R. 874,
  C.A. 405
Somers & Somers *v.* Doncaster Corpn. (1965) 16 P. & C.R. 323, Lands Tribunal 735
Somershield *v.* Robin [1946] 1 K.B. 244; 174 L.T. 181; 62 T.L.R. 196; [1946] 1 All
  E.R. 218 172

Somma *v.* Hazelhurst [1978] 2 All E.R. 1011; 37 P. & C.R. 391; 122 S.J. 280; [1978] 2
    All E.R. 1011; [1978] J.P.L. 554; *sub nom.* Somma *v.* Hazlehurst; Somma *v.*
    Savelli (1978) 246 E.G. 311, C.A. 5, 17, 20, 21, 23, 24
Sonnenthal *v.* Newton (1965) 109 S.J. 333, C.A. 309
Sopwith *v.* Stutchbury (1984) 17 H.L.R. 50, C.A. 416
Sotheby *v.* Grundy [1947] 2 All E.R. 761 227
South Kensington Co-operative Stores, *Re* (1881) 17 Ch.D. 161; 50 L.J.Ch. 446; 44
    L.T. 471; 29 W.R. 662 204
South Tottenham Land Securities *v.* R. & A. Millett (Shops) Ltd. [1984] 1 W.L.R.
    710; 128 S.J. 365; [1984] 1 All E.R. 614; 269 E.G. 630; 48 P. & C.R. 159;
    (1984) 81 L.S.Gaz. 1999, C.A.; *affirming* (1983) 127 S.J. 510 .... 183, 184, 194
South West Water Authority *v.* Palmer (1983) 268 E.G. 357, 443, C.A.; 263 E.G.
    438 766
—— *v.* Rumble's [1985] 2 W.L.R. 405; 129 S.J. 130; [1985] 1 All E.R. 513; 83
    L.S.Gaz. 297; 25 R.V.R. 66; [1985] J.P.L. 476; 82 L.S.Gaz. 1173, H.L. 113
Southern Portland Cement Ltd. *v.* Cooper [1974] A.C. 623; [1974] 2 W.L.R. 152;
    sub nom. Southern Portland Cement *v.* Cooper (1973) 118 S.J. 99; [1974] 1
    All E.R. 87, P.C. 366
Southgate B.C. *v.* Watson [1944] K.B. 541; 113 L.J.K.B. 337; 171 L.T. 26; 60
    T.L.R. 392; 108 J.P. 207; 42 L.G.R. 219; [1944] 1 All E.R. 603 14
Southport Old Links *v.* Naylor (1985) 273 E.G. 767 .... 684, 686
Sowler *v.* Potter [1940] 1 K.B. 271; 109 L.J.K.B. 177; 56 T.L.R. 142; 162 L.T. 12; 84
    S.J. 115; [1939] 4 All E.R. 478 81
Spafax *v.* Harrison [1980] I.R.L.R. 442, C.A. 746
Sparham-Souter *v.* Town & Country Developments (Essex) Ltd. [1976] 1 Q.B.
    858; [1976] 2 W.L.R. 493; 120 S.J. 216; [1976] 2 All E.R. 65; 74 L.G.R. 355,
    C.A. 372
Spectrum Investment Co. *v.* Holmes [1981] 1 W.L.R. 221; 125 S.J. 47; [1981] 1 All
    E.R. 6; 41 P. & C.R. 133 .... 337, 379
Spencer's Case (1583) 5 Co.Rep. 16a; 1 Sm.L.C. (13th ed.) 51; [1558–1774] All
    E.R.Rep. 68 .... 317, 319
Sperry Ltd. *v.* Hambro Life Assurance Ltd. (1982) 265 E.G. 223 751
Spindlow *v.* Spindlow [1979] Ch. 52; 9 Fam.Law 22; [1979] 1 All E.R. 169; [1978] 3
    W.L.R. 777; 122 S.J. 556, C.A. 444
Sport International Bussum B.V. *v.* Inter-Footwear Ltd. [1984] 1 W.L.R. 776; 128
    S.J. 383; [1984] 2 All E.R. 321; 81 L.S.Gaz. 1992; 134 New L.J. 568, H.L.;
    affirming [1984] 1 All E.R. 376, C.A. 351
Spyer *v.* Phillipson [1931] 2 Ch. 183; 100 L.J.Ch. 109; 144 L.T. 626; [1930] All
    E.R.Rep. 457 58
Stacey *v.* Hill [1901] 1 K.B. 660; 69 L.J.Q.B. 796; 70 L.J.K.B. 435; 84 L.T. 410; 49
    W.R. 390; 7 Mans. 399; 8 *ibid.* 169 331
Stack *v.* Church Commissioners for England [1952] 116 J.P. 334; [1952] 1 All E.R.
    1352, C.A. 128
Stagg *v.* Brickett [1951] K.B. 648; [1951] 1 T.L.R. 82; 95 S.J. 14; [1951] 1 All E.R.
    152, C.A. 475
Stait *v.* Fenner [1912] 2 Ch. 504; 81 L.J.Ch. 710; 107 L.T. 120; 56 S.J. 669 ..... 138, 348
Standen *v.* Chrismas (1847) 10 Q.B. 135; 16 L.J.Q.B. 265; 11 Jur. 694; 74 R.R.
    224 283
Stanfield (Ben) (Carlisle) *v.* Carlisle C.C. *The Times*, October 30, 1982 43
Stanhope *v.* Haworth (1886) 3 T.L.R. 34 197
Stansfield *v.* Portsmouth (Mayor) (1858) 4 C.B.(N.S.) 120; 27 L.J.C.P. 124; 4
    Jur.(N.S.) 440 60
Stanley *v.* Compton [1951] 1 All E.R. 859, C.A. 465
Starrokate Ltd. *v.* Burry (1983) 265 E.G. 871, C.A. 290, 352
Starside Properties *v.* Mustapha [1974] 1 W.L.R. 816; 118 S.J. 388; [1974] 2 All E.R.
    567; 28 P. & C.R. 95, C.A. 2

Stavely Iron & Chemical Co. *v.* National Coal Board [1950] W.N. 273; 66 T.L.R. (Pt. 1) 1075; 94 S.J. 255 340

Steadman *v.* Steadman [1976] A.C. 536; [1974] 3 W.L.R. 56; 118 S.J. 480; [1974] 2 All E.R. 977; 29 P. & C.R. 46, H.L.; *affirming* [1974] Q.B 161; [1973] 3 W.L.R. 695; 117 S.J. 794; [1973] 3 All E.R. 977; 26 P. & C.R. 249, C.A. 87

Stedman *v.* Moore (1874) 10 L.T.(o.s.) 289; 12 J.P. 39, N.P. 57

Stein *v.* Pope [1902] 1 K.B. 595; 71 L.J.K.B. 322; 86 L.T. 283; 50 W.R. 374; 9 Mans. 125 205

Stening *v.* Abrahams [1931] 1 Ch. 470; 100 L.J.Ch. 278; 145 L.T. 18 305

Stephens *v.* Balls (1957) 107 L.J. 764; [1957] C.L.Y. 1154, Cty.Ct. 762

Stephenson (Robert) & Co. Ltd., *Re*, Poole *v.* The Company [1915] 1 Ch. 802; 84 L.J.Ch. 563; 113 L.T. 230; 59 S.J. 429; 31 T.L.R. 331 299

Sterling Land Office Developments *v.* Lloyd's Bank (1984) 271 E.G. 894 186

Stevenson & Rush (Holdings) Ltd. *v.* Langdon (1979) 38 P. & C.R. 208; 249 E.G. 743; 122 S.J. 827, C.A. 655

Stewart *v.* Higgins (1951) 157 E.G. 470, Cty.Ct. 441

Stile Hall Properties *v.* Goods [1980] 1 W.L.R. 62; [1979] 3 All E.R. 848; 39 P. & C.R. 173, C.A. 676, 688, 691

Stickney *v.* Keeble [1915] A.C. 386 95

Stocker *v.* Planet Building Society (1879) 27 W.R. 877 286

Stockdale *v.* Ascherberg [1902] 1 K.B. 447; 73 L.J.K.B 206; 90 L.T. 111; 52 W.R. 13, 289; 68 J.P. 241; 1 L.G.R. 548; 20 T.L.R. 235 114

Stokes *v.* Mixconcrete (Holdings) (1978) 38 P. & C.R. 488, C.A.; *affirming* (1978) 36 P. & C.R. 427, D.C. 99

——— *v.* Whicher [1920] 1 Ch. 411; 89 L.J.Ch. 198; 123 L.T. 23; 64 S.J. 292 83

Stokes (Insp. of Taxes) *v.* Costain Property Investments [1984] 1 W.L.R. 763; [1984] C.I.L.L. 83; 128 S.J. 190; [1984] 1 All E.R. 849; [1984] S.T.C. 204, C.A.; *affirming* [1983] 1 W.L.R. 907 56

Stoke Lands *v.* Sears (1951) 151 E.G. 196 123

Stone *v.* Whitcombe (1980) 40 P. & C.R. 296; 257 E.G. 929, C.A. 766

Stone (J. & F.) Lighting and Radio Ltd. *v.* Levitt [1947] A.C. 209; [1947] L.J.R. 65; 176 L.T. 1; 62 T.L.R. 737; [1946] 2 All E.R. 653, H.L. 399

Stoneman *v.* Brown [1973] 1 W.L.R. 459; 117 S.J. 109; [1973] 2 All E.R. 225; 25 P. & C.R. 297, C.A. 786

Storer *v.* Manchester C.C. [1974] 1 W.L.R. 1403; 118 S.J. 599; [1974] 3 All E.R. 824; 73 L.G.R. 1, C.A. 574

Strahan *v.* Smith (1827) 4 Bing. 91; 12 Moore, C.P. 289; 5 L.J.(o.s.)C.P. 95; 130 E.R. 703 165

Strand & Savoy Properties Ltd., *Re* [1960] Ch. 582; [1960] 3 W.L.R. 1; 104 S.J. 491; [1960] 2 All E.R. 327 .... 38, 54

Strand Securities Ltd. *v.* Caswell [1965] Ch. 958; [1965] 2 W.L.R. 958; 109 S.J. 131; [1965] 1 All E.R. 820, C.A. 145

Stratford *v.* Syrett [1958] 1 Q.B 107; [1957] 3 W.L.R. 733; 101 S.J. 850; [1957] 3 All E.R. 363, C.A. 14, 66, 456

Stream Properties *v.* Davies [1972] 1 W.L.R. 645; 116 S.J. 274; [1972] 2 All E.R. 746; 23 P. & C.R. 294 679

Street *v.* Mountford [1985] A.C. 809; [1985] 2 W.L.R. 877; 129 S.J. 348; [1985] 2 All E.R. 289; 50 P. & C.R. 258; 274 E.G. 821; 17 H.L.R. 402; 135 New L.J. 460; 82 L.S.Gaz. 2087, H.L. 5, 10, 15, 16, 17, 20, 21, 22, 23, 24, 25, 26, 28, 30, 31, 357, 475, 653, 654, 761

——— *v.* Union Bank (1885) 30 Ch.D. 156; 55 L.J.Ch. 31; 53 L.T. 262; 33 W.R. 901; 1 T.L.R. 554 741

Stroud Building Society *v.* Delamont [1960] 1 W.L.R. 431; 104 S.J. 329; [1960] 1 All E.R. 749 69

Strutt *v.* Pointer [1953] 1 Q.B. 397; [1953] 2 W.L.R. 406; 97 S.J. 130; [1953] 1 All E.R. 445, C.A. 406

Stuart *v.* Joy and Nantes [1904] 1 K.B. 362; 73 L.J.K.B. 97; 90 L.T. 78 324
Stubbs *v.* Slough B.C. [1980] L.A.G.Bull. 16 622
Stuchberry *v.* General Accident Assurance Corp. [1949] 2 K.B. 256; [1949] L.J.R.
    1238; 65 T.L.R. 329; 93 S.J. 301; [1949] 1 All E.R. 1026, C.A. 664
Sturcke *v.* Edwards (S. W.) (1972) 23 P. & C.R. 185 234
Sturge *v.* Hackett [1962] 1 W.L.R. 1257; 106 S.J. 568; [1962] 3 All E.R. 166; [1962] 1
    Lloyd's Rep. 626, C.A. 103
Sturolson & Co. *v.* Weniz (1984) 17 H.L.R. 140; 272 E.G. 326, C.A. 17, 20
Sutton *v.* Begley [1923] 2 K.B 694; 92 L.J.K.B. 1086; 129 L.T. 773; 68 S.J. 82;
    21 L.G.R. 679 382
—— *v.* Dorf [1932] 2 K.B. 304; 101 L.J.K.B. 536; 147 L.T. 171; 96 J.P. 259;
    30 L.G.R. 312; 76 S.J. 359; 48 T.L.R. 430 .... 330, 405
Stylo Shoes *v.* Wetherall, Bond Street, W.1 (1974) 237 E.G. 343, C.A. 179
Sudbrook Trading Estate Ltd. *v.* Eggleton [1983] 1 A.C. 444; [1982] 3 W.L.R. 315;
    126 S.J. 512; [1982] 3 All E.R. 1; 44 P. & C.R. 153; 79 L.S.Gaz. 1175; 265
    E.G. 215, H.L. 143, 179
Suffield *v.* Brown (1864) 4 De G.J. & Sm. 185; 3 New Rep. 340; 33 L.J.Ch. 249; 9
    L.T. 627; 10 Jur.(N.S.) 111; 12 W.R. 356; 36 E.R. 888, L.C. 106
Summerfield *v.* Hampstead B.C. [1957] 1 W.L.R. 167; 121 J.P. 72; 101 S.J. 111;
    [1957] 1 All E.R. 221; 55 L.G.R. 67 530
Summers *v.* Salford Corpn. [1943] A.C. 283; 112 L.J.K.B. 65; 168 L.T. 97; 59 T.L.R.
    78; 107 J.P. 35; 41 L.G.R. 1; 86 S.J. 391; [1943] 1 All E.R. 68 242
Sumnall *v.* Statt (1985) 49 P. & C.R. 367; (1984) 271 E.G. 628, C.A. 123, 789
Sun Life Assurance Society *v.* Davidson [1957] 3 W.L.R. 362; 101 S.J. 590; [1957] 2
    All E.R. 760; [1957] T.R. 171; 50 R. & I.T. 530; (1957) 37 T.C. 330; 36
    A.T.C. 152, H.L.; *affirming* [1956] Ch. 524 211
Sunlight House, Quay Street, Manchester *Re*, (1959) 173 E.G. 311 709
Sutherland (Dowager Duchess) *v.* Sutherland (Duke) [1983] 3 Ch. 169; 62 L.J.Ch.
    946; 69 L.T. 186; 42 W.R. 12; 3 R. 650 63
Sutton L.B.C. *v.* Swann *The Times*, November 30, 1985, C.A. 565, 574
Swallow Securities *v.* Brand (1983) 45 P. & C.R. 328; 260 E.G. 63 .... 284, 285
—— *v.* Isenberg (1985) 274 E.G. 1028, C.A. 12, 464
Swansea Corpn. *v.* Thomas (1882) 10 Q.B.D. 48; 52 L.J.Q.B. 340; 47 L.T. 657; 31
    W.R. 506; 47 J.P. 135 165
Swanson *v.* Forton [1949] Ch. 143; [1949] L.J.R. 632; 65 T.L.R. 178; [1949] 1 All
    E.R. 135; *sub nom.* Swanton *v.* Forton 92 S.J. 731, C.A. 311
Swanson's Agreement, *Re* Hill *v.* Swanson [1947] L.J.R. 169; 176 L.T. 25; 62 T.L.R.
    719; 90 S.J. 643; [1946] 2 All E.R. 628 310
Sweet & Maxwell Ltd. *v.* Universal News Services Ltd. [1964] 2 Q.B 699; [1964] 3
    W.L.R. 356; 108 S.J. 478; [1964] 3 All E.R. 30, C.A. 82, 84, 93, 302
Swift *v.* Macbean [1942] 1 K.B 375; 111 L.J.K.B. 185; 166 L.T. 87; 58 T.L.R. 110;
    [1942] 1 All E.R. 126 .... 40, 153
Swiss Bank Corpn. *v.* Lloyd's Bank Ltd. [1982] A.C. 584; [1981] 2 W.L.R. 893; 125
    S.J. 495; [1981] 2 All E.R. 449, H.L.; *affirming* [1980] 3 W.L.R. 457, C.A. 2, 13
Sykes *v.* Land (1984) 271 E.G 1264, C.A. 782

T. & E. Homes Ltd. *v.* Robinson [1979] 1 W.L.R. 452; 123 S.J. 164; [1979] 2 All E.R.
    522; [1979] S.T.C. 351; [1979] T.R.19; [1981] T.C. 567, C.A. 157, 159
Talbot *v.* Talbot [1968] A.C. 1; [1967] 3 W.L.R. 438; [1967] 2 All E.R. 920; *sub nom.*
    Talbot, *Re*, Talbot *v.* Talbot (1967) 111 S.J. 278, C.A.; *affirming* [1967] 1
    All E.R. 601 143
Tandon *v.* Trustees of Spurgeon's Homes [1982] A.C. 755; [1982] 2 W.L.R. 735; 26
    S.J. 260; [1982] 1 All E.R. 1086; 44 P. & C.R. 307; 263 E.G. 349; [1983]
    H.L.R. 15, H.L. 506
Tanner *v.* Tanner [1975] 1 W.L.R. 1346; 119 S.J. 391; [1975] 3 All E.R. 776; 5
    Fam.Law 193 11

Tarjomani *v.* Panther Securities Ltd. (1983) 46 P. & C.R. 32 .... 655, 675
Tarry *v.* Ashton (1876) 1 Q.B.D. 314; 45 L.J.Q.B. 260; 34 L.T. 97 369
Taylor *v.* Beal (1591) Cro. Eliz. 222; 1 Leon. 237 254
—— *v.* Caldwell (1863) 3 B. & S. 826; 32 L.J.Q.B 164; 8 L.T. 356; 11 W.R.
    726 .... 36, 152
—— *v.* Jackson (1846) 2 C. & K. 22 16
—— *v.* Knowsley B.C. (1985) 17 H.L.R. 376, C.A. 251
—— *v.* Liverpool Corpn. [1939] 3 All E.R. 329 257
—— *v.* Twinberrow [1930] 2 K.B 16; [1930] All E.R. 342; 99 L.J.K.B. 313; 142 L.T.
    648, D.C. 337
—— *v.* Webb [1937] 2 K.B 283; 106 L.J.K.B. 480; 156 L.T. 326; 53 T.L.R. 377; 81
    S.J. 137; [1937] 1 All E.R. 590; *reversed* [1937] 2 K.B. 290 ...... 225, 254, 255, 256
Taylor Fashions *v.* Liverpool Victoria Friendly Society, Old & Campbell *v.* Same
    [1981] Q.B 133; [1981] 2 W.L.R. 576; [1981] 1 All E.R. 897; [1981] Com.L.R.
    34; (1979) 251 E.G. 159 .... 12, 145
Teasdale *v.* Walker [1958] 1 W.L.R. 1076; 102 S.J. 757; [1958] 3 All E.R. 307,
    C.A. 642, 650
Tebb *v.* Cave [1900] 1 Ch. 642; 69 L.J.Ch. 282; 82 L.T. 115; 48 W.R. 318 131
Tegardine *v.* Brooks (1977) 121 S.J. 155; 36 P. & C.R. 261; 245 E.G. 51,
    C.A. 342, 684
Telegraph Properties (Securities) Ltd. *v.* Courtaulds Ltd. (1981) 257 E.G. 1153 182
Tendler *v.* Sproule [1947] 1 All E.R. 193, C.A. 123
Terrell *v.* Murray (1901) 17 T.L.R. 570 224
Terunnanse *v.* Terunnanse [1968] A.C. 1086; [1968] 2 W.L.R. 1125; [1968] 1 All
    E.R. 651; 112 S.J. 134, P.C. 11
Tetragon Ltd. *v.* Shidasb Construction Co. Ltd. (1981) 7 H.L.R. 113 408
Texaco *v.* Benton & Bowles (Holdings) (1983) 127 S.J. 307; 267 E.G. 355 679
Thames Manufacturing Co. *v.* Penotts (Nichol & Peyton) (1984) 128 S.J. 447; 49
    P. & C.R. 1; 271 E.G. 284; 81 L.S.Gaz. 1362 .... 219, 315
Thatcher *v.* Pearce (C. H.) & Sons (Contractors) Ltd. [1968] 1 W.L.R. 748; 112 S.J.
    379; 19 P. & C.R. 682 197
Thomas *v.* Fryer [1970] 1 W.L.R. 845; 114 S.J. 190; [1970] 2 All E.R. 1; 21 P. & C.R.
    398; 214 E.G. 131, C.A. 456, 457
—— *v.* Hammond-Lawrence [1986] 1 W.L.R. 456; 130 S.J. 284; [1986] 2 All E.R.
    214; 278 E.G. 414; 83 L.S.Gaz. 785; 136 New L.J. 463, C.A. 679, 682
—— *v.* Hayward (1869) L.R. 4 Ex. 311; 38 L.J.Ex. 175; 20 L.T. 814; [1861–73] All
    E.R.Rep. 290 318
—— *v.* National Farmers Union Mutual Insurance Society [1961] 1 W.L.R. 386; 105
    S.J. 233; [1961] 1 All E.R. 363; [1960] 2 Lloyd's Rep. 444 803
Thomas *v.* Sorrell (1673) Vaughan 330 .... 9, 15
Thompson *v.* Gibson (1841) 7 M. & W. 456; 9 Dowl. 717; 10 L.J.Ex. 330 368
—— *v.* McCullough [1947] K.B. 447; 176 L.T. 493; 63 T.L.R. 95; 91 S.J. 147; [1947]
    1 All E.R. 265, C.A. 89, 348
—— *v.* Lapworth (1868) L.R. 3 C.P. 149; 37 L.J.C.P. 74; 17 L.T. 507; 16 W.R.
    312 115
Thompson *v.* Park [1944] K.B. 408 .... 11, 360
—— *v.* Rolls [1926] 2 K.B. 426; 95 L.J.K.B 901; 135 L.T. 446; 24 L.G.R. 531; 42
    T.L.R. 582; 70 S.J. 775 .... 451, 695
—— *v.* Thompson [1976] Fam. 25; [1975] 2 W.L.R. 868; 119 S.J. 255; [1975] 2 All
    E.R. 208; 30 P. & C.R. 91; 5 Fam. Law 162; 73 L.G.R. 488, C.A. 577
—— *v.* Tottenham & Forest Gate Ry. Co. (1892) 67 L.T. 416; 57 J.P. 181; 8 T.L.R.
    602; 36 Sol.Jo. 542 721
—— *v.* Ward [1953] 2 Q.B 153; [1953] 2 W.L.R. 1042; 97 S.J. 352; [1953] 1 All E.R.
    1169, C.A. 371, 404, 405
Thompsons (Funeral Furnishers) *v.* Phillips [1945] 2 All E.R. 49 .... 28, 33

Thorn *v*. Madden [1925] Ch. 847; 95 L.J.Ch. 52; 135 L.T. 91; 70 S.J. 75; 41 T.L.R.
628 123
Thorn EMI Pension Trust Ltd. *v*. Quinton Hazell plc (1983) 269 E.G. 414 ...... 180, 181
Thorne *v*. Smith [1947] K.B. 307; [1947] L.J.R. 596; 63 T.L.R. 55; 91 S.J. 54; [1947] 1
All E.R. 39, C.A. 752
Thornton *v*. Kirklees M.B.C. [1979] Q.B 626; [1979] 3 W.L.R. 1; 77 L.G.R. 417; *sub
nom*. Thornton *v*. Kirklees M.D.C. 123 S.J. 285; [1979] 2 All E.R. 349; [1979]
J.P.L. 459, C.A. 629
Threlfall, *Re, ex p*. Queen's Benefit Building Society (1880) 16 Ch.D. 274; 44 L.T. 74;
29 W.R. 128; *sub nom*. *Re* Threlfall, *ex p*. Blakey 50 L.J.Ch. 318, C.A. 345
Thresher *v*. East London Water Works Co. (1824) 2 B. & C. 608; 4 D. & R. 62; 2
L.J.(o.s.)K.B. 100; 26 R.R. 486 56
Thurrock U.D.C. *v*. Shina (1972) 23 P. & C.R. 205; 70 L.G.R. 301, D.C. 474, 607
Thursby *v*. Plant (1670) 1 Wms.Saund. 237; 85 E.R. 268 294
Tichborne *v*. Weir (1892) 67 L.T. 735; 4 R. 26; [1891–94] All E.R.Rep. 449 ... 320, 337
Tickner *v*. Buzzacott [1965] Ch. 426; [1965] 2 W.L.R. 154; 109 S.J. 74; [1964] 1 All
E.R. 131 198
—— *v*. Hearn [1960] 1 W.L.R. 1406; 104 S.J. 1076; [1961] 1 All E.R. 65, C.A. 409
—— *v*. Mole Valley D.C. [1980] L.A.G.Bull. 187 612
Tideway Investment and Property Holdings Ltd. *v*. Wellwood [1952] Ch. 791; [1952]
2 T.L.R. 365; 96 S.J. 579; [1952] 2 All E.R. 514, C.A. 407, 449, 467, 468
Tilling *v*. Whiteman [1980] A.C. 1; [1979] 2 W.L.R. 401; 123 S.J. 202; [1979] 1 All
E.R. 737; 38 P. & C.R. 341; 250 E.G. 51; [1979] J.P.L. 834, H.L. 459
Timmins *v*. Moreland Street Property Co. Ltd. [1958] Ch. 110; [1957] 3 W.L.R. 678;
101 S.J. 815; [1957] 3 All E.R. 265, C.A. 84–85
—— *v*. Rowlinson (1765) 1 W.Bl. 533; 3 Burr. 1603 342
Tingey *v*. Sutton [1984] 1 W.L.R. 812; [1984] 3 All E.R. 561; 272 E.G. 555; 17
H.L.R. 11; 81 L.S.Gaz. 2294, C.A. 422
Titterton *v*. Cooper (1882) 9 Q.B.D. 473; 51 L.J.Q.B. 472; 46 L.T. 870; 30 W.R. 866;
[1881–85] All E.R. Rep. 757 .... 204, 331
Tiverton Estate Ltd. *v*. Wearwell Ltd. [1975] Ch. 146; [1974] 2 W.L.R. 176; 117 S.J.
913; [1974] 1 All E.R. 209; 27 P. & C.R. 24, C.A. 83
Toby *v*. Major (1899) 43 S.J. 778 747
Tolhurst *v*. Associated Portland Cement Manufacturers (1900); Tolhurst *v*. Associ-
ated Portland Cement Manufacturers (1900) and Imperial Portland Cement
Co. [1903] A.C. 414; 72 L.J.K.B. 834; 89 L.T. 196; 52 W.R. 143; 19 T.L.R.
677, H.L. 10
Tomlinson *v*. Plymouth Argyle Football Co. and Plymouth City Council [1960]
C.L.Y. 2701; 8 R.R.C. 218; [1961] J.P.L. 263, Lands Tribunal 186
Tool Metal Manufacturing Co. Ltd. *v*. Tungsten Electric Co. Ltd. [1955] 1 W.LR.
761; 99 S.J. 470; [1955] 2 All E.R. 657; 72 R.P.C. 209, H.L. 359
Torbett *v*. Faulkener [1952] 2 T.L.R. 659; 96 S.J. 747, C.A. 14, 17, 20
Tormes Property Co. Ltd. *v*. Landau [1971] 1 Q.B 261; [1970] 3 W.L.R. 762; 114
S.J. 769; [1970] 3 All E.R. 653; 21 P. & C.R. 923; [1971] J.P.L. 112,
D.C. 422, 425, 426
Torminster Properties Ltd. *v*. Green [1983] 1 W.L.R. 676; 127 S.J. 391; [1983] 2 All
E.R. 457; 45 P. & C.R. 391; 267 E.G. 256, C.A.; [1982] 1 W.L.R. 751; 126
S.J. 208; 43 P. & C.R. 369; 263 E.G. 65 .... 161, 183, 184, 335, 336
Torrens *v*. Walker [1906] 2 Ch. 166; 75 L.J.Ch. 645; 95 L.T. 409; 54 W.R. 584 230
Torridge D.C. *v*. Jones (1985) 276 E.G. 1253 552
Total Oil Great Britain Ltd. *v*. Thompson Garages (Biggin Hill) Ltd. [1972] 1
Q.B. 318; [1971] 3 W.L.R. 979; 115 S.J. 848; [1971] 3 All E.R. 1226,
C.A. 111, 126
Touche Ross & Co. *v*. Secretary of State for the Environment (1982) 46 P. & C.R.
187; 265 E.G. 982, C.A. 180, 181, 182
Tourret *v*. Cripps (1879) 48 L.J.Ch. 567 85

Tovey v. Tyack [1955] 1 Q.B 57; [1954] 3 W.L.R. 570; 98 S.J. 733; [1954] 3 All E.R.
210, C.A. 385, 398
Town Investments Ltd. v. Department of the Environment [1978] A.C. 359; [1977]
2 W.L.R. 450; 121 S.J. 203; [1977] 1 All E.R. 813; 34 P. & C.R. 48,
H.L. 643, 644, 647
Town Investments Underlease Ltd., Re, McLaughlin v. Town Investments
Ltd. [1954] Ch. 301; [1954] 2 W.L.R. 355; 98 S.J. 162; [1954] 1 All E.R.
585 .... 121, 311
Trayfoot v. Lock [1957] 1 W.L.R. 351; 101 S.J. 171; [1957] 1 All E.R. 423, C.A. 440
Tredway v. Machin (1904) 91 L.T. 310; 20 T.L.R. 726 365
Trego v. Hunt [1896] A.C. 7; [1895–9] All E.R.Rep. 804; 65 L.J.Ch. 1; 73 L.T. 514;
44 W.R. 225; 12 T.L.R. 80, H.L.; *reversing* [1895] 1 Ch. 462, C.A. 739, 742
Treloar v. Bigge (1874) L.R. 9 Ex. 151; 43 L.J.Ex. 95; 22 W.R. 843 314
—— v. Nute [1976] 1 W.L.R. 1295; [1977] 1 All E.R. 230; 120 S.J. 590, C.A. 337
Treseder-Griffin v. Co-operative Insurance Society Ltd. [1956] 2 Q.B 127; [1956] 2
W.L.R. 866; 100 S.J. 283; [1956] 2 All E.R. 33; [1956] 1 Lloyd's Rep. 377,
C.A. 155, 193
Trim v. Sturminster R.D.C. [1938] 2 K.B. 508; 107 L.J.K.B. 687; 159 L.T. 7; 54
T.L.R. 597; 102 J.P. 249; 36 L.G.R. 319; 82 S.J. 313; [1938] 2 All E.R. 168 103
Trinity College, Cambridge v. Caines (1984) 272 E.G. 1287 794
Trow v. Ind Coope (West Midlands) Ltd. [1967] 2 Q.B. 899; [1967] 3 W.L.R. 633;
111 S.J. 375; [1967] 2 All E.R. 900, C.A.; *affirming* [1967] 2 Q.B., sub nom.
Trow v. Ind Coope [1966] 3 W.L.R. 1300 107
Trust House Forte Albany Hotels Ltd. v. Daejan Investment Ltd. (1980) 256 E.G.
915 183
Trustees of National Deposit Friendly Society v. Beatties of London (1985) 275 E.G.
54 .... 82, 141, 693, 706
Trustees of Smith's (Henry) Charity v. Wilson [1983] Q.B 316; [1983] 2 W.L.R. 77;
126 S.J. 673; [1983] 1 All E.R. 73; 45 P. & C.R. 377, C.A. 195, 305, 344,
448, 463, 464
Trustees of the Property of Smith's Charity v. Hemmings (1983) 265 E.G. 383;
80 L.S.Gaz. 99, C.A.; *affirming*, sub nom. Smith's (Henry) Charity Trustees
v. Hemmings (1981) E.G. 178 425
Tulk v. Moxhay (1848) 2 Ph. 774; 78 R.R. 289 .... 13, 75
Tummon v. Barclays Bank Trust Co. (1979) 39 P. & C.R. 300; 250 E.G. 980, Bodmin
County Court 776
Tunstall v. Steigman [1962] 2 Q.B 593; [1962] 2 W.L.R. 1045; 106 S.J. 282; [1962] 2
All E.R. 417, C.A. 643
Turley v. Panton (1975) 119 S.J. 236; 29 P. & C.R. 397, D.C. 419, 477
Turner v. Allday (1836) Tyr. & G. 819 159
—— v. Barnes (1862) 2 B. & S. 435; 31 L.J.Q.B 170; 9 Jur.(N.S.) 199; 10 W.R. 561 .. 43
—— v. Watts (1927) 97 L.J.K.B 403; 44 T.L.R. 105, 337 340
Turner & Bell v. Searles (Stanford-le-Hope) (1977) 33 P. & C.R. 208; 244 e.g. 1023,
C.A. 695
Turone v. de Walden (Howard) Estates (1982) 263 E.G. 1189, C.A. 708, 714

U.D.S. Tailoring Ltd. v. B.L. Holdings Ltd. (1982) 261 E.G. 49 .... 186, 681
Uniproducts (Manchester) v. Rose Furnishers [1956] 1 W.L.R. 45; 100 S.J. 15;
[1956] 1 All E.R. 146 .... 235, 250
United Dominions Corp. (Jamaica) Ltd. v. Shoucair (Michael Mitri) [1969] 1 A.C.
340; [1968] 3 W.L.R. 893; sub nom. United Dominions Corp. (Jamaica) v.
Shohcair (1968) 112 S.J. 482; [1968] 2 All E.R. 904, P.C. 84
United Scientific Holdings v. Burnley B.C.; Cheapside Land Development Co. v.
Messels Service Co. [1978] A.C. 904; [1977] 2 W.L.R. 806; 121 S.J. 223; 33 P.
& C.R. 220; 75 L.G.R. 407; 243 E.G. 43, H.L.; sub nom. United Scientific
Holdings v. Burnley Corp. (1976) 238 E.G. 487, C.A. . 81, 138, 156, 180, 181, 182

Unity Joint Stock Mutual Banking Association *v.* King (1858) 25 Beav. 72; 27
    L.J.Ch. 585; 31 L.T.(o.s.) 128; 4 Jur.(n.s.) 470; 6 W.R. 264; 53 E.R. 563   12
University of Reading *v.* Johnson-Houghton (1985) 276 E.G. 1353   654
Upfill *v.* Wright [1911] 1 K.B. 506; 80 L.J.K.B. 254; 103 L.T. 834; 55 S.J. 189; 27
    T.L.R. 160   81
Upsons Ltd. *v.* Robins (E.) Ltd. [1956] 1 Q.B 131; [1955] 3 W.L.R. 584; 99 S.J. 779;
    [1955] 3 All E.R. 348, C.A. 704, 709

Valliant *v.* Dodemede (1742) 2 Atk. 546   295
Vancouver Malt and Sake Brewing Co. Ltd. *v.* Vancouver Breweries Ltd. [1934]
    A.C. 181; [1934] All E.R.Rep. 38; 103 L.J.P.C. 58; 150 L.T. 503; 50 T.L.R.
    253; 78 Sol.Jo. 173, P.C.   743
Vaudeville Electric Cinema, Ltd. *v.* Muriset [1923] 2 Ch. 74; 92 L.J.Ch. 558; 129
    L.T. 466; 67 S.J. 595   58
Vaughan *v.* Hampson (1875) 33 L.T. 15   10
Venner's Electrical Cooking & Heating Appliances *v.* Thorpe [1915] 2 Ch. 404; 84
    L.J.Ch. 925; 113 L.T. 1137; 60 S.J. 27; [1915] H.B.R. 201   204
Verfall *v.* Farnes [1966] 1 W.L.R. 1254; 110 S.J. 406; [1966] 2 All E.R. 808   761
Verrall *v.* Great Yarmouth B.C. [1981] Q.B 202; [1980] 3 W.L.R. 258; [1980] 1 All
    E.R. 839, C.A. 11, 96, 360
Vicker's Lease, *Re*, Pocock *v.* Vickers [1947] Ch. 420; [1948] L.J.R. 69; 177 L.T. 637;
    91 S.J. 294; [1947] 1 All E.R. 707, C.A.   106
Victoria Square Property Co. *v.* Southwark B.C. [1978] 1 W.L.R. 463; (1977) 121
    S.J. 816; [1978] 2 All E.R. 281; (1977) 76 L.G.R. 349; 34 P. & C.R. 275;
    [1978] J.P.L. 243; (1977) 247 E.G. 989, C.A.   268
Vienit *v.* Williams (W.) & Son (Bread Street) Ltd. [1958] 1 W.L.R. 1267; 102 S.J.
    916; [1958] 3 All E.R. 621 ....   307, 310
Villenex Co. *v.* Courtney Hotel (1969) 20 P. & C.R. 575   116
Vine Products *v.* Mackenzie (No. 2) [1969] R.P.C. 1; [1967] F.S.R. 402   741
Viola's Lease, *Re* Humphrey *v.* Stenbury [1909] 1 Ch. 244; 78 L.J.Ch. 128; 100 L.T.
    33 ....   138, 348
Voli *v.* Inglewood Shire Council and Lockwood (1963) 37 A.L.J.R. 25; 56 Q.L.R.
    256   36

Wadham *v.* Postmaster-General (1871) L.R. 6 Q.B. 644; 40 L.J.Q.B. 310; 24 L.T.
    545; 19 W.R. 1082   658
Wainwright *v.* Leeds City Council (1984) 270 E.G. 1289; 82 L.G.R. 657; 13 H.L.R.
    117; 81 L.S.Gaz. 2000, C.A. 226, 245, 246, 543
Waite *v.* Jennings [1906] 2 K.B. 11; 75 L.J.K.B. 542; 95 L.T. 1; 54 W.R. 511   661
Walker *v.* Hatton (1842) 10 M. & W. 249; 2 Dow.(n.s.) 263; 11 L.J.Ex. 361; 62 R.R.
    600   222
—— *v.* Hobbs (1889) 23 Q.B.D. 458; 59 L.J.Q.B. 93; 61 L.T. 688; 38 W.R. 63   240
—— *v.* Ost [1970] 2 All E.R. 106   741
Walker (James), Goldsmith & Silversmith Ltd. [1948] 1 K.B. 257; [1948] L.J.R. 343;
    91 S.J. 614; [1947] 2 All E.R. 789 ....   299, 307
Wall *v.* Rederiaktiebolaget Luggude [1915] 3 K.B 66; 84 L.J.K.B 1663; 114 L.T. 286;
    31 T.L.R. 487; 21 Com.Cas. 132   171
Wallis *v.* Hands [1893] 2 Ch. 75; 62 L.J.Ch. 586; 68 L.T. 428; 41 W.R. 471; 5 R.
    370 ....   129, 339
—— *v.* Harrison (1838) 4 M. & W. 538; 5 *ibid* 142; 1 H. & H. 405; 2 Jur. 1019; 8
    L.J.Ex. 148   11
Walsh *v.* Griffiths-Jones and Durant [1978] 2 All E.R. 1002 ....   5, 20, 21
—— *v.* Lonsdale (1882) 21 Ch.D. 9; 52 L.J.Ch. 2; 46 L.T. 858; 31 W.R. 109,
    C.A. 92, 94, 157
Walter *v.* Ashton [1902] 2 Ch. 282; 71 L.J.Ch. 839; 87 L.T. 196; 51 W.R. 131; 18
    T.L.R. 445   741

Walter *v.* Selfe (1851) 4 De G. & S. 315; 20 L.J.Ch. 433; 17 L.T.(o.s.) 103; 15 Jur.
416; 64 E.R. 849 125
Wamford Investments Ltd. *v.* Duckworth [1979] Ch. 127; [1978] 2 W.L.R. 741;
(1977) 122 S.J. 63; [1978] 2 All E.R. 517; (1977) 76 P. & C.R. 295 .... 322, 331
Wansbrough *v.* Malton (1836) 4 A. & E. 884; 43 R.R. 510; 5 L.J.K.B. 150; 2 H. &
W. 37 57
Ward *v.* Gold (1969) 211 E.G. 155 103
—— *v.* Kirkland [1967] Ch. 194; [1966] 1 W.L.R. 601; 110 S.J. 289; [1966] 1 All E.R.
609 12
Warder *v.* Cooper [1970] 1 Ch. 495; [1970] 2 W.L.R. 975; [1970] 1 All E.R. 1112;
(1969) 21 P. & C.R. 336; *sub nom.* Wardell *v.* Cooper 114 S.J. 244 ..... 477, 609,
610
Wareing *v.* White (1985) 274 E.G. 488; 17 H.L.R. 433, C.A.; (1984) 270 E.G. 851 426
Waring *v.* Foden; Waring *v.* Booth Crushed Gravel Co., Ltd. [1932] 1 Ch.
276; [1931] All E.R.Rep. 291; 101 L.J.Ch. 33; 146 L.T. 107; 75 Sol.Jo. 852,
C.A. 105
Warlock *v.* Saws (1981) 260 E.G. 920 257
Warmington *v.* Miller [1973] Q.B 877; [1973] 2 W.L.R. 654; 117 S.J. 166; [1973] 2 All
E.R. 372; 25 P. & C.R. 340, C.A. 94
Warner *v.* Lambeth L.B.C. (1984) 15 H.L.R. 42, D.C. 263
—— *v.* Sampson [1959] 1 Q.B. 297; [1959] 2 W.L.R. 109; 103 S.J. 91; [1959] 1 All
E.R. 120, C.A. 357
Warr & Co. Ltd. *v.* L.C.C. [1904] 1 K.B. 713; 73 L.J.K.B. 362; 90 L.T. 368; 68 J.P.
335; 20 T.L.R. 346; 2 L.G.R. 723; 52 W.R. 405 32
Warren *v.* Keen [1954] 1 Q.B 15; [1953] 3 W.L.R. 702; 97 S.J. 742; [1953] 2 All E.R.
1118, C.A. 218, 282, 283
Warriner, *Re*, Brayshaw *v.* Ninnis [1903] 2 Ch. 367; 72 L.J.Ch. 701; 88 L.T. 766; 62
J.P. 351; 19 T.L.R. 543; 1 L.G.R. 765 114
Warwick R.D.C. *v.* Miller-Mead [1962] Ch. 441; [1962] 2 W.L.R. 284; 126 J.P. 143;
[1962] 1 All E.R. 212; 60 L.G.R. 29; *sub nom.* Warwick R.D.C. *v.* Miller-
Read, 105 S.J. 1124, C.A.; *affirming sub nom.* Warwick R.D.C. *v.* Miller-
Mead; Miller-Mead *v.* Warwick R.D.C. [1961] Ch. 590; [1961] 3 W.L.R. 737;
125 J.P. 640; [1961] 3 All E.R. 542; leave to appeal to H.L. dismissed [1962] 1
W.L.R. 424 264
Warwick & Warwick (Philately) *v.* Shell (U.K.); Chipperfield *v.* Shell (U.K.) (1980)
125 S.J. 99; (1981) 42 P. & C.R. 1360; (1980) 257 E.G. 1042, C.A. 708
Waters *v.* Weigall (1795) 2 Anst. 757 254
Wates *v.* Rowland [1952] 2 Q.B. 12; [1952] 1 T.L.R. 488; [1952] 1 All E.R. 470,
C.A. 227
Watkins *v.* Emslie (1982) 261 E.G. 1192, C.A. 690
Watling *v.* Rees (1914) 84 L.J.K.B. 1122 263
Watney *v.* Boardley [1975] 1 W.L.R. 857; 119 S.J. 391; [1975] 2 All E.R. 644; 29 P. &
C.R. 294 .... 340, 674
Watney, Combe, Reid & Co. *v.* Ewart 86 L.T. 242; 18 T.L.R. 426, H.L.; *sub nom.*
Fryer *v.* Ewart [1902] A.C. 187; 71 L.J.Ch. 433; 9 Mans. 281; *affirming* S.C.
sub nom. Ewart *v.* Fryer [1901] 1 Ch. 499, C.A. 353
Watson *v.* Charlesworth [1905] 1 K.B 74; 74 L.J.K.B 155; 92 L.T. 46 169
—— *v.* Lucas [1980] 1 W.L.R. 1493; 124 S.J. 513; [1980] 3 All E.R. 647; 40 P. &
C.R. 531; 256 E.G. 1171, C.A. 442, 579
Watts *v.* Spence [1976] Ch. 165; [1975] 2 W.L.R. 1039; 119 S.J. 168; [1975] 2 All E.R.
528; 29 P. & C.R. 501 95
Webb *v.* Bevis (Frank) [1940] 1 All E.R. 247 60
—— *v.* Nightingale March 8, 1957 (unreported); 107 L.J. 359 104
—— *v.* Pollmount Ltd. [1966] Ch. 584; [1966] 2 W.L.R 543; 109 S.J. 1029; [1966] 1
All E.R. 481; [1965] C.L.Y. 2179 145
—— *v.* Stockport Corpn. (1962) 13 P. & C.R. 339; Lands Tribunal 735

Webber *v.* Smith (1689) 2 Vern. 103; 23 E.R. 676 356
Webb's Lease, *Re*, Sandom *v.* Webb [1951] Ch. 808; 95 S.J. 367; *sub nom. Re* Webb,
    Sandom *v.* Webb [1951] 2 All E.R. 131; *sub nom.* Sandom *v.* Webb [1951] 2
    T.L.R. 530, C.A. 106
Wedd *v.* Porter [1916] 2 K.B. 91; 85 L.J.K.B. 1298; 115 L.T. 243, C.A. 282
Wedderburn *v.* Wedderburn (No. 4) (1856) 22 Beav. 84; 25 L.J.Ch. 710; 28
    L.T.(O.S.) 4; 2 Jur.(N.S.) 674; 52 E.R. 1039 740
Weg Motors *v.* Hales [1962] Ch. 49; [1961] 3 W.L.R. 558; 105 S.J. 610; [1961] 3 All
    E.R. 181, C.A.; *affirming* [1961] Ch. 176; [1960] 3 W.L.R. 964; 104 S.J. 1057;
    [1960] 3 All E.R.762 .... 38, 54, 141
Weigall *v.* Waters (1795) 6 T.R. 488 .... 234, 254
Weinbergs Weatherproofs Ltd. *v.* Radcliffe Paper Mill Co. Ltd. [1958] Ch. 437;
    [1958] 2 W.L.R. 1; 102 S.J. 15; *sub nom. Re* Bleachers' Associations Leases,
    Weinbergs Weatherproofs *v.* Radcliffe Paper Mill Co. [1957] 3 All E.R.
    663 .... 139, 675, 686
Welch *v.* Birane (1974) 29 P. & C.R. 102 195
—— *v.* Nagy [1950] 1 K.B. 455; 66 T.L.R. (Pt. 1) 278; [1949] 1 All E.R. 868, C.A. ... 499
Weller *v.* Akehurst [1981] 3 All E.R. 411; (1981) 42 P. & C.R. 320; (1980) 257 E.G.
    1259 182
West *v.* Lascelles (1601) Cro.Eliz. 851 165
West (H. & Sons) Ltd. *v.* Brecht (1982) 261 E.G. 156 .... 180, 182
West Country Cleaners (Falmouth) Ltd. *v.* Saly [1966] 1 W.L.R. 1485; 110 S.J. 634;
    [1966] 3 All E.R. 210; 119 E.G. 563, C.A. 140
West Ferry Road, *Re*, Poplar, London [1955] 1 W.L.R. 751; 119 J.P. 467; 99 S.J. 472;
    [1955] 2 All E.R. 638; 5 P. & C.R. 265; 53 L.G.R. 488, C.A.; *affirming* [1955]
    1 W.L.R. 439 722
West Ham Central Charity Board *v.* East London Waterworks [1900] 1 Ch. 624; 69
    L.J.Ch. 257; 82 L.T. 85; 48 W.R. 284 281
West Layton Ltd. *v.* Ford (Executrix of the Estate of Joseph, decd.) [1979] Q.B 593;
    [1979] 3 W.L.R. 14; [1979] 2 All E.R. 657; (1978) 38 P. & C.R. 304, *sub nom.*
    West Layton *v.* Joseph (1979) 123 S.J. 233; 250 E.G. 345, C.A. 309, 311
West Midland Baptist (Trust) Association (Inc.) *v.* Birmingham Corpn. *See*
    Birmingham Corpn. *v.* West Midland Baptist (Trust) Association (Inc.).
Westbury Property & Investment Co. Ltd. *v.* Carpenter [1961] 1 All E.R. 481; *sub*
    nom. Westerbury Property & Investment Co. Ltd. *v.* Carpenter [1961] 1
    W.L.R. 272; 105 S.J. 155 684
Western Heritable Investment Co. *v.* Husband [1983] A.C. 849; [1983] 3 W.L.R.
    429; 127 S.J. 551; [1983] 3 All E.R. 65; 268 E.G. 266; 133 New L.J. 847; 80
    L.S.Gaz. 2443, H.L. 425, 426
Westlake *v.* Page [1926] 1 K.B. 298; 95 L.J.K.B. 456; 134 L.T. 612 808
Westminster City Council *v.* British Waterways Board [1985] A.C. 676; [1984] 3
    W.L.R. 1047; 128 S.J. 783; [1984] 3 All E.R. 737; 272 E.G. 1279; (1985) 83
    L.G.R. 113; 49 P. & C.R. 117; [1985] J.P.L. 102; (1984) 81 L.S.Gaz. 3501,
    H.L.; *affirming* (1983) 82 L.G.R. 44; [1984] J.P.L. 507; (1983) 268 E.G. 145,
    C.A. 704
—— *v.* Peart (1968) 112 S.J. 543; 19 P. & C.R. 736; 66 L.G.R. 561; *sub nom.* City of
    Westminster *v.* Peart 207 E.G. 140, D.C. 608
—— *v.* Select Managements Ltd. [1985] 1 W.L.R. 576; 129 S.J. 221; [1985] 1 All
    E.R. 897; [1985] I.C.R. 353; 83 L.G.R. 409; [1985] I.R.L.R. 344; 82
    L.S.Gaz. 1091, C.A.; *affirming* [1984] 1 W.L.R. 1058; [1984] I.C.R. 488;
    128 S.J. 580; [1984] 1 All E.R. 994; 81 L.S.Gaz. 2850 365
Westminster (Duke) *v.* Store Properties [1944] Ch. 129; 113 L.J.Ch. 157; 171 L.T. 7;
    60 T.L.R. 146; 88 S.J. 68; [1944] 1 All E.R. 118 178
—— *v.* Swinton [1948] 1 K.B. 524; 92 S.J. 97; [1948] 1 All E.R.248 .... 111, 121
Wetherall *v.* Smith [1980] 1 W.L.R. 1290; (1980) 124 S.J. 543; [1980] 2 All E.R. 530;
    40 P. & C.R. 205; 256 E.G. 163, C.A. 758, 759

Wettern Electric Ltd. *v.* Welsh Development Board [1983] Q.B 796; [1983] 2
    W.L.R. 897; [1983] 2 All E.R. 629; (1984) P. & C.R. 113 .... 9, 10
Wheeldon *v.* Burrows (1879) 12 Ch.D. 31; 48 L.J.Ch. 853; 39 L.T. 558; 27 W.R. 165,
    C.A. 106
Wheeler *v.* Mercer [1957] A.C. 416; [1956] 3 W.L.R. 841; 100 S.J. 836; [1956] 3 All
    E.R. 631, H.L. 16, 44, 45, 641
White *v.* Bayley (1861) 10 C.B.(N.S.) 227; 30 L.J.C.P. 263; 7 Jur.(N.S.) 948 27
—— *v.* Bijou Mansions Ltd. [1938] Ch. 351; 107 L.J.Ch. 212; 158 L.T. 338; 54
    T.L.R. 458; 82 S.J. 135; *affirming* [1937] Ch. 610 .... 75, 76
—— *v.* Greenish (1861) 11 C.B.(N.S.) 209; 8 Jur.(N.S.) 563; 142 E.R. 776; *sub nom.*
    Greenish *v.* White 31 L.J.C.P. 93 166
White Hudson *v.* Asian Organisation [1964] 1 W.L.R. 1466; 108 S.J. 937; [1965] 1 All
    E.R. 1040; [1965] R.P.C. 45, P.C. 741
Whitehead *v.* Bennett (1858) 27 L.J.Ch. 474; 6 W.R. 351 60
Whiteley *v.* Wilson [1953] 1 Q.B 77; [1952] 2 T.L.R. 802; 96 S.J. 901; [1952] 2 All
    E.R. 940, C.A. 381, 392
Whiteminster Estates *v.* Hodges Menswear (1974) 232 E.G. 715 311
Whitham *v.* Bullock (1939) 55 T.L.R. 617 320
Whitley *v.* Stumbles [1930] A.C. 544 52
Whitmore *v.* Lambert [1955] 1 W.L.R. 495; 99 S.J. 316; [1955] 2 All E.R. 147,
    C.A. 378
Whittaker *v.* Howe (1841) 3 Beav. 383; 49 E.R. 150 746
Whittam *v.* Kershaw (1886) 16 Q.B.D. 613; 54 L.T. 124; 34 W.R. 340 293
Whitton *v.* Bye (1618) Cro.Jac. 486; 79 E.R. 415; *sub nom.* Wooton *v.* Bye, Poph.
    136; *sub nom.* Mitton *v.* By, J.Bridg. 123 154
Whitty *v.* Scott-Russell [1950] 2 K.B. 32; 66 T.L.R. (Pt. 1) 1003; 94 S.J. 319; [1950] 1
    All E.R. 884, C.A. 379, 499
Wickington *v.* Bonney (1984) 47 P. & C.R. 655; (1983) 266 E.G. 434 783
Wigginton & Milner Ltd. *v.* Winster Engineering Ltd. [1978] 1 W.L.R. 1462; 122 S.J.
    826; [1978] 3 All E.R. 436; (1977) 36 P. & C.R. 203, C.A. 104
Wilchick *v.* Marks and Silverstone [1934] 2 K.B. 56; 103 L.J.K.B. 372; 151 L.T. 60;
    50 T.L.R. 281; 78 S.J. 277 .... 42, 369
Wilkes *v.* Goodwin [1923] 2 K.B. 86; 92 L.J.K.B. 580; 129 L.T. 44; 39 T.L.R. 262; 67
    S.J. 437; 21 L.G.R. 239 401
Wilkins *v.* Leighton [1932] 2 Ch. 106; 101 L.J.Ch. 385; 147 L.T. 495; 76 S.J. 232 369
Wilkinson *v.* Hall (1835–37) 1 Bing.N.C. 713; 3 Bing.N.C. 508; 6 L.J.C.P. 82; 4 Scott
    301; 3 Hodges 56; 43 R.R. 728 102
—— *v.* Middlesborough B.C. (1983) 45 P. & C.R. 142; (1982) 261 E.G. 673; [1982]
    J.P.L. 306, C.A.; 39 P. & C.R. 212; (1979) 250 E.G. 867 730
Williams *v.* Bartholomew (1798) 1 Bos. & P. 326; 4 R.R. 816 166
—— *v.* Earle (1868) L.R. 3 Q.B. 739; 37 L.J.Q.B. 231; 19 L.T. 238; 16 W.R. 1041;
    9 B. & S. 740 317
—— *v.* Evans (1875) L.R. 19 Eq. 547; 44 L.J.Ch. 319; 32 L.T. 359; 23 W.R. 466 87
—— *v.* Greatrex [1957] 1 W.L.R. 31; 101 S.J. 48; [1956] 3 All E.R. 705, C.A. 97
—— *v.* Khan (1982) 43 P. & C.R. 1; (1981) 258 E.G. 554, C.A.; *affirming* (1980) 255
    E.G. 1208 425
—— *v.* Mate (1983) 46 P. & C.R. 43; [1983] H.L.R. 15; (1982) 263 E.G.883, C.A. ... 397
—— *v.* Staite [1979] Ch. 291; [1978] 2 W.L.R. 825; (1977) 122 S.J. 333; [1978] 2 All
    E.R. 928; 36 P. & C.R. 103, C.A. 11, 360
—— *v.* Williams [1970] 1 W.L.R. 1530; 114 S.J. 826; [1970] 3 All E.R. 988; 21 P. &
    C.R. 915, C.A. 440
Williams Deacon's Bank *v.* Catlow [1928] E.G.D. 286 452
Willmott *v.* Barber (1880) 15 Ch.D. 96; 49 L.J.Ch. 792; 43 L.T. 95; 28 W.R.
    911 .... 12, 313
—— *v.* London Road Car Co. [1910] 2 Ch. 525; 80 L.J.Ch. 1; 103 L.T. 447; 54 S.J.
    873; 27 T.L.R. 4 306

Willson v. Greene, Moss (Third Party) [1971] 1 W.L.R. 635; [1971] 1 All E.R. 1098;
22 P. & C.R. 697 104
Wilson v. Croft [1971] 1 Q.B 241; [1970] 3 W.L.R. 1; 114 S.J. 456; [1970] 2 All E.R.
623; 21 P. & C.R. 878, C.A. 490
—— v. Earl Spencer's Settlement Trustees (1985) 274 E.G. 1254 795
—— v. Finch-Hatton (1877) 2 Ex.D. 336; 46 L.J.Q.B. 489; 36 L.T. 473; 25 W.R.
537 239
—— v. Fynn [1948] W.N. 242; 92 S.J. 324; [1948] 2 All E.R. 40 307
—— v. Liverpool Corpn. [1971] 1 W.L.R. 302; (1970) 114 S.J. 932; 22 P. & C.R.
282; *sub nom.* Wilson (Personal Representatives of Wilson) v. Liverpool
City Council [1971] 1 All E.R. 628, C.A. 732
—— v. Rosenthal (1906) 22 T.L.R. 233 305
Winchester Court v. Holmes (1941) 165 L.T. 396; 57 T.L.R. 595; 85 S.J. 333; [1941] 2
All E.R. 542 346
Windmill Investments (London) Ltd. v. Milano Restaurant Ltd. [1962] 2 Q.B 373;
[1962] 3 W.L.R. 651; 106 S.J. 689; [1962] 2 All E.R. 680 195
Winter Garden Theatre (London) Ltd. v. Millenium Productions Ltd. [1948] A.C.
173; [1947] L.J.R. 1422; 177 L.T. 349; 63 T.L.R. 529; 91 S.J. 504; [1947] 2 All
E.R. 331, H.L. 358, 359
Wisbech St. Mary Parish Council v. Lilley [1956] 1 W.L.R. 121; [1956] 1 All E.R.
301, C.A. 357
Wise v. Perpetual Trustee Co. [1903] A.C. 139; 72 L.J.P.C. 31; 87 L.T. 569; 51 W.R.
241; 19 T.L.R. 125, P.C. 72
Wix v. Rutson [1899] 1 Q.B 474; 68 L.J.Q.B. 298; 80 L.T. 168 317
Wolf v. Crutchley [1971] 1 W.L.R. 99; (1970) 114 S.J. 807; [1971] 1 All E.R. 520; 22
P. & C.R. 146, C.A. 507
Wolfe v. Clarkson [1950] W.N. 427; 66 T.L.R. (Pt. 2) 694; [1950] 2 All E.R. 529,
C.A. 202
—— v. Hogan [1949] 2 K.B. 194; [1949] 1 All E.R. 570, C.A. 380, 381, 499
Wolmer Securities v. Corne [1966] 2 Q.B. 243; [1966] 2 W.L.R. 1381; 110 S.J. 350;
[1966] 2 All E.R. 691, C.A. 198
Wolveridge v. Steward (1833) 1 C. & M. 644; 3 Tyr. 637; 3 Moo. & S. 561; 3 L.J.Ex.
360; 38 R.R. 701 322
Wombles v. Wombles Skips [1975] F.S.R. 488 741
Wonderland, Cleethorpes, *Re. See* East Coast Amusement Co. v. British Transport
Board.
Wong v. Beaumont Property Trust Ltd. [1965] 1 Q.B 173; [1964] 2 W.L.R. 1325; 108
S.J. 237; [1964] 2 All E.R. 119, C.A. 105
Wood v. Leadbitter (1845) 13 M. & W. 838; 14 L.J.Ex. 161; 9 Jur. 187; 4 L.T.(o.s.)
433; 67 R.R. 831 36
—— v. Manley (1839) 11 A. & E. 34; 9 L.J.Q.B. 27; 3 P. & D. 5; 3 Jur. 1028;
[1835–42] All E.R. Rep. 128 .... 11, 358
—— v. South Western Co-operative Housing Society (1982) 4 H.L.R. 101; 44 P. &
C.R. 198, C.A. 595
Woodall v. Clifton [1905] 2 Ch. 257; 74 L.J.Ch. 555; 93 L.T. 257; 54 W.R. 7 .141, 142,
318
Woodar Investments Developments Ltd. v. Wimpey Construction U.K. Ltd. [1980]
1 W.L.R. 277; 124 S.J. 184; [1980] 1 All E.R. 571, H.L. 133, 251
Woodhouse v. Hooney [1915] 1 Ir.R. 296 173
Woodhouse (Edwin) Trustee Co. Ltd. v. Sheffield Brick Co. plc (1984) 270 E.G.
548 181
Woods v. Wise [1955] 2 Q.B 29; [1955] 2 W.L.R. 734; 119 J.P. 254; 99 S.J. 234; [1955]
1 All E.R. 767, C.A. 428
Woods (L. H.) & Co. v. City & West End Properties (1921) 38 T.L.R. 692; 93 S.J.
791; [1949] 2 All E.R. 709 158

Woodward *v.* Docherty [1974] 1 W.L.R. 966; 118 S.J. 443; [1974] 2 All E.R. 844; 28
P. & C.R. 62, C.A. 402
—— *v.* Dudley (Earl of) [1954] Ch. 283; [1954] 1 W.L.R. 476; 98 S.J. 162; [1954] 1
All E.R. 559; 52 L.G.R 269 800
Woolfson *v.* Strathclyde Regional Council (1978) 38 P. & C.R. 521; [1979] J.P.L.
169; [1978] S.L.T. 159; 248 E.G. 777, H.L. 733
Woollerton and Wilson *v.* Costain (Richard) [1970] 1 W.L.R. 411; 114 S.J. 170 103
Woolworth (F. W.) & Co. Ltd. *v.* Lambert [1937] Ch. 37; 106 L.J.Ch. 15; 155 L.T.
236; 52 T.L.R. 732; 80 S.J. 703; [1936] 2 All E.R. 1523 121
Woozley *v.* Woodall Smith [1950] 1 K.B. 325; 94 S.J. 13; [1949] 2 All E.R. 1055,
C.A. 399
Worcester Diocesan Trust *v.* Taylor (1947) 177 L.T. 581, C.A. 393
Wright *v.* Dean [1948] Ch. 686; [1948] L.J.R. 1571; 64 T.L.R. 467; 92 S.J. 393; [1948]
2 All E.R. 415 142
—— *v.* Howell (1948) 92 S.J. 26 .... 386, 387
—— *v.* Lawson (1903) 19 T.L.R.510; 68 J.P. 34; *affirming* 19 T.L.R. 203 231
—— *v.* Macadam [1949] 2 K.B. 744; 93 S.J. 646; [1949] 2 All E.R. 565, C.A. .. 88, 104
Wright (A Bankrupt), *Re, ex p.* Landau *v.* Trustee [1949] Ch. 729; 65 T.L.R. 564; 93
S.J. 679; [1949] 2 All E.R. 605 .... 299, 303, 331
Wringe *v.* Cohen [1940] 1 K.B. 299; 109 L.J.K.B. 227; 56 T.L.R. 101; 161 L.T. 366;
[1939] 4 All E.R. 241 368
Wuta-Ofei *v.* Danquah [1961] 1 W.L.R. 1238; 105 S.J. 806; [1961] 3 All E.R. 596,
P.C. 371
Wycombe Area Health Authority *v.* Barnett (1982) 264 E.G. 619 .... 244, 245, 283
Wykes *v.* Davis [1975] Q.B 843; [1975] 2 W.L.R. 131; (1974) 119 S.J. 84; [1975] 1 All
E.R. 399; (1974) 30 P. & C.R. 338, C.A. 788
Wyness D.C. *v.* Poole [1979] L.A.G.Bull. 166 .... 612, 621
Wynn *v.* Conway Corporation [1914] 2 Ch. 705; 78 J.P. 380; 59 S.J. 43; 30 T.L.R.
666 47

X.L. Fisheries *v.* Leeds Corporation [1955] 2 Q.B 636; [1955] 3 W.L.R. 393; 119 J.P.
519; 99 S.J. 560; [1955] 2 All E.R. 875; 53 L.G.R. 505, C.A. 683

Yates *v.* Morris [1951] 1 K.B. 77; [1950] W.N. 409; 66 T.L.R. (Pt. 2) 707; [1950] 2 All
E.R. 577, C.A. 450, 452, 468
Yelloly *v.* Morley (1910) 27 T.L.R. 20 .... 283, 658
Yellowly *v.* Gower (1855) 11 Ex. 274; 24 L.J.Ex. 289 281
Yewbright Properties *v.* Stone (1980) 124 S.J. 311; (1980) 40 P. & C.R. 402; (1980)
254 E.G. 863, C.A. 450
Yoland *v.* Reddington (1982) 263 E.G. 157, C.A. 449
Yorkbrook Investments *v.* Batten (1985) 276 E.G. 493 .... 172, 237
Young *v.* Ashley Gardens Property Ltd. [1903] 2 Ch. 112; 72 L.J.Ch. 520; 88 L.T.
541 309
—— *v.* Hargreaves (1963) 186 E.G. 355, C.A. 44
Young, Austen & Young *v.* British Medical Association [1977] 1 W.L.R. 881; 121
S.J. 492; [1977] 2 All E.R. 884; 33 P. & C.R. 437; 244 E.G. 303 .... 693, 749
Youngs *v.* Thanet D.C. (1980) 78 L.G.R. 474 624
Youngmin *v.* Heath [1974] 1 W.L.R. 135; (1973) 117 S.J. 795; [1974] 1 All E.R. 461;
(1973) 26 P. & C.R. 570, C.A. 326, 327, 328

Zarraga *v.* Newcastle upon Tyne Corpn. (1968) 19 P. & C.R. 609; [1968] J.P.L.
346, Lands Tribunal 737
Zbytniewski *v.* Broughton [1956] 2 Q.B 673; [1956] 3 W.L.R. 630; 100 S.J. 631;
[1956] 3 All E.R. 348, C.A. 394, 410
Zouch *d.* Abbott and Hallet *v.* Parsons (1765) 3 Burr. 1794; 1 Wm.Bl. 575; 95 E.R.
1103 339

TABLE OF STATUTES

1267	Statute of Marlebridge (52 Hen. 3, c. 23)	281
1677	Statute of Frauds (29 Car. 2, c. 3)	86
	s. 4	83
1689	Distress for Rent Act (2 & 3 Will. & Mar., sess. 1, c. 5)—	
	s. 3	201
1709	Landlord and Tenant Act (8 Anne, c. 14) (c. 18 in the Statutes Revised)	204
	s. 1	204
1730	Landlord and Tenant Act (4 Geo. 2, c. 28)	193
	s. 1	335
	s. 5	166
1737	Distress for Rent Act (11 Geo. 2, c. 19)	201
	s. 14	193
1774	Fires Prevention (Metropolis) Act (14 Geo. 3, c. 78)—	
	s. 83	120, 234
	s. 86	120, 234
1833	Fines and Recoveries Act (3 & 4 Will. 4, c. 74)—	
	s. 41	755
1838	Pluralities Act (1 & 2 Vict. c. 106)	393
1845	Lands Clauses Consolidation Act (8 & 9 Vict. c. 18)—	
	s. 121	728
1852	Common Law Procedure Act (15 & 16 Vict. c. 76)	408
	s. 210 .... 196, 197, 198	
	ss. 211, 212	197
	s. 214	193
1859	Law of Property Amendment Act (22 & 23 Vict. c. 35)—	
	ss. 1, 2	298
1870	Apportionment Act (33 & 34 Vict. c. 35)—	
	ss. 2, 3	165
1873	Judicature Act (36 & 37 Vict. c. 66)	92
	s. 25 (11)	92
1875	Judicature Act (38 & 39 Vict. c. 77)	92
1875	Public Health Act (38 & 39 Vict. c. 55)	115
1881	Conveyancing Act (44 & 45 Vict., c. 41)—	
	s. 14	299
	(1), (2)	299
	(6) (i)	300
1891	Stamp Act (54 & 55 Vict. c. 39)	88
	s. 14	88
	s. 75 (1)	527
	Sched. 1	527
1907	National Trust Act (7 Edw. 7, c. cxxxvi)—	
	s. 21	514
1908	Law of Distress Amendment Act (8 Edw. 7, c. 53)—	
	s. 4A	200
1914	Bankruptcy Act (4 & 5 Geo. 5, c. 59)—	
	s. 9 (1)	203
	s. 35 (1)	203
	s. 53	329
	s. 54	330
	(1)	330
	(2)	331
	(6)	331
	s. 129	330
	s. 167	329
1915	Increase of Rent and Mortgage (War Restrictions) Act (5 & 6 Geo. 5, c. 97)	376, 637
1919	Statement of Rates Act (9 & 10 Geo. 5, c. 31)—	
	s. 1 (1)	163
	ss. 2, 3	163
	s. 11 (2)	163
1920	Increase of Rent and Mortgage Interest (Restrictions) Act (10 & 11 Geo. 5, c. 17)	376
	s. 2 (1) (d) (ii)	221
1922	Law of Property Act (12 & 13 Geo. 5, c. 16)—	
	s. 145	46
	Sched. 15, paras. 1, 2.	141
	para. 7	141, 142
	para. 9	38
1925	Settled Land Act (15 & 16 Geo. 5, c. 18) . 62, 65, 169, 762	
	s. 1	62

1925 Settled Land Act—*cont.*

s. 4	62
s. 7	63
s. 19	62
s. 20	62
(1) (iv)	41
s. 23	62
s. 29 (1)	67
s. 41	63
s. 42	63, 763
(1)	63
(4)	63
(5)	64
(ii)	63
s. 43	63
s. 44	63
(2)	167
s. 45	63, 168
ss. 46–48	63
s. 55	63
s. 101	63
(5)	64
s. 106	63
s. 107 (1)	64
s. 109	64
s. 110	763
(1)	64
s. 117 (1) (i)	301

Trustee Act (15 & 16 Geo. 5, c. 19)—

s. 25	71
s. 26	328
(2)	329
s. 27	328
s. 30 (2)	72
s. 34	62
(1), (2)	72

Law of Property Act (15 & 16 Geo. 5, c. 20) | 66, 637

s. 1	1, 2
(1)	9, 12, 37, 38, 45, 51
(2) (*a*)	51
(3)	38
(5)	39
s. 2 (1)	65
s. 7 (1)	38
s. 8	77
s. 22 (1)	315
s. 27 (2)	64
s. 28	763
(1)	65
s. 29	66, 763
(2)	66
s. 30	763
s. 34 (2)	62, 71
s. 35	63, 71

1925 Law of Property Act—*cont.*

s. 40	56, 84, 85, 94, 338
(1)	83
(2)	87
s. 41	95
s. 44 (2)	66, 76, 78, 313
(3)	313
(4)	77, 78, 313
(5)	76, 77, 79, 313
(10)	79
s. 45 (2)	79, 314, 321
(3)	314, 321
s. 50 (2)	75
s. 52	51, 55, 324, 338
(1)	75, 87, 93, 314
(2) (*c*)	339
(*d*)	338
s. 53 (1)	338
s. 54 (2)	20, 55, 71, 87, 88, 315, 338
s. 61	344
s. 62	88, 104, 105
(4)	105
s. 76 (1), (2)	321
s. 77	321
s. 79	294, 303, 317
(1)	299
s. 84	128
s. 85 (1)	7
s. 86	304
(1)	304
s. 87	304
(1)	39
s. 98 (1)	69
s. 99	67, 68, 337
(5), (6)	68
(8)	68
(11)	68
(13)	68
(17)	68
s. 100	337
s. 109 (2)	69
s. 121	166
s. 123	77
s. 135	281
s. 136	10, 166
s. 139	336, 341, 465, 764
s. 140	325
(2)	326
s. 141	163, 169, 317, 324, 325
(1)	152
s. 142	317, 324, 325
(1)	141
s. 143	298, 661
s. 144	306, 661
s. 145	141

1925 Law of Property Act—*cont.*
  s. 145—*cont.*
    (11) 351
  s. 146 .... 98, 112, 147, 284, 289,
            290, 300, 335, 352–356,
            408, 637, 790, 808
    (1) 290, 291, 299
    (2) 292, 352, 354
    (3) 352
    (4) ... 198, 319, 336, 355, 356,
            463, 674, 764
    (8) 356
    (9) 356, 790
    (10) 356, 790
    (11) 356
    (12) 357
  s. 147 .... 98, 290, 292, 352, 637
    (2) 292
  s. 48 313
  s. 149 371
    (3) 38, 54, 108, 139
    (5) 53
    (6) .. 41, 81, 88, 297, 335, 792
  s. 150 (1)–(4) 336
  s. 151 (1) 163
  s. 152 .... 64, 763
  s. 185 674
  s. 196 .... 146, 290, 349
    (1) 349
  s. 198 .... 76, 79
    (1) 75
  s. 199 (1) 76, 94
  s. 202 141
  s. 205 (1) (ii) 88, 104
        (iii) 301
        (ix) 103, 800
        (x) 763
        (xix) 55
        (xxi) 75
        (xxiii) 55
        (xxvii) ... 3, 36, 38, 43,
                335
  Sched. 2, Pts. I, II 321
  Pt. IX 321
  Land Registration Act (15 &
    16 Geo. 5, c. 21) 103
  s. 8 89
    (2) 88, 301
  s. 18 (1) (c) 51
      (e) 62
  s. 19 .... 88, 324
    (2) 88
  s. 20 (1) (a) 75
  s. 21 324
    (1) 301
      (b) 51

1925 Land Registration Act—
  cont.
  s. 21—*cont.*
    (1)—*cont.*
      (d) 62
  s. 22 88
    (1) 324
    (2) 88
  s. 41 (4) 326
  s. 48 .... 89, 94, 301
  s. 59 569
  s. 70 (1) (g) . 88, 94, 145, 146, 405
      (k) 88, 94, 145
  s. 75 (2) 337
  s. 110 75
  s. 123 89
  Administration of Estates
    Act (15 & 16 Geo. 5, c.
    23)—
  s. 1 163
  s. 2 163
    (2) 66
  s. 3 163
  s. 9 .... 326, 439
  s. 33 66
  s. 36 326
  s. 39 66
  s. 55 (1) (xv) 326
1926 Law of Property (Amend-
    ment) Act (16 & 17 Geo.
    5, c. 11)—
  ss. 7, 8 329
  Sched. 38, 329
1927 Landlord and Tenant Act (17
    & 18 Geo. 5, c. 36) .. 639, 748
  Pt. I 638, 640, 663–665,
            668, 734, 807
  s. 1 638
    (1) 665, 668, 670
      (b) 670
    (2) 670
    (3) 671
  s. 2 638
    (1) 638, 665
      (b) 671
    (3) 668, 671
  s. 3 .... 638, 666, 807
    (1) 666, 667
    (2) 667
    (4)–(6) 667
  s. 4 .... 638, 747
    (1) (b) 638
  s. 5 .... 638, 747
    (3) 638
  s. 6 638
  s. 8 .... 666, 667

1927 Landlord and Tenant Act—
cont.
  s. 8—*cont.*
    (1) 286
  s. 9 666
  s. 10 668
  s. 11 671
    (2) 164
  s. 17 .... 638, 663
    (1) 52, 664
    (2)–(4) 664
  s. 18 .... 284, 285
    (1) 288
    (2) 353
  s. 19 .... 298, 300, 301, 308, 660
    (1) 127, 338, 662
      (*a*) 306
      (*b*) 301
    (2) 121, 127, 663
    (3) 127
    (4) 301, 769
  s. 21 .... 639, 807
  s. 23 147
  s. 25 649
    (1) 664, 665
1929 Law of Property (Amend-
ment) Act (19 & 20 Geo.
5, c. 9)—
  s. 1 356
1930 Land Drainage Act (20 & 21
Geo. 5, c. 44)—
  s. 26 164
1935 Housing Act (25 & 26 Geo. 5,
c. 40)—
  s. 2 221
1936 Public Health Act (26 Geo. 5
& 1 Edw. 8, c. 49) ... 116, 164,
                        259
  s. 92 .... 261, 262
    (1) 259, 262
  s. 93 .... 262, 263, 264, 544
  s. 94 .... 263, 264
    (2) 263, 544
  s. 95 .... 263, 264
  s. 96 264
  s. 99 .... 263, 264, 544
  s. 100 264
  s. 141 259
  s. 259 (1) (*a*), (*b*) 259
  s. 268 (2) 259
  s. 343 259
    (1) 263
1938 Trade Marks Act (1 & 2 Geo.
6, c. 22) 741
  s. 2 741

1938 Leasehold Property (Repairs) Act (1 & 2 Geo. 6,
c. 34) 284, 285, 289, 290,
                        352, 416
  s. 1 .... 284, 290, 292
    (1) 290
    (3) 284, 290
    (5) 290, 291
1939 London Building (Amend-
ment) Act (2 & 3 Geo. 6,
c. xcvii)—
  s. 62 273
  s. 107 669
  s. 141 285
  Landlord and Tenant (War
Damage) Act (2 & 3
Geo. 6, c. 72) 137
1941 Liabilities (War Time Adjustment) Act (4 & 5
Geo. 6, c. 14) 175
  Landlord and Tenant (War
Damage) (Amendment)
Act (4 & 5 Geo. 6, c.
41)—
  s. 7 175
1944 Landlord and Tenant (Requisitioned Land) Act (7
& 8 Geo. 6, c. 5) 137
  Validation of War-Time
Leases Act (7 & 8 Geo.
6, c. 34) 40
  s. 7 (2) 41
  Liabilities (War Time Ad-
justment) Act (7 & 8
Geo. 6, c. 40) 175
1946 Furnished Houses (Rent
Control) Act (9 & 10
Geo. 6, c. 34) 473
1948 National Assistance Act (11
& 12 Geo. 6, c. 29)—
  s. 21 (1) 610
    (*a*) 611, 618
  Agricultural Wages Act (11 &
12 Geo. 6, c. 47)—
  s. 17 (1) 279
  Agricultural Holdings Act
(11 & 12 Geo. 6, c.
63) . 301, 334, 340, 393, 548, 756
  s. 2 (1), (2) 648
  s. 3 341
  s. 13 60
    (2), (3) 60
    (4A) 60
  s. 15 170
  s. 17 283
  s. 22 164

1948	Agricultural Holdings Act—	
	cont.	
	ss. 23, 24	756
	s. 25	756
	(1) (*a*)	782
	s. 92	47, 349
	s. 96	763
1949	Consolidation of Enactments	
	(Procedure) Act (12, 13	
	& 14 Geo. 6, c. 33)	377
1950	Arbitration Act (14 Geo. 6, c.	
	27)	147
	s. 19A	183
	s. 20	183
	s. 27	182
1951	Leasehold Property (Tem-	
	porary Provisions) Act	
	(14 & 15 Geo. 6, c. 38)	639
1952	Magistrates' Courts Act (15	
	& 16 Geo. 6 & 1 Eliz. 2,	
	c. 55)—	
	s. 126 (2)	263
1953	Accommodation Agencies	
	Act (1 & 2 Eliz. 2, c. 23)	432
	s. 1	432
	Licensing Act (1 & 2 Eliz. 2,	
	c. 46)—	
	s. 18 (4)	164
	Sched. IV, Pt. II	164
1954	Agriculture (Miscellaneous	
	Provisions) Act (2 & 3	
	Eliz. 2, c. 39)—	
	s. 6	781
	Landlord and Tenant Act (2	
	& 3 Eliz. 2, c. 56)	5, 94, 142,
		342, 640–642, 666, 747
	Pt. I	343, 399, 430, 497, 498,
		500, 607, 637
	Pt. II	10, 16, 19, 32, 33, 44, 45,
		52, 53, 60, 90, 139, 140, 161,
		189, 316, 326, 342, 343, 381,
		393, 398, 496, 549, 555, 607,
		640, 642, 645, 646, 649, 650,
		654, 655, 664, 668, 673–675,
		678, 682, 684, 690, 692, 693,
		695, 703, 728, 730, 736, 758
	Pt. III	640, 663
	s. 2 (1)	498, 500, 501
	(2)	500
	(4), (5)	498
	(7)	498
	s. 3 (1)	465, 499
	(2) (*a*), (*b*)	499
	s. 4	342, 343, 519
	(1)	465, 499, 500
	(2)	501

1954	Landlord and Tenant Act	
	—*cont.*	
	s. 4—*cont.*	
	(3)	500, 501
	s. 5	344, 501
	s. 6 (1), (2)	501
	s. 7	501, 502
	(2)	501
	s. 8	502
	s. 9	503
	s. 12 (1)	501
	(*a*)	501
	s. 16 (1)	502
	(2)	502, 519
	(3), (4)	502
	s. 17	498
	s. 19	498
	s. 21	501
	s. 22 (3)	499
	s. 23	644, 645
	(1)	52, 641–643, 645
	(2)	646, 647
	(3)	645, 702
	(4)	642, 648
	s. 24	44, 334, 674, 677, 683, 686,
		687, 689, 728
	(1)	656, 673–677, 688, 689,
		691
	(2)	673, 674, 677
	(*b*)	674
	(3)	343
	(*a*), (*b*)	678
	s. 24A	679, 681, 706
	(1)	679, 680
	(2)	682
	(3)	680, 681
	s. 25	342, 676, 677, 682–690,
		692, 696, 703, 706–708, 749
	(2)	343, 673, 675, 685
	(3)	684
	(*b*)	685
	(4)	684
	(5)	676
	(6)	685, 692
	s. 26	668, 677, 688–692, 696,
		703, 706–708
	(1)	682, 689
	(2)	690, 691
	(3)	673, 690, 691
	(4)	677, 689
	(6)	692, 749
	s. 27	656, 675, 677, 689
	(1)	343, 677, 687
	(2)	343, 673, 677
	s. 28	683, 688, 689, 692
	(2)	687

1954 Landlord and Tenant Act
—*cont.*
s. 29 .... 674, 677
(1) 689, 707
(2) 676, 687–689
(3) 688, 691
s. 30 (1) .. 685, 686, 692–694, 709,
729, 749, 751
(*a*)–(*c*) 694
(*d*) 695, 707
(*e*) 694, 696, 707, 748,
749
(*f*) 555, 693, 697, 701,
702, 704, 705, 707, 709,
728, 748, 749, 751, 784
(*g*) 697, 701–704, 709,
748, 749, 751
(2) 677, 697, 703
(3) 703
s. 31 (1) 686, 707
(2) 707
s. 31A 701
(1) 698, 700
(*a*) 701
(2) 699
s. 32 (1) 710
(3) 711
s. 32A (1) 711
s. 33 .... 708, 709
s. 34 .... 188, 669, 681, 713, 715
(1) 679, 711
(*a*) 711
(*d*) 711
(2) 669, 679, 712
(3) 715
s. 35 .... 501, 714–716
s. 36 68
(1) 717
(2) 707, 708
(3) 708
(4) 68
s. 37 693
(1) 748, 749, 751
(2) 750
(*a*), (*b*) 750
(3) 750
(*a*), (*b*) 750
(4) 749
(5)–(7) 751
s. 38 .... 16, 641
(1) 338, 655, 656, 675
(4) 641, 655, 656
(*a*), (*b*) 655
s. 39 (3) 728
s. 41 (1) 644
(2) 702

1954 Landlord and Tenant Act
—*cont.*
s. 41A 644
s. 42 (1) 643, 645, 703
(3) 703
s. 43 342
(1) (*a*) 648
(*b*) 649
(*d*) 646, 649, 664
(2) 650
(3) 652, 690
s. 44 763
(1) 683, 696
s. 46 649
s. 47 668
s. 48 (1) 666
s. 49 666
s. 51 289
s. 53 122
(1) 307
s. 54 349
s. 55 .... 696, 705, 751, 752
s. 56 (3) 644
s. 57 650
s. 58 651
(2) 651
(3), (4) 652
s. 63 706
s. 64 .... 678, 687, 708
(1), (2) 708
s. 66 (4) 147
s. 69 (1) 641, 648
(2) 687
Sched. 1 502
Sched. 2 503
Sched. 3 502
Sched. 6, para. 2 717
paras. 3–7 718
1955 Requisitioned Houses and
Housing (Amendment)
Act (3 & 4 Eliz. 2, c.
24)—
s. 4 14
1956 Clear Air Act (4 & 5 Eliz. 2, c.
52)—
s. 16 259
s. 28 669
1957 Occupiers Liability Act (5 & 6
Eliz. 2, c. 31) 249, 365, 367
s. 2 .... 257, 366
(3) 366
s. 3 366
Cheques Act (5 & 6 Eliz. 2, c.
36)—
s. 3 163

1957 Housing Act (5 & 6 Eliz. 2, c. 56) 488
    s. 6 221
    s. 9 (1) 272
        (1A) 272
    s. 11 272
        (3) 271, 272
    s. 14 116
    s. 113 (5) 533, 577
1958 Costs of Leases Act (6 & 7 Eliz. 2, c. 52)—
    s. 1 .... 90, 147, 717
1959 County Courts Act (7 & 8 Eliz. 2, c. 22)—
    s. 74 253
    Mental Health Act (7 & 8 Eliz. 2, c. 72) 514
1960 Charities Act (8 & 9 Eliz. 2, c. 58)—
    s. 29 .... 67, 594
        (2) 67
    s. 45 (3) 67
    Sched. 2 67
    Noise Abatement Act (8 & 9 Eliz. 2, c. 68) 259
1961 Land Compensation Act (9 & 10 Eliz. 2, c. 33)—
    s. 5 .... 730, 732
    s. 7 732
    s. 9 732
    s. 31 721
    s. 32 725
    Factories Act (9 & 10 Eliz. 2, c. 34) 365
    s. 169 122
    s. 170 113
    Land Drainage Act (9 & 10 Eliz. 2, c. 48)—
    s. 32 164
    Sched. 1, Pt. 1, para. 5 164
    Housing Act (9 & 10 Eliz. 2, c. 65)—
    s. 15 276
    s. 32 486
        (1) 236
1962 Recorded Delivery Service Act (10 & 11 Eliz. 2, c. 27) 146, 290, 349
    Landlord and Tenant Act (10 & 11 Eliz. 2, c. 50)—
    s. 1 163
1963 London Government Act (c. 33)—
    s. 43 273

1963 Children and Young Persons Act (c. 37)—
    s. 1 .... 200, 611
    Offices, Shops, and Railway Premises Act (c. 41) . 189, 365
    s. 73 .... 113, 122
        (2) 669
1964 Perpetuities and Accumulations Act (c. 55)—
    s. 9 (1) 143
1965 Industrial and Provident Societies Act (c. 12) . 585, 591, 595
    Compulsory Purchase Act (c. 56) 720, 738
    s. 2 727
    ss. 4, 5 720
    s. 6 721
    s. 8 (1) 721
    s. 9 722
    s. 11 (1) 725–728
    s. 20 .... 724, 727, 728, 733
        (1) 724
    s. 22 723
    s. 23 722
    s. 39 728
    Sched. 5 722
    Sched. 7 728
    New Towns Act (c. 59) 275
    Rent Act (c. 75) 411
1966 Docks and Harbours Act (c. 28)—
    s. 34 669
1967 Misrepresentation Act (c. 7) . 148
    s. 1 149
    s. 2 (1) 95, 149
        (2) 149
    General Rate Act (c. 9)—
    s. 2 113
    s. 16 112
    s. 26 (3) (a) 392
    s. 58 .... 113, 164
    s. 59 117
    s. 68 390
    Agriculture Act (c. 22)—
    s. 29 (1) 797
    Leasehold Reform Act (c. 88) 311, 498, 522, 546
    Pt. I 430
    s. 1 503
        (1) 505, 506, 513
            (a) 508
            (b) 510–512
        (2) 511, 512, 546
            (b) 512
        (3), (4) 508

1967	Leasehold Reform Act— *cont.*	
	Pt. I—*cont.*	
	s. 1—*cont.*	
	(4A)	508
	(5) (*a*), (*b*)	509
	(6)	509
	s. 2 (1)	505
	(2)	506
	(3)	507
	(4)	508
	(5)	507
	(6)	508
	s. 3 (1)–(3)	510
	(5)	510
	(6)	507
	s. 4 (1)	511
	(*b*), (*c*)	511
	(5)	511
	s. 5	512, 513
	(1)	513, 514
	(2)	514
	(6)	518
	ss. 6, 7	512
	s. 8 (1)	513, 514
	s. 9 (1)	504, 515
	(*b*), (*c*)	516
	(1A)	515, 516
	(1B)	515
	(3)	518
	(4)	517
	s. 10	514
	s. 14	504
	s. 15 (2) (*a*)	504
	s. 16 (1)	652
	(*a*), (*b*)	504
	(*c*)	504, 652
	(*d*)	652
	s. 17	504
	(1), (2)	504
	s. 18	518
	s. 19	519
	(1)	519
	(8)	519
	(10)	520
	s. 20	514
	s. 21	517
	s. 23	503
	(3)	503
	s. 25	513, 514
	s. 26	514
	s. 27	515
	(2)	515
	s. 28	501, 514
	(1) (*a*), (*b*)	518
	(5)	518

1967	Leasehold Reform Act— *cont.*	
	s. 29	514, 518
	ss. 31–33	514
	s. 37 (1) (*f*)	512
	s. 38	501
	s. 39	503
	Sched. 1	513
	para. 2	514
	paras. 3, 4	513
	para. 5 (1)	513
	(3), (4)	513
	para. 7 (1) (*b*)	514, 517
	para. 7A	517
	Sched. 2	516, 518
	para. 5	504
	Sched. 3, Pt. II	513
	paras. 1, 2	510, 519
	para. 4 (1)	519
	(4)	502, 519
	paras. 7–9	513
	Sched. 5	503
1968	Capital Allowances Act (c. 3)—	
	s. 47	207
	Rent Act (c. 23)	29, 377, 378
	s. 3 (1) (*a*)	378
	s. 85	378
	Prices and Incomes Act (c. 42)—	
	s. 12	177
	Caravan Sites Act (c. 52)—	
	Pt. I	380
1969	Housing Act (c. 33)—	
	s. 89	271–272
	Law of Property Act (c. 59)	640, 644, 698
	s. 1	669
	(1)	712
	s. 5	656
	s. 6	643
	s. 7 (1)	699
	s. 11	751
	s. 23	76
	s. 25	76, 77
	(9)	76
	(*b*)	77
	Expiring Laws Act (c. 61)—	
	s. 1	432
1970	Taxes Management Act (c. 9)—	
	s. 106	115
	Income and Corporation Taxes Act (c. 10)—	
	s. 4 (1)	212
	s. 67	115

1970 Income and Corporation
Taxes Act—*cont.*
s. 67—*cont.*
(1) 205, 206
(2) 206
s. 68 115
s. 69 (1), (2) 212
s. 70 115
(1), (2) 212
s. 71 115
(2) 209
s. 72 (1), (2) 208
(3)–(7) 209
s. 80 .... 91, 115, 213, 671
(1) 214
(2)–(4) 213
(5) 214
(6) 215
s. 81 .... 213, 215
s. 82 .... 213, 216
(3) 216
s. 83 .... 213, 215, 672
s. 84 213
(3A) 214
s. 85 213
s. 87 115
(1) 205
(2) 206
s. 90 (2) 213
s. 125 206
s. 134 672
s. 168 207
s. 171 207
s. 174 207
s. 180 757
s. 265 741
s. 304 211
s. 386 (3) 741
s. 491 211
(4) 211
(8) 211
s. 533 213
Sched. 3 214
Administration of Justice Act
(c. 31)—
s. 1 326
s. 40 530
Sched. 2 (5) 326
Agriculture Act (c. 40)—
Pt. III 794
Chronically Sick and Dis-
abled Persons Act (c.
44) 566
s. 3 .... 525, 526

1971 Powers of Attorney Act (c.
27)—
s. 9 71
Sched. 1 71
Attachment of Earnings Act
(c. 32) 529, 559
Fire Precautions Act (c. 40)—
s. 28 .... 113, 122
Tribunals and Inquiries Act
(c. 62) 422
s. 12 (1) 479
s. 13 422
Finance Act (c. 68)—
s. 47 207
Town and Country Planning
Act (c. 78)—
s. 22 73
(1) 547, 658
(2) 547
s. 23 73
(2)–(10) 73
s. 52 74
s. 87 73
ss. 112, 113 719
Banking and Financial Dealings Act (c. 80)—
s. 1 159
1972 Defective Premises Act (c.
35) 249, 257, 365, 371
s. 1 371
(1) 249
(4) 249
(5) 249, 371
s. 2 371
(7) (*b*) 249
s. 3 (1), (2) 371
s. 4 .... 37, 241, 244, 249, 250, 367,
368
(1) 236, 249, 284
(2) 236, 249
(3) 249
(4) 236, 249
(5) 236
(6) 249
s. 6 (1), (2) 249
(3) 236, 249
Finance Act (c. 41)—
s. 80 211
s. 81 (3) 213
(6) 213
s. 125 (3) 527
Housing Finance Act (c. 47) 7,
377, 597, 605
Pt. III 417
Land Charges Act (c. 61) ... 13, 79,
290

1972 Land Charges Act—*cont.*
    s. 2 (4) 338
          (iv) 88, 94, 145
          (5) 75, 77
    s. 4 (6) 76, 145
    Local Government Act (c. 70)—
    s. 121 719
    s. 123 70
    s. 128 (1), (2) 70
    s. 214 565
    s. 222 264
    s. 270 70
1973 Counter Inflation Act (c. 9) 389, 431
    s. 14 .... 455, 458
    Costs in Criminal Cases Act (c. 14) 545
    Matrimonial Causes Act (c. 18)—
    s. 24 .... 445, 533, 538, 551, 569, 577–579
    Sched. 1 444
    Land Compensation (c. 26) 720, 734
    Pt. I 733
    s. 29 602
          (3), (4) 602
          (7) 545
    s. 30 (1) 603
    s. 32 (1), (2) 603
    s. 37 734
          (1), (2) 603
    s. 38 .... 603, 734
    s. 39 (1) 527
          (*b*) 545
          (9) 545
    s. 44 732
    s. 47 .... 728–730, 736, 738
    s. 70 735
    Water Act (c. 37)—
    s. 30 113
    s. 32A 113
    Powers of Criminal Courts Act (c. 62)—
    s. 35 545
1974 Legal Aid Act (c. 4)—
    s. 2 (4) 545
    Local Government Act (c. 7)—
    s. 38 113
    Finance Act (c. 30)—
    s. 49 (1) 527
    Sched. II 527
    Health and Safety at Work, etc. Act (c. 37) 365

1974 Consumer Credit Act (c. 39) . 200
    s. 132 (1) 2
    Control of Pollution Act (c. 40)—
    s. 57 259
    s. 58 .... 127, 259
    s. 59 .... 127, 259, 544
    ss. 60–74 259
    Housing Act (c. 44) 273, 274
    Pt. VIII 806
    s. 2 (1), (2) 594
          (4) 594
    s. 118 (1) 509
          (2) 519
          (4) 516
    Sched. 8, para. 1 (2) 508
        para. 2 509
    Rent Act (c. 51) 377, 473
1975 Housing Rents and Subsidies Act (c. 6) 377
    Mobile Homes Act (c. 49)—
    s. 2 249
    Inheritance (Provision for Family and Dependants) Act (c. 63)—
    s. 2 .... 326, 569
    Sex Discrimination Act (c. 65) 526
    s. 1 7
          (1) 526
    s. 2 (1) 526
    s. 29 7
    s. 30 (1), (2) 526
    s. 31 .... 310, 526, 661
    Children Act (c. 72)—
    s. 8 579
    Local Land Charges Act (c. 76)—
    s. 2 74
1976 Water Charges Act (c. 9)—
    s. 2 113
    Domestic Violence and Matrimonial Proceedings Act (c. 50)—
    s. 11 (1) (*c*) 444
    Agriculture (Miscellaneous Provisions) Act (c. 55)—
    Pt. II 792
    Local Government (Miscellaneous Provisions) Act (c. 57)—
    s. 8 (1), (2) 270
    Land Drainage Act (c. 70)—
    s. 8 114
    s. 18 114
    s. 19 (6) 114

1976 Land Drainage Act—*cont.*
s. 19—*cont.*
    (7) 114
s. 63 114
    (3) 114
s. 72 (5) 114
Race Relations Act (c. 74) 526
s. 21 (1) 526
s. 24 .... 310, 661
s. 78 (1) 526
Rent (Agriculture) Act (c.
  80) 279, 447, 454, 465, 475,
      482, 483, 607, 609, 620
s. 1 483
s. 2 (1) 483
    (3) 484
    (4) 483
s. 3 (2), (3) 484
s. 4 (1) 483, 486
    (3), (4) 484
s. 5 485
s. 7 (2) 488
s. 8 .... 201, 487
s. 9 490
    (2) 491
s. 10 (2) 486, 487
    (3) 487
s. 11 487
    (2) 487
s. 12 487
    (9) 487
s. 13 487
s. 14 (2) 487
s. 15 487
s. 16 .... 483, 487
ss. 20, 21 487
s. 23 485
    (2) 485
    (4), (5) 485
    (7) 485
s. 27 (1) 488
    (2) 489
s. 28 (1) 489
    (3) 489
    (6) 489
    (6A) 489
    (7), (8) 488
    (9) 489
    (11) 489, 490
    (14) 490
s. 29 489
s. 32 487
Sched. 1 483
Sched. 2 484
  paras. 1, 2 .... 484, 485
  para. 3 484

1976 Rent (Agriculture) Act—*cont.*
Sched. 3, paras. 1, 2 483
  para. 3 486
  para. 4 483
  para. 12 783
Sched. 4, Pt. I 465, 491
Pt. II 487
Case XIII 488
Sched. 5, paras. 1, 2 486
  paras. 4–9 486
  para. 11 487
Sched. 6 487
Sched. 9 395
  para. 3 484
1977 Agricultural Holdings
  (Notices to Quit) Act (c.
  12) 791, 792
s. 1 343
s. 9 326
Rent Charges Act (c. 30)—
ss. 2, 3 152
Torts (Interference with
  Goods) Act (c. 32)—
s. 1 201
Control of Office Develop-
  ment Act (c. 40) 74
Rent Act (c. 42) . 2, 4, 5, 10, 16, 21,
    22, 29, 44, 45, 60, 158, 167, 172,
    173, 175, 177, 192, 195, 198,
    202, 241, 249, 267, 269, 270,
    285, 325, 377–379, 410, 411,
    607, 637, 646, 649, 676
Pt. I 484
Pt. II 7, 457
Pt. III 457, 534
Pt. V 379, 380, 383, 457, 533,
              534, 590
Pt. VI 587, 588
Pt. VII 5, 394
Pt. VIII 417
s. 1 .. 378–380, 383, 386, 393, 408,
              545
s. 2 . 5, 44, 344, 407, 463, 579, 580
    (1) 198
      (*a*) 406, 408, 443
    (2) 198
    (3) 408
s. 3 (1) 410
    (2) 218, 452
    (3) 344, 410
    (4) 448
s. 4 .... 388, 393, 408, 587
    (2) 389–391
    (3) 391, 490
s. 5 ... 399, 428, 466, 484, 498, 587

1977   Rent Act—*cont.*
    s. 5—*cont.*
        (1) 399, 400
        (4), (5) 400
    s. 6 392
    s. 7 .... 401, 403, 477, 484
        (1) 400
        (2) 400, 401, 475
    s. 8 .... 398, 477
        (1) 461
    s. 9 .... 380, 402, 461
    s. 10 .... 393, 484
    s. 11 .... 393, 431
    s. 12 .. 66, 383, 395, 396, 463, 476,
                                          534
        (1) (*a*) 395
              (*b, (c*) 396
        (2) 397
    s. 13 395
    s. 14 .... 395, 476, 485, 534, 557
    s. 15 .... 395, 587, 591
        (1) 586
        (2) (*b*) 590
        (3) 587
        (4) 586
    s. 16 .... 395, 584, 587
    s. 16A 398
    s. 18 411
        (3) 417
    s. 19 279
        (2) 474, 593
        (4) 475
        (5) 533, 593
              (*a*) 475, 476
              (*aa*) 560
              (*b*) 476
              (*c*), (*d*) 475, 485
              (*e*) 476, 590, 593
        (6) 474
        (7) 475
        (8) 474, 477
    s. 20 .... 404, 476
    s. 21 .... 66, 385, 398, 404, 476
    s. 22 .... 50, 383–385, 398
        (1) 383
        (3) 383
        (5) 383
        (6) 383, 384
        (7) 383
        (8) 384
    s. 24 (3) 381, 393, 646, 649
    s. 25 .... 399, 475
        (1) 508
        (2) 391, 508
        (3) 389, 508
        (4) 389

1977   Rent Act—*cont.*
    s. 26 392
        (1), (2) 392
    s. 27 417
    s. 29 292
    s. 33 292
    s. 44 (1) 414, 418
        (2) 414, 415
    s. 45 (1) 417
    s. 46 417
    s. 47 .... 135, 417
    s. 49 424
        (4) 424
    s. 51 .... 416, 477, 493
        (1) (*b*) 414, 416
        (3) 416
        (1), (4) 414, 416
    s. 52 418
        (3) 418
        (5) 418
    s. 54 (1) 416
        (2) 414
    s. 56 177
    s. 57 (3) 415, 416
    s. 60 419
    s. 67 .... 587, 588
        (1)–(3) 419
        (5) 415, 419
    s. 68 .... 418, 590
        (2) 419
    s. 69 .... 415, 481, 482, 494, 588
        (1) (*b*) (ii) 415
        (3) 481
        (4) 415
    s. 70 .... 424, 479, 488
        (2) 425
    s. 71 .... 588, 590
        (1), (2) 423
        (4) 135, 423
    s. 72 588
        (1) 421
        (3) 421
    s. 73 415
        (1) 417
        (1A) 415
        (4) 417
    s. 75 (1) 425
    s. 77 .... 480, 481, 533
        (1) 477
        (2) 478
    s. 78 (1) 478
        (2) 478, 479
    s. 79 480
        (3) 479
    s. 80 481
        (2) 479, 480

1977 Rent Act—*cont.*
s. 81 479
   (3) 479
   (4) 469, 479
s. 81A 480
s. 85 (3) 477
s. 86 398
   (2) 587
s. 87 (2) 588, 590
    (*a*) 588
   (6) 588
s. 88 (1) 588
   (4) 588
   (5) 589
s. 89 589
   (2) 589
s. 92 (1) 587
s. 93 .... 177, 589
   (5) 177
s. 94 (1), (2) 588
   (4), (5) 588
s. 98 .... 196, 347, 360, 407, 410,
      448, 456, 491, 695
   (1) ... 198, 292, 449, 456, 464,
       466, 553, 623, 782
    (*a*) 450
   (2) 458
s. 99 .... 410, 465, 489
   (2) 464, 491
   (3) 491
s. 100 .... 201, 443, 451, 467
   (3) 468
   (4A), (4B) 444
s. 101 394
   (1) 410
s. 102 .... 455, 457, 490
s. 102A 4, 10
s. 103 .... 480, 481
   (2) 480
s. 104 .... 480, 481
   (1) 481
   (3), (4) 481
s. 105 481
s. 106 481
   (2)–(4) 481
s. 106A 474, 482, 534
   (3) 482
s. 113 (1), (2) 579
s. 119 .... 428, 435, 436
   (1)–(4) 428
s. 120 .... 61, 435, 437, 438
   (1) 429
   (3) 436
    (*a*), (*b*) 429
    (*d*) 429
   (5) 431, 436

1977 Rent Act—*cont.*
s. 122 .... 435, 438, 477, 480
ss. 123, 124 .... 428, 438
s. 125 437
   (1) 428, 436
   (2) 428
s. 126 428
   (1) 429
   (4)–(6) 429
s. 127 .... 430, 431
   (2) (*b*) 430
   (3B) 431
   (3D) 430
   (5) 430
s. 128 (1) 61, 430, 435
s. 131 (*b*) 395
s. 137 ...... 393, 464–465, 470, 491,
        494, 499
   (1) 464
   (2), (3) 465, 466
   (5) 465, 466
   (6) 465, 499
s. 138 465
s. 139 463
s. 141 .... 420, 478
   (3)–(5) 467
ss. 143, 144 404
s. 146 498
s. 147 201
s. 148 .... 218, 452
s. 151 146
Sched. 1 .... 5, 406, 438, 579
   paras. 1, 2 439
   para. 3 440
   para. 7 .... 440, 579
   para. 12 410
   para. 13 .... 404, 433
   para. 14 438
Sched. 2 465
   para. 1 397
    (*a*)–(*c*) 397
   paras. 2, 3 397
   paras. 4, 5 396
Sched. 4 417
Sched. 8 .... 424, 589
   para. 2 423
Sched. 9 177
Sched. 10, paras. 5, 6 421
Sched. 11, para. 1 420
   paras. 3–5 420
   para. 7 421
   para. 9 421
Sched. 15 .... 292, 298, 350, 458,
     488, 491, 493, 502, 553, 554,
       622, 623, 695, 782
   para. 1 .... 456, 783

1977 Rent Act—*cont.*
Sched. 15—*cont.*
para. 2 .... 450, 458, 492
para. 3 .... 450, 451
para. 4 .... 450, 488
para. 5 .... 450, 488, 553
para. 5 (1) (*a*), (*b*) 450
Case 1 .... 198, 449, 451, 467
Case 2 452
Case 5 453
Case 6 .... 449, 453, 466
Case 8 .... 449, 454, 623
Case 9 .... 449, 455, 490
Case 10 .... 457, 467
Case 11 ..... 68, 397, 458, 467, 493
Case 12 .... 68, 397, 460
Cases 13, 14 461
Case 15 .... 393, 461, 467
Cases 16–18 491
Case 20 .... 462, 467
Sched. 16 487
Case 1, paras. 1, 3 450
Sched. 18, Pt. I 431, 436
Pt. I, para. 2 437
para. 5 437
Pt. II 431
Sched. 24 395
para. 7 408
Protection from Eviction Act
(c. 43) . 132, 467, 471, 473, 482,
483, 545, 607, 637
s. 1 .... 360, 485, 607
(2) 608
(3) 560, 608
(4) 560
(6) 608
s. 2 ..... 53, 194, 361, 448, 541, 609
s. 2A 19
s. 3 .... 53, 360, 448, 482, 485, 593,
609
(1) 454, 489, 609
(2A) 379
(3) 609
s. 4 .... 468, 485, 489, 607
(1)–(3) 489
(4) 490
(7) 490
(8) 489
(9), (10) 490
s. 5 .... 45, 482, 532
(1) 342, 343, 448, 560
s. 8 (1) 607, 609
(2) 454, 485, 489, 609
s. 9 .... 361, 609
Criminal Law Act (c. 45)—
s. 6 .... 360, 467, 607

1977 Criminal Law Act—*cont.*
s. 6—*cont.*
(3) 360
s. 31 267
Housing (Homeless Persons)
Act (c. 48) 560, 610, 631
National Health Service Act
(c. 49)—
s. 54 (1) 736
Sched. 10, para. 1 (1) 736
Unfair Contract Terms Act
(c. 50)—
s. 1 366
s. 2 (1), (2) 366
1978 Domestic Proceedings and
Magistrates' Courts Act
(c. 22)—
s. 16 577
Finance Act (c. 42)—
s. 30 207
Civil Liability (Contribution)
Act (c. 47) 369
1979 Capital Gains Tax Act (c.
14)—
s. 3 91
s. 5 91
s. 10 (1) 546
ss. 28–34 90
s. 35 .... 90, 91
s. 36 90
s. 37 .... 90, 92
ss. 38–43 90
s. 101 91
s. 106 115
s. 107 91
s. 115 .... 91, 207
s. 121 207
s. 124 207
s. 126 207
s. 136 207
s. 191 741
Sched. 3 115
para. 1 .... 91, 92
para. 2 90
(2) 91
paras. 3, 5 91
para. 8 (3)–(5) 91
1980 Child Care Act (c. 5)—
s. 1 .... 200, 611
Limitation (Amendment)
Act (c. 24)—
s. 3 (3) 173
Magistrates' Courts Act (c.
43)—
s. 50 544
s. 94 (2) 544

1980 Magistrates' Courts Act—
    cont.
  s. 95 (1) 544
  s. 143 (1) 544
Finance Act (c. 48)—
  s. 39 207
  s. 79 207
Housing Act (c. 51) 377, 444
  Pt. I 545, 590
  Pt. II 589
  s. 27 (3) 564
  s. 32 451
  s. 47 545
  s. 52 (1) 492
        (*a*) 492, 494
        (*b*) 493
        (*c*) 494
      (2) 493, 495
      (3) 493
      (5) 492
  s. 53 494
      (1), (2) 492
  s. 54 (1) 494
      (2) 332, 494
      (3) 494
  s. 55 .... 494, 495
      (1) 492, 493, 495
      (2) 494
  s. 56 .... 398, 649, 695
      (1) 496
      (3) 398, 496
      (4) 398
      (6) 399, 496
      (7) 399
  s. 57 496
  s. 60 .... 419, 424
      (1) 487
      (2) 419
      (3) 487
      (5) 589
      (7) 589
  s. 61 421
      (3) 588
  s. 62 415
  s. 63 395
  s. 64 417
  s. 65 397
      (1) 396
      (2) 397, 465
      (3) 397
      (5) 397, 465
      (7) 397
  s. 66 .... 68, 458, 460
  s. 67 .... 462, 491
  s. 68 (2) 418
  s. 69 .... 379, 474, 480, 482, 609

1980 Housing Act—*cont.*
  s. 69—*cont.*
      (2) 474, 482
      (3) 4, 593
      (4) 397
  s. 70 479
  s. 71 480
  s. 72 .... 397, 478
  s. 73 .... 395, 399, 483
      (2) 476
      (3) 485
  s. 74 586
      (1) 586
  s. 75 622
      (2) 468
      (3) 474
  s. 76 484
      (1) 439
  s. 77 589
  s. 78 430
      (3) 430
      (4) 430, 431
  s. 79 .... 430, 435
  s. 81 .... 121, 282
  ss. 82, 83 121
  s. 88 (1), (2) 471
      (4) 471
  s. 89 .... 468, 490
  s. 140 520
  s. 142 517
  s. 149 262
  s. 152 .... 177, 577
  Sched. 5 .... 496, 649
  Sched. 7 .. 397, 458, 460, 487, 491
  Sched. 8, Pt. II 483
    para. 4 428
  Sched. 10 589
    para. 5 570
  Sched. 21 517
    para. 1 512
    para. 2 508
    para. 3 510
    para. 6 517
  Sched. 22 517
  Sched. 25 .... 177, 577
    para. 7 455
    para. 36 .... 476, 533, 593
    para. 58 450
    para. 61 471
    para. 75 399
  Sched. 26 .... 424, 587
Limitation Act (c. 58)—
  s. 15 (1) 173, 337
      (6) 44, 173
  s. 19 .... 173, 202
  Sched. 1, para. 5 ..... 44, 173, 337

1980 Limitation Act—*cont.*	
Sched. 1—*cont.*	
para. 6	173
(1)	173
Local Government, Planning and Land Act (c. 65)—	
s. 193	748
Sched. 33, para. 4 (2)	748
Highways Act (c. 66)	285
ss. 205–218	164
1981 Local Government and Planning (Amendment) Act (c. 41)—	
Sched. 1, para. 1	73
Supreme Court Act (c. 54)	11
s. 31	422, 527, 628
s. 37	258, 294
(1)	258
s. 38	197
s. 49	92
s. 461	197
Compulsory Purchase (Vesting Declarations) Act (c. 66)	723
s. 2 (1), (2)	725
s. 3 (4)	724
s. 4 (1)	723
s. 5 (2)	723
s. 6 (1)	724
s. 7 (1) (ii)	725
Acquisition of Land Act (c. 67)	720
1982 Social Security and Housing Benefits Act (c. 24)	529, 597
s. 36 (4)	423
Local Government (Miscellaneous Provisions) Act (c. 30)—	
s. 26 (1)	259
s. 29	273
s. 33	74, 75
Forfeiture Act (c. 34)—	
s. 2 (7)	5
Finance Act (c. 39)—	
s. 50	207
s. 86	92
Criminal Justice Act (c. 48)—	
s. 37	544
s. 38 (1) (b)	544
Sched. 3	267
Transport Act (c. 49)—	
s. 14 (1)	651
1983 Matrimonial Homes Act (c. 19)	159, 442, 443, 607, 620
s. 1	249
(1) (a), (b)	442

1983 Matrimonial Homes Act—*cont.*	
s. 1—*cont.*	
(2), (3)	443
(5)	159, 332, 443, 444
(6)	443, 546
(10)	443
s. 2 (5)	336
(7)	331
s. 7	444, 445, 557
s. 9 (1)	443
s. 10 (1)	442
s. 24	444
Sched. 1	322, 444, 445, 551
para. 2	538
(2)	332
paras. 5, 8	332
Mental Health Act (c. 20)	514, 566
Mobile Homes Act (c. 34)	449
ss. 1, 2	380
s. 5 (1)	380
1984 Occupiers' Liability Act (c. 3)—	
s. 1	366
Trade Marks (Amendment) Act (c. 19)	741
County Courts Act (c. 28)—	
s. 18	361
s. 21	361
s. 22	122
s. 23 (d)	94
s. 38	94
ss. 41, 42	202
s. 77	266
s. 102	202
s. 111	362
(2)	468
s. 138 (2)	198
(4), (5)	198
(7), (8)	198
(9A–9C)	198
s. 147 (2), (3)	361
Sched. 2, para. 23	122
Housing and Building Control Act (c. 29)	520
Food Act (c. 30)—	
s. 13 (4), (5)	669
Agricultural Holdings Act (c. 41)	10
s. 8	775
s. 8A	775
Matrimonial and Family Proceedings Act (c. 42)—	
Pt. III	445
s. 22	332, 445

1984	Finance Act (c. 43)—	
	s. 49	206
	Sched. 11	206
	para. 2	207
	paras. 4, 5	207
	Capital Transfer Tax Act (c. 51)—	
	s. 43 (3)	81
	Building Act (c. 55)—	
	Pts. III, IV	273
	s. 76	264
	s. 77	272
	ss. 78, 79	272
	s. 86	273
	s. 98	285
1985	Companies Act (c. 6)—	
	s. 35	14, 70, 655
	(1), (2)	14
	s. 36	69
	s. 521	204
	s. 523	204
	s. 525 (2)	203, 204
	s. 618	330, 331
	s. 619	330, 331
	s. 736	644
	Sched. 20, Pt. I	330, 331
	Rent (Amendment) Act (c. 24)—	
	s. 1	458
	Finance Act (c. 54)—	
	s. 55	207
	s. 59	207
	s. 69	207
	Sched. 17	207
	Administration of Justice Act (c. 61)—	
	s. 55	198
	Insolvency Act (c. 65)—	
	s. 91 (1), (4), (5)	205
	s. 153	204
	s. 161 (1), (4)–(6)	205
	Housing Associations Act (c. 69)	587, 595
	s. 1	594
	(1)	583
	(2)	587, 591
	s. 2	590, 594
	s. 3 (1)	585
	s. 4 (1), (2)	585
	s. 5 (1)	585, 586
	(4)	585
	s. 6 (2)	585
	(4)	586
	s. 8 (1)–(3)	594
	s. 9 (1), (2)	594
	(3)	595

1985	Housing Associations Act—*cont.*	
	s. 10 (1)	594
	s. 11	594
	s. 45 (1)	586
	s. 60 (1)	586
	Sched. 2	594
	Landlord and Tenant Act (c. 70)—	
	s. 1	431
	s. 3 (1)	300, 324
	s. 4	431, 432, 469
	s. 7	432
	s. 8	221
	(1)	240, 241, 289
	(3) (b)	240
	(4)–(6)	240
	s. 10	241, 242
	s. 11	134, 237, 246, 248, 285, 423, 528, 539, 542, 543
	(1)	243, 244, 246
	(a)	245, 247
	(2)	244
	(4)	244
	(6)	244
	ss. 11–16	237
	s. 12	237, 528, 542
	(2)	244
	s. 13	134, 237, 528, 542
	(1)	248
	(2) (b), (c)	248
	s. 14	237, 528, 542
	(4), (5)	248
	s. 15	237, 528, 542
	s. 16	237, 528, 542
	s. 17	253, 255, 293
	s. 18	134, 135, 172
	s. 19	135, 172, 434
	(1), (3)	135
	s. 20	135, 172
	(2), (3)	135
	s. 21	135, 172
	ss. 22–25	135, 172
	s. 26	135, 136, 172
	s. 27	135, 172
	ss. 28–30	135, 172
	s. 32	245
	Housing (Consequential Provisions) Act (c. 71)—	
	s. 2	549, 552, 568, 569, 570
	s. 4	546
	Sched. 2, para. 35	587, 594
	para. 56	546
	Sched. 4, para. 9	533
	Housing Act (c. 68)	394, 425

1985 Housing Act—*cont.*
    Pt. III 449, 559, 604, 611,
                     614, 627, 630
    Pt. IV 4, 70, 528, 542, 591, 630
    Pt. V ... 4, 528, 542, 567, 575, 576,
                          591
    Pt. VII 275, 602, 806
    Pt. VIII 274
    Pt. IX 274, 602
    Pt. X 394, 555
    Pt. XIII 530
    Pt. XV 538
    s. 2 614
    s. 4 (3) 585
    s. 5 .... 585, 594, 595, 615
        (1) 583
        (2) 591
    s. 6 .... 585, 590, 594
        (1) (*c*) 615
    s. 8 (1), (2) 525
    ss. 9, 10 585
    s. 14 585
        (4), (5) 218
    s. 15 (3) 585
    s. 16 585
    s. 19 (1) 615
    s. 20 258
    s. 21 .... 258, 558, 560, 561
    s. 22 .... 258, 526, 561
    s. 23 .... 258, 561
    s. 24 .... 258, 522, 558, 561
        (1) 530
        (2) 531
        (4) 585
    s. 25 .... 258, 531, 561, 589
        (3) (*a*), (*b*) 531
            (*c*) 532
        (4) (*b*), (*c*) 532
    s. 26 .... 258, 561, 585, 594, 605
    s. 32 .... 70, 585
    s. 35 (4) 533
    s. 43 70
    s. 44 (1) 70
    s. 58 584
        (1), (2) 619
        (3), (4) 620
    s. 59 618
        (1) 618
            (*a*) 618
        (2) 618
    s. 60 .... 584, 621–624, 627
        (1) 620, 625
        (2) 620
        (3) 621, 624
        (4) 621
    s. 61 (1) 584, 617

1985 Housing Act—*cont.*
    s. 61—*cont.*
        (2), (3) 617
    s. 62 628
        (1)–(3) 611
    s. 63 547
        (1) 612
    s. 64 (1) 547, 628
        (4) 628
    s. 65 .... 526, 527, 616, 617, 628
        (2) 613, 614, 616, 618, 626
        (3) 547, 613
            (*b*) 613
        (4) 613
    s. 66 628
        (2) 613, 614
        (3) 613
        (4) 614
    s. 67 (1) 613
        (2) 615, 616
        (3) (*a*), (*b*) 616
    s. 68 .... 526, 527
        (1) 547, 616
        (2) 616
        (3) 547, 616, 628
    s. 69 (1) 614
    s. 70 604
    s. 71 (1) 618
    s. 76 394
    s. 77 614
    s. 79 .... 332, 520, 550, 591
        (1) 545
        (3) 4, 10, 19, 379, 545
        (4) 4, 545
    s. 80 .... 520, 550, 594
        (1), (2) 595
    s. 81 .... 520, 534, 546, 550, 551
    s. 82 (1) 542, 550
        (3) 194, 199, 542, 550, 552
    s. 83 535
        (1) 550, 552, 556
        (2) 552
        (3) (*a*) 552
        (4) 552
        (5) 550, 552
    s. 84 292
        (1) 550, 552
        (2) 553
            (*a*) 554
            (*b*) 555
            (*c*) 555, 593
        (3) 552
    s. 85 (1), (2) 557
    s. 86 542
        (1) 194, 199, 542, 550–552
            (*b*) 542

1985 Housing Act—*cont.*
  s. 86—*cont.*
    (2) 542
  s. 87 .... 440, 550, 578
    (b) 556, 579
  s. 88 (1) 550, 578, 579
    (c) 550
    (2) 579
    (3) 579
    (4) 580
  s. 89 .... 533, 538, 556
    (1) 442, 550
    (2) 577
    (a) 578
    (b) 579
  s. 90 (2) 550, 551
    (3) 578
    (b) 578, 580
  s. 91 .... 534, 577
    (1) 533, 536, 550, 551
    (2) 533, 551
    (3) 533
    (b) 577
    (c) 538
  s. 92 .... 533, 535, 550, 551, 554,
             555, 579, 591
    (1) 535, 591
    (2) 535
    (3) 536, 592
    (4)–(6) 536
  s. 93 .... 305, 534
    (1) 532
    (a) 534
    (b) 532, 534
    (2) 532, 534, 551
  s. 94 305
    (2) 532, 533
    (3) 533
    (5) 536
    (6) (a), (b) 533
  s. 95 534
    (1), (2) 551
  s. 96 .... 255, 256, 539
    (1) 539
    (2) (a), (b) 539
    (5) 539
  s. 97 .... 280, 282
    (1)–(3) 537
  s. 98 280
    (1), (2) 537
    (4) (a), (b) 537
  s. 99 280
    (1), (2) 537
    (4) 537
  s. 100 280
    (1), (2) 538

1985 Housing Act—*cont.*
  s. 101 280
    (1) 538
    (3), (4) 538
  s. 102 .... 177, 528, 589
    (1) 532
    (a) 528
    (3) 177
    (b) 589
    (4) 550
  s. 103 .... 177, 528
    (1) 532
    (3)–(5) 528, 532
    (6) 529, 532
  s. 104 .... 7, 542
    (1), (2) 528
  s. 105 (1) 561
    (2) 561, 562
    (3) 562
    (5) (a), (b) 562
  s. 106 527
    (5) 527
  s. 108 543
    (3), (4) 543
    (5) (d), (e) 544
  s. 109 591
  s. 110 536
    (1) 533, 537
    (2) 537
    (b) 533
  s. 112 (1), (2) 545
  s. 113 .... 442, 520, 580, 581
    (1), (2) 580
  s. 114 (1) 591
  s. 115 546
  s. 118 .... 520, 586
    (1) 545, 595
    (a) 562
    (b) 520, 521, 562, 563
    (2) 564
  s. 119 520
    (1) 562
  s. 120 565
  s. 121 (1) 545, 564
    (2) 564
  s. 122 .... 565, 568
    (1) 570
    (2) 567
    (3) 573
  s. 123 (1) 564, 570
    (2) (b) 564
  s. 124 .... 566, 567
    (1) 570
    (3) 567
  s. 125 .... 568, 570, 576
    (4) 570

1985   Housing Act—*cont.*
      s. 126 (1) 567
      s. 127 (1)–(3) 567
      s. 128 568
      s. 129 .... 520–522, 568
      s. 130 (1)–(4) 568
      s. 131 .... 521, 568
      s. 132 520
         (1) 569, 595
            (b) 595
      s. 133 (1) 569
         (4) 469
      s. 134 574
         (1), (2) 571
         (4) 571
      s. 135 (1) 571
         (2), (3) 572
      s. 136 (1), (2) 571
         (6), (7) 571
      s. 138 (1) 574
         (2), (3) 564
      s. 139 (1) 570
         (2) 549
         (3) 569
      s. 140 (1), (2) 572
         (3) (c) 572
      s. 141 (1)–(4) 573
      s. 142 .... 521, 574
         (1) 572, 595
            (c) 574
         (4) 572, 573
         (5) (a) 572
      s. 143 ...... 341, 520, 521, 572, 573,
                                           584
      s. 144 .... 521, 574
         (3) 521
         (5) 521
      s. 145 (2) (3) 521
      s. 148 521
      s. 151 521
         (1) 521
         (2) 341, 521, 549
      s. 153 .... 520, 572, 574, 584
      s. 154 (1) 569
      s. 155 .... 568, 569
         (2) 569
      s. 156 (3) 569
      s. 159 .... 522, 569
      s. 160 523
         (1) 569
      s. 164 574–576
         (3)–(6) 575
      ss. 165, 166 575
      ss. 167–169 575
      s. 170 .... 574, 576
      s. 172 (1) 522

1985   Housing Act—*cont.*
      s. 173 522
      s. 175 522
      s. 176 (1) 570
      s. 178 605
      s. 179 567
      s. 181 (1), (2) 570
      s. 183 (2) 522, 562
         (a)–(c) 562
         (3) 563
      s. 185 (1) 545
      s. 186 564
         (1), (2) 580
      s. 189 .... 265, 266
         (1) 265, 272
      s. 190 (1) 271
         (a), (b) 270, 272
      s. 191 .... 267, 271
         (3) 272
      s. 192 .... 267, 268
      s. 206 265
      s. 207 .... 266, 535
      s. 209 276
      s. 210 116
         (1) 275
      s. 211 (1)–(5) 277
      s. 212 116
         (1) 278, 279
         (2) 279
      s. 213 .... 277, 279
      s. 214 (1)–(3) 277
         (4), (5) 278
      s. 216 (1), (2) 277
      s. 217 .... 116, 278
      s. 218 278
      s. 220 (1)–(3) 278
         (6) 278
      s. 223 278
      s. 224 (1), (2) 278
      s. 225 (1), (2) 278
      s. 227 (1) 278
      s. 228 278
      s. 232 (2) 275
      s. 234 (1)–(3) 276
      s. 236 116
         (2) 278
      s. 237 275
      ss. 239–246 274
      s. 247 274
         (2) 342
      s. 248 274
      s. 249 274
         (2) 342
      ss. 250–259 274
      s. 264 .... 265, 268
         (1) 265, 267

1985	Housing Act—*cont.*	
	s. 264—*cont.*	
	(4)	267
	(*b*)	267
	(5), (6)	267
	s. 265 (2)	268
	(*b*)	268
	s. 266	268
	s. 268 (1)	268
	s. 269	268, 269
	(2)	268
	s. 270	268
	(1)	269
	(3)	269, 394
	(5)	269
	s. 271	268
	(1)	269
	s. 272	268
	(1), (3)	269
	s. 273	268
	s. 274	268
	(1)	269
	(5)	269
	s. 275	268
	s. 276	269
	s. 278 (1)	269
	ss. 289–298	274
	s. 300	268
	(2)	268
	s. 304	268
	ss. 325, 326	394
	s. 327 (1)	394
	ss. 328, 329	394
	s. 331	394
	s. 435 (1)	278
	s. 438 (1)	569
	s. 508	275
	s. 585	268
	(1)	732
	s. 586	268
	s. 610	128
	s. 612	557, 558, 593
	s. 622	573
	Sched. 1	546, 550
	para. 2 (2)–(4)	546
	para. 5	548
	para. 6 (*a*)	548
	para. 12	591, 595
	Sched. 2	199, 535, 536, 552, 592
	Pt. I	292, 553, 554
	Pt. II	553, 555
	Ground 11	556, 592
	para. 2	553
	Pt. III, Ground 14	556, 592
	Pt. IV	553
	Ground 5, para. (*b*)	535
1985	Housing Act—*cont.*	
	Pt. IV—*cont.*	
	Ground 6	535
	Ground 11	592
	Ground 14	536, 592
	Ground 15	536
	Ground 16	580
	Sched. 3	535, 536, 592
	Ground 6	592
	Ground 8	536, 592
	Ground 9	536
	Sched. 4	562
	para. 2	563
	(*a*)	564
	paras. 3, 4	563
	para. 5	568
	Sched. 5	565
	paras. 1, 3	595
	para. 4	521, 562
	para. 8	565
	para. 9 (*b*)	566
	para. 14	521
	Sched. 6	521, 570
	Pt. II, para. 11	563
	para. 12	521, 563, 567
	para. 16 (*a*), (*b*)	521
	para. 18	570
	Sched. 7	521, 569
	Sched. 8	521
	para. 1	521
	paras. 2, 3	522
	para. 4 (2), (3)	522
	para. 5	522
	para. 6 (1)	522
	(3)	523
	para. 9	522
	(2)	522
	para. 11	522
	Sched. 9	521
	Sched. 10, paras. 6, 7	278
	Sched. 22	720
	Sched. 23	268
1986	Agricultural Holdings Act	
	(c. 5)	10, 607, 648, 757, 761, 763, 764, 797, 799
	s. 1	648, 779
	(1)	758, 764
	(2)	759
	(*c*)	759
	(3)	759
	(4) (*a*)	757, 758
	s. 2	649, 762, 779
	(1)	760, 765
	(2)	761
	(*a*)	760
	(3)	764, 765

1986 Agricultural Holdings Act—
        cont.
      s. 2—cont.
          (4) 762, 766
      s. 3 .... 766, 779
          (1) 760, 767
          (3) 792
      s. 4 (2) 767
      s. 5 .... 760, 766, 767
          (1) 760
          (3) 767
      s. 6 769
          (2), (5) 770
      s. 7 720
          (3) 773
      s. 8 761
          (2), (3) 773
          (4) 774
          (5) 774
      s. 6 (2), (3) 774
      s. 8 (6) 773
      s. 9 774
      s. 10 812
      s. 11 770
          (2) 770
      s. 12 (1) 774
          (2), (3) 775
          (4) 774
      s. 13 .... 774, 807
          (1), (4) 776
      s. 14 771
          (2) 771
          (12) 68
      s. 15 (1) 771
          (3) 772
          (4), (5) 771
      ss. 16–19 200
      s. 18 .... 200, 201
      s. 21 762
          (1) 762
      s. 22 .... 771, 811
      ss. 23, 24 774
      s. 25 (1) 759, 760, 779
          (2) 779
              (a) 790
              (b) 784, 800
              (c) 792, 799
          (3) 779
          (4) 785
      s. 26 (1) .. 779, 780, 782, 793, 799,
                                            808
      s. 27 780
          (1) 782
          (2) (f) 800
          (3) (a), (b) 782
              (c)–(f) 783

1986 Agricultural Holdings Act—
        cont.
      s. 27—cont.
          (4), (5) 783
          (6) (b) 783
      s. 28 (1), (2) 789
          (4), (5) 789
      s. 29 799
      s. 31 800
          (1), (2) 800
      s. 32 .... 808, 809
          (2) 800
      s. 33 .... 774, 777
          (1) 777
      s. 34 (1) 797
              (a), (b) 792
      s. 36 (2) 793
              (b) 793
          (3) 794
              (b) 795
          (4) 794
      s. 37 794
          (2) 794
          (6) 798
      s. 38 (1) 793
          (2) 798
          (4), (5) 794, 797
      s. 39 (1) 793, 794
          (2) 794, 796
          (4)–(7) 796
          (9) 796
          (10) 793
      s. 40 (1), (2) 796
      s. 41 795
          (1) (b) 795
          (6) 795
      s. 43 (1) 793
              (b) (i) 793
      s. 44 (1) 793, 796
          (5)–(7) 793
      s. 45 (1) 796
      s. 47 796
      s. 48 796
          (3), (4) 798
          (5) 796, 798
          (6), (7) 798
          (8) 796, 798
          (9)–(12) 798
      s. 49 (1) 797
              (b) 797
          (3) 797
      s. 50 (1) 797
      s. 51 (1) 797, 798
          (2) 798
          (3) 797
          (4), (6) 798

1986 Agricultural Holdings Act—
cont.

s. 53	797
(3)	797
(5)–(8)	798
s. 54 (1), (2)	798
s. 55	798
(6)	798
s. 56 (2), (3)	798
s. 57	798
(3), (4)	798
s. 60	791, 808, 810
(1) (b)	808
(2)	791, 809
(3)	809
(b)	810
(4)	779, 810
(5)	809, 810
(6)	802, 810, 811
(a)	810
s. 61 (1)	809
(2)–(4)	810
s. 62	811
s. 63 (1)	802, 808
(2), (3)	809
s. 64 (1), (4)	802
s. 65 (1)	802
(2)	803
s. 66 (1)	807
(2)	805
(5)	805, 807
s. 67	806
(1)	806
(2)	807
(3)	806
(4), (5)	807
s. 68 (1)	805
s. 69	708
(2), (3)	807, 808
s. 70	791
(2)	791, 811
s. 71	815, 816
(1)	814–816
(2)	814
(3)	814–816
(5)	814, 815
s. 72	815, 816
(4)	816
s. 73	816
s. 74	808
s. 77 (1)	802
s. 78	791
s. 78 (1)	802, 808, 811
s. 79 (1)	812
(2)	813
(3)–(5)	812

1986 Agricultural Holdings Act—
cont.

s. 80	813
(1)	812
(3)–(5)	813
s. 81 (1)	812
(2)	812, 813
s. 83	811
(1)	816
(2)	803, 810
(3)	810, 815
(6)	804
s. 84	804
s. 93 (3)	792
(5)	803
s. 96	803
(1)	757, 773, 802
(2)	791
Sched. 1	769, 774
para. 9	797
Sched. 2, para. 1	775
para. 1 (3) (a)–(c)	776
(a), (b)	775
para. 2 (1)	776
para. 3	776
para. 4	774
(2)	774
(c)	777
Sched. 3, Pt. I	780
Case B	784, 800, 811
Case C	785, 790
Case D (a), (b)	785
Case F	790
Case G	767, 792
Case H	797
Pt. II	780
para. 8	783
para. 9 (2)	785
para. 10	785
(1) (a)	788
(c)	787
para. 12	792
Sched. 4, para. 7	799
Sched. 6	795
para. 2	794
paras. 3, 4	795
para. 6	795
para. 10	795
para. 14	797
Sched. 7	805
Pt. I	805
Pt. II	806
Pt. I	805, 813
Pt. II	803
Sched. 9	802

1986 Agricultural Holdings Act—
    cont.
    Sched. 10 812
    Sched. 11 .... 781, 804
        para. 1 (6) 775
        para. 21 781
        para. 26 786

1986 Agricultural Holdings Act—
    cont.
    Sched. 11—*cont.*
        para. 27 781
        para. 28 (1), (2) 781
    Sched. 14, para. 12 68
        para. 21 648

PART I

THE GENERAL LAW

In this Part the following abbreviations are used:

H.A.	Housing Act
L. & T.A.	Landlord and Tenant Act
L.C.A.	Land Charges Act
L.P.A.	Law of Property Act
S.L.A.	Settled Land Act
T.A.	Trustee Act

Books

Challis: H.W. Challis, *The Law of Real Property* (3rd ed.), by C. Sweet.
Co.Litt: *Coke Upon Littleton* (19th ed.), with notes by F. Hargrave & C. Butler.
Emmet: *Emmet on Title* (17th ed.), by J. Gilchrist-Smith & J. T. Farrand.
Evans: *Landord & Tenant*, by D, Ll. Evans, (2nd ed. by P. Smith).
Farrand: *Contract and Conveyance* (3rd ed.), by J. T. Farrand.
Foa: *Edgar Foa, Law of Landlord and Tenant* (8th ed.), by H. Heathcote Williams.
Halsbury: *Halsbury's Laws of England* (4th ed.) (3rd ed. where specified).
Hanbury & Maudsley: Hanbury & Maudsley, *Modern Equity* (12th ed.), by J.E. Martin
Hill & Redman: *Hill and Redman's Landlord and Tenant* (17th ed.), by M. Barnes, L. Dennis, G. Lockhart-Mummery & J. Gaunt.
Megarry & Wade: *The Law of Real Property* (5th ed.). by Sir Robert Megarry & H. W. R. Wade.
Partington: *Landlord and Tenant* (2nd ed.), by M. Partington.
Platt: *Law of Leases*, by Thomas Platt.
Woodfall: *William Woodfall's Landlord and Tenant* (28th ed.), by V. G. Wellings and G. N. Huskinson.

CHAPTER 1

LANDLORD AND TENANT

I. The Context of Landlord and Tenant
.... 1

II. Rights of Occupation 4

III. The Flexibility of the Term of Years
.... 6

I. THE CONTEXT OF LANDLORD AND TENANT

English law tends to regard the hiring of land entirely differently from the hiring of chattels. The former is dealt with as a branch of real property law (even though a lease is technically regarded as personal rather than real property), the latter as part of the law of bailment, contract and tort. In English law a lease constitutes an estate in the land which has an existence independent either of physical possession of the land itself, or of any other third party rights in it. Consequently, the creation or transfer of other interests in the land cannot affect the validity of a prior, properly granted lease. Under the name of "a term of years absolute" it is one of the two legal estates in land permitted by the Law of Property Act 1925, s.1, although it must not be forgotten that it also has a contractual aspect.[1]

There can, however, be no "estate" in a chattel, and the hiring of a chattel is thus primarily a contract, by which the owner permits the other party to use the article hired in consideration of some kind of hire charge. Notwithstanding this difference, however, hirings of both land and chattels have certain features in common. Both the landlord and the owner of a chattel to be hired stipulate for payment (usually in money, but sometimes in money's worth)[2] in return for parting with possession of their properties. Since the parting with possession will normally last over some period of time which is either fixed or capable of being fixed under the terms of the agreement, the consideration paid will generally bear some relation to the length of that period, and will therefore be more likely to consist of a series of periodic payments than a single lump sum. Also, a person who takes a lease of land and buildings is, like his counterpart in the case of chattels, under an obligation not to cause deliberate or negligent harm to the subject-matter of his contract, and to return it to the landlord or owner at the end of the agreed period. Subject to proper observance by the tenant

---

[1] See *post*, Chaps. 3 and 4.

[2] For hire payments other than in money see: Palmer & Yates [1979] C.L.J. 180 at pp. 187–189 and Palmer, *Bailment* pp. 718–719; for rental payments under leases in consideration other than money see: *Pitcher* v. *Tovey* (1692) 4 Mod. 71; *Duke of Marlborough* v. *Osborn* (1864) 5 B. & S. 67; *Doe d. Edney* v. *Benham* (1845) 7 Q.B. 976. See also *C.H. Bailey* v. *Memorial Enterprises* [1974] 1 All E.R. 1003, *per* Lord Denning M.R. at p. 1007.

or hirer of the terms of his contract, he is entitled to the use and enjoyment of the land or chattel for the period agreed by the parties. Both leasing and hiring, therefore, enable the commercial exploitation of property by its owner.

Despite these and other similarities between leasing land and hiring chattels[3] however, the two have, as a matter of jurisprudence, always been regarded as distinct, having by and large their own separate rules. Chattels can be the subject of absolute ownership, land cannot. English real property theory decrees that all land is vested in the Crown and an individual freehold "owner" is simply a person holding in perpetuity and rent-free, as tenant-in-chief of the Crown. The freeholder's interest in the land is an estate of fee simple absolute in possession, which signifies a kind or degree of ownership in land related to the duration of the estate owner's interest.

Since 1925 only two estates in land have been permitted: the fee simple absolute in possession, and the term of years absolute or lease.[4] In theory the leasehold estate is inferior to the freehold estate since it might not last for as long as the fee simple. An estate in fee simple is capable of virtually perpetual duration, subject only to the interest coming to an end should the tenant for the time being die leaving no lineal or collateral descendants without having devised his estate. An estate for a term of years absolute is certain to come to an end at the expiry of the term granted and does not have the potential for perpetual duration. However, this theoretical superiority of the fee simple estate must, today, give way to practicality since, in economic terms, long leases at low rents, or short leases with statutory security of tenure granted to the tenant,[5] are at least as secure and valuable in many cases as a freehold estate.

So, the holder of a fee simple in possession, frequently referred to simply as "the freeholder," is the nearest English law gets to the absolute owner of land. The freehold landowner has a right to dispose of the property and his rights in respect of the property will form part of his estate on his death, and his assets during life. His death will not terminate the interest he has in land he owns as a freeholder, nor will the simple expiration of a period of years. He has a right at all times to occupy the property himself, or to receive the rents from a tenant in the property. He pays no rent himself to any landlord. The

---

[3] It may be possible to create third party incumbrances that attach to some chattels, binding those persons into whose hands the chattel comes, most notably restrictive covenants: see *Lord Strathcona SS Co.* v. *Dominion Coal Co.* [1926] A.C. 108; *Swiss Bank Corporation* v. *Lloyds Bank Ltd.* [1980] 2 All E.R. 449. *Cf.* Diplock J. in *Port Line Steamers* v. *Ben Line Ltd.* [1958] 2 Q.B. 146; see also Palmer [1978] J.B.L. 369–372. The provisions for relief against forfeiture may also be similar in cases of leases of land and chattels: *Barton Thompson & Co Ltd.* v. *Stapling Machine Co. Ltd.* [1966] Ch. 499; *Starside Properties Ltd.* v. *Mustapha* [1974] 2 All E.R. 567; *Cf. Millichamp* v. *Jones* [1982] 1 W.L.R. 1422; Consumer Credit Act 1974, s.132(1). See also Palmer & Yates [1979] C.L.J. 180.

[4] L.P.A. 1925, s.1.

[5] As, for example, under the Rent Act 1977; see *post*, Chap. 10.

leaseholder, on the other hand, does pay rent. He will only be granted the right to occupy and enjoy the property for a definite number of years, months or weeks as the case may be (a person owning a leasehold estate is still said to own "a term of years absolute" even though he may only be granted his lease for one week),[6] depending upon his agreement with the freeholder. He may have a tenancy for one week, or for 999 years. Or he may hold under a periodic tenancy of indefinite duration until ended by a notice to quit. In any case, however, in theory, at the end of the period the landlord will be entitled to the property freed from the tenant's rights. For this reason the landlord is said to own "the reversion" in the property, for at the end of the tenancy the property "reverts" to him. The terms "lease" and "tenancy" tend to be used interchangeably and they do not have separate technical meanings, although the word "lease" is frequently also used to describe the document or deed under which the tenant's interest is granted. Again, the landlord may himself either be a freeholder, or another tenant holding for a term of years absolute himself (in which case there will be what is called a "sub-letting," the intermediate landlord being known, technically, as the "mesne" landlord).

The characteristics of the leasehold estate are similar to those of the freehold estate, save that the former will determine after a fixed and certain period and also the tenant will be required to pay rent to his landlord. Aside from this, however, the leaseholder has a right to dispose of his interest (technically known as an assignment). He has the right to occupy or receive rents and profits if he has sub-let. The tenancy will form part of his estate on his death and can be passed on by his will provided that the term for which it was expressed to be granted has not expired.

Not everyone who has a right to occupy property of which he is not the freeholder will be a tenant. He may simply be someone with permission to be on the land. In law, this is called a bare licence. The licensee has no legal estate in land, but simply a right to be there that prevents him from being regarded as a trespasser. Lawyers have argued long over the differences between leases and licences, and the issue is an extremely complex one in which decisions frequently turn on very technical points. Several factors must be taken into account, discussed more fully in the next chapter. Suffice it to say here that a person who enjoys merely temporary use of land, such as a hotel resident, a lodger, or a cinema-goer, is regarded as a licensee. He is permitted to be there, but he has no lease of the property which the law can protect.

---

[6] L.P.A. 1925, s.205(1) (xxvii).

II. Rights of Occupation

The dominant characteristic of a tenant is that he is entitled to *exclusive* occupation. The tenant must be entitled to exclusive occupation, as against his landlord, of at least part of the premises he is renting. Although this is not decisive,[7] it is a consideration of the first importance. It may be possible to explain exclusive occupation on some ground inconsistent with the existence of a tenancy, and, for this reason, exclusive occupation cannot be the only factor. The most common explanation is that the occupant was entitled to occupy the premises for the purposes of performing his employer's work, rather than for his own individual benefit. The physical situation of the premises might indicate that only a licence was intended, for example, a kiosk in an hotel foyer. The arrangement may be so obviously temporary in nature that it is only explicable on the basis that the parties intended a licence, for example, where a charity is offered a shop in the high street "between tenants," or an organisation hires a large hall to put on an antique dealers' fair.

A number of consequences flow from the distinction. Because a licence did not create an estate in land it was, until recently, regarded merely as incident to a personal agreement between two parties. As such it created no proprietary rights capable of binding third parties, and, where a licence was revoked in breach of contract, the licensee had contractual remedies only, *i.e.* damages and occasionally the injunction and specific performance. However, in recent times this distinction has become somewhat blurred in that the courts have held that certain licences, notably licences by estoppel, can in suitable circumstances bind third parties.[8] Thus, although they are not estates in land, some licences have now taken on some of the characteristics of property rights.

Other important consequences attach to the distinction between leases and licences. Aside from the Agricultural Holdings Act, some sections of the Rent Act 1977[9] and the Housing Act 1985, Pts. IV & V,[10] the various statutory provisions that afford wide-ranging protections to tenants do not extend to licensees. So, the commercial exploitation by a landowner of his land may not necessarily involve renting it out within the landlord and tenant relationship. Owners of property used for hypermarkets housing different trading units may often find it convenient to create licences in favour of different commercial organisations occupying the trading floor, giving them limited trading rights in defined areas. One current advantage of this

[7] See Chap. 2, *post.*
[8] See *post*, Chap. 2.
[9] ss.76–85, 103–106 (repealed as to agreements made after October 3, 1980: Rent Act 1977, s.102A; Housing Act 1980, s.69(3)).
[10] Licensees of residential accommodation from a local authority or housing association may still be treated as secure tenants under the Housing Act 1985, s.79(3), (4).

is to avoid the security given to business tenants by the Landlord and Tenant Act 1954.[11] Owners of residential accommodation occupied as "bed-sitters" frequently took tortuous steps to create licences and sharing arrangements, again designed to move the relationship outside the ambit of the law of landlord and tenant and much of the security afforded to residential tenants by the Rent Acts.[12] Because of the opportunities thus provided for extensive avoidance of statutory provisions, the distinction between leases and licences arouses the intense interest of conveyancing draftsmen and close scrutiny by the judiciary.

It is clearly established that the label which the parties have placed on the relationship between them, perhaps in a document that they have called "a licence agreement," is irrelevant. If the occupancy bears all the marks of a tenancy, then in law it is a tenancy, and is not turned into a licence merely by calling it one.[13] Conversely, the label "tenant" may also be misleading, in that it appears to denote a person who holds a legal estate in land—a term of years absolute. However, under the Rent Act 1977, a tenant who remains in occupation after his lease has expired or been terminated by the service of a notice to quit from his landlord, takes on the status of what the legislation terms "a statutory tenant."[14] This gives him both security of tenure, in that he can only be removed on certain specified grounds,[15] and permits his statutory tenancy to be transmitted, twice, on the death of the previous occupant.[16] Although the statute calls him a "tenant," and he has the status of irremovability and his interest is, in some cases, transmissible on death, it nevertheless remains personal to the so-called "tenant." He loses all protection once he ceases to occupy the property himself and he does not have an estate in land. The consequence is that the statutory tenancy is not assignable, cannot be settled on trust or be bequeathed by will. It is a type of statutory "half-way house" being neither purely personal, as is a licence, nor exclusively proprietary, as is a contractual tenancy. Such creations are likely to become more common as the law of property moves further away from its feudal origins in the doctrines of estates.[17]

---

[11] *Shell-Mex and B.P. Ltd.* v. *Manchester Garages Ltd.* [1971] 1 W.L.R. 612.
[12] *Walsh* v. *Griffiths-Jones* [1978] 2 All E.R. 1002; *Somma* v. *Hazelhurst* [1978] 2 All E.R. 1011. These decisions have been overruled by the House of Lords and it is now much more difficult to avoid the Rent Act 1977 by attempting to create a licence, at least where the contract confers exclusive possession on the occupant: *Street* v. *Mountford* [1985] 2 All E.R. 289, and see *post*, Chap. 2. Easier methods of partial avoidance are now available: see the discussion of shorthold tenancies *post*, Chap. 14.
[13] *Addiscombe Garden Estates Ltd.* v. *Crabbe* [1958] 1 Q.B. 513.
[14] Rent Act 1977, s.2, Sched. 1.
[15] *Ibid.* Pt. VII.
[16] *Ibid.* Sched. 1, Pt. 1.
[17] See for instances, the development of property rights out of "mere equities" in the law of succession—see *Re Leigh's Will Trusts* [1970] Ch. 277. In the context of the Forfeiture Act 1982, s.2(7), see *Re K* [1985] 1 All E.R. 403, and the development of licences by estoppel, see Chap. 2. See also Hand [1980] Conv. 351.

III. The Flexibility of the Term of Years

Tenants, by virtue of having estates in land can, as we have seen, sub-let or assign their interests. A landlord too can simply transfer his reversion and the transferee will then take over the landlord's estate, standing in his shoes and finding himself bound by leases granted by his predecessor in title, even if unaware of their existence when he acquired the transferor's interest. The rights, duties and obligations created by a tenancy will bind successors to the interests of either landlord or tenant.

The ability of a tenant to transfer his entire interest, or to carve out lesser ones, has significant commercial consequences. It facilitates large-scale commercial or domestic developments, producing smaller occupational units which are readily marketable. For example, a landowner whose site is ripe for commercial development might grant a long lease, at a nominal rent, to the developer. The lease will contain a break clause or rent revision clause which can be implemented when the development is complete. The developer will agree to build a substantial block, comprising offices, shops and possibly some residential units. On completion of the development the site owner will receive a larger rent. The head tenant or developer will, at the same time, let off the several units, often in as large a block as possible, to sub-tenants. For example, all the office accommodation may be let off to one entrepreneurial tenant, such as a bank, which has no immediate need for such extensive accommodation for its own use. Consequently it will occupy only such parts as it needs, reducing its own overall financial liabilities, and making a small profit by sub-letting the rest to a company which, possibly for commercial reasons, does not want to acquire a long-term interest in the property. As these short leases come to an end, the bank has the choice of taking over more office accommodation itself for its own expanding business, or re-letting on further short terms. The several shops will ultimately be let to non-competing traders. So a development is carried out that neither the landowner nor the individual traders could have mounted, and smaller units which enjoy greater market flexibility have been created. A further commercial result of the use of tenancies in connection with large-scale development is that the estate owner can control the management of the whole development over a period of years. This will be done not only in his own best financial interests but also for the preservation of adequate standards of maintenance, repair and control over the use of the individual units.

Conversely, the device of a tenancy may be used to raise a lump sum rather than annual income. A trader running a business on his own fully developed property or farm may sell his own premises and take a lease back to himself as tenant. He may find that the advantages in releasing his own capital outweigh the benefits of owning the premises.

In all these cases the relationship of landlord and tenant is a commercially exploitative device. Indeed, it was the contractual and commercial aspects of the creation of leasehold interests that set them apart and prevented their absorption into the feudal structure of English land law.[18] As a commercial device today the lease, in addition to simply providing for the enjoyment, occupation or use of another's property in return for rent, is also a useful tool of commerce, being available as a way of providing security by mortgage in return for a loan,[19] or of providing additional security by means of attornment clauses.[20] It has been used for raising capital, as we have seen, in the sale and lease-back transaction.[21]

However, not every lease is necessarily granted to make a profit from land ownership. Leases can be used to regulate the provision of free housing accommodation for favoured friends or relatives for their respective lives. Aside from the politically sensitive and very brief flirtation with the profit element under the Housing Finance Act 1972, the provision of local authority housing, much of which is made available to tenants on somewhat one-sided tenancy agreements,[22] is not a profit-making activity.[23] Even in the diminishing private sector, the ability of a landlord to take advantage of the market scarcity in renting out residential property has been severely curtailed by the Rent Acts.[24]

In the context of residential accommodation the lease is resorted to, not so much for flexibility as a matter of necessity. Low income or lack of regular income or employment, or minimal capital resources, deprives some sectors of the population from access to such funds as are available, usually through the building societies, to finance house purchase. The recent massive inflation in house prices has compounded this problem. The only realistic alternative to house purchase is, frequently, to rent. Some groups meet different difficulties in trying to buy a house. Notwithstanding legislation making such discrimination illegal,[25] single women, even if their earnings are good, sometimes find difficulty obtaining loans from building societies.[26] Similarly, it may be more difficult for members of racial minorities to

---

[18] see Simpson, *An Introduction to the History of the Land Law,* pp. 87–89, 135–145, 255–261.
[19] L.P.A. 1925, s.85(1).
[20] See *post,* Chap. 3.
[21] Formerly portions could be raised for the younger children of the family by means of terms of years granted to portion term trustees (usually distinct from the trustees of the settlement): see *Megarry & Wade,* p. 630.
[22] See *Liverpool City Council* v. *Irwin* [1977] A.C. 239, but see also Housing Act 1985, s.104.
[23] See *post,* Chap. 16.
[24] Rent Act 1977, Pt. II.
[25] Sex Discrimination Act 1975, ss.1,29.
[26] Coote & Gill, *Women's Rights: A Practical Guide,* pp. 260–264; Boddy, *The Building Societies,* pp. 60–72.

obtain finance for house purchase.[27] So, for some groups, low-income families, women, ethnic minorities, the chances of buying the freehold interest in their houses are very much reduced. The only way in which such persons can secure a roof over their heads is to rent, either from a private landlord or from a local authority or housing association.

There is no simple pattern for all tenancies. Part of the law has been derived from the law of real property, *i.e.* that principally affecting land, and part has come from the law relating to personalty, *i.e.* assets other than land. Attempts were made to assimilate the law of landlord and tenant with the rest of the law affecting land, culminating in the 1925 property legislation. However, on top of that theoretical and conceptual purity have been laid, almost annually, layers of complex statutory provisions to protect tenants, tax landlords, control rents and returns from land, vary liabilities and responsibilities for repair, assist the spouses of deserting tenants and to enable certain tenants to buy out their landlords' reversions. This list is and will continue to be endless so long as the exploitation of property rights by landlords and tenants remains a politically sensitive area.[28]

---

[27] *Select Committee on Race Relations and Immigration, Report on Housing* (HMSO, H.C. 508–I/1970–71), Chaps. 4 & 10; McKay, *Housing and Race in Industrial Society*, Chaps. 4 & 6.
[28] See Denman, *The Place of Property, passim.*

CHAPTER 2

LEASES AND LICENCES[1]

I. The Need to Determine the Nature of an Occupier's Interest 9	(1) Service Occupancy 27
	(2) Lodgings 28
II. Characteristics of Leases and Licences 13	(3) Other Factors 31
A. Power to Create Leases 13	G. Uncertainty as to Grant of Exclusive Possession 32
B. Possession to the Exclusion of the Landlord 15	H. The Relevance of Duration . . 36
C. Intention 17	(1) Leases for a fixed term of years 38
D. Intention and Sham Transactions 20	(2) Periodic Tenancies 42
E. Intention to Enter into Legal Relations 24	(3) Tenancies at Will 43
	(4) Tenancies at Sufferance . 45
F. The Special Factors 26	(5) Perpetually renewable Leases 46

I THE NEED TO DETERMINE THE NATURE OF AN OCCUPIER'S INTEREST

A person entitled merely to some temporary use of land or some part of it, such as the lodger, cinema-goer or organisation that uses local authority-provided sports facilities for a few hours a week, is regarded as a licensee. A licensee is merely permitted to be there, so that his presence, which would otherwise be a trespass, is made lawful.[2] However, he has neither a fee simple abolute in possession nor a term of years absolute, and so has no legal estate in the land.[3] Several consequences follow. Between the parties to a lease, the law implies certain covenants in order to give the tenant the full benefit of his legal estate[4] and in order to give reasonable protection of the landlord's reversion.[5] Although, as a matter of contract, it is possible for licensors and licensees to incur obligations to each other, these obligations, with the possible exception of restraints upon revocation, to be effective, must normally be express. It was thought that the law would not generally imply covenants in the licence arrangement since the licensee has no estate in land needing protection. However, recently the Court of Appeal has implied a term into a contractual licence so as to confer on occupiers the right to quiet enjoyment of their rooms,[6] and in *Wettern Electric Ltd.* v. *Welsh Development*

---

[1] See generally Dawson & Pearce, *Licences Relating to the Occupation of Use of Land, passim.* Robson & Watchman [1980] Conv. 27.

[2] *Thomas* v. *Sorrell* (1673) Vaugh. 330, *per* Vaughan C.J. at p. 351.

[3] L.P.A. 1925, s.1(1).

[4] Such as the covenants for quiet enjoyment and non-derogation from grant.

[5] Such as the covenants to pay rent, rates and other outgoings, and to use premises in a tenant-like manner. These implied covenants are discussed in Chaps. 4–6, *post.*

[6] *Smith* v. *Nottinghamshire County Council, The Times,* November 3, 1981.

Board [7] the Court implied a term as to fitness or suitability for purpose into a licence agreement for a factory.

Because a tenant has an estate in land, a landlord commits a trespass if he enters without the tenant's permission and without authority under the lease. If only a licence is granted, the licensor, by entering, may commit a breach of contract, but not a trespass. Also, with few exceptions,[8] the various statutory provisions designed to grant security of tenure to residential tenants,[9] to secure the grant of new tenancies to tenants of business premises whose former tenancy has terminated,[10] and to enable residential tenants to get "fair" rents fixed for their occupation of the property,[11] do not protect licensees. For this reason alone, therefore, the distinction is of the first importance, since it provides the potential, depending upon how vigilant the courts are in detecting a "sham,"[12] for wholesale avoidance of the various statutory provisions.[13]

A licence is *prima facie* personal to the licensee,[14] who consequently has no power to sub-let.[15] A licence that is regarded as personal to the licensee carries with it an implied restriction on assignment,[16] so that the benefit of the contractual right of occupation cannot then be assigned in equity or under section 136 of the Law of Property Act 1925. However, a licence coupled with the grant of an interest, such as a right to enjoy a *profit à prendre* or other incorporeal hereditament,[17] is capable of assignment[18] and where the circumstances surrounding the grant of the licence are such as to lead to the inference that it was not intended to be purely personal, as is the case with many commercial licences,[19] then the licence may well be assignable in accordance with its express or implied terms.[20]

---

[7] [1983] Q.B. 796.

[8] *e.g.* Rent Act 1977, s.102A; Agricultural Holding Act 1986; Housing Act 1985, s.79(3).

[9] Rent Act 1977, *post*, Chap. 13.

[10] Landlord and Tenant Act 1954, Pt. II, *post*, Chap. 22.

[11] Rent Act 1977, *post*, Chap. 11.

[12] *Samrose Properties Ltd.* v. *Gibbard* [1958] 1 W.L.R. 235; *Street* v. *Mountford* [1985] 2 All E.R. 289.

[13] For business occupations see, *e.g. Shell-Mex and B.P. Ltd.* v. *Manchester Garages Ltd.* [1971] 1 W.L.R. 612. For residential occupants see: *Appah* v. *Parncliffe Investments Ltd.* [1964] 1 W.L.R. 1064; *Abbeyfield (Harpenden) Society Ltd.* v. *Woods* [1968] 1 W.L.R. 374; *Luganda* v. *Service Hotels Ltd.* [1969] 2 Ch. 209; *Marchant* v. *Charters* [1977] 1 W.L.R. 1181. *cf. Demuren & Adefope* v. *Seal Estates Ltd.* (1978) 249 E.G. 440, *Street* v. *Mountford* [1985] 2 All E.R. 289, *per* Lord Templeman at p. 291.

[14] *Isaac* v. *Hotel de Paris Ltd.* [1960] 1 W.L.R. 239, *per* Lord Denning at p. 245 and see (1960) 104 S.J. 245.

[15] *Errington* v. *Errington and Woods* [1952] 1 K.B. 290.

[16] *Tolhurst* v. *Associated Portland Cement Manufacturers (1900) Ltd.* [1902] 2 K.B. 600, *per* Collins M.R. at p. 668; *Kemp* v. *Baerselman* [1906] 2 K.B. 604.

[17] *Vaughan* v. *Hampson* (1875) 33 L.T. 15; *Hounslow London Borough* v. *Twickenham Garden Developments Ltd.* [1971] Ch. 233.

[18] As, for instance, the licence to prospect for and carry away metals in *Muskett* v. *Hill* (1839) 5 Bing., N.C. 694.

[19] Such as the right to a stall or "lock-up" in a privately run and managed "covered market."

[20] *Dorling* v. *Honnor Marine Ltd.* [1964] Ch. 560, *per* Cross J. at p. 568, confirmed on this point at [1965] Ch. 1.

Unlike a lease, a licence to occupy land terminates on the licensee's death and there is consequently nothing capable of forming part of his estate. A licensee's rights of occupation are not transmissible on his death.[21] By virtue of the personal nature of licences, and the fact that the licensee has no legal estate in land it was thought that he had no proprietary interest capable of protection against third parties, so that a licence would terminate on the death of the licensor or on the assignment of the licensor's interest, binding neither the licensor's estate nor his successors in title.[22] However, in recent years, largely as a result of the intervention of equity in what was, for centuries, regarded as the province of common law, some licences have come to be regarded as irrevocable by the licensor.[23] Once it became possible to protect a licensee against arbitrary ejection by the licensor, it was a short step to protect him against ejection by a third party to whom the licensor had transferred his interest. Discussion of the problems associated with revocation of licences will be found in Chapter 8 alongside consideration of the requirements for proper termination of leases.

Most of the recent cases concerning the irrevocability of licences have concerned the doctrine of estoppel. At common law a licensor will be estopped from revoking a licence if he has permitted or induced the licensee to act to his detriment on the understanding that the licence was irrevocable.[24] In equity, the doctrine of proprietary

---

[21] *Coleman* v. *Foster* (1856) 1 H. & N. 37; *Roberts* v. *Rose* (1863–1864) 3 H. & C. 162; *Wallis* v. *Harrison* (1838) 4 M. & W. 538; *Roffey* v. *Henderson* (1851) 17 Q.B. 574.

[22] *Terunnanse* v. *Terunnanse* [1968] A.C. 1086; *National Provincial Bank Ltd.* v. *Ainsworth* [1965] A.C. 1175.

[23] A gratuitous licence is revocable by notice. The right to revoke a contractual licence depends upon the terms of the contract. In the case of joint ownership, any one of the joint owners may terminate a licence which, on its terms, is revocable: *Annen* v. *Rattee* (1985) 273 E.G. 503. There may be an express or implied term not to revoke which the court will, by virtue of the Judicature Acts (now Supreme Court Act 1981), regard as specifically enforceable. Hence, there are now circumstances in which a contractual licence will be irrevocable accordingly to its express or implied terms: *Hurst* v. *Picture Theatres Ltd.* [1915] 1 K.B. 1; *Thompson* v. *Park* [1944] K.B. 408; *Winter Garden Theatre (London) Ltd.* v. *Millenium Productions Ltd.* [1946] 1 All E.R. 678, *per* Lord Greene M.R. at p. 684 (reversed on other grounds, [1948] A.C. 173); *Hounslow L.B.C.* v. *Twickenham Garden Developments Ltd.* [1971] Ch. 233; *Verrall* v. *Great Yarmouth B.C.* [1981] Q.B. 202. In a number of informal family arrangements the court has been prepared to find an implied contract which prevented or restricted the revocation of a licence: *Tanner* v. *Tanner* [1975] 1 W.L.R. 1346; *Hardwick* v. *Johnson* [1978] 1 W.L.R. 683; *Re Sharpe* [1980] 1 W.L.R. 219. *cf. Chandler* v. *Kerley; Horrocks* v. *Forray* [1976] 1 W.L.R. 230. See also *Williams* v. *Staite* [1979] Ch. 291. A licence coupled with an interest or grant is also irrevocable: see *James Jones & Sons Ltd.* v. *Earl of Tankerville* [1909] 2 Ch. 440; *Doe d. Hanley* v. *Wood* (1819) 2 B. & Ald. 724; *Wood* v. *Manley* (1839) 11 A. & E. 34.

[24] *Hopgood* v. *Brown* [1955] 1 W.L.R. 13.

estoppel[25] permits the court to fulfil, either wholly[26] in part[27] an expectation, encouraged or acquiesced in, which is subsequently acted upon.[28] If the licensor induces the licensee to rely upon an expectation that the licence will not be revoked, it is regarded by equity as unconscionable to deny a remedy should the licensor subsequently purport to deny or revoke the licence. This issue of unconscionability is composed of two elements.[29] First, there must have been action by the licensee in reliance on an expectation, otherwise no equity can arise. Secondly, the licensor must have created that expectation of irrevocability, either by active encouragement, or by standing idly but knowingly by while the licensee acted in reliance on the expectation.[30]

However, the fact that a licensee's right of occupation may be protected against revocation, either by the licensor or by third parties, does not *necessarily* mean that some licensees have proprietary interests. If a licence does create an interest in land (necessarily equitable, since the Law of Property Act 1925, s.1(1), would prevent it from being legal), then it follows that the licence would bind third parties, subject, of course, to special factors relating to the destruction of equitable interests by a bona fide purchaser of the legal estate for value without notice,[31] to registration of charges, to over-reaching, and to other factors relating to minor interests in registered land.[32] In *National Provincial Bank Ltd.* v. *Ainsworth*[33] Lord Upjohn said: "To create a right over the land of another that right must (apart from statute) create a burden on the land, *i.e.* an equitable estate or interest in the land. . . . An equity to which a subsequent purchaser is subject must create an interest in land." That this may be so in the case of licences creating life interests,[34] or in the case of licensees claiming an

---

[25] See Briggs [1981] Conv. 221, [1983] Conv. 285; Thompson [1983] Conv. 50, 471, (1983) 42 C.L.J. 257; Naresh (1980) 96 L.Q.R. 534 at pp. 539–542; Moriarty (1984) 100 L.Q.R. 376; Crane (1967) 31 Conv.(N.S.) 323; Todd [1981] Conv. 347; Martin [1980] Conv. 207.

[26] *Dillwyn* v. *Llewelyn* (1862) 4 De D. G. & J. 517; *Plimmer* v. *Wellington Corp.* (1884) 9 App.Cas. 699; *Pascoe* v. *Turner* [1979] 1 W.L.R. 431; *Chalmers* v. *Pardoe* [1963] 1 W.L.R. 677.

[27] *Unity Joint Stock Mutual Banking Association* v. *King* (1858) 25 Beav. 72; *Duke of Beaufort* v. *Patrick* (1853) 17 Beav. 60; *Jackson* v. *Cator* (1800) 5 Ves. 688; *Cotching* v. *Bassett* (1862) 32 Beav. 101; *Inwards* v. *Baker* [1965] 2 Q.B. 29; *Dodsworth* v. *Dodsworth* (1973) 228 E. G. 1115; *Griffiths* v. *Williams* (1977) 248 E.G. 947. See also Murphy & Clarke, *The Family Home*, p. 119.

[28] *Armstrong* v. *Sheppard & Short Ltd.* [1959] 2 Q.B. 384; *Ward* v. *Kirkland* [1967] Ch. 194; *Ives (E.R.) Investment Co.* v. *High* [1967] 2 Q.B. 379; *Crabb* v. *Arun District Council* [1976] Ch. 179; *Greasley* v. *Cooke* [1980] 1 W.L.R. 1306; *Salvation Army Trustee Co. Ltd.* v. *West Yorks Metropolitan County Council* (1981) 41 P. & C.R. 179.

[29] A contraction of what are sometimes referred to as "the five probanda": see Fry J. in *Willmott* v. *Barber* (1880) 15 Ch.D. 96 at pp. 105–106; see also *Crabb* v. *Arun District Council* [1976] Ch. 179; *Shaw* v. *Applegate* [1977] 1 W.L.R. 970; *Swallow Securities Ltd.* v. *Isenberg* (1985) 2 74 E.G. 1028.

[30] *Taylor Fashions Ltd* v. *Liverpool Victoria Friendly Society* [1981] 1 All E.R. 897; *Habib Bank Ltd.* v. *Habib Bank A.C. Zurich* [1981] 2 All E.R. 650 *per* Oliver J. at p. 666; *Amalgamated Investment & Property Co. (in liquidation)* v. *Texas Commerce International Bank Ltd.* [1982] Q.B. 84; *Pacol Ltd.* v. *Trade Lines Ltd.* [1982] 1 Lloyd's Rep. 456.

[31] See Hanbury and Maudsley, *Modern Equity* (12th ed.), pp. 833 *et seq.*

[32] *Ibid.* p. 662.

[33] [1965] A.C. 1175 at p. 1239.

[34] *e.g. Bannister* v. *Bannister* [1948] 2 All E.R. 133; *Binions* v. *Evans* [1972] Ch. 359; *Hussey* v. *Palmer* [1972] 1 W.L.R. 1286; *cf.* Martin (1972) 36 (Conv N.S.) 266.

interest under the doctrine of proprietary estoppel[35] is not sufficient reason for characterising all irrevocable licences as proprietary interests,[36] and indeed, Lord Upjohn adverted to this difficulty himself.[37]

The fact that equity may be prepared to intervene to prevent revocation of a licence by granting an equitable remedy against the licensor, or even against an assignee from him who takes with notice of the agreement, does not automatically result in the translation of rights *in personam* into rights *in rem*. The process is, perhaps, more gradual and we are at present experiencing the transition through the medium of equitable remedies. Exactly the same slow process can be observed in the history of the development of restrictive covenants, from the decision in *Tulk* v. *Moxhay* [38] in 1838 to the case of *Swiss Bank Corporation* v. *Lloyds Bank Ltd*[39] 130 years later, in which there is some sign that, in appropriate circumstances (although this case was not one) the court may be prepared to create a proprietary interest out of a restrictive covenant imposed upon a chattel. However, there is no cause for over-hasty development or unnecessary assumptions about the nature of any property interests created by licences. The impact of such developments, especially upon the 1925 property legislation, must be carefully considered. One difficulty is that if a licence is to be considered as an interest in land, it would come very much nearer to resembling a lease, or an estate contract, but at the same time it would possibly be a stronger and better safeguarded interest.[40] Perhaps the better view is that at present a licence, *vis-à-vis* a purchaser for value with notice, is not an interest in land but somewhere between a right *in rem* and a right *in personam*, protected by the availability of equitable remedies.[41]

II. Characteristics of Leases and Licences

A. Power to Create Leases

As a general rule a tenancy cannot be granted by a grantor who has no

---

[35] *e.g. Dillwyn* v. *Llewelyn* (1862) 4 De G.F. & J. 517; *Plimmer* v. *Wellington Corporation* (1884) 9 App.Cas. 699; *Siew Soon Wah* v. *Yong Tong Hong* [1973] A.C. 836; *Pascoe* v. *Turner* [1979] 2 All. E.R. 945; *Re Sharpe (A Bankrupt)* [1980] 1 W.L.R. 219.

[36] Cheshire (1953) 16 M.L.R. 1; Bondali (1973) 37 Conv.(N.S.) 402; Thompson [1983] C.L.J. 275.

[37] [1965] A.C. 1175 at pp. 1239–1240. See also *Hounslow L.B.C.* v. *Twickenham Garden Developments* [1971] Ch. 233; *cf. Mayfield Holdings* v. *Moana Reef* [1973] 1 N.Z.L.R. 309.

[38] (1848) 2 Ph. 774.

[39] [1982] A.C. 584.

[40] Unlike an "estate contract," it would not be registrable under the Land Charges Act 1972 and would therefore be subject to the pre-1925 rules concerning notice.

[41] *cf.* a right of re-entry in *Shiloh Spinners Ltd.* v. *Harding* [1973] A.C. 691.

power to grant a tenancy. So, in *Torbett* v. *Faulkener*[42] a company that had no estate or interest in a house that was vested in a director of the company was held, when the company granted a right of occupation, to have created only a licence since the grantor lacked any sufficient estate or power to create a lease. Similar problems arose where government departments requisitioned property under war-time emergency powers. The requisitioning authority did not have all the powers of an estate owner, and hence a person permitted to occupy requisitioned premises was necessarily no more than a licensee, no tenancy being created between him and the authority,[43] even by estoppel.[44]

One possible way of creating "judge proof" licences,[45] therefore, is to arrange matters so that the grantor lacks the legal capacity to create a lease.[46] This can be achieved by ensuring that the grantor, who should be a company with appropriately limited capacity, expressly purports to grant a mere licence and not a lease. The company should have a clause in its memorandum of association expressly restricting its powers to dealing in licences and sub-licences over land.[47] All that a landowner need do is form such a company and allow it to permit residential and/or business occupancy for suitable payments; tenancies would then be *ultra vires* the company's powers and, as a matter of law, incapable of being granted.[48]

However, one reservation must be made. Under section 35(1) of the Companies Act 1985, where a person is dealing with a company in good faith, any transaction decided on by its directors shall be deemed to be within the capacity of the company, irrespective of any restrictions in the memorandum or articles of association. By virtue of section 35(2) a third party who enters into a contract with the company's directors is not bound to enquire about the capacity of the company to enter into it and, unless the contrary is proved, the third party will be deemed to have acted in good faith. This means that a person who has taken a tenancy from a company following a decision of its directors to grant it, where the company has no power to grant leases can, nevertheless, relying on section 35, claim to be a tenant and will not be fixed with constructive notice of the fact that the

[42] [1952] 2 T.L.R. 659; *cf. Calladine* v. *Webster* [1951] E.G. D300.
[43] *Minister of Aircraft Production* v. *Hunt* [1945] L.J.N.C.C.R. 1; *Southgate Borough Council* v. *Watson* [1944] K.B. 541. But see Requisitioned Houses and Housing (Amendment) Act 1955, s.4.
[44] See *post*, Chap. 3, and also *Minister of Agriculture and Fisheries* v. *Hunkin* [1948] E.G.D. 195; *Minister of Agriculture and Fisheries* v. *Matthews* [1950] 1 K.B. 148.
[45] The phrase is that of a former learned editor of *The Conveyancer*, see (1976) 40 Conv.(N.S.) 6.
[46] This purpose will not be achieved simply by some superior owner imposing an effective restriction upon leasing powers, because there will still be the likelihood of a tenancy by estoppel: see further Chap. 3 and also *Stratford* v. *Syrett* [1958] 1 Q.B. 107.
[47] For a precedent see *Precedents for the Conveyancer*, Form 5–1.
[48] See *Minister of Agriculture and Fisheries* v. *Matthews* [1950] 1 K.B. 148; *Lewisham Metropolitan Borough* v. *Roberts* [1949] 2 K.B. 608; *Finbow* v. *Air Ministry* [1963] 1 W.L.R. 697; *cf. Epsom & Ewell Borough Council* v. *C. Bell (Tadworth) Ltd.* [1983] 1 W.L.R. 379. See also *Torbett* v. *Faulkener* [1952] 2 T.L.R. 659; *cf.* Pettit [1980] Conv. 112.

transaction is *ultra vires*. So, the landowner who sets up his own company for the purposes of granting licences only must ensure that, in his capacity as director, he never decides that the company should enter into any lease. However, since there is now a risk that any occupation agreement granting an occupant exclusive possession will be treated as a tenancy unless it falls into a special category such as a lodging contract or service occupancy,[49] the fact that there may be no decision on the part of the directors to grant a tenancy may not be enough. Accordingly, as a double safeguard, it is perhaps appropriate for the licence agreement itself to recite the objects clause of the company. In that way the grantee would be unable to argue that he acted in ignorance of the company's limited powers to grant occupation rights.[50]

B. Possession to the Exclusion of the Landlord

It is an essential characteristic of a lease that the tenant should be given the right to exclude all other persons, including his landlord, from the premises.[51] A right of occupation granted for a fixed period cannot be a tenancy if the person granting the right remains in general control. This will normally be the case with rooms in an hotel or boarding house, so that a lodger is usually a mere licensee and not a tenant.[52] In *Street* v. *Mountford*[53] Lord Templeman put the matter thus:[54]

> "There can be no tenancy unless the occupier enjoys exclusive possession; but an occupier who enjoys exclusive possession is not necessarily a tenant. He may be owner in fee simple, a trespasser, a mortgagee in possession, an object of charity or a service occupier. To constitute a tenancy the occupier must be granted exclusive possession for a fixed or periodic term certain in consideration of a premium or periodic payments. The grant may be express or may be inferred where the owner accepts weekly or other periodic payments from the occupier."

[49] *Street* v. *Mountford* [1985] 2 All E.R. 289.
[50] *cf. International Sales and Agencies Ltd.* v. *Marcus* [1982] 2 C.M.L.R. 46.
[51] *Thomas* v. *Sorrell* (1673) Vaugh. 330. *Addiscombe Garden Estates Ltd.* v. *Crabbe* [1958] 1 Q.B. 513; *Errington* v. *Errington & Woods* [1952] 1 K.B. 290; *Grand Junction Co.* v. *Bates* [1954] 2 Q.B. 160; *Oakley* v.*Wilson* [1927] 2 K.B. 279; *Lynes* v. *Snaith* [1899] 1 Q.B. 486; *Street* v. *Mountford* [1985] 2 All E.R. 289.
[52] *Smith* v. *St. Michael's, Cambridge, Overseers* (1860) 3 E. & E. 383; *Appah* v. *Parncliffe Investments Ltd.* [1964] 1 W.L.R. 1064; *Luganda* v. *Service Hotels Ltd.* [1969] 2 Ch. 209; *Mayflower Cambridge* v. *Secretary of State for the Environment* (1975) 30 P. & C.R. 28; *Bradley* v. *Baylis* (1881) 8 Q.B.D. 195; *Helman* v. *Horsham & Worthing Assessment Committee* [1949] 2 K.B. 335; *Douglas* v. *Smith* [1907] 2 K.B. 568; *Allan* v. *Liverpool Overseers* (1874) L.R. 9 Q.B. 180, *per* Blackburn J. at pp. 191–192.
[53] [1985] 2 All E.R. 289.
[54] *Ibid.* p. 294.

However, a person described as a lodger or licensee will frequently still be a tenant if he is, in fact, given exclusive possession of some definite part of the premises together with the right to exclude all other people including the landlord,[55] even if the landlord lives on the premises,[56] and notwithstanding the presence of a clause in the agreement expressly negating any tenancy.[57]

Whether or not the grantee has exclusive possession is, therefore, a consideration of the first importance in deciding whether the grantor has granted a lease or a licence.[58] It was formerly thought that the overriding consideration was the intention of the parties, *i.e.* to create a tenancy the parties must have intended a tenancy—an intention on the part of the grantor to grant and on the part of the grantee to take exclusive possession as a consequence of the grant of a term of years absolute.[59] It now seems to be the case, at least for residential tenancies but possibly all tenancies,[60] that a person who is let into exclusive possession is *prima facie* to be regarded as a tenant[61] in the absence of special circumstances negating any intention to create legal

[55] *Addiscombe Garden Estates Ltd.* v. *Crabbe* [1958] 1 Q.B. 513; *Street* v. *Mountford* [1985] 2 All E.R. 289.
[56] *Kent* v. *Fittall* [1906] 1 K.B. 6.
[57] *Facchini* v. *Bryson* [1952] 1 T.L.R. 1386; *Street* v. *Mountford* [1985] 2 All E.R. 289.
[58] *Street* v. *Mountford* [1985] 2 All E.R. 289, approving *Addiscombe Garden Estates* v. *Crabbe* [1958] 1 Q.B. 513, *per* Jenkins L.J. at p. 528. The earlier cases seem to be unclear upon whether what is required is exclusive possession in fact (more preferably referred to as exclusive occupation) and exclusive possession as a matter of legal right: see Cullity, (1965) 29 Conv.(N.S.) 336.
[59] *Brewer* v. *Hill* (1794) 2 Anstr. 413; *Doe d. Hughes* v. *Derry* (1840) 9 C. & P. 494; *Mayhew* v. *Suttle* (1854) 4 E. & B. 347; *Taylor* v. *Jackson* (1846) 2 C & K. 22.
[60] *Street* v. *Mountford* [1985] 2 All E.R. 289, *per* Lord Templeman at p. 293. It may be argued that, despite the general nature of some of his comments, his Lordship's observations (which receive the unanimous endorsement of Lords Scarman, Keith of Kinkel, Bridge and Brightman) are, by context and, on occasion, express words, confined to leases and licences of residential accommodation. To apply the presumption of intention to grant a tenancy from the fact of exclusive possession in the case of commercial lettings would certainly frustrate the entire base and commercial purpose of many business licence arrangements and one wonders whether their Lordships really thought through this aspect of the matter. Although Lord Templeman cites both *Isaac* v. *Hotel de Paris Ltd.* [1960] 1 W.L.R. 239, and *Shell-Mex & B.P. Ltd.* v. *Manchester Garages Ltd.*, [1971] 1 W.L.R. 612, and appears to suggest that, even in the case of agreements falling within the Landlord and Tenant Act 1954, Pt. II, the sole test of the lease/licence question is whether or not exclusive possession has been granted (at p. 298), the policy issues in respect of Pt. II of the 1954 Act might seem to call for a more flexible approach to the lease/licence issue, since not only is contracting out of the 1954 Act expressly permitted (see Landlord and Tenant Act 1954, Pt. II, s.38 and *Hagee (London) Ltd.* v. *A.B. Erikson & Larson* [1976] Q.B. 209 *per* Lord Denning M.R. at p. 213) but tenancies at will are also excluded from the ambit of the Act: *Wheeler* v. *Mercer* [1957] A.C. 416; *Manfield Sons Ltd.* v. *Botchin* [1970] 2 Q.B. 612. Neither factor pertains to the Rent Act 1977. Indeed, at one point (p. 295) Lord Templeman appears himself to be confused as to the precise circumstances when a licence rather than a lease will be created. He refers to the special relationship between a vendor and purchaser as giving rise to a licence whereas a purchaser who goes into possession after contract and pending completion is generally regarded as a tenant at will, at least under an open contract: *Chamberlain* v. *Farr* [1942] 2 All E.R. 567; *Ball* v. *Cullimore* (1835) 2 Cr. M. & R. 120.
[61] *Street* v. *Mountford* [1985] 2 All. E.R. 289; *Addiscombe Garden Estates* v. *Crabbe* [1958] 1 Q.B. 513, *per* Jenkins L.J. at p. 528; *Radaich* v. *Smith* (1959) 101 C.L.R. 209; *Errington* v. *Errington & Woods* [1952] 1 K.B. 290, *per* Denning L.J. at p. 296, as explained in *Street* v. *Mountford*, *infra*, pp. 295–296 *per* Lord Templeman; *Eastleigh Borough Council* v. *Walsh* [1985] 2 All E.R. 112, *per* Lord Bridge at pp. 116–117. *cf. Doe d. Hull* v. *Wood* (1845) 14 M. & W. 682; *Lynes* v. *Snaith* [1899] 1 Q.B. 486; *Glenwood Lumber Co.* v. *Phillips* [1904] A.C. 405, *per* Lord Davey at p. 408.

relations or a tenancy.[62] In other words, in the absence of special factors, the intention to create a tenancy will be presumed from the fact of exclusive possession. In *Street* v. *Mountford*[63] the House of Lords held that those cases in which grantees have been found to be licensees notwithstanding the fact that they had exclusive possession *vis-à-vis* the grantor, were either wrongly decided,[64] or were based upon some special factor in the relationship between grantor and grantee, such as family connections, friendship, charity, employment and such like, which negatived an intention either to create legal relations at all, or to create a tenancy.

Notwithstanding that it is possible in special circumstances for a licensee to be granted rights of exclusive use and enjoyment, it is now the case that if an agreement confers on the occupier the right to exclusive use of the premises, the normal presumption will be, assuming the arrangement was intended to have legal consequences at all, that a tenancy has been created. The grantor may, of course, (and frequently does) reserve certain rights to enter, *e.g.* to inspect the condition of the premises, or to carry out repairs which he is contractually obliged to carry out. Such a reservation is not inconsistent with a grant of exclusive possession. Indeed, as Lord Templeman observed in *Street* v. *Mountford*:[65] "any express reservation to the landlord of limited rights to enter and view the state of the premises and to repair and maintain the premises only serves to emphasise the fact that the grantee is entitled to exclusive possession and is a tenant." The thinking is, presumably, that if exclusive possession had not been granted the reservation would be unnecessary, since the grantor would then enjoy such rights of entry anyway.[66]

C. Intention

Before 1985 it was thought that the question of whether the grantor had created a lease or a licence depended, in part, or even mainly, on the intention of the parties. " ... Did the circumstances and the

---

[62] *Errington* v. *Errington & Woods* [1952] 1 K.B. 290; *Cobb* v. *Lane* [1952] 1 All E.R. 1199; *Torbett* v. *Faulkener* [1952] 2 T.L.R. 659; *Booker* v. *Palmer* [1942] 2 All E.R. 674, *per* Lord Greene M.R. at p. 677; *Bramwell* v. *Bramwell* [1942] 1 K.B. 370; *Foster* v. *Robinson* [1951] 1 K.B. 149; *Marcroft Wagons* v. *Smith* [1951] 2 K.B. 496; *Isaac* v. *Hotel de Paris* [1960] 1 W.L.R. 239; *Facchini* v. *Bryson* [1952] 1 T.L.R. 1386, *per* Denning L.J. at pp. 1389–1390; *Abbeyfield (Harpenden) Society Ltd.* v. *Woods* [1968] 1 W.L.R. 374; *Shell-Mex & B.P. Ltd.* v. *Manchester Garages Ltd.* [1971] 1 W.L.R. 612; *Heslop* v. *Burns* [1974] 1 W.L.R. 1241; *D. H. N. Food Distributors* v. *Tower Hamlets London Borough Council* [1976] 1 W.L.R. 852.

[63] [1985] 2 All E.R. 289. ·

[64] *Murray Bull & Co. Ltd.* v. *Murray* [1953] 1 Q.B. 211; *Somma* v. *Hazelhurst* [1978] 1 W.L.R. 1014; *Aldrington Garages Ltd.* v. *Fielder* (1978) 37 P. & C.R. 461; *Sturolson & Co.* v. *Weniz* (1984) 272 E.G. 326. Doubt was also expressed about the reasoning, though not the conclusion, of Lord Denning M.R. in *Marchant* v. *Charters* [1977] 1 W.L.R. 1181 at p. 1185.

[65] [1985] 2 All E.R. 289 at p. 293.

[66] *Addiscombe Garden Estates Ltd.* v. *Crabbe* [1958] 1 Q.B. 513.

conduct of the parties show that all that was intended was that the occupier should have a personal privilege with no interest in the land?"[67] If so, the arrangement was likely to be a licence.[68] In *Marcroft Wagons Ltd.* v. *Smith*[69] the tenant of a house, protected by the Rent Acts, died and his widow and daughter continued to occupy the house, paying rent, until the widow's death. The daughter thereafter remained in occupation but the landlords, while accepting rent, refused to allow her name to be entered in the rent book. Six months later possession proceedings were brought and the Court of Appeal held that the arrangement constituted a licence agreement and not a tenancy. Roxburgh J., sitting as a Lord Justice of Appeal, said:[70]

> "Here the landlords could quite easily create a tenancy, and the question is . . . whether they were merely leaving the defendant in occupation while they and she considered their respective positions or whether they agreed to leave her in occupation until they should actually require the premises for use for an employee. I think, on the whole, that that is the question to which the county court judge directed his mind, and that what he has really found is that the landlords intended the defendant to remain for the time being in occupation of the premises for a consideration but without becoming a tenant. Such a conclusion, which is one of fact, was in my view permissible in law in a Rent Act case, and . . . one at which . . . he could properly arrive. . . . "[71]

The concluding part of this *dictum* raises a further complication with regard to the parties' intentions and that is the obvious desire grantors may have in avoiding, where possible, the unfavourable consequences of legislation designed to protect the interests of tenants. Were the courts to pay too much regard to what the landlord claims to have been his intention at the time of the grant we might, in the words of Denning L.J. in *Facchini* v. *Bryson*,[72] "find all landlords granting licences and not tenancies, and we should make a hole in the Rent Acts through which can be driven—I will not in these days say a coach and four, but an articulated vehicle."[73] Against this assumption that the courts ought to place little reliance on the intention of the

[67] *Cobb* v. *Lane* [1952] 1 All E.R. 1199, *per* Denning L.J. at p. 1202.
[68] *Errington* v. *Errington & Woods* [1952] 1 K.B. 290.
[69] [1951] 2 K.B. 496; see also *Gorham (Contractors) Ltd.* v. *Field* [1952] C.P.L. 266; *Isaac* v. *Hotel de Paris Ltd.* [1960] 1 W.L.R. 239; *Finbow* v. *Air Ministry* [1963] 1 W.L.R. 697. For a criticism of the view that the parties' purposes and intentions should influence the lease/licence question see: Hargreaves (1953) 69 L.Q.R. 466—an example of heresy becoming orthodoxy! See also Cullity, (1965) 29 Conv. (N.S.) 336.
[70] [1951] 2 K.B. 496 at p. 508.
[71] See also *Doe d. Cheny* v. *Batten* (1775) 1 Cowp. 243, *per* Lord Mansfield at p. 245: "The question therefore is, *quo animo* the rent was received, and what the real intention of both parties was?"
[72] [1952] 1 T.L.R. 1386 at p. 1389.
[73] See also *Hess* v. *Gitliss* [1951] E.G.D. 154; *Calladine* v. *Webster* [1951] E.G.D. 300.

grantor where there is evidence of an attempt deliberately to evade legislative provisions, must be set the fact that the very circumstance that a licence falls outside most of the legislative protection conferred on tenants[74] is some ground for arguing that the grantor did not intend to grant a tenancy in the first place.[75] Despite occasional twinges of judicial conscience about the grave social consequences of permitting landowners, by careful and explicit drafting, to escape the provisions of legislation designed to protect tenants,[76] changes in approach were slow in coming. In *Marcroft Wagons Ltd.* v. *Smith*[77] in 1951, Denning L.J. said:[78]

> "It must be remembered that at common law the landlords would have had a clear, indisputable right to turn the [occupant] out; and, even if they did allow her to stay on and accepted rent from her, the consequences would not be serious because the landlords could always get rid of her by giving her a week's notice to quit. In that state of affairs, it was very proper to infer a tenancy at will, or a weekly tenancy, as the case may be, from the acceptance of rent. But it is very different when the rights of landlords are obscured by the Rent Restriction Acts. Seeing that the house was within the Acts, the landlords had no clear right to turn the defendant out. They could not have done so except by proving to the county court that she was not protected by the Acts. And the consequences of granting her a contractual tenancy would be very far-reaching, because she would then be clothed with the valuable status or irremovability conferred by the Rent Acts.... In these circumstances, it is no longer proper for the courts to infer a tenancy at will, or a weekly tenancy, as they would previously have done from the mere acceptance of rent.... If the acceptance of rent can be explained on some other footing than that a contractual tenancy existed ... then a new tenancy should not be inferred."

Similar judicial approaches have been displayed with regard to arrangements held to fall outside the protection given to business tenants by the Landlord and Tenant Act 1954, Pt. II,[79] and echoes of an almost innate reluctance to find against a grantor who had made it

---

[74] Residential licensees now have protection against eviction without a court order: Protection from Eviction Act 1977, s.2A, and in the public sector licensees who, but for the fact that they occupy under a licence, would have been secure tenants, are entitled to the same rights and protections as secure tenants: Housing Act 1985, s.79(3).

[75] *Hyde* v. *Littlefield* [1949] E.G.D. 116.

[76] *e.g. Samrose Properties Ltd.* v. *Gibbard* [1958] 1 W.L.R. 235.

[77] [1951] 2 K.B. 496.

[78] *Ibid* pp. 505–506. Denning L.J.'s views in this regard were reiterated as late as 1979: see *Longrigg, Burrough & Trounson* v. *Smith* (1979) 251 E.G. 847.

[79] *Shell-Mex and B.P. Ltd.* v. *Manchester Garages Ltd.* [1971] 1 W.L.R. 612; *Matchams Park (Holdings)* v. *Dommett* (1984) 272 E.G. 549.

obvious to the grantee that his intention was to avoid the operation of protective legislation are found in the cases throughout the last thirty years.[80]

D. Intention and the Sham Transaction

As explained in the next chapter, certain formalities are required to create a lease of more than three years' duration. If the tenancy is to be for not longer than three years and takes effect in possession there is no need for a deed or any form of writing if the rent is the best that can be obtained without taking a premium.[81] However, where statutory formal requirements for the creation of a lease are not complied with, it does not follow that a licence is created, for the law frequently treats a purported lease that does not fulfil the formal requirements as an agreement for a lease which, being specifically enforceable, is nevertheless still a lease, in equity.[82] Thus, there are circumstances in which a term of years absolute can be created orally or in writing, without the need for a deed.

If the agreement is oral, its terms will, in the event of a dispute, have to be proved as questions of fact.[83] Once these terms are ascertained, then it will be a "question . . . of construction . . . whether the rights of the occupier are those of a tenant or a licensee."[84] Precisely the same considerations apply where the agreement is written, save that the terms will not need to be proved since the agreement itself can be produced. A written agreement will normally be conclusive[85] evidence of what is intended by the parties. Assuming there is no dispute as to whether or not the document accurately represents the intentions of the parties, then the question of whether or not it amounts to a tenancy or a licence is one of construction of the document.[86] If the essentials of a tenancy are found in the document[87] then, in the absence of the special circumstances explained below,[88] the document

---

[80] *Appah* v. *Parncliffe Investments Ltd.* [1964] 1 W.L.R. 1064; *Abbeyfield (Harpenden) Society Ltd.* v. *Woods* [1968] 1 W.L.R. 374; *Luganda* v. *Service Hotels Ltd.* [1969] 2 Ch. 209; *Barnes* v. *Barratt* [1970] 2 Q.B. 657; *Horford Investments Ltd.* v. *Lambert* [1976] Ch. 39; *R.* v. *South Middlesex Rent Tribunal, ex p. Beswick* (1976) 32 P. & C.R. 67; *Marchant* v. *Charters* [1977] 1 W.L.R. 1181; *Walsh* v. *Griffiths-Jones* [1978] 2 All E.R. 1002; *Somma* v. *Hazelhurst* [1978] 2 All E.R. 1011, *per* Cumming-Bruce L.J. at p. 1018–1020; *Aldrington Garages* v. *Fielder* (1978) 37 P. & C.R. 461; *Sturolson & Co.* v. *Weniz* (1984) 272 E.G. 326 (these last three cases being overruled by *Street* v. *Mountford* [1985] 2 All E.R. 289).

[81] L.P.A. 1925, s.54(2).

[82] See *post*, Chap. 3(V) E.

[83] *Torbett* v. *Faulkener* [1952] 2 T.L.R. 659, *per* Romer L.J. at p. 661.

[84] *Ibid.*

[85] For rectification see *post*, Chap. 3(VI).

[86] *Street* v. *Mountford* [1985] 2 All E.R. 289, *per* Lord Templeman at p. 300.

[87] A lessor and a lessee, ascertained or ascertainable subject-matter, which must be land, buildings or parts of buildings, a reversion, a certain term and exclusive possession and an intention to be legally bound.

[88] See *post*, Chap. 2(II) F.

will be construed as creating a lease and not a licence.[89] If there is no written agreement then, in similar fashion and regardless of how the parties refer to it, it is the facts of what has been agreed which must be so construed.

However, in construing the agreement the court "must look not so much at the words as the substance of the agreement."[90] The relationship of the parties "is determined by the law and not by the label which they choose to put on it,"[91] so that "parties cannot turn a tenancy into a licence merely by calling it one."[92] Thus, especially where the finding that a licence was intended rather than a lease would enable the grantor to avoid protective legislation, such as the Rent Act 1977, the courts have, particularly in recent years, been prepared to apply the doctrine of sham transactions, finding that the real intention of the parties was not the declared intention acquiesced in by the grantee. In effect, therefore, where the parties have attached a "false label"[93] to their transaction, the court can scrutinise any arrangements and determine what they are in substance, regardless of the appearance created by the language used in the agreement.[94]

Most of the cases on sham licences have involved what are called non—exclusive occupation agreements. The object of such devices from the grantor's standpoint is to prevent the occupant securing the exclusive use essential to establish exclusive possession and thus a tenancy. Normally there will be several contemporaneous grants, to different people, perhaps a cohabiting couple or a group of students, each of whom will, under the agreement, obtain merely a right to use and share the premises in common with such other persons as the grantor may allow. They will not be granted, either individually or collectively, exclusive use of any particular part of the premises. The grantor will further reserve the right to nominate replacement occupiers should any of the original group leave[95] and he will usually also reserve the right to come and share the premises himself.

In *Demuren* v. *Seal Estates*[96] there were two occupiers of a flat occupying under non-exclusive occupation agreements which purported to be licences determinable on a week's notice by the landlord

---

[89] *Street* v. *Mountford* [1985] 2 All E.R. 289; *Eastleigh Borough Council* v. *Walsh* [1985] 2 All E.R. 112.

[90] *Smith* v. *St. Michael, Cambridge Overseers* (1860) 3 E. & E. 383 at p. 390.

[91] *Facchini* v. *Bryson* [1952] 1 T.L.R. 1386, *per* Denning L.J. at p. 1390.

[92] *Errington* v. *Errington and Woods* [1952] 1 K.B. 290, *per* Denning L.J. at p. 298.

[93] *R.* v. *Rent Officer for London Borough of Camden, ex p. Plant* (1981) 257 E.G. 713.

[94] *Snook* v. *London and West Riding Investments Ltd.* [1967] 2 Q.B. 786; *Walsh* v. *Griffiths-Jones* [1978] 2 All E.R. 1002; *Buchman* v. *May* [1978] 2 All E.R. 993; *Demuren* v. *Seal Estates* (1978) 249 E.G. 440; *O'Malley* v. *Seymour* (1978) 250 E.G. 1083; *McHale* v. *Daneham* (1979) 249 E.G. 969. *cf. Somma* v. *Hazelhurst* [1978] 1 W.L.R. 1014, overruled by *Street* v. *Mountford* [1985] 2 All E.R. 289. For the evidential rules to be observed in such cases see Arden & Partington, *Housing Law*, pp. 55–56.

[95] Thus attempting to prevent the occupiers, jointly, having complete control over the use of the premises.

[96] (1978) 249 E.G. 440.

and, if not determined, to last for a year. Both occupants were to be liable only for their respective shares of the rent, and a year's rent was taken from each of them in a number of post-dated cheques. The county court judge found that the two occupants were together in exclusive possession of the flat. He concluded that they were joint tenants and entitled to the protection of the Rent Act 1977. The Court of Appeal agreed, observing that while a joint tenancy with each of the joint tenants liable for only one half of the rent could create a logical inconsistency, it did not rule out a joint tenancy in this case since, in fact, the landlord had already secured the whole of the year's rent from the occupants. There was, therefore, a contemporaneous oral agreement for a joint tenancy, against which the written licence agreements should be regarded as shams.

In *O'Malley* v. *Seymour*[97] a non-exclusive occupation agreement had been entered into for a flat by a single occupant. The Court of Appeal held that the so-called licence agreement was a sham and that there had been a prior oral agreement for a tenancy inconsistent with the so-called licence agreement. Although the *written* agreement contemplated sharing the premises with others, the landlord did not, *in fact*, contemplate requiring the respondent to share with anyone else at all.

It now seems that an express finding of sham may well be unnecessary in a future case arising on facts similar to those in *O'Malley* v. *Seymour*.[98] In *Street* v. *Mountford*[99] the owner of a flat granted to the occupier under what purported to be a licence agreement, the right to occupy two rooms at a weekly "licence fee" of £37 per week and subject to 14 days' notice of termination. The grantee also understood and accepted that "this personal licence is not assignable" and that "a licence in the above form does not and is not intended to give me a tenancy protected under the Rent Acts." It was conceded that the occupier had exclusive possession but the landlord nevertheless sought a declaration, in the face of the grantee's application to have a fair rent registered for the rooms, that the grantee occupied under a licence and not a tenancy. The county court judge held that the appellant was a tenant entitled to Rent Act protection, but the Court of Appeal[1] held that she was a licensee since, despite the fact of exclusive possession, the agreement bore all the hallmarks of a licence and the parties had in fact only intended, as the contract openly and clearly expressed, to create a licence. A unanimous House of Lords restored the decision of the county court judge, holding that, with the exception of a limited range of special categories, such as lodging contracts and service occupancies, the sole

[97] (1978) 250 E.G. 1083.
[98] *Ibid.*
[99] [1985] 2 All E.R. 289.
[1] (1984) 271 E.G. 1261.

test was whether the agreement granted the occupier exclusive possession. If it did (and such was conceded by the landlord in the instant case), then that was the end of the matter, and the intention of the parties, as evidenced by the agreement (or, indeed, any other factors falling short of the special circumstances previously referred to) that a licence only was to be created, or that the agreement was not to be subject to the Rent Acts, was irrelevant. In the colourful, if somewhat agricultural, metaphor of Lord Templeman: "If the agreement satisfied all the requirements of a tenancy, then the agreement produced a tenancy and the parties cannot alter the effect of the agreement by insisting that they only created a licence. The manufacture of a five-pronged implement for manual digging results in a fork even if the manufacturer, unfamiliar with the English language, insists that he intended to make and has made a spade."

However, a more difficult case arises where the non-exclusive occupation agreement involves more than one occupant. If the device of a sham is not to be used by the court, then it becomes less easy to find a lease rather than a licence in such cases. In *Somma* v. *Hazelhurst*[2] a single room was let under two separate agreements to a man and a woman living together. The landlady retained the right to share the premises with them, and to nominate replacement occupiers should one of them leave. The Court of Appeal found that the written agreement was not a sham and did not offend public policy. The court refused to treat the occupants as joint tenants, and found that the liability to share the room with the landlady, and other persons nominated by her, prevented either occupant from obtaining a right to exclusive occupation of the room. In *Street* v. *Mountford*[3] the House of Lords held this case to be wrongly decided. Whatever the agreement in form provided, it was clearly the case in fact that the landlady would not exercise her right to live in the room herself or nominate another occupier to share with either of the grantees, should one leave. In actuality, therefore, the grantees enjoyed exclusive possession and, since the arrangement was not in one of the special categories where a licence with exclusive occupation may be created, the agreement should have been regarded as creating a joint tenancy.

Although Lord Templeman accuses the Court of Appeal of being "diverted" by the terms of the non-exclusive occupation agreement,[4] it is submitted that the real difference between the Court of Appeal in *Somma* v. *Hazelhurst*[5] and the House of Lords in *Street* v. *Mountford*[6] lies in the fact that the former tribunal seemed to regard the test of exclusive possession as one of law, *i.e.* did the "real" agreement

[2] [1978] 1 W.L.R. 1014.
[3] [1985] 2 All E.R. 289.
[4] *Ibid.* p. 299.
[5] [1978] 1 W.L.R. 1014.
[6] [1985] 2 All E.R. 289.

between the parties, and not the sham one, confer on the grantee or grantees the legal right to exclude all other persons from the premises? Clearly, once it is held that a written agreement which confers a right to share a room with another occupier (who has received a like right under a separate agreement), the landlady retaining the right to choose a new occupier should one of the couple leave, is not a sham, it is impossible to find a tenancy. The grant of a licence is the only conclusion, if one takes the view that it is exclusive possession *in law* that determines the matter. However, if the real issue is whether the occupants enjoy exclusive possession *in fact*, regardless of what the agreement, real or sham, says on the matter, which appears to be the view taken by the House of Lords in *Street* v. *Mountford*[7], and one further takes the view that it is only in exceptional, defined and specialised classes of case that such exclusive possession will not be decisive in favour of a lease, then there will be very few so-called "licence agreements," let alone non-exclusive occupation agreements, that will henceforth avoid being classified as leases.

One difficulty that may still remain, however, is where there is more than one grantee and each grantee receives his grant under a non-exclusive occupation agreement made on a different day. Although separate liability for a proportion only of the total rental outgoings on the premises is no longer fatal to a joint tenancy,[8] the absence of one of the four unities surely is. Occupants whose interests in the premises commence at different times and run for different terms cannot be regarded as joint tenants. If the written agreements are a sham, and there was, in fact, a prior oral agreement under which all the occupants were granted their interests from the same date and for the same periods, then the fact of exclusive possession will presumably, in the normal case, make them joint tenants. However, if the consecutive written agreements are genuine, and the court refuses to find a sham then, even though the occupants collectively might in fact, but not as of right, enjoy exclusive possession, it is hard to see how they can be tenants, joint or otherwise, *Street* v. *Mountford*[9] notwithstanding.

E. Intention to Enter into Legal Relations

It may well be asked, in the light of the decision in *Street* v. *Mountford*[10], what is the fate of those cases, discussed earlier in this

[7] *Ibid.*

[8] *Demuren* v. *Seal Estates* (1978) 249 E.G. 440; *cf. Somma* v. *Hazelhurst* [1978] 1 W.L.R. 1014.

[9] [1985] 2 All E.R. 289. *Quaere* the possibility of the occupiers being tenants in common, the only indispensable unity being unity of possession, which these occupiers could have. They may be regarded as enjoying their interests in "undivided shares," with exclusive possession as against the landlord. That their interests must be equitable would not seem to affect this argument, though it may well create "conveyancing difficulties."

[10] *Ibid.*

chapter, which appear to suggest that whether or not a lease or a licence has been created is largely a matter of intention,[11] given, of course, that the grantee has exclusive possession. They have not been overruled by the House of Lords, but they have been explained in a way that is somewhat different from the interpretation formerly put upon them. Instead of being treated as cases in which the parties had expressed a real and genuine intention to create a licence rather than a lease, notwithstanding the granting of exclusive possession, they are now to be regarded as cases in which the court was merely seeking to ascertain whether the parties intended to be legally bound at all, *i.e.* whether they intended to create legal relations.[12] If they did not, then clearly no lease could have been granted, though presumably a gratuitous licence could still have been given.

There is considerable difficulty with this interpretation of the earlier cases, and it must be doubted whether this is really what the judges in those earlier cases meant when they referred to "the parties' intentions." The major difficulty is that, if there is no intention to create legal relations in some of those cases, then not only is there no lease, but there can be no contractual basis for any licence either. However, it can hardly be doubted that the Court of Appeal in *Errington* v. *Errington & Woods,* [13] for example, held that the licensees in that case had a contractual right to remain in possession so long as they paid the mortgage instalments. Similarly, in *Marcroft Wagons Ltd.* v. *Smith*[14] Denning L.J. said[15]: "In such cases I think that the landlord can give such a person permission to occupy and receive a weekly payment from him without necessarily creating a tenancy." Roxburgh J. said:[16] " ... the plaintiffs intended the defendant to remain for the time being in occupation of the premises for a consideration, but without becoming a tenant." The inference clearly is that the relationship was contractual, the consideration being the weekly payments, but that there was no intention to enter into the relationship of landlord and tenant. Again, in *Isaac* v. *Hotel de Paris Ltd.*[17] there appears to be no doubt in the minds of the members of the Privy Council that the owner of the hotel was entitled to the "rent" paid and payable by the occupier, even though he was held to be merely a licensee. Again, the inference is that the arrangement had a contractual basis. It was not so much a question of no intention to enter into legal relations, as no intention on the part of the grantor to

[11] *Marcroft Wagons Ltd.* v. *Smith* [1951] 2 K.B. 496; *Gorham (Contractors) Ltd.* v. *Field* [1952] C.P.L. 266; *Isaac* v. *Hotel de Paris Ltd.* [1960] 1 W.L.R. 239; *Cobb* v. *Lane* [1952] 1 All E.R. 1199; *Errington* v. *Errington & Woods* [1952] 1 K.B. 290; *Booker* v. *Palmer* [1942] 2 All E.R. 674; *Heslop* v. *Burns* [1974] 1 W.L.R. 1241.
[12] *Street* v. *Mountford* [1985] 2 All E.R. 289, *per* Lord Templeman at pp. 294–298.
[13] [1952] 1 K.B. 290.
[14] [1951] 2 K.B. 496.
[15] *Ibid.* p. 507.
[16] *Ibid.* p. 508.
[17] [1960] 1 W.L.R. 239.

accept the grantee as a tenant—a matter of which the grantee was fully aware. The other cases cited by Lord Templeman, in support of his suggestion that the question of intention really goes to the issue of legal relations rather than to the question of whether a lease or a licence was intended, are all cases in which the grantors were, as acts of charity or friendliness, allowing the grantees to live in residential accommodation rent free.[18] In these cases it may well be true, given the non-commercial flavour of the transactions, that there was no intention shown by the parties to enter into legal relations and it is, in any event, rather more difficult here to find consideration to support a contractual licence. But these charitable or domestic arrangements are rather different and it does seem, therefore, that the House of Lords were laying down new law, or rather reverting to very old law, in deciding that in many cases, even where the arrangement is purely commercial and an "occupation payment" has been agreed, intention is only relevant to determine whether or not the parties intended legal consequences to flow from their arrangement. The consequence of this is that, once such an intention is manifested then, if the grantee obtains exclusive possession, he will be a tenant and further attempted refinements of that intention, even when openly expressed and agreed to with no element of sham, will, it seems, now be irrelevant. While this will certainly prevent many of the abuses designed to avoid Rent Act protection it may well, as was adverted to earlier, cause difficulties in relation to business lettings and certainly does not square with the normal rules governing intention in other areas of contract law.[19]

F. The Special Factors

In *Street* v. *Mountford*[20] Lord Templeman said:[21]

> "Exclusive possession is of first importance in considering whether an occupier is a tenant; exclusive possession is not decisive because an occupier who enjoys exclusive possession is not necessarily a tenant. The occupier may be a lodger or service occupier or fall within the other exceptional categories mentioned by Denning L.J. in *Errington* v. *Errington*."

Denning L.J. in *Facchini* v. *Bryson*[22] said[23] that "in all cases where an

---

[18] *Booker* v. *Palmer* [1942] 2 All E.R. 674; *Cobb* v. *Lane* [1952] 1 All E.R. 1199; *Heslop* v. *Burns* [1974] 1 W.L.R. 1241.
[19] See *Rearden-Smith Line Ltd.* v. *Hansen-Tangen* [1976] 1 W.L.R. 989, and the cases cited therein.
[20] [1985] 2 All E.R. 289.
[21] *Ibid.* p. 297.
[22] [1952] 1 T.L.R. 1386.
[23] *Ibid.* p. 1389.

occupier has been held to be a licensee there has been something in the circumstances, such as a family arrangement, an act of friendship or generosity, or such like, to negative any intention to create a tenancy." What, then, are these special factors or circumstances surrounding the grant of a right of occupation, even sometimes with exclusive possession, that, in themselves, operate against the normal inference of tenancy?

(1) *Service Occupancy*

One of the most common examples of exclusive use and occupation which is nevertheless inconsistent with the existence of a tenancy is the service occupancy, which is invariably treated as a licence and not a lease.[24] The most common explanation for this is that the occupant was entitled to occupy the premises for the purpose of performing his employer's work, rather than for his own individual benefit. Generally an employee who is allowed to occupy premises belonging to his employer for the more convenient performance of his duties, is not a lessee, even if he is also allowed to use the premises for carrying on his own independent business as well.[25] Where an employee occupies his employee's premises, as part-remuneration for his services, the question will often be whether the occupation is subservient and necessary to the employment: if it is, the occupation may be considered to be, vicariously, that of the employer; if it is not, the occupation will probably be that of the tenant.[26] To justify the inference of a licence and not a tenancy the employee must be *required* to occupy in performance of his contract of employment.[27] However, "required" in this context means that the residence must be ancillary and necessary to the performance of the employee's duties, and not merely required as an arbitrary regulation on the part of the employer.[28] Strong considerations of convenience are often as effective for this purpose as actual necessity, so that the test would seem to be whether it is either necessary to live in the premises in question to carry out the duties of the job or whether residence is so required by the employment contract for the better performance of

---

[24] Special provisions apply to service tenants and service occupiers employed in agriculture and forestry. They are explained *post*, Chap. 14(II).

[25] *White* v. *Bayley* (1861) 10 C.B.(N.S.) 227. See also *R.* v. *Stock* (1810) 2 Taun. 339; employee occupying cottage rent-free, with less wages on that account, not considered a tenant. Also: *Mayhew* v. *Suttle* (1854) 4 E. & B. 347; *R.* v. *Shipdam* (1823) 3 D. & R. 384; *R.* v. *Cheshunt* (1818) 1 B. & A. 473; *Bertie* v. *Beaumont* (1812) 16 Ea. 33.

[26] *R.* v. *Spurrell* (1865) L.R. 1 Q.B. 72.

[27] *Hughes* v. *Chatham Overseers* (1843) 5 Man. & G. 54. It is not sufficient that, as a term of his contract, the employee is required to leave the house at the termination of employment: *Royal Philanthropic Society* v. *County, The Times*, November 9, 1985.

[28] *Smith* v. *Seghill Overseers* (1875) L.R. 10 Q.B. 422. See also *Dobson* v. *Jones* (1844) 5 Man. & G. 112.

those duties and not merely as an arbitrary whim[29] or as an additional means of controlling the employee.[30]

In *Thompsons (Funeral Furnishers)* v. *Phillips* [31] a chauffeur was required to live at certain premises and to be present there to take instructions, for which he was to receive 15s. less each week in wages. He was held to occupy as an employee licensee and not as a tenant, notwithstanding his exclusive occupation of this living accommodation, and that actually he was paid his wages in full and he paid back 15s. each week which was entered in a rent book. The acceptance of two further payments of 15s after his employment ceased and he had been required to go, was held not to be evidence of any intention to create a tenancy from that time. The need for residence in the house, therefore, must arise out of the nature of the employee's duties, and the employee must have exclusive occupation of the premises for the purpose of performing more conveniently his employment obligations on those premises, rather than occupying for his own purposes.[32]

(2) *Lodging*

A lodger, who does not have exclusive possession of his room, has only a licence to live in the house. An occupier of apartments cannot be a tenant unless he has exclusive possession of them.[33] Whether or not an occupier is merely a lodger, or whether rooms have been let to him in such a way as to create a tenancy will be dependent upon the circumstances of each case, but if the landlord retains general control of a house, with a right to interfere with the occupier's use of it as he thinks fit, the person who occupies part of that house would seem to be a lodger.[34] The presumption will be that an occupier is a lodger, in the absence of further evidence to the contrary, where the landlord also resides in the house and allows the occupier to live in some of the rooms, though the issue of whether the landlord intended to abandon control of those rooms is, ultimately, one of fact.[35] In *Helman* v. *Horsham & Worthing Assessment Committee*[36] the court appears to be

---

[29] See *Gray* v. *Holmes* (1949) 30 T.C. 467.
[30] *Ford* v. *Langford* [1949] L.J.R. 586; *Fox* v. *Dalby* (1874) L.R. 10 C.P. 285; *Glasgow Corporation* v. *Johnstone* [1965] A.C. 609; *Hirst* v. *Sargant* (1967) 65 L.G.R. 127; *Northern Ireland Commissioner of Valuation* v. *Fermanagh Protestant Board of Education* [1969] 1 W.L.R. 1708; *Chapman* v. *Chapman* (1978) 128 New L.J. 611. *cf. Scrimgeour* v. *Waller* (1981) 257 E.G. 61.
[31] [1945] 2 All E.R. 49; see also *Hunt* v. *Colson* (1833) 3 Moo. & S. 790; *cf. Reed* v. *Cattermole* [1937] 1 K.B. 613, *per* Lord Wright at pp. 618, 619.
[32] See *Dover* v. *Prosser* [1904] 1 K.B. 84.
[33] *Cook* v. *Humber* (1861) 11 C.B.(N.S.) 33, 43; *Street* v. *Mountford* [1985] 2 All E.R. 289.
[34] *Bradley* v. *Baylis* (1881) 8 Q.B.D. 195.
[35] *Helman* v. *Horsham & Worthing Assessment Committee* [1949] 2 K.B. 335; *Douglas* v. *Smith* [1907] 2 K.B. 568. See also *Abbeyfield (Harpenden) Society* v. *Woods* [1968] 1 W.L.R. 374.
[36] [1949] 2 K.B. 335.

of the view that it is possible for an occupier to be a lodger for rating purposes while being a tenant for the purposes of the Rent Acts.

In *Appah* v. *Parncliffe Investments*[37] a building was divided into individual, lockable rooms. The management undertook responsibility for cleaning, bed-making and laundry, and also emptied the gas meters. Occupiers were not allowed to take in unauthorised guests, and visitors were required to leave by 10.30 p.m. The Court of Appeal held that an occupier of one of the rooms who had been offered a choice of a daily or a weekly rate and who chose the weekly rate, but who could leave at any time on any day so long as the payments were not in arrears, was not a tenant but a licensee lodger. In *Abbeyfield (Harpenden) Society* v. *Woods*, [38] although a resident of an old people's home had exclusive possession of his bed-sitting room, the arrangement as a whole was so personal in nature as to show that the occupier was intended to be a licensee only. Similarly, in *Barnes* v. *Barratt*[39] a married couple, who were given exclusive occupation of three rooms and a kitchen in part of a house in return for paying fuel bills for the whole house and undertaking cleaning and cooking duties for the grantor, were held to be licensees and not tenants of part of the property, since none of the other normal incidents of a tenancy, such as a fixed rent, a fixed or periodic term and an assignable interest, was present.

In *Marchant* v. *Charters*[40] the plaintiff grantor owned a house split up into seven bed-sitting rooms, each of which was let off individually, sparsely furnished and provided with a sink, hot and cold water, a gas ring, grill, cooking utensils, crockery and cutlery. A resident housekeeper cleaned the rooms daily and provided clean linen weekly. All occupants shared bathroom and lavatory. The defendant had made a successful application to the rent officer under the Rent Act 1968 (now 1977) to fix a fair rent. The rent officer could only do this if the occupant had a tenancy of his room and not a mere licence. The plaintiff sought a court order evicting the defendant and would succeed if the occupant was a mere licensee and not a Rent Act protected tenant. The Court of Appeal took the view that the defendant was simply a licensee lodger. Lord Denning M.R. said:[41]

> "What is the test to see whether the occupier of one room in a house is a tenant or a licensee? It does not depend on whether he or she has exclusive possession or not. . . . It does not depend on whether the occupation is permanent or temporary. it does not depend on the label which the parties put on it. All these are

[37] [1964] 1 W.L.R. 1064.

[38] [1968] 1 W.L.R. 374.

[39] [1970] 2 Q.B. 657.

[40] [1977] 1 W.L.R. 1181; *cf. Guppys (Bridport)* v. *Brookling* (1984) 269 E.G. 846 at p. 942.

[41] *Ibid.* p. 1185

factors which may influence the decision but none of them is conclusive. All the circumstances have to be worked out. Eventually the answer depends on the nature and quality of the occupany. Was it intended that the occupier should have a stake in the room or did he have only permission for himself personally to occupy the room, whether under a contract or not, in which case he is a licensee?"

In *Street* v. *Mountford*[42] Lord Templeman added the following gloss on Lord Denning M.R.'s *dictum*:[43] " . . . in order to ascertain the nature and quality of the occupancy and to see whether the occupier has or has not a stake in the room or only permission for himself personally to occupy, the court must decide whether on its true construction the agreement confers on the occupier exclusive possession," though elsewhere in his speech he did appear to suggest that a lodger, who might nevertheless obtain exclusive enjoyment of his room, could constitute a general exception to the conclusiveness of exclusive possession as a mark of a tenancy. In doing so he quoted with approval the definition of a lodger provided by Blackburn J. in *Allan* v. *Liverpool Overseers*:[44]

"A lodger in a house, although he has the exclusive use of rooms in the house, in the sense that nobody else is to be there, and though his goods are stored there, yet he is not in exclusive occupation in that sense, because the landlord is there for the purpose of being able, as landlords commonly do in the case of lodgings, to have his own servants to look after the house and the furniture, and has retained to himself the occupation, though he has agreed to give the exclusive enjoyment of the occupation to the lodger."

Lord Templeman summed the matter up thus:[45]

"An occupier of residential accommodation at a rent for a term is either a lodger or a tenant. The occupier is a lodger if the landlord provides attendance or services which require the landlord or his servants to exercise unrestricted access to and use of the premises. A lodger is entitled to live in the premises but cannot call the place his own."

A court may also be influenced, in arriving at its view of the occupier's status, by whether or not at the time of the transaction the occupier

---

[42] [1985] 2 All E.R. 289.
[43] *Ibid.* p. 293.
[44] (1874) L.R. 9 Q.B. 180 at pp. 191–192.
[45] *Street* v. *Mountford* [1985] 2 All E.R. 289 at p. 293.

already had possession of the premises. As Megarry has observed:[46] "The inferences to be drawn where the transaction gives *de novo* the right of exclusive possession are prima facie very different from those to be drawn where the occupant had, *e.g.* lived on the premises with a previous tenant for many years and has an arguable right to remain." In the former case a tenancy will normally arise whereas in the latter case it is less difficult to infer a licence,[47] although if the occupier pays rent, the longer the relationship continues "the more likely it is that the court will infer that a new tenancy has been in fact created."[48]

(3) *Other Factors*[49]

Sometimes it may appear from the surrounding circumstances that the right to exclusive possession is referable to a legal relationship other than a tenancy, such as office holding, a family arrangement, or an act of friendship or generosity.[50] Thus, the courts have held licences to exist where a father permitted his son to occupy a house in return for paying the building society instalments[51]; where a sister purchased a house for her brother to occupy free of payment[52]; where tenants who were temporarily absent from a house left friends in occupation, even though the friends made regular payments for their accommodation and, in fact, enjoyed exclusive possession[53]; where the flat in question had direct access to premises upon which the former employers of the occupier carried on confidential work[54]; where a charitable society had converted a big house into an old people's home with 12 rooms, with a resident housekeeper and common dining room[55]; and where an owner of a cottage agreed to allow a friend to install an evacuee in the cottage rent free for the duration of the war.[56]

Other factors might also counter the normally conclusive force of exclusive occupation. The physical situation of the premises might indicate that only a licence was intended, *e.g.* a kiosk in an hotel or a

[46] Megarry, *The Rent Acts* (10th ed.), Vol. 1, p. 59.
[47] *Marcroft Wagons Ltd.* v. *Smith* [1951] 2 K.B. 496 at pp. 504, 507, *per* Evershed M.R. and Denning L.J. respectively.
[48] *Ibid.* p. 507, *per* Denning L.J.
[49] For an extensive list see Megarry, *The Rent Acts* (10th ed.), Vol. 1, pp. 58–59.
[50] *Street* v. *Mountford* [1985] 2 All E.R. 289 at p. 295.
[51] *Errington* v. *Errington and Woods* [1952] 1 K.B. 290.
[52] *Cobb* v. *Lane* [1952] 1 All E.R. 1199.
[53] *E. Moss Ltd.* v. *Brown* [1946] 2 All E.R. 557.
[54] *Murray Bull & Co. Ltd.* v. *Murray* [1953] 1 Q.B. 211, described by Megarry, *op.cit.* p. 59, n. 32 as "a strong decision," and regarded as wrongly decided by the House of Lords in *Street* v. *Mountford* [1985] 2 All E.R. 289, *per* Lord Templeman at p. 296.
[55] *Abbeyfield (Harpenden) Society Ltd.* v. *Woods* [1968] 1 W.L.R. 374.
[56] *Booker* v. *Palmer* [1942] 2 All E.R. 674.

theatre foyer.[57] The arrangement may be so obviously temporary that, notwithstanding exclusive occupation, it can be explained only on the basis that the parties intended a licence, *e.g.* where a charity is offered a shop in the high street "between tenants," or an organisation hires a large hall to put on a trade exhibition.[58]

The factors at work were neatly illustrated in *Shell-Mex and B.P. Ltd.* v., *Manchester Garages Ltd.*[59] A filling station was owned by the plaintiffs and the defendants were given occupation under a document called "a licence." The agreement specified that it was solely for the purpose of selling the plaintiffs' brand of fuel oil, was to last for one year, and required the defendants to "use every endeavour and due diligence to sell and foster the sale" of the plaintiffs' products. The defendants also promised, in the agreement, not to interfere with the plaintiffs' employees "in the exercise by them of the [plaintiffs'] rights of possession and control of the premises" and to give them reasonable assistance and facilities "for the alteration at any time of the layout, decoration and equipment of the premises." The plaintiffs asked the defendants to leave when the agreement expired but the defendants refused, claiming that they were tenants of business premises entitled to the protection of the Landlord and Tenant Act 1954, Pt. II. The Court of Appeal disagreed, holding that, even though the fact that the parties had called their agreement a licence was not conclusive, there were other factors that indicated a licence agreement rather than a lease. These were first, that the agreement provided for the retention of possession and control of the premises by the plaintiffs which was inconsistent with the granting of a tenancy; secondly, the agreement was essentially personal, in that its purpose was the promotion and sale of the plaintiffs' products, which was dependent upon the personal capabilities of the defendants; it was thus not assignable and a characteristic of a lease is that it can be assigned.[60]

G. Uncertainty as to Grant of Exclusive Possession

If a grantor grants a right to occupy land or premises to another, and there is real uncertainty whether the parties intended a lease or a licence, the court may often scrutinise the terms of the agreement to certain whether they can, taken together, be regarded as "badges of

[57] *Warr & Co. Ltd.* v. *L.C.C.* [1904] 1 K.B. 713; *Isaac* v. *Hotel de Paris* [1960] 1 W.L.R. 239; *Clore* v. *Theatrical Properties Ltd.* [1936] 3 All E.R. 483.
[58] *Rendell* v. *Roman* (1893) 9 T.L.R. 192.
[59] [1971] 1 W.L.R. 612. See also *Matchams Park (Holdings)* v. *Dommett* (1984) 272 E.G. 549.
[60] See also *Barnes* v. *Barratt* [1970] 2 Q.B. 657, *per* Sachs L.J. at p. 661. But the power to assign may be excluded or qualified by the express covenant in the lease: see *post*, Chap. 7.

a tenancy"[61] such as to lead to the inference that the landlord intended to grant a lease. The most obvious "badge" is the right of the grantee to exclusive occupation. This matter has already been discussed earlier in this chapter. However, it may be unclear whether or not exclusive occupation has been granted until other factors have been analysed. Another such badge is the payment of rent. An agreement for payment of money in return for the right to occupy property *prima facie* indicates a tenancy,[62] although it is not conclusive,[63] even where the payments are termed "rent."[64] The occupier may be a licensee whether the payments are merely the amount of the outgoings[65] or a fixed sum.[66] However, the provision of a rent book is some indication that a tenancy was intended, especially when the parties make use of statutory machinery applicable to tenancies to fix the rent.[67] However, if services or other value in money's worth are rendered by the occupier in return for the grant, the conclusion of tenancy is not so easily drawn. It is well settled that services can constitute rent at common law, but where it is not clear from other evidence that the parties intended a tenancy, the court will not infer one, and certainly not a tenancy falling within the Rent Acts, from the fact of payment in anything other than money.[68]

Perhaps the best summary of the relevance of the terms of the agreement to the establishment of lease is to be found in the decision of the Court of Appeal in *Addiscombe Garden Estates* v. *Crabbe*.[69] A tennis club occupied the club house and tennis courts under an agreement, which purported to be a "licence," for a period of two years. At the end of this period, the club refused to vacate the premises, claiming statutory security of tenure under the Landlord and Tenant Act 1954, Pt. II. This they could only do if they had a lease and not a mere licence. The Court of Appeal held that, notwithstanding the description attached to the arrangement by the parties, it was a lease. The determining factors were contained in the agreement itself, and were clearly set out by Jenkins L.J.[70]:

"Looking at the substance of the matter, what do the grantees get? By clause 1 they are licensed and authorized 'to enter upon use

---

[61] This term is borrowed from Megarry, *The Rent Acts* (10th ed.), Vol. 1, p. 56, and see *Cobb* v. *Lane* [1952] 1 All E.R. 1199, especially at p. 1200.

[62] *E. Moss Ltd.* v. *Brown* [1946] 2 All E.R. 557, *per* Somervell L.J. at p. 554.

[63] *Isaac* v. *Hotel de Paris Ltd.* [1960] 1 W.L.R. 239.

[64] *Ibid.* See also *Marcroft Wagons Ltd.* v. *Smith* [1951] 2 K.B. 496, *per* Denning L.J. at p. 506.

[65] *Loyds (Building Investments) Ltd.* v. *Brown* (1949) 153 E.G. 120.

[66] *E. Moss Ltd.* v. *Brown* [1946] 2 All E.R. 557.

[67] *Calladine* v. *Webster* [1951] E.G.D. 300. *cf. Rice* v. *Mitchman* (1954) 163 E.G. 680; *Thompsons (Funeral Furnishers)* v. *Phillips* [1945] 2 All E.R. 49.

[68] *Hornsby* v. *Maynard* [1925] 1 K.B. 514; *Barnes* v. *Barratt* [1970] 2 Q.B. 657.

[69] [1958] 1 Q.B. 513; see also: *O'Malley* v. *Seymour* (1978) 250 E.G. 1083; *Aldrington Garages* v. *Fielder* (1978) 37 P. & C.R. 461.

[70] [1958] 1 Q.B. 513 at pp. 522 *et seq.*

and enjoy' the items mentioned; and it seems to me that those words, taken together, are apt to give to the tenant something in the nature of an interest in the land. I would next observe that in clause 2 provision is made for the licence, as it is called, extending for the fixed period of two years from May 1 1954. There is thus a term certain which would be appropriate to the grant of a tenancy. Then in clause 3 it is provided that: 'The grantees shall have the use and enjoyment of the premises in consideration' of a payment. The payment is described as a payment of 'court fees'; it is fixed at the sum of £37.10s. per month, and it has to be paid in advance on the first day of each month. In all but name that appears to me to be a rent or reddendum in consideration of the right to 'enter upon, use and enjoy' the premises which is granted by clause 1.

So far, it seems to me that the rights expressed to be conferred on the grantees are, in substance, the rights of a tenant as distinct from the rights of a mere licensee; and, as I have said, there is the correlative obligation of making monthly payments which, although not so called, are in fact, it seems to me, in the nature of rent. Then there are the various agreements by the grantees with the grantors in clause 4, beginning with the agreement to make the monthly payment of the court fees very much like the agreement to pay rent which is always to be found in a tenancy agreement. There is a significant provision in sub-clause (iii) under which the grantees agree 'to repair and maintain the club house'. It seems inappropriate that a mere licensee should be saddled with an obligation to repair. Then one finds as to repairs that the items mentioned are to be maintained 'in good tenantable repair'.... That, one cannot help thinking, to some extent supports the view that the grantees are tenants, although I do not attach very much weight to it.... But, for what it is worth, that is, I think it, if anything, an indication in favour of tenancy rather than licence.

Then under sub-clause (iv) there is the obligation to maintain the tennis courts. In sub-clause (v) there is a provision which, I think, is not without significance. That is the provision under which the grantees shall not 'without the grantors' previously written consent cut down or injure any plants trees bushes or hedges or remove from the said property any soil clay sand or other materials and not make any excavations thereon except for the purpose of maintaining the [tennis courts] in accordance with the agreement and conditions hereinbefore contained.' The significance of that is that it should be thought necessary expressly to prohibit the grantees from doing certain things which, quite plainly, if they were mere licensees, they would have no right or power to do.[71] What business could a licensee have to cut down or injure plants, trees, bushes or hedges, or to do any other of these things, including the removal of 'soil clay sand or other materials'? In a similar sense one may note that provision in sub-clause (vi): 'not to erect any building or other structures upon the said property except such as shall be approved by the grantors.' . . .

The next provision of importance is the agreement to permit 'the grantors and their agents at all reasonable times to enter the said premises to inspect the condition thereof and for all other reasonable purposes'. The importance of that is that it shows that the right to occupy the premises conferred on the grantees was intended as an exclusive right of occupation, in that it was thought necessary to give a special and express power to the grantors to enter. The exclusive character of the occupation granted by a document such as this has always been regarded, if not as a decisive indication, at all events as a very important indication to the effect that a tenancy, as distinct from licence, is the real subject-matter of a document such as this.

In sub-clause (xii) there is provision 'to deliver up the said premises at the termination of this licence in a condition consistent with the foregoing provisions.' 'To deliver up' seems to me to be an expression more appropriate to a tenant with an interest in the land than to a person who has a mere contractual right to be on the land; it is an expression univerally used, I think, in all tenancy agreements and leases. The provision as to insurance points in the same direction; it would, I think, be curious if a mere licensee, with no interest in the premises, was made liable for insurance. Then in clause 5, sub-clause (ii) there is what is practically a common form convenant for quiet enjoyment such as is found in every tenancy agreement or lease; and it seems to me that this clause points strongly in the direction of tenancy agreement here. In clause 6, sub-clause (i), there is the provision: 'that the grantors may re-enter and determine the licence in the event of non-payment of any of the said payments of court fees for fourteen days (whether formally demanded or not) or on breach of any of the grantees' stipulations'. Those references to re-entry and 'non-payment of any of the said payments of court fees for fourteen days (whether formally demanded or not)' are provisions wholly appropriate to a tenancy agreement—and I should have thought that a reference to re-entry was really inappropriate to the case of a licence; the

---

[71] A warning against the indiscriminate use of a common "belt and braces" drafting policy, *i.e.* making express in the agreement that which the law already implies! *cf. O'Malley* v. *Seymour* (1978) 250 E.G. 1083.

conception of re-entry is the resumption of possession by the
landlord, and the determination of the interest of the tenant.

Taking all those considerations together, I am of the opinion
that the judge was perfectly right in holding ... that this was a
tenancy."

The relevance of factors such as these will clearly vary with the
circumstances, and it may not be common in an agreement that calls
itself a licence, to find all these terms present together. However, as
Buckley L.J. observed in *Shell-Mex & B.P. Ltd.* v. *Manchester Garages
Ltd.,*[72] if none of these features is present in the agreement the chances
are that it will be construed by the court as a licence and not a tenancy.

H. The Relevance of Duration

Whilst it is in theory possible to grant a lease for any certain period,
for a week or for 3,000 years—both are equally valid[73]—there is some
indication that the courts tend to treat grants of very short periods as
more likely to have been intended to be licences than leases. So, the
hire of a concert hall for several days for the purposes of public
performances,[74] a permission given to view a race[75] or a cinema
peerformance,[76] and permission to use the front part of a shop at night
for the sale of tickets for a night club carried on in the basement,[77]
were all held to be licences.[78]

In the Irish case, *Boylan* v. *Mayor of Dublin*,[79] a hall was hired for
the evening by the organisers of a charity whist drive. A participant
was injured when a flag-pole fell. The question of liability in
negligence was arguably dependent, in part, upon whether the hall had
been leased to the organisers or merely hired under a licence
agreement. It was conceded that the arrangement was a licence but
nevertheless Black J. felt compelled to observe[80]: "I doubt whether the
shortness of the hiring matters. Can there not be a tenancy for three
days, and if so, why not for three hours?" In the Australian case, *Voli*
v. *Inglewood Shire Council*[81] the plaintiff brought an action for

---

[72] [1971] 1 W.L.R. 612 at p. 618.
[73] A term of less than one year can still be "a term of years absolute": L.P.A. 1925, s.205(1) (xxvii);
but see *Re Land and Premises at Liss, Hants* [1971] Ch. 986, *per* Goulding J. at p. 990: "That
definition ... shows that the legislature considered that the expression 'terms of years' without
explanation would not necessarily include a term of less than a year."
[74] *Taylor* v. *Caldwell* (1863) 3 B. & S. 826.
[75] *Wood* v. *Leadbitter* (1845) 13 M. & W. 838.
[76] *Hurst* v. *Picture Theatres Ltd.* [1915] 1 K.B. 1.
[77] *Jackson* v. *Simons* [1923] 1 Ch. 373.
[78] See also *Isaac* v. *Hotel de Paris* [1960] 1 W.L.R. 239.
[79] [1949] I.R. 60.
[80] *Ibid.* p. 73.
[81] (1963) 37 A.L.J.R. 25.

damages in respect of injuries sustained as a result of the collapse of the stage in a hall hired for a meeting. The council's liability again turned, in part, upon whether the hall had been leased or simply hired under a licence agreement. Commenting on the observations of Black J. in *Boylan's* case,[82] Windeyer J. said[83]: "Possibly there could be [a tenancy for three hours] in some cases. But in this case the letting of the hall to the association for the purpose of holding its meeting was no more than the grant of a sole licence to have the use of it for a brief time."

A more positive statement of principle is to be found in another Irish case, *Kelly* v. *Woolworth & Co.*[84] Rooms had been hired for a whist drive and charity dance. The plaintiff tripped on linoleum while dancing. She sought damages in negligence from the owners of the rooms and the success of her claim was dependent upon the nature of the hirer's interest. In a peremptory dismissal of any suggestion that the organisers secured a lease of the rooms, Ronan L.J. observed[85]: "It is absurd to think that by a hiring for four hours for a dance the parties intended that an estate should pass."

These difficulties will no longer arise in precisely this form under English law since Parliament has now abolished the former rule[86] that a landlord's liability, being contractual, did not cover injury to the tenant's family or visitors.[87] That being so the question of the liability of the owner of premises in negligence, who hires those premises out for short periods for functions and meetings, will not turn upon whether he grants a lease or a licence. For this reason the policy considerations that prompted statements such as that by Ronan L.J. in *Kelly's* case[88] may now be different. Nevertheless, it may still be true that in determining whether a grant of a period of less than one week creates a lease or a licence, the duration of the right of occupation is relevant, at least in so far as it may lead to an inference as to what the parties intended.

It is, however, the case that in order to create a legal estate which can rank as a term of years absolute within section 1 (1) of the Law of Property Act 1925, its duration must be clearly marked out. A lease must have a certain beginning and a certain maximum duration and if it purports to be a lease for an indefinite period instead of for a fixed term it will fail as a lease and be, at most, a licence.

---

[82] [1949] I.R. 60.
[83] (1963) 37 A.L.J.R. 25 at p.30.
[84] [1922] 2 I.R. 5.
[85] *Ibid.* p. 10.
[86] *Cavalier* v. *Pope* [1906] A.C. 428.
[87] Defective Premises Act 1972, s.4.
[88] [1922] 2 I.R. 5.

(1) *Leases for a Fixed Term of Years*

Since 1925 a term of years absolute is the only leasehold interest that is capable of existing as a legal estate.[89] All other leasehold interests take effect in equity.[90] So, a specifically enforceable contract for a lease creates an equitable lease.[91] Further, a lease, like any other property, may be held upon trusts, by trustees, for a person or persons absolutely or by way of succession. In this case the beneficiary will hold an equitable interest in the lease. Problems of creating equitable interests by grants of a lease for life are discussed below.

Provided that the grant has a certain beginning and a certain maximum duration it can be a term of years. A monthly tenancy and one for 100 years are equally "terms of years" since, as we have seen, the definition includes terms of less than one year. The word "absolute" seems to have an obscure meaning, for the definition expressly includes terms which are liable to terminate through notice to quit, by operation of law, or by re-entry.[92]

A right of re-entry is inserted in a lease in order to enable the grantor to bring about its premature forfeiture for breach of some convenant. So, those factors which might prevent a fee simple from being absolute[93] do not do so in the case of a lease.

There is no requirement that the lease shall be in possession. So, a lease granted today to take effect in possession next year may be a legal estate. Before 1925 the law placed no restriction on the length of time that might elapse before the "reversionary leases," as they are called, began. A lease could be granted in 1900 to commence in 1950.[94] The perpetuity rule was not infringed because the tenant took a vested interest immediately, albeit not in possession. Now, as a result of the Law of Property Act 1925, section 149 (3), the grant of a term at a rent or in consideration of a fine,[95] limited to take effect more than 21 years from the date of the instrument creating it, is void. A contract to grant such a term which is agreed to take effect more than 21 years from *the date of the grant of the lease* is also void.

A contract to grant a lease more than 21 years *from the date of the contract*, is valid, for otherwise an option for renewal contained in any lease granted for more than 21 years would be unenforceable.[96] However, any contract made after 1925 to renew a lease for over 60 years, after the termination of the current lease, is void.[97]

---

[89] L.P.A. 1925, ss.1(1), 205(1) (xxvii).
[90] *Ibid.* s.1(3).
[91] See *post*, Chap. 5.
[92] L.P.A. 1925, s.205(1) (xxvii).
[93] *Megarry & Wade*, pp. 126–130; L.P.A. 1925, s.7(1), as amended by L.P.A. 1926, Sched.
[94] *Mann, Crossman & Paulin Ltd.* v. *Registrar of the Land Registry* [1918] 1 Ch. 202.
[95] Otherwise known as "a premium." This is a capital sum demanded by the landlord as consideration for the grant of the term to the tenant.
[96] *Re Strand & Savoy Properties Ltd.* [1960] Ch. 582; *Weg Motors* v. *Hales* [1962] Ch. 49.
[97] L.P.A. 1922, Sched. 15, para. 9.

If a lessee transfers to another person the whole of the unexpired term of his lease, the transaction is called an "assignment."[98] So, if A leased land in 1970 to B for 20 years and in 1980 B transferred all the remaining term of 10 years to C, an assignment has been made. C now becomes the owner of the lease and holds of A.

If, however, B transfers to a person a period less in duration, even by a single day, than the unexpired term he holds himself, the transaction is called a sub-lease. If he, for instance, in 1980 granted to D a term of nine years, or even 10 years less one day, D would take a sub-lease. In that case D would hold of B, who would continue to hold of A, although only D would be entitled to present possession of the land. In such circumstances A, if he owns the fee simple, is said to hold the "freehold reversion"[99] while B holds a "leasehold reversion," although it is, in this case, only of one day's duration. If A assigns his interest the transaction is simply a conveyance or transfer of his fee simple which entitles the purchaser to receive the rent from B, or from B's assignee if B has assigned his interest.

Another type of arrangement is the concurrent lease. Suppose A, having granted B a 20–year term, wishes to raise a loan of money on the security of his freehold reversion. One way in which he can do this is to mortgage his reversion to the lender, such as a bank, under a sub-lease or an ordinary charge by way of legal mortgage.[1] This may carry disadvantages. First, the reversion, being subject to an existing lease, will have a relatively low capital value and thus a low security value. Secondly, if the mortgagee has doubts about the mortgagor's ability to meet the monthly repayments, he may not be prepared to lend. One possible way out is to utilise the concurrent lease. It is possible for a reversion upon a legal lease itself to be leased concurrently with the existing lease. A concurrent lease is one that begins before the expiration of an existing lease of the same property to another person. Such a lease operates as a lease of the reversion. It has the effect of substituting the new tenant of the reversion as the landlord in relation to the existing lease for as long as the two interests last concurrently. As security for money lent this scheme has a double advantage. First, the amount of capital monies lent can be related to the amount of money being received by the reversioner in rent, rather than solely on the capital value of the reversion, and secondly, the new tenant of the reversion, *i.e.* the lender, will receive the rent direct from the tenant under the existing lease, rather than rely on the solvency of the borrower to meet all the repayments out of his own resources.

It can therefore be seen that it is possible to create any number of concurrent leasehold estates in the same land. However, in all cases

[98] See *Milmo* v. *Carreras* [1946] 1 All E.R. 288.
[99] Despite this convenient designation, the landlord's estate is not a "reversion." He has a *present* estate: see L.P.A. 1925, s.1(5).
[1] L.P.A. 1925, s.87(1).

where fixed term lettings are used, the duration of the term must be certain, as must its commencement. The term may commence immediately upon the grant, or from a past or future date, but the date of commencement must be stated with certainty, or be ascertainable, otherwise the lease or contract to create it is void. In *Marshall* v. *Berridge*[2] Lush L.J. said[3]: "It is essential to the validity of a lease that it shall appear either in express terms or by reference to some writing which would make it certain on what day the term is to commence. There must be a certain beginning and a certain ending, otherwise it is not a perfect lease. . . . " The law will not imply that the tenancy will commence within a reasonable time, if no starting date is specified.[4] In the absence of anything which indicates a contrary intention, where the agreement is under seal, the term begins from the date when the deed is delivered.[5] However, where a tenant enters into possession under an instrument not under seal, the lease commences from the date of entry.[6]

The maximum duration of the term must either be fixed by specifying the number of years in the first instance or be expressed by reference to a collateral matter which can be looked at, *at the time when the lease takes effect*, to ascertain the latest date on which the term must end.[7] So, in *Gwynne* v. *Manistone*[8] a lease under an instrument whereby the tenant should pay certain specified sums at the end of every three years up to a specified date, and from and after that date "should pay the clear annual rental of £9 till the end of the lease," without mentioning any period at which the lease was to terminate, was held good only up to the specified date.

The requirement of certain duration can cause inconvenience. After some initial judicial disagreement[9] it was finally settled that a lease granted during wartime "for the duration of the war" is void for uncertainty at common law.[10] This decision caused so much uncertainty and would have created so much inconvenience during the Second World War that such leases were converted by statute into terms of 10 years, determinable after the end of the war by (usually) one month's notice.[11] The Act was severely limited in scope, being

[2] (1881) 19 Ch.D. 233.
[3] *Ibid.* p. 245.
[4] *Harvey* v. *Pratt* [1965] 1 W.L.R. 1025; *cf. Re Lander & Bayley's Contract* [1892] 3 Ch. 41.
[5] *Doe d. Phillip* v. *Benjamin* (1839) 9 A. & E. 644; *Furness* v. *Bond* (1888) 4 T.L.R. 457; *Sandhill* v. *Franklin* (1875) L.R. 10 C.P. 377; *Ladyman* v. *Wirral Estates* [1968] 2 All E.R. 197.
[6] *Martin* v. *Smith* (1874) L.R. 9 Ex. 50; *Kemp* v. *Derrett* (1814) 3 Camp. 510.
[7] *Lace* v. *Chantler* [1944] K.B. 368. The period of the fixed term need not, however, be continuous. Occupation may not be permitted on certain days of the week, or the letting may be for one or more specified weeks in a year or number of years: this arrangement is colloquially referred to as "time sharing": see *Cottage Holiday Associates Ltd.* v. *Customs & Excise Commissioners* [1983] Q.B. 735; See *Woodfall*, para. 1–0517/1.
[8] (1828) 3 C. & P. 302.
[9] *Great Northern Railway* v. *Arnold* (1916) 33 T.L.R. 114; *Swift* v. *Macbean* [1942] 1 K.B. 375.
[10] *Lace* v. *Chantler* [1944] K.B. 368.
[11] Validation of War-Time Leases Act 1944.

confined only to the Second World War.[12] It did not at all affect
tenancies for other uncertain periods, such as the duration of a
partnership, which were, and remain, void. So, for example, a lease
may be required while other premises are being redeveloped, or a
tenant may need a tenancy for the duration of his stay in London, but
he may not know precisely how long this will be. In all these cases, if a
lease is intended, a definite term must be granted. The difficulty can
be avoided by granting a definite term for longer than is likely to be
necessary, adding a proviso that the term can be ended by three
months' notice on the happening of the future uncertain event.

Should a lease at a rent or in a consideration of a premium be
granted for the duration of someone's life, or until a person marries,
or be granted for a term of years determinable upon death or
marriage, this takes effect as a lease for 90 years. It is, however,
terminable after such death or marriage by either party by one
month's written notice to end it on one of the quarter days applicable
to the tenancy, or, if there are none, on one of the usual quarter days.[13]

The general effect of this provision is simply to equip such leases
with a maximum duration without affecting the substantial intentions
and rights of the parties. The grantor must beware, when granting
short fixed periods, that the provision does not frustrate his
intentions. Thus, if a grant is made for five years should the tenant live
so long and he confounds medical prognosis by surviving for a longer
period, the grantor will find himself with a sitting tenant whom he will
be unable to evict.

The application of this principle only where a rent or premium is
taken is aimed at drawing a sharp line between a profit-making
business arrangement to grant a life term which leaves the fee simple
still in possession, and one which is a truly gratuitous family or non-
commercial arrangement which in reality pushes the fee simple into
remainder, thus creating an element of succession. The latter case,
such as a grant to the tenant for 100 years if he should live so long, free
of rent or premium, creates a settlement. Such a lease is clearly
equivalent in every substantial respect to a life interest. The lessee
then becomes a tenant for life under section 20 (1) (iv) of the Settled
Land Act 1925.[14]

A lease for a fixed term, that is from one certain date to another
certain date, will end automatically by effluxion of time, without the
need for the landlord to serve the tenant with a notice to quit. Again,
the tenancy can be expressed to end "on or before"[15] a certain date, or
the agreement may state that the tenant will give up possession "by" a

---

[12] *Ibid.* s.7(2).
[13] L.P.A. 1925, s.149(6).
[14] But see *Re Catling* [1931] 2 Ch. 359.
[15] *cf. Dagger* v. *Shepherd* [1946] K.B. 215.

stated date.[16] The lease may provide for termination before the expiration of the term on notice given by one party or the other to terminate the tenancy at given intervals during its currency. These options to terminate are commonly known as "break-clauses" and are frequently found in leases of 14 years or more, expressed to be exercisable at intervals of seven years, frequently coinciding with rent reviews.

(2) *Periodic Tenancies*

As we have seen, in a fixed-term tenancy, the total duration is fixed. In periodic tenancies there is no initial limitation on their total duration, but instead they continue automatically from period to period until determined by the appropriate notice to quit given by one party to the other.[17] They can arise by implication, whenever a person occupies land with the owner's consent, and with the intention of creating a lease, where rent is paid and accepted by reference to fixed periods of a week, a month, a quarter or a year as the case may be. The express provision in the tenancy that it is to be determinable by some specified period of notice, *e.g.* a quarter's notice, may also raise the inference of a periodic tenancy.[18] Alternatively, they can arise expressly, where the landlord expressly grants a weekly, monthly, quarterly or yearly tenancy. These tenancies are not affected by the rule against leases of uncertain maximum duration, for whatever period is employed is bound to be the minimum duration of the tenancy. The lease is, therefore, treated initially as a grant for the period only, which, if not determined at the end of the period, will automatically and without any new letting, run for another period, and so on from week to week, month to month, year to year.[19] So, whatever period is initially granted, that must be the minimum duration of the tenancy, although until notice to quit is given, its total duration will not be certain.

In one case a periodic tenancy arises automatically by statute. The Housing Act 1985, s.86, provides that when a fixed term "secure tenancy"[20] expires, a periodic tenancy automatically arises unless the landlord has granted a renewal to begin immediately on the expiry of the previous tenancy. The periods are the same as those for which rent was last payable under the first tenancy.

---

[16] *Joseph* v. *Joseph* [1967] Ch. 78.

[17] The problems associated with notices to quit are discussed *post*, Chap. 8.

[18] *Kemp* v. *Derrett* (1814) 3 Camp. 510. This is subject to any contrary indication, as in a yearly tenancy with a special period of notice: See *post*, Chap. 8.

[19] *Centaploy Ltd.* v. *Matlodge Ltd.* [1974] Ch. 1; *Bowen* v. *Anderson* [1894] 1 Q.B. 164; *Wilchick* v. *Marks* [1934] 2 K.B. 56; *Re Midland Railway Co.'s Agreement* [1971] Ch. 725. Because it is regarded as one continuous tenancy, it should not be confused with a renewable lease.

[20] This term is defined *post*, Chap. 16.

Any provision which is repugnant to the nature of a periodic tenancy, such as attempted restrictions on the rights of one or other of the parties to serve a notice to quit, will be void and unenforceable.[21] However, a restriction is repugnant only if it would remove the right altogther. So, in *Breams Property Investment Co. Ltd.* v. *Strougler*[22] an agreement by the landlord not to serve notice to quit during the first three years of the tenancy unless he required the premises for his own occupation, was held not to be repugnant to the quarterly periodic letting, but merely an addition to its normal term as to notice. The methods of creation of periodic tenancies, both expressly and by implication, are discussed in the next chapter.[23]

(3) *Tenancies at Will*

A tenancy at will arises whenever a tenant, with the consent of the owner, occupies land as tenant (and not merely as employee, agent or other licensee[24]) "at the will" of the landlord, *i.e.* on the terms that either party can bring the tenancy to an end at any time. The lessee, consequently, has no defined estate in the land, so that a tenancy at will is not within the definition of a term of years absolute.[25] Since the tenant has no certain estate, the interest is determinable simply by a demand for possession, or by implication of law from other acts or events, such as the death of either party,[26] or the transfer of the landlord's reversionary interest, with notice to the tenant,[27] or a mortgage of the reversion.[28] However, in the case of a joint tenancy at will, the death of one joint tenant does not determine the tenancy which accrues, by right of survivorship, to the other, who remains liable for the whole rent.[29]

When asked to do so, the tenant must leave immediately. However, because the concept of a tenancy at will was originally developed for tenant farmers who had no fixed term or formal lease, some

---

[21] *Doe d. Warner* v. *Browne* (1807) 8 Ea. 165.

[22] [1948] 2 K.B. 1; see also, *Re Midland Railway Co.'s Agreement* [1971] Ch. 725.

[23] See *post*, Chap. 3.

[24] *Mayhew* v. *Suttle* (1854) 4 E. & B. 347.

[25] L.P.A. 1925, s.205(1)(xxvii). There is a suggestion that a tenancy at will must now be an equitable interest rather than a term of years absolute within the statutory definition. The arguments for and against are summarised in Foa, *Law of Landlord and Tenant*, (8th ed.), p. 2, n. (i) and *Megarry and Wade*, pp. 654–655.

[26] *Doe d. Stanway* v. *Rock* (1842) Car. & M. 549; *James* v. *Dean* (1804–08) 11 Ves.Jr. 383, 391; *Att.-Gen.* v. *Foley* (1753) 1 Dick. 363 at p. 366; *Turner* v. *Barnes* (1862) 2 B.& S. 435 at p. 452; *Scobie* v. *Collins* [1895] 1 Q.B. 375; *cf. Morton* v. *Woods* (1869) L.R. 4 Q.B. 293 at p. 306.

[27] *Disdale* v. *Illes* (1673) 2 Lev. 88; *Doe d. Goody* v.*Carter* (1847) 9 Q.B. 863. A tenancy at will has also been held to expire when a prohibition notice, preventing user of the premises, served by a local authority who were also the landlords, expired: *Ben Stanfield (Carlisle)* v. *Carlisle City Council, The Times,* October 30, 1982; (1983) 99 L.Q.R. 178.

[28] *Jarman* v. *Hale* [1899] 1 Q.B. 994. other circumstances that will result in determination of a tenancy at will see *Woodfall*, para. 1–0652.

[29] *Henstead's Case* (1594) 5 Co. Rep. 10a.

peculiarities survive. So, for example, a tenant at will who has quitted his holding nevertheless has a right to re-enter upon the land within a reasonable time thereafter to remove his goods or his crops.[30] Unless the parties agree that the tenancy shall be rent free, the landlord is entitled to claim from a tenant at will compensation for the "use and occupation" of his land.[31] If rent is agreed upon, the landlord can distrain for it.[32] If a tenancy at will is created without any agreement as to payment of rent, and rent is subsequently paid and accepted upon some regular periodical basis, a yearly, monthly or other periodical tenancy will be created.[33]

A tenancy at will arises if a tenant holds over at the end of a lease with the implied consent of his landlord, although if the former lease was a "protected tenancy" within the Rent Act 1977, a tenant holding over becomes, not a tenant at will, but a statutory tenant under that Act.[34] Similarly a tenant of business premises within the Landlord and Tenant Act 1954, Pt. II who holds over under the terms of that Act is deemed to be a tenant under the original lease, and not a tenant at will.[35] A tenancy at will can also arise where a purchaser goes into possession pending completion,[36] or a prospective tenant goes into possession during negotiation for a lease.[37]

Under the Limitation Act 1980 section 15(6) and Schedule 1 para. 5, a landlord's title is extinguished by adverse possession after 12 years' uninterrupted rent-free occupation, from the time the tenancy at will comes to an end. There is, therefore, no longer a special rule for acquisition by adverse possession of a landlord's interest in the case of tenancies at will. The tenancy is no longer deemed to end one year after its commencement and 13 years' rent-free occupation by a tenant at will no longer amounts, in itself, to adverse occupation.[38]

The line between a tenancy at will and a licence is often difficult to

---

[30] *Doe d. Nicholl* v. *M'Kaeg* (1830) 10 B. & C. 721 (goods); *Oland* v. *Burdwick* (1595) Cro.Eliz. (1) 460; *Buliver* v. *Buliver* (1819) 2 B. & A. 470 (crops); and see *Woodfall*, Chap. 21.

[31] *Howard* v. *Shaw* (1841) 8 M. & W. 118; see *post*, Chap. 5.

[32] *Anderson* v. *Midland Railway* (1861) 3 E. & E. 614; see *post, loc. cit.*

[33] *Young* v. *Hargreaves* (1963) 186 E.G. 355, although if the tenancy at will was created expressly, it will not be converted into a periodic tenancy by periodical rental payments: *Manfield & Sons Ltd.* v. *Botchin* [1970] 2 Q.B. 612.

[34] Rent Act 1977, s.2 *cf. Artisans, Labourers and General Dwellings Co. Ltd.* v. *Whittaker* [1919] 2 K.B. 301. The same reasoning applies to a tenancy at sufferance: *infra.*

[35] Landlord and Tenant Act 1954, s.24 *cf. Wheeler* v. *Mercer* [1957] A.C. 416; *Hagee (London)* v. *Erikson & Larson* [1976] Q.B. 209.

[36] It seems that a tenancy at will at a rent arises even though the rent be calculated as interest on the purchase money: *Francis Jackson Developments* v. *Stemp* [1943] 2 All E.R. 74. However, this will not be so if the payments are referable merely to the contract for sale: *Dunthorne & Shore* v. *Wiggins* [1943] 2 All E.R. 678. (Sums covering outgoings and mortgage instalments and also reducing the balance of the purchase price were paid as rent.) Normally the agreement between the parties for the sale under which occupation is allowed expressly provides for a licence instead of a tenancy; see National Conditions of Sale (20th ed), No. 8, and Law Society's Conditions of Sale 1984 Revision, No. 18.

[37] *British Railways Board* v. *Bodywright Ltd.* (1971) 22 E.G. 651.

[38] *cf. Heslop* v. *Burns* [1974] 1 W.L.R. 1241.

draw.[39] There was a time when a court would readily infer a tenancy at will from the fact that an occupant was in possession, paying periodic sums for his continued right to remain there.[40] The courts are increasingly reluctant, as we have seen earlier in this chapter, to infer a tenancy at will from exclusive possession or occupation, and at least one judge has suggested that the tenancy at will can now serve only one legal purpose, and that is to protect the interests of an occupier during a period of transition before firmer and more permanent arrangements are concluded.[41] The major reason for this change has been the advent of protective legislation, notably the Rent Acts.[42] It seems a tenancy at will can still be a protected tenancy within the Rent Act 1977 since, notwithstanding the fact that it may not be a legal estate within section 1 (1) of the Law of Property Act 1925, it still invokes the relationship of tenure.[43] Notwithstanding this, presumably because no proper notice to quit is required to terminate a tenancy at will, section 5 of the Protection from Eviction Act 1977, which requires a minimum of four weeks' notice to quit a dwelling, is inapplicable to a tenancy at will.

(4) *Tenancies at Sufferance*[44]

A tenancy at sufferance arises where a tenant, once in lawful possession of land, holds over on the termination of his previous tenancy without his landlord's consent. It is different from a tenancy at will in that the landlord does not consent to the holding over. No rent can be paid under a tenancy at sufferance since, if rent is accepted by the landlord he will be deemed to have consented and a new lawful tenancy will arise, either periodic or at will. However, the landlord can bring an action in respect of mesne profits for use and occupation of the property from his tenant at sufferance.[45]

A tenancy at sufferance is not really a tenancy at all but essentially a legal device to protect the tenant from being treated as a trespasser. They are, in practice, now extremely rare since most tenants of dwellings have statutory rights which permit them to remain in possession, notwithstanding the landlord's opposition and, in the case

---

[39] See *Binions* v. *Evans* [1972] Ch. 359; *Heslop* v. *Burns* [1974] 1 W.L.R. 1241.

[40] *Marcroft Wagons Ltd.* v. *Smith* [1951] 2 K.B. 496, *per* Denning L.J. at p. 507.

[41] *Heslop* v. *Burns* [1974] 1 W.L.R. 1241, *per* Scarman L.J. at p. 1152.

[42] The business tenancy code under the Landlord and Tenant Act 1954, Pt. II, does not protect tenants at will, and so the distinction between their interests and those of mere licensees is, perhaps, of less significance; see *Wheeler* v. *Mercer* [1957] A.C. 416; *Hagee (London)* v. *Erikson & Larson* [1976] Q.B. 209.

[43] *Chamberlain* v. *Farr* [1942] 2 All E.R. 567.

[44] For a detailed consideration of these tenancies, see *Megarry and Wade*, pp. 655–657.

[45] See *post*, Chap. 5.

of business lettings, holding over creates a statutory extension of the original letting.[46]

(5) *Perpetually Renewable Leases*

A perpetually renewable lease was one of which the tenant could demand a renewal on the same terms, *i.e.* including the clause for renewal.[47] This must be distinguished from a lease which is merely expressed to be renewable, for in this case the original lease does not give the right to demand a lease which is the mirror image of itself, but simply another lease, minus the renewal clause.

Perpetually renewable leases existing at the end of 1925 were, by the Law of Property Act 1922, s.145, converted into leases for 2,000 years calculated from the time when the existing term began. Fines, otherwise known as premiums, payable on renewal, became payable as additional rent. A purported grant of, or a contract for, such a lease after 1925 takes effect as a term of 2,000 years, or contract therefor, as the case may be, but free from any obligation to pay renewal money. The converted lease is on the same terms and conditions as the original lease other than those relating to renewal, but subject to a number of important modifications made necessary by the conversion into a fixed term of such length. These are:

(i) The lessee for the time being may end the lease by giving at least 10 days' notice in writing before any date at which it would have expired had there been no conversion and if it has not been renewed.

(ii) The lessee must register every assignment or devolution with the lessor or his agent within six months.

(iii) A lessee who assigns the term ceases to be liable on the covenants even though privity of contract still exists between him and the lessor.

A lease will be construed as perpetually renewable where the language used shows that to have been the unequivocal intention of the parties, even though that intention may not be expressly stated.[48] A renewal covenant in a seven-year lease providing that a renewed lease must contain a covenant for renewal for a further term of seven years when the renewed term expired, was held not to be a perpetually renewable lease. The tenant was entitled only to a double renewal.[49]

---

[46] See footnote 97 *supra*.
[47] *Hare* v. *Burges* (1857) 4 K. & J. 45; *Parkus* v. *Greenwood* [1950] Ch. 644; *Re Hopkins Lease* [1972] 1 W.L.R. 372; *Northchurch Estates Ltd.* v. *Daniels* [1947] Ch. 117.
[48] *Parkus* v.*Greenwood* [1950] Ch. 644.
[49] *Marjorie Burnett Ltd.* v. *Barclay* (1980) 258 E.G. 642.

The court will, in the absence of a clear and express covenant to that effect in the lease, lean against a construction that would result in the lease being perpetually renewable.[50] An option for a renewal of a lease at the same rent and on the same terms as the current lease, "including this present covenant,"[51] or "on identical terms and conditions,"[52] is sufficient, and a lease for a period of 21 years renewable as often as every 11 years of the term should expire, has been held to create a perpetually renewable lease.[53] The substantial position of the parties is unchanged. So the lessee has complete control over his future occupation, since the landlord is not entitled to serve the statutory notice ending the lease.

---

[50] *Ibid.*
[51] *Hare* v. *Burges* (1857) 4 K. & J. 45.
[52] *Northchurch Estates* v. *Daniels* [1947] Ch. 117.
[53] *Wynn* v. *Conway Corp.* [1914] 2 Ch. 705.

CHAPTER 3

CREATION OF LEASES

I. What is Being Let? 50
   A. The Identity of the Property . 50
   B. Lettings Involving Intermittent
      Use 50
   C. Grants of Rights Only 51
   D. Concurrent Leases and Leases
      in Reversion 53
   E. Fixtures and Fittings 55
II. Who Can Create Leases and For How
     Long? 62
   A. Sole Owners 62
   B. Trustees and Beneficiaries . . . 62
   C. Charity Trustees 66
   D. Mortgagor and Mortgagee . . . 67
   E. Trading Companies 69
   F. Local Authorities 70
   G. Agents and Attorneys 71
III. Who Can Take Leases? 71

IV. Preliminary Steps to the Granting of
     a Lease 72
   A. Can the Property be Used for
      the Tenant's Purpose? 72
   B. Can the Landlord Grant the
      Tenancy? 78
   C. The Contract for a Lease . . . 80
   D. Formal Creation of the Lease . 87
V. Failure to Complete the Contract . 92
   A. Introduction 92
   B. Effect of Entry Before Agree-
      ment Reached 93
   C. Entry Following Agreement or
      Under Void Lease 93
   D. Damages for Failure to Com-
      plete 94
   E. Actions for Specific Perform-
      ance 96

Introduction

Before a tenancy is created, the parties have negotiated and agreed terms. Each party has made enquiries about the other. The tenant needs to know what he is taking, how much it will cost him and on what terms. The landlord will be concerned that the tenant is responsible, financially sound and agrees to the terms of the proposed letting.

It is likely that in the letting of a lock-up garage on a weekly basis, the preliminaries will be concluded in a perfunctory manner. If the lease is of a farm, or a large office suite or a shop, for example, and will involve the tenant in a substantial outlay during the proposed term, then more thorough enquiries will be made, and the negotiations are likely to be more detailed. However, a written agreement for the grant of a tenancy tends to be the exception rather than the rule. This does not matter if disputes do not arise about what has been agreed. But often it is important to decide first if an enforceable agreement was reached to take a lease, and secondly what were the terms of that agreement.

It is proposed to review the preliminary matters that both parties should ideally consider before agreeing to the grant of a tenancy, how the agreement should be made and completed, and the position if there is either an alleged breach or failure to perform that agreement.

I. What is Being Let?

A. The Identity of the Property

The original details of the property are likely to be contained in the estate agent's particulars. The estate agent's description will not be the same as the one contained in the lease.[1] The tenant should ensure that what is described as Number 4 Short Street does include all he hopes to take in the lease, for example, that the landlord does intend to let the garden, and all the garages; that he will not be excluding a boxroom for storage of his own personal effects; which boundary walls and fences are included in the letting, and further that there are no disputes brewing with the neighbours about the way the property is used or maintained, or about the provision of joint access or drainage services.

If the landlord is letting only part of his property, the tenant must make sure either that the common parts giving him access are let to him, or that he obtains sufficient rights over the hallways, passages and staircases to enable him to use his premises whenever he wishes. It cannot be assumed, merely because the premises are on or above the first floor of a building, that the tenant will automatically get a right of way over the staircase leading to them.[2] He should normally have a right of way of necessity over a staircase providing his sole means of access. But it will not be assumed that the staircase is let to him, even if he is the only person who is likely to use it.[3] If rooms are to be shared, the tenant will want to know if they are included in the letting to him, and are subject to rights of enjoyment in favour of others, or whether he has merely rights of enjoyment over rooms let to other tenants.[4]

B. Lettings Involving Intermittent Use

The tenant's exclusive possession in the sense that he can exclude his landlord from occupying the property does not necessarily mean that the tenant has a correlative right to occupy the property himself physically all the time. Leases frequently envisage that the tenant will occupy only intermittently. For security reasons, access to an office suite in bank premises may be limited to certain hours of weekdays. Sports stadiums are often subject to concurrent leases of different

---

[1] For a discussion on the interpretation of the parcels to a lease, see *post*, Chap. 4(I)E.
[2] *Chappell* v. *Mason* (1894) 10 T.L.R. 404 (C.A.).
[3] *Altmann* v. *Boatman* (1963) 186 E.G. 109.
[4] A residential tenant is regarded as having a tenancy of a separate dwelling-house comprising all the essential living rooms, bathroom, kitchen and bedroom, etc., even if he has a right only to share, for example, the kitchen. R.A. 1977, s.22.

parts, *e.g.* the dog track, totalisator, kennels and supporters' club may be let to one lessee, and the football or rugby pitch in the middle and the training gymnasium let to a second lessee, both being given joint permission to use the stands. The owner of playing fields[5] will often let to a football or cricket club reserving to himself grazing rights, either out of season, or when the ground is not being used for playing purposes. In all these cases, it is essential for the tenant to obtain rights of enjoyment sufficiently extensive for his purposes. There must be also some workable mechanism to resolve possible conflict between the different tenants wanting to use their own properties at the same time.

C. Grants of Rights Only

An owner or tenant may require access over a neighbour's land for domestic, commercial or sporting purposes. The owner of the land to be burdened with the proposed access (known as the servient owner), may be unwilling or unable to grant a right of way for more than a limited number of years.[6] Obviously if the servient owner is himself a tenant he cannot carve interests out of his property that will outlast his own interest.

A right of way or other easement is a right appurtenant to a corporeal hereditament[7] or incorporeal hereditament. Its owner has a legal interest in land that will bind subsequent owners and tenants of the servient tenement. The owner of a right of way does not have an estate in the land.[8] The easement cannot exist as a proprietary right by itself.[9] For example, one cannot grant a lease of a right of way simply, either to an individual or to a group, *e.g.* a rambling club, that will automatically bind the subsequent owners of the burdened land.[10] The grant must be for the benefit of a corporeal hereditament or an incorporeal hereditament owned by the persons to whom the enjoyment of the easement is granted.[11] The owner of a corporeal hereditament owns an estate in the land,[12] either as the freeholder or as the tenant of the land. An incorporeal hereditament consisting in a *profit à prendre, e.g.* a right of fishing,[13] or a right to shoot over and

---

[5] For example, see *Encyclopedia of Forms and Precedents*, (4th ed.), Vol. 12, pp. 1056 *et seq.*
[6] And see L.R.A. 1925, ss.18(1)(*c*) and 21(1)(*b*).
[7] Strictly, it is not itself an incorporeal hereditament, see 40 Halsbury's Laws (4th ed.), p. 4, para. 4, and notes where the authorities are collected. In Challis's *Real Property* (3rd ed., 1911), p. 55 Charles Sweet wrote "...for over a century easements have been treated as incorporeal hereditaments by text-writers of authority... and their view has been adopted by the courts."
[8] L.P.A. 1925, s.1(2)(*a*).
[9] *Ackroyd* v. *Smith* (1850) 10 C.B. 164.
[10] The servient tenement.
[11] It must be created by deed, L.P.A. 1925 s.52.
[12] L.P.A. 1925, s.1(1).
[13] *Hanbury* v. *Jenkins* [1901] 2 Ch. 401 at p. 422.

take game away from another's land may be owned "in gross," *i.e.* irrespective of any dominant tenement benefited thereby. The *profit à prendre* may itself be properly the subject of a lease.[14]

The grant of a right of way for a number of years can be commercially very important. It now seems to be the law that the tenant of such a lease will not be able to enjoy the benefits of provisions for security given to other commercial tenants. The right of way does not amount to premises "occupied for the purposes of a business."[15] In *Land Reclamation Co. Ltd.* v. *Basildon D.C.*[16] the plaintiffs owned derelict farmland and mudflats of impermeable clay suitable for dumping toxic wastes. The area was approached by a road over the defendants' land. A lease granted a right of way over the road from 1969 until 1977. Conservationists objected to the plaintiffs' use of the land, and the Council were unwilling to renew the lease unless legally compelled. Brightman J. refused to compel the authority, holding[17] that "the company uses the roadway for the purposes of its business but it does not occupy either the easements or the roadway." He took the view that Part II of the Landlord and Tenant Act 1954 "has no application to a mere right of way standing by itself because such a right is not property or premises capable of being occupied for the purposes of a business, or indeed for any other purpose."

The best that such a tenant can do is to obtain a lease for as long as possible at the outset, and before he is too heavily involved in capital expenditure. However, it is far more likely that he will be able to obtain merely a bare licence or permission,[18] effective only between himself and the licensor.[19]

In some cases the Courts have regarded a grant of what prima facie seemed intermittent rights to be a grant of a lease of the land over which the rights are enjoyed. This was done in the curious case of *Bracey* v. *Read.*[20] Here a right to exercise and train racehorses on gallops on the Berkshire Downs was regarded as a lease of the strips of land comprising the gallops, subject to extensive rights of crossing in favour of the owner. This seems to be a benign construction. In most cases, it is suggested, a person who is given intermittent rights will have at best a lease of an easement, if it benefits his land, at the worst, more often, a mere licence.

---

[14] *Hooper* v. *Clark* (1867) L.R. 2 Q.B. 200; *Bird* v. *Great Eastern Railway Co.* (1865) 19 C.B., (N.S.) 268.
[15] L. & T.A. 1954, s.23(1), *cf.* the earlier position under L.& T.A. 1927, s.17(1), where the business premises had to be "used," and also *Whitley* v. *Stumbles* [1930] A.C. 544 (involving compensation for a right of fishing).
[16] [1978] 2 All E.R. 1162, affd. [1979] 2 All E.R. 993; *cf. Long (Nevill) & Co. (Boards)* v. *Firmenich and Co.* (1984) 47 P. & C.R. 59 (C.A.).
[17] [1978] 2 All E.R. 1162 at p. 1167.
[18] See before Chap. 2.
[19] Chap. 2(I).
[20] [1963] Ch. 88.

D. Concurrent Leases and Leases in Reversion[21]

Normally a tenant takes a lease with a view to occupying the property from the specified date. But the property might already be let. Either the landlord can grant a second lease to start before the end of the first one. This is a concurrent lease. It is a lease of the landlord's reversion. Alternatively, the second lease might be granted to start at the end of the first. This is a grant of a lease in reversion. In this case the second tenant's rights of enjoyment are intended to start when the first lease comes to an end. This may be done because the second tenant wants to tie the landlord down straight away and is prepared to offer the landlord more favourable terms than the landlord is currently receiving from the first existing lease. A lease in reversion might be granted either to the same or another tenant, again with a view to granting him immediately a legal estate which he will be able to enjoy at the end of the current tenancy.

These arrangements made particular sense when tenants could reasonably be expected to leave the property at the end of the term granted. Before statutory intervention a tenant who overstayed his term could in the last resort be physically evicted. It is now unlawful to evict residential tenants except under a court order.[22] In the case of business property the effect of Part II of the Landlord & Tenant Act 1954, is in most cases to continue the contractual tenancy beyond the end of the agreed term until the tenancy is ended either in accordance with the Act, or by agreement between the parties. In both cases, the statutory provisions are likely to interfere with the enjoyment the parties anticipated from the concurrent lease, or the lease in reversion, as the case may be.[23]

(1) *Concurrent Leases*

A concurrent lease may be for either a shorter or longer period than the original lease. It is more likely to be for a longer period. During the continuance of the original lease, the tenant under the concurrent lease is entitled to exercise all the rights and remedies of the original landlord against the original tenant under the first tenancy. The grant of the concurrent lease operates as an assignment of the landlord's interest for the duration of the concurrent lease.[24] The second tenant steps into the landlord's shoes in relation to the first tenant, receiving

---

[21] See Chap. 2(H).
[22] Protection from Eviction Act 1977, ss.2, 3.
[23] *Bowes-Lyon* v. *Green* [1963] A.C. 420; *Skelton and Son* v. *Harrison & Pinder* [1975] Q.B. 361.
[24] L.P.A. 1925, s.149(5).

rent from the first tenant, and enforcing the covenants in the first lease against him.[25]

A concurrent lease is frequently used in flat development. First the developer will grant long leases to the purchasers of the several flats in the building. He will then grant to a management company a concurrent lease for at least as long as the original leases. The individual flat owners will generally be members of the management company, and will pay their ground rent and service charges to the management company, which assumes the developer's responsibility for the maintenance of the shell of the building, provision of the services and enforcement of covenants in the leases of the individual flat owners. The original developer retains the ultimate reversion expectant on the determination of all the leases and an immediate right to a small ground rent. The effect of this is to relieve the developer of a continuing responsibility to maintain and manage, and to place the management of the flats under the control of a third person, the management company, itself subject to the direction of the individual flat owners.[26]

(2) *Leases in Reversion*

Here the second tenant's enjoyment of the property not only starts in the future, but after the end of the current tenancy. The grant of the lease in reversion does not affect the landlord's rights in respect of the current tenancy.[27] The commencement date must not be more than 21 years after the date of the instrument purporting to create the term. If it is to take effect at a later date more than 21 years in the future, the instrument is void.[28] Section 149(3) of the Law of Property Act 1925 also provides that "any contract made after [December 31, 1925] to create such a term is likewise void."

At first sight this provision would seem to strike at an option to renew a tenancy contained in a lease for more than 21 years. If the option is exercised the second term must start more than 21 years after the option was originally granted. However, the section does not bear that restrictive interpretation, as Buckley J. explained in *Re Strand & Savoy Properties Ltd.*[29] Here an option to renew was given in a 35 year lease. The landlords argued that the option was invalid, struck down by statute. Buckley J. held that the section was confined "as far as contracts are concerned, to contracts to create terms which, when created, will only take effect more than twenty one years from

---

[25] *Birch* v. *Wright* (1786) 1 T.R. 378; [1775–1802] All E.R. Rep. 41, and see *Re Moore & Hulm's Contract* [1912] 2 Ch. 105.
[26] See further George & George, *Sale of Flats* (5th ed.).
[27] *Smith* v. *Day* (1837) 2 M. & W. 684; [1835–42] All E.R. Rep. 521.
[28] L.P.A. 1925, s.149(3).
[29] [1960] Ch. 582, and see *Weg Motors* v. *Hales* [1962] Ch. 49.

the dates of the instruments creating them; that is to say, it invalidates contracts for the granting of leases which will, when granted, be reversionary leases, the postponement of the commencement of the term being for more than twenty one years from the date of the lease." A lease in reversion must be created by deed[30] if it is to be effective in law. The exception[31] which validates leases created orally, applies only if they take effect *in possession* for a term not exceeding three years at the best rent which can be reasonably obtained without taking a fine[32] (*i.e.* a premium). Whether a concurrent lease taking effect immediately and for less than three years can be orally created is a matter of some doubt.[33] As soon as the tenant under a concurrent lease is entitled to receive the rents from the first tenant, then he will of course be regarded as being "in possession."[34]

E. Fixtures and Fittings

An in-coming tenant needs to know what fixtures and fittings on the premises when he inspects them will form part of the demise to him. An out-going tenant needs to know what fixtures like fitted cupboards, shelving, light and curtain fittings, fitted carpets, kitchen machinery and so forth he can remove or sell to the in-coming tenant. These questions are of particular importance to business tenants where trade fittings, plant and machinery are either already in the premises or likely to be added during the tenancy.

(1) *Fixtures Installed at the Time of the First Letting*

In the case of commercial letting of public houses, garages or factories fitted out with basic machinery, or shops with display units useful to the in-coming tenant, he has doubtless asked specifically what fixtures and fittings are to be included in the letting. They may well be valued and scheduled. If the agreement specifies the fittings included in the letting, it follows that those not listed are deemed excluded. In *Hare* v. *Horton* [35] there was a mortgage of two dwelling-houses and an iron foundry and appurtenances, together with other specified fixtures in or about the two dwelling-houses. It was held that the mortgage did not include cranes, boilers and other machinery to the value of £600 in the foundry. Taunton J.[36] said:

[30] L.P.A. 1925, s.52.
[31] L.P.A. 1925, s.54(2).
[32] L.P.A. 1925, s.205(1)(xxiii) contains a definition of a "fine."
[33] *Woodfall*, para 1–0612.
[34] L.P.A. 1925, s.205(1)(xix).
[35] (1833) 5 B. & Ad. 715.
[36] At p. 728.

"it is very plain, that if the granting part of the deed had only mentioned the foundry, messuages and dwellinghouses, the foundry fixtures, as well as those in the dwellinghouses, would have passed. There are many cases which shew this. But as the deed goes on to say 'together with all grates, boilers, bells and fixtures in and about the said two dwellinghouses,' I think mention of these fixtures excluded those in the foundry, on the principle 'expressio unius est exclusio alterius.' "

If the agreement had been for the mortgaging of the houses and the foundry without reference to any of the fixtures, then all the fixtures would have passed as part of the property let.[37]

If the landlord is proposing to sell the fixtures and fittings outright to the tenant, which commonly occurs in letting public houses, there should be a separate term in the agreement to that effect. It is obviously more satisfactory if it is part of a written agreement, but this is not essential.[38] As will be seen[39] the agreement for a lease is an agreement for a disposition of an interest in land, and so covered by section 40 of the Law of Property Act 1925. It should be evidenced in writing if it is to be enforceable by action. As fixtures do not constitute an interest in land, they can be sold orally.

(2) *What are Fixtures?*

A fixture is quite simply anything that is attached to or fastened to or connected with the freehold, *e.g.* a curtain rail, fitted carpet, fitted kitchen cupboard, gas fire or petrol pump. The significance of the fact of attachment lies in two rules. The first is that whatever is attached to the freehold automatically becomes part of it and belongs to the owner of the freehold rather than the person who paid for and installed "the fixture."[40] The second rule, which has been described as quite different and separate, is that "whatever once becomes part of the inheritance cannot be severed by a limited owner, whether he be owner for life or for years."[41] If the article supplied by the tenant is not a fixture there is no problem about removing it. If it is a fixture, then it may nevertheless be removable if it falls within the complex exceptions relating to trade, ornamental and domestic fixtures.[42] There are detailed statutory provisions affecting agricultural fix

---

[37] *Thresher* v. *The East London Waterworks Company Co.* (1824) 2 B. & C. 608.

[38] *Lee* v. *Gaskell* (1876) 1 Q.B.D. 700.

[39] See below, (IV) C.

[40] *Climie* v. *Wood* (1868) L.R. 3 Ex. 257; affd. (1869) L.R. 4 Ex. 328; [1861–73] All E.R. Rep. 831. "Quicquid plantatur solo, solo cedit." And see *Stokes (Insp. of Taxes)* v. *Costain Property Investments* [1984] 1 W.L.R. 763 (C.A.).

[41] *Bain* v. *Brand* (1876) 1 App.Cas. 762, *per* Lord Cairns at p. 767.

[42] See later, at (I) E (6).

tures.[43] If the fixture belongs to the landlord, either because it was his at the outset or because he provided it, then it is known as a "landlord's fixture." In the absence of an express agreement obviously such objects cannot be removed by the tenant.

If a tenant wants to know if he can remove things provided or paid for by him, there are two questions. First is the item a fixture; has it been attached to the land in such a way as to make it part of the land? If the answer is yes, then has the article been attached so that it can be enjoyed or used more easily, or was the intention to make it part of the freehold? At this stage the argument tends to become a little circular. To determine the intent one has to look at the extent and mode of annexation.

(3) *Have the Things Been Attached to the Freehold?*

If the things rest on the ground by their own weight, and are not attached they are unlikely to be fixtures, *e.g.* moveable sheds,[44] barns[45] simply resting on brick foundations, moveable warehouse hoist jibs[46] and removable commercial greenhouses.[47] Yet even here intention can intrude.

> "Thus blocks of stone placed one on top of another without any mortar or cement for the purpose of forming a drystone wall would become part of the land, though the same stones, if deposited in a builder's yard and for convenience sake stacked on the top of each other in the form of a wall, would remain chattels.... Perhaps the true rule is, that articles not otherwise attached to the land than by their own weight are not to be considered as part of the land, unless the circumstances are such as to show that they were intended to be part of the land, the onus of showing that they were so intended lying on those who assert that they have ceased to be chattels, and that, on the contrary, an article which is affixed to the land even slightly is to be considered as part of the land, unless the circumstances are such as to show that it was intended all along to continue a chattel, the onus lying on those who contend it is a chattel."[48]

Hence in *Pole-Carew* v. *Western Counties & General Manure Co.*[49] a

[43] *Ibid.*
[44] *Stedman* v. *Moore* (1874) 10 L.T. (O.S.) 289; 12 J.P. 39, N.P.
[45] *Wansbrough* v. *Maton* (1836) 4 Ad. & E. 884.
[46] *Davis* v. *Jones* (1818) 2 B. & A. 165.
[47] *H. E. Dibble Ltd. (trading as Mill Lane Nurseries)* v. *Moore* [1970] 2 Q.B. 181 (holding that such greenhouses were not included in the sale of a market garden).
[48] *Holland* v. *Hodgson* (1872) L.R. 7 C.P. 328 at p. 335, Blackburn J.; [1861–73] All E.R. Rep. 237.
[49] [1920] 2 Ch. 97; [1920] All E.R. Rep. 274.

substantial free-standing chemical plant and towers for the manufacture of sulphuric acid were, therefore, regarded as an integral part of a building permanently annexed to the freehold.

(4) *Were the Items Intended to Become Landlord's Fixtures?*

If the circumstances clearly show the purpose of the attachment was only to fasten the thing temporarily for its better enjoyment, then that is clear evidence that the article was to continue as a chattel and it will be removable as such. In the "ordinary instance given of a carpet nailed to the floor of a room, the nature of the thing sufficiently shows it is only fastened as a chattel temporarily, and not affixed permanently as part of the land."[50] If the object was attached "for the more complete enjoyment and user of it as a chattel," then this is evidence that it was not intended to become part of the landlord's property.[51] Light bulbs,[52] chairs screwed to the floor of a theatre,[53] panelling and chimney pieces,[54] pictures, curtain rails, kitchen shelving, gas fires and plumbed in washing machines are all attached for their more convenient use, and not for the permanent improvement of the freehold. The nature of the thing may itself demonstrate that it was intended to become part of the property after it was attached, *e.g.* windows, doors, fastenings,[55] in certain circumstances fireplaces, immersion heaters and fan extractors.

(5) *Mode of Attachment*

It is here that the argument becomes circular. There are cases that suggest one looks at the mode of attachment to discover the intention of the person who made the attachment. It is true that the court is apprehensive about investigating the motive of the person who annexed the chattel as opposed to seeking the object and purpose of the attachment.[56] The court will also avoid a consideration whether the screws used were "one inch, or two or three inches long, whether

---

[50] *Holland* v. *Hodgson* (1872) L.R. 7 C.P. 328 at p. 335, Blackburn J.
[51] *Elliott* v. *Bishop* (1854) 10 Ex. 496, 508.
[52] *British Economical Map Co. Ltd.* v. *Empire Mile End Ltd.* [1913] 29 T.L.R. 386; *cf. Vaudeville Electric Cinema* v. *Muriset* [1923] 2 Ch. 74.
[53] *Lyon & Co.* v. *London City & Midland Bank* [1903] 2 K.B. 135; [1900–3] All E.R. Rep. 598.
[54] *Spyer* v. *Phillipson* [1931] 2 Ch. 183; [1930] All E.R. Rep. 457, and see also *Re De Falbe, Ward* v. *Taylor* [1901] 1 Ch. 523, affd: *sub nom. Leigh* v. *Taylor* [1902] A.C. 157; [1900–3] All E.R. Rep. 520.
[55] *Liford's Case* (1614) 11 Co.Rep. 46b; [1558–1774] All E.R. Rep. 73.
[56] *Re De Falbe, Ward* v. *Taylor* [1901] 1 Ch. 523 at p. 535, Vaughan Williams L.J. (tapestries, period fireplaces and chimney glasses).

there were half-a-dozen or a dozen of them, or whether they did or did not penetrate into the plaster of the wall."[57]

In *Hellawell* v. *Eastwood*[58] the issue was whether cotton spinning machinery partly screwed into wooden floors, and partly fixed into stone flooring and secured by molten lead remained the tenant's property. Parke B.[59] pointed out that it was a question of fact, depending principally on two considerations

> " . . . first, the mode of annexation to the soil or fabric of the house, and the extent to which it is united to them, whether it can easily be removed, integre, salve, et commode, or not, without injury to itself or the fabric of the building; secondly, on the object and purpose of the annexation, whether it was for the permanent and substantial improvement of the dwelling . . . or merely for a temporary purpose, or the more complete enjoyment and use of it as a chattel."

(6) *Removal*

If the chattels are not fixtures, they remain the tenant's property, will pass to his trustee in bankruptcy, in certain circumstances can be taken by the landlord as distress for unpaid rent, and can be removed by the tenant without further ado. If the chattels have become fixtures, then at least for the time being they lose their character of chattels and become part of the land.[60] They will therefore pass to the landlord's mortgagee and prima facie cannot be removed by the tenant. The inconvenience that would result from complete inability to remove items regarded as fixtures is obvious. There are therefore three principal exceptions. First, domestic items either of ornament or domestic utility can be removed by the outgoing tenant. So also can trade fixtures. Furthermore there are specific rules affecting agricultural fixtures. Chattels in these three groups are known as "tenant's fixtures."

Domestic items may include, for example, pictures, wall hangings, mirrors, kitchen stoves[61] and grates. Today the list would probably cover plumbed in household washing machines, refrigerators and fitted cookers, kitchen furniture and cupboards, but probably not built in bedroom suites, immersion heaters and gas geysers. There is obvious scope for argument over the modern fitted kitchen with separately built in grills, hot plates and ovens.

---

[57] *Ibid.* Rigby L.J. at p. 531.
[58] (1851) 6 Ex. 295.
[59] At p. 312.
[60] *Lee* v. *Risdon* (1816) 7 Taun. 188; *Gibson* v. *Hammersmith & City Ry.* (1863) 2 Dr. & Sm. 603.
[61] *Grymes* v. *Boweren* (1830) Bing. 437, and see further Amos and Ferard on *Fixtures* (3rd ed.).

The reason behind the exception in favour of trade fixtures is to encourage trade.[62] If tenants who installed expensive machinery and utensils were unable to remove them on giving up possession, this would be a strong disincentive either to capital investment or the taking of tenancies. Trade fixtures, infinite in their variety, include sheds,[63] machinery, petrol pumps,[64] engines, plant, vats, but not substantial buildings.[65]

For many years the exception for trade fixtures did not include agricultural fixtures, *i.e.* fixtures installed for the purposes of farming.[66] Section 10 of the Agricultural Holdings Act 1986 gives the tenant the right to remove engines, machinery, fencing or other fixtures of whatever description and buildings up to two months after the end of the tenancy. The right to remove is extended to fixtures whether affixed for the purposes of agriculture or not.[67] The tenant must have complied with his part of the lease and given to the landlord at least one month's written notice before he removes the items at the end of the tenancy.[68] The landlord can elect to purchase the items at a fair value.[69] The tenant's right does not extend to fixtures affixed or buildings erected in pursuance of some obligation in that behalf, or to buildings in respect of which he was entitled to compensation.

The fixtures which the tenant can remove should be removed before the end of his original term.[70] Once the term has ended, he has no right to go back and remove his fixtures unless the notice ending his tenancy allows too little time to complete the removal.[71] His right to remove items continues during what has been called "an excrescence on the term."[72] For some time it was not clear if the tenant could remove his fixtures when he remained in possession as tenant by holding over, or under the Rent Act 1977, or an extension of a lease of business premises under Part II of the Landlord and Tenant Act 1954. *New Zealand Government Property Corporation* v. *H.M. & S.* clearly establishes that the tenant retains his right of removal so long as he is in possession.[73]

"If the tenant surrenders his lease and vacates the premises

---

[62] And see *Elwes* v. *Maw* (1802) 3 Ea.38; [1775–1802] All E.R. Rep. 320.
[63] *Webb* v. *Frank Bevis Ltd.* [1940] 1 All E.R. 247.
[64] *Smith* v. *City Petroleum Co. Ltd.* [1940] 1 All E.R. 260.
[65] *Whitehead* v. *Bennett* (1858) 27 L.J. Ch. 474.
[66] *Elwes* v. *Maw* above. The agricultural tenant has the same right to enjoy trade fixtures as a business tenant.
[67] Agricultural Holdings Act 1986, s.10(1)(*a*).
[68] Agricultural Holdings Act 1986, s.10(3).
[69] *Ibid.* s. 10(4).
[70] *Barff* v. *Probyn* (1895) 64 L.J.Q.B. 557; [1895–9] All E.R. Rep. 1038.
[71] *Stansfield* v. *Portsmouth Corporation* (1858) 4 C.B., N.S. 120.
[72] *Mackintosh* v. *Trotter* (1838) 3 M. & W. 184, Parke B.
[73] [1982] Q.B. 1145 (C.A.).

without removing the tenant's fixtures, then he is held to have abandoned them. But if he surrenders his lease, either expressly or by operation of law, and remains in possession under a new lease, it is a question of construction of the instrument of surrender whether or not he has also given up his right to remove his fixtures. If nothing is said, then the common law rule applies, and he retains his right to remove the fixtures so long as he is in possession as a tenant."[74]

But difficulties can arise if at the end of the term the old tenant sells his fixtures to a new tenant, who takes a new tenancy. As the old tenant did not remove the fixtures before the end of his term, they will become his landlord's property and form part of the property let to the new tenant. The incoming tenant will be unable either to sell or remove the fixtures, unless the landlord agrees that they retain their characteristic of being removable tenant's fixtures.[75] The tenant's ability to remove fixtures may be restricted by the terms of his lease. If he has agreed to yield up the premises at the end of the term with all fittings and fixtures he will have to leave behind his tenant's fixtures[76] including his trade fixtures.[77] "If the landlord wishes to restrict his tenant's ordinary right to remove trade fixtures attached to the demised premises . . . the landlord must say so in plain language. If the language used leaves the matter doubtful, the ordinary right of the tenant to remove trade fixtures will not be affected."[78] A tenant should make sure that the covenant to yield up expressly excludes "tenant's fixtures."

Damage caused by removal should be made good. If the tenant is removing, for example, special light fittings that replaced fittings originally on the premises, then the originals should be replaced or something like them substituted if they no longer exist. If the premises are left in a damaged condition, the landlord can sue for damages either under the repairing covenant, or in tort for waste.[79]

---

[74] *Ibid. per* Dunn L.J. at p. 1161.

[75] Rent Act 1977, s.120, makes it a criminal offence for an assigning tenant to charge the incoming tenant a sum exceeding a reasonable amount for the fixtures he has provided or improved which he cannot remove as against the landlord. There is also a restriction on charging an excessive price for furniture, s.123, and furniture includes fittings, s.128(1).

[76] *Burt* v. *Haslett* (1856) 18 C.B. 162, affd. at p. 893.

[77] *Leschallas* v. *Woolf* [1908] 1 Ch. 641, where the tenant covenanted to yield up "with all and singular the fixtures and articles belonging thereto."

[78] *Lambourn* v. *McLellan* [1903] 2 Ch. 268, Vaughan Williams L.J. at p. 277, where a tenant's boot and shoe machinery could be removed as it was not of the same kind as items contained in a list comprising "doors, locks, keys, stoves, hearths . . . pipes, pumps . . . and all other fixtures."

[79] *Mancetter Developments Ltd.* v. *Garmanson Ltd and Givertz* [1986] 1 All E.R. 449..

II. WHO CAN CREATE LEASES, AND FOR HOW LONG?

A. Sole Owners

It is a normal incident of the freeholder's estate that its owner can create tenancies. The Land Registration Act 1925, s.18(1)(*e*), expressly states that a registered owner of the freehold may grant leases. A tenant similarly has the power to create sub-tenancies.[80] The Land Registration Act 1925, s.21(1)(*d*), states this to be a right of the registered proprietor of a leasehold interest. The tenant's right to create sub-tenancies is frequently excluded or restricted by the terms of his lease. In any event the sub-tenancy must be for a shorter period than the tenant's own term of years. An individual owner's rights may be affected by personal disabilities,[81] *e.g.* an unsound mind, bankruptcy, etc.

B. Trustees and Beneficiaries

Whenever an estate is to be enjoyed by more than one person either consecutively or concurrently one, of two forms of trust apparatus must be used. If the estate is to be enjoyed consecutively then traditionally the estate owner would make a settlement under the machinery of the Settled Land Act 1925. Sometimes it is provided on divorce that the house shall be enjoyed by the wife during her life and by the children when she is dead. Here again use may be made of the machinery of the Settled Land Act 1925.[82] The fee simple, or if the settlement comprises a leasehold, the term of years absolute, will usually be vested[83] in the tenant for life. A tenant for life is the beneficiary of full age currently entitled to the income[84] or the person who is entitled to exercise his powers.[85] If there is no such person, then the trustees as the statutory owners can exercise the tenant for life's powers.[86]

If the property is to be enjoyed concurrently, *e.g.* when spouses, partners or others acquire a property together, then the legal estate must be held by not more than four persons[87] upon trust to sell.[88] The net proceeds of sale and the profits until sale are held for the

[80] *Leith Properties* v. *Byrne* [1983] Q.B. 433.
[81] *Woodfall*, paras. 1–0150, 1–0160.
[82] S.L.A. 1925, s.1, sets out the circumstances where there are settlements within the Act.
[83] S.L.A. 1925, ss.4, 5.
[84] He is identified in S.L.A. 1925, s.19.
[85] S.L.A. 1925, s.20.
[86] S.L.A. 1925, s.23, save where the settlement has nominated some person of full age to exercise the powers of a tenant for life.
[87] T.A. 1925, s.34.
[88] L.P.A. 1925, s.34(2).

beneficial owners either jointly or in shares.[89] The trust for sale can be used to enable beneficiaries to enjoy property consecutively. In most cases, *e.g.* where husbands and wives acquire property, the trustees or nominal owners will hold the proceeds of sale for themselves. They will therefore be both the trustees or the nominal owners of the legal estate and also own the beneficial interest. For historical reasons it is easier to consider the leasing ability of tenants for life, trustees for sale and beneficiaries under a trust in that order.

(1) *Tenants for Life*

The tenant for life has the right to call for the legal estate to be vested in him.[90] He then can exercise the statutory leasing powers.[91] He may create:

(1) A building lease[92] or a forestry lease[93] for 999 years.
(2) A mining lease for 100 years.[94]
(3) Other leases for 50 years.[95]

Generally the lease must be by deed[96] at the best rent reasonably obtainable[97] bearing in mind any capital premium receivable,[98] and improvements undertaken by the tenant. It must contain a covenant to pay rent and a right of re-entry if the rent is not paid after a specified period not exceeding 30 days, the counterpart executed by the lessee has to be handed over to the tenant for life, and the tenancy has to commence within 12 months of the lease.[99] The best rent is not necessarily the highest rent, for a lower rent which is more likely to be paid may be a better rent than a higher one from someone likely to default.[1]

Notice of an intended transaction has to be given to the settlement trustees[2] unless the lease is for less than 21 years at the best rent that

---

[89] L.P.A. 1925, s.35. Frequently the precise beneficial interest will be set out in a separate detailed declaration of trust.

[90] S.L.A. 1925, s.7.

[91] S.L.A. 1925, ss.41–48. By s.106 if the settlement contains any prohibition or limitation or inducement against exercise of the powers, the provision is void so far as it might have that effect.

[92] S.L.A. 1925, s.44.

[93] S.L.A. 1925, s.48.

[94] Part of the rent has to be capitalised, S.L.A. 1925, s.47.

[95] S.L.A. 1925, s.41.

[96] Unless it is for less than three years, when it can be in writing, S.L.A. 1925, s.42(5)(ii). And see [1979] Conv. 258 (M. Dockray).

[97] An exception exists in the case of leases for public and charitable purposes, S.L.A. 1925, s.55.

[98] This is payable as capital money to the trustees of the settlement, S.L.A. 1925, s.42(4).

[99] Unless it is a reversionary lease, when it must start within seven years; *quaere* whether the power extends to a concurrent lease, S.L.A. 1925, s.42(1).

[1] *Sutherland* v. *Sutherland* [1893] 3 Ch. 169, 195. Compare the duties of trustees to obtain the best price on a sale, see Samuels (1975) 39 Conv. (N.S.) 177, and Taylor (1968) 32 Conv. (N.S.) 412.

[2] S.L.A. 1925, s.101.

may reasonably be obtained without a premium.[3] In agreeing terms
and entering into a lease, the tenant for life has to have regard not only
to his own interest but also those of the settlement as a whole. For this
purpose he is regarded as having the duties and liabilities of a trustee
for the other beneficiaries.[4] The prospective tenant need not enquire if
the tenant for life has given notice to the trustees,[5] and provided that
the tenant has acted in good faith he is conclusively presumed, as
against the other beneficiaries under the settlement, to have paid the
best rent.[6] Of course the statutory powers may have been expressly
extended by the settlement.[7]

If the lease is patently ouside the tenant for life's powers it can be
attacked by the other parties to the settlement and declared to be
invalid. In *Kisch* v. *Hawes Bros. Ltd.*[8] a 21-year lease was forfeited
after 14 years had run because it took effect in possession more than
12 months after its commencement. But a lease by the tenant for life
invalid because of failure to comply with the terms of his powers may
be regarded as a valid agreement for a lease under the Law of Property
Act 1925, s.152. This section is of wide application. It applies
whenever a lease is invalid as a result of failure to comply with leasing
powers conferred by an Act of Parliament or by any other instrument,
for example such leases by tenants for life, trustees, local authorities[9]
and mortgagors.[10] To obtain the benefit of the section the tenant has to
show that he made the lease in good faith. It seems he will not be able
to do this if being challenged on this point he cannot show that the
rent is the best obtainable.[11]

(2) *Trustees for Sale and Personal Representatives*

The trustees hold the legal estate be it freehold or leasehold and as
such owners they can create leases in the same way as a sole owner.[12]
All the trustees who hold the legal estate must be parties to the lease.
Unless a capital premium is payable, a sole surviving trustee can
validly let the property. If there is to be a premium, then it must be
paid to at least two trustees or a trust corporation.[13] The rights of the
beneficiaries where they are not the same people as the trustees, are

[3] S.L.A. 1925, s.42(5).
[4] S.L.A. 1925, s.107(1).
[5] S.L.A. 1925, s.101(5), and see *Davies* v. *Hall* [1954] 2 All E.R. 330.
[6] S.L.A. 1925, s.110(1).
[7] S.L.A. 1925, s.109.
[8] [1935] 1 Ch. 102.
[9] *Readymix Concrete* v. *Farnborough U.D.C.* [1972] C.L.Y. 2020.
[10] *Pawson* v. *Revell* [1958] 2 Q.B. 360.
[11] *Davies* v. *Hall* [1954] 1 All E.R. 330, and see *Chandler* v. *Bradley* [1897] 1 Ch. 315, where a lease
    was granted in return for a bribe.
[12] See before, s.II, A, *ante.*
[13] L.P.A. 1925, s.27(2).

over-reached.[14] They have to look exclusively to the trustees to account for the rents or capital money. Trustees also have all the Settled Land Act powers of the tenant for life and settlement trustees in relation to the management of lands,[15] including the powers of leasing which have just been considered. These powers of leasing are by some considered to limit their inherent powers as estate owners. To avoid this limitation, the trustees' powers of disposal and leasing will often be expressly extended by the document creating the trust. This will declare that the trustees have all the powers of an absolute owner to mortgage, sell or lease the property.

One thing trustees cannot do is to let property to themselves.[16] This is logical but inconvenient. Partners often own their own premises but may not want them to be part of the partnership asset. Strictly they are unable to let the premises as owners to themselves as partners. Indeed the suggestion that they could do so was described by Viscount Simonds as fanciful and whimsical, and such a purported lease was "a monstrous child."[17] The reason is that they are as owners entitled to possession, and can hardly enforce covenants against themselves, but the inability to determine their rights as owners against themselves as partners causes difficulties when one of the partners leaves the firm either on death or retirement. It is obviously more satisfactory if the rights of the estate of the deceased or retiring partner can be clearly delineated in respect of non-partnership property at the time the original agreement is reached. No problem arises when there is not complete identity between all the owners and the partners.

In a number of situations the sole legal and apparently beneficial owner may be regarded by the law as holding the land on trust for sale. This will ordinarily arise where there has been a contribution towards the costs of acquisition by the owner's wife or other relation[18] or *a fortiori* by a stranger. Again this does not affect his leasing powers or the validity of any lease he creates provided that the tenant acts in good faith. Letting the property in these circumstances may render the sole owner liable to an action for breach of trust at the suit of the persons claiming to be entitled to a share in the proceeds of sale.[19]

(3) *Beneficiaries*

Trustees for sale can delegate their powers of management in creating leases to anyone who is entitled to the benefit of the rents and profits

---

[14] L.P.A. 1925, s.2(1).
[15] L.P.A. 1925, s.28(1).
[16] *Rye* v. *Rye* [1962] A.C. 496.
[17] *Ibid.* p. 506.
[18] See Snell's *Equity* (28th ed.), pp. 179 *et seq.*; Hanbury and Maudsley, pp. 252. *et seq.*
[19] *Peffer* v. *Rigg* [1977] 1 W.L.R. 285.

of the land during his life.[20] The appointment has to be in writing and is revocable. The beneficiary has to exercise the power in the names of all the trustees.[21] If the trustees are asked to delegate and refuse, then the beneficiary can apply to the court for an order directing delegation. Formal delegation is unusual. But the situation often occurs where trustees hold a house on trust for sale with power to permit the late owner's widow or other beneficiary to live there rent free for life. The widow may be one of the trustees and often will create tenancies of part of the property.[22] A tenancy so created will bind both parties to it by estoppel,[23] but will not bind the trustees who can take steps to remove the tenant, for example on the widow's death. Furthermore, if the tenancy is brought to a premature end, the tenant may well be remediless. He may be unable to sue on the covenants express or implied, for quiet enjoyment as he has been disturbed by someone from whom his landlord claims, and not from someone claiming from his landlord.[24] A further aggravation is that the right of the prospective tenant to see the freehold title is statutorily restricted.[25] An inquiring, cautious, prospective tenant may be unable to find out what really is the position.[26]

Personal representatives, *i.e.* executors or administrators, have the same powers of dealing with property as trustees for sale for the purposes of winding up the estate, or during a beneficiary's infancy or a life interest.[27] Furthermore, where they hold the estate on trust for sale, which they do on an intestacy,[28] they have the same detailed powers as trustees for sale that are contained in the Law of Property Act 1925. These include the leasing powers just considered. Like trustees they all have to join in the creation of leases.[29]

C. Charity Trustees

It is not possible to consider the leasing powers of all charity trustees collectively. The powers of charity trustees often depend on the nature of the trust which is being administered. There are specialised rules relating to ecclesiastical charities.[30] The nature of the powers depend

---

[20] L.P.A. 1925, s.29.
[21] L.P.A. 1925, s.29(2).
[22] Rent Act protection is substantially diminished when the dwelling is shared with the landlord, R.A. 1977, ss.12, 21.
[23] *Stratford* v. *Syrett* [1958] 1 Q.B. 107.
[24] See *Jones* v. *Lavington* [1903] 1 K.B. 253 and *Markham* v. *Paget* [1908] 1 Ch. 697, and see *post* on the implied covenants for quiet enjoyment, Chap. 4(IV)E.
[25] L.P.A. 1925, s.44(2).
[26] If the transaction is proceeding formally and is governed by the Law Society's or National Conditions of Sale, then there may be a contractual right to see the paramount title: see *post*, (IV).
[27] A.E.A. 1925, s.39.
[28] A.E.A. 1925, s.33.
[29] A.E.A. 1925, s.2(2).
[30] *Woodfall*, para 1–0227.

on the nature of the lessor, or lessors—the Bishop, incumbent, trustees of a special Church of England trust, of a Methodist Circuit,[31] or of a Roman Catholic Convent. In this last case it is not unusual to find the assets vested in the trustees for the time being apparently as beneficial owners. There are also specialised rules affecting the older educational colleges and foundations,[32] but what might be called ordinary charity trustees have the same leasing powers as a tenant for life or trustees of settled land.[33] However the trustees may have to obtain the Charity Commissions's consent to the letting in the circumstances contained in section 29 of the Charities Act 1960. Here consent is needed only if the lease is for more than 22 years, unless a premium is receivable and either the land being let is part of the permanent endowment of the charity[34] or has been occupied for purposes of the charity.[35]

Section 29 of the Charities Act 1960 contains additional dispensing powers.[36] The lease should state that the land is held on charitable trusts and the tenants should ensure that the necessary consents have been obtained.[37] If the formalities are not observed, the lease of land occupied for the purposes of the charity is still valid in favour of a tenant who "in good faith acquires an interest in the land for money."[38] This clearly includes an honest but ignorant tenant. It is doubtful if it includes one who knew that he was dealing with charity trustees.

D. Mortgagor and Mortgagee

The open market value of rented residential property where the tenant has the benefit of a regulated tenancy is generally about half its vacant possession value. Building society mortgages therefore contain a provision restricting the statutory power of mortgagors in possession to create leases,[39] by a requirement that they first obtain the society's consent. That consent will be forthcoming if the mortgagor is likely to

---

[31] The land is likely to be held on the Trusts contained in the Model Trust Deed. A copy of this can be found in *Encyclopedia of Forms and Precedents* (4th ed.), Vol. 8, p. 270.

[32] *Woodfall*, paras. 1–0242 *et seq.* For Housing Trusts, see Chap. 17, *post.*

[33] S.L.A. 1925, s.29(1).

[34] Charities Act 1960, s.45(3). Land is permanent endowment if the proceeds of sale cannot be spent as income.

[35] This covers functional land used by the charity, although it is not easy to predict when the Charity Commission will regard land as "occupied" for the purposes of a charity. *cf.* the discussion on "occupied for the purposes of a business" in *Groveside Properties* v. *Westminster Medical School* (1984) 47 P. & C.R. 507 (C.A.).

[36] In relation to "exempt charities," set out in Charities Act 1960 Sched. 2, and transactions that are authorised by other Acts of Parliament.

[37] S.L.A. 1925, s.29(1). If the consents have not been obtained and the land forms the charity's "permanent endowment," the lease will be void, *Bishop of Bangor* v. *Parry* [1891] 2 Q.B. 277.

[38] Charities Act 1960, s.29(2).

[39] Contained in L.P.A. 1925, s.99.

be able to recover possession without conspicuous difficulty. This will cover the situation of the owner-occupier going abroad.[40] Alternatively if the locality where the property is situated has changed so that the property can be usefully managed only in multiple occupation then again consent may be given. However, if a development can be exploited only by the granting of tenancies, *e.g.* commercial offices or a block of flats then a mortgage of the whole block will not restrict the creation of tenancies by the mortgagor under the statutory power.

The statutory power, contained in section 99 of the Law of Property Act 1925, is conferred on mortgagors and mortgagees respectively in possession. When in possession they can create agricultural or occupation leases not exceeding 50 years, and building leases not exceeding 999 years. The lease has to take effect in possession within 12 months of its date,[41] be at the best rent reasonably obtainable,[42] and contain a covenant to pay rent and a proviso for re-entry for non-payment after 30 days.[43] A counterpart must be executed by the lessee,[44] and if the lease is entered into by the mortgagor, the counterpart has to be sent to the mortgagee, although failure to do so does not invalidate the lease.[45] If the lease is granted under these powers it will be binding on the other party to the mortgage. To prevent such leases becoming binding, the statutory power of leasing is usually restricted or excluded. This is permitted by section 99(13). But a mortgagor of agricultural land cannot be deprived of his statutory powers of leasing.[46] However, if he creates a tenancy contrary to the terms of his mortgage and without observing the statutory requirements this may still amount to a breach of the terms of the mortgage agreement entitling the lender to take steps to call in the mortgage.[47] And a new lease of business premises agreed or granted under section 36 of the Landlord and Tenant Act 1954 will also be binding on a mortgagee despite any agreement in the mortgage restricting the statutory leasing power.[48]

If the property is already let before the mortgage is created, then of course the lease will bind the mortgagee. The tenant continues to pay rent to the mortgagor who can enforce the terms of the lease. If the

---

[40] When possession can be recovered under R.A. 1977, Sched. 15, Case 11, and see also Case 12; Housing Act 1980, s.66, and Chap. 13, *post.*
[41] L.P.A. 1925, s.99(5).
[42] L.P.A. 1925, s.99(6), no premium must be taken. And see *Lloyds Bank Ltd.* v. *Marcan* [1973] 3 All E.R. 754.
[43] This requirement may be inappropriate in the case of a short periodic tenancy, and see L.P.A. 1925, s.99(17) and *cf. Davies* v. *Hall* [1954] 2 All E.R. 330 at pp. 333, 334.
[44] L.P.A. 1925, s.99(8).
[45] L.P.A. 1925, s.99(11). Failure may cause the power of sale under the mortgage to be immediately exercisable, *Public Trustee* v. *Lawrence* [1912] 1 Ch. 789; [1911–1913] All E.R. Rep. 670.
[46] A.H.A. 1986, Sched. 14, para. 12.
[47] *Rhodes* v. *Dalby* [1971] 1 All E.R. 1144.
[48] L. & T.A. 1954, s.36(4).

mortgagee wants the rent to be paid to him and also to enforce the terms of the lease he has to give notice to the tenant.[49]

Despite the express provisions in their mortgages, borrowers do in fact often create tenancies of all or part of the mortgaged property. If the borrower is only prevented from exercising the statutory power of creating leases then it is still possible for him to create, under his common law powers as an estate owner,[50] a valid tenancy binding at least on himself. It will not be binding on the mortgagee. The mortgagee can regard the tenant as a trespasser,[51] and it follows that as against the mortgagee the tenant cannot claim any of the protection afforded by the Rent Acts[52] to residential tenants. In fact the restrictions on creation of leases in most building society mortgages expressly prohibit also sharing arrangements and licences. Although the lease is not initially binding on the mortgagee, if he accepts rent from the tenant without qualification, or directs the tenant to pay rent to him, then he may be treated as accepting the situation,[53] so that the tenancy will then bind him. This will cause problems if the tenant claims Rent Act protection when the mortgagee tries to obtain vacant possession before selling.

E. Trading Companies

There are no statutory restrictions on a registered company's ability to hold lands. Generally the company's Memorandum of Association expressly states that the company can buy and sell land, take and grant leases and enter into mortgages to further the declared objects of the company.[54] There is a statutory presumption in favour of persons dealing with the company in good faith that it has the legal ability to enter into any transaction decided on by the directors, free of any limitation there may be in the Memorandum or Articles of Association. Such a person dealing with the company is not bound to enquire

---

[49] L.P.A. 1925, s.98(1).

[50] *Iron Trades Employers' Insurance Assn.* v. *Union of House and Land Investors, Ltd.* [1937] Ch. 313.

[51] *Hughes* v. *Waite* [1957] 1 All E.R. 603.

[52] *Dudley and District Benefit Building Society* v. *Emerson* [1949] Ch. 707. Lord Evershed left open whether a statutory tenancy would bind the mortgagee, and see Peter Smith (1977) 41 Conv. (N.S.) 197 arguing they should be binding, based on *Jessamine Investment Co.* v. *Schwartz* [1976] 3 All E.R. 521. In practice mortgagees do not seem to have any difficulty in obtaining possession orders, unless there is collusion between mortgagor and mortgagee, as in *Quennel* v. *Maltby* [1979] 1 W.L.R. 318.

[53] *Stroud Building Society* v. *Delamont* [1960] 1 All E.R. 749; *Chatsworth Properties Ltd.* v. *Effiom* [1971] 1 All E.R. 604. The mortgagee should appoint a receiver as the mortgagor's agent under L.P.A. 1925, s.109 (2). The receiver can collect rent expressly as the mortgagor's agent without making the tenancy binding on the mortgagee, *cf. Lever Finance Ltd.* v. *Needleman's Trustee and Kreutzer* [1956] Ch. 375.

[54] Companies Act 1985, s.36.

about the company's capacity, and his good faith is presumed.[55] Nevertheless, cautious tenants will still make enquiries and searches to satisfy themselves that the company has power to grant the lease, and has not created any prior charges over the land.

F. Local Authorities

Apart from creating council house tenancies local authorities are significant landlords. Frequently they will own and manage industrial, shopping and commercial estates. They have always had a marked reluctance to dispose of their freeholds. On the development of an industrial estate or block of flats the developer needs the security of a long term so that he can recoup his outlay over a number of years, from 21 to 99. He may possibly want to be in a position to grant long leases at low rents and substantial premiums so as to recover his capital investment. A "principal" council[56] can only dispose of land by way of a short tenancy, and for the best consideration that can be obtained, unless the consent of the Secretary of State for the Department of the Environment has been obtained.[57] Consents can be and are given under the powers contained in section 128(1) of the Local Government Act 1972. The consent can be given either for particular transactions or classes of transactions, conditionally or unconditionally, and for local authorities generally, particularly, or for a class. Most local authority dwellinghouses have to be let on secure tenancies within Part IV of the Housing Act 1985. This requirement can be relaxed[58]. A grant without the necessary ministerial consent will be void unless in favour of an individual.[59] In non-housing cases, a failure by a local authority to obtain consent does not invalidate a lease in favour of the tenant, who is not concerned to see if the consent has been obtained.[60] Agreements for the grant of long leases from local authorities are generally expressly subject to the necessary ministerial consents being obtained. One should be careful when dealing with agreements for leases to ensure that the relevant official signing on behalf of a local authority has the legal power to bind his authority.

---

[55] Companies Act 1985, s.35.
[56] Defined in Local Government Act 1972, s.270, as amended, so as to cover non-metropolitan county councils, district councils and London Borough Councils.
[57] Local Government Act 1972, s.123.
[58] Housing Act 1985, s.43, and see also s.32.
[59] Housing Act 1985, s.44(1), and see generally, *post*, Chap. 16.
[60] Local Government Act 1972, s.128(2). The authority would be estopped from denying it had obtained the necessary consents, *cf. Lever Finance Ltd.* v. *Needleman's Trustee and Kreutzer* [1956] Ch. 375.

G. Agents and Attorneys

Agents are of course extensively used in the management and letting of property. The extent of the agent's authority depends on the terms of his agreement with his principal. He may have to refer matters for ultimate decision to his principal or he may be authorised to negotiate terms, agree to grant leases, serve notices to quit and initiate proceedings on the owner's behalf. Even if the agent has acted without authority his principal may subsequently ratify what he has done. If the agent is to grant leases in his principal's name then his authority will have to be under seal if the lease is to be under seal.[61] If the tenancy can be created orally,[62] it is sufficient if the agent's authority was given to him orally.[63]

Powers of attorney are frequently extracted from owners who are likely to be working abroad for extended periods and want their property managed and let in their absence. There are no great difficulties in the case of sole owners and a simple general form[64] will enable the attorney to deal satisfactorily with the property. More detailed forms can spell out and delimit the attorney's powers. But a difficulty arises where the property is owned jointly, for example by a husband and wife. They hold the property as trustees and can delegate their powers[65] by power of attorney granted under section 9 of the Powers of Attorney Act 1971.[66] The power cannot last for more than 12 months and so if a tour of duty abroad lasts longer, it will have to be renewed. The amended section is wider than its forerunner. Before 1971 a trustee could appoint an attorney only if he was going to be out of the United Kingdom for more than a month.

III. WHO CAN TAKE LEASES?

There are no particular difficulties in stating legal competence to be a tenant. Persons of full age and sound mind are competent tenants. Not more than four persons can jointly hold the legal estate.[67] The estate will be held either on express trust for sale, or more commonly subject to the statutory trust for sale in section 35 of the Law of Property Act 1925.

Frequently sporting clubs want to take leases either of playing areas or club headquarters. The membership of the club will be continually

---

[61] *Powell* v. *London & Provincial Bank Ltd.* [1893] 2 Ch. 555.
[62] *e.g.* under L.P.A. 1925, s.54(2).
[63] *Coles* v. *Trecothick* (1804) 9 Ves.Jr. 234; [1803–1813] All E.R. Rep. 14 (an action to enforce a contract for the sale of land signed by an auctioneer verbally authorised to sign).
[64] As in Powers of Attorney Act 1971, Sched. 1.
[65] See *ante* (II)B(2).
[66] Replacing T.A. 1925, s.25.
[67] L.P.A. 1925, s.34(2).

changing and numerous. In such a situation the club will have to appoint nominees or trustees to hold the tenancy and generally other property for the members of the club as a whole. Again not more than four trustees can have the tenancy vested in them.[68] Each will be personally liable to the landlord for breaches of the terms of the lease. They will however have a right to be indemnified and reimbursed out of the club assets for any financial liabilities personally incurred.[69] Individual members of the club will themselves be responsible only to the extent of their annual subscriptions, or other payments which they have contracted to make. In *Wise* v. *Perpetual Trustee Co.*[70] trustees of a club in Sydney, New South Wales took a 10 year lease at £555 per annum. The trustees in the end were liable to pay £5,000 to the lessors in rent and under the terms of the lease. They sought an indemnity from the former members of the club, as the club's assets were insufficient. The Privy Council held that though the trustees were entitled to indemnity out of the club property nevertheless "the feature which distinguished [clubs] from other societies is that no members of such become liable to pay to the funds of the Society or to anyone else any money beyond the subscriptions required by the rules of the Club to be paid so long as he remains a member. It is upon this fundamental condition, not usually expressed but understood by everyone, that clubs are formed." The court said that the decision might be hard on the trustees, but they only had themselves to blame for their imprudence and in not seeing to their own safety. It is always open to trustees to try to contract on the basis that they will only be liable to the extent of the funds out of which they can claim an indemnity.[71] Such a limited covenant might not appeal to a landlord.[72]

IV. PRELIMINARY STEPS TO THE GRANTING OF A LEASE

A. Can the Property be Used for the Tenant's Purposes?

After the premises and landlord have been identified, the prospective tenant will want to know if he can use the premises for the purposes he has in mind. This involves a consideration of the planning position, any restrictive covenants affecting the property, the title of the landlord to grant the proposed lease, the physical suitability of the premises and the likely cost of complying with the covenants proposed. "It is the business of the tenant, if he does not protect

---

[68] T.A. 1925, s.34(1) and (2). For exemptions from this restriction see s.34(3).
[69] T.A. 1925, s.30(2).
[70] [1903] A.C. 139 (J.C.).
[71] See the form in *Ency. of Forms and Precedents* (4th ed.), Vol. 12, at p. 1238.
[72] *Fiduciary* landlords could hardly consider the proposal.

himself by an express warranty, to satisfy himself that the premises are fit for the purpose for which he wants to use them, whether such fitness depends on the state of the structure or the state of the law or any other relevant circumstances."[73]

(1) *Planning and Restrictive Covenants*

(a) Planning

Enquiries will have to be made of both the lessor and the planning authority to ascertain the permitted use for the premises. Enquiry is made of the local planning authority by submitting a local land charge search form and the standard additional enquiries. The search in the register will reveal charges registered under the Local Land Charges Act 1975. The additional enquiries should reveal extant planning permissions and their conditions and details of refusals of applications for permission to develop, information relating to proposals likely to affect the land as a result of highway, planning, or housing schemes, whether the road is adopted by the highway authority, and also if it is likely that the property is drained into a public sewer. If formal enquiries do not resolve outstanding queries, they should be followed by correspondence with or attendances on the planning department.

Planning enquiries should be made when taking a lease[74] of a house, but they are particularly important in commercial leases. In the case of erected premises the permitted use will either be that granted by a planning permission, or established by long user since before December 31, 1963.[75] In commercial premises latitude is granted by the Town and Country Planning (Use Classes) Order 1972[76] to change the use of a building within the ambit of one of the Use classes. For example, a shop can be changed from a hairdresser's to a grocer's without permission, or offices can be used for different types of business, or a light industrial building used by different types of business provided they are carrying on what is defined as light industry. But if the change involves substantial construction works,[77] or a shift from one class of uses to another then planning permission will be necessary. If the physical development involves an extension of less than 10 per cent. of the existing cubic volume or specified changes from certain Use Classes to other Use Classes then the development may be covered by blanket permission granted by the

---

[73] Devlin J. in *Edler* v. *Auerbach* [1950] 1 K.B. 359 at p. 374.

[74] They are unlikely to be made in the case of short periodic tenancies.

[75] T. & C.P.A. 1971, ss.23(2–10), 87, as substituted by Local Government and Planning (Amendment) Act 1981, Sched. 1, para. 1.

[76] S.I. 1972 No. 1385, as amended by S.I. 1983 No. 1614.

[77] *i.e.* development requiring permission under T. & C.P.A. 1971, ss.22, 23.

Town and Country Planning (General Development) Order 1977.[78]
Any physical alterations will have to be completed in accordance with
planning conditions and building regulations. Commercial developers
of factories or industrial premises must further have regard to specific
regulations governing those developments.[79]

When local authorities are involved in development schemes they
can impose negative restrictions and positive obligations on the
developer. The former restrict the uses to which the land can be put,
and the latter may require the observance of numerous provisions in
connection with the development. Both negative restrictions and
positive obligations can be registered as local land charges. As such
they can be enforced directly against individual estate owners of the
affected land from time to time, and irrespective of whether the
individual who has taken the land burdened with the land charge is
himself at fault. The negative restrictions are registrable under section
52 of the Town and Country Planning Act 1971, and the positive
obligations under section 33 of the Local Government (Miscellaneous
Provisions) Act 1982.[80]

(b) Restrictive covenants

(i) *Grant by freeholder*

On the grant of a lease, the prospective tenant is concerned with
restrictive covenants in two ways. Most obviously, are the terms of the
proposed lease likely to interfere with tenant's plans? Does the lease
restrict the user to that of a private dwelling-house only? If business
user is permitted, is user restricted to certain trades or businesses?
Will the restrictions affect natural developments of the tenant's
business or make it difficult for him to dispose freely of the lease?
These are matters for negotiation, and the extent and effect of such
covenants for user are considered later.[81] Less obviously, the freeholder himself may be bound by covenants restrictive of the user of his
estate imposed for the benefit of other adjoining or neighbouring land.
If the tenant uses the property contrary to the terms of those
covenants could the owners of the benefit of the covenant restrain the
tenant's user?

The tenant will be bound by restrictive covenants affecting his
freehold landlord only if he has notice of them. First of all the
covenants must be negative in nature if not in form. They are not

---

[78] S.I. 1977 No. 289.
[79] T. & C.P. (Industrial Development Certificates) Regulations 1979 (S.I. 1979 No. 838), and see
further *Encyclopedia of Planning*, and Heap's *Outline of Planning Law* (8th ed.).
[80] Local authority attempts to make these matters registrable when they appear as covenants in
leases to developers seem misconceived in the light of Local Land Charges Act 1975, s.2, but the
practice of registering covenants in leases is common.
[81] *Post* Chap. 4(IV)D.

negative in nature if they oblige the person who has to observe them to spend money.[82] The burden of positive covenants does not automatically run with the land so as to bind successive owners.[83] But in the case of restrictive covenants "nothing could be more inequitable than that the original purchaser should be able to sell the property the next day for a greater price, in consideration of the assignee being allowed to escape from the liability which he had himself undertaken."[84] Secondly, therefore, to be bound the tenant must have notice. It is at this point that difficulties in relation to lettings of property arise. If the lessor's title is registered the restrictive covenants or their existence should either be contained in or noted in the Charges register. That registration constitutes actual notice to all persons dealing with the land whether they have searched the register or not.[85] However, to inspect the register one needs the registered proprietor's authority. But there is no statutory obligation on the freehold lessor to give this authority to the prospective tenant.[86] Simonds J. said[87]:

> " ... it appears to me to be clear beyond all doubt that, when notice of an incumbrance has been entered on the register, it is notice to all the world, though it may be, and I recognise it as perhaps a blot, that the lessee, unless he makes some bargain to that effect, is not permitted to inspect the register. The answer is: He is at liberty, if he thinks fit, to make such a bargain, and refuse to enter into any contract or lease, unless first he obtains the permission of the lessor, who can grant it to him, to inspect the register."

Much the same result is reached if the title is unregistered. If the covenant has been entered into since 1925 then it should be registered against the freeholder who covenanted to observe it as a Class D (ii) land charge.[88] Registration constitutes actual notice to all persons and for all purposes connected with the land.[89] If the covenant has not been registered, then it will not be binding on a purchaser[90] even if he

---

[82] *Haywood* v. *Brunswick P.B.S.* (1881) 8 Q.B.D. 403.
[83] Unless they are registered as local land charges under Local Government (Miscellaneous Provisions) Act 1982, s.33, and see further Report on Positive Covenants (1965) Cmnd. 2719.
[84] *Tulk* v. *Moxhay* (1848) 2 Ph. 774; [1843–60] All E.R. Rep. 9, Lord Cottenham L.C. (preventing development of the garden in Leicester Sq.).
[85] L.R.A. 1925, ss.20(1)(*a*), 50(2), 52(1), and see *White* v. *Bijou Mansions Ltd.* [1937] Ch. 610, affd. [1938] Ch. 351.
[86] L.R.A. 1925, s.110.
[87] In *White* v. *Bijou Mansions Ltd.*, above at p. 621 (covenant to build dwelling-house and use as a private residence, later conversion by tenant to single room flatlets).
[88] L.C.A. 1972, s.2(5).
[89] L.P.A. 1925, s.198(1).
[90] "Purchaser" includes lessee, L.P.A. 1925, s.205(1)(xxi).

has notice of it.[91] If the covenant was entered into before 1925, then a tenant taking a lease since that date will only be bound by the pre-1925 covenant if he had actual notice of it. The duty of proving that the tenant had notice is on the person seeking to enforce the covenant.[92]

The tenant's position is therefore that he is bound by post-1925 restrictive covenants which have been registered as land charges. However he may not be in a position to discover their existence. Section 44(2) of the Law of Property Act 1925 provides that: "Under a contract to grant or assign a term of years, whether derived or to be derived out of freehold or leasehold land, the intended lessee or assign shall not be entitled to call for the title to the freehold." It is probably true to say that unless a substantial premium is being paid, or the lease is for more than 21 years, prospective tenants will not ask to see the freehold title, although they may ask if there are any covenants affecting the freehold that will restrict the proposed user. Strictly, the tenant should ask for both the freehold title and the names of the estate owners since 1925. On the grant of a lease by the freeholder, the prospective tenant should ask for the freehold title to be deduced for a period of not less than 15 years before the date of the contract up to the date of the grant of the lease.[93] Although this does not theoretically give the tenant all the information he needs,[94] he is in practice unlikely to be disturbed by a covenant imposed before the root of his title and not mentioned at all in the documents of the title deduced.[95]

(ii) *Grant by leaseholder*

A sub-tenant is likely to be affected by three sets of restrictive covenants:

(1) those affecting the freehold title;
(2) those contained in the lease between the freeholder and the intermediate landlord;
(3) those contained in his under-lease.

---

[91] L.P.A. 1925, s.199(1); L.C.A. 1972, s.4(6), declares the covenant void against the tenant who takes a legal estate, see *Midland Bank Trust Co. Ltd.* v. *Green* [1981] A.C. 513 (H.L.).

[92] *Shears* v. *Wells* [1936] 1 All E.R. 832 (1852 covenant against permitting noisy or offensive business not binding on tenant who took a lease in 1931 to repair motors).

[93] The length of title for unregistered conveyancing was reduced to 15 years by L.P.A. 1969, s.23. S.25 contains machinery for compensating purchasers adversely affected by land charges registered against the name of persons not parties to the transactions in the title, and of which the purchaser had no actual knowledge. Actual knowledge is determined without reference to L.P.A. 1925, s.198. The section does not apply to the grant of a term of years out of the freehold, L.P.A. 1969, s.25(9).

[94] He should still have the names of all post-1925 estate owners.

[95] It seems unlikely that a prospective tenant can neglect to ask for the freehold title, rely on L.P.A. 1925, s.44(5), and argue that he does not have actual notice of registered covenants, *cf. White* v. *Bijou Mansions Ltd.* [1937] Ch. 610.

If he is a sub-under-tenant then he may be affected by those in his immediate landlord's lease. If the restrictive covenants affecting the freehold are registered as Class D (ii) land charges they will bind all the sub-tenants.[96] The same is true of covenants noted on or contained in the charges register where the title is registered. Restrictive covenants contained in the lease between the freeholder and his tenant cannot be registered as land charges.[97] When the head tenant proposes to grant an under-lease the prospective under-tenant should ask to see his lease.[98] If he does not he is still nevertheless regarded as having notice of its contents and is bound by its restrictive covenants.[99] And a prospective under-tenant's solicitor who fails to ask to see the lease is likely to be liable in negligence for any consequential loss.[1]

However, the position becomes more complicated on further sub-letting. If the under-tenant grants a sub-under-lease, he ought to disclose his own under-lease, and in any event the sub-under-tenant is regarded as having constructive notice of its contents and so is bound by restrictive covenants therein.[2] The prospective sub-under-tenant does not have the right to ask for sight of the lease between the freeholder and the head tenant[3] and is not regarded as having notice of anything in it.[4] If he does not have notice of the covenants, he is not bound by them. This position may be altered by contract between the parties, and if as a result the sub-under-tenant does have notice of covenants in the head lease he will be bound by them. The position is much the same in the case of land with registered title. However, if the head-lease or indeed any subsequent lease is to last for more than 21 years title to it may be registered,[5] and if the land is in an area of compulsory registration and the lease is for more than 40 years title to it must be registered.[6] The effect of registration is to give actual notice of restrictive covenants to all persons dealing with the land, even if they do not have authority to inspect the register.

---

[96] A sub-tenant who is adversely affected by the existence of a registered land charge and who can bring himself within the protection of L.P.A. 1969, s.25 (see above n. 93) may be able to claim compensation under that section, see L.P.A. 1969, s.25(9) (*b*).

[97] L.C.A. 1972, s.2(5).

[98] He has a right to see it, see *Woodfall*, para. 1–1719, *Megarry and Wade*, p. 725.

[99] *Patman* v. *Harland* (1881) 17 Ch.D. 353.

[1] *Hill* v. *Harris* [1965] 2 Q.B. 601 (business use restricted in lease to boot and shoe makers and dealers, sub-tenant prevented by freeholder from trading as confectioner and tobacconist).

[2] *Patman* v. *Harland* (1881) 17 Ch.D. 353.

[3] L.P.A. 1925, s.44(4).

[4] L.P.A. 1925, s.44(5). See further *Megarry and Wade*, pp. 723–727.

[5] L.R.A. 1925, s.8.

[6] L.R.A. 1925, s.123.

(2) *Dilapidations Survey and Inventory*

A prospective tenant, like a purchaser, will satisfy himself about the physical condition and suitability of the property. The nature and extent of the tenant's and landlord's covenants to repair are considered later.[7] Normally the tenant will not have to leave the property in a better state of repair than it is when let to him. If the lease is a substantial one or the repairing covenant likely to be onerous, a dilapidations survey should be made before the lease, and the disrepair itemised and agreed at that stage. The survey should obviously be repeated at the end of the lease by a surveyor who knows the various repairing liabilities. A schedule should also be made of the landlord's fittings, fixtures and contents either if they are being let to and have to be replaced by the tenant, or if they are being sold to him. If the items are being let the inventory should be agreed at the outset, and at the end of the term the items should again be compared with the descriptions in the inventory.

B. Can the Landlord Grant the Tenancy?

(1) *The Landlord's Title*

More often than not the landlord's title is neither investigated nor questioned. Indeed section 44(2) of the Law of Property Act 1925 provides that an intended assignee or grantee of a term of years derived or to be derived out of the freehold or leasehold has no right to call for the title to the freehold reversion. In other words on the grant of the head lease of the whole building the original tenant cannot ask to see the freehold title. The same restriction applies to his assignees and under-tenants. If after the head lease of the whole building has been granted and assigned, a subsequent assignee intends to grant an under-lease of a whole floor, he must produce the original instrument of lease, and prove that the lease is still valid and has been properly assigned to him. He will prove title by producing the assignments normally for the last 15 years before the proposed sub-lease. If the matter is taken one stage further, and the under-lessee of the whole floor proposes to grant a sub-under-lease of a suite of rooms on that floor, then he will have to produce his title. He should begin with the lease of the whole floor and again deduce subsequent assignments, if there are any. But section 44(4) of the Law of Property Act 1925 restricts the right of the intended sub-under-lessee of the suite of rooms to call for the title of the head tenant of the whole

---

[7] See *post*, Chap. 6.

building although he should see a copy of the head lease. The statutory provisions can be altered by agreement,[8] but where they apply, the prospective tenant is not to be affected with notice of matters he might have known about had he required the landlord to produce his title.[9]

Title should and will generally be asked for on the grants of long leases. The leasehold title will generally be asked for on the grant of under-leases. The tenant granting the under-lease should be asked for confirmation that so far as he is aware no covenant or condition in the lease has been broken. In any event he should be asked to produce the receipt for the last payment of rent.[10] A sub-tenant is particularly concerned to ensure that there are no restrictions on the creation of the sub-lease and the subsequent assignments of it. If there are, this may cause a forfeiture of the superior lease, and his own may fall with it.[11]

(2) *Tenancy by Estoppel*

One reason why the lack of investigation of title does not frequently give rise to difficulty between the landlord and the tenant is that both parties are prevented from denying the validity of the creation of the tenancy.[12] The landlord cannot argue that he was unable to create the tenancy,[13] and the tenant cannot avoid liability under the tenancy by adducing evidence that the landlord was incapable of creating it. Harman J. in *E. H. Lewis & Son Ltd.* v. *Morelli*[14] pointed out that the inability of the tenant to question his landlord's title cannot strictly operate by estoppel as it applies even where there is no deed and the tenancy is created either in writing or orally. He said that the doctrine also applies where the tenant knows of the defects in the landlord's title but nevertheless enters and pays rent. The inability of the tenant to challenge lasts as long as the tenant is in possession unless he is evicted by someone with a title paramount or its equivalent. And it is now clear that the tenant cannot deny his landlord's title after he has gone out of possession unless he is confronted by an adverse claim to the property by a third person. In *Industrial Properties (Barton Hill) Ltd.* v. *Associated Electrical Industries*[15] the tenants were alleged to be

---

[8] L.P.A. 1925, s.44(10).

[9] L.P.A. 1925, s.44(5). He will still be affected by land charges which have been registered under L.C.A. 1972, see L.P.A. 1925, s.198, and by incumbrances registered in the Charges Register.

[10] L.P.A. 1925, s.45(2).

[11] *Becker* v. *Partridge* [1966] 2 Q.B. 155 (reversioner's consent to sub-letting not obtained, as required by the under-lease).

[12] See generally Jill Martin [1978] Conv. (N.S.) 137.

[13] Unless the grant is *ultra vires* as in *Minister of Agriculture and Fisheries* v. *Matthews* [1950] 1 K.B. 148, where the Minister had no statutory powers to grant leases of requisitioned land.

[14] [1948] 2 All E.R. 1021.

[15] [1977] Q.B. 580.

in breach of repairing covenants. After they had gone out of possession they discovered that their landlords could not in law have granted the lease. They argued unsuccessfully that this could be a defence to a claim for dilapidations. But it is open to a tenant to show that his interest has determined, and to stop paying rent, unless he has made payments after knowing the true facts.[16]

A landlord may indeed have a defective title at the time when he grants the lease, *e.g.* he may create a tenancy at a time when he has only contracted to purchase the freehold, or when he has mortgaged the property and agreed not to create tenancies. If the defects of the title are removed, in the first instance by acquiring the freehold and in the second by paying off the mortgage, then this will automatically enure for the benefit of the tenant. The tenant's title by estoppel is said to be "fed" by the lessor's perfected title without the need for any further documentation or agreement.[16]

C. The Contract for a Lease

It is not possible to classify exhaustively agreements leading to a lease, but they are likely to fall into one of the four following categories. (i) Often in the case of short lettings at lower rentals there will have been discussions reaching agreement on rent, both its amount and frequency, how long the tenancy is to last and when it is to start. (ii) If the parties are conducting their affairs slightly more formally they may have written to each other or signed a memorandum setting out the heads of their arrangement. (iii) It is particularly common in arrangements for the lettings of smaller commercial properties to find that the parties have reached their agreement partly orally, partly in correspondence, and that they have agreed that the terms of the lease should be drawn up by a solicitor and approved by the parties. (iv) Lastly, where the term is longer and the rent more substantial and possibly a premium is being taken as well, there will usually be a formal written agreement for the grant of the lease, the agreed terms of which are annexed to the document.

In most cases the tenant will take possession, the lease will be granted and no difficulty arises, but it may be that one or other party will deny that a binding agreement was reached, or if reached declines to implement it, or alleges a breach. It will then be essential to decide if they have reached a binding agreement and what are its terms. It will be seen that the oral agreement in the first category is likely to be valid but unenforceable because evidential requirements have not been observed. The second agreement contained in correspondence or

---

[16] *National Westminster Bank Ltd.* v. *Hart* [1983] Q.B. 773.
[17] *Church of England Building Society* v. *Piskor* [1954] Ch. 553, and see A. M. Pritchard (1964) 80 L.Q.R. 370.

a signed memorandum is likely to be valid and enforceable, but possibly not on the terms that both parties would have preferred. In the third arrangement, as the precise terms of the lease still have to be agreed, there is no complete agreement at all. In the last instance, that of the formal agreement, again there is a binding and enforceable agreement. In each case there are both the contractual and the formal or evidential requirements to be satisfied for there to be a binding and enforceable contract for a lease.

(1) *The Requirements of a Valid Contract*

A contract for a lease has the same contractual ingredients as any ordinary binding contract. The parties must have legal capacity and be identifiable,[18] they must intend to enter into legal relations.[19] There must be consideration. A gratuitous offer to permit someone to occupy property cannot amount to a contract to grant a lease, unless at the very least the occupant agrees to undertake responsibilities in respect of the property.[20] The letting must not be for a purpose regarded by the law as unlawful.[21] In addition to the normal contractual requirements, the rent to be paid must be agreed, or at least there must be agreement on the machinery to be used for fixing the rent.[22] The parties must also agree how long the tenancy is to last, *e.g.* weekly, quarterly, yearly or for a specified number of years. It is not sufficient if it is for an uncertain duration,[23] *e.g.* for so long as a student continues his studies, or for so long as someone is alive.[24] Although "The simple statement of the law that the maximum duration of a term must be certainly known in advance of its taking effect cannot . . . have direct reference to periodic tenancies."[25] It will be sufficient if it is known when the term can be ended, although if a periodic tenancy can be ended only by the tenant, this may be repugnant to the interest the parties are trying to create.[26]

[18] *cf. Sowler* v. *Potter* [1940] 1 K.B. 271, where a lease was declared void *ab initio* the landlord having been misled as to the tenant's identity, Denning L.J. considered the lease should have been voidable. *Solle* v. *Butcher* [1950] 1 K.B. 671, 691, 693.

[19] *Jones* v. *Padvatton* [1969] 2 All E.R. 616 (agreement to let daughter occupy house and maintain herself as bar student out of rents).

[20] *Richards* v. *Powell* (1966) 110 S.J. 330.

[21] *Upfill* v. *Wright* [1911] 1 K.B. 506 (lease of flat for mistress); *Alexander* v. *Rayson* [1936] 1 K.B. 169 (agreement designed to deceive rating authority).

[22] *Buswell* v. *Goodwin* [1971] 1 All E.R. 418 (tenant agreeing to pay "proper" rent after modernisation). There is no requirement that the rent has to be certain at the date it falls due, *United Scientific Holdings* v. *Burnley B.C.* [1978] A.C. 904.

[23] *Lace* v. *Chantler* [1944] K.B. 368 (for duration of the war).

[24] Such a lease would take effect as a lease for 90 years determinable after the death, L.P.A. 1925, s.149(6), and constituted the creation of a settlement for C.T.T. purposes, Capital Transfer Tax Act 1984, s.43(3). see Chap. 2E(1) for notice to quit under s.149(6).

[25] *Re Midland Ry. Co.'s Agreement; Charles Clay & Sons Ltd.* v. *British Railways Board* [1971] Ch. 725 (Russell L.J. at p. 732).

[26] *Centaploy Ltd.* v. *Matlodge Ltd* [1974] Ch. 1.

Furthermore there must be agreement on the starting date.[27] It will not be assumed that the tenancy is to start within a reasonable time,[28] although it will be sufficient if the starting date has been ascertained by reference to a future event, even if it was a long time in coming, *e.g.* when the flat becomes vacant.[29] The most common reason why the parties have failed to reach a binding contract is because they have not unequivocally agreed on all the terms. This often occurs if the negotiations are conducted on a "subject to contract" basis. "It is ... clearly established by authority that negotiations subject to contract for the grant of a lease remain in a state of negotiation until exchange of lease and counterpart. The authority for that is *Eccles* v. *Bryant*.[30]"[31] Where "parties negotiate on a basis 'subject to contract' everybody knows there is a risk that, at the end of the day, either side may back out of the negotiations, up to the point where leases are exchanged."[32] There may, exceptionally, be evidence of an express or implied agreement that the qualifying words "subject to contract" be expunged.[33] There may also be clear evidence of a later, separate and distinct agreement, replacing an earlier one which was "subject to contract."[34] Numerous variations of the formula have been litigated.[35] But if the parties have agreed all the necessary terms, and only want it put into more formal language, then there is authority for saying they have concluded their negotiations and made a bargain.[36] The same result is reached if the agreement provides "the lease shall contain such other covenants and conditions as shall be reasonably required by" the lessor.[37] The court in such a case can decide if the landlord's requirements are reasonable.[38]

[27] *Marshall* v. *Berridge* (1881) 19 Ch.D. 233.
[28] *Harvey* v. *Pratt* [1965] 2 All E.R. 786. And see *Trustees of National Deposit Friendly Society* v. *Beatties of London* (1985) 275 E.G. 55, where a very lenient attitude to uncertainty of rent, commencement and terms was shown.
[29] *Brilliant* v. *Michaels* [1945] 1 All E.R. 121.
[30] [1948] Ch. 93 (correspondence between solicitors for sale of land).
[31] *Per* Buckley J. in *D'Silva* v. *Lister House Development Ltd.* [1971] Ch. 17, and see A. M. Pritchard (1974) 90 L.Q.R. 55, H. W. Wilkinson (1979) 95 L.Q.R. 7.
[32] *Derby & Co. Ltd.* v. *I.T.C. Pension Trust Ltd.* [1977] 2 All E.R. 890, Oliver J. at p. 896.
[33] *Cohen* v. *Nessdale* [1982] 2 All E.R. 97.
[34] *Alpenstow* v. *Regalian Properties* [1985] 1 W.L.R. 721.
[35] See further *Woodfall*, para. 1–0321.
[36] *Branca* v. *Cobarro* [1947] K.B. 854 ("provisional agreement until full legalised agreement drawn up" for sale of mushroom farm).
[37] *Sweet & Maxwell Ltd.* v. *Universal News Services Ltd.* [1964] 2 Q.B. 699.
[38] *cf. Caney* v. *Leith* [1937] 2 All E.R. 532 (agreement for assignment of lease "subject to purchaser's solicitor approving the lease," no enforceable contract until approved in the absence of bad faith or unreasonable conduct).

(2) *Form of a Valid Contract*

(a) Contracts evidenced in writing

Before an action can be brought for damages for breach of the contract to grant a lease,[39] it is necessary to show that the fact of agreement has been evidenced in writing.[40] It is not necessary for the agreement to have been made in writing, but the writing must contain not only all the terms agreed on, but also all the terms that are necessary to make a binding contract for a lease. The writing must be signed either by the defendant or his lawfully authorised agent.[41] The necessity for writing originally appeared in section 4 of the Statute of Frauds 1677 and is now contained in section 40(1) of the Law of Property Act 1925 which provides:

> "No action may be brought upon any contract for the sale or other disposition of land or any interest in land, unless the agreement upon which such action is brought, or some memorandum thereof, is in writing, and signed by the party to be charged or by some other person thereunto by him lawfully authorised."

Failure to satisfy this much litigated section goes more often to enforceability than validity.[42] The section does not prevent the formation of a valid oral or partly written contract. But if the section is specifically pleaded it is a defence to an action for damages for breach of the contract to grant a lease where either there is no signed memorandum or it fails to contain the necessary terms.[43] If the agreement is contained in a formal document signed by the defendant then it must contain the following essential terms[44]: the names of the landlord and tenant, or their respective agents, or at least sufficient means of identifying them[45]; a sufficient description of the property to enable it to be identified[46]; the length of term to be granted and when it is to start[47]; the rent to be paid and any other terms agreed on between the parties.[48] It is not necessary for the parties to agree any additional

---

[39] *Lavery* v. *Pursell* (1888) 39 Ch.D. 508.
[40] *Tiverton Estate Ltd.* v. *Wearwell Ltd.* [1975] Ch. 146; *cf. Daulia Ltd.* v. *Four Millbank Nominees Ltd.* [1978] 2 All E.R. 557.
[41] *Eccles* v. *Bryant* [1948] Ch. 93; *D'Silva* v. *Lister House Development Ltd.* [1971] Ch. 17 ("letters written by solicitors acting as solicitors relating to a proposed grant of a lease . . . are letters written by agents who have no authority to conclude a contract").
[42] *Leroux* v. *Brown* (1852) 12 C.B. 801.
[43] The position where there is an action for specific performance of an inadequately evidenced contract to grant a lease where there is an act of part performance is considered at (V)E later.
[44] For collections of cases on these points see *Woodfall*, paras. 1–0332 *et seq.* and *Megarry & Wade* pp. 556–558.
[45] *Stokes* v. *Whicher* [1920] 1 Ch. 411.
[46] *Dolling* v. *Evans* (1867) 36 L.J. Ch. 474, and see *Ogilvie* v. *Foljambe* (1817) 3 Mer. 53 ("Mr. Ogilvie's house").
[47] *Marshall* v. *Berridge* (1881) 19 Ch.D. 233, and see before at note 26.
[48] *Hawkins* v. *Price* [1947] Ch. 645.

terms, *e.g.* as to repairs, use, restrictions on assignment, as certain very basic terms can be implied. As Harman L.J. said " . . . if A agrees with B to grant him a lease at such a rent on such and such terms beginning on such a day, and no more, that is a specifically enforceable agreement, and the court will insert in it what are called 'Usual' covenants. Those were defined in a case before Sir George Jessel M.R.[49] being very jejune covenants."[50] However, if the documentation produced shows that there are still outstanding counter-proposals which have not been agreed, there is no concluded agreement or contract.[51] The parties are still in a state of negotiation.

(b) Variation and waiver

Oral variation of written terms can similarly render the agreement unenforceable. If the parties orally agree to change the starting date, or vary the rent for the initial period and the variation is not evidenced in writing, there is no complete record of the contract.[52] The contract is only partly in writing and that is not sufficient. However, if the oral variation is for the benefit of the plaintiff, then it may be possible to obtain an order enforcing the contract either with or without the oral variation, at the defendant's option.[53]

If a term has been left out altogether, the party who has the benefit of the term may be able to waive it and enforce the contract as it stands. The simplest example of this is an agreement to pay all or part of the plaintiff's costs.[54] If the term is for the other party's benefit, *e.g.* to pay the defendant's costs, then the defect may be cured by the plaintiff's offer to comply with the unwritten term,[55] unless the term is of material importance, *e.g.* that vacant possession will be given.[56] It is not easy to suggest a test to settle the question whether a given term is of material importance.

(c) Joinder and signature

Often the issue in section 40 disputes is not whether all the relevant terms are contained in the letters passing between the parties or their solicitors and in the cheques and receipts they may have signed, but whether it is possible to establish a link between the various documents and transactions that the negotiations have generated. The matter was discussed by the Court of Appeal in *Timmins* v. *Moreland*

[49] *Hampshire* v. *Wickens* (1878) 7 Ch.D. 555 at p. 561.
[50] *Sweet & Maxwell Ltd.* v. *Universal News Services Ltd.* [1964] 2 Q.B. 699 at p. 726, see *post*, (V)E(4).
[51] *Honeyman* v. *Marryatt* (1855) 21 Beav. 14.
[52] *Goss* v. *Lord Nugent* (1833) 5 B. & Ad. 58; [1824–34] All E.R. Rep. 305.
[53] *Morris* v. *Baron & Co.* [1918] A.C. 1; *United Dominions Corporation (Jamaica) Ltd.* v. *Shoucair* [1969] 1 A.C. 340.
[54] *North* v. *Loomes* [1919] 1 Ch. 378; [1918–1919] All E.R. Rep. 936.
[55] *Scott* v. *Bradley* [1971] 1 Ch. 850, and see also R.E.M. (1951) 67 L.Q.R. 300.
[56] *Hawkins* v. *Price* [1947] Ch. 645.

Street Property Co. Ltd.[57] The plaintiff vendor unsuccessfully attempted to link a cheque signed by the defendant company in favour of his solicitors, his employers, with a receipt he signed and gave to the defendants setting out the terms of the sale of freehold property for £39,000. Jenkins L.J. said[58]:

> "I think it is still indispensably necessary, in order to justify the reading of documents together for this purpose, that there should be a document signed by the party to be charged which, while not containing in itself all the necessary ingredients of the required memorandum, does contain some reference, express or implied, to some other document or transaction. Where any such reference can be spelt out of a document so signed, then parol evidence may be given to identify the other document referred to, or, as the case may be, to explain the other transaction, and to identify any documents relating to it. If by this process a document is brought to light which contains in writing all the terms of the bargain so far as not contained in the document signed by the party to be charged, then the two documents can be read together so as to constitute a sufficient memorandum for the purposes of s.40 of the Law of Property Act, 1925. The laying of documents side by side may no doubt lead to the conclusion as a matter of *res ipsa loquitur* that the two are connected; but before a document signed by the party to be charged can be laid alongside another document to see if between them they constitute a sufficient memorandum, there must, I conceive, be found in the document signed by the party to be charged some reference to some other document or transaction."[59]

The requirement that the memorandum has to be signed raises two issues. Has the defendant put on the document something which can amount to a "signature," and if anyone else has signed, was he "lawfully authorised" so to do? Signature has been interpreted very liberally, initials,[60] marks,[61] and printed names[62] having all been accepted, but the "signature" must indicate an acceptance by the defendant of the transaction. More serious difficulties surround the issue of the agent's authority. In many cases, it is alleged that the memorandum can be constructed out of the correspondence passing between the parties' solicitors. Was the solicitor authorised to sign a section 40 memorandum?

---

[57] [1958] Ch. 110.
[58] At p. 130.
[59] And see R.E.M. (1958) 74 L.Q.R. 22.
[60] *Hill* v. *Hill* [1947] Ch. 231 (landlord initialling rent book).
[61] *Selby* v. *Selby* (1817) 3 Mer.2.
[62] *Tourret* v. *Cripps* (1879) 48 L.J. Ch. 567.

"It is no doubt correct (and there are cases in which it was so held) that the mere fact of the relationship of solicitor and client being constituted in regard to a particular purchase does not by implication give a solicitor any authority to make a contract or to sign a memorandum, and I may refer to *Forster* v. *Rowland*[63] and *Smith* v. *Webster*.[64] But that is not a hard and fast rule which is not capable of alteration. On the facts of the case, as it seems to me, from the way in which the instructions are given to the solicitor, he may by implication be entitled to sign a memorandum which will bind his client."[65]

Subject to the terms of their instructions solicitors do not have authority to conclude a contract for a lease, or to sign a binding memorandum in the course of negotiations.[66] But a distinction seems to be drawn between making a contract and providing evidence of it. If all the solicitor is doing is carrying into effect a completed oral contract, then he may be regarded as having sufficient authority to sign a memorandum.[67] As the authority can be implied, it obviously need not itself be in writing. Indeed it need not even exist until after the memorandum has been signed, if the client accepts the situation and is prepared to ratify the memorandum.[68]

(d) Contracts evidenced by part performance

"Soon after the Statute of Frauds was enacted, the Court of Chancery laid down the principle that should A be sued by B on a parol contract disposing of an interest in land, A could not be allowed to rely on the absence of a written memorandum of the contract·in order to defeat B's claim if there had been part performance of the contract. This was because it would be unconscionable in such circumstances for A to seek to take advantage of the statute. For example, if B had performed his obligations under the parol contract, the benefit of which had been accepted by A, it would clearly be an abuse of the statute if A were then allowed to take the point that the contract was

---

[63] (1861) 7 H. & N. 103.
[64] (1876) 3 Ch.D. 49.
[65] *Gavaghan* v. *Edwards* [1961] 2 Q.B. 220, *per* Danckwerts L.J. at p. 226 (solicitor acting for both parties, he went on to refer to *Rosenbaum* v. *Belson* [1900] 2 Ch. 267 (estate agent authorised to sign on facts).
[66] *D'Silva* v. *Lister House Development Ltd.* [1971] Ch. 17.
[67] *Horner* v. *Walker* [1923] Ch. 218. The authority point was raised by counsel in *Law* v. *Jones* [1974] Ch. 112, but not apparently dealt with by the court. And see *North* v. *Loomes* [1919] 1 Ch. 378.
[68] *Maclean* v. *Dunn* (1828) 4 Bing. 722.

unenforceable against him when sued by B to perform his corresponding contractual obligations."[69]

The act of performance has to be that of the plaintiff himself.[70] And furthermore it seems that the acts done by the plaintiff must in themselves be referable to some contract concerning the property affected by the agreement,[71] *e.g.* taking possession with the lessor's consent,[72] consenting to the tenant taking possession,[73] plaintiff tenant spending money on improvements and repairs,[74] plaintiff landlord spending money on improvements after agreement with tenant.[75] Payment of rent in advance cannot by itself be a sufficient act of part performance,[76] but may be sufficient if taken with other acts.[77] Simply remaining in possession is not adequate evidence of an agreement for a new lease,[78] but staying in possession and paying the new rental is sufficient.[79] Once there is an admissible act of part performance "that is sufficient to warrant the admission of oral evidence to prove what the exact terms of the contract were."[80]

D. Formal Creation of the Lease

(1) *Formalities*

The object of a contract for a lease is to secure the formal grant of a lease on the agreed terms. A deed[81] must be used to create the legal estate of a term of years absolute if the term is to exceed three years.[82] If the tenant is granted immediate possession for a term not exceeding three years at the best rent which can be reasonably obtained without taking a fine, the tenancy can be created orally,[83] and will frequently

---

[69] *Steadman* v. *Steadman* [1976] A.C. 536, Lord Salmon at p. 566 (payment of £100 in conjunction with announcement of oral agreement to justices that wife would surrender her interest in the matrimonial home for £1,500, together with husband's abandonment of claim to remission for maintenance arrears and his taking conveyancing steps to complete agreement amounted to sufficient part performance), and see L.P.A. 1925, s.40(2).

[70] *Williams* v. *Evans* (1875) L.R. 19 Eq. 547.

[71] *Steadman* v. *Steadman* [1976] A.C. 536; *Re Gonin (deceased)* [1977] 2 All E.R. 720, and see further *Megarry & Wade*, pp. 589 *et seq.*, and *Hanbury & Maudsley*, pp. 665 *et seq.*

[72] *Morphett* v. *Jones* (1818) 1 Wils. Ch. 100; [1814–23] All E.R. Rep. 612; *Brough* v. *Nettleton* [1921] 2 Ch. 25.

[73] *Smallwood* v. *Sheppards* [1895] 2 Q.B. 627.

[74] *Broughton* v. *Snook* [1938] Ch. 505.

[75] *Rawlinson* v. *Ames* [1925] Ch. 96.

[76] *Chaproniére* v. *Lambert* [1917] 2 Ch. 356; [1916–17] All E.R. Rep. 1089.

[77] *Steadman* v. *Steadman* [1976] A.C. 536.

[78] *Re National Savings Bank Assn.* (1867) 15 W.R. 753.

[79] *Miller & Aldworth Ltd.* v. *Sharp* [1899] 1 Ch. 622.

[80] *Kingswood Estate Co.* v. *Anderson* [1963] 2 Q.B. 169. Willmer L.J. at p. 181.

[81] *i.e.* a document which is signed, sealed and delivered by the executing parties.

[82] L.P.A. 1925, s.52(1). Failure to comply renders the document void at law, and see later (V).

[83] L.P.A. 1925, s.54(2).

be created in an agreement under hand only.[84] Weekly tenancies are often granted orally. A periodic tenancy, made orally or in writing,[85] that in the event lasts for longer than three years has still been validly created.

If the transaction is formally completed the landlord will execute the lease, and the tenant will execute an exact copy, the counterpart. If the lease is liable to stamp duty,[86] then both documents should be submitted to the stamp office for stamping,[87] and the landlord retains possession of the counterpart and the tenant retains possession of the lease.[88] If the title to the land is unregistered, there are no further formal steps to be taken.[89] The same is true if the title is registered, or the land is in an area where registration of title is compulsory and the term granted does not exceed 21 years.[90] The tenant's rights in these cases bind successors to the land automatically as "overriding interests," under section $70(1)(k)$[91] of the Land Registration Act 1925, unless a fine was taken on the granting of the lease. The same also applies if the lease contains an absolute prohibition against assignment.[92] Such a restriction is invariably found when a lease at a nominal rental is being used to provide a favoured beneficiary "rent free" accommodation for life.[93] Again if he is "in actual occupation of the land"[94] the tenant's rights, even where merely equitable, are protected as overriding interests against other persons dealing with the land.

If a registered proprietor of either the freehold title or the immediate leasehold title is granting a lease for more than 21 years then the transaction is not completed until the tenant has been registered as the proprietor of the newly created term.[95] If a new lease is granted for not less than 40 years in an area of compulsory registration, the lease has to be submitted for first registration within

---

[84] Such a valid written agreement is a conveyance within L.P.A. 1925, s.205(1)(ii), and s.62, for the purpose of creating implied legal easements in favour of the tenant, *Wright* v. Macadam [1949] 2 K.B. 744 (access to coal shed).

[85] L.P.A. 1925, s.54(2).

[86] Stamp Act 1891, and see *Woodfall*, App. A1.

[87] Apart from the liability to pay penalty stamps, the sanction is that the document is not admissible in evidence if not properly stamped, Stamp Act 1891, s.14.

[88] *Hall* v. *Ball* (1841) 3 Man. & G. 242.

[89] If the agreement contains options to purchase or renew they should be registered as land charges to bind purchasers of the lessor's interest, L.C.A. 1972, s.2(4)(iv), and see *post*, Chap. 4(V).

[90] L.R.A. 1925, ss.19,22.

[91] In s.70(1)(k) "granted" means granted at law: see *City Permanent B.S.* v. *Miller* [1952] Ch. 840. And see the same case on the meaning of a "fine" in s.70(1)(k).

[92] L.R.A. 1925, s.8(2).

[93] The lease is granted for longer than the beneficiary is likely to live, subject to prior determination on notice following his death, and see L.P.A. 1925, s.149(6).

[94] L.R.A. 1925, s.70(1)(g), save where enquiry is made of the tenant and his rights are not disclosed. See Taylor (1971) New L.J. Vol. 121, p. 784 and p. 821.

[95] L.R.A. 1925, ss. 19(2), 22(2).

two months of its grants[96] even if the superior title is unregistered.[97] A failure to do so renders the lease void as a grant of the legal estate. If the lease is for more than 21 and yet less than 40 years and will not be protected as an overriding interest, then it should be protected by the registration of a notice under section 48 of the Land Registration Act 1925. On the registration of a head lease, the tenant will usually be registered with a good leasehold title, unless the freehold title out of which the term is granted is approved at the same time by the registrar.[98]

Many developments often require a system of private registration. Head lessors commonly require the registration of the grant and assignments of derivative terms so that they can maintain up-to-date records of owners and occupiers of the various lesser interests in the property.

Deeds are usually taken to be delivered and therefore legally effective from the date when they are stated to be made. The legal estate cannot commence earlier than the date the lease is executed.[99] In most cases the lease and counterpart will be executed a few days before the date the deed bears. The executing party will generally deliver the deed to his solicitor subject to the other party executing his part of the lease, the matter being completed by the exchange of lease and counterpart within a reasonable time[1] of that agreed between the parties. If that is the situation the deed is known as an "escrow." The deed will become automatically effective on the happening of the specified event or the occurrence of the specified condition.[2] On that date the legal term will automatically vest. However, the fulfilment of the condition has a retroactive effect. The date properly to be inserted as the date of the deed is the date it was delivered as an escrow. This may be important when determining the date from which rent and other obligations become due.[3]

(2) *Costs*

Market forces are such that the lessor can generally obtain the tenant's agreement that his solicitor's charges and out payments, including sometimes the surveyor's charges, be met by the tenant. This

---

[96] An extension can be asked for and will be granted if there is a reasonable explanation for the delay. If the extension is not granted a new lease will have to be executed.
[97] L.R.A. 1925, s.123.
[98] L.R.A. 1925, s.8, and further Hayton *Registered Land* (3rd. ed.), Curtis and Ruoff, *Registered Conveyancing* (2nd. ed.).
[99] *Bradshaw* v. *Pawley* [1980] 1 W.L.R. 10.
[1] *Kingston* v. *Ambrian Investment Co. Ltd.* [1975] 1 All E.R. 120; *Glessing* v. *Green* [1975] 2 All E.R. 696.
[2] *Thompson* v. *McCullough* [1947] K.B. 447; *Beesly* v. *Hallwood Estates* [1961] Ch. 105.
[3] *Alan Estates Ltd.* v. *W.G. Stores Ltd.* [1981] 3 W.L.R. 892, but see the criticism of this case by P.H. Kenny [1982] Conv. 409.

agreement is not enforceable unless it is contained in writing,[4] and generally it will be a term of the lease itself.[5] The tenant is unlikely to have to pay the landlord's legal costs when the lease is renewed under the Landlord and Tenant Act 1954, Part II[6]

(3) *Premiums and Capital Gains Tax*

A premium in the form of a lump sum is often taken by a lessor in addition to rent on the grant of long leases. This is particularly common in the case of developments involving multiple occupation such as flats. The landlord wants to recoup his outlay as quickly as possible. The tenant wants to acquire an appreciating asset, and the most effective way of managing a development that is in multiple occupation is by means of the grant of leases. In that way positive covenants can be enforced more readily against successive owners of the individual units.

In the past premiums were frequently taken to avoid income tax on the receipt of rent. There are now detailed rules for taxing part of the premium as income when the lease has been granted for not more than 50 years. These provisions are considered in Chapter 5[7] but they do not bring into charge to tax the whole of a premium on a lease for less than 50 years, or indeed any of it when the term is for more than 50 years. As most premiums are charged by builders or other dealers in land on the disposal of part of their stock in trade, then the receipt comes into their trading accounts and is subject either to income tax or corporation tax.[8]

But exceptionally, a lease will be granted at a premium by an individual who is not a builder, or a dealer or trader in land. The grant of such a lease amounts to a part disposal of a capital asset by the grantor.[9] It is a part disposal because he still retains the reversion expectant on the determination of the lease and the right to receive the rent in the meantime. The extent of a capital gain that is taxable is normally calculated by subtracting the expenditure involved in acquiring the asset from either the price received on disposal, or if it is a gratuitous transaction, its value on disposal.[10] Subject to important

---

[4] Costs of Leases Act 1958, s.1.
[5] For a specimen clause see *Encyclopedia of Forms and Precedents* (4th ed.). Vol. 11. p. 279.
[6] *Cairnplace* v. *C.B.L. (Property Investment) Co.* [1984] 1 W.L.R. 696, and see Chap. 22, *post*.
[7] See *post*, Chap. 5(VIII)H.
[8] An excellent introduction to the law on this topic still remains Park and Landau's "The taxation of leaseholds" (1969) 6 B.T.R. 265, 368, and see also *Woodfall*, para. 1–1368.
[9] Capital Gains Tax Act 1979, Sched. 3, para. 2.
[10] Capital Gains Tax Act 1979, ss.28–43.

exemptions[11] and reliefs[12] the resulting balance is charged to tax at 30 per cent.[13] The normal method of calculating a capital gain is inappropriate where there is a part disposal only. The chargeable part of the gain is calculated according to a formula:

$$\frac{\text{A (consideration for disposal)}}{\text{A + B (market value of property remaining undisposed)}}[14]$$

The value of the property undisposed of includes the right to receive the rent, and the value of that right is assessed at the time of the part disposal[15] Although capital gains tax is obviously likely to be charged on the grant at a premium of a lease or sub-lease, it is also, but less obviously, chargeable on the surrender of the term or variation of the terms where sums become payable by the tenant otherwise than in the form of rent.[16]

Leases that do not exceed 50 years receive different treatment as they are regarded as wasting assets.[17] The reason is that their capital value not only wastes to nothing over the 50 years, but does so much quicker in the last 11 years than it does in the previous 39 years. The statutory rate of depreciation does not follow a straight line in this instance.[18] Part of the premium on the grant of a lease for less than 50 years is brought into tax under section 80 of the Income and Corporation Taxes Act 1970.[19] That part is left out of account in calculating any liability to capital gains tax.[20] Subject to that, if a lease for a period not exceeding 50 years is granted out of the freehold at a premium, then the calculation of the capital gain is made in the same way as on the grant of a longer lease. The lease is not regarded as lasting any longer than the earliest date on which it can by its terms be ended by the landlord.[21] If the lease contains a rent review clause operative by the landlord and a break clause operative by the tenant at the same time, then the lease is regarded as having been granted only up to that time.[22] Apart from that, the lease is regarded as lasting for as long as the tenant can extend it by notice.[23]

The acute complications arise when a lease for less than 50 years is

---

[11] For present purposes the exemption on the disposal of private residences is possibly the most important, Capital Gains Tax Act 1979, s.101.
[12] There are important reliefs on an individual's first £6,300 gains, *ibid.* s.5, as amended, roll-over relief on the replacement of business assets s.115, and a variation of that relief on small part disposals, where the consideration is less than £20,000, s.107.
[13] Capital Gains Tax Act 1979, s.3.
[14] Capital Gains Tax Act 1979, s.35.
[15] Capital Gains Tax Act 1979, Sched. 3, para. 2(2).
[16] Capital Gains Tax Act 1979, Sched. 3, para. 3.
[17] Capital Gains Tax Act 1979, Sched. 3, para. 1.
[18] See Capital Gains Tax Act 1979, Sched. 3, Table.
[19] See Chap. 5(VIII)H, *post.*
[20] Capital Gains Tax Act 1979, Sched. 3, para. 5.
[21] Capital Gains Tax Act 1979, Sched. 3, para. 5.
[22] *Ibid.* para. 8(3), (4).
[23] *Ibid.* para. 8(5).

acquired subject to a short sub-lease, and the head lease is disposed of at a premium on the falling in of the sub-lease, and again where there are grants at premiums of short leases out of a lease which is itself a wasting asset, *i.e.* likely to last for less than 50 years. In these cases, a complex formula is used. In working out the grantor's expenditure the calculation has to take into account the fact that the interest has been taken out of an asset that has itself depreciated at a variable rate since its acquisition.[24]

Where a lease not exceeding 50 years is acquired, and later disposed of, on the payment of a premium, this also gives rise to a charge to capital gains tax. Again, the fact that one is dealing with a wasting asset has to be taken into account in calculating the taxable gain or less.[25] The final complication to these already confused calculations is that indexation relief may apply to disposals of property since 6th April 1982.[26]

V. FAILURE TO COMPLETE THE CONTRACT

A. Introduction

There can be a failure to execute a proper lease in accordance with the contract either before or after possession has been taken, and either by the landlord or the tenant. The failure might result from apathetic inactivity, wrongful refusal to proceed, or from a consideration that the other party has already broken his part of the agreement thereby ending it. Much of the case law comes from the middle of the last century when property was built extensively to let and before many of the procedural reforms culminating in the Judicature Acts 1873 and 1875. For these purposes, the effect of those Acts was that the plaintiff could ask for specific performance of the contract whether he took proceedings in the Queen's Bench Division or the Chancery Division.

More significantly, the parties to the contract could argue correctly as a result of section 25(11) of the Judicature Act 1873[27] and *Walsh* v. *Lonsdale*[28] that, because of their right to request specific performance, they should be regarded as being in the same position as if such a claim had been made and a lease for the requisite number of years executed.[29] As Cotton L.J. said in *Lowther* v. *Heaver*[30]:

[24] Capital Gains Tax Act 1979, Sched. 3, para. 1.
[25] *Ibid.* and ss. 37 *et seq.*
[26] F.A. 1982, s.86 as amended.
[27] See now Supreme Court Act 1981, s.49.
[28] (1882) 21 Ch.D. 9.
[29] See further Hanbury & Maudsley, *Modern Equity*, pp. 14–17.
[30] (1889) 41 Ch.D. 248 at p. 264.

"A tenant holding under an agreement for a lease of which specific performance would be decreed stands now in the same position as if the lease had been granted. He is entitled only in equity it is true to a lease, but being entitled in equity to have a lease granted, his rights ought, in my opinion, to be dealt with in the same way as if a lease had been granted to him, and do not depend upon its actually having been granted."

As a result, in the majority of cases, if the tenant is in possession it makes no difference to the parties whether they have properly completed their agreement or not. Actions for specific performance for breach of contracts to grant leases are not very common. The working relationship of landlord and tenant is likely to be uncomfortably difficult if it begins with hostile litigation. Alternatively, a party has the common law right to sue for damages, but these actions seem to be even more unusual. This may be because the parties are not worth powder and shot, or because the damages might be so low as to make a law suit uneconomical. The parties' time and money might well be better utilised on finding other tenants or alternative accommodation as the case may be.

B. Effect of Entry Before Agreement Reached

It is not unusual to find that the prospective landlord has permitted the tenant to take possession before the parties' respective solicitors have agreed terms. Agreement sometimes is not reached, and that means that there is no binding contract between the parties for a lease at all. In this case acts that would have amounted to part performance if there had been an agreement are irrelevant and the "tenant" is not entitled to be in occupation.[31] If, however, in the meantime he has improved the premises with the knowledge and acquiescence of the prospective landlord he may be entitled to compensation on the basis of restitution.[32]

C. Entry Following Agreement or Under Void Lease

The parties may have entered into a valid and enforceable agreement for a lease which has not been completed by a valid lease, or they may have signed a document purporting to be a lease for more than three years which is void at law because it is not under seal.[33] If rent has

---

[31] For a case where it was argued that this should happen see *Sweet & Maxwell Ltd.* v. *Universal Services Ltd.* [1964] 2 Q.B. 699.
[32] *Preeper* v. *Preeper* (1978) 84 D.L.R. (3d) 74, Nova Scotia Sup. Ct.
[33] L.P.A. 1925, s.52(1).

been paid periodically as agreed, the tenant is likely to be regarded at law as a yearly tenant.[34] This may well be of importance to a tenant if, following a change of landlord, he has to rely on the statutory security provisions for business or residential tenants. He may not have the legal estate he sought but he has a sufficient interest to bring him within the protection of the Rent Acts[35] or the Landlord and Tenant Act 1954.[36] Apart from that the *Walsh* v. *Lonsdale*[37] rule may apply. Where it does apply, it applies equally to landlord and tenant, and each can enforce against the other all the terms that should have been in the lease. The principle however only applies if the tenant is still entitled to specific performance.[38] This will not be the situation if there are unperformed conditions precedent,[39] or there is a subsisting breach[40] or the effect of an order against the landlord would render him liable to an action for forfeiture of his own interest.[41] If the principle applies it can be used equally to defeat an action for possession as to ground a claim for specific performance.[42]

A tenant claiming the benefit of the principle is claiming the benefit of an estate contract under section 2(4)(iv) of the Land Charges Act 1972. If the tenant does not protect his claim by registration as a class C(iv) charge then it will not bind a purchaser of the lessor's interest if the title is unregistered, even if the purchaser knows about the contract.[43] If the title is registered, the tenant's rights will be protected if he is "in actual occupation of the land."[44]

D. Damages for Failure to Complete

Damages can be claimed only if there is a contract binding at law because it is properly evidenced in writing within section 40 of the Law of Property Act 1925.[45] If the plaintiff has to rely on acts of part performance to prove his contract he can claim only the discretionary remedy of specific performance.[46] Damages are limited if the contract cannot be completed because of a defect in the landlord's title, *e.g.* if

---

[34] *Berrey* v. *Lindley* (1841) 3 Man. & G. 498; *Bell Street Investments* v. *Wood* (1970) 216 E.G. 585.
[35] See *post*, II.
[36] See *post*, III.
[37] (1881) 21 Ch.D. 9.
[38] See *Walsh* v. *Lonsdale* (1881) 21 Ch.D. 9 at p. 21, Sir George Jessel M.R.
[39] *I.R.C.* v. *Earl of Derby* [1914] 3 K.B. 1186; *Cornish* v. *Brook Green Laundry Ltd.* [1959] 1 Q.B. 394 (failure to complete specified works).
[40] *Coatsworth* v. *Johnson* (1886) 55 L.J.Q.B. 220; [1886–90] All E.R. Rep. 547 (non-payment of rent).
[41] *Warmington* v. *Miller* [1973] Q.B. 877.
[42] *Kingswood Estate Co.* v. *Anderson* [1963] 2 Q.B. 169. See now County Courts Act 1984, ss.23(*d*), 38.
[43] L.P.A. 1925, s.199(1).
[44] L.R.A. 1925, s.70(1)(*g*). Where he is not covered by s.70(1)(*g*) or (*k*) he should protect his interest by entry of a notice on the Charges register under the L.R.A. 1925, s.48, and see Chap. 4(V)F.
[45] *Lavery* v. *Pursell* (1888) 39 Ch.D. 508.
[46] See *post*, (V)E.

the landlord does not have capacity to grant the lease, or the grant would result in a breach of covenants affecting the landlord.

"The measure of damages in a case of this kind has been settled for two hundred years, the rule having been laid down in *Flureau* v. *Thornhill*[47] which is discussed at length in *Bain* v. *Fothergill.*[48] The plaintiffs are entitled to the return of the deposit, to interest on the deposit, and to the expenses incurred by them in investigating the title ... If the difficulty is one which can be removed by the payment of money, it is the vendor's duty to remove it."[49]

Damages for loss of bargain may be recovered if it can be shown that the defendant has not used his best endeavours to remove a blot on his title.[50] Damages can be recovered in deceit if it can be shown that the lessor has acted fraudulently, *e.g.* where he knows he has no reasonable ground for thinking he would be able to create a valid lease.[51] If the action is for breach of a careless, but innocent, misrepresentation,[52] the recoverable damages are measured in tort, but still likely to be limited to his expenses.[53] But delay in completion gives rise to conspicuous aggravation and frustration, especially where the tenant proposes to move in and start trading. Generally provisions as to time in the contract are not of the essence,[54] *i.e.* failure to observe them does not entitle the innocent party automatically to repudiate the agreement or sue for damages. A naturopath did successfully claim damages for the loss his practice suffered as a result of a six weeks' delay in *Phillips* v. *Lamdin.*[55] The House of Lords in *Raineri* v. *Miles*[56] has held that expenses incurred as a result of a delay in completion can be recovered. Before this decision, the passing of the completion date was sometimes noted with interest, but no greater urgency. Since this decision, completion dates are as a rule observed, rather than regarded as hopeful target dates.

---

[47] (1776) 2 W. Bl. 1078.
[48] (1874) L.R. 7 H.L. 158.
[49] *J. W. Cafes Ltd.* v. *Brownlow Trust Ltd.* [1950] 1 All E.R. 894, Lord Goddard C.J. at p. 897. See further Angela Sydenham (1971) 41 Conv. (N.S.) 341, C.T. Emery [1978] Conv. (N.S.) 338.
[50] *Malhotra* v. *Choudhury* [1980] Ch. 52.
[51] *Bain* v. *Fothergill, ante* at p. 207, Lord Chelmsford.
[52] Under Misrepresentation Act 1967, s.2(1).
[53] *Sharneyford Supplies Ltd.* v. *Edge* [1985] 1 All E.R. 976 not following *Watts* v. *Spence* [1976] Ch. 165.
[54] L.P.A. 1925, s.41, and see *Stickney* v. *Keeble* [1915] A.C. 386.
[55] [1949] 2 K.B. 33.
[56] [1981] A.C. 1050, and see M. P. Thompson [1982] Conv. 191, C. Harpum [1983] Conv. 435.

E. Actions for Specific Performance

Either party can take proceedings to obtain an order that the contract for the lease be specifically performed. The remedy is discretionary. Sometimes it will not be ordered because of the circumstances surrounding the contract or the conduct of the parties or because damages would be an adequate remedy. Damages can be given either in lieu of an order for specific performance, or in addition to it. If the court orders specific performance it may also have to settle the terms of the lease to be executed. There are detailed rules relating to the remedy which are discussed elsewhere.[57] It is proposed to concentrate here only on the more salient features of the remedy.

(1) *The Circumstances Surrounding the Contract*

The fact that it is envisaged that the tenancy or licence will only last a short time is not a bar to the grant of specific performance.[58] It may be a reason for refusing to grant it. But it may well be that one could now obtain specific performance of an agreement to grant a short periodic tenancy of residential accommodation where the tenant would secure statutory protection.[59] Generally if the remedy would not be equally available to both parties it will not be granted, but the rule is not invariable.[60] The remedy is not likely to be readily available if the court would have to supervise one party in carrying out his part of the contract,[61] although the courts now seem to be far more flexible on this point.

(2) *The Conduct of the Parties*

The plaintiff's conduct may put him out of court. If illegality would result from the grant, it will not be ordered.[62] Further, if the defendant has entered into the contract for the lease relying on a misrepresentation made by the plaintiff, this can be a defence to the action for specific performance.[63] It is further said that generally equity aids the vigilant, and that delay defeats equity. However, these general statements are not much help. Delay is regarded less seriously if the

[57] *Snell,* pp. 570, 576; *Hanbury & Maudsley,* pp. 683, 842; *Woodfall,* paras. 1–0353 *et seq.*
[58] *Verrall* v. *Great Yarmouth Borough Council* [1981] Q.B. 202.
[59] *cf. Kingswood Estate Co.* v. *Anderson* [1963] 2 Q.B. 169.
[60] *Price* v. *Strange* [1977] 3 All E.R. 371.
[61] *C. H. Giles & Co. Ltd.* v. *Morris* [1972] 1 All E.R. 960; *Jeune* v. *Queens Cross Properties Ltd.* [1974] Ch. 97.
[62] *Edler* v. *Auerbach* [1950] 1 K.B. 359 (proposed use would involve breach of the Defence Regulations).
[63] *Laurence* v. *Lexcourt Holdings Ltd.* [1978] 2 All E.R. 810 (that office premises have valid planning permission for the full duration of lease).

tenant is in fact in possession, or if the delay can be explained by the other party's acquiescence.[64] If neither of these applies he should pursue his remedies promptly, and even a few months' delay may have to be satisfactorily explained.

(3) *Damages in Lieu or in Addition*

If the contract is evidenced in writing the plaintiff can either sue in law for damages of ask for specific performance. He should elect before judgment which remedy he wants. If he elects for damages then he is accepting the other party's repudiation of the contract and cannot afterwards seek specific performance. If the order for specific performance is not complied with, the party who obtained it can either apply to the court for enforcement of the order or may apply to the court to dissolve the order and ask the court to put an end to the contract and for an order for damages. Damages are awarded on the same basis in equity as at common law, *i.e.* to place the innocent party in the same position, so far as money can do so, as if the contract had been performed.[65] Damages can take into account an increase in property values up to the date the contract is aborted, and is clearly lost,[66] and can include loss of business profits.[67] Damages can be ordered in addition to specific performance,[68] and can be awarded for delay even when the contract has been completed by the hearing date.[69]

(4) *Settling the Terms of the Lease*

If a contract for the lease has not precisely specified the terms of the lease, the court will order execution of a lease containing what is known as the "usual" covenants. The same result follows if the contract has provided that the lease is to contain the usual and proper covenants.[70] In a technical sense, the usual covenants are limited to those set out in the judgment of Jessel M.R. in *Hampshire* v.

---

[64] See generally *Williams* v. *Greatrex* [1956] 3 All E.R. 705, where there was a 10 year delay on a contract to buy.
[65] *Johnson* v. *Agnew* [1980] A.C. 376 (H.L.).
[66] *Ibid.*
[67] *Malhotra* v. *Choudhury* [1979] 1 All E.R. 186 (sale of house and doctor's surgery).
[68] *Grant* v. *Dawkins* [1973] 3 All E.R. 897 (plaintiff purchaser taking conveyance subject to mortgages, additionally entitled to damages to cover the amount his liability under the mortgages exceeded the original price).
[69] *Oakacre Ltd.* v. *Claire Cleaners (Holdings) Ltd.* [1981] 3 W.L.R. 761.
[70] *Blakesley* v. *Whieldon* (1841) 1 Hare 176.

Wickens.[71] They are covenants:

    (a) to pay rent,
    (b) to pay rates and taxes,
    (c) to keep and deliver up in repair,
    (d) to allow the lessor to enter and view the state of repair,
    (e) and the usual qualified covenant for quiet enjoyment.

It is often argued that "usual" should also include those in ordinary use.[72] In *Chester* v. *Buckingham Travel Ltd.*,[73] Foster J. considered that it was a question of fact to be determined by the court, not necessarily on the view of conveyancing counsel, but by looking at the nature of the premises, their situation, the purpose for which they were being let, the length of term, the evidence of conveyancers and the books of precedents. In a letting for 14 years from 1971 of a garage and workshop in a residential area of London, he agreed that, in 1971, the following covenants would be usual:

    (a) not to alter the building except with consent,
    (b) not to block windows or permit the acquisition of easements over the property,[74]
    (c) a covenant restricting user, and change of use except with consent, such consent not to be unreasonably withheld,
    (d) a covenant not to permit or allow nuisance or annoyance, on the premises, and
    (e) a proviso for re-entry for breach of covenant or non-payment of rent, but not for bankruptcy.

He disallowed:

    (a) a covenant prohibiting auction sales,[75]
    (b) a covenant restricting assignment and the creation of sub-leases, except with consent, coupled with a provision that sub-lessees enter into direct covenants with the landlord, and
    (c) a covenant to pay the landlord's legal and surveyor's costs in respect of notices served under sections 146 and 147 of the Law of Property Act 1925.

The most important clause disallowed was that restricting assignment. The underlying reason seems to be that there are so many variations of these clauses that it is impossible to say they are "usual." It is submitted that a simple restriction on assignment except with consent should have passed the "usual" test. The appropriate form of order is that the defendant is to execute a lease, such lease to be settled

---

[71] (1878) 7 Ch.D. 555.
[72] *Flexman* v. *Corbett* [1930] 1 Ch. 672.
[73] [1981] 1 All E.R. 386.
[74] Not such a common covenant, one would have thought.
[75] This was originally inserted to prevent retail sales premises being used for mock auction sales.

by the judge if the parties fail to agree.[76] The court is unwilling to include in the lease terms that have not been clearly covered by the parties' agreement.[77]

---

[76] *Charalambous* v. *Ktori* [1972] 3 All E.R. 701.
[77] *Stokes* v. *Mixconcrete (Holdings)* (1978) 36 P. & C.R. 427; affd. (1978) 38 P. & C.R. 488.

CHAPTER 4

THE LEASE

I. The Premises	102	E. For Quiet Enjoyment 128
A. Operative Words	102	F. Covenants in Flats Schemes . 133
B. The Parcels	102	V. The Provisos and Options 136
C. Exceptions and Reservations .	105	A. Proviso for the Suspension of
II. The Habendum	107	Rent 137
A. Grants for a Definite Number		B. Break Clauses 138
of Years	107	C. Option to Renew 139
B. Grants of Periodic Terms ...	108	D. Option to Purchase 140
C. Grant for Definite and then		E. Rights of Pre-emption 144
Periodic Terms	109	F. Protection of Options to Re-
III. The Reddendum	110	new, Purchase and Rights of
IV. The Covenants	110	Pre-emption 145
A. To Pay Rates, Taxes, etc. ...	112	G. Service of Notices 146
B. To Insure	117	H. Arbitration Clauses 147
C. Not to Alter the Physical State		I. Costs 147
of the Building	120	VI. Remedies 148
D. To Use in Specified Ways ...	122	

The formal parts of a lease by deed are 1. *The premises*, these include the date, parties, the words effecting the grant of the lease, otherwise known as the operative words, a description of the property let, the parcels, and the parts or rights excepted or reserved out of the property let for the benefit of the lessor or the adjoining owners; 2. *The habendum* which defines the length of the term; 3. *The reddendum* which states the rent reserved; 4. *The covenants* undertaken by the tenant and the landlord. In some cases these are implied either by common law or statute; 5. *The provisos and options.* The provisos state what is to happen in the event of failure to pay rent or observe the covenants, or destruction of the property; or may provide in other ways for premature ending of the term. The options may grant the tenant a right to renew the lease or to purchase the reversion.[1]

We have seen from the last chapter the circumstances in which a formal lease by deed is necessary to create a legal estate in the land in favour of the tenant. But the function of a well drawn lease should be to state what are the various parties' rights both in the circumstances that exist at the time the grant is made and on the occurrence of various events that are likely to occur during the term. If the parties' rights and liabilities are stated in some detail and with clarity then the scope for disagreement between the original parties or their successors is reduced. It follows that leases are nearly always lengthy documents. Furthermore as two properties are rarely "identical," the terms of

---

[1] An option may give the tenant a right to initiate purchase or merely give him preference should the landlord decide to sell. *i.e.* a right of pre-emption. See *post*, (V).

standard forms of precedents have to be adapted to the individual characteristics of the property being let and the circumstances of the individual parties to the lease. The tenant has to ask himself if the terms of the lease will enable him and any likely successor to use the property not only in the way he wants to use it, but also in any way he is likely to want to use it in the future. He also needs to satisfy himself, in view of his limited interest in the property, that his potential liabilities are not disproportionate to his likely enjoyment. The landlord needs to satisfy himself that the terms of the lease do not enable the tenant to use the property in such a way as may cause nuisance or annoyance to the adjoining occupiers or damage his interest in reversion.

I. THE PREMISES

A. Operative Words

There is no magic formula for creating a lease.

> "Whatever words are sufficient to explain the intent of the parties, that the one shall divest himself of the possession, and the other come into it for such a determinate time, such words, whether they run in the form of a licence, covenant, or agreement, are of themselves sufficient and will, in construction of law, amount to a lease for years as effectually as if the most proper and pertinent words had been made use of for that purpose."[2]

The most common expressions used are "demise," "grant and demise," "let," or in a tenancy agreement for not more than three years "agree to let."[3] As was pointed out in Chapter 2 the important consideration is the parties' intention, and not the words they have used either to express or, in some cases, to disguise it.[4]

B. The Parcels

The parcels of a lease are usually inconspicuous because of their brevity. In leases of houses and shops the parcels are often simply "all that house situate and known as No. 24 Main Street . . . together with

---

[2] *Wilkinson* v. *Hall* (1837) 3 Bing., N.C. 508 at p. 533, *per* Tindall C.J. referring to Bacon's Abridgement, Leases, K.
[3] *Duxbury* v. *Sandiford* (1898) 80 L.T. 552, where in fact the agreement was for 10 years.
[4] *Addiscombe Garden Estates* v. *Crabbe* [1958] 1 Q.B. 513, and see further Chap. 2, *ante.*

the outbuildings and appurtenances."[5] And a shop will often have as brief a description, as "All that lock-up shop known as No. 32 Bridge Street . . . ." Descriptions improve in the case of more commercial properties, particularly where part only of a property is being let. Leases of agricultural property frequently have a schedule of the fields described by reference to their cultivation and ordnance survey numbers and to a plan. Leases of parts of modern buildings, either for commercial or residential purposes, often contain detailed scale plans and descriptions. The same is true if the lease is to be registered under the Land Registration Act 1925, unless it is a demise of all the property in a previously registered title when there will be a reference to the relevant title number.

If the description includes the word "land," the extended definition given to this word by the Law of Property Act 1925, s.205 (1) (ix), can be relied on, although this is unlikely by itself to resolve any dispute about what is included in the demise. A lease of premises will normally include the external walls.[6] And so the tenant can stop the landlord from placing advertisement hoardings on the outside walls of the demised premises.[7] Furthermore, the demise of a flat will extend to at least the underside of the floor joists to which the ceiling of the flat is attached[8] If false ceilings have been inserted, the demise may include all the space between the floor of the flat demised and the underneath of the floor above.[9] A lease of shop premises also includes the airspace above it, and so the landlord and others can be stopped from erecting hoardings that take up airspace above the demised premises.[10] And a conveyance of "All that dwellinghouse . . . " included a cellar immediately beneath it although access to it was from the former owner's adjoining house.[11] The same would presumably apply on a lease. But the letting of a suite of rooms on the top floor of a block of flats is unlikely to include the common roof over all the flats.[12]

Difficulties often arise about the ownership of boundary walls and fences, where they are situated and who has to repair them.

---

[5] Nothing, it seems, is likely to pass as a result of the use of the word "appurtenances" which are mere surplusage, *Trim* v. *Sturminster R.D.C.* [1938] 2 K.B. 508; *Methuen-Campbell* v. *Walters* [1979] 2 W.L.R. 113.

[6] *Graystone* v. *Margulies* (1984) 47 P. & C.R. 472 (C.A.).

[7] *Goldfoot* v. *Welch* [1914] 1 Ch. 213; [1911–13] All E.R. Rep. 652 (demise of "rooms").

[8] *Sturge* v. *Hackett* [1962] 1 W.L.R. 1257. See also *Campden Hill Towers* v. *Gardner* [1977] Q.B. 823.

[9] *Graystone* v. *Margulies* (1984) 47 P. & C.R. 472 (C.A.) (tenant removed false ceilings and constructed mezzanine floors in the space).

[10] *Kelsen* v. *Imperial Tobacco Co. (of Great Britain & Ireland) Ltd.* [1957] 2 Q.B. 334; *Woollerton and Wilson* v. *Richard Costain* [1970] 1 W.L.R. 411 (interference from jib of tower crane). *cf. Ward* v. *Gold* (1969) 211 E.G. 155 (interference from pipework too trivial to justify injunction).

[11] *Cockburn* v. *Smith* [1924] 2 K.B. 119. (C.A.) (landlord liable to remedy defects of common roof retained), and see *Douglas-Scott* v. *Scorgie* [1984] 1 All E.R. 1086 (landlord under statutory duty to repair regardless of whether roof formed part of the premises).

[12] *Grigsby* v. *Melville* [1974] 1 W.L.R. 80.

Frequently the lease is adorned with a plan "for identification purposes only," but neither the plan nor the description may take matters any further. Often these qualifying words are meaningless but are "frequently used in conveyances in which the parcels are described in the body of the deed. In such cases the plan is merely to assist identification, and, in the event of any inconsistency arising, is subordinate to the verbal description."[13] In these cases, although extrinsic evidence cannot be given to contradict a written document, the court can take into account evidence of the surrounding circumstances in an attempt to dispel the vagueness.[14]

In many cases the Law of Property Act 1925, s.62, will operate to include in the grant the various matters referred to in the first two subsections. The section was designed to render it unnecessary for conveyancers to have to write out lists of items likely to be included in the property. The section applies to conveyances, which include leases[15] for more than three years and written agreements for tenancies for not more than three years, but not to agreements for leases for longer than three years.[16]

The grant of a lease creates a new estate, and the section operates to create new easements and rights for the tenants, even out of privileges that were previously only permissive. Jenkins L.J. in *Wright* v. *Macadam* said[17]:

> "First, the section is not confined to rights which, as a matter of law, were so annexed or appurtenant to the property conveyed at the time of the conveyance as to make them actual legally enforceable rights. Thus, on the severance of a piece of land in common ownership, the quasi easements de facto enjoyed in respect of it by one part of the land over another will pass although, of course, as a matter of law, no man can have a right appendant or appurtenant to one part of his property exercisable by him over the other part of his property. Secondly, the right, in order to pass, need not be one to which the owner or occupier for the time being of the land has had what may be described as a permanent title. A right enjoyed merely by permission is enough."

The tenants of a flat acquired a right to use a coal shed when they were granted a new tenancy of the flat and an additional room. Previously, they had only used the coal shed with permission. The importance of

[13] *Webb* v. *Nightingale* (March 8, 1957) unreported, *per* Romer L.J. quoted in *Willson* v. *Greene, Moss (Third Party)* [1971] 1 W.L.R. 635.
[14] *Willson* v. *Greene, Moss (Third Party)* [1971] 1 W.L.R. 635; *Wigginton & Milner Ltd.* v. *Winster Engineering Ltd.* [1978] 3 All E.R. 436.
[15] L.P.A. 1925, s.205(1)(ii).
[16] *Borman* v. *Griffith* [1930] 1 Ch. 493.
[17] [1949] 2 K.B. 744 at p. 748. *cf. Green* v. *Ashco Horticulturist Ltd.* [1966] 1 W.L.R. 889 at p. 897.

this decision is that the tenant can acquire considerably more extensive rights than the landlord intends him to have. This is a situation that is particularly likely to occur where the tenant occupied part of the landlord's premises, and his lease is renewed.[18] If the landlord does not want permissive rights previously enjoyed by the occupier of the premises to become transmuted *eo instanti* into indefeasible legal rights then the lease should clearly say so.[19]

Even if the lease is silent about the grant of a specific easement and the Law of Property Act 1925, s.62, cannot be prayed in aid, a tenant may still be able to claim an easement if it is essential to the intended enjoyment of the premises,[20] *e.g.* access through halls and staircases to upper floors. And in *Wong* v. *Beaumont Property Trust Ltd.*[21] the tenants of a basement Chinese restaurant successfully claimed a right to erect an external ventilation duct so that they could comply with the food hygiene regulations and avoid causing a nuisance to the adjoining occupiers.

C. Exceptions and Reservations

(1) *Exceptions*

Often a landlord will want to exclude from the lease some part of the property which apparently would form part of the property let. For example, a landlord may want to retain passages and staircases in a building granting the tenant only rights of access over them. Or, for security reasons, he may want to retain a back yard serving his and other tenants' properties, again only giving limited rights of access over it. An exception is often made of mines and minerals. This, it seems, will include all substances capable of being worked for profit below the top surface of the land including sand, gravel and clay.[22] Such an exception would also normally include all the rights strictly necessary to work the minerals and remove them.[23] Another frequent exception is of timber, which again will carry with it the necessary rights to cut, remove and, of course, sell.[24] The subject matter of a valid exception must be part of the property demised and in existence

---

[18] The problem can also arise on an original grant. It would not seem to be necessary to have diversity of occupation before section 62 can operate, and see Peter Smith [1978] Conv. 449, where many of the references to the relevant literature on that point are collected.
[19] L.P.A. 1925, s.62(4).
[20] *Pwllbach Colliery Co. Ltd.* v. *Woodman* [1915] A.C. 634.
[21] [1965] 1 Q.B. 173.
[22] *O'Callaghan* v. *Elliott* [1966] 1 Q.B. 601, *cf. Waring* v. *Foden, Waring* v. *Booth Crushed Gravel Co. Ltd.* [1932] 1 Ch. 276; [1931] All E.R. Rep. 291.
[23] *Cardigan (Earl)* v. *Armitage* (1823) 2 B. & C. 197; [1814–23] All E.R. Rep. 33.
[24] *Liford's Case* (1614) 11 Co. Rep. 46b; [1558–1774] All E.R. Rep. 73.

at the time of the grant, and its extent will be strictly construed in favour of the tenant and against the landlord.[25]

(2) *Reservations*

Formerly, these had a very technical meaning and extended only to some new thing issuing or coming out of the thing granted in favour of the landlord, such as, *e.g.* rent.[26] But nowadays after the property in the lease has been described it will normally continue "Excepting and Reserving to the landlord ... " or other the owners and occupiers of nearby property specified rights of way, drainage and other easements for the enjoyment of that nearby property over or under the demised property. This "reservation" amounts to a grant by the tenant to his landlord of the specified rights, even though the tenant does not execute the lease.[27] If the landlord wants to reserve these rights over or under the land let then they should be expressly mentioned in the lease. In *Re Webb's Lease, Sandom* v. *Webb* [28] a landlord claimed unsuccessfully a right to maintain advertisements on the outside walls of a hairdressing salon that had been let. Jenkins L.J. said that

> "as a general rule a grantor, whether by way of conveyance or lease, of part of a hereditament in his ownership, cannot claim any easement over the part granted for the benefit of the part retained unless it is expressly reserved out of the grant[29].... There are, however, certain exceptions to the general rule. Two well-established exceptions relate to easements of necessity and mutual easements such as rights of support between adjacent buildings."

When the landlord does reserve easements in his own favour their terms will be restrictively interpreted against him[30]. A reservation of a right of way over a path expressly to gain access to a well does not entitle the grantor or his successors to use the path for general purposes of access.[31] This is based on the principle that the grantor should not derogate from his grant. In *Re Vicker's Lease, Pocock* v.*Vickers*[32] the landlord inserted in a lease of fishing rights for 21 years a statement that it was understood and agreed that she would "retain

[25] *Cardigan (Earl)* v. *Armitage* (1823) 2 B. & C. 197; [1814–23] All E.R. Rep. 33.
[26] *Doe d. Douglas* v. *Lock* (1835) 2 Ad. & E. 705; [1835–42] All E.R. Rep. 13.
[27] L.P.A. 1925 s.65, and see *St. Edmundsbury and Ipswich Diocesan Board of Finance* v. *Clark (No. 2)* [1975] 1 W.L.R. 468.
[28] [1951] Ch. 808.
[29] He referred to *Suffield* v. *Brown* (1864) 4 De G.J. & S. 185; *Crossley & Sons Ltd.* v. *Lightowler* (1867) 2 Ch.App. 478; *Wheeldon* v. *Burrows* (1879) 12 Ch.D. 31.
[30] *St. Edmundsbury and Ipswich Diocesan Board of Finance* v. *Clark (No. 2)* [1975] 1 W.L.R. 468.
[31] *Liddiard* v. *Waldron* [1934] 1 K.B. 435.
[32] [1947] Ch. 420.

for her own use a rod in the said fishing." The failure to use the technical words "exception," "reservation" or "re-grant" prevented the words being construed as an exception or reservation in the technical sense, and the Court of Appeal decided that the words used did nothing more than enable the landlord personally to come and fish, which right ended on the death of the landlord.[33]

II. THE HABENDUM

A. Grants for a Definite Number of Years

"To hold the same unto the Tenant from the 1st day of April 1986 for the term of five years . . . " is a typical habendum. It states the date from which the term is to run and specifies its duration. It has already been stated that it is essential if the legal estate of a term of years is to be created that the term granted must be certain.[34] In this habendum it is obvious that the tenant could expect to be given possession on April 1. It is not however possible to be absolutely certain simply from reading the habendum whether the tenancy ends on March 31, 1991, or April 1 of that year.[35] A term will normally start at midnight after the date it is granted, *i.e.* in this case midnight April 1–2 and end on April 1. "The general understanding is that terms for years last during the whole anniversary of the day from which they are granted. Indeed, if this were otherwise, the last day, on which rent is almost uniformly made payable, would be posterior to the lease."[36] The reasoning on which that conclusion is based falls to the ground if the rent is payable in advance on April 1 and at the beginning of each subsequent quarter, as occurred in *Ladyman* v. *Wirral Estates Ltd.*[37] One therefore has to look at all the terms of the lease to decide if the normal rule has been displaced.

It seems that if the lease states the term is to start "on" a specified date, then the term will include that date.[38] The question of dates becomes important not at the start of the lease but at the end of it. In the case of a fixed term lease, the tenant needs to know when he must give up possession. In the case of a periodic tenancy a notice to quit must expire either on the anniversary of the term granted, or at the end of a period of the tenancy.[39]

---

[33] See further on this principle *Megarry and Wade*, p. 857.
[34] See *ante,* Chap 2, (II) E, and Chap. 3,(IV) C(1).
[35] *Brakspear (W.H.) & Sons Ltd.* v. *Baron* [1924] 2 K.B. 88.
[36] *Ackland* v. *Lutley* (1839) 9 Ad. & E. 879 at p. 894, Lord Denman C.J.
[37] [1968] 2 All E.R. 197.
[38] *Trow* v. *Ind Coope (West Midlands) Ltd.* [1967] 2 Q.B. 899, and see also *Sidebotham* v. *Holland* [1895] 1 Q.B. 378.
[39] This matter is discussed in Chap. 8, *post.*

If no starting date is specified in the lease, then the term will usually start from the date the lease is delivered. Often the date from which the term is stated to run has already passed. This is likely when a number of long leases are granted of flats in a newly erected building. It is more convenient for administrative purposes for all the leases to have the same term and the same rent days, and in the case of commercial properties let in the same block with rent review clauses, for all to operate at the same time. If the term does ante-date the lease, then the duration of the tenant's interest is computed from the stated date, but the tenant's estate and liability under the lease cannot, in the absence of agreement to the contrary,[40] ante-date its execution. He will not be liable for disrepair suffered before the lease was granted,[41] and he cannot rely on the earlier date in the habendum to claim that he is a tenant for the full specified term of years.[42] If the term is to take effect at a later date than the lease, which is the normal situation, then that date must not be more than 21 years from the date of the deed.[43]

B. Grants of Periodic Terms

There is often difficulty over the construction of the habendum granting periodic tenancies. If the tenant wants a yearly tenancy, it is often necessary to determine if the initial grant is for one year, or for a minimum of two years. "A tenancy from year to year is essentially a tenancy for an indefinite period which runs on from year to year until it is stopped by a notice to quit expiring at the end of some year, which may be the first or any later year but very often is a year much later than the first."[44] If the term is for "one year and thereafter from year to year" a tenancy of at least two years has been created,[45] and this is so even if the words "until determined by three months' notice" are added.[46] If the lease is simply "for one year" or "for one year certain," the lease has been created for only one year. A notice to quit will not be necessary in this case as a periodic tenancy has not been created.[47]

In many of these cases tenants of agricultural, residential or business property will continue to have statutory occupational rights

[40] *Bradshaw* v. *Pawley* [1979] 3 All E.R. 273 at p. 279.
[41] *Shaw* v. *Kay* (1847) 1 Ex. 412.
[42] *Roberts* v. *Church Commissioners for England* [1972] 1 Q.B. 278 (tenant unsuccessfully claiming he had a lease exceeding 21 years).
[43] L.P.A. 1925, s.149(3), and see *ante,* Chap. 3,(I) D(2), and see also *Northcote Laundry* v. *Frederick Donnelly* [1968] 1 W.L.R. 562 (the tenant's interest will start from the date of the lease, even though the term commences later). For a consideration of the problems caused by L.P.A. 1925, s.149(3) to time-sharing arrangements, see Woodfall, para. 1–0517/1.
[44] *Lower* v. *Sorrell* [1963] 1 Q.B. 959 at p. 978, Pearson L.J.
[45] *Cannon Brewery* v. *Nash* (1898) 77 L.T. 648.
[46] *Doe d. Chadborn* v. *Green* (1839) 9 Ad. & E. 658.
[47] *Cobb* v. *Stokes* (1807) 8 Ea. 358.

of varying qualities.[48] In view of the difficulties that can be encountered in construing the precise length of term granted it is surprising that not more use is made in drafting leases of a formula that provides for the term to run from one stated date to another stated date, *e.g.* "until March 31, 1990."[49] It might be more sensible if a reasonable time of the day were selected also for the end of the term—"until Midday on . . . ," which would avoid reliance on the presumption that time runs from midnight. This formula is adopted in a number of standard forms, and seems favoured by housing trusts and local authorities.

C. Grants for Definite and then Periodic Terms

It is not unusual for a tenant to ask for a definite term, *e.g.* six months or a year, and then to provide that the tenancy is to continue as a yearly periodic tenancy until determined by three or six months' notice as agreed. A tenant starting a new venture is likely to find this a convenient arrangement if he does not want to commit himself for a longer period. In *Addis* v. *Burrows*[50] premises were let: "from Jan. 1 1944 to June 30 1945 for the term of one year and so on from year to year until the tenancy be determined at the end of the first or any subsequent year by one of the parties giving to the other of them 6 calendar months' previous notice in writing." In *H. & G. Simonds Ltd.* v. *Heywood*[51] a beer house was let "from July 4 1935 until Oct. 3 1935 and afterwards from year to year (but subject to the determination of the tenancy hereby created as hereinafter mentioned) at the yearly rent of £40 payable by equal monthly instalments." There was a proviso that "either of the said parties hereto shall be at liberty to put an end to and determine these presents at any time on or after Oct. 3 1935 on giving to the other of them . . . three calendar months' previous notice thereof in writing without reference to the commencement of the said tenancy any law or usage to the contrary notwithstanding." The precise length of the initial term granted was in issue in both cases. In the first case, the Court of Appeal held that the agreement created a fixed term of 18 months and thereafter a tenancy from year to year, which could be determined by the requisite notice at the end of any of those years. In the second case, Lynskey J. considered that the tenancy could have been ended at any time after October 3, 1935, on three months' notice by either party. He saw nothing repugnant in the parties agreeing to terminate a "yearly

---

[48] See *post*, (II–IV).
[49] But see *Addis* v. *Burrows* [1948] 1 K.B. 444, where there was an unfortunate reference to both dates and period.
[50] [1948] 1 K.B. 444.
[51] [1948] 1 All E.R. 260.

tenancy" in the first year of the tenancy, by analogy with "break" clauses.[52]

Break clauses are not generally an integal part of the habendum.[53] They are options given to either party to determine the lease on specified periods of notice during the term. In a 21-year term, the tenant may have an option to determine it after seven or 14 years. He may negotiate for this right if he thinks there is a possibility that he might be unable either to continue to use the premises profitably himself or to assign them to anyone else.[54] It is trite to say, but nevertheless essential to remember that the length of term created in any tenancy depends on the precise wording of the tenancy agreement as a whole.

III. THE REDDENDUM

"Paying during the term hereby granted the yearly rent of £1,200 (without any deductions except only such as the tenant may be by law entitled to make notwithstanding any contract to the contrary) by equal quarterly payments to be made on the usual quarter days the first payment to be made on the First day of May next...." The reddendum reserves the rent to the landlord.[55]

IV. THE COVENANTS

The covenants spell out the liabilities of the parties to the lease, and although prolixity is rarely welcome it can prove a virtue in this instance. An express covenant is a binding agreement made by deed. The tenant will covenant with the landlord either to do something, or to do something in a particular way or refrain from doing something. The landlord's covenants with the tenant are generally very much more restricted than the tenant's. In a lease the usual word is "covenant," but often one will find: "The parties hereby agree and declare...." Provided that the intention is clear the precise words are not significant.

In addition to the express covenants, there may be included by law in the agreement certain implied covenants. If the tenancy agreement is under hand only, for a term not exceeding three years, then the parties' mutual obligations are usually expressed in the form of agreements: "The Tenant hereby agrees with the Landlord..." but

[52] He distinguished *Mayo* v. *Joyce* [1920] 1 K.B. 824.
[53] *cf. Goodright d. Hall* v. *Richardson* (1789) 3 Term. 462 where a 1785 lease for three, six or nine years was held to be a lease for nine years determinable at the end of three or six years on reasonable notice.
[54] Break clauses are considered *post*, s.V,B.
[55] See further, Chap. 5.

the legal effect will be the same as if they were covenants. The one distinction which does have to be made is between covenants and conditions. "Condition" has a very technical meaning.

> "At Common law, a condition is a qualification annexed to an estate, whereby the latter shall either be created (condition precedent), enlarged, or defeated (condition subsequent), upon its performance or breach. The main distinction between a condition subsequent for the cesser of the term of a lease upon the happening of a certain event and a lessee's covenant is that (subject to any right of relief from forfeiture given to the lessee) upon breach of a condition the lessor may re-enter, because the estate of the lessee is determined; whereas a breach of covenant only gives him the right to recover damages (or to obtain an injunction) unless the right to re-enter is expressly reserved to him, by the lease. Foa's *Landlord and Tenant* (7th ed.), pp. 311, 312."[56]

The remedies for breach of covenant are actions for damages, specific performance or injunction. It will be seen[57] that, both in relation to covenants to repair and covenants against physical alterations, the measure of damages is the amount "the plaintiff has really suffered from the breach."[58] In both cases the measure of damages suffered by the landlord will usually be the amount by which the value of the landlord's reversion has diminished. If he cannot prove that the value of his interest has been reduced because of the breach then his damages will be nominal.[59] The parties often attempt to avoid the difficulties of this rule by providing that the tenant will pay the landlord either his actual expenses of remedying the tenant's breaches of a repairing covenant,[60] or a specified amount on each breach of covenant.[61] Obviously the parties will seek the discretionary remedy of specific performance if they want to compel compliance with the terms of the lease, although it will not be granted if damages are an adequate remedy. An injunction is likely to be sought to restrain the tenant from using the premises contrary to the terms of his covenants. A breach of covenant by itself will not bring the term to an end.[62] But the next part of the lease, The Provisos,[63] will contain conditions subsequent. These enable the lessor to take steps for the

---

[56] *Bashir* v. *Commissioner of Lands* [1960] A.C. 44 (J.C.P.C. quoting with approval Sir Kenneth O'Connor in the Court of Appeal for Eastern Africa [1958] E.A. C.A. 45 at p. 53).
[57] *Post*, Chap. 6(VI)B.
[58] *Westminster (Duke)* v. *Swinton* [1948] 1 K.B. 524 (intermediate landlord entitled to recover part of likely cost of future reinstatement).
[59] *Espir* v. *Basil Street Hotel Ltd.* [1936] 3 All E.R. 91.
[60] For example, see *Hamilton* v. *Martell Securities* [1984] Ch. 266, discussed *post*. Chap. 6(VI)B.
[61] As in *Hurst* v. *Hurst* (1849) 4 Ex. 571 (£1 for every tree cut down).
[62] And see *Total Oil Great Britain* v. *Thompson Garages (Biggin Hill)* [972] 1 Q.B. 318.
[63] See *post*, (V).

premature determination of the lease by providing that if the covenants on the tenant's part are not observed and performed[64] the landlord can re-enter the premises and the demise will absolutely determine. It will be seen that the provisos do not have the devastating effect that one might suppose they have from a literal reading, because the Courts of Equity have for many years been prepared to grant relief against forfeiture, a jurisdiction which statute has largely confirmed, extended and regulated.[65]

A typical lease may contain the following covenants by the tenant:

(1) to pay rent,
(2) to pay rates, taxes, etc.,
(3) to repair and yield up in repair,
(4) to paint,
(5) to permit the landlord to enter and inspect,
(6) to permit the landlord to enter and repair,
(7) either to insure, or not to avoid the landlord's insurance,
(8) not to alter the physical state of the buildings,
(9) not to assign, underlet, or part with possession,
(10) to use only for specified purposes, and in specified ways,
(11) to pay the expenses of notices under the Law of Property Act 1925, s.146,
(12) to comply with statutory notices and forward them to the landlord.

And the landlord is likely to covenant:

(1) for repair,
(2) for quiet enjoyment by the tenant,
(3) for insurance and reinstatement.

A. To Pay Rates, Taxes, etc.

(1) *Rates*

The General Rate Act 1967, s.16, provides that every occupier of lands, houses, mines and sporting rights enjoyed separately from the occupation of land "shall be liable to be assessed to rates in respect of the hereditament ... according to the rateable value ... of that hereditament...." Hence the liability to the general rate which over the years replaced a large number of specific rates levied by precept by local authorities to provide for the estimated expenditure they are

---

[64] These words seem to be interchangeable, *Ayling* v. *Wade* [1961] 2 Q.B. 228.
[65] See Chap. 8 for the effect of forfeiture clauses.

likely to incur.[66] In addition the occupier will probably have the benefit of a water supply and sewerage disposal and will be liable to charges for those services.[67]

The Water Act 1973,[68] s.32A, enables water authorities to agree with rating authorities that the latter shall collect the water rate along with the general rates. If the lease is silent about who pays the rates the occupying tenant of premises separately assessed for rating purposes will have to bear and pay the rates, and is not entitled to deduct the payment from his rent. An exception to this is contained in the General Rate Act 1967, s.58, which entitles the tenant to deduct rates he has paid when the premises have been let for a term not exceeding three months.[69]

In most cases there will be an express agreement by the tenant to pay rates.[70] but often the clause may by design or inadvertence go much further. In addition to raising rates, local authorities may issue notices requiring the making up of roads if they are not already maintained by the public at large; requiring the provision of fire escapes, the installation of fire alarms and fire resistant materials; the remedying of a wide range of defects, *e.g.* both in the structure of the property which may have become dangerous, or in the drainage from it, or demanding payment for their attention to these matters. A tenant for a short term, *e.g.* three years, may not unreasonably want to avoid liability for what amounts to capital improvements that are likely to be of more benefit to his landlord and subsequent tenants.

A number of statutes[71] that permit the imposition of liabilities also contain a mechanism whereby the parties can apply to the county court for apportionment of the expenses. But the language used in the lease may clearly have provided who is to bear the expense. In *Monro v. Burghclere*[72] the tenant agreed to pay rates, etc., and additionally agreed to execute works directed or required by local or public authorities under the direction of Acts of Parliament. At the time of the grant of the 21-year lease in 1903 the Factories Acts already

---

[66] General Rate Act 1967, s.2.

[67] Water Act 1973, s.30, as amended by Water Charges Act 1976, s.2. Properties not connected to mains drainage are not subject to charges for sewerage but are to the "environmental service charge," and see *South West Water Authority* v. *Rumble's* [1985] 2 W.L.R. 405, (H.L.) (Occupier of ground floor lock-up shop has "use" of, and liable to pay for, drainage from roof of block).

[68] This is contained in Local Government Act 1974, s.38.

[69] Strictly this applies to weekly tenancies irrespective of how long they last, *Hammond* v. *Farrow* [1904] 2 K.B. 332. If such a tenant has agreed to pay rates then he will pay them by weekly instalments to his landlord, who suffers cash flow problems as he has to pay the rates in two instalments.

[70] This will include the water rate, *King* v. *Cave-Browne-Cave* [1960] 2 Q.B. 222.

[71] *e.g.* Factories Act 1961, s.170 Office, Shops and Railway Premises Act 1963 s.73; Fire Precautions Act 1971, s.28. In the last two Acts there is power to modify the terms of the lease "so far as concerns rent payable in respect of the premises." And see *Monk* v. *Arnold* [1902] 1 K.B. 761; *Horner* v. *Franklin* [1905] 1 K.B. 479 at p. 488.

[72] [1918] 1 K.B. 291. In *Howe* v. *Botwood* [1913] 2 K.B. 387 the tenant agreed to pay outgoings and the landlord external repairs, and as a result the landlord had to bear the expense of complying with a notice to reconstruct the outside drainage system.

provided for installation of fire escapes. Legislation in 1905 extended this to certain residential property and contained apportionment provisions. On appeal it was held that the county court could only order the tenant to pay as the lessee must be presumed to have contemplated the passing of a similar Act imposing like obligations to those affecting factories.

Covenants by the tenant to comply with statutory notices requiring the execution of works must be considered with some circumspection. But there is a common principle affecting both the interpretation of these clauses and exceptionally wide clauses to pay rates, taxes and other outgoings affecting the property. Neither clause will make the tenant liable to an entirely new sort of rate, tax or outgoing of a type not contemplated when the tenancy was granted. In *Mile End Vestry* v. *Whitby*[73] the tenant was not liable to pay the Lee Valley Drainage rate introduced by an Act of Parliament in 1892 four years after the start of his tenancy. But subject to that qualification, if the agreement throws liability on the tenant, then he will have to pay even though he has a very short term and will not benefit from his expenditure.[74]

Owners and occupiers of properties in rural areas are also likely to be concerned with drainage rates raised by internal drainage boards under the Land Drainage Act 1976, s.63. The rate can be an "occupier's drainage rate" which is used to pay for new works, or improve existing ones or contribute towards the costs of water boards. The responsibility of water boards is primarily toward the maintenance of what are designated as "main rivers," their banks and drainage works in connection with them.[75] The other rate is the "occupier's drainage rate" which is used for defraying other expenses or charges. Both these rates are assessed and levied on the occupier,[76] and the tenant will have to pay both of them if he has agreed to pay all rates due in respect of the premises[77] If there is no agreement by the tenant to pay the rates, then the tenant will bear the occupier's rate for the time he occupied, but can recover the owner's rate by deduction from the rent.[78]

(2) *Taxes*

A liability to pay taxes is often included in the tenant's covenant to

[73] (1898) 78 I.T. 80, and see *Smith* v. *Smith* [1939] 4 All E.R. 312, where Hallett J. surmised that a covenant to pay taxes might not apply to a latter day window tax.
[74] *Foulger* v. *Arding* [1902] 1 K.B. 700; *Stockdale* v. *Ascherberg* [1903] 1 K.B. 873 affd. [1904] 1 K.B. 447; *Re Warriner, Brayshaw* v. *Ninnis* [1903] 2 Ch. 367; *Lowther* v. *Clifford* [1927] 1 K.B. 130 (tenant who held over liable to pay costs of making up lane); and see also Land Drainage Act 1976, s.19(6)(7), in respect of notices under s.18.
[75] Land Drainage Act 1976, s.8.
[76] Land Drainage Act 1976, s.63(3).
[77] *Smith* v. *Smith* [1939] 4 All E.R. 312.
[78] Land Drainage Act 1976, s.72(5).

pay rates, etc., but it is easier to say what it does not cover than what it does. It does not cover items normally called "rates,"[79] neither will it cover the landlord's liability to pay income tax on the rents receivable[80] by him. Rents are assessable to income tax under Schedule A on a current year basis. To calculate the net gains subject to tax the landlord is entitled to make a number of deductions,[81] the most important being for repairs, insurance, maintenance, management and services and rates properly payable by the landlord. The landlord can be given relief if he cannot obtain payment of rent.[82] If the landlord does not pay the tax, then the collector can look to the tenant, but his liability cannot exceed the amount of rent payable by him for the relevant period.[83] The tenant sets off the amount he has paid in respect of the landlord's tax against subsequent payments of rent, and any agreement that he pays the rent in full without allowing any deduction for tax is void.[84] If the tenant pays a premium for the grant of a tenancy not exceeding 50 years, then this is regarded as capitalised rent, and the landlord is assessed to income tax on a proportion of it.[85] Capital gains tax is likely to catch the proportion of the premium not covered by the these provisions, or the whole premium if the lease is for more than 50 years.[86]

(3) *Assessments, Duties and Outgoings*

One hundred years ago there was considerable concern about the lack of paving, proper streets and the existence of privies and cess-pools in the major urban areas. A number of statutes were passed like the Public Health Act 1875 enabling authorities to issue notices either requiring the removal of these defects, or providing for the assessment of charges on owners and occupiers to cover the cost of the remedial works. There were innumerable cases between landlords and tenants to decide on whom the financial burden was thrown by the language which they had used. Collins M.R. in *Foulger* v. *Arding*[87] lamented the waste of judicial time and power involved in examining all the similar decisions, which created a "labyrinth of cases." The current line of authority flows from *Thompson* v. *Lapworth*[88] where a liability to pay "all taxes, rates duties and assessments . . . " covered paving charges.

[79] *Smith* v. *Smith* [1939] 4 All E.R. 312, and see generally *Brewster* v. *Kidgell* (1698) Carth. 438.
[80] Income and Corporation Taxes Act 1970, ss.67, 68. This topic is considered in detail in Chap. 5,(VIII) *post.*
[81] Income and Corporation Taxes Act 1970, ss.71 *et seq.*
[82] Income and Corporation Taxes Act 1970, s.87.
[83] Income and Corporation Taxes Act 1970, s.70.
[84] Taxes Management Act 1970, s.106.
[85] Income and Corporation Taxes Act 1970, s.80.
[86] Capital Gains Tax Act 1979, s.106, Sched. 3, and see *ante*, Chap. 3, (IV)D(3).
[87] [1902] 1 K.B. 700.
[88] (1868) L.R. 3 C.P. 149. Willes J. interpreted "assessments" widely at p. 158.

And in *Farlow* v. *Stevenson*,[89] Lindley M.R. said of an almost identical phrase that he could not imagine wider words. "Duties" clearly covered the liability to execute substantial works of drainage construction and improvement in *Budd* v. *Marshall*.[90] and in the more recent case of *Villenex Co.* v. *Courtney Hotel*,[91] Willis J. held the tenants of a hotel liable for the cost of installing a new fire escape required by the Public Health Act 1936 on the basis that "Duties" covered non-recurring payments. The cost of the fire escape to the tenants was £1,983, only slightly more than the annual rental. It seems therefore that the words duties and outgoings and impositions are interchangeable and wide enough to catch non-recurrent liabilities that arise during the tenancy.[92] The tenant can escape if the liability arose before the tenancy began.[93]

The compulsory improvement of sub-standard tenanted property can now be dealt with by the service of notices under the Housing Act 1985, ss.210 and 212. Section 210 applies if the dwellings are in general improvement areas and housing action areas, and section 212 if they are not. In either case, the notice is served on the "person having the control of the dwelling." He will either be the owner or a tenant for a term exceeding 21 years, who is not himself the landlord of a similar tenant.[94] If the person having control does not himself carry out the works, the local authority may do it, and charge him. But there are apportionment provisions. The person having control can appeal to the county court on receiving the improvement notice. One of the grounds of appeal is that some other person holding an estate or interest in the dwelling[95] will derive benefit from the execution of the works and so ought to pay for all or part of them.[96]

It seems that the person with whom it is sought to share the charge must have a proprietary estate or interest. In *Harrington* v. *Croydon Corporation*[97] Russell L.J. was clearly of the opinion that a statutory tenant protected by the Rent Act did not come within this category[98] and Salmon L.J. thought it "fantastic in the case of a statutory tenant or of an ordinary weekly, monthly or yearly tenant that, in addition to an increase in rent, he should be asked to make some contribution towards the capital expense, since he can have no real interest in the capital value of the land."

---

[89] [1900] 1 Ch. 128 (drainage works).
[90] (1880) 5 C.P.D. 481.
[91] (1969) 20 P. & C.R. 575.
[92] *Foulger* v. *Arding* [1902] 1 K.B. 700.
[93] *Lumby* v. *Faupel* (1904) 90 L.T. 140.
[94] Housing Act 1985, s.236. If the occupying tenant is an agricultural worker residing in the property as part of his terms of employment, the person having control will be his employer.
[95] Whether or not that person occupies it.
[96] Housing Act 1985, s.217.
[97] [1968] 1 Q.B. 856 (application to share cost of grant installed bathroom under Housing Act 1957, s.14).
[98-99] See *post*, Pt.II for a discussion of the nature of a statutory tenant's interest.

Where the tenanted premises are not separately assessed, or there is a low rateable value the landlord may agree to pay the rates and charge the tenant an inclusive rental. Under such an agreement, the landlord will normally have to pay the domestic water rate[1], but he can pass directly to the tenant water rates that may be charged for commercial purposes, *e.g.* for the consumption of water in a cafe.[2] If the tenant has to pay the rates because the landlord defaults, he can deduct the payment from his rent,[3] or if necessary sue the landlord to recover the payment.[4]

B. To Insure

A policy of insurance is a contract to indemnity. An insured person can recover from his insurance company only to the extent that he has suffered loss. If he suffers no loss, he cannot normally recover. If he has taken out insurance cover for more than his loss he will only be paid out what he has lost. If he has insured for less than what is likely to be the full amount of the loss, then the policy moneys payable to him on making a claim are likely to be reduced on the "subject to average" basis. An owner occupier who insures will normally be expected to take out cover that will be enough to pay for reinstatement of the property. That sum will usually be substantially more than the market value of the property. If he insures for its market value only, say £20,000, and half the property is damaged but it will cost £15,000 to repair, then his insurance company is likely to pay him only a percentage of this sum if, *e.g.* they estimate that the cost of full replacement would have been nearer £30,000. Conversely, if the premises are totally destroyed and he has been insuring them for the full replacement value of £30,000 he will only recover from the insurance company the market value of the property, say £20,000, less the value of the site.[5]

Initially the parties to a lease can only take out insurance to cover their liability under the terms of the lease, and their interest in the property. For the tenant this means his liability to repair, if any, and the value of his interest in the property. If the premises are used for commercial purposes the tenant will also want to insure against loss of profits that would flow from a destruction of the property, and the dislocation of his business, and the landlord may be concerned to insure against loss of rent. If the premises are extensive and would not be reinstated in the event of serious damage, *e.g.* the mode of

[1] *Bourn and Tant* v. *Salmon & Gluckstein Ltd* [1907] 1 Ch. 616.
[2] *Re Floyd, Floyd* v. *J. Lyons & Co. Ltd* [1897] 1 Ch. 633.
[3] General Rate Act 1967, s.59.
[4] *Graham* v. *Tate* (1813) 1 M. & S. 609; [1803–13] All E.R. Rep. 378.
[5] See *Leppard* v. *Excess Insurance Co.* [1979] 1 W.L.R. 512 for a recent application of these well-established principles.

construction of Georgian and even Victorian buildings makes them prohibitively expensive to replace, then consideration has to be given to insuring against the cost of site clearance and reinstatement with modern buildings. If both parties take out policies to cover their separate interests and there is a claim, this can lead to a dispute between the insurers about how the loss is to be shared between them. Often the better course of action is for one policy only to be taken out either in the joint names of both parties, or if it is in one party's name only, for the interest of the other to be noted on the policy.[6]

> "When a policy of fire insurance of a building (as distinct from goods) is taken out, the names of all the persons interested therein, or for whose benefit it is made must be inserted in the policy. No person can recover thereon unless he is named therein and then only to the extent of his interest.... If, therefore, the tenant insures in his own name alone, the policy is good only to the extent of his interest. True it is that, when he is bound by covenant to repair his interest extends to cover his liability; and thus he recovers the cost of reinstatement (see *Castellain* v. *Preston, per* Bowen L.J.)[7] Nevertheless it is the tenant's interest alone which is covered; he alone is entitled to the policy moneys, and the landlord has no claim on them: see *Simpson* v. *Scottish Union Insurance Co.*[8] where Sir Hugh Cairns, in the course of his successful argument put the law most neatly: '... the insurance was in the tenant's name, and could only be good to the extent of the tenant's interest. It could not cover the landlord's interest unless his interest appeared on the face of the policy.' "[9]

The tenant's covenant to insure is therefore linked with the covenant to repair, and it may specify insurance in a particular sum, or "to the full value," or the "full insurable value." Here, it seems that if the insuring party seeks and takes the insurance company's advice about the level of cover, then there can be no liability if the cover turns out to be inadequate.[10] Insurance may have to be effected either with a named company, or "reputable" company or through the landlord's managing agent, and there is likely to be a requirement that the policy is effected in the joint names of landlord and tenant, and that the receipt for the last premium is to be produced on request. In other cases, and particularly if there are a number of tenants in the

---

[6] The insurer cannot by subrogation sue a person whose interest is noted on a policy on property, for breach of his duty to the insured, either in negligence, or, for example, for breach of his repairing covenants, *Petrofina (U.K.) Ltd.* v. *Magnaload Ltd.* [1984] 1 Q.B. 127.

[7] (1883) 1 Q.B.D. 380 at p. 400.

[8] (1863) 1 Hem. & M. 618 at p. 624.

[9] *Per* Lord Denning, M.R. in a dissenting judgment in *Re King, Robinson* v. *Gray* [1963] Ch. 459.

[10] *Mumford Hotels Ltd.* v. *Wheler* [1964] Ch. 117.

same building, the landlord may covenant to effect insurance and exact an insurance "rent" from the tenant varying with the premium for the time being.[11] A tenant who pays an insurance rent is intended to benefit from the insurance cover. Even if his interest is not noted on the policy, the insurers cannot sue him, by subrogation, in negligence for causing the loss[12]

The landlord will often reserve the right to insure on the tenant's failure.[13] If the landlord is insuring, the tenant will usually covenant to do nothing to vitiate the policy or cause an increase in the premiums.[14] Whoever is insuring, there will generally be an agreement for abatement of rent for so long as the premises are unusable as a result of damage from an insurable risk,[15] provided that the policies have not been vitiated as a result of the acts or defaults of the tenant. The duration and amount of the abatement may have to be settled by agreement after the disaster, and failing agreement, by arbitration.

A well drawn insurance clause will provide that the insurance moneys are to be laid out in reinstatement, probably with a provision for making up any deficiency out of the covenantor's own funds unless the covenantee specifies the level of cover. It should also provide for the destination of the policy moneys should reinstatement be impossible, *e.g.* because it is agreed to be unreasonably expensive, or impossible either because planning permission or the necessary materials cannot be obtained. Where the landlord insures, the tenant has no equity to compel him to pay out the money in reinstatement,[16] in the absence of express agreement. However, that is not the end of the matter. The tenant may be paying an insurance rent as in *Mumford Hotels Ltd.* v. *Wheler.*[17] In that event, as Harman L.J. said[18]: " . . . the true implication is that the landlord's obligation to insure, done as it was at the tenant's expense, was an obligation intended to enure for the benefit of both parties, and that the landlord cannot simply put the money in her pocket and disregard the tenant's claim. She must, therefore, if called on by the tenants so to do use the money as far as it will go towards reinstatement of the property."

There is no universally established principle which governs the beneficial ownership of a policy of insurance effected in the joint

---

[11] The tenant cannot complain if he can obtain a much cheaper quotation on equally satisfactory terms, *Bandar Property Holdings Ltd.* v. *J. S. Darwen (Successors) Ltd* [1968] 2 All E.R. 305. And see *post*, Chap. 5(III)H(7).

[12] *Mark Rowlands Ltd* v. *Berni Inns* [1985] 3 All E.R. 473.

[13] For the position of the landlords who voluntarily assumed responsibility for cover, and then let it lapse without telling the tenants, see *Argy Trading Development Co. Ltd.* v. *Lapid Developments Ltd.* [1977] 1 W.L.R. 444.

[14] The landlord is under no similar implied obligation in respect of the tenant's policy, *O'Cedar* v. *Slough Trading Co.* [1927] 2 K.B. 123.

[15] If there is no such agreement the full rent remains payable even if the premises are totally destroyed, and see *Matthey* v. *Curling* [1922] 2 A.C. 180.

[16] *Leeds* v. *Cheetham* (1827) 1 Sim. 146.

[17] [1964] Ch. 117.

[18] At p. 126 (Harman L.J. was sitting as an additional judge of the Chancery Division).

names by a landlord or a tenant, under a covenant in the lease. To determine the destination of money not used in reinstatement, one has to ascertain the parties' intentions by reference to all the terms of the lease and the policy. This may well lead one to conclude that, in the absence of express ageement, it is to be implied that the benefit of the policy moneys belong to the parties to the lease in shares proportionate to the value of their interests in the premises immediately before the fire.[19]

Finally, either party has a statutory right under the Fires Prevention (Metropolis) Act 1774, s.83,[20] to direct people who have to pay moneys to an insured in respect of premises to expend those moneys in a particular way. Despite its title the Act is of general and not just local application.[21] It was passed to deter fraudulent people from arson, and not to provide a solution of the difficulties arising out of rival claims to the policy moneys.[22] The section provides that any person interested in, or entitled to, any house or houses or other buildings which have been burnt down or damaged by fire may give notice to the governors or directors of the insurance offices calling on them to expend the insurance moneys upon reinstating the premises burnt down, instead of paying the money over to the insured. The application has to be made before the insurance company settles the claim and pays out.

C. Not to alter the Physical State of the Building

The form of the traditional covenant was "not to cut maim or injure any walls or timber.... " In *L.C.C.* v. *Hutter*[23] this was held to be broken by cutting holes six inches deep in the walls to hold brackets for a large electric light advertisement. Covenants of that nature are still found, but more frequently the tenant will covenant "Not to make any structural alterations or structural additions to the demised premises.... " Sometimes the covenant is absolute, and on other occasions, it will be qualified by the words "without the previous consent in writing of the landlord." A typical alteration often desired by tenants is demolition of internal walls, either to provide larger living accommodation or a through-lounge, or, in shop premises, a larger selling space. An alteration carried out ill-advisedly can lead to physical collapse of the premises. But in any event, it can lead to a significant destruction of the identity of the premises, *e.g.* when the

---

[19] *Beacon Carpets Ltd.* v. *Kirby* [1984] 3 W.L.R. 489.
[20] s.86 provides that no action lies against any person in whose house a fire should accidentally begin. There is no defence if the fire is started negligently, as in *Balfour* v. *Barty-King* [1957] 1 Q.B. 496 (use of blow-lamp to thaw frozen felt lagged pipes in loft).
[21] *Sinnott* v. *Bowden* [1912] 2 Ch. 414; [1911–13] All E.R. Rep. 752.
[22] *Portavon Cinema Co. Ltd.* v. *Price and Century Insurance Co. Ltd.* [1939] 4 All E.R. 601.
[23] [1925] Ch. 626. *cf. Joseph* v. *L.C.C.* (1914) 111 L.T. 276.

tenant wants to extend the rented property into a larger unit with adjoining property which he either owns, or rents separately. Tenants often seek to carry out alterations to modernise shop fronts. If the clause is an absolute one, and the landlord refuses his consent, then nothing can be done.[24]

If the alterations can be carried out with consent, the Landlord and Tenant Act 1927, s.19(2),[25] provides that the covenant shall be subject to a proviso that consent is not to be unreasonably withheld.[26] But the landlord has the right to ask for payment of a reasonable sum in respect of damage to or diminution in the value of the premises or any neighbouring premises belonging to him, and for the payment of the legal costs involved in giving his consent. If the alteration does not add to the letting value of the property, he can, if it is reasonable to do so, ask for an undertaking that the tenant shall reinstate the premises at the end of the tenancy.

If the tenant is convinced that consent has been unreasonably refused, he may proceed without it.[27] But in doing so he does run the risk that he may be proved wrong in a subsequent action by the landlord for damages and possibly forfeiture. The measure of damages may be the cost of reinstatement.[28] Alternatively, the tenant can take proceedings for a declaration that consent has been unreasonably withheld, and that he is entitled to proceed without consent. In *Lambert* v. *F.W. Woolworth & Co. Ltd.* (No. 2),[29] Slesser L.J. said that the "onus of proving that the withholding is unreasonable is on the tenant, but if the landlord gives no reason, but merely refuses, that in itself, ... puts upon him the duty of showing that his action was reasonable...." The "refusal is unreasonable if no grounds are given at all and none can be shown.... Many considerations, aesthetic, historic or even personal, may be relied upon as yielding reasonable grounds for refusing consent."[30] There Woolworth Ltd. wanted to enlarge their shop premises in Bournemouth, and also replace "a sordid front of late-Victorian architecture" with "the erection of a kind of Assyrian facade, appropriate to, and possibly copied from, an archaic heathen temple," which Slesser L.J. thought

---

[24] *F. W. Woolworth & Co. Ltd.* v. *Lambert* [1937] Ch. 37.

[25] The Act refers to covenants against improvements, but these are in practice unknown, and the section is taken to refer to covenants against alterations, *Balls Bros. Ltd.* v. *Sinclair* [1931] 2 Ch. 325.

[26] s.19(2) is replaced for most Rent Act tenancies by a separate code, which makes it a term of such tenancies that the tenant will not effect improvements, which are defined, without the landlord's consent, such consent not to be unreasonably withheld, the onus being on the landlord to show he was not unreasonable, Housing Act 1980, ss 81–83.

[27] *Balls Bros. Ltd.* v. *Sinclair* [1931] 2 Ch. 325; *Commissioner for Railways* v. *Avrom Investments Proprietary Ltd.* [1959] 1 W.L.R. 389.

[28] *Eyre* v. *Rea* [1947] K.B. 567; *Westminster (Duke)* v. *Swinton* [1948] 1 K.B. 524. *cf. James* v. *Hutton* [1950] K.B. 9.

[29] [1938] Ch. 883.

[30] It has been argued that it would be reasonable to refuse consent if to grant it would conflict with the proper management of the landlord's estate,'*Re Town Investments Underlease* [1954] Ch. 301.

might or might not have been "in accordance with the spirit of the age." However, more importantly, the case also decided that whether an alteration is an improvement must be considered from the tenant's point of view, having regard to the demised premises, and not in relation to the tenant's other premises.

In addition to the court being asked if the landlord has been unreasonable in refusing his consent, it can also be asked if he has been unreasonable in demanding too large a figure for the probable damage to his property. The court can also be requested to determine what would be a reasonable figure. Applications for these declarations can be made either to the High Court, or to the county court. Normally the county court can only make declarations and determine whether a sum is reasonable if the property is within its financial jurisdiction;[31] but the Landlord and Tenant Act 1954, s.53, gives the county court unlimited jurisdiction to make declarations on the question of whether consent has been unreasonably withheld in respect of sublettings and assignments, the making of improvements (alterations) and changes of use, and at the same time the court can be asked either to declare that the sum claimed is unreasonable, or to determine what would be a reasonable sum.[32] If the only issue between the parties is the amount to be paid by the tenant, it seems that section 53 does not operate to extend the normal county court jurisdiction.

Occupiers of property can be required to alter and improve their property under a wide range of safety and welfare legislation. A number of the Acts involved provide a mechanism for applying to the county court for modification of tenancy agreements if they would otherwise prohibit the required improvements.[33]

D. To Use in Specified Ways

(1) *The Covenants*

We have already seen[34] that the ways in which a tenant can use the property are affected by enforceable restrictive covenants binding on the property and also by extant planning permissions. But most leases go further. If the property is to be used for private residential purposes only, then there is likely to be a covenant "Not to use the premises otherwise than as a single private dwellinghouse." This will be broken

---

[31] County Courts Act 1984, s.22 (when the rateable value of the property does not exceed £1,000).
[32] And see County Courts Act 1984, Sched. 2, para. 23.
[33] *e.g.* Factories Act 1961, s.169; Offices, Shops and Railway Premises Act 1963, s.73; Fire Precautions Act 1971, s.28.
[34] *Ante,* Chap. 3, (IV).

by subletting,[35] taking in paying guests,[36] or using the premises as a solicitor's office.[37] The covenant may be expressed in a positive form, and may even require the personal occupation of the tenant. This last provision is more likely to be found in a lease designed to afford the tenant subsidised accommodation for the rest of his life. In *Lloyds Bank* v. *Jones*[38] such a provision was held to be broken when the trustees of the deceased tenant's will failed personally to occupy Lower Onibury Farm, the tenanted property. The covenant to use as a private dwelling-house only is often strengthened by a further covenant not to use the premises for any trade, business or profession. It is not always easy to decide when this covenant is broken, *e.g.* does the use of a room in the house by a tenant who is an artist, script-writer, solicitor or builder constitute a breach? It is suggested that if the use involves communication from the property on a regular basis either by telephone or by callers, then there may be good reasons for arguing that the premises are being used for trade or business purposes.[39]

If the premises are being let for business purposes, the extent of the covenant will often depend on whether the property is the only one owned in the area by the landlord, or if it is part of his commercial estate. Further considerations apply if it is part of a chain of retail outlets for the landlord's goods. If it is an isolated property belonging to the landlord, the covenant will be designed by the landlord to preserve what he considers to be his financial interest in that property. There may be no overriding objection to a shop being changed from one trade to another,[40] and indeed a restriction in this respect is likely to reduce the marketability of the lease at the outset. But the landlord may want to guard against trades he might consider to be offensive, or against the property moving from one Town and Country Planning Use Class to another,[41] and even a change within the Class. There might therefore be a covenant "Not to use the premises except for the purposes of a retail florist's and greengrocer's and not for any other purposes except with the lessor's written consent." The covenant may be expressed in positive terms.[42] As will be seen[43] a covenant in these terms gives the landlord unfettered control to decide what trades

---

[35] *Barton* v. *Keeble* [1928] Ch. 517.
[36] *Thorn* v. *Madden* [1925] Ch. 847; *Tendler* v. *Sproule* [1947] 1 All E.R. 193; *Segal Securities Ltd.* v. *Thoseby* [1963] 1 Q.B. 887.
[37] *Angell* v. *Burn* (1933) 77 S.J. 337.
[38] [1955] 2 Q.B. 298; and see *Sumnal* v. *Statt* (1985) 49 P. & C.R. 367 (broken by imprisonment).
[39] *cf. Stoke* v. *Sears* (1951) 151 E.G. 196 (private hire service).
[40] *cf. Horwitz* v. *Rowson* [1960] 1 W.L.R. 803 (not to make a material change in use without written consent).
[41] See *ante*, Chap. 3, (IV)A.
[42] As in *Creery* v. *Summersell and Flowerdew & Co.* [1949] Ch. 751 (tenant's agreement to use premises as offices in connection with his business of surveyor and valuer, broken when he sub-let to law agents).
[43] See *post* (3).

might be carried on in the future, and it may become apparent after a short time that any florist's and greengrocer's business run from the premises is likely to be doomed to financial obscurity.

If a tenant is taking a lease of a shop in part of a commercial estate, then he may want to be sure that a competitor in exactly the same line of business will not be given a tenancy in the same row of shops. The landlord may also want to attempt to prevent his tenants from running competing businesses. It is a matter for some speculation whether the proximity of competitors encourages more customers generally or divides up business so that it ceases to be profitable. If the landlord does decide to have a policy of letting to non-competing businesses, then the covenants are likely to be drawn with some particularity. Such covenants are not registrable restrictions under the control of the restrictive trades practices legislation, at least in the absence of a trading nexus between the parties.[44]

There is no room for implying that the landlord will not let to competing businesses.[45] There must be an express covenant by him to that effect, and such covenants are very strictly construed. A landlord's covenant "Not to let any other shop on the Housing Estate for the purpose of a General Hardware Merchant and Ironmonger" cannot be enlarged into a covenant "not to permit the premises to be used" for a particular purpose. Where the landlords let further premises for use as a foodhall, they were not in breach of their covenants when the tenants of the foodhall later on sold a wide range of items that were also sold by the ironmongers.[46] The landlords had not let the premises for competing purposes.

If the tenant wants to avoid this difficulty, he should take a covenant from his landlord that the latter will not let for specified competing purposes, and will not "permit or suffer" his other premises to be used by those competing businesses. "Permit" normally connotes some form of control,[47] and "a man may permit the continuance of an act if he can prevent it by taking legal proceedings and refrains from doing so.[48] There is no need for him to take proceedings if there is a reasonable doubt about their likely success. "Suffer," it seems, is an even wider word.[49] Tenants have some difficulty in enforcing covenants against letting to competing businesses where the objectionable trading is only a peripheral part of

[44] *Re Ravenseft Properties Application* [1978] Q.B. 52.
[45] *Port* v. *Griffith* [1938] 1 All E.R. 295.
[46] *Rother* v. *Colchester Corporation* [1969] 1 W.L.R. 720.
[47] *Sefton (Earl of)* v. *Tophams* (No. 2) [1967] 1 A.C. 50. *cf. Leicester (Earl of)* v. *Wells-next-the-Sea U.D.C.* [1973] Ch. 110.
[48] *Berton* v. *Alliance Economic Investment Co.* [1922] 1 K.B. 742 at p. 758, *per* Atkin L.J.
[49] *Barton* v. *Reed* [1932] 1 Ch. 362.

the other tenant's business.[50]

In most leases, whatever the other covenants relating to user, there is a covenant by the tenant that he will not do anything on the premises which may be to the annoyance, nuisance or disturbance of the landlord or the owners, tenants, lessees and occupiers of any adjoining or neighbouring property. The production of excessive noise[51] or smells and the use of premises for immoral purposes[52] commonly give rise to grounds of complaint. "What is a nuisance or annoyance will continue to be determined by the courts according to robust and common-sense standards."[53]

The last type of covenants that restrict the use of land to be considered are those that tie the tenant to take supplies of beer, petrol or other commodities from the landlord—hence the tied house, or the petrol station subject to a solus agreement. The agreement usually specifies minimum supplies to be taken by the tenant, and prudently should either specify the maximum amount the landlord is obliged to supply, or require all supplies to be sold by retail on the premises.[54]

These agreements were subject to considerable litigation during the scramble for retail petrol outlets. A number of traders bound by ties sought to obtain supplies elsewhere and argued that their agreements were in restraint of trade and so illegal and unenforceable. The issue was discussed at length in *Esso Petroleum Co. Ltd.* v. *Harper's Garage (Stourport) Ltd.*[55] A distinction seems to be drawn between the tenant who is already in possession of the land before he enters into a tie, and the trader who is out of possession and is then let into it by a lease from the supplier.[56] The tie in the first case may be affected by the doctrine vitiating contracts in unreasonable restraint of trade. In the second case: "A person buying or leasing land had no previous right to be there at all, let alone to trade there, and, when he takes possession of that land subject to a negative restrictive covenant, he gives up no right or freedom which he previously had."[57] But a supplier may have some difficulty in obtaining an injunction to enforce a tie if it is

---

[50] *A. Lewis & Co. (Westminster) Ltd.* v. *Bell Property Trust Ltd.* [1940] Ch. 345 (sale of cigarettes in tea-shop no breach of covenant not to use the premises as a tobacconist's); *Labone* v. *Litherland U.D.C.* [1956] 1 W.L.R. 522 (sale of bread by grocer no breach of covenant not to let to competing businesses in a lease to baker and confectioner).

[51] *Hampstead and Suburban Properties Ltd.* v. *Diomedous* [1969] 1 Ch. 248.

[52] *Central Estates (Belgravia) Ltd.* v. *Woolgar (No. 2)* [1972] 1 W.L.R. 1048.

[53] *Hampstead and Suburban Properties Ltd.* v. *Diomedous* [1969] 1 Ch. at p. 258, Megarry J. and see *Walter* v. *Selfe* (1851) 4 De G. & Sm. 315.

[54] *cf. Sky Petroleum Ltd.* v. *V.I.P. Petroleum Ltd.* [1974] 1 W.L.R. 576.

[55] [1968] A.C. 269.

[56] And see *Cleveland Petroleum Co. Ltd.* v. *Dartstone Ltd.* [1969] 1 W.L.R. 115. The corporate veil may be pierced to discover the realities of the situation, *Alex Lobb (Garages) Ltd.* v. *Total Oil G.B. Ltd.* [1985] 1 All E.R. 303.

[57] *Esso Petroleum Co. Ltd.* v. *Harper's Garage (Stourport) Ltd.* [1968] A.C. at p. 298; *cf. Amoco Australia Pty. Ltd.* v. *Rocca Bros. Motor Engineering Co. Pty. Ltd.* [1975] A.C. 561, where the view was expressed that there was no difference between an unenforceable promise contained in a contract and one contained in a lease.

operating unfairly and unreasonably. In *Shell U.K. Ltd.* v. *Lostock Garage Ltd.*,[58] Shell were selling to the defendant at the contract price but offering discounts to other Shell garages in the neighbourhood. The defendant sought supplies elsewhere, and Shell for the time being were unable to enforce the tie. However, a breach by the supplier in this respect does not entitle the tenant to regard the tie provisions as a dead letter and either repudiate that part of them, or the lease itself.[59] In any event, a void covenant may be severed if there is sufficient consideration to support the rest of the agreement.[60]

(2) *Enforcement*

Enforcement is by action for damages, injunction or forfeiture, but in most cases what the plaintiff wants is to stop the offending activity and to stop it quickly, generally by means of an interlocutory injunction. If he acts promptly he should be entitled to one. Megarry J. in *Hampstead and Suburban Properties Ltd.* v. *Diomedous*,[61] said:

> "Where there is a plain and uncontested breach of a clear covenant not to do a particular thing, and the covenantor promptly begins to do what he has promised not to do, then in the absence of special circumstances it seems to me that the sooner he is compelled to keep his promise the better . . . I see no reason for allowing a covenantor who stands in clear breach of an express prohibition to have a holiday from the enforcement of his obligations until the trial."

But an injunction will not be granted where the plaintiff has sat back for some time, acquiescing in the breach,[62] and as will be seen,[63] it is not possible to enforce forfeiture if the breach has been waived by demand and receipt of rent in full knowledge of the breach.[64]

Tenants would often like to enforce covenants entered into by their landlord with their neighbours in identical terms to those in their own leases. One tenant may want to take steps to stop another tenant's use of his flat for business purposes, or to prevent a breach of covenant not to carry on a particular competing trade. In most cases, the tenant will be unable to take direct action against the erring tenant, unless he

[58] [1976] 1 W.L.R. 1187.
[59] *Total Oil Great Britain Ltd.* v. *Thompson Garages (Biggin Hill) Ltd.* [1972] 1 Q.B. 318. And see *Esso Petroleum Co.* v. *Kingswood Motors (Addlestone)* [1974] Q.B. 142.
[60] *Alec Lobb Ltd.* v. *Total Oil G.B. Ltd.* [1985] 1 All E.R. 303.
[61] [1969] 1 Ch. 248 (loud music from licensed restaurant caused annoyance to neighbours).
[62] *Barret* v. *Blagrave* (1800) 5 Ves.Jr. 555; [1775–1802] All E.R. Rep. 118.
[63] *Post*, Chap. 8.
[64] *Central Estates (Belgravia) Ltd.* v. *Woolgar* (No. 2) [1972] 1 W.L.R. 1048.

can either establish the covenants amount to a building scheme,[65] or letting scheme,[66] or that the way the development was carried out indicates that all the parties must be regarded as having a common interest and intent that the covenants should be mutually enforceable.[67] It is not unusual to find a declaration expressly denying the existence of such a mutual intent or a provision permitting the landlord to consent to variations of the scheme.[68] If the tenant is simply complaining about noise from his neighbours then he might be well advised to galvanise the local authority into activity under the Control of Pollution Act 1974, s.58, or if that fails to take proceedings himself under s.59. In other cases he may have grounds for taking proceedings in nuisance.

(3) *Variation*

It is not easy to vary covenants in leases controlling the use of land. If the covenant is absolute, or provides for variation only with the lessor's consent, then there are no grounds for implying that the lessor has to be reasonable in refusing his consent. A simple refusal to give his consent cannot be challenged.[69] There is no statutory proviso that the landlord is not to withhold his consent unreasonably, as there is in the cases of covenants against assigning and under-letting, etc., and altering the premises without consent.[70] There is a curious provision in the Landlord and Tenant Act 1927, s.19(3), which prevents the landlord from asking for a lump sum or increased rent[71] as a condition of granting his consent to an alteration of the permitted user. But he can ask for a reasonable sum[72] to compensate for any damage to or loss of value of the property, or any of his neighbouring properties. The prohibition does not apply if consent is also necessary to carry out alterations. Alterations are very likely if the incoming tenant is changing the nature of the business carried on in the demised premises, and where consent is required for change of use and alterations, there is no restriction on the amount the landlord can ask for his consent.[73] In view of these difficulties, tenants will often

---

[65] *Elliston* v. *Reacher* [1908] 2 Ch.374, affd. 665, and see *Megarry and Wade*, pp. 790 *et seq.*
[66] *Hudson* v. *Cripps* [1896] 1 Ch. 265 (change from flats to club restrained); *Newman* v. *Real Estate Debenture Corpn. Ltd.* [1940] 1 All E.R. 131 (flats to showroom and offices restrained); *cf. Kelly* v. *Battershell* [1949] 2 All E.R. 830; *Ashby* v. *Wilson* [1900] 1 Ch. 66 (no scheme on lettings of shops in a row).
[67] *Re Dolphin's Conveyance* [1970] 1 Ch. 654; *Brunner* v. *Greenslade* [1971] Ch. 993.
[68] *Pearce* v. *Maryon-Wilson* [1935] Ch. 188.
[69] *Comber* v. *Fleet Electrics Ltd.* [1955] 1 W.L.R. 566.
[70] Landlord and Tenant Act 1927, s.19(1)(2) and see *Guardian Assurance Co.* v. *Gants Hill Holdings* (1983) 267 E.G. 678 (no proviso at common law).
[71] *Jenkins* v. *Price* [1907] 2 Ch. 229; [1908] 1 Ch. 10.
[72] For the determination of this issue, see *ante*, (IV)C.
[73] See *ante*, (IV)C for the position where the tenant is only seeking consent to alterations.

endeavour to negotiate that the covenant restricting user will be subject to a proviso that the use can be changed with consent "such consent not to be unreasonably withheld." If that is done, then the position is the same as in the case of covenants against assigning and altering without consent.

A number of older, larger properties are let on long leases with restrictions designed to maintain them in the occupation of one family. Both the size of the properties concerned and changes in the neighbourhood can make maintenance of these covenants unrealistic. The Housing Act 1985, s.610, provides a means of obtaining the consent of the County Court to a modification of the covenants to enable conversion[75] of the property into flats. Furthermore, changes in a neighbourhood can also be a ground for the Land Tribunal modifying a restrictive covenant because it is obsolete, on the application of a tenant with a term of more than 40 years after 25 years of his term have expired.[76]

E. For Quiet Enjoyment

(1) *The Nature of the Covenant*

Tenants frequently enquire if anything can be done when their enjoyment and use of the property has been diminished by the behaviour of the landlord or of someone they consider can be connected with him. In extreme cases, the conduct complained of amounts to harassment calculated to drive the tenant out, and succeeds in that object. In other situations, the landlord's use of property still retained by him prevents the tenant from using the demised property in the way he thought was contemplated by both. There are a number of strings to the tenant's bow:

    (a) he may sue the landlord for breach of the covenant for quiet enjoyment contained in the lease, or for breach of the implied covenant if there is no express one, as in an oral tenancy;

    (b) he may sue the landlord for breach of the implied covenant that the landlord will not derogate from his grant;

    (c) he may be able to sue the person who is causing the difficulty either in nuisance or trespass;

    (d) he may be able to sue the person at fault for breach of a restrictive covenant that the offender should have observed, and which he is entitled to enforce, as a result, *e.g.* of a letting

[74] And see *post*. Chap. 7 (II)C.
[75] *Stack* v. *Church Commissioners for England* [1952] 1 All E.R. 1352.
[76] L.P.A. 1925, s.84, as amended, and see further Woodfall, paras. 1–1227 *et seq.*

scheme affecting a whole block of flats. This may include an action against the landlord if he has permitted the situation to arise.[77]

The normal express covenant by the landlord will be in the following terms, or a variation of them:

"The Landlord hereby covenants with the tenant that the tenant paying the rent hereby reserved and performing and observing the several covenants on his part herein contained shall peaceably hold and enjoy the demised premises during the term without any interruption by the landlord or any person rightfully claiming under or in trust for him."

If there is no express covenant, then one in similar terms will be implied by the use of the word "demise," which word "imports a covenant in law on the part of the lessor that he has good title, and that the lessee shall quietly enjoy during the term, and, therefore, if the lessee be ousted during the term, an action of covenant will lie by him against the lessor."[78] Even where the word "demise" is not used the covenant will be implied by the mere creation of the relationship of landlord and tenant.[79] But the implied covenant is in some respects wider than the express one, and will include an obligation on the landlord's part to give possession at the beginning of the lease.[80] In other respects the implied covenant is narrower, in that it is coterminous with the lessor's estate,[81] which may end before the lease. Like the express qualified covenant for title it only gives the tenant a right of action against the landlord in respect of lawful and not unlawful interruptions by third persons for whom the landlord might be responsible.[82] In such a case the tenant is left to his action in tort against the third party.

If there is an express covenant then that displaces entirely any reliance on the implied covenant,[83] and this may include the obligation to give possession.[84] The express covenant usually cuts down the landlord's implied obligations to responsibility for those claiming from him. The tenant therefore will be remediless if he is dispossessed by the true owner of the property because it turns out

---

[77] *Jaeger* v. *Mansions Consolidated Ltd.* (1902) 87 L.T. 690 (action against landlord for permitting flat to be used for immoral purposes).
[78] *Burnett* v. *Lynch* (1826) 5 B. & C. 589; [1824–34] All E.R. Rep. 352, Littledale J.
[79] *Budd-Scott* v. *Daniel* [1902] 2 K.B. 351.
[80] *Coe* v. *Clay* (1829) 5 Bing. 440; *Jinks* v. *Edwards* (1856) 11 Ex. 775.
[81] *Adams* v. *Gibney* (1830) 6 Bing. 656.
[82] *Wallis* v. *Hands* [1893] 2 Ch. 75; and see *Kenny* v. *Preen* [1963] 1 Q.B. 499 at p. 512, Pearson L.J.
[83] *Line* v. *Stephenson* (1838) 4 Bing., N.C. 678, affd. 5 Bing., N.C. 183; *Grosvenor Hotel Co.* v. *Hamilton* [1894] 2 Q.B. 836.
[84] *Miller* v. *Emcer Products Ltd.* [1956] Ch. 304 (unsuccessful action for damages for breach of right to use lavatory granted by underlease).

that the landlord had no right to create the tenancy at all.[85] The same is true if the tenant is dispossessed by a superior landlord unless there was an express covenant by the landlord to observe the terms of the head lease.[86] On the credit side, the covenant will last for the whole duration of the lease and binds the landlord's successors in title.[87] The express covenant, despite appearances to the contrary, is not dependent on the tenant paying the rent and observing his covenants. It is independent of the tenant's obligations. A tenant in default can still sue.[88]

Because of the poor protection of a tenant under the covenant for quiet enjoyment as normally qualified, or under the implied covenant, wherever practicable a prospective tenant who is paying a substantial premium or heavy rent in advance or who contemplates a large outlay on improvements, should request proof of the prospective landlord's title. Where the land is registered he will need only the proprietor's consent to search the register. If consent is refused he can still make local searches. Where land is unregistered he can and should still make local and central land charge searches. By such means he can diminish his risk if, despite the landlord's refusal to show title, he chooses to take the tenancy.[89]

(2) *Acts Causing a Breach of the Covenant*

The cases are full of general statements of what conduct constitutes a breach of covenant. In *Browne* v. *Flower*,[90] Parker J. said: "It appears to me that to constitute a breach of such a covenant there must be some physical interference with the enjoyment of the demised premises, and that a mere interference with the comfort of persons using the demised premises by the creation of a personal annoyance such as might arise from noise, invasion of privacy, or otherwise is not enough." In *Hudson* v. *Cripps*,[91] North J. said: "I do not understand the stipulation for quiet enjoyment to be one which means that the plaintiff is to enjoy the premises without the nuisance of a noise in the neighbourhood. A covenant for quiet enjoyment is a covenant for freedom from disturbance by adverse claimants to the property." But

---

[85] See, for example, *Celsteel Ltd.* v. *Alton House Holdings Ltd.* (No. 2) [1986] 1 All E.R. 598. (grant by earlier landlord of rights of way effectively prevented enjoyment of lease granted by his successor—no breach of covenant for quiet enjoyment).

[86] *Kelly* v. *Rogers* [1892] 1 Q.B. 910, *cf. Cohen* v. *Tannar* [1900] 2 Q.B. 609 (where the mesne landlord submitted to judgment unnecessarily for forfeiture of the head lease and was liable to his tenant for loss of the estate); *Queensway Marketing* v. *Associated Restaurants* (1984) 271 E.G. 1106 (definition clause extended covenant to cover acts of superior lessor). And see Russell (1976) 40 Conv. (N.S.) 427.

[87] As in *Sampson* v. *Hodson-Pressinger* [1981] 3 All E.R. 710.

[88] *Dawson* v. *Dyer* (1883) 5 B. and Ad. 584; *Edge* v. *Boileau* (1885) 16 Q.B.D. 117.

[89] See further Chap. 3 (IV)B, *ante.*

[90] [1911] 1 Ch. 219 at p. 228.

[91] [1896] 1 Ch. 265.

applying general statements to particular situations has proved more difficult. The cases are, however, clear that whether quiet enjoyment has been interrupted is a question of fact.[92]

The covenant has been broken when the plaintiff's land was flooded as a result of the proper use by another of the landlord's tenants of badly constructed drains[93]; when it was flooded and damaged because the landlord failed to maintain and keep clear a culvert on his retained land.[94] Damages have been recovered by a physician tenant whose chimneys smoked into the rooms after the landlord erected tall flats on the adjoining site[95]; by a printer whose premises had to be demolished following vibrations from pumping equipment • and machines operated by his landlord in the next building.[96] The covenant is broken if the superior landlord unjustifiably requires his tenant's own tenants to pay their rents direct to himself.[97] It could be broken if the landlord sanctions building works which generate noise and dust making the tenanted property unusable,[98] or if the scaffolding for the works physically hinders the tenant's customers from getting to his shop window.[99] A landlord was liable for unreasonable noise in the demised flat resulting from the normal use of a poorly constructed tiled terrace above it.[1] But the erection of an outside staircase which reduces the tenant's privacy has been held not to be actionable.[2]

The covenant is proving increasingly useful in cases where the landlord is behaving in such a way as to drive the tenant out, *e.g.* removing the doors and windows[3]; cutting off the gas and electricity[4]; failing to pay the electricity bill so that it is cut off[5]; knocking on the tenant's door and shouting threats of physical eviction[6]; putting out the tenant's belongings and changing the locks.[7] If the landlord physically evicts the tenant he may be able to sue for the tort of trespass in addition to bringing an action in contract for breach of the covenant for quiet enjoyment. One thing the tenant cannot do is to

---

[92] *Owen* v. *Gadd* [1956] 2 Q.B. 99.
[93] *Sanderson* v. *Berwick-upon-Tweed Corpn.* (1884) 13 Q.B.D. 547.
[94] *Booth* v. *Thomas* [1926] Ch. 397.
[95] *Tebb* v. *Cave* [1900] 1 Ch. 642, a decision regarded with some suspicion in *Davis* v. *Town Properties Investment Corporation Ltd.* [1903] 1 Ch. 797 (where the smoke-affected tenant failed against the landlord who developed on a site acquired after the date of the lease).
[96] *Grosvenor Hotel Co.* v. *Hamilton* [1894] 2 Q.B. 836, *cf. Lyttleton Times Co. Ltd.* v. *Warners Ltd.* [1907] A.C. 476.
[97] *Edge* v. *Boileau* (1885) 16 Q.B.D. 117. But note that there is no "physical interference" here.
[98] *cf. Matania* v. *National Provincial Bank Ltd.* [1936] 2 All E.R. 633, where in fact the landlord's consent had not been obtained.
[99] *Owen* v. *Gadd* [1956] 2 Q.B. 99.
[1] *Sampson* v. *Hodson-Pressinger* [1981] 3 All E.R. 710.
[2] *Browne* v. *Flower* [1911] 1 Ch. 219.
[3] *Lavender* v. *Betts* [1942] 2 All E.R. 72.
[4] *Perera* v. *Vandiyar* [1953] 1 W.L.R. 672.
[5] *McCall* v. *Abelesz* [1976] Q.B. 585.
[6] *Kenny* v. *Preen* [1963] 1 Q.B. 499.
[7] *Drane* v. *Evangelou* [1978] 1 W.L.R. 455; and see (1979) 42 M.L.R. 223.

bring an action for breach of the statutory duty contained in the Protection from Eviction Act 1977 making harassment a criminal offence[8] If the premises are requisitioned, this does not amount to an eviction. In such a case a tenant of the Crown can neither withhold rent nor sue for breach of the implied covenant for quiet enjoyment.[9]

Actions for breach of covenant for quiet enjoyment are often linked with actions for breach of the implied covenant that the landlord will not derogate from his grant. These are actions to stop the landlord taking away with one hand what he is giving with the other and are directed to restraining the landlord from misusing adjoining land retained by him or to claiming damages for its misuse. The tenant will argue that the way the landlord is using the adjoining premises frustrates the purpose of the lease, *e.g.* operating pumping machines that cause the demised premises to be destroyed,[10] erecting buildings for a Cornish tin mine so close to the demised explosive magazines that they could no longer be legally used for that purpose.[11] But carrying out alterations that will make the demised flat less comfortable to live in[12] or commercial premises more expensive to operate have been held not to frustrate the purposes of the lease or to amount to a derogation from the lessor's grant.[13]

(3) *Damages*

The plaintiff is entitled to general damages for his immediate loss, but these are not likely to be significantly large.[14] If he can establish special loss, *e.g.* show that the interference put him to extra expense, *e.g.* removal expenses, or demonstrate a loss of profits to his business resulting from the breach, then he can claim for these items.[15] If he can show that the defendant has acted in cynical disregard[16] for the plaintiff's rights, the court may award exemplary or punitive damages "to teach a wrongdoer that tort does not pay."[17] A a result in *Drane* v. *Evangelou*[18] an award of £1,000 for the "monstrous behaviour" of the landlord who put out the tenant's belongings and changed the locks was upheld by the Court of Appeal. And it seems that damages in the action for breach of contract would be given not only for the tenant's inconvenience but also for the distress and inconvenience of

---

[8] *McCall* v. *Abelesz* [1976] Q.B. 585.
[9] *Crown Lands Commissioners* v. *Page* [1960] 2 Q.B. 274.
[10] *Grosvenor Hotel Co.* v. *Hamilton* [1894] 2 Q.B. 836.
[11] *Harmer* v. *Jumbil (Nigeria) Tin Areas Ltd.* [1921] 1 Ch. 200.
[12] *Kelly* v. *Battershell* [1949] 2 All E.R. 830.
[13] *O'Cedar* v. *Slough Trading Co. Ltd.* [1927] 2 K.B. 123.
[14] *e.g.* £2 was awarded in both *Owen* v. *Gadd* [1956] 2 Q.B. 99 and *Kenny* v. *Preen* [1963] 1 Q.B. 499.
[15] *Grosvenor Hotel Co.* v. *Hamilton* [1894] 2 Q.B. 836; *Cruse* v. *Mount* [1933] Ch. 278.
[16] *Rookes* v. *Barnard* [1964] A.C. 1129 at p. 1226, Lord Devlin.
[17] *Ibid.* p. 1227.
[18] [1978] 1 W.L.R. 455.

his wife and family.[19] If the action can be framed in tort, *e.g.* trespass or nuisance;[20] then clearly "exemplary"[21] or "punitive" and "aggravated"[22] damages can be awarded where aggravating circumstances have been proved.

F. Covenants in Flats Schemes

(1) *Flat Schemes*

There is no restriction on the length of terms that the freehold owners and managers of flats can create. Leasehold owners will be restricted by the length of their own term. The length of term will depend on the financial objectives of the owners; the restrictions that might be imposed on them by the provisions in their own head leases, if any, or the current financial climate which might encourage the disposal of all the flats at substantial premiums and low rents. The choice of scheme also depends on the state of the local housing market. But whichever type of development[24] is chosen, it is likely that the lessor will retain the shell of the building, including the main walls, drains, foundations and common parts and a responsibility to maintain them. The normal scheme will provide for costs of repair and maintenance of the retained parts, as well as costs of the management and insurance of the whole block, to be divided amongst the tenants for the time being and to be recovered from them as a service charge in the same way as rent. The scheme will usually provide for a fixed part of the service charge to be paid at the beginning of the rental year on account of the year's total charge.

If the scheme is proceeding by way of the grant of long leaseholds, *e.g.* for 125 years, then it is likely that the immediate landlord will be a management company limited either by shares or guarantee[25] and that all the long leaseholders will be members of the company and in effective control of it. Such a scheme gives power of management over the whole building to all the tenants for the time being. The scheme may also provide that the management company is not to undertake the discharge of liabilities in excess of a specified figure until the management company has been put into funds.

---

[19] *McCall* v. *Abelesz* [1976] Q.B. 585; *cf. Woodar Investment Development Ltd.* v. *Wimpey Construction U.K. Ltd* [1980] 1 All E.R. 571 (H.L.) especially pp. 576, 585, 588, and 590–591.
[20] *Guppys (Bridport) Ltd.* v. *Brookling; Same* v. *James* (1984) 269 E.G. 846 and 942 (C.A.).
[21] *Cruise* v. *Terrell* [1922] 1 K.B. 664.
[22] *Lavender* v. *Betts* [1942] 2 All E.R. 72.
[23] *Asghar* v. *Ahmed* (1984) 17 H.L.R. 25 (C.A.). And see *McMillan* v. *Singh* (1984) 17 H.L.R. 120; *Millington* v. *Duffy* (1984) 17 H.L.R. 232.
[24] See generally George and George, *The Sale of Flats* (5th ed.).
[25] This facilitates changes in membership; share certificates can be dispensed with.

Problems of an acute nature can arise where the proprietor or his company are managing a building let on shorter terms which is either subject to rapidly escalating management costs or very substantial bills for major items of repair. The cost of servicing lifts has given rise to considerable concern in a number of schemes, and repair to roofs, central heating systems and the plumbing can produce bills comparable to the annual rent. If the tenancy is for less than seven years[26] the tenant may be able to shelter behind the Landlord and Tenant Act 1985, s.11.[27] This imposes a liability on the landlord for repair of the structure and exterior of the property (including drains, gutters and external pipes) and to installations in the flat for the supply of water, hot and cold, space heating, gas, electricity, and sanitation. The landlord cannot recover service charges in respect of these items. The section does not apply to a main central heating boiler outside the flat.

Flat schemes also contain detailed provisions controlling how the flats can be used. Frequently, the management reserve the right to vary the regulations from time to time both in respect of new and existing tenants. It seems that there is nothing inherently objectionable in this provided that the new regulations do not attempt to impose new onerous burdens on the tenants. The scheme may amount to a "letting scheme."[28]

(2) *Service Charges*

In addition to rent, most tenants will pay a service charge, usually to the management company. It can only be called and treated as a payment of rent if the payee is the landlord. In the better founded schemes the management company will also be the immediate landlord, holding either the reversion, or at least a concurrent lease. There is a limit on the items which can be properly included in a service charge. They are the costs or estimated costs for services, repairs, maintenance, insurance or the landlord's costs of management,[29] including overheads. A number of common expenses do not feature in this list—notional cost of the caretaker's accommodation, damages the management company may have to pay in litigation, payments in respect of the management company's management profits. Not all these items can be covered by the heading "overheads." If the leases omit to charge for items which should be included, like management costs, or interest on pre-payments,[30] then

---

[26] L. & T.A. 1985, s.13.
[27] See *post*, Chap. 6. (III) C.
[28] See *ante*. (IV)D(2).
[29] L. & T.A. 1985, s.18.
[30] *Boldmark Ltd.* v. *Cohen, Financial Times*, November 20, 1985.

it is practically impossible to change the scheme to include them.[31] The Landlord and Tenant Act 1985, sections 18–30, provides a mild form of control over the amounts which can be properly charged. The enforcement of these provisions will generally require an active and interested tenants' association. The statutory requirements provide that service charges should be limited to costs reasonably incurred or likely to be incurred in the provision of services or works, which should be of a reasonable standard.[32] If the work will cost more than £500 or £25 times the number of flats, whichever is the greater, then two estimates for the work have to be obtained, one of them from a firm unconnected with the landlord.[33] One month's notice has to be given to each of the tenants and their association of work to be done, and their observations invited.[34] The landlord cannot obtain the tenant's prior consent to the reasonableness of the work and charges.[35] It is not possible for the service charge agreement to provide that the landlord's surveyor's decision "shall be final and binding on the parties," because he cannot be expected to hold the balance impartially between the landlord and tenant.[36] Such a surveyor's decision will always be open to challenge, and so cannot be "final."

The tenant is entitled to a written summary of how the costs have been calculated certified by a qualified accountant to whom receipts and vouchers have to be produced.[37] The scheme may sensibly provide for a sinking fund for the replacement of expensive capital items, *e.g.* lifts, boilers, major roof repairs. This spreads the cost of such items over a number of years. If the scheme does provide for a sinking fund, then it is better for it to be held in the form of a trust fund, so that it is not part of the management company's general fund and available to a liquidator.[38] The scheme should state clearly to whom the funds belong. If possible one wants to avoid outgoing tenants making claims in respect of their payments, and incoming tenants being faced with disproportionately large charges to remedy deficiencies.

Rent Act tenants whose rents are registered are not entitled to the benefit of these provisions unless their rents have been registered with services entered as a variable amount.[39] Local authority tenants are outside the provisions altogether unless they have a long tenancy, *i.e.*

---

[31] If the physical circumstances change so radically as to make the scheme unfair, *e.g.* change in floor area used to calculate heating charge, the court may intervene and do what is fair, *Pole Properties v. Feinberg* (1982) 43 P. & C.R. 121.

[32] L. & T.A. 1985, s.19(1).

[33] L. & T.A. 1985, s.20(2), (3).

[34] L. & T.A. 1985, s.20(3).

[35] L. & T.A. 1985, s.19(3).

[36] *Concorde Graphics v. Andromeda Investments SA* (1983) 265 E.G. 386.

[37] L. & T.A. 1985, s.21.

[38] *Re Chelsea Cloisters (In Liquidation)* (1980) 41 P. & C.R. 98.

[39] L. & T.A. 1985, s.27, and see Rent Act 1977, ss.47, and 71(4), and *post* Chap. 11.

for more than 21 years.[40] In many cases, the express provisions for the payment of service charges will themselves entitle the tenants to call for certified accounts.

V. THE PROVISOS AND OPTIONS

The last part of the lease contains the provisos and other general administrative provisions for the smoother running of the relationship of landlord and tenant. A "proviso" is the same as a "condition" strictly so called, *e.g.* "Provided if the tenant fails to pay the rent hereby reserved . . . " observe the covenants, or becomes bankrupt, then the landlord can re-enter and end the lease. This is a forfeiture clause,[41] and it is in the landlord's interest to make sure the lease has one. Again the lease may provide that: "If the premises are destroyed by fire . . . " or other causes then the rent is to be abated. This is a clause for the abatement of rent. The tenant should make sure this is included. The lease may provide that: "If the tenant is desirous . . . " of either renewing the lease or purchasing the landlord's interest, he can so do so long as certain further conditions are observed. This is an option to renew or to purchase. Again, there may be a "break clause," which is more commonly drawn for the benefit of tenants than landlords, as follows: "If either the tenant or the landlord shall be desirous of determining the term hereby granted at the expiration of the 7th. 14th . . . years" then he can do so by serving notice on the other party, subject to the observance of detailed conditions.

Except in the case of the proviso for the abatement of rent, the effect of the proviso will be to end the tenant's interest in the case of forfeiture or break clauses, or enlarge it in the case of options to renew or purchase. In each case the operation of the proviso is triggered off by the happening of a future uncertain event. The following are the provisos and other terms some at least of which are likely to be found in the final part of leases:

(a) proviso for abatement or suspension of rent,
(b) proviso for forfeiture for non-payment of rent, etc.,
(c) break clauses,
(d) options to purchase and renew,
(e) provisions for the service of notices,
(f) arbitration clauses,
(g) agreement for the payment of legal costs.

[40] L. & T.A. 1985, s.26.
[41] These are considered in Chap. 8, *post*.

A. Proviso for Suspension of Rent

It will be seen that the payment of rent[42] must continue throughout the duration of the tenant's estate, irrespective of the condition of the property unless it is destroyed by war damage,[43] or the lease provides for abatement of rent. Parke B. said in *Hart* v. *Windsor*[44] that

> "the tenant can neither maintain an action, nor is he exonerated from the payment of rent, if the house demised is blown down, or destroyed by fire: *Monk* v. *Cooper*,[45] *Belfour* v. *Weston*[46] and *Pindar* v. *Ainsley and Rutter*[47]; or gained upon by the sea: *Richards le Tavener's Case*[48]; or the occupation rendered impracticable by the king's enemies: *Paradine* v. *Jane*[49]; or where a wharf demised was swept away by the Thames: *Carter* v. *Cummins*.[50] In all these cases, the estate of the lessor continues, and that is all the lessor impliedly warrants."

Later examples would include the destruction of warehouse premises as a result of overloading by another tenant,[51] and the destruction of the premises by fire during their requisitioning.[52] It might be argued that many of these cases would not be decided in the same way today in view of developments in the doctrine of frustration.[53] The more prudent tenant will consider what physical changes to the property might foreseeably frustrate the purposes for which he is taking the tenancy, and what economic or political changes might occur with a similar effect. To safeguard himself against adverse physical changes he will negotiate for the insertion of a clause providing for abatement or suspension of rent for so long, or to such an extent, as might be agreed between the parties, or failing agreement settled by an architect, surveyor or arbitrator. To counter possible economic or political changes he might want to give consideration to insertion of a break clause enabling him to determine the lease prematurely.

---

[42] See *post*, Chap. 5(I) and (IV).
[43] Landlord and Tenant Act (War Damage) Act 1939, enabling disclaimer.
[44] (1844) 12 M. & W. 68; [1843–60] All E.R. Rep. 681 (whether house unfit because of "bugs").
[45] (1727) 2 Ld. Ray. 1477.
[46] (1786) 1 Term. 310.
[47] (1767) cited 1 T.R. 312.
[48] (1544) 1 Dy. 55 b.
[49] (1647) Aleyn 26; [1558–1774] All E.R. Rep. 172.
[50] (1665) cited in 1 Cas. in Ch. 84.
[51] *Manchester Bonded Warehouse Co. Ltd.* v. *Carr* (1880) 5 C.P.D. 507.
[52] *Matthey* v. *Curling* [1922] A.C. 180. A tenant may have a right to disclaim under the Landlord and Tenant (Requisitioned Land) Act 1942 if the land is requisitioned.
[53] *National Carriers Ltd.* v. *Panaplina (Northern) Ltd.* [1981] A.C. 675, discussed in Chap. 5, (I), *post*.

B. Break Clauses

The lease will often contain a proviso giving either or both parties the option to serve a notice at specified times indicating the party's intention to determine the lease. It is not unusual for 21-year leases to contain an option enabling the tenant to break at the end of the seventh and fourteenth years. The exercise of the option is usually subject to a proviso that up to the determination of the lease the tenant shall pay the rent and observe the covenants and that at the expiration of the notice the demise shall cease and be void but without prejudice to the rights and remedies of either party against the other in respect of antecedent claims or breaches of covenant.

Problems similar to those encountered in construing the habendum where the grant is for a fixed term followed by a periodic term are met in construing break clauses.[54] It is not always easy to state the earliest time when the notice can be given.[55] But if notice is given at the correct time, then clerical errors relating to the effective date will not vitiate if they do not mislead.[56] A party who wishes to operate a break clause must do so at the specified time, as time is of the essence in these clauses.[57] If the lease is silent as to the parties who can exercise the option, the normal rule of construction adopted is that most favourable to the lessees, and so consequently the option will be exercisable only by the tenant.[58] If there are two of them, both will have to exercise it.[59] The benefit of the option runs with the legal estate of the party entitled to exercise it.[60] Therefore after assigning the lease the original tenant cannot exercise the option to determine, even though, as will be seen,[61] he is likely to remain liable under the covenants of the lease during the whole term.[62]

Compliance with the terms of the lease is a condition precedent to effectiveness of the notice. In other words, if the tenant has served the notice he must have complied with the terms of the lease at latest by the date when the notice expires.[63] This is so even if the break clause

---

[54] See *ante*, s(II).

[55] *cf. Associated London Properties Ltd.* v. *Sheridan* [1946] 1 All E.R. 20; and *British Iron & Steel Corporation Ltd.* v. *Malpern* [1946] K.B. 171.

[56] *Carradine Properties Ltd.* v. *Aslam* [1976] 1 W.L.R. 442 (notice in 1974 provided for termination on September 27, 1973 and not 1975); *cf. Hankey* v. *Clavering* [1942] 2 K.B. 326.

[57] *United Scientific Holdings* v. *Burnley Borough Council*; *Cheapside Land Development* v. *Messels Service Co.* [1978] A.C. 904. The inter-relationship of a break clause with a rent review provision may also make time of the essence in the latter, as in *Al Saloom* v. *Shirley James Travel Services* (1981) 42 P. & C.R. 81; *Legal and General Assurance (Pension Management)* v. *Cheshire County Council* (1984) 269 E.G. 40, C.A.

[58] *Dann* v. *Spurrier* (1803) 3 Bos. & Pul. 399; [1803–13] All E.R. Rep. 410; *Price* v. *Dyer* (1810) 17 Ves.Jr. 356; [1803–13] All E.R. Rep. 61.

[59] *Re Viola's Lease, Humphrey* v. *Stenbury* [1909] 1 Ch. 244.

[60] *Stait* v. *Fenner* [1912] 2 Ch. 504 (equitable assignee unable to exercise option).

[61] *Post*, Chap. 7(IV)A.

[62] *Stait* v. *Fenner* [1912] 2 Ch. 504.

[63] *Simons* v. *Associated Furnishers Ltd.* [1931] 1 Ch. 379.

reserves rights of action for antecedent breaches.[64] And indeed actions can be brought for antecedent breaches whether the right to sue in respect of them is reserved or not.[65] But the service of the notice may have the happy result for the tenant of absolving him from liabilities in respect of repairs and dilapidations that he would have to attend to in the last year of the term granted. And so the tenants in *Dickinson* v. *St. Aubyn*[66] did not have to paint the flat in the last quarter of the term granted as they had agreed.

If the landlord exercises his rights to serve a notice under a break clause the notice may have only a limited effect. The effect of the notice may be to put an end to the term of years granted and to a number of the tenant's rights under the terms of the lease, but it may not necessarily by itself entitle the landlord to possession if the tenant has the benefit of the statutory protection afforded to the majority of business, agricultural and residential tenants.[67] If special statutory forms have to be used to terminate the tenant's statutory rights, *e.g.* under Part II of the Landlord and Tenant Act 1954, then the service by the landlord of such a notice is likely to end the term granted by the lease. One looks to the intention of the party serving the notice rather than to the form he has used.[68]

C. Option to Renew

A typical option to renew provides that if the tenant wants a further term of years from the end of the original term, and gives notice to that effect not less than six months nor more than 12 months from the end of the original lease[69] then, provided he has paid the rent and observed the terms of the lease, the landlord will grant him a new term for a specified number of years from the end of the first term.[70] When rents were relatively stable it was not unusual for the option to provide that the lease was to be renewed at the same rent. Unless the initial term is for a very short period, *e.g.* a year or 18 months and the renewed term is to be as short, then the option will provide for the term to be renewed at a new rent, not less than the existing rent, and ascertainable as provided by the agreement. The option clause will generally provide machinery for assessment of increased rent, *e.g.* by

---

[64] *Grey* v. *Friar* (1854) 4 H.L. Cas. 565.
[65] *Blore* v. *Giulini* [1903] 1 K.B. 356.
[66] [1944] K.B. 454.
[67] *Weinbergs Weatherproofs Ltd.* v. *Radcliffe Paper Mill Co. Ltd.* [1958] Ch. 437.
[68] *Scholl Mfg. Co. Ltd.* v. *Clifton (Slim-Line) Ltd.* [1967] Ch. 41; *Keith Bayley Rogers & Co. (A Firm)* v. *Cubes* (1975) 21 P. & C.R. 412.
[69] A failure to restrict the length of the notice to renew does not enable the tenant to serve the notice a short time after the grant of the original lease, *Biondi* v. *Kirklington & Piccadilly Estates Ltd.* [1947] 2 All E.R. 59 (ineffective notice to renew served one month after grant of 35 year term in 1911).
[70] L.P.A. 1925, s.149(3) (restricting the commencement date of leases) is considered at Chap. 3 (I) D.

agreement between the parties, or their valuers, or by reference to an arbitrator or umpire, who may be required to calculate the rent by reference to current market rentals. The option clause may provide for the new rent to be fixed by reference to the Index of Retail Prices. The option should also provide for renewal on the same terms, with the exception of the renewal clause.

Strict observance of the terms of the existing lease is a condition precedent to the service of a valid notice to renew. A failure to paint a ceiling once in every three years, and also the interior of what were in any event premises in a fair decorative state in the last year of the term was fatal in *West Country Cleaners (Falmouth) Ltd.* v. *Saly.*[71] A better drawn clause will provide for renewal where rent has been paid and the terms reasonably performed.[72] A landlord may have waived his right to object to the renewal by accepting further payments of rent.[73]

The criteria adopted to determine the new rent can often give rise to the same difficulty as that encountered in operating rent review clauses.[74] The parties often fail to apply their minds to the problem of how improvements to the property are to be treated. Are they to be disregarded or taken into account in determining the new rent, and if taken into account, then to what extent? If the lease provides for the payment of an "open market rent" or a "reasonable rent", then the rent to be fixed is likely to be the market rent determined objectively without reference to the parties' or to tenants' improvements.[75] This can produce a harsh result, and a different one from where Landlord and Tenant Act 1954, Part II operates.[76] If the lease is to be renewed "at a rent to be agreed between the parties ... or in default ... determined by a single arbitrator", the courts incline to the view that a fair rent, taking into account the parties' improvements should be determined.[77] This will be a reasonable rent as between the parties, as opposed to an objectively reasonable or market rent rent. If the parties have inserted no criterion and no arbitration mechanism for determining rent in default of agreement, they run the risk that the option may be held to be unenforceable for uncertainty,[78] but the

---

[71] [1966] 1 W.L.R. 1485; and see *Finch* v. *Underwood* (1876) 2 Ch.D. 310. *cf. Kitney* v. *Greater London Properties* (1984) 272 E.G. 786.

[72] And see *Bassett* v. *Whiteley* (1983) 45 P. & C.R. 87 (C.A.) (rent withheld until landlord repaired, rent paid by end of term).

[73] *Gardner* v. *Blaxill* [1960] 1 W.L.R. 752.

[74] see *post*, Chap. 5(V).

[75] *cf. Cuff* v. *J. & F. Stone Property Co. Ltd.* [1979] A.C. 87; *Ponsford* v. *H.M.S. Aerosols Ltd.* [1979] A.C. 63.

[76] See *post*, Chap. 5(V)B. and Chap 22.

[77] *Lear* v. *Blizzard* [1983] 3 All E.R. 662, and see *Bates (Thomas) & Son* v. *Wyndham's (Lingerie)* [1981] 1 W.L.R. 505.

[78] *King's Motors (Oxford) Ltd.* v. *Lax* [1970] 1 W.L.R. 426, and *cf. King* v. *King* [1981] 41 P. & C.R. 311 (a rent review clause).

court will be reluctant to be driven to that conclusion.[79] There is no power on the exercise of an option for renewal for a rent review clause to be inserted into the renewed term if none has been agreed,[80] and no power to order the payment or a premium to compensate for the absence of rent reviews even on a 21-year term.[81] The fact that the formula the parties have agreed on produces a figure which is higher than the currently legally recoverable rent, because of the Rent Acts or anti-inflation legislation, will not make the option clause unenforceable.[82]

Covenants for the renewal of leases are outside the rule against perpetuities.[83] The reason is that they are regarded as covenants running with the land, and "perpetuity has no application to covenants which run with the land, because they are so annexed to the land as to create something in the nature of an interest in the land."[84] The fact that options to renew run with the land has been described as anomalous, but it is well established.[85] The effect of the option to renew running with the land is that the benefit of the covenant will pass automatically to the tenant for the time being, and the burden will also pass automatically with the lessor's interest by virtue of the Law of Property Act 1925, s.142(1).[86] Personal representatives, volunteers and trustees in bankruptcy will be bound whether they have actual notice or not. The extent to which purchasers for money or money's worth of a legal estate in the land leased will be bound is considered later.[87]

The major hazard to be avoided in drafting options to renew is using words that make the lease perpetually renewable. A lease will be perpetually renewable if the landlord grants an option to renew and also agrees that the renewed lease will contain all the original covenants "including this option to renew." The disastrous consequence of doing this is to grant the tenant a demise for 2,000 years,[88] even if the circumstances indicate that it was unlikely that the landlord intended to sterilise his interest for so long. In *Parkus* v. *Greenwood*[89] a lease for three years of a tailor's premises at a rent of £383 a year with an option to renew "(including the present covenant for renewal)" was held to take effect as a demise for 2,000 years

---

[79] *Brown* v. *Gould* [1972] Ch. 53; *Trustees of National Deposit Friendly Society* v. *Beatties of London* (1985) 275 E.G. 55.

[80] *National Westminster Bank* v. *B.S.C. Footwear* (1981) 42 P. & C.R. 90.

[81] *Lear* v. *Blizzard* [1983] 3 All E.R. 662.

[82] *Newman* v. *Dorrington Developments Ltd.* [1975] 1 W.L.R. 1642.

[83] *Rider* v. *Ford* [1923] 1 Ch. 541 but the renewed term cannot be for more than 60 years, L.P.A. 1922, Sched. 15, para. 7.

[84] Per Farwell J. in *Muller* v. *Trafford* [1901] 1 Ch. 54 at p. 61.

[85] *Woodall* v. *Clifton* [1905] 2 Ch. 257.

[86] *Weg Motors Ltd.* v. *Hales* [1962] Ch. 49.

[87] *Post* (V) F.

[88] By reason of the operation of Law of Property Act 1922, s.145, and Sched. 15, paras. 1, 2; L.P.A. 1925, s.202 and see *ante* Chap. 2(II)H(5).

[89] [1950] Ch. 644; and see *Caerphilly Concrete Products Ltd.* v. *Owen* [1972] 1 W.L.R. 372.

despite the fact that it seemed clearly against the parties' intention. The court avoided this result in *Plumrose* v. *Real and Leasehold Estates Investment Society*[90] holding that it had jurisdiction to cut down the words in the lease by looking at the surrounding circumstances and the correspondence between the parties.

Much of the significance of options to renew has diminished with the increase in statutory protection given to residential tenants and the statutory continuation of the contractual tenancy of most business tenants. But the existence of an option clause is still very important for business tenants who may want to dispose of their businesses as going concerns towards the end of their contractual terms. An option to renew is more marketable than rights under the Landlord and Tenant Act 1954. And again options to renew are particularly significant in building leases where substantial development may be carried out in phases, initially on the grant of short terms together with an option for the grant of much longer terms on satisfactory completion of the building works in each phase.

D. Option to Purchase

The landlord may give the tenant an option to purchase his reversion. Although this option does not run automatically with the land,[91] its existence may be protected,[92] so as to make it enforceable against purchasers of the grantor's estate. But in any case the original lessor remains liable under his contract granting the option. If the option is unenforceable for want of effective protection against the grantor's successors, then the original grantor of the option may be liable in damages to the disappointed owner of the option.[93] The grantor of the option may be able to recover those damages from the present landlord under the terms of an indemnity clause.[94]

The two important questions affecting the benefit of the option are who can exercise it and for how long does it remain valid? The option may be expressly restricted to the original tenant. But if not, then it does constitute a property interest.[95] As such it may be assigned separately from the lease, but normally will pass with an assignment of the lease itself.[96] How long the option remains valid becomes important either when there is a renewal of the original term, or the

---

[90] [1970] 1 W.L.R. 52. But the *renewed* term cannot be for more than 60 years, L.P.A. 1922, Sched. 15, para. 7.

[91] *Woodall* v. *Clifton* [1905] 2 Ch. 257.

[92] See *post*, at F.

[93] *Wright* v. *Dean* [1948] Ch. 686; *Cottrill* v. *Steyning and Littlehampton Building Society* [1966] 1 W.L.R. 753 (damage may include loss of profit from prospective development).

[94] *Eagon* v. *Dent* [1965] 3 All E.R. 334.

[95] *Re Button's Lease, Inman* v. *Button* [1964] Ch. 263.

[96] *Griffith* v. *Pelton* [1958] Ch. 205.

tenant holds over, or is statutorily protected, and then wants to exercise the option. There is authority for saying that the option lasts for so long as the relationship of landlord and tenant, unless the contrary is expressed in the option itself.[97] But it is suggested that the better view is that the option will not normally survive for the benefit of a tenant who holds over,[98] and certainly not if he is holding over as a statutory tenant.[99] A simple extension of the term by endorsement will not extend the option,[1] unless the renewal clause provides for renewal "on the same terms and conditions in all respects" as in the original lease.[2] And options in leases enabling the tenant or his successors in title to purchase the reversion for valuable consideration not later than one year after the end of the leases are not affected by the rule against perpetuities.[3]

It was not unusual for options to be granted at a fixed price and this is still done if the landlord wishes to benefit his tenant gratuitously and cause consequential tax complications all round. Normally the option provides for the price to be determined at the time the option is exercised. If the option is to purchase "at a reasonable valuation" an inquiry can be directed to fix the price.[4] If an option is given to purchase "at such price not being less than £12,000 as may be agreed upon by two valuers..." the court will regard this as an agreement for the sale and purchase at a fair and reasonable price. If the mechanics of fixing the price break down, the court may regard this as the failure of a subsidiary and non-essential part of the agreement, and substitute machinery to prevent the contract failing.[5] But a failure to specify the criteria and mechanism for determining the price may render the agreement unenforceable for uncertainty. If the parties have agreed to pay a price by reference to fair market values then it is likely that the price must be settled by reference to vacant possession values, leaving out of account the effect of the lease.[6] If the landlord is to grant an option to purchase, he should consider whether he wants the property to be valued with vacant possession or subject to the lease and the tenant's statutory rights, if any, and also on the basis that both parties have complied with all the terms of the lease.

[97] *Rider* v. *Ford* [1923] 1 Ch. 541.
[98] *Re Leeds & Batley Breweries & Bradbury's Lease, Bradbury* v. *Grimble & Co. Ltd.* [1920] 2 Ch. 548.
[99] *Longmuir* v. *Kew* [1960] 1 W.L.R. 862.
[1] *Sherwood* v. *Tucker* [1924] 2 Ch. 440.
[2] *Batchelor* v. *Murphy* [1926] A.C. 63; *Hill* v. *Hill* [1947] Ch. 231.
[3] Perpetuities and Accumulations Act 1964, s.9(1).
[4] *Talbot* v. *Talbot* [1968] A.C. 1.
[5] *Sudbrook Trading Estate Ltd.* v. *Eggleton* [1983] 5 A.C. 444.
[6] *Re Nagel's Lease, Allen* v. *Little Abbey School (Newbury) Ltd.* [1974] 1 W.L.R. 1077.

E. Rights of Pre-emption

A landlord may not be prepared to grant his tenant an option to purchase, but may be willing to give him a right of pre-emption, *i.e.* a right of first refusal. In this case, the initiative lies with the landlord. If he wishes to sell, he must first notify the tenant of his intention to sell. The right of pre-emption may provide for the landlord to make an offer of the property at a fixed or ascertainable price. It is then up to the tenant to decide if he wants to accept that offer. Alternatively, the clause may envisage the tenant making the offer to the landlord, leaving the landlord to decide whether or not to accept it. If a contract is not concluded, the landlord will be free to offer the property elsewhere, subject to the existence of the lease.

There are a number of problems to be considered when either granting or drafting a right of pre-emption. The right is often expressed to be exercisable "when the landlord wishes to sell." This is an imprecise expression, leaving it far from clear when the landlord must notify the tenant that he is minded to sell. On a rising market the timing could make a substantial difference to the price. It is also unclear if the pre-emption is expended should the tenant not exercise his rights successfully on the first occasion the property is offered to him. The problem is more acute if the property is not sold at all on the first occasion. Is the landlord still bound by the right if he is later minded to sell? Again assuming that the right is protected[7] and not exercised when the landlord sells, can a subsequent purchaser ignore it, or does the tenant continue to be the person to whom the property must first be offered? These points can be dealt with by careful drafting.

The clause may provide that if the tenant wants to buy the property, then the landlord will sell it to him at a price to be agreed. There are a number of variations on this formula but they are all generally characterised by their vagueness about how the price is to be quantified and agreed. Since *Smith* v. *Morgan*,[8] however, the court is likely to strive to avoid holding the provision unenforceable for uncertainty. The right to purchase was exercisable at a "figure to be agreed upon." Brightman J. held that the vendor was bound to make an offer bona fide at the price for which she was in fact willing to sell. That price was to be either the reserve price if she was intending to sell by auction, or the advertised price if she was intending to sell by private treaty.

---

[7] Considered in the next section F.
[8] [1971] 1 W.L.R. 803, see *ante*, at D, and also *Brown* v. *Gould* [1972] Ch. 53.

F. Protection of Options to Renew, Purchase, and Rights of Pre-emption

The position is straightforward if the title to the land is unregistered. All these rights will only bind purchasers for money or money's worth of a legal estate in the land leased if their existence has been protected by registration at Class C (iv) land charges against the name of the estate owner who granted the right before completion of the first purchase of his estate.[9]

The position is more complicated where the title is registered. Initially a distinction has to be made between options to renew and purchase on the one hand, and rights of pre-emption on the other. Options to renew and purchase can and should be protected by entry of notice or caution against the grantor's title. It is suggested that it is safer, even if not technically necessary, to take this step when the lease containing the option is substantively registered.[10] It is prudent to protect options by caution or notice even where they are overriding interests and so part and parcel of the rights of a tenant who is in actual occupation or in receipt of the rents and profits, unless enquiry has been made of him and the rights not disclosed.[11] Leases for any term[12] not exceeding 21 years granted[13] at a rent without taking a fine are also overriding interests[14] binding on purchasers. But it is not clear[15] to what extent that protection will extend to options to renew or purchase contained in such leases. It is obviously better to rely on an express registration of a caution or notice than the protection given to overriding rights.

The protection of rights of pre-emption in respect of registered land is even more complex. *Murray* v. *Two Strokes, Ltd.*[16] decided that this right was a mere contractual right, and unlike an option to purchase, did not constitute an interest in land. As a result it could not be protected by caution. This view has been criticised,[17] but the Court of Appeal in *Pritchard* v. *Briggs*[18] agreed that a right of pre-emption does not create an interest in land. When it is exercised, it becomes an

---

[9] Land Charges Act 1972, ss.2(4)(iv) 4(6), and see *Beesly* v. *Hallwood Estates Ltd.* [1961] Ch. 105; *cf. Taylor Fashions* v. *Liverpool Victoria Friendly Society; Old & Campbell* v. *Same* [1981] Q.B. 133 (Equitable estoppel can bind landlord, if it would be "dishonest and unconscionable" for him to argue otherwise).

[10] See further Ruoff and Roper, *Registered Conveyancing* (3rd ed.), pp. 751, 752.

[11] L.R.A. 1925, s.70(1)(*g*); and see Russell L.J. in *Strand Securities Ltd.* v. *Caswell* [1965] Ch. 958 at p. 983; and also *City Permanent Building Society* v. *Miller* [1952] Ch. 840; *Webb* v. *Pollmount Ltd.* [1966] Ch. 584.

[12] This seems to include a lease of the reversion or a lease effective in reversion.

[13] "Granted" means granted at law, *City Permanent Building Society* v. *Miller* [1952] Ch. 840.

[14] L.R.A. 1925, s.70(1)(*k*).

[15] See Ungoed-Thomas J. in *Webb* v. *Pollmount Ltd.* [1966] Ch. 584 at p. 593, and Farrand, *Contract and Conveyance* (3rd ed.). pp. 149, 152.

[16] [1973] 1 W.L.R. 823.

[17] Michael Alberry Q.C. (1973) 89 L.Q.R. 462.

[18] [1980] 1 All E.R. 294.

option and so creates an equitable interest, which is an overriding interest within section 70(1)(g) of the Land Registration Act 1925.[19] In the case of unregistered land it may enjoy some protection if it is registered as a land charge. It will bind successors of the grantor's estate, but its priority as an equitable interest in land, only operates from the date it becomes exercisable. In any event, *Peffer* v. *Rigg*[20] may afford some degree of protection to holders of unregistered minor interests against purchasers who can be shown to have acted in bad faith.

Grantors of options frequently specify that they should become void unless protected by registration within three months of their grant. In any event, if a grantee's solicitor fails to take steps to register an option as a land charge or protect it by registering a notice or caution, he is liable to be sued for negligence.[21]

G. Service of Notice

In the absence of agreement or statutory provisions, notices have to be served in such a way that they can be proved to have come to the knowledge of the person concerned. This is particularly important in connection with the service of notices to quit, which are considered in Part I, Chapter 8. To avoid difficulties that arise in establishing whether or when notices have been served, a well-drawn lease will usually contain a clause providing for the incorporation of the Law of Property Act 1925, s.196. This provides that notices required or authorised to be served under that Act shall be in writing and shall be sufficiently served if left at the last-known place or abode[22] of the landlord or tenant, or in the case of a notice to be served on a lessee if it is affixed or left for him on the land or any house or building comprised in the lease. Further, notices are sufficiently served if sent by registered post addressed to the landlord or tenant at his place of abode, business or office. The Recorded Delivery Service Act 1962 extends the benefit of service by registered letter to the recorded delivery service, where the certificate of delivery is signed either by a recipient at the address or by the delivering postman. This provision can be helpful in all leases and tenancy agreements. Considerable difficulty can be experienced if the lease provides for personal service of certain notices and the prospective recipient is either deliberately evasive, temporarily lost or even simply working irregular periods away from his "abode."[23] The Rent Act 1977, s.151, does provide for

---

[19] *Kling* v. *Keston Properties* (1985) 49 P. & C.R. 212.
[20] [1977] 1 W.L.R. 285.
[21] And see *Midland Bank Trust Co. Ltd.* v. *Hett, Stubbs & Kemp (A firm)* [1978] 3 W.L.R. 167.
[22] And see *Italica Holdings S.A.* v. *Bayadea* (1985) 273 E.G. 888.
[23] And see *Hogg* v. *Brooks* (1885) 15 Q.B.D. 256.

the effective service by tenants of notices required or authorised by that Act on their landlords if served either on the landlord's agent named as such in the rent book or similar document, or on the actual recipient of the rent.[24] There is no correlative provision for the service of notices by landlords.

H. Arbitration Clauses

Leases often contain a standard arbitration clause. This provides that if there is any dispute between the parties about the operation or construction of the lease, or the rights and liabilities of the parties under the lease, then the issue is to be settled by a single arbitrator in accordance with the Arbitration Act 1950. The clause usually provides for the arbitrator to be appointed by the president of the local law society or institute of surveyors. The value of the clause is that it will normally prevent effective challenge of the validity of renewal or rent review clauses on the basis that the parties have not come to any certain agreement. It is in these areas, and especially in relation to agricultural properties, that references to arbitrators are most common.[25]

I. Costs

A lease usually contains a number of provisions for the payment of legal costs. There will often be a covenant that the tenant is to pay the legal and surveyor's costs of the preparation and service of a notice under the Law of Property Act 1925, s.146, relating to breaches of covenant and want of repair. Options to renew and sell may also provide for the allocation of the lessor's costs. So far as the payment of the lessor's solicitor's costs of the preparation and completion of the lease are concerned, the theory is that each party should pay his own charges unless there is a written agreement to the contrary.[26] That agreement will be either in the agreement for the lease or the lease itself. It is the rule rather than the exception that the tenant pays either the landlord's solicitor's charges, or his reasonable charges, or a fixed contribution towards them, which reduces argument about whether they are fair and reasonable within the Solicitor's Remunera-

---

[24] And see also Agricultural Holdings Act 1985, s.93, providing for service by the landlord or tenant of notices by leaving, delivering or posting them to the relevant address either of the other party or of a servant or agent of either party having the control of the management or farming. And see Landlord and Tenant Act 1927, s.23; L. & T.A. 1954, s.66(4).

[25] See *post*, Pt. (IV) and see also A. M. Pritchard (1977) 41 Conv. (N.S.) 427.

[26] Costs of Leases Act 1958, s.1, and see *Cairnplace Ltd.* v. *C.B.L. (Property Investment) Co.* [1984] 1 W.L.R. 696.

tion Order 1972. Whether the tenant agrees to pay the costs is often determined by the state of the market between landlords and tenants.

VI. REMEDIES

After the parties have entered into their contract for a lease, or the lease itself, one or other party may consider that he has not received what he thought he bargained for. He may aver that he has been misled about the existence of planning permission, the likely profitability of the business he is proposing to run, the state of the drains or the undisclosed existence of onerous covenants. A landlord may complain that he was misled about the precise identity of the tenant or the nature of his business. After the lease has been executed, one of the parties may argue that it does not represent accurately the agreement they reached, and so should be rectified, or that it was entered into by both parties under the same mistake of fact, and so should either be set aside or corrected. These problems involve the application of general principles in the law of contract to specific instances of fact arising out of the relationship of landlord and tenant. These are matters discussed in detail in the standard works on the law of contract, to which reference should be made. Here it is proposed to indicate in outline only the nature of the problems that can arise and of the remedies that may be available.

There are three different but not always distinct stages in the formation of the relationship of landlord and tenant, each of which may give rise to its quota of contract problems. First of all there will be the negotiations, leading secondly to the agreement for the lease, and finally there should be the execution of the lease itself. Until 1967 a tenant under a lease was in most cases remediless if he considered that he had been seriously misled by a statement of fact made in good faith by the landlord into entering into the contract for the lease, unless the statement was itself one of the terms of the contract. The tenant of a house in Chelsea could neither recover damages nor avoid a three-year lease when his family became ill because of the defective state of the drains, although the landlord had told him that he thought they were all right.[27] This led parties to contend vigorously either that the statements were part of the contract, generally unsuccessfully, or that they formed a separate contract by themselves, collateral to the main contract.[28]

This unsatisfactory situation was largely remedied by the Misrepresentation Act 1967. This enables the person who has entered into a lease relying on a misstatement of fact to take steps to rescind it

[27] *Angel* v. *Jay* [1911] 1 K.B. 666.
[28] *City and Westminster Properties (1934) Ltd.* v. *Mudd* [1959] Ch. 129.

providing he acts promptly on discovering the true position, and provided that the rescission would not prejudice third parties.[29] In that connection, it is suggested that it is too late to take steps for rescission after the original landlord has disposed of his reversion to an innocent purchaser without notice of the tenant's rights to take proceedings. Instead of ordering rescission, the court can order the defendant to pay damages in lieu, which will often be a more satisfactory remedy.[30] Furthermore, unless the defendant can prove that he had reasonable ground to believe and did believe, up to the time the contract was made, that the facts he represented were true, then he may be liable to pay damages for what is conveniently known as negligent misrepresentation.[31]

Successful proceedings have been taken where the defendants represented that planning permission was available for offices for the full duration of a lease[32]; that a lease would be for 21 years, when the lessor could grant it for only 18 years[33]; and that a rent review notice had not been served in connection with a contract to sell the lease.[34] The Act is frequently relied on in practice, and it is suggested that most claims or actions are settled. Perhaps the most compelling motive for settling this type of action is that it is either totally won or lost; it cannot be drawn, and that makes losing very expensive. A fundamental mistake of fact[35] shared by both parties can also be a ground for seeking rescission. A mistake by one party alone will not, it seems, be sufficient.[36]

The intermediate action is one for rectification of the lease. If the lease clearly does not represent what the parties agreed, then it is likely to be rectified by agreement, evidenced either by an agreed exchange of letters, or a formal deed of rectification. But if the matter is in dispute, proceedings may be taken for rectification. This usually happens when the landlord insists on the terms of the written lease, and the tenant denies liability, arguing that the written terms do not represent the agreement the parties reached. Rectification will be ordered if there is a mutual mistake of both parties,[37] and it can be clearly proved that the lease does not represent the common intention

---

[29] s.1.
[30] s.2(2).
[31] s.2(1). Plaintiffs who cannot rely on the 1967 Act may be able to rely on the principle in *Hedley Byrne & Co. Ltd.* v. *Heller & Partners Ltd.* [1964] A.C. 465, as in *Esso Petroleum Co. Ltd.* v. *Mardon* [1976] Q.B. 801 (statement as to likely turnover of petrol filling station).
[32] *Laurence* v. *Lexcourt Holdings Ltd.* [1978] 1 W.L.R. 1128.
[33] *Mapes* v. *Jones* (1974) 232 E.G. 717.
[34] *F. & H. Entertainments* v. *Leisure Enterprises* (1976) 120 S.J. 331.
[35] *Grist* v. *Bailey* [1967] Ch. 532 (contract for sale of property thought incorrectly to be subject to Rent Act protected tenancy). A mistake of law is not sufficient, *Solle* v. *Butcher* [1950] 1 K.B. 671.
[36] *Riverlate Properties Ltd.* v. *Paul* [1975] Ch. 133 (landlord failed to ensure that lease shared costs of repairing the structure with the tenant, as he had intended). *cf. Paget* v. *Marshall* (1884) 28 Ch.D.255.
[37] *Mortimer* v. *Shortall* (1842) 2 Dr. & War. 363; [1835–42] All E.R. Rep. 229.

of both parties.[38] It can also be ordered where the tenant executes a lease which contains no rent review clause, knowing that his landlord mistakenly believes it to contain one.[39] The right to claim rectification can pass to a purchaser of the landlord's interest.[40]

[38] *City and Westminster Properties (1934) Ltd.* v. *Mudd* [1959] Ch. 129.
[39] *Bates (Thomas) & Son* v. *Wyndham's (Lingerie)* [1981] 1 W.L.R. 505, *Central & Metropolitan Estates* v. *Compusave* (1983) 266 E.G. 900.
[40] *Boots the Chemist* v. *Street* (1983) 268 E.G. 817.

CHAPTER 5

THE OPERATION OF THE LEASE—RENT

I. Nature 151
II. Services or Goods in Lieu of Rent . 157
III. Payment 159
  A. Time of Payment 159
  B. Manner of Payment 160
  C. By Whom Rent is Payable .. 161
  D. To whom Rent is Payable ... 162
  E. Receipts for Rent 163
  F. Deductions 164
  G. Apportionment of Rent 165
  H. Estoppel by Payment of Rent . 165
  I. Different Kinds of Rent and Other Periodical Payments Distinguished 166
IV. Non-payment 173
  A. Effect of Non-payment 173
  B. Suspension of Rent 174
  C. Reduction of Rent 174
  D. Waiver 176
V. Rent Increases, Rent Reviews and Index-Linked Clauses 177
  A. Rent Increases 177
  B. Rent Review Clauses 178

  C. Factors that Determine Rent Levels 185
  D. Index-Linked Clauses 191
VI. Payment for Occupation in Lieu of Rent at Expiration of Lease 192
VII. Landlord's Remedies for Non-payment of rent 194
  A. Forfeiture 194
  B. Distress 200
  C. Actions for Non-payment .. 202
  D. Bankruptcy and Liquidation . 202
VIII. Taxation of Rental Income 205
  A. The Charge to Tax Under Schedule A 205
  B. Rents from Furnished Lettings 206
  C. Furnished Holiday Lettings . 206
  D. Deductions and Expenses .. 208
  E. Pooling of Expenses 209
  F. Management Expenses 210
  G. Sale and Lease Back 211
  H. Assessment and Collection . 212
  I. The Taxation of Premiums as Rent 212

I. NATURE

A lease or tenancy agreement will generally contain an express covenant by the tenant to pay rent. This will be inserted to back up the formal reservation of rent, or *reddendum*, inserted in the lease by the use of such words as "yielding up and paying" or "rendering" the sum agreed. However, although usual, an express covenant to pay rent is not essential. An obligation to pay will be implied from the fact that the deed contains a valid reservation of rent, on execution of the counterpart lease by the tenant.[1] However, if the landlord relies on an implied covenant to pay rent, he cannot claim in respect of any period arising before the tenant has gone into occupation, nor in respect of any period following a valid assignment of the residue of the term.[2] A good reservation of rent will be construed out of any form of words

---

[1] *Giles* v. *Hooper* (1690) Carth. 135; *Iggulden* v. *May* (1804) 9 Ves.Jr. 325. Since the covenant arises on a construction of the wording of the *reddendum*, it has been argued that the covenant is not implied, but express: see *Newton* v. *Osborn* (1653) Sty. 387; *Porter* v. *Swetman* (1653) Sty. 406; *Hellier* v. *Casbard* (1665) 1 Sid. 266. However, the better view seems to be that it is implied: see *Platt on Covenants*, p. 53; 2, *Platt on Leases*, p. 87.

[2] *Paradine* v. *Jane* (1647) Aleyn 26.

showing an intention to create an agreement to pay rent, such as "at and under the rent of £80."[3]

Rent reserved by a lease is properly called rent-service, because there is tenure and privity of estate arising between landlord and tenant. It therefore differs from a rent charge, which is a sum of money charged on land for a term or in perpetuity[4] but in respect of which the owner has no reversion in the land charged. Rent-service reserved by a lease, however, is annexed and incident to and goes with the reversionary estate in the land immediately expectant on the term granted by the lease.[5] This medieval view of the nature of rent as a service rendered by the tenant to the landlord has, however, been increasingly displaced by the modern view of rent as an ordinary contractual and commercial payment of money.

The traditional view of rent is that it is "the recompense paid by the lessee to the lessor for the exclusive possession of corporeal hereditaments".[6] The rent is compensation for the occupation of land rather than buildings, and thus liability for rent will continue, unless expressly excepted, even where the premises themselves are destroyed. Particular problems in this respect, may arise with multistorey flats and office blocks in which the tenant rents premises above ground floor level. He rents a strip of airspace on, say, the second floor, depending for his support on another landowner or tenant who occupies the ground floor and the land upon which it stands, and for his protection on those owning or renting the floors above. In the event of destruction of the building his liability for rent continues but, unlike the ground floor tenant, who at least still has the land to occupy upon which the building stood, if he so chooses, the tenant of the upper floors now has strips of airspace only which, for almost all purposes, are totally useless until the building is reconstructed. In practice this eventuality will be guarded against either by an express exception against payment of rent should the premises be destroyed, or by insurance.[7]

Of course, if the contractual aspects of a lease are emphasised, rather than the tenurial consequences, such a problem may be solved by the contractual doctrine of frustration, as in the case of licenses.[8] In *Cricklewood Property and Investment Trust Ltd.* v. *Leighton's Investment Trust Ltd.*[9] the House of Lords held that a building lease for 99 years was not frustrated by war-time building restrictions, but

---

[3] *Doe d. Raines* v. *Kneller* (1829) 4 C. & P. 3.
[4] Under Rentcharges Act 1977, s.2, the creation of new rent charges (with certain limited exceptions) is prohibited and s.3 contains machinery for the extinguishment over a period of 60 years of existing rent charges.
[5] L.P.A. 1925, s.141(1).
[6] *Hill & Redman*, p. 308.
[7] See George & George, *The Sale of Flats* (5th ed.), Chap. 6.
[8] *Taylor* v. *Caldwell* (1863) 3 B. & S. 826.
[9] [1945] A.C. 221.

Viscount Simon L.C. made observations[10] that if by legislation building on the land were permanently forbidden, frustration might occur. The Court of Appeal, in *Denman* v. *Brise*,[11] however, four years later, took a different view, holding that a lease can never be frustrated. In view of the observations of at least two members of the House of Lords in the *Cricklewood* case,[12] however, the matter was still open to argument.

In *National Carriers Ltd.* v. *Panalpina (Northern) Ltd.*[13] the House of Lords accepted that the doctrine of frustration did apply to executed leases, although the circumstances in which this might be so were said to be very rare. It is thus now probably the case that where the performance of a particular stipulation in the lease has, since the date of the lease and without the fault of either party, become impossible, and no provision[14] has been made for that eventuality in the lease, the lease may be frustrated. In the *National Carriers* case[15] itself the House rejected the tenant's claim of frustration and held that rent remained payable where a local authority had closed the only road giving access to the demised warehouse, thus rendering it useless for a likely period of 20 months in the middle of a 10 years lease. The question was treated as one of degree, so that a longer interruption, or a very much shorter lease, might have resulted in frustration.

A demise must have some subject-matter to which it can relate. That subject-matter may either be corporeal, such as land, or incorporeal, such as an easement. If the subject-matter of the lease is entirely destroyed, it is difficult to see how the lease can continue. Indeed, in *National Carriers Ltd.* v. *Panalpina (Northern) Ltd.*[16] several of their Lordships[17] appeared to be of the view that if, through some act of nature, a piece of land ceases to exist, for example by falling into the sea as a consequence of coastal erosion, any lease of that land would thereby be frustrated.[18] Such reasoning appears to be

---

[10] At p. 229.

[11] [1949] 1 K.B. 22; see also *London & Northern Estates* v. *Schlesinger* [1916] 1 K.B. 20; *Matthey* v. *Curling* [1922] 2 A.C.180; *Eyre* v. *Johnson* [1946] 1 All E.R. 719; *Swift* v. *Macbean* [1942] 1 All E.R. 126.

[12] Viscount Simon L.C. at p. 229 and Lord Wright at p. 241.

[13] [1981] A.C. 675.

[14] Such as an insurance clause, a suspension of rent clause or a repairing covenant. It must be remembered that there can be no frustration by events that have been expressly contemplated and provided for by the parties: *Joseph Constantine S.S. Line Ltd.* v. *Imperial Smelting Corp. Ltd.* [1942] A.C. 154, *per* Lord Simon at p. 163; *Krell* v. *Henry* [1903] 2 K.B. 740, *per* Vaughan Williams L.J. at p. 752; *National Carriers Ltd.* v. *Panalpina (Northern) Ltd* [1981] A.C. 675 *per* Lord Wilberforce at pp. 697–698.

[15] *Supra.*

[16] *Supra.*

[17] *Per* Lord Hailsham L.C. at p. 691 and Lord Russell of Killowen, dissenting, at p. 709, and Lord Simon at pp. 700–701, 704.

[18] See *Cricklewood Property Investment Trust Ltd.* v. *Leighton's Investment Trust Ltd.* [1945] A.C. 221, *per* Lord Simon L.C. at p. 229; *Highway Properties Ltd.* v. *Kelley, Douglas & Co. Ltd.* (1971) 17 D.L.R. (3d) 710 *per* Laskin J. at p. 721; *Firth* v. *Halloran* (1926) 38 C.L.R. 261, *per* Isaacs J. at p. 269.

entirely consistent with those provisions allowing for an apportionment of rent in the event of the total loss of part only of the land demised.[19] The mere destruction of buildings on land would not, however, except in special cases, amount to a frustration of the lease since technically the subject-matter of the demise, the land itself[20] still survives and performance by either side has not, therefore, become impossible. The rent is paid for the occupation of land, rather than buildings, under the terms of most leases, and this must mean that destruction of the building will not normally frustrate the lease and, in the absence of a suspension of rent clause, payments must be maintained.

Different considerations might, however, apply where a tenant rents a strip of airspace, the occupation of which by the tenant is necessarily dependent upon the continued existence of a building or structure. A demise of part of a building above the ground requires the delineation of the subject-matter of the lease by walls, floors and ceilings, it being difficult to envisage the possibility of a lease of unbounded airspace. Thus, any demise of floors above ground level would be frustrated by the destruction of the upper stories.[21] Such a possibility appears to have been contemplated in all of the speeches in the *National Carriers* case[22] and certainly such a course provides "an expedient escape from injustice,"[23] at least in those cases where there was no landlord's covenant to reinstate and the tenant has paid no premium for the lease.

Rent must be a profit (in the sense of a return) on the land enuring for the benefit of the landlord, and no-one else. If it is reserved to a third party, traditional learning has it that it is not a true rent, even though the third party can recover the payment by action, the doctrine of privity of contract notwithstanding.[24] Similarly no rent can be reserved on the assignment of a lease, since no reversion remains in the assignor, although the courts have held that the reservation is good as a straightforward contract to pay the money.[25] Further, the rent must be reserved out of a corporeal and not an incorporeal

---

[19] *Infra*, Chap. 5, (III) F.

[20] Since a lease is a grant of an estate in land, the lessee will receive his estate despite the destruction of buildings.

[21] Even here, it is not entirely clear whether the entire lease is frustrated, or merely the obligation to pay rent, the tenant's legal estate in the airspace remaining in being for the duration of the term. If the landlord is under an obligation to reinstate then, depending upon the length of the term, the rent obligation may simply be suspended, no frustration being possible in the event of circumstances contemplated by covenants and provisos in the lease: see *Balfour* v. *Weston* (1786) 1 T.R. 310; *Matthey* v. *Curling* [1922] 2 A.C. 180, *cf. Izon* v. *Gorton* (1839) 5 Bing.N.C. 501, a case of partial, not total destruction.

[22] *Supra, per* Lords Hailsham L.C. at pp. 690–691, Wilberforce at pp. 694–695, Simon at p. 701, Russell at p. 709 (dissenting), Roskill at pp. 713–714.

[23] *National Carriers Ltd.* v. *Panalpina (Northern) Ltd.* [1981] A.C. 675, *per* Lord Simon at p. 701.

[24] *Jewel's Case* (1588) 5 Co.Rep 3a; *Oates* v. *Frith* (1615) Hob. 130; *Cole* v. *Sury* (1627) Lat. 264; *Deering* v. *Farrington* (1674) 1 Mod.Rep. 113; see also Littleton's *Tenures*, s.346; Co.Litt. 143b.

[25] *Whitton* v. *Bye* (1618) Cro.Jac. 486; *Cooper's Case* (1768) 2 Wils. 375; *Parmenter* v. *Webber* (1818) 8 Taun. 593; *Langfor* v. *Selmes* (1857) 3 K. & J. 220.

hereditament. While it is possible for an incorporeal hereditament to be the subject of a lease.[26] any periodical payments reserved in respect of it will not, technically, be rent.[27] They are, nevertheless, recoverable by action on the contract.

Again it is always said[28] that, to be rent, the payments must be certain, or must be so stated that they can afterwards be ascertained with certainty. In *Treseder-Griffin* v. *Co-operative Insurance Society Ltd.*[29] tenants were required, under a lease, to pay "either in gold sterling or Bank of England notes to the equivalent value of gold sterling the rent of £1,900." It was held that a certain rent had been reserved of £1,900 payable in £1 notes. The rent may be fixed by arbitration,[30] and a provision to increase the rent on notice does not make it uncertain.[31] Therefore the requirement of certainty is met if by calculation and on the happening of certain events the payment becomes certain, and provided it can be so ascertained from time to time, an objection that the rent is of fluctuating amounts must fail. Two instances, one of some antiquity and the other modern, may serve to illustrate this principle. An early text[32] gives as an example of a lease having the requisite certainty as to rent, the service of shearing "all the sheep pasturing within the lord's manor." In *Blumenthal* v. *Gallery Five Ltd.*[33] a rent calculated by reference to the monthly Index of Retail Prices was held to be sufficiently certain.[34]

Most of these characteristics of the traditional view of the nature of rent, *i.e.* that it must be certain, be reserved out of a corporeal hereditament, be annexed and incident to a reversionary interest and so on, arise from the peculiar availability of one particular remedy for non-payment—namely distress. Distress is the right of a landlord to enter the premises and impound a tenant's goods to the value of the rent owed. If the tenant continues to default, the landlord may proceed to sell the goods, though any excess in value over and above the amount owed must be repaid to the tenant.[35] So, our definitional problems concerning the nature of rent nearly all flow from the fact that, to constitute rent, it must be possible to levy distress for the payment. If, however, distress could be regarded not as a "badge" of rent, but merely as a possible remedy for its non-payment, available

---

[26] See Chap. 3, *supra*.

[27] *Butt's Case* (1600) 7 Co.Rep. 23a; see also Co.Litt. 47a.

[28] See, *e.g. Halsbury's Laws of England* (4th ed.), Vol. 27, pp. 165–166; *Hill & Redman*, p. 311.

[29] [1956] 2 Q.B. 127.

[30] *Daly* v. *Duggan* (1839) 11 Eq.R. 311.

[31] *Greater London Council* v. *Connolly* [1970] 2 Q.B. 100.

[32] Co.Litt. 96a; see also *Kendall* v. *Baker* (1852) 11 C.B. 842 (rent varying with the price of wheat); *Att.-Gen. for Ontario* v. *Canadian Niagara Power Co.* [1912] A.C. 852 (rent to vary with the amount of electrical power generated).

[33] (1971) 220 E.G. 31.

[34] For a discussion of differential rents and similar schemes see *post*.

[35] The common law right to levy distress is now considerably circumscribed by statute: see (VII), B, *infra*.

only provided that conditions relating to certainty and so on are met, then the need to characterise rent as a service, an incident of tenure in accordance with its historical origins, could be replaced by a more modern approach which recognises the contractual nature of rent as the consideration for the grant of occupation rights.

During the last 10 years, this conceptual revolution has begun. In *C. H. Bailey* v. *Memorial Enterprises*[36] a rent review clause in a lease provided that "if on September 21, 1969, the market rental value shall be found to exceed the rent of [£x] there shall be substituted from such date [rent at the market value]." It was held by the Court of Appeal that September 21 was the date *by reference to which* the new rent was to be ascertained but that *it did not have to be determined* on that date. The rent as so ascertained was to be paid retrospectively from that date. Lord Denning M.R. said[37]: "It is time to get away from the medieval concept of rent . . . . The time and manner of the payment is to be ascertained according to the true construction of the Contract; and not by reference to outdated relics of medieval law." In the same vein, Sir Eric Sachs said[38]: "It seems to me that, whatever the position in the last century, the word 'rent' today can often simply refer to a contractual sum to which a landlord becomes entitled for the use of his land . . . . There are nowadays many instances where a rental cannot be quantified until after the relevant quarter day had passed, and yet the sum that becomes due from the tenant can properly be styled rent." This rejection of the so-called "medieval" thinking on the nature of rent was reiterated by the House of Lords, at greater and reasoned length, in *United Scientific Holdings Ltd.* v. *Burnley Borough Council*.[39] Lord Diplock, who appears to receive the support of his brother Law Lords in their speeches,[40] said[41]:

> "The mediaeval concept of rent as a service rendered by the tenant to the landlord has been displaced by the modern concept of a payment which a tenant is bound by his contract to pay to the landlord for the use of his land. The mediaeval concept has, however, left as its only surviving relic the ancient remedy of distress. To attract the remedy of distress rent must be certain at the time that it falls due. *Re Knight, ex parte Voisey*[42] was a case about the validity of a distress for a fluctuating rent and what was said there about the necessity for certainty in the amount payable

---

[36] [1974] 1 W.L.R. 728; *cf. Re Essoldo (Bingo) Ltd.'s Underlease* (1971) 23 P. & C.R. 1: "It is established beyond doubt that rent can only be effectually charged under a lease if the amount is or has been rendered certain at the due date for payment," *per* Pennycuick V.-C.
[37] [1974] W.L.R 728, p. 732.
[38] *Ibid* p. 735.
[39] [1977] 2 All E.R. 62; see also Smith [1979] Conv. 10.
[40] Viscount Dilhorne at p. 80; Lord Simon at p. 86; Lord Salmon at p. 93, Lord Fraser at p. 99.
[41] [1977] 2 All E.R. 62, p. 76.
[42] (1882) 21 Ch.D. 442.

was [said] in relation to what may be conveniently referred to as 'distrainable rent' in order to distinguish it from any other part of the rent (in its modern sense) that the tenant has agreed to pay the landlord for the use of his land, but for which the remedy of distress is not available. In the famous case of *Walsh* v. *Lonsdale*[43] . . . there were two elements in the rent, one part was fixed in advance and was certain at the time that it accrued, the other part was fluctuating and could not be ascertained until the end of the period in respect of which it was payable. The actual decision of the Court of Appeal was that the fixed part or minimum rent could be distrained for, but that the fluctuating part could not. It was taken for granted that the fluctuating amount could be sued for once it has been ascertained."

Thus it seems that, other than for the purposes of the remedy of distress, the expression "rent" should, in accordance with modern judicial analysis, be construed as meaning the contractual sum payable under the terms of a lease.[44] There is no legal requirement that, to be recoverable, the amount of rent must be certain at the date when it falls due for payment.[45] In *T & E Homes Ltd.* v. *Robinson*[46] the Court of Appeal held that the absence of the power to distrain for money payable under a lease (because, for instance, the "rent" takes the form of a royalty for minerals extracted from the land) did not exclude the money payment being regarded as rent for the purposes of Schedule A income tax.[47]

II. SERVICES OR GOODS IN LIEU OF RENT

Rent need not consist of the payment of money. In the absence of any other arrangement a covenant to pay rent is to pay it in cash,[48] but it has long been settled that rent may be payable in kind.[49] So, rent may consist of chattels,[50] or the performance of services, such as the cleaning of the parish church[51] or a synagogue.[52]

---

[43] (1882) 21 Ch.D. 9.
[44] See also *Bradshaw* v. *Pawley* [1980] 1 W.L.R. 10 (rent payable under contract for period before lease took effect).
[45] For an interesting comment on the different approaches of lawyer and economist to the concept of rent see Partington, pp. 239–242.
[46] [1979] 2 All E.R. 522.
[47] *Infra* (VII).
[48] *Henderson* v. *Arthur* [1907] 1 K.B. 10.
[49] Co.Litt. 142 (a).
[50] *e.g.* bottles of wine in *Pitcher* v. *Tovey* (1692) 4 Mod.Rep. 71.
[51] *Doe d. Edney* v. *Benham* (1845) 7 Q.B. 976.
[52] *Montague* v. *Browning* [1954] 2 All E.R. 601. See also *Doe d. Tucker* v. *Morse* (1830) 1 B. & Ad. 365 (carrying coals); *Duke of Marlborough* v. *Osborn* (1864) 5 B. & S. 67 (team work with horses and cart).

For the purposes of the Rent Acts the Courts have, on occasion adopted a somewhat wider view of rent. Rent has been construed as the entire sum payable to the landlord in money,[53] or in goods or services quantified in money,[54] as rent both for the dwelling and any articles or services provided by the landlord with it.[55] However, whereas under the common law services or chattels can, *per se*, constitute rent, it seems that unless there is an agreed monetary quantification of the services or chattels, or an agreed method of quantifying them, they cannot constitute rent for the purposes of the Rent Act 1977. Presumably, therefore, a tenancy would not be at a rent, within the meaning of that word in the Rent Act 1977, if the goods or services were not susceptible of monetary quantification.[56] This does not mean the agreement is necessarily void, since there can still be a perfectly proper rent at common law. Provided that the chattels or services are clearly agreed upon, their incapacity for precise valuation will not prevent them being regarded as rent at common law. A contract for the grant of a tenancy at a rent will not be void at common law on the ground of lack of quantification unless that rent is expressed "to be agreed" with no mechanism for quantification.[57] Further, if the rent is to be fixed "having regard to the market value," again the tenancy will not be void.[58] A provision entitling the landlord to increase or reduce the rent to any sum he wishes is not void for uncertainty.[59] What is required is that the rent should be ascertained or ascertainable at the time when payment is due.[60] Once a lease has been granted the court will endeavour to give meaning to indefinite provisions about rent. Thus, where the rent was fixed for the first five years of a 10 years lease and was thereafter to be "as agreed," it was held that a reasonable rent[61] was payable for the second five years, to be assessed as at the commencement of that period.[62]

---

[53] *Hornsby* v. *Maynard* [1925] 1 K.B. 541 at pp. 524, 525.
[54] *Montague* v. *Browning* [1954] 2 All E.R. 601.
[55] *Property Holding Co. Ltd.* v. *Clark* [1948] 1 K.B. 630. See also *L. H. Woods & Co. Ltd.* v. *City & West End Properties Ltd.* (1921) 38 T.L.R. 98.
[56] *Barnes* v. *Barratt* [1970] 2 Q.B. 657, approved in *Heslop* v. *Burns* [1974] 1 W.L.R. 1241.
[57] *King's Motors (Oxford) Ltd.* v. *Lax* [1970] 1 W.L.R. 426; *Foley* v. *Classique Coaches* [1934] 2 K.B. 1; *cf. King* v. *King* (1980) 41 P. & C.R. 311.
[58] Even if the tenancy provides no machinery for fixing the rent: *Brown* v. *Gould* [1972] Ch. 53.
[59] *Greater London Council* v. *Connolly* [1970] 2 Q.B. 100.
[60] *Ibid.*
[61] Not necessarily the open market rent, but the rent upon which the parties might be expected to agree: *Thomas Bates & Son Ltd.* v. *Wyndham's (Lingerie) Ltd.* [1981] 1 W.L.R. 505.
[62] *Beer* v. *Bowden* [1981] 1 W.L.R. 522.

III. PAYMENT

A. Time of Payment

Rent becomes due on the morning of the day specified in the lease or tenancy agreement for payment, although no cause of action accrues to the landlord for non-payment until midnight on that day.[63] Rent may be made payable on a Sunday, but rent falling due on a Bank Holiday is not payable until the following day.[64] Tenants sometimes pay their rents ahead of time but this can carry a danger. A tenant paying his rent before the day appointed in the lease will find his obligation to pay rent has not been discharged as against anyone who, in the meantime, acquires the landlord's reversion, unless the tenant can show he had no notice of the assignment before the day appointed for payment.[65]

The tenant will remain liable for the rent even though the amount owing has been paid by a third party under a contract of guarantee,[66] although acceptance of the money by the landlord from the guarantor could possibly constitute an implied waiver.[67] However, a husband or wife with statutory rights of occupation under the Matrimonial Homes Act 1983, may pay rent on behalf of the other spouse.[68] In the normal way, in order that a tenant may obtain a good discharge, the rent must be paid by him or by his agent for and on his account.[69]

If there is no express agreement between the parties as to the rental periods, a yearly rent will be implied at Common Law,[70] the rent being due annually in arrear. Rent is always payable in arrear unless expressly agreed to be payable in advance. Agreements to pay rent in advance are always strictly construed, against the landlord.[71] Since a year's rent is likely in many cases to be a large amount, both for the tenant to find and for the landlord to receive as a lump sum, yearly tenancies often expressly make rent payable quarterly, the quarters being calculated from the date of the agreement unless the lease specifies payment on the usual quarter days.

---

[63] *Duppa* v. *Mayo* (1668) 1 Saund. 275; *Dibble* v. *Bowater* (1853) 2 E. & B. 564; *Re Aspinall* [1961] Ch. 526. It is a general principle of law that where a person under an obligation to do a particular act has to do it on or before a particular date, he has the whole of that day to perform his duty: *Aforos Shipping Co. S.A.* v. *Pagnan* [1983] 1 W.L.R. 195.
[64] Banking and Financial Dealings Act 1971, s.1.
[65] *De Nicolls* v. *Saunders* (1870) L.R. 5 C.P. 589.
[66] *London & County (A & D) Ltd.* v. *Wilfred Sportsman Ltd.* [1971] Ch. 764.
[67] *Re Hawkins* [1972] Ch. 714.
[68] s.1(5).
[69] *Simpson* v. *Eggington* (1855) 10 Ex. 845; *Smith* v. *Cox* [1940] 3 All E.R. 546. Where a third party tenders the rent, the landlords are entitled to reject the tender so long as they are unaware that the third party tenders as agent for the tenant; *Richards* v. *De Freitas* (1974) 29 P. & C.R. 1.
[70] *Turner* v. *Allday* (1836) Tyr. & G. 819.
[71] *Holland* v. *Palser* (1817) 2 Star. 161.

These are: Lady-day   (March 25)
            Midsummer   (June 24)
            Michaelmas   (September 29)
            Christmas Day   (December 25)

Rent calculated on a weekly or monthly basis in a short periodic tenancy may be construed as an agreement to pay rent weekly, or monthly, as the case may be.

B. Manner of Payment

Payment should be made in cash, unless any other mode of payment, *e.g.* by cheque, is authorised by custom, or by the previous course of dealing between the parties. So, if the landlord has earlier agreed to accept a cheque, or has been in the habit of taking cheques from his tenants in the past, then tender by cheque will be proper payment, although if a landlord accepts a cheque, payment of rent is conditional upon its being honoured. Where the normal method of payment is by cheque, the rent is conditionally paid when the cheque is posted.[72]

If the obligation to pay rent is express, then it is the duty of the tenant to seek the landlord out, wherever he may be, and to make the payment to him.[73] This is sometimes easier said than done. It may be that a tenant is unable to pay his rent regularly and properly because the landlord has either disappeared or refuses to accept tender. This situation most frequently arises when the landlord is trying to evict the tenant or some other dispute has arisen between them. Technically, a tenant who does not find his landlord to tender the rent due will be in breach of an express covenant to pay rent[74] but, provided the tenant does not spend the rent elsewhere and is able to call upon the whole sum outstanding when asked for it, such a breach is unlikely to have any serious practical consequences. The tenant will be able to tender on demand, or offer to tender forthwith in any proceedings brought by the landlord to recover the arrears or possession of the property. The court is also almost certain to grant relief against forfeiture to any tenant who, in these circumstances, can instantly produce the money to discharge the accumulated arrears, especially where the landlord has, in the meantime, deliberately made himself scarce. Where the obligation to pay rent is not express, but implied, then the proper place for payment is the land itself and, if the landlord does not present himself there for payment, the tenant is under no obligation to seek him out. If the rent is remitted by post, this is done at the risk of the tenant, unless the landlord has expressly or impliedly

---

[72] *Beevers v. Mason* (1978) 37 P. & C.R. 452.
[73] *Haldane v. Johnson* (1853) 8 Ex. 689.
[74] See *infra.*

authorised such method of payment[75] but, even here, the tenant must exercise due care in posting, ensuring that the envelope is properly addressed, that cash is sent only by registered post and so on.[76]

C. By Whom Rent is Payable

Although it is the contractual tenant who is prima facie liable to pay the rent and from whom the landlord must accept payment, the landlord is also bound to accept rent from a permitted assignee if he tenders it. The original lessee is thereby *pro tanto* discharged.[77] Payment or other satisfaction of the rent due by a third party does not discharge the tenant unless that third party is the tenant's assignee or his agent acting with prior authority or on subsequent ratification.[78]

Payment of arrears by a guarantor does not discharge the lessee.[79] In *Junction Estates* v. *Cope*[80] a guarantor covenanted that the tenant would pay the rent reserved in the manner stipulated in the lease. It was held, as a matter of construction, that such a guarantee did not survive the expiry of the fixed term of the lease, notwithstanding that the tenancy was thereafter statutorily extended under the provisions of the Landlord and Tenant Act 1954, Pt. II. Clear words are necessary if the guarantor is to be taken to have assumed the kind of indefinite liability argued for by the landlords in the *Junction Estates* case.[81] However, where a tenant fails to yield up possession following forfeiture, the guarantor will be liable for mesne profits.[82] An assignee of the reversion cannot take the benefit of a guarantee of rent and covenants given to the assignor without an express assignment.[83]

Of course, on an assignment of a lease the original tenant remains in a position somewhat similar to that of the guarantor, in that, since an assignment of the lease does not destroy the privity of contract existing between the original tenant and the landlord, the tenant remains liable on all his covenants in the lease.[84] It seems, however, that the original tenant will even be bound by any variation of the

---

[75] *Norman* v. *Ricketts* (1886) 3 T.L.R. 182; *Luttges* v. *Sherwood* (1895) 11 T.L.R. 233; *Pennington* v. *Crossley & Son* (1897) 13 T.L.R. 513.

[76] *Hawkins* v. *Rutt* (1793) Pea. 248.

[77] *Re House Property and Investment Co.* [1954] Ch. 576, *per* Roxburgh J. at p. 586.

[78] *Smith* v. *Cox* [1940] 2 K.B. 558; *Simpson* v. *Eggington* (1855) 10 Ex. 845; *Matthews* v. *Dobbins* [1963] 1 W.L.R. 227.

[79] *London County (A.D.)* v. *Wilfred Sportsman* [1969] 1 W.L.R. 1215; reversed on another ground [1971] Ch. 764; *Richards* v. *De Freitas* (1974) 29 P. & C.R. 1.

[80] (1974) 27 P. & C.R. 482; *A. Plesser & Co.* v. *Davis* (1983) 267 E.G. 1039. In *Torminster Properties Ltd.* v. *Green* [1983] 1 W.L.R. 676, guarantors were held liable to pay an increased level of rent resulting from a rent review, even though the lease was surrendered after the period affected by the review had started to run and review was not completed until after the surrender date.

[81] *Supra.*

[82] *Associated Dairies* v. *Pierce* (1983) 265 E.G. 127.

[83] *Pinemain* v. *Welbeck International* (1984) 272 E.G. 116.

[84] *Baynton* v. *Morgan* (1888) 22 Q.B.D. 74.

lease effected by agreement between landlord and assignee, and the relationship is not to be treated as one of suretyship. In *Centrovincial Estates plc* v. *Bulk Storage Ltd.*[85] Harman J. held that where an assignee agrees a rent increase with the landlord subsequent to assignment, the estate, as altered, binds the original tenant, who can therefore be called upon to pay the increased rent in the event of the assignee's default. In *Selous Street Properties Ltd.* v. *Oroneal Fabrics Ltd.*[86] Hutchinson J. held that such a rent increase attributable to alterations carried out to the property by the assignee in breach of covenant would also bind the original tenant and his guarantor. Thus, it seems that the original tenant, and his guarantor, will be bound by any alteration to the lease, even if the alteration was not envisaged by the terms of the original contract. It would appear, however, that these two cases proceeded upon the misassumption that the original tenant's liability depends upon privity of estate, whereas it in fact depends upon privity of contract. Privity of estate ceases to exist between the original tenant and the landlord on assignment. Thus, if the original tenant is to be bound by alterations or variations in the lease subsequent to assignment, it ought to be a requirement that those variations lie within the contemplation of the original contract. For the original tenant to be liable for rent increases agreed after assignment, therefore, the rent review must, on general principle, be one which the tenant had originally agreed to. It is doubtful that a review occasioned by an assignee's breach of contract falls within this principle,[87] and to this extent it would appear that recent decisions to the contrary are wrongly decided.[88]

D. To Whom Rent is Payable

The rent is payable either to the landlord or to his agent having express or implied authority to receive it. This may be a person whom the tenant has been specifically directed to pay on the landlord's behalf, or a person whom the tenant has previously paid with the approval of the landlord, such as the landlord's wife,[89] or it may be the landlord's managing agent. The tenant is entitled to continue paying the landlord's agent until he has notice of the fact that the agent's authority to receive the rents on the landlord's behalf has been withdrawn.[90] On the landlord's death the rent is payable to his

---

[85] (1983) 268 E.G. 59. See also *Allied London Investments Ltd.* v. *Hambro Life Assurance Ltd.* (1984) 269 E.G. 41.

[86] (1984) 270 E.G. 643.

[87] See McLoughlin [1984] Conv. 443.

[88] Presumably, until these decisions are reversed, prudent assignors should insert suitable assignees' undertakings in deeds of assignment for the protection of assignors.

[89] *Browne* v. *Powell* (1827) 4 Bing. 230.

[90] *cf. Drew* v. *Nunn* (1879) 4 Q.B.D. 661.

personal representatives until the reversion becomes vested by their
assent or by conveyance in some other person.[91] Upon an assignment
of the reversion the assignee becomes entitled to receive the rent. A
tenant is not prejudiced if he continues to pay the assignor unless he
has received notice of the assignment.[92]

E. Receipts for Rent

A landlord is not, at common law, required to give his tenant a written
receipt for rent paid. However, if the landlord is prepared to accept a
cheque from his tenant, when the cheque appears to have been paid
by the banker on whom it is drawn, it is evidence of payment by the
payer of the sum payable by the cheque.[93] Section 4 of the Landlord
and Tenant Act 1985 requires a landlord to provide a rent book,
containing certain statutorily prescribed information, to any tenant
paying weekly rent for residence.[94] There does not seem to be any legal
requirement that the rent book be kept up to date, in that it may not
actually record all rental payments made by the tenant. However, in
so far as a rental payment is noted in the rent book, that can operate as
a receipt for rent.

Every document containing a demand or a receipt for rent that
includes any sum paid by the landlord for rates, must be accompanied
by a statement giving the annual half-yearly, quarterly, monthly or
weekly amount of such rates calculated in accordance with the last
rating demand sent to the landlord.[95] The words "demand for rent" or
"receipt for rent" will, therefore include a rent book, rent card, and
any document used for the notification or collection of rent or for the
acknowledgement of its receipt.[96] It is not clear whether a landlord is
automatically required to furnish this statement to any tenant paying
an inclusive rent by cheque since, as was observed earlier, payment of
the cheque by the banker is, under section 3 of the Cheques Act 1957,
"evidence of the receipt by the payee of the sum payable by the
cheque." The matter is not entirely academic since failure to provide
the statement of rates is a crime.[97]

---

[91] Administration of Estates Act 1925, ss.1–3.
[92] L.P.A. 1925, ss.141, 151(1).
[93] Cheques Act 1957 s.3.
[94] Failure to provide a rent book does not make the rent irrecoverable: *Shaw* v. *Groom* [1970] 2 Q.B. 504.
[95] Statement of Rates Act 1919, s.1(1).
[96] *Ibid.* s.2. The Act does not apply to weekly lettings at inclusive rentals in any market established under or controlled by statute (*ibid.* s.11(2)).
[97] *Ibid.* s.3.

F. Deductions

Most leases will contain a covenant by the tenant to pay rates and other outgoings. If no express covenant has been given, one may nevertheless be implied by law, since rates are more usually payable by the occupier of premises, rather than the owner, and, in the absence of special circumstances, the rating authority will not be concerned with questions of title. In the absence of any covenant on the part of the tenant to pay rates, or in cases in which the landlord has expressly undertaken liability for rates, a tenant is authorised to deduct from his rent any rate payments he has himself made to the rating authority. Section 58 of the General Rate Act 1967 allows a tenant to deduct the amount he has paid by way of general rate from his rent where the premises are let to him for a term not exceeding three months. A weekly or monthly tenancy will, therefore, fall within this section.[98] There are other provisions which permit tenants to make deductions from their rents where they have been statutorily required to make payments which are their landlords', rather than their own, liability.[99]

In the case of sub-tenancies it may be that a sub-tenant learns that a superior landlord has demanded rent which has remained unpaid and, in order to protect his own rights of occupation, he has himself discharged the outstanding liability. An underlessee is entitled to deduct from the rent payable to the underlessor arrears of rent due to a superior landlord which have been demanded from the sub-tenant and which he has paid. This right of deduction only applies, of course, in respect of payments which the underlessor should have made himself.[1]

It is usual to find in written leases a provision that attempts to limit the tenant's right to make deductions from his rent. This is done by drafting the reservation of rent so as to be free from specified deductions, such as taxes, charges and impositions.[2] It may even be expressed to be free from deductions generally, or all deductions, in which case it is known as a "net rent." In this case the tenant is prevented from making any deductions which, statute aside, he would otherwise have been able to make.[3]

---

[98] *Hammond* v. *Farrow* [1904] 2 K.B. 332.
[99] *e.g.* Owner's drainage rate: Land Drainage Act 1930, s.26; Land Drainage Act 1976, s72(5). Sums payable by way of compensation; see *e.g.* Manorial Incidents (Extinguishment) Rules 1925 (S.R. & O. 1925 No. 810) Sched. r. 6; Agricultural Holdings Act 1986, s.17; Licensing Act 1953, s.18(4), Sched. IV. Pt. II; Landlord and Tenant Act 1927 s.11(2). Certain Local Authority improvement expenses; see Public Health Act 1936; Highways Act 1980, ss.205–218.
[1] *O'Donoghue* v. *Coalbrook and Broadoak Co.* (1872) 26 L.T. 806.
[2] *Giles* v. *Hooper* (1690) Carth. 135.
[3] *Bradbury* v. *Wright* (1781) 2 Doug.(K.B.) 624; *Bennett* v. *Womack* (1828) 7 B. & C. 627.

G. Apportionment of Rent

It may be that a landlord assigns only a part of his reversion to a third party, or that the landlord's entire reversionary interest is divided up amongst several people. In both cases, if the division is made by court order, for instance by way of financial provision on the breakdown of the landlord's marriage, or is made with the tenant's consent, then the rent can be apportioned among the various new holders of the original reversion.[4] Alternatively, where a tenant gives up or loses part of his land (for example, by surrender, eviction by a superior owner or by erosion by the sea), the tenant has a right to demand that the rent be apportioned between the amount retained and the amount lost, on the basis of the value of the lost land. The rent may then be reduced accordingly.[5]

Apportionment of rent may also take place on the basis of time. Section 2 of the Apportionment Act 1870 provides that rent and other periodical payments shall "be considered as accruing from day to day." Therefore, should the tenancy be forfeited by the landlord, or otherwise brought to an end prematurely, only a proportionate part of the rent for that rental period will be due. Section 3 provides that even though there is an apportionment, liability for the portion payable shall not, as a result, arise any sooner than it would otherwise have done.

H. Estoppel by Payment of Rent

Although payment of rent does not, by itself, create a tenancy, a tenant may either by mistake or for some other reason, pay rent to a person who is in no position to grant the tenancy.[6] Suppose a sub-lessor has a prohibition in his head lease against sub-letting but nevertheless purports to sub-let to the sub-lessee, who goes into possession and pays rent to the sub-lessor. In these circumstances can the sub-lessee later question the sub-lessor's right to grant the tenancy? It has been long established that payment of rent is a recognition by the payor of the title of the payee, and operates as an estoppel against the tenant if he later disputes this title.[7] The only exceptions seem to be where the tenant did not originally receive possession from the person to whom he is now paying the so-called "rent," or where the payee's title has expired before the payments. In either case it seems that if the tenant is able to show that the payment

---

[4] *West* v. *Lascelles* (1601) Cro.Eliz. (1) 851; *Swansea Corp.* v. *Thomas* (1882) 10 Q.B. 48.
[5] There are various other statutory provisions for permitting apportionment "in respect of estate," as this is known: see *Woodfall*, paras. 1–0764 to 1–0765 (pp. 306–307).
[6] *Strahan* v. *Smith* (1827) 4 Bing. 91; *cf. Meredith* v. *Gilpin* (1816) 6 Pr.Exch. 146.
[7] See *Doe d. Jackson* v. *Wilkinson* (1824) 3 B. & C. 413; *Cooper* v. *Blandy* (1834) 1 Bing.N.C. 45; *Cooke* v. *Rickman* [1911] 2 K.B. 1125.

has been made by mistake or as a result of fraud or misrepresentation, and that the real title is in someone else, no estoppel can be raised against him.[8] Where rent has been paid to a person not entitled to the reversion, the only estoppel operates against the tenant to prevent him impugning the purported landlord's title. So, the tenant is liable to pay the rent over again to the true reversioner,[9] unless the reversioner is himself estopped from claiming, as where he has represented that the actual payee was entitled to receive the money.[10]

I. Different Kinds of Rent and Other Periodical Payments Distinguished

(1) *Rent Service, Rent Charge and Rent-Seck*

The difference between a rent service, *i.e.* the obligation to make a money payment arising out of the relationship of tenure and privity of estate between landlord and tenant, and a rent charge, *i.e.* a sum of money charged on land in which the owner of the charge has no reversion, has been noted earlier.[11] Of all the periodic payments issuing out of land, only a rent-service can be distrained for by the landlord at common law, and, in many cases, it is the relationship of tenure, giving rise to privity of estate, that enables an obligation to pay a rent-service to be enforceable not only against the original parties but also, unlike many other periodical payments,[12] against an assignee of the tenant. A rent-seck, sometimes known as a barren rent, is a type of rent charge under which the chargee has reserved no power to levy distress. It has been a difference without distinction since 1730,[13] when statute gave a power to chargees to distrain for unpaid rent charges or rents-seck.

(2) *Peppercorn Rent*

A peppercorn rent is a nominal rent, often reserved with no intention, on either side, that it should be paid, from a common though erroneous view that the reservation of some rent is necessary to constitute a valid lease.[14] It is most frequently found in building

---

[8] *Sergeant* v. *Nash, Field & Co.* [1903] 2 K.B. 304.
[9] *Williams* v. *Bartholomew* (1798) 1 Bros. & Pul. 326.
[10] *White* v. *Greenish* (1861) 11 C.B., N.S. 209.
[11] *Supra*, Chap. 5(I).
[12] Contractual obligations to pay sums of money have to be expressly assigned as choses in action, either in equity or under L.P.A. 1925, s.136.
[13] Landlord and Tenant Act 1730, s.5 now Law of Property Act 1925, s.121.
[14] See *Beer* v. *Bowden* (1975) 237 E.G. 41.

leases,[15] in which it is usually reserved for the first few years of the term only, during which the houses, shops or offices to be built will be in the course of erection, and therefore not yet profitable to the lessee.

(3) *Rack-rent*

A rack-rent is a rent of the full annual value of the property, or near to it.[16] It must be determined according to the value at the time of the letting.[17] Where the rent obtainable on the open market would exceed the maximum legal rent recoverable because, for instance, a fair rent has been registered for the premises under the Rent Act 1977, then the rack-rent will be the maximum legally recoverable rent.[18]

(4) *Equity Rent*

The rent payable by a tenant may be made to vary with the rents which he receives, or ought to receive, from time to time, from subtenants and other occupiers of the premises.[19] This is known as an "equity rent."

(5) *Progressive Rent*

It is very common for leases of business premises to contain rent review clauses[20] intended to provide for periodic increases in the rent during the term in an attempt to keep pace with inflation and rising values. They will be valid and binding on the tenant provided the review clause contains machinery for making the new rental payment certain in amount. This is commonly done in one of three ways. In shorter leases the parties may be prepared to fix the figure for each period definitely, as for example, in a lease of six years "at a rent of £5,000 p.a. for the first three years, and £6,000 p.a. thereafter." In longer leases, the rents for all periods after the first may be made ascertainable either by reference to a multiplier of the first period's rent, (a type of clause known as an "escalator"), or by a provision for

---

[15] See Settled Land Act 1925, s.44(2), which authorises a peppercorn rent for the first five years of any building lease granted by the tenant for life.

[16] *Re Sawyer & Withall* [1919] 2 Ch. 333.

[17] *Corporation of the City of London* v. *Cusack-Smith* [1955] A.C. 337.

[18] *Rawlance* v. *Croydon Corporation* [1952] Q.B. 803; *Gidlow-Jackson* v. *Middlegate Properties* [1974] 1 Q.B. 361; *Newman* v. *Dorrington Developments* [1975] 1 W.L.R. 1642; *cf. Compton Group* v. *Estates Gazette* (1978) 36 P. & C.R. 148.

[19] For example see *British Railways Board* v. *Elgar House* (1969) 209 E.G. 1313; *Freehold & Leasehold Shop Properties* v. *Friendly Provident Life Office* (1984) 271, E.G. 451, where the judge at first instance referred to such provisions as "Delphic" clauses.

[20] These are discussed in detail below: see *post*, (V).

arbitration, in default of agreement between the parties when the time comes. So, *e.g.* under a 21 year lease, one might find a specified rent for the first seven years, and provision for the rent to increase by 25 per cent. and 50 per cent., or for a rent review, at the end of the seventh and fourteenth years respectively. The lapse of time between reviews depends much on the state of the market when the lease is granted. A rent that is made to rise by amounts, and at times specified in the lease is called a "progressive rent."

(6) *Sliding Scale Rents*

A sliding scale rent is one that provides for the division of profit and loss between landlord and tenant by a rent that rises and falls with the price of the produce of the property let. So, *e.g.* section 45 of the Settled Land Act 1925, specifically authorises sliding scale rents in mining leases, to vary in accordance with the price of the mineral being worked. Rents may be made to rise or fall with the cost of living as expressed in the Government index of wholesale or retail prices,[21] or the tenant's trade, such as his turnover, his net profits or gross profits.

(7) *Insurance Rent*

Where the landlord insures the demised premises the lease will generally make provision for an insurance rent equal to the premiums (or a relevant portion of them if the tenant does not rent the whole of the premises covered by the policy) paid by the landlord. In cases where these insurance rents are paid, the lease will not always contain a covenant by the landlord to insure, and one is not necessarily implied at common law.[22]

(8) *Net Rent*

As was explained earlier,[23] a net rent is a sum to be paid to the landlord clear of all deductions that would otherwise be permitted by common law or statute.

---

[21] *Blumenthal* v. *Gallery Five Ltd.* (1971) 220 E.G. 31.
[22] See *e.g. Mumford Hotels* v. *Wheler* [1964] Ch. 117; *Argy Trading Developments Co.* v. *Lapid Developments* [1977] 1 W.L.R. 444.
[23] *Supra,* Chap. 5(III)E.

(9) *Dead Rent*

Mining leases frequently stipulate for two rents: first, a dead rent, *i.e.* a rent payable whether the mines be worked or not; and secondly, a royalty, *i.e.* a payment of so much per ton of the mineral mined and/or sold. Clearly the dead rent will be fixed,[24] whereas the royalty payment (which is still rent if properly reserved under the lease) will vary with production.[25]

(10) *Best Rent*

A best rent is the highest rent that can reasonably be obtained for the duration of the lease. Under the Settled Land Act 1925, a tenant for life exercising his power of leasing must, with certain exceptions, reserve the best rent that can reasonably be obtained.[26]

(11) *Ground Rent*

A ground rent is a rent that is substantially less than the full market rent of the property, but which is greater than, and not intended to be, a nominal or peppercorn rent. The difference between the ground rent and the full market rent will have been taken by the landlord, at its "capitalised value," as a premium on the grant of the lease (see below). It is a rent for the "bare" site.

(12) *Penal Rent*

Sometimes a landlord will endeavour to compel payment of rent and performance of covenants in a lease or agreement for a lease by providing that, in the event of rent remaining unpaid or a covenant being broken, an additional sum will forthwith become payable by the tenant. The landlord's right to demand such a penal rent will pass with the reversion, and can be enforced against an assignee of the term.[27] It seems that a penal rent may be waived by the landlord by acceptance of the rent.[28]

When a breach of a covenant in the lease occurs, the landlord may

---

[24] *Marquis of Bute* v. *Thompson* (1844) 13 M. & W. 487; *Jervis* v. *Tomkinson* (1856) 1 H. & N. 195, 208; *Watson* v. *Charlesworth* [1905] 1 K.B. 74; *O'Callaghan* v. *Elliott* [1966] 1 Q.B. 601; *Earl of Lonsdale* v. *Att.-Gen.* (1982) 45 P. & C.R. 1.

[25] See *T & E Homes Ltd.* v. *Robinson* [1979] 2 All E.R. 522.

[26] *Supra*, Chap. 3, (II) B(1).

[27] *Brendloss* v. *Philips* (1602) Cro.Eliz. (1) 895; *Egerton* v. *Sheafe* (1606) Lutw. 1151; and see L.P.A. 1925, s.141.

[28] *Doe d. Cheny* v. *Batten* (1775) Cowp. 243.

sue either for the penal rent or for general damages. Where he elects to sue for the penal rent he must first allege that the penal rent has not been paid, otherwise there will be no sufficient breach and only general damages can be recovered.[29] If, on the other hand, the landlord elects to sue for general damages, he cannot afterwards maintain an action for the penal rent. He will, however, be able to recover his proved actual loss, whether that be greater or less than the amount of the penal rent.[30]

A penal rent may take the form of a genuine attempt to pre-estimate the landlord's loss flowing from the breach by the tenant of his covenant or covenants. In this case the penal rent clause will be drafted as a liquidated damages clause, and will be recoverable as rent.[31] This type of penal rent is commonly found as an addition to covenants restrictive of the user of the property let. The tenant will agree to pay additional rent if he uses the premises for purposes other than those specified.[32] It must be remembered, however, that a breach remains a breach, notwithstanding a provision in the lease for the payment of an increased rent in that event. Thus a penal rent provision does not, of itself, entitle the tenant to break the covenant and pay the increased rent,[33] and an injunction may therefore still be obtained to restrain a breach in respect of which a single sum is payable.[34] Nevertheless, if the agreement provides that the additional rent should not take the form of a single payment, but be payable for the remainder of the term, the court is likely to construe the clause as giving to the tenant the option to break the covenant and pay the increased rent.

The penal rent may, on the other hand, take the form of a straightforward penalty, specified to be payable in the event of breach, but being quite arbitrary in nature. In this case the sum fixed upon will be sufficiently high to operate as a deterrent to the tenant against breach, but will bear no relation to the true or likely loss sustained by the landlord. A penal rent in the form of a penalty will not always be enforced by the court because of Equity's view that a landlord acts unconscionably if he demands a sum which, though certainly fixed by agreement, is disproportionate to the injury.[35] The rule here therefore is that a landlord who brings an action for the enforcement of a penalty can recover compensation only for the damage he has in fact suffered. He is not entitled to recover the sum stated in the lease if he

[29] *Reindel* v. *Schell* (1858) 4 C.B.(N.S.) 97.
[30] See *Kemble* v. *Farren* (1829) 6 Bing. 141.
[31] In the case of agricultural holdings, liquidated damages for breach of covenant were abolished by s.15 of the Agricultural Holdings Act 1948. See now Agricultural Holdings Act 1986, s.24.
[32] Although planning controls may restrain the change of user in any event, at whatever additional cost by way of rent.
[33] *French* v. *Macale* (1842) 2 Dr. & War. 269; *Hanbury* v. *Cundy* (1887) 58 L.T. 155.
[34] *Jones* v. *Heavens* (1877) 4 Ch.D. 636.
[35] Story, *Equity Jurisprudence*, ss.1316 *et seq.*

has not in fact suffered so much loss. Where, however, the stipulated sum does not compensate for the actual loss suffered, the landlord has an election. Either he may sue on the penalty clause, in which case he cannot recover more than the stipulated sum; or he may sue for breach of covenant and recover general damages in full.[36]

It is, therefore, a question of some importance whether the penal rent is liquidated damages or a penalty, and the terminology used in the lease is by no means conclusive. In *Dunlop Pneumatic Tyre Co. Ltd.* v. *New Garage & Motor Co. Ltd.*[37] Lord Dunedin[38] set out the now accepted test for distinguishing between a penalty and liquidated damages. The essence of a penalty is a payment of money intended, on account of the expense, to put the tenant in fear of breach; the essence of liquidated damages is a genuine covenanted pre-estimate of damage. The question is one of construction, to be decided upon the terms and inherent circumstances of each particular contract, judged as at the time of making it. Where it is impossible at the date of the contract to foresee the extent of injury which might be sustained by its breach, or the cost and difficulty of proving it, but the sum made payable by way of penal rent is reasonable in amount, it will be treated as liquidated damages.[39] However, if the sum stipulated for is extravagant in amount in comparison with the greatest loss that could conceivably be proved to have followed from the breach, or if a very large sum is made payable in consequence of the non-payment of a very small sum, it is likely to be held a penalty. Payments made proportionate to the extent of the actual damage will be regarded as liquidated damages but where stipulations of varying degrees of importance, such as covenants for rent, repair, user, requirements of notice and so on, are all followed by an agreement for payment of the same sum for breach of any of those stipulations, the presumption is that the parties intended the sum to be a penalty.

(13) *Service Charge*

The landlord, who will be construed to include the holder of a concurrent lease,[40] may reserve separate sums on account of the cost of providing services to the tenant, such as porterage or lifts or carrying out repairs to the property in which the premises leased are

---

[36] *Wall* v. *Rederiaktiebolaget Luggade* [1915] 3 K.B. 66.
[37] [1915] A.C. 79; see also *Chitty on Contracts* (25th ed.), Vol. 1, paras. 1724 *et seq.*
[38] At p. 86.
[39] *Clydebank Engineering & Shipbuilding Co.* v. *Yzquierda* [1905] A.C. 6.
[40] *Adelphi Estates* v. *Christie* (1984) 269 E.G. 221.

comprised,[41] or in respect of management costs of the building.[42] A service charge clause does not, however, permit the landlord to charge the cost of insurance on the building unless this is expressly provided for.[43] The whole amount reserved as rent by the landlord will be distrainable as rent although, where the charge relates in part to future services, the amount agreed may be an advanced rental on account of the provision of furniture or services by the landlord.[44] These sums, even when specified as separate payments in respect of services, furniture, fitments, management costs, etc., are treated as rent both at common law and under the Rent Act 1977.[45] The ascertainment of the amount due from time to time on the service charge will frequently be a matter for the landlord's surveyor, though his certificate cannot be conclusive on matters of law.[46] The certificate of an independent surveyor may, however, be conclusive and a tenant who pays under a mistake of law cannot recover the excess.[47] In *Finchbourne* v. *Rodrigues*[48] a lease provided for the sums payable by the tenant to be certified by the landlord's surveyor and the landlord and the surveyor were the same person. It was held that the certificate given by him was invalid and a term was implied into the lease that the charges were to be "fair and reasonable." This term was explained by the Court of Appeal in *Pole Properties* v. *Feinberg*[49] where the lease provided for the costs of heating a building to be apportioned according to floor area. Following the installation of a new heating system it was argued that the circumstances had changed so radically that the original formula was no longer applicable. The Court of Appeal, applying the test of what was "fair and reasonable" held that the tenant's contribution should be calculated on the basis of the use he made of the heating system and not according to floor area.[50] There are special statutory provisions relating to service charges for flats.[51]

---

[41] A clause imposing maintenance obligations on the landlord "subject to the lessees paying to the maintenance contribution" does not create a condition precedent, absolving the landlord from his obligation in the absence of payment; *Yorkbrook Investments* v. *Batten,* (1985) 276 E.G. 493.

[42] An entitlement to charge management costs may be implied, at least where the landlord is a management company formed by the tenants: *Embassy Court Residents' Association Ltd.* v. *Lipman* (1984) 271 E.G. 545.

[43] *Property Holding & Investment Trust* v. *Lewis* (1969) 20 P. & C.R. 808.

[44] *Newman* v. *Anderton* (1806) 2 B. & P.N.R. 224; *Rousou* v. *Photi* [1940] 2 K.B. 379; *Somershield* v. *Robin* [1946] 1 K.B. 244.

[45] *Sidney Trading Co.* v. *Finsbury Corp.* [1952] 1 T.L.R. 512; *Property Holding Co.* v. *Clark* [1948] 1 K.B. 630; *cf. O'May* v. *City of London Real Property Co.* [1983] 2 A.C. 726.

[46] *Re Davstone Estates* [1969] 2 Ch. 378.

[47] *Concorde Graphics* v. *Andromeda Investments S.A.* (1983) 265 E.G. 386.

[48] [1976] 3 All E.R. 581.

[49] (1981) 43 P. & C.R. 121.

[50] As to whether monies paid by the tenant constitute a trust fund, see *Re Chelsea Cloisters (in Liquidation)* (1980) 41 P. & C.R. 128.

[51] *Supra,* Chap. 4 (IV) F and see also Landlord and Tenant Act 1985, ss.18–30.

(14) *Premium*

In granting a lease, part of the rent is sometimes capitalised and paid in a lump sum to the landlord at the time the lease is granted. This is called a fine or premium and, although it represents capitalised rent, it is not, except in certain limited circumstances, treated in law as rent.[52] In some cases, however, notably where the landlord is attempting to evade the statutory restrictions of the Rent Act 1977, the court may be prepared to regard the label placed upon the alleged capital payment as a sham and treat the premium as rent paid in advance.[53]

IV. NON-PAYMENT

A. Effect of Non-payment

A tenant from year to year, without any lease in writing[54] gains, after paying no rent for 12 years, a title by adverse possession under sections 15(1) and 15(6), and Schedule 1, para. 5, of the Limitation Act 1980.[55] A mere licensee, however, gains no title under the 1980 Act merely through non-payment of rent, nor does a tenant at will. If the licence or tenancy at will has not been terminated, or if the owner visits the land after such termination in the character of owner and exercises rights of ownership with a view to recovering possession, such visits may prevent the Limitation Act running in favour of the occupant.[56]

The effect of non-payment of rent with a lease in writing is very different. Where the lease is in writing the tenant himself cannot begin to acquire a good title against his landlord as long as the lease continues. He can do so, however, when it expires. The only effect of non-payment of rent is to bar recovery of each instalment of rent after six years, as a contract debt.[57] If the lease is in writing and the rent amounts to £10[58] a year or upwards, and that rent is paid to a third person for 12 years, then that person acquires a title to the reversion as against the lessor, by virtue of Schedule 1, para. 6(1), of the Limitation Act 1980. So, receipt of rent by the person wrongfully claiming is deemed to be adverse possession of the land.

---

[52] *Regor Estates Ltd.* v. *Wright* [1951] 1 K.B. 689.

[53] *Samrose Properties* v. *Gibbard* [1958] 1 W.L.R. 235.

[54] The provision of a rent book does not turn the lease into "a lease in writing": *Moses* v. *Lovegrove* [1952] 2 Q.B. 533.

[55] Technically the effect of limitation is not to give title to the adverse possessor as such, but to extinguish the landlord's right to bring an action to recover the land.

[56] *Woodhouse* v. *Hooney* [1915] 1 Ir.R. 296.

[57] Limitation Act 1980, s.19.

[58] Figure raised from £1 by the Limitation (Amendment) Act 1980, s.3(3), replaced as from May 1, 1981, by Limitation Act 1980, s.15(6) and Sched. 1, para. 6.

B. Suspension of Rent

A tenant is not liable in respect of any rent accruing due after he has been evicted from the premises whether by the landlord or by a person lawfully claiming by superior title, so long as the eviction continues. He remains liable, however, for rent due before the eviction. If the tenant is evicted by someone other than his landlord or a person claiming by virtue of superior title, he remains liable for the rent accruing during the period of his eviction. Thus, expulsion by a trespasser does not relieve the tenant from liability.[59]

To constitute an eviction for this purpose it is not necessary that the tenant be physically put out of possession of any part of the premises. Any act of the landlord, done with the intention of depriving the tenant of his enjoyment of the whole or part of the premises, will suffice.[60] So, there will be an eviction if the landlord enters and uses the premises, even if the tenant remains in possession,[61] although a mere trespass by the landlord is not sufficient.[62]

A tenant who simply abandons the premises does not cease to be liable for rent. If, however, the landlord then enters and uses the premises for his purposes[63] or re-lets them,[64] this is equivalent to an eviction and the landlord cannot from that point recover any further rent from his tenant. A landlord is allowed to protect his premises, *e.g.* by putting in a caretaker, once they have been abandoned by a tenant, without losing his right to continue to look to him for rent.[65]

C. Reduction of Rent

It may be that a tenant, whose business is no longer prospering, finds that he is unable to continue to afford the rental payments he originally agreed to make. It may also be, however, that the landlord does not wish to lose this particular tenant, perhaps because the property is difficult to let. For this reason the landlord may be prepared to consider a rent reduction. If the lease is in writing, an agreement for a reduction in the rent must also be in writing.[66] Unless the agreement to reduce the rent is under seal, it will also need to be supported by consideration, although a gratuitous promise by the

---

[59] *Paradine* v. *Jane* (1647) Aleyn 26.
[60] *Baynton* v. *Morgan* (1888) 22 Q.B.D. 74.
[61] *Smith* v. *Raleigh* (1814) 3 Camp. 513.
[62] *Newby* v. *Sharpe* (1878) 8 Ch.D. 39, although the landlord may, nevertheless, be in breach of his covenant for quiet enjoyment: see *supra*, Chap. 4.
[63] *Bird* v. *Defonvielle* (1846) 2 Car. & K. 415.
[64] *Hall* v. *Burgess* (1826) 5 B. & C. 332.
[65] *Griffith* v. *Hodges* (1824) 1 C. & P. 419; *cf. Old Grovebury Manor Farm Ltd.* v. *Seymour Plant Sales & Hire Ltd.* [1979] 1 All E.R. 573.
[66] *Hilton* v. *Goodhind* (1827) 2 C. & P. 591.

landlord to accept a lower rent may still operate as a waiver.[67] The mere payment and acceptance of a new rent does not, it seems, operate to create a new lease unless it has been brought about by a threat on the part of the tenant to leave. In such a case the court will sometimes construe the arrangement as a surrender of the old and creation of a new tenancy at the reduced rent.[68] Statutory provisions have, at various times, operated to effect rent reductions.[69] Most important is now the Rent Act 1977 under which the full contractual rent may not always be recoverable by the landlord.[70]

In some cases a rent reduction may be demanded by the tenant under the terms of the original lease itself. It is common practice to insert in most professionally drafted leases a proviso that the rent shall be suspended or extinguished in case of damage by fire. Although it has been argued earlier in this chapter that, at least in the case of total destruction of multi-storey property in multi-occupation, a lease may be frustrated,[71] the conventional view is that in the event of loss of, or damage to the premises by fire, the tenant remains liable for the full rent at least in the absence of an appropriate proviso. The insertion of a proviso, which can take several different forms, to deal with loss or damage through fire, would seem to indicate that such a consequence was within the contemplation of the parties, thus precluding the operation of the doctrine of frustration in that event also.[72] Words such as "damage by fire excepted" do not entitle the tenant to a complete suspension of rental payments, but only to an abatement in proportion to the damage.[73] If, on the other hand, the proviso refers to "suspension" of rent, then the tenant's liability to pay rent will not arise until the damage has been put right. In *Saner* v. *Bilton*[74] the lease contained a proviso that if the premises or any part thereof "should be destroyed or damaged by fire, flood, storm, tempest, or other inevitable accident" the rent should cease or abate. The court held that an exclusion of the tenant from the premises by the landlord executing repairs in pursuance of his covenant so to do contained in the lease, did not fall within the proviso, and hence the tenant's liability to pay the rent was not suspended, though, depending upon the length of the lease and the duration of the interruption

---

[67] See *post* (IV) D.

[68] *Parker* v. *Briggs* (1893) 37 S.J. 452 at p. 452.

[69] See the Liabilities (War Time Adjustment) Acts 1941 and 1944; the Landlord and Tenant (War Damage) (Amendment) Act 1941, s.7.

[70] See *post*, Chap. 11.

[71] Following *National Carriers Ltd.* v. *Panalpina (Northern) Ltd.* [1981] A.C. 675, esp. Lords Hailsham L.C. at pp. 690–691, Wilberforce at pp. 694–695, Simon at p. 701 and Russell at p. 709 (dissenting).

[72] See, *e.g. Joseph Constantine S.S. Line Ltd.* v. *Imperial Smelting Corp. Ltd.* [1942] A.C. 154, *per* Lord Simon L.C. at p. 163.

[73] *Bennett* v. *Ireland* (1858) E.B. & E. 326.

[74] (1878) 7 Ch.D 815.

it could, in appropriate circumstances, amount to frustration.[76]

D. Waiver

A landlord who has promised his tenant, even in the absence of consideration, that he will accept a reduction in the rent, cannot afterwards go back upon his promise and claim from the tenant the difference between the reduced rent and the full rent formally reserved in the lease. Equity will restrain the landlord from acting inconsistently with his promise if it was intended to affect the existing legal relationship between the parties, to be acted upon by the tenant and was in fact acted upon or relied upon by him. Reliance upon the landlord's undertaking to accept a reduced rent can frequently be shown by a tenant who has remained in possession and not assigned or surrendered his interest knowing that he could no longer afford to continue as tenant at the full rent.

The leading case is *Central London Property Trust* v. *High Trees House*.[76] A lease under seal of a block of flats was executed at a rent of £2,500 per annum. The landlord company agreed to a reduction of £250 in the rent since the tenant company found itself unable to sub-let profitably because of the war. At the end of the war the landlord's receiver sued for the full rent then due under the lease and also for the arrears of some of the amount abated during the last part of 1945. Denning J. considered what the position would have been had the landlord sued for the full arrears of the amount abated during the war and suggested that the landlord's promise to accept a lower rent was a promise which the parties intended to be binding, which the tenant had acted upon and which the landlord intended the tenant to act upon. It was therefore binding upon the landlord even though there was no consideration and no period had been stated for the duration of the reduction, although the evidence showed that the period was to last until the property was fully let once more, which was likely to be the end of the war. So the landlord would have been estopped from setting up the enforceability of the tenant's promise to pay the full rent as contained in the lease for the duration of the war. The landlord company was, however, entitled to revoke its promise to accept a reduced rent once the special circumstances had ceased, by giving reasonable notice of intention to demand payment in full of the rent reserved, in the future. Service of the writ was effective notice to the tenant for that purpose.

It should be noted, however, that his principle of quasi, equitable or promissory estoppel, as it is variously known, can operate only by way

---

[75] *National Carriers Ltd.* v. *Panalpina (Northern) Ltd. (supra).*
[76] [1947] K.B. 130; *cf. Brikom Investments Ltd.* v. *Carr* [1979] 2 All E.R. 753.

of defence.[77] The courts have not gone so far as to give the tenant a cause of action in damages against the landlord for breach of such gratuitous promises, although they have refused to allow the party making them to act inconsistently with them.[78]

V. Rent Increases, Rent Reviews and Index-Linked Clauses

A. Rent Increases

Unless there is provision for it by statute[79] or in the lease itself, or the existing tenancy is terminated by effluxion of time or the service of a notice to quit and a new, higher rent agreed for the new tenancy, rent increases can be demanded by the landlord only with his tenant's agreement. As increased rent can be agreed upon verbally, provided that the landlord provides some consideration. This is most likely to take the form of improvements to the premises carried out by the landlord. However, this extra rent, being secured by an agreement collateral to the main lease, is not part of the rent reserved by the lease and therefore does not pass with the reversion unless expressly assigned with it.[80] The only exception is where the agreement can be construed as a surrender of the old and the creation of a new tenancy at the increased rent.[81] This will be a question of the construction of the new rental agreement, although, as in the case of a rent reduction, a mere change in the amount of rent paid does not operate as a new demise.[82]

In the absence of special provision in the lease or tenancy agreement, the only cases in which a landlord can increase the rent unilaterally without first terminating the existing tenancy are those in which the landlord is a local authority[83] or a housing association,[84] or where the rent has been increased in accordance with the machinery of the Rent Act 1977.[85] It has been suggested, relying on a dictum of Goff J. in *Gable Construction Co. Ltd.* v. *I.R.C.*[86] that an *ad hoc*

---

[77] *Combe* v. *Combe* [1951] 2 K.B. 215.

[78] See *Mitas* v. *Hyams* [1951] 2 T.L.R. 1215.

[79] *e.g.* Housing Act 1985, ss. 25, 102,103.

[80] *Hoby* v. *Roebuck & Palmer* (1816) 7 Taun. 157.

[81] See *Lambert* v. *Norris* (1837) 2 M. & W. 333; *cf. Burrowes* v. *Gradin* (1843) 1 Dow. & L. 213.

[82] See the discussion of this point by Buckley J. In *Jenkin R. Lewis & Son Ltd.* v. *Kerman* [1970] 1 All E.R. 833 at pp. 838–839.

[83] Housing Act 1985, ss. 25, 102–103.

[84] Rent Act 1977, s.93. The section does not, however, authorise an increase in rent above the registered rent limit (subs. 5); Housing Act 1985, s.102(3).

[85] s.56; Sched. 9. See *post*, Chap. 11. A tenant of residential accommodation faced with a rent increase may be able to obtain financial assistance from the local authority in the form of housing benefit: see *post*, Chap. 18.

[86] [1968] 2 All E.R. 968.

increase in rent can be imposed by a landlord, without terminating the existing lease, where the lease is by parol.[87] However, this does not seem to be so since, in that case, Goff J. appears to be referring to the possibility of varying orally a lease which, originally, was not created by deed. Understandably, he concedes that this is possible,[88] but nothing in his judgment appears to affect the requirement that such oral variation requires the consent and agreement of the tenant.

B. Rent Review Clauses[89]

Many professionally drafted modern leases, especially of business premises, contain rent review clauses, the purpose of which is to ensure that the rent keeps pace with inflation. The usual practice is to provide that there shall be reviews of rent at regular intervals, usually of five years, throughout the duration of the term, although intervals of seven or even three years are not uncommon. The periods are likely to depend on the view which the landlord's advisers take as to the time-scale in which increases in market rents are likely.[90] It is less common for the lease itself to fix the rental figure for each period definitively, although this is sometimes done in shorter leases. A lease for six years may, for instance, provide for "a rent of £1,000 p.a. for the first three years, and £1,400 p.a. thereafter."

A rent review clause may run the risk of being void for uncertainty[91] unless it clearly defines the rent review periods and provides a formula for assessing the rent in each of those periods, usually by reference to the open market rent at the beginning of each period. In addition to providing a formula, however, the clause must also define the machinery to be employed in assessing the new rent. This machinery will usually be "by agreement of the parties in writing, or in default of such agreement, by arbitration." Where arbitration agreements are used, it is usual for a clause to provide for the appointment of a surveyor by each party, or by the President of the Royal Institute of Chartered Surveyors in the event of a tenant's default, and for the appointment of an umpire should the arbitrators

---

[87] See Evans, *The Law of Landlord and Tenant* (2nd ed. by P. F. Smith), p. 111.

[88] At pp. 971–972; see also *Donellan* v. *Read* (1832) 3 B. & Ad. 899; *Duke of Westminster* v. *Store Properties Ltd.* [1944] Ch. 129.

[89] See Bernstein, *Handbook of Rent Review*; for valuation principles see Baum, *Statutory Valuations*, pp. 31 *et seq.* The clearest and most comprehensive discussion of the law is to be found in Clarke and Adams, *Rent Reviews and Variable Rents* (2nd ed.), *passim*.

[90] See Westlake & Birkett 23 E.G. 996; *Precedents for the Conveyancer*, 5–61A, and R.I.C.S./Law Society Model Rent Review Clause (1985 ed.).

[91] *Brown* v. *Gould* [1972] Ch. 53. See also *T. Bates & Sons* v. *Wyndham's (Lingerie)* (1979) 39 P. & C.R. 517 (no provision for calculating rent to be agreed); *Beer* v. *Bowden* [1981] 1 W.L.R. 522 (note).

fail to agree.[92] It is, however, by no means clear to what extent the certainty principle, as formerly understood, may still be relied upon. It seems that if the machinery specified in the lease breaks down, it is possible that the court will substitute its own machinery; it has done this in regard to the machinery for fixing the price on the exercise of an option to purchase the reversion[93] and there seems no reason in principle why a similar approach should not be adopted in the case of a rent review clause. Certainly if the parties fail to provide for any machinery to determine the price in an option, the court will determine the question itself,[94] and a rent review clause or option to renew a lease at "a rent to be agreed" is valid and enforceable.[95] It seems, therefore, to be the case that if uncertainty in a review clause may result in that particular clause being void, the court will substitute its own review machinery, but the uncertainty will not invalidate the entire lease.

In view of the very large amount of litigation on rent review clauses over the last 20 years, it would seem that many of them were not well-drawn.[96] Some rent reviews may, of course, be automatic, in that the clause may provide that if, by the date of the review, the rent reserved is no longer the market rent, then the new rent shall be whatever is found to be the market rent,[97] or they may be semi-automatic. One particular problem encountered is that many rent reviews require the landlord to furnish his tenant with a notice of review by a particular date, as a means of bringing the review into operation,[98] or require a review to take place *on* a particular date, yet the review clause fails to make clear what is to happen if the landlord fails to serve the "trigger" notice duly, or the review does not take place on time. At least in those cases where the only direction in which the rent can go is upward, the courts used to regard time as being of the essence in rent review clauses. In a series of cases[99] a distinction was drawn between the landlord who had the option whether or not to operate the rent review—in which case time was of the essence—and the landlord who did not, in which case the rent review procedure was automatic, did not depend upon the will of the parties and did not create time limits which were of the essence. This somewhat artificial distinction was

[92] See *Estates Projects* v. *Greenwich Borough Council* (1979) 251 E.G. 851, on the arbitrator's role in rent review cases.
[93] *Sudbrook Trading Estate Ltd.* v. *Eggleton* [1983] 1 A.C. 444.
[94] *Brown* v. *Gould* [1972] Ch. 53.
[95] *Beer* v. *Bowden* [1981] 1 W.L.R. 522.
[96] See *Woodfall*, para. 1–0703/1 *et seq.*
[97] *C. H. Bailey Ltd.* v. *Memorial Enterprises Ltd.* [1974] 1 W.L.R. 728.
[98] The so-called "trigger notice."
[99] *Samuel Properties (Developments)* v. *Hayek* (1972) 1 W.L.R. 1296; *C. Richards & Son* v. *Karenita* (1972) 221 E.G. 25; *Fousset* v. *27 Welbeck Street* (1973) 25 P. & C.R. 277; *Stylo Shoes* v. *Wetherall Bond Street* (1974) 237 E.G. 343; *Accuba* v. *Allied Shoe Repairs* [1975] 1 W.L.R. 1559; *Mount Charlotte Investments* v. *Leek & Westbourne Building Society* [1976] 1 All E.R. 890; *Cheapside Land Development Co.* v. *Messels Service Co.* (1976) 120 S.J. 554; *Davstone Holdings* v. *Al-Rifai* (1976) 32 P. & C.R. 18.

swept away by the House of Lords in *United Scientific Holdings* v. *Burnley Borough Council*,[1] which held that there is a presumption that time is not of the essence. This is so whether the clause stipulates a timetable for determining the new rent or requires the new rent to have been ascertained by a particular date.[2] The analogy with options, which had formed the basis of earlier decisions on the point, was said to be misleading and inappropriate.

In this case, the lease provided that during the year preceding the first review period the parties were to agree, or failing agreement, were to determine by arbitration, the rack rent of the demised premises; the landlord had taken no steps to agree or determine that rent until after the start of the review period. The House of Lords held that this did not prevent the landlord from serving his notice late and still enjoying the review. A further time stipulation that in the event of a failure by the parties to agree, the matter shall be referred to arbitration before a certain date, was not of the essence either, so that a failure to comply with the limits did not invalidate the rent review.

The question is, then, one of interpretation of the clause, albeit under the presumption that time is not of the essence. The House of Lords did make it clear, however, that the parties may always decide the question for themselves by expressly providing that time shall or shall not be of the essence.[3] The Courts will give effect to such an express provision. If time is not of the essence, the tenant may make it so by a reasonable notice served on the landlord.[4]

Their Lordships also considered instances where time may be of the essence by implication. There may be some other provision in the lease that demands it in order to give that other provision efficacy. The example given was an option to determine the lease (known as a "break clause") made to operate when the new rent became known, and itself subject to a time limit. As the option has to be strictly interpreted, its purpose, which is to allow a tenant who cannot afford the new rent an opportunity to terminate early, would be frustrated if

---

[1] [1978] A.C. 904.

[2] See also *Dean and Chapter of Chichester Cathedral* v. *Lennards Ltd.* (1977) 35 P. & C.R. 309; *H. West & Sons Ltd.* v. *Brecht* (1982) 261 E.G. 156; *Amherst* v. *James Walker (Goldsmith & Silversmith) Ltd.* [1983] Ch. 305; *Lewis* v. *Barnett* (1982) 264 E.G. 1079.

[3] Use of phrase "shall serve" will not make time of the essence; *Kenilworth Industrial Sites Ltd.* v. *E. C. Little & Co. Ltd.* [1975] 1 W.L.R. 143; failing agreement, there should be reference to a surveyor "as soon as practicable, but in any event not later than three months" held not to make time of the essence in: *Touche Ross & Co.* v. *Secretary of State for the Environment* (1982) 46 P. & C.R. 187; *Thorn EMI Pension Trust Ltd.* v. *Quinton Hazell plc.* (1984) 269 E.G. 414. However, a clause making detailed provision for exactly what was to happen on failure to observe a time limit, by automatically resolving the dispute by "deeming" provisions applying a market rent, was held to make time of the essence in *Henry Smith's Charity Trustees* v. *A.W.A.D.A. Trading and Promotion Services Ltd.* (1983) 47 P. & C.R. 607; *cf. Mecca Leisure Ltd.* v. *Renown Investments (Holdings) Ltd.* (1984) 49 P. & C.R. 12.

[4] *United Scientific Holdings Ltd.* v. *Burnley Borough Council* [1978] A.C. 904.

the rent review was delayed for so long that the option period passed.[5] However, time will not always be of the essence in a rent review clause simply because it is associated with a tenant's break clause. Obviously if there is no correlation between the review and the break clause (where, for instance, they are drafted to operate independently on different dates) or where there is an express provision dealing with the matter, then time will not be of the essence, nor would it be if the lease provided for an automatic extension of the period within which the break clause could be exercised in the event of a delay in the rent review procedure.[6] If the rent review is not initiated by notice to which time limits apply, or there are no stated limits as to when application for independent determination in default of agreement may be made, then even the presence of strict time limits on a break clause would not make time of the essence in the rent review, since there are no limits specified in the review clause which could be made of the essence. It may not be inferred from the fact that time is specified to be of the essence in one stage of the review procedure that it was so intended for all stages. Indeed, the reverse is probably the case in that failing expressly to mention that time is of the essence in relation to any other stage will lead to the inference that the omission was deliberate.[7]

Lord Diplock in the *United Scientific Holdings* case[8] also made it clear that there could be other cases where time might be of the essence. One such case, turning on the wording of the particular review clause, arose in *Drebbond Ltd.* v. *Horsham District Council.*[9] Here the lease required the amount of the new rent, if not agreed, to be referred to arbitration within three months, "but not otherwise." Megarry V.-C. decided that those words made time of the essence for service of this notice and a notice served out of time was, therefore, ineffective. The Court of Appeal, in *Touche Ross & Co.* v. *Secretary of State for the Environment,*[10] where the review was, failing agreement, to be referred to a surveyor "as soon as practicable but in any event not later than three months," held that time was not of the essence,

---

[5] *Metrolands Investments* v. *Dewhurst* (1985) 49 P. & C.R. 334. See also *Al Saloom* v. *Shirley James Travel Services Ltd.* (1981) 42 P. & C.R. 181; *Legal and General Assurance (Pension Management) Ltd.* v. *Cheshire County Council* (1984) 269 E.G. 40. *Cf. Edwin Woodhouse Trustee Co.* v. *Sheffield Brick Co.* (1984) 270 E.G. 548.

[6] *Edwin Woodhouse Trustee Co. Ltd.* v. *Sheffield Brick Co. plc.* (1984) 270 E.G. 548.

[7] *Accuba Ltd.* v. *Allied Shoe Repairs Ltd.* [1975] 1 W.L.R. 1559; *Amherst* v. *James Walker (Goldsmith and Silversmith) Ltd.* (1980) 254 E.G. 123; *London and Manchester Assurance Co. Ltd.* v. *G. A. Dunn & Co.* (1982) 265 E.G. 33 and 131, especially *per* Slade L.J. at p. 134; *Laing Investment Co.* v. *G. A. Dunn & Co.* (1981) 262 E.G. 879. A provision that the rent payable at the expiration of the review time limits shall be the rent payable immediately before the review date, leads to the inference that time is of the essence: *Greenhaven Securities* v. *Compton* (1985) 275 E.G. 628.

[8] [1978] A.C. 904.

[9] (1978) 37 P. & C.R. 237.

[10] (1982) 46 P. & C.R. 187. See also *Thorn EMI Pension Trust Ltd.* v. *Quinton Hazell plc.* (1984) 269 E.G. 414.

but would not express a view upon whether the *Drebbond* case was rightly decided, simply pointing out the differences in wording in the clauses in the two cases. Dillon L.J. observed[11]: "Obviously it is undesirable that questions of whether time is of the essence of a rent review clause should depend on minute differences of language," but despite these sentiments, it would appear that such constructions are required by the cases.

Where time is of the essence, then service of any notice out of time, whether it be a trigger or arbitration notice, will render the notice ineffective and prevent the review operating.[12] There is no jurisdiction or power in a court to relieve the defaulting party from the consequences of this and the right to review will therefore be lost.[13] If the landlord fails to catch the review date in such circumstances, it seems that the old rent remains payable.[14]

Where time is not of the essence, Lord Diplock suggests in the *United Scientific Holdings* case[15] that where the landlord takes no action to initiate proceedings, the tenant can force the issue, but not until the date for serving notice of the increase has passed. Then he in his turn can serve reasonable notice on the landlord requiring him to operate the revision clause or abandon his right to do so. If the period of notice is indeed reasonable, this makes time of the essence. If the landlord, by representation of word or conduct, has led the tenant to believe that the rent review will not be proceeded with, he is estopped from pursuing the claim at a later date, even if time is not of the essence, where to do so would be detrimental to the tenant.[16] Also a rent review may possibly be lost where the tenant produces evidence of the landlord's unreasonable delay[17] or abandonment of the review.[18]

The Arbitration Act 1950, s.27 gives power to the High Court to extend the time for commencing arbitration proceedings if undue

---

[11] At p. 193.
[12] If the delay in service is due to causes outside the landlord's control, such delay may not be fatal to the review: *Touche Ross & Co.* v. *Secretary of State for the Environment* (1982) 46 P. & C.R. 187.
[13] *Beer* v. *Bowden* [1981] 1 All E.R.1070.
[14] *Weller* v. *Akehurst* [1981] 3 All E.R.411.
[15] [1978] A.C. 904, at p. 928. See also Viscount Dilhorne at p. 939; Lord Fraser at p. 958.
[16] *Amherst* v. *James Walker (Goldsmith and Silversmith) Ltd.* (No. 2) [1983] Ch. 305; *James* v. *Heim Gallery* (1980) 41 P. & C.R. 269; *cf. Esso Petroleum* v. *Anthony Gibbs Financial Services Ltd.* (1982) 262 E.G. 661.
[17] *London & Manchester Assurance Co. Ltd.* v. *G. A. Dunn & Co.* (1982) 265 E.G. 33 & 131 *per* Oliver L.J. at p. 42, although in *Amherst* v. *James Walker (Goldsmith and Silversmith) Ltd.* (No. 2) [1983] Ch. 305, overruling *Telegraph Properties (Securities) Ltd.* v. *Courtaulds Ltd.* (1981) 257 E.G. 1153, the Court of Appeal said that mere delay, however lengthy, did not necessarily destroy the contractual right to a review. The matter was one of construction of the clause. In *Million Pigs* v. *Parry* (1983) 46 P. & C.R. 333, Goulding J. appears to suggest that gross delay causing prejudice to the tenant would destroy the right to the review.
[18] *London & Manchester Assurance Co. Ltd.* v. *G. A. Dunn & Co.* (1982) 265 E.G. 33 & 131, *per* Slade L.J. at p. 135; *H. West & Son Ltd.* v. *Brecht* (1981) 261 E.G. 156; *Printing House Properties Ltd.* v. *J. Winston & Co. Ltd.* (1982) 263 E.G. 725; *cf. Amherst* v. *James Walker (Goldsmith and Silversmith) Ltd.* (No. 2) [1983] Ch. 305, *per* Oliver L.J. at p. 316.

hardship would be caused by adhering to the time limit, and this section has been held to apply to a rent review clause where time is expressly or impliedly made of the essence.[19] The provision applies to any time limit in a review clause relating to the appointment of the arbitrator or any step in that process. Where such a clause is construed so as to bar arbitration if notice is not given in the time allowed, then the clause should be read as subject to the court's power to extend the time limit.[20]

The other important question on timing in connection with rent review clauses is to determine from exactly when the new rent is to date. If the rent is revised on time, this may not cause any difficulty; but if the review is delayed it will be important to know whether the rent can date back. Where time is not of the essence a well-drafted rent review clause should make it clear whether or not the revised rent is to date back to the date of review.[21] In *C. H. Bailey* v. *Memorial Enterprises Ltd.*[22] the Court of Appeal made it clear that rent provisions in leases are to be interpreted literally, without the doctrinal restraints of ancient rules that require rent to be ascertained in amount before becoming payable.[23] These rules, the court felt, have modern application only in relation to the remedy of distress and are not appropriate today in other contexts. If, therefore, the lease clearly states that as soon as the amount of the new rent is known it is to date back to the review date, then effect will be given to this. Presumably, however, such back-dated additional rent could not be the subject of a distraint and interest is not presumed to be payable on a back dated rent[24] in the absence of an express provision in the lease.

Two types of back-dating clause are commonly used,[25] and in at least one particular their effects may differ. On the one hand a clause may simply state that as from a certain date the rent shall be the sum ascertained in accordance with the rent review clause. On the other hand, there are clauses which provide that once the new rent is decided, then an additional lump sum of rent is payable to cover the balance between the old and the new figures for the period between

---

[19] *S.I. Pension Trustees Ltd.* v. *William Hudson Ltd.* (1977) 242 E.G. 689; *Edlingham Ltd.* v. *M.F.I. Furniture Centres Ltd.* (1981) 259 E.G. 421.

[20] *Ibid.* See also: *Chartered Trust* v. *Maylands Green Estate Co.* (1984) 270 E.G. 845.

[21] See *South Tottenham Land Securities* v. *R & A Millett (Shops) Ltd.* [1984] 1 All E.R. 614, *per* O'Connor L.J. at p. 618. A rent does not have to be certain at the date from which it is payable, even where the lease is surrendered not long after the review date: *Torminster Properties Ltd.* v. *Green* [1983] 1 W.L.R. 676.

[22] [1974] 1 W.L.R. 728.

[23] See, *e.g. Torminster Properties Ltd.* v. *Green, supra.*

[24] *Trust House Forte Albany Hotels Ltd.* v. *Daejan Investment Ltd.* (1980) 256 E.G. 915, *sed quaere* the application of ss.19A and 20 of Arbitration Act 1950, providing for the payment of interest on an arbitral award.

[25] See *Encyclopaedia of Forms and Precedents*, 4–25; *Kelly's Draftsman*, (14th ed.), form 14; *The Conveyancer and Property Lawyer: Precedents for the Conveyancer*, 5–57; R.I.C.S./Law Society Model Forms of Rent Review, 1979 version, clause 3(6); 1980 version, clause 4(D); 1985 version, clause 4, Variations A, B & C.

the date when the review should have taken place and the date of actual review. The practical difference between these two forms becomes apparent if the lease is assigned during the period between the stated and actual rent review dates. If the new rent payments are back-dated by a clause in the lease, the assignor should, it may be argued, be responsible for all rent due before he parted with his interest, even if the amount of it was only known later. On the other hand, an assignee of a lease under which extra rent is payable on the rent day after the new rent level is fixed, would find himself responsible for the whole of the surplus, even though much of it really referred to a period before he took over.[26]

The issue will, in most cases, be one of construction of the review clause. In *South Tottenham Land Securities Ltd.* v. *R. & A. Millett (Shops) Ltd.*[27] a rent review of rent with effect from 25 March 1980, payable in arrear, was subject to an arbitrator's award on 30 October of that year, notice to the tenants being sent on November, 6. On 26 November the landlords forfeited the lease for non-payment of rent increases attributable to the June and September quarter days. The landlords could only do this (the lease providing for forfeiture if the rent was more than twenty-one days in arrear), if the rent became due on the date of publication of the award, notwithstanding the fact that the lease was actually silent on the issue of late determination. The Court of Appeal, however, held that, in the absence of a clear provision, the reddendum (which provided for rent payments on the usual quarter days) should prevail and that accordingly no increases were due until the December quarter day. The forfeiture was therefore wrongful and the landlords were required to pay damages on that account as well as being unable to recover rent for the period due in December 1980. However, the increased rent for the earlier quarters in September and June was still recoverable because the liability to pay had arisen before the forfeiture occurred.[28] O'Connor L.J. said[29] that an arbitral award of rent is published and binding on the parties when the arbitrator notifies them that he has made his award, whether or not they have notice of its contents. Accordingly, it was unfair and objectionable to have the rent falling due on the date of publication, since the tenant cannot be expected to pay an amount he may not know about, and this was a further reason for holding, in the absence of an express statement on the matter in the lease, that the rent fell due on the next quarter day.

---

[26] See *Bradshaw* v. *Pawley* [1979] 3 All E.R. 273, *per* Megarry V.-C. at pp. 277–278. These points appear to have been lost sight of in *Centrovincial Estates plc* v. *Bulk Storage Ltd.* (1983) 268 E.G. 59; *Allied London Investments Ltd.* v. *Hambro Life Assurance Ltd.* (1984) 269 E.G. 41; *Selous Street Properties Ltd.* v. *Oroneal Fabrics Ltd.* (1984) 270 E.G. 643, discussed *supra*, Chap. 5(III) C.

[27] [1984] 1 All E.R. 614.

[28] *Torminster Properties Ltd.* v. *Green* [1983] 1 W.L.R. 676.

[29] [1984] 1 All E.R. 614, p. 618.

C. Factors that Determine Rent Levels

The setting of rent levels is largely a matter of valuation, more the field of the valuer than the lawyer. A valuer with experience of the properties in a particular locality is likely to have first-hand knowledge of the market, drawing on his experience of recent lettings of comparable properties in the area. Valuation is usually carried out on a square foot basis, relying on values current for comparable properties, where available. In the case of commercial properties, trading figures, in the form of balance sheets, profit and loss accounts and turnover figures of previous occupiers will be helpful in indicating the trading capacity of the premises to a potential lessee, and may thus be a factor affecting valuation of the rent.[30]

The rateable value of the premises might be thought significant in arriving at a market rental, but seldom is. Gross value, which is the valuation figure upon which rateable values are based, means the rent at which a property might reasonably be expected to be let from year to year if the tenant undertook to pay all usual tenant's rates and taxes, and if the landlord undertook to bear the cost of repairs and insurance, and the other expenses, if any, necessary to maintain the property in a state to command that rent. It is rare, today for the terms of a tenancy, both as to duration and to liability for repairs, to be comparable with those underlying the basis of rating assessment. For this reason alone, therefore, rateable value is unlikely to have much impact on rent valuation. Even where comparison is close, it will often be found in practice that the rating assessment was made some time prior to the rental valuation. Even an assessment recently brought into force may be suspect as it may have been made some time considerably earlier.

There are a variety of phrases commonly found in the precedents indicating that the full open market rental value will be the rent payable under the lease after review. The review clause may, unusually, specify the actual rent to be charged at each stage of the escalator, or may provide for a percentage of full rental value to be charged upon review where a premium reflecting this advantage has been paid by the tenant at the start of the lease. Normally, however, the review will be upward only [31] to the "rack rental value," the "open market rental value," or "the yearly rent having regard to open market rental values current at the relevant review date."

The amount of rent payable as a result of a rent review is normally also a valuation question, but there is some authority on the interpretation to be put upon the formulae for rent fixing normally

---

[30] *Pivot Properties v. Secretary of State for the Environment* (1979) 39 P. & C.R. 386 (statutory right to a new lease a relevant factor); *Plinth Property Investments v. Mott, Hay & Anderson* (1979) 38 P. & C.R. 361 (covenants in lease relevant).
[31] *cf. Jane's (Gowns) Ltd. v. Harlow Development Corporation* (1980) 253 E.G. 799.

found in leases. Many of these formulae talk of what would be payable as rent in the open market by a willing lessor to a willing lessee, having regard to the terms of the tenancy (other than those relating to rent). In *F. R. Evans (Leeds) Ltd.* v. *English Electric Co. Ltd.*[32] the question was how to apply such a formula when the premises were of a kind that made the tenant to whom the premises were in fact let the only possible tenant. The reason in this case was size of premises, but clearly the same situation might arise for other reasons, such as the specialist nature of the buildings or the monopoly position of the tenant, particularly in the case of nationalised industries. The Court of Appeal were of the view that the "'willing lessor" and the "willing lessee" were strictly hypothetical people, unaffected by personal ills such as cash-flow crises, mortgages, the need to let or lease, or governmental pressure to maintain employment in the area. Circumstances affecting the real landlord and tenant were only relevant if they would also affect their hypothetical counterparts. None of the motives of the parties involved in the transaction, whether it be desire to let the premises or compulsion to take them, should be allowed to influence the fixing of a new "full market rental," unless the factors spring from the premises rather than from the parties themselves.

A review clause may assume that the premises are fit for immediate occupation and use, that the tenant has not diminished the rental value of the premises and that the tenant's covenants have been duly performed.[33] This is clearly designed to prevent the tenant or landlord benefitting in the review from his own wrongdoing. Should the lease contain a clause restrictive of the user of the property demised, this will normally produce a rent on a review lower than the full rental value, dependent upon the nature of the restriction. In *U.D.S. Tailoring Ltd.* v. *B.L. Holdings Ltd.*[34] the user restriction was "for the purposes of business of men's and women's bespoke and ready-to-wear tailors and outfitters," and a *10 per cent.* reduction in rent was awarded by the court to allow for this. In *Plinth Property Investment Ltd.* v. *Mott, Hay and Anderson*[35] property was let subject to a restriction on the tenants "not to use the demised premises or any part thereof or suffer the same to be used otherwise than as offices . . . in connection with the lessee's business of consulting engineers." It was agreed that the effect of the restriction was to reduce the market rental value from £130,455 to £89,200. The Court of Appeal held that, in arriving at his valuation, the arbitrator must adhere to the strict terms

---

[32] (1978) 245 E.G. 657; see also *I.R.C.* v. *Clay* [1914] 3 K.B. 466; *Tomlinson* v. *Plymouth Argyle Football Club Ltd.* [1960] C.L.Y. 2701.

[33] *Harmsworth Pension Fund Trustees* v. *Charrington's Industrial Holdings* (1985) 49 P. & C.R. 297.

[34] (1982) 261 E.G. 49. The review clause may, on its construction, require the user restriction to be disregarded: *Sterling Land Office Developments* v. *Lloyd's Bank* (1984) 271 E.G.894; see also *Scottish & Newcastle Breweries* v. *Sir Richard Sutton's S.E.* (1985) 276 E.G. 77.

[35] (1979) 38 P. & C.R. 361. See also *Law Land Co. Ltd.* v. *Consumers' Association Ltd.* (1980) 255 E.G. 617.

of the lease and not speculate upon the likelihood of the restrictions being relaxed by the landlord.[36]

It would also appear that the valuer or arbitrator must disregard any excess rental value created by the use by the tenant of the premises in an illegal manner.[37] A common instance of this is the use of part-residential premises wholly as offices without planning consent. In such a case an illegal user should be ignored in the assessment of rent at review, unless there appears to be a real prospect of permission being forthcoming.

If the tenant occupies adjoining premises through which he gains access to the demised premises, the review clause should provide that the presence of an alternative access be assumed for the purposes of the rent review, so as to defeat the argument that the demised premises are incapable of being let to anyone else.[38] If the review clause does not provide for valuation on the basis of vacant possession the question of whether this should be implied is one of construction, having regard to the circumstances of the original letting. It may, for example, be asked whether it was the parties' intention that the tenant would sub-let, and whether there was a sub-letting in existence at the time of the lease.[39] In *F. R. Evans (Leeds) Ltd.* v. *English Electric Co. Ltd.*[40] Donaldson J. defined the term "vacant possession" in the context of the rent review hypothetical letting as meaning that the tenant would be deemed to have moved out of and never to have occupied the premises. This is, of course, favourable to the landlord because it ignores the fact that, in reality, the landlord would incur considerable costs and professional fees on a new letting, be responsible for security of the premises and bear the cost of any void periods. Two further consequences,[41] which could operate in favour of either party, is that the tenant's fixtures would also be deemed to have been removed and that a sub-letting would be ignored in arriving at the revised rent.

Improvements can also present a problem in fixing a revised rent. If the landlord has paid the capital costs of making them, he naturally expects to obtain additional rent as a result. If it is the tenant who has paid for their installation, he may feel that to have his rent increased

---

[36] It may be different if the lease contains a provision for variation in user with the landlord's consent. Here it might be argued that the arbitrator should proceed on the assumption that the landlord is likely to want to maximise his return on the premises and thus a higher rent could be fixed to take account of this relative benefit to the tenant: *Bocardo S.A.* v. *S & M Hotels* [1980] 1 W.L.R. 17, but see *Guardian Assurance Co.* v. *Gants Hill Holdings* (1983) 267 E.G. 678, rejecting the view that "such consent not to be unreasonably withheld" may be implied into user clauses permitting change of use with consent, and Vinelott J. in *Pearl Assurance* v. *Shaw* (1985) 274 E.G. 492.

[37] *Compton Group Ltd.* v. *Estates Gazette Ltd.* (1977) 244 E.G. 799; *Molton Builders Ltd.* v. *Westminster City Council* (1975) 234 E.G. 115. See also the impact of gaming or justices' licences in *Daejan Investments* v. *Cornwall Coast Country Club* (1985) 50 P. & C.R. 157.

[38] In some circumstances this will be implied: see *Jeffries* v. *O'Neill* (1984) 269 E.G. 131.

[39] *Avon C.C.* v. *Alliance Property Co.* (1981) 258 E.G. 1181.   [40] (1978) 245 E.G. 657.

[41] See *99 Bishopsgate Ltd.* v. *Prudential Assurance Co. Ltd.* (1985) 273 E.G. 984.

as a result of the improvements is to require him to pay for the same thing twice over. In *Cuff* v. *J. & F. Stone Property Co.*[42] a rent review clause provided that the rent should be "such sum as shall be assessed as a reasonable rent for the demised premises." The tenants contended that the valuation should take account of the fact that they themselves had improved the premises. Megarry V.-C. held that the question was a matter of valuation alone as to what rent was reasonable for those premises, and the provenance of any improvements should be disregarded.

This view has recently been confirmed by the House of Lords in *Ponsford* v. *H.M.S. Aerosols.*[43] A 21-year lease of industrial premises contained a rent review clause stating that the rent for the second and third seven-year-periods was to be £9,000 or "a reasonable rent for the demised premises" to be assessed by an independent surveyor. Shortly after the lease was granted, the premises burnt down. The landlords granted the tenants a licence to make improvements, and it was a term of the licence that all the tenants' covenants and conditions in the lease were to apply to the premises as and when altered. At the end of the first seven years, a dispute arose as to the basis on which the reasonable rent was to be fixed. A majority of the House of Lords held "a reasonable rent for the demised premises" meant a rent which it was reasonable for *that* tenant to pay. It is always open to parties to make special provision to avoid the consequences of this rule but, unless they do so, the rent is to be assessed for the premises as they stand at the date of the rent review. That is to say, any improvements incorporated at that point are to be reflected in the rent. Who paid for those improvements is irrelevant. In the particular case the improvements had been made during the current lease, but the same principle ought to apply to improvements made under a previous lease.

This somewhat draconian solution to the problem may not always be as harsh as it might at first appear. Whether improvements should be counted in the rent review valuation is really not as simple as merely dividing them according to which party paid for them. After all, if the tenant's rent was reduced at the start of the lease to take account of the fact that he would be making improvements, the cost of them would then be effectively transferred to the landlord, who has foregone rent he would otherwise have received. However, it may equally be the case that at the start of the lease the tenant pays the full rental value of the demised premises. He immediately carries out improvements and at the first review the value of these improvements is included in the new rent. At the second review it is again included in the rent. At the end of the lease, however, section 34 of the

---

[42] [1978] 3 W.L.R. 241 (note).
[43] [1978] 3 W.L.R. 241; for a discussion of the valuation problems created by this decision, see *G.R.E.A. Real Property Investments* v. *Williams* (1979) 250 E.G. 651.

Landlord and Tenant Act 1954, if applicable, will operate and the rent payable under the new lease will exclude the value of improvements carried out during the last lease or last 21 years. Consequently the rent will be reduced, in real terms, until the next review.[44] In determining the rent level for a new tenancy awarded under the Landlord and Tenant Act 1954, Pt. II, the courts are specifically ordered by section 34 to disregard the effect on rent of any improvement. Again, various statutory provisions allow for apportionment between the landlord and tenant of the cost of improvements that have to be made to comply with legal requirements.[45] It may, as the above examples illustrate, be equally unjust on the landlord or the tenant were the law to take account of who paid for the improvements in assessing a new market rent. The solution, of course, is for the well-drawn rent revision clause to state just how improvements should be dealt with on a valuation. Such a clause was incorporated in the lease in *G.R.E.A. Real Property Investments Ltd.* v. *Williams*[46] in which the methods used by the valuer in disregarding improvements at review were the subject of close scrutiny. The tenant had taken a lease of an unfinished office building and completed it. At the review the value of the tenant's improvements was to be disregarded. Comparable evidence of rental on an uncompleted building was, unsurprisingly, difficult to come by and the parties' valuers were forced to consider means of assessing the rental value of the shell. Forbes J. made it clear that the valuer should consider carefully the effect of inflation both on the shell and the improvements, but not necessarily to the same extent. This is of particular relevance where a valuation requires the calculation of the rental value of the completed premises before making a deduction for the value of improvements.

Where the lease contains a particularly unusual term, such as rent free periods, the rent review clause should deal expressly with the question of whether it should be taken into account in fixing the revised rent.[47] A clause requiring a disregard of the rent review provisions themselves must, however, be avoided. To require a valuer to consider, on a first review, a hypothetical letting of, say, ten or fifteen years without further reviews would raise questions of a premium rent, and it is likely that the rent would be higher, on account of the fact that no further review was contemplated, than would be the case if the rent was to be revised to the market value every five years. This point arose in *Pugh* v. *Smiths Industries Ltd.*[48]

---

[44] See *Euston Centre Properties Ltd.* v. *H & T Wilson Ltd.* (1982) 262 E.G. 1079.
[45] *e.g.* Offices, Shops and Railway Premises Act 1963.
[46] (1979) 250 E.G. 651. See also *Estates Projects Ltd.* v. *Greenwich L.B.C.* (1979) 251 E.G. 851
[47] See *Guys 'n' Dolls Ltd.* v. *Sade Bros. Catering Ltd.* (1984) 269 E.G. 129; *99 Bishopsgate Ltd.* v. *Prudential Assurance Co. Ltd.* (1985) 273 E.G. 984.
[48] (1982) 264 E.G. 823; see also *Safeway Food Stores Ltd.* v. *Banderway Ltd.* (1983) 267 E.G. 850; *National Westminster Bank plc.* v. *Arthur Young McCleland Moores & Co.* (1985) 273 E.G. 402; *Equity and Law Life Assurance Society plc.* v. *Bodfield Ltd.* (1985) 276 E.G. 1157.

The valuation of the revised rent was to be on "'the residue of the term hereby granted and on the basis that the Lessee would be obliged to perform and observe the covenants and conditions on the part of the Lessee contained herein but excluding therefrom the provisions of this clause." The term of the lease was twenty-three years and there were to be reviews in the third and thereafter every fifth year. Goulding J. held that the clause, on its construction, required the hypothetical letting to be for a term equal to the residue without reviews. Thus the revised rent was £36,750, the independent valuer having determined that, were there to be five yearly reviews, and were they to be taken into account the rent would have been £30,000.[48a]

Rent reviews are sometimes encountered in which the review period of the formula or hypothetical letting exceeds what would be normal on a new letting of the premises at the time of review. A lease with reviews every fourteen years may, for example, require the valuer or arbitrator to assume that the terms of the hypothetical letting are those of the lease. This would result in the determination of the market value rent on the basis of a fourteen year review period, despite the fact that it was generally accepted that a new lease of the premises granted at the review date would contain five yearly reviews. There would naturally be a tendency on the part of valuers and arbitrators in such cases to determine a higher rent for the longer review period on the ground that, in the open market, tenants would be prepared to pay for a significantly longer review-free period.

However, Tudor Evans J. in *Lear* v. *Blizzard*[49] cast considerable doubt on the validity of such a valuation "uplift" during the early years of the review period. The case did not, in fact, concern a rent review, but an option to renew. The new lease was for a term of twenty-one years at a rent to be agreed between the parties or, in default of agreement, at a rent to be determined by an arbitrator. Extensive improvements had been carried out by a predecessor of the tenant. Tudor Evans J. held that the rent was to be assessed on a subjective basis, having regard to what was fair as between the particular landlord and tenant, rather than on an objective basis, *i.e.*, by determining what was fair for the demised premises as they stood, including the improvements.

This, of course, then raises the question of the extent, if any, to which the tenant's improvements were to influence the valuation. The tenant argued that, since his predecessor in title had paid for the improvements, they should be wholly disregarded when determining the rent. The learned judge held, however, that it was for the tenant to

---

[48a] This "literal" approach has now been rejected, and recent decisions suggest that the landlord should not, under the "disregarding provisions as to rent" formula, obtain a rent additionally inflated by the unreal and uncontemplated factor of a disregard of rent reviews: *Datastream International Ltd.* v. *Oakeep Ltd.* [1986] 1 W.L.R. 404; *M.F.I. Properties Ltd.* v. *B.I.C.C. Group Pension Trust Ltd.* [1986] 1 All E.R. 974; *British Gas Corp.* v. *Universities Superannuation Scheme Ltd.* [1986] 1 W.L.R. 398.
[49] [1983] 3 All E.R. 662.

demonstrate that when he took the lease he paid the cost of the whole or part of the improvement and the arbitrator should then take this into account. Finally, Tudor Evans J. had to decide what, if any, "uplift" to the rent should be given to take account of the hypothetical 21 years term without rent review—a point similar to that raised on a rent review where a long review period must be assumed. In *National Westminster Bank Ltd.* v. *B.S.C. Footwear Ltd.*[50] the Court of Appeal had held that there is no power for an arbitrator determining the open market rent to include a rent review clause in a lease being granted pursuant to an option. In the light of this, Tudor Evans J. in *Lear's* case[51] held that the introduction of an "uplift" on what otherwise would be the open market rent would, in effect, be contrary to the earlier Court of Appeal decision. On the other hand, it is arguable that the Court of Appeal were considering whether, by means of a rent review clause, the arbitrator could in some way award the landlord the "fruits of inflation."[52] This is rather different from providing a means to cater for an arbitrator's finding of fact that tenants would pay a higher rent for a longer review schedule, and the situation may, therefore, be distinguishable on this ground.[53]

D. Index-Linked Clauses

The landlord's desire to protect his rental income against inflation can be met by a type of sliding scale rent. The rent can be linked to the rise or fall in the cost of living as expressed in the official index of wholesale or retail prices, published from time to time by the Department of Trade and Industry. The clause requires the tenant to pay "by way of additional rent a sum of £x per annum for each point the Retail Prices Index published by the Department of Trade and Industry rises above the figure of Y, being the figure at which the said Index stands at the date hereof."[54] This avoids the difficulty inherent in gold clauses, once a favoured way of dealing with the problem of inflation, that the Court may treat such clauses as permitting payment in gold to the value of the figure specified in the lease, rather than payment in money that varies with the value of gold.[55]

[50] (1980) 257 E.G. 277. See also *Bracknell Development Corporation* v. *Greenlees Lennards Ltd.* (1981) 260 E.G. 501.

[51] [1983] 3 All E.R. 662.

[52] The phrase is that of Templeman J. in *National Westminster Bank Ltd.* v. *B.S.C. Footwear Ltd.* (1980) 257 E.G. 277.

[53] See Stapleton, (1984) 269 E.G. 1232. Another valuation theory to deal with the problem of "uplift" and "front-loaded" rents is developed by Baum & Mackmin, *The Income Approach to Property Valuation* (2nd ed.), pp. 140 *et seq.* See also Baum, *Statutory Valuations*, pp. 36–40 (discussing the constant rent theory).

[54] See *Blumenthal* v. *Gallery Five* (1971) 220 E.G. 31.

[55] In *Multiservice Bookbinding* v. *Marden* [1979] Ch. 84, the Court upheld the validity of mortgage payments index-linked to the exchange rate of the Swiss Franc and the Pound Sterling.

Gold clauses, that is clauses linking the reservation of rent to the rise (or fall) in the price of gold, are now very rare, largely because of their failure to achieve their aim, which is to protect the lessor from the loss due to the fall in the value of money during the term. It will be recalled from the discussion earlier in this chapter of *Treseder-Griffin* v. *Co-operative Insurance Society*[56] that the lease reserved rent in the following terms: "paying either in gold sterling or Bank of England notes to the equivalent value in gold sterling the yearly rental of ... £1,900 ... to be payable by equal quarterly payments on the usual quarter days." The Court of Appeal held that the lessee's obligation was to pay £1,900 yearly by equal quarterly payments, the words "either in gold sterling or in Bank of England notes to the equivalent value in gold sterling" merely defining alternative modes of paying that amount. The obligation was to pay £1,900 and that could be discharged by payment of £1,900 in bank notes of that value. If a money rent is reserved, it must be expressed in terms of a sum in lawful currency.[57]

VI. PAYMENT FOR OCCUPATION IN LIEU OF RENT AT EXPIRATION OF LEASE

Situations can arise in which the legal relation of landlord and tenant exists without any arrangement at all for the payment of rent properly so-called since none has been reserved. Analogous to this are cases in which the law implies from the conduct of the parties a promise to compensate the owner for his loss by reason of occupation of his premises. So, a tenant, or his assignee, who holds over after his tenancy has expired or been determined by a notice to quit, will fall into this class, provided the landlord has acted so as to raise a presumption of a continued tenancy, and not an intention to treat the tenant as a mere trespasser. Similarly, if any sub-tenant refuses to quit at the end of the term, *his* landlord, *i.e.* the tenant, will continue to be liable for use and occupation so long as his sub-tenant holds over, but no longer.[58] A person who has entered into possession under a mere agreement for a lease, which has not yet been granted, is liable to be sued for use and occupation. So too can a purchaser who goes into possession, as a tenant at will, pending completion.[59]

---

[56] [1956] 2 Q.B. 127.

[57] *Ibid. per* Lord Denning M.R. at pp. 148–149.

[58] There is an exception in the case of a tenant of a dwelling-house who has lawfully sub-let a portion of the premises and given notice to the landlord to determine the tenancy, and also notice to the sub-tenant to determine the sub-tenancy at the same time, and has left the premises at the expiration of his notice. Such a person will not be liable to the landlord for use and occupation because the sub-tenant remains in possession as a statutory tenant under the Rent Act 1977, where the tenant has done everything legally possible to get rid of him: *Reynolds* v. *Bannerman* [1922] 1 K.B. 719; *Watson* v. *Saunders-Roe* [1947] K.B. 437.

[59] *Howard* v. *Shaw* (1841) 8 M. & W. 118.

The action which can, in these cases, be maintained by the "landlord" is not one to recover rent, but damages due on an implied agreement to pay for the use of the landlord's property. In *Dean and Chapter of Rochester* v. *Pierce*[60] Lord Ellenborough said: "the action for use and occupation does not necessarily suppose any demise; it is enough that the defendant used and occupied the premises by the permission of the plaintiff." This form of action could not be maintained at common law where there had been an actual lease, but by virtue of the Distress for Rent Act 1737, s.14, proof at the trial of a lease will not prejudice the plaintiff unless it be by deed. It might be thought odd that where a lease is proved, which reserves a rent, an action for use and occupation can still be maintained. The rule here is that the rent reserved is used as a measure of the quantum of damages payable to the plaintiff and, where present, will usually be decisive.[61]

It is frequently said that an action for use and occupation is always founded upon some contract or promise, express or implied,[62] but this is not strictly correct, as all that the law says is that the proof of an express contract of demise does not put an end to an action for use and occupation. It may be more correct to say that the defendant must have held or occupied the premises as tenant to the plaintiff, or by his permission or sufferance. In the absence of an express lease or agreement for a lease at a fixed rent, where the premises have been used or occupied by the defendant by the permission or sufferance of the plaintiff, the law will imply a contract or promise by the defendant to pay the plaintiff a reasonable sum for such use and occupation. This is so, notwithstanding that there is an existing lease, even one in writing, save that if the lease is under seal, compensation for use and occupation cannot be claimed unless that lease has expired or been terminated.[63]

---

[60] (1808) 1 Camp. 466.

[61] *Gretton* v. *Mees* (1878) 7 Ch.D. 839. *c.f. Official Custodian for Charities* v. *Mackey (No. 2)* [1985] 1 W.L.R. 1308.

[62] See, *e.g.* Hill & Redman, p. 352. See also *Gibson* v. *Kirk* (1841) 1 Q.B. 850. Note that a court will not make an interim award in respect of mesne profits under the R.S.C.Ord. 29, r. 18 where the defendant has a bona fide counterclaim against the plaintiff which exceeds the amount of the claim for mesne profits: *Old Grovebury Manor Farm Ltd.* v. *W. Seymour Plant Sales & Hire Ltd.* [1979] 1 All E.R. 573.

[63] See Distress for Rent Act 1737, s.14; *Beer* v. *Bowden* (1975) 237 E.G. 41. Note that a landlord cannot sue for damages for use and occupation once he has commenced proceedings for ejectment, since he is considered as having thereby elected to treat the tenant as a trespasser. Instead, his remedy is an action for double value under the Landlord and Tenant Act 1730. Alternatively, the landlord may claim mesne profits which shall or might have accrued from the date of the expiration or termination of the tenancy (*e.g.* re-entry) down to the time of judgment, and thereafter down to the day of delivery of possession, under the Common Law Procedure Act 1852, s.214. Note also that an action for use and occupation is not precluded where a deed of lease is delivered as an escrow and the condition has not been performed: *Gudgen* v. *Besset* (1856) 6 E. & B. 986.

VII. Landlord's Remedies for Non-Payment of Rent

A. Forfeiture

(1) *Forfeiting the Lease*

Most leases and tenancy agreements contain a clause stating that the landlord shall be entitled to re-enter and end the tenancy if any term of the agreement is broken by the tenant. The agreement will confer on the landlord the right to take this action in a number of different specified circumstances. It may, for instance, arise if the rent is more than 21 days in arrear. It may arise when the tenant has become bankrupt or a judgment creditor has levied execution on his goods to satisfy an unpaid judgment debt. The lease will usually enable the landlord to forfeit if the tenant is demonstrably likely to fail financially or if the tenant has broken the other terms that he has agreed to observe in the lease. It is however, essential for there to be some provisions in the lease which enables the landlord to retake the premises and put an end to the lease, at a date earlier than it would otherwise end by a notice to quit or expiration of the term, because the breach of an obligation by the tenant does not, by itself, have the consequence of automatic forfeiture.[64]

Whether the right is secured by the landlord in the form of making performance by the tenant of his covenant a condition precedent to the continuance of the lease, or as a proviso for re-entry annexed to the covenants, the lease will not come to an end until the landlord has either re-entered or (more usually) commenced proceedings for possession. In the normal way service of a writ for possession[65] will be regarded as equivalent to actual re-entry but, in the case of premises let as a dwelling, the Protection from Eviction Act 1977, s.2, makes it unlawful to enforce a forfeiture otherwise than by action for possession, while any person is lawfully residing there. The courts have interpreted this as excluding re-entry as a means of forfeiture altogether and hence it is the court order for possession, and not the service of the writ, that effects the forfeiture.[66] If a landlord acts prematurely by purporting to forfeit the lease before a right to forfeit has actually arisen, the tenant may be able to claim damages for wrongful forfeiture.[67]

There is no need for the landlord to forfeit merely because the tenant is not carrying out his obligation. He can continue to accept

---

[64] *Clays Lane Housing Co-operative* v. *Patrick* (1985) 40 P. & C.R. 72.

[65] But not issue of the writ: see *Canas Property Co. Ltd.* v. *K.L. Television Services Ltd.* [1970] 2 Q.B. 433; *Associated Deliveries Ltd.* v. *Harrison* (1984) 272 E.G. 321.

[66] *Borzak* v. *Ahmed* [1965] 2 Q.B. 320. The same effect is produced by Housing Act 1985, ss.82(3), 86(1) in the case of secure tenancies (explained *post*, Chap. 16).

[67] *South Tottenham Land Securities* v. *R. & A. Millett (Shops)* [1984] 1 All E.R. 614.

rent and simply sue for damages for breach. However, the landlord's right to forfeit will then probably be lost by waiver. As Parker J. observed in *Matthews* v. *Smallwood*[68]: "Waiver of a right of re-entry can only occur where the lessor, with knowledge of the facts upon which his right to re-enter arises, does some unequivocal act recognising the continued existence of the lease." Such an unequivocal act may be demand or acceptance of rent whether by the landlord or by his agent.[69] Moreover, demand or acceptance of rent can constitute waiver even if it is demanded or accepted "without prejudice."[70] The point here is that acceptance of rent with full knowledge of the facts is the strongest affirmation that the tenancy is meant to continue owing to the special position of rent in contractual tenancies as an acknowledgement of the tenurial relationship.[71]

In a number of instances the facts that would entitle a landlord to take forfeiture proceedings are known to a managing agent, but not to the landlord himself, or are known only to one part of the organisation managing the property. Those in charge of the computerised rent roll pour out their demands in happy ignorance of the circumstances that could give rise to proceedings for forfeiture. However, it is clear that the consequences of a demand for rent are a matter of law and it is irrelevant with what intention the rent was demanded.[72] Swanwick J. pointed out in *David Blackstone Ltd.* v. *Burnetts (West End) Ltd.*[73] that in his judgment and without the guidance of direct authority

> "the knowledge required to put a landlord to his election is knowledge of the basic facts that in law constitute a breach of covenant entitling him to forfeit the lease. Once he or his agent knows these facts, an appropriate act by himself or any agent will in law effect a waiver of a forfeiture. His knowledge or ignorance of the law is . . . irrelevant. If it were not so, a vast gap would be opened in the administration of the law of landlord and tenant, and a facile escape route for landlords would be provided."

Where a landlord wishes to forfeit the lease for non-payment of rent,

---

[68] [1910] 1 Ch. 777 at p. 786.

[69] *Central Estates (Belgravia) Ltd.* v. *Woolgar (No. 2)* [1972] 1 W.L.R. 1048. See also Sainer, *Waiver of Forfeiture by Demand or Acceptance of Rent* (1975) 235 E.G. 811; *Expert Clothing Service & Sales* v. *Hillgate House* [1985] 3 W.L.R. 359.

[70] *Segal Securities Ltd.* v. *Thoseby* [1963] 1 Q.B. 887, *per* Sachs L.J. at p. 898. The right to forfeit is not lost by a demand for rent where there is a continuing breach of covenant, and the breach continues after the demand: *cf. Chelsea Estates Ltd.* v. *Kadri* [1970] E.G. D. 425.

[71] The position may be different in the case of statutory tenancies under the Rent Act 1977; *cf. Harvey* v. *Staff* (1977) 247 E.G. 463.

[72] *Windmill Investments (London) Ltd.* v. *Milano Restaurant Ltd.* [1962] 2 Q.B. 373; *Legal & General Assurance Society Ltd.* v. *General Metal Agencies Ltd.* (1969) 20 P. & C.R. 953; *Central Estates (Belgravia) Ltd.* v. *Woolgar (No. 2)* [1972] 1 W.L.R. 1048.

[73] [1973] 1 W.L.R.1487; and see *Welch* v. *Birrane* (1974) 29 P. & C.R. 102; *Trustees of Henry Smith's Charity* v. *Wilson* [1983] Q.B. 316; *cf. Peyman* v. *Lanjani* [1985] 2 W.L.R. 154, *per* Stephenson L.J. at p. 181.

he must first make a formal demand for the rent, or else be exempted from doing so by a suitable phrase in the lease permitting forfeiture whether the landlord has formally demanded the rent or not. The rules for formal demand are exacting and must be strictly complied with. The demand must be made by the landlord or his duly authorised agent, at the place specified in the lease for payment or, if none is, then on the demised premises. The demand must be made before sunset, on the last day for payment and only in respect of the sum due in respect of the last rental period. From this it will be seen that it is always desirable to incorporate in a forfeiture clause a proviso dispensing with the formal demand, for no landlord would willingly risk grappling with the complexities of the common law in this regard.

By the Common Law Procedure Act 1852, s.210, a formal demand may be dispensed with if half a year's rent is in arrear and if any goods found on the premises, available for distress, are insufficient to satisfy the amount due.

(2) *Relief Against Forfeiture*

A tenant has always been entitled to obtain relief from forfeiture in equity by paying off all arrears of rent and the landlord's expenses. Relief is discretionary but is commonly granted because of the equitable view that a right of re-entry, in substance, is security for the payment of rent. The matter is now, to some extent, governed by statute and the position in the High Court and the county court is substantially the same. The county court has jurisdiction when the rateable value of the premises does not exceed £1,000, or by agreement. However, in the case of residential tenancies protected by the Rent Act 1977, an order for possession under section 98 must be obtained, in addition to the order terminating the contractual tenancy for forfeiture. Since the section 98 order will be made by the county court in most instances, it is clearly desirable for the forfeiture issue to be heard by the same court.[74]

(3) *High Court*

If the landlord brings an action for possession, the tenant has a statutory right to have the action terminated, provided that he[75] pays

---

[74] *Peachey Property Corporation* v. *Robinson* [1967] 2 Q.B. 543. If the landlord proceeds in the High Court in these circumstances, he is unlikely to get his costs: *Lircata Properties Ltd.* v. *Jones* [1967] 3 All E.R. 386. The court has an inherent jurisdiction to grant relief to an equitable chargee of the lease: *Ladup* v. *Williams & Glyns Bank* [1985] 1 W.L.R. 857. *Smith* v. *Metropolitan Properties* (1985) 277 E.G. 753.

[75] Payment by a third party will probably not suffice: see *Matthews* v. *Dobbins* [1963] 1 W.L.R. 227.

all arrears of rent and costs before the trial.[76] However, at least half a year's rent must be in arrear and due from the tenant before he has this right to stay proceedings. Should he owe less than six months' arrears, or be unable to pay before the trial, he must fall back upon the inherent jurisdiction of the court to grant relief. In this case, even though the landlord has forfeited, equity will allow the tenant to go back into possession and take up his lease again,[77] provided that he pays all rent due, together with the landlord's costs, and the court considers it just and equitable to grant relief. The court will refuse relief on the ground of justice and equity if, in the meantime, the landlord has let the premises to a third party.[78] The court has power under R.S.C.Ord. 29, r. 10, to make orders for interim payments when a landlord issues a writ claiming forfeiture but the tenant remains in occupation.[79]

Originally equity imposed no time limit on the tenant within which he could ask for relief against forfeiture, except for the general equitable doctrine of laches.[80] The obvious inconvenience created by this latitude is, in part, obviated by sections 210–212 of the Common Law Procedure Act 1852 which provide that where the landlord has obtained judgment for possession in circumstances which allowed him to dispense with the formal demand for rent, an application for relief must be made within six months of execution of the judgment. In other cases, the equitable jurisdiction to grant relief is unimpaired by statutory time limits.[81] Where the county court has allowed relief against forfeiture on the basis that the tenant pays arrears of rent, and he fails to do so, there is no further jurisdiction in the High Court to grant relief.[82] Where a landlord issues a writ claiming forfeiture and the tenant remains in possession, there is no inherent jurisdiction in the court to make an order for interim payments.[83]

Where a lease is forfeited, any underleases created out of it automatically come to an end, for "every subordinate interest must perish with the superior interest on which it is dependent."[84] However, an underlessee or mortgagee has the same right of applying for relief against forfeiture of the lease as has the tenant under the

---

[76] Common Law Procedure Act, s.212.
[77] See *Howard* v. *Fanshawe* [1895] 2 Ch. 581; Supreme Court Act 1981, s.38. *Belgravia Insurance Co. Ltd.* v. *Meah* [1964] 1 Q.B. 436.
[78] *Stanhope* v. *Haworth* (1886) 3 T.L.R. 34.
[79] *cf. Felix* v. *Shiva* [1982] Q.B. 82.
[80] *i.e.* unconscionable delay by the tenant in asking the court for relief: see *Abbey National Building Society* v. *Maybeech Ltd.* [1985] 1 Ch. 190.
[81] See *Lovelock* v. *Margo* [1963] 3 Q.B. 786. The court may, nevertheless, adopt a similar time limit by analogy, but a few days either way are unlikely to matter: *Thatcher* v. *C. H. Pearce & Sons (Contractors) Ltd.* [1968] 1 W.L.R. 748, *per* Simon P. at p. 756. See also *Di Palma* v. *Victoria Square Properties Co.* [1985] 2 All E.R. 676.
[82] *Di Palma* v. *Victoria Square Properties Co.* [1985] 2 All E.R. 676.
[83] *Moore* v. *Assignment Courier Ltd.* [1977] 2 All E.R. 842; *cf. Smith* v. *Metropolitan City Properties Ltd.* (1985) 277 E.G. 753, and see Smith (1986) 136 N.L.J. 339.
[84] *Bendall* v. *McWhirter* [1952] 2 Q.B. 466, *per* Romer L.J. at p. 487. See *post*, Chap. 8(VI) D.

head lease.[85] Relief cannot be applied for by a person who has no legal interest in the term created by the lease, such as a squatter.[86]

(4) *County Court*

The county court provisions are similar to those for the High Court. They provide for the end of the action on payment of rent and costs not less than five days before the hearing.[87] However, in many cases, tenants will promise to discharge the arrears within a reasonably short time, and, if full payment is made within the period of suspension, the original lease continues.[88] If the tenant does not either within the period specified in the order or within that period as extended pay into court all the rent in arrear and costs of the action the order is to be enforceable in the prescribed manner, and so long as the order remains unreversed, the tenant shall be barred from all relief.[89] However a tenant, including a sub-tenant or chargee, whose landlord has forfeited or who is subject to an order made under section 138(3), may still be able to secure relief or further relief, provided that he applies to the county court within six months of the date on which the landlord recovered possession. The court is empowered to grant relief, which may include restoring the applicant to possession for the remainder of the term, on such terms and conditions as it thinks fit.[89a] In the case of tenancies protected by the Rent Act 1977, forfeiture under any of these provisions ends only the contractual tenancy.[90] It will not by itself entitle the landlord to possession automatically, as the tenant will be entitled to stay on as a statutory tenant.[91] The court can make an order for possession of the premises and so end the statutory tenancy if it considers that to make such an order would be reasonable.[92] In such a case, a history of bad payment by the tenant will clearly be a relevant factor.[93]

In the case of local authority or housing association tenancies

---

[85] Common Law Procedure Act 1852, s.210; *Doe d. Wyatt* v. *Byron* (1845) 1 C.B. 623. Relief may also be sought by an underlessee under L.P.A. 1925, s.146(4), but only before re-entry: *Rogers* v. *Rice* [1892] 2 Ch. 170; *Belgravia Insurance Co. Ltd.* v. *Meah* [1964] 1 Q.B. 436.

[86] *Tickner* v. *Buzzacott* [1965] Ch. 426.

[87] County Courts Act 1984, s.138(2).

[88] *Ibid.* s.138(5).

[89] *Ibid.* s.138(7), though this does not debar him from seeking an extension under s.138(4) or further relief under s.138(9A): s.138(7), (8); it does, however, debar him from seeking any relief in the High Court: *Di Palma* v. *Victoria Square Property Co.* [1985] 2 All E.R. 676, overruling *Jones* v. *Barnett* [1984] Ch. 500.

[89a] County Courts Act 1984 s.138(9A)–(9C), as inserted by Administration of Justice Act 1985 s.55 and reversing the effect of, but not the decision in, *Di Palma* v. *Victoria Square Properties Co.* [1985] 2 All E.R. 676.

[90] *Wolmer Securities* v. *Corne* [1966] 2 Q.B. 243; and see *post* Chap. 13.

[91] Rent Act 1977, s.2(1), (2).

[92] *Ibid.* s.98(1), Sched. 15, Pt. 1, Case 1. For a detailed consideration of the grounds upon which the court may order possession of a tenancy protected by the Rent Act 1977 see *post*, Chap. 13.

[93] *Dellenty* v. *Pellow* [1951] 2 K.B. 858.

coming within the definition of "secure tenancies" in the Housing Act 1985, the position is similar. Forfeiture of the tenancy will not give the landlord possession but will merely terminate the contract under section 82(3) of the Housing Act 1985. Thereupon a periodic tenancy automatically arises under section 86(1), for periods the same as those for which rent was last payable under the earlier tenancy. In order to recover possession the landlord will then have to terminate the periodic tenancy and claim possession on one of the grounds set out in Schedule 2 of the 1985 Act. Forfeiture proceedings in such cases, therefore, unless coupled with proceedings for possession under the Act on the ground of non-payment of rent, will be fruitless. Although not available to assist with payments of arrears, a rent allowance may be obtainable by the tenant from the local authority to help meet the cost of current rental payments.[94]

(5) *Assistance in Forestalling Forfeiture*

A tenant in receipt of housing benefit will normally receive, as part of that benefit, an allowance for rent. In the case of council tenants, the housing benefit will include a rent rebate which will automatically be set off against the rent payable. Private or housing association tenants get a rent allowance which is normally paid to them monthly or weekly, but can be paid direct to the landlord in some circumstances. These matters are dealt with later in Chapter 18.

Tenants in receipt of supplementary benefit may be able to receive lump-sum payments for rent arrears in exceptional cases, for instance where no housing benefit has already been paid and there is no other way of averting eviction and the break-up of a family. In general, however, lump-sum payments are not given for rent which has been included in the tenant's benefit but not paid over by him to the landlord. When it is learned that a person receiving supplementary benefit has fallen into arrears with his rent, he is seen and advised that he must pay his rent regularly. If he still does not make regular payments, and there are accumulated rent arrears of at least four times the full weekly rent, part of the supplementary benefit, representing charges for amenities (such as heating, hot water lighting and cooking) and an amount representing part of the arrears, may be paid directly to the landlord. However, for this to occur the rent must be in arrears for at least thirteen weeks, and the landlord must have requested direct payment, or the adjudication officer, acting on behalf of the Secretary of State for Health and Social Security, must have

---

[94] See *post*, Chap. 18. Tenants on supplementary benefit receive an element for rent in their benefit payments.

decided that the direct payment is in the overriding interests of the claimant and his family.[95]

The Child Care Act 1980, s.1 gives social service authorities the power to use authorities' money to prevent children from being taken into care.[96] This power may be used to clear rent arrears and to provide rent guarantees.[97]

B. Distress[98]

Distress is an ancient remedy of self-help by which a landlord may enter the premises as soon as rent is due and not paid and take possession of goods to the value of the rent owed. If the tenant does not pay within five days, the goods may be sold. Certain goods are exempt from distress and special provision is made for the goods of third parties. A landlord who does not distrain in person is required to employ a certificated bailiff.[99]

Under the Law of Distress Amendment Act 1908[1] most third parties are able to protect their goods, which are on the tenants' premises, by making a written declaration in a prescribed form to the landlord. Special provisions for the protection of goods subject to hire purchase and conditional sale agreements were also added by the Consumer Credit Act 1974.[2] There are also statutory provisions as to stock and machinery of third parties on agricultural holdings.[3]

Many classes of goods, even if they belong to the tenant, are privileged against distress.[4] For example, things in actual use and perishables may not be taken at all; and tools and implements of trade and certain farm animals may be taken only if there is no other sufficient distress on the premises. Fixtures may not be taken, even though they may be removable as tenants' fixtures,[5] since in law they are land, not chattels.[6] Similarly growing crops could not be distrained at common law, nor could sheaves of corn, which could not be

[95] Supplementary Benefit (Claims and Payments) Regulations, 1981, reg. 15B. See also *Berg* v. *Markhill* (1985) 17 H.L.R. 455, as to the possibility of a landlord obtaining an interlocutory order requiring a tenant to pay his housing benefit towards rent.
[96] See Freeman [1980] J.S.W.L. 84. s.1 of the 1980 Act is not yet in force. The current provision, to the same effect, is the Children and Young Person Act 1963, s.1.
[97] See *R.* v. *Local Commissioner for Administration for the North and East Area of England, ex p. Bradford Metropolitan Borough Council* [1979] Q.B. 287.
[98] See Hill-Smith [1983] Conv. 444.
[99] See generally *Woodfall* paras. 1–0896—1–0901.
[1] s.4A
[2] See *Woodfall*, paras. 1–0860—1–0863. See also *Lawrence Chemical Co Ltd.* v. *Rubenstein* [1982] 1 W.L.R. 284; *Perdana Properties Bhd.* v. *United Orient Leasing Co. Sdn. Bhd.* [1981] 1 W.L.R. 1496.
[3] Agricultural Holdings Act 1986, s.18.
[4] For a detailed analysis see Foa, *Landlord and Tenant*, p. 485; see also Agricultural Holdings Act 1986, ss.16–19. See also *Woodfall*, paras. 1–0843—1–0880.
[5] *Supra*, Chap. 3.
[6] *Provincial Bill Posting Co.* v. *Low Moor Iron Co.* [1909] 2 K.B. 344.

returned to the tenant in the same state as they were taken should he pay the rent owing; both privileges were removed by statute.[7] In the case of agricultural holdings distress must be made within a year of the default.[8] There are general rules as to time of distress; it may not be levied between dusk and dawn, nor on a Sunday.

The landlord may impound the goods, that is secure them for safe custody either on the premises themselves, or elsewhere. If the tenant interferes with them he commits "pound-breach" and becomes liable to an action for treble damages under section 3 of the Distress for Rent Act 1689. If the distress is illegal because, for instance, the tenant in fact owes no rent, or irregular, because the procedure required by law has not been complied with,[9] or excessive,[10] the landlord is liable for wrongful interference with goods.[11] In the case of illegal (but not irregular or excessive) distress, the tenant has two other remedies; he may "rescue," that is re-take his goods, provided they are not yet impounded, or he may "replevy," that is obtain in the county court an order for the return of the goods on his giving security for the rent and costs due, and undertaking to bring an action for wrongful interference against the landlord.

Distress for rent has been described as an archaic remedy which has largely fallen into disuse,[12] and its abolition has been recommended by the Law Commission[13] and by the Committee on Enforcement of Judgment Debts.[14] It is still used occasionally by local authorities who, having been persuaded that eviction is an unsatisfactory way of dealing with rent arrears,[15] for some reason regard distress (which may frequently be irregular as a result of the interests of third parties in many of the tenant's chattels) as an acceptable alternative. There are also some signs that distress is undergoing something of a revival as a remedy for non-payment of rent in commercial leases.

Under the Rent Act 1977, s.147, a distress may not be levied for the rent of a dwelling-house let on a protected tenancy[16] or subject to a statutory tenancy[17] except by leave of the county court. In dealing with applications for leave, the county court has powers to adjourn, stay, suspend or postpone the proceedings.[18] This enables the court to

---

[7] Distress for Rent Acts 1689 and 1737.
[8] Agricultural Holdings Act 1986, s.16.
[9] *e.g.* the goods are sold before the five days (allowed to the tenant to pay the rent owing and recover his goods) have expired.
[10] *i.e.* where more goods are seized than are reasonably necessary to satisfy the rent and costs.
[11] See Torts (Interference with Goods) Act 1977, s.1; Sacks (1978) 41 M.L.R. 713.
[12] See Lord Denning M.R. in *Abingdon R.D.C.* v. *O'Gorman* [1968] 3 All E.R. 79 at p. 92.
[13] Law Com. No. 5.
[14] Cmnd. 3909, paras. 912–932 (1969).
[15] See Department of the Environment Circular No. 83/72.
[16] For an explanation of this term see *post*, Chap. 10. There are similar provisions applying to distress for rent on a dwelling house subject to a protected occupancy or statutory tenancy within the meaning of the Rent (Agriculture) Act 1976, s.8.
[17] *Ibid.* These limitations do not, however, apply to "restricted contracts."
[18] See Rent Act 1977, s.100.

determine such matters as whether the unpaid rent is lawfully due and whether the tenant is ready to pay off the arrears.[19]

C. Actions for Non-payment

An action for arrears of rent may be brought whether the obligation to pay rent is contained in an express covenant under seal, or in an express agreement not under seal, or arises by implication. By virtue of privity of estate, assignees of the reversion and of the lease can sue and be sued respectively on the covenant, as may a surety of the tenant by the original landlord.[20] The action is a normal one for the recovery of a debt,[21] but is subject to section 19 of the Limitation Act 1980, which provides that no action may be brought to recover arrears of rent after the expiration of six years from the date when the rent became due.

As from March 1, 1972, it has been possible to recover arrears of rent by a rent action in the county court.[22] This procedure provides for the recovery of rent from a tenant who is still in occupation. Upon application to the county court a summons for arrears will be issued against the tenant. The hearing will then follow and judgment will be given at that hearing whether the tenant appears or not, unless the tenant files some substantial defence. Once judgment has been entered the tenant can pay into court either in satisfaction or on account of the arrears, in accordance with terms settled by the court. If he fails to comply, the landlord may take enforcement proceedings, such as by asking the court for an attachment of earnings order.

D. Bankruptcy[23] and Liquidation

A limited company tenant winding up or reducing its capital is not relieved of any liability for rent to any landlord, and the landlord may be able to claim rent which may become due to him in the future, where necessary obtaining an injunction to restrain the company from

---

[19] Distress levied under the County Courts Act 1984, s.102, does not require the leave of the court. This procedure enables the landlord to distrain for a limited amount of arrears; see *County Court Practice* notes to s.102.

[20] *Associated Dairies Ltd.* v. *Pierce* (1983) 265 E.G. 127.

[21] A county court has jurisdiction where the claim does not exceed £5,000. Sections 41 and 42 of the County Courts Act 1984 give wide powers to the High Court and County Court respectively to transfer the proceedings to the High Court. These provisions contain no minimum financial limits; either party may apply for the transfer. A claim for rent exceeding £5,000 due in respect of premises to which the Rent Act 1977 applies can be brought in a county court if the tenancy is statutory, but not if it is contractual; *A. J. Smith & Co.* v. *Kirby* [1947] 1 All E.R. 459; *Wolfe* v. *Clarkson* [1950] 2 All E.R. 529.

[22] County Court (New Procedure) Rules 1971, r. 17 (S.I. 1971 No. 2152), now C.C.R. 1981. Ord. 24, Pt. 11.

[23] See also *post*, Chap. 7(IV) g.

distributing its assets and dissolving without making proper pro-vision.[24] In the case of a liquidation a landlord can refuse to accept a surrender of the lease but may instead enter a claim for the whole of the future rent,[25] and have the *assets* of the company impounded to meet this claim,[26] but not its dividends to creditors.[27] If the landlord prefers to treat the lease as determined, he can prove at once for his loss. The liquidator cannot, in such a case, accept proof only of rent actually accrued due, for this might enable him to apply all the assets in paying other creditors large dividends, leaving nothing available for payment of the landlord's future rent. To prevent such injustice the landlord is permitted to prove his *entire* loss.[28] However, in *Re House Property and Investment Co.*[29] the court held that where the lease had been assigned, in the liquidation, to a substantial assignee, the landlord could not demand that a sum be set aside to meet future rent liabilities, although the court could, nevertheless, so decree in appropriate cases. The court is required to approach such an order with caution since, where a valuable lease is assigned for value, the orders would constitute a serious clog on the statutory right of a solvent company to go into liquidation and to dispose of its assets within a reasonable time. The landlord might well finish up with more than the compensation to which he is entitled. A landlord is therefore required to lodge a proof in the winding up for the difference between the value of the lease with and without the benefit of the original lessee's covenant to pay future rent.

The landlord's right to distrain for rent, when the tenant becomes bankrupt, is limited to six months' prior to the adjudication. If any more arrears are due, they must be proved for.[30] Distress for arrears of up to six months may be levied without the leave of the court.[31] If the trustee in bankruptcy remains in possession and does not disclaim liability under the lease, all rent accruing due after the adjudication may be distrained for, again without leave.[32]

When a winding-up order has been made, or a provisional liquidator been appointed, no action or proceeding may be com-menced or continued against the company tenant except by leave of the court, and subject to such terms as the court may impose.[33] The

[24] *Oppenheimer* v. *British Exchange Bank* (1877) 6 Ch.D. 744; *cf. Re Midland Coal, Coke and Iron Co. (Craig's Claim)* [1895] 1 Ch. 267.
[25] *Re New Oriental Bank Corp. (No. 2)* [1895] 1 Ch. 753; *cf. Hardy* v. *Fothergill* (1888) 13 App.Cas. 351.
[26] *Re Haytor Granite Co.* (1865) L.R. 1 Ch. 77.
[27] *Re London & Colonial Co.* (1868) L.R. 5 Eq. 561.
[28] *Re Panther Lead Co.* [1896] 1 Ch. 978.
[29] [1954] Ch. 576.
[30] Insolvency Act 1985, s.180(1).
[31] *Ex p. Till, re Mayhew* (1873) L.R. 16 Eq. 97.
[32] *Ex p. Hale, re Binns* (1875) 1 Ch.D. 285; *cf.* Insolvency Act 1985, s.132(1); it seems distress is not a "legal process" within the meaning of that section, see *Woodfall*, 1–0831.
[33] Companies Act 1985, s.525(2).

court also has power, after the presentation of a winding-up petition, and before the order is made, to stay or restrain any action or proceeding against the company, including distress, upon the application of the company, any creditor or contributory.[34]

Where the tenant company is being wound up by the court or under the court's supervision, any distress levied against the company's property after the commencement of the winding up is void,[35] unless leave has been given.[36] To obtain leave the landlord must show either some special equity,[37] or that the rent ought to be paid as one of the expenses of the winding up.[38]

Leave will not be given to distrain for rent accrued due from the company before the winding-up order. This is provable in the winding-up itself.[39] For rent due before the presentation of the petition—to which the winding-up order has relation back[40]—the landlord must prove, with the other creditors, in the winding up. Where an execution is levied prior to the presentation of a petition for winding up, the sheriff has a right under the Landlord and Tenant Act 1709,[41] on demand, to pay the rent due to the landlord in full.[42]

In *Re Bellaglade*[43] Oliver J. said that the court will not, at the instance of the liquidator, restrain further proceedings under a distress levied before winding-up commenced, but not completed by sale, unless there are special reasons, rendering it inequitable to allow the distress to go on.[44] If the company remains in possession after the winding-up order, for instance, to obtain a better price from an assignee, then the court will normally grant leave to distrain.[45] The mere fact that the liquidator has not endeavoured to surrender the property of which the company is the tenant is not, of itself sufficient ground for giving leave to distrain.[46]

On the tenant's bankruptcy, the trustee in bankruptcy, in whom the lease automatically vests on his appointment,[47] becomes liable unless and until he disclaims the lease, for rent; that liability is personal, although he has a right to be indemnified out of the assets.[48] The trustee in bankruptcy, or liquidator in the case of a corporate tenant,

---

[34] *Ibid.* s.521.
[35] *Ibid.* s.523. This provision does not apply to a voluntary liquidation.
[36] Under s.525(2): see footnote 33, *supra.*
[37] For instance that of a mortgagee.
[38] *Re Exhall Coal Mining Co.* (1864) 33 L.J. Ch. 569.
[39] *Re Progress Assurance Co.* (1870) L.R. 9 Eq. 370.
[40] *Re South Kensington Co-operative Stores* (1881) 17 Ch.D. 161.
[41] s.1.
[42] *Re British Salicylates Ltd.* [1919] 2 Ch. 155.
[43] [1977] 1 All E.R. 319.
[44] See also *Venner's Electrical Cooking & Heating Appliances* v. *Thorpe* [1915] 2 Ch. 404; *Re Herbert Berry Associates* [1977] 1 W.L.R. 617.
[45] *Re A.B.C. Coupler & Engineering Co. (No. 3)* [1970] 1 W.L.R. 702; *Re Downer Enterprises* [1974] 1 W.L.R. 1460.
[46] *Re Oak Pits Colliery Co.* (1882) 21 Ch.D. 322.
[47] Insolvency Act 1985, s.153.
[48] *Titterton* v. *Cooper* (1882) 9 Q.B.D. 473.

may disclaim the property by writing signed by him at any time within 28 days of an application by the landlord enquiring if disclaimer will be made, but the period may be extended by the court. The notice of disclaimer must be served on every person claiming under the tenant as underlessee or mortgagee.[49] Where the act of bankruptcy is the assignment of a lease, and the trustee disclaims, the assignee is liable for rent accrued due before the adjudication in bankruptcy.[50] The trustee or liquidator's obligation to pay rent continues, in all cases, until the date of the notice of disclaimer to the landlord. The landlord can, therefore, claim in bankruptcy for the full rent until disclaimer of the lease, even in those cases where the tenancy has been kept on foot with a view to it being realised as an asset.[51] Where the trustee or liquidator keeps the lease on foot and then subsequently disposes of it to an assignee, the landlord is entitled to claim the full rent due up to assignment.[52] He can then, of course, seek payment subsequent to assignment from the assignee.

VII. TAXATION OF RENTAL INCOME[53]

A. The Charge to Tax under Schedule A

Section 67(1) of the Income and Corporation Taxes Act 1970, charges income tax under Schedule A on the "annual profits or gains" to which "a person becomes entitled" in respect of, *inter alia*, rents under leases of land. The fact that the section taxes "annual profits or gains" means that the charge relates solely to receipts of an income, rather than a capital nature. Therefore, while pure rental income falls within this definition, premiums, which represent capitalised rental income, do not, and are dealt with under special provisions.[54] The word "entitled" indicates that the charge to tax arises on rental income which the landlord ought to receive, irrespective of whether he actually receives it. However, amounts receivable but not actually received may be taken out of account provided that the taxpayer can satisfy one of two conditions.[55] These are either that the non-receipt is

---

[49] Insolvency Act 1985, ss.91(1),(4),(5), 161(1)(4)(5)(6).

[50] *Stein* v. *Pope* [1902] 1 K.B. 595.

[51] *Re H.H. Realisations Ltd.* (1975) 31 P. & C.R. 249.

[52] *Ibid.* It is disputed whether the landlord can, in such circumstances claim the full rent up to assignment or merely compensation for loss, proved as a debt in the bankruptcy: see *Re Panther Lead Co.* [1896] 1 Ch. 978; *Re House Property & Investment Co.* [1954] Ch. 576.

[53] This section is only an outline of the taxation principles applicable to rental income. For a detailed consideration of the rules see: *Butterworth's U.K. Tax Guide*, Chap. 9. *Simon's Taxes* (3rd ed.), Vol. A.4, B.7.

[54] *Infra.*

[55] Income and Corporation Taxes Act 1970, s.87(1).

attributable to default by the tenant and the taxpayer has taken reasonable steps to enforce payment, or that the landlord has waived payment, without consideration, and has done so reasonably in order to avoid hardship.[56] If an amount relieved under this provision is later received, the landlord must within six months inform his Inspector of Taxes in writing of its receipt. The receipt is then related back to the year of entitlement. Lease, in this context, includes an agreement for a lease and any form of tenancy, even a tenancy at will.

B. Rents from Furnished Lettings

The component of rent under a furnished letting attributable to the use of furniture is assessable, not under Schedule A, but Case VI of Schedule D. Section 67(1), para. 4 of the Income and Corporation Taxes Act 1970 provides that the rent itself is also to be charged under Case VI, unless the landlord elects to exclude the provision, in which case the rent will be charged under Schedule A while payment for the use of furniture continues to be charged under Case VI. The election must be made by notice in writing to the Inspector within two years after the end of the chargeable period.[57] The landlord of furnished premises is likely to make the election if the Schedule A provisions with regard to expenditure and losses would be more favourable than those governing Case VI.

Tax under Case VI is charged on the full amount of the rent *received* (not receivable) in the year of assessment.[58] There is no express provision in the Act for deduction of expenses under this provision but it seems clear from the fact that the charge is levied on "profits or gains" that it is limited to the excess of rental payments over such expenses as are necessary to keep the property going. In practice Inspectors often allow the landlord of furnished lettings a deduction for depreciation on furnishings in the form of an annual percentage of about 10 per cent. of the gross rents received.

C. Furnished Holiday Lettings

The Finance Act 1984, section 49 and Schedule 11 imposed special rules for the taxation of income from furnished holiday lettings. Although still taxable under Schedule D Case VI, receipts from such lettings are treated for some purposes as trading income rather than property rental income. The rules apply for income tax for 1982–83 and later years and for corporation tax for the financial year 1982 and

---

[56] This relief is extended to premiums: s.87(2).
[57] Income and Corporation Taxes Act 1970, s.67(2).
[58] *Ibid.*, s.125.

later. There are also some special capital gains tax provisions applying to furnished holiday lettings.[59] These operate as if the "trade" of letting furnished holiday property were carried on throughout the year and the property used only for such purposes, save where the accommodation is neither let commercially nor available to be so let (ignoring periods of reconstruction or repair).[60] The purpose of this rule is to withhold the capital gains relief if there is a period of owner-occupation. Provision is also made for the situation in which, on a taxable disposition and replacement, the house being replaced was eligible for exemption from capital gains tax as an only or main residence.[61] The new rules apply for roll-over relief,[62] to acquisition of new assets on or after April 6, 1982 and, for all other capital gains tax purposes, to disposals on or after that date.

The new rules, especially those dealing with rental income, are designed to bring a measure of certainty to this area, and result in tax being paid in two equal instalments on 1 January and 1 July. The loss relief rules otherwise applicable to trades under Schedule D Case 1 apply,[63] and the income is to be treated as earned income, and expenditure is deductible, as if the letting were a trade. The retirement annuity contract rules apply,[64] capital allowances are available,[65] and relief is given for pre-trading expenditure.[66]

An adapted[67] version of the three years' carry back rule for trading losses in the first three years of trade under the Finance Act 1978, section 30, is also available.

There are stringent conditions to be satisfied before a letting is treated as a furnished holiday letting under these provisions, though if these conditions are not met, the taxpayer may still be able to argue that he is carrying on a trade and to come within Schedule D Case 1.[68] To qualify under the new rules the property must be in the United Kingdom and must be let on a commercial basis with a view to profit. The tenant must be entitled to use the furniture and the property must be available for letting to the general public during a season of not less than 140 days, of which at least 70 days must be actual letting. For a period of at least seven months the property must not normally be in the same occupation for continuous periods exceeding thirty-one

---

[59] "Roll-over" relief: Capital Gains Tax Act 1979, ss.115 and 121; retirement relief: Finance Act 1985, s.69; relief for gifts of business assets: Finance Act 1980, s.79, Capital Gains Tax Act 1979, ss.124, 126; bad debt relief for loans to traders: *ibid.*, s.136.

[60] Finance Act 1984, Sched. 11, para. 4.

[61] *Ibid.* para. 5.

[62] See footnote 59, *supra.*

[63] Income and Corporation Taxes Act 1970, ss.168, 171 and 174; Finance Act 1978, s.30.

[64] *See Simon's Taxes*, Vol. E 7.201.

[65] Finance Act 1971, s.47; Capital Allowances Act 1968, s.47; Finance Act 1985, ss.55, 59 and Sched. 17.

[66] Finance Act 1980, s.39; Finance Act 1982, s.50; Income and Corporation Taxes Act 1970, ss.168, 171 and 174.

[67] Finance Act 1984, Sched. 11, para. 2.

[68] *Griffiths* v. *Pearman* [1983] B.T.C. 68.

days. Where these conditions are fulfilled in relation to one property but not another the landlord may elect to have the properties averaged. So, if the first property is let for 82 days and the second property for 66 days, an average would yield a letting of 74 days for each property, and since this is above the statutory minimum it would be worth the landlord's while to elect for averaging. These conditions must be satisfied by reference to periods of twelve months.[69] If the accommodation was not within the rules in the previous year the twelve months' period runs from the date of the first letting.

D. Deductions and Expenses

Clearly as a manager of premises available to rent, the landlord is likely to incur certain expenditure in the management, maintenance and repair of the property. He may also provide his tenant with services for which he receives an additional payment, and he may be called upon to pay rates, or rent to a superior landlord, the costs of which are not passed on to the sitting tenant. All these items, together with the cost of insurance premiums on the property, are deductible from the receivable rents in order to produce a figure upon which tax will be charged.[70]

However, payments made by a landlord in respect of the premises may only be deducted from rent payable in respect of those premises, and must represent expenditure incurred during the currency of the lease or, in the case of a payment for maintenance or repairs, must be incurred by reason of dilapidation attributable to a period falling within the currency of the lease.[71] From this it will be apparent that difficulties can arise in connection with the deduction of expenditure in respect of deferred repairs to property which has been recently acquired. A purchasing landlord may not deduct expenditure incurred to make good dilapidations referable to a period of previous ownership.[72] This rule is supported on two grounds: first, that such expenditure is not sufficiently related to the earning of the purchaser's rental income from which the deduction is sought; and secondly, that although expenditure on repairs is prima facie of a revenue nature, in such circumstances it would be treated as an outgoing on capital account as an addition to the purchase price of the property.

In relation to the taxation of profits from a trade, taxable under Case 1 of Schedule D, this position has been somewhat modified. In

---

[69] This is the year of assessment for an individual and the accounting period of a company.
[70] Income and Corporation Taxes Act 1970, s.72(1).
[71] *Ibid.* s.72(2).
[72] See *Law Shipping Co. Ltd.* v. *I.R.C.* (1924) 12 T.C. 621. Pre-acquisition expenses are allowed if the acquisition was by a surviving spouse on the death of the other spouse and the expense was incurred by that other: Extra-statutory Concession A21 (1980).

Odeon Associated Cinemas Ltd. v. *Jones*[73] the taxpayer purchased a cinema in 1945 which, owing to war time restrictions on building, had not been kept in repair. Some years later the taxpayer carried out repairs which were outstanding at the time when the cinema was purchased. There was no element of improvement in the repairs and the price paid for the cinema was diminished on their account. The Court of Appeal held that the cost of the repairs was deductible as revenue expenditure, since it was not necessary for the repairs to be carried out *before* the cinema could be used as a profit-earning asset. The assumption that such repairs would always be charged to capital account did not necessarily conform to modern accountancy practice.

The anomaly now, therefore, exists that there is a more extensive right to deduct expenditure in respect of pre-acquisition dilapidation for Schedule D purposes that for Schedule A. The Law Commission recommended, in 1971, that this anomaly be abolished and that the Schedule A provision be made at least as favourable to the landlord as that pertaining to Schedule D.[74] Legislative action is still awaited.

There is an exception to the general principle in the case of a lease at a full rent,[75] when a deduction is allowed for expenditure incurred prior to the start of the lease in what the Act calls "a previous qualifying period," *i.e.* when a previous lease at a full rent with the same landlord was subsisting, or when no lease was subsisting and the landlord was entitled to possession (called a "void period").[76] Thus, where a landlord grants successive leases at a full rent, the allowable expenditure may be carried forward and deducted from the future rent: the right to carry forward expenditure is lost only by a period of owner-occupation or by a letting which is not at a full rent.[77]

E. Pooling of Expenses

In the case of properties let at a full rent (henceforth called "commercial leases") there are provisions which allow expenses to be "pooled" in certain circumstances. A distinction must be drawn, however, between commercial leases under which the tenant is responsible for all or substantially all repairs, and other commercial leases.[78] Full pooling applies only to the latter. In the nature of things, a landlord's expenditure is unlikely, in the case of a tenant's repairing lease, ever to exceed the income from the same property; if,

---

[73] (1971) 48 T.C. 257.
[74] Law Com. No. 43, paras. 31–33.
[75] This does not mean the best obtainable rent, but is defined in the Income and Corporation Taxes Act 1970, s.71(2), to mean a rent sufficient, taking one year with another, to cover the landlord's outgoings.
[76] Income and Corporation Taxes Act 1970, s.72(3)–(7).
[77] There are special rules for furnished holiday lettings: *supra*, Chap. 5(VIII) C.
[78] *Ibid.* s.72(4).

exceptionally, it does, the excess may be deducted from the rental income of the landlord's other rented properties, *i.e.* the pool income. That arrangement is not, however, reciprocal; if the expenditure on the other properties exceeds the available pool income, the excess must be carried forward and cannot be deducted at once from available income from tenants' repairing leases.

Expenditure on commercially let properties in the pool may exceed the pool income, and in that case the excess is normally carried forward in full. The carry-forward is, nevertheless, restricted if a property leaves the pool, either on sale or on its ceasing to be commercially let. Expenditure may only be deducted from pool income if it is lawfully deductible from the income of the particular property on which the expenditure was incurred; and since the owner of the pooled properties cannot, in a subsequent year, deduct the earlier expenditure on a property which has left the pool from any income from that property arising in such subsequent year, he cannot deduct that expenditure *from the pool income* for such subsequent year.

The calculation of this restriction is complicated, but an example may serve to show how it works. Suppose a landlord has two pooled properties, Blackacre, with a rental income of £500, and Whiteacre, with a rental income also of £500. In a particular year his expenditure on them respectively is £1,250 and £250, so there is a pool loss of £500. He sells Blackacre. He is allowed to set the whole of the pool income (£1,000) against expenditure on Blackacre, but the £250 balance on Blackacre is not carried forward.

In this matter, then, it will be seen that the taxpayer is seriously disadvantaged. Expenditure incurred shortly before sale is likely to affect the sale price, and so the amount of any capital gain subject to tax. There is no relief against the tax on that gain in respect of the excess expenditure unrelieved for Schedule A purposes. If the expenditure is not incurred by the vendor, but the dilapidations are afterwards made good by the purchaser, he may not get relief either. The position is, to say the least, somewhat unsatisfactory.[79]

F. Management Expenses

A company which owns tenanted property as an investment bears corporation tax on its annual profits or gains arising in respect of rents, computed under the rules applicable to Schedule A; and, in particular, may deduct the cost of managing the properties. In addition, tax relief is allowed in respect of the cost of managing the company, by way of deduction in computing the profits liable to

---

[79] There are special rules for furnished holiday lettings: *supra*, Chap. 5(VIII) C.

corporation tax.[80] A proportion of directors' fees may be claimed as management expenses, but these will be closely scrutinised.[81] Agents' fees and stamp duty paid on a sale of the properties are not allowable management expenses[82] and, in one case, the taxpayer unsuccessfully claimed to deduct a loss arising when rents were misappropriated by an agent who had been appointed to manage the premises.[83]

G. Sale and Lease Back

A long-established tax avoidance device is the sale and lease-back transaction. This scheme has the advantage that the profit on the sale (ideally to a charity or other exempt person) ranks as a capital receipt, and the rent under the lease is deductible in computing the appropriate charge to income or corporation tax, usually as a trading expense. At one time it was possible to optimise the utility of the device by arranging for a high rent in the early years of the lease. However, section 491 of the Income and Corporation Taxes Act 1970 puts an end to this by limiting the permissible deduction in a sale and lease-back transaction to a "commercial rent,"[84] defined as the rent negotiable in the open market at the time when the lease was created.[85]

A variation of this scheme was utilised by businesses which occupied premises under a long lease at a very old (low) rent, assigning the lease to an institution and taking a sub-lease back for which they would pay rent at a market value. They would thus have received a capital sum and also, since the new rent would be deductible, tax relief on the rent. This practice has now been struck down by section 80 of the Finance Act 1972 which charges tax on a fraction of the capital sum received on the assignment or surrender of the lease. There are, however, three preconditions that must be fulfilled before the section can bite: the original lease must have no more than 50 years to run; the lease-back must be for a term not exceeding 15 years; and the lessee must be entitled to tax relief on the rent he pays under the new lease. The fraction brought into charge is

$$\frac{(16 - n)}{15}$$

where n is the term of the new lease expressed in years.

---

[80] Income and Corporation Taxes Act 1970, s.304.

[81] See *Berry Investments* v. *Attwooll* (1964) 41 T.C. 547.

[82] *Capital & National Trust* v. *Golder* (1949) 31 T.C. 265; *Sun Life Assurance Society* v. *Davidson* (1957) 37 T.C. 330.

[83] *Pyne* v. *Stallard-Penoyre* (1964) 42 T.C. 183.

[84] Income and Corporation Taxes Act 1970; s.491(4).

[85] *Ibid.* s.491(8).

H. Assessment and Collection

Tax under Schedule A is assessed on a current year basis.[86] Thus, tax in the year 1980–81 is levied on the annual profits or gains from rents in the year ended April 5, 1981. Since, however, tax for 1980–81 is due on or before January 1, 1981, and assessments have to be made in advance of this date, the assessment has to be provisional, followed by adjustment when the profits of the year are finally agreed. The provisional assessment is to be made on the basis that all sources of income and all amounts relevant in computing profits or gains are the same as for the last preceding year of assessment.[87] A person who ceases to own property after the beginning of a year for assessment may have this excluded from the provisional assessment of the following year by notifying the Inspector in writing before January 1 in that year. It will not be excluded, however, unless the taxpayer can show that his provisional assessment will be less than it would have been if he had not ceased to possess the property.[88]

If the landlord defaults in paying Schedule A tax, section 70(1) of the Income and Corporation Taxes Act 1970 empowers the Revenue to recover the tax due from the tenants or the landlord's agent. The Collector of Taxes serves a notice on the tenant of the defaulting landlord, requiring him to pay the tax due within a specified time. The amount demanded must not exceed the amount the tenant is liable to pay the landlord as rent in the remaining rental periods. The tenant in receipt of the notice is, in turn, allowed to deduct any sum paid to the Revenue from any subsequent payment he may be required to make to the landlord. The Collector is similarly empowered by subsection (2) to recover any unpaid Schedule A tax charged on a defaulter from any agent who collects rental payments on the landlord's behalf. The agent must pay over any sums in his hand held to the account of the defaulter at the date of the notice, as well as any future sums he receives on behalf of the landlord, until the tax due has been fully paid. The agent incurs a penalty on every failure to comply with these requirements.

I. The Taxation of Premiums as Rent

(1) *What is a Premium?*

Since Schedule A taxes only the annual profits and not the capital gains arising from land, the payment of a premium by a tenant to his

[86] *Ibid.* s.4(1).
[87] *Ibid.* s.69(1).
[88] *Ibid.* s.69(2).

landlord would escape Schedule A even though this resulted in a lower rent and thus a lower income to the taxpayer. To prevent this means of avoidance, sections 80 to 85 of the Income and Corporation Taxes Act 1970, bring certain premiums into charge to income tax as rent, chargeable on the landlord. To the extent that these premiums are brought into charge for income tax purposes, double taxation is avoided by taking them outside the capital gains tax provisions.[89]

For this purpose a premium includes the payment of any like sum of money to the immediate or a superior landlord, or a person connected with either of them.[90] Any sum of money, other than rent, paid on or in connection with the granting of a tenancy is presumed to have been paid by way of premium except in so far as the taxpayer can show some reason for payment other than the grant of the lease.[91] A number of other items are also taxed as if they were premiums. There are[82]:

(i) where the lease *requires* the tenant to carry out work on the premises, the consequent increase in value of the landlord's interest immediately after the commencement of the lease;

(ii) sums payable in lieu of rent, or as consideration for surrender of the lease;

(iii) sums payable by the tenant, otherwise than by way of rent, as consideration for the variation or waiver of any of the terms of the lease.[93]

(2) *Duration of Term*

A premium on a lease for a term exceeding 50 years escapes the charge to tax under Schedule A. However, the definition of a 50 year lease has been statutorily modified.[94] Thus, if a lease of less than 50 years contains an option to extend it for a further period, taking it over the 50 year limit, then account must be taken of the circumstances making it likely that the lease will be so extended. Likewise if a tenant or a person connected with him has the right not to extend the existing lease but to demand a further new lease of the same premises or part of them, the term may be treated as not expiring before the end of the further lease. Both these provisions favour the landlord but, in one case, what may at first sight appear to be a premium that avoids Schedule A, is caught. If any of the terms of the lease (such as an

---

[89] *Supra*, Chap. 3.

[90] "Connected persons" are defined in Income and Corporation Taxes Act 1970, s.533, as extended by the Finance Act 1972, s.81(3), (6); *cf. Elmdene Estates Ltd.* v. *White* [1960] A.C. 528.

[91] Income and Corporation Taxes Act 1970, s.90(2); see Beattie [1963] B.T.R. 245.

[92] *Ibid.* s.80(2)–(4).

[93] See *Banning* v. *Wright* [1972] 1 W.L.R. 972.

[94] Income and Corporation Taxes Act 1970, s.84.

"escalator" clause), or any other circumstances, make it unlikely that the lease will continue beyond a date falling short of the expiry of the term of the lease, the lease shall be treated as if it ended not later than that date, provided that the premium would not have been substantially greater had the lease been expected to run its full term. Thus, a 51 year lease with an option to the landlord to terminate it after 10 years, would be treated as a 10 year lease. The same would apply to a lease which provided that the rent should be doubled every five years. Where an Inspector has reason to believe that a person (other than a solicitor acting for a client) has information relevant to the ascertainment of the duration of the lease, such as an estate agent or surveyor, then he may by notice in writing require that person to disclose the information in his possession.[95]

(3) *The Charge*

If a premium is payable in respect of a lease not exceeding 50 years, it is treated as payable by way of rent and so falls within Schedule A, unless it is payable to someone other than the landlord, in which event it falls under Schedule D, Case VI as that person's income.[96] The landlord or other person is treated as becoming entitled when the lease is granted.[97]

If this were the limit of the rule, a sharp financial distinction would be drawn between a 49 year lease and a 51 year lease. To provide for this, the taxable element is the whole premium less two per cent. thereof for each year of the lease other than the first. A premium for a 21 year lease is thus taxable as to 60 per cent., and one for a seven year lease as to 88 per cent. The object of this is to provide a tapering relief, thus avoiding too sharp a contrast between a 49 and a 51 year lease.

It would be rather draconian to tax a landlord on an entire premium in a single year, since a substantial sum, which is really attributable to the number of years the lease is expected to run, is being treated as the income of one year and taxed at high rates. Schedule 3 of the Income and Corporation Taxes Act 1970, therefore, entitles an individual (not a company) to a complicated form of relief known as "top slicing," the object of which is to spread the amount of the premium chargeable to tax (*i.e.* the premium as discounted by two per cent. for each year of the lease, other than the first) over the period of the lease. In this way the landlord is taxed in each year of the duration of the lease on one year's proportion of the chargeable sum, on the assumption that it forms the top slice of his income. That amount is then multiplied by the number of years over which the sum has been

---

[95] *Ibid.* s.84(3A).
[96] *Ibid.* s.80(1), (5).
[97] It is not clear how this provision bites in the case of agreements for leases at a premium.

spread to produce the amount the landlord must pay in tax in the year of assessment. This is not the same as deeming the premium to be spread over the duration of the lease, since that would permit the landlord to pay year by year at the rates then in force, and to defer the payment of tax due in respect of money he has already received.

There is one case in which the tax may be paid by instalments and that is where the premium itself is payable by instalments. In these circumstances the landlord may, if he satisfies the Revenue that he would otherwise suffer undue hardship, have each instalment treated as rent as it accrues.[98] However, instalments may only be spread over a maximum of eight years or the duration of the lease, if shorter, and if this option is exercised, there can be no discounting of the lease in accordance with the two per cent. per year principle.

(4) *Relief for Sub-Lessor*

The position of the tenant who has paid such a premium, and who may wish to recover some or all of it from his sub-tenant, is affected by section 83 of the Income and Corporation Taxes Act 1970. He is treated for income tax purposes as if he were paying in each year an additional sum by way of rent equal to the sum charged on his landlord by way of premium, spread over the term of the lease. If he therefore grants a sub-lease, that "rent" is deductible from the rent received by him, for the purposes of his own liability to tax under Schedule A.

(5) *Assignment of Lease granted at an Undervalue*

Section 81 of the Income and Corporation Taxes Act deals with leases not exceeding 50 years which have been granted at an undervalue. The point of this section can only be understood if it is appreciated that the normal Schedule A charge on premiums arises on the *grant* of a lease but not on its *assignment*. It would therefore be a simple matter for a landlord, wishing to grant a lease to his tenant at a premium of £1,000, to avoid tax by granting the lease to a collaborator at a small premium of £100, on the understanding that the collaborator would then assign the lease to the intended tenant at a premium of £900. The remedy imposed by section 81 is to provide that where a premium obtained on the grant of a lease is less than the premium obtainable on a transaction at arm's length, "the amount foregone" may be recovered on subsequent assignments of the lease. Each assignor is chargeable under Case VI of Schedule D on a

---

[98] Income and Corporation Taxes Act 1970, s.80(6).

notional premium equal to the difference between the consideration he paid and the consideration he received, until the amount foregone is fully recouped. The notional premiums may be reduced in accordance with the two per cent. per year discounting formula, and each assignor is entitled to top-slicing relief.

(6) *Sale with Right of Reconveyance*

A landlord might suppose that he could exact the equivalent of a premium by the device of conveying his entire interest to the purchaser and reserving to himself, in the deed of conveyance, transfer or assignment, a right to reacquire the property at some future date. So, instead of giving his tenant a seven year lease at a premium of £5,000, the landlord could convey his entire fee simple estate to the "tenant" for £8,000 and reserve a right to buy it back from him for £3,000 after seven years. However, section 82 of the Income and Corporation Taxes Act 1970 is framed to apply when the terms subject to which an estate or interest is sold provide that it shall or may be required to be reconveyed to the grantor or to a person connected with him. The amount by which the sale price exceeds the repurchase price is charged *to the vendor* under Schedule D, Case VI. The amount is charged, not at the time of repurchase, but at the time of the original sale.

Should the terms of the sale provide that the purchaser is to lease the property back to the vendor, rather than reconvey it, a notional premium may arise. If the lease is granted and begins to run within one month of the sale—a provision designed to exempt the normal commercial sale and lease-back transaction—then no tax liability arises on the notional premium. If, however, the lease is later, then the lease-back is treated as a reconveyance of the property at a price equivalent to the sum of the amount of the premium (if any) for the lease-back, and the value at the date of the sale of the right to receive a conveyance of the reversion immediately after the lease begins to run. Therefore, the notional premium charged to tax is the original sale price less the value of the reversion on the lease and any premium paid on the lease-back.[99]

[99] *Ibid.* s.82(3).

Chapter 6

REPAIR AND MAINTENANCE OF THE TENANTED PROPERTY

I. Express and Implied Provisions . . 217
II. Construction of Express Covenants . 219
   A. To Keep in Repair 219
   B. To Leave in Repair 219
   C. To Put in Repair 220
   D. Good, Habitable or Tenantable
      Repair 220
   E. Covenants to Paint 223
   F. Repairing Buildings Erected
      During the Term 224
   G. Exception of Fair Wear and
      Tear 224
   H. Repair, Improvement and Re-
      newal 226
   I. Liability to Repair in Case of
      Fire 233
   J. Landlord's Express Covenants
      234
III. Landlord's Implied Obligations as to
   Repair or Condition 238
   A. Condition of the Housing Stock
      238
   B. Fitness for Habitation 239
   C. Duty to Repair Structure . . . 243
   D. Duty of Care to Ensure Safe
      Premises 248

IV. Enforcement of Landlord's Repairing
   Obligations 250
   A. Damages for Breach of Coven-
      ant 250
   B. Specific Performance 253
   C. Declaration 253
   D. Set-off against Rent 254
   E. Settlement of Action and Un-
      dertaking 257
   F. Negligence Action 257
   G. Appointment of Receiver . . 258
   H. Complaint to the Local Au-
      thority 259
V. The Tenant's Implied Obligations . 280
   A. Waste 280
   B. Tenant-like User 282
VI. Enforcement of Tenant's Repairing
   Obligations 283
   A. Exercise of Right of Entry to
      Repair 283
   B. Action for Damages 286
   C. Forfeiture 291
   D. Specific Performance 293
   E. Remedies for Waste 293
   F. Liability of Former Tenants . 294
VII. Remedies in Respect of Fixtures . 295

I. Express and Implied Provisions

Leases of buildings usually contain a covenant by the tenant to repair and *keep* the tenanted property in repair during the term, and also a distinct covenant to repair defects within a specified time (usually three months) after written notice of disrepair has been served on the tenant. The latter covenant is generally coupled with a covenant by the tenant to permit the landlord and his agents to enter and view the state of the premises at all reasonable times during the currency of the term.

Repairing covenants depend largely on the length of the lease and the type of premises demised. In their own financial interests landlords have, in the past, endeavoured to make tenants of terms as short as three years, even of dwelling-houses, responsible for inside

217

and outside repairs. As will be explained later in this chapter,[1] in this respect at least Parliament has intervened in the case of residential tenancies for less than seven years,[2] and for all tenancies of seven years or more there are certain checks on the landlord's right of action should the tenant break his covenant to repair.

The extent of a tenant's liability depends upon a number of variable factors. Weekly and monthly tenants will generally only agree to keep the premises "in a tenant-like manner."[3] This involves turning off the water during prolonged absences, cleaning windows, mending fuses, unstopping drains and sinks, attending to jammed locks and so on. It requires the tenant to attend to those everyday jobs about the premises which a reasonable occupier would normally do. It goes without saying that he must not wilfully damage the property.[4]

Tenants of residential property with seven-year leases will usually agree to repair the interior, and also to redecorate in the fifth year. Most business tenants, and residential tenants for more than seven years, will generally agree to keep both the inside and outside in good, or tenantable, or reasonable repair "fair wear and tear excepted." They will also generally agree to deliver up the premises at the end of the term in that state. In addition to inside painting, they will agree to attend to the outside painting every three years.

If a lease or tenancy agreement is silent on the question of repairs, then the obligations of the tenant to repair are founded entirely in the common law. Under the common law, the tenant has an implied duty not to commit waste, and is under an implied obligation to use the premises in a tenant-like manner. Where a landlord is under any express or statutorily implied obligation to repair, the tenant is under a duty to allow the landlord to enter and inspect the premises.[5] It is a condition of a protected tenancy under the Rent Act 1977 that the tenant must afford his landlord access and all reasonable facilities for carrying out repairs which the landlord is entitled to execute[6]; this is also a condition of a statutory tenancy.[7]

---

[1] See *post* (III) B, C .

[2] Unless the tenancy is granted *to* an educational institution, local authority, housing association or the Crown: Housing Act 1985, ss.14(4), (5).

[3] *Warren* v. *Keen* [1954] 1 Q.B. 15.

[4] *Ibid. per* Denning L.J. at p. 20.

[5] *Mint* v. *Good* [1951] 1 K.B. 517; *Saner* v. *Bilton* (1878) 7 Ch.D. 815; *Granada Theatres* v. *Freehold Investment (Leytonstone)* [1959] 1 W.L.R. 570; *McGreal* v. *Wake* (1984) 269 E.G. 1254; *Regional Properties Ltd.* v. *City of London Real Property Co. Ltd.* (1980) 257 E.G. 65, *per* Oliver J. at p. 66.

[6] Rent Act 1977, s.148.

[7] *Ibid.* s.3(2). See *post*, Chap. 10.

II. CONSTRUCTION OF EXPRESS COVENANTS

A. To Keep in Repair

A tenant who has covenanted to keep the demised premises in repair during the term will commit a breach if the premises are allowed to fall out of repair at any time during the continuance of the tenancy.[8] So, this covenant actually imposes quite onerous obligations on the tenant. He can hardly keep the premises in repair if they are in a state of disrepair at the commencement of the term. A tenant who has agreed to keep premises in repair must therefore put them into repair when the tenancy begins.[9] This covenant is usually linked with another to the effect that the tenant will leave the premises in repair at the end of the term. In fact such precise drafting is usually superfluous verbiage, for the simple covenant to keep in repair binds the tenant to leave the premises in repair when he yields up possession.

B. To Leave in Repair

An express covenant by the tenant to leave the premises in repair at the end of the term means that the tenant must put them into repair before he leaves, regardless of their prior state. In short leases this is often the only express covenant to repair given by the tenant and, in such cases, no liability can arise until the end of the tenancy. As has been observed, it is unnecessary to couple this covenant with an express covenant to keep in repair since the latter embraces the former. There is, however, one situation in which the presence of both covenants may be advantageous to the landlord. The existence of both covenants may give the landlord two independent causes of action against a recalcitrant tenant. A previous judgment in an action for failure to keep in repair does not estop the landlord from bringing an action at the end of the term upon the covenant to leave the premises in repair, although it may affect the amount of damages.[10] In the absence of a release, a tenant remains liable to his landlord in respect of a covenant to repair notwithstanding that the tenant's interest has been assigned to another.[11]

---

[8] *Luxmore* v. *Robson* (1818) 1 B. & A. 584.
[9] *Proudfoot* v. *Hart* (1890) 25 Q.B.D. 42. Tenants may, instead of covenanting to repair, agree to contribute towards the cost of repairs carried out by the landlord. A covenant on the part of a tenant to pay contributions towards the maintenance of the premises may also contain an implied term that the contribution should be fair and reasonable: *Finchbourne Ltd.* v. *Rodrigues* [1976] 3 All E.R. 581; *cf. Concorde Graphics Ltd.* v. *Andromeda Investments S.A.* (1982) 265 E.G. 386.
[10] *Ebbetts* v. *Conquest* (1900) 82 L.T. 560.
[11] *Thames Manufacturing Co.* v. *Perrotts* (1985) 49 P. & C.R. 1.

C. To Put in Repair

Where a tenant takes premises in a serious state of disrepair at the start of the term, he may covenant to put them in repair at the beginning of the lease. This additional expense incurred by the tenant will frequently be reflected in the rent negotiated by the parties. A covenant "forthwith" to put premises in repair must receive a reasonable construction, and is not limited to any specific time. It is a question of fact, to be decided upon the evidence of each case, whether the tenant has done what he reasonably ought in performance of it. "There is no doubt that the word 'forthwith' means with all reasonable celerity, and not necessarily immediately."[12] A tenant who covenants to put premises in repair usually agrees also to a specific state of repair, *e.g.* good, habitable or tenantable repair.

D. Good, Habitable or Tenantable Repair

Usually the word "repair" in a covenant will be qualified by some such expression as "good," "habitable" or "tenantable." Lord Esher in *Proudfoot* v. *Hart*[13] seemed to suggest that these expressions mean much the same thing and, in *Calthorpe* v. *McOscar*[14] Scrutton L.J. saw no difference in meaning between "repair," "repair reasonably and properly," "keep in good repair," "sufficient repair" or "tenantable repair." Such factors as the length of the term and other circumstances of the lease may affect the construction of words used in a particular covenant, so that a definition of the expression "tenantable" or "habitable repair" laid down in one case is not necessarily to be imputed to every other case where the same or similar words are used. In *Firstcross Ltd.* v. *Teasdale*[15] McNeill J. held that a covenant by a tenant in a lease of furnished premises "to keep the flat . . . in good and tenantable condition throughout the said term," where the letting was for a period of three months or less, involved the tenant in the obligation only to use the premises in a "husband-like or tenant-like manner," and did not impose a general obligation of repair. Had the landlord wished to impose general repairing obligations, then the word "repair" would need to be used, as in the phrase "good habitable or tenantable repair." Unless some special or unusual words or expression is to be found in an express covenant, the general standard of repair required by such words as "habitable repair," "tenantable repair," "sufficient repair" *etc.* will be, by and large, the same.

---

[12] *Burgess* v. *Boetefeur* (1844) 7 Man. & G. 481 at p. 494; *Roberts* v. *Brett* (1865) 11 H.L.C. 337 at p. 355.
[13] (1890) 25 Q.B.D. 42 at p. 51.
[14] [1924] 1 K.B. 716 at p. 729.
[15] (1983) 265 E.G. 305.

This contrasts sharply with the use of similar words in statutory provisions. A covenant by the tenant to keep the premises in good and tenantable repair imposes a higher standard of repair than that imposed on a landlord by section 8 of the Landlord and Tenant Act 1985 to keep a house let at a low rent[16] fit for human habitation. In *Jones* v. *Green*[17] the tenant had given such an express covenant but the house also fell within the forerunner of section 8,[18] so that the landlord was not responsible for the whole of the repairs which partially fell to the lot of the tenant within the terms of his express covenant.

What, then, is the standard of repair under these express covenants? In *Proudfoot* v. *Hart*,[19] a case of a three years' tenancy, Lord Esher M.R. defined "good tenantable repair" as being:

"... such repair as, having regard to the age, character and locality of the house, would make it reasonably fit for the occupation of a reasonably-minded tenant of the class who would be likely to take it. The age of the house must be taken into account, because nobody could reasonably expect that a house 200 years old should be in the same condition of repair as a house lately built; the character of the house must be taken into account, because the same class of repair as would be necessary to a palace would be wholly unnecessary to a cottage; and the locality of the house must be taken into account, because the state of repair necessary for a house in Grosvenor Square would be wholly different from the state of repair necessary for a house in Spitalfields. The house need not be put into the same condition as when the tenant took it; it need not be put into perfect repair ... I agree that a tenant is not bound to re-paper simply because the old paper has become worn out, but I do not agree with the view that under a covenant to keep a house in tenantable repair the tenant can never be required to put up a new paper. Take a house in Grosvenor Square; if when the tenancy ends the paper on the walls is merely worse than when the tenant went in, I think the mere fact of it being in a worse condition does not impose upon the tenant any obligation to re-paper under the covenant, if it is in such a condition that a reasonably-minded tenant of the class who takes houses in Grosvenor Square would not think the house unfit for his occupation. But suppose the damp had caused the paper to peel off the walls and it is lying on the floor, so that such a tenant would think it a disgrace. I should say, then, that the tenant was bound, under his covenant to leave the premises in

---

[16] See *post*.
[17] [1925] 1 K.B. 659.
[18] Housing Act 1935, s.2; Increase of Rent and Mortgage Interest (Restrictions) Act 1920, s.2(1)(*d*)(ii); Housing Act 1957, s.6.
[19] (1890) 25 Q.B.D. 42 at pp. 52–54.

tenantable repair, to put up a new paper. He need not put up a paper of a similar kind—which I take to mean equal value to the paper which was on the walls when the tenancy began. He need not put up a paper of a richer character than would satisfy a reasonable man within the definition."

However, the lease in *Proudfoot* v. *Hart* was for three years only, and while the words of Lord Esher M.R. may be accepted as an authoritative definition of what is, in general, meant by "good tenantable repair," caution must be exercised in applying it to a case in which the facts are different. For example, during the period of a longer lease, the character of the neighbourhood may change substantially. It may then be a difficult question to decide whether to apply a standard determined by the neighbourhood as it was at the time the lease commenced, or as it is in the changed circumstances prevalent when the dispute arose.

In *Calthorpe* v. *McOscar*[20] it was sought to apply the definition explained in *Proudfoot* v. *Hart* literally to a lessee's obligation in a 95-years' lease to "well and sufficiently repair" the premises. At the beginning of the term the houses were country houses; by the end of the term the district was so built up that the only tenants likely to occupy the houses were tenants taking short leases who would not demand high standards of repair. It was contended that the lessee's obligation was to do only such repairs as would make the premises reasonably fit for the occupation of a tenant of the kind *now* likely to take them. The Court of Appeal held that this was not the true test, and that the defendants were liable for the cost of putting the premises into that state of repair in which they would be found if they had been managed by a reasonably minded owner. Regard was to be had to the age, character and ordinary uses of the premises, or the requirements of the type of tenant likely to take a lease of the property, at the time of the original demise.

It would seem, therefore, that a general covenant to repair must be construed to have reference to the condition of the premises at the time when the covenant *begins* to operate. For this reason, identical covenants in a head lease and a sub-lease made at different times are capable of imposing different liabilities to repair.[21] Nevertheless, while the condition of the premises at the time of the demise provides a useful indication of the standard of repair contemplated by the parties, the covenantor's obligation depends primarily on the words of his covenant. As has already been observed,[22] a covenant to keep and

[20] [1924] 1 K.B. 716.
[21] *Walker* v. *Hatton* (1842) 10 M. & W. 249; *Brew Bros.* v. *Snax (Ross) Ltd.* [1970] 1 Q.B. 612; *Ravenseft Properties Ltd.* v. *Davstone (Holdings) Ltd.* [1979] 1 All E.R. 929.
[22] Chap. 6 (II) A, B. Note that a failure on the part of a landlord to keep the premises watertight in breach of a repairing obligation, may amount to a breach of the implied covenant for quiet enjoyment: *Gordon* v. *Selico* (1985) 275 E.G. 628.

leave in repair requires the tenant first to put the premises in repair if they are out of repair at the time of the demise, since he cannot otherwise keep and deliver them up in repair. The fact that they were out of repair when the covenant was made does not relieve the tenant from his obligation.

E. Covenants to Paint

Leases of business premises, and long leases of houses, usually contain a covenant to paint the outside and inside wood and ironwork in a certain manner at stated times, besides other covenants such as to whitewash ceilings, paper or distemper walls, and carry out such other works of repair and maintenance as the parties may agree. Repairing covenants are often worded with great stringency as to the frequency and materials with which such works are to be carried out. For example, covenants often specify the use of oil-based paints—a material that is, incidentally, no longer commercially available.

Notwithstanding the frequent presence of express covenants to paint, some degree of painting is still included in the mere term "repair" found in general repairing covenants. In *Monk* v. *Noyes*[23] the court held that under a covenant to "substantially repair, uphold and maintain" a house, the tenant was bound to keep up the inside painting. It has been laid down, however, that the painting which a tenant is bound to do under a general repairing covenant is such painting as is necessary for the prevention of decay and not painting for mere ornamentation.[24] In *Crawford* v. *Newton*[25] the Court of Appeal went so far as to hold that a tenant who agreed to keep the inside of the premises in tenantable repair, and then occupied them for 17 years without having papered or painted, was bound to paint and paper only so as to prevent the house from falling into decay.

Perhaps the determining factor is the weight the courts are prepared to attach to words such as "good" or "tenantable," in relation to repair. In *Proudfoot* v. *Hart*[26] the Court of Appeal held that the words "good tenantable repair" do not bind the tenant to do repairs which are merely decorative, yet on the other hand he is bound to re-paper, paint and whitewash ceilings if the condition of the house in those respects is such that it would not be taken by a reasonably minded tenant of the class likely to take the house. It is a question of construction what liability for painting is imposed by a covenant, and a question of fact whether that liability has been satisfied.

[23] (1824) 1 C. & P. 265. Note that a landlord's obligation to effect repairs carries with it an obligation to make good any consequential damage to decorations: *Bradley* v. *Chorley B.C.* (1985) 17 H.L.R. 305. The same principle would presumably operate in the case of a tenant's covenant.
[24] *Proudfoot* v. *Hart* (1890) 25 Q.B.D. 42.
[25] (1886) 36 W.R. 54.
[26] (1890) 25 Q.B.D. 42.

F. Repairing Buildings Erected During the Term

Covenants to repair and leave in repair generally extend to all buildings put up on the property leased during the term.[27] Each case depends, however, on the terms of the particular covenant.[28] Where, in a lease of land with buildings on it, the covenant was to repair "the buildings demised," and to rebuild them if necessary, and to keep the fences in repair, it was held that the tenant was not bound to keep in repair additional buildings erected by the tenant on other parts of the land.[29] Where the covenant to keep in repair is limited by its terms to buildings on the site at the time of the demise, the fact that a covenant to yield up in good repair is in wider terms does not enlarge the covenant to keep in repair.[30] It has been suggested,[31] however, that where such disparities occur, the terms of the covenant to keep in repair may well affect the construction of the covenant as to yielding up, on the principle of giving a sensible meaning to the lease as a whole.

G. Exception of Fair Wear and Tear

Liability under a repairing covenant is frequently limited by the exception of dilapidations caused by fair or reasonable wear and tear. The effect of this exception, often (but not exclusively) found in short fixed term or periodic tenancies, is to relieve the tenant from liability for disrepair arising both from the normal action of time and weather, and from normal and reasonable use by the tenant for the purpose for which the premises were let.[32] In *Miller* v. *Burt*[33] the covenant to repair contained an exception of fair wear and tear. The court laid down the principle that while the tenant was responsible for repairs necessary to maintain the premises in the same state as when he took them, yet if the elements had a greater effect on the premises, having regard to their character, than if the premises had been sound, the tenant was not bound so to repair as to meet the extra effect of the dilapidations so caused. Reasonable wear and tear does not include destruction by a catastrophe never contemplated by either party, even if it results from reasonable use of the premises. The exception will excuse a tenant from liability for repairs that become necessary as a result of normal

---

[27] *Dowse* v. *Cale* (1690) 2 Vent. 126; *Hudson* v. *Williams* (1878) 39 L.T. 632. Covenants to reinstate, *e.g.* as a result of fire, are probably not covenants to repair: *Re King dec'd* [1962] 1 W.L.R. 632, *per* Buckley J. at p. 645; nor are covenants to lay out insurance monies on re-building: *Farimani* v. *Gates* (1984) 271 E.G. 887.
[28] *Cornish* v. *Cleife* (1864) 3 H. & C. 446.
[29] *Doe d. Worcester School Trustees* v. *Rowlands* (1841) 9 C. & P. 734.
[30] Smith v. Mills (1899) 16 T.L.R. 59.
[31] *Woodfall*, para. 1–1448, fn. 100.
[32] *Terrell* v. *Murray* (1901) 17 T.L.R. 570.
[33] (1918) 63 S.J. 117.

use, but will not protect him against damage from misuse, such as overloading a warehouse floor, causing it to collapse.[34]

In *Gutteridge* v. *Munyard*[35] Tindall C.J. stated the effect of a repairing covenant containing an exception of reasonable use and wear in these words:

> "What the natural operation of time flowing on effects, and all that the elements bring about in diminishing the value, constitute a loss, which, so far as it results from time and nature, falls upon the landlord. But the tenant is to take care that the premises do not suffer more than the operation of time and nature would effect; he is bound by seasonable applications of labour to keep the house as nearly as possible in the same condition as when it was demised."

In *Haskell* v. *Marlow*[36] it was held that to bring dilapidations within an exception of reasonable wear and tear, two things must be shown. First, that the dilapidations for which exemption from liability to repair is claimed were caused by normal human use or by the normal action of the elements. Secondly, that they are reasonable in amount, having regard to the terms of the contract to repair and the other circumstances of the case.[37] Talbot J. said[38]:

> "... it lies on the tenant to show that it comes within the exception. Reasonable wear and tear means the reasonable use of the house by the tenant and the ordinary operation of natural forces. The exception of want of repair due to wear and tear must be construed as limited to what is directly due to wear and tear, reasonable conduct on the part of the tenant being assumed. It does not mean that if there is a defect originally proceeding from reasonable wear and tear the tenant is released from his obligation to keep in good repair and condition everything which it may be possible to trace ultimately to that defect. He is bound to do such repairs as may be required to prevent the consequences flowing originally from wear and tear from producing others which wear and tear would not directly produce."

This statement of principle was expressly affirmed by the House of Lords in *Regis Property Co. Ltd.* v. *Dudley*,[39] where a rent-controlled flat was let to a tenant on a monthly tenancy under an agreement by which the tenant undertook internal repairs, "fair wear and tear

---

[34] *Manchester Bonded Warehouse Co.* v. *Carr* (1880) 5 C.P.D. 507.
[35] (1834) 1 Moo. & R. 334.
[36] [1928] 2 K.B. 45.
[37] On the second point, *cf. Taylor* v. *Webb* [1937] 2 K.B. 283.
[38] *Ibid.* pp. 58–59.
[39] [1959] A.C. 370.

excepted," and the exterior repairs and all interior repairs covered by the fair wear and tear exception, were undertaken by the landlord. Under section 1 of the Rent Act 1957 the rent limit was determined by taking the 1956 gross value of the flat and multiplying it by the "appropriate factor." This multiplier varied in accordance with the extent of the landlord's repairing obligations, and it was therefore necessary to ascertain the extent of the dilapidations affected by the fair wear and tear exception in order to put a figure on the "appropriate factor." The House of Lords held, *inter alia*, that the exception for fair wear and tear in the tenant's repairing covenant did not exempt the tenant from the responsibility for taking steps to avoid further damage deriving from a defect of repair which was itself due, originally, to fair wear and tear. Lord Denning said[40]:

> "I have never understood that in an ordinary house, a fair wear and tear exception reduced the burden of repairs to practically nothing at all. It exempts a tenant from liability for repairs that are decorative and for remedying parts that wear or come adrift in the course of reasonable use, but it does not exempt him from anything else. If further damage is likely to flow from the wear and tear, he must do such repairs as are necessary to stop that further damage. If a slate falls off the roof through wear and tear and in consequence the roof is likely to let through the water, the tenant is not responsible for the slate coming off but he ought to put in another one to prevent further damage."

H. Repair, Improvement and Renewal[41]

The precise extent of the tenant's obligation will depend on the wording of the covenant, but it may be that, as a result of bad design, construction or neglect, a basic part of the building may need replacing. A covenant to repair does not involve a duty to improve the property by the introduction of something different in kind from that which was to be found in the property leased, however beneficial or even necessary that improvement may be by modern standards. In *Pembery* v. *Lamdin*[42] a landlord of old premises not constructed with a dampcourse or with waterproofing for the outside walls was not bound by his repairing covenant to make the place dry by waterproofing the walls. If a defect in design has given rise to dry-rot, the elimination of that existing rot and the replacement of affected timber is an obligation imposed by a covenant to repair, but there is no obligation to undertake the structural alteration which is needed to

---

[40] *Ibid.* p. 410.
[41] See generally: Smith [1979] Conv. 429.
[42] [1940] 2 All E.R. 434. See also *Wainwright* v. *Leeds City Council* (1984) 270 E.G. 1289.

prevent a recurrence of the rot, for that is improvement and not repair.[43]

So, when an old house is let, the tenant, by his repairing covenant, is bound only to keep up the house as an old house, and not give back to the landlord a new one. If an old house built with defective foundations can be saved from demolition only by an operation of underpinning and putting in new foundations, that is an improvement and not the liability of the tenant under a covenant to repair.[44] In order to determine the standard of repair imposed by the covenant, the age and general condition of the premises when demised may be taken into account, but the court is not concerned with matters of detail as to the exact state of repair of the premises at the start of the lease. The question of fact which the court has to decide was expressed by Tindal C.J. in *Gutteridge* v. *Munyard*[45]:

" . . . [Have the lessees] done what was reasonably to be expected of them, looking to the age of the premises, on the one hand, and to the words of the covenant which they have chosen to enter into, on the other?"

However, as Ackner L.J. observed in *Elmcroft Developments Ltd.* v. *Tankersley-Sawyer*[46] in considering a landlord's covenant "to maintain and keep the exterior of the building and the roof, the main walls, timbers and drains thereof in good and tenantable repair and conditon," in a lease of a basement flat suffering from rising damp, "the question [is] one of degree." In this case the flat was in a Victorian building providing high class accommodation in a sought-after and fashionable area of London. By requiring the landlords to insert a damp-proof course in performance of their repairing covenant, the court was not requiring the landlords to provide the tenant with a new or wholly different thing from that demised, nor would it change the nature and character of the flats. It was also regarded as relevant that an old, slate damp course actually existed in the building even though it had been long-since bridged. The principles in the case would be equally applicable to the construction of a tenant's covenant.

Time and weather are nevertheless bound to result in some unavoidable deterioration which could be remedied only by building a new house. This the covenantor is not obliged to do. He must, however, undertake all repairs which are possible to make good and protect against damage caused by time and the elements (subject to

---

[43] *Wates* v. *Rowland* [1952] 2 Q.B. 12.
[44] *Sotheby* v. *Grundy* [1947] 2 All E.R. 761.
[45] (1834) 1 Moo. & Rob. 334 at p. 335.
[46] (1984) 270 E.G. 140 at p. 141 *cf. Gordon* v. *Selico* (1985) 275 E.G. 628.

any exception for fair wear and tear),[47] for his duty is to take care that the premises do not suffer more than is unavoidably brought about by those agencies.

Repair does, however, include renewal of subordinate parts. As Buckley L.J. said in *Lurcott* v. *Wakeley*[48]:

> "Repair is restoration by renewal or replacement of subsidiary parts of a whole. Renewal, as distinguished from repair, is reconstruction of the entirety, meaning by the entirety not necessarily the whole but substantially the whole subject-matter under discussion."

When, during the currency of the lease, the premises become unsafe by reason of some inherent defect in their construction, the covenantor is bound, by a repairing covenant, to make the premises safe if that can be done by renewal or replacement of subsidiary or monetarily trivial parts of the whole. Where the security of the premises can be achieved only by the reconstruction of substantially the whole subject-matter of the covenant, or by making a substantial alteration in the design or structure of the building, he is not obliged to undertake that reconstruction or improvement unless that is within the clear contemplation of the parties when the repairing covenant was agreed upon.[49] It is a question of degree whether the works the covenantor is asked to carry out or to pay for can properly be described as repairs, so as to fall within a covenant to repair, or whether, in the case of a tenant's covenant, it involves giving back to the landlord a wholly different thing from that demised, in which case the work would not fall within a repairing covenant. So, in *Ravenseft Properties Ltd.* v. *Davstone (Holdings) Ltd.*[50] Forbes J. held that the insertion of expansion joints into the concrete cladding of a building did not amount to changing the character of the building so as to take that work out of the ambit of express covenants to repair and pay for the cost of repairs, for the joints formed a trivial part only of the whole building. The cost of inserting them was slight compared to the value of the building.

But, if the cost of the repairs is likely to be high in relation to the cost of re-building the entire premises, and if the defect was known to the landlord, but not the tenant, at the time of letting, and there was no way in which the tenant could know when he leased the building

---

[47] *Supra.*
[48] [1911] 1 K.B. 905 at p. 924.
[49] *Smedley* v. *Chumley & Hawke Ltd.* (1982) 261 E.G. 775.
[50] [1979] 1 All E.R. 929. See also *Elmcroft Developments Ltd.* v. *Tankersley-Sawyer* (1984) 270 E.G. 140.

that it was inherently defective, it is unlikely that the court will regard rectification as falling within a tenant's covenant to repair.[51]

It does not follow that, if the works required to remedy an inherent defect in a building do not amount to repair or renewal of the whole, they are necessarily repair within the meaning of a repairing covenant. Disrepair must relate to the physical condition of the property, not to lack of amenity, and a covenant to repair can only come into operation where there has been damage to that part of the property covered by the covenant. If there has been such damage caused by an inherent defect, and if the only way to deal with that damage is to improve the building, then such works will fall within the repairing covenant, provided they do not amount to a complete renewal. If the only damage caused, however, is to property or parts of the building falling outside the ambit of the repairing covenant (such as interior, where the only obligation is to repair structure) then the remedying of an inherent defect would not fall within the covenent to repair.[52]

In *Lister* v. *Lane*[53] the tenant of a house at least 100 years old covenanted that he would "well, sufficiently and substantially repair, uphold, sustain, maintain, amend and keep" the premises, and yield them up in that condition at the end of the term. The foundation of the house was a timber platform resting on boggy soil. Owing to the timber rotting, the platform sank and one of the walls bulged so badly that the house was condemned and had to be demolished. The Court of Appeal held that the tenant was not liable for the cost of rebuilding the house. Lord Esher M.R. said[54]:

> " . . . if a tenant takes a house which is of such a kind that by its own inherent nature it will in course of time fall into a particular condition, the effects of that result are not within the tenant's covenant to repair. However large the words of the covenant may be, a covenant to repair a house is not a covenant to give a different thing from that which the tenant took when he entered into the covenant. He has to repair that thing which he took—he is not obliged to make a new and different thing, and, moreover, the result of the nature and condition of the house itself, the result of time upon that state of things, is not a breach of the covenant to repair."

However, it was clear in that case that the defect in the construction of the premises was one which could be remedied only by the

---

[51] *Halliard Property Co. Ltd.* v. *Nicholas Clarke Investments Ltd.* (1984) 269 E.G. 1257 (unsupported rear wall of "jerry-built" structure attached to premises collapsed; nothing to indicate wall in imminent danger of collapse, and cost of rebuilding more than one third of cost of rebuilding entire premises).
[52] *Quick* v. *Taff-Ely Borough Council* [1985] 3 All E.R. 321.
[53] [1893] 2 Q.B. 212.
[54] *Ibid.* pp. 216–217.

reconstruction of the entire house. In the words of Lord Esher M.R.[55]: "If it is a timber house, the lessee is not bound to repair it by making a brick or a stone house." This principle was followed in *Torrens* v. *Walker*[56] where the lessor had covenanted to keep "the outside of the premises" demised in good and substantial repair, and the London County Council served a dangerous structure notice in respect of the front and back walls, which constituted almost the entirety of "the outside of the premises." The tenant at once informed the landlord of this notice and required him to repair the walls, but by the time the landlord received this notice, nothing could be done to make the walls safe without rebuilding. It was held that the landlord was not liable for the damage caused to the tenant by the council taking down the walls themselves and leaving the place uninhabitable.

Where, on the other hand, the defect of construction can be remedied without rebuilding the entire structure, the words of Lord Esher M.R. must be read with rather more caution. In *Lurcott* v. *Wakeley*[57] the tenant of a 200 years' old house covenanted that he would substantially repair and keep in thorough repair and good condition the whole of the demised premises and deliver up the same so repaired and kept. Shortly before the end of the lease the ubiquitous London County Council served a dangerous structure notice on the owner and occupiers, requiring them to take down the front external wall to the ground-floor level. The landlord called upon the tenants to comply with this notice, which they failed to do. At the end of the lease the landlord, in compliance with the demolition order, took down the offending wall and rebuit it in accordance with the then current building requirements. The dangerous condition of the old wall was due to decay caused by old age, and the wall could not have been repaired without rebuilding it. Nevertheless, the Court of Appeal held that the tenants were liable for the cost of taking down and rebuilding it. Buckley L.J. observed[58]: "The test is whether the act to be done is one which in substance is the renewal or replacement of defective parts, or the renewal or replacement of substantially the whole." In this case the house, the subject of the covenant, could be put into repair by rebuilding a subsidiary part of it. Fletcher-Moulton L.J. pointed out[59] that the tenant had entered into three separate covenants, to repair and to keep in thorough repair and good condition. The duty to keep the premises in good condition was, apart from the duties to repair and to keep in thorough repair, a wide one involving the replacement of part after part, if necessary, until the

---

[55] *Ibid.* p. 216.
[56] [1906] 2 Ch. 166.
[57] [1911] 1 K.B. 905.
[58] *Ibid.* p. 924.
[59] *Ibid.* pp. 915 *et seq.*

whole was replaced, in order to maintain the building in good condition.

In *Lurcott* v. *Wakeley*[60] the tenants' obligation could be satisfied by replacing the defective part by new construction substantially similar to what was there before. If, however, the tenant is obliged, possibly as a result of local authority intervention, to take down part of the existing structure, but because, for instance, of standards imposed by current building regulations, he cannot rebuild it as it was before, there is no obligation by virtue of a repairing covenant to rebuild something different which will comply with present regulations,[61] although presumably the premises must still be made wind and water tight.

In *Brew Bros.* v. *Snax (Ross)*[62] the landlords leased premises for a period of 14 years on terms that included a covenant by the tenant "during the said term as often as occasion shall require well and substantially to repair uphold support maintain cleanse and keep in repair the demised premises ... " Some 17 months after the start of the lease the flank wall of the premises cracked and tilted towards a neighbour's building, and had to be shored up as it was in a dangerous condition. The condition of the wall was caused by a shift in the foundations which, though adequate when the wall was built, had been affected by seepage of water from certain drains which had been defective for many years, and by the removal of a tree from the pavement opposite the wall, subsequent to the grant of the lease. A scheme of works involving underpinning so as to make the wall safe was devised, costing some £8,000. It was found that, by the date of the lease, a serious subsidence had already occurred and the works, which were subsequently realised to be necessary to make the building safe, were also necessary for that purpose at the date the lease was granted. The cost of a new building on the site, of the same size and general specification would have been about £9,000 to £10,000 and the value of the existing building, if it had been in good repair, would have been between £7,500 and £9,500.

On the question of whether the necessary works did or did not fall within the scope of the repairing covenant, the Court of Appeal, having stated that such a question was one of degree in every case, held by a majority that the correct approach was for the court to conclude, on a fair interpretation of the precise terms of the lease in relation to the state of the property at the date of the lease, whether the work could fairly be called repair or not.[63] In coming to its

---

[60] [1911] 1 K.B. 905.
[61] *Wright* v. *Lawson* (1903) 19 T.L.R. 510.
[62] [1970] 1 Q.B. 612.
[63] In *Smedley* v. *Chumley & Hawke Ltd.* (1982) 261 E.G. 775, the Court of Appeal expressed the view that the test was to compare the premises contemplated by the parties at the date of the lease with the premises as changed by the works actually done. If these two factors were substantially the same, the works are likely to fall within a repairing covenant.

conclusion the court must look at the work required as a whole, rather than considering the component parts of repair of foundations and drains, and the rebuilding of the wall. The majority concluded that when approached on this basis, the works went far beyond what any reasonable person would contemplate by the word "repair" and fell well on the renewal side of the line. Phillimore L.J. clearly had the cost of the works in mind when he stated, as part of the reason for his decision[64]:

> "Suppose some busybody had said to these parties when signing the contract: 'You realise, of course, that it might be necessary within 18 months to spend between £8,000 and £9,000 to render this building safe. If that happened would you both regard that as repair?' I suspect even a landlord (unless utterly unreasonable) would have replied: 'Of course not.' "

Sachs L.J. recounted[65] how a number of varying phrases had been used by judges in an attempt to express the distinction between the end-product of work which constituted repair and that of work which did not (*e.g.* "improvement," "important improvement," "different in kind," "different in character," "different in substance" and so on). He also recounted how another set of phrases had been used in seeking to define the distinctive quality of the fault to be rectified (*e.g.* "inherent nature," "radical defect in the structure," "inherent defect," "inherent vice"). He concluded, however, that it was not much use looking at individual phrases which necessarily dealt only with one of the infinitely variable sets of circumstances that can arise. The correct approach was "to look at the particular building, to look at the state which it is in at the date of the lease, to look at the precise terms of the lease, and then to come to the conclusion as to whether, on a fair interpretation of those terms in relation to that state, the requisite work can fairly be termed repair. However large the covenant is it must not be looked at *in vacuo*."

It may, of course, be that rebuilding is within the contemplation of the covenant by virtue of the special circumstances of the letting. In *Smedley* v. *Chumley & Hawke Ltd.*[66] a landlord of a new building, which was let as a restaurant on terms which required the tenant to open for the public within three months of the date of the lease, covenanted to keep the main walls and roof in good structural repair and condition throughout the term and to make good all defects due to faulty materials or workmanship. Within four years the foundations failed, necessitating extensive rebuilding work. The Court of

[64] *Ibid.* p. 607.
[65] *Ibid.* p. 602.
[66] (1982) 261 E.G. 775.

Appeal held that this fell within the landlord's repairing obligations. Cumming-Bruce L.J. said[67]:

> "It is important to distinguish the extent of the obligations where the lessor has let to the lessee an old house which has gradually deteriorated, through the inevitable effect of the passage of time, from the extent of the obligations imposed in connection with the lease of premises recently constructed.... Secondly, in order to discover whether there is an obligation to do work made necessary in order to correct the effect of defects in design, it is necessary to examine carefully the whole lease and to decide the intention to be collected therefrom, and in this lease the intention was to place upon the landlords an unqualified obligation to keep the walls and roof in good structural condition."

In this case, therefore, it appeared that from the outset, such extensive works lay within the parties' contemplation.[68]

I. Liability to Repair in Case of Fire

It has been remarked earlier in this book that the current emphasis given by the courts to the contractual rather than the tenurial aspect of leases has resulted in the possible application of the contractual doctrine of frustration to leases. In *National Carriers Ltd.* v. *Panalpina (Northern) Ltd.* Lords Hailsham L.C. and Russell of Killowen[69] both appeared to suggest that the doctrine might apply when the premises that are the subject of the demise are totally destroyed.[70] However, in the case of destruction by fire frustration will normally be excluded by virtue of the fact that risk of damage or destruction by fire will be specifically allocated by repairing or insurance covenants, or both. As Lord Wilberforce points out in the *National Carriers* case,[71] the lease cannot be frustrated where the risk concerned was within the mutual contemplation of the parties when the demise was made. The conventional view is that a tenant who covenants to repair the demised premises during the term, must rebuild the premises if burned down by accident, negligence or

[67] *Ibid.* p. 776.
[68] In *Post Office* v. *Aquarium Properties* (1985) 276 E.G. 923, Hoffman J. held, in deciding whether remedial water-proofing works fell within a covenant "to keep in good and substantial repair," that it was legitimate to take into account the commercial relationship between the parties, including the length of the tenant's underlease (22 years) as against that of the landlord's head-lease (125 years), the substantiality of the works, and their probable cost in relation to the annual market rental value and capital value of the building. In the light of these factors, the works in question were not repairs but were structural alterations and improvements.
[69] [1981] A.C. 675 at pp. 690–691, and p. 709 respectively.
[70] *Supra*, Chap. 5.
[71] [1981] A.C. 675 at p. 695.

otherwise,[72] unless he is exonerated from liability by the use of such words as "damage by fire excepted."[73] He continues to be liable for rent notwithstanding the fire,[74] and it has been held to make no difference that the landlord has received insurance money and not laid it out in rebuilding.[75] In *Sturcke* v. *S. W. Edwards*[76] the premises were so badly damaged by fire that they could not be repaired without planning permission. It was held that, notwithstanding the refusal of planning permission, the tenant was still liable for breach of the repairing covenant and the covenant to yield up in repair. Even where the tenant's covenant to repair contains an express exception of damage by fire and tempest, whereby he is relieved of the obligation to rebuild, it seems that this exception casts no obligation on the landlord to rebuild or repair in the event of loss or damage by fire or tempest, and that only an express covenant by the landlord to repair will cast such an obligation on him.[77] A covenant for quiet enjoyment during the term is not sufficient.[78] If the tenant has given a covenant to keep the premises in repair, and also a covenant to insure them for a specific amount against fire, on their being burnt down the tenant's liability on the former covenant is not limited to the amount to be insured under the latter.[79]

Section 86 of the Fires Prevention (Metropolis) Act 1774 provides that no action shall be maintained against any person in whose house, chamber, stable, barn or other building, or on whose estate any fire shall accidentally begin, nor shall any recompense be made by such person for any damage suffered thereby, provided "that no contract or agreement made between landlord and tenant shall be hereby defeated or made void." The section does not, therefore, affect the liability of a tenant to reinstate, in case of fire, under a repairing covenant.

J. Landlord's Express Covenants

A landlord may, of course, agree to do all or part of the repairs during the currency of the lease by an express covenant or promise to that effect. However, in the absence of any such stipulation he is not

---

[72] *Bullock* v. *Dommitt* (1796) 2 Chit. 608; *Earl of Chesterfield* v. *Duke of Bolton* (1738) Com. 627; *Poole* v. *Archer* (1684) Skin. 210; *Clarke* v. *Glasgow Assurance Co.* (1854) 1 Macq. 668.
[73] See *Bennett* v. *Ireland* (1858) E.B. & E. 326.
[74] *Supra*, Chap. 5.
[75] *Leeds* v. *Cheetham* (1827) 1 Sim. 146; *Lofft* v. *Dennis* (1859) 1 E. & E. 474; but see Fires Prevention (Metropolis) Act 1774, s.83, *supra*, Chap. 4, (IV) B.
[76] (1972) 23 P. & C.R. 185.
[77] *Weigall* v. *Waters* (1795) 6 T.R. 488.
[78] *Brown* v. *Quilter* (1764) Amb. 619.
[79] *Digby* v. *Atkinson* (1815) 4 Camp. 275; *cf. Re King* [1963] Ch. 459; *Beacon Carpets* v. *Kirby* (1984) 48 P. & C.R. 445.

usually liable at common law to do any repairs.[80] Statute has, over the years, remedied this and landlords are now under substantial and important implied obligations to repair, which are discussed later in this chapter. Where a landlord does give an express covenant to repair, many of the principles of construction already discussed in relation to tenants' covenants have equal application to those of landlords. However, there are some special factors peculiar to landlords' covenants.

(1) *Requirement of Notice*

Where a landlord covenants to do repairs a condition is implied that the tenant must give notice of want of repair before the landlord's obligation arises.[81] The rule applies equally to the landlord's implied obligations to repair arising under statute.[82] The principle that a landlord's repairing covenant is to be construed as a covenant to repair on notice appears to arise from the fact that without notice from the tenant, the landlord had no means of ascertaining the state of repair. On that basis one might assume that if the landlord has the means of acquiring the requisite knowledge notice is not necessary. This does not, however, seem to be the case, and the rule still applies both where the tenant has agreed that the landlord may enter and inspect,[83] and where the defect existed when the premises were first let.[84] The rule does not apply to a covenant by the lessor to repair a part of the premises retained by him in his own control, such as access routes, stairways, rubbish chutes, etc., in blocks of flats. In this case no notice is required to render the landlord liable.[85]

A landlord will be taken to have had notice of disrepair if, for instance, his employee knows that the premises are showing signs of defects. In *Sheldon* v. *West Bromwich Corporation*[86] a plumber employed by the defendant corporation discovered, while investigating complaints, by the tenant of a council house, of noises in the water pipes, that the cold water tank, some 30 to 40 years old, was discoloured. It was not, however, "weeping." The council did nothing

---

[80] So that, for example, there is no implied obligation on a landlord to maintain a drain, running partly under the premises demised and partly under the landlord's adjoining premises: *Duke of Westminster* v. *Guild* (1984) 48 P. & C.R. 42; *cf. Cockburn* v. *Smith* [1924] 2 K.B. 119.

[81] *O'Brien* v. *Robinson* [1973] A.C. 912; *McGreal* v. *Wake* (1984) 269 E.G. 1254: the landlord's liability arises "when the landlord learns or perhaps is put on inquiry that there is a need for such repairs," *per* Donaldson M.R., so that action taken by the local authority under its powers in the Housing Act 1985 after a tenant's complaint can trigger a landlord's repairing obligations by acting as notice; see Reynolds (1974) 37 M.L.R. 377; Robinson (1976) 39 M.L.R. 43.

[82] See *post.*

[83] *Morgan* v. *Liverpool Corporation* [1927] 2 K.B. 131; *McCarrick* v. *Liverpool Corporation* [1947] A.C. 219.

[84] *Uniproducts (Manchester)* v. *Rose Furnishers* [1956] 1 W.L.R. 45.

[85] *Melles & Co.* v. *Holme* [1918] 2 K.B. 100; *Liverpool City Council* v. *Irwin* [1977] A.C. 239.

[86] (1973) 25 P. & C.R. 360.

by way of repair or replacement. Subsequently the tank burst, damaging the tenant's property. The tenant brought proceedings against the corporation for failure to observe their implied covenant under section 32(1) of the Housing Act 1961 to keep the supply of water in repair. The Court of Appeal held that, in view of the time during which discoloration had existed in this old tank, it had to be repaired or replaced by the corporation as soon as they had notice of the state of discoloration and, possibly, decay in the metal which had been reached at the time of inspection. Notice to the plumber was, for these purposes, notice to the landlord.

Now, however, tenants (and, indeed, third parties) who suffer damage as a result of a landlord's failure to carry out those repairs which he has expressly or impliedly covenanted to do, will have an action in tort against the landlord for breach of the latter's duty of care, even though he has no actual notice of the defect. For by section 4(1) of the Defective Premises Act 1972, where premises are let either under a tenancy which places on the landlord an obligation to the tenant for the maintenance or repair of premises,[87] or under a tenancy which gives the landlord an express or implied right to enter to maintain or repair,[88] then the landlord owes, to all persons (including the tenant) who might reasonably be expected to be affected by defects in the premises, a duty to take reasonable care to see that they and their possessions are reasonably safe from injury or damage caused by such defects. Further, the duty is owed not merely where the landlord knows of the defect (through notification by the tenant or otherwise) but also where he ought to have known of it.[89] This is considerably wider than the "notice" element required for a contractual claim for breach of repairing covenants. The landlord cannot exclude this liability in the tenancy agreement.[90]

(2) *Structural Repairs*

It is quite usual under a lease, especially a lease of a building in multiple occupation, containing covenants for repair, for the landlord to assume responsibility for structural repairs, or external structural repairs, and for the tenant to be responsible for all other repairs. Such covenants are usually made conditional upon the tenant contributing

---

[87] Including statutory obligations to repair: Defective Premises Act 1972 s.4(5).
[88] *Ibid.* s.4(4). A tenant successfully sued his landlord under this sub-section in *Smith* v. *Bradford Metropolitan Council* (1982) 44 P. & C.R. 171; *cf. McDonagh* v. *Kent Area Health Authority* (1984) 134 New L.J. 567.
[89] *Ibid.* s.4(2).
[90] *Ibid.* s.6(3). See further on this Act, *post.* Chap. 9 (III).

towards the cost.[91] A covenant to do structural repairs of a substantial nature places on the landlord an obligation to do any considerable repairs to the structure including the replacement of slates on the roof, and the removal of defective cement rendering, repair of brickwork and replacement of the rendering.[92] A covenant to repair the external parts of the demised premises includes a partition wall,[93] but will not extend to the repair of windows in an ordinary house with the normal amount of windows,[94] although it may be otherwise in the case of a building with walls largely of glass.[95] A covenant to do "outside" repairs has been held to include the mending of broken windows, as being part of the "skin" of the house.[96] Vaisey J. defined "structural repairs" in *Granada Theatres* v. *Freehold Investments (Leytonstone)*[97] as meaning repairs of, or to, a structure. This, in itself, is not especially helpful. In a covenant excepting structural repairs to the foundations, roof, main walls and drains, "structural" was held to mean "substantial."[98] It is arguable that the landlord's covenant for structural repairs does not apply to minor works to the structure, such as repairing cracks, but is confined to matters essential to preserving the structure as such, *e.g.* the stability of the walls or the repairing of the roof. The contrary view, finding some support in the judgment of Vaisey J. mentioned above, is that all repairs are either structural or decorative, and if the repair is of or to those parts of the building which are the structure (*i.e.* walls, roof, foundations, etc.) it is a structural repair, however minor. Advocates of this interpretation are far from numerous.[99]

In leases of houses for less than seven years there are implied certain covenants to repair, *inter alia*, structure, on the part of the landlord. There is some case-law on what is meant by structure in this context, discussed later in this chapter.[99a]

---

[91] For a precedent see George & George: *The Sale of Flats* (5th ed.), p. 345. A clause making the landlord's obligations "subject to the lessees paying the maintenance contribution" does not create a condition precedent absolving the landlord from his obligation in the absence of payment: *Yorkbrook Investments* v. *Batten* (1985) 276 E.G. 493.

[92] *Granada Theatres Ltd.* v. *Freehold Investments (Leytonstone) Ltd.* [1959] Ch. 592.

[93] *Green* v. *Eales* (1841) 2 Q.B. 225.

[94] *Holiday Fellowships Ltd.* v. *Viscount Hereford* [1959] 1 All E.R. 433.

[95] See *Boswell* v. *Crucible Steel Co.* [1925] 1 K.B. 119.

[96] *Ball* v. *Plummer* (1879) 23 S.J. 656.

[97] [1959] 1 W.L.R. 570 (reversed on other points by the Court of Appeal).

[98] *Blundell* v. *Obsdale Ltd.* (1958) 171 E.G. 491.

[99] See *Woodfall*, para. 1–1460; Hill & Redman, p. 245; and see *Pearlman* v. *Keepers and Governors of Harrow School* [1979] Q.B. 56.

[99a] Landlord and Tenant Act 1985, ss.11–16; *infra*.

III. Landlord's Implied Obligations as to Repair or Condition

A. Condition of the Housing Stock

Not only housing property can fall into decay or disrepair. Office and business accommodation can be equally neglected by the landlord and, as a result, provide unsatisfactory premises for the tenant. However, because of its obvious social importance, it is property let for housing purposes that has received the scrutiny of Parliament. Because landlords formerly and frequently imposed unfair repairing burdens on their tenants under rental agreements, and because in many informal tenancy arrangements there was no provision for repairs at all,[1] there has been a gradual increase in the amount of statute law casting repairing obligations on the landlord.

Besides, preservation of the existing housing stock is obviously in the public interest. This interest suffers if repairs are not carried out, since houses then decay and deteriorate. On the other hand, tenants, particularly the poorer tenants who, more and more, occupy the property in the privately rented market, will clearly suffer if their repairing obligations are too onerous and too rigidly enforced. One must also bear in mind that many small private landlords are too poor to carry out major repairs, and enforcement is frequently complicated by a long chain of landlords and tenants, created as a result of subletting, producing consequent confusion as to who is responsible for repairs. The role that the law can play in producing an even balance between these points of view is, therefore, far from clear.

At the time of the 1981 House Condition Survey in England there were 1.1 million unfit houses, compared with an estimated 794,000 when the 1976 survey was undertaken.[2] Unfitness, for this purpose, is judged by reference to the statutory standard in the Housing Act 1985.[3] Nine hundred thousand dwellings lacked one or more basic amenities such as exclusive use of a w.c., fixed bath, wash basin, kitchen sink, or a hot and cold water system. One million dwellings required repairs costing more than £7,000. It was estimated that the total number of dwellings in poor repair was in the region of 2 million. If a threshold of £2,500 is used to indicate disrepair, then numbers of dwellings in poor condition escalate to 4.3 million.

In London the problem is far worse. In 1984 it was found that one in six homes was built over 100 years ago and that 1 in 3 was constructed before the First World War. The total bill for putting London's housing into good repair is estimated at £9.8 billion,

---

[1] Thus throwing upon the tenant the common law duties relating to waste and tenant-like user: see *post* (V)

[2] English House Conditions Survey, 1981, Report of the Social Survey.

[3] See *post*, (B)(2).

increasing at a rate of £210 million per annum. Nearly one in four of London's homes is unfit, lacking in amenities, or in serious disrepair.[4] Outside London, it is estimated that repair costs for a substantial amount of housing in the large conurbations of Birmingham, Sheffield, Leeds, Manchester and Liverpool have already exceeded the 1981 estimates, with properties falling into disrepair faster than existing disrepair can be remedied. Significant numbers of houses in disrepair will be found in the public sector.[5] It is against this background of enormity, both in cost and in levels of disrepair, that the laws imposing extensive repairing obligations on landlords must be viewed.

B. Fitness for Habitation

(1) *The Implied Obligations*

At common law there is generally no implied term that the premises will be suitable for any purpose, whether that be residence, business or agriculture, that the tenant may have in view.[6] So there is no implied undertaking at common law on the letting of an unfurnished house or land that it is reasonably fit for habitation, or that it is physically fit for the purpose for which it is let.[7] However, in a letting of a *furnished* house there is a common law implied obligation that it is fit for habitation at the commencement of the tenancy. If this condition is not fulfilled, the tenant is allowed to repudiate the tenancy agreement forthwith.[8] The tenant does not need to give the landlord an opportunity to carry out repairs before repudiating and, on repudiation, the tenant ceases to be liable for rent or for use and occupation.[8a] The tenant can also recover damages for any loss.[8b] To fulfil the condition it is not enough that the landlord believes the house to be in a fit state for habitation; it must in fact be reasonably habitable.[9] The implied condition will be broken if there are substantial defects in the drainage[10] or if the house is infested with vermin[11], or if there has been

---

[4] *Capital Decay* (2nd ed.), a report by SHAC, 1985.
[5] *Defects in Housing*, a report by the Association of Metropolitan Authorities, Pt. 2 (1984), Pt. 3 (1985).
[6] See the discussion in *Rimmer* v. *Liverpool City Council* [1984] 1 All E.R. 930.
[7] *Lane* v. *Cox* [1897] 1 Q.B. 415; *Cruse* v. *Mount* [1933] Ch. 278; *Bottomley* v. *Bannister* [1932] 1 K.B. 458; *Davies* v. *Foots* [1940] 1 K.B. 116.
[8] *Smith* v. *Marrable* (1843) 11 M. & W. 5.
[8a] *Wilson* v. *Finch Hatton* (1877) 2 Ex.D. 336.
[8b] *Harrison* v. *Malet* (1886) 3 T.L.R. 58.
[9] *Charsley* v. *Jones* (1889) 53 J.P. 280.
[10] *Wilson* v. *Finch Hatton* (1877) 2 Ex.D. 336.
[11] *Campbell* v. *Lord Wenlock* (1866) 4 F. & F. 716 (in this case the tenant failed to establish a sufficiently serious degree of infestation).

recent infectious illness and the house has not been properly disinfected.[11a]

The implied obligation at common law relates only to the sate of the premises at the start of the tenancy. There is no term implied by the common law that they should continue fit for habitation throughout the term.[12] But where lettings are at a low rent statute has intervened and whether the letting be of a furnished or unfurnished house, there is implied by section 8(1) of the Landlord and Tenant Act 1985 an undertaking by the landlord that the house is fit for human habitation at the start of the tenancy and that it will be kept fit throughout the duration of the letting. The undertaking applies to a letting of part only of a house, and any garden, yard or outhouse.[13] A house is regarded as let at a low rent where it is let for human habitation at a rent not exceeding £40 in London or £26 elsewhere, if the letting was made before July 6, 1957. If the contract for letting was made on or after July 6, 1957 the rental limits are £80 in London and £52 elsewhere.[14] Rent for this purpose means the actual contractual rent paid by the tenant to his landlord irrespective of the liability of either party to pay rates.[15] These remarkably low and unamended rent limits have been the subject of critical judicial comment.[16]

The implied undertaking is excluded where the house is let for a term of three years or more, not determinable either by the landlord or the tenant within that time, upon the terms that the *tenant* shall put the property into a condition fit for human habitation.[17] Where the landlord's obligation is implied, he, or any person authorised by him in writing, may, at reasonable times of the day and on giving 24 hours' notice in writing, enter for the purpose of viewing the state and condition of the house.

The effect of this statutorily implied term is to cast on the landlord a duty to execute such repairs as are necessary to keep the premises fit for human habitation throughout the tenancy. If a house is not fit for human habitation, the tenant may leave without paying rent and can sue the landlord for damages for breach of the term.[18] Damages may be recovered for personal injury or loss of property or such other loss as is occasioned by the breach. Since the condition operates only in

---

[11a] *Bird* v. *Lord Greville* (1884) Cab. & Ell. 317; *Collins* v. *Hopkins* [1923] 2 K.B. 617. There is no corresponding undertaking on the part of the intending tenant that he is not suffering from an infectious disease: *Humphreys* v. *Miller* [1917] 2 K.B. 122.

[12] *Sarson* v. *Roberts* [1895] 2 Q.B. 395.

[13] Landlord and Tenant Act 1985, s.8(6).

[14] *Ibid.*, s.8(4).

[15] *Rousou* v. *Photi* [1940] 2 K.B. 379.

[16] *Quick* v. *Taff-Ely Borough Council* [1985] 3 All E.R. 321 at p. 324 *per* Dillon L.J. at p. 324 and Lawton L.J. at pp. 327–328.

[17] Landlord and Tenant Act 1985, s.8(3)(b), (5).

[18] *Walker* v. *Hobbs* (1889) 23 Q.B.D. 458.

contract, *i.e.* between the landlord and tenant, strangers to the contract, such as members of the tenant's family or visitors, cannot rely on it.[19] Liability to such persons may, however, arise under the Defective Premises Act 1972, s.4.[20]

In *McCarrick* v. *Liverpool Corporation*[21] the House of Lords held that notice to the landlord of want of repair was a condition precedent to liability under the forerunner of the Landlord and Tenant Act 1985, s.8(1). The landlord's obligation under this section is, however, restricted to cases where the house is capable of being made fit for human habitation at reasonable expense. In *Buswell* v. *Goodwin*[22] a landlord had purchased property which already had a sitting tenant. Indeed, the tenant introduced his prospective landlord to the assignor of the reversion and was assured, by the prospective landlord, that the property, which was very dilapidated, would be put into good repair and that, in return for his good offices in assisting the landlord to buy the reversion, the tenant would be charged a lower rent. The repairs were not carried out and the local authority made a closing order. The Court of Appeal held that the dilapidated state of the premises did not result from the breach of a contractual duty because the parties had never reached agreement on the rent to be paid and there was, therefore, no concluded bargain between them which could support a contractual duty to keep the premises reasonably fit for human habitation. So far as the statutory duty under the forerunner of section 8(1) was concerned, the court held that this was restricted to cases where the house was capable of being made fit for human habitation at reasonable expense, which, on the evidence, was not possible in that case—a decision that effectively emasculates the section in all but trivial cases.[23]

(2) *Meaning*

The Landlord and Tenant Act 1985, s.10, provides a list of matters to which regard must be had in considering whether a house is unfit for human habitation within the meaning of that Act. Some confusion

---

[19] *Ryall* v. *Kidwell* [1914] 3 K.B. 135.
[20] Outlined earlier in this Chapter and discussed *post*, Chap. 9.
[21] [1947] A.C. 219.
[22] [1971] 1 W.L.R. 92.
[23] The attempt to draw a distinction between a contractual obligation and a statutory one in this case is curious. S.8(1) clearly sees the obligation as one implied into the agreement, and long-standing authority has held the implied obligation to be contractual: see *Ryall* v. *Kidwell* [1914] 3 K.B. 135. The decision is also unfortunate in another respect. If the landlord fails to honour his obligations and allows the premises to fall into such a state of disrepair that a closing order is necessary, the tenant loses his home and his security of tenure under the Rent Act 1977. He may have suffered loss or damage to himself or his possessions. The more serious the neglect, the less likely it is that the repairs can be carried out at reasonable expense and the less likely, therefore, that the landlord will be found to have failed in his statutory duty; see Reynolds (1974) 37 M.L.R. 377.

has surrounded this definition because it operates for two purposes, namely in relation to repair and in relation to the action a local authority can take in respect of an unfit house. In determining whether a house is unfit for human habitation, regard must be had to its condition in respect of the following matters:

1. repair;
2. stability;
3. freedom from damp;
4. natural lighting;
5. ventilation;
6. water supply;
7. drainage and sanitary conveniences;
8. facilities for the preparation and cooking of food and for the disposal of waste water;
9. internal arrangement.

The house is deemed unfit for human habitation within the 1985 Act only if it is so far defective in one or more of the matters listed that it is not reasonably suitable for occupation in that condition. Section 10 contains what is often called the "nine-point standard." It is an exhaustive list rather than a descriptive list of examples, and therefore does not necessarily coincide with other standards of fitness, such as the common law obligation in respect of furnished lettings.[24]

The interpretation of the standard is, in many ways, subjective although it is regarded by the courts as a question of fact. In *Hall* v. *Manchester Corporation*[25] it was decided that whether a house is unfit for human habitation is a question of fact to be determined by reference to the standards of an ordinary reasonable man. Atkin L.J. commented further in *Morgan* v. *Liverpool Corporation*[26]:

> "If the state of repair of a house is such that by ordinary use damage may naturally be caused to the occupier, either in respect of personal injury to life or limb or injury to health, then the house is not in all respects reasonably fit for human habitation."

Atkin L.J.'s views were approved by the House of Lords in *Summers* v. *Salford Corporation*,[27] in which Lord Atkin himself also gave judgment. The plaintiff, an elderly woman of 64 had been for 34

---

[24] *Supra*. The contents of the forerunner of Landlord and Tenant Act 1985, s.10 were considered by the Standards of Fitness Sub-Committee of the Central Housing Advisory Committee, and their report (*Our Older Homes: A Call for Action*) reprinted in the Appendix to the Min. of H. and L.G. Circular No. 69/67. The report discusses the nine point standard and advises on the decision as to whether or not a house is unfit for human habitation within that standard.

[25] (1915) L.J. 84 Ch. 732.

[26] [1927] 2 K.B. 131 at p. 145.

[27] [1943] A.C. 283, *per* Lord Wright at p. 295 and, *per* Lord Romer at p. 299.

years the tenant of a house in Salford at a weekly rent of 10s. It was an old house of two storeys, with two rooms back and front on the ground floor, and two bedrooms back and front on the first floor. In February 1940 one of the sash cords of the top sash in the only window in the front room broke, and the plaintiff gave notice of this to the council. Nothing was done. The damaged sash window eventually collapsed onto the plaintiff's hands when she was cleaning the lower window, causing serious injury. Lord Atkin said[28]:

> "In the present case the breaking of one sash-cord necessarily involved the strong probability that its fellow cord, especially with the extra strain imposed upon it, would also break, with the further certainty of danger to anyone handling the window at the time of the break; and with the further certainty still that until repair that window must either remain permanently closed or permanently open. Either event would prevent that room from being reasonably fit for occupation; and as this room was one of only two bedrooms, it appears to me clear that until repair the whole house would properly be described as unfit for occupation. . . . "

Lord Romer was of opinion that it was "legitimate and proper" to treat the statutory provision as imposing upon the landlord a duty to:

> " . . . keep the house in all respects reasonably ventilated. It equally imposes upon him the duty of seeing that the house does not get too much ventilation or get in such a damp condition by the impossibility of keeping the windows closed when necessary, and that the rooms of the house do not in course of time become too dark for comfort by reason that the windows cannot be cleaned. If the windows in a room cannot be opened or shut or cleaned that room is not, in my opinion, reasonably fit for human habitation. It is even more unfit for human habitation if the occupant of the house can only open or shut or clean the windows at the risk of serious injury to himself. Further, if the room forms a substantial part of the house, it must be held that the house as a whole is not in all respects reasonably fit for human habitation."[29]

C. Duty to Repair Structure

The Landlord and Tenant Act 1985, s.11(1), provides that, in any lease of a dwelling-house to which that section applies there is an implied

[28] *Ibid.* p. 289.
[29] *Ibid.* pp. 297–298.

covenant by the landlord: (i) to keep in repair the structure and exterior of the dwelling-house including drains, gutters and external pipes; and (ii) to keep in repair and proper working order the installations for the supply of water, gas, electricity and sanitation, including basins, sinks, baths and sanitary conveniences, and installations for space and water heating. The covenant implied by virtue of section 11(1) does not require the landlord to carry out repairs for which the tenant is liable by virtue of his duty to use the premises in a tenant-like manner,[30] nor to rebuild or reinstate the premises in case of destruction or damage by fire, tempest, flood or other inevitable accident. He does not have to keep in repair or maintain anything which the tenant is entitled to remove from the house.[31] Any covenant by the tenant to repair shall be of no effect so far as it relates to the listed matters[32] and the parties cannot contract out of the statutory obligations. However, the county court may, with the consent of the parties, exclude or modify the statutory repairing obligations of the landlord if it is considered reasonable to do so.[33]

In order to enable a landlord to carry out his obligation, there is an implied covenant on the part of the tenant that the landlord or an authorised agent may inspect the premises at a reasonable time of the day on giving twenty-four hours' notice in writing.[34] The landlord is not obliged to carry out repairs unless he has actual notice of the need for them.[35] This means that a landlord will frequently not be liable for latent defects. Notice of a defect given to a resident caretaker may be sufficient where, by the appointment of a caretaker, the landlord has given him ostensible authority to receive complaints. This will be so in the absence of any express direction from the landlord to the tenant concerning notice.[36] Notice of disrepair will, however, frequently be imputed by virtue of section 4 of the Defective Premises Act 1972.[37] This places a duty of care on landlords for defects in the state of the premises let where the agreement places an obligation on the landlord to remedy such defects. He has constructive notice of the defect *vis-à-vis* the tenant from the moment when he is in a position to exercise his right of entry to carry out the work.

Most of the matters within section 11(1) are self-evident but there has, recently, been some significant litigation, much of it being brought about by recalcitrant local authority landlords, although the

---

[30] *Ante*, (I)B; *post* (V) B; and see *Wycombe Area Health Authority* v. *Barnett* (1982) 264 E.G. 619.
[31] Landlord and Tenant Act 1985, s.11(2).
[32] *Ibid.* s.11(4).
[33] *Ibid.* s.12(2). Any covenant in the lease whereby the tenant agrees to pay a service charge to reimburse the landlord for his expenditure incurred in maintaining the listed items will be construed, to that extent, as of no effect: *Campden Hill Towers Ltd.* v. *Gardner* [1977] Q.B. 823.
[34] *Ibid.* s.11(6).
[35] *O'Brien* v. *Robinson* [1973] A.C. 912; see also *Sheldon* v. *West Bromwich Corporation* (1973) 25 P. & C.R. 360.
[36] *Daejan Properties Ltd.* v. *Elliott* [1977] L.A.G. Bull 208.
[37] *Supra.*

courts have maintained that local authority landlords owe no higher duties than other landlords in this respect.[38] A path and steps leading to the front of a house have been held to be within the meaning of structure and exterior,[39] but slabs in a back yard are not, as not being a necessary means of access.[40] Generally the statutorily implied covenant does not extend to keeping in repair necessary means of access, including lifts and stairways, in multi-storey flat accommodation[41] but such a covenant will, nevertheless, still frequently be implied at common law.[42] It has also been said that a landlord is in breach of his obligations under section 32 to maintain sanitary conveniences when water closets in flats are in such a condition that they overflow when flushed. The duty placed on the landlord is an absolute one and it is no defence to assert that the cisterns are of bad design.[43] There is no obligation arising under the section, however, to lag pipes, and the landlord is not impliedly obliged to carry out works which are the tenant's responsibility by virtue of his duty to use the premises in a tenant-like manner.[44] The onus of proof that breaches of the obligation exist is on the tenant.[45] In *McGreal* v. *Wake*[46] the Court of Appeal held, however, that the landlord's implied obligation to repair structure carries with it an obligation to make good any consequential damage to decorations, and this is so regardless of whether the tenant is responsible, under the lease, for internal decoration, or whether the landlord has, or has not defaulted on his repairing obligation.[47]

In *Campden Hill Towers Ltd.* v. *Gardner*[48] the Court of Appeal was called upon to decide, *inter alia*, whether the obligation to keep the structure and exterior in repair and the obligation to keep the installations in repair extended to structure and installations which were not part of, or contained in the property actually let (in this case a third floor flat in a block of flats). The Court of Appeal held that in determining which parts of the building came within the obligations it was necessary to treat structure differently from installations.

So far as the obligation to keep the structure and exterior in repair is concerned, the Court of Appeal felt that this was a question of fact and degree but was not limited to physical objects which were part of the flat itself. While the word "dwelling-house" in section 11(1)(*a*) meant

[38] *Wainwright* v. *Leeds City Council* (1984) 270 E.G. 1289; *Quick* v. *Taff-Ely B.C.* [1985] 3 All E.R. 321.

[39] *Brown* v. *Liverpool Corporation* [1969] 3 All E.R. 1345.

[40] *Hopwood* v. *Cannock Chase District Council* [1975] 1 W.L.R. 373; *cf. Smith* v. *Bradford Metropolitan Council* [1983] H.L.R. 86.

[41] *Campden Hill Towers Ltd.* v. *Gardner* [1977] 3 Q.B. 823.

[42] *Liverpool City Council* v. *Irwin* [1977] A.C. 239.

[43] *Ibid.*

[44] *Wycombe Area Health Authority* v. *Barnett* (1982) 264 E.G. 619.

[45] *Foster* v. *Day* (1968) 208 E.G. 495.

[46] (1984) 269 E.G. 1254. *cf. Quick* v. *Taff-Ely B.C.* [1985] 3 All E.R. 321.

[47] *Bradley* v. *Chorley Borough Council* (1985) 17 H.L.R. 305.

[48] [1977] 1 Q.B. 823.

the particular part of the building let to the defendants rather than the whole block of flats as a single building, the obligation imposed on the landlord to keep the structure and exterior in repair included anything which could, in the ordinary way, be regarded as an essential, integral part of the structure or exterior of the flat. This would include the outside walls of the flat, even though they might, technically, have been excluded from the letting.[49] It would also cover the outside of the inner party walls of the flat, the horizontal divisions between the demised flat and the flats above and below it, the structural framework and supporting beams and so on. It did not, however, include any part of the structure of the building as a whole which could not, at any given moment, be taken as affecting the stability or usability of the particular flat demised.

In *Douglas-Scott* v. *Scorgie*[50] the Court of Appeal held that, even though a demise of a top floor flat did not, unless specifically referred to, include a demise of the roof,[51] yet a roof, provided it contained no special features such as a loft or a large void between ceiling and roof that were not part of the premises let, could be regarded as an integral part of the tenant's dwelling and thus subject to the obligation to repair under section 11. Slade L.J. said[52]:

> "I can see no reason in principle why the roof above such a flat [*i.e.* a top floor flat] should not be capable in some circumstances of falling within the scope of [s.11(1)] para. *a*. To take the simplest case by way of example, if the ceiling and roof of a particular top floor dwelling all formed part of one flat, inseparable, structural unit, it would seem to me *prima facie* that in the ordinary use of words, the roof and ceiling would be regarded as part of the structure or exterior of that dwelling, as much as its outside walls, inner party walls and so forth. On the other hand, I do not think one can go so far as to say that the roof, or part of the roof, which lies above *any* so-called top floor flat necessarily will fall within the definition in para. *(a)* of the subsection.... Everything must depend on the particular facts of the case."

It also seems clear that the landlord cannot be required to remedy design inefficiency of the structure. The mere fact, for example, that the premises suffer from severe condensation problems on account of the design and construction of the fabric of the building does not mean that the building is in need of structural repair. Unless the

[49] It would not, however, include an obligation to instal a damp course, since in the normal way, that is going beyond structural repair: *Wainwright* v. *Leeds City Council* (1984) 270 E.G. 1289.
[50] [1984] 1 All E.R. 1086.
[51] Although a duty to take reasonable care of retained parts may be implied, as in *Cockburn* v. *Smith* [1924] 2 K.B. 119.
[52] [1984] 1 All E.R. 1086 at p. 1090.

condensation is caused by actual damage to or disrepair of the structure or exterior of the building, it will not be covered by the implied obligation in section 11(1)(*a*).[53]

The obligation to keep in repair and proper working order "installations in the dwelling house" was given a more restrictive application in the *Campden Hill Towers* case. It was limited to installations which were within the physical confines of the flat and did not extend to installations situated outside the flat. This interpretation can seriously limit a tenant's right to demand that water and heating services be effectively maintained to his flat. For example, in the case of a central heating system fired by a main boiler in the basement of the block, the obligation would cover the radiators, thermostats, valves and piping within the flat, but not the boiler and external piping which was situated outside it.

In such a case, however, as a result of a decision of the House of Lords, the tenant might be able to rely on a very limited obligation imposed on a landlord to maintain structure and installations at common law. In *Liverpool City Council* v. *Irwin*[54] the tenants of council maisonettes on the ninth and tenth floors of a 15–storey tower block of flats claimed damages from the local authority landlords for breach of an implied obligation to repair and maintain the common parts of the building of which the authority had retained control, including lifts, staircases, rubbish chutes and passages. The House of Lords took the view that in relation to such common parts there had to be implied an easement for the tenants and their licensees to use the stairs, a right in the nature of an easement to use the lifts and an easement to use the rubbish chutes. It was also therefore necessary to read into the tenancy agreements such obligations as were required to give the contracts efficacy. Where an essential means of access to units in a building in multiple occupation was retained in the landlord's occupation, then, unless the obligation to maintain that means of access was placed, in a defined manner, on the tenants individually or collectively (*e.g.* by means of covenants to repair or covenants to pay service charges), the nature of the contract and the circumstances called for it to be placed on the landlord. But, the implied obligation is not absolute. The standard of obligation in this case was to do that which was reasonably necessary to keep the means of access in reasonable repair and usability, with the corresponding recognition that the tenants themselves had their responsibilities also. It was therefore reasonable for the landlords to expect the tenants to do what a reasonable set of tenants would do for themselves (*e.g.* taking care not to block rubbish chutes by throwing down unsuitable material).

The decision in *Irwin's* case must be approached with some

---

[53] *Quick* v. *Taff-Ely Borough Council* [1985] 2 All E.R. 321 and *supra,* Chap. 6 (11) H.
[54] [1977] A.C. 239; *cf. Duke of Westminster* v. *Guild* (1984) 48 P. & C.R. 42.

circumspection. It concerned the letting of flats in a high-rise block where the use of communal facilities such as lifts was essential for the use of the flats demised and where the tenancy agreement contained no clear reference to or limit on the duty of repair. The House of Lords did not go so far as to lay down a general implied obligation on landlords to keep the common parts attached to the demised premises in repair. Indeed the Court of Appeal held in *Duke of Westminster* v. *Guild*[55] that a covenant would not be implied at common law requiring the landlord to keep clear and in repair a drain running under his land but serving the adjacent demised premises. *Irwin's* case was distinguished on the ground that there was here a formally executed lease, apparently representing the totality of the agreement between the parties, and there were no special factors, such as the peculiar high-rise structure in multiple occupation in *Irwin's* case, requiring a term to be implied in order to give the arrangement efficacy.

One limitation not operative on the common law implied term, but clearly imposed in relation to the obligation created by section 11 of the Landlord and Tenant Act 1985, relates to the duration of the lease. The covenant contained in section 11 applies only to leases granted after October 24, 1961, for a term of less than seven years.[56] A lease is treated as being for less than seven years if the landlord has an option to determine it in less than seven years.[57] This does not include an option to determine a long lease on the death of the landlord.[58] Where the tenant has an option to renew the lease for a period which, when added to the original period, exceeds seven years, the statutorily implied obligation is excluded.[59]

D. Duty of Care to Ensure Safe Premises

A landlord owes a duty to all persons, including the tenant,[60] who might reasonably be expected to be affected by defects in the state of the premises, to take such care as is reasonable in all the circumstances to see that they are reasonably safe from personal injury or

---

[55] (1984) 48 P. & C.R. 42.
[56] Landlord and Tenant Act 1985, s.13(1).
[57] *Ibid.* s.13(2)(*b*).
[58] *Parker* v. *O'Connor* [1974] 1 W.L.R. 1160. "Lease" includes an agreement for a lease, so that if the tenant has an equitable lease for a period of seven years or more, the implied obligations in s.11 will not apply, even where the formally executed lease refers to a demise of less than seven years: *Brikom Investments Ltd.* v. *Seaford* [1981] 1 W.L.R. 863, unless the landlord had, throughout the term, acknowledged that he was liable for s.11 repairs by, for example, accepting an enhanced rent, in which case he will be estopped from denying his responsibility: *ibid.*
[59] Landlord and Tenant Act 1985, s.13(2)(*c*). The implied obligation does not apply in the case of lettings to certain educational institutions, registered housing associations, local authorities or the Crown: Landlord and Tenant Act 1985, s.14(4), (5).
[60] *Smith* v. *Bradford Metropolitan Council* [1983] H.L.R. 86, *cf. McDonagh* v. *Kent Area Health Authority* (1984) 134 N.L.J. 567.

from damage to their property caused by a relevant defect.[61] This duty arises where premises are let under a tenancy which imposes on the landlord an obligation, whether contractual or statutory, to repair or maintain premises, or where the landlord has an express or implied right to enter the premises for repair or maintenance purposes.[62] The duty applies to all types of lease or tenancy (including tenancies at will and at sufferance, and statutory tenancies under the Rent Act 1977).[63] It also applies where a right of occupation is granted by contract or by statute.[64] Any attempt to restrict or exclude the duty is void.[65] The duty comes into effect when the landlord knows of the relevant defect as a result of being notified by the tenant, or if he ought to have known of it in the circumstances (because, for instance, he had a right of entry and inspection which he has negligently failed to exercise).[66] A "relevant defect" means a defect in the state of the premises arising from, or continuing because of, a breach by the landlord of his repairing obligations. This duty owed under the Defective Premises Act 1972, is additional to any duty owed in law.[67] A landlord may still be liable in nuisance,[68] or as the legal occupier under the Occupiers Liability Act 1957,[69] or, as is explained below, as a negligent designer or builder at common law.

Where the landlord has himself built the dwelling or undertaken any work in connection with its provision (a case most likely to arise with council housing built for renting by the council's direct works department), he is under a duty to see that the work is properly done, with appropriate materials, and so that the dwelling will, as regards the work, be fit for human habitation.[70] This applies both to a new building and to the conversion or enlargement of an existing building, perhaps into flats. It applies whether the landlord does the work himself or employs an outside contractor. The duty is owed to every person acquiring an interest in the dwelling, and extends to dwellings compulsorily acquired by a local authority from a private occupier; any work done by the occupier is to be treated as having been done by the authority.[71] The Court of Appeal has also held that, regardless of

---

[61] Defective Premises Act 1972, s.4.
[62] *Ibid.* s.4(1)–(4).
[63] *Ibid.* s.6(1).
[64] *Ibid.* s.4(6). Rights of occupation given by contract include contractual licences, the right of occupation conferred on spouses under the Matrimonial Homes Act 1983, s.1, and rights of occupation granted under the Mobile Homes Act 1983, s.1.
[65] *Ibid.* s.6(3).
[66] *Ibid.* s.4(2).
[67] *Ibid.* s.6(2).
[68] *Brew Bros.* v. *Snax (Ross) Ltd.* [1970] 1 Q.B. 612.
[69] *Harris* v. *Birkenhead Corporation* [1976] 1 W.L.R. 279.
[70] Defective Premises Act 1972, s.1(1), (4), see Gravells [1979] Conv. 97.
[71] *Ibid.* s.2(7)(*b*). It is specifically provided that any cause of action arising under the Act is deemed to have accrued on the date of completion of the work, or completion of further work, if such be needed to rectify work originally done: *ibid.*, s.1(5); see *Alexander* v. *Mercouris* [1979] 1 W.L.R. 1270; *cf. Rimmer* v. *Liverpool City Council* [1984] 1 All E.R. 930.

statute, a local authority landlord owes, at common law, a duty of care, as designer or builder of premises, to all persons (including the tenant) who might reasonably be expected to be affected by the design or construction of the premises. This duty is to take reasonable care to see that such persons do not suffer injury as a result of faults in the design or construction of the premises, and the fact that the tenant or other person knows of the defect will not exonerate the landlord/builder from liability.[72]

IV. Enforcement of Landlord's Repairing Obligations

A. Damages for Breach of Contract

What if the landlord fails to maintain the lift, or provides furnished accommodation that is damp and uninhabitable, or fails to repair a leaking roof that lets the rain in? The tenant will complain to his landlord. If the landlord fails to take any action to remedy the defect the tenant may, in some circumstances, leave the property and cease to be liable for rent. This drastic step, however, may do more harm to the tenant than to the landlord, especially if the property is residential accommodation, for the tenant may then be left without a home and the landlord be free of a complaining tenant. What other steps can the tenant take? The oldest established remedy is an action by the tenant against his landlord for damages for breach of covenant.[73]

Where the landlord is guilty of a breach of an express or implied covenant to repair, he will not be liable to compensate for any damage suffered by the tenant before he received notice to repair or before he has been put on inquiry as to the want of repair.[74] Prima facie the measure of damages is the difference in value, to the tenant, between the premises in their condition at the time of assessment, and their value if the landlord had fulfilled his repairing obligations on receipt of notice of disrepair,[75] but the prima facie rule must give way to the particular facts of the case. Compensation is payable for the period between the date of notice of disrepair down to the date of assessment of damages. The tenant is also entitled to recover for damage to his

---

[72] *Rimmer* v. *Liverpool City Council* [1984] 1 All E.R. 930.

[73] A tenant's action for damages does not appear to be registrable as a land charge: see *Reagan & Blackburn Ltd.* v. *Rogers* [1985] 2 All E.R. 180, distinguishing *Selim Ltd.* v. *Bickenhall Engineering Ltd.* [1981] 3 All E.R. 210.

[74] *McCarrick* v. *Liverpool Corporation* [1947] A.C. 219; *Uniproducts (Manchester) Ltd.* v. *Rose Furnishers Ltd.* [1956] 1 All E.R. 146; *O'Brien* v. *Robinson* [1973] A.C. 912; *McGreal* v. *Wake* (1984) 269 E.G. 1254, unless the action is one for breach of the duty of care pursuant to the Defective Premises Act 1972, s.4 when implied notice will suffice.

[75] *Hewitt* v. *Rowlands* (1924) L.J. 93 K.B. 1080.

chattels during the same period,[76] and to damages for injury to himself arising from the want of repair.[77]

The Court of Appeal has recently considered the case of the tenant who is forced, by reason of the disrepair, to seek alternative accommodation. In *Calabar Properties Ltd.* v. *Stitcher*[78] the premises became damp and uninhabitable as a consequence of the landlord's failure to repair. The tenant, who had taken a long lease on the property with the intention of living permanently there, was obliged to rent alternative accommodation until the repairs were carried out. The tenant sought damages for diminution in market value, based on the cost of repair, and also for discomfort, ill health and loss of enjoyment. These heads of damage were regarded as unexceptionable. However, the tenant also sought to recover the outgoings on the flat during the period of enforced absence, and the loss of rental value while it was uninhabitable. The Court of Appeal pointed out that there will be cases where diminution of market value may not necessarily provide an adequate measure of damages. The test must be based upon the difference in value *to the tenant*,[79] so that, if the flat was, to the landlord's knowledge, bought for resale or subletting, then the measure of damage would be the loss in market value or the loss in rental value. This would not, however, provide an adequate measure for a tenant who had taken a lease of premises in order to live in them himself. In that case, it was quite proper to take the cost of repairs and decorations (and cleaning up debris etc. after the repairs have been done[80]), without any reduction for betterment.[81] The tenant's claim to outgoings failed but, it seems, had they been claimed, she could have recovered the reasonable costs of alternative accommodation.[82] The subject-matter of leases for the provision of living accommodation (though probably not for other types of land and premises), is so fundamentally important and emotive that a tenant may now also be able to recover for the mental distress and disappointment suffered by himself (though perhaps not by the members of his family[83]) as a result of the landlord's breach. The provision of unsatisfactory living accommodation is likely to involve the tenant and his family in considerable distress and disappointment should their expectations not be fulfilled. That being so, cases in which the courts have awarded damages for emotional distress, disturbance and disappointment as a

---

[76] *Ibid.*

[77] *Porter* v. *Jones* [1942] 2 All E.R. 570.

[78] [1984] 1 W.L.R. 287; see also *Bradley* v. *Chorley Borough Council* (1985) 17 H.L.R. 305.

[79] *McCoy & Co.* v. *Clark* (1982) 13 H.L.R. 89, see also *Taylor* v. *Knowsley Borough Council* (1985) 17 H.L.R. 376.

[80] *McGreal* v. *Wake* (1984) 269 E.G. 1254.

[81] *Harbutt's 'Plasticine' Ltd.* v. *Wayne Tank & Pump Co. Ltd.* [1970] 1 Q.B. 447 at pp. 468, 473 and 476.

[82] *McGreal* v. *Wake* (1984) 269 E.G. 1254; *cf. Green* v. *Eales* (1841) 2 Q.B. 225.

[83] *Woodar Investments Developments Ltd.* v. *Wimpey Construction U.K. Ltd.* [1980] 1 All E.R. 571, *per* Lord Wilberforce at pp. 576–577, *per* Lord Russell at p. 585, *per* Lord Keith at p. 588.

result of a promisor's failure to provide holiday, entertainment, recreational or employment facilities in accordance with his promise, may well be relevant in considering a landlord's liability for serious breaches of his covenants to repair, at least in the case of living accommodation.[84] The type of damage suffered is likely to be the same, save that mental distress is likely to be greater when one's home is seriously out of repair than when one's holiday is spoilt.

In assessing damages for the landlord's breach of covenant, damage due to defects which the landlord is not bound to remedy, except consequent redecoration and cleaning, must be excluded. However, it is irrelevant to take into account whether the execution of the repairs is to the commercial advantage or disadvantage of the landlord.[85] If the landlord does some work, for instance "patching up" a leaking roof, but it is insufficient to effect the repair in accordance with the covenant, then it seems that he will be liable in damages for the sum which would have been necessary to put the premises into the covenanted state of repair.[86]

If the landlord does not carry out the necessary repairs within a reasonable time of receiving notice, the tenant can sue him for damages to compensate for his loss without first incurring the expense of doing the repairs himself,[87] although the tenant carries the burden of proving the breach of covenant and consequent damage.[88] If the tenant has prevented the landlord's builder from gaining access to the property, then he cannot recover damages from the landlord.[89] The matter essentially turns on the reasonableness of the tenant's conduct, although a court would not regard him as acting unreasonably if he continues to use the premises pending or even during the execution of repairs, however much this inconveniences the builder.[90] This is always provided, of course, that the tenant's continued presence in the building does not prevent the repairs from being carried out altogether.[91]

Although the usual contractual remedy for breach of covenant is damages, this will not, from the tenant's point of view, achieve the purpose of the repairing covenant, which is repair of the property. There are, however, other avenues open to the tenant likely to

---

[84] *Diesen* v. *Sampson*, 1971 S.L.T. 49; *Jarvis* v. *Swan's Tours Ltd.* [1973] 1 Q.B. 233; *Jackson* v. *Horizon Holidays Ltd.* [1975] 1 W.L.R. 1468; *Cox* v. *Phillips Industries Ltd.* [1976] 1 W.L.R. 638; *Heywood* v. *Wellers* [1976] Q.B. 446; *Buckley* v. *Lane Herdman & Co.* [1977] C.L.Y. 3143; *McNally* v. *Welltrade International* [1978] 1 R.L.R. 490; *McCall* v. *Abelesz* [1976] 1 All E.R. 727.

[85] *Hewitt* v. *Rowlands* (1924) L.J. 93 K.B. 1080; affirmed *ibid.* p. 1080.

[86] *Granada Theatres Ltd.* v. *Freehold Investments (Leytonstone) Ltd.* [1959] Ch. 592.

[87] *Ibid.* See also the discussion of *Lee–Parker* v. *Izzet* [1971] 1 W.L.R. 1688, *post.*

[88] *Foster* v. *Day* (1968) 208 E.G. 495.

[89] *Granada Theatres Ltd.* v. *Freehold Investments (Leytonstone) Ltd.* [1959] Ch. 592.

[90] *Porter* v. *Jones* [1942] 2 All E.R. 570.

[91] But see the comments on this in *McGreal* v. *Wake* (1984) 269 E.G. 1254, *per* Donaldson M.R. at p. 1257.

produce a more positive effect on the condition of the rented premises.

B. Specific Performance

A far more efficacious remedy, although it is always discretionary, is for the tenant to obtain a mandatory injunction compelling the landlord to carry out the repairs. Originally this was a High Court matter, for the county court had no power to grant such an order save as "ancillary" to a cause of action otherwise within its jurisdiction, such as an action for damages for breach of covenant.[92] However, in *Jeune* v. *Queens Cross Properties Ltd.*[93] it was held that the court did have power to make an order compelling a landlord to do some work under a covenant to repair.

Statutory effect is given to this decision by section 17 of the Landlord and Tenant Act 1985 enabling the court, at its discretion, to order specific performance of the landlord's repairing covenants. This power relates only to covenants to repair "dwellings" and cannot be used to obtain specific performance of repairing covenants in leases of business property, where recourse must be had to the inherent jurisdiction of the High Court, unless the relief is sought as "ancillary" to some other cause of action. The section 17 power is, however, extensive. It applies whether or not the breach relates to the part of the premises let to the tenant. It might, therefore, be used to compel repair of common parts, or a roof, even though these are not let to the tenant under the terms of his lease. It further applies "notwithstanding any equitable rule restricting the scope of [the] remedy [of specific performance], whether on the basis of lack of mutuality or otherwise."[94]

C. Declaration

A declaration, like an injunction, is a discretionary remedy and may be obtained from the county court if coupled with a claim for damages. It may be asked what useful purpose such an order serves. The answer is that there may well be circumstances in which it is to the tenant's advantage to have a clear statement from the court that the landlord is in breach of his repairing obligation. Where a tenant cannot get, or is refused, an injunction, he may seek a declaration

---

[92] See *Kenny* v. *Preen* [1963] 1 Q.B. 499; County Courts Act 1984, s.38.
[93] [1974] Ch. 97. A landlord's obligation to repair is not to be regarded as frustrated by reason of the landlord's insolvency rendering performance financially impossible. The hardship caused to the landlord does not prevent a decree of specific performance being made: *Francis* v. *Cowcliffe* (1976) 33 P. & C.R. 368.
[94] See *Peninsular Maritime* v. *Padseal* (1981) 259 E.G. 860.

from the court that the landlord is in breach of his repairing covenant, and that the tenant is entitled to do the work necessary to put right the disrepair and recover the cost by withholding rent.[95] A tenant who then proceeds to act within the terms of the declaration will not be in breach of his covenant to pay rent by withholding payment from the landlord.[96]

This declaration will not, of course, require the landlord to undertake any of the repairs himself. Thus, if the cost of the repairs is substantial, a declaration may be of little value since the amount of rent the tenant pays and can withhold will probably not meet the cost of repairs for a very long time. Nevertheless, where withholding of rent to pay for repairs is an economic proposition for the tenant, action *after* obtaining an appropriate declaration is probably a safer expedient. Although the common law does permit a tenant to carry out repairs and deduct their cost from future rental payments without the need for a declaration, there are risks inherent in such a course of action.[97]

D. Set-off against Rent[98]

In *Lee-Parker* v. *Izzet*[99] Goff J. held that a tenant is entitled, at common law, on giving the landlord notice of disrepair, to have the work done and to deduct the proper cost of repairs carried out by him within the express or implied repairing covenants from future payments of rent. The tenant will not be liable for rent to the extent of any such proper costs. He will have a defence to an action for non-payment of rent should he be sued on his covenant by the landlord.

Although Goff J. states this proposition of law in emphatic terms, he relies exclusively on authorities of some antiquity.[1] These authorities while clearly relevant, contain only dicta, and there is some authority the other way.[2] *Lee-Parker* v. *Izzet* must therefore be regarded with some circumspection and, in any event, the case is silent as to whether the common law provision can be excluded by contrary words in the lease or tenancy agreement itself. Many local authority tenancy agreements, for instance, contain clauses in the following terms: "The council will not accept responsibility for orders which are given by the tenant direct to statutory undertakings or any

---

[95] *Lee-Parker* v. *Izzet* [1971] 1 W.L.R. 1688; see *post*. See the tenant's proposed course of action in *Brikom Investments Ltd.* v. *Seaford* [1981] 1 W.L.R. 863.
[96] *Ideal Film Co.* v. *Nielsen* [1921] 1 Ch. 575.
[97] See the discussion of *Lee–Parker* v. *Izzet* [1971] 1 W.L.R. 1688, *post*; see also (1972) 36 Conv.(N.S.) 48; *post*, Chap. 7.
[98] See Rank, (1976) 40 Conv.(N.S.) 196; Waite, [1981] Conv. 199; [1983] Conv. 373.
[99] [1971] 1 W.L.R. 1688.
[1] *Taylor* v. *Beal* (1591) Cro.Eliz. (1) 222; *Waters* v. *Weigall* (1795) 2 Anst. 575.
[2] *Weigall* v. *Waters* (1795) 6 T.R. 488; *Taylor* v. *Webb* [1937] 2 K.B. 283.

other bodies or persons, and any charges arising from such orders will be the tenant's liability." The operation of such clauses may not affect the *Lee-Parker* principle in that the liability of the landlord for the cost of the repairs arises by virtue of his implied covenant, not by virtue of him accepting or repudiating a liability incurred by the tenant to an outside contractor.[3] However, it is not settled whether a sufficiently clear and precisely drafted form of words could prevent a tenant from setting-off the cost of repairs against rent.

Even more problematic is the question whether the tenant has any right of set-off against the rent in respect of any *damages* caused by breach of the landlord's repairing covenants. In *Lee-Parker* v. *Izzet*[4] Goff J. seems to suggest that the tenant's common law right to deduct the cost of his doing the landlord's repairs from future rent is a right unconnected with set-off, in the technical sense. Goff J. also held that the nexus between rent due to mortgagees in possession and the cost of repairs that fell outside the landlord's covenants in the lease, was too tenuous to permit a set-off. The case does not, however, actually decide the question of set-off between landlord and tenant, although reservations are expressed about its availability.

Goff J.'s doubts as to whether a set-off is permissible seem to be based on two cases. The first is *Government of Newfoundland* v. *Newfoundland Railway Co.*,[5] where the question arose whether assignees of contractual rights had a set-off against the plaintiffs, who were original parties. Since the parties' cross-claims arose out of the same contract, the House of Lords held that a set-off was permissible, notwithstanding the fact that the defendants were assignees. The other authority that causes difficulty is *Taylor* v. *Webb*.[6] Here du Parcq J. held that the covenants to pay rent and to do repairs are independent, in that an action in respect of one may be maintained in spite of the plaintiff's breach of the other. Thus, a landlord's failure to repair does not discharge a tenant from liability to pay rent. What it does is enable the tenant both to pay future rent by doing the landlord's repairs for him,[7] and to bring a counterclaim for damages,[8] and for specific performance.[9] The need for the claim and counterclaim to be dependent, before set-off is permissible, might prevent it in the situation under discussion.

It is submitted that the fears of Goff J. were ill-founded.[10] The

---

[3] The Housing Act 1985, s.96, empowers the Secretary of State to make regulations permitting secure tenants to carry out works of repair for which the landlord is responsible, recouping the cost from the landlord: *post*, Chap. 16, and Secure Tenancies (Right to Repair Scheme) Regs. 1985, S.I. 1985 No. 1493.
[4] [1971] 1 W.L.R. 1688.
[5] (1888) 13 A.C. 199.
[6] [1937] 2 K.B. 283.
[7] *Lee–Parker* v. *Izzet* [1971] 1 W.L.R. 1688.
[8] *Hart* v. *Rogers* [1916] 1 K.B. 646.
[9] *Jeune* v. *Queen's Cross Properties* [1974] Ch. 97; Landlord and Tenant Act 1985, s.17, *supra*.
[10] See Arden [1979] L.A.G.Bull. 210.

Newfoundland case only requires the cross-claims to arise *out of the same contract.* Clearly the tenant's covenant to pay rent and the landlord's covenant to repair satisfy this requirement. The matter of set-off was not specifically discussed in *Taylor* v. *Webb*[11] at all. Further, under the Rules of the Supreme Court, Orders 15, r. 2 and 18, r. 17, a defendant in any action may set-off or set up by way of counterclaim against the claims of the plaintiff, any right or claim, whether such set-off or counterclaim sounds in damages or not, and such set-off or counterclaim has the same effect as a cross-action. It would therefore seem that mutual set-offs are permissible between landlord and tenant provided that claim and counterclaim arise out of the same contract. The fact that arrears of rent are debt and the set-off is of damages would seem to be immaterial.[12]

In *British Anzani (Felixstowe) Ltd.* v. *International Marine Management (U.K.) Ltd.*[13] Forbes J. accepted that the *Lee-Parker* case contained an accurate (if slightly too wide) statement of the common law right of set-off against rent. He suggested, however, that at common law set-off could only be used if the amount in issue was certain, and not capable of dispute by the landlord. This will generally only be the case if the tenant has already paid the money out on repairs, acknowledged by the landlord, or the sum has been the subject of some prior determination, such as arbitration or a declaration. However, in equity he felt the position to be different. If, instead of paying for the repairs himself, the tenant cross-claims for damages for breach of the repairing covenant, even though there may be no common law defence because the amount is unliquidated, nevertheless there is, in equity, a possibility of setting off the unliquidated sum. Of course, the set-off must arise under the lease or tenancy and, being equitable and therefore discretionary, it will not be available in every case where a tenant has a claim against a landlord. The court must be satisfied that it would be unconscionable to allow the landlord to recover the rent, or the full amount claimed, in the face of the tenant's claim. It is unlikely that this obstacle would prevent a set-off by a tenant against a landlord who was claiming the full rent while failing at the same time to provide the full consideration contracted for in terms of repairs. Under the Housing Act 1985, section 96[14] the Secretary of State is empowered to make regulations permitting a local authority or housing association secure tenant to carry out works falling within a landlord's repairing covenant, and to

---

[11] [1937] 2 K.B. 283.
[12] See *British Anzani (Felixstowe) Ltd.* v. *International Marine Management (UK) Ltd.* [1979] 2 All E.R. 1063.
[13] *Ibid.* See also; *Asco Developments* v. *Gordon* (1978) 248 E.G. 683; *Melville* v. *Grapelodge Developments Ltd.* (1979) 39 P. & C.R. 179.
[14] See *post*, Chap. 16.

recover the cost from the landlord, local authority or housing association. A scheme giving effect to these rights has been prepared.[15]

E. Settlement of Action and Undertaking

A tenant who has commenced proceedings for damages against a landlord, for failure to carry out repairs, may be able to secure a settlement of the action which includes an undertaking by the landlord to the court to do the repairs. If the landlord then breaks the undertaking, the judge has jurisdiction to direct the tenant to do the work and order the landlord to pay the cost.[16]

F. Negligence Action

It may be open to a tenant to establish damage as a result of the landlord's negligence. The most obvious area in which this may be done is in relation to the landlord's duty of care under the Defective Premises Act 1974.[17] There are, however, other cases. A landlord who lets premises but retains control of other premises, such as common parts, which he knows to be in a dangerous condition and which he negligently fails to make safe, will be liable to the tenant or members of the tenant's family for any damage caused by that part of the building which remains in the landlord's control.[18] Anyone, whether landlord, builder or other third party who carries out work on premises, is under a general duty to use reasonable care for the safety of those whom he knows, or ought reasonably to have known, might be affected by those works or who were lawfully in the vicinity of the works.[19] Where the landlord of the dwelling is also the designer or the builder, and the design or construction was done negligently, the builder or designer/landlord will be liable for damage caused to the tenant[20], even though the acts of negligence might have occurred before the lease was granted.[21]

[15] See Secure Tenancies (Right to Repair Scheme) Regulations 1985, S.I. No. 1493.
[16] *Mortimer* v. *Wilson* (1885) 33 W.R. 927.
[17] *Supra.*
[18] *Cunard* v. *Antifyre* [1933] 1 K.B. 551; *Taylor* v. *Liverpool Corp.* [1939] 3 All E.R. 329; Occupiers' Liability Act 1957, s.2.
[19] *A.C. Billings & Son* v. *Rider* [1958] A.C. 240.
[20] *Anns* v. *Merton L.B.C.* [1978] A.C. 728; *Batty* v. *Metropolitan Property Realisations Ltd.* [1978] Q.B. 554; *Balcomb* v. *Wards Construction* (1981) 259 E.G. 765; *Warlock* v. *Saws* (1981) 260 E.G. 920; *Rimmer* v. *Liverpool City Council* [1984] 1 All E.R. 930.
[21] See [1974] L.A.G. Bull. 71.

G. Appointment of Receiver

The court has jurisdiction to appoint a receiver and manager of the property at the instigation and request of the tenants pursuant to the enforcement of the landlord's covenants (including the covenant to repair). In *Hart* v. *Emelkirk*[22] the landlord of a block of flats had neglected for three years to collect rents and perform his covenants to repair and insure. Goulding J. held that the court could exercise its power under the Supreme Court Act 1981, section 37(1), to appoint a receiver, by interlocutory or final order, where justice and convenience so required. The court could confer on the receiver such powers as were necessary to preserve the property. In the instant case the receiver could be appointed and give a good receipt for rents and service charges, and to manage the property in accordance with the landlord's rights and obligations under the lease. The funds received could, of course, lawfully be applied for these purposes. Justice and convenience required, in this case, the appointment of a chartered surveyor as receiver, until trial of the action or further order, because there were covenants to be enforced and urgent action to be taken to preserve the property. The decision was applied by Harman J. in *Daiches* v. *Bluelake Investments*,[23] where again a receiver was appointed to carry out substantial repairs to the property. Although the landlord had not abandoned the property (a block of flats), he had failed to respond to tenants' requests to carry out the urgently needed repairs. He had also failed to maintain a reserve fund against future repairing liabilities, despite contributions to such a fund by the tenants. Since the tenants were prepared to finance a receiver, and since urgent, necessary major works were required to the property if it was to continue in use as flats, it was regarded as just and convenient that a receiver and manager be appointed. However, in *Parker* v. *Camden London Borough Council*[24] the Court of Appeal held that, although it had a general and unlimited jurisdiction to appoint a receiver and manager under the Supreme Court Act 1981, section 37, it was obliged to exercise its discretion judicially. Accordingly, where Parliament had expressly conferred powers and imposed duties on a local authority, such as the powers and duties of management conferred upon local housing authorities in respect of council housing by the Housing Act 1985, sections 20 to 26, the court cannot abrogate those statutory powers and duties by appointing a receiver, since such an appointee would be the agent of the court, and not of the local housing authority.

[22] [1983] 3 All E.R. 15.
[23] [1985] 275 E.G. 462.
[24] [1985] 2 All E.R. 141. See also *Gardner* v. *London Chatham and Dover Rly. Co. (No. 1)* (1867) L.R. 2 Ch.App. 201.

H. Complaint to the Local Authority

(1) *Statutory Nuisance*

It is possible for the local authority (or the tenant himself if the local authority will not act), to take out a summons to the magistrates' court asking the magistrates to issue an order compelling the landlord to carry out necessary repairs. The summons will allege that the disrepair constitutes a statutory nuisance under the Public Health Act 1936.

Several matters can constitute a statutory nuisance. Any premises[25] that are in such a state as to be prejudicial to health[26] or to constitute a nuisance, will be a statutory nuisance, within section 92(1) of the Act.[27] The phrase "prejudicial to health" was considered at length in *Coventry City Council* v. *Cartwright*.[28] The local authority had allowed indiscriminate tipping of building materials, scrap iron and broken glass on a piece of vacant land they owned. Some household rubbish was tipped, but the local authority had periodically removed this. The justices found that the material deposited could encourage rodent infestation and rats had been seen on land near the site. Children played on the site and used it as a short cut to a nearby school. The justices held that a statutory nuisance existed, in that the materials were dangerous to health and limb, especially to the children, and that as the site was in a residential area the visual impact could constitute a nuisance. Accordingly the justices made a nuisance order. The local authority appealed by way of case stated, the question for the Divisional Court being whether inert matter, such as builders' rubble, without any putrescible matter attached to it, fell within the ambit of the Public Health Act 1936, s.92(1).

The Divisional Court considered that the justices had taken too wide a view of the section. The case turned on the phrase "prejudicial

---

[25] Public Health Act 1936, s.343.
[26] *Ibid.* s.92(1) as amended by Local Government (Miscellaneous Provisions) Act, 1982, s.26(1).
[27] The following also constitute "statutory nuisances":
   (i)   any animal kept in such a place or manner as to be prejudicial to health or constitute a nuisance;
   (ii) any accumulation or deposit which is prejudicial to health or constitutes a nuisance;
   (iii) any dust or effluvia caused by any trade, business, manufacture or process which is injurious or likely to cause injury to the public health or a nuisance;
   (iv) any workplace, which is not provided with sufficient means of ventilation or in which sufficient ventilation is not maintained, or which is not kept clean or free from noxious effluvia, or which is so overcrowded while work is carried on as to be prejudicial to the health of those employed in it;
   (v)   any other matter declared by any provision of the Public Health Act 1936 (see ss.141, 259(1)(*a*), (*b*), 268(2)) to be a statutory nuisance; Public Health Act 1936, s.92(1). See also Clean Air Act 1956, s.16, Control of Pollution Act 1974, ss.57–74, and Noise Abatement Act 1960.
[28] [1975] 1 W.L.R. 845.

to health." Lord Widgery C.J. said: "that which is struck at is an accumulation of something which produces a threat to health in the sense of a threat of disease, vermin or the like."[29] He concluded that all the relevant cases reinforced him in the view that[30]: "the general purpose of the Act is to stop accumulations which have a public health consequence, which tend to create smell or smoke or other emanations of that kind," and there was no justification for holding that the visual impact of tipped rubbish could be a statutory nuisance. Ashworth J. said[31] that the case was borderline and that if there had been more evidence about the effect of the rubbish, and whether the rubbish had set up an infestation of rats, the justices would have had grounds for their decision. It should be remembered, however, that premises may be prejudicial to health even when they are not occupied and the nuisance will not, therefore, be abated by the simple expedient of removing the occupants.[32]

One thing is clear from the cases. A tenant who wishes to utilise these Public Health Act provisions against a landlord who is failing to carry out his repairing obligations must distinguish between simple lack of repair and prejudice to health. It is not the defect in premises, but the result of the defect, that is important. For example, a defective roof or guttering does not make premises a statutory nuisance, but the fact that water thereby penetrates the fabric of the building into the living accommodation does. It is the severity of the condition of the premises that is decisive. A minor defect would not, of itself, warrant classification of the premises as a statutory nuisance but a multiplicity of minor defects and the resultant interference with living conditions would. However, in relation to dwellings the arguments used in the *Cartwright* case should be viewed with care. The land on which the inert matter was accumulated was owned by the council, and a person unauthorised to enter has, as a trespasser, limited rights in respect of injury, or likely injury, incurred by entering on the land. The occupier of a dwelling has no alternative but to enter, and if there are conditions that may cause physical injury, it is more than a possibility that the case would cross the borderline, and the dwelling be "prejudicial to health."

The problem of condensation in the context of premises "prejudicial to health" has been held, in *Dover District Council* v. *Farrar*,[33] to be capable of constituting a statutory nuisance in an appropriate case.

---

[29] *Per* Lord Widgery C.J. at p. 849. See also: *Great Western Railway* v. *Bishop* (1872) L.R. 7 Q.B. 550; *Bishop Auckland Local Board* v. *Bishop Auckland Iron & Steel Co. Ltd.* (1882) 10 Q.B.D. 138; *Morrissey* v. *Galer* [1955] 1 W.L.R. 110 (*sub. nom. Galer* v. *Morrissey* [1955] 1 All E.R. 380).
[30] At p. 851.
[31] *Ibid.*
[32] *Lambeth London Borough Council* v. *Stubbs* (1980) 78 L.G.R. 650; *Coventry City Council* v. *Doyle* [1981] 2 All E.R. 184.
[33] (1982) 2 H.L.R. 32.

If the condensation is caused by a defective heating system, or one that is inadequate or unsuitable, or is caused by the absence of a system altogether, in a building so unusually constructed that it is prone to condensation, then a nuisance order might lie, even if this meant that the landlord would be required to instal a new or even an original system.[34] However, if the condensation is due to the tenant's failure to use the existing heating system (for example, on the grounds of expense) but, had it been in full use, no condensation problem would have arisen, then the Court of Appeal has expressed the view that no statutory nuisance arises.[35]

The term "nuisance" is not defined in the Public Health Act 1936, although there is some case law on its meaning within the context of section 92. To be a nuisance within that section the act, omission or situation complained of must be such as to constitute a nuisance at common law in relation to public or private nuisances. In *Betts* v. *Penge U.D.C.*[36] a wider meaning was given, and it was held that the conduct of a landlord in harassing a tenant by removing the front door and some window sashes constituted a nuisance, since the landlord's acts resulted in an interference with the personal comfort of the occupiers.[37]

In *National Coal Board* v. *Neath Borough Council*[38] a house was in a state of disrepair, with defective windows, guttering and skirting boards. The justices held themselves bound by *Betts* v. *Penge U.D.C.*[39] and issued a nuisance order. It was held that this was contrary to the notion of a nuisance at common law, which denotes an interference as emanating from outside the occupied premises. Watkins J. said[40]: "A nuisance cannot arise if what has taken place affects only the person or persons occupying the premises where the nuisance is said to have taken place. A nuisance coming within the meaning of the Public Health Act must be either a private or public nuisance as understood by common law."

This, of course, severely limits the efficacy of the statutory nuisance remedy for dealing with disrepair. Where the letting is of part only of the property, with the landlord retaining part, such as common accessways to flats or offices, or a garden or a garage forecourt, and the nuisance emanates from the part retained by the landlord, then it

---

[34] *G.L.C.* v. *London Borough of Tower Hamlets* (1983) 15 H.L.R. 57. "A landlord is required to apply his mind to the necessity of ventilation and, if need be, to insulation and heating. The landlord must provide a combination of these factors to make a house habitable for the tenant": *ibid. per* Griffiths L.J. at p. 61.

[35] *Dover District Council* v. *Farrar* (1982) 2 H.L.R. 32.

[36] [1942] 2 K.B. 154.

[37] Some members of the House of Lords have expressed the view that this case makes an unwarranted extension of the meaning of the term "nuisance" in s.92: see *Salford City Council* v. *McNally* [1976] A.C. 379.

[38] [1976] 2 All E.R. 478.

[39] [1942] 2 K.B. 154.

[40] [1976] 2 All E.R. 478 at p. 482.

seems section 92 may be used. Where, on the other hand, the tenant has rented the entire property, or the nuisance emanates from the part that is subject to the lease, then it will affect "only the person or persons occupying the premises where the nuisance is said to have taken place," and no statutory nuisance has been occasioned (although the defects may still produce consequences that are "prejudicial to health," and can therefore be dealt with under section 92 on this ground). The effects of this ruling have been substantially reduced by the Housing Act 1986, section 190, which empowers local authorities to serve notices requiring persons in control of dwellings to repair them where the condition of the house is such that, although it is not unfit for human habitation, it materially interferes with the personal comfort of the occupying tenant. To invoke this power the council must have received representations from the occupying tenant.

Further, an act, omission or situation, to be a nuisance, must in some way be concerned with the health of the person who is affected by the alleged nuisance. The nuisance does not have to be "injurious to health," since that is covered by the first limb of section 92(1). In *Bishop Auckland Local Board* v. *Bishop Auckland Iron and Steel Co. Ltd.*[41] Stephen J. referred to a nuisance as either interfering with personal comfort or being injurious to health.[42] The use of the words "personal comfort" was considered "appropriate" by Lord Wilberforce in *Salford City Council* v. *McNally*.[43] In *National Coal Board* v. *Neath Borough Council*[44] the court agreed that "nuisance" in the Public Health Act 1936, s.92, should come within the spirit of the 1936 Act as a whole, and must be directed to the question of the health of the person who claims to be or has been affected by the nuisance.

A tenant who complains to the Environmental Health Department of his local authority that a lack of repair constitutes a statutory nuisance, is entitled to have his complaint investigated by the authority. Where a local authority are satisfied of the existence of a statutory nuisance, it serves a notice, called an "abatement notice."[45] The notice is served on the person by whose act, default or sufferance the nuisance arises or continues. If that person cannot be found, the notice is served on the owner or occupier of the premises on which the nuisance arises. This is further qualified by the proviso that where the nuisance arises from a defect of a structural character, the notice must be served on the owner of the premises. So, for the purposes of dealing

---

[41] (1882) 10 Q.B.D. 138.
[42] At p. 141.
[43] [1976] A.C. 379 at p. 389.
[44] [1976] 2 All E.R. 478.
[45] Public Health Act 1936, s.93. As to the meaning of the words "*shall* serve" in this section, see *Nottingham City District Council* v. *Newton* [1974] 1 W.L.R. 923, *per* Lord Widgery C.J. at p. 926.

with housing conditions, the local authority will normally serve the abatement notice on the owner[46] of the house.

The abatement notice must be in writing, specifying the nuisance and *may* also require the execution of such works as are necessary to abate the nuisance.[47] If the person on whom the notice has been served fails to comply with the requirements of the notice, or has complied in such a manner that the local authority feel that the statutory nuisance is likely to recur, then the local authority are required to apply for a summons to the magistrates' court.[48] If the magistrates are satisfied that the nuisance exists, or did exist and is likely to recur, they must make an order requiring the defendant to comply with all or any of the requirements of the abatement notice, within a specified time. The magistrates may also, where appropriate, specify works the defendant must carry out to prevent a recurrence.[49] If the magistrates are satisfied that the nuisance is so serious that it renders the premises unfit for human habitation, then they may prohibit the premises from being used for human habitation.[50] This prohibition will continue until the court are satisfied that the premises have been rendered fit. A tenant making use of the statutory nuisance procedure should, therefore, be aware that in extreme cases there is a risk that he may have to vacate the premises.

At the time of making a nuisance order the court also has power to impose a fine on the defendant, and to make a compensation order against the defendant in favour of the occupier. The fine increases by a further figure, not to exceed £50, for each day on which the nuisance continues beyond the time specified for its abatement. The local authority may, if the nuisance continues unabated, abate the nuisance by carrying out any necessary works specified in the magistrates' order.[51] The local authority are also empowered to recover from the

---

[46] Public Health Act 1936, s.343(1), defines "owner" as the person for the time being receiving the rackrent of the premises, whether on his own account or as agent or trustee for any other person, or who would receive the same if those premises were let at a rackrent. See also *Warner* v. *London Borough of Lambeth* (1984) 1'5 H.L.R. 42: where a "person aggrieved" takes action in respect of a statutory nuisance under s.99, the information laid should, at least in summary form, contain the details that would have been included in an abatement notice issued under s.93, and the steps required to abate the alleged nuisance. This is because the landlord should know the case to be answered.

[47] Public Health Act 1936, s.93. See also *Millard* v. *Wastall* [1898] 1 Q.B. 342; *Watling* v. *Rees* (1914) 84 L.J.K.B. 1122. The notice must specify a reasonable time limit within which the works are to be completed: *Bristol Corporation* v. *Sinnott* [1918] 1 Ch. 62.

[48] Public Health Act 1936, s.94. *cf. Nottingham City District Council* v. *Newton* [1974] 1 W.L.R. 923. Application for a summons is made by way of laying information: Magistrates' Courts Act 1980, s.150(2); Magistrates' Courts Rules 1981, r. 4; see also *Northern Ireland Trailers Ltd.* v. *Preston Corporation* [1972] 1 W.L.R. 203.

[49] Public Health Act 1936, s.94(2). As to the discretion the magistrates have when making the order to take into account, *inter alia*, the other housing powers of the local authority, see: *Nottingham City District Council* v. *Newton* [1974] 1 W.L.R. 923, *per* Lord Widgery C.J. at pp. 928–929; *Salford City Council* v. *McNally* [1976] A.C. 379.

[50] Public Health Act 1936, s.94(2).

[51] *Ibid.* s.95.

person on whom the order was made, the expenses of obtaining the order and of carrying out any necessary works of abatement.[52]

There is a streamlined procedure open to a local authority under section 76 of the Building Act 1984, if it appears to the local authority that the premises are in such a state as to be prejudicial to health or to constitute a nuisance, and unreasonable delay in remedying the defective state would result from using the standard procedure in sections 93–95 of the 1936 Act. In this case the authority may serve a notice stating that the authority intends to remedy the defect itself. Unless a counter-notice is then served on the authority, the council may, after nine days, carry out the necessary works and recover the cost of doing so from the person on whom the notice is served. If a counter-notice is served within seven days, stating that the owner intends to remedy the defect himself, the council cannot take action unless either the works are not started within a reasonable time, or they are proceeding too slowly.[53]

The Public Health Act 1936, s.99, allows a person aggrieved by a statutory nuisance (and this would clearly include a tenant) to lay an information himself. The proceedings are criminal in nature and the burden of proof is that appropriate for criminal proceedings.[54] Section 99 applies not only to statutory nuisances caused by private persons, such as private landlords, but also to nuisances caused by local authorities,[55] even where the authority are using their housing powers to improve the housing in a particular neighbourhood.[56] If an information is laid under section 99, the same procedure and actions are available to a magistrates' court as if the information had been laid by a local authority following default in complying with an abatement notice.

(2) *Unfit for Human Habitation*

The definition of a house "unfit for human habitation" has been considered earlier in this chapter.[57] A tenant who believes that, as a result of landlord neglect, his house is unfit for human habitation, can complain to his local authority, through the Environmental Health Department. Where a local authority are satisfied that a house is unfit for human habitation they must[58] take action to deal with that

---

[52] *Ibid.* s.96.

[53] If the local authority feel that the magistrates' court proceedings are inadequate, they may take action in their own name through the High Court: Public Health Act 1936, s.100; Local Government Act 1972, s.222. See also *Warwick R.D.C.* v. *Miller-Mead* [1962] 2 W.L.R. 284.

[54] *R.* v. *Newham JJ., ex p. Hunt* [1976] 1 W.L.R. 420.

[55] *R.* v. *Epping (Waltham Abbey) JJ., ex p. Burlinson* [1948] 1 K.B. 79; see *post*, Chap. 16.

[56] *Salford City Council* v. *McNally* [1976] A.C. 379. See also (1976) 27 N.I.L.Q., 1.

[57] *Supra*, (III)B, (2). See H.A. 1985, ss. 282, 604.

[58] The duty is mandatory: see *R.* v. *Kerrier District Council, ex p. Guppy's (Bridport) Ltd.* (1976) 32 P. & C.R. 411.

unfitness. The duty is contained in two separate sections. Section 189(1) of the Housing Act 1985 requires the local authority to take action in respect of houses repairable at reasonable expense. Section 264(1) of that Act requires them to take action in respect of houses not repairable at reasonable expense.[59]

The decision whether the action to deal with the unfitness is taken under section 189(1) or under section 264(1) centres on the interpretation of "reasonable expense."[60] In determining whether a house can be rendered fit for human habitation at reasonable expense, regard must be had to the estimated cost of the works considered necessary to render it fit and the value which it is estimated that the house will have when the works are completed.[61] The main cases considering reasonable expense have allowed a wide interpretation.[62] It is not always necessary for the local authority to draw up detailed estimates, though they may sometimes be desirable. The local authority decide what is reasonable expense and what are the estimated costs and values, not the owner. Their estimate should include the cost of making good decorations and other works disturbed as a result of any structural works, as well as the costs of those structural works.[63] In determining the value the house will have when the works are completed the authority must consider the amount the house will fetch on the open market.[64] Any method that demonstrates reasonably conclusively whether repairs will be an economic proposition will suffice.[65]

As a starting point a house will not be considered repairable at reasonable expense if the cost of the works is greater than the difference in value between the property in its unrepaired and repaired states,[66] value being, generally, not investment value but open market value.[67] It is the freehold interest which is to be valued for this purpose, not the particular interest of the person upon whom the notice is served.[68] Although an unfit house will normally have at least site value, in some circumstances (for example, in the case of flats or maisonettes, where the unfit ground floor unit owes easements

[59] See Morgan [1979] Conv. 414.
[60] Where the only person having a relevant interest in the house is the local authority itself, that local authority is not required to apply the provisions of sections 189 and 264 of the 1985 Act to itself: *R.* v. *Cardiff City Council, ex p. Cross* [1982] R.V.R. 270.
[61] Housing Act 1985, s.206.
[62] See *Bacon* v. *Grimsby Corporation* [1950] 1 K.B. 272, and the cases cited therein.
[63] *Ellis Copp & Co.* v. *London Borough of Richmond-upon-Thames* (1976) 245 E.G. 931.
[64] *Inworth Property Co.* v. *London Borough of Southwark* (1977) 33 P. & C.R. 186.
[65] *e.g.* the interest returned on the current market value of the house if that amount were to be invested in gilt-edged securities for five years. *Quaere* whether any grant-aid available should be taken into account; see *Harrington* v. *Croydon Corporation* [1968] 1 Q.B. 856. The value is value with vacant possession: *Hillbank Properties Ltd.* v. *Hackney London Borough Council* [1978] Q.B. 998.
[66] *Kimsey* v. *London Borough of Barnet* (1976) 3 H.L.R. 45.
[67] *Inworth Property Co. Ltd.* v. *London Borough of Southwark* (1977) 33 P. & C.R. 186.
[68] *Bacon* v. *Grimsby Corp.* [1950] 1 K.B. 272; *cf. Lesley Maurice & Co. Ltd.* v. *Willesden Corp.* [1953] 2 Q.B. 1.

of support to the upper floors) the value may be nil.[69] An authority or court may take into account loss of rental over the period during which works are being carried out, as well as any interest payable on the capital outlay involved.[70] The presence of a sitting tenant will be relevant, though there is no fixed rule whether valuation should proceed on the basis of vacant possession or of sitting tenants. The court tends to pay particular regard to the personal characteristics of the individual tenants in occupation, if any, and any other factor which would influence the minds of a hypothetical willing vendor and willing purchaser.[71]

However, the values are only elements in defining reasonable expense. The expense must still be reasonable and other elements may suggest that what is arithmetically reasonable is not actually so. It may, for example, be reasonable to offset against the cost of repairs the amount that the person served with the notice might otherwise have to spend in demolition costs if demolition would be the appropriate alternative to repairs.[72] It must also be remembered that appeal lies from the county court to the Court of Appeal only on a point of law in these cases,[73] and it must therefore be shown, in any appeal, that a county court has erred in law, and this will not be established merely by showing that a county court preferred one approach to the test of "reasonable expense" rather than another, unless that approach is manifestly and wholly wrong.[74]

The Housing Act 1985, s.189 requires that if the authority consider that the house is unfit, then, unless they are satisfied that it is not possible to make it fit at reasonable expense, they must serve upon the person having control of the house, a notice requiring the execution of works specified which, in the authority's opinion, will render the house fit. The notice must also specify a reasonable time (being not less than 21 days) within which the works must be completed. Generally speaking, in the case of tenanted property, this notice will be served on the landlord.[75] After the expiration of the time specified

---

[69] *Kimsey* v. *London Borough of Barnet* (1976) 3 H.L.R. 45.

[70] *F.F.F. Estates* v. *London Borough of Hackney* [1981] Q.B. 503.

[71] *Bacon* v. *Grimsby Corp* [1950] 1 K.B. 272; *Hillbank Properties Ltd.* v. *Hackney London Borough Council* [1978] Q.B. 998; *Dudlow Estates Ltd.* v. *Sefton Metropolitan Borough Council* (1979) 249 E.G. 1271; *F.F.F. Estates* v. *London Borough of Hackney* [1981] Q.B. 503; *Phillips* v. *Newham London Borough Council* (1982) 48 P. & C.R. 54.

[72] *Dudlow Estates Ltd.* v. *Sefton Metropolitan Borough Council, supra.*

[73] County Courts Act 1984, s.77.

[74] *Kenny* v. *Royal Borough of Kingston-upon-Thames* (1985) 274 E.G. 395. But see *R.* v. *Ealing London Borough ex parte Richardson* (1982) 265 E.G. 691.

[75] The person who receives the rack-rent of a house, whether on his own account or as agent or trustee for any other person, or who would so receive it if the house were let at a rack-rent, is deemed to be the person having control of the house, "rack-rent" meaning a rent not less than two-thirds of the full net annual value of the house: Housing Act 1985, s.207. See also *Pollway Nominees Ltd.* v. *Croydon London Borough Council* [1985] 3 W.L.R. 564: the Court of Appeal held that where the notice is served upon a person who is not and cannot be deemed to be a person having control of the house (because, *e.g.* it is served on the freeholder who has let the property to an occupying tenant on a long lease at a ground rent below a rack-rent) the notice is a nullity.

in the notice the local authority themselves may enter to carry out the works specified in the notice, and recover the cost of doing so from the person upon whom the notice was served.[76]

The procedure where unfit houses are not repairable at reasonable expense is complex, and allows consultation with the owner, and others interested in the house, before making a decision on the action necessary to deal with the condition. Section 264(1) requires a local authority, which is satisfied that a house is unfit for human habitation and cannot be made fit at reasonable expense, to serve on the person having control of it,[77] upon any other person who is an owner of it and, so far as reasonably practicable to ascertain such persons, upon every mortgagee, notice of the time (not less than 21 days after service) and place at which discussions may take place. These discussions will cover the condition of the house and any offer with respect to the carrying out of future works, or the future user of the house (which cannot be used for human habitation until the works have been done) which the person(s) upon whom the notice was served may wish to propose.[78]

The local authority may, after the consultation, accept an undertaking if it either provides for the carrying out, within a reasonable time, of works that will make the house fit, or provides that the house will not be used for human habitation. An owner who has given an undertaking that the premises will not be used for human habitation may obtain possession, since it is expressly stated that the Rent Act 1977 does not apply to such premises (a point to be borne in mind by tenants complaining to the local authority that the premises are unfit).[79] Any person who, knowing that an undertaking has been given that premises will not be used for certain purposes specified in the undertaking, uses premises in contravention of that undertaking or permits them to be so used, is liable to a fine of £2,000 and an additional £5 for every day the offence continues.[80] The local authority, on being satisfied that the house has been rendered fit, can cancel the undertaking.[81]

If the local authority are not offered, or do not accept, an undertaking, or are satisfied that the agreed works are not being carried out within the specified time, they must forthwith[82] make a demolition order for the premises. They must also do this if they are

---

[76] There is an appeals procedure available to a person receiving a notice: see Housing Act 1985, ss.191, 192.
[77] See footnote 75, *supra*.
[78] Housing Act 1985, s.264(1), (4).
[79] Housing Act 1985, s.264(5). There appear to be few limits on the type of undertaking regarding works to be done: much depends upon the circumstances: *Johnson* v. *Leicester Corporation* [1934] 1 K.B. 638.
[80] Housing Act 1985, s.264(6). See also: the Criminal Law Act 1977, s.31 and the Criminal Justice Act 1982, Sched. 3.
[81] *Ibid.* s.264(4)(b).
[82] See *London Borough of Hillingdon* v. *Cutler* [1968] 1 Q.B. 124.

satisfied that the house is being occupied in contravention of an undertaking. Where, however, the local authority consider it inexpedient to make a demolition order, having regard to the effect of the demolition of a house on any other house or building, they may make a closing order instead.[83] A closing order is made in respect of a building which is part of a terrace or which is semi-detached. It is also made in respect of a part of a building, *e.g.* an attic which cannot be made fit at reasonable expense, or an underground room,[84] and in respect of buildings listed for preservation because of architectural or historic interest.[85]

If the local authority feel that the house is, or can be, rendered capable of providing accommodation which is adequate for the time being, instead of making a demolition order or a closing order, they may purchase the house.[86] Notice of their decision to purchase is given, under section 300(2) of the Housing Act 1985, to the same persons to whom they are required to give notice under section 268(1) and the amount of compensation paid to the owner is assessed at the value of the vacant site ready for redevelopment.[87] If the house has been well-maintained, the local authority, on acquisition, will be required to make a well-maintained payment. The amount is equal to eight times the rateable value of the house, but is in any case not to exceed the amount by which the full market value (*i.e.* the value of the house if not affected by a compulsory purchase order or declared unfit) exceeds the site value.[88] This sometimes means that although the payment is approved, no payment, or a low payment, is made, because the site value is higher than, or at least equal to, the market value of the house.

Once the local authority have decided to make either a closing order or a demolition order, or to purchase the house, they must send copies of the order or notice of intention to purchase to everyone notified under section 264. A demolition order must state the period in which the premises are to be vacated (not less than 28 days) and that the premises must be demolished within six weeks after the end of that period. The time limit may be extended by the local authority.[89]

The local authority are required[90] to notify the *occupiers* of the effect of a demolition order, of the date by which the building must be

---

[83] Housing Act 1985, s.265(2).
[84] *Ibid.* s.266.
[85] *Ibid.* s.265(2)*(b)*, 304.
[86] *Ibid.* s.300. This procedure cannot be used to acquire permanent housing stock nor in substitution for the procedure in s.192: *Victoria Square Property Co.* v. *Southwark London B.C.* [1978] 1 W.L.R. 463; *cf. R.* v. *City of Birmingham Corp exp. Sale* (1983) 9 H.L.R. 35.
[87] *Ibid.* s.585.
[88] *Ibid.* s.586 and Sched. 23.
[89] Housing Act 1985, ss.270–275. For the appeals procedure, see Housing Act 1985, s.269. A statutory tenant is not able to appeal (s.269(2)): *Brown* v. *Minister of Housing and Local Government* [1953] 1 W.L.R. 1370.
[90] See *R.* v. *Epsom and Ewell Corp., ex p. R.B. Property Investments (Eastern)* [1964] 2 All E.R. 832.

vacated, and of the requirement that the occupier must quit the building before that date or before the expiration of 28 days from the service of the notice, whichever is the later.[91] Once a demolition order is in force, any protection given to the occupiers by the Rent Act 1977, is removed,[92] and if the owner does not recover possession the local authority may do so, and recover any expense incurred. It is an offence for anyone knowingly to occupy or allow occupation of premises to which a demolition order applies.[93]

If an owner fails to demolish the building within the period specified, the local authority can themselves demolish it and sell any materials.[94] If they are left with outstanding expenses they can recover them as a civil debt from the owner.[95] Any surplus from the sale of materials must be returned to the owner.[96] An owner may apply to the local authority for an extension of the period allowed for demolition on the ground that he wishes to improve or reconstruct the building.[97] The authority may extend the time limit as appropriate if satisfied with the proposed works and their progress. If the work, when completed, makes the house fit for human habitation the demolition order must be revoked.[98]

A closing order, while prohibiting the use of the whole, or part, of the premises for human habitation, should allow them to be used for other reasonable purposes. If the authority are satisfied that the premises have been made fit for human habitation, they must revoke the order; they must also revoke it so far as it relates to part of the premises, on being satisfied that the part has been rendered fit for human habitation (*e.g.* in the case of the whole house being made fit except for an attic, the order can be revoked in relation to the fit part of the house, leaving the attic subject to the closing order).[99] Nothing in the Rent Act 1977 prevents possession being obtained by the owner of premises subject to a closing order,[1] even where the unfit state of the premises is due to the landlord's breach of his repairing obligations.[2] If it appears to the local authority that any unoccupied premises in their area, in respect of which a closing order is in force, are not effectively secured against unauthorised entry or are, or are likely to become, a danger to public health, the authority may, after giving the owner not less than 48 hours' notice, do such works in connection with the premises as they think fit to make them secure or

---

[91] Housing Act 1985, s.270(1).
[92] *Ibid.* s.270(3).
[93] *Ibid.* s.270(5).
[94] *Ibid.* s.271(1).
[95] *Ibid.* s.272(1).
[96] *Ibid.* s.272(3).
[97] *Ibid.* s.274(1).
[98] *Ibid.* s.274(5).
[99] *Ibid.* s.278(1). For rights of appeal see Housing Act 1985, s.269.
[1] *Ibid.* s.276.
[2] *Buswell* v. *Goodwin* [1971] 1 W.L.R. 92.

to prevent the public health danger.[3] Under the Housing Act 1985, s.190(1)(b), on a representation by a qualifying tenant, a local authority may serve a repair notice in respect of houses in disrepair where the condition of the house is such as to interfere materially with the comfort of the tenant. This procedure is described below.

(3) *Houses in Disrepair*

The Housing Act 1985, s.190(1)(a), contains provisions allowing local authorities to require repair of houses which are not unfit but which are, nevertheless, in a state of disrepair. Where a local authority are satisfied that a house is in such a state of disrepair that, although it is not unfit for human habitation, substantial repairs are required to bring it up to a reasonable standard, having regard to its age, character and locality, they may serve a notice upon the person having control of the house.[4]

In *Hillbank Properties Ltd.* v. *Hackney London Borough Council*[5] the Court of Appeal emphasised the importance of the section 190(1)(a) power. The court pointed out the social undesirability of owners allowing houses to fall into gross disrepair and to become unfit for human habitation, thus depriving tenants of their homes by relieving them of their security of tenure under the Rent Act 1977. Lord Denning said[6]:

> "It seems to me that the policy of Parliament was to make the owners of houses keep them in proper repair. Not only so as to keep up the stock of houses but also to see that protected tenants should be able to have their houses properly kept up. It would be deplorable if there were no means of compelling owners of old houses keeping them in proper repair; or if the owners could let them fall into disrepair—as a means of evicting tenants. Of course, if the state of a house is so bad that it should be condemned—whoever was occupying it—then let it be demolished or closed or purchased. But if it is worth repairing, then it should be repaired, no matter whether it is occupied by a protected tenant or an unprotected tenant."

---

[3] Local Government (Miscellaneous Provisions) Act 1976, s.8(1), (2).
[4] The notice only need contain sufficient information to enable the owner to have the work costed out by a reasonably competent builder; there is no need for the notice to spell out in minute precision what has to be done. The notice may properly leave to the owner matters for the exercise of individual judgment as to what is necessary to put the building back into a satisfactory state of repair: *The Church of Our Lady of Hal* v. *Camden London Borough Council* (1980) 40 P. & C.R. 472.
[5] [1978] Q.B. 998.
[6] *Ibid.* p. 1009.

However, there is clearly room for debate on the degree to which this issue of policy can determine the question under section 190(1)(a), especially when the cost of the repairs far exceeds the increase in value of the property attributable to them. However, as the Court of Appeal pointed out in *Kenny* v. *Royal Borough of Kingston upon Thames*[7] this is essentially a matter for the judgment of the tribunal of first instance should an appeal be lodged[8] on the local authority's notice, and if, in the exercise of that judgment, it appears that the landlord is attempting, by the disrepair, to force the tenant to leave, policy should sometimes override economics. As Ackner L.J. observed[9]:

> "(The Learned judge) drew the inference ... that (the landlord) was adopting a policy of inactivity for the express purpose of allowing the premises to run down, with a view to her thereby obtaining vacant possession and obtaining the financial benefit which that would bring. The learned judge was entitled to draw the conclusion that it would not be long before the tenant ... found it impossible to go on living at these premises because of their state of repair and accordingly, if the notice was not adhered to, the housing stock would suffer and the tenant would lose the benefit of being able to occupy his flat. In a situation in which there is no suggestion that to carry out the repairs would involve [the landlord] in any financial problems, the learned judge was ... perfectly entitled to place strong emphasis on the policy considerations and the consequences which would follow if this repair work was not carried out. He bore in mind that this was a case where the ultimate value of the building would exceed the cost of repairs and therefore it was not one of those glaring cases where the excess of cost of repairs over the increase in value was so pronounced as to make it ... financial folly to incur the expenditure necessary to comply with the notice."

Although the local authority's powers to require repairs under section 190(1)(a) are not expressed to depend upon whether the work can be effected "at reasonable expense,"[10] in *Hillbank Properties Ltd.* v. *Hackney London Borough Council*[11] the Court of Appeal held that this condition nevertheless operated in respect of a section 190(1)(*a*) notice. It is by no means clear that the Court of Appeal is correct in this assertion. Section 11(3) of the Housing Act 1957, (the forerunner of the 1985 Act), was specifically amended by the Housing Act 1969,

---

[7] (1985) 274 E.G. 395.
[8] Under Housing Act 1985, s.191.
[9] At p. 397.
[10] Instead it appears that the standard of repair is to be considered, having regard to the "age, character and locality."
[11] [1978] Q.B. 998.

section 89,—the Act which first introduced what is now section 190(1)(*a*) of the 1985 Act into the Housing Act 1957. The relevant part of section 11(3), with the amendment added in 1969 in square brackets, reads as follows:

> " . . . where the judge allows an appeal [under section 9(1) of this Act[12]] requiring the execution of works to a house, he shall, if requested by the local authority so to do, include in his judgment a finding whether the house can or cannot be rendered fit for human habitation at reasonable expense."[13]

Had repair at reasonable expense been intended by the legislature to be a factor to take into account on the issue of a section 190(1)(*a*) notice, it is strange that consequent reference was not made to section 9(1A), the forerunner of s.190(1)(*a*), in relation to the appeals procedure in section 11(3), especially as section 11(3) was expressly amended to include a reference only to section 9(1), at the same time and under the same amending statute as introduced section 9(1A) into the law. The Housing Act of 1985 was intended merely as a consolidation of the earlier Housing Acts. Nevertheless, the relevance of "reasonable expense" to section 190(1)(*a*) notices has been recognised in subsequent cases, although in *Kenny* v. *Royal Borough of Kingston upon Thames*[14] the Court of Appeal do suggest that it is only one relevant consideration to take into account and it may be overridden by other factors, including those policy considerations adverted to earlier.

By virtue of section 190(1)(*b*) of the Housing Act 1985, where a local authority receive a representation from a qualifying tenant, they may serve a repair notice where the condition of the house is such that, although it is not unfit for human habitation, it materially interferes with the personal comfort of the occupying tenant.

(4) *Dangerous or Ruinous Structures*

If it appears to a local authority that any building or structure is in such a condition, or is used to carry such loads, as to be dangerous, the authority can apply to a court of summary jurisdiction under the Building Act 1984, s.77, and the court may make an order requiring the owner to execute such work as may be necessary to obviate the danger. Alternatively, the owner may elect to demolish the whole or

---

[12] This is in substitution for "against a notice" which could, originally, only have meant a s.9(1) notice, since that is the only notice against which an appeal could lie under the original s.11. S.9(1) is now s.189(1) of the 1985 Act.

[13] With minor amendments in wording, this provision now appears in s.191(3) of the 1985 Act.

[14] (1985) 274 E.G. 395.

any part of the building, and remove any rubbish resulting from the demolition. Emergency powers where immediate action is required are conferred on local authorities by the Building Act 1984, s.78, under which prior notice only has to be given "if it is reasonably practicable so to do." Powers in relation to ruinous or dilapidated buildings are given by section 79 of the 1984 Act. Section 79 provides for dealing with a building or structure which is, by reason of its ruinous or dilapidated condition, seriously detrimental to the amenities of the neighbourhood.[15]

(5) *Unoccupied Premises*

Section 29 of the Local Government (Miscellaneous Provision) Act 1982 contains provisions to deal with unoccupied premises. If it appears to a local authority that an occupier of a building in their area is temporarily absent, and it appears also that the building is not effectively secured against unauthorised entry or is likely to become a danger to public health, the local authority may undertake works in connection with the building for the purpose of preventing unauthorised entry to it or, as the case may be, for the purpose of preventing it becoming a danger to public health.

(6) *Area Action*[16]

Besides giving local authorities powers to deal with individual complaints from, *inter alia*, tenants whose landlords have neglected their obligations to repair, Parliament has also empowered local authorities to deal generally with areas of bad or inadequate housing conditions. These powers start with the means of holding or controlling any further deterioration pending action by the local authority, and finish with the drastic and comprehensive demolition of the area. Historically, the range of these powers has varied and developed, priorities switching from one to the other. With the Housing Act of 1974, central government shifted the priority from one of almost wholesale demolition, to one of rehabilitation—the comprehensive repair of the structure of existing houses, together with the installation of amenities. Gradual renewal lies somewhere between these two extremes. It involves a mixture of demolition and rehabilitation on an area basis—some houses being demolished and

---

[15] An appeal lies to the Crown Court under s.86 of the 1984 Act in relation to certain orders, determinations and other decisions of a magistrates' court under Pts. III and IV of the Building Act 1984. Neither s.78 nor s.79 of the 1984 Act apply to Inner London, which is covered by powers contained in the London Building (Amendment) Act 1939, s.62, as applied by the London Government Act 1963, s.43.

[16] See Hetzel (1974) J.P.L. 646, 735; *cf.* Hadden [1979] J.P.L. 725.

replaced with new dwellings, others being rehabilitated for short periods (to be demolished later), still others being rehabilitated with a view to 30 or 40 years' further life. The changes in priorities have reflected not only the lack of available finance for housing, but also a growing recognition and appreciation of the community as a unit which should be preserved. The current powers are contained in the Housing Act 1985, Parts VIII and IX.

The local authority have the power to declare three different types of action areas. The clearance area is aimed at those areas of housing which have served their useful life, where the structure of the houses has become worn out, and where rehabilitation would not be feasible either practically or financially. It involves the comprehensive demolition of all the buildings in the designated area, save those that are determined not unfit for human habitation or dangerous or injurious to health.[17]

Housing action areas[18] are aimed at areas where the physical and social factors combine to create housing stress. The existence of such areas is ascertained by studying reports detailing the physical state of the housing in the area studied, and analysing the social conditions in the area. These reports may be prepared either by the local authority or by other interested parties, such as neighbourhood councils, residents' associations, housing associations and so on. If a council is satisfied that declaring the area a housing action area will, within five years, improve the housing accommodation, the well-being of the residents, and the management of the residential property, then it may so declare. The effect of the declaration is to give the local authority additional powers to improve the physical and social conditions of the area. They have extensive powers of compulsory purchase, building, conversion, repairing and upgrading, management and even of furnishing, as well as providing financial assistance to owner-occupiers.

General improvement areas[19] may be designated when a report (prepared by the same kind of interested persons as may submit reports for housing action areas), dealing with a predominantly residential area, concludes that living conditions in the area can best be dealt with by the improvement of the amenities or dwellings or assisted by the exercise, by a local authority, of its powers under the Housing Act 1985[19a]. If satisfied by the report, the local authority can designate the area a general improvement area, although it must not include within its boundaries either part of a housing action area or part of a clearance area. Once a general improvement area has been effectively designated, the local authority must publish information

---

[17] Housing Act 1985, ss.289–298.
[18] Housing Act 1985, ss.239–252.
[19] Housing Act 1985, ss.253–259.
[19a] *Ibid.*

and notify residents of the action the authority proposes to take, and of the availability of house renovation grants. The authority also has extensive powers to require compulsory improvements and to assist in improvement of land not owned by them, as well as compulsory purchase powers and powers to improve the general environment by landscaping and closing certain areas to traffic.

(7) *Compulsory Improvement*

The Housing Act 1985, Pt. VII contains a full range of powers available to local authorities to deal with unsatisfactory conditions in individual houses by providing for the compulsory improvement of dwellings in general improvement areas and housing action areas. In addition, provision is made for a tenant to initiate the process for compulsory improvement of dwellings which are outside general improvement areas and housing action areas.

(a) Local authority action

Under section 210(1) of the Housing Act 1985, local authorities have power to serve[20] what is called a "provisional notice" on the person having control of a dwelling (who, in the case of rented property, will generally be the landlord). The dwelling must lie within the boundaries of a general improvement area or a housing action area and have been built (or converted for residential use) before October 3, 1961. The dwelling must be without one or more of the standard amenities. A dwelling is without one of the standard amenities if it has only shared use of a bathroom and inside W.C.[21] The full list of standard amenities is[22]:

1. a fixed bath or shower (this amenity should be provided within a bathroom, but if this is not reasonably practicable it may be provided in any other part of the dwelling, except a bedroom;
2. a supply of hot and cold water to the fixed bath or shower;
3. a wash hand-basin;
4. a supply of hot and cold water to the wash hand-basin;
5. a sink;
6. a supply of hot and cold water to the sink;
7. a water closet. If reasonably practicable, the water closet should be within, and accessible from within, the dwelling; otherwise it must be at least readily accessible from the dwelling, preferably with access under permanent cover.

---

[20] No notice may be served in respect of dwellings owned by a local authority, Commission for the New Towns, the Housing Corporation, a registered housing association, a development corporation under the New Towns Act, 1965, or a housing trust: Housing Act, 1985, s.232(2).
[21] *F.F.F. Estates* v. *Hackney London Borough Council* [1981] Q.B. 503.
[22] Housing Act 1985, ss.237, 508.

The dwelling, in order to be the subject of a provisional notice to improve, must also be capable, at reasonable expense,[23] of improvement to either of two standards, referred to as the "full standard" or the "reduced standard."[24]

The full standard requires satisfaction of five points. These are that the dwelling:

1. is provided with all the standard amenities for the exclusive use of its occupants;
2. is in reasonable repair (disregarding the state of internal decorative repair) having regard to its age and character, and the locality in which it is situated;
3. conforms with such requirements with respect to thermal insulation as may for the time being be specified by the Secretary of State[25];
4. is in all other respects fit for human habitation;
5. is likely to be available for use as a dwelling for a period of 15 years or such other period as may, for the time being, be specified by the Secretary of State.

If it appears to a local authority to be reasonable to do so, it may dispense wholly or in part with any of the requirements of the above standard, in which case the dwelling is said to attain a reduced standard.[26] However, under section 352 of the Housing Act 1985 the authority have power, in certain cases, to compel the execution of certain works by the landlord and where that power extends to compelling a landlord or tenant to install the standard amenities, the authority is not permitted to adopt the reduced standard by dispensing with the requirement that the dwelling meet point 1 above. The requirement that the dwelling be fit for human habitation is, for obvious reasons, in practice rarely waived.

The provisional notice to improve served on the landlord must specify several things. It must specify the works which, in the opinion of the local authority, are necessary to improve the dwellings to the full or reduced standard, as the case may be.[27] It must also indicate a date (not less than 21 days after the service of the notice), a time and a place at which a meeting will be held to discuss the local authority's proposals, any alternative proposals, any proposed permanent or temporary rehousing for the occupying tenant (during and after the

---

[23] The meaning of this phrase is discussed *supra.*
[24] Housing Act 1985, s.209.
[25] *Ibid.* s.234(1).
[26] *Ibid.* s.234(2), (3).
[27] Failure to comply with the statutory requirements for the notice (such as a failure to provide an estimate of costs) renders the purported improvement notice wholly bad: *Canterbury City Council v. Bern* (1982) 44 P. & C.R. 178. The defect cannot be cured by amendment of the notice: *ibid.*

work),[28] and the views and interests of the occupying tenant, and any other relevant matters.[29]

At the meeting the local authority can accept an undertaking given in writing from anyone having an interest in the dwelling who has a right to carry out works. The undertaking must specify the works to be carried out, and a time limit within which those works will be completed, which must not be less than nine months from the date of acceptance of the undertaking. The occupying tenant must counter-sign the undertaking. If an undertaking is accepted and subsequently, the local authority learn that the circumstances have changed in relation to the housing arrangements for the occupying tenant, they must cancel the undertaking. They may also cancel if any of the other circumstances relating to the improvement have changed.[30]

If any of the requirements and conditions in the undertaking are not met, or there is, in the opinion of the authority, no prospect of meeting them, or indeed, if no undertaking is given or accepted at all, then the local authority may serve an improvement notice.[31] The notice must be served within 9 months of the service of the provisional notice or, where an undertaking to carry out the works has been given, within 6 months of the expiry of the period specified in the undertaking.[32] Before serving this notice, the authority must be satisfied that the dwelling lacks at least one standard amenity, was built or converted before October 3, 1961, and is capable of improvement at reasonable expense. They must also be convinced that it is unlikely that the dwelling will be improved unless they serve the notice, and that the occupying tenant has not unreasonably refused to agree to any temporary or permanent housing arrange-ments offered. The authority are also required to ascertain that all the necessary housing arrangements for the occupying tenant have been made and can be satisfied.[33]

The improvement notice must specify the works required, the local authority's estimated cost for carrying out those works,[34] and a time limit (which must not be more than 12 months) within which the works are to be carried out. The works specified in the notice may differ from those given in the provisional notice, except that if the local authority originally accepted a reduced rather than a full standard, they cannot require the full standard in the improvement notice.[35] The notice takes effect six weeks after the date of service or

---

[28] For permanent rehousing, see *post*, Chap. 15.
[29] Housing Act 1985, s.213.
[30] *Ibid.* s.211(1)–(5).
[31] *Ibid.* s.214(1).
[32] *Ibid.* s.214(3).
[33] *Ibid.* s.214(2).
[34] Failure so to specify results in the notice being bad: *Canterbury City Council* v. *Bern* (1982) 44 P. & C.R. 178.
[35] *Ibid.* s.216(1), (2).

on the determination or withdrawal of any appeal.[36] Copies of the improvement notice must be sent to the occupying tenant, and details of the notice must be entered in the register of local land charges.[37]

When the time period specified in the improvement notice has expired, there may still be works outstanding. Alternatively, the landlord may have informed the local authority that he cannot, or will not, carry out the works. In these cases the authority can complete, or carry out the works themselves, and recover expenses from the landlord,[38] if necessary through the county court.[39] An authority may agree with the landlord to carry out the necessary works at his expense.[40] The local authority may (before the expiry of the time given in the improvement notice, but not earlier than six months from the coming into operation of the notice) inquire of the landlord whether he intends to comply. If no adequate reply is given within 21 days, then again the authority may complete or carry out the works.[41]

The 1985 Act contains powers to enable local authorities to make loans to assist persons who incur expense as a result of the compulsory improvement provisions.[42] The landlord may, instead of carrying out the works, require the local authority to purchase the dwelling,[43] and any occupying tenant then becomes the tenant of the local authority. After written requests have been submitted to the occupying tenant, the landlord has the right to enter the premises to survey and estimate the costs of the works. Once the landlord has given the undertaking to improve, or has received an improvement notice, he has a right to enter to enable him to comply with the undertaking or notice.[44] There are penalties for preventing the landlord from executing the works.[45]

(b) Occupying tenant action

The Housing Act 1985, s.212(1), allows an occupying tenant to write to the local authority requesting them to take action under its compulsory improvement powers. A tenant can do this provided that the dwelling is *not* in a housing action area or general improvement area, is without at least one standard amenity, and was built or converted before October 3, 1961.

The "occupying tenant"[46] is the person who is not an owner occupier, but who:

---

[36] *Ibid.* s.218. For appeals, see Housing Act 1985, s.217.
[37] *Ibid.* s.214(4), (5).
[38] *Ibid.* s.220(1), (2), (6) and Sched. 10.
[39] *Ibid.* Sched. 10, para. 6. The costs became a charge on the property: *ibid.* para. 7.
[40] *Ibid.* s.225(1), (2).
[41] *Ibid.* s.220(3).
[42] *Ibid.* ss.228, 435(1).
[43] *Ibid.* s.227(1).
[44] *Ibid.* s.224(1), (2).
[45] *Ibid.* s.223.
[46] Housing Act 1985, s.236(2).

1.   occupies or is entitled to occupy the dwelling as a lessee; or
2.   is a statutory tenant of the dwelling within the meaning of the Rent Act 1977[47]; or
3.   occupies the dwelling as a residence under a restricted contract within the meaning of the Rent Act 1977, s.19[48]; or
4.   is employed in agriculture (as defined in the Agricultural Wages Act 1948, s.17(1)) and occupies or resides in the dwelling as part of the terms of his employment; or
5.   is a statutory tenant of the dwelling, within the meaning of the Rent (Agriculture) Act 1976.[49]

On receipt of a written representation under section 212(1) of the 1985 Act, the authority must notify the landlord or owner of its receipt.[50] They must then investigate the representation, ascertaining that it has, in fact, been made by someone who is an occupying tenant within the Act, and that it complies with the other conditions necessary to be fulfilled before the occupying tenant can make a valid representation. They must also investigate whether the dwelling is capable of being improved to the full standard or, if appropriate, to a reduced standard, at reasonable expense. The authority must further consider whether, having regard to all the circumstances, the dwelling ought to be improved and whether it is unlikely to be improved unless the local authority take action.[51]

Having satisfied themselves on all these points, there are two courses of action open to the local authority. They can serve on the landlord a provisional notice to improve, sending copies to the occupying tenant, in which case the procedures already described above with regard to local authority action for compulsory improvement are followed. Alternatively, they can notify the occupying tenant that they do not intend to serve the provisional notice, and give a written statement of their reasons for reaching that decision.[52]

(8) *Which Course to Follow?*

If a local authority decide that premises are unfit, they may take various steps to deal with the situation, such as requiring the owner to make good the defects, or making a demolition or closing order. If the premises are one of a number of houses unfit for human habitation, the local authority may declare a clearance area. However, if the premises also constitute a statutory nuisance, because they are in such

[47] See *post*, Chap. 11.
[48] *Ibid.*
[49] See *post*, Chaps. 12 & 15.
[50] Housing Act 1985, s.212(2).
[51] *Ibid.* s.212(3).
[52] *Ibid.*

a state as to be prejudicial to health or a nuisance, remedying that situation may take priority if the local authority or a person aggrieved invokes the procedures to abate a statutory nuisance. There are cases[53] where this has been the situation when individuals have invoked the statutory nuisance procedures in order to repair and improve houses already subject to the determinations of local authorities using their powers under the Housing Act.

In *Salford City Council* v. *McNally*[54] Lord Wilberforce said[55]:

> "The Housing Acts and Public Health Acts are dealing with different matters and setting different standards, which may in any individual case have to be separately met . . . a house may well be 'unfit for human habitation' in the statutory sense without being either 'prejudicial to health' or a 'nuisance.' "

Unfitness is a higher standard, including more clearly defined aspects of housing conditions and amenities and requiring a higher standard of works, whereas "statutory nuisance" is more applicable to premises with a life of less than five years or so, and relies more on patch-repairs to relieve the situation.

V. THE TENANT'S IMPLIED OBLIGATIONS

The liability of a tenant for the maintenance and repair of the premises depends, in the absence of express agreement, partly on the doctrine of waste and partly on an implied covenant to use the premises in a tenant-like manner.

A. Waste

Waste is any act of spoil or destruction to the land or premises which alters the nature of the property demised. The obligation of a tenant not to commit waste is a tortious one, independent of contract or implied covenant.[56] Waste can be ameliorating, voluntary, permissive or equitable. Ameliorating waste consists of doing acts or works which improve the value of the land. Voluntary waste is the doing of some act which tends to the destruction of the premises, such as pulling down buildings or removing fixtures, or altering the premises in some

---

[53] *e.g. Salford City Council* v. *McNally* [1976] A.C. 379.

[54] [1976] A.C. 379.

[55] *Ibid.* p. 388.

[56] So, for example, it cannot be assigned: *Defries* v. *Milne* [1913] 1 Ch. 98. A term giving the tenant a qualified right to carry out improvements is implied into certain agreements for letting dwelling-houses: see Housing Act 1985, ss.97–101.

way.[57] Permissive waste implies an omission to carry out works whereby damage results to the premises, as where premises are allowed to fall into decay. Equitable waste consists of extreme acts of deliberate or wanton damage. It is an aggravated form of voluntary waste, and the distinctive name is relevant only where a tenancy is granted "without impeachment of waste." Such a licence is never granted to leaseholders and, in practice, concerns only tenants for life, as part of the law of "settlements."[58]

To constitute voluntary waste by destruction of the premises, the destruction must be deliberate or negligent; it is not waste if the premises are destroyed whilst in the course of reasonable use. The use will be considered reasonable if it is for a purpose for which the property was intended to be used. However, the mode and extent of the user must be apparently proper, having regard to the nature of the property and what the tenant knows of it and, in the case of business premises, to what, as an ordinary businessman, he ought to know of it.[59]

A tenant at will is not liable for either voluntary or permissive waste as such, though, since voluntary waste terminates the tenancy and makes him liable in trespass,[60] he is in fact liable for damage to the premises caused by his own wilful acts. The tenant at will is not, however, liable for permissive waste.[61] A tenant at sufferance is liable for voluntary waste, but not for permissive waste.[62]

Lessees for years or from year to year, and other periodic tenants (such as weekly or monthly) are liable for voluntary waste, whether it be committed by themselves or by a third party. Acts of voluntary waste committed by third parties are always the periodic tenant's responsibility, since he is deemed to be in a position to prevent them.[63]

There is some doubt as to whether lessees for years are liable for permissive waste, although the better opinion seems to hold that they are.[64] They are consequently liable to do such repairs as are necessary to preserve the premises in as good a state as at the beginning of the tenancy. The same would seem to apply to tenants from year to year. Weekly and monthly tenants are not liable for permissive waste. All tenants are liable for voluntary waste.

Carrying out alterations on the premises, such as putting in a new

---

[57] See *West Ham Central Charity Board* v. *East London Waterworks Co.* [1900] 1 Ch. 624.
[58] L.P.A. 1925, s.135.
[59] *Manchester Bonded Warehouses Co.* v. *Carr* (1880) 5 C.P.D. 507.
[60] *Countess of Shrewsbury's Case* (1600) 5 Co.Rep. 13
[61] *Harnett* v. *Maitland* (1847) 16 M. & W. 257.
[62] *Burchell* v. *Hornsby* (1808) 1 Camp. 360.
[63] *Attersoll* v. *Stevens* (1808) 1 Taun. 183. The liability on a covenant to repair and the liability for voluntary waste are distinct: *Edge* v. *Pemberton* (1843) 12 M. & W. 187.
[64] Statute of Marlebridge (1267) (52 Hen. 3, c. 23); 2 Co.Inst. 145; *Harnett* v. *Maitland* (1847), 16 M. & W. 257; *Davies* v. *Davies* (1888) 38 Ch.D. 499. *cf. Jones* v. *Hill* (1817) 7 Taun. 392; *Yellowly* v. *Gower* (1855) 11 Ex. 274.

staircase, or a new shop window, etc., is technically waste, unless it has been expressly sanctioned by the landlord.[65] In the case of acts which may technically be waste, but in fact improve the value of the landlord's reversion—termed ameliorating waste—the court will not interfere to restrain them by injunction.[66] Nor will they be a ground for forfeiting the lease where there is a provision for forfeiture on commission of waste in the lease.[67] Generally speaking, a court will not award damages against a tenant who commits ameliorating waste, since the reversioner has suffered no loss. So, although ameliorating waste may be a breach of a tenant's obligations as to waste, it will often be a breach without a penalty. Usually the position will be regulated by express covenants, and a breach of an express covenant against making alterations, or erecting new buildings, will be enforced by injunction and, where appropriate, may carry the sanction of damages.

B. Tenant-like User

In the absence of any express stipulation as to repairs, and apart from his liability for waste, every tenant is subject to an implied obligation to use the premises in a tenant-like manner. This means that he must take proper care of the premises,[68] and this is the full extent of the liability of a weekly tenant.[69]

It has been held that a tenant from year to year must keep the premises wind and water tight,[70] and make fair and tenantable repairs.[71] However, in *Warren* v. *Keen*[72] the Court of Appeal felt that such expressions added little to the understanding of a tenant's obligations, and were without much meaning. It would seem that a tenant from year to year is liable for minor repairs only and not for those of a substantial nature, nor is he answerable for mere wear and tear of the premises.[73] Tenants for years are, it seems, liable for permissive waste,[74] and it would therefore seem to be their duty to make such timely repairs as would enable them to give up the

---

[65] *Meux* v. *Cobley* [1892] 2 Ch. 253. See Housing Act 1980, s.81 providing that the landlord's consent is always needed by a protected or statutory tenant who wishes to carry out improvements, such consent not to be unreasonably withheld. There is a similar provision operative in the case of secure tenancies: Housing Act 1985, s.97.

[66] *Jones* v. *Chappell* (1875) L.R. 20 Eq. 539; *Doherty* v. *Allman* (1878) 3 App.Cas. 709.

[67] *Doe d. Darlington (Earl)* v. *Bond* (1826) 5 B. & C. 855.

[68] *Marsden* v. *Heyes (Edward) Ltd.* [1927] 2 K.B. 1.

[69] *Warren* v. *Keen* (1954) 1 Q.B. 15.

[70] *Wedd* v. *Porter* [1916] 2 K.B. 91.

[71] *Gregory* v. *Mighell* (1811) 18 Ves.Jr. 328.

[72] [1954] 1 Q.B. 15.

[73] *Supra*.

[74] *Supra*.

premises in the same tenantable condition as when first let, allowance being made for the natural decay of time.

The obligation of a weekly (and probably monthly) tenant to use the premises in a tenant-like manner would seem to mean that he must not commit voluntary waste and must repair damage occasioned, whether wilfully or negligently, by himself, his family or guests. Beyond this his responsibility is simply to take proper care of the place, doing the little jobs which a reasonable tenant would do.[75] In *Wycombe Area Health Authority* v. *Barnett*[76] the Court of Appeal held that the tenant of a dwelling house is not expected, in fulfilment of his obligation of tenant-like user, to lag internal water pipes or to keep the premises heated during winter as a precaution against freezing. However, if the climate is particularly cold, or the tenant is going to be absent for a long period during inclemently cold weather, he may be required to turn off the water or even to drain down the system.[77]

Treating the obligation of tenant-like user as an implied covenant, it was laid down in *Standen* v. *Christmas*[78] that no such contract is to be implied where the tenant has expressly contracted to repair. Lord Denning, on the other hand, in *Regis Property Co.* v. *Dudley*,[79] expressed it as a common law obligation of the tenant, separate and distinct from that imposed by a covenant to repair (whether express or implied) and giving rise to separate and distinct remedies, which are accordingly cumulative.

VI. ENFORCEMENT OF TENANT'S REPAIRING OBLIGATIONS

A. Exercise of Right of Entry to Repair

A provision in the lease that the landlord (who has no common law right to enter the leased premises for any purpose whatever other than to distrain for rent in arrear),[80] may enter for the purposes of viewing the state of repair, is very commonly inserted in leases.[81] A further stipulation often found permits the landlord to execute the necessary repairs at the tenant's expense, should the tenant fail to observe his repairing obligations. This provision is designed to enable the landlord to recoup the repair costs from the tenant.

[75] *Warren* v. *Keen* [1954] 1 Q.B. 15.
[76] (1982) 264 E.G. 619; *cf. Mickel* v. *M'Coard* 1913 S.C. 896.
[77] *Ibid.* See also *Warren* v. *Keen* [1954] 1 Q.B. 15; *Regis Property Co.* v. *Dudley* [1954] A.C. 370, *per* Lord Denning at p. 407.
[78] (1847) 10 Q.B. 135.
[79] [1959] A.C. 370 at p. 407; *cf. Buswell* v. *Goodwin* [1971] 1 W.L.R. 92 for a corresponding view of the landlord's statutory obligations to repair.
[80] *Yelloly* v. *Morley* (1910) 27 T.L.R. 20.
[81] See also Agricultural Holdings Act 1986, s.23.

However, such a device may prove to be a trap for the unwary landlord. It may be that the landlords' claim to recover the cost of the repairs from the tenant will be regarded as the equivalent of a claim for damages for breach of the tenant's repairing covenant, thus raising the potential applicability of the Leasehold Property (Repairs) Act 1938 and also the Landlord and Tenant Act 1927, s.18.[82] Since one of the objects of such an express term in the lease is to obviate the need to pay regard to such statutory provisions, much of the usefulness of the device might disappear. The law on this matter is in a considerable state of uncertainty. In *Swallow Securities* v. *Brand*[83] McNeill J. held that unliquidated payments of the kind stipulated for in the type of covenant under discussion fell full square within the mischief with which the Leasehold Property (Repairs) Act 1938, s.1, was designed to deal and hence a landlord's claim for reimbursement of the cost of repairs should be treated as a claim for damages for breach of repairing covenant. Accordingly, a landlord who enters with a view to carrying out the works at the tenant's expense without first serving a notice under the Law of Property Act 1925, s.146 and then securing the leave of the court under the 1938 Act[84] will be unable to recoup the costs of the repairs from his tenant who may thus, by virtue of his own default in repair, be presented with a most unmeritorious windfall.[85] Further, as a result of the Defective Premises Act 1972, s.4(1)[86] the existence of the right to enter and carry out repairs might involve the landlord in liability to third parties injured as a result of the premises being out of repair, without the landlord's having any effective remedy against the tenant.

In *Hamilton* v. *Martell Securities Ltd.*[87] Vinelott J. found these arguments persuasive and, as a consequence, refused to follow *Swallow Securities* v. *Brand*,[88] a decision he held to have been given *per incuriam*.[89] He also felt that there was a sufficient disincentive to landlords to perpetrate those abuses on their tenants at which the 1938 Act and the Landlord and Tenant Act 1927, s.18 were aimed, in the fact that the lessor must initially meet the cost of carrying out repairs. In the view of Vinelott J. a claim under a clause in a lease to recover moneys actually expended by the landlord in remedying disrepair occasioned by a tenant's breach of a repairing covenant should not be treated as a claim for damages for breach of contract but

---

[82] *Post*, Chap. 6 (VI) B.
[83] (1983) 45 P. & C.R. 328.
[84] Assuming that the tenant has served a counter notice under the Leasehold Property (Repairs) Act 1938, s.1(3).
[85] *S.E.D.A.C. Investments* v. *Tanner* [1982] 1 W.L.R. 1342.
[86] *Infra*.
[87] [1984] Ch. 266.
[88] *Supra*.
[89] The important cases to which McNeill J. had not been referred were *Bader Properties Ltd.* v. *Linley Property Investment Ltd.* (1968) 19 P. & C.R. 620 and *Middlegate Properties Ltd.* v. *Gidlow-Jackman* (1977) 34 P. & C.R. 4.

as a claim for debt. Accordingly, it fell outside the 1938 Act (and, presumably, section 18 of the 1927 Act also) and the lessor was entitled to sue without obtaining or seeking any leave from the court.[90] He did not, however, consider how a tenant could then defend a claim from a landlord for a fixed sum when the landlord had carried out a "de luxe" repair going far beyond the extent of the tenant's covenant.

It is submitted that the view of Vinelott J. is, on balance, to be preferred. The combined effect of *Swallow Securities* v. *Brand*[91] and *S.E.D.A.C. Investments Ltd.* v. *Tanner*[92] (a case which Vinelott J. regarded as unusual but not wrongly decided) was to turn clauses permitting landlords to re-enter and repair in the event of tenant default, recouping costs from the defaulting tenant, into dangerous and useless traps for landlords acting in good faith and in the best interests of good estate management practice and safety. In *Colchester Estates (Cardiff)* v. *Carlton Industries plc*[93] Nourse J. was required, effectively, to choose which authority to follow. He elected to apply *Hamilton's* case because "I am not convinced that Vinelott J. was wrong in not following McNeill J." After "full and careful arguments on both sides, each of which was almost certainly fuller than the arguments on the same side in either of the earlier cases,"[94] Nourse J. chose to resolve the matter by recourse to technical rules of precedent, holding that, in the case of conflict between two first instance decisions, the second decision should normally be followed. He urged that "further debate or expression of judicial view" should be at "the level of the Court of Appeal."[95] A resolution of this difficult point by a higher tribunal is, therefore, now awaited.

Access and reasonable facilities for repairs are an implied condition of a regulated tenancy under the Rent Act 1977.[96] A landlord who is subject to the obligations implied by section 11 of the Landlord and Tenant Act 1985, has a statutory right to enter and view on 24 hours' notice in writing to the occupier.[97]

The landlord has an implied right to enter for the purpose of complying with his own repairing obligations.[98] Beyond this, and except where there is a statutory right of entry, he has no right to enter his tenants' premises to repair them, in the absence of a distinct stipulation in the lease to that effect. Even though the tenant is clearly in breach, and though the landlord may himself be liable to forfeiture

---

[90] See Martin, [1984] Conv. 231.
[91] *Supra.*
[92] *Supra*, see footnote 84.
[93] [1984] 2 All E.R. 601.
[94] *Ibid.* p. 605.
[95] *Ibid.*
[96] *Post*, Chap. 11.
[97] *Supra*. See also The London Buildings Acts (Amendment) Act 1939, s.141; Building Act 1984, s.98; Highways Act 1980, s.304.
[98] *Granada Theatres* v. *Freehold Investment (Leytonstone) Ltd.* [1959] 1 W.L.R. 570. See also: *Duke of Westminster* v. *Guild* (1983) 267 E.G. 762; *McGreal* v. *Wake* (1984) 269 E.G. 1254.

for non-repair under a superior lease, if he enters to repair, he will commit a trespass which may be restrained by injunction.[99]

B. Action for Damages

(1) *Quantum*

An action for damages for non-repair may be brought by the landlord at any time during the term, and after its expiry.[1] The proper measure of damage was, at common law, the amount by which the reversion depreciated in market value by the premises being out of repair[2]—an amount which must be influenced by the length of time the lease has yet to run. By section 8(1) of the Landlord and Tenant Act 1927 damages for the breach of a covenant to keep or put in repair during the currency of a lease may not exceed the amount (if any) by which the value of the reversion is diminished owing to the breach of covenant. This provides a ceiling on the amount of damages recoverable, but does not alter the method of assessing them. The date for assessing damages for breach of the covenant to repair and deliver up in repair is the date of the writ of forfeiture.[3]

When action is brought at the termination of the lease the "value of the reversion" means the value of the property which has reverted.[4] Where the landlord has re-entered for the breach of covenant, the damages are the difference between the value of the property as it stands and the value it would have had if the tenant had carried out his obligations under the covenant, without regard to any gain which may accrue to the landlord from the acceleration of the falling in of the reversion.[5] In some cases the amount which has been, or would have to be, spent on putting the premises into the state in which they should have been put by the tenant will provide prima facie evidence of damage to the value of the reversion, and of the extent of such

---

[99] *Stocker* v. *Planet Building Society* (1879) 27 W.R. 877; *Regional Properties Ltd.* v. *City of London Real Property Co. Ltd.* (1980) 257 E.G. 64; although if the landlord gained entry and carried out repairs, under threat of forfeiture by a superior landlord, he may be able to recover his expenses from the sub-tenant: *Colley* v. *Streeton* (1823) 2 B. & C. 273.

[1] This is so even if the landlord had no title to grant the lease and the estoppel binding the tenant as a matter of law ceases when the term ends: *Industrial Properties (Barton Hill)* v. *Associated Electrical Industries* [1977] Q.B. 580. The landlord may make representations that the cost of the repairs will not be charged to the tenant. In such a case the landlord will be estopped from claiming damages, or indeed any other remedy for breach of the repairing covenant: *Brikom Investments Ltd.* v. *Carr* [1979] 2 All E.R. 753.

[2] *Mills* v. *East London Union* (1872) L.R. 8 C.P. 79. See also *Family Management* v. *Gray* (1979) 253 E.G. 369.

[3] *Associated Deliveries* v. *Harrison* (1984) 272 E.G. 321.

[4] *Hanson* v. *Newman* [1934] Ch. 298.

[5] *Ibid.*

damage.[6] The fact that the landlord actually has had, or intends to have, the repairs carried out is a strong case for the award of the actual or estimated cost of the works, in an action brought at or after the end of the lease. In *Jones* v. *Herxheimer*[7] rooms had been let for residential purposes. The landlord intended to let them again for the same purposes, once the repairs had been carried out. The cost of repairs done to make good the failure of the previous tenant to repair, and to make a new letting possible, was taken as the measure of the damage to the reversion. Where, however, there is little or no likelihood of the landlord doing the repairs, the cost provides very little evidence of the existence of damage or its quantum,[8] and evidence must be given (usually the expert evidence of a valuer) of an actual diminution in the value of the reversion through being out of repair, in order to entitle the landlord to more than nominal damages.[9]

In *Drummond* v. *S. & U. Stores Ltd.*[10] Glidewell J. said, however, in considering the extent to which certain dilapidations[11] in retail premises left empty for a number of years had diminished the value of the reversion:

> "It is apparent that evidence of the value of the premises in their state of disrepair may be difficult to come by, because of course, since most leases, particularly of commercial premises, envisage the premises being let in repair, or at any rate subject to the liability of a previous tenant to repair, the majority of comparable evidence relates to lettings of property in repair rather than in disrepair. Thus it may be very difficult indeed to obtain and put forward evidence of a comparable property in disrepair. . . . Thus it follows that evidence of the cost of putting the property into the state of repair required by the lease is relevant evidence and will very often be *prima facie* evidence, or at any rate the starting point, from which the amount of the diminution in the value of the reversion may be deduced."

The injury to the reversion from lack of repair while the term has still a substantial time to run is likely to be less than the damage would be from the same dilapidations at the end of the term. In some cases,

---

[6] *Joyner* v. *Weeks* [1891] 2 Q.B. 31; *Smiley* v. *Townshend* [1950] 2 K.B. 311; *Harrison* v. *Wells* [1967] 1 Q.B. 263.
[7] [1950] 2 K.B. 106.
[8] *Smiley* v. *Townshend* [1950] 2 K.B. 211.
[9] *Espir* v. *Basil Street Hotel* [1936] 3 All E.R. 91; *James* v. *Hutton* [1950] K.B. 9 *cf. Family Management* v. *Gray* (1979) 253 E.G. 369.
[10] (1981) 258 E.G. 1293.
[11] The need for clearing away rubbish and redecorating, repairing floorboards, erecting a firescreen round a staircase, checking and repairing electricity circuits, and determining that the tenant must meet the landlord's liability to V.A.T. on the cost of the repairs. See also *Smiley* v. *Townshend* [1950] 2 K.B. 311, *per* Denning L.J. at pp. 319, 322 and Singleton L.J. at p. 328.

to assess damages when the term has a relatively short time to run, the court may, where it would have awarded the cost of carrying out the works had the reversion fallen in, adopt a simple formula. This involves reducing the cost of carrying out the repairs to such sum as, invested at the rate of interest for the time being allowed on judgments, would yield a sum equal to that cost at the end of the term.[12] However, in times of high inflation, when the cost of repairs is likely to increase significantly over as short a period as six months, this solution is not especially beneficial to the landlord.

The landlord is not bound to expend the damages recovered in repairing the premises. He continues to have the benefit of the covenant where the term continues to run, and he may sue on it again if the tenant persists in breaking it. In the second action he can recover damages for the diminution in the value of the reversion by reason of the breaches then existing, credit being given, however, for the amount of any previous judgment.[13]

Under section 18(1) of the 1927 Act, no damages are recoverable by the landlord for a failure to leave or put premises in repair at the end of a lease, if it is shown that the premises would, at or shortly after the termination of the tenancy, have been demolished or undergone such structural alterations as would render the repairs in question valueless. The question is whether the landlord had such an intention to demolish or structurally alter at the actual date when the covenant fell to be performed, that is, at the termination of the lease, not at some earlier or later date.[14]

In *Hibernian Property Co.* v. *Liverpool Corporation*[15] the tenant, a local authority, was in breach of the covenant to repair to such an extent that the premises became unfit for human habitation and were included in a clearance area. The result was that the landlords, on compulsory purchase, became entitled only to site value compensation. In an action by the landlords for damages for breach of the repairing covenants the defendant authority claimed that, by virtue of section 18(1) of the Landlord and Tenant Act 1927 the landlords were not entitled to recover damages because it had been shown that shortly after the termination of the lease the house would be pulled down. Caulfield J. held that the landlords had suffered damage as a result of the local authority's breach of covenant in that the value of their reversion had been diminished. The relevant provision of section 18(1) had no application to the instant case because, *inter alia*, the section contemplated the lessor making a decision to pull down or so structurally alter the premises that any repairs necessary to comply with the lease would have been nugatory. It could not be construed as

---

[12] See *Kent* v. *Conniff* [1953] 1 Q.B. 361, *per* Slade J.
[13] *Ebbetts* v. *Conquest* [1895] 2 Ch. 377.
[14] *Salisbury* v. *Gilmore* [1942] 2 K.B. 38; *Keats* v. *Graham* [1959] 3 All E.R. 919.
[15] [1973] 1 W.L.R. 751.

enabling a local authority, by its own failure to comply with the repairing covenant, so that the house had to be demolished, to claim relief in an action for damages for breach of covenant.[16]

(2) *Sub-leases*

The damages for breach of covenant to repair in a sub-lease will be governed by the diminution in value of the sub-lessor's reversion. Where the sub-lessee has notice that there is a superior landlord, the sub-lessor's liability to the superior landlord must be taken into account.[17] Even without such notice, if the effect of the sub-lessee's breaches is to convert his landlord's reversion into a liability, the amount of which may be measured by the sum he would have to pay someone to take it over, the sub-tenant will be liable in damages for that amount.[18] Where, however, the sub-lessor has only a nominal reversion and there is no liability owed to the superior landlord, as where the reversion on the head lease has become vested in the sub-lessee, no more than nominal damages can be recovered.[19]

The covenants in a sub-lease may differ from those in the head lease, or the covenants may be different in effect from having been entered into at a different time. Where this is so the damages may not necessarily be the same, and the head lessee may not necessarily (in the absence of a covenant of indemnity) be able to recover the costs of the lessor's action against him.

(3) *Leasehold Property (Repairs) Act 1938*

This Act, as extended by section 51 of the Landlord and Tenant Act 1954, provides considerable protection to tenants of terms of seven years or longer. Quite often when a tenant acquires the end of a lease, he finds that he has to pay for all the repairs which the earlier tenants should have carried out. If the tenancy has still at least three years to run of a term that was originally for more than seven years, the 1938 Act requires the landlord to serve a notice on the tenant under section 146 of the Law of Property Act 1925. This notice must specify the particular covenant to repair which, in his view, has been broken. The notice must require the tenant to remedy the situation by specifying which repairs must be carried out, assuming the breach can be remedied. Finally, it must require the tenant to pay compensation in

[16] *cf.* the attitude of the court towards extreme landlord default under the Landlord and Tenant Act 1985, s.8(1): *Buswell* v. *Goodwin* [1971] 1 W.L.R. 92.
[17] *Ebbetts* v. *Conquest* [1895] 2 Ch. 377; affd. [1896] A.C. 490; *Ellis* v. *Viscountess Torrington* [1920] 1 K.B. 399.
[18] *Lloyds Bank* v. *Lake* [1961] 1 W.L.R. 884.
[19] *Espir* v. *Basil Street Hotel* [1936] 3 All E.R. 91.

money for the breach. The tenant must be given a reasonable time to comply with the notice.

The landlord cannot enforce a right to damages for breach of a covenant to repair,[20] in a lease to which the 1938 Act applies, unless he has served on the tenant, not less than one month before commencement of the action, a notice in accordance with section 146(1) of the Law of Property Act 1925.[21] The notice will not be valid unless it contains a statement, in characters no less conspicuous than those used in any other part of the notice, to the effect that the lessee is entitled to serve a counter-notice claiming the benefit of the 1938 Act. The landlord's notice must also inform the tenant of his rights with respect to the time and manner of service of the counter-notice, and the name and address of the landlord where such counter-notice can be served.[22] It is essential that these requirements are strictly complied with.[23]

If the tenant, within 28 days of the date of service upon him of the landlord's notice, serves on the landlord a counter-notice to the effect that he claims the benefit of the Leasehold Property (Repairs) Act 1938, then no proceedings can be taken by the lessor, either for damages (or forfeiture)[24] for breach of the covenant in question, otherwise than with the leave of the court.[25] Section 1(5) provides that leave shall not be given unless the landlord proves:

"(a) that the immediate remedying of the breach is requisite for preventing substantial diminution in the value of his reversion, or that the value thereof has been substantially diminished by the breach;

(b) that the immediate remedying of the breach is required for giving effect in relation to the premises to the purposes of

---

[20] Not every obligation in the repairing covenant will be an obligation "to keep or put in repair" within s.1(1) of the 1938 Act. Thus, in *Starrokate Ltd.* v. *Burry* (1983) 265 E.G. 871, an obligation to cleanse a lavatory was not an obligation to repair to which s.1(1) applied, even though it was found amongst the repairing covenants in the lease. A covenant to lay out insurance monies on rebuilding is not a repairing covenant within s.1(1), although it may be different in the case of a covenant to reinstate: *Farimani* v. *Gates* (1984) 271 E.G. 887, but, on this last point, see *contra* Buckley J. in *Re King dec'd* [1962] 1 W.L.R. 632 at p. 645.

[21] Leasehold Property (Repairs) Act 1938, s.1. Costs or expenses incurred by the landlord in or in contemplation of any proceedings under Law of Property Act 1925, ss.146 or 147 and recoverable under an express covenant in the lease are not damages; thus no leave under the 1938 Act is necessary: *Bader* v. *Linley Property Investments* (1968) 19 P. & C.R. 620; *Middlegate Properties* v. *Gidlow-Jackson* (1977) 34 P. & C.R. 4.

[22] For a form of notice see *Woodfall*, Vol. 1.A.3.

[23] See *Middlegate Properties* v. *Messimeris* [1973] 1 W.L.R. 168. For details of proper service see the Law of Property Act 1925, s.196; Recorded Delivery Service Act 1962; *Sidnell* v. *Wilson* [1966] 2 Q.B. 67. For a s.146 notice to be validly served so as to comply with the 1938 Act it is necessary that the notice is served before the breach of covenant in question has been remedied: *S.E.D.A.C. Investments* v. *Tanner* [1982] 1 W.L.R. 1342.

[24] See *post.*

[25] Leasehold Property (Repairs) Act 1938, s.1(3). A landlord's application under s.1(3) for leave to commence action for breach of a repairing covenant is registrable as a pending land action under the Land Charges Act 1972: *Selim* v. *Bickenhall Engineering Co. Ltd.* [1981] 3 All E.R. 210.

any enactment, or of any by-law or other provision having effect under any enactment, or for giving effect to any order of a court or requirement of any authority under any enactment or any such by-law or provision as aforesaid;

(c) where the lessee is not in occupation of the whole premises as respects which the covenant or agreement is proposed to be enforced, that the immediate remedying of the breach is required in the interests of the occupier of those premises or of part thereof;

(d) that the breach can be immediately remedied at an expense that is relatively small in comparison with the much greater expense that would probably be occasioned by postponement of the necessary work; or

(e) special circumstances which in the opinion of the court render it just and equitable that leave should be given."

The landlord has only to show what Lord Denning M.R. has called a "*prima facie* case,"[26] and what Diplock L.J. called "an arguable case" of such a breach by the tenant. The application for leave should not constitute a full-scale hearing, although the landlord must adduce some admissible evidence of a breach which satisfies one or more of paragraphs (a) to (e) listed above. The court may, in granting or refusing leave, impose such terms and conditions on either party as it may think fit. The court's discretion to grant leave on any of the grounds in section 1(5) of the 1938 Act is interlocutory, but there is a complete discretion to grant or refuse leave.[27]

Where a tenant fails to repair and the landlord, relying upon a covenant in the lease, carries out the necessary repair works himself and then seeks repayment of the costs thereof under the terms of the lease, there is conflicting authority as to whether the 1938 Act applies. These cases have been discussed in detail earlier in this chapter.[28]

C. Forfeiture

A landlord may only forfeit the lease for disrepair if he has reserved the right to forfeit for breach of repairing covenants in the lease. The way in which a landlord can set out to forfeit for non-repair is statutorily circumscribed by section 146(1) of the Law of Property Act

---

[26] *Sidnell* v. *Wilson* [1966] 2 Q.B. 67. See also *Land Securities plc.* v. *Receiver for Metropolitan Police District* [1983] 2 All E.R. 254, *per* Megarry V.-C. at p. 258.

[27] *Land Securities plc.* v. *Receiver for Metropolitan Police District, supra.*

[28] *Supra,* Chap. 6 (VI) A.

1925. As with a claim for damages, he must give the tenant notice.[29] He must tell the tenant what he is complaining about, demand that the situation be remedied if it is capable of remedy,[30] and require a sum from the tenant as compensation for the breach. The tenant must be given a reasonable time to comply with the notice. The tenant may regard the notice, or the time allowed, as unreasonable, or he may dispute that there has been a breach. If the landlord proceeds to forfeit, then the tenant can apply to the court for relief against forfeiture.[31] There is a wide discretion to grant relief and the court must have regard to the parties' conduct and to all the other circumstances.[32] If the tenant's breach relates to internal decorations, then any tenant who is threatened with forfeiture can apply to the court for relief from liability for such repairs.[33] There are circumstances in which the court cannot grant relief, *e.g.* if the repairs are needed to keep the house fit for human habitation, or structurally sound, or sanitary[34] but, apart from that, the court can grant either partial or complete relief.[35]

The position of tenants of terms of seven years or longer is given the same especial consideration with regard to forfeiture as in actions for damages. The requirements for service of notice and counter-notice in the case of tenancies that still have at least three years to run of terms that were originally for more than seven years, apply equally to forfeiture as to damages actions.[36] Similarly, if the tenant serves a counter-notice the landlord cannot forfeit without the court's leave, granted on the five limited grounds discussed above in relation to claims for damages.

Even if the lease is forfeited, the tenant of residential property may still be able to stay on as a statutory tenant, where his tenancy is protected by the Rent Act 1977,[37] or if he is a "secure" tenant under the Housing Act 1985, he may still remain in possession on forfeiture.[38] Forfeiture will not, in these cases, by itself entitle the landlord to possession. The residential statutory or secure tenancy will still have to be ended by court order. The court will have to be

---

[29] The notice must be served on the tenant for the time being. If the lease has been assigned the notice must be served on the assignee even if the assignment has taken place without the consent of the landlord as required by the lease: *Old Grovebury Manor Farm Ltd.* v. *Seymour Plant Sales & Hire Ltd.* (No. 2) [1979] 3 All E.R. 504.

[30] See *Expert Clothing Service & Sales* v. *Hillgate House* [1985] 3 W.L.R. 359.

[31] Law of Property Act 1925, s.146(2). In considering relief, the court must still have regard to judicial practice prior to 1873, though probably not in respect of the s.146(2) power: *G.M.S. Syndicate Ltd.* v. *Gary Elliott Ltd.* [1982] Ch. 1.

[32] *Hyman* v. *Rose* [1912] A.C. 623. For a general discussion of forfeiture other than for non-payment of rent, see *post*, Chap. 8.

[33] Law of Property Act 1925, s.147.

[34] *Ibid.* s.147(2).

[35] Leasehold Property (Repairs) Act 1938, s.1, *supra.*

[36] See *post*, Chap. 11.

[37] ss.29, 33. See *post*, Chap. 16.

[38] Rent Act 1977, s.98(1), Sched. 15, Case 3; Housing Act 1985, s.84, Sched. 2, Pt. 1, ground 3.

satisfied both that it is reasonable to make an order for possession and that the condition of the house has deteriorated as a result of the tenant's breaches of repairing covenants.[39]

D. Specific Performance

In *Hill* v. *Barclay*[40] Lord Eldon stated emphatically[41] that a tenant cannot be compelled by mandatory injunction or decree of specific performance to comply with his repairing covenants. In *Jeune* v. *Queens Cross Properties*[42] Pennycuick V.-C. did not feel that Lord Eldon's words were operative to prevent an order of specific performance being made against a landlord to compel him to carry out his repairing obligations. Indeed, the power to compel performance by a landlord has now been given statutory effect.[43] Logically, where the repairs required to be done are sufficiently specific, the principle of mutuality might require that no distinction in the matter of granting a decree of specific performance should be drawn between landlord and tenant. However, unless and until *Hill* v. *Barclay*[44] is overruled on this point, it would appear to be the case that a landlord cannot secure an order compelling his tenant actually to carry out repairs in accordance with his covenant. As recently as 1980 Oliver J. appeared to infer that it was unlikely that specific performance could be obtained of a tenant's repairing covenant.[45]

E. Remedies for Waste

A tenant who is liable for waste may be sued for damages by the landlord, the measure of damage being the diminution in the value of the reversion, less a discount for immediate payment.[46] There is older authority[47] for the proposition that in very gross cases, what have been called "vindictive damages" may be given.[48] It is hardly conceivable

---

[39] (1810) 16 Ves.Jr. 402.
[40] *Ibid.* p. 405.
[41] Even though the lease is determined by service of the writ of forfeiture, it is retrospectively re-instated if relief is granted. Where a relief application is pending, the landlord's covenants remain enforceable by the tenant during the "limbo" period: *Peninsular Maritime Ltd.* v. *Padseal Ltd.* (1981) 259 E.G. 860. The landlord, however, having elected to end the lease, would be unable to enforce the tenant's covenants. The tenant's covenants cannot subsist after the writ of forfeiture: see *Associated Deliveries* v. *Harrison* (1984) 272 E.G. 321.
[42] [1974] Ch. 97.
[43] Landlord and Tenant Act 1985, s.17; mutuality is not required.
[44] (1810) 16 Ves.Jr. 402.
[45] *Regional Properties* v. *City of London Real Property Co.* (1980) 257 E.G. 64
[46] *Whitham* v. *Kershaw* (1886) 16 Q.B.D. 613.
[47] *Ibid. per* Bowen L.J.
[48] See *Woodfall*, Vol. 1, p. 651.

that such awards survive the House of Lords' decisions in *Rookes* v. *Barnard*[49] and *Broome* v. *Cassell & Co.*[50]

In an action for voluntary waste the plaintiff may claim an injunction against repetition or continuance of the injury complained of, and an interlocutory injunction may be granted where justified.[51] Where a tenant commits acts of waste for which merely nominal damages would be given, an injunction will not be granted if it appears that the tenant does not contemplate committing any further waste.[52] The remedy by injunction is ordinarily the most effective to deal with tenants committing acts of waste, as it prevents that injury which after it is done, can only be compensated for by other remedies. It seems that no injunction will issue, however, to restrain acts of permissive waste.[53]

F. Liability of Former Tenants

A tenant who assigns his tenancy to a new, incoming tenant does not thereby cease to be liable on any express covenant to repair which he may have given. The original tenant is liable for all breaches of covenant (though only, of course, in damages),[54] throughout the term of the lease, even after he has assigned, because there is still privity of contract between him and the landlord.[55] However, an assignee of the lease is liable only for breaches committed while the lease was vested in him,[56] since his liability depends upon privity of estate, and privity of estate exists only while the estate is held.[57] Some covenants, nevertheless, are such that, if broken, the breach is a continuing one, and covenants to repair (as opposed to covenants to leave in repair at the end of the term) are of this kind.[58] In these circumstances, an assignee of the term will be liable for breaches of repairing covenants occurring *before* the lease was assigned to him. He will not, however, be liable for breaches committed after he has himself assigned the lease.[59]

---

[49] [1964] A.C. 1129.
[50] [1972] A.C. 1027.
[51] Supreme Court Act 1981, s.37.
[52] *Doran* v. *Carroll* (1860) 111 Ch.R. 379.
[53] *Powys* v. *Blagrave* (1854) 4 De. G.M. & G. 448.
[54] There are special rules in respect of rent, so that the original lessee may be liable to pay an increased rent resulting from a rent review carried out after assignment: see *Centrovincial Estates* v. *Bulk Storage* (1983) 46 P. & C.R. 393; *Selous Street Properties* v. *Oronel Fabrics* (1984) 270 E.G. 643; *Allied London Investments* v. *Hambro Life Assurance* (1984) 269 E.G. 41. These difficult cases are discussed *supra*, Chap. 5(III) C.
[55] *Thursby* v. *Plant* (1670) 1 Wms.Saund. 230; *John Betts & Sons Ltd.* v. *Price* (1924) 40 T.L.R. 589; Law of Property Act 1925, s.79.
[56] *Chancellor* v. *Poole* (1781) 2 Doug. 764.
[57] Megarry & Wade, pp. 743–744.
[58] *Granada Theatres Ltd.* v. *Freehold Investment (Leytonstone) Ltd.* [1959] Ch. 592.
[59] *Paul* v. *Nurse* (1828) 8 B. & C. 486.

If a covenant is broken while the lease is vested in an assignee of the original tenant, that assignee's liability for this breach will continue despite any subsequent assignment of the tenancy he may make.[60] So, while the original lessee of a lease containing onerous covenants to repair cannot divest himself of liability for future breaches, an assignee can do so by assigning the lease, even if the new assignee has no funds to meet his liability.[61]

VII. Remedies in Respect of Fixtures[62]

A landlord has an action for damages for waste in respect of any fixtures wrongfully removed by the tenant when he leaves. He can also apply for an injunction to restrain such an act. Only where damages would be an inequitable or unconscionable remedy will a mandatory injunction be granted to replace a fixture wrongfully removed. In *Phillips* v. *Lamdin*[63] the plaintiff contracted with the defendant to take an assignment of the defendant's lease of a house. When viewing the house before the contract to purchase, the plaintiff noticed an ornate door, matching a mantel-piece, attributed to the design of Adam. On taking possession, however, she found that the door had been removed and replaced by one of plain white wood. Croom-Johnson J. said[64]:

> " . . . the defendant, in the teeth of his contract, has removed something which is not a mere trifle. I entertain no doubt that he is liable to replace the door. You cannot make a new Adam door. In these times you cannot re-fashion a door or make a copy. It seems to me that it is proper to order the defendant to return the door to where it belongs and to pay the expenses of so doing. I do not see how damages can be an adequate remedy, and I do not mean, if I can avoid it, to give the defendant the opportunity of paying damages in lieu."

It seems that a tenant who lawfully removes tenants' fixtures also commits waste if he fails to make good damage (such as holes made by the fixtures) which affect the structure of the building.[65]

---

[60] *Harley* v. *King* (1835) 2 Cromp.M. & R. 18.
[61] *Valliant* v. *Dodemede* (1742) 2 Atk. 546. For a detailed consideration of the position on assignment, see *post*, Chap. 7.
[62] See the discussion *supra*, Chap. 3.
[63] [1949] 2 K.B. 33.
[64] *Ibid.* p. 35.
[65] *Mancetter Developments Ltd.* v. *Garmanson Ltd., Financial Times*, January 22, 1986. Where a company director instructs his company to remove tenant's fixtures without making good, he may be personally liable to the landlord for the company's acts of waste: *ibid.*

CHAPTER 7

TRANSFER

I. Introduction 297
II. Can the Tenant Part with his Interest? 301
    A. The Right to Assign 301
    B. Restrictions on the Right to Dispose 302
    C. Consent to Disposals 306
III. Effecting Assignments and Subtenancies 313
    A. The Contract 313
    B. The Assignment 314
    C. Sub-leases 315
IV. The Position after Assignment, Transfer and Sub-lease 315
    A. Original Landlord and Tenant 315
    B. Landlord and Assignee 316
    C. Original Tenant and Assignee . 321
    D. Sub-lessors, Sub-lessees and their Assigns 322
    E. Original Lessors and their Transferees 324
    F. Transfer on Death 326
    G. Transfer on Bankruptcy 329
    H. Transfer following Divorce .. 332

I. INTRODUCTION

When a landlord creates a tenancy he wants to make sure that the tenant is likely to be sufficiently responsible to carry out the contractual obligations and also financially able to do so. There is always the possibility that the original tenant may want to dispose of his interest during the term voluntarily, by assigning his whole interest, sub-letting part of the property or creating occupational licences. The extent to which the landlord prohibits these activities, or places limited restrictions on them will depend on the terms negotiated between the original parties. In general, the longer the lease, the less likely a tenant will be to agree to restrictions on his power to dispose of his interest. The shorter the term, the more likely the landlord will be able, in his own financial and property interests, to insist on some control over the choice of an incoming tenant or sub-tenant.

An absolute prohibition against assignment in the following terms: "Not to assign underlet or part with the possession of the property or any part thereof" is commonly found in two cases. First, where the landlord is providing what is in effect rent free accommodation for a favoured relative, employee or friend for the rest of his life. This is done by creating a lease for, say, 21 years at a nominal rent terminable by notice following the death of the tenant.[1] Secondly, the restriction will be found in lettings by owner-occupiers who are letting their houses, most commonly while they are working abroad for a year or longer, and want to let in such a way that on their return they can

---

[1] The restriction on creating a lease for a life is contained in L.P.A. 1925, s.149(6). For a specimen lease for years terminable on death, see *Encyclopedia of Forms and Precedents* (4th ed.), Vol. 11, p. 522.

297

recover possession readily from their tenants who will be unable to claim Rent Act protection.[2] But even these express restrictions on voluntary assignments will not prevent the devolution of the tenant's interest involuntarily that may happen on death or bankruptcy.

The next type of covenant will provide: "Not without the written consent of the landlord to assign. . . . " It will be seen that the landlord has to act reasonably in the granting or withholding of his consent,[3] and, indeed, that may be expressed in the covenant itself by the addition of the words: "Such consent not to be unreasonably withheld in the case of a responsible and respectable person." A long lease, especially one granted at a premium, may well contain no restrictions on assignment or sub-letting but a requirement that dealings with the tenant's interest be registered with the landlord's agents. The purpose of this is to ensure that the agents know who are the tenants for the time being, to whom the landlord can look in the first instance for compliance with the terms of the lease.

The covenant against assignment is likely to be reinforced either by a specific condition that the term will come to an end if it is broken or by a general proviso for re-entry and forfeiture of the tenant's term on breach of his covenants. Forfeiture for non-payment of rent has already been discussed[4] and forfeiture generally is considered in the following chapter. But forfeiture for breach of a covenant against assigning was a very potent weapon that has been blunted by a succession of legislative changes. It is helpful to bear in mind the Parliamentary "state of play" at the date of any specific decision which is being considered, as it does seem that the courts leaned more towards a tenant's construction of a covenant against assignment when relief from forfeiture was less likely to be given.

Until 1859 landlords were reluctant to grant their consent to assignments because of *Dumpor's Case*.[5] The effect of that decision was to treat the covenant against assignment as entire. Once the landlord had given his consent to an assignment he could never again during the continuance of the lease enforce that covenant restricting assignment or sub-letting. This grotesque interpretation was changed by the Law of Property Amendment Act 1859, ss.1 and 2, now the Law of Property Act 1925, s.143. Perhaps traces of the decision still survive in that formal licences to assign still frequently provide that the consent applies only to the specific proposed assignment and not to future assignments generally, although these words seem to be added on the "belt and braces" principle.

The two common defences to actions for forfeiture were first that

---

[2] *e.g.* a letting under Rent Act 1977, Sched. 15, Case 11. Lettings under cases 12–20 will also contain similar restrictions.
[3] Landlord and Tenant Act 1927, s.19 and see *post*, (II)C.
[4] *Ante*, Chap. 5 (VII).
[5] (1603) 4 Co. Rep. 119b.

the terms of the covenant did not apply to the person attempting to assign, and secondly that the activity complained of did not fall within the precise words of the covenant. When a tenant covenanted on behalf of himself and his assigns, this was held in 1815 not to include assigns who took by operation of law. The covenant would not bind the tenant's trustee in bankruptcy.[6] The Law of Property Act 1925, s.79(1), settles that issue for covenants entered into after 1925 by providing that:

"A covenant relating to any land of a covenantor or capable of being bound by him, shall, unless a contrary intention is expressed, be deemed to be made by the covenantor on behalf of himself, his successors in title and the persons deriving title under him or them, and, subject as aforesaid, shall have effect as if such successors and other persons were expressed."

This section was new in 1925. It is a word saving section and obviates the need for the draftsman to specify all the persons who will be bound by the covenant. The second defence, that the activity complained about is not covered by the words used, is still the subject of much litigation and depends on the true construction of the clause in relation to the facts. As a general principle covenants against assignment are restrictively interpreted "having been always construed by courts of law with the utmost jealousy to prevent the restraint from going beyond the express stipulation."[7]

In 1947 Lord Goddard C.J. with characteristic clarity, set out the history of relief from forfeiture in the following terms[8]:

"Before the Act of 1925, so far as courts of law were concerned, the Conveyancing Act 1881, s.14, contained the relevant provisions on this matter. Section 14(1), which was similar to s.146(1) of the Act of 1925, deprived the landlord of the right of re-entry unless he complied with the requirements of the subsection,[9] and s.14(2) conferred on the court power to grant relief against forfeiture—a power which had hitherto only been exercised by courts of equity. Section 14 of the Act of 1881 did not, however, apply to covenants against assignment or underlett-

---

[6] *Doe d.Goodbehere* v. *Bevan* (1815) 3 M. & S. 353; [1814–23] All E.R. Rep. 706. It is clear that the trustee in bankruptcy is now regarded as a successor in title, and so bound by the covenant, *Re Wright (a Bankrupt), ex p. Landau* v. *The Trustee* [1949] Ch. 729. And see also *Re Robert Stephenson & Co. Ltd., Poole* v. *The Company* [1915] 1 Ch. 802 (where the "The Lessees" were expressed to include executors and administrators, and were held to include an assignee company).

[7] *Per* Lord Eldon L.C. in *Church* v. *Brown* (1808) 15 Ves.Jr. 258; [1803–13] All E.R. Rep. 440.

[8] *House Property and Investment Co. Ltd.* v. *James Walker, Goldsmith & Silversmith Ltd.* [1948] 1 K.B. 257 at p. 260.

[9] Service of notice specifying breach, and requiring remedy if appropriate, and claiming compensation.

ing or parting with the possession of property[10] without the consent of the landlord (s.14(6)(i)), and, therefore, the courts had no power to grant relief in such cases. In spite of the limitation which was placed on the powers of the courts by the Act of 1881, in *Barrow* v. *Isaacs & Son*[11] it was held that, in certain circumstances, a court of equity could still give relief, but not where it was a mere matter of neglect and mistake, and therefore in the latter circumstances the tenant could get relief neither at law nor at equity.

"The Conveyancing Act, 1881, was repealed *in toto* by the Law of Property Act 1925, except for a few immaterial provisions, and one object of s.146 of the Act of 1925 was to extend the powers of the courts which had been limited by the earlier Act. Section 146 of the Act of 1925, however, applies to any breach of covenant, and, therefore, it applies equally to covenants against assignment or underletting without consent as it does to any other breach."

The only other important legislative change to bear in mind throughout is that made by section 19 of the Landlord and Tenant Act 1927. This applies where there is a covenant "Not to assign etc. without the consent of the landlord," or similar variations on that theme. In these cases, the section implies a proviso that such licence or consent is not to be unreasonably withheld.[12] No such proviso is implied at common law in the case of covenants not to assign or alter, except with consent.[13]

Just as the tenant may wish to dispose of his interest, the landlord may well want to transfer his reversion, or again there may be an involuntary disposition on death or bankruptcy. The landlord's interest need not be assigned as a whole. He can dispose of part of his interest in the tenanted property, *e.g.* half the farm. But in all these cases one is concerned to establish the rights of the original parties and their successors, and in particular the duration and extent of the liability of successors to the landlord's and tenant's estates. There are no restrictions on the landlord's right to dispose of his interest, although his interest may well be affected by the grant of an option to purchase, or right of pre-emption.[14] Within two months of the transfer of the landlord's interest in a dwelling, the new landlord has to give the tenant written notice of the assignment, and his name and address.[15]

---

[10] This expression seems to have covered parting with possession or part of the property, *Abrahams* v. *Macfisheries Ltd.* [1925] 2 K.B. 18, not following *Russell* v. *Beecham* [1924] 1 K.B. 525.
[11] [1891] 1 Q.B. 417.
[12] This is discussed *post*, (II).
[13] *Pearl Assurance* v. *Shaw* (1985) 274 E.G. 492.
[14] See *ante*, Chap. 4(V) C, D.
[15] Landlord and Tenant Act 1985, s.3(1).

II. Can the Tenant Part with his Interest?

A. The Right to Assign

The right to assign a leasehold interest is a normal incident of the leasehold estate, unless the right is restrained.[16] A registered proprietor of a leasehold estate has an express statutory right both to transfer his interest and create underleases.[17] Where there is a partial restriction in the lease the register must contain an entry for preventing dealings in contravention of that restriction.[18] Where the lease contains an absolute prohibition against all *inter vivos* dealings it is not possible to register it at all.[19] If the covenant permitting assignment with consent only is contained in a building lease[20] for more than 40 years then it may automatically be subject to a statutory proviso that the consent is not needed if the assignment, underletting, charging or parting with possession is effected more than seven years before the end of the term,[21] provided that the lessor is given notice within six months of any assignment, etc. Tenants of building leases will be resistant in any event to agreeing to restrictions on their right to create subsidiary interests or to dispose of their own, because they obviously hope to recover their capital outlay by exploitation of the development. Opposition to restrictions is likely to be more successful in the case of a development consisting of houses which the purchasers will want to mortgage than one of offices, shops and flats involving multiple occupation of the same unit. In any event the relieving statutory proviso does not apply when the landlord is a Government department, local or public authority or a statutory or public utility. This can be of some importance as local authorities especially are often involved as landlords in building schemes in inner cities and usually want to retain considerable overall control. In all these cases, the prospective tenant has to consider if the restrictions will reduce the commercial viability of his project.

When the parties have agreed that the lease shall contain such terms restricting the tenant's disposal as the landlord might reasonably

---

[16] *Church* v. *Brown* (1808) 15 Ves.Jr. 258.

[17] L.R.A. 1925, s.21(1).

[18] L.R.A.1925, s.8(2).

[19] L.R.A. 1925, s.8(2). Because the L.R.A. is a "conveyancing" statute there would be no point in providing for substantive registration of a non-transferable estate. But protective registration by entry of a notice under section 48 against the lessor's registered title is necessary.

[20] This covers a lease made wholly or partially in consideration of the erection, substantial improvement, addition or alteration of buildings. See L.P.A. 1925, s.205(1)(*iii*) and S.L.A. 1925, s.117(1)(*i*).

[21] L. & T.A. 1927, s.19(1)(*b*). These particular provisions do not apply to mining leases, and section 19 as a whole does not apply to leases of agricultural holdings, within the Agricultural Holdings Act 1986, see L. & T.A. 1927, s.19(4), as amended.

require,[22] the court can spell out the precise terms of the covenant. But the court cannot insert a covenant restricting assigning and under-letting in a lease if the parties have agreed that the lease will contain the "usual covenants." The covenant restricting assignment and underletting although common and normal is not technically "usual."[23]

B. Restrictions on the Right to Dispose

"Not to assign underlet or part with the possession of the property or any part thereof. . . . "

These are three separate covenants, but they are not mutually exclusive. The extent to which they overlap is still not entirely clear.[24]

(1) *"Assign"*

"Assign" means a formal legal assignment. The covenant is not broken by an equitable assignment giving a charge on the property,[25] or by a deposit of the lease by way of security,[26] or by the tenant's declaration that he holds the lease on trust for his creditors.[27] A difficult situation can arise when there is a change in the members of a partnership who trade in leasehold premises, and the lease prohibits assignments. But again so long as the lease is not assigned when new partners are taken in, there will be no breach of the covenant even if the lease is part of the partnership property.[28] The same is true on a dissolution. A formal assignment to the continuing partners will be a breach,[29] an unexecuted agreement to assign will not.[30]

An assignment involves a parting with the whole of the tenant's term of years. A simple covenant against assigning is not therefore broken simply by a normal sub-letting of all or part of the property.[31] But if the tenant creates a purported sub-lease for the entire term and of the entire property then this will amount to an assignment and be in

---

[22] *Sweet & Maxwell, Ltd.* v. *Universal News Services, Ltd.* [1964] 2 Q.B. 699.
[23] *Church* v. *Brown* (1808) 15 Ves.Jr. 258; [1803–13] All E.R. Rep. 440; *Hampshire* v. *Wickens* (1878) 7 Ch.D. 555; *Chester* v. *Buckingham Travel Ltd.* [1981] 1 W.L.R. 96. and see *ante*, Chap. 3(V) E(4).
[24] *Marks* v. *Warren* [1979] 1 All E.R. 29.
[25] *Bowser* v. *Colby* (1841) 1 Hare 109; [1835–42] All E.R. Rep. 478.
[26] *Doe d.Pitt* v. *Hogg* (1824) 4 Dow. and Ry. 226.
[27] *Gentle* v. *Faulkner* [1900] 2 Q.B. 267; and see *Pincott* v. *Moorstons, Ltd.* [1937] 1 All E.R. 513 (where the parties proposed to carry out a prohibited assignment by means of a declaration of trust).
[28] *Singh (Gian) & Co.* v. *Nahar* [1965] 1 W.L.R. 412.
[29] *Langton* v. *Henson* (1905) 92 L.T. 805.
[30] *Bristol Corporation* v. *Westcott* (1879) 12 Ch.D. 461, describing covenants against assignment as "seldom artistically drawn" and "very often meaningless."
[31] *Church* v. *Brown* (1808) 15 Ves.Jr. 258; [1803–13] All E.R. Rep. 440.

breach of the covenant against assigning.[32] Of course, the covenant against assigning rarely stands by itself and an underletting of this nature will usually be covered by the other parts of the covenant. The covenant against assigning prohibits only voluntary assignments. It does not catch the passing of the estate on death to the tenant's personal representatives[33] or to his trustee in bankruptcy.[34] Neither will there be a breach of the covenant when the lease is subject to a compulsory purchase order,[35] or when it is taken in execution under a judgment order.[36] But it is not uncommon to find in the forfeiture clause a proviso that the lease will come to an end on the bankruptcy of the tenant, or on the liquidation of a tenant company except for the purposes of voluntary reconstruction, or on the tenant suffering a distress or execution.[37] In any event the liquidator of the company will himself be subject to the terms of the covenant,[38] and, it is suggested, the effect of section 79 of the Law of Property Act 1925 is now to make the covenant binding on trustees in bankruptcy.[39]

(2) *"Sub-letting"*

"Sub-letting" is the creation of an underlease of all or part of the demised property. The tenant who is sub-letting must retain a reversion, even if only a nominal one of a day if he is to retain a legal estate in the premises. If he "sub-lets" the entire property for the rest of his term then this constitutes in law an assignment of his term. One effect of this is that his landlord becomes the so-called sub-tenant's landlord, and in this instance there is privity of estate between the original landlord and the so-called sub-tenant. Lord Greene M.R. explained this in *Milmo* v. *Carreras*,[40] where in fact the sub-letting for longer than the original term was accidental. He said:

> "Where a lessee, by a document in the form of a sub-lease, divests himself of everything that he has (which he must necessarily do if he is transferring to his so-called sub-lessee an estate as great as, or purporting to be greater than, his own) from that moment he is a stranger to the land, in the sense that the relationship of landlord and tenant, in respect of tenure, cannot any longer exist between him and the so-called sub-lessee. That relationship must

[32] *Langford* v. *Selmes* (1857) 3 K. & J. 220, and see (1967) 31 Conv. (N.S.) 159, Paul Jackson.
[33] *Crusoe d.Blencowe* v. *Rugby* (1771) 3 Wils. 234; (1963) 27 Conv. (N.S.) 159, D. G. Barnsley.
[34] *Re Riggs, ex p. Lovell* [1901] 2 K.B. 16 (tenant filed his own petition).
[35] *Slipper* v. *Tottenham and Hampstead Junction Railway Co.* (1867) L.R. 4 Eq. 112.
[36] *Crusoe d.Blencowe* v. *Rugby* (1771) 3 Wils. 234.
[37] And see *post*, (IV) G.
[38] *Re Farrow's Bank, Ltd.* [1921] 2 Ch. 164.
[39] And see *Re Wright (A Bankrupt), ex p. Landau* v. *The Trustee* [1949] Ch. 729; *cf. Doe d.Goodbehere* v. *Bevan* (1815) 3 M. & S. 353; [1814–23] All E.R. Rep. 706.
[40] [1946] K.B. 306 at p. 310.

depend on privity of estate. I find it impossible to conceive of a relationship of landlord and tenant which has not got that essential element of tenure in it, which implies that the tenant holds of his landlord. He can only do that if the landlord has a reversion. . . . The position would appear to be that, when this document (the purported sub-lease) was executed, Colonel Carreras became the assignee of Captain Milmo's term. He became, therefore, tenant of the Haversham Estates under the head lease which expired on Nov. 28, 1944."

Covenants restricting a tenant's right to dispose of his interest in the property often restrict his right to assign. They do not always restrict his right to underlet. And as Browne-Wilkinson J.[41] has recently pointed out:

"It is an open question . . . whether a covenant against underletting alone precludes an assignment. Woodfall on *Landlord and Tenant* states that it does.[42] But in my judgment the decision of the Irish Court of Appeal in *Re Doyle and O'Hara's Contract*[43] shows that it is by no means a concluded question and it very much depends on the actual words used in each covenant."

Since 1925 mortgages of leaseholds can only be created either by sub-demise (sub-letting) or by a charge by way of legal mortgage,[44] which is expressed by statute to have the same effect.[45] It seems to be clear that if the tenant creates a mortgage of his interest that will cause a breach of the covenant against underletting, and possibly, of the covenant against assigning, even though the mortgage will be created by a technical sub-demise or charge.[46] One of the reasons behind this is that if the tenant could mortgage without breaking the covenant, the covenant could easily be circumvented, as the tenant could then readily consent to the mortgagee taking possession. If the lease provides that the landlord's consent is required for a sub-demise by way of mortgage, then the Law of Property Act 1925, s.86(1), provides that "such licence shall not be unreasonably refused."

Covenants against underletting do not always expressly prohibit underletting part of the property. Sometimes, the covenants against sub-letting are limited in their terms, but the limits have to be carefully observed. The creation of a periodic tenancy is a breach of a

---

[41] *Marks* v. *Warren* [1979] 1 All E.R. 29 at p. 31.
[42] He referred to (27th ed.), Vol. 1, para. 1219, see (28th ed.), para. 1–1195.
[43] [1899] 1 I.R. 113.
[44] L.P.A. 1925, ss.86 and 87.
[45] L.P.A. 1925, s.87; *Grand Junction Co. Ltd.* v. *Bates* [1954] 2 Q.B. 160.
[46] *Serjeant* v. *Nash, Field & Co.* [1903] 2 K.B. 304; [1900–03] All E.R. 525. Upjohn J. did not comment on the view that the position might be different if the mortgage were by charge in *Grand Junction Co. Ltd.* v. *Bates, supra.*

covenant against sub-letting "except for a term not exceeding six calendar months in any one year."[47] And mildly illogical though it may seem, it has been held that a covenant against underletting is not broken by an underletting of part only,[48] although a covenant prohibiting underletting or assignment "of any part" will prevent an assignment or underletting of the whole.[49] If there are separate underlettings of parts of the property resulting in the whole property being underlet, then that will amount to a breach of the covenant against underletting.[50]

There is a clear distinction between an underletting and a licence. The grant of a licence permitting limited occupation of the premises will not be a breach of the covenant against underletting. In *Jackson* v. *Simons*[51] the defendant tenant tobacconist allowed a nightclub owner to use part of his shop between 10.30 p.m. and 2 a.m. for the sale of entrance tickets to his club. This was held to be no breach of the covenant against assigning, underletting or parting with possession. As a result covenants restricting the tenant's right to dispose of the property are sometimes extended to prevent him from creating licences of all or part of the property without consent.

(3) *"Part with Possession"*

Whether the covenant "not to part with possession" has been broken is, as Farwell J. pointed out in *Stening* v. *Abrahams*,[52] a question of fact, and the construction of the particular document. There permission to erect an advertisement hoarding for seven years was not a breach of the covenant. But this does not entitle one to assume that the creation of a licence can never be a breach of this covenant. Farwell J. said[53]:

> "But, in my view, a lessee cannot be said to part with the possession of any part of the premises unless his agreement with his licensee wholly ousts him from the legal possession of that part. If there is anything in the nature of a right to concurrent user there is no parting with possession. Retention of a key may be a

---

[47] *Trustees of Smith's (Henry) Charity* v. *Wilson* [1983] Q.B. 316.
[48] *Wilson* v. *Rosenthal* (1906) 22 T.L.R. 233; *Cook* v. *Shoesmith* [1951] 1 K.B. 752; *Esdaile* v. *Lewis* [1956] 1 W.L.R. 709; *cf. Rhodes* v. *Dalby* [1971] 1 W.L.R. 1325 (covenant restricting granting of "Tenancy in respect of the property" contained in a mortgage, whether broken by tenancy of part.) .
[49] *Field* v. *Barkworth* [1986] 1 All E.R. 362..
[50] *Chatterton* v. *Terrell* [1923] A.C. 578. Secure tenants cannot sub-let or part with possession of part of the dwelling house, except with consent, which is not to be unreasonably withheld, Housing Act 1985, ss.93, 94.
[51] [1923] 1 Ch. 373.
[52] [1931] 1 Ch. 470.
[53] *Ibid.* p. 473.

negative indication, and the authorities show that nothing short of a complete exclusion of the grantor or licensor from the legal possession for all purposes amounts to a parting with possession. The fact that the agreement is in the form of a licence is immaterial, as the licence may give the licensee so exclusive a right to legal possession as to amount to a parting with possession."[54]

It seems as if the covenant can be broken if there is a parting with possession of only part of the property.[55]

C. Consent to Disposals

If there is to be a restriction on the tenant's right to dispose, the least stringent clause the tenant can hope for is one that prevents him from assigning "without the written consent of the landlord such consent not to be unreasonably withheld in the case of a respectable and responsible person." Here the landlord can still reasonably object even to a respectable and responsible person,[56] unless he has incautiously covenanted that consent "will not be withheld in the case of a respectable and responsible person."[57] In that event the landlord cannot object to a proposed assignment if it is to a respectable and responsible person. This can include a limited company that is "worthy of respect"[58] and has the financial capacity to undertake "the amount of rent and the burden of the covenants and other obligations contained in the lease."[59]

We have already seen that if the covenant only goes so far as to prevent assignments, etc., without the consent of the landlord, then the Landlord and Tenant Act 1927, s.19(1)(a), automatically implies a proviso that such consent shall not be unreasonably withheld. The proviso is implied "notwithstanding any express provision to the contrary." The landlord cannot make the grant of his consent conditional on the payment of a fine or sum of money, other than reasonable legal expenses.[60] A tenant's agreement to make such a payment cannot be enforced against him,[61] but if the payment is

---

[54] And see *Chaplin* v. *Smith* [1926] 1 K.B. 198 (no breach where tenant carried on business on premises through his own controlled companies, the tenant both keeping a key and stipulating that he should remain in possession as tenant).

[55] *Abrahams* v. *Macfisheries Ltd.* [1925] 2 K.B. 18; *cf. Russell* v. *Beecham* [1924] 1 K.B. 525.

[56] *Bates* v. *Donaldson* [1896] 2 Q.B. 241; [1895–9] All E.R. Rep. 170.

[57] *Moat* v. *Martin* [1950] 1 K.B. 175; *Re Cooper's Lease, Cowan* v. *Beaumont Property Trusts* (1968) 19 P. & C.R. 541.

[58] *Willmott* v. *London Road Car Co. Ltd.* [1910] 2 Ch. 525, at 537, Farwell L.J.

[59] *Re Greater London Properties Ltd.'s Lease, Taylor Bros. (Grocers) Ltd.* v. *Covent Garden Properties Co. Ltd.* [1959] 1 W.L.R. 503, Danckwerts J.

[60] L.P.A. 1925, s.144, L. & T.A. 1927, s.19(1)(a).

[61] *Comber* v. *Fleet Electrics Ltd.* [1955] 1 W.L.R. 566.

made, then it cannot be recovered from the landlord.[62] Some longer leases provide quite properly that a percentage of any premium paid by the incoming tenant shall be paid to the landlord.

However, even if it seems inevitable to the tenant that the landlord must grant consent, it is still clearly his duty to ask for consent.[63] A failure to do so may render the tenant liable to an action for damages,[64] and possibly forfeiture, although relief is likely to be given if the omission arose from neglect or mistake.[65]

(1) *Refusal of Consent*

A tenant faced with a refusal by his landlord to consent to an assignment has two options. Either he can assign without consent,[66] assuming the assignee agrees, or ask the court for a declaration that consent has been unreasonably refused. The risks of the first course of action are that the landlord may have reasonable grounds for refusing consent despite the responsibility and respectability of the proposed assignee.[67] This could result in an action for damages against the tenant and the assignee's loss of his estate in forfeiture proceedings. Unfortunately the delays inherent in getting cases to court may mean the loss of a prospective assignee who is not prepared to wait and is unenthusiastic about being shackled to an unwilling landlord. The tenant can take proceedings, usually by way of originating summons, either in the High Court or the county court irrespective of the value of the property.[68] But only the parties to the action are bound by the judgment; so if an assignment needs the consent of the immediate and head landlord both must be made parties.[69]

(2) *Avoiding the Statutory Provisions*

Most attempts by landlords to grant tenants the right to assign with consent in one clause, and in the next to take it away without recourse to the courts have been unsuccessful, *e.g.* a provision that the landlord can refuse his consent if for any reason he considers the proposed

---

[62] *Andrew* v. *Bridgman* [1908] 1 K.B. 596, at least if the payment was not made under protest.
[63] *Wilson* v. *Fynn* [1948] 2 All E.R. 40.
[64] *Cohen* v. *Popular Restaurants Ltd.* [1917] 1 K.B. 480.
[65] *House Property and Investment Co. Ltd.* v. *James Walker, Goldsmith and Silversmith Ltd.* [1948] 1 K.B. 257, *cf.* the pre-1925 decisions of *Barrow* v. *Isaacs & Son* [1891] 1 Q.B. 417; *Ellis* v. *Allen* [1914] 1 Ch. 904.
[66] *Ideal Film Renting Co.* v. *Nielsen* [1921] 1 Ch. 575.
[67] *Wilson* v. *Fynn* [1948] 2 All E.R. 40.
[68] L. & T.A. 1954, s.53(1).
[69] *Vienit* v. *W. Williams & Son (Bread Street) Ltd.* [1958] 1 W.L.R. 1267. The requirement that an estate needs consent of both immediate and head landlords for its assignment has a significantly depreciatory effect on its value.

assignee undesirable[70]; or that a refusal to consent is not to be deemed unreasonable if accompanied by an offer to accept a surrender.[71] It does, however, seem that if the tenant has agreed that "if the tenant desires to assign he shall first by irrevocable notice in writing to the landlord offer to surrender this lease," then he can be held to that agreement.[72] The clause constitutes a condition precedent to the application for consent. Such a clause is ineffective if the lease is within the business tenancy code.[73] Of course, if landlords can so enforce surrenders they can nullify the policy behind the Landlord and Tenant Act 1927, s.19. Their financial incentive to attempt to do so is very strong. The effect of inflation is to make market rents fixed only a short time ago look ridiculously cheap. If the landlord can obtain a surrender, he can re-let at a current market rent and if he has not done so insert a regular rent review clause. If he fails to obtain a surrender, his tenant will obviously assign for a substantial premium capitalising the difference between the reserved and current market rentals. It has been suggested[74] that absolute bars against assignment are invalid as they nullify the effect of section 19, but the point has not been directly litigated, and seems difficult to sustain.

(3) *Has Consent been Reasonably Refused?*

A number of attempts have been made to reconcile the cases and set out the relevant propositions of law that govern this area.[75] Some matters are clear. The objects of covenants restricting transfer are to protect the landlord from having his premises used or occupied in an undesirable way or by an undesirable tenant.[76] He can object to prevent that occuring, he cannot object with the ulterior motive of regaining possession of the property,[77] or on grounds that have nothing to do either with the personality of the proposed assignee or to the subject-matter of the lease.[78] It might, therefore, be reasonable for him to object on the grounds of the purpose for which the proposed assignee intended to use the premises, even though that purpose was not forbidden by the lease.[79] But two difficult areas

---

[70] *Creery* v. *Summersell and Flowerdew & Co. Ltd.* [1949] Ch. 751.

[71] *Re Smith's Lease, Smith* v. *Richards* [1951] 1 All E.R. 346.

[72] *Adler* v. *Upper Grosvenor Street Investments Ltd.* [1957] 1 W.L.R. 227; *Bocardo S.A.* v. *S. & M. Hotels Ltd.* [1979] 3 All E.R. 737, C.A. disagreeing with observations in *Greene* v. *Church Commissioners for England* [1974] Ch. 467.

[73] *Allnatt London Properties Ltd.* v. *Newton* [1984] 1 All E.R. 423, and see Chap. 22, *post.*

[74] *Property and Bloodstock Ltd.* v. *Emmerton; Bush* v. *Property and Bloodstock Ltd.* [1968] Ch. 94.

[75] *Pimms Ltd.* v. *Tallow Chandlers Co.* [1964] 2 Q.B. 547; *International Drilling Fluids Ltd.* v. *Louisville Investments (Uxbridge) Ltd.* (1985) 277 E.G. 62.

[76] *Bates* v. *Donaldson* [1896] 2 Q.B. 241.

[77] *Ibid.; Bromley Park Garden Estates Ltd.* v. *Moss* [1982] 2 All E.R. 890.

[78] *Houlder Brothers & Co. Ltd.* v. *Gibbs* [1925] Ch. 575.

[79] *Bates* v. *Donaldson, supra.*

remain. How far can the landlord bear in mind the interests of good estate management, or the good management of his estate? To what extent does one have regard to the consequences to the tenant if consent is not given? Dunn L.J. considered the first point in *Bromley Park Garden Estates Ltd.* v. *Moss.*[80] He thought it had been established[81] that one should look at the covenant in the context of the lease, and ascertain the purpose of the covenant in that context. "If the refusal of the landlord was designed to achieve that purpose then it may not be unreasonable, even in the case of a respectable and responsible assignee; but if the refusal is designed to achieve some collateral purpose wholly unconnected with the terms of the lease ... then it would be unreasonable, even though the purpose was in accordance with good estate management."[82] If the landlord considers that he is likely to want to rely on principles of good estate management, perhaps the covenant should give some indication that the property is part of a larger holding, the management interests of which will be relevant on any proposed assignment. The second point, the extent to which the landlord has to consider the tenant's interests, was discussed by Balcombe L.J. in *International Drilling Fluids Ltd.* v. *Louisville Investments (Uxbridge) Ltd.*[83] He considered that the landlord needed usually only to consider his own relevant interests, although there might be cases where there was such a disproportion between the benefit to the landlord and the detriment to the tenant if consent were withheld that it was unreasonable to refuse consent.

"It is not necessary for the landlords to prove that the conclusions which led them to refuse consent were justified, if they were conclusions which might be reached by a reasonable man in the circumstances."[84] The landlord need not, it seems, state his reasons for refusing consent,[85] and the onus is on the tenant to establish unreasonableness.[86] But it is a matter of common sense that if the landlord is relying on less apparent reasons than the unsuitability of the tenant or his proposed use of the premises then he should say so. The landlord is not, it seems, restricted to the reasons he initially gives,[87] but he is only permitted to rely on reasons which did actually influence his mind at the time he refused his consent.[88] The covenant should be looked at in the light of the circumstances

---

[80] [1982] 2 All E.R. 890.
[81] By *West Layton Ltd.* v. *Ford* [1979] Q.B. 593.
[82] [1982] 2 All E.R. 890 at p. 901.
[83] (1985) 277 E.G. 62.
[84] *Per* Danckwerts L.J. in *Pimms Ltd.* v. *Tallow Chandlers Co.* [1964] 2 Q.B. 547 at p. 564.
[85] *Young* v. *Ashley Garden Properties Ltd.* [1903] 2 Ch. 112.
[86] *Shanly* v. *Ward* (1913) 29 T.L.R. 714.
[87] *Parker* v. *Boggon* [1947] K.B. 346, and see R.E.M. (1963) 79 L.Q.R. 479, and *Sonnenthal* v. *Newton* (1965) 109 S.J. 333.
[88] *Per* Slade L.J., *Bromley Park Garden Estates Ltd.* v. *Moss* [1982] 2 All E.R. 890, at p. 902.

and law as they exist when consent is requested. This allows significant changes in statutory protection given to tenants to be taken into account.[89]

In the following instances the landlord has been held to have withheld his consent unreasonably:

Where the proposed tenant was a Turkish diplomat, and would be protected by diplomatic immunity[90];
Where the proposed assignee company was substantially indebted to its holding company Allied Bakeries Ltd. which was not prepared to act as guarantor, but was otherwise "responsible" having regard to its disclosed trading profits[91];
Where the sub-lessors refused their consent because their superior lessors withheld their consent[92];
Where the landlord insisted that the proposed sub-lessee enter a covenant to pay the rent of £700 reserved by the lease, although the best rent obtainable was only £450 which the sub-lessee proposed to pay[93];
Where the assignment of the last seven and a half months of a five year term by a tenant with Rent Act protection would create a new protected tenancy, but this was not the ulterior motive for the assignment and the premises could only be re-let at the same rent[94];
Where the proposed assignee, Roneo Ltd., would move out of other property owned by the same landlord and that other property would be difficult to re-let[95];
Where the landlord objected, unsuccessfully, to the proposed assignee as not being responsible and respectable, and also on the ground that he had already commenced forfeiture proceedings against the tenant company because of its liquidation[96];
Where the landlords apprehended a likely breach of the user covenant following assignment as the premises could only be used as a printers, but this would not be a necessary consequence of the granting of consent[97];
Where the result of refusing consent probably would have been the

---

[89] *Leeward Securities* v. *Lilyheath Properties* (1983) 271 E.G. 279.
[90] *Parker* v. *Boggon* [1947] K.B. 346. The Race Relations Act 1976, s.24, makes it unlawful to withhold consent on racial grounds unless the landlord or a near relative resides and intends to reside on the premises which are not large enough to accommodate more than seven people or two households, and accommodation would have to be shared with the tenant. Accommodation for access and storage purposes is discounted. See also Sex Discrimination Act 1975, s.31.
[91] *Re Greater London Properties Ltd.'s Lease* [1959] 1 W.L.R. 503.
[92] *Vienit Ltd.* v. *W. Williams & Sons (Bread Street) Ltd.* [1958] 1 W.L.R. 1267.
[93] *Balfour* v. *Kensington Gardens Mansions Ltd.* (1932) 49 T.L.R. 29.
[94] *Thomas Bookman Ltd.* v. *Nathan* [1955] 1 W.L.R. 815; and see *Swanson's Agreement Re Hill* v. *Swanson* [1946] 2 All E.R. 628.
[95] *Re Gibbs and Houlder Bros. & Co. Ltd.'s Lease* [1925] Ch. 575.
[96] *Pakwood Transport* v. *15 Beauchamp Place* (1978) 36 P. & C.R. 112.
[97] *Killick* v. *Second Covent Garden Property Co. Ltd.* [1973] 1 W.L.R. 658.

destruction of the tenancy, and the reduction of the premises into sole occupation.[98]

The landlord has been held to have withheld his consent reasonably:

Where the tenant's references were unsatisfactory[99];
Where the proposed assignee's use of the premises would damage the landlord's own trading interests, as the assignee would run a rival business next door to the landlord's own premises[1];
Where the landlords considered that their property interests would be damaged because they would be landlords of two competing neighbouring businesses[2];
or because the assignment would have the effect of creating a statutorily protected tenant[3];
or because one result of the assignment would be to enable the tenant to acquire the lessor's freehold interest under the Leasehold Reform Act 1967 which could interfere with the proper management of the lessor's estate as a whole[4];
or because the proposed under-lease was at a substantial premium and low rent, which would have the effect of depreciating the value of the property let[5];
or because the proposed assignment of a restaurant was to a property company whose object was to share in the profits arising from the landlord's proposed scheme of redevelopment.[6]

These cases are simply illustrations of how the courts have decided whether in fact the consent has or has not been unreasonably withheld.

"Seeing that the circumstances are infinitely various, it is impossible to formulate strict rules as to how a landlord should exercise his power of refusal. The utmost that the courts can do is to give guidance to those who have to consider the problem. As one decision follows another, people will get to know the likely result, in any given set of circumstances. But no one decision will be a binding precedent as a strict rule of law. The reasons given by

[98] *Bromley Park Garden Estates Ltd.* v. *Moss* [1982] 2 All E.R. 890.
[99] *Shanly* v. *Ward* (1913) 29 T.L.R. 714.
[1] *Whiteminster Estates* v. *Hodges Menswear* (1974) 232 E.G. 715.
[2] *Premier Confectionery (London) Co. Ltd.* v. *London Commercial Sale Rooms Ltd.* [1933] Ch. 904.
[3] *Lee* v. *K. Carter Ltd.* [1949] 1 K.B. 85 (assignment by limited company to one of its directors); *Swanson* v. *Forton* [1949] Ch. 143 (assignment by non-resident tenant 12 days before expiry of term); *West Layton Ltd.* v. *Ford* [1979] Q.B. 575 (sub-letting of flat over shop). But see *dicta* in *Leeward Securities Ltd.* v. *Lilyheath Properties Ltd.* (1983) 271 E.G. 279.
[4] *Bickel* v. *Duke of Westminster* [1977] Q.B. 517; *Norfolk Capital Group Ltd.* v. *Kitway Ltd.* [1977] Q.B. 506.
[5] *Re Town Investments Ltd.'s Underlease, McLaughlin* v. *Town Investments Ltd.* [1954] Ch. 301.
[6] *Pimms, Ltd.* v. *Tallow Chandlers in the City of London* [1964] 2 Q.B. 547.

the judges are to be treated as propositions of good sense—in relation to the particular case—rather than propositions of law applicable to all cases."[7]

And once given, consent cannot be withdrawn if further unpalatable facts come to light about the proposed assignee.[8]

(4) *Waiver*

Even though the assignment may have been executed without obtaining the landlord's consent, the landlord can obviously adopt the situation and waive the breach of covenant. This can be done simply by expressly accepting the assignee as his tenant. But even if this is not done expressly, the landlord by his conduct may be held to have accepted the assignment and be bound by it. Lord Herschell L.C. said[9]:

> "Whether the assignees have been accepted by the landlord in the place of the assignors must, as it seems to me, be determined as a question of fact upon a review of all the circumstances. The fact that possession has been given to the assignees with the knowledge of the landlord and without objection on his part is no doubt an important element, but it is not the only element to be taken into consideration. Where . . . the landlord did not intend to accept the assignees in lieu of the assignors, . . . and intimated the contrary intention, I cannot think that the mere absence of objection to the possession of the assignees is conclusive that the landlord has accepted them and discharged the assignors."

The issue has been raised a number of times in connection with the creation of binding sub-tenancies that would be protected by the Rent Acts. In those cases the waiver only operates to make the sub-letting lawful from the date of the waiver, and does not relate back to the creation of the sub-tenancy.[10] It will be seen that a demand for rent by a landlord or his agent with knowledge of the true situation will be regarded as a waiver of the right to take proceedings for forfeiture.[11] But the waiver does not destroy the effect of the covenant for the future. Like the grant of a licence to assign, which for evidential

---

[7] *Per* Lord Denning M.R. *Bickel* v. *Duke of Westminster* [1977] Q.B. 517 at p. 524.

[8] *Mitten* v. *Fagg* (1978) 247 E.G. 901 (convictions under Food Hygiene Regs. of future assignee of baker's shop).

[9] *Elphinstone (Lord)* v. *Monkland Iron & Coal Co.* (1886) 11 App. Case 332, 344; and see *O'Toole* v. *Lyons* [1948] I.R. 115.

[10] *Muspratt* v. *Johnston* [1963] 2 Q.B. 383.

[11] See *ante*, Chap. 5, s.VII, G, A(1), and also *Hyde* v. *Pimley* [1952] 2 Q.B. 506.

reasons should be in writing,[12] the waiver operates to excuse only the breach which has occurred and does not operate as a general waiver of covenant.[13]

Where the lease is assigned without consent, then it seems that the assignment will operate to vest the remainder of the term in the assignee[14] It has been pointed out that unless the tenant could effectively assign in breach of the covenant, then there would never be a breach of the covenant against assigning.[15] If there is an absolute prohibition against assignment then it is suggested that no estate at all passes by virtue of the assignment[16] on the ground that the tenant has no power to assign without consent. It is submitted that the best that the assignee can hope for in these cases is that his interest will be protected by estoppel. The assignor is estopped from denying the validity of his assignment, and if it is adopted by the landlord, then he will also be prevented from denying the existence of the relationship of landlord and tenant between himself and the assignee. Of course later events could lead to the acquisition of an estate by the assignee under the doctrine of "feeding the estoppel."[17]

III. EFFECTING ASSIGNMENTS AND SUB-TENANCIES

A. The Contract

In relation to the agreement to assign or sub-let a person taking an assignment or sub-lease is contractually in a similar situation to a prospective tenant taking an original lease, whose position has been discussed already.[18] Despite the statutory restrictions on investigating title,[19] the prudent assignee or sub-lessee will want to make additional enquiries to satisfy himself that the tenant can indeed either assign or sub-let, that the covenants in the lease out of which the interest is being derived have not been broken, especially in relation to dilapidations, and that the lessor's consent to the disposition has been obtained. It is the duty of the tenant who is granting the assignment or

---

[12] *Willmott* v. *Barber* (1880) 15 Ch.D. 96.
[13] L.P.A. 1925, s.148.
[14] *Old Grovebury Manor Farm Ltd.* v. *W. Seymour Plant Sales & Hire Ltd. (No. 2)* [1979] 3 All E.R. 504; *Peabody Donation Fund* v. *Higgins* [1983] 1 W.L.R. 1091.
[15] *Ibid.* Lord Russell at 506.
[16] *Elliott* v. *Johnson* (1866) L.R. 2 Q.B. 120. In *Peabody Donation Fund* v. *Higgins, supra,* there was no absolute prohibition on assignment of the secure tenancy.
[17] See *ante,* Chap. 3 (IV) B(2).
[18] *Ante,* Chap. 3(III).
[19] L.P.A. 1925, s.44(2)–(5), see *ante,* Chap. 3 (IV) B.

sub-lease to obtain the necessary[20] consents.[21] The Law of Property Act 1925, s.45(2), provides that where land sold is held by lease[22] the purchaser shall assume that the lease was duly granted, and on production of the receipt for the last payment due for rent before completion that the covenants have been observed up to the date of completion. This obviously does not apply if there is evidence that the lease was not properly granted or that its terms have been broken. This may be apparent either from an inspection of the property or from correspondence passing between the landlord and the tenant.

Often an assignee is taking over a business as well as the remainder of a lease. Obviously in that case close consideration should be devoted to making sure that the business is as sound as it has been represented to be, and that the books of account do indeed reflect the true position of the business. It is not uncommon for the sale agreement to contain a clause stating that the purchaser has inspected the books and has satisfied himself that they accurately reflect the position of the business, and for the vendor to represent that he is not aware of any facts or developments that would make reliance on the accounts unsafe. The assignee will usually be paying a capital sum when a business is taken over, for the goodwill and other assets in the business, and in many cases a premium for the assignment of the lease as well. Some of the taxation aspects of this last payment have already been considered.[23]

B. The Assignment

If the assignment is to transfer the legal estate it must be by deed.[24] Until an assignment is executed, the former tenant will remain liable under the terms of the lease. "[A] mere equitable assignee as such who has entered into possession and paid rent is not thereby rendered liable upon the covenants of the lease or, amongst other things, for the payment of rent. No privity of estate is created between himself and the landlord by those facts . . . "[25] But the surrounding circumstances may be such that the assignee is estopped from denying that the legal estate has been assigned to him, and so may be unable to deny liability.[26] If the lease which has been assigned has been substantively

---

[20] "Necessary" in Condition 11(5) of the *National Conditions of Sale* (20th ed.) means necessary under the terms of the lease, and not in the light of the parties' conduct, *Bickel* v. *Courtenay Investments (Nominees) Ltd.* [1984] 1 W.L.R. 795; *cf. Treloar* v. *Bigge* (1874) L.R. 9 Ex. 151.

[21] *Lloyd* v. *Crispe* (1813) 5 Taun. 249, and see Law Society's Conditions of Sale (1984 Revision), Condition 8(4), and Condition 11(5), National Conditions of Sale (20th ed.).

[22] And *mutatis mutandis* where the property is held by under-lease, L.P.A. 1925, s.45(3).

[23] See *ante*, Chap. 5, (VIII) H. For "Goodwill," see Chap. 24.

[24] L.P.A. 1925, s.52(1).

[25] *Rodenhurst Estates, Ltd.* v. *W. H. Barnes, Ltd.* [1936] 2 All E.R. 3, at p. 6, Sir Boyd Merriman P.

[26] *Ibid.*

registered, then the assignment is not completed until itself registered.[27]

Exceptionally, a problem can arise where the assignor intended to
create a sub-lease but does so in such a way that he disposes of his
entire interest in the property. As we have seen, such a sub-lease
amounts to an assignment.[28] The problem here is that though the
assignment has to be by deed, it may well be possible to create a valid
sub-lease orally for longer than the residue of the sub-lessor's own
term by relying on section 54(2) of the Law of Property Act 1925. The
illogicalities involved in describing this as an assignment by operation
of law have been discussed elsewhere.[29]

C. Sub-leases

This heading is put in only for completeness. The formalities
surrounding the creation of a sub-lease are the same as for a head
lease. Attention does have to be paid to the precise way by which the
parties intend to ensure observance of covenants in the head lease.
Both the common forms of precedent and practice reveal a conspicuous lack of uniformity over the extent of the obligations which the
parties to the underlease undertake in relation to observance of the
covenants in the head lease. The likely extent of the parties' liabilities
is considered in the next section.

IV. THE POSITION AFTER ASSIGNMENT, TRANSFER AND SUB-LEASE

A. Original Landlord, Tenant and Guarantor

The original parties to the lease are bound to each other not only
because they are landlord and tenant of the same estate in the land,
but because they have entered into a contract with each other.
Liability under the terms of that contract lasts for as long as the lease.
This may be for longer than the duration of the tenant's personal
enjoyment for he may assign his estate. In that event although the
tenant is still liable, the landlord is most likely to look initially to the
assignee for the time being.

After assignment, the original tenant, and his guarantors will be
liable for all breaches of covenant, even when it is difficult for them to
ensure compliance, *e.g.* failure to repair, and to yield up.[30] The

---

[27] L.R.A. 1925, s.22(1).
[28] *Ante*, (II)B(1) and see *Milmo* v. *Carreras* [1946] K.B. 306.
[29] *Megarry & Wade* 665, and see also (1967) 31 Conv. (N.S.) 159, Paul Jackson.
[30] *Thames Manufacturing Co.* v. *Perrotts (Nichol & Peyton)* (1985) 49 P. & C.R. 1.

original tenant will be liable for increased rents following rent reviews agreed with the assignee,[31] even when the increases result from the assignee's unauthorised improvements.[32] The original tenant's liability is direct and primary,[33] but if sued, of course, he can seek indemnity from the defaulting assignee.[34] The liability might also extend after the nominal term of years has ended if the provisions of Part II of the Landlord and Tenant Act 1954 apply to extend the lease,[35] or if the original term has been extended by the exercise of an option given to the tenant to extend the lease.[36] The liability may be made coterminous with the tenant's personal enjoyment of the estate. This can occur when the landlord agrees to join in the assignment to release the original tenant in consideration of fresh covenants taken directly from the assignee, with whom there is then privity of contract as well as estate.[37] The landlord is also contractually liable to his original tenant for the duration of the lease, which is why he may be liable in damages for breach of an option to purchase that is unenforceable against his successor in title for want of protection by registration.[38]

The original guarantor's liability to the original landlord is essentially contractual. If the landlord disposes of his interest, this will not automatically pass the right to enforce the original guarantee. If it is intended that the guarantee should benefit the landlord's successor, then it should be expressly assigned to him.[39]

B. Landlord and Assignee

The fundamental rule of contract that only the parties to a bargain can enforce its terms and are bound by its obligations affects the rights and liability of assignees of the tenant's interest and transferees of the landlord. The exceptions to the privity rule that apply in relation to the observance and enforcement of covenants restrictive of the user of land have already been considered.[40] But those covenants are essentially negative and are regarded as running in equity. Successors

---

[31] *Centrovincial Estates* v. *Bulk Storage* (1983) 46 P. & C.R. 393.

[32] *Selous Street Properties* v. *Oronel Fabrics* (1984) 270 E.G. 643, 743. It has been convincingly argued that this decision confuses the original tenant's liability in contract with his successor's liability arising out of privity of estate, P. McLoughlin [1984] Conv. 443.

[33] *Allied London Investments* v. *Hambro Life Assurance* (1985) 50 P. & C.R. 207, following *Baynton* v. *Morgan* (1888) 22 Q.B.D. 74.

[34] *Moule* v. *Garrett* (1872) L.R. 7 Ex. 101; [1861–73] All E.R. Rep. 135 (recovery of cost of repairs).

[35] See *post*, pt. III.

[36] *Baker* v. *Merckel; Anson (Third Party)* [1960] 1 Q.B. 657.

[37] *J. Lyons & Co. Ltd.* v. *Knowles* [1943] 1 K.B. 366, where there were covenants by successive assignees with the landlords, although no releases.

[38] *Ante*, Chap. 4, (V), F.

[39] *Pinemain* v. *Welbeck International* (1984) 272 E.G. 1166, and see *In Re Distributors and Warehousing Ltd.*, *Financial Times*, November 19, 1985.

[40] *Ante*, Chap. 3 (IV) A.

to the tenant's estate are bound by most of the terms in the lease in law because there is no privity of estate between the assignee and his landlord. They are not bound by privity of contract, unless they have directly covenanted with the lessor to observe the terms of the lease.[41] Conversely, assignees can enforce most of the terms of the lease against the landlord. The two essential questions are which covenants are enforceable because of privity of estate, and secondly, precisely what is meant by an assignee?

(1) *Covenants Binding the Assignee and Enforceable by Him*

A number of phrases are used to describe the calibre of covenant that runs at law for the benefit and burden of the assignee. The covenant may be said to touch and concern the thing demised,[42] or relate to the land of the covenantor,[43] or have reference to the subject-matter of the lease.[44] The observations in Cheshire's *Modern Real Property* (5th ed.), pp. 214–5,[45] were accepted by Scott L.J. as supplying the true test,[46] where it is stated:

> "If a simple test is desired for ascertaining into which category a covenant falls, it is suggested that the proper enquiry should be whether the covenant affects either the landlord qua landlord or the tenant qua tenant. A covenant may very well have reference to the land, but, unless it is reasonably incidental to the relationship of landlord and tenant, it cannot be said to touch and concern the land so as to be capable of running therewith or with the reversion."

No difficulty arises in connection with the tenant's covenants to pay rent,[47] rates,[48] to repair and leave in repair,[49] to replace tenant's fixtures and fixed machinery,[50] to build on the demised land,[51] and to rebuild in the case of destruction,[52] or the covenants to insure or the covenants both positive and negative controlling the use of the demised land, including sole supply covenants,[53] and covenants

---

[41] As in *J. Lyons & Co. Ltd.* v. *Knowles* [1943] 1 K.B. 366.
[42] *Spencer's Case* (1583) 5 Co. Rep. 16a; [1558–1774] All E.R. Rep. 68.
[43] L.P.A. 1925, s.79.
[44] L.P.A. 1925, ss.141, 142.
[45] Now see Cheshire and Burns (13th ed.), p. 431.
[46] In *Breams Property Investment Co. Ltd.* v. *Stroulger* [1948] 2 K.B. 1 at p. 7.
[47] *Parker* v. *Webb* (1703) 3 Salk. 5.
[48] *Wix* v. *Rutson* [1899] 1 Q.B. 474.
[49] *Martyn* v. *Clue* (1852) 18 Q.B. 661.
[50] *Williams* v. *Earle* (1868) L.R. 3, Q.B. 739.
[51] *Spencer's Case* (1583) 5 Co. Rep. 16a.
[52] *Re King (Deceased), Robinson* v. *Gray* [1963] Ch. 459.
[53] *Clegg* v. *Hands* (1890) 44 Ch.D. 503 (beer); *Regent Oil Co. Ltd.* v. *J. A. Gregory (Hatch End) Ltd.* [1966] Ch. 402 (petrol). The running of these covenants depends on their precise interpretation.

restricting assignment.[54] The usual covenant by the landlord for quiet enjoyment,[55] and unusual ones to provide attendance,[56] to supply water,[57] and not to build in front of the building line on the adjoining premises also run with the land.[58] Successors to the landlord and tenant's respective estates can enforce and are bound by these covenants because of the privity of estate that exists between them. The benefit and burden of these covenants are said to run at law. But the benefit of the tenant's guarantor's covenant does not automatically run, and should be expressly assigned.[59]

It has already been seen that both the benefit and burden of covenants to renew are regarded anomalously as running with the tenant's estate, and subject to the necessary protection by registration are enforceable against the successors to the landlord's estate.[60] The treatment of these covenants is anomalous because the covenants are not essentially connected with the relationship of landlord and tenant. Covenants and options to purchase apparently fall on the other side of the dividing line. The benefit of the covenant may pass automatically on an assignment of the tenant's estate,[61] but the option can be separately assigned, unless the terms in which it was granted preclude its separation from the tenant's estate.[62] The burden of such a covenant will not pass automatically to the successors of the landlord's estate,[63] but much the same effect may be achieved if the option or covenant has been protected by registration.[64]

Many of the landlord's covenants that have been held not to run with the land are frequently covenants that are beneficial to the tenant as tenant, but are regarded as not running because they do not affect the land that has been demised. For this reason in *Thomas* v. *Hayward*[65] a tenant's successor of the Mill Hill Tavern could not enforce a covenant by the landlord that the latter would not erect or keep a house for the sale of spirits or beer within the distance of half a mile of the tavern.

The more difficult and common situation arises where there is a sub-lease. The sub-lessee will normally extract a covenant from the sub-lessor that he will observe and perform the covenants in the head lease, as a failure to do so is likely to result in forfeiture of the estate

---

[54] *Cohen* v. *Popular Restaurants Ltd.* [1917] 1 K.B. 480.
[55] *Lewis* v. *Campbell* (1819) 8 Taun. 715; (1820) 3 B. & A. 391.
[56] *Barnes* v. *City of London Real Property Co. Ltd.* [1918] 2 Ch. 18, (housekeeper).
[57] *Jourdain* v. *Wilson* (1821) 4 B. & A. 266.
[58] *Ricketts* v. *Enfield (Churchwardens)* [1909] 1 Ch. 544, and see further Woodfall, paras. 1–1130, 1–1131.
[59] *Pinemain* v. *Welbeck International* (1984) 272 E.G. 1166.
[60] *Ante*, Chap. 4, (V)F.
[61] *Griffith* v. *Pelton* [1958] Ch. 205.
[62] *Re Button's Lease* [1964] Ch. 263.
[63] *Woodall* v. *Clifton* [1905] 2 Ch. 257.
[64] This has been discussed *ante*, Chap. 4 (V) F.
[65] (1869) L.R. 4 Ex. 311; [1861–73] All E.R. Rep. 290.

created by it, and loss of the term created by the sub-lease.[66] The sub-lessor's successors will not be automatically bound by the covenant to observe the covenants in the head lease and to indemnify the sub-tenant in the event of loss flowing from breach of that covenant. In *Dewar* v. *Goodman*[67] a head tenant failed to comply with the repairing covenants in a lease of some 211 houses, as a result of which the sub-tenant of two of them was evicted following proceedings for forfeiture and also failed to recover damages from the defaulting sub-lessor's successor. The covenant clearly affected the sub-tenant's estate, but related to land that was not the subject of the demise. It similarly follows that a covenant by the landlord to build on other land he retains will not run.[68] And a covenant by a tenant to replace chattels and machinery that are not fixtures cannot be enforced by the landlord against the tenant's assignees as it in no way relates to the land demised.[69]

(2) *What is Meant by an Assignee?*

If the whole of the tenant's estate has been assigned by deed, then there will be privity of estate between the landlord and the assignee. It follows that the covenants that do run with the land can be enforced by and against the persons who are for the time being landlord and tenant. If the person in possession is holding as a sub-lessee of the tenant, and not as an assignee, there is no privity of estate between him and the head landlord.[70] There is also no privity of estate if the legal estate has not been assigned by a properly completed assignment by deed. In that case the assignee holds under an equitable assignment. He may have rights to take proceedings to compel the execution of a deed to transfer the outstanding estate of the tenant, but for the time being it will not be vested in him. He will not be liable to the landlord on the covenants in the lease.[71]

However, both parties may be estopped by their conduct from denying that they stand in the relationship of landlord and tenant to each other. This will be so where the landlord has not objected to the equitable assignee taking possession, and has demanded and received the rent from him.[72] But those facts by themselves do not necessarily prevent the person in occupation from showing that he was in law

---

[66] The sub-tenant has a right to apply for relief under L.P.A. 1925, s.146(4), but this can involve the sub-tenant in considerable expense. The matter is considered *post*, D.

[67] [1909] A.C. 72.

[68] *Spencer's Case* (1583) 5 Co. Rep. 16a; [1558–1774] All E.R. Rep. 68.

[69] *Gorton* v. *Gregory* (1862) 3 B. & S. 90 (tools of a calico printer).

[70] *Hand* v. *Blow* [1901] 2 Ch. 721. This is the position of mortgagees of the tenant's estate; *Bonner* v. *Tottenham and Edmonton Permanent Building Society* [1899] 1 Q.B. 161.

[71] *Robinson* v. *Rosher* (1841) 1 Y. & C. Ch. 7.

[72] As in *Rodenhurst Estates, Ltd.* v. *W. H. Barnes, Ltd.* [1936] 2 All E.R. 3.

occupying as sub-tenant and not as an equitable assignee, and that he was paying the rent only to preserve his estate as sub-tenant. In that event the person in possession can deny that he is bound by the covenants in the head lease.[73]

A more complicated situation arises where the original lease is split among separate assignees who each take part of the property originally demised for the rest of the original term. This happens in the simplest case where there is a term of 90 years of two houses. Sometime later the tenant disposes of one house for the rest of the term to *A*, and the second house to *B*. Of course, if the landlord agrees to join in then the original rent can be legally apportioned and separate covenants entered into by *A* and *B* with the landlord, and so each property can be considered separately from the other. But if this has not been done then the assignees' position is either unclear or unsatisfactory.

The landlord can levy distress for non-payment of rent, subject to the usual restrictions on that right,[74] on the assets of either assignee for the rent due in respect of the whole property.[75] It is not clear if an assignee of part can be liable to an action for arrears of rent in respect of the whole,[76] although it is well established that he is liable for the proportion of rent attributable to the part of which he is tenant.[77] He is also liable under the other covenants, such as repair, to the extent that they affect the property held under his part of the split lease.[78] However, an assignee of part is likely to pay the whole rent if he is threatened with forfeiture proceedings that would result in the ending of the term in respect of all the property. If he does, then it seems that he can recover from the other assignee(s) the sum he paid in respect of the other property, because of the community of interest that both assignees have in keeping the original lease on foot.[79] But this will not help the assignee of part if repairs still remain to be done to the other property in the original lease, for he has no right of entry on to that other part. Further, if forfeiture proceedings are taken, the assignee of part has only indistinct rights to claim relief from forfeiture.[80]

It follows that the assignee of a split lease is liable because of privity of estate in respect of the covenants so far as they relate to the property he holds, and that his estate is at risk as a result of the non-compliance by other assignees of the covenants in respect of the property which he does not hold. Often, of course, the split lease

---

[73] *Official Trustee of Charity Lands* v. *Ferriman Trust, Ltd.* [1937] 3 All E.R. 85, and see also *Tichborne* v. *Weir* (1892) 67 L.T. 735; [1891–4] All E.R. Rep. 449.
[74] See *ante*, Chap. 5 (VII) B.
[75] *Curtis* v. *Spitty* (1835) 1 Bing., N.C. 756.
[76] *Whitham* v. *Bullock* [1939] 2 K.B. 81.
[77] *Gammon* v. *Vernon* (1678) 2 Lev. 231.
[78] *Congham* v. *King* (1630) Cro.Car. (3) 221.
[79] *Whitham* v. *Bullock* [1939] 2 K.B. 81, and see (1967) 31 Conv. (N.S.) 38 (P. St. J. Langan) where the problems of contribution are discussed.
[80] See further (1961) 25 Conv. (N.S.) 384, Bernard Rudden.

situation will arise not from the simple instance of an original lease of two adjoining properties, but from an original lease of a large block of properties.

C. Original Tenant and Assignee

In many cases, the parties to an assignment will first have entered a written agreement stating the terms on which the assignment is to take place. This agreement should also deal with the potential liablity for any breaches of covenant that are subsisting at the date of the agreement and assignment.[81] This is particularly important where the premises are not in a complete state of repair, or if the covenants relating to decorations have not been observed. If there is no express agreement on these points, then the issue will be left to be determined by an application of the covenants that are statutorily implied in an assignment for valuable consideration, where the assignor expressly transfers his estate as beneficial owner.

The statutory covenants for title that the assignor gives are implied by the Law of Property Act 1925, s.76(1), (2), and contained in Parts I and II to the Second Schedule of the Act. These covenants are detailed and have been discussed at length elsewhere.[82] They are that the assignor has power to convey, that the assignee will have quiet enjoyment from persons claiming through the assignor, or from whom the assignor claims otherwise than by purchase for value, that the estate is free from incumbrances, except as may be expressly mentioned, and that the assignor will obtain the execution of further assignments to perfect the title if necessary. There is also an implied covenant that the lease is still valid and has not become void or voidable, and that its terms have been observed.[83]

The correlative obligations by the assignee to pay the rents, observe the covenants and indemnify the tenant, or the assignee as the case may be in respect of liability for any breaches of the covenants are set out in the Law of Property Act 1925, s.77, and Part IX of the Second Schedule. The precise operation of these covenants is not entirely free from doubt. The assignee who is the tenant for the time being will be primarily responsible.[84] He will however be responsible to the landlord for the rent accruing due and other breaches that occur only while he is tenant, and not for those that arise after he has assigned

---

[81] *cf.* General Condition 8(5), Law Society's General Conditions of Sale (1984 Revision), General Conditions 11(7), National Conditions of Sale (20th ed.).

[82] Emmet on *Title* (18th ed.).

[83] L.P.A. 1925, s.45(2), provides the purchaser shall assume the lease was duly granted and on production of the last receipt for rent that its terms have been duly observed. L.P.A. 1925, s.45(3), deals with sales of land held by under-leases.

[84] *Moule* v. *Garrett* (1872) L.R. 7 Ex. 101; [1861–73] All E.R. Rep. 135.

away his term,[85] unless he has entered into a direct covenant with the landlord undertaking liability for the rest of the term.[86]

If there is no express agreement on how liabilities are to be borne, then it is suggested that if they arise after the date of the assignment responsibility will lie with the assignee. If liability occurs before the date of the assignment, responsibility rests with the assignor, unless the liability arises under the covenant to repair. It seems that the assignee will be responsible for both existing and future breaches of the covenant to repair without any recourse against the assignor under the covenants for title. Conversely, the assignee is liable to indemnify the assignor if the landlord sues the assignor for antecedent breaches of the repairing covenant.[87] The price the assignee agrees to pay is likely to reflect this potential liability.

The original tenant has two strings to his bow if he has to pay rent[88] because of the default of a subsequent assignee. First, he can sue the defaulting assignee because he has been compelled to discharge that assignee's legal liability, as in *Moule* v. *Garrett*.[89] Secondly, he can sue his own immediate assignee, who can join in his assignee, and so on down the line.[90] The line can be broken if an intermediate assignee is a company in liquidation. And here the situation can only be retrieved if, before the final dissolution of the company, the benefit of the covenant to indemnify taken by the company is assigned to the company's own assignor.[91] This will save the contractual chain of indemnities from being broken.

D. Sub-lessors, Sub-lessees and their Assigns

A typical situation where sub-tenancies are created is where there is a head lease for, say, 21 years by the landlord to a tenant of a block of offices in three floors, and the tenant occupies the ground floor and sub-lets on short terms to separate sub-tenants the first and second floors. For the purposes of the present section, the landlord of the block will be called "the landlord," and the tenant of the block "the tenant/landlord," and the sub-tenants "the sub-lessees." The tenant/landlord will want to make sure that the sub-lessee observes the covenants in the head lease to the extent that they affect what is to be

---

[85] *Wolveridge* v. *Steward* (1833) 1 Cromp. & M. 644.
[86] As in *J. Lyons & Co. Ltd.* v. *Knowles* [1943] K.B. 366.
[87] *Middlegate Properties Ltd.* v. *Bilbao, Caroline Construction Co. Ltd. (Third Party)* (1972) 24 P. & C.R. 329; and see also *Butler* v. *Mountview Estates, Ltd.* [1951] 2 K.B. 563.
[88] The original tenant's liability arises from the date each payment of rent becomes due, and he may be liable for interest on unpaid rent from that date, and not from when he knew arrears were owing, *Allied London Investments* v. *Hambro Life Assurance* (1985) 50 P. & C.R. 207.
[89] (1872) L.R. 7 Ex. 101; [1861–73] All E.R. Rep. 135.
[90] And see the discussion in *Warnford Investments Ltd.* v. *Duckworth* [1978] 2 W.L.R. 741.
[91] As in *Butler Estates, Ltd.* v. *Bean* [1942] 1 K.B. 1. A trustee in bankruptcy of an assignee may similarly agree to assign the benefit of the covenant for indemnity on terms.

done, or not to be done on the floor of the building that is sub-let. The sub-lessee wants to make sure that the tenant/landlord pays the rent for the whole building and observes the covenants in the head lease, which will affect not only the floor sub-let to him but the other two floors as well.

It has already been seen that as between the three original parties first of all there is no privity of estate or contract between the landlord and the sub-lessee, and therefore the latter cannot be liable to the former.[92] Secondly, if the sub-lease is silent about the observance of the covenants in the head lease, then the tenant/landlord will not be liable to the sub-lessee under the usual restricted express covenant for quiet enjoyment if forfeiture proceedings are taken by the head landlord.[93] Thirdly, if the sub-lease is silent about the covenants in the head lease, the sub-lessee will not be responsible for the tenant/landlord's loss under the terms of the head lease, but only for the loss arising under the covenants in the sub-lease itself.[94]

If the tenant/landlord has covenanted with the sub-tenant to observe the covenants in the head lease and to indemnify the sub-tenant against the same then he can be liable in damages to the sub-tenant or his assignee for a breach of the covenant, *e.g.* to repair contained in the head lease, whether or not the head landlord has done anything about the breach. In *Ayling* v. *Wade*[95] the tenant/landlord incautiously contracted in these terms and was responsible when his disrepair of a skylight caused £38 damage to the restaurant business conducted on the premises of his sub-lessee's assignee. In this case, there would have been no liability if the covenant had been simply for indemnity, because the head landlord had not sued. Neither would there have been liability if the tenant/landlord had assigned his own interest. For in that case, the covenant although relating to the estate of the sub-lessee would not have touched and concerned the land the subject of the sub-lease.[96] And so the burden of it would not have passed to the tenant/landlord's assignee, except to the extent that it related to the actual land sub-let.

Sub-lessees can often be forced into a difficult position either resulting from the failure of the tenant/landlord to observe the terms of the head lease, or from a failure of one of the other sub-lessees to observe the terms of his lease. In either case, a sub-lessee may take it on himself to assume compliance with the liabilities that have been broken with a view to preserving his own estate. It is not clear if he can recover the costs of launching the lifeboat for the benefit of the sub-lessees from them. On the one hand, he has discharged legal

---

[92] *Bonner* v. *Tottenham and Edmonton Permanent Investment Building Society* [1899] 1 Q.B. 161.
[93] *Kelly* v. *Rogers* [1892] 1 Q.B. 910, and *ante*, Chap. 4 (IV) E.
[94] *Clare* v. *Dobson* [1911] 1 K.B. 35; *Lloyds Bank Ltd.* v. *Lake* [1961] 1 W.L.R. 884.
[95] [1961] 2 Q.B. 228.
[96] *Dewar* v. *Goodman* [1909] A.C. 72.

liabilities when he was under no legal compulsion so to do and so has acted gratuitously. On the other hand, his action has benefited all the other sub-lessees who should as a matter of convenience and equity be bound to contribute for the benefit received. The matter is unresolved, but common sense argues in favour of contribution.[97]

E. Original Lessors and their Transferees

Whether the landlord's estate is freehold or leasehold it can, of course, only be transferred by deed.[98] If the title to the estate is registered, transfer of the landlord's estate will not be completed until registration of the transfer.[99] However, the original landlord remains bound by his contract to the original tenant, and to the extent that the benefit of those covenants can run, to the original tenant's successors in title even after he has assigned his reversion.[1] His position mirrors that of the original tenant. The passing of the benefit of covenants in the lease is the subject of the Law of Property Act 1925, s.141, and the passing of the burden is the subject of section 142.

Section 141 provides:

> "(1) Rent reserved by a lease,[2] and the benefit of every covenant or provision therein contained, having reference to the subject-matter thereof, and on the lessee's part to be observed or performed, and every condition of re-entry and other condition therein contained, shall be annexed and incident to and shall go with the reversionary estate in the land, or in any part thereof, immediately expectant on the term granted by the lease, notwithstanding severance of that reversionary estate, and without prejudice to any liability affecting a covenantor or his estate.
>
> (2) Any such rent, covenant or provision shall be capable of being recovered, received, enforced, and taken advantage of, by the person for the time being entitled, subject to the term, to the income of the whole or any part, as the case may require, of the land leased.
>
> (3) Where that person becomes entitled by conveyance or otherwise, such rent, covenant or provision may be recovered,

---

[97] And see (1967) 31 Conv. (N.S.) 38, P. St. J. Langan.

[98] L.P.A. 1925, s.52. If the tenanted property is a dwelling, the new landlord will have to give the tenant notice under Landlord and Tenant Act 1985, s.3(1). A transfer may be effected by the creation of a concurrent lease, *ante*, Chap. 3 (I) D.

[99] L.R.A. 1925, ss.19, 21, 22(1). And see *Naumann* v. *Ford* (1985) 275 E.G. 542.

[1] *Stuart* v. *Joy* [1904] 1 K.B. 362.

[2] This does not extend to a covenant to pay rent by the tenant's guarantor, which covenant does not appear to run with the land, *Pinemain* v. *Welbeck International* (1984) 272 E.G. 1166. The benefit of such a covenant should be expressly assigned.

received, enforced or taken advantage of by him notwithstanding that he becomes so entitled after the condition of re-entry or forfeiture has become enforceable, but this subsection does not render enforceable any condition of re-entry or other condition waived or released before such person becomes entitled as aforesaid."[3]

The nature of the covenants that run has already been considered. But one difficulty that remained unresolved for many years was whether the landlord's transferee could sue for breaches of covenant that occurred before he became landlord, *e.g.* breaches of covenant to repair. And whether he could sue for breaches of the covenant to pay rent that accrued due before the transfer of the landlord's estate. In both cases the answer seems to be that the transferee can sue. The issue relating to covenants to repair and other continuing covenants was determined by the Court of Appeal in *Re King (deceased).*[4] It follows that on assignment the transferring landlord loses his rights of action against the tenant. And Russell L.J. has observed in the Court of Appeal[5]: "It has been established in this court that an assignee of the reversion can claim, against the lessee, arrears of rent accrued prior to the assignment, and to re-enter on the ground of the failure to have paid such arrears by force of section 141 of the Law of Property Act 1925: see *London and County (A. & D.) Ltd.* v. *Wilfred Sportsman, Ltd. (Greenwoods (Hosiers and Outfitters), Ltd. third party)."*[6] Obviously the parties to the transfer should apply their minds to the question of subsisting breaches by the tenant when reaching agreement on the price to be paid.

The Law of Property Act 1925, s.142, contains similar provisions for the passing of the burden of covenants entered into by the lessor "with reference to the subject-matter of the lease." But a particular problem may arise where the reversionary estate is split.[7] A simple example is where the freehold of a house and garden, let as a whole to a single tenant, is divided between two brothers. The tenant now has two separate landlords, where before he only had one, but somewhat paradoxically only one tenancy. The split will not affect any statutory protection he enjoys.[8] Section 140 provides that where the reversionary estate is split[9] then so also are all the covenants, conditions and

---

[3] (4) is not reproduced.
[4] *Re King, Robinson* v. *Gray* [1963] Ch. 459, and see (1966) 30 Conv. (N.S.) 429, D. Macintyre.
[5] In *Arlesford Trading Co. Ltd.* v. *Servansingh* [1971] 1 W.L.R. 1080 at p. 1082.
[6] [1971] Ch. 764.
[7] *Jelley* v. *Buckman* [1974] Q.B. 488 (tenant not deprived of Rent Act protection in respect of his garden, outbuildings and outside lavatory accommodation that devolved to a separate landlord); and see *William Skelton & Son* v. *Harrison & Pinder Ltd.* [1975] Q.B. 361.
[8] *Jelley* v. *Buckman, supra; Nevill Long & Co. (Boards)* v. *Firmenich* (1984) 47 P. & C.R. 59 (business tenancy protection).
[9] A severance is not affected by transferring part of the property to trustees for the original landlord, *Persey* v. *Bazley* (1984) 47 P. & C.R. 37.

rights of re-entry as if the land in each severed part had been the only land let. However, if the landlord of part serves a notice to determine the tenancy as respects his part of the land, the tenant can by a counter notice served within one month end his tenancy of the other part at the same time.[10] The rent payable to the two new landlords is apportionable between them, and this has already been considered.[11] The apportioned rent will usually be paid separately to each landlord.

F. Transfer on Death

(1) *Devolution of Estate*

When a tenant dies his estate has to be wound up, *i.e.* the assets collected, debts paid, and the balance distributed amongst the beneficiaries either according to the terms of the will if the deceased has left one, or under the statutory provisions relating to an intestacy.[12] The assets of the tenant include his leasehold interests, even of course if it is only a weekly tenancy.[13] If the deceased has left a will appointing executors, their title relates back to the date of death, but they must obtain a grant of probate to transfer the tenant's legal estate.[14] If the tenant dies intestate, or the executors he appoints are unwilling or unable to take a grant of probate, then the administration of the estate will be carried out by his administrators, and their title to the property will only date from the grant of letters of administration.[15] In the intervening period the estate is vested in the President of the Family Division.[16] This provision enables the landlord to serve notices effectively before the grant of letters of administration. Persons who claim to be entitled to a leasehold estate under the terms of the will or intestacy have no legal right to it until the estate has been legally vested in them, by an assent. This must be in writing signed by all the personal representatives,[17] and it will usually be under seal and contain covenants by the beneficiary to indemnify the personal

---

[10] L.P.A. 1925, s.140(2). There are special provisions where notices are given to quit an agricultural holding, Agricultural Holdings Act 1986, s.32, but none affecting business tenancies protected by L. & T.A. 1954, Pt. II, see the discussion in *William Skelton & Son* v. *Harrison & Pinder Ltd.,* above.

[11] *Ante,* Chap. 5 (III).

[12] An application for an order transferring the tenancy to a dissatisfied dependant may be made under Inheritance (Provision for Family and Dependants) Act 1975, s.2.

[13] As in *Youngmin* v. *Heath* [1974] 1 W.L.R. 135.

[14] *Re Crowhurst Park, Sims-Hilditch* v. *Simmons* [1974] 1 W.L.R. 583.

[15] *Hilton* v. *Sutton Steam Laundry* [1946] K.B. 65; *Long (Fred) & Sons Ltd.* v. *Burgess* [1959] K.B. 115.

[16] Administration of Estates Act 1925, s.9, 55(1)(xv) and Administration of Justice Act 1970, s.1, Sched. 2(5).

[17] Administration of Estate Act 1925, s.36. If the title is registered, then the beneficiary must be registered as proprietor, L.R.A. 1925, s.41(4).

representatives from future liability under the terms of the lease. The same mechanics apply to the devolution of the lessor's estates.

A personal representative cannot choose to administer some parts of the estate, and wash his hands of the rest. If the assets include leaseholds pregnant with contingent liabilities for arrears of rent and repairs the personal representative must decide initially whether he is prepared to accept the administration of the whole estate including the leases, or renounce his right to administer entirely.[18] If a person intermeddles with an estate, by taking steps to wind it up without obtaining a grant, he can be regarded as an executor *de son tort* and become irretrievably saddled with the burden of winding it up.

(2) *Death of Original Tenant*

(a) Representative liability of the personal representative

The estate of the original tenant, like the original tenant himself, is liable in contract to the landlord for the duration of the lease. In *Youngmin* v. *Heath*[19] a personal representative argued unsuccessfully that she was not liable in a representative capacity for arrears of rent of a weekly tenancy. Stamp L.J. said[20]:

> "It is axiomatic that a personal representative does not automatically become liable for the liabilities of the deceased except to the extent of the assets of the estate, and, unless he enters into possession of the property held under the lease, there is no privity of estate between the landlord and the personal representative, and the personal representative does not become personally liable to pay the rent payable under the lease . . . The personal representative of a deceased is, however, bound to perform all the contracts of the deceased if he has assets, and is accordingly bound to discharge any contractual liability of the deceased under a tenancy."

But to limit his liability to the extent of the assets of the deceased, the personal representative must plead the state of the administration of the estate.[21]

(b) Liability as assignee

The personal representative can be regarded as an assignee if he has

---

[18] *Rubery* v. *Stevens* (1832) 4 B. & Ad. 241, 244.
[19] [1974] 1 W.L.R. 135.
[20] At p. 137.
[21] For a case where this was not done with apparently disastrous results, see *Midland Bank Trust Co. Ltd.* v. *Green (No. 2)* [1979] 1 All E.R. 726.

either physically entered the premises, or demanded rent for them from a sub-tenant. "If Mr. Heath had entered into the premises himself and had used them or taken the benefit of them, he would be liable *personally*[22] for the rent from the time from which he took possession. Even if there were no assets, he would be liable for the rent up to the annual value of the premises: see *Rendall* v. *Andreae.*[23]"[24] His liability under the covenant for repairs and other covenants cannot be so limited. Although here an assignment will put a time limit at least on the extent of that liability.[25] It follows that a personal representative of an original tenant can be liable in two distinct ways; first of all he can be liable in a representative capacity and secondly he can be liable as an assignee, by reason of the privity of estate between himself and the landlord.

(3) *Death of Assignee Tenant*

The potential liabilities of a deceased tenant who was himself an assignee are much smaller than if he was the original tenant. Liability can usually[26] only arise during the time the estate is held by the tenant or his personal representative. Again the personal representative can be liable in both a representative capacity and as an assignee. His clear duty in the interests of the estate as a whole is to dispose of the leasehold as soon as possible, if continuing to hold it is likely to involve the deceased's estate in increasing liabilities.[27]

(4) *Distribution of the Estate*

The object of the administration is the distribution of the estate to the beneficiaries, but a personal representative will be reluctant to dispose of assets if that is going to leave him in the position where he is likely to be sued by a landlord and have no assets out of which to claim an indemnity. The Trustee Act 1925, s.26, assists the distribution where there is representative liability. It applies, *inter alia*, where the personal representative is liable "as such" in respect of any rent, covenant or agreement reserved by or contained in any lease. The personal representative can distribute if he satisfies accrued liabilities which have been claimed,[28] and sets aside a sufficient fund in respect

---

[22] Italics in the original.
[23] (1892) L.J. 61 Q.B. 630, a curious rule limiting the liability of the personal representative as assignee only in respect of rent.
[24] *Per* Lord Denning M.R. in *Youngmin* v. *Heath* [1974] 1 W.L.R. 135 at p. 137.
[25] See *ante*, this Chap. (IV)C.
[26] There is always the possibility of liability under an indemnity given by the deceased tenant.
[27] *Rowley* v. *Adams* (1839) 4 Myl. & Cr. 534.
[28] He should advertise for claims under Trustee Act 1925, s.27.

of fixed or ascertained sums the lessee has agreed to lay out, *e.g.* to pay £200 towards the cost of redecorations at the end of the lease. After he distributes the estate, which will involve either assigning the lease to a beneficiary or purchaser as the case may be, he will not be liable in respect of subsequent claims under the lease made against him in his representative capacity. This includes claims that might arise under an indemnity given by the deceased tenant as an assignee in respect of any rent or covenant in the lease. This distribution does not prevent the lessor, or his successors, from following the assets into the hands of other beneficiaries to satisfy any other claims that might arise in the future.[29]

The potential liability which a personal representative can incur as an assignee because he has entered the property can be minimised in two ways at least. First, he can take an indemnity on assignment of the lease. Secondly, he can set aside an indemnity fund to cover possible future claims.[30] If there is difficulty about the size of sum to be set aside, it can be determined by the court. But the sum must be set aside before the property is disposed of by way of assent.[31] The fund set aside will be held until all claims are statute barred, and then it should be distributed among the beneficiaries, to whom of course it belongs.[32]

G. Transfer on Bankruptcy

Most leases will contain a proviso enabling the landlord to take steps to forfeit the lease in the event of the tenant's bankruptcy, submission to distress or, in certain cases, his removal of goods from the demised premises.[33] This covenant runs with the land and so becomes operative on the bankruptcy of the tenant for the time being.[34] Where a tenant is adjudicated bankrupt during the currency of a tenancy, the tenancy vests under the Bankruptcy Act 1914, s.53, in the trustee in bankruptcy. The bankrupt thereupon ceases to be the tenant, and the trustee in bankruptcy becomes the tenant as a person deriving title under him. This applies to all the tenant's contractual tenancies, including those protected by the Rent Acts.[35] It does not apply to a statutory tenancy protected by the Rent Acts, because it is not "property" within the Bankruptcy Act 1914, s.167, but merely a

---

[29] Trustee Act 1925, s.26(2), as amended by Law of Property (Amendment) Act 1926, ss.7, 8 and Sched. and see generally Parry and Clark, *The Law of Succession* (8th ed.), pp. 220 *et seq.*.

[30] *Re Owers, Public Trustee* v. *Death and Mount Vernon Hospital* [1941] Ch. 389.

[31] *Re Bennett, Midland Bank Executor and Trustee Co. Ltd.* v. *Fletcher* [1943] 1 All E.R. 467. Assignment to the beneficiaries may require the lessor's consent, see *ante*, (II)B.

[32] *Re Lewis,·Jennings* v. *Hemsley* [1939] Ch. 232 (fund paid into court in 1891).

[33] The operation of forfeiture clauses is considered in Chap. 8.

[34] *Smith* v. *Gronow* [1891] 2 Q.B. 394.

[35] *Reeves* v. *Davies* [1921] 2 K.B. 486; *Smalley* v. *Quarrier* [1975] 1 W.L.R. 938. The Rent Acts are considered in Pt. II, *post*.

personal right of the tenant.[36] This assignment to the trustee in bankruptcy does not amount to a breach of the covenant against assignment as it is involuntary.[37]

The trustee in bankruptcy has an option either to disclaim the lease if it is likely to be more of a liability than an asset, or to realise it, most probably by sale. A lease can in every case be disclaimed with the leave of the court. There are special statutory provisions[38] enabling liquidators of companies to disclaim with leave. Leave will more readily be granted if the disclaimer will not affect the rights of guarantors, either where the lease has no premium which could benefit them, or their liability under the guarantee has not been effectively transferred to the present lessor.[39] But the combined effect of the Bankruptcy Act 1914, s.54, and the Bankruptcy Rules 1952, r. 278[40] permits disclaimer of a lease without leave:

"(a) where the bankrupt has not sub-let the demised premises or any part thereof or created a mortgage or charge on the lease; and

   (i) the rent reserved and the real value of the property leased, as ascertained by the gross assessment for (rating purposes) are less than £20 per annum; or

   (ii) the estate is administered in a summary manner under section 129 of the Act. [This can only be done if the debtor's property is likely to be less than £4,000.]; or

   (iii) the trustee serves the lessor with notice of his intention to disclaim, and the lessor does not within seven days after the receipt of such notice give notice to the trustee requiring the matter to be brought before the court.

(b) Where the bankrupt has sub-let the demised premises or created a mortgage or charge upon the lease, and the trustee serves the lessor and the sub-lessee or the mortgagees with notice of his intention to disclaim, and neither the lessor nor the sub-lessee or the mortgagees, or any of them, within fourteen days after the receipt of such notice, require or requires the matter to be brought before the court."[41]

It is not possible to summarise what in practice usually happens as this obviously depends on the value of the property, the extent of the bankruptcy, and whether the lease is at the time of the bankruptcy

---

[36] *Sutton* v. *Dorf* [1932] 2 K.B. 304.

[37] *Re Riggs, ex p. Lovell* [1901] 2 K.B. 16 (bankruptcy following tenant's own petition).

[38] Companies Act 1985, ss.618, 619, Sched. 20, Pt. I.

[39] *Re Distributors and Warehousing Ltd.*, *Financial Times*, November 19, 1985.

[40] S.I. 1952 No. 2114.

[41] Applications to disclaim should generally be made within 12 months of the trustee's appointment, Bankruptcy Act 1914, s.54(1). The provisions considered in this section will be altered and replaced when the Insolvency Act 1985, ss. 153, 161 and 232 are brought into force

more beneficial to the landlord than the tenant. But from the landlord's point of view, unless the terms of the lease are particularly advantageous to him there are considerable benefits in disclaimer by the trustee, especially if the property is freely marketable on terms similar to those in the lease. The landlord is saved the trouble of making forfeiture proceedings. The disclaimer crystallises the amount he may have to claim against the bankrupt's estate for current arrears of rent,[42] and he can re-let on new terms.

The effect of disclaimer in every case is to release the estate of the bankrupt, but it does not affect the rights and liabilities of other persons.[43] Its effect on the leasehold estate itself depends on whether the bankrupt tenant was the original tenant or an assignee. If the original lessee becomes bankrupt, disclaimer ends the lease, and also the liability of the guarantor.[44] If the landlord can only re-let at a lower rental, he can claim in the bankruptcy for this loss. If a subsequent assignee becomes bankrupt and his trustee disclaims, the lease continues in existence, rent still falls due, and the landlord can claim against the original lessee who can prove for it in the bankruptcy. The original lessee or any other person claiming an interest in the lease may apply for an order vesting[45] the lease in himself so that he can deal again with the legal estate. Under an express or implied covenant for indemnity[46] the original lessee may also be able to claim against his own assignee for rent which he has had to pay. If the trustee decides not to disclaim he will be personally liable as an assignee by virtue of the privity of estate between himself and the lessor under the covenants in the lease.[47] And if the tenant needs the lessor's consent to an assignment, then the trustee in bankruptcy will have to obtain it.[48]

The position on the liquidation of a company is much the same. The estate does not vest in the liquidator personally, but he has power to disclaim[49] onerous property, or he can continue to hold and realise it as an asset of the company for the benefit of the creditors. The liquidation of a company can breach the contractual chain of indemnities from assignee to assignee. Before the final dissolution of the company the circumspect can meet this difficulty by taking an assignment of the benefit of the covenant to indemnify.

---

[42] See further Chap. 5.
[43] Bankruptcy Act 1914, s.54(2). It will, however, prevent a wife making any application for the transfer to her under the matrimonial legislation, Matrimonial Homes Act 1983, s.2(7), and see *post* (H).
[44] *Stacey* v. *Hill* [1901] 1 K.B. 660.
[45] Bankruptcy Act 1914, s.54(6).
[46] See the discussion in *Warnford Investments Ltd.* v. *Duckworth* [1978] 2 W.L.R. 741 (claim against original lessee on liquidation of subsequent assignee).
[47] *Re Soloman, ex p. Dressler* (1878) 9 Ch.D. 252; [1874–80] All E.R. Rep. 1194; *Titterton* v. *Cooper* (1882) 9 Q.B.D. 473; [1881–5] All E.R. Rep. 757.
[48] *Re Wright, Landau* v. *The Trustee* [1949] Ch. 729.
[49] Companies Act 1985, ss.618, 619, Sched. 20, Pt. I.

H. Transfer following Divorce

The court has a statutory power to order the transfer of a protected or statutory tenancy or a secure tenancy[50] or a protected shorthold[51] from one spouse to the other, or from the joint ownership of both spouses to one of them. The order can be made where one at least of the spouses occupies a dwelling-house either in his own right or with the other spouse. The order for transfer can be made when the marriage is ended by divorce or a decree of nullity and by the court that grants the decree.[52] It can also be made when there is an application during a marriage for financial relief.[53] The order operates by itself to effect the transfer. The transferee spouse is subject to the rights and liabilities attaching to the former spouse's estate. The former spouse who has lost his estate is relieved from future liability to the landlord in respect of liability for matters to be performed or discharged after the date on which the decree is made absolute.[54] This seems to mean that he is relieved from the liabilities that would remain with an original tenant who voluntarily assigns. He seems to be in a similar category as an assignee who assigns. Consequential orders may be made for the discharge and performance by either or both of the spouses of liabilities which have accrued at the time of the order.[55] The provisions only apply to certain tenancies within the Rent Acts, and the landlord may not take kindly to the proposed arrangements. The landlord has a right to be heard before the order is made.[56]

---

[50] *i.e.* within Housing Act 1985, s.79, see Chap. 16, *post.*
[51] Housing Act 1980, s.54(2).
[52] Matrimonial Homes Act 1983, Sched. 1. Section 1(5) enables the non-estate owing spouse to make effective rent payments during the marriage.
[53] Matrimonial and Family Proceedings Act 1984, s.22.
[54] Matrimonial Homes Act 1983, Sched. 1, para. 2(2).
[55] Matrimonial Homes Act 1983, Sched. 1, para. 5.
[56] Matrimonial Homes Act 1983, Sched. 1, para. 8.

CHAPTER 8

TERMINATION

I. Introduction 333
II. Expiration of Term 334
III. Surrender 335
  A. Nature and Effect 335
  B. Capacity to Make and Accept a
    Surrender 337
  C. Methods of Effecting a Sur-
    render 338
IV. Merger 340
V. Notice to Quit 341
  A. Types of Tenancy when neces-
    sary 341
  B. Formal Requirements of a No-
    tice to Quit 342
  C. The Effect of a Notice 350
VI. Forfeiture 351
  A. The Need for a Forfeiture
    Clause 351

  B. Formal Requirements 351
  C. Service and Effect of Notice . 353
  D. Effect on Sub-tenants 354
  E. Covenants Outside the Pro-
    visions 356
  F. Avoidance of the Relief Pro-
    visions 357
VII. Disclaimer 357
VIII. Termination of Contractual Li-
  cences by Notice 357
IX. Recovery of Possession 360
  A. Self-help 360
  B. Proceedings in the County
    Court 361
  C. Proceedings in the High
    Court 362

I. INTRODUCTION

Leases and licences can come to an end in a variety of ways. A lease for a fixed term can simply expire at the end of the term; both parties may agree to end the relationship prematurely with the acquisition of the other's outstanding estate; either party may give notice to the other to end the periodic tenancy or licence of uncertain duration, or circumstances may arise where the landlord can claim that the tenant's misconduct has caused him to forfeit the lease.

Termination has given rise to a large amount of detailed law, much seemingly founded on the little quirks and niceties. But until it is certain that the relationship has ended, the landlord cannot deal with his estate without at least the possibility of a claim that the tenant still has an outstanding legal estate in the land which will take priority over further interests that might be created.[1] Licensees are also wont to make similar claims, which can paralyse further dispositions until the situation is resolved. Similarly, the tenant faces the possibility of a claim that he is still liable under the terms of the lease, especially for rent and repairs, until the estate created by the lease has ended.

[1] See *Public Trustee* v. *Westbrook* [1965] 1 W.L.R. 1160.

II. EXPIRATION OF TERM

There is no need to serve a notice to quit to end a term for a fixed number of years. A tenancy for 10 years from October 10, 1977, will not automatically expire until October 11, 1987. The tenant ought to quit the minute after midnight of October 10/11.[2] The tenant may, and in most cases will, remain lawfully in possession, if he is a business tenant under a statutory continuation of his tenancy[3]; if he is a residential tenant under the protection of the Rent Acts[4] or the Housing Act 1985 or if he is a farmer by virtue of the Agricultural Holdings Act 1986.[5] If the landlord still wants to rent the premises and the tenant is satisfactory, a continuation of the present arrangements at an increased rent is likely to suit both parties.

The tenant holding over after the expiration of a fixed number of years initially holds as a tenant on sufferance.[6] But the circumstances of the holding over may give rise to the implication that a new tenancy from year to year has been created. The parties may have had a formal written agreement for one year certain, the rent payable monthly. Before the end of the first year they may agree that the tenancy is to continue at an increased monthly rental. It can be a matter of some difficulty to decide if the tenant is holding over as a yearly tenant, and so unable to leave before the end of the year on giving his landlord a month's notice. The question is: what was the real intention of the parties when they made the new arrangement?[7] At the time of the parties' discussion it would have been in the tenant's interest to argue that he had the security of a fixed rent for a further year. However in the case of residential tenancies protected by the Rent Acts: "If the acceptance of rent can be explained on some other footing than a contractual tenancy, as, for instance, by reason of an existing or possible statutory right to remain, then a new tenancy should not be inferred."[8]

If the tenant with statutory protection stays on and loses the benefit thereof then he ceases "to be clothed with the garment of a tenant."[9] and of course, has to pay for the privilege of remaining.[10] If the

[2] *Cutting* v. *Derby* (1776) 2 Wm.Bl. 1075.
[3] Under L. & T.A. 1954, s.24, and see *post.* Pt. III.
[4] See *post.* Pt. II.
[5] See *post.* Pt. IV.
[6] See *ante,* Chap. 2 (II)H (4).
[7] *Doe d.Cheny* v. *Baten* (1775) 1 Cowp. 243; [1775–1802] All E.R. Rep. 594; *Legal & General Assurance Society, Ltd.* v. *General Metal Agencies, Ltd.* (1969) 20 P. & C.R. 953.
[8] *Marcroft Wagons, Ltd.* v. *Smith* [1951] 2 K.B. 496, Denning L.J. at p. 506, and see also *Dealex Properties, Ltd.* v. *Brooks* [1966] 1 Q.B. 542; *Lewis* v. *M.T.C. (Cars) Ltd.* [1975] 1 W.L.R. 457 (where sub-tenants unsuccessfully argued that they had acquired a new tenancy as a result of the payment of rent).
[9] Edmund Davies L.J.'s colourful description of an unhappy business tenant who lost his statutory protection and right to apply for a new tenancy by being hopelessly out of time in *Meah* v. *Sector Properties Ltd.* [1974] 1 W.L.R. 547.
[10] See Chap. 5 (VI) *ante.*

original tenancy was more than a weekly or quarterly tenancy and he wilfully holds over, in theory at least, he can be required to pay rent at the rate of double the yearly value of the premises if the landlord has served him with a notice that he requires possession.[11]

We have seen that often the parties want to create a term for an uncertain period, *e.g.* for so long as *A* lives,[12] or for so long as *B* is posted in the United Kingdom or until *C* returns from working abroad, and that this objective can be achieved by the grant of a term of years terminable on notice following the happening of the uncertain event. The lease is subject to a determinable limitation. The satisfying of the condition usually followed by notice will automatically operate to determine the term.[13] However, unsuccessful attempts have been made to extend this doctrine so as to bring the lease to an automatic end either on the financial failure of the tenant or his surety,[14] or his non-observance of what in effect are covenants to build[15] and repair and at the same time to deprive the tenant of the benefit of the statutory relief against forfeiture[16] contained in the Law of Property Act 1925, s.146.[17] The fact that the lease is subject to a conditional limitation and so liable to end following the occurrence of an uncertain event does not prevent the term of years from being "absolute."[18]

III. Surrender

A. Nature and Effect

" '*Surrender' sursum redditio*, properly is a yielding up an estate for life or yeares to him that hath an immediate estate in reversion or remainder, wherein the estate for life or yeares may drowne by mutuall agreement betweene them."[19] The landlord agrees to the premature ending of his tenant's estate. An effective surrender does not relieve the tenant or his surety[20] from liability for breaches of covenant existing at the date of the surrender. His liability for repair,[21]

---

[11] Landlord and Tenant Act 1730, s.1, and see further Woodfall, paras. 1–2092 *et seq.* The means whereby the landlord recovers possession is considered *post* (VIII).
[12] L.P.A. 1925, s.149(6), and *ante*, Chap. 2 (II) H (1).
[13] But see the doubts on this point in (1963) 27 Conv. (N.S.) 111, F. R. Crane.
[14] *Halliard Property Co. Ltd.* v. *Jack Segal, Ltd.* [1978] 1 W.L.R. 377.
[15] *Bashir* v. *Commissioner of Lands* [1960] A.C. 44.
[16] Discussed *post* (VI).
[17] For a similarly unsuccessful attempt using a surrender executed in escrow on the grant of the lease, see *Plymouth Corporation* v. *Harvey* [1971] 1 W.L.R. 549.
[18] L.P.A. 1925, s.205(1) (xxvii).
[19] Co.Litt. 337b.
[20] *Torminster Properties* v. *Green* [1983] 1 W.L.R. 676.
[21] *Richmond* v. *Savill* [1926] 2 K.B. 530.

and to pay increased rent for a period before the surrender, but determined after it,[22] will survive, unless the circumstances are such as to show that the landlords have either waived or released their legal rights or that there has been accord and satisfaction.[23] The surrender operates as a release from future liability. A spouse cannot, however, defeat his wife's statutory occupational rights by surrendering his tenancy of what is, or has been the matrimonial home.[24]

(1) *Effect of Surrender on Sub-lessees*

A surrender does not affect the validity of an effectively granted sub-lease.[25] The branch does not fall with the tree. The sub-tenant looks to the landlord to whom the intermediate estate has been surrendered. This is so even if the estate has been surrendered under threat of forfeiture.[26] A sub-tenant is in a much better position where the intermediate estate has been surrendered than where it has been forfeited. For if the intermediate estate has been forfeited the sub-tenant has only the right to make an application under the Law of Property Act 1925, s.146(4), for all or part of his landlord's estate to be vested in him on terms.[27]

Following the surrender the superior landlord may grant a new lease either to the surrendering tenant or to a third party altogether. The sub-leases still continue.[28] But the rights and liabilities of the sub-tenant and the new intermediate landlord under the sub-lease take effect as if the original lease had remained on foot and had not been surrendered.[29] This arrangement is not uncommon and is often found where an intermediate tenant's term is coming to an end and he would like the security of a longer term before embarking on a scheme of capital expenditure. He may therefore propose to his landlord that he surrenders the rest of his term and takes a new longer lease on terms that make the arrangement attractive to the landlord. The statutory provisions enable the re-arrangement to proceed without having to drag in the sub-tenants and extract their respective consents.[30]

---

[22] *Torminster Properties* v. *Green, supra.*
[23] *Dalton.* v. *Pickard* [1926] 2 K.B. 545n.
[24] Matrimonial Homes Act 1983, s.2(5).
[25] L.P.A. 1925, s.139.
[26] *Great Western Ry. Co.* v. *Smith* (1876) 2 Ch.D. 235.
[27] See *post* (VI) D.
[28] L.P.A. 1925, s.150 (1) (2).
[29] L.P.A. 1925, s.150 (3) (4).
[30] A brief but illuminating history of the difficulties that used to prevail is contained in *Re Grosvenor Estates, Westminister (Duke)* v. *McKenna* [1932] 1 Ch. 232.

(2) *Effect of Surrender on Squatters*

A squatter who has successfully completed 12 years' adverse possession[31] acquires a certain degree of immunity from successful action to
remove him.[32] The person who has the right to remove the squatter of
tenanted property is the tenant himself, for he is the person who has
the right to possession of it. The landlord, having no right to
possession, has no right of action until the lease has ended.[33] In the
meantime there is no privity of estate between squatter and
landlord.[34] The time when the landlord is entitled to possession can be
accelerated by a surrender of the tenant's estate. The landlord will
then have 12 years from that time to take proceedings to recover
possession from the squatter.[35] If the leasehold title is registered, the
squatter can apply to be registered as the proprietor of it.[35] If he does
successfully apply, and is registered as the leasehold proprietor, a
purported surrender by the former registered tenant is ineffective to
defeat the squatter's title.[36]

B. Capacity to Make and Accept a Surrender

Sole owners who are either the original tenant or assignees can effect
surrenders,[37] but if there are joint tenants for the time being then all
must join in the surrender, or alternatively the joint tenants effecting
the surrender must have the express authority of the others.[38] The
capacity of mortgagors in possession to accept surrenders is peculiarly
circumscribed. Strictly, they can only accept surrenders[39] for the
purpose of enabling the creation of a further lease authorised by the
Law of Property Act 1925, s.99. If the section applies and is not
complied with, then the original lease continues and the purported
surrender is void.[40] However, usually the statutory power of granting
leases is expressly restricted.[41] The statutory power of mortgagors to
accept surrenders is more properly related to the situation when the
mortgage would be discharged out of rents from statutorily permitted

---

[31] For a discussion on this expression, see *Treloar* v. *Nute* [1976] 1 W.L.R. 1295.
[32] Limitation Act 1980, s.15(1), Sched. I, para. 5 states the date from which time runs in the case of a tenancy from year to year, or other period, not being in writing (from the end of the first year, or other period). Payment of rent extends the period.
[33] *Fairweather* v. *St. Marylebone Property Co. Ltd.* [1963] A.C. 510.
[34] *Tichborne* v. *Weir* (1892) 67 L.T. 735.
[35] L.R.A. 1925, s.75(2).
[36] *Spectrum Investment Co.* v. *Holmes* [1981] 1 W.L.R. 221, and see further P. H. Kenny [1982] Conv. 201.
[37] *Taylor* v. *Twinberrow* [1930] 2 K.B. 16.
[38] *Leek & Moorlands Building Society* v. *Clark* [1952] 2 Q.B. 788 (ineffective surrender by husband alone, joint tenant with his wife).
[39] See L.P.A. 1925, s.100.
[40] *Barclays Bank Ltd.* v. *Stasek* [1957] Ch. 28.
[41] *Ante*, Chap. 3 (II)D.

leases, rather than out of the general income of the mortgagor/land-lord. If the mortgagee hopes to be paid out of the rents, then he is obviously concerned with the continuity of tenanted occupation.

C. Methods of Effecting a Surrender

(1) *Express Surrenders*

The most effective and unequivocal form of surrender is by deed.[42] Like a conveyance of freeholds the surrender should take immediate effect, and it will be invalid if it is expressed to take effect at some time in the future.[43] Irrespective of the length of the original term, an express surrender of the legal estate should always be by deed.[44] But if the tenant purports to give up his tenancy in writing, then the writing may operate to dispose of the tenant's beneficial interest in the tenancy to his landlord, assuming that the landlord does not reject this attempted surrender.[45] Part only of the property may be surrendered,[46] but to be effective the surrender must be for the rest of the duration of the lease.[47]

A formal contract to surrender a lease is unusual but if one is to be enforceable then it has to be evidenced in writing in the same way as a contract to grant a lease, or sell the land.[48] It ought also to be protected by registration as a land charge if it is to bind purchasers of the respective estates involved.[49] It is not uncommon to find a covenant in leases requiring the tenant to offer to surrender his term if he wants to assign. Doubt has been cast on the efficacy of this device as a means of avoiding the Landlord and Tenant Act 1927, s.19(1),[50] but it does seem to be valid[51] for those purposes. But if the covenant is in a business lease, and would have the effect of depriving the tenant of his statutory protection, then it will be void and unenforceable.[52]

(2) *Surrender by Operation of Law*

Most leases are effectively surrendered by operation of law, and

---

[42] L.P.A. 1925, s.52.
[43] *Doe d.Murrell* v. *Milward* (1838) 3 M. & W. 328.
[44] L.P.A. 1925, s.52. There is no express exception in favour of the surrender of terms that may have been created otherwise than by deed under L.P.A. 1925, ss.52(2)(*d*), 54(2).
[45] L.P.A. 1925, s.53(1).
[46] *Jenkin R. Lewis & Son Ltd.* v. *Kerman* [1971] Ch. 477, following *Baynton* v. *Morgan* (1888) 22 Q.B.D. 74.
[47] *Burton* v. *Barclay* (1831) 7 Bing. 745; [1824–34] All E.R. Rep. 437.
[48] *i.e.* L.P.A. 1925, s.40 applies.
[49] Land Charges Act 1972, s.2(4).
[50] *Greene* v. *Church Commissioners for England* [1974] Ch. 467.
[51] *Bocardo S.A.* v. *S. & M. Hotels Ltd.* [1979] 3 All E.R. 737.
[52] It contravenes L. & T.A. 1954, s.38(1), *Allnatt London Properties* v. *Newton* [1984] 1 All E.R. 423, and see *post* Chap. 22.

without any writing being used at all.[53] Tearing up,[54] or writing "cancelled" on a lease[55] will not amount to an effective express surrender but in most cases, taken with the other actions of the parties it will be possible to establish a surrender by operation of law. The most common evidence of an effective surrender is that the landlord has accepted back possession after agreeing that the term will come to an end.[56] When both parties act in such a way as can only be explained on the basis that there has been a surrender, they are estopped from denying that the tenancy has been surrendered.[57]

It follows that accepting the key "without prejudice" to see if the premises can be re-let,[58] or changing the locks on the premises to make them secure after the tenant has left,[59] or simply being the passive and unwilling recipient of the key[60] are not acts which estop the landlord from denying that a surrender has taken place. The simple fact that there has been a grant of a new lease to a third party even with the existing tenant's consent does not amount to a surrender, unless it is accompanied at the same time by a change of possession preceding or following the lease.[61]

To establish a surrender of the old lease is seldom difficult where it has been replaced by the grant of a new one to the same tenant.[62] However, the surrender of the old lease in this situation will be effective only if the new lease has been validly granted.[63] This is even so even if the first lease was expressly surrendered by the lease granting the new term[64] but not if the surrender is by a separate deed.[65] A variation of the terms of the existing lease may amount to a surrender and new grant. An alteration that extends the original term will operate in this way.[66] The same result may follow where there is an agreement to pay an increased rent, but a strict application of the principle that the old lease has been surrendered is often inconvenient and has been avoided by arguing that the additional payment is

[53] L.P.A. 1925, s.52(2)(*c*).
[54] *Doe d.Courtail* v. *Thomas* (1829) 9 B. & C. 288.
[55] *Doe d.Berkeley (Earl)* v. *York (Archbishop)* (1805) 6 Ea. 86; [1803–13] All E.R. Rep. 248.
[56] *Phenè* v. *Popplewell* (1862) 12 C.B. (N.S.) 334 (putting up board to let and painting out tenant's name).
[57] *Lyon* v. *Reed* (1844) 13 M. & W. 285; [1843–60] All E.R. Rep. 178; *Foster* v. *Robinson* [1951] 1 K.B. 149 (tenancy surrendered on agreement to allow tenant to live rent free for rest of his life; agreement acted on).
[58] *Re Panther Lead Co.* [1896] 1 Ch. 978.
[59] *Relvok Properties* v. *Dixon* (1973) 25 P. & C.R. 1.
[60] *Cannan* v. *Hartley* (1850) 9 C.B. 634.
[61] *Wallis* v. *Hands* [1893] 2 Ch. 75.
[62] *Lyon* v. *Reed* (1844) 13 M. & W. 285; [1843–60] All E.R. Rep. 178.
[63] *Zouch d.Abbott and Hallett* v. *Parsons* (1765) 3 Burr. 1794; [1558–1774] All E.R. Rep. 161.
[64] *Doe d. Earl of Egremont* v. *Courtenay* (1848) 11 Q.B. 702; [1843–60] All E.R. Rep. 685 (surrender contained in new lease that was beyond the landlord's powers to grant); *Barclays Bank Ltd.* v. *Stasek* [1957] Ch. 28.
[65] *Rhyl Urban District Council* v. *Rhyl Amusements Ltd.* [1959] 1 W.L.R. 465.
[66] *Re Savile Settled Estates, Savile* v. *Savile* [1931] 2 Ch. 210; *Baker* v. *Merckel, Anson (Third Party)* [1960] 1 Q.B. 657 (variation giving option to extend).

merely a collateral payment and not strictly rent,[67] that the rule is inconvenient, ill-founded and unreasonable[68]; and finally that in any event the rule is inapplicable to lettings subject to and within the statutory framework of the Agricultural Holdings Act 1986.[69]

The fact that the tenant has agreed to purchase his landlord's interest does not automatically at that time cause a surrender of the lease, although on the facts of the particular agreement the contract may have this effect.[70] The point becomes important when the sale goes off and the vendor/landlord wants to recover possession. He will obviously have considerably less difficulty in doing so if he is dealing with a defaulting purchaser rather than a non-paying tenant. For this reasons options to purchase may be so drafted as to effect a surrender of the lease on their exercise.[71]

IV. MERGER

This is the mirror situation of that seen in a surrender. Here the tenant acquires the reversion immediately expectant on his own term. Theoretically that would make him his own landlord, a situation manifestly fraught with difficulty if it ever came to enforcing covenants against himself.[72] At common law merger of the two estates took place automatically in those cases where both estates were held in the same capacity, *e.g.* both beneficially, or both as trustees of the same estate. But automatic merger of estates can often defeat the intention of the parties.[73] The equitable rule was that merger would only occur if that was what the party acquiring both estates intended. This is now the general rule.[74]

Most tenants acquire their landlord's estate with a view to ending the lease. But it is more satisfactory for the assignment of the reversion or transfer of the freehold to state expressly that a merger is intended. If there is no such statement the court can look at the surrounding circumstances. These may clearly indicate that no merger was contemplated, as when the tenant first mortgaged his leasehold estate and then acquired the freehold reversion and to raise the purchase money mortgaged that as well.[75] Evidence of merger can be

---

[67] *Donellan* v. *Read* (1832) 3 B. & Ad. 899; [1824–34] All E.R. Rep. 639.

[68] *Gable Construction Co. Ltd.* v. *Inland Revenue Comrs.* [1968] 1 W.L.R. 1426.

[69] *Jenkin R. Lewis & Son Ltd.* v. *Kerman* [1971] Ch. 477.

[70] *cf. Turner* v. *Watts* (1927) L.J. 97 I.J. K.B. 92 and *Nightingale* v. *Courtney* [1954] 1 Q.B. 399; *Leek & Moorlands Building Society* v. *Clark* [1952] 2 Q.B. 788.

[71] *Watney* v. *Boardley* [1975] 1 W.L.R. 857.

[72] *Rye* v. *Rye* [1962] A.C. 496.

[73] *Silsby* v. *Holliman* [1955] Ch. 552 is an example of where a "merger" would have defeated a statutory tenant's objective in becoming his own landlord's mortgagee.

[74] L.P.A. 1925, s.185, and see *Stavely Iron & Chemical Co.* v. *National Coal Board* [1950] W.N. 273; [1947–1951] C.L.C. 6268.

[75] *Capital & Counties Bank, Ltd.* v. *Rhodes* [1903] 1 Ch. 631.

obtained from a later transaction, *e.g.* a mortgage by the tenant who has acquired the freehold.[76] Where the transfer or conveyance is silent on the point, such a mortgagee would be well advised to make sure that the mortgage contains a statement that both estates had merged. But if there is no evidence at all, and it is not possible to state whether merger was in the interest of the tenant or intended by him, then it does seem as if a merger will be presumed.[77]

A merger may have the unexpected result of destroying restrictive covenants in the original lease binding other land of the former landlord.[78] It does not however have any effect on a sub-lease, the obligations of which are then enforceable by and against the person in whom the estates have merged.[79]

V. NOTICE TO QUIT

A. Types of Tenancy when Necessary

"A notice to quit may be the subject of express agreement; it may be required by law in the absence of agreement, as in the case of a weekly, monthly, or yearly tenancy."[80] The ability of either party to determine any periodic tenancy by the service of a notice to quit is an inherent characteristic of a periodic tenancy.[81] If by the terms of the agreement one party cannot serve a notice, then either that term is repugnant to the periodic tenancy created, or a term greater than a periodic tenancy has been created. If the term preventing one party from serving a notice is repugnant, then it is void and can be disregarded.[82] It is however possible for one party to agree to a curb on his right to serve a notice, *e.g.* that he cannot serve a notice for 10, 20 or 50 years.[83]

It is unusual for a lease for a fixed term to require also the service of a notice to quit, but the provision is sometimes met. In its absence the term will automatically expire. An exception occurs in relation to agricultural tenancies protected by the Agricultural Holdings Act 1986. Section 3 of the Act provides that leases for two years and

---

[76] *Re Fletcher, Reading* v. *Fletcher* [1917] 1 Ch. 339 (tenants who acquired freehold later mortgaged both their freehold and leasehold interests separately to secure a loan. There was no merger).
[77] *Re Attkins, Life* v. *Attkins* [1913] 2 Ch. 619.
[78] *Golden Lion Hotel (Hunstanton) Ltd.* v. *Carter* [1965] 1 W.L.R. 1189.
[79] L.P.A. 1925, s.139. Merger occurs when a "secure tenant" acquires a shared ownership under the Housing Act 1985, s.143. s.151(2) of the 1985 Act extends L.P.A. 1925, s.139 to the secure tenant's sub-tenants. And see further Chap. 16 *post*.
[80] *P. Phipps & Co. (Northampton and Towcester Breweries), Ltd.* v. *Rogers* [1925] 1 K.B. 14 at p. 27, Atkins L.J.
[81] *Lower* v. *Sorrell* [1963] 1 Q.B. 959.
[82] *Centaploy Ltd.* v. *Matlodge Ltd.* [1974] Ch. 1 (purported weekly tenancy "to continue until determined by the lessee").
[83] *Re Midland Railway Co.'s Agreement, Clay (Charles) & Sons, Ltd.* v. *British Railways Board* [1971] Ch. 725.

upwards do not automatically expire at the end of their term, but continue as tenancies from year to year unless a notice was served at least one year before the end of the term.[84] It will be seen that the Landlord and Tenant Act 1954 automatically continues certain residential tenancies granted for more than 21 years[85] and certain business tenancies granted for a fixed term of more than six months.[86] In either case a notice has to be served to end what starts as apparently a fixed term lease.

B. Formal Requirements of a Notice to Quit

(1) *Common Law and Statutory Requirements*

There appear to be no common law requirements that the notice should be in writing, at least where the tenancy was orally created.[87] Oral notices are common and are often given by tenants. A written notice at least reduces the field of conflict by eliminating the issue of whether there is a notice, still leaving for argument validity of its service and terms. However, the statutory provisions that pepper this area require in most cases not merely written notice but often the utilisation of specific forms,[88] and the tenancy agreement itself will often expressly provide for the service of written notices.

A notice served by either landlord or tenant to quit a dwelling must be in writing.[89] Moreover, it must contain prescribed information,[90] which is that proceedings must be taken before a residential tenant can be lawfully evicted, and an indication that he may have additional security of tenure under the Rent Acts. A notice to end the statutory continuation of a business tenancy protected by Part II of the Landlord and Tenant Act 1954 also has to be in a specified form which sets out in detail the tenant's rights.[91] And there are detailed rules prescribing appropriate forms for notices to quit agricultural holdings.[92]

Whatever form is used, the notice must be clear and unambiguous.

---

[84] See Pt. (IV), *post.*

[85] See Pt. (II) *post*, and L. & T.A. 1954, s.4.

[86] See Pt. III, *post*, and L. & T.A. 1954, ss.25, 43.

[87] *Timmins* v. *Rowlinson* (1765) 3 Burr. 1603 *cf. Johnstone* v. *Hudlestone* (1825) 4 B. & C. 922.

[88] See *post*, Pt. II–IV.

[89] Protection from Eviction Act 1977, s.5(1).

[90] The Notices to Quit (Prescribed Information) (Protected Tenancies and Part VI Contracts) Regulations 1980 (S.I. 1980 No. 1624). See *Post*, pt. II. If the property is in a housing action area, the local authority have to be notified under Housing Act 1985, s.247(2) and 249(2).

[91] s.25, and see *post*, Pt. III. It will not necessarily be fatal to its validity if the notice differs in minor respects from the currently prescribed form, if it does not mislead: *Tegerdine* v. *Brooks* (1977) 36 P. & C.R. 261 *cf. Earthcare Cooperative* v. *Troveworth*, May 13, 1985, Durham Cty Ct. [1985] C.L.Y. 1854.

[92] See Pt. IV, *post.*

In *Gardner* v. *Ingram*[93] a tenant expected some difficulty if certain repairs were carried out and wrote to his landlord: "Kindly, therefore, take notice that I intend to surrender to you the tenancy of this house, on or before Sept. 29 next." It was held that the notice was uncertain. Lord Coleridge C.J. said: "A notice to quit must be absolute in its terms. Although no particular form need be followed, there must be plain, unambiguous words claiming to determine the existing tenancy at a certain time." And in *Phipps & Co.* v. *Rogers*[94] Lush J. commented that the notice "must indicate with reasonable clearness when possession will be demanded or given, so that the other party may know what is required of him."

(2) *Length of Notice Required*

The length of notice needed to end a periodic tenancy depends both on the period of the tenancy and the overriding statutory provisions. A notice to quit any premises let as a dwelling must in any event be given not less than four weeks before the date on which it is to take effect.[95] A longer notice may be necessary. In respect of business tenancies protected by Part II of the Landlord and Tenant Act 1954 the notice by the landlord must be not less than six nor more than 12 months before its effective date.[96] If the business tenant wants to give up possession at the end of a fixed term he has to give notice three months before the end of the term.[97] If the term is statutorily continued the tenant has to give not less than three months' notice ending on any quarter day.[98] At least 12 months' notice has to be given to quit a protected agricultural holding.[99] Long tenancies at low rents[1] are protected by Part I of the Landlord and Tenant Act 1954. Such a residential tenant's term does not automatically expire at the end of the term of years, but is statutorily continued. To end that state of affairs a landlord has to serve a notice of not less than six months nor more than 12 months,[2] and the tenant has to serve a notice of not less

---

[93] (1889) 61 L.T. 729 at 730; [1886–90] All E.R. Rep. 258 at 260. The validity of this decision but not the dicta is doubted in Woodfall, para. 1–2011.

[94] [1924] 2 K.B. 45 at 49 affd. [1925] 1 K.B. 14.

[95] Protection from Eviction Act 1977, s.5(1); *Schnabel* v. *Allard* [1967] 1 Q.B. 627 (this means inclusive of the day of service and exclusive of the day of expiry).

[96] s.25(2). Not less than three nor more than six months' notice is needed to end a fixed term that has been statutorily continued but ceases to enjoy the protection of the Act, *e.g.* because the premises are no longer used for business purposes, L. & T.A. 1954, s.24(3).

[97] L. & T.A. 1954, s.27(1).

[98] L. & T.A. 1954, s.27(2).

[99] Agricultural Holdings Act 1986, s.25. There are exceptions where the tenant is bankrupt, or the landlord requires possession for non-farming purposes and has reserved a right to enter for that purpose.

[1] Originally granted for more than 21 years, with a rental of less than two-thirds the rateable value.

[2] L. & T.A. 1954, s.4.

than one month.[3] For an ordinary residential tenant under the Rent Acts in possession as a statutory tenant[4] after the end of the contractual tenancy, the length of notice that he proposes to give up possession is either that required under the provisions of the original contract, or not less than three months if no notice would have been required.[5]

In most cases, before serving a notice to quit, it will be necessary to consider the relevant statutory provisions as they are likely to supersede both the common law requirements on the length of notice to be given and any express agreement the parties may have made. But in the absence of statutory requirements the length of notice usually corresponds to the period of the tenancy. Weekly, monthly[6] and quarterly tenancies will usually require a week's, month's or quarter's notice. It is, of course, quite competent for the parties expressly to provide for either shorter or longer notice.

The difficulties in relation to the length of notices to end periodic tenancies cluster more thickly around yearly tenancies. A yearly tenancy needs half a year's notice, usually ending with the first year, or its subsequent anniversary.[7] A mistake in the service of such a notice generally involves a further year's delay at least before the position can be retrieved. The three main problems are (1) Is the tenancy a yearly one, or for a shorter period; (2) How long is half a year's notice, and (3) What is the correct date for the expiration of the notice?

(a) Is the tenancy a yearly one?

The construction of express grants of periodic terms, and of definite and then periodic terms has already been considered.[8] If the length of the proposed periodic tenancy is not expressly mentioned one would first look at any provisions for the giving of notices in an attempt to decide if a yearly tenancy had been created. If a tenancy can be ended expressly at any time on either three months', or one month's notice, then in the first case a quarterly,[9] and in the second a monthly tenancy[10] will have been created. Secondly one would look at the agreement to pay rent. If a yearly rental is agreed, this is an indication that a yearly tenancy is initially intended even though the rent is paid quarterly, monthly or weekly. However, if the tenant stays in possession after the end of the first year it then becomes necessary to

---

[3] L. & T.A. 1954, s.5.
[4] Rent Act 1977, s.2.
[5] Rent Act 1977, s.3(3). Strictly, his liabilities continue until either notice is given or a court order made, *Trustee of Smith's Charity* v. *Wilson* [1983] Q.B. 316; and see *Boyer* v. *Warbey* [1953] 1 Q.B. 234.
[6] "Month" means calendar month in deeds coming into effect after January 1, 1926, L.P.A. 1925, s.61. In deeds effective before that date but often still operative it was construed as a lunar month.
[7] *Doe d. Shore* v. *Porter* (1789) 3 Term. 13; [1775–1802] All E.R. Rep. 575.
[8] *Ante*, Chap. 4(II) B, C.
[9] *Kemp* v. *Derrett* (1814) 3 Camp. 510.
[10] *Doe d. Peacock* v. *Raffan* (1806) 6 Esp. 4.

decide as a matter of law whether he is holding over as a yearly tenant, or as a weekly, monthly or quarterly tenant. To find an implication of a yearly tenancy after the determination of a letting for a year or for a term of years it is essential that the rent should be expressed as an annual sum.[11] It seems that if the facts are equivocal then the court will lean in favour of the landlord and find that no yearly tenancy was intended. In any event, if the tenant's continuation in possession can be justified on statutory rather than contractual grounds, then it seems that the court will so decide.[12]

(b) How long is half a year's notice?

Half a year is at least 183 days. But if the tenancy can be ended on one of the usual quarter days (Lady Day, March 25; Midsummer, June 24; Michaelmas, September 29 and Christmas Day, December 25) then two quarters' notice is needed although between Michaelmas and Lady Day there are less than 183 days,[13] and there are more than 183 days between Lady Day and Michaelmas.

(c) What is the correct date for the expiration of the notice?

It will normally be at the end of the year, or its anniversary. But the parties can vary this by agreement.[14] They can agree that only three months' notice will be needed, and further that the notice can expire at any time during the year, or a combination of these two. So the tenancy may be determinable at any time on three months' notice, and this will not be repugnant to holding that a yearly tenancy has been created.[15] Furthermore it seems as if it is possible to draft the agreement as a yearly tenancy terminable during the first year on, say, three months' notice.[16] It is quite common to have a notice served during the first year terminating the tenancy at its first anniversary. In one situation the relevant anniversary is the date the initial grant ended and not the date it commenced. This occurs where the tenant holds over on a yearly tenancy after the expiration of an original grant for a fixed period of years and a further fraction of a year, *e.g.* a grant of 18 months, from July in one year to the end of December of the

---

[11] See Jenkins L.J. in *Adler* v. *Blackman* [1953] 1 Q.B. 146 at p. 151 commenting on observations of Maugham J. in *Ladies' Hosiery & Underwear Ltd.* v. *Parker* [1930] 1 Ch. 304 (in both cases a weekly rent was paid).

[12] *Marcroft Wagons, Ltd.* v. *Smith* [1951] 2 K.B. 496; *Dealex Properties, Ltd.* v. *Brooks* [1956] 1 Q.B. 542; *Lewis* v. *M.T.C. (Cars) Ltd.* [1975] 1 W.L.R. 457 at p. 462, Russell L.J.; *Longrigg, Burrough & Trounson* v. *Smith* [1979] 251 E.G. 847.

[13] *Morgan* v. *Davies* (1878) 3 C.P.D. 260; and see *Doe d. Shore* v. *Porter* (1789) 3 Term. 13; {1775–1802] All E.R. Rep. 575.

[14] *Re Threlfall, ex p. Queen's Benefit Building Society* (1880) 16 Ch.D. 274, holding one could have an annual tenancy terminable at any time without notice.

[15] *King* v. *Eversfield* [1897] 2 Q.B. 475; *H. & G. Simonds, Ltd.* v. *Heywood* [1948] 1 All E.R. 260.

[16] See the observations of Lynskey J. in *H. & G. Simonds, Ltd.* v. *Heywood* [1948] 1 All E.R. 260, especially at p. 263.

next year. In that event the anniversary would fall at the end of December and not June.[17]

(3) *The Operational Date for the Notice*

The operational date is the date when the tenant's estate ends. That date must be the end of a current period of the tenancy. Lush J. in *Queen's Club Garden Estates, Ltd.* v. *Bignell*[18] said: "I think the true view is that in any periodic tenancy, whether it be yearly, quarterly, monthly, or weekly, the notice to quit must expire at the end of the current period." Considerable difficulty has been experienced in stating accurately the "anniversary" of a tenancy when its starting date is known, *a fortiori* when it is not. This area has provided many a field day for the technically minded lawyer.

Although it is agreed that a tenancy ends on the "anniversary" of its creation, it has not always been clear when the term in law started. Stable J. in *Winchester Court, Ltd.* v. *Holmes*[19] was concerned with a notice to quit a tenancy that ran from January 1, 1937. He considered the authorities established that "the term began at that moment of time when January 1 merges into January 2, the very first tick on January 2, 1937, and, accordingly, the end of the third year of this agreement—at which moment, by the prescribed notice, the tenant could determine the tenancy if he wished—came at midnight on Jan. 1 1940." He also commented, with apparent feeling, that he had "no doubt that there is hardly a form of words or a collocation of words in the English language which cannot be twisted so as to make an absurdity, but that is not the attitude of mind in which the court has to construe the written word which passes from hand to hand in everyday life."

Not surprisingly it has been argued that a tenancy that starts "on" a specified day, has a different ending from a tenancy "from" the same day, the former having its anniversary one day earlier than the latter. However, it has been sensibly if somewhat belatedly settled that there should be no difference in construing an agreement beginning "at," "on," "from," or "on and from" a specified date, and that a notice to quit either on the last day of the current period, or on the "anniversary" of the day should both be good.[20] This rule holds also for a weekly tenancy, and so a tenancy that starts on a Saturday can be ended by a notice expiring either on the Friday, the last day of the

---

[17] *Croft* v. *William F. Blay, Ltd.* [1919] 2 Ch. 343, *cf. Rhyl U.D.C.* v. *Rhyl Amusements, Ltd.* [1959] 1 W.L.R. 465 where the dates of the half-yearly rent days constrained Harman J. to reach a different conclusion.

[18] [1924] 1 K.B. 117 at p. 124 approved in *Lemon* v. *Lardeur* [1946] K.B. 613.

[19] [1941] 2 All E.R. 542.

[20] *Sidebotham* v. *Holland* [1895] 1 Q.B. 378; [1891–94] All E.R. Rep. 617; *cf. Ladyman* v. *Wirral Estates, Ltd.* [1968] 2 All E.R. 197.

current term, or a Saturday, the "anniversary" of the commencement of the period.[21] Further, a notice to quit "by"[22] a certain date will be construed as one to quit "on or before" a date, and that formula is valid. Such a notice indicates that the landlord would accept a premature surrender.[23]

Often no-one knows when the tenancy was started, especially where a weekly tenancy has continued for years. If a residential statutory tenancy protected by the Rent Acts has succeeded a contractual tenancy, then strictly no notice by the landlord is required at all before he takes proceedings for possession.[24] In most cases in practice notice will be given. To avoid difficulties caused by uncertainty of either the starting date of the tenancy or its correct finishing date an almost standard formula is used. This requires the tenant to quit and deliver up the premises on a specified date, which the landlord or his agent hopes will be the correct one "or at the expiration of the week, month, quarter, etc. of your tenancy which shall expire next after the expiration of 'one week, four weeks, one month or one quarter (as the case may be)' from the service of this notice."[25]

This formula may require the tenant to read his tenancy agreement, if any, and consult a calendar, and it may involve him in interpreting his tenancy agreement. However, the landlord cannot serve a valid notice which involves the tenant in a complex calculation involving interlocking questions both of law and fact.[26] A notice to quit "at the earliest possible moment" seems, regrettably, to be invalid,[27] although in *Allam & Co. Ltd.* v. *Europe Poster Services Ltd.*[28] a similarly brief formula was held valid to terminate some 218 different licences of advertising sites. There the notice required the licensee "to cease occupation of the sites referred to at the earliest date after the service of this notice that such agreement . . . can lawfully be terminated." The agreements were expressly stated to be terminable on 12 months' notice on either side. Buckley J. considered[29] that *Phipps & Co.* v. *Rogers*[30] "clearly establishes that where a formula is used in a notice of this kind which involves reference to some other document, in order to ascertain the date at which the notice is intended to operate, and some question of law arises upon the interpretation of that other

[21] *Crate* v. *Miller* [1947] K.B. 946.
[22] *Easthaugh* v. *Macpherson* [1954] 1 W.L.R. 1307.
[23] *Dagger* v. *Shepherd* [1946] 1 K.B. 215.
[24] *Morrison* v. *Jacobs* [1945] K.B. 577; Rent Act 1977, s.98.
[25] *Addis* v. *Burrows* [1948] 1 K.B. 444.
[26] See Asquith L.J.'s observations in *Addis* v. *Burrows*, above, on the notice that failed in *P. Phipps & Co.* v. *Rogers* [1925] 1 K.B. 14; (notice to quit by reference to the dates of special transfer sessions).
[27] The form was held valid in *May* v. *Borup* [1915] 1 K.B. 830, but that case was not approved in *P. Phipps & Co.* v. *Rogers* [1925] 1 K.B. 14.
[28] [1968] 1 W.L.R. 638.
[29] *Ibid.* p. 650.
[30] [1925] 1 K.B. 14.

document relevant to ascertaining the date, that fact is not of itself necessarily fatal to the validity of the notice." Neither will an obvious clerical error in the date be fatal[31] if the notice is quite clear to a reasonable tenant reading it.

But if the notice is expressed to expire other than at the proper time, then it will be invalid. A clear example of this occurred in *Bathavon Rural District Council* v. *Carlile*.[32] The council served a notice that purported to end a weekly tenancy that began on a Monday. The notice required the tenant to quit "by noon on Monday, July 1, 1957." The notice was invalid, although the objectives of the council were eminently sensible and totally unambiguous. A notice in the Bathavon form can only be served if the period of the tenancy is expressed in the tenancy agreement to end at say, noon, on any Monday after service of a notice to quit.

(4) *Authority to Serve, Authenticity and Service*

"A notice to quit is a notice given by an existing landlord to an existing tenant; if that view be right, a person cannot give a valid notice to quit before he has become a landlord and the recipient of his notice has become the tenant."[33] A prospective purchaser cannot serve a notice[34] neither can one be served on someone who is a sub-tenant.[35] It seems that one of two joint landlords can serve an effective notice to end a periodic tenancy, as the tenancy continues only for as long as both shall please.[36] There is authority that one of the occupying joint tenants can give the landlord an effective notice to quit[37] even when he does not have the express or implied authority of his co-tenants. But the matter is not free from doubt.[38]

Most notices are served by agents on behalf of the landlord, and it can be important to determine if the agent had sufficient authority to serve the notice. Agents who are concerned with the general letting and management of the property have sufficient authority and can serve notices in their own name.[39] Other agents, *e.g.* solicitors

---

[31] *Carradine Properties, Ltd.* v. *Aslam* [1976] 1 W.L.R. 442 (1974 notice specified a date in 1973 instead of 1975), distinguishing *Hankey* v. *Clavering* [1942] 2 K.B. 326.

[32] [1958] 1 Q.B. 461.

[33] *Lower* v. *Sorrell* [1963] 1 Q.B. 959, at p. 975, Donovan L.J.

[34] *Thompson* v. *McCullough* [1947] K.B. 447.

[35] *Pleasant (Lessee of Hayton)* v. *Benson* (1811) 14 Ea. 234.

[36] *Doe d. Aslin* v. *Summersett* (1830) 1 B. & Ad. 135; *Parsons* v. *Parsons* [1983] 1 W.L.R. 1390 (agricultural tenancy). *cf. Re Viola's Indenture of Lease* [1909] 1 Ch. 244, where the terms of the lease prevented such a conclusion.

[37] *Greenwich London Borough Council* v. *McGrady* (1983) 46 P. & C.R. 233 (secure tenancy), applying dicta in *Leek and Moorlands Building Society* v. *Clark* [1952] 2 Q.B. 788.

[38] It has been argued that the recent decisions overlook *Howson* v. *Buxton* (1928) 27 L.J.K.B. 749, see F. Webb [1983] Conv. 194, and also *Featherstone* v. *Staples* (1985) 49 P. & C.R. 273.

[39] *Jones* v. *Phipps* (1868) L.R. 3 Q.B. 567 (valid notice by beneficiary in his name to whom management of estates had been delegated); *cf. Stait* v. *Fenner* [1912] 2 Ch. 504.

instructed to recover possession, require authority to serve notices and should do so either in the landlord's name or on his behalf. In *Harmond Properties Ltd.* v. *Gajdzis*[40] an effective notice was served by solicitors expressly on behalf of Mr. R. P. Harvey who was a director of and held to be general agent for the plaintiff landlord company. A husband has no general authority to serve a notice in his own name in respect of his wife's property[41] simply because he is the husband.

A notice is effectively served if it can be shown that it should have come to the tenant before the period of the notice starts to run. Personal service is obviously effective but unusual. Service by delivery to the tenant's wife or employees at the premises is effective.[42] A notice physically left at the premises must be shown to have come to the tenant's notice before the period began and not spent six months lurking unseen beneath the front doormat[43], unless the statutory requirements about service apply.[44] The recorded delivery service is still optimistically used, the postman's certificate of delivery being accepted as sufficient evidence of service. But most standard form tenancy agreements and other written tenancy agreements and leases will incorporate the provisions of the Law of Property Act 1925, s.196, as to service. This first provides that notices must be in writing.[45] Secondly, it provides that notices will be effectively served if addressed to the tenant, by that designation without his name, and either left at his last known place of abode or business, or in the case of a notice to be served on a tenant, affixed or left at the premises, or posted to him by name at his place of abode or business by registered post—or by the recorded delivery service.[46]

Obviously if section 196 has been incorporated it avoids problems that might otherwise arise when a tenant dies intestate or without having appointed executors and leaves the premises empty. The notice can be left at the premises. If section 196 does not apply then the notice should be directed to the President of the Family Division of the High Court[47] unless either letters of administration have been obtained, when service can be effected on the administrators, or someone has been left in possession, when they can be served.[48]

If the premises have been deserted and vacated for six months and the landlord can show unsuccessful attempts to communicate with the non-paying tenant, then he can apply to the county court under the Landlord and Tenant Act 1954, s.54, for an order determining the

[40] [1968] 1 W.L.R. 1858.
[41] *Lemon* v. *Lardeur* [1946] K.B. 613.
[42] *Mason* v. *Bibby* (1864) 2 H. & C. 881 at p. 886.
[43] *Alford* v. *Vickery* (1842) Car. & M. 280; but see *Newborough (Lord)* v. *Jones* [1975] Ch. 90 (where the notice spent six months under linoleum).
[44] *e.g.* L.P.A. 1925, s.196, or A.H.A. 1986, s.93.
[45] L.P.A. 1925, s.196(1).
[46] Recorded Delivery Service Act 1962.
[47] And see Practice Direction, [1985] 1 All E.R. 832.
[48] *Harrowby* v. *Snelson* [1951] 1 All E.R. 140.

tenancy. The more difficult situation arises where the tenant has disappeared, not having paid his rent, and leaving furniture on the premises. This will invariably turn out to comprise priceless antiques, despite its unpromising junklike appearance, if the landlord without the benefit of a possession order, obtained by substituted service, puts the items into the garden or a shed where they are damaged or lost. The landlord may well be responsible for the resulting loss to the tenant who will surprisingly reappear.[49]

C. The Effect of a Notice

At common law the expiration of an effective notice to quit marks the end of the relationship of landlord and tenant and the term of years absolute.[50] It will be seen in later parts of this book that in many cases the service of the notice often marks the start of a statutorily regulated *pas de deux*. However, subject to the statutory rights that do come into play at this point, landlords and sometimes tenants, occasionally seek to "withdraw" a notice before the operational date, or "waive" its effect afterwards.

Although service of a notice is essentially a unilateral act, withdrawal must be consensual to be effective.[51] The effect of agreement is that another tenancy is created replacing the one that has been ended by the notice. The old tenancy does not continue unaffected by the notice.[52] A waiver may be deduced from the parties' behaviour. The service of a further notice by itself is not sufficient evidence of a waiver or withdrawal.[53] Demand and payment of rent may be evidence of an agreement to waive,[54] but payment of rent by itself will only be evidence of a new tenancy in favour of the tenant if there are other circumstances showing that this is what the parties intended.[55] Certainly, a landlord's demand for payment and receipt of mesne profits at a rate equal to the rent and without prejudice to the effect of the notice to quit will not amount to a waiver of his rights. "The question therefore is, quo animo the rent was received, and what the real intention of both parties was?"[56]

---

[49] cf. *Mitchell* v. *London Borough of Ealing* [1978] 2 W.L.R. 999.
[50] *Clarke* v. *Grant* [1950] 1 K.B. 104.
[51] But a Rent Act protected tenant may still retain his protection if he fails to leave after giving a notice to quit unless the landlord can show that he has agreed to sell, or re-let the property or is otherwise seriously prejudiced by failing to obtain possession, Rent Act 1977, Sched. 15, Case 5, *post*, Pt. II.
[52] *Freeman* v. *Evans* [1922] 1 Ch. 36; *Lower* v. *Sorrell* [1963] 1 Q.B. 959, and see (1963) 27 Conv. (N.S.) 335, D. G. Barnsley.
[53] *Lowenthal* v. *Vanhoute* [1947] K.B. 342.
[54] And see (1976) 40 Conv. (N.S.) 327, E. L. G. Tyler.
[55] *Clarke* v. *Grant* [1950] 1 K.B. 104.
[56] Lord Mansfield in *Doe d. Cheny* v. *Batten* (1775) 1 Cowp. 243 at 245; [1775–1802] All E.R. Rep. 594, 595.

VI. FORFEITURE

A. The Need for a Forfeiture Clause

Most leases will contain a proviso for forfeiture. This will normally provide that if either the rent is in arrears for 21 days, whether formally demanded or not, or there is any breach by the tenant of any of his covenants or if the tenant becomes bankrupt or being a company goes into liquidation except for the purposes of reconstruction or amalgamation then the landlord can re-enter the property and thereby determine the demise.

There is no implied proviso for forfeiture, and so if the lease contains no express proviso for forfeiture the landlord cannot take steps to bring the lease to a premature end. He can only bring an action for damages or rent or to restrain the breach as the case may be. Even if there is a breach he cannot act peremptorily in the way a literal reading of the proviso might suggest. "The Court of Equity . . . always regarded the condition of re-entry as being merely security for payment of the rent, and gave relief if the landlord could get his rent."[57] And notice has already been taken of the general principles surrounding the operation of forfeiture clauses and in particular of the operation of the proviso with regard to non-payment of rent[58] and to covenants restricting assignments.[59] The proviso is of considerable assistance in securing compliance with the terms of the lease especially where continuing breach is likely to prejudice the landlord seriously. This can obviously happen where there is a breach of building covenants in a building lease and where there is a breach of covenants restricting user and disposal. An unchecked breach by a sub-tenant may well lead to the loss of the landlord/tenant's own estate.

B. Formal Requirements

It will be recollected that there is no statutory requirement for making a formal demand for rent before forfeiture proceedings are instituted for non-payment.[60] It may be that the rent itself should be "formally"

---

[57] *Chandless-Chandless* v. *Nicholson* [1942] 2 K.B. 321 at p. 323, Lord Greene M.R.; and see also Farwell L.J. in *Dendy* v. *Evans* [1910] 1 K.B. 263. It is doubtful if the jurisdiction can be widened to other commercial contracts of a leasing nature, *Scandinavian Trading Tanker Co. A.B.* v. *Flota Petrolera Ecuatoriana, The Scaptrade* [1983] Q.B. 329, C.A. affd. [1983] 2 A.C. 694, H.L. (time charter); *Sport International Bussum B.V.* v. *Inter-Footwear Ltd.* [1984] 1 All E.R. 376, C.A. affd. [1984] 1 W.L.R. 776, H.L. (licence to use trade marks).

[58] *Ante*, Chap. 5 (VII)A.

[59] *Ante*, Chap. 7 (I) and the requirement of the service of notices is considered in Chap. 6 (VI) C, in relation to repairing covenants.

[60] L.P.A. 1925, s.146(11).

demanded unless the proviso for forfeiture expressly exempts the landlord from this mildly legalistic pantomime.[61] It nearly always does. But in the case of almost all the other covenants the Law of Property Act 1925, s.146, obliges the landlord to serve what is in effect a statutory letter before action.

(1) *The Contents of a Section 146 Notice*

The notice must:

(a) specify the particular breach[62] complained of;
(b) require the tenant to remedy it, if it is capable of remedy;
(c) in any case, require the tenant to make compensation in money for the breach.

If the tenant fails to remedy the breach within a reasonable time, and to make reasonable compensation in money to the landlord's satisfaction then the landlord can take steps to enforce the forfeiture. If the landlord is attempting to forfeit for disrepair[63] the notice will usually consist of a schedule of dilapidations prepared by a surveyor or builder; it may, but need not, contain[64] a statement of the remedial work required; it can but need not contain a claim for compensation but should give the tenant a reasonable time in which to complete the repairs. Additionally, the landlord may have to serve a notice on the tenant of the tenant's rights under the Leasehold Property (Repairs) Act 1938.[65] The expenses of preparing and serving a notice that either results in forfeiture[66] or in relief from or waiver of the forfeiture[67] can be recovered from the tenant. But an express agreement in the lease is necessary if the landlord is to be able to recover the expenses incurred in taking steps to prepare a threatened notice or one which is in the event complied with. The lease will often contain a covenant that such costs are recoverable from the tenant as a debt.

---

[61] See *ante*, Chap. 5 (VII).
[62] It must be unremedied at the time the notice is served, *SEDAC Investments Ltd.* v. *Tanner* [1982] 1 W.L.R. 1342, distinguished on other grounds *Hamilton* v. *Martell Securities Ltd.* [1984] Ch. 266.
[63] Relief from forfeiture for decorative disrepair can be granted under s.147 where the court considers the notice unreasonable.
[64] *Fox* v. *Jolly* [1916] 1 A.C. 1; and see the discussion in *Silvester* v. *Ostrowska* [1959] 1 W.L.R. 1060.
[65] See *ante*, Chap. 6 (VI) C. Not needed for a cleaning covenant, *Starrokate Ltd.* v. *Burry* (1983) 265 E.G. 871, and see also *Farimani* v. *Gates* (1984) 271 E.G. 887.
[66] L.P.A. 1925, s.146(2).
[67] L.P.A. 1925, s.146(3).

(2) *Irremediable Breaches*

Some breaches are incapable of remedy, although they may be capable of relief. In those circumstances, the landlord need not require the tenant to remedy the situation, or if he does, he need give him only a nominal time in which to do so. The cases were discussed at length in *Scala House and District Property Co., Ltd.* v. *Forbes*.[68] It was held that the breach of a covenant against assignment, sub-letting or parting with possession was a once and for all breach, and that whatever events follow they could not wipe the slate clean. The same is true where a notice is served following bankruptcy of an individual tenant[69] or the voluntary liquidation of a corporate one.[70] The issue also frequently arises in relation to negative covenants[70a] and especially those restricting immoral user, prostitution,[71] or illegal user, *e.g.* gambling,[72] or the sale of obscene material.[73] In these instances it is not fatal to the validity of the notice if it does not ask for compensation if the landlord does not want it.[74]

C. Service and Effect of Notice

The formalities surrounding service of section 146 notices are much the same as those for notices to quit.[74a] But if there is more than one tenant, then all and not just one must be served.[75] If the landlord is purporting to forfeit because of the surety's bankruptcy, then notice still has to be served on the tenant.[76] Once the reasonable time has expired either for remedying the breach or for the tenant to consider his position following an irremediable breach, then the landlord can commence his proceedings for forfeiture. It has already been seen that if the landlord wants to end both the common law estate and any

---

[68] [1974] Q.B. 575.
[69] *Civil Service Co-operative Society, Ltd.* v. *McGrigor's Trustee* [1923] 2 Ch. 347 (14 days sufficient notice).
[70] *Horsey Estate, Ltd.* v. *Steiger* [1899] 2 Q.B. 259 (liquidation for reconstruction); *Watney, Combe, Reid & Co.* v. *Ewart* [1902] 86 L.T. 242.
[70a] And see *Expert Service & Sales Ltd.* v. *Hillgate House Ltd.* [1985] 3 W.L.R. 359.
[71] *Rugby School (Governors)* v. *Tannahill* [1935] 1 K.B. 87; *Egerton* v. *Esplanade Hotels, London, Ltd.* [1947] 2 All E.R. 88, *cf. Glass* v. *Kencakes, Ltd.* [1966] 1 Q.B. 611 (notice to tenant about sub-tenant's activities was in respect of a remediable breach, but doubt was cast on this in *Scala House and District Property Co., Ltd.* v. *Forbes* [1974] Q.B. 575). And see *British Petroleum Pension Trust* v. *Behrendt* (1985) 276 E.G. 199.
[72] *Hoffman* v. *Fineberg* [1949] Ch. 245.
[73] *Dunraven Securities* v. *Holloway* (1982) 264 E.G. 709.
[74] *Lock* v. *Pearce* [1893] 2 Ch. 271; *Rugby School (Governors)* v. *Tannahill* [1935] 1 K.B. 87.
[74a] See *ante* (V) and for the service of notices in respect of repairing covenants, see L. & T.A. 1927, s.18(2).
[75] *Blewett* v. *Blewett* [1936] 2 All E.R. 188. If relief is sought both must apply, *T. M. Fairclough & Sons, Ltd.* v. *Berliner* [1931] 1 Ch. 60.
[76] *Halliard Property Co., Ltd.* v. *Jack Segal, Ltd.* [1977] 1 W.L.R. 377.

statutory protection afforded by the Rent Acts, then the proceedings must be instituted in the county court.[77]

The significance of section 146 lies in the statutory right it gives both lessees and sub-lessees to apply for relief. The lessee's right to apply is contained in section 146(2) and enables the lessee to apply either in the lessor's action for forfeiture or in any action brought by himself for relief. The court may grant or refuse relief "as the court, having regard to the proceedings and conduct of the parties . . . and to all the other circumstancs, thinks fit." Relief can be granted on such terms as the court also thinks fit.

The House of Lords in *Hyman* v. *Rose*[78] has stated that the discretion is very wide, and that rigid rules should not be laid down guiding its exercise. The tenant must be prompt in applying for relief, and it is too late to make an application after the landlord has re-entered.[79] The fact that the tenant has remedied the situation or undertakes to do so or that the breach occurred without his knowledge or consent[80] are all factors that can be urged on the court in favour of the exercise of its discretion.[81] It seems that relief can be granted even if there is a breach of the covenant not to use the premises in an immoral way,[82] although such conduct may be regarded as a stigma that has a depreciating effect on the value of the property. The court has jurisdiction to order possession of that part of the premises used for immoral purposes and to grant relief from forfeiture for the remainder.[83] It is likely that the landlord will be granted an indemnity[84] as to his costs even where the tenant is legally aided.[85]

D. Effect on Sub-tenants

The normal rule is that the branch falls with the tree, and the ending of the tenant's estate would also have the effect of ending the sub-tenant's estates. This can obviously have a catastrophic effect, especially if they are sub-lessess in a technical sense being mortgagees or charges of the tenant's estate.[86] Sub-lessees do not have to be

---

[77] *Ante* Chap. 5 (VII) A (4).
[78] [1912] A.C. 623.
[79] *Quilter* v. *Mapleson* (1882) 9 Q.B.D. 672; *Pakwood Transport Ltd.* v. *15 Beauchamp Place* (1978) 36 P. & C.R. 112.
[80] *Glass* v. *Kencakes, Ltd.* [1966] 1 Q.B. 611; *cf. Borthwick-Norton* v. *Romney Warwick Estates, Ltd.* [1950] 1 All E.R. 798.
[81] But see *Bathurst (Earl)* v. *Fine* [1974] 1 W.L.R. 905.
[82] *Central Estates (Belgravia) Ltd.* v. *Woolgar (No. 2)* [1972] 1 W.L.R. 1048.
[83] *GMS Syndicate* v. *Elliott (Gary) Ltd.* [1982] Ch. 1.
[84] *Egerton* v. *Jones* [1939] 2 K.B. 702.
[85] *Factors (Sundries) Ltd.* v. *Miller* [1952] 2 All E.R.630.
[86] *Grand Junction Co. Ltd.* v. *Bates* [1954] 2 Q.B. 160 (chargee relieved after tenant guilty of running a brothel, and disrepair).

served with the section 146 notice.[87] But they do have an independent right under section 146(4), to ask for relief. The court can "make an order vesting, for the whole term of the lease or any less term, the property comprised in the lease or any part thereof in any person entitled as under-lessee to any estate or interest in such property upon such conditions . . . as the court thinks fit." The court's discretion is again unlimited, although it cannot grant the applicant a longer term than he had under his original sub-lease.[88] A sub-lessee who cannot bring himself within the statutory provisions, because judgment has already been executed, may still be able to rely on the inherent jurisdiction of the court.[89] Sub-lessees include equitable mortgagees, even though such mortgages are not entitled to possession without a further court order, and so therefore are not automatically under any obligation under the terms of the lease.[90] The term granted under section 146(4) is an entirely new one, and not a reinstatement of the forfeited term. As a result rents from the property between forfeiture and the grant of a new term do not belong to the person obtaining relief.[91] This can mean a significant loss to a morgagee where the mortgagor/tenant's interest has been lost.

In most cases the sub-lessee can come to court as an innocent party, which is an advantage. If he is not, because he has caused or contributed to the breach, there is likely to be some reluctance to grant him relief.[92] Of course, if the lessee is granted relief that is the end of the sub-lessee's application.[93] If the sub-lessee's estate extends to the whole property then he is likely to have to undertake all the outstanding obligations of the defaulting tenant.

An acute problem however arises where there is a lease of property sub-let in numerous units. This can arise in commercial flat development or in the development of office and shop accommodation. Head lessors may be amenable to agreeing to the deletion of the usual proviso for forfeiture for bankruptcy, but are likely to insist on the retention of the proviso for breach of the other covenants. A prospective sub-tenant of a small unit could therefore be faced with the necessity of applying for relief from forfeiture of the head lease should the head lessor take steps to forfeit it, either because of default

---

[87] *Egerton* v. *Jones* [1939] 2 K.B. 702; *Church Commissioners for England* v. *Ve-ri-best Manufacturing Co. Ltd.* [1957] 1 Q.B. 238.

[88] *Factors (Sundries) Ltd.* v. *Miller* [1952] 2 All E.R. 630; and see *Cadogan* v. *Dimovic* [1984] 2 All E.R. 168 (court has statutory jurisdiction where a business tenant occupies by virtue of the protection given by the business tenancy code).

[89] *Abbey National Building Society* v. *Maybeech* [1984] 3 All E.R. 262; *c.f. Smith* v. *Metropolitan Properties* (1985) 277 E.G. 753.

[90] *Ladup Ltd.* v. *William & Glyn's Bank plc* [1985] 2 All E.R. 577.

[91] *Official Custodian for Charities* v. *Mackey* [1984] 3 All E.R. 689. It does not follow, however, that the rents belong automatically to the landlord, *Official Custodian for Charities* v. *Mackey (No. 2)* [1985] 2 All E.R. 1016.

[92] *Matthews* v. *Smallwood* [1910] 1 Ch. 777.

[93] *Hurd* v. *Whaley* [1918] 1 K.B. 448.

in respect of the rent or because of substantial want of repair of the structure. Head lessors sometimes agree to the insertion in the lease of a clause entitling sub-tenants to relief from forfeiture if they agree to undertake their proportionate part of the outstanding liabilities.[94] If the lease is silent on the point, then it is not entirely clear whether sub-lessees applying for relief will be required to undertake all the defaulting head tenant's obligations or only a proportionate part of them.[95] It is suggested that relief may be given on a proportionate basis, but the court must consider the difficulties the landlord might find himself in if only some of the sub-tenants apply for relief. The landlord could find it impossible to deal legally with the physical unit as a single entity.

E. Covenants outside the Provisions

Undetected pre-1926 breaches of covenants restricting assignments are outside the provisions of section 146, and so also are breaches of covenants enabling lessors of mines to enter and inspect the books and workings.[96] More importantly it does not apply to forfeiture following bankruptcy where there is a lease of agricultural land, mines and minerals, furnished dwelling-houses or any lease where the personal qualifications of the tenant are important for the preservation of the property.[97] The section also does not affect the law of forfeiture for non-payment of rent, and in that case no notice has to be served under section 146.[98] But in all these instances sub-tenants still have a right to apply for relief under section 146(4).

In the other leases where the tenant becomes bankrupt, the section has a delaying effect for one year, if the tenant makes application for relief. If the tenant's interest is sold within the year, then the section will in practice operate so as to deprive the landlord of the right to forfeit altogether.[99] The statutory provisions for relief following bankruptcy displace the inherent jurisdiction of the court to grant relief from forfeiture to tenants.[99a]

---

[94] See, for example, *Precedents for the Conveyancer*, 5–91.

[95] *Webber* v. *Smith* (1689) 2 Vern. 103 (6 out of 100 sub-tenants who applied for relief had to undertake all liabilities) quoted with apparent approval in *Belgravia Insurance Co. Ltd.* v. *Meah* [1964] 1 Q.B. 436; *cf. Chatham Empire Theatre (1955) Ltd.* v. *Ultrans, Ltd.* [1961] 1 W.L.R. 817.

[96] L.P.A. 1925, s.146(8).

[97] L.P.A. 1925, s.146(9).

[98] L.P.A. 1925, s.146(11).

[99] L.P.A. 1925, s.146(10); *Civil Service Co-operative Society, Ltd.* v. *McGrigor's Trustee* [1923] 2 Ch. 347. The effect of the tenant's bankruptcy is also considered in Chap. 7 (IV) G, *ante.*

[99a] *Official Custodian for Charities* v. *Parway Estates Developments Ltd.* [1984] 3 All E.R. 679. The position of their sub-lessees or mortgagees is saved by Law of Property (Amendment) Act 1929, s.1.

F. Avoidance of Relief Provisions

Section 146(12) expressly provides that the section applies "notwithstanding any stipulation to the contrary." Nothing daunted conveyancers have tried to avoid the provisions for relief. They have required the tenant to execute a surrender in escrow which was to come into effect on a tenant's breach of covenant.[99b] They have provided for the premature determination of the term on the service of a short notice to quit following a breach.[99c] The attempts to deny the court the opportunity to grant relief have been singularly unsuccessful.

VII. DISCLAIMER

This is a peculiar method of ending a lease, and is more in the nature of a legal curiosity. It is mentioned for the sake of completeness only, and occurs in relation to a periodic tenancy when the tenant disclaims or denies his landlord's title. The landlord need not accept the repudiation, but he can treat it as an act putting an end to the tenancy. Recent actions by landlords claiming that the lease has come to an end in this way have not been significantly successful.[99d] Disclaimer of the lease by the tenant's trustee in bankruptcy has already been considered.[99e]

VIII. TERMINATION OF CONTRACTUAL LICENCES BY NOTICE

The nature of a licence has been considered in Chapter 2. Sometimes the parties enter into a licence with the motive of avoiding the statutory restrictions on the recovery of possession.[99f] Sometimes a transaction can only be carried out by using a licence. This may occur when an owner enters into a complex building agreement[99g] with a building contractor, or a house owner agrees to take a lodger, or a ticket is sold for the use of a cinema seat,[99h] or simpler agreements are made to permit the erection and maintenance of advertisements,[99i] rediffusion cables, or telegraph lines.[1]

[99b] *Plymouth Corporation* v. *Harvey* [1971] 1 W.L.R. 549.
[99c] *Richard Clarke & Co. Ltd.* v. *Widnall* [1976] 1 W.L.R. 845.
[99d] *Wisbech St. Mary Parish Council* v. *Lilley* [1956] 1 W.L.R. 121; and see *Warner* v. *Sampson* [1959] 1 Q.B. 297, and Woodfall, paras. 1–2045 *et seq.*
[99e] Chap. 7 (IV) G.
[99f] *Shell-Mex and B.P. Ltd.* v. *Manchester Garages Ltd.* [1971] 1 W.L.R. 612; *Street* v. *Mountford* [1985] 2 All E.R. 289. (residential sharing agreement).
[99g] *Hounslow London Borough Council* v. *Twickenham Garden Developments, Ltd.* [1971] Ch. 233; *cf. Mayfield Holdings* v. *Moana Reef* [1973] 1 N.Z.L.R. 309.
[99h] *Hurst* v. *Picture Theatres Ltd.* [1915] 1 K.B. 1.
[99i] *King* v. *David Allen & Sons, Billposting Ltd.* [1916] 2 A.C. 54.
[1] *Canadian Pacific Rail Co.* v. *R.* [1931] A.C. 414.

The licence may be expressly or impliedly non-revocable, at least until the object of the agreement has been achieved. The parties may expressly provide what length of notice is required.[2] Alternatively the circumstances may be such as to indicate that the licence cannot be revoked for so long as the licensee observes his contractual obligations, *e.g.* for so long as he continues building operations satisfactorily[3]; or until he has removed the goods sold from the licensor's land,[4] or seen the film show.[5]

When the agreement is silent on the length of notice, there are two views on what notice is required. There is authority for arguing that one may need reasonable notice ending by a specified date, a dated notice, to terminate the contractual licence. But in the majority of cases, the notice itself ends the licence, although the licensee must be given a reasonable time either to pack and leave or to re-arrange his affairs.[6] In *Canadian Pacific Railway Co.* v. *R.*[7] the Privy Council decided that it was a

> "case in which the licence can only be effectively ended after notice has been served upon the appellant determining the licence on such a specified date in the future, as will give the appellant an interval of time between the service of the notice and the specified date, sufficient not only to allow the removal of the poles and wires from off the property of the Crown, but also to enable the appellant to make arrangements for the continuance of the telegraph line by the erection of poles and wires elsewhere than on Crown property."

The Privy Council decided that the Crown would have to serve a dated notice, and fix the length of the notice at its own risk.

Such a conclusion can produce a totally unsatisfactory situation. In the case of a periodic tenancy advice can be given with reasonable certainty on the length of notice required. If a dated notice is required for a licence, then there is a real possibility that the court's view may differ from that of the person advising the licensor, and furthermore the fact that more than a reasonable time will have elapsed before the issue is litigated will not remedy the defective dated notice. However, the fortunes of the *Canadian Pacific Railway* case have been dismal. Lord Greene M.R. in *Minister of Health* v. *Bellotti*[8] considered that the only principle that could be extracted from the *Canadian* case was a pellucid observation that any and what restrictions on the

---

[2] *Allam & Co. Ltd.* v. *Europa Poster Services Ltd.* [1968] 1 W.L.R. 638.
[3] *Hounslow L.B.C.* v. *Twickenham Garden Developments Ltd.* [1971] Ch. 233.
[4] *Wood* v. *Manley* (1839) 11 Ad. & E. 34; [1835–42] All E.R. Rep. 128.
[5] *Hurst* v. *Picture Theatres Ltd.* [1915] 1 K.B. 1.
[6] *Winter Garden Theatre (London) Ltd.* v. *Millenium Productions, Ltd.* [1948] A.C. 173.
[7] [1931] A.C. 414.
[8] [1944] K.B. 298.

revocability of a licence depend on the circumstances of each case. And the House of Lords in *Tool Metal Manufacturing Co. Ltd.* v. *Tungsten Electric Co. Ltd.*[9] considered the facts of the *Canadian Railway* case to be singular in the extreme and that it was not helpful in establishing the relevant principles.

The Privy Council returned to the question of the length of notice to end a licence in *Australian Blue Metal Ltd.* v. *Hughes*[10] where licensees with the benefit of a mining concession were given two notices, one to end immediately, and the second given two months later on October 16, 1957, to leave the land by the end of the month. Lord Devlin observed:

> "The question whether a requirement of reasonable notice is to be implied in a contract is to be answered in the light of the circumstances existing when the contract is made. The length of the notice, if any, is the time that is deemed to be reasonable in the light of the circumstances in which the notice is given. That does not mean that the reasonable time is the time during which one party or the other could reasonably wish for the contract to continue."

The validity of the notices were upheld. The contract was negotiated between two commercial ventures and they had decided not to insert any provision for notice. The Privy Council considered the arrangement was determinable at will subject to a period of grace to leave. Even if reasonable notice were required it had long since expired. The trend does seem to be to uphold shorter notices of licences. Seven days' notice was sufficient to end a licence to run a commercial bar in a hotel,[11]; a boat repairing business,[12] and an occupational licence to use flats.[13] A county court has expressed the opinion that 21 days' notice would be reasonable to end a residential licence enjoyed for a year,[14] and a month's notice to coincide with the end of the shooting season was sufficient to end the grant of shooting rights in *Lowe* v. *Adams*.[15] The amount of time the licensee needs to rearrange his affairs and his contractual obligations entered into as a result of the licence are relevant considerations,[16] as also is the fact that he has not stipulated for a minimum period of notice. If a licence is terminated by a local authority in the exercise of its powers, it may

---

[9] [1955] 1 W.L.R. 761.
[10] [1963] A.C. 74.
[11] *Isaac* v. *Hotel de Paris, Ltd.* [1960] 1 W.L.R. 239.
[12] *Iveagh (Earl)* v. *Martin* [1961] 1 Q.B. 232 (no evidence of any likely interference with existing repairing contracts).
[13] *Minister of Health* v. *Bellotti* [1944] K.B. 298.
[14] *Roach* v. *Johannes* [1976] C.L.Y. 1549.
[15] [1901] 2 Ch. 598.
[16] *Winter Garden Theatre (London) Ltd.* v. *Millenium Productions Ltd.* [1948] A.C. 173.

have to observe the principles of natural justice, and give the licensee both prior notification and an opportunity to be heard.[17] An effective notice may be given by one of two joint owners to terminate an oral licence.[18]

An attempt to revoke a contractual licence that is either expressly or impliedly irrevocable for an ascertainable period may be restrained by an injunction, at least if the agreement is one that could be specifically enforceable.[19] But if it is impossible for the court to supervise the performance of the agreement,[19a] or if the party seeking relief has himself behaved in an unreasonable way,[20] this form of holding relief may not be forthcoming. In other cases the remedy is damages, and so only recoverable if a resultant loss can be properly proved.[21]

IX. RECOVERY OF POSSESSION

A. Self-help

Although this course of action has a number of superficial attractions for some, it should be avoided. The Criminal Law Act 1977, s.6, makes it an offence for any person, without lawful authority, to use or threaten violence for the purpose of securing entry into any premises when to his knowledge there is someone present on those premises who is opposed to the entry. A defence is available to the displaced residential occupier who, for example, returns from holiday to find that squatters have moved in.[22] Furthermore, attempts to harrass a residential occupier, be he tenant or licensee, into leaving prematurely, *e.g.* by turning off his gas, water and electricity, or attempting to evict him unlawfully, are also offences under the Protection from Eviction Act 1977, s.1. Section 3 makes it unlawful for the owner to enforce his right to recover possession of premises let as a dwelling against any person who is lawfully residing in them at the end of the tenancy without taking court proceedings. This section applies when the tenancy was not a statutorily protected tenancy. Section 98 of the Rent Act 1977 gives statutory security of tenure where there is either a statutory or protected tenancy under the Rent Acts. This is considered

[17] *R.* v. *Wear Valley District Council, ex p. Binks* [1985] 2 All E.R. 699 (street trader operating hot-food take-away caravan).
[18] *Annen* v. *Rattee* (1985) 273 E.G. 503.
[19] *Hounslow L.B.C.* v. *Twickenham Garden Developments Ltd.* [1971] Ch. 233. And see *Verrall* v. *Great Yarmouth B.C.* [1981] Q.B. 202.
[19a] *Thompson* v. *Park* [1944] 1 K.B. 408 (a school sharing arrangement).
[20] *cf. Williams* v. *Staite* [1978] 2 W.L.R. 825 (whether an *equitable* residential licence could be terminated because of bad behaviour).
[21] *C. & P. Haulage (a firm)* v. *Middleton* [1983] 1 W.L.R. 1461 (loss flowed from bad bargain rather than breach).
[22] Criminal Law Act 1977, s.6(3). The defence is also open to one acting on his behalf.

in Part II. Finally, the Protection from Eviction Act 1977, s.2, makes it unlawful to enforce a right of re-entry or forfeiture to premises let as a dwelling otherwise than by court proceedings while any person is lawfully residing on them. Apart from criminal sanctions, the measure of damages payable for breach of the covenant for quiet enjoyment by landlords who help themselves has already been considered.[23] These provisions do not mean that before the landlord can recover possession there must be court proceedings every time a tenancy is ended. In very many cases the tenant will peaceably give up possession to the landlord.

B. Proceedings in the County Court

Proceedings to recover possession of dwellings must be taken in the county court if the rateable value of the premises brings them within the county court jurisdiction.[24] The county court has jurisdiction where the net annual value for rating does not exceed £1,000.[25] If the premises exceed that value the parties may still agree that the court is to have jurisdiction.[26] The value is that at the time when the proceedings are started, and is ascertained by referring to the current valuation list.[27] If the property is not separately rated, which is quite common with property in multiple occupation, its net rateable value is taken to be not more than that of the whole building of which it forms part, and equal to its value by the year.[28]

The normal county court procedure is then followed. The plaintiff files a request for the issue of a summons together with the particulars of claim, and copies for service on each defendant, and pays the correct fees. The court prepares the summons which is generally served by post, together with the particulars of claim.[29]

The defendant has 14 days in which to deliver a defence,[30] which can be done quite informally by completing the pro forma attached to the summons. Time in this respect is not vital, and will readily be extended right up to and including the hearing, if a reasonable excuse can be proffered. Any persons who are in possession, *e.g.* deserted wives, sub-tenants, etc., can apply to appear and defend.[31] If the matter is contested, then there can be a pre-trial review, which affords the Registrar the opportunity of giving interlocutory directions, *e.g.* as

---

[23] See *ante*, Chap. 4 (IV) E. and see *post.*, Chap. 19 (II).
[24] Protection from Eviction Act 1977, s.9.
[25] County Courts Act 1984, s.21 (in Rent Act cases in Greater London the limit is £1,500).
[26] County Courts Act 1984, s.18.
[27] County Courts Act 1984, s.147(2).
[28] County Courts Act 1984, s.147(3).
[29] C.C.R. Ord. 3, r. 3; Ord. 6, r. 3; Ord. 7, r. 1.
[30] C.C.R. Ord. 9, r. 2.
[31] C.C.R. Ord. 15, r. 13.

to production and service of lists of documents, and their admission.

In every case, unless there is a formal admission[32], the plaintiff will have to prove his right to an order. If judgment for possession is given the plaintiff then has to apply for a warrant for possession when the time expressed by the judgment for the defendant to give up possession has expired.[33] The warrant may extend to all persons on the premises at the time of its execution,[33a] and should preferably be framed to extend to the tenant's furniture and possessions.[34] Otherwise, although the former tenant may be outside, all his possessions, no doubt subject to hire purchase agreements, are still inside. The warrant is executed by the bailiffs, subject to their other commitments, and the owner or his representative should be in attendance, in order to change the locks, for reasons that are too obvious to state. The plaintiff should apply to have the warrant executed within one year, but an application can be made for its renewal.[35]

C. Proceedings in the High Court

The High Court does not have jurisdiction in relation to residential tenancies within the county court limits. In relation to other tenancies the jurisdictions overlap. However, a successful High Court plaintiff may only be given an order for costs on the county court scale if proceedings should have been brought in the inferior courts.

High Court proceedings are started by writ which should name and be served on all the tenants and sub-tenants who are lawfully in possession. Unless the writ is specially indorsed with the statement of claim, it must state concisely the relief claimed.[36] It also has to contain further information designed to establish that the Rent Acts do not apply. It has to state if the claim relates to a dwelling-house, and if so, that the rateable value for the property puts it outside the Rent Acts limits.[37] The correct response to a writ is to return to the court office the form of acknowledgement of service. A defence should be delivered, obviously, if the defendant intends to defend. The advantage of High Court procedure is that the plaintiff can proceed to judgment if the defendant fails to give notice of intention to defend.[38] The application for judgment in default is by summons and must be

---

[32] In Rent Act cases, there can be no valid judgment by consent, unless it is conceded that the Acts do not apply, *R.* v. *Bloomsbury and Marylebone County Court, ex p. Blackburne* (1985) 275 E.G. 1273.

[33] C.C.R. Ord. 26, r. 17.

[33a] *R* v. *Wandsworth County Council, ex p. Wandsworth London Borough Council* [1975] 1 W.L.R. 1314, *cf. Hawkin* v. *Heathcote* [1976] C.L.Y. 371, (County Court).

[34] *cf.* County Courts Act 1984, s.111.

[35] C.C.R. Ord. 26, r. 6.

[36] R.S.C. Ord. 6, r. 2.

[37] R.S.C. Ord. 6, r. 2(1)(*c*).

[38] R.S.C. Ord. 13, r. 4.

supported by an affidavit from a plaintiff acting in person or certificates from his solicitors verifying that the claim is not for possession of a dwelling-house by a mortgagee and as to the relevant rateable limits. Even if the defendant has given a notice of intention to defend, the plaintiff may still apply for summary judgment under Order 14. But the original claim for possession must be on the grounds either that the tenant has held over, or is liable to forfeiture for non-payment of rent. Again, the application is made by summons, supported by affidavit not only verifying the facts but also stating the plaintiff's belief that there is no defence to the claim.[39] Summary judgment will not be given if the defendant can show that there are grounds for disputing the claim, and he may be given leave to defend either conditionally or unconditionally. Even if judgment is signed under Order 14 there can still be an application to set it aside on grounds being shown,[40] and in any event the defendant can still apply for relief.[41]

If the matter is contested and comes to trial after the parties have marched each other through the various standard procedural formalities the plaintiff has to prove his title and case. This may involve the landlord in proof of the various matters discussed earlier in this chapter in connection with claims for termination for forfeiture or following service of a notice to quit. If judgment for possession is eventually given, then it is enforced by making an application for the court's leave for the issue of a writ of possession.[42] The writ of possession is a formal order of the court to the Sheriff authorising him to take steps to secure possession of the property for the plaintiff. Application for the writ is made *ex parte* on affidavit, which has to show details of notice of the proceedings given to the various occupiers of the property. The affidavit is designed to do two things. First it must establish that all persons in actual possession have had sufficient notice of the proceedings to enable them to apply for relief. Secondly, it must contain sufficient detailed and specified information that will enable the Master to be satisfied that the Rent Acts do not apply, by declaring whether any part of the property is a dwelling-house, and if so its rateable value.[43] If the order for possession has been suspended on terms, which have been broken, then application for leave to issue execution will have to be made by summons, supported by affidavit, and served on the defendant.[44] In many cases the writ of possession will contain also authority to enforce the judgment in respect of unpaid rent, mesne profits and the costs of the execution itself.

[39] R.S.C. Ord. 14, r. 2.
[40] R.S.C. Ord. 14, r. 11.
[41] R.S.C. Ord. 14, r. 10.
[42] R.S.C. Ord. 45, r. 3.
[43] No. P.F. 94.
[44] R.S.C. Ord. 46, r. 4.

CHAPTER 9

THE TENANTED PROPERTY AND THIRD PARTIES

I. Liability to Third Parties for Use and
   Disrepair 365
     A. Liability of Landlord 365
     B. Liability of Tenant 369

II. Rights of Landlords Against Third
    Parties 369

III. Rights of Tenants Against Third
     Parties 370

I. LIABILITY TO THIRD PARTIES FOR USE AND DISREPAIR

A. Liability of Landlord

As a general principle, one might think that the tenant, and not the landlord, is the person liable to third parties for any accident or injury suffered while visiting or staying at the rented premises. However, there are circumstances when the landlord will be liable in tort, either in negligence or nuisance, to persons other than the tenant. At common law there is no duty, apart from contract, on the owner of unfurnished premises, as between him and his tenant, to see that the house is let to the tenant in a safe condition at the beginning of the term.[1] If the tenant, or his customer, guest or employee, suffer injury from the unsafe state of the property, no action for negligence will lie against the owner.[2] Statute has made substantial inroads into this general proposition of the common law. Some statutory inroads, such as the Factories Act 1961, the Offices, Shops and Railway Premises Act 1963 and the Health and Safety at Work Act 1974, are aimed at encouraging and compelling landowners, who are also employers, to provide healthy, safe and acceptable conditions of work for their employees.[3] Others, such as the Occupiers' Liability Act 1957 and the Defective Premises Act 1972 are of more general application.

(1) *Negligence*

The occupier of premises owes to all his visitors the "common duty of care," that is the duty to make certain that visitors will be reasonably

[1] *Tredway* v. *Machin* (1904) 91 L.T. 310 *Bottomley* v. *Bannister* [1932] 1 K.B. 458.
[2] *Ball* v. *L.C.C.* [1949] 2 K.B. 159, unless the landlord is also the builder or designer, see *Anns* v. *Merton London Borough Council* [1978] A.C. 728; at common law a landlord who designs or builds premises owes a duty of care to persons who may reasonably be expected to be affected by the condition of the premises to see that they are reasonably safe from personal injury: *Rimmer* v. *Liverpool City Council* [1985] Q.B. 1.
[3] See *Westminster City Council* v. *Select Managements Ltd.* [1985] 1 All E.R. 897.

safe in using the premises for the purposes for which they were invited
or permitted to be there.[4] If the landlord retains any control over any
part of the building, such as the entrance hall, lifts, forecourt,
lavatories or other common parts, he will be under that duty as
occupier. The landlord may attempt to restrict, modify or exclude this
statutory duty by agreement, notice or any other means at his
disposal.[5] However, any such exclusion or modification must be
shown to be "reasonable,"[6] and in so far as an occupier purports to
exclude or restrict liability for death or personal injury, this will be
ineffective.[7]

The degree of care required to satisfy the duty of care is relative to
the particular visitor, so that, for instance, he must be prepared for
children to be less careful than adults.[8] But he is entitled to expect that
a person, in the exercise of his calling (for instance a window-cleaner
or a decorator who may be clambering about the building) will
appreciate and guard against any special risks ordinarily incident to
that calling.[9]

A landlord was not liable to trespassers under these provisions
unless the harm caused to them was deliberately inflicted (for instance
by the use of dangerous devices designed to deter intruders).
Trespassing children were always treated more favourably by the
courts if their presence could be regarded as having been tolerated on
the premises. So, if no steps were taken to exclude them where they
are known to be on, or likely to frequent the premises, the occupier's
duty of care survived.[10] The occupier is regarded as having discharged
his duty if the danger has been caused as a result of faulty work by an
independent contractor employed by him in carrying out any
construction, maintenance or repairs, provided that he can show that
he had taken such steps as could reasonably be expected of him in
order to satisfy himself that the contractor was competent and that the
work had been properly done.[11]

However, as a consequence of the Occupiers' Liability Act 1984,
s.1, the duty of care has been extended to trespassers, as from May 13,
1984. To owe such a duty to a trespasser the occupier must know of
the danger or have reasonable grounds for believing that it is present.
He must also know or have reasonable grounds for believing that the
trespasser is in the area of the danger or may come within the vicinity
of it, and the risk must be one against which, in all the circumstances

---

[4] Occupiers' Liability Act 1957, s.2.
[5] *Ibid.* s.3.
[6] Unfair Contract Terms Act 1977, ss.1, 2(1); see Mesher [1979] Conv. 58.
[7] *Ibid.* ss.1, 2(2).
[8] *British Railways Board* v. *Herrington* [1972] A.C. 877.
[9] Occupiers' Liability Act 1957, s.2(3); *cf. Salmon* v. *Seafarer Restaurants Ltd.* [1983] 3 All E.R. 729.
[10] *British Railways Board* v. *Herrington* [1972] A.C. 877; *Southern Portland Cement Ltd.* v. *Cooper*
[1974] A.C. 623.
[11] Occupiers' Liability Act 1957, s.2(3).

of the case, he may reasonably be expected to offer the trespasser protection. The duty owed by the occupier is to take such care as is reasonable in all the circumstances to ensure that the trespasser does not suffer injury as a result of the danger. In this context, injury means death or personal injury but not damage to property. This duty may be discharged by taking all reasonable steps to warn the trespasser of the danger and to discourage people from incurring the risk. No duty of care is owed under the Act to any person in respect of risks willingly incurred by that person. The question of whether a risk was so accepted is decided by reference to the normal tort principles of *volenti non fit injuria*.

If the landlord has let off the whole of the premises, retaining no part himself, then he ceases to be the occupier for the purposes of the Occupiers' Liability Act 1957 and the burden falls upon the tenant. However, under the Defective Premises Act 1972, s.4, the landlord remains under a duty of care to *all* persons[12] who might reasonably be expected to be affected by defects in the premises. This duty arises when under the tenancy the landlord is either under an obligation to the tenant (whether it is statutory or otherwise) for the maintenance or repair of the premises, or else he is or can become entitled to enter the premises to maintain or repair them.[13] The duty is, however, owed only if the defect falls within the landlord's obligation or right to maintain or repair, and he knows, or ought to have known of the defect.

(2) *Nuisance*

When a landlord lets property in a state which constitutes a nuisance, and he is himself responsible for its being in such a state, he is liable in tort to anyone thereby injured.[14] If the landlord remains liable under the lease for repairs of or to the part of the property creating the nuisance, that is evidence of his continuing the nuisance.[15] The tenant's obligation to repair, on the other hand, is nearly always conclusive evidence that the landlord is not liable.[16] Where a nuisance is caused by the act of a tenant, the landlord is not usually liable unless the nuisance is the inevitable result of the purpose for which the land was let, such as a noxious trade, unsuited to the environment of the premises.[17] So, if the act is one expressly contemplated in and

[12] This will include the tenant: *Smith* v. *Bradford Metropolitan Council* (1982) 44 P. & C.R. 171.
[13] *Supra*, Chap. 6.
[14] *Metropolitan Properties* v. *Jones* [1939] 2 All E.R. 202; *Sampson* v. *Hodson-Pressinger* [1981] 3 All E.R. 710.
[15] *Pretty* v. *Bickmore* (1873) L.R. 8 C.P. 401.
[16] *Gwinnell* v. *Eamer* (1875) L.R. 10 C.P. 658.
[17] *Smith* v. *Scott* [1973] Ch. 314.

authorised by the lease, the landlord may be liable, as well as the tenant, for any injury caused thereby.[18]

Where a continuing nuisance is created on land occupied by a tenant from year to year, the landlord is liable for damage caused by it if it is shown that, since the creation of the nuisance and before the damage, the tenancy was renewed. It has been held that when a landlord might have given notice to quit and did not, such continuance of the tenancy is equivalent to a re-letting.[19] It is not clear, however, whether this principle applies to periodic lettings of less than a year.[20]

A special responsibility rests on the landlord in the case of a public nuisance caused by premises bordering on the highway getting into a state of disrepair. A distinction must be drawn between the state of disrepair caused by the landlord's failure to repair and a state of disrepair caused by a trespasser or a latent defect.[21] Where the state of disrepair is caused by a lack of repair there is no necessity for the landlord to have express notice of the particular lack of repair which has caused damage, as he must know that if he does not carry out repairs the property will become dangerous.[22] So, a landlord has been held liable where he has agreed with the tenant to repair the premises[23]; also where between himself and the tenant he has not agreed to repair but has expressly reserved the right to enter and repair,[24] and where between himself and the tenant he has not agreed to repair nor has he expressly reserved the right to enter and repair, but such right has been impliedly reserved,[25] *e.g.* in the case of premises let on a weekly tenancy.[26]

When the state of disrepair arises not from lack of repair but from some other cause, then the landlord will only be liable if he adopts the nuisance,[27] or when he should have known of the state of affairs giving rise to the nuisance.[28] Despite old authority to the contrary,[29] it now seems unlikely that a landlord can escape liability to third parties for public nuisance simply by taking a repairing covenant from a tenant.[30] A landlord will also be liable if he is responsible for a nuisance

---

[18] *Ibid.*; see also *Harris* v. *James* (1876) L.J. 45 Q.B. 545; *Sampson* v. *Hodson-Pressinger* [1981] 3 All E.R. 710.
[19] *Thompson* v. *Gibson* (1841) 7 M. & W. 456.
[20] See the undelivered judgment of the Exchequer Chamber in *Gandy* v. *Jubber* (1864–65) 9 B. & S. 15; *quaere* the precedent value of an undelivered judgment.
[21] *Mint* v. *Good* [1951] 1 K.B. 517, *per* Somervell L.J. at p. 524.
[22] *Heap* v. *Ind, Coope & Allsopp* [1940] 2 K.B. 476.
[23] *Wringe* v. *Cohen* [1940] 1 K.B. 229.
[24] *Heap* v. *Ind, Coope & Allsopp* [1940] 2 K.B. 476.
[25] See Defective Premises Act 1972, s.4.
[26] *Mint* v. *Good* [1951] 1 K.B. 517.
[27] *Sedleigh-Denfield* v. *O'Callaghan* [1940] A.C. 880; *Leakey* v. *National Trust* [1980] 1 All E.R. 17.
[28] *Slater* v. *Worthington's Cash Stores* [1941] 1 K.B. 488 (snow on roof); *Leanse* v. *Lord Egerton* [1943] K.B. 323 (air-raid damages).
[29] *Pretty* v. *Bickmore* (1873) L.R. 8 C.P. 401.
[30] *Mint* v. *Good* [1951] 1 K.B. 517, *per* Denning L.J. at p. 528.

adjoining the highway and someone is injured by it when accidentally deviating from the highway,[31] but the deviation must be accidental; if it is deliberate, then the landlord will not be liable in nuisance.[32]

B. Liability of Tenant

Except to the extent that the landlord may be liable in accordance with the principles discussed above, it is generally the tenant, as occupier, upon whom liability to injured parties is likely to fall. As occupier the tenant is liable in respect of any nuisance created upon the premises during his occupancy, or of any nuisance which he allows to continue when he knows or ought to know of its existence.[33] In addition to the occupier's duty to prevent or abate a nuisance, he is also under a duty to take reasonable care that his property does not get into such a state as to be dangerous to adjoining property or persons lawfully thereon. An action for negligence lies for any breach of this duty.[34]

In the case of public nuisance, both owners and occupiers are under a strict duty towards passers-by on the highway.[35] The fact that the landlord may also be liable[36] does not exclude the liability of the tenant for a public nuisance on premises occupied by him.[37] On the other hand, an occupier who neither created the nuisance nor, with knowledge of its existence, permitted its continuance, is under no liability.[38]

II. RIGHTS OF LANDLORDS AGAINST THIRD PARTIES

Once a lease is granted to him the tenant acquires, by virtue of his estate, almost all the proprietary rights in the land that are capable of being damaged by third parties. Since the tenant has enjoyment of the land it is generally his interests that are likely to be interfered with by third parties. A landlord will, therefore, only have good cause for complaint if his *reversionary* interest is threatened or injured. So, for a

---

[31] *Barnes* v. *Ward* (1850) L.J. 19 C.P. 195.
[32] *Jacobs* v. *London County Council* [1950] A.C. 361.
[33] *Wilkins* v. *Leighton* [1932] 2 Ch. 106; *Sampson* v. *Hodson-Pressinger* [1981] 3 All E.R. 710.
[34] *Cunard* v. *Antifyre* [1933] 1 K.B. 551. In the case of both landlord and tenant being liable in respect of the same damage (though not necessarily on the same cause of action), where only one of them is sued by the injured third party, the one sued will have a right of contribution against the other under the Civil Liability (Contribution) Act 1978. See also *Sampson* v. *Hodson-Pressinger*, *supra*.
[35] *Ibid.*; *Tarry* v. *Ashton* (1876) 1 Q.B.D. 314.
[36] *Supra*, note. 34.
[37] *Wilchick* v. *Marks* [1934] 2 K.B. 56.
[38] *Barker* v. *Herbert* [1911] 2 K.B. 633; *Caminer* v. *Northern & London Investment Trust* [1951] A.C. 88.

landlord to be able to maintain an action for damage to the reversion against a third party, he would have to show injury of such a permanent nature as to affect the value of his reversion adversely. This is only likely to be sustainable if the tenant is, or would be, unable to deliver up the land, at the end of the term, as it was at the commencement of the tenancy.[39] In many of such cases, however, the landlord would probably prefer to proceed against the tenant for breach of his express or implied covenant for redelivery, rather than hazard an action in tort against the third party.[40]

Similarly, in the case of nuisance a landlord will only have cause of action against a third party when some permanent injury has been caused to the reversion. Noxious smells and noise are not normally of a kind likely to cause such injury, although a landlord has been granted an injunction against a third party to restrain the carrying on of works which caused structural damage to the property let.[41]

III. RIGHTS OF TENANTS AGAINST THIRD PARTIES

In almost all cases it is the person in occupation of land and premises who is prima facie entitled to maintain an action for an injury done to the property, even where the wrongful act has also injured the person entitled to the reversion, so as to allow him a concurrent right to sue.[42] An action may even be brought by a tenant against a wrongdoer even though his lease is void (because, for example, the landlord had no right to grant it), provided that the "tenant" is in possession.[43] A periodic tenant, at the expiry of his lease, can also maintain an action for trespass on the land before his lease was ended. But where a tenant's interest is determined, and he is absent from the premises, and does no act indicating an intention to remain in possession (such as leaving his furniture or office equipment behind), he is presumed to be out of possession and therefore cannot sue in respect of a subsequent trespass.[44] In one case, however, even where a tenant remained in possession after termination of his interest on assignment, the court held that he had no cause of action for nuisance on adjoining premises.[45] The emphasis on the need for possession by the tenant may well have arisen from the old doctrine of *interesse termini*, which resulted in a tenant being unable to sue a trespasser until he had gone into possession under his lease. After entry, however, his right to

---

[39] *Jones* v. *Llanrwst Urban District Council* [1911] 1 Ch. 393; *cf. Family Management* v. *Gray* (1979) 253 E.G. 369.
[40] *Phillimore* v. *Lane* (1925) 133 L.T. 268.
[41] *Shelfer* v. *City of London Electric Light Co.* [1895] 1 Ch. 287.
[42] *Harker* v. *Birkbeck* (1764) 3 Burr. 1556.
[43] *Graham* v. *Peat* (1801) 1 Ea. 244.
[44] *Brown* v. *Notley* (1848) 3 Ex. 219.
[45] *Metropolitan Properties* v. *Jones* [1939] 2 All E.R. 202.

maintain an action then related back to the time at which the right to enter accrued (normally the commencement of the lease). The doctrine of *interesse termini* was abolished by the Law of Property Act 1925, s.149. Since that time courts, in determining whether a tenant can maintain an action for trespass, appear to have been more concerned with the nature of the interest the tenant is seeking to protect, rather than the fact of actual occupation.[46]

Under the Defective Premises Act 1972 a tenant of a dwelling may, in certain circumstances, have a right to sue a building contractor, architect or other professional person concerned in the construction of the dwelling if in breach of the duty established by section 1 of the Act. This is so even where the building or construction contract in question was not made with the tenant. Section 1 imposes on any person taking on work for or in connection with the provision of a dwelling, whether by original construction, or by conversion or enlargement of an existing building, a duty to see that the work which he takes on is done:

(a) in a workmanlike or professional manner;
(b) with proper materials for the job;
(c) and so that as regards that work the dwelling will be fit for human habitation.

The duty will fall primarily upon builders, developers, local authorities, architects and civil engineers. It will not fall on suppliers or manufacturers of *general* building materials (as against specialist materials such as lifts), nor will it fall on persons carrying out work under a scheme approved by the Minister.[47] Such a scheme is that organised by the National House Builders Registration Council, whereby a registered member of the Council obtains a "guarantee" of the work by a certificate issued after inspection by the council's surveyor. Landlords most likely to be affected by this duty are local authorities, housing associations and property companies and property owners who themselves carry out or commission work in the course of a conversion of large premises into smaller units. Breach of the duty will give a right of action to any tenant (or purchaser) whose tenancy commenced (or, as the case may be, who bought) on or after January 1, 1974,[48] against the person who owed that duty, for the recovery of damages. Liability under the Act continues for six years after the dwelling is completed,[49] and will not cease merely because the person owed the duty was the owner and subsequently sold or let

[46] See footnote 45, *supra.* Also: *Wuta-Ofei* v. *Danquah* [1961] 1 W.L.R. 1238 (which refused to follow *Brown* v. *Notley* (see footnote 44, *supra*)); *Thompson* v. *Ward* [1953] 2 Q.B. 153.
[47] Defective Premises Act 1972, s.2; see Gravells [1979] Conv. 97.
[48] *Ibid.* s.3(2).
[49] *Ibid.* s.1(5).

the house.[50] As a result of recent decisions, it now seems that similar obligations arise at common law.[51]

[50] *Ibid.* s.3(1).
[51] *Dutton* v. *Bognor Regis United Building Co. Ltd.* [1972] 1 All E.R. 462; *Anns* v. *Merton London Borough Council* [1978] A.C. 728, although at common law time will not begin to run until the damage resulting from the defect is discovered: *Cartledge* v. *Jopling & Sons Ltd.* [1963] A.C. 758, *per* Lord Reid at p. 772; *Sparham-Souter* v. *Town & Country Developments (Essex) Ltd.* [1976] 1 Q.B. 858; *Anns* v. *Merton London Borough Council* [1978] A.C. 728, especially Lord Salmon at pp. 769–771; *Rimmer* v. *Liverpool City Council* [1985] Q.B. 1. *cf. Peabody Donation Fund* v. *Sir Lindsay Parkinson & Co.* [1985] A.C. 210.

PART II

RESIDENTIAL TENANCIES

In this Part the following abbreviations are used:

Legislation

H.A.	Housing Act.
H.B.regs	Housing Benefit Regulations 1985 S.I. 1985 No. 677.
H.A.A.	Housing Associations Act
L. & T.A.	Landlord and Tenant Act
P.E.A.	Protection from Eviction Act 1977
R.A.	Rent Act
T. & C.P.A.	Town and Country Planning Act

Books

Arden & Partington: *Housing Law* by A. Arden & M. Partington
Emmet: *Emmet on Title* (18th ed.), by J. T. Farrand.
Evans: *Landlord and Tenant*, by D. Ll. Evans, (2nd ed. by P. Smith).
Farrand: *The Rent Act 1977*, by J. T. Farrand.
Halsbury: *Halsbury's Laws of England* (4th ed.) (3rd ed. where specified).
Hill and Redman: *Hill and Redman's Landlord and Tenant* (17th ed.), by M. Barnes, L.
    Dennis, G. Lockhart-Mummery & J. Gaunt.
Megarry & Wade: *The Law of Real Property* (5th ed.), by Sir Robert Megarry & H. W.
    R. Wade.
Partington: *Landlord and Tenant* (2nd ed.) by M. Partington.
Pettit: *The Rent Act 1977*, by P. H. Pettit.
Woodfall: *William Woodfall's Landlord and Tenant* (28th ed.), by V. G. Wellings and
    G. N. Huskinson.

CHAPTER 10

ESTABLISHING THE STATUS FOR PROTECTION

I. The History of Residential Tenant
Protection 375
  A. The Background 375
II. Protected Tenancies 378
  A. There must be a Tenancy under
    which a Dwelling-house is let as
    a Separate Dwelling 378
  B. The Dwelling-house must have
    a Rateable Value which does
    not exceed Prescribed Limits
    on Particular Dates 388

  C. The Tenancy must not come
    within any of the Various
    Categories of Exempt Agree-
    ments 391
III. The Statutory Tenant 404
  A. Nature 404
  B. Commencement 406
  C. Terms and Conditions 410
  D. Determination 410
IV. Regulated Tenancies 411

I. THE HISTORY OF RESIDENTIAL TENANT PROTECTION[1]

A. The Background

At the turn of the century, the great majority of houses in Britain were rented from private landlords. By 1947 the proportion had fallen to 61 per cent. and by 1972 it was no more than 13 per cent. Since the end of the First World War, the place of the private landlord has increasingly been taken by local authorities and by the growth in owner-occupation. For over 150 years, the privately rented sector dominated the British housing scene, but its recent decline has been very rapid. Unlike the situation in many European countries and North America, virtually no new housing has been built for short-term private letting since before the Second World War, and even between the wars the numbers built were very small indeed. The reasons for this dramatic decline have been most ably described elsewhere[2] and it is beyond the scope of this book to re-examine that ground. Suffice it to say that government intervention, through housing standards and rent control, coupled with changing economic circumstances, slum clearance and redevelopment, and the growth of alternative forms of tenure, have resulted in a vast and complex body of law regulating an ever-decreasing share of the housing market.

The present statutory framework regulating the relationship between a landlord and tenant of residential accommodation has been imposed on an existing structure of rules, both common law and statutory. The common law of landlord and tenant was founded

---

[1] For a concise and useful account see Murie, Niner and Watson, *Housing Policy and the Housing System*, Chap. 6.
[2] *Ibid.* pp. 179–189; see also Berry, *Housing: The Great British Failure, passim.*

largely on the concept of freedom of contract, based on the presupposition of equality of bargaining power in both parties. This presupposition, it transpired, was erroneous, and subsequent legislative endeavours to redress the balance have produced the present legislative maze.

Before the First World War, the majority of dwellings had been built for letting by landlords who were interested in investment: the tenant could reasonably expect security of tenure with little alteration in the rent he had agreed to pay. Changes in economic and social conditions, however, weakened the position of the tenant, who could be put out of his home (which would then be let to a new tenant at a higher rent) by the simple expedient of serving upon him a notice to quit. The demand for houses in the early years of the first war, particularly in the industrial towns and cities, exceeded supply and caused rents to rise. The inability of tenants to afford higher rents, except by demanding higher wages, and the lack of security of tenure and alternative accommodation, caused social and political unrest, which began to affect the production of munitions. This forced Parliament to intervene. The Increase of Rent and Mortgage Interest (War Restrictions) Act 1915 imposed rent control by restraining landlords of property within specified rateable value and annual rent limits from increasing rents or recovering possession from tenants. As its name implies, the Act of 1915 was designed to deal with war-time difficulties and its operation was restricted to the duration of the war and six months thereafter. The Act was amended in 1917 and 1918 and two new Acts were passed in 1919. The end of the war did not, however, bring an end to the housing shortage. The problem increased. Consequently, the initial legislation was consolidated and amended by the Increase of Rent and Mortgage Interest (Restrictions) Act 1920, which extended rent control to a wider range of houses by increasing the rateable value and annual rent limits. The result was that a large proportion of houses let to tenants were subject to full control. The 1920 Act marked the start of virtually continuous rent restriction in the private housing market. This history of the legislation from 1920 to the present day is one of a series of attempts to match the degree of restriction to current perceptions of housing shortage, against a general background of housing policies developed by the major political parties.[3]

The effect of these policies, brought about by and large by sudden shifts in thinking as a result of changes in the political colour of the government of the day, has meant there is no longer a free market in private rented accommodation in the sense that such accommodation now remains the only choice for prospective occupiers who are unable to become owner-occupiers, council tenants or the tenants of housing

---

[3] See Cullingworth, *Essays on Housing Policy,* Chap. 4.

associations and like bodies. This group of persons, which includes single persons, young married persons, immigrants, students and divorcees, is increasing in size and thus adding more pressure to an already difficult situation. It was the need to protect such persons in the declining market which persuaded the Government to extend full Rent Act protection to furnished tenants, even though such an extension might diminish the amount of accommodation available to them. At present, therefore, rent restriction and security of tenure can be seen as something of a stop-gap system designed to curb the worst excesses of a market where demand exceeds supply, but incapable in itself of increasing the supply of houses. As such, it ought to remain an important part of the legal system until such time as an adequate provision is made for the housing of all citizens. The view has been expressed in some quarters that a change in the law can, of itself, do something to increase the supply of houses for rent. That this should be the case in a time when more property is falling into decay for want of repair and fewer new houses are being built than at any time since the war, seems remarkable, but it explains the thinking behind the new form of shorthold tenancy created by the Housing Act 1980 and discussed later in this Part.

The bulk of the current legislation is contained in the Rent Act 1977. This Act is a consolidating act and, as such, is subject to the presumption that the law was not intended to be changed, so that regard may be had to decisions on the construction of the earlier enactments which are repealed and re-enacted by the consolidating Act, even though the words are not identical. The effect of most consolidating acts is to achieve improved arrangement and ease of reference, but in the process of consolidation it is inevitable that the arrangement of the former Acts and the harmonisation of their language should to some extent alter the law. The Consolidation of Enactments (Procedure) Act 1949 provides that in the process of consolidation there may be made such corrections and finer improvements as may be judged expedient, being amendments whose effect is confined to resolving ambiguities, removing doubts, bringing obsolete provisions into conformity with modern practice or removing unnecessary provisions and anomalies which are not of substantial importance; it also allows amendments designed to facilitate improvement in the form or manner in which the law is stated, including such transitional provisions as may be necessary in consequence of such amendments. The Rent Act 1977 consolidated (with a number of amendments) the Rent Act 1968 and the legislation which extended its scope and amended it, namely, the Housing Finance Act 1972, the Rent Act 1974, and the Housing Rents and Subsidies Act 1975. So far as the Rent Act 1968 is concerned, however, it cannot be said with certainty that the Act simply replaced the earlier law. The Act contained three separate sets of provisions, namely, provisions dealing with controlled tenancies, provisions introduced in 1965 to provide for regulated tenancies and harassment and illegal eviction, and the provisions governing furnished tenancies. While reference to decisions on the previous legislation may be useful, it would seem that the safest course with the Rent Act 1968 was first to read the provisions of the Act giving them their plain meaning and only to seek assistance from decisions on earlier Acts to resolve ambiguities.[4]

II. Protected Tenancies

The application of the Rent Act 1977 to residential tenancies is determined by three distinct requirements, which must be fulfilled before a tenancy can be regarded as "protected" within the meaning given to that term by the legislation.

A. There must be a Tenancy under which a Dwelling-House is Let as a Separate Dwelling

The legislation[5] "makes it clear that a protected tenancy is merely shorthand for a tenancy of a dwelling-house which qualifies for inclusion as being let as a separate dwelling and having a rateable value within the limits laid down by the Act; and a protected tenant is simply the (contractual) tenant of such a dwelling-house."[6] The legislation will, therefore, confer protection only where the relationship of landlord and tenant exists between the parties. This will depend on the essential requirements of a lease being present, including either the formal creation of a lease, or an enforceable agreement for a lease, or an enforceable act of part-performance.[7] The word "tenancy" is not defined by the Rent Act 1977 but, as the cases show,[8] it includes all known forms of tenancy, including terms of years, periodic tenancies, tenancies at will, at sufferance, and

---

[4] See Lord Simon in *Maunsell* v. *Olins* [1975] 1 All E.R. 16 at pp. 26–27; James L.J. in *Avenue Properties Ltd.* v. *Aisinzon* [1976] 2 All E.R. 177 at p. 181; see also Lord Wilberforce in *Farrell* v. *Alexander* [1976] 2 All E.R. 721, where the House of Lords held that the penal character of the Rent Act 1968, s.85, which prohibited the charging of a premium by "any person" as a condition of the grant, renewal or continuance of a tenancy—was not sufficiently ambiguous to require the application of the general presumption that no change in the previous law had been intended. It has also been held that the enactment in the Rent Act 1968, s.3(1)(*a*), of rules governing the commencement of statutory tenancies was not intended to change the existing law: *Roland House Gardens* v. *Cravitz* (1975) 235 E.G. 683 at p. 685; *Smalley* v. *Quarrier* [1975] 2 All E.R. 688 at p. 692.
[5] R.A. 1977, s.1.
[6] *Smalley* v. *Quarrier* [1975] 2 All E.R. 688, *per* Stephenson L.J. at p. 693; *Fletcher* v. *Davies* (1981) 257 E.G. 1149.
[7] *Supra*, Chap. 3.
[8] See *Rees* v. *Marquis of Bute* [1916] 2 Ch. 64 at p. 72; *Francis Jackson Developments Ltd.* v. *Stemp* [1943] 2 All E.R. 74; *Remon* v. *City of London Real Property Co. Ltd.* [1921] 1 K.B. 49 at p. 59; *Whitmore* v. *Lambert* [1955] 1 W.L.R. 495.

tenancies by estoppel.[9] However, the Rent Act 1977 does not accord the status of "protected tenancy" to an occupation of premises governed by a licence.[10] This is a rule developed by the courts to deal with a variety of situations where no true tenancy could be said to exist and where the existing presumptions which gave rise to a tenancy at common law had to be reconsidered in the light of the judiciary's view of the purposes of the Rent Acts. It has unfortunately produced a morass of litigation, the main result of which has been to point the way to landlords to indulge in wholesale avoidance, to the detriment of some residential occupants, of considerable portions of the Rent Act 1977. The question has been fully discussed in Chapter 2 of this book and further reference to the problem is made below in Chapter 13.[11]

(1) *A House or Part of a House*

The Rent Act 1977, s.1, provides that a protected tenancy is restricted to the letting of a dwelling-house which may be a house or part of a house. These words are not defined in the statute but in most cases their meaning will be obvious. However, the meaning of "house" for the purpose of section 1 is wider than the ordinary normal house or flat residence. Two separate flats, if let together as a dwelling, may constitute a house,[12] as may a house and adjacent cottage similarly let.[13] Part of a house may also be a dwelling, and this may be a single room, provided it contains essential living accommodation. A single house, therefore, in the popular sense, may contain several dwelling-houses for the purposes of the Rent Act 1977.[14]

Difficulties arise where premises are not permanent, such as caravans and houseboats, or not primarily intended as residences, such as stables or workshops. Case law on this is scarce, but it is suggested that one relevant factor will be the intention the parties had at the time of the letting. If it was intended to be used as a residence, then it can be a "house," provided it has a sufficient degree of permanence. It has been held that a stationary, but not immobile, caravan is outside full protection,[15] yet it has also been held that a caravan let furnished where it was not intended to be moved was

---

[9] *Supra*, Chap. 3, and see *Spectrum Investment v. Holmes* [1981] 1 All E.R. 6.
[10] Although residential licensees within R.A. 1977, Pt. V, may not now be evicted without a court order: Housing Act 1980, s.69, amending the Protection from Eviction Act 1977, s.3(2A); *cf.* Housing Act 1985, s.79(3), which affords the same protection to licensees as is granted to "secure" tenants in the public sector: *post*, Chap. 16.
[11] Readers should consult those chapters for further discussion of the issues raised for owners and occupiers of residential accommodation by the distinction between leases and licences.
[12] *Langford Property Co. Ltd. v. Goldrich* [1949] 1 K.B. 511.
[13] *Whitty v. Scott-Russell* [1950] 2 K.B. 32.
[14] *Abrahart v. Webster* [1925] 1 K.B. 563.
[15] *Morgan v. Taylor* (1949) 153 E.G. 3.

within the scope of what is now the Rent Act 1977, Pt. V.[16] Following
the extension of Rent Act protection to all qualifying tenants, whether
their premises be furnished or unfurnished[17] there would seem to be
no reason why a stationary and immobile caravan, which is let
together with a site, should not be a dwelling-house for the purposes of
the Rent Act 1977, s.1.[18] Indeed, in *R.* v. *Nottinghamshire Registration Area, ex parte Allen*[19] Farquharson J. appeared to suggest that this
was so, even though, in the case before him, the fact that the caravan
was moved from time to time and the services connected in a way to
facilitate removal pointed to the inference that the caravan was not, in
this case, "a house."

(2) *Let as a Separate Dwelling*

(a) The purpose of the letting

The word "let" in the Rent Act 1977, s.1, in addition to indicating
the need for a tenancy, also qualifies the words "as a separate
dwelling," which means that if the premises are let for some other
purpose, the fact that there is a tenancy will not result in protection.
The purpose of the letting is, therefore, vital. The rules governing the
purpose of the letting were discussed in *Wolfe* v. *Hogan.*[20] The
defendant took a sub-tenancy of a large room in premises in Chelsea
which, when let, contained articles of furniture and junk. There was
no water supply and no lavatory, although the landlord arranged with
other tenants for the defendant to use their lavatory and bathroom.
There was no express prohibition against using the room as a
dwelling, but all the negotiations between the parties had proceeded
on the footing that the defendant was taking the room for use as an
antique shop. During the blitz the landlord gave the defendant
permission to sleep in the room, but he did not have full knowledge
that she was using the room as a residence. In proceedings to recover
possession it was held that although there had been a change of user,
there was not such full knowledge of the change by the landlord as to
show that the premises were let as a separate dwelling. Denning L.J.
said[21]:

---

[16] See *post, R.* v. *Guildford Area Rent Tribunal, ex p. Grubey* [1951] E.G.D. 286.
[17] After the Rent Act 1974.
[18] *N.B.* R.A. 1977, s.9, relating to holiday lettings: *post.* Comprehensive protection against
harassment and eviction for residential occupiers of caravans on a protected site is provided by
the Caravan Sites Act 1968, Pt. 1. The Mobile Homes Act 1983 provides that the owner of a
protected site has a duty to offer a statutory agreement (s.2) to a person who intends to occupy a
mobile home (s.5(1)) on that site as his only or main residence (s.1).
[19] (1985) 275 E.G. 251. See also Kenny & Wilson, [1984] J.P.L. 853.
[20] [1949] 2 K.B. 194.
[21] *Ibid.* p. 204.

" . . . if there is no express provision, it is open to the courts to look at the circumstances of the letting. If the house is constructed for use as a dwelling house, it is reasonable to infer the purpose was to let it as a dwelling. But if, on the other hand, it is constructed for the purpose of being used as a lock-up shop, the reasonable inference is that it was let for business purposes. If the position were neutral, then it would be proper to look at the actual user. It is not a question of implied terms. It is a question of the purpose for which the premises were let."[22]

Where the terms of the tenancy express that the premises are to be used for a particular purpose, that purpose is the essential factor, not the nature of the premises or the actual use made of them.[23] In such cases the court will not admit oral evidence to disprove the clear terms of the written lease. Consequently, where the tenancy expressly states that the premises are let for business or non-residential purposes, the tenant cannot claim a protected tenancy simply because he lives there.[24] If, however, residential use is not specifically prohibited, in general the courts will lean in favour of applying the Rent Act.[25] It is possible for the parties themselves to change the user by subsequent agreement: in such cases the change of user will be the one relied on by the court in determining whether the Rent Act applies. There must be definitive evidence that user has been changed by agreement, and the mere acceptance of rent by the landlord, with knowledge of a change of user, will not, of itself, suffice.[26]

The courts will also consider the circumstances of the letting to determine its purpose where no express provision on purpose is present.[27] In cases of this kind the courts will often infer the purpose of the letting from any description of the premises, *e.g.* "all that shop, garage and premises"[28]—in the tenancy agreement. The circumstance of the letting may contemplate no one purpose and the nature of the premises may be apt for a number of different purposes, including residence. If there is no description of the premises given in the lease which would assist the court in deciding the matter, then the matter is a question of fact for the judge. In *Whiteley* v. *Wilson*[29] the Court of

---

[22] See *St. Catherine's College* v. *Dorling* [1979] 3 All E.R. 253 at pp. 253–254.
[23] *Barrett* v. *Hardy Bros. Ltd.* [1925] K.B. 220, *per* Scrutton L.J. at p. 227; *Wolfe* v. *Hogan* [1949] 2 K.B. 194, *per* Evershed L.J. at p. 203; *Russell* v. *Booker* (1982) 263 E.G. 513 where the principles of *Wolfe* v. *Hogan (supra)* are concisely summarised.
[24] *Gardiner* v. *Deptford Liberal Club* [1924] E.G.D. 55.
[25] *Epsom Grand Stand Association Ltd.* v. *Clarke* (1919) 35 T.L.R. 525 *per* Bankes L.J. at p. 526. If the premises are *let* for mixed business and residential user, different considerations apply where such premises would otherwise be subject to a regulated tenancy. Here the matter is removed from the R.A. 1977 and made subject to the Landlord and Tenant Act 1945, Pt. II, which gives security to business tenants: R.A. 1977, s.24(3); *post*, and Chap. 20.
[26] *Wolfe* v. *Hogan* [1949] 2 K.B. 194.
[27] *Ibid.*
[28] *Grant & Partners* v. *Lines* (1952) 102 L.J. 416; see also *Ponder* v. *Hillman* [1969] 3 All E.R. 694.
[29] [1953] 1 Q.B. 77.

Appeal held that the judge should determine whether the premises should, in a broad sense, be considered as business premises with a dwelling added, or as a dwelling partly used as a shop.

In *St Catherine's College* v. *Dorling*[30] the Court of Appeal took the view that for the premises to be let as a separate dwelling the tenant in occupation should have the right to go to any part of the premises he chooses. Eveleigh L.J. said[31]:

> "It may well be that a tenant who takes a separate dwelling house will sub-let so as to preclude himself, vis-à-vis the sub-lessee, from entering another part of the premises for the period of the sub-letting: but that is something which occurs after the lease has been entered into and in no way detracts from the right of the tenant vis-à-vis the landlord to go to another room. The existence of someone able to go of his own right to all the rooms of the premises is one of the hall-marks of a dwelling-house."

In that case, the court had to consider whether a tenancy granted to the college for use "as private residence" by students of the college, was a protected tenancy. The college permitted five undergraduates to occupy the house, each student being assigned one room, and sharing kitchen and bathroom. The Court of Appeal held that no protected tenancy arose. The phrase "used as private residence" did not mean that the college had been granted the premises "to be used as a private residence," but merely meant that the premises should be used for residential purposes. The college had, therefore, merely been granted a tenancy of a building which contained a number of units of habitation, and the arrangement contemplated with the landlord and the student occupants was inconsistent with the whole building itself being described as a separate dwelling.

(b) Shared premises

The dwelling-house must be "let as a separate dwelling" in the sense of being a distinct dwelling rather than being physically separated or partitioned-off from other dwellings. Part of a house may, therefore, be a separate dwelling without being a self-contained flat. Before 1945 the fact that a dwelling did not have all domestic offices within the part separately let, but that the tenant shared some of these with other persons, did not prevent a separate letting from arising.[32] However, in *Neale* v. *Del Soto*[33] a new doctrine emerged to the effect that if accommodation was shared, there could be no letting as a separate

[30] [1979] 3 All E.R. 250.
[31] *Ibid.* p. 255.
[32] *Sutton* v. *Begley* [1923] 2 K.B. 694.
[33] [1945] K.B. 144.

dwelling to constitute a protected tenancy. This view was approved by the House of Lords in *Goodrich* v. *Paisner*.[34] A distinction between sharing with a landlord and sharing with the other tenants is to be found in the Rent Act 1977. The former receives protection under Part V of the Act,[35] while the latter receives full protection for his separate part, and some protection in relation to the shared part.[36] Most cases of sharing with the landlord will be covered by the rules governing resident landlords. These rules no longer depend on sharing but on whether the landlord is resident within the terms of the Rent Act 1977, s.12. This question is discussed later in Chapter 14. However, since the Rent Act 1977, s.12, does not affect protected tenancies already existing on August 14, 1974, and since not all cases of sharing with landlords will be a sharing with a resident landlord as defined in the Act, the provisions governing sharing with landlords remain important and are discussed later in this chapter in relation to the various exceptions from full Rent Act protection.

The Rent Act 1977, s.22, deals with the position where a tenant shares with persons other than the landlord and applies where a tenant has the exclusive occupation of any accommodation (referred to as "the separate accommodation"), the terms of his lease including the use of other, shared accommodation (referred to as "the shared accommodation") with persons other than the landlord. If it is only the use of his shared accommodation which prevents the separate accommodation being deemed a dwelling-house let on or subject to a protected tenancy, then the separate accommodation is, as it were, severed off and deemed to be subject to a protected tenancy.[37]

If, while the tenant is in possession of the separate accommodation, a term or condition of his tenancy contract purports to modify or terminate his right to the use of any of the shared accommodation which is living accommodation, this term or condition is void.[38] While the tenant is in possession of the separate accommodation, no order can be made for possession of any of the shared accommodation unless the court is also able and willing to grant possession of the separate accommodation[39] The county court may, on the application of the landlord, make any order which it thinks just, either terminating the right of the tenant to use a part or the whole of the shared accommodation other than living accommodation, or modifying his right to use the whole or part of the shared accommodation.[40] A proviso is however added[41] that no such order can be made which

---

[34] [1957] A.C. 65.
[35] Otherwise known as "restricted contracts"—see *post*, Chap. 14.
[36] R.A. 1977, ss.1, 22.
[37] R.A. 1977, s.22(1).
[38] *Ibid.* s.22(3).
[39] *Ibid.* s.22(5). See *post*, Chap. 13.
[40] R.A. 1977, s.22(6).
[41] By R.A. 1977, s.22(7).

could not be effected under the terms of the contract of tenancy. The construction of this proviso has caused difficulty, and its meaning is certainly obscure. In *Lockwood* v. *Lowe*[42] Denning L.J. said[43]:

> "Incidentally, I may say in passing that I find it difficult to understand the proviso . . . but I am inclined to think that its principal object is to see that, on any change of occupants, the hours during which the tenant can use the shared accommodation are not diminished or altered to his disadvantage. At any rate, the proviso should not be so construed as to nullify the operative part of [section 22(6)]."

In the context of section 22, "living accommodation" means accommodation of such a nature that the fact that it is included in the shared accommodation is sufficient, in itself, to prevent the tenancy constituting a protected tenancy of a dwelling-house.[44] The courts have held that if living accommodation is shared then there could be no separate dwelling, aside from the provisions of section 22.[45] In *Neale* v. *Del Soto*[46] a tenant, by oral agreement, was let two unfurnished rooms in a seven-roomed house together with the use jointly with the landlord of the garage, kitchen, bathroom, lavatory, coal-house and conservatory. In proceedings for the apportionment of rent it was held by the county court judge that the letting of the two rooms was not a letting of part of a house as a separate dwelling. This was upheld by the Court of Appeal which ruled that such a degree of sharing excluded the application of the Rent Acts. On this basis a kitchen has been held to be a living room, while a bathroom and lavatory are not.

While the test of living accommodation will determine the matter in ordinary cases, it cannot assist the court in unusual or extraordinary cases. In these the court must go back to section 1 and ascertain whether or not the particular premises were let as a separate dwelling.

Lord Radcliffe observed in *Goodrich* v. *Paisner*[47]:

> "The truth is that a living room is not something which can be identified objectively without regard to the situation of its particular occupant, occupants or users. What, indeed, may be a living room if in single occupation, as for instance, a kitchen, is not necessarily a living room if it has to be made available for the use of several distinct households: and I should say the same of a bathroom and, again, a spare bedroom."

[42] [1954] 2 Q.B. 267.
[43] *Ibid.* p. 270.
[44] R.A. 1977, s.22(8).
[45] *Cole* v. *Harris* [1945] K.B. 474.
[46] [1945] K.B. 144.
[47] [1957] A.C. 65 at pp. 91–92.

A right to share premises is a personal right and does not appear to be assignable.[48] It therefore has the character of a mere licence, but not every licence is a sharing right. It will only become a sharing right when the accommodation is shared for living purposes and when the sharing prevents a letting of a separate dwelling.[49]

If the tenancy is excluded from protection for any reason save that the tenant is required to share with others, then section 22 does not bring it within protection. The material time for applying this test is the date of action for possession. In *Tovey* v. *Tyack*[50] the defendant took a tenancy in 1948 of part of a house which included the right to share the use of the kitchen with the plaintiff, to whom the landlord had let the remainder of the house. The plaintiff was the landlord's son and in 1951 the landlord granted his interest absolutely to his son who, as the new landlord, subsequently sought possession because at the time when the action commenced, the defendant was sharing accommodation with his landlord and not, therefore, entitled to the assistance of what is now the Rent Act 1977, s.21. The question of timing under this section is, however, exactly the same as that applicable to actions within section 22.

The importance of sharing rights under the Rent Act 1977, s.22, is illustrated by *Lockwood* v. *Lowe*.[51] A house was let by the owner to two tenants on terms that they should each occupy half and share the use of a kitchen and bathroom. The occupier of the lower half moved out, but the defendant stayed on and continued to use the kitchen and bathroom. The Court of Appeal held that while both tenants were in occupation the premises were protected under what is now the Rent Act 1977, s.22. When one tenant left, that did not alter the nature of the tenancy of the remaining tenant, as under the sharing arrangements the landlord did not have the right to enter and share except by court order. The effect of this decision is to construe sharing arrangements as excluding the landlord unless the terms are wide enough to enable the landlord to enter and share when one tenant leaves.[52]

So, the protection afforded by section 22 is twofold. The separate accommodation is completely protected and the shared accommodation is also protected in the sense that no order can be made for possession of the shared accommodation, unless an order is also made for possession of the separate accommodation. However, the contract may confer on the landlord a power to vary the terms of sharing arrangements, unless that relates to living accommodation, where the

---

[48] *Dakyns* v. *Pace* [1958] 1 K.B. 22.
[49] *Hayward* v. *Marshall* [1952] 2 Q.B. 89.
[50] [1955] 1 Q.B. 57.
[51] [1954] 2 Q.B. 267.
[52] In which case R.A. 1977, s.21, will apply: see *post*, and *Isaacs* v. *Titus* [1954] 1 W.L.R. 398.

landlord is unable to terminate or modify any rights in respect of the shared living accommodation.

(c) Dwelling

For there to be a protected tenancy the premises must be let as a single dwelling. More than one house can be let as a separate dwelling,[53] but the words "a dwelling" in the Rent Act 1977, s.1, must be given a singular meaning.[54] At first sight the word "dwelling" may seem to be superfluous, given that section 1 requires "*a* dwelling-house," let as a separate dwelling and given that the meaning of "dwelling-house" is wider than that contemplated by ordinary usage. The word "dwelling" directs attention to the fact that, whatever kind of structure is let, it must have the capacity to be a dwelling in that it can be used for normal residence activities. In *Wright* v. *Howell*[55] the Court of Appeal held that the word "dwelling" included all the major activities of life such as sleeping, cooking and eating. The case concerned the letting of an unfurnished room which had no cooking arrangements nor water supply, and was not used by the tenant for sleeping. In deciding that the tenant was unprotected, emphasis was laid on the fact that such an important aspect of living as sleeping was carried on elsewhere.[56]

If someone sleeps on the premises, but that is just about the only use made of them, it is unlikely that the tenancy will be protected. In *Curl* v. *Angelo*[57] a householder let two rooms in his house to the proprietor of an adjacent hotel. The rooms were used by the hotelier as sleeping accommodation for his guests and employees. The Court of Appeal held that it was impossible to attribute the character of a dwelling to rooms where a tenant carries on only one of the many domestic activities that go to make up everyday living and residence, while others are carried on elsewhere. For premises to be a dwelling, more than one residential activity must be carried on.

The question is raised as a result of this decision whether a letting of premises to a person who already has a home elsewhere can constitute a "dwelling." In *Langford Property Co. Ltd.* v. *Tureman*[58] the defendant, who owned a cottage in the country, took a tenancy of a flat in London in order to have a place to stay while on business visits. He slept in the flat on average two nights a week, but rarely had a meal there. On the termination of the tenancy, the landlord sought to recover possession. The Court of Appeal held that the defendant was a

---

[53] Interpretation Act 1978, s.6(c).
[54] *Whitty* v. *Scott-Russell* [1950] 2 K.B. 32; *Horford Investments Ltd.* v. *Lambert* [1974] 1 All E.R. 131; *Regalian Securities Ltd.* v. *Ramsden* [1981] 1 W.L.R. 611. *cf. St. Catherine's College* v. *Dorling* [1979] 3 All E.R. 250.
[55] (1948) 92 S.J. 26.
[56] *cf. Wolfe* v. *Hogan* [1949] 2 K.B. 194, *supra.*
[57] [1948] 2 All E.R. 189.
[58] [1949] 1 K.B. 29.

protected tenant. He was in personal occupation of the flat and there was nothing in the Rent Acts to prevent a person having more than one home, especially where his profession or occupation required it. *Curl* v. *Angelo*[59] was not cited, and it is not clear how far these two cases conflict. It could be argued that the tenant in *Tureman's* case satisfied the requirements of residential user on the occasions when he occupied the premises and, in any case, the flat itself clearly had the full capacity to be used for residential purposes, which alone would distinguish the case from *Curl* v. *Angelo*[60] and *Wright* v. *Howell*.[61] This distinction appears to be borne out by the decision of the House of Lords in *Hampstead Way Investments* v. *Lewis-Weare*.[62] In this case the tenant of a flat married and went to live with his wife and stepchild in a nearby house. However, he retained the flat to sleep in five nights a week after finishing night work so as not to disturb the family, and his adult step-son also lived there. The tenant paid all the outgoings, had his mail directed there but never ate there. The House of Lords held that, while it was possible for a person to occupy two houses as his residence (indeed, that had properly been so held in the *Langford Property* case) the question was one of fact and degree. In this case the tenant made only limited use of the flat, and then only for part of his daily living, since he did not eat there. The tenancy was not, therefore, protected.

It may be that, where a tenant occupies two homes, he occupies neither independently as his residence, but both together as a combined residential unit. In *Kavanagh* v. *Lyroudias*[63] the tenant had been let a house adjacent to another residential property. He slept in the adjacent house and used one of the rooms there as a study, but he kept his clothes in the house which he rented, and used the bathroom and living room, as well as eating there. It was, however, held by the Court of Appeal that he was not using the rented house as a residence, even though it clearly had the full capacity to be used as such. Although the nature and *capacity* for use as a residence are important, the *actual* use of the premises is of equal significance.[64] In *Kavanagh's* case the premises were not used as a complete home, but as part of a larger unit.

It is also important to note in any event, that the Act requires the premises to be let "as *a* separate dwelling," so that the contemplated user must be for premises to be used as one dwelling, even if made up of two or more. In *Grosvenor (Mayfair) Estates* v. *Amberton*[65] there was a single sub-letting of two adjacent self-contained flats, subject to

---

[59] [1948] 2 All E.R. 189.
[60] *Ibid.*
[61] (1948) 92 S.J. 26.
[62] [1985] 1 W.L.R. 164.
[63] (1984) 269 E.G. 629.
[64] See the discussion of statutory tenancies, *post.*
[65] (1983) 265 E.G. 693.

a covenant that the property demised should not be used except as a private residence. However, at the time of the sub-letting one of the flats was subject to a non-exclusive occupation agreement, thus preventing use of the two flats as a single, unitary dwelling. Since, at the date of the letting, there was no clear intention that the flats would be required for use as *a* separate dwelling (there being no real prospect of the user covenant actually being complied with) the claim to protection failed. The user covenant could not prevail over what the court took to be the clear intention of the parties at the time of the letting. It would, however, have been different if there had been a real prospect of the non-exclusive occupation agreement coming to an early end, for then the intentions of the parties at the time of letting could not have been so readily assumed and the user covenant might then have been regarded as the paramount expression of that intention. Had the parties, therefore, had it in contemplation to let the two flats as one single dwelling, it would have been protected.

In deciding whether premises constitute a "dwelling," and thus whether the tenancy is protected, it is immaterial whether the tenant resides in the premises or allows an employee or sub-tenant to do so.[66] The fact that it is not the tenant himself who resides in the premises, but someone else lawfully authorised by the tenant to reside there, does not prevent the corporate or employing tenant, for example, from claiming that the premises are let as a separate dwelling, nor prevent protection from being conferred by the Rent Act 1977.[67] However, it is necessary either for the tenant himself or the person he has authorised to live in the accommodation, to have access to all parts of the premises, or at least to all those parts necessary to carry out the activities of everyday living.[68]

B. The Dwelling-House must have a Rateable Value which does not Exceed Prescribed Limits on Particular Dates

(1) *The "Appropriate Day"*

For the tenancy to be protected, it must be a tenancy of a dwelling whose rateable value does not exceed the limits prescribed by the Rent Act 1977, s.4, on what the Act calls "the appropriate day." The appropriate day is March 23, 1965, in relation to any dwelling-house which was, or was part of premises, shown in the valuation list on that

---

[66] Although it is a vital consideration in deciding whether the tenant is a "statutory" tenant, where actual occupation by the tenant is essential: see *post.*
[67] *Carter* v. *S.U. Carburettor Co.* [1942] 2 K.B 288; *Anspach* v. *Charlton Steam Shipping Co. Ltd.* [1955] Q.B. 21; *Feather Supplies Ltd.* v. *Ingham* [1971] 2 Q.B. 348.
[68] *St. Catherine's College* v. *Dorling* [1979] 3 All E.R. 250.

date. In relation to premises not within this category, the appropriate day means the date on which the rateable value is or was first shown in the valuation list.[69] If the valuation list is altered after this date, but the effect of the alteration is backdated to some time before or on the appropriate day, then the rateable value on the appropriate day becomes the value as altered.[70] This provision is, however, strictly applied. In *Rodwell* v. *Gwynne Trusts Ltd.*[71] the lease of a flat in the Greater London area was purchased by the appellant on November 1, 1963, on which date its rateable value was £430. In July 1967 the local valuation court reduced the rateable value to £388. The valuation list was altered accordingly, and the alteration took effect from April 1, 1965. The appellant then applied to the rating authority for a partial refund of rates in respect of the period from November 1, 1963 to March 31, 1965. A refund was calculated on the basis of a rateable value of £388 *for the whole period in question*, notwithstanding that the alteration in the valuation list only took effect from April 1, 1965. When the appellant's lease expired, the respondent landlord claimed possession and the question arose whether on March 23, 1965 (the appropriate day), the rateable value of the flat for the purposes of the Rent Acts was £430 or £388. If the latter, the appellant was a protected tenant. The House of Lords held that since the figure of £430 was the rateable value *shown in the valuation list* on March 23, 1965, there was no protected tenancy. What is now the Rent Act 1977, s.25 (4), had no application in the case of a partial refund of rates, as anything not entered or recorded in the valuation list was outside its scope.

(2) *"Appropriate Day" Falling before March 22, 1973*

Where the appropriate day fell before March 22, 1973,[72] the tenancy will be a protected tenancy if the rateable value was equal to or less than *any* of the figures given in the Rent Act 1977, s.4(2), Class C, on the dates specified. These are:

(i) £400 in Greater London; £200 elsewhere *on the appropriate day; or*
(ii) £600 in Greater London; £300 elsewhere *on March 22, 1973; or*
(iii) £1,500 in Greater London; £750 elsewhere *on April 1, 1973.*

For example, a house was built in London before 1965, and

---

[69] R.A. 1977, s.25 (3).
[70] *Ibid.* s.25 (4).
[71] [1970] 1 All E.R. 314.
[72] The date of the passing of the Counter-Inflation Act 1973.

assessed in the valuation list on March 23, 1965, at £450, assessed on March 22, 1973, at £570 and April 1, 1973, at £1,400. The tenancy was not a protected tenancy on the appropriate date of March 23, 1965, because the rateable value exceeded £400. It is now a protected tenancy because the rateable value did not exceed £600 on March 22, 1973, or, alternatively, because it did not exceed £1,500 on April 1, 1973. If the rateable value had exceeded £600 on March 22, 1973, but was £1,400 on April 1, 1973, the tenancy would be protected from April 1, 1973.

(3) *"Appropriate Day" Falling on or after March 22, 1973*

Where the appropriate day fell on or after March 22, 1973, but before April 1, 1973,[73] the tenancy will be a protected tenancy if the rateable value was equal to or less than *any* of the figures given in the Rent Act 1977, s.4 (2), Class B, on the dates specified. These are:

(i) £600 in Greater London; £300 elsewhere *on the appropriate day; or*
(ii) £1,500 in London; £750 elsewhere *on April 1, 1973.*

For example, a house was built in London in December 1972 and assessed in the valuation list on March 29, 1973, at £650 and on April 1, 1973, at £1,500. The tenancy would not have been a protected tenancy on the appropriate day of March 29, 1973, because the rateable value of the dwelling exceeded the original limit of £600. However, it becomes a protected tenancy on April 1, 1973, because on that date the rateable value does not exceed the new limit of £1,500.

(4) *"Appropriate Day" Falling on or after April 1, 1973*

Where the appropriate day falls on or after April 1, 1973 the position is governed by the Rent Act 1977, s.4(2), Class A, and the tenancy will be protected if the rateable value was equal to or less than £1,500 in Greater London and £750 elsewhere on the appropriate day. For example, a house was built in London in 1975 and first assessed at £1,600 on October 1, 1975, which is the appropriate day. As its rateable value exceeds £1,500 on the appropriate day, a tenancy in respect of it will not be protected.

---

[73] The date when new rating assessments under the General Rate Act 1967, s.68, took effect.

(5) *Deeming Provisions*

A dwelling-house is deemed to be within the limits set out in the Rent Act 1977, s.4(2), unless the contrary is shown.[74] The presumption so raised can be rebutted by obtaining a certificate from the clerk to the rating authority showing that the rateable value on the appropriate day is outside the prescribed limits. The statutory presumption in respect of rateable values operates "if any question rises in any proceedings."[75] In *R.* v. *Westminster (City) London Borough Rent Officer, ex p. Rendall*[76] it was held that an application to a rent officer to fix a fair rent and the ensuing steps were "proceedings" within section 4(3) of the Rent Act 1977. "Proceedings" covered any proceedings of a legal nature, even though they did not take place in a court of law. The rent officer had made his own informal assessment of the rateable value on the ground floor flat of a six floor house which was assessed for rates as a whole. On this assessment he assumed jurisdiction and determined a fair rent. An order of certiorari was granted by the Divisional Court on the ground that the rent officer had no jurisdiction to apportion rateable values which, by virtue of the Rent Act 1977, s.25 (2), can be done only by the county court, and accordingly the rent officer had no jurisdiction to register a fair rent. The Court of Appeal allowed an appeal from this order on the ground that the Rent Act 1977, s.4 (3), gave the rent officer jurisdiction unless the assumption that the property was within the rateable value limits was challenged by the landlord at the time when it was made. In such a case, apportionment would then be a matter for the county court.

C. The Tenancy must not come within any of the Various Categories of Exempt Agreements

Even where a dwelling is within the prescribed rateable value limits, and is let as a separate dwelling, the tenancy is not protected unless it falls outside the various categories of tenancies excepted from the application of the Rent Act 1977. The exceptions can be grouped into three classes,[77] namely, those where the nature of the premises is material, those where the status of the landlord is material and those where the terms of the tenancy are material.

---

[74] R.A. 1977, s.4 (3).
[75] *Ibid.*
[76] [1973] 3 All E.R. 119.
[77] Following Megarry, *The Rent Acts* (10th ed.). p. 93.

(1) *The Nature of the Premises*

(a) Houses let with a substantial quantity of land

The Rent Act 1977, s.6, provides that a tenancy is not a protected tenancy if the dwelling-house which is subject to the tenancy is let together with land, *other than the site of the dwelling.* However, certain land let with the dwelling can be ignored (and therefore the exception will not apply). The Rent Act 1977, s.26 (1), provides that any land or premises *let together with* a dwelling (unless it consists of agricultural land exceeding two acres in extent) is to be treated as part of the dwelling-house. Section 26 presupposes that a dwelling-house has been let as a separate dwelling, and together with such a dwelling-house, other land or premises are also let. The extent of such other land is immaterial, unless it is agricultural land exceeding two acres.[78] The combined entity constitutes a protected tenancy.[79] If, however, the position is reversed, so that instead of the house being let with land, land is let which happens to have a dwelling-house upon it, then the exception in section 6 operates and neither land nor dwelling can comprise a protected tenancy.

The material words in section 6 and 26 are "let together with." The question of whether the land is "let together with" the dwelling-house or the dwelling-house is "let together with" the land is a question of fact, and the material time for the determination is when the landlord seeks to recover possession. There is no need for a single letting, or even for a single rent, for the two entities to be let together, but there must be some physical propinquity between them and some coincidence in the terms on which they are let. The intention of the parties is relevant in determining whether there is one tenancy or two.[80] In determining whether sections 6 or 26 apply in the case of composite lettings, the nature and purpose of the lettings is a material consideration. In the absence of express provisions as to the purpose of the letting, considerations of the relative size and composition of the entities, arrived at in a commonsense way, will determine the question.[81]

(b) Mixed business and residential regulated tenancies

Use of part of premises comprised in a dwelling-house for business

---

[78] R.A. 1977, s.26(2); General Rate Act 1967, s.26(3)(*a*). This does not include land kept or preserved mainly or exclusively for the purposes of recreation or sport, such as a paddock kept for equestrian activities: *Bradshaw* v. *Smith* (1980) 255 E.G. 699.

[79] Provided it falls within the rateable value limits, which it may not do if substantial amounts of land are let.

[80] *Metropolitan Properties Co. (F.G.C.) Ltd.* v. *Barder* [1968] 1 All E.R. 536; *Jelley* v. *Buckman* [1973] 3 All E.R. 853.

[81] *Feyereisel* v. *Turnidge* [1952] 2 Q.B. 29; *Whiteley* v. *Wilson* [1953] 1 Q.B. 77; *Horford Investments Ltd.* v. *Lambert* [1974] 1 All E.R. 131.

purposes prevents it from being subject to a protected tenancy.[82]
Where the tenancy would be a regulated tenancy, but where it is also
within the ambit of the Landlord and Tenant Act 1954, Pt. II,[83] the
tenancy is treated as a business tenancy, protected under the 1954 Act
not under the Rent Act 1977.[84]

(c) Agricultural holdings occupied by the farmer

A tenancy is not a protected tenancy if the dwelling-house is
comprised in an agricultural holding (within the meaning of the
Agricultural Holdings Act 1986[85]) and is occupied by the person
responsible for the control (whether as a tenant or as an employee or
agent of the tenant) of the farming of the holding.[86] The object of the
exception is to exclude from protection dwelling-houses on farms,
which are generally subject to separate protection under the Agricultural Holdings Act 1986.[87] A sub-tenant of part of such premises will not
be protected either under the Rent Act 1977, as against the superior
landlord.[88]

(d) Public houses

A tenancy of a dwelling-house which consists of, or comprises,
premises licensed for the sale of intoxicating liquors for consumption
on the premises will not be a protected tenancy.[89]

(e) Parsonage houses

Where a dwelling-house belongs to an ecclesiastical benefice of the
Church of England for the occupation of the incumbent, the premises,
if let to a tenant, are outside the scope of the Rent Act 1977. This is
because they are subject to their own system of control under the
Pluralities Act 1838 and the Rent Act 1977 is excluded from
operation because it is in conflict with this earlier legislation.[90]
Dwelling-houses let to other ministers of religion may be subject to a
protected tenancy if they come within the Rent Act 1977, ss.1 and 4.[91]

---

[82] A letting of premises for the purpose of sub-letting is not a letting for business purposes: *Carter* v.
   S.U. Carburettor Co. [1942] 2 K.B. 288.
[83] *Post*, Chap. 20.
[84] R.A. 1977, s.24(3); *post*.
[85] *Post*, Chap. 25.
[86] R.A. 1977, s.10.
[87] *Post*, Chaps. 25, 26.
[88] R.A. 1977, s.137; *Sherwood* v. *Moody* [1952] 1 All E.R. 389; *Maunsell* v. *Olins* [1975] 1 All E.R.
   16.
[89] R.A. 1977, s.11.
[90] *Bishop of Gloucester* v. *Cunningham* [1943] 1 K.B. 101. The exception applies only to true
   parsonage houses: see *Worcester Diocesan Trust* v. *Taylor* (1947) 177 L.T. 581.
[91] But see R.A. 1977, Sched. 15, Case 15.

(f) Overcrowded or insanitary dwellings

The Rent Act 1977, s.101, provides that at any time when a dwelling-house, to which the section applies, is overcrowded within the meaning of the Housing Act 1985, Part X, in such circumstances as to render the occupier guilty of the offence of overcrowding, nothing in the Rent Act 1977, Pt. VII,[92] prevents the immediate landlord of the occupier from obtaining possession of the dwelling. The effect of this provision is to deprive the tenant of security of tenure[93] while the overcrowding lasts, but he is still protected in relation to rent.[94] The material time is the date of the hearing, so that if, before that date, the overcrowding has ceased, or the tenant has applied to the local authority for suitable alternative accommodation (a wise tactic for tenants fearing a loss of security of tenure on this ground), or the local authority has licensed the overcrowding,[95] there will be no jurisdiction to make an order for possession[96]

The landlord commits the offence[97] if the premises become overcrowded, and he then permits them to be used, having been served with an overcrowding notice by the local authority. If such a notice is served, the landlord is under an obligation to bring the tenancy to an end, if he is able to do so, and to take proceedings for possession. If there is no way of bringing the contractual tenancy to an end,[98] then no offence will be committed by the landlord. The tenant may, however, be committing an offence both during and after the contractual tenancy.[99] That offence is of occupying premises which are overcrowded, although in practice it is rarely prosecuted.

Overcrowding is defined in the Housing Act 1985.[1] Premises are overcrowded when the number of persons sleeping in them is *either* such that any two of those persons, being 10 years old or more and of opposite sexes, and not being persons living together as husband and wife, must sleep in the same room, *or* is in excess of the permitted number of occupants, taking account of the number of rooms in the premises and their floor areas.

Similar principles apply in the case of unfit premises, in respect of which a closing order[2] or demolition order has been made.[3] The only difference is that to avoid committing the offence, the landlord is not obliged to serve a notice to quit. At the end of the contractual period

[92] *Post*, Chap. 13.
[93] *Post*, Chap. 13.
[94] *Post*, Chap. 11.
[95] H.A. 1985, ss.328, 329.
[96] *Zbytniewski* v. *Broughton* [1956] 2 Q.B. 673.
[97] H.A. 1985, s.331.
[98] *e.g.* because it is a fixed term letting.
[99] H.A. 1985, s.327(1).
[1] H.A. 1985, ss.325, 326.
[2] H.A. 1985, s.276; *Marela* v. *Machorowski* [1953] 1 Q.B. 565; *F.W.R. Leaseholders* v. *Childs* (1962) 102 S.J. 307; *Buswell* v. *Goodwin* [1971] 1 All E.R. 418.
[3] H.A. 1985, s.270(3).

of the tenancy it is sufficient for him simply to withdraw his permission for the tenant to remain.

(2) *The Status of the Landlord*

(a) Crown property

The Rent Act 1977, s.13, as amended by the Housing Act 1980, s.73, provides that a tenancy is not a protected tenancy at any time when the interest of the landlord under the tenancy belongs to the Crown, or a government department, or is held in trust for the Crown for the purposes of a government department, unless the landlord's interest is vested in the Crown Estate Commissioners. A tenancy excluded from protection by this provision is not protected while the Crown interest subsists. If the reversion is transferred to a private individual, the tenancy will become protected, and if a Crown tenant sub-lets the whole or part of the dwelling-house, the sub-tenant will also be protected. A person cannot be a statutory tenant if the interest of his immediate landlord belongs to the Crown[4]

(b) Houses let by an exempt body

The Rent Act 1977, ss.14–16, provide that tenancies granted by a number of public and quasi-public bodies will not be protected tenancies. The most important of these are tenancies granted by local authorities[5] and housing associations.[6] They are discussed later.[7]

(c) Dwelling-house let by a resident landlord[8]

A tenancy will not be a protected tenancy if it was granted on or after August 14, 1974[9] by a landlord who is resident in the premises.[10] For the exemption to operate the dwelling-house must form part only of a building and, except where the dwelling itself also forms part of a flat, the building must not be a purpose-built block of flats.[11] A

---

[4] R.A. 1977, s.131 (b). The protection granted to tenants of the Crown Estate Commissioners is not retrospective: *Crown Estate Commissioners* v. *Wordsworth* (1982) 44 P. & C.R. 302.

[5] R.A. 1977, s.14.

[6] *Ibid.* s.15.

[7] See *post*, Chaps. 16 and 17.

[8] See comments on R.A. 1977, s.12, in Farrand, *The Rent Act 1977*.

[9] The commencement date of the R.A. 1974.

[10] R.A. 1977, s.12, as amended by Housing Act 1980, s.63. A furnished tenant, who would on August 14, 1974, have become a protected tenant, did not do so where there was a resident landlord. This provision does not apply to unfurnished tenancies which were in operation before this date, so, for this purpose, the distinction between a furnished and an unfurnished tenancy remains material: R.A. 1977, Sched. 24, paras. 6 & 7; *Christophides* v. *Cumming* (1976) 239 E.G. 275; *Mann* v. *Cornella* (1980) 254 E.G. 403. By the Rent (Agriculture) Act 1976, Sched. 9, paras. 1 & 2, a licence or tenancy created before or after January 1, 1979, will not become a protected occupancy where there is a resident landlord.

[11] R.A. 1977, s.12(1)(*a*).

"purpose-built" block is defined as a building which, as constructed, contained and still contains two or more flats. A flat is a dwelling-house which forms part only of a building and is separated horizontally from another dwelling-house which forms part of the same building.[12] The circumstances normally covered by the exemption are where a two or three storey dwelling-house constructed as a single dwelling, is divided into two or more flats and the landlord resides in one flat.[13] In each case it is a question of fact. A landlord living in an extension structurally tied to a house, but with no internal communication between the house and the extension, has been held not to be living in part of the same building, and so does not come within the exception.[14]

The exception can operate only if the tenancy was granted by a person who, at the time he granted it, occupied as his residence another dwelling-house in the same building or flat.[15] Residential occupation of the landlord for this purpose is defined as being subject to the same conditions as are necessary to keep a statutory tenancy[16] in being.[17] Broadly speaking these are personal residence by the tenant himself, although periods of absence, where there is an intention of returning coupled with physical manifestations of retention of possession, are permissible. Constructive residence, except through wives, is insufficient. On the other hand, a tenant is not prevented from being a statutory tenant by having two homes, even where there is only a small amount of residence in the dwelling in issue.[18]

The difficulty about applying these criteria to resident landlords is that, in relation to their application to tenants, the courts have generally been willing to extend the residence requirements to preserve a statutory tenancy, but under section 12 the same tests must be used to justify an exception to protection. It is not clear whether the statutory provision that the analogy is to be applied only "so far as the nature of the case allows"[19] covers the matter, since it is unlikely these words would enable a court to avoid applying the main principles evolved for statutory tenants.

Generally speaking the tenancy will only be exempt from protection if, at all times since the tenancy was granted, the interest of the landlord has belonged to a person who satisfies the residence rules.[20] The requirement is relaxed in specified cases by the Rent Act 1977,

[12] *Ibid.* Sched. 2, para. 4.
[13] *Barnes* v. *Gorsuch* (1982) 43 P. & C.R. 294.
[14] *Bardrick* v. *Haycock* (1976) 31 P. & C.R. 420; *cf. Griffiths* v. *English* (1982) 261 E.G. 257 (tenant living in extension but regarded as one building).
[15] R.A. 1977, s.12(1)(*b*), as amended by Housing Act 1980, s.65 (1). Joint landlords need not all be resident for the exception to operate: *Cooper* v. *Tait* (1984) 271 E.G. 105.
[16] *Post*, Chap. 10(III).
[17] R.A. 1977, Sched. 2, para. 5.
[18] *Bevington* v. *Crawford* (1974) 232 E.G. 191.
[19] R.A. 1977, Sched. 2, para. 5.
[20] *ibid.* s.12(1)(*c*) as amended by Housing Act 1980, s.65(1).

s.12(2), and certain gaps in residence will not prevent the exception operating, although during such gaps possession cannot be recovered except under the rules which govern recovery of possession for regulated tenancies.[21]

Section 12(2)[22] provides that the exception will not operate where the tenancy is granted to a person who, immediately before it was granted, was a protected or statutory[23] tenant of the same dwelling-house or of any other dwelling-house in the same building. A landlord cannot, therefore, benefit from the exception by offering the tenant a different flat in the same premises.

So long as the tenancy is precluded from being a protected tenancy by virtue of the resident landlord exception, the tenancy is treated as a "restricted contract," and these tenancies constitute the major group subject to the jurisdiction of rent assessment committees, sitting as rent tribunals.[24]

Certain gaps in the landlord's residence will not prevent the exceptions from operating. This is to enable a transfer of ownership in the building to take place where the new owner wishes to take up residence. A period of 28 days may be disregarded, beginning on the date when the landlord's interest vests without his becoming resident on that date.[25] The landlord during the 28 days may give written notice to his tenants extending this period for up to six months.[26] A gap of two years in residence may be disregarded where the interest of the landlord becomes vested in his personal representatives.[27] This enables the exception to remain open following the death of the landlord during the period while his estate is being administered.[28] It will, in any event, be rare for a successor to want to go into residence anyway, since he will frequently already have his own house. If he does not go into residence, the tenant is irremovable by the successor (though not, of course, by the personal representatives[29]), and the house cannot be sold with vacant possession, unless the new owner can claim possession under the Rent Act 1977, Sched. 15, Cases 11 and 12.[30] If the property is vested in a beneficiary, and he takes up residence, then the resident landlord exception again applies.[31]

---

[21] *Post*, R.A. 1977, Sched. 2, paras. 1 & 3 as amended by Housing Act 1980, s.65(2).

[22] As substituted by Housing Act 1980, s.69(4).

[23] *Post*, Chap. 14.

[24] Housing Act 1980, s.72.

[25] R.A. 1977, Sched. 2, para. 1(*a*), as amended by Housing Act 1980, s.65(3).

[26] *Ibid*. Sched. 2, para. 1(*b*), as amended by Housing Act 1980, s.65(3).

[27] *ibid*. Sched. 2, para. 1(*c*), as amended by Housing Act 1980, s.65(3).

[28] In the case of a pre-28 November, 1980 tenancy, the notice to quit may be referred to a rent tribunal, who may suspend its operation beyond the 2 years period, effectively giving the tenant a protected tenancy, see Chap. 14(I) *post*, and *Williams* v. *Mate* (1983) 46 P. & C.R. 43.

[29] R.A. 1977, Sched. 2, para 2; H.A. 1980, s.65(5), (7).

[30] Housing Act 1980, s.65 and Sched. 7; *post*, Chap. 13.

[31] As in *Beebe* v. *Mason* (1980) 254 E.G. 987 (failure to execute assent irrelevant in circumstances).

(d) Tenancies granted by educational institutions

A tenancy is not protected if it is granted to a person who is pursuing or intends to pursue a course of study provided by certain specified educational institutions, and the tenancy is granted either by that institution or by another specified institution or body.[32] The specified institutions are all universities or other colleges of further education, together with certain foundations specifically established to provide accommodation for students.[33]

(e) Tenants sharing with landlords[34]

Most cases of sharing with landlords will be covered by the rules governing resident landlords discussed in (c) above. However, not all cases of sharing[35] will fall within the rules of the resident landlord exception. The Rent Act 1977, s.21, therefore applies where a tenant is in exclusive occupation of part of his accommodation and shares other living accommodation with his landlord. In this circumstance, the tenancy will not be a protected tenancy.[36] The material time to discover whether in fact the tenant shares accommodation with his landlord is the time when the action for possession is commenced.[37]

(f) Assured tenancies

Assured tenancies were created by the Housing Act 1980, s.56 and, while not expressly excluded from being restricted contracts,[38] are exempt from protected tenancy status.[39] A tenancy will be assured if it would, when created, have been a protected tenancy or a housing association tenancy[40] and the following conditions were satisfied[41]:

(i) the interest of the landlord has, since the creation of the tenancy, belonged to a body approved by order of the Secretary of State[42]; and

---

[32] R.A. 1977, s.8.

[33] See the Protected Tenancies (Exceptions) Regulations 1974 (S.I. 1974 No. 1336), as amended by S.I. 1975 No. 1054, reg. 4(5); Protected Tenancies (Further Exceptions) Regulations 1976 (S.I. 1976 No. 905); both continued in force by R.A. 1977, s.22. The letting of premises for sub-occupation by students, so that the letting is not as a separate dwelling and is thus outside protection (see *St. Catherine's College* v. *Dorling* [1980] 1 W.L.R. 66), may be a letting within the business tenancy code under the Landlord and Tenant Act 1954, Pt. II: *Groveside Properties Ltd.* v. *Westminster Medical School* (1984) 47 P. & C.R. 507.

[34] *cf. ante,* the discussion of R.A. 1977, s.22.

[35] For an explanation of sharing see *ante,* on the definition of "separate dwelling."

[36] Although it will be a restricted contract; *post,* Chap. 14.

[37] *Tovey* v. *Tyack* [1955] 1 Q.B. 57.

[38] See *post,* Chap. 14, *cf. Lambeth B.C.* v. *Udechuka* (1980) 41 P. & C.R. 200, as to the possible significance of this.

[39] R.A. 1977, s.16A.

[40] *i.e.* falling within R.A. 1977, s.86, see *post,* Chap. 17.

[41] Housing Act 1980, s.56(3).

[42] *Ibid.* s.56 (4). Bodies are approved by statutory instrument and include building societies, pension funds, housing associations, and similar investment bodies.

(ii) the dwelling-house is, or is part of, a building which was erected, and on which construction work first began, after August 8, 1980; and

(iii) before the tenant first occupied the dwelling-house under the tenancy, no part of it had been occupied by any person as his residence except under an assured tenancy; and

(iv) the landlord did not, before the tenancy was granted, give the tenant a valid notice, in the prescribed form, stating that the tenancy is to be a protected or housing association tenancy.[43]

(3) *The Terms of the Tenancy*

(a) Tenancies at a low rent

A tenancy at a low rent is not a protected tenancy if no rent is payable under the tenancy at all or the rent payable is less than two thirds of the rateable value,[44] although such tenancies may enjoy the benefit of the provisions of Part 1 of the Landlord and Tenant Act 1954 and/or the Leasehold Reform Act 1967.[45] For this purpose the letting will not qualify for protection if the rent is less than two-thirds of the rateable value *on the appropriate day*, as determined in accordance with section 25 of the 1977 Act[46]; it is *not* the rateable value on the date of the letting. The assessment of whether the tenancy is at a low rent must be made in accordance with the facts as they are at the date the issue is raised.[47] Thus, a tenancy can move into and out of the ambit of protection according to fluctuations in the rent payable,[48] though not for variations in rateable values, since this part of the ratio is fixed at a particular date, *i.e.* the appropriate day.

Rent, in this context, means the total sum the tenant is obliged to pay, not the amount received by the landlord after payment of rates and taxes.[49] The Act does not actually define rent, and this might pose a difficulty with regard to service charges. Such charges usually fluctuate with the actual cost of the services provided by the landlord.

---

[43] Housing Act 1980, s.56(6), (7). Assured tenancies are discussed in more detail *post*, Chap. 14(IV).

[44] R.A. 1977, s.5(1). See *Barnes* v. *Barratt* [1970] 2 All E.R. 483, and the discussion of "rent" *supra*, Chap. 5.

[45] *Post*, Chap. 15.

[46] Explained *ante*, B. There are special provisions relating to tenancies which became protected tenancies, or would but for their low rent have become protected tenancies, by virtue of H.A. 1980, s.73 (tenants of Crown Estate Commissioners *etc.*). In such cases, s.5 of the 1977 Act applies as if, in relation to the dwelling house in question, the appropriate day was 28th November 1980: H.A. 1980, Sched. 25, para. 75.

[47] *J. & F. Stone Lighting and Radio Ltd.* v. *Levitt* [1947] A.C. 209.

[48] *Mackworth* v. *Hellard* [1921] 2 K.B. 755; *Woozley* v. *Woodall Smith* [1949] 2 All E.R. 1055; *Sidney Trading Co.* v. *Finsbury Borough Council* [1952] 1 All E.R. 460.

[49] *Mackworth* v. *Hellard* [1921] 2 K.B. 755; *Sidney Trading Co. Ltd.* v. *Finsbury Borough Council*, *supra*. It may even include a premium, where it can be established that the premium is really commuted rent: *Samrose Properties Ltd.* v. *Gibbard* [1958] 1 W.L.R. 235.

If such charges are regarded as part of the rent, and such decisions as have been given on the meaning of "rent" in section 5(1) of the Act would seem to indicate that they should be so regarded,[50] then variations in the service charges (these days, usually upwards) are likely to bring some tenancies, formerly outside the Act, into protection. In the case of long tenancies[51] certain service charges are, however, to be disregarded under section 5(4). These sums, expressed in the lease to be payable as such, "in respect of rates, services, repairs, maintenance, or insurance."

(b) Lettings with board or attendance

The Rent Act 1977, s.7(1), provides that a tenancy is not protected if the dwelling is let, bona fide, at a rent which includes payment in respect of board or attendance. Section 7(2) enacts that this requirement cannot be met unless the amount of rent fairly attributable to attendance (though not board, which is not mentioned in the sub-section) forms a substantial part of the whole rent, having regard to the value of the attendance to the tenant. The dwelling must be "*bona fide* let," which means that sham transactions are excluded (for example where the tenancy makes reference to board and attendance which is not, in fact, provided).[52]

Viscount Simon, in *Palser* v. *Grinling* explained attendance thus[53]:

> "It means service personal to the tenant performed by an attendant provided by the landlord in accordance with his covenant for the benefit or convenience of the individual tenant in his use or enjoyment of the demised premises. 'Service' is a wider word than attendance. Attendance, being personal in its nature, may be dispensed with by an individual tenant at his pleasure, though it is not on that account excluded from what the tenant pays for when the landlord has covenanted to supply it. But services common to others (*e.g.* the heating of a communal water supply, or the cleaning of passages, hall, etc., outside the demised premises) will not constitute attendance. It follows from the above that a landlord's covenant to supply someone to carry up coals to a flat or to carry down refuse from the flat is a covenant to provide attendance. Similarly, the provision of a house-maid or valet to discharge duties in connection with the flat would be the provision of attendance, but a covenant by the

---

[50] The fact that specific service charges are to be ignored in "long leases" under s.5(4) would also seem to indicate that, but for the specific exclusion, service charges are to be treated as "rent" for the purposes of s.5(1).

[51] Defined in R.A. 1977, s.5(5) as tenancies granted for terms exceeding 21 years with no "break" clause permitting earlier termination.

[52] See, *e.g. Palser* v. *Grinling* [1948] A.C. 291, *per* Viscount Simon at p. 310.

[53] *Ibid.*

landlord to provide a resident porter or housekeeper for a block of flats would not."

"Board" is not defined in the Rent Act 1977, but it would not seem to involve provision of full meals, merely of sufficient food to exclude the *de minimis* principle or to avoid the allegation that the transaction is a sham.[54]

For the purposes of section 7, "rent" means the total amount of money paid under the letting. The payments in respect of board or attendance must be part of the rent and not merely a collateral contract, but the mere fact that separate payments in respect of each item are provided for and they are not inclusive in the rental figure is not fatal. The question is whether the payments are genuinely part of the rent.[55]

The Rent Act 1977, s.7(2), which applies only in the case of attendance, introduces restrictions on the meaning of "bona fide let": the amount of rent must be "fairly attributable to attendance"; regard must be paid "to the value of the attendance to the tenant"; and the amount of rent so attributed and regarded must form "a substantial part of the whole rent." The matters to be determined here are essentially questions of fact, but some guidance on the provisions was given by Viscount Simon in *Palser* v. *Grinling*[56]:

"Now comes the question of how to arrive at 'the amount of rent which is fairly attributable to attendance . . . regard being had to the value of the same to the tenant . . .' A question of some difficulty arises as to the meaning of the 'tenant'—does the expression refer to the particular individual whose lease is in question, or does it refer to the average or normal tenant of that class of property? I think the phrase refers to the actual tenant whose lease is under examination. . . . It is the value to him . . . which must be taken into account. But in taking this view, it is of the utmost importance to observe that 'regard shall be had' to the value to the tenant, and not that the value to such tenant is to govern the calculation absolutely. . . . In the present case the direction that regard is to be had to the value to the tenant, i.e., that such value must not be overlooked but must be suitably allowed for, is made clear by the main direction that the amount of rent is to be such as 'is fairly attributable to' the item in question. Other factors have to be duly weighed and allowed for. In some cases the parties to the lease may themselves have placed a value upon various elements which enter into the total rent.

---

[54] *Wilkes* v. *Goodwin* [1923] 2 K.B. 86.
[55] *Property Holding Co. Ltd.* v. *Clark* [1948] 1 K.B. 360; *Artillery Mansions* v. *Macartney* [1949] 1 K.B. 164; *Alliance Property Co. Ltd.* v. *Shaffer* [1949] 1 K.B. 367.
[56] [1948] A.C. 291 at pp. 314–318.

Even so, the statement of these respective values in the lease is not a conclusive distribution, though it may be strong evidence of what the proper distribution would be. Nevertheless, the amount to be arrived at is the amount which is 'fairly attributable' to the item, not the amount which is actually attributed to it in the lease . . .

A number of factors may be relevant in arriving at the proper figure. The governing consideration is the word 'fairly.' The questions involved are to be answered by commonsense considerations rather than by any formula which can be laid down by this House.

What does 'substantial portion' mean? It is plain that the phrase requires a comparison with the whole rent, and the whole rent means the entire contractual rent payable by the tenant in return for the occupation of the premises together with all the other covenants of the landlord. 'Substantial' in this context is not the same as 'not unsubstantial,' i.e. just enough to avoid the *de minimis* principle. One of the primary meanings of the word is equivalent to considerable, solid or big . . . Applying the word in this sense, it must be left to the discretion of the judge of fact to decide as best he can according to the circumstances in each case, the onus being on the landlord . . . To say that everything over 20 per cent[57] of the whole rent should be regarded as a substantial portion of that rent would be to play the part of a legislator: if Parliament thinks fit to amend the statute by fixing percentages, Parliament will do so."

This approach was reinforced by the Court of Appeal in *Woodward* v. *Docherty*,[58] where it was stressed that the courts should also bear in mind changing social and economic conditions, such as shortage of housing. Although the case was concerned with furniture, the principles stated are equally applicable to attendance. The question is essentially one of valuation.[59]

(c) Holiday homes[60]

The Rent Act 1977, s.9, exempts from protected tenancy status a dwelling let for the purpose of holiday occupation. This provision has undoubtedly encouraged landlords to let premises, ostensibly for a holiday, in such unlikely places as Walsall and Scunthorpe, simply to avoid the protection of the Act. The general principles for distinguish-

---

[57] The figure settled on by the Court of Appeal.
[58] [1974] 2 All E.R. 844; *Mann* v. *Cornella* (1980) 254 E.G. 403. See also the discussion of *Marchant* v. *Charters* [1977] 3 All E.R. 918, *supra,* Chap. 2.
[59] See Megarry, *The Rent Acts* (10th ed.), p. 149.
[60] See Lyons [1984] Conv. 286.

ing between genuine and sham transactions discussed in Chapter 2 of this book have equal application here.[61]

In *Kemp* v. *Cunningham*[62] a county court judge dismissed the landlord's claim under what is now section 7 when it was pleaded that the tenants had no other home. They had, with the landlord's consent, moved their own furniture into the premises and the location of the premises (Baron's Court) was not noted as a holiday area. Notwithstanding the statement in the tenancy agreement that it was for holiday purposes, the court gave the tenancy full protected status.

In *Buchmann* v. *May*[63] a landlord had let a house to a tenant and his wife (who were resident in England on visitors' permits) by a series of short-term furnished tenancies. The wife eventually signed, without reading, a tenancy agreement granting her a tenancy for three months containing the following: "It is mutually agreed and declared that the letting hereby made is solely for the purpose of the tenant's holiday in the London area." At the end of the tenancy she refused to vacate, claiming that she was a protected tenant. The Court of Appeal held that the purpose of the tenancy was to be deduced from the written agreement, unless this was a sham. The court would be astute to detect a sham where it appeared in the context of the Rent Acts, but the burden was on the tenant to prove it and that burden had not been discharged in the present case. The tenant was a visitor from overseas, whose permit would expire at the end of the year, and she had told the landlord that her stay would be for two months or just over. The Court also indicated that in the absence of a statutory definition of "holiday," the dictionary definition of "a period of cessation from work or a period of recreation" would be a workable definition if not too narrowly construed. In *R.* v. *Rent Officer for London Borough of Camden, ex p. Plant*[64] the rent officer refused to hold a hearing on the plaintiffs' application for registration of a fair rent because he took the view that the county court should determine the status of the tenancy, which was expressed to be for a holiday. In fact the tenants and fellow occupants were student nurses and all parties were aware of the occupants' permanency. The court took the view that since the landlord knew that the tenants did not require the premises for the purposes of a holiday, he had in fact, by requiring the tenants to put their names to an agreement purporting to be a holiday letting, put a "false label" on the letting, regardless of how willingly or voluntarily the parties had entered into it. In fact, in this case, the tenancy in question was a renewal of an earlier holiday letting. Certainly, any knowledge that the landlord has acquired as to the true purpose of the occupation during the first letting, will be admissible in evidence as to

---

[61] See [1975] L.A.G.Bull 100.
[62] [1975] L.A.G.Bull 192.
[63] [1978] 2 All E.R. 993. See also *McHale* v. *Daneham* (1979) 249 E.G. 969.
[64] (1981) 257 E.G. 713.

the sham nature of a subsequent letting or renewal. The burden of proof is on the tenant to rebut the prima facie evidence of the declaration in the written agreement that the letting is for holiday purposes. The tenant will therefore have to show that the landlord knew, or must be taken to have known, that the tenant was not on holiday and in this regard, knowledge gained from an earlier letting will be relevant. Once a sham is established, however, nothing further will be necessary for the court to disregard the false label attached to the letting.

(d) Tenancies exempt by ministerial order

The Rent Act 1977, s.143, empowers the Secretary of State to exempt, by reference to rateable value limits, certain dwellings from rent regulation if he is satisfied that, in the whole area to which his order relates, there is not scarcity. As one commentator has observed[65]: "Since this power has never been exercised perhaps it may be assumed that scarcity persists everywhere." Section 144 empowers the Secretary of State to release from certain restricted contract provisions[66] certain dwellings, by reference to their rateable values. Since the power does not apply to the most important group of restricted contracts[67] it will almost certainly remain unexercised.

III. THE STATUTORY TENANCY[68]

A. Nature

A statutory tenancy is not an interest in property, but a "status of irremoveability," or a personal right, conferred by the Rent Act 1977 to enable a tenant, whose tenancy has expired, to remain in possession of his dwelling.[69] A statutory tenancy cannot be assigned or transferred, except under the limited provisions of the Rent Act 1977, Sched. 1, para. 13.[70] A statutory tenancy cannot be disposed of by will and does not vest in the tenant's personal representatives,[71] unlike the contractual tenancy, on the termination of which the statutory

---

[65] Farrand, *The Rent Act 1977*, comment to section 143.
[66] *Post*, Chap. 14.
[67] Resident landlords and shared accommodation, *i.e.* R.A. 1977, ss.20 & 21.
[68] For a judicial view of the imprecise nature of the statutory tenancy see *Gofor Investments Ltd.* v. *Roberts* (1975) 29 P. & C.R. 366, *per* Lawton L.J. at p. 374. *cf.* Hand [1980] Conv. 351.
[69] See *Keeves* v. *Dean* [1924] 1 K.B. 685; *Thompson* v. *Ward* [1953] 2 Q.B. 153; *Atyeo* v. *Fardoe* (1978) 37 P. & C.R. 494. The right must be enjoyed by a "person" in the non-technical sense. Occupation by a company will not do. *cf. Feather Supplies* v. *Ingham* [1971] 2 Q.B. 348.
[70] *Post*, Chap. 12; *Maxted* v. *McAll* [1952] C.P.L. 185; *Atyeo* v. *Fardoe* (1978) 37 P. & C.R. 494.
[71] *Lovibond & Sons* v. *Vincent* [1929] 1 K.B. 687.

tenancy arises.[72] Similarly, a statutory tenancy cannot vest in a trustee in bankruptcy.[73] It cannot be sub-let as a whole, because the tenant has no estate out of which to create such an interest,[74] and because retention of possession of at least part of the dwelling is, as we shall see, essential to the maintenance by the tenant of his statutory tenancy. The mere sub-letting of part of the premises, however, does not necessarily remove protection from that part.[75]

The emphasis on personal occupation by the tenant enables him to defend or assert his right of occupation against unlawful interference. A statutory tenant can obtain damages for trespass or unlawful re-entry by the landlord[76] and an injunction to restrain a trespass or a threatened trespass.[77] If he loses his status as a statutory tenant, however, his right to maintain an action for trespass is also lost.[78] A statutory tenant can recover damages for breach of the covenant for quiet enjoyment.[79] and for unlawful eviction,[80] together with an order restoring him to possession in such circumstances.[81] However, he will not be able to claim protection against a person claiming by title paramount, if the contractual tenancy out of which the statutory tenancy arose would not be a protected tenancy.[82] So, if a mortgagee holds a charge and there is a clause in it whereby there are to be no tenancies granted or surrendered except with the written consent of the mortgagee, any tenancy granted by the mortgagor without such consent will not be binding on the mortgagee, and is not capable of being a protected or statutory tenancy within the Rent Act 1977.[83] However, the court can look behind the formal legal relationship of mortgagor and mortgagee and, should the mortgagee seek possession from the tenant, it will not be granted unless it is sought bona fide and reasonably, for the purpose of enforcing the security. Possession will not be granted where the mortgagee is simply doing the landlord a favour to enable him to circumvent the Rent Act.[84]

An important difference between a statutory tenancy and a contractual tenancy is that a statutory tenancy subsists only in relation to the dwelling-house, whereas a contractual tenancy of a house on land is a tenancy of the land to which the house is annexed. This means that if the house is destroyed, the statutory tenancy will

---

[72] *Lawrence* v. *Hartwell* [1946] K.B. 553.
[73] *Sutton* v. *Dorf* [1932] 2 K.B. 304.
[74] *Solomon* v. *Orwell* [1954] 1 W.L.R. 624.
[75] *Post.* Because a statutory tenancy is not an interest in property it has been suggested that the actual occupation of the tenant is not an overriding interest under the L.R.A. 1925, s.70(1)(*g*).
[76] *Cruise* v. *Terrell* [1922] 1 K.B. 664.
[77] *Maynard* v. *Maynard* [1969] 1 All E.R. 1.
[78] *Thompson* v. *Ward* [1953] 2 Q.B. 153.
[79] *Perera* v. *Vandijar* [1953] 1 W.L.R. 672; *supra*, Chap. 4.
[80] *Post*, Chap. 19.
[81] *Olidowura* v. *Fulmuk* [1975] C.L.Y. 1929.
[82] *Dudley & District Benefit Building Society* v. *Emerson* [1949] Ch. 707.
[83] *Ibid.* but *cf.* Smith (1977) 41 Conv. 197 and Chap. 3(II)D, *supra*.
[84] *Quennell* v. *Maltby* [1979] 1 All E.R. 568.

come to an end.[85] A contractual tenancy, on the other hand, will continue until determined, regardless of the condition of the premises,[86] unless the premises are flats.[87] The mere occurrence of damage rendering the house uninhabitable will not necessarily destroy the statutory tenancy unless the damage is so considerable that the house has substantially ceased to exist.[88] Presumably the statutory tenancy will also be lost, even when damage is not so substantial, if the tenant abandons the premises or fails to show the required *animus revertendi.*[89]

B. Commencement

When a protected tenancy has been brought to an end, either by the landlord or by effluxion of time,[90] the person who, immediately before the termination, was the protected tenant, becomes the statutory tenant if and so long as he occupies the house as his residence.[91] Where a protected tenancy is granted to joint tenants and one of them leaves the premises before the expiry of the contractual term, the tenant remaining on the premises is entitled to become a statutory tenant of the premises at the end of the contractual term.[92] So, a statutory tenancy comes into existence only if three conditions are satisfied: the tenant is holding over from a contractual tenancy which has terminated; the contractual tenancy was a protected tenancy when it terminated; and the tenant continues to occupy the house or flat as his residence.

(1) *Holding Over from a Contractual Tenancy*

No statutory tenancy can arise while a contractual tenancy remains in existence.[93] While the contractual tenancy continues, the rights and duties of the parties are governed by the terms and conditions of their agreement or by terms implied in their agreement by law, except in so far as such rights are affected by the tenant's status as a protected tenant. The statutory tenancy arises regardless of the consent of the

---

[85] *Ellis & Sons Amalgamated Properties* v. *Sisman* [1948] 1 K.B. 653; *Hemns* v. *Wheeler* [1948] 2 K.B. 61. See *Woodfall*, para. 3–0049.
[86] *Denman* v. *Brise* [1949] 1 K.B. 22. If, after the house has ceased to exist the contractual tenancy is determined, no statutory tenancy can arise because there is no house to which it can attach: *East End Dwellings Co. Ltd.* v. *Finsbury Borough Council* [1952] A.C. 109.
[87] See the discussion of the doctrine of frustration in relation to leases, *supra*, Chap. 5.
[88] *Morleys (Birmingham) Ltd.* v. *Slater* [1950] 1 K.B. 506.
[89] *Post.*
[90] *Supra*, Chap. 8.
[91] R.A. 1977, s.2(1)(*a*).
[92] *Lloyd* v. *Sadler* [1978] 2 W.L.R. 721.
[93] *Strutt* v. *Panter* [1953] 1 Q.B. 397, *per* Evershed M.R. at p. 399. But see R.A. 1977, Sched. 1.

landlord, whose common law rights are curtailed by the Rent Act 1977. This has affected the attitude taken by the courts to the relationship between contractual and statutory tenancies, and has led to tight control of the circumstances in which a holding over will give rise to a statutory tenancy.

No inference of a new contractual tenancy will be made from the payment and acceptance of rent at the end of the contractual period,[94] because in the case of a protected tenancy the landlord has no choice but to continue to accept rent by virtue of the Rent Act 1977.[95] The prior protected tenancy must have been lawful, and not void for illegality, or voidable on the ground of some other vitiating factor.[96] For a statutory tenancy to arise, the contractual tenancy must have remained vested in the person who holds over at the moment of its determination. Consequently, if at that time the contractual tenancy has become vested in another person (*e.g.* the tenant's trustee in bankruptcy), the continued occupation of the person who had been the contractual tenant cannot give rise to a statutory tenancy.[97]

(2) *Determination of the Contractual Tenancy*

Apart from certain very limited circumstances,[98] the mode by which a contractual tenancy comes to an end is immaterial, since the purpose of the Rent Act 1977, s.2, is to confer a statutory tenancy on a contractual tenant whose tenancy has determined. So, for example, a tenant whose contractual tenancy has terminated by forfeiture for breach of an obligation, will become a statutory tenant, even though the breach may give the landlord a ground for possession under the Rent Act.[99] The object of the Act is to ensure that possession will be granted only to a landlord who satisfies the conditions for recovery of possession.[1] The onus of proof is on the party who asserts that a statutory tenancy has arisen to show not only that the contractual tenancy has terminated, but that the tenant is holding over from it.[2] The determination of the contractual tenancy is largely a question of fact,[3] but it may involve such questions of law as, for example, the

---

[94] As would be the case at common law: *supra,* Chap. 2.
[95] *Morrison* v. *Jacobs* [1945] K.B. 577.
[96] *cf. Solle* v. *Butcher* [1950] 1 K.B. 671; *Grist* v. *Bailey* [1966] 2 All E.R. 875.
[97] *Smalley* v. *Quarrier* [1975] 2 All E.R. 688.
[98] *e.g.* surrender, disclaimer and merger.
[99] *Tideway Investment and Property Holdings Ltd.* v. *Wellwood* [1952] Ch. 791 at p. 818.
[1] R.A. 1977, s.98; *post,* Chap. 13.
[2] *Mount* v. *Childs* (1948) 64 T.L.R. 559.
[3] See *Smalley* v. *Quarrier* [1975] 2 All E.R. 688, *per* Sir John Pennycuick at pp. 694–695.

validity of notices to quit,[4] the capacity to forfeit and whether waiver has occurred, and compliance with general statutory provisions.[5]

For a statutory tenancy to arise the contractual tenancy must have been a protected tenancy at the moment of its determination.[6] It is necessary, therefore, as *at that moment* to consider whether the contractual tenancy was within the financial and other requirements of the Rent Act 1977, ss.1 and 4.[7] Any holding over from a tenancy which does not meet the requirements for protection or which is an excepted tenancy, will not create a statutory tenancy. Since it is the moment of termination of the contractual tenancy that is important, cases have held, transitional provisions aside,[8] that a statutory tenancy will arise where a tenant has held over from an unprotected tenancy until a new Act conferred protection, even though at the time the action commenced the tenancy was unprotected,[9] although recent Court of Appeal qualification to this principle suggests that this matter must be governed by the express wording of the legislation making the operation of the Act retrospective[10]

(3) *The Tenant Continues to Occupy the Dwelling-House as his Residence*

The requirement[11] of continued occupation is essentially a question of fact,[12] although the courts have attempted to formulate some rules of guidance as to how the evidence should be assessed. Since a statutory tenancy is a personal right conferred by the Rent Act to enable a tenant to remain in his dwelling, it can be enjoyed only by a tenant who continues to reside there from the moment his contractual tenancy ends and who, should he go away for a period of temporary absence, intends to return.[13]

The legal personality of some tenants may render them incapable of residing and thus of becoming statutory tenants. This is especially true of limited liability companies, who cannot plead vicarious residence for this purpose.[14] The question may also arise whether the

---

[4] *Post*, Chap. 13.

[5] *e.g.* the Common Law Procedure Act 1852, ss.210–212; L.P.A. 1925, s.146. See *supra*, Chaps. 5, 6 & 8.

[6] R.A. 1977, s.2(1)(*a*).

[7] *Supra.*

[8] See R.A. 1977, Sched. 24, para. 7.

[9] *Remon* v. *City of London Real Property Co. Ltd.* [1921] 1 K.B. 49; *Hutchinson* v. *Jauncey* [1950] 1 K.B. 574.

[10] *Harrison* v. *London Borough of Hammersmith & Fulham* [1981] 1 W.L.R. 650.

[11] Defined in R.A. 1977, s.2 (3).

[12] *Gofor Investments Ltd.* v. *Roberts* (1975) 29 P. & C.R. 366, *per* Lawton L.J. at pp. 373–374.

[13] *Skinner* v. *Geary* [1931] 2 K.B. 546, *per* Scrutton L.J. at pp. 561–562.

[14] *Hiller* v. *United Dairies (London) Ltd.* [1934] 1 K.B. 57; *Firstcross Ltd.* v. *East West Ltd.* (1980) 255 E.G. 355; the letting to the company may be a sham, so that it is then the individual who is the tenant; *cf. Tetragon Ltd.* v. *Shidasb Construction Co. Ltd.* (1981) 7 H.L.R. 113.

premises themselves have retained their residential character, or still come within the requirements of being let as a separate dwelling. This is particularly a problem with premises let for mixed user; if the residential user has ceased by the time the contractual tenancy determines, no statutory tenancy arises.[15]

If the tenant has sub-let the whole of the premises, then clearly he will not be in possession of them at the time the contractual tenancy comes to an end and there will be no statutory tenancy.[16] The position where only part of the premises has been sub-let is rather more complicated. In *Crowhurst* v. *Maidment*[17] it was held that if a tenant sub-lets parts of his dwelling-house which he has never occupied and never intends to occupy, then he loses his statutory protection in respect of those parts. In *Berkeley* v. *Papadoyannis*,[18] however, the Court of Appeal decided that sub-letting part would deprive the tenant of his statutory tenancy only where he had positively and clearly decided never to re-occupy the parts sub-let. If he merely suspends his decision on the matter until the sub-tenant vacates, he can still argue for his statutory tenancy of that part.[19]

The requirement of continuous residence will not be infringed if a tenant is temporarily absent from his dwelling, provided he shows an intention of resuming occupation on his return.[20] Absence abroad on business or for the education of the children of the family,[21] or absence during a long illness,[22] will not be sufficient to defeat the evidence of residence, providing the tenant can show a clear intention to return to the premises. Where, however, primary use as a residence has ceased and the tenant normally resides elsewhere, returning only occasionally to his former residence as a temporary expedient, statutory residence ceases.[23] At the end of the day the question will be decided by the weight the judge attaches to the tenant's evidence of that intention.

Ceasing to reside in the premises because of their bad condition will not, of itself, justify a claim to be a statutory tenant, but absence due to a sudden calamity (such as burst water pipes) will not result in a loss of the statutory tenancy, so long as the intention to return as soon as possible can be shown.[24] A statutory tenancy can still arise even if

---

[15] *John M.Brown Ltd.* v. *Bestwick* [1951] 1 K.B. 21.
[16] *Haskins* v. *Lewis* [1931] 2 K.B. 1; *Horford Investments Ltd.* v. *Lambert* [1974] 1 All E.R. 131, *per* Scarman L.J. at p. 139.
[17] [1953] 1 Q.B. 23.
[18] [1954] 2 Q.B. 149.
[19] *Regalian Securities* v. *Ramsden* [1981] 1 W.L.R. 611.
[20] *Brown* v. *Brash* [1948] 2 K.B. 247, *per* Asquith L.J. at pp. 254–255; *Skinner* v. *Geary* [1931] 2 K.B. 546; *Roland House Gardens Ltd.* v. *Cravitz* (1975) 29 P. & C.R. 432; see also the discussion of *Atyeo* v. *Fardoe* (1978) 37 P. & C.R. 494, *post*, Chap. 12, and *Richards* v. *Green* (1983) 11 H.L.R. 1.
[21] *Gofor Investments Ltd.* v. *Roberts* (1975) 23 P. & C.R. 366.
[22] *Regalian Securities Ltd* v. *Scheuer* (1982) 263 E.G. 973.
[23] *Tickner* v. *Hearn* [1960] 1 W.L.R. 1406.
[24] *Ibid. cf. Hoggett* v. *Hoggett* (1979) 39 P. & C.R. 121.

the tenant is deprived of his security of tenure by reason of overcrowding or a closing order.[25]

C. Terms and Conditions

The general provisions governing the terms and conditions of statutory tenancies are contained in the Rent Act 1977, s.3(1), which states that so long as the statutory tenant retains possession, he is to observe and be entitled to the benefit of all the terms and conditions of the original contract of tenancy,[26] so far as they are consistent with the provisions of the Rent Act 1977. So, a statutory tenant is entitled to the benefit of the implied covenant for quiet enjoyment,[27] repairing covenants, and covenants to supply services[28] and he must comply with his own covenants as to user, to repair and so on.[29] The main types of inconsistent terms and conditions are those which relate to rent, recovery of possession and covenants against assignment and sub-letting. A statutory tenant is liable to pay only the rent provided by the Rent Act 1977 and it is under that Act, rather than under a covenant in the lease, that a statutory tenant pays his rent. Terms requiring the tenant to give up possession at the end of his tenancy are clearly inconsistent with Rent Act protection and, since the statutory tenancy cannot be assigned or sub-let as a whole, provisions in the contract which deal with this are excluded. Options for purchase or for a further lease are likewise inconsistent.

D. Determination

A statutory tenancy determines if the court makes an order for possession.[30] Also, any unequivocal act by which the statutory tenant gives up possession to his landlord will bring the tenancy to an end. The tenant must here, however, comply with the Rent Act 1977, s.3 (3), which provides that a statutory tenant is entitled to give up possession if, and only if, he gives such notice to the landlord as would have been required under the original contract or, if no notice was required, on giving not less than three months notice.

Special provision is made by the Rent Act 1977, Sched. 1, para. 12, for payments demanded by statutory tenants either as a condition of giving up possession, or in payment for furniture or other articles. A

[25] *Bushford* v. *Falco* [1954] 1 W.L.R. 672.
[26] R.A. 1977, s.101(1) *supra, Zbytniewski* v. *Broughton* [1956] 2 Q.B. 673.
[27] See *Oxley* v. *Regional Properties Ltd.* [1944] 2 All E.R. 510; reversed on another point: [1945] A.C. 347.
[28] *Lavender* v. *Betts* (1942) 167 L.T. 70.
[29] *Engvall* v. *Ideal Flats Ltd.* [1945] K.B. 205.
[30] R.A. 1977, ss.98 & 99; *post*, Chap. 13.

statutory tenant who, as a condition of giving up possession, asks for or receives payment from anyone other than the landlord, is guilty of an offence and may be made to pay the money back. If the statutory tenant demands that furniture or effects be purchased as a condition of giving up possession, the person on whom the demand is made can request that the price be quoted in writing and, if it exceeds a reasonable price, the excess is treated in the same way as payments for giving up possession, with the same penalties.[31]

IV REGULATED TENANCIES

The system of rent regulation, introduced by the Rent Act 1965 and now contained in the Rent Act 1977, is discussed in detail in the next chapter. It embodies two separate features. First, it establishes rent limits, *i.e.* the maximum rent levels that a tenant can be required to pay at any given time. As a general principle, this will be either the contractual rent negotiated between the parties or a "fair rent" fixed by a rent officer or a rent assessment committee. Secondly, it establishes the criteria and procedures for fixing fair rents. Central to the understanding of both features, however, is the regulated tenancy. This will be either a protected tenancy or a statutory tenancy.[32] A tenancy falling within this definition is still regulated even though the rent for it is established solely by reference to the first feature described above, *i.e.* the rent has not actually been referred to a rent officer.

---

[31] See *Sheridan* v. *Dickson* [1970] 3 All E.R. 1049.
[32] R.A. 1977, s.18.

CHAPTER 11

RENT CONTROL

I. Introduction	413	B. Prohibition of Associated Payments	428
II. Rent Limits on New Grants	414	C. Permitted Premiums	430
A. No Previous Registered Rent	414	D. Rent Books	431
B. Previous Registered Rent	414	E. Accommodation Agencies Act 1953	432
III. Varying the Rent	416		
A. By Agreement	416		
B. By Obtaining a Registered Rent	418		
IV. Anti-avoidance Provisions	428		
A. Prohibited Premiums on Grants	428		

I. INTRODUCTION

The basic scheme of rent control for regulated tenancies is simple. On the grant of a new tenancy the parties can agree on whatever rent they choose if no rent has been registered for the property let. Either party is at liberty to refer the rent to the rent officer to determine a fair rent. In determining a fair rent, the rent officer has to have regard to the state of the property, its location and the terms of the tenancy, and has to disregard a number of specified factors. The most important factor to be disregarded is the distorting effect on market rentals that may be caused by demand exceeding supply for the particular type of tenanted property under consideration. The rent determined as fair is registered.

If there is dissatisfaction with the rent officer's decision, then either party can ask for the matter to be referred to the rent assessment committee, who will either determine a different fair rent, or confirm the rent officer's figure. Again the rent they fix will be registered. A rent, once registered, will govern the maximum that can be charged either in that tenancy or on the grant of a new one. A registered rent can be altered by further application to the rent officer. Increases in registered rents are generally phased over two years, and applications to reconsider the rent can only be made at intervals of two years. It is possible for the parties to agree to a cancellation of the registration, and its replacement by a formalised rent agreement.

If no rent is registered, then in the case of a protected, *i.e.* contractual, tenancy, it can be altered by a written agreement. This must state the tenant's rights to apply for a fair rent to be determined. If the contractual tenancy has been replaced by a statutory tenancy, then an application to the rent officer will generally be necessary before the rent is altered. Use of premiums to avoid the rent control provisions is prohibited.

II. RENT LIMITS ON NEW GRANTS

A. No Previous Registered Rent

There are no restrictions on the rent levels the parties may agree on the grant of a new tenancy to a new tenant. A new grant to an existing tenant, or someone who could succeed him as a statutory tenant,[1] has to observe certain formalities,[2] if the agreed rent is to be fully enforceable.[3] But if those formalities are observed, then again there is no limit on the rent the parties can agree.[4]

B. Previous Registered Rent

If there is an earlier, uncancelled registered rent, then that figure will control the maximum recoverable rent on any new tenancy.[5] The parties may agree on a higher rent·and quite often do, but the registered rent will be the maximum recoverable until it has been properly changed.[6] That the rent was registered a long time ago, or that both parties were totally ignorant of it, is irrelevant. Registered rents, like registered land charges, bind successive estate owners whether or not they have searched the registers.[7]

Where there is a difference in the property let, *e.g.* the subsequent letting comprises additional accommodation[8] or there is a material change in the particulars of the tenancy, *e.g.* it is a furnished letting[9] instead of an unfurnished one, then, it is submitted, the earlier registration will not apply. Substantial alterations and improvements may be sufficient to effect a substantial change in identity[10] of the property let, and enable one to argue that the registered rent does not

---

[1] R.A. 1977, s.51(1) (*b*).

[2] R.A. 1977, s.51(1)(4).

[3] R.A. 1977, s.54(2).

[4] But obviously if the tenant thinks he is paying too much he can apply to the rent officer.

[5] R.A. 1977, s.44(1).

[6] R.A. 1977, s.44(2).

[7] *Feather Supplies Ltd.* v. *Ingham* [1971] 2 Q.B. 348.

[8] *Langford Property Co. Ltd.* v. *Batten* [1951] A.C. 223 (addition of garage to letting of flat), and see *Gluchowska* v. *Tottenham Borough Council* [1954] 1 Q.B. 439 (later letting of part of controlled premises was outside original controlled rent).

[9] *cf. Metrobarn Ltd.* v. *Gehring* [1976] 1 W.L.R. 776; *Kent* v. *Millmead Properties* (1983) 266 E.G. 899.

[10] *Langford Property Co. Ltd.* v. *Batten* [1951] A.C. 223, and especially Lord Porter.

relate to the "dwelling-house" subsequently let. Minor changes in the terms of the letting do not have the same effect.

When the parties have agreed a rent in excess of a registered rent, then the excess is irrecoverable from the tenant,[11] irrespective of anything in any agreement. Furthermore, the tenant has a right to recover the excess over the old registered rent from the landlord up to two years after the date of payment.[12]

A prospective landlord faced with an out-of-date registration can apply for its cancellation provided that in most cases it is two years since the date the last registration took effect,[13] there is no current regulated tenancy and he would be landlord if the house were let.[14] If the prospective landlord wants to go one step further and find out what would be the fair or maximum recoverable rent, he can apply for a certificate of fair rent, under the Rent Act 1977, s.69. This is designed for and used by persons contemplating physical alterations or improvements to their properties, or who are considering letting their property. It is commonly used by flat developers to ascertain what rents they could charge if they decide to let, and often an application will be made in respect of one type of unit, and not in respect of all the units in a block. No application can be made if a rent has been registered for the unit in the last two years.[15] The certificate specifies what the rent officer, or rent assessment committee, considers would be a fair rent under a regulated tenancy for the property after the proposed alterations (if any) have been effected, and on the proposed terms. If the landlord lets the property in the next two years, he can apply for the rent to be registered in accordance with the certificate.[16] There is no need for him to make the application. Presumably the tenant could apply for a rent to be registered lower than that in the certificate on the basis that the alterations had been badly done, or because the premises suffered from defects not apparent when the certificate was granted. In any event, it is always open to a private landlord to ask his tenant to pay a rent lower than the registered rent.

[11] R.A. 1977, s.44(2).
[12] R.A. 1977, s.57(3), as amended.
[13] R.A. 1977, ss.67(5), 73, Housing Act 1980, s.62.
[14] R.A. 1977, s.73(1A), Housing Act 1980, s.62.
[15] R.A. 1977, s.69(1)(*b*)(ii), as amended.
[16] R.A. 1977, s.69(4), as amended.

III. VARYING THE RENT

A. By Agreement

(1) *Contractual or Protected Tenancies*

Landlords and tenants can, and frequently do, agree to increase the rent by agreement. If the increase is to be enforceable[17] the agreement must be in writing and made at a time when there is no registered rent.[18] Further it must state "in characters not less conspicuous[19] than those used in any other part of the agreement"[20] that the tenant's security will not be affected if he refuses to enter into the agreement; that in any event he can apply at any time for a fair rent to be registered, and that if the increase had been determined on an application for registration, then the increase would be phased.[21] These provisions are probably ignored as often as they are observed, but the consequences of failure to comply with section 51 are not only that the increase is irrecoverable, but also that the tenant can recover so much of the increase as he has paid in the last year.[22] The operation of a rent review clause is not affected by section 51 if it is in a lease to a new tenant who does not enjoy existing security of tenure at the time of the grant.[23] He can, of course, always apply to the rent officer.

(2) *Statutory Tenancies*

A statutory tenancy exists when the tenant's rights to remain arise from the provisions of the Rent Acts and not the parties' contract. This occurs when there has been a notice to quit, or forfeiture proceedings or the person holding as tenant does so because of the provisions relating to statutory succession[24] If no rent has been registered for the property, the parties can again agree an increase in rent, provided they observe the same formalities as mentioned in the last subsection. However, the agreement here will effect the grant of a new tenancy,[25] as it will when the agreement is made with a new

---

[17] R.A. 1977, s.54(1).
[18] R.A. 1977, s.51(3).
[19] *Middlegate Properties* v. *Messimeris* [1973] 1 W.L.R. 168 (requirements of notice under similar provisions in Leasehold Property (Repairs) Act 1938 satisfied if the notice was "equally readable"). The notice must appear at the head of the agreement.
[20] R.A. 1977, s.51(4), as amended.
[21] R.A. 1977, s.51(4), as amended.
[22] R.A. 1977, s.57(3), as amended.
[23] *Sopwith* v. *Stutchbury* (1984) 17 H.L.R. 50.
[24] A notice of increase of rent will also operate to end the contractual tenancy, but in that case a rent would have been registered, and the present provisions for altering rent by agreement would be inapplicable.
[25] R.A. 1977, s.51(1)(*b*). If the current tenant is a first or second statutory successor, the landlord is more likely to seek an increase by applying for registration.

tenant who might have succeeded the present tenant as a statutory tenant.[26]

Apart from these provisions it is not possible to vary the rent limit of a statutory tenancy by agreement. The rent limit is tied to the rent for the last contractual period.[27] The rent can be adjusted to take into account changes in the rates the landlord has to pay for the property[28] and differences in the services or furniture provided by him.[29]

(3) *Where the Rent has been Registered*

There is machinery enabling parties who agree an increased rent where the earlier rent has been registered to make a joint application to the rent officer for the cancellation of the existing registration. Two years must have elapsed since the earlier registration became effective and under the terms of the new agreement the landlord must be unable to end the tenancy within 12 months of the application for cancellation.[30] The rent officer can only cancel if he is satisfied that the highest rent payable under the agreement does not exceed a fair rent.[31] There are few incentives for either party to use this procedure. It could be of interest to a tenant if he thought he was being offered a rent distinctly lower than that likely to be determined by the rent officer. So far as the landlord is concerned, if the application fails, should he still wish to increase the rent he must start again with a fresh application.

(4) *Where the Tenancy was Formerly Controlled*

The rent under controlled tenancies was approximately twice the 1956 gross rateable value,[32] and this would often work out at less than £2 per week. Tenancies moved from the controlled to the fair rent sector as a result of a number of provisions,[33] becoming in the process regulated tenancies. An agreement that purports simply to increase

---

[26] Because of his relationship to the old tenant.

[27] R.A. 1977, s.45(1).

[28] R.A. 1977, s.46.

[29] R.A. 1977, s.47. Failing agreement to the alteration by the parties, the matter can be referred to the county court. It is more likely that the difference will precipitate an application to register a fair rent.

[30] R.A. 1977, s.73(1), as amended.

[31] R.A. 1977, s.73(4).

[32] See generally R.A. 1977, s.27, and Sched. 4, now repealed. For practical purposes, any tenancies still in this category will have been created before July 6, 1957. The species is rare but not extinct. Their ancestry is traced at p. 305 of the First edition of this book.

[33] Principally on the grant of qualification certificates following improvement of the property, R.A. 1977, Pt. VIII; increases in rateable values under Housing Finance Act 1972, Pt. III; following death of first successor, R.A. 1977, s.18(3), and finally on implementation of Housing Act 1980, s.64.

the rent of such a tenancy is void.[34] An agreement that amounts to the grant of a new tenancy is valid as a grant. But if no rent has been registered at that time, the landlord cannot recover the excess over the rent limit that applied to the earlier tenancy.[35] To obtain a rent increase, the landlord is forced to seek registration. The application will often provoke a counter-application to the local authority to operate the Public Health Act machinery because of the dilapidated state of the property.[36] After registration, then the same procedures governing cancellation that have already been discussed apply. The taint of a controlled tenancy does not affect a new tenancy granted to someone who was neither the old tenant nor a person who might have succeeded him as a statutory tenant.[37]

B. By Obtaining a Registered Rent

(1) *First Registration*

If there is no registered rent for the property, then either party can at any time apply for a fair rent to be registered. Tenants often make an application when they discover from others living in the locality that they are paying a rent which is significantly higher than the current going-rate or local levels of registered rents. The fact that they have only recently agreed to pay that higher rent, possibly for a fixed period, is irrelevant. If a fair rent is registered which is lower than the contractual rent, then the registered rent becomes the maximum recoverable rent,[38] despite the fact that the tenant may, for example, have agreed to pay a higher rent for three years. But the reverse is not true. If the registered rent is higher than the contractual rent for the agreed period of time, the landlord can nevertheless be held to his contract, and cannot serve a notice of increase until the term granted has ended. Local authorities can also initiate references for the determination of fair rents.[39] These applications are common, being made when an apparently high rent has been agreed, which is being substantially met out of housing benefit. Rent officers, it would seem,

---

[34] R.A. 1977, s.52, Housing Act 1980, s.68(2).
[35] R.A. 1977, s.52(3), as amended.
[36] See *ante* Chap. 6(IV)H.
[37] R.A. 1977, s.52(5), as amended.
[38] R.A. 1977, s.44(1), and see *Crofton Investment Trust* v. *Greater London Rent Assessment Committee* [1967] 2 Q.B. 955.
[39] R.A. 1977, s.68. If they act frivolously, capriciously or vexatiously then they may be held to have acted *ultra vires* in making the reference, *R.* v. *Barnett and Camden Rent Tribunal, ex p. Frey Investments, Ltd.* [1972] 2 Q.B. 342.

cannot register a rent higher than the agreed rent.[40] Rent Assessment Committees are not so constrained.[41]

(2) *Re-registration*

Normally an application for a re-registration cannot be made within two years[42] from the date when the last registration took effect.[43] Landlords only can submit their applications three months before that date, although any rent determined will not have any effect before the end of the initial two year period.[44] However, either party can make an interim application if he can establish to the rent officer's satisfaction[45] that there has been a significant change in the condition of the house, the terms of the tenancy, the amount and condition of the furniture or other circumstances taken into consideration when the rent was last registered. The changes must be such as to render the registered rent no longer a fair rent.[46] Inflation by itself does not seem to be a sufficient reason to reconsider the rent. A reason often relied on for making an interim application is the extraordinary escalation of heating costs where these are included in the services covered by the rent. Once the rent officer accepts jurisdiction he is not limited to altering the rent to cover the factors that gave rise to the interim application, but can consider the whole question of the fair rent afresh.[47]

(3) *Procedural Matters*

Applications to the rent officer for registration of the rent are made in writing on prescribed forms.[48] The application can be made by landlord or tenant or both jointly.[49] The prescribed form requires the

[40] R.A. 1977, s.68(2).
[41] Rent Regulation (Local Authority Applications) Regs. 1982, (S.I. 1982 No. 1015), reg. 15(1).
[42] R.A. 1977, s.67(3), as amended.
[43] R.A. 1977, s.67(5), as amended. If the last rent was determined by a rent officer and registered before the commencement of H.A. 1980, s.60, then three years must elapse before re-registration or cancellation, H.A. 1980, s.60(2). It seems to be irrelevant that the rent was later determined by a Committee after the commencement of s.60.
[44] R.A. 1977, s.67(3), as amended.
[45] *London Housing and Commercial Properties* v. *Cowan* [1977] Q.B. 148 (acceptance of jurisdiction by rent officer determined that issue for the committee).
[46] R.A. 1977, s.67(3).
[47] *London Housing and Commercial Properties* v. *Cowan* [1977] Q.B. 148 (change in rent level not limited to cost of replacement boiler).
[48] R.A. 1977, s.67(1), (2), as amended. Details of expenditure on services must be specified, and see Rent Act 1977 (Forms etc.) Regs. 1980 (S.I. 1980 No. 1697, as amended by S.I. 1984 No. 1391), Form 5. These requirements are directory and not mandatory, *Druid Development Co. (Bingley)* v. *Kay* (1982) 44 P. & C.R. 76.
[49] R.A. 1977, s.67(1). All joint tenants, or joint landlords, must join in the application, *Turley* v. *Panton* (1975) 29 P. & C.R. 397 (a rent tribunal case).

supply of detailed information relating to the terms of the tenancy, its creation and history and the property, furniture and services comprised in the letting. The applicant must state also his proposed rent, or an effective formula which can be used to produce a rental figure,[50] otherwise the application will be a nullity.[51] Either party can be asked for additional information,[52] and if the application is not made jointly, the other party must be invited within a time limit to state if he wants the rent officer to consider what rent should be registered in a joint consultation with himself and the party making the application.[53] If a consultation is not requested, then the rent officer will either determine the rent himself, or give notice that he proposes to hold a meeting of the parties to consider the rent.[54] After hearing what the parties or their representatives have to say, assuming they bother to attend, the rent officer either determines a fair rent, or confirms the existing registered rent as fair. He must notify both parties of his decision and also their right within 28 days to require him to refer the matter to the rent assessment committee.[55] The criteria for determining fair rents are considered in the next subsection, but rent officers pay particular attention to rent assessment committee decisions and also their own decisions in respect of comparable properties.[56]

Rent officers are often faced with an initial query about their jurisdiction. It may be argued that the agreement only amounts to a licence; that not all the tenants have joined in the application; or that there is a resident landlord, and so only a restricted contract. Often arguments about jurisdiction are at the best delaying tactics, and at the worst blatant attempts to deprive tenants of Rent Act protection. The mechanical answer is that section 141 of the Rent Act 1977 enables either party to refer that question of jurisdiction to the county court. The rent officer will in practice be faced with the question whether there is a valid and simple question of jurisdiction which he can[57] reasonably and properly attempt to solve, or whether there is a real issue between the parties which they should be given the opportunity[58] at least of having resolved by the county court. He is

---

[50] *R.* v. *London Rent Assessment Committee, ex p. Braq Investments* [1969] 1 W.L.R. 970.

[51] *Chapman* v. *Earl* [1968] 1 W.L.R. 1315.

[52] R.A. 1977, Sched. 11, para. 1. Procedure is governed by the Regulated Tenancies (Procedure) Regs. 1980 (S.I. 1980 No. 1696), which modified Sched. 11.

[53] R.A. 1977, Sched. 11, para. 3 as amended.

[54] R.A. 1977, Sched. 11, para. 3A.

[55] R.A. 1977, Sched. 11, para. 5.

[56] And see *R.* v. *Brighton Rent Officers, ex p. Elliott* (1975) 29 P. & C.R. 456 (no need for the rent officer to disclose the comparable rents he relies on either at or before the consultation).

[57] *R.* v. *Kensington and Chelsea L.B.C. Rent Officer, ex p. Noel* [1978] Q.B. 1, explaining *R.* v. *Brent London Borough Rent Officer, ex p. Granatra* [1976] Q.B. 576.

[58] *R.* v. *Croydon and South West London Rent Tribunal, ex p. Ryzewska* [1977] Q.B. 876 (where the opportunity to go to the county court was declined), and see also *R.* v. *City of London Rent Tribunal, ex p. Honig* [1951] K.B. 641; *R.* v. *Fulham, Hammersmith and Kensington Rent Tribunal, ex p. Zerek* [1951] 2 K.B. 1.

under a duty to consider the question, and must proceed with his determination if he is satisfied that there is a protected tenancy.[59]

Rent assessment committees are drawn from panels covering groups of counties. The committee usually consists of three,[60] comprising a surveyor, lay person and legally qualified chairman.[61] Both parties are asked if they want to make written or oral representations, and quite often make both. They can be asked to produce additional information,[62] within a time limit. The committee have the benefit of the rent officer's report.[63] If no hearing has been requested, the committee will endeavour to inspect the property and familiarise itself with any properties likely to be relied on as comparable. The committee has to disclose to both parties copies of documents it receives from the rent officer, letters and documents submitted by the parties, and copies of documents containing information relevant to their decision and prepared for the purposes of the reference.[64] If the committee relies on its own selection of comparables, these have to be disclosed before either the hearing or the decision meeting. If a hearing has been requested, its course will depend on which parties appear. Generally, the landlord, if he is the applicant, will be asked to explain his rent proposals, and he will be questioned by the tenant. The tenant will then be asked for his representations, and again be subject to questioning by the landlord. The individual members of the committee are likely to ask both parties additional questions.[65]

The committee's function is a simple one. They have to confirm the rent officer's figure if it appears to them to be fair. If not, they have to determine a fair rent themselves. They are not concerned with questions of jurisdiction if the matter has been properly referred to them.[66] Their decision has to be communicated to the parties and the rent officer.[67] The registration of the rent determined by the committee normally takes effect from the date when the committee made their decision.[68]

---

[59] *R. v. Rent Officer for Camden, ex parte Ebiri* [1981] 1 All E.R. 950. He should *not*, in such a case, adjourn pending resolution by the county court.

[60] R.A. 1977, Sched. 10, para. 6, permits a direction that the committee's functions may be discharged by the chairman alone with the parties' consent.

[61] R.A. 1977, Sched. 10, para. 5.

[62] R.A. 1977, Sched. 11, para. 7.

[63] Rent officers as a matter of practice but not law do not give evidence to the committee, and so are not subject to cross-examination. It has been argued relying on observations of Megarry J. in *English Exporters (London) Ltd.* v. *Eldonwall* [1973] Ch. 415 that such evidence should be inadmissible, and its reception can amount to a breach of the principles of natural justice.

[64] Rent Assessment Committees (England and Wales) Regulations, 1971 (S.I. 1971 No. 1065, as amended) paras. 5, 6.

[65] And see generally The Rent Assessment Committees (England and Wales) Regulations 1971 (S.I. 1971 No. 1065), as amended.

[66] *London Housing and Commercial Properties* v. *Cowan* [1977] Q.B. 148.

[67] R.A. 1977, Sched. 11. para. 9.

[68] R.A. 1977, s.72(1), as amended by H.A. 1980, s.61. If the application has been made in the 3 months before the end of the two year period from the last registration, it will take effect at the end of the two year period, R.A. 1977, s.72(3).

It is not unusual to find that by the time the matter reaches the committee the premises have been vacated. An objection referred to the committee cannot be unilaterally withdrawn. Even if both parties consent to its withdrawal, the committee can still proceed with the matter if they consider that its withdrawal could be prejudicial to the public interest,[69] but in most cases they will agree to the withdrawal.

The committee's decision has to be given in writing[70] but reasons only have to be given if requested.[71] A party who is dissatisfied on a point of law can appeal under the Tribunal and Inquiries Act 1971 to the Divisional Court and also ask for the issue of orders of mandamus, prohibition and certiorari, for a case to be stated or judicial review.[72] He cannot appeal to the county court.[73] Frequent causes for complaint are the paucity of the committee's reasons; that they have relied on information or knowledge not adduced in evidence and subject to cross-examination; that they have rejected arguments and evidence justifying higher rents without explaining why, and lastly that they have not explained precisely how they have arrived at their final figure. Unless the purported reasons are so inadequate as not to amount to reasons at all then most of these attacks are likely to fail.

"If they (the committee) have decided, having carefully weighed the evidence, that they must reject one approach and adopt another, then all they need to do is to say that in the exercise of their discretion and relying on their skill and judgment they prefer the method which in fact they do prefer. If they say that, it cannot be said against them that their decision is invalidated by the fact that no further or more detailed explanation of why they prefer method A and reject method B is given."[74]

If reasons are given they must be intelligible and should deal with the substantial matters raised, but subject to that the committee can

---

[69] *Hanson* v. *Church Commissioners for England* [1978] Q.B. 823 and see also *R.* v. *Lambeth Rent Officer, ex p. Fox* (1977) 35 P. & C.R. 65 (where the rent officer mistakenly declined to determine a fair rent, considering that the tenant who had left had abandoned his application).

[70] Rent Assessment Committees (England and Wales) Regulations 1971, reg. 10. A majority decision can be given, but this fact should not be disclosed.

[71] Rent Assessment Committees (England and Wales) Regulations 1971, reg. 10A.

[72] Tribunals and Inquiries Act 1971, s.13; Supreme Court Act 1981, s.31; and see *Ellis and Son Fourth Amalgamated Properties* v. *Southern Rent Assessment Panel* (1984) 270 E.G. 39; P. Q. Watchman [1979] Conv. 205.

[73] *Tingey* v. *Sutton* [1984] 1 W.L.R. 812.

[74] *Per* Lord Widgery C.J. *Guppys (Bridport) Ltd.* v. *Sandoe* (1975) 30 P. & C.R. 69, and see also *Tormes Property Co. Ltd.* v. *Landau* [1971] 1 Q.B. 261 and *Mason* v. *Skilling* [1974] 1 W.L.R. 1437, especially Lord Reid, pp. 1439–1440 and *cf. Albyn Properties* v. *Knox* [1977] S.L.T. 41, 1st Div., indicating that a more exacting standard is expected of committees north of the Border; and see P. Q. Watchman [1985] Conv. 199.

rely on its own knowledge and experience without further explanation of how they reached their figure.[75]

The rent determined and registered is a rent exclusive of rates,[76] irrespective of the agreement between the parties. But the rent may also include a figure for furniture and services provided by the landlord. Common items of service are porterage, central heating, provision of gardening services, lighting and cleaning of common parts, and less usually, the provision of common laundry or other communal rooms. The amount attributable to services has to be separately mentioned in the register, unless it amounts to less than 5 per cent. of the registered rent.[77]

The tenancy agreement may provide a formula for automatically adjusting the amount to be paid for the services. This is a common provision in leases of flats and in housing association tenancies, especially of sheltered accommodation. The committee has to consider whether or not the terms or mechanics of altering and apportioning the charge for services are reasonable. They have to bear in mind that if variable services are registered, then they are subject to Schedule 19 of the Housing Act 1980,[78] and said to be subject to a "fair and reasonable" check.[79] They are clearly not, however, subject to control either by the rent officer or rent assessment committee. If the terms are not unreasonable, then a variable rent should be registered.[80] This is so even if the list of "services" includes substantial items of repair which should more properly be borne by the landlord.[81]

When assessing services, the committee is generally concerned with the value of the services to the tenant rather than their cost to the landlord.[82] In the normal situation the actual cost of the services will be powerful evidence as to what the future cost of services should be.[83] If the cost formula produces a seriously distorted charge to the tenant, then the court can intervene and do what is fair and reasonable.[84] If the committee is basing itself on costs, then the landlord is entitled to an amount in respect of depreciation and

---

[75] *Guppys Properties* v. *Knott (No. 3)* (1981) 258 E.G. 1083; *Midmanbury Properties (Southampton)* v. *Houghton, T. Clerk & Son* (1981) 259 E.G. 565.
[76] R.A. 1977, s.71(2).
[77] R.A. 1977, s.71(1), Sched. 8, para. 2; Social Security and Housing Benefits Act 1982, s.36(4).
[78] See *ante* Chap. 4(IV)F.
[79] *Finchbourne* v. *Rodrigues* [1976] 3 All E.R. 581.
[80] Rent Act 1977, s.71(4): and see *Firstcross Ltd.* v. *Teesdale* (1982) 265 E.G. 305, and *Re Heathview Tenants' Co-operative Ltd.* (1980) 258 E.G. 644, and J. T. Farrand (1983) 265 E.G. 286.
[81] Because of the provisions of L. & T.A. 1985, s.11, see *ante* Chap. 6 (III)C. It is suggested that the rent register should state precisely what items are covered by the variable provisions.
[82] *Metropolitan Properties Co.* v. *Noble* [1968] 1 W.L.R. 838 (inefficient heating system).
[83] *R.* v. *London Rent Assessment Panel, ex p. Cliftvylle Properties* (1983) 266 E.G. 44.
[84] *Pole Properties* v. *Feinberg* (1982) 43 P. & C.R. 121 (central heating costs based on floor areas, total let floor areas later increased).

replacement of, for example, boilers, lifts, carpets, oil-storage tanks, etc., and for his profit in respect of the services provided.[85]

If the landlord is not prevented by the terms of the contractual tenancy from increasing the rent, and he wants to increase it, he must serve a notice of increase in a specified form.[86] Before the landlord can increase the rent of a protected tenant, that contractual tenancy will have had to be ended, either by a notice to quit, or more usually by the notice of increase itself. The notice of increase operates to change the protected tenancy into a statutory one where the contractual tenancy could have been ended by a notice to quit which became effective before the date specified for the increase.[87] If the tenancy is already a statutory one, then the effective date for increasing the rent must not be earlier than the date on which registration took effect, nor four weeks before the service of the notice of increase.[88] The increase is subject to phasing over two years.[89]

(4) *Determining a Fair Rent*

The Rent Act contains no indication how a fair rent has to be determined. It merely indicates certain factors to which in particular regard shall be had, and what matters have to be disregarded.[90] Nor does the Act define a fair rent, and unfortunately, unlike the elephant, it is not always possible to recognise one. However, the matter can be approached in a common sense way, relying but not too much on the skills of the valuer member of the committee.

In determining a fair rent, one has to have regard to all the circumstances, and in particular:

(a) the age, character, state of repair and locality[91] of the dwelling-house, and
(b) the furniture provided for use under the tenancy, its quantity, quality and condition;

And one must disregard:

---

[85] *Perseus Property Co.* v. *Burberry* (1985) 273 E.G. 405.

[86] Rent Act 1977, s.49. Rent Act 1977 (Forms etc.) Regulations 1980 (S.I. 1980 No. 1697) (as amended), Forms 1 (rent), and 4 (rates). Use of the proper forms is mandatory and defects cannot be waived, *Aristocrat Property Investments* v. *Harounoff* (1982) 43 P. & C.R. 284.

[87] R.A. 1977, s.49(4).

[88] Rent Regulations (Forms, etc.) Regulations 1978, forms 3, 4. There is no need in this instance for the rent increase to coincide with the next rent day, *Avenue Properties (St John's Wood) Ltd.* v. *Aisinzon* [1977] Q.B. 628.

[89] R.A. 1977, Sched. 8, as amended by H.A. 1980, s.60. The full increase for services is not subject to phasing.

[90] R.A. 1977, s.70, as amended by H.A. 1980, Sched. 26.

[91] And see *Metropolitan Property Holdings Ltd.* v. *Finegold* [1975] 1 W.L.R. 349 (effect of a recently built school specifically for Americans, on rent levels in a small locality).

(a) disrepair or other defects attributable to the failure of the tenant or his predecessors[92] to comply with the terms of the tenancy;

(b) the improvements by the tenant or his predecessors, either to the property or the furniture unless they were done as one of the terms of the tenancy;

(c) deterioration to the furniture resulting from ill-treatment of it by the tenant, persons residing with him, or his sub-tenants.

These matters will be noted on an inspection of the property, and the checking and valuation of the inventory. Tenant's improvements are often extensive and include construction of kitchens, installation of hot water systems, immersion heaters, installation of power points, and construction of outhouses and garages. Unless an identical unimproved house can be inspected at the same time it is often difficult to disregard entirely the effect of a tenant's improvements. Tenant's improvements do not include anything the tenant has done by way of redecoration or repair, *e.g.* rewiring.[93] The bad state of repair will often have a depreciatory effect, and a landlord's promises that repairs are likely to be done will probably be ignored unless redeemed by the time the committee inspects.[94]

The most important factor to be disregarded is the scarcity element. Section 70(2) provides that one has to assume "that the number of persons seeking to become tenants of similar dwelling-houses in the locality on the terms (other than those relating to rent) of the regulated tenancy is not substantially greater than the number of dwelling-houses in the locality which are available for letting on such terms." One does not have to assume a nil demand, but simply try to value out any distorting effect scarcity has on rent and vacant possession values.[95] Scarcity is a matter of evidence or experience,[96] but it does not always exist and does not always distort the pattern of values. Often committees and valuers will make a 10–40 per cent. deduction from the figures they are using to allow for the "scarcity element."[97] Indeed it is often argued that a fair rent should be the market rent less the distorting effect of scarcity.[98]

The approved method of determining a fair rent is by the use of

---

[92] *Trustees of the Property of Smith's Charity* v. *Hemmings* (1983) 265 E.G. 383.

[93] Rent Act 1977, s.75(1).

[94] *cf. Nicoll* v. *First National Developments* (1972) 226 E.G. 301. The committee need not fix a nominal rent simply because a closing order has been made under Housing Act 1985, *Williams* v. *Khan,* (1982) 43 P. & C.R. 1.

[95] And see Lord Widgery C.J. in *Metropolitan Property Holdings Ltd.* v. *Finegold* [1975] 1 W.L.R. 349, 352; *Western Heritable Investment Co.* v. *Husband* [1983] A.C. 849, and P. Q. Watchman [1985] Conv. 199, Lee (1984) 4 Oxf.J. of Legal Studies 287.

[96] *Crofton Investment Trust Ltd.* v. *Greater London Rent Assessment Committee* [1967] 1 Q.B. 955.

[97] Care has to be taken not to make the deduction twice, as in *Anglo-Italian Properties* v. *London Rent Assessment Panel* [1969] 1 W.L.R. 730.

[98] See *Tormes Property Co. Ltd.* v. *Landau* [1971] 1 Q.B. 261 at p. 267, *per* Lord Parker C.J.

existing registered fair rents for comparable properties.[99] This involves making adjustments to take into account the different sizes and
types of property and locality, etc.[1] Until the contrary is proved one is
entitled to assume that the registered rents were rightly ascertained.[2]
But this simple and effective method has a number of drawbacks. The
passing of time with inflation and changes in market direction can
make even recently registered rents look out-of-date. Although
inflation which has occurred since the registration of rents relied on
has to be considered,[3] it is not satisfactory to increase the existing
registered rent by the historic rates of inflation, or to take into account
forecasted rates.[4]

One approach often adopted is "the contractor's theory." Lord
Reid in *Mason* v. *Skilling*[5] said that: "A fair rent should be fair to the
landlord as well as fair to the tenant and it can be regarded as fair to
the landlord that he should receive a fair return on his capital."
Following that decision calculations are produced arguing that the
prospective rent should be a percentage of the vacant possession
value, discounted because of scarcity. The true contractor's method
relies on the cost of building or replacing the dwelling-house. In either
case this method can only produce a ceiling,[6] and has been described
as a "notoriously unreliable method of valuation."[7] Invariably the
calculations ignore that whether the house be rented or not, its capital
value has increased and is likely to increase substantially during the
period of registration. Indeed, it has been held that the possibility of
capital appreciation is irrelevant,[8] although it is a factor considered by
most investors.

Rent committees rely on a number of additional methods to help
them determine fair rents. "Spot valuation" is the least scientific. This
involves individual members of the committee asking themselves
what they subjectively would estimate a fair rent to be as a matter of
impression and experience. Some attention is paid to rateable values,
but they do not usually help. Rateable values are often relied on by
landlords who detect that existing registered rents are the result of
multiplying rateable values by a certain figure. But this is not an
approach usually adopted by committees. Rateable values often

---

[99] *Tormes Property Co. Ltd* v. *Landau*, above, and see *Mason* v. *Skilling* [1974] 1 W.L.R. 1437.
[1] "Extrapolating" rents, usually on a price per square foot or metre.
[2] *Mason* v. *Skilling* [1974] 1 W.L.R. 1437, *per* Lord Reid at p. 1439; *R.* v. *London Rent Assessment Committee, ex p. St. George's Court (No. 2)* (1983) 267 E.G. 253.
[3] It is one of the "circumstances" and see Widgery J. in *Metropolitan Properties Co. (F.G.C.) Ltd.* v. *Lannon* [1968] 1 W.L.R. 815 at p. 836, reversed in part on another point [1969] 1 Q.B. 577.
[4] And see *Guppy's (Bridport) Ltd.* v. *Carpenter* [1973] R.V.R. 573; *Kovats* v. *Corporation of Trinity House* (1982) 262 E.G. 445. The court will not lay down how inflation should be approached, *Wareing* v. *White* (1985) 274 E.G. 488.
[5] [1974] 1 W.L.R. 1437 at p. 1440.
[6] *Tormes Property Co. Ltd.* v. *Landau* [1971] 1 Q.B. 261 at p. 266, *per* Lord Parker C.J.
[7] *Per* Lord Keith in *Western Heritable Investment Co.* v. *Husband* [1983] A.C. 849 at p. 857.
[8] *Midmanbury Properties (Southampton)* v. *Houghton* and *T. Clerk & Son* v. *Heathfield* (No. 2) (1982) 263 E.G. 792.

overlook individual characteristics of the subject property, especially its state of repair and location. In any event, district valuers seem to approach their valuation exercise more strictly on a price per square foot/metre basis, than rent assessment committees. District valuers also seem to be concerned with the "tone of the list," which seems to involve a concentration on its inherent consistency. Fair rents reflect market values, and therefore are not ultimately susceptible to such a rigorous mathematical approach.

Attention will be paid to evidence of how the market is operating at a particular time. Although inflation seems to increase or at least continue inexorably each year, the same is not true of the property market. At times, prices and market rents escalate rapidly, especially when finance is more freely available and employment prospects are increasing. Conversely, if rents are determined in an area of high general unemployment, when money is tight, or where there is a surfeit of the type of property the subject of the hearing, then the committee may determine that market rents have either reached a plateau, or may be falling back. In such circumstances, landlords argue that "fair rents" should nevertheless be increased in line with rates of inflation, so that the increased cost of repairs, management, etc., are covered, even though the evidence of market rents does not support such an increase.

One of the major problems rent assessment committees face is a lack of hard evidence, *e.g.* what are current vacant possession prices for comparable properties; what has been spent on repairs, etc.; how often do tenants change and for how long is the property left empty ("voids")? In the last resort, the committee have to stand back from their various calculations based on price per square foot, comparable registered rents, products of old registered rents and price indices, vacant possession values, etc., and exercise a collective judgment on whether they consider their proposed rent fair to both parties in all the circumstances.[9] In doing this, they are likely to consider what will be the total cost of the accommodation to the tenant, bearing in mind his liability for rates. The committee may consider what sort of accommodation the tenant could secure in other parts of the housing market, *e.g.* if he took a flat, instead of a house, or bought on mortgage, with the benefit of tax relief on his interest payments.

---

[9] Excluding the "personal circumstances," the most important being the poverty of the tenant, the inability of the landlord to meet his bills, and his actual investment and borrowing costs.

IV. ANTI-AVOIDANCE PROVISIONS

A. Prohibited Premiums on Grants

An obvious way of avoiding the rent control legislation would be to let at or below the registered rent, but to demand in addition a lump sum, as a premium, or "key-money" as a condition of making the grant. In many localities market conditions are such that prospective tenants would be willing to pay premiums, or agree to other variations on the same theme. Section 119 of the Rent Act 1977 makes it a criminal offence to require a premium or the making of a loan as a condition of the granting, continuance or renewal of a protected tenancy.[9] It is a further offence to receive[10] a premium, which may be ordered to be repaid on conviction.[11] The provisions do not catch agreements where, *e.g.* a licence is created as opposed to the grant of a tenancy. Nor do they apply to tenancies unless they are "protected" where the rent must be at least two-thirds of the rateable value.[12] The offending payment need not be to the landlord, and may be to an agent, or an outgoing tenant surrendering his tenancy.[13] The effect of the payment does not vitiate the whole agreement, which may in the court's discretion remain specifically enforceable.[14] But in any event, the premium is recoverable,[15] or the loan repayable on demand.[16]

B. Prohibition of Associated Payments

(1) *Excessive Price for Furniture*

If it can be established that an excessive price was required or paid, then it is treated as a premium. It can be recovered if paid.[17] One is not concerned simply with the sale-room price for the items, but an appropriate figure bearing in mind that the incoming tenant would

---

[9] R.A. 1977, s.119(1). There is a limited exception until 1990 in favour of some tenancies held of the Crown Estates Commissioners, H.A. 1980, Sched 8, para. 4.

[10] R.A. 1977, s.119(2), (3).

[11] R.A. 1977, s.119(4).

[12] R.A. 1977, s.5. A lump sum payment may be a genuine pre-payment of rent, and not a lump sum for granting a protected tenancy, *Woods* v. *Wise* [1955] 2 Q.B. 29, but in that event, R.A. 1977, s.126, may apply. And see *Regor Estates Ltd.* v. *Wright* [1951] 1 K.B. 689.

[13] *Farrell* v. *Alexander* [1977] A.C. 59 (recovery of excessive sum to outgoing and surrendering tenant).

[14] As in *Ailion* v. *Spiekermann* [1976] Ch. 158 (excessive sum payable to assigning tenant for furniture).

[15] R.A. 1977, s.125(1).

[16] R.A. 1977, s.125(2). See also Chap. 12 (II) *post*.

[17] R.A. 1977, s.123: An offence is also committed, s.124. And see *Adair* v. *Murrell* (1982) 263 E.G. 66.

have to acquire and install furniture, and that the outgoing tenant would have to remove it.[18]

(2) *Payments on Assignments*

The prohibition on taking premiums on grants is extended to assignments of protected tenancies, to defeat both assigning tenants who enjoy tenancies at favourable rents and devious landlords,[19] who might be disposed to initiate sham grants. There are exceptions to the blanket prohibition.[20] The commonly used exceptions permit apportionments of outgoings[21]; payment to the outgoing tenant for reasonable costs of structural alterations or improvement or installation of fixtures the tenant cannot remove[22]; or genuine[23] payments for goodwill, where a business is passing as well.[24]

(3) *Pre-payments of Rent*

A stringent and often overlooked prohibition relates to advance payments of rent. Section 126(1) of the Rent Act 1977 prohibits requirements that rent be paid before the start of the rental period it covers, and that payments be made more than six months in advance. If the prohibition is broken an offence is committed,[25] and the rent paid is recoverable.[26] The landlord cannot recover rent for a rental period where parties have agreed that it should be paid before its commencement.[27] This does not affect an agreement to pay rent in advance at the start of a rental period. In practice, this is more likely to affect a requirement to make the initial payment in advance. The prohibition does not prevent the landlord from requiring the tenant to pay a deposit to cover services and depreciation.[28]

---

[18] *Eales* v. *Dale* [1954] 1 Q.B. 539 at p. 548, *per* Denning L.J.
[19] R.A. 1977, s.120(1).
[20] See (C) *post.*
[21] R.A. 1977, s.120 (3) (*a*).
[22] R.A. 1977, s.120(3)(*b*), and see *Nock* v. *Munk* (1982) 263 E.G. 1085 (reasonable and lawful payments of £16,460 for furniture and £23,540 for alterations etc.,).
[23] *Lower* v. *Porter* [1956] 1 Q.B. 325 (no genuine business at all).
[24] R.A. 1977, s.120(3) (*d*).
[25] R.A. 1977, s.126(4).
[26] R.A. 1977, s.126(5), recovery may be effected by deduction from subsequent rent, s.126(6).
[27] In *R.* v. *Ewing* (1977) 65 Cr.App.R. 4, a payment made the day before the tenancy started for the first month's rent was not caught by this provision.
[28] *R.* v. *Ewing* (1977) 65 Cr.App.R. 4.

(4) *Other Payments*

Premiums are widely defined to include "any fine or other like sum" and "any other pecuniary consideration in addition to rent."[29] Possible permutations are almost infinite. In *Elmdene Estates Ltd.* v. *White*[30] the tenant was persuaded to sell his house at £500 less than its market value to obtain the tenancy from the landlord, which sum was recoverable. Deposits will be regarded as premiums unless they do not exceed one-sixth of the annual rent and are reasonable in relation to the potential liability they are meant to cover.[31]

C. Permitted Premiums

(1) *On Grant*

Premiums are most commonly taken when a developer grants long leases of flats on low rentals and subject to a service charge. These tenancies are outside the ambit of the Rent Acts. But occasionally there will be grants of long leases of protected tenancies within Part I of the Landlord and Tenant Act 1954.[32] A premium can be taken[33] provided: (1) the tenancy is not and cannot be ended by notice to the tenant within 20 years of the grant; (2) the rent cannot be varied[34] under the terms of the tenancy within the first 20 years of the grant, and thereafter not more often than once in every 21 years; (3) the terms of the tenancy do not inhibit both assignment and underletting of the whole.[35] If the long lease is created after July 15, 1980, then the conditions are more relaxed. Here provisions can be inserted for varying the rent after the first six years, and thereafter, once in every seven years. But the lease must provide that as a result of the variation the sums payable will not exceed two-thirds of the rateable value of the house when the variation is made. One leaves out of account payments for rates, repairs, services, and maintenance, when calculating if the limit has been exceeded.[36]

---

[29] R.A. 1977, s.128(1), as amended. It is possible that a contribution required from a tenant for the lessor's legal costs could be caught by these provisions.

[30] [1960] A.C. 528. And see also *Samrose Properties Ltd.* v. *Gibbard* [1958] 1 W.L.R. 235.

[31] Housing Act 1980, s.79.

[32] See *post*, Chap. 15.

[33] R.A. 1977, s.127, and see H.A. 1980, s.78.

[34] Payments for rates, services, repairs, maintenance and insurance can be varied. The restriction on rental variation does not apply to tenancies under Part I, Leasehold Reform Act 1967 or to tenancies granted before July 25, 1977, s.127(2)(*b*).

[35] What is meant by inhibiting is contained in H.A. 1980, s.78(3), adding to R.A. 1977, s.127(5).

[36] R.A. 1977, s.127(3D); H.A. 1980, s.78(4).

(2) *On Assignment*

Tenants who have properly paid a premium on the grant or assignment to them of their term can find that subsequent changes in the law prevent them from charging a premium when they come to assign the remainder of their term. Three groups of tenants are caught and partially relieved. Tenants who would have come in the category just considered[37] but for their failure to satisfy any of the three conditions about variation of rent, termination or assignment can gain partial relief. So can tenants whose regulated protected tenancies were granted at a premium at a time one could be lawfully demanded,[38] and tenants whose leases were granted before March 8, 1973, but because of their high rateable values were brought into the Rent Acts as a result of the Counter-Inflation Act 1973.[39] Some of the details of the relief are complex. The principle in all cases is that the tenant on assigning can charge a premium which is part of the amount he paid, and calculated by reference to the unexpired period of the lease. He therefore cannot make a profit, but the loss he would otherwise suffer is made good. The previous restrictions are deemed never to have applied at all to long tenancies granted at low rents before July 16, 1980, if the premium was lawfully required and paid and the lease does not inhibit both assignment and underletting of the whole.[40]

D. Rent Books

Tenants who pay their rent weekly have to be provided by their landlord with rent books or similar documents.[41] The rent books have to contain prescribed information which can be found in The Rent Book (Forms of Notice) Regulations 1982[42] Sched., Pt. II. Apart from information about the name and address of the landlord[43] and his agent and details of the rent, the prescribed information tells the tenant of his basic protection, the possibility of help from rent and rate assistance schemes, and refers him to Departmental booklets, his local authority and Citizens Advice Bureau, etc., for further information, advice and assistance. The information now required to be given is minimal. Failure to provide a rent book, when necessary, amounts

---

[37] *i.e.* tenants of protected long leases, R.A. 1977, s.127. They gain relief under R.A. 1977, Sched. 18, Pt. II.
[38] R.A. 1977, s.120(5). Relief is given under R.A. 1977, Sched. 18, Pt. I.
[39] R.A. 1977, s.11. Relief is granted under R.A. 1977, Sched. 18, Pt. II.
[40] R.A. 1977, s.127(3B); H.A. 1980, s.78(4). See Chap. 12 (II) C *post.*
[41] L. & T.A. 1985, s.4.
[42] S.I. 1982 No. 1474.
[43] See also L. & T.A. 1985, s.1.

to a criminal offence,[44] but it does not render the contract or rent unenforceable.[45]

E. Accommodation Agencies Act 1953

It was apprehended that considerable profits were being made by persons collecting lists of addresses of accommodation to rent and then providing those lists at a fee, or registering the requirements of prospective tenants, again at a fee. Obviously, the situation was open to considerable abuse. Equally obviously it is the proper function of estate agents to find tenants for their client landlords, and properties for their client tenants. The 1953 Act[46] makes it an offence to demand or accept payment in consideration of registering the name or requirements of a prospective tenant. It is also an offence to supply lists of houses to let on payment, and to issue lists of houses to let without the authority of the owner or his agent. The main force of the Act is against charging for supplying lists, and does not attack transactions in which an agent is appointed and paid for finding accommodation. It is not always easy to be certain on which side of the line any particular arrangement may fall.[47]

---

[44] Landlord and Tenant Act 1985, s.7.
[45] *Shaw* v. *Groom* [1970] 2 Q.B. 504.
[46] s.1. The Act has an extended life because of the Expiring Laws Act 1969, s.1.
[47] And see *Saunders* v. *Soper* [1975] A.C. 239.

CHAPTER 12

TRANSFERS

I. Transfers *Inter Vivos* and on Death . 433
II. Premiums on Assignment 434
   A. Meaning 434
   B. Prohibition 435
   C. Lawful Payments 436
   D. Effect on Tenancy of Illegal
      Premium 437

   E. Restricted Contracts 438
   F. Statutory Tenancies 438
   G. Payments for Furniture 438
III. Involuntary Transfers 438
   A. Statutory Tenants by Succes-
      sion 438
   B. The Matrimonial Home 442

I. TRANSFERS INTER VIVOS AND ON DEATH

As long as the contractual tenancy lasts, it may be assigned by the tenant in the normal way, if there is no ban on assignment and, where necessary, the landlord's consent has been obtained. The common law governing assignment of leases is discussed earlier in this book.[1] A contractual fixed-term tenancy will, until the contractual period expires, form part of the protected tenant's estate at his death and the residue of the term can be passed on by his will, although, as we shall see later, it may be in abeyance during the continuance of a transmitted statutory tenancy. The same applies to a periodic tenancy, unless the landlord has served a notice to quit operative before or at the time of the tenant's death.

A statutory tenancy is not, as such, freely assignable, and by virtue of the fact that the tenancy will last only for as long as the statutory tenant remains in possession, it cannot form part of his estate on his death and be transmitted by will, although there is, as we shall see, some provision in the Rent Act 1977 for limited statutory succession.[2] Special provision is, nevertheless, made by the Rent Act 1977, Sched. 1, para. 13, for the transfer of a statutory tenancy by agreement. The agreement must be in writing and be between the outgoing tenant, the incoming tenant and the landlord. If the consent of any superior landlord would have been required to the assignment of the previous contractual tenancy, then that superior landlord must be a party to the agreement of transfer as well. Without such participation in the agreement of transfer by the landlord(s), the transfer is wholly ineffective. This can produce curious results.

In *Atyeo* v. *Fardoe*[3] the first defendant was the tenant of a bungalow. The plaintiff landlord gave him notice to quit, whereupon he became

---

[1] *Supra*, Chap. 7.
[2] *Post*.
[3] (1978) 37 P. & C.R. 494.

a statutory tenant. Because of the poor condition of the bungalow, and his wife's pregnancy, the tenant wished to move out for the winter of 1977/78 and return in the spring. He came to an arrangement with the second defendant, his son, whereby the son would move into the bungalow for the winter and carry out works to the property to make it more habitable. The first defendant purported to transfer his statutory tenancy to his son, the intention being that it would be re-transferred back to him in the spring, when he returned. The plaintiff was not a party to this transfer. The first defendant moved out, leaving a substantial quantity of his effects behind. The landlord then sought possession. The Court of Appeal held that, since the first defendant's absence during the winter months on account of his wife's condition did not amount to giving up possession, as he retained the clear intention to return,[4] and since the purported transfer of the statutory tenancy was a nullity (the landlord not being a party), it could have no effect in law on the position of the first defendant, who remained a statutory tenant capable of defeating the landlord's claim. It would, of course, have been otherwise if the statutory tenant had given up possession to the purported transferee, retaining no intention to return, for then the statutory tenancy would simply have terminated.[5]

The need for the landlord's participation places him in a better position than where his consent is required to the assignment of a contractual tenancy. For by the Landlord and Tenant Act 1927, s.19, consent to assignment of the contractual tenancy may not be unreasonably withheld. However, refusal of consent may be reasonable where the assignment would result in the creation of a statutory tenancy.[6] If an effective agreement for transferring the statutory tenancy is made, the incoming tenant takes the place of the outgoing tenant as a statutory tenant. The outgoing tenant may charge the incoming tenant for apportioned outgoings, structural alterations or improvements to fixtures, and similar charges paid by him on an assignment of the previous contractual tenancy. He may not, however, charge a premium.[7]

II. PREMIUMS ON ASSIGNMENT[8]

A. Meaning

From their inception the Rent Acts have contained prohibitions

[4] *Supra*, Chap. 10.
[5] See also *Maxten* v. *McAll* [1952] C.P.L. 185.
[6] *Thomas Bookman Ltd.* v. *Nathan* [1955] 1 W.L.R. 815 at p. 819; *Brann* v. *Westminster Anglo-Continental Investment Co. Ltd.* (1976) 240 E.G. 927.
[7] See *post*.
[8] Premiums on the grant of tenancies are discussed *supra*, Chap. 11.

against the charging of premiums on the grant or renewal of protected tenancies. The object of such prohibitions was to ensure that landlords could not exploit the housing shortage and avoid the rent limits by charging tenants additional sums of money as a pre-condition for the grant or renewal of a tenancy. By the same reasoning tenants, or landlords whose consent to an assignment was necessary, should not be permitted to charge assignees premiums on the transfer of tenancies. The Rent Act 1977, s.120, prohibits premiums on the assignment of protected tenancies and section 122 prohibits premiums for both grants and assignments of restricted contracts.[9]

A premium is defined[10] as including any fine or other like sum, and any other pecuniary consideration in addition to rent. Its general meaning is any sum of money which is paid for the granting or assignment of the lease, and it is clear that the Rent Act 1977 generally contemplates premiums as money payments. However, the words "pecuniary consideration" are wide enough to cover any form of consideration having a money value. Foregoing a debt or selling a house at less than its value, if required by the landlord as a condition of a grant, can constitute a premium.[11] In determining whether a money payment or other pecuniary consideration is a premium, the courts look to the substance of the transaction and not to its form.[12] The taking of a deposit, even if returnable, is an illegal premium unless it is reasonable in relation to the potential liability in respect of which it is paid, *and* does not exceed one-sixth of the annual rent.[13]

B. Prohibition

The Rent Act 1977, s.120, prohibits both the requiring and the receiving of a premium on the assignment of a protected tenancy. The assignment of a tenancy is the disposition by the tenant of the whole of his interest in the property. However, if the tenancy is surrendered to the landlord by a tenant who receives some consideration for that surrender from the new tenant, (to whom a lease is subsequently granted), the premium is still illegal by virtue of section 119, which makes it unlawful for "any person" to receive a premium in connection with the grant, renewal or continuance of a protected

[9] See Chap. 14, *post.*

[10] In R.A. 1977, s.128(1), as amended by Housing Act 1980, s.79.

[11] *Elmdene Estates Ltd.* v. *White* [1960] A.C. 528. A returnable deposit is not "pecuniary consideration": *R.* v. *Ewing* (1977) 65 Cr.App.R. 4. By virtue of R.A. 1977, s.128(1), as now amended by Housing Act 1980, s.79, a deposit may, in certain circumstances, constitute an illegal premium: see above.

[12] *Samrose Properties Ltd.* v. *Gibbard* [1958] 1 W.L.R. 235.

[13] R.A. 1977, s.128(1), as amended. It may be easier for a landlord to establish that a returnable deposit is reasonable if it is paid into a separate tenants' deposit account, thus protecting the money against interception by the landlord's creditors should he become bankrupt: *Re Chelsea Cloisters Ltd. (in liquidation)* (1981) 41 P. & C.R. 98.

tenancy.[14] In *Farrell* v. *Alexander*[15] a tenant wished to assign her lease but was subject to a condition that she first had to offer it to the landlords without consideration. It was agreed between the tenant and the plaintiff that if the plaintiff paid the defendant £4,000 for fixtures and fittings, the tenant would surrender the lease to the landlords. The landlords were willing to grant a new lease to the plaintiff, subject to an interview and satisfactory references. In due course the tenant surrendered the lease and the £4,000 was paid. The landlords granted a new lease to the plaintiff who, on discovering the value of the fixtures and fittings to be only £1,002, claimed the balance from the defendant as an illegal premium.[16] The House of Lords held that the words "any person" in the Rent Act 1977, s.119, were wide enough to cover landlords, tenants, agents and any other "middle-men" who had received capital payments on a change of tenancy, and that the excess payment was, therefore, an illegal premium and could be recovered.

C. Lawful Payments

The Rent Act 1977, s.120(3), makes provision for the assignor of a protected tenancy to require or receive some payment from the assignee. Where the assignor would, apart from the general ban on taking premiums on assignment, be able to secure some payment to cover expenditure on outgoings, structural alterations, and improvements,[17] these payments are permitted. Section 120 (5) also provides that in the circumstances set out in the Rent Act 1977, Sched. 18, Pt. I, certain premiums can be lawfully required or received. The circumstances in which this is possible are:

(i) a premium was lawfully required and paid, or lawfully received, in respect of the grant, continuance or renewal of a protected regulated tenancy[18]; and

(ii) since the grant, continuance or renewal of the tenancy the landlord has not granted a tenancy to someone other than the tenant who paid the premium; and

(iii) the rent is a registered rent which is higher than the former controlled rent under the tenancy.

---

[14] A tenant who wishes to avoid the prohibition against charging a premium on assignment may do so by granting a sub-tenancy which is not a protected tenancy, provided the transaction is not a sham: *Brann* v. *Westminster Anglo-Continental Investment Co. Ltd.* (1976) 240 E.G. 927.

[15] [1976] 2 All E.R. 721.

[16] An illegal premium may be recovered by the party who has paid it under R.A. 1977, s.125(1).

[17] This includes liabilities incurred though not discharged at the date of assignment: *Adair* v. *Murrell* (1982) 263 E.G. 66.

[18] *i.e.* before the ban on such premiums was introduced or before the tenancy became a protected tenancy.

If these conditions are fulfilled, a premium calculated in accordance with a statutory formula can be required or received on the assignment of the protected tenancy.[19]

D. Effect on Tenancy of Illegal Premium

If the contract to assign, or the assignment itself, makes provision for the payment of an illegal premium, does this render the contract or assignment itself void for illegality? In *Ailion* v. *Spiekermann*[20] the tenant occupied a flat under a protected tenancy expiring in December 1976. In April 1974 the tenant agreed to assign the residue of his lease on payment by the assignees of £3,750 for certain chattels. All parties were aware that this was an overvalue. Before completion the assignees were allowed into possession as licensees, subject to a condition that they would vacate the flat on demand if they failed to complete. The assignees could not raise the money and failed to complete on the appointed day. The assignor served notice to complete and revoked the assignees' licence. The assignees refused to leave and refused to pay the contract sum, but offered instead to complete by paying a reasonable sum, on valuation of the chattels. The assignor claimed possession and rescission of the contract, and the assignees counterclaimed for specific performance.

Templeman J. held that the effect of the Rent Act 1977, s.120, was not to make the contract or the assignment illegal *ex turpi causa*, but only the receipt by the assignor of the premium. There was a clear division between the legal and illegal elements in the contract and they could, therefore, be severed. Since the purchasers could have completed and then recovered the excessive price of the chattels under section 125,[21] the vendor's claim was dismissed and specific performance of the contract was ordered without payment of the illegal premium.

---

[19] The formula is

$$\frac{P \times A}{G}$$

where P is the premium originally paid, A is the length of the period beginning on the date on which the assignment takes effect, and ending on the relevant date, and G is the length of the period beginning on the date of grant, continuance or renewal in respect of which the premium was paid, and ending on the relevant date. The "relevant date" depends on the length of the term granted. If the tenancy was granted for a term exceeding seven years, the relevant date is the date when the term expires. In any other case, it is the date of the expiry of seven years from the commencement of the term: R.A. 1977, Sched. 18, Pt. I, paras. 2 & 5.

[20] [1976] 1 All E.R. 497.

[21] See note 15, *supra*.

E. Restricted Contracts

It is illegal to require, (though not to receive unsought), premiums on the assignment of restricted contracts whose rents have been registered by a rent tribunal.[22] This matter is discussed in Chapter 14.

F. Statutory Tenancies

Statutory tenancies cannot, in the normal way, be assigned, and therefore do not come within the provisions of the Rent Act 1977, s.120. However, a statutory tenancy can be surrendered and arrangements made for a new tenancy to be granted on terms which include the payment of money to the outgoing tenant or to the landlord. Indeed, such devices are often resorted to by landlords who wish to recover possession from statutory tenants who cannot, lawfully, be evicted. These payments are not illegal. As discussed earlier there is one circumstance in which a statutory tenancy can be transferred *inter vivos* with the concurrence of the landlord, and the payment of pecuniary consideration for such a transfer is illegal, except in the case of certain permitted charges.[23]

G. Payments for Furniture

By the Rent Act 1977, s.123, which applies both to protected tenancies and restricted contracts, where the purchase of any furniture has been required as a condition of grant, renewal, continuance or assignment, any excess in the price over the reasonable price of the furniture may be treated as a premium and recovered. There are criminal penalties for offering furniture in such circumstances at an inflated value, and also for failing to supply a written inventory, giving itemised values, on request.[24]

III. INVOLUNTARY TRANSFERS

A. Statutory Tenants By Succession

The Rent Act 1977, Sched. 1 relaxes the general principle that a statutory tenancy represents no more than a personal, non-assignable, status of irremovability by providing that such a tenancy may,

[22] R.A. 1977, s.122.
[23] R.A. 1977, Sched. 1, Pt. II, para. 14.
[24] *Ibid.* s.124.

following the tenant's death, be succeeded to, or transmitted, twice—once to the successor, and then again to qualified persons on that successor's death. The transmission operates in favour of a resident surviving spouse or, if there is none, a member of the deceased's family able to show six months' residence.[25] As noted earlier in this chapter, this succession to a statutory tenancy can occur on the death of a *protected* tenant,[26] *i.e.* the contractual tenancy may devolve separately under the ordinary law and will then rest in abeyance, while the transmitted statutory tenancy is enjoyed by the appropriate successor.

In *Moodie* v. *Hosegood*,[27] Moodie was tenant of a house from 1937 to his death in 1950. He died intestate and the tenancy thereupon vested in the Probate Judge under the Administration of Estates Act 1925, s.9. His widow, who was residing with him at the time of his death, continued to reside in the house. Shortly after Moodie's death the respondent acquired the freehold and served notice to quit on the Probate Judge. This determined the contractual tenancy. He then brought an action to recover possession from the appellant. She claimed to be in lawful possession as a successor to a transmitted protected tenancy, and the House of Lords held that she was entitled to remain in possession. Lord Morton observed[28]: "It would be capricious in the extreme to extend the protection of the Acts to a widow whose husband's contract of tenancy had been determined in his lifetime, and to withhold it from the widow whose husband's contract of tenancy was still subsisting at his death." The effect of this reasoning is not to render the contractual tenancy void or inoperative. As Lord Morton explained[29]:

> "If a contractual tenancy is still subsisting at her husband's death, and devolves on someone other than the widow, it is not destroyed, but the rights and obligations which would ordinarily devolve upon the successor in title of the contractual tenant are suspended, so long as the widow retains possession of the dwelling-house."

This may produce an anomalous situation, because during the existence of the statutory tenancy the tenant is bound to observe only such terms and conditions of the original contractual tenancy as are consistent with the Rent Act 1977, yet the contractual tenancy, unlike the normal situation of statutory transmission, is still in existence. Will the contractual tenant therefore be liable for any breaches of

[25] Rent Act, Sched. 1, para. 2 as amended by Housing Act 1980, s.76(1).
[26] R.A. 1977, Sched. 1, para. 1.
[27] [1952] A.C. 61.
[28] At p. 71.
[29] At p. 74.

terms in the contractual tenancy which are not incorporated into the statutory tenancy, but are committed by the statutory tenant?

In order to succeed to a statutory tenancy the spouse must be residing with the statutory or protected tenant at the time of his death. If there is no qualifying surviving spouse, but a member of the deceased tenant's family wishes to claim, a requirement of six months' residence, in the period immediately before the tenant's death, is imposed.[30] Whether a person was "residing with" the tenant is essentially a question of fact. In *Foreman* v. *Beagley*[31] the defendant's mother was the statutory tenant of a flat as first successor to her husband, the original tenant. From 1965 to her death in 1968 she had been confined to hospital. In 1967 the defendant moved into the flat and lived there until his mother's death. His intention was to look after the flat during his mother's absence and to care for her in the event she was discharged from hospital. It was held that, despite these intentions, as a matter of fact, the defendant had not "resided with" his mother and thus could not become a successor. The Court of Appeal held that, while it was unwise to generalise, the words "residing with" must import the idea of family living or membership of a household. In this case there was no community of living, nor was there evidence of an agreement to establish such community during the relevant period.

Specific provision is made where more than one member of the tenant's family qualifies as successor.[32] There can only be one successor and the expression "a member of the original tenant's family" means one member only, thus precluding any succession by joint tenants.[33] If there is more than one qualified successor, they can come to an agreement as to which one of them shall be the successor. The landlord has no right to be a party to the agreement, and cannot object to the person chosen. If the members of the family cannot agree, the successor will be chosen by the county court. The Act does not indicate the grounds on which the county court judge makes such a choice, but the cases seem to establish that a decision should be reached after putting all the competing factors into the scales, including the wishes of the deceased (which should not, however, be conclusive of the matter).[34]

In determining which persons constitute members of the deceased tenant's family, the courts have held on a number of occasions that the word "family" in this context is not a technical term, but is used in its ordinary or popular sense.[35] It is generally accepted that children,

---

[30] *cf.* Housing Act 1985 s.87, where the period of residence is 12 months in the case of "secure" tenancies; see *post,* Chap. 16.

[31] [1969] 3 All E.R. 838. *cf. Morgan* v. *Murch* [1970] 2 All E.R. 100.

[32] R.A. 1977, Sched. 1, paras. 3 & 7.

[33] *Dealex Properties* v. *Brooks* [1966] 1 Q.B. 542.

[34] *Williams* v. *Williams* [1970] 1 W.L.R. 1530; *Trayfoot* v. *Lock* [1957] 1 W.L.R. 351.

[35] *Brock* v. *Wollams* [1949] 2 K.B. 388; *Langdon* v. *Horton* [1951] 1 K.B. 666.

including adopted, illegitimate and step-children qualify,[36] as do brothers and sisters, including in-laws of a deceased tenant,[37] the husband of a female tenant,[38] nephews and nieces by blood or marriage,[39] grandchildren, and persons to whom the deceased tenant was *in loco parentis*.[40] In giving the word "family" its ordinary meaning, one must take care not to extend that meaning too far. In *Carega Properties S.A.* v. *Sharratt*,[41] Viscount Dilhorne said[42]: "When used in a statute [the word 'family'] has not in my opinion the same meaning as the word 'household.' While a household may consist only of members of a family, it can include persons not capable of being so regarded. I accordingly cannot accept the argument that 'family' in the Act can be read as meaning 'household.' " Therefore, although "family" was not limited to cases of a familial nexus in the strict sense, it still required a broadly recognisable *de facto* familial nexus. Two adults who lived together in a platonic relationship could never establish a sufficient familial nexus by acting, for example, as brother and sister or father and daughter.

The cases are not, however, completely clear on the question of whether a woman, living with the tenant at his death but not married to him, is a member of that tenant's family for this purpose. In *Hawes* v. *Evenden*[43] the Court of Appeal held that a mistress who had been living with the tenant for 12 years prior to his death, and had two children by him, was a member of his family. In *Dyson Holdings* v. *Fox*[44] a mistress had lived with the tenant for 40 years and had taken his name. In 1940 they went to live in a house and after the tenant's death in 1961, the woman continued in residence, paying the rent. The Court of Appeal held that she was a member of the tenant's family and, therefore, entitled to remain in possession. The court held that the meaning of "family" had changed in step with major changes in family law, and was not restricted to blood relationships and those created by the marriage ceremony, at least in cases where the relationship is more than platonic.[45] However, relationships of a casual or intermittent character, and those bearing indications of impermanence, would not normally come within the meaning of the word "family." In *Helby* v. *Rafferty*[46] a man who had been living, and

---

[36] *Brock* v. *Wollams* [1949] 2 K.B. 388.
[37] *Stewart* v. *Higgins* (1951) 157 E.G. 470.
[38] *Gammans* v. *Ekins* [1950] 2 K.B. 328.
[39] *Jones* v. *Whitehill* [1950] 2 K.B. 204; *cf. Carega Properties S.A.* v. *Sharratt* [1979] 2 All E.R. 1084.
[40] *Ross* v. *Collins* [1964] 1 W.L.R. 425.
[41] [1979] 2 All E.R. 1084.
[42] At p. 1087.
[43] [1953] 1 W.L.R. 1169.
[44] [1975] 3 All E.R. 1030.
[45] See *Carega Properties S.A.* v. *Sharratt* [1979] 2 All E.R. 1084. *cf. Helby* v. *Rafferty* [1979] 1 W.L.R. 13, where the Court of Appeal appeared to reject the notion that the meaning of the word "family" could change with times, preferring the view that it should have the meaning applicable when first used by Parliament in the legislation.
[46] [1979] 1 W.L.R. 13.

sharing living expenses for five years, with a female tenant who had deliberately not taken his name was held not to be a member of her family as the relationship lacked permanence and that appeared to be the wish of the deceased tenant. On the other hand, in *Watson* v. *Lucas*[47] a man who had never divorced his wife, was held to be a member of the family of the deceased female tenant, with whom he had lived for nearly twenty years. The Court of Appeal felt the case sufficiently similar to *Dyson* v. *Fox*[48] for that decision to be binding upon them in the instant case. In summary, the overriding considerations would seem to be the establishment of a relationship that is more than purely platonic and which is permanent. The use of a common name, the length of time the relationship has lasted and the presence of children of the relationship are, while not essential, useful items of evidence in support of the family relationship. However, the courts appear to be unwilling, as yet, to accord the status of "family" to a relationship between persons of the same sex who are unrelated by blood or marriage, even where that relationship extends beyond the merely platonic.[49]

B. The Matrimonial Home

Both husband and wife have a right to occupy the rented matrimonial home and to use the furniture in it.[50] If the house is let to both spouses on a joint tenancy, both will be entitled to remain in occupation of it by virtue of the legal estate. If the husband is the sole tenant (whether protected or statutory), the wife has a common law right of occupation by virtue of her right to maintenance and consortium. The Matrimonial Homes Act 1983 gives the non-tenant spouse a statutory right of occupation. If she is in occupation of the rented home, she has a right not to be evicted or excluded from any part of it by the tenant except by court order; if she is out of occupation she has a right to apply for an order permitting her to enter and occupy.[51] This right extends to any yard, garden, garage, or outhouse forming part of the tenancy.[52] The Act does not, however, apply to any house which has never been the spouses' matrimonial home; consequently, although a spouse

---

[47] [1980] 1 W.L.R. 1493.

[48] *Supra.*

[49] See *Harrogate Borough Council* v. *Simpson* (1985) 25 R.V.R. 10, a case under the Housing Act 1985, s.89(1). The circumstances of statutory succession under this Act for "secure" tenancies are different, in that s.113 defines a member of the family rather restrictively. The Court of Appeal decided that a lesbian couple were not a family since they did not, as the Act required, "live together as husband and wife." It is still, therefore, possible for the Court to come to a different conclusion on a statutory succession claim under R.A. 1977, since in that Act "a member of the family" is not defined.

[50] *National Provincial Bank Ltd.* v. *Ainsworth* [1965] A.C. 1175.

[51] Matrimonial Homes Act 1983, s.1(1)(*a*), (*b*).

[52] *Ibid.* s.10(1).

leaving the matrimonial home as a result of constructive desertion will be protected, that person has no right to occupy the house into which the other spouse has later moved.[53]

So long as a spouse has a right of occupation, either party may apply to the court for an order declaring, enforcing, restricting or terminating it.[54] The court may make such order as it thinks just and reasonable, and it must have regard to all the circumstances, including the spouses' conduct towards each other, their needs and resources, and the needs of the children.[55] Either of the parties may apply to the court for an order prohibiting, suspending or restricting the exercise by the other of the right to occupy the dwelling or requiring either spouse to permit the exercise by the other of that right.[56] These orders can also be obtained where the tenancy of the matrimonial home is jointly held by the husband and wife so that a wife who has been granted a joint tenancy can obtain a discretionary order under the Matrimonial Homes Act 1983.[57]

The provisions of the Rent Act 1977, s.2(1)(*a*),[58] make it clear that only an occupying tenant can become or remain a statutory tenant. In consequence, residence by other members of the tenant's family, employees or other licensees cannot, prima facie, be used as constructive residence by the tenant in order to claim a statutory tenancy.[59] There is, however, an exception in the case of spouses. The Matrimonial Homes Act 1983,[60] provides that one spouse's occupation is to be treated as that of the other for the purposes of the Rent Act 1977. The same Act requires the landlord to accept rent from the spouse, notwithstanding that he or she is not the tenant.[61] A spouse who is left in the rented accommodation is, therefore, adequately protected, provided the rent is paid and the other obligations of the tenancy are observed. This last provision is vital. It may sometimes happen that for example, where the wife is left in possession of the matrimonial home, she does not exercise her right to pay the rent because she is under the impression that her husband is still paying it. If the rent in fact remains unpaid, the landlord (possibly in collusion with the husband) may get an order for possession. The court normally has the power to suspend a possession order in such circumstances, on receiving appropriate undertakings concerning payment of rent and arrears.[62] The deserted wife, however, formerly could not obtain suspension of the order. By granting the possession

---

[53] *Ibid.* s.1(10).
[54] *Ibid.* s.1(2).
[55] *Ibid.* s.1(3).
[56] *Ibid.* s.1(2).
[57] *Ibid.* s.9(1) *cf. Phillips* v. *Phillips* [1973] 1 W.L.R. 615.
[58] *Supra*, Chap. 10.
[59] *Cove* v. *Flick* [1954] 2 All E.R. 441.
[60] s.1(6).
[61] *Ibid.*, s.1(5).
[62] R.A. 1977, s.100.

order the court terminated her husband's tenancy. Her rights under what is now the Matrimonial Homes Act 1983, s.1(5),[63] only operated if her husband "is entitled to occupy" the property. His rights, and therefore her rights, terminated on the making of the order for possession and she had no *locus standi* to claim a suspension of the order.[64] However, the Housing Act 1980 provided an amendment to the Rent Act 1977.[65] Where proceedings are brought for possession and the tenant's spouse or former spouse, with rights of occupation under the 1983 Act, is still in occupation, that spouse has the same rights in relation to any adjournment of proceedings, or stay, suspension or postponement of the order for possession, as he or she would have had if the rights of occupation under the 1983 Act had not been lost by termination of the tenancy.

This right to take over and preserve rights under a protected or statutory tenancy is available only to a spouse, and not to other family members. It is not available to a women who has lived with a statutory tenant as his wife, even if she has borne his children.[66] This is in contrast with the provisions for transmission of statutory tenancies to a member of the deceased tenant's family, operative on death.[67]

If the marriage is terminated, a tenant's spouse would, in the normal way, lose the security of tenure since it was the status of marriage which allowed that spouse to maintain, through his or her presence in the property, the tenant's possession. The Matrimonial Homes Act 1983, s.7,[68] provides that the court on pronouncing a decree nisi of divorce or nullity or judicial separation or at any time thereafter, may make an order transferring a protected or statutory tenancy from one to the other. The court may, in place of this power, order transfers of tenancies as transfers of property under the Matrimonial Causes Act 1973, section 24.[69] This is, in practice, the more generally used provision. However, in the case of statutory tenancies it might be advisable to utilise the 1983 Act since statutory tenancies are specifically mentioned in that Act,[70] whereas there is

---

[63] Formerly, the Matrimonial Homes Act 1967, s.1(5).

[64] *Penn* v. *Dunn* [1970] 2 Q.B. 686; *cf.* Law Com. No. 86, paras. 2.42–2.46; Finer Report (Cmnd. 5629), para. 6.44(3).

[65] Housing Act 1980, s.75(3), inserting new subs. (4A) and (4B) to R.A. 1977, s.100(4).

[66] *Colin Smith Music Ltd.* v. *Ridge* [1975] 1 W.L.R. 463.

[67] *Supra, cf,* Domestic Violence and Matrimonial Proceedings Act, 1976, s.1(1)(c); *Spindlow* v. *Spindlow* [1979] 1 All E.R. 169.

[68] And Sched. 1, where the substantive provisions are to be found. This does *not* reverse the effect of *Metropolitan Properties Co.* v. *Cronan* (1982) 44 P. & C.R. 1. The provisions are not retrospective: *Lewis* v. *Lewis* [1985] A.C. 459. It seems that the statutory provision permitting transfer after decree absolute cannot be used to revive a statutory tenancy which has ceased to exist (perhaps because termination of the marriage has ended the "representative" occupation by the wife, thus bringing the statutory tenancy to an end: see, *e.g. Brown* v. *Draper* [1944] K.B. 309) *before* the application for transfer: *Lewis* v. *Lewis, supra.* In such cases, therefore, application under the 1983 Act will still need to be made before decree absolute.

[69] See Hayes & Battersby [1981] Conv. 404.

[70] See Sched. 1.

some doubt as to whether they are "property" within section 24 of the 1973 Act.[71]

---

[71] See also Matrimonial and Family Proceedings Act 1984, s.22, which provides that where leave is granted to apply for financial relief under Pt. III of the 1984 Act, the court has the same powers to order a transfer to the applicant of a protected or statutory tenancy as it has under the Matrimonial Homes Act 1983, s.7 and Sched. 1 on or after a decree of divorce, nullity or judicial separation.

CHAPTER 13

SECURITY OF TENURE

I. Terminating the Tenancy 447
II. Discretionary Grounds for Posses-
sion 449
  A. Suitable Alternative Accommo-
dation 450
  B. Non-payment of Rent or Other
Breaches 451
  C. Nuisance, Immoral or Illegal
User 452
  D. Deterioration of Dwelling-
house 453
  E. Deterioration of Furniture . . 453
  F. Tenant's Notice to Quit 453
  G. Assignment or Sub-letting of
Whole Without Consent 453
  H. Premises Required for an Em-
ployee 454
  I. Premises Required for Land-
lord or Family 455
  J. Overcharging Sub-tenants . . . 457
III. Mandatory Grounds for Possession . 458
  A. Dwelling-house Let by an
Owner-Occupier 458
  B. Landlord's Retirement Home . 460

  C. Out of Season Lettings 461
  D. Vacation Lettings 461
  E. Letting of Dwellings for Minis-
ters of Religion 462
  F. Lettings by Servicemen 462
IV. Sub-tenants 463
  A. Lawful Creation of Sub-tenan-
cies 463
  B. Statutorily Protected Sub-ten-
ancies 464
V. Procedural Matters 467
  A. Jurisdiction 467
  B. Orders and Suspended Orders 468
  C. Enforcement 468
VI. Attempts to Avoid Rent Act Protec-
tion 469
  A. Disregard of the Registered
Rent 469
  B. Licences 469
  C. The Unlawful Sub-tenant or
Licensee 470
  D. The "Holiday-Let" 470
  E. "Bed and Breakfast" Lets . . . 470
  F. Rental Purchase 471

The Rent Act 1977 and the Rent (Agriculture) Act 1976 contain restrictions on the landlord's normal rights to recover possession where a dwelling is let on a protected tenancy, or is subject to a statutory tenancy, or is a protected occupancy or statutory tenancy under the Rent (Agriculture) Act 1976.[1] Certain of these restrictions allow the court a discretion to award the landlord possession if he can make out the necessary statutory grounds; certain of them are mandatory, in that if the landlord makes out the appropriate statutory ground, then the court must grant him possession.

I. TERMINATING THE TENANCY

While a contractual tenancy subsists, the rights and duties of the parties are governed by the terms of the contract. This is particularly important when the landlord seeks to recover possession from a contractual tenant. He will be able to do so only if the terms of the tenancy provide a means of bringing it to an end, such as forfeiture for breach of terms or conditions, or notice to quit. Otherwise the tenancy

---

[1] *Post.* The security of tenure provisions for agricultural occupiers are discussed in Chap. 14.

will continue until it terminates by effluxion of time or one of the other modes of termination discussed earlier in this book.[2] If the tenancy provides for forfeiture upon breach of terms or conditions, the landlord must show that a breach exists within the manner specified and that the breach has not been waived.[3] If the tenancy is determinable by notice to quit, either expressly or by operation of the special rules governing periodic tenancies,[4] then the appropriate period of notice must be given. By the Protection from Eviction Act 1977, s.5(1), no notice by a landlord or a tenant to quit any premises let as a dwelling is valid unless it is in writing, and is given not less than four weeks before the date on which it is to take effect. It must also contain certain information, prescribed by statutory instrument,[5] designed to put tenants on notice that they may have rights to remain in possession. Once the contractual tenancy has been duly determined, the landlord must then show that he has satisfied the grounds for possession under the Rent Act 1977, s.98. In no circumstances can the landlord dispense with the need for a court order. Neither can he obtain judgment by consent unless the tenant concedes that the Rent Acts do not apply to the tenancy.[6] By the Protection from Eviction Act 1977, s.2, where any premises are let as a dwelling on a lease which is subject to a right of re-entry or forfeiture, it is illegal to enforce that right otherwise than by proceedings in court. Section 3 of that Act makes it unlawful to recover possession from a residential occupier otherwise than by court order.

Once the contractual tenancy has come to an end, the tenant's position changes. His right to remain in possession arises solely by virtue of his statutory tenancy under the Rent Act 1977[7] and accordingly he can retain possession for only so long as that Act operates to deprive the landlord of possession. If the statutory tenancy comes to an end for any reason,[8] the landlord can commence proceedings for possession under the Rent Act 1977 immediately and is not required to give the statutory tenant any notice to quit.[9] Normally, any holding over after the due determination of a contractual tenancy will give rise to a statutory tenancy, but there are circumstances where a new contractual tenancy may be created.[10] In such a case, the new tenancy will also have to be determined in the

---

[2] *Supra,* Chap. 8.
[3] Waiver is a common law concept of limited application to a statutory tenancy, *Trustees of Smith's (Henry) Charity* v. *Wilson* [1983] Q.B. 316.
[4] *Supra.* Chap. 2.
[5] The Notices to Quit (Prescribed Information) Regulations 1980 (S.I. 1980 No. 1624).
[6] *R.* v. *Bloomsbury and Marylebone C.C. ex p. Blackburne* (1984) 14 H.L.R. 56.
[7] *Supra,* Chap. 10.
[8] *Ibid.*
[9] R.A. 1977, s.3(4).
[10] See *Errington* v. *Errington* [1952] 1 K.B. 290; *Murray, Bull & Co. Ltd* v. *Murray* [1953] 1 Q.B. 211.

proper way before the court would make an order for possession under the Rent Act 1977.[11]

II. DISCRETIONARY GROUNDS FOR POSSESSION

Certain of the grounds (here referred to as the "discretionary grounds") upon which the landlord can claim possession of a statutory tenancy are discretionary in that the court should not make the order for possession unless it "considers it reasonable to make such an order."[12] This discretion must be exercised "in a judicial manner, having regard on the one hand to the general scheme and purpose of the Act, and on the other to the special conditions, including to a large extent matters of a domestic and social character."[13]

Directions on how the discretion should be exercised were given by Lord Greene M.R. in *Cummings* v. *Danson*.[14]

"In considering reasonableness... it is, in my opinion, perfectly clear that the duty of the judge is to take into account all relevant circumstances as they exist at the date of the hearing. That he must do in what I venture to call a broad, common sense way as a man of the world, and come to his conclusion giving such weight as he thinks right to the various factors in the situation. Some factors may have little or no weight, others may be decisive, but it is quite wrong for him to exclude from his consideration matters which he ought to take into account."

Relevant considerations might include consideration of other legislation affecting the issue,[15] and whether planning permission for a change of use would be available in cases where alternative accommodation is offered by way of a sub-lease of part of existing premises,[16] and sentimental[17] and social matters.[18] It has also been held that environmental matters should be taken into account where relevant.[19]

---

[11] *Marcroft Wagons Ltd.* v. *Smith* [1951] 2 K.B. 496 at p. 507.
[12] R.A. 1977, ss.98(1). It is not possible to appeal on any question of fact in relation to this "reasonableness" issue, when it arises in claims for possession under Cases 1–6, and 8 and 9 of Sched. 15, R.A. 1977 (see *post*), County Courts Act 1984, s.77 (6).
[13] *Per* Macardie J. in *Chiverton* v. *Ede* [1921] 2 K.B. 30 at pp. 44–45.
[14] [1942] 2 All E.R. 653 at p. 655; see also *Rhodes* v. *Cornford* [1947] 2 All E.R. 601; *Cresswell* v. *Hodgson* [1951] 2 K.B. 92; *Dellenty* v. *Pellow* [1951] 2 K.B. 858; *Tideway Investment & Property Holdings Ltd.* v. *Wellwood* [1952] 1 Ch. 791.
[15] *e.g.* rights of occupation under the Matrimonial Homes Act 1983, the Mobile Homes Act 1983, overcrowding and other matters under the Housing Act 1985, and current Code of Guidance issued in respect of Pt. III of H.A. 1985.
[16] *Allen* v. *Jacobs* (1949) 100 L.J. 16; *Schaffer* v. *Griffith* (1955) 105 L.J. 188.
[17] *Battlespring* v. *Gates* (1983) 268 E.G. 355 (family home for 35 years).
[18] *Yoland* v. *Reddington* (1982) 263 E.G. 157 (tenant enjoyed living with sub-tenants of his choice).
[19] *Redspring Ltd.* v. *Francis* [1973] 1 All E.R. 640.

The conduct of the parties or their agents will be relevant, especially where the case concerns non-payment of rent or other breaches of covenant[20]

There are 11[21] discretionary grounds for possession.

A. Suitable Alternative Accommodation

The court may make an order for possession if it is satisfied that suitable alternative accommodation is available to the tenant, or will be available to him when the order for possession takes effect.[22] There are two methods open to a landlord to show the existence of suitable alternative accommodation. First, he can produce a certificate from the housing authority for the district in which the dwelling is situated certifying that the authority will provide suitable alternative accommodation by the date specified in the certificate. Such a certificate is conclusive evidence that suitable alternative accommodation is available.[23] The difficulty with reliance upon this method is that, as local authority accommodation becomes scarcer and waiting lists longer, many authorities are now reluctant to accept the additional burden of tenants who are already protected in the private sector.

The alternative is for the landlord to find and offer alternative accommodation himself.[24] He will be deemed to have done so if

(i)   there would be a protected tenancy or equivalent security of the new accommodation,[25] *and*

(ii) the working place needs of the tenant and his family would be suited,[26] *and*

(iii) the rent would be satisfactory in the light of local authority rent levels or in the light of the tenant's means,[27] *and*

(iv) the accommodation would be either similar in extent to local authority housing or suitable in extent and character to the needs[28] of the tenant and his family,[29] *and*

(v)   where appropriate, similar or suitable furniture would be provided.[30]

---

[20] See *Yates* v. *Morris* [1951] 1 K.B. 77.
[21] For agricultural occupiers see *post*, Chap. 14.
[22] R.A. 1977, s.98 (1) (*a*); Sched. 16, Case 1, para. 1.
[23] R.A. 1977 Sched. 15, Pt. IV, para. 3; Sched. 16, Case 1, para. 3.
[24] R.A. 1977, Sched. 15, para. 4.
[25] This requirement will not be satisfied if any of the mandatory grounds for possession can apply to the new tenancy offered: Housing Act 1980, Sched. 25, para. 58 amending R.A. 1977, Sched. 15, Pt. IV, para. 4.
[26] *Ibid.* para. 5, see *Yewbright Properties* v. *Stone* (1980) 254 E.G. 863.
[27] *Ibid.* para 5(1)(*a*), (*b*), 2.
[28] "needs" means housing needs, as opposed to enjoyment of a certain lifestyle, needing, for example, a stable, *Hill* v. *Rochard* [1983] 1 W.L.R. 478.
[29] *Ibid.*
[30] *Ibid.*

Any separation of rooms between buildings, or an element of sharing, will disqualify the accommodation from being "suitable."[31]

The accommodation offered must be suitable to the needs of the tenant and his family. It must be environmentally suitable[32] and suitable for the work of the members of the household.[33] It does not need to be in a different building to constitute "alternative" accommodation,[34] and indeed suitable alternative accommodation may, in appropriate cases, be constituted by part only of the tenant's present accommodation.[35]

The alternative accommodation must give the tenant either full security of tenure under the Rent Act or its equivalent. The grant of a fixed term of years of reasonable length will satisfy this requirement but a periodic tenancy will not, unless protected.[36] Earlier cases have held that the grant of a council tenancy will not do, since council tenants enjoyed no security of tenure.[37] It is doubtful whether these cases survived the enactment of the Rent Act 1977, Sched. 15, Pt. IV, para. 3. They certainly cannot survive the Housing Act 1985, s.82, which gives some security of tenure to council tenants. Similar reasoning applies to offers of accommodation from housing associations.

B. Non-Payment of Rent or Other Breaches[38]

A landlord may claim possession on the ground of non-payment by the tenant of the lawfully due rent. In general, the discretion of the court under this head will be exercised in a manner similar to the exercise of the jurisdiction to grant relief from forfeiture.[39] In consequence, possession will not normally be granted where the tenant has paid off the arrears due either before the action or before judgment. If the arrears are not paid off until later, the tenant's situation will fall within the case, but it may nevertheless be unreasonable for the court to make the possession order.[40] In any event, the court has a discretion under the Rent Act 1977, s.100,[41] to suspend the operation of a possession order on conditions. To establish a ground for possession on account of non-payment of rent,

[31] *Selwyn* v. *Hamill* [1948] 2 All E.R. 70; *Barnard* v. *Towers* [1953] 1 W.L.R. 1203.
[32] *Redspring Ltd.* v. *Francis* [1973] 1 All E.R. 640. This requirement does not extend to such matters as the society of friends and cultural matters: *Siddiqui* v. *Rashid* [1980] 3 All E.R. 184.
[33] *MacDonnell* v. *Daly* [1969] 1 W.L.R. 1482.
[34] *Thompson* v. *Rolls* [1926] 2 K.B. 426.
[35] *Mykolyshyn* v. *Noah* [1970] 1 W.L.R. 1271.
[36] *Scrace* v. *Windust* [955] 1 W.L.R. 475.
[37] *e.g. Sills* v. *Watkins* [1956] 1 Q.B. 250.
[38] R.A. 1977, Sched. 15, Pt. I, Case 1.
[39] *Supra*, Chap. 5.
[40] *Hayman* v. *Rowlands* [1957] 1 W.L.R. 317.
[41] *Post*.

the landlord must show that an obligation to pay some rent has arisen and not been discharged (*i.e.* that it is "lawfully due") and that such rent remains neither paid nor tendered.[42]

A landlord can also claim possession for other breaches of covenant. These include breaches of obligations imposed on protected or statutory tenants by the Rent Act 1977 (*e.g.* failure to allow the landlord access and reasonable facilities for carrying out repairs[43]); breach of obligations in the contractual tenancy (*e.g.* user[44] and repairing covenants, covenants not to assign or sub-let); and breaches of obligations in a statutory tenancy (which probably includes breaches of implied obligations[45]).

C. Nuisance, Immoral or Illegal User[46]

A court may award a landlord possession where the tenant or any person residing with him or any sub-tenant of his has been guilty of conduct which is a nuisance[47] or annoyance to adjoining occupiers[48] or, where he has been convicted of using the dwelling-house or allowing it to be used for immoral or illegal purposes. This ground for possession can cover an extensive range of conduct, and there is here clearly room for large differences of opinion between landlord, tenant and neighbours. The question of nuisance or annoyance is dependent essentially on the type of neighbourhood and the attitude of the people who live in it.[49]

So far as illegal or immoral user is concerned, the landlord must show that the tenant or one of the other relevant occupiers has been convicted of *using* the house, or allowing it to be used, for an illegal or immoral purpose.[50] The crime must have been committed on the premises.[51] Where such user is established, an order for possession should prima facie be made, although the court has a discretion.[52]

---

[42] *Bird* v. *Hildage* [1948] 1 K.B. 91.
[43] R.A. 1977, ss.3 (2), 148.
[44] *Florent* v. *Horez* (1983) 48 P. & C.R. 166 (restriction on business user broken by running non-profit making organisation).
[45] *cf. Williams Deacons Bank* v. *Catlow* (1928) E.G.D. 286; *Chapman* v. *Hughes* (1923) 129 L.T. 223.
[46] R.A. 1977, Sched. 15, Pt. I, Case 2.
[47] "Nuisance" has a narrower meaning than "annoyance" and is confined to an interference with the ordinary comfort of the adjoining occupiers. Annoyance is a wider expression and covers everything which an ordinary sensible person would deem to be an unreasonable disturbance: *Chapman* v. *Hughes* (1923) 129 L.T. 223.
[48] "Adjoining" extends to "neighbouring," *Cobstone Investments Ltd.* v. *Maxim* [1984] 3 W.L.R. 563.
[49] See Megarry, *The Rent Acts* (10th ed.). pp. 270–272.
[50] *Schneiders & Sons Ltd.* v. *Abrahams* [1925] 1 K.B. 301.
[51] *Abrahams* v. *Wilson* [1971] 2 All E.R. 1114.
[52] See *Yates* v. *Morris* [1950] 1 K.B. 77.

D. Deterioration of Dwelling-House[52a]

If the condition of the property[52b] has, in the opinion of the court, deteriorated owing to acts of waste[52c] by, or the neglect or default of, the tenant, the court may grant the landlord possession of the dwelling. Where the responsibility for the waste or neglect can be laid at the door of lodger or sub-tenant, the court may nevertheless grant possession if it is satisfied that the tenant has not taken such steps as he ought reasonably to have taken to get the lodger or sub-tenant out of the property.

E. Deterioration of Furniture[52d]

Where the condition of any furniture provided for use under the tenancy has, in the opinion of the court, deteriorated owing to ill-treatment by the tenant, it may order possession. Again, if the responsibility for the damage is that of a lodger or sub-tenant, the court may order possession unless the tenant takes all reasonable steps to remove the person responsible.

F. Tenant's Notice to Quit[53]

The landlord may claim possession if the tenant has given notice to quit and, in consequence of that notice, the landlord has contracted to sell or let the dwelling-house or has taken other steps as a result of which he would, in the court's opinion, be seriously prejudiced if he could not obtain possession. This Case is designed to deal with a tenant who, having given his landlord a notice to quit, changes his mind and wishes to stay on in the property. If, in the meantime, the landlord, in reliance on the notice, has committed the property elsewhere, he may be able to secure possession.

G. Assignment or Sub-Letting of Whole Without Consent[54]

A landlord may claim possession where, without his consent,[55] the tenant has, at any time after:

[52a] R.A. 1977, Sched. 15, Pt. I, Case 3.
[52b] Including the state of the garden: *Holloway* v. *Povey* (1984) 271 E.G. 195.
[52c] *Supra*, Chap. 6.
[52d] R.A. 1977, Sched. 15, Pt. I Case 4.
[53] R.A. 1977, Sched. 15, Pt. I Case 5.
[54] *Ibid.* Case 6.
[55] "Consent" here means the consent of the tenant's immediate landlord, and it can be given either expressly or by implication: *Regional Properties Co. Ltd.* v. *Frankenschwerth* [1951] 1 K.B. 631.

(i)   March 22, 1973, in the case of a tenancy which became a
      regulated tenancy by virtue of the Counter-Inflation Act 1973,
      s.14;

(ii) August 14, 1974, in the case of a regulated furnished tenancy;
      or

(iii) December 8, 1965, in the case of any other tenancy,

assigned or sub-let the whole of the dwelling or sub-let part, the
remainder being already sub-let.

This Case was originally provided at a time when it had not been
established that a statutory tenancy could not be assigned,[56] and when
the rules on the requirement of residence for statutory tenants[57] had
not been fully developed. In the case of statutory tenants, any
assignment or sub-letting of the whole premises will put the tenant
outside the protection of the Rent Act 1977, and possession can be
recovered without reference to this Case at all. The Case is,
accordingly, only appropriate in relation to a contractual tenant where
there are no specific prohibitions in the lease prohibiting assignment
or sub-letting[58] The landlord may, on the assumption that it is
reasonable, recover possession because his tenant has assigned or sub-
let, even in cases where the assignment or sub-letting is lawful but he
has not given his consent to it.[59]

H. Premises Required for an Employee[60]

This Case (which does not apply to agricultural occupiers[61]) enables a
landlord to recover possession from a service tenant where the
premises are required for a new employee. It applies only to service
tenancies; service occupancies or licences are governed by the general
law.[62] To recover on this ground the landlord, apart from the general
question of reasonableness, has to show that the dwelling is reasonably required as a residence for a person engaged in his whole-time
employment, or in the whole-time employment of one of his tenants.
Or he may show that the dwelling is required for a prospective
employee with whom a contract has been made, conditional upon

---

[56] *Supra*, Chap. 12.
[57] *Supra*, Chap. 10.
[58] If there are, the landlord can proceed under Case 1 without the need to rely on Case 6.
[59] *Regional Properties Co. Ltd.* v. *Frankenschwerth* [1951] 1 K.B. 631, *per* Evershed M.R. at p. 673,
      and see *Leith Properties Ltd.* v. *Byrne* [1983] Q.B. 433.The assignee or sub-tenant should be heard
      on the question of reasonableness.
[60] R.A. 1977, Sched. 15, Case 8.
[61] *Post*, Chap. 14.
[62] *Supra*, Chap. 2, aside from the need to obtain a court order to recover possession: Protection from
      Eviction Act 1977, ss.3(1), 8(2) and the case of agricultural occupiers under the Rent (Agriculture)
      Act 1976: *post*, Chap. 14.

housing being provided. Apart from the question of the new employee, the landlord must also show that the existing tenant was in his employment or the employment of a former landlord, that the dwelling-house was let to him in consequence of that employment, and that he has ceased to be in that employment.

It is cesser of employment in these circumstances that brings the contractual tenancy to an end, so that any continued occupation by the tenant will be as a statutory tenant and will not, therefore, give rise to any inference that a new tenancy has been created. The landlord does not have to show that the new employee will become a tenant, but merely that he will occupy the dwelling as his residence.[63] Where a landlord obtains an order for possession on this ground and it is subsequently made to appear to the court that the order was obtained by misrepresentation or concealment of material facts, the court may order the landlord to pay to the former tenant such sum as appears sufficient as compensation for damage or loss sustained by the tenant as a result of the order.[64]

I. Premises Required for Landlord or Family[65]

A landlord may recover possession of a dwelling-house let on a protected or statutory tenancy if he can show that it is reasonably required[66] for occupation as a residence for:

(i)   himself, or
(ii) any son or daughter of his over 18, or
(iii) his father or mother, or
(iv) the father or mother of the landlord's spouse.

To maintain the ground the landlord must show that he did not become landlord by purchasing the dwelling or any interest in it after:

(a) in the case of a controlled tenancy, November 7, 1956[67];
(b) in the case of a tenancy which became regulated by virtue of the Counter-Inflation Act 1973, s.14, March 8, 1973;
(c) in the case of a regulated furnished tenancy, May 24, 1974; or
(d) in the case of any other tenancy, March 23, 1965.

Whether or not the dwelling is "reasonably required" for occupa-

---

[63] *Benninga (Mitcham) Ltd.* v. *Bijstra* [1946] K.B. 58; *Royal Crown Derby Porcelain Co. Ltd.* v. *Russell* [1949] 2 K.B. 417; *Harvard* v. *Shears* (1967) 111 S.J. 683.
[64] R.A. 1977, s.102.
[65] *Ibid.* Sched. 15 Pt. I Case 9.
[66] See *Kenneally* v. *Dunne* [1977] 2 All E.R. 16.
[67] This date is unchanged by the Housing Act 1980: see Sched. 25, para. 7.

tion as a residence by one of the persons mentioned above is a question of fact to be determined at the date of the hearing, and the onus of proving it is on the landlord.[68] The issue turns on the needs of the landlord and the other designated persons, and considerations such as their present living conditions, financial circumstances, proximity to place of work and availability of accommodation.[69] The word "landlord" includes joint landlords if they require the house for their joint occupation.[70] If the matter goes on appeal, the Court of Appeal is only concerned with the circumstances as at the county court hearing, and should ignore a later change of circumstances.[71] Nevertheless, a suspended order can be made in anticipation that the property will shortly be required.[72]

The object of excepting from the Case landlords by recent purchase,[73] is to prevent people from buying houses over the heads of sitting tenants and then evicting them without giving them alternative accommodation.[74] The limitation operates only where there is a protected tenant in occupation at the time of purchase. Consequently if a person buys a house with vacant possession and then lets it to a tenant without first living in it himself, he will not be precluded from recovering possession by reason of this limitation.[75]

The Rent Act 1977, Sched. 15, Pt. III, para. 1, states that a court shall not make an order for possession on this ground unless it is satisfied that, having regard to all the circumstances, including the question of whether other accommodation is available for the landlord or the tenant, greater hardship would be caused by refusing the order than granting it. The object of this "greater hardship" qualification is to give the judge discretion to consider all the circumstances of both the landlord and the tenant before making an order for possession. The onus is on the tenant to show greater hardship,[76] but it is not clear how much this qualification adds to the general duty placed upon the court by the Rent Act 1977, s.98(1), to be satisfied that it is reasonable to make the order for possession. The

---

[68] *Epsom Grand Stand Association Ltd.* v. *Clarke* (1919) 35 T.L.R. 525. The question is separate from the general requirement of reasonableness under the R.A. 1977, s.98. See also *Kenneally* v. *Dunne* [1979] 2 All E.R. 16.

[69] *Rowe* v. *Truelove* (1976) 241 E.G. 533.

[70] *Baker* v. *Lewis* [1947] K.B. 186. Personal representatives requiring possession for themselves and infant beneficiaries can use this ground, *Patel* v. *Patel* [1981] 1 W.L.R. 1342, but generally trustees cannot use the ground: *Parker* v. *Rosenberg* [1947] K.B. 371; see also *Stratford* v. *Syrett* [1958] 1 Q.B. 107.

[71] *Fuggle* v. *Gasden* [1948] 2 Q.B. 236; see further *Woodfall*, para. 3–0147.

[72] *Kidder* v. *Birch* (1983) 46 P. & C.R. 362.

[73] "Purchase" here means "buying," rather than its technical meaning of acquisition otherwise than as a volunteer: *Thomas* v. *Fryer* [1970] 2 All E.R. 1.

[74] *Littlechild* v. *Holt* [1950] 1 K.B. 1 , *per* Denning L.J. at p. 7.

[75] *Epps* v. *Rothnie* [1945] K.B. 562.

[76] *Sims* v. *Wilson* [1946] 2 All E.R. 261.

judge has a duty to consider greater hardship at the date of the hearing and not on the basis of prior admissions by the parties.[77]

Asquith L.J.[78] has characterised the "greater hardship" qualification thus:

> " . . . the county court judge should take into account hardship to all who may be affected by the grant or refusal of an order for possession—relatives, dependants, lodgers, guests, and the stranger within the gates—but should weigh such hardship with due regard to the status of the persons affected and their 'proximity' to the tenant or landlord, and the extent to which, consequently, hardship to them would be hardship to him. The inability to take in a guest for the weekend would no doubt be assessed by the judge as nil. The exclusion of a loved and trusted relation, whether dependent or not, would weigh heavily in the scales."

Where a landlord obtains an order for possession on this ground by means of misrepresentation or concealment of material facts, he may be ordered to compensate the tenant thus injured.[79]

J. Overcharging Sub-Tenants[80]

A court may grant the landlord possession if it is satisfied that the rent charged by the tenant:

(i) for any sub-let part of the dwelling-house, is or was in excess of the maximum rent for the time being recoverable for that part, having regard to the provisions of the Rent Act 1977, Pts. II or III[81]; or

(ii) for any sub-let part of the dwelling-house which is subject to a restricted contract,[82] is or was in excess of the maximum (if any) which is lawfully recoverable by the lessor having regard to the Rent Act 1977, Pt. V.[83]

---

[77] *Smith* v. *McGoldrick* (1976) 242 E.G. 1047.
[78] In *Harte* v. *Frampton* [1948] 1 K.B. 73 at p. 79; see also: *Rhodes* v. *Cornford* [1947] 2 All E.R. 601; *Bailey* v. *Purser* [1967] 2 All E.R. 189; *McDonnell* v. *Daly* [1969] 3 All E.R. 851 at p. 854; *Thomas* v. *Fryer* [1970] 2 All E.R. 1.
[79] R.A. 1977, s.102.
[80] *Ibid.* Sched. 15, Pt. I Case 10.
[81] *Supra*, Chap. 11.
[82] This term is explained *post*, Chap. 14.
[83] *Ibid.*

III. MANDATORY GROUNDS FOR POSSESSION

In the case of regulated tenancies, certain grounds upon which the landlord can obtain possession are set out in the Rent Act 1977, Sched. 15, Pt. II. These are mandatory grounds, in that if the landlord can make out any of the grounds detailed in Cases 11–15, the court is obliged to make the order, without regard to the question of whether it is reasonable to do so.[84]

A. Dwelling-House Let by an Owner-Occupier[85]

Where a person who lets the dwelling-house on a regulated tenancy had at any time[86] before letting it occupied it as his residence, and not later than the date of commencement of the tenancy[87] the landlord gave notice in writing to the tenant that possession might be recovered on this ground, *and* the dwelling has not since:

(i)   March 22, 1973, in the case of a tenancy which became a regulated tenancy by virtue of the Counter-Inflation Act 1973, s.14;

(ii) August 14, 1974, in the case of a regulated furnished tenancy; or

(iii) December 8, 1965, in the case of any other tenancy,

been let by the owner-occupier on a protected tenancy without this notice being served, then the court must order possession if satisfied that:

(a)   the dwelling is required as a residence for the owner-occupier or any member of his family who resided with him when he last occupied the property as his residence; or

(b)   the owner has died, and the dwelling is required as a residence for a member of his family who was living with him at the date of his death. The member of the family need never have lived in the house of which possession is sought unless the landlord died before section 66 of the Housing Act 1980[88] was brought into force; or

---

[84] R.A. 1977, s.98 (2).

[85] *Ibid.* Sched. 15, Pt. II Case 11, as amended by Housing Act 1980, s.66 & Sched.7; and Rent (Amendment) Act 1985, s.1 overturning the effect of *Pocock* v. *Steel* [1985] 1 W.L.R. 229.

[86] Even if only intermittently, *Naish* v. *Curzon* (1985) 273 E.G. 1221.

[87] Unless created before December 8, 1965, when the relevant date for the notice is June 7, 1966; if a furnished tenancy created before August 14, 1974, the relevant date is February 13, 1975; if the tenancy became a regulated tenancy by virtue of the Counter-Inflation Act 1973, s.14, and the previous contractual tenancy was created before March 22, 1973, the relevant date is September 22, 1973: R.A. 1977, Sched. 15, Pt. III, para. 2.

[88] November 28, 1980.

(c) the owner has died and the dwelling-house is required by a successor in title as his residence or for the purpose of disposing of it with vacant possession. This is not limited to successors to the landlord's beneficial interest, and can therefore be used by personal representatives who wish to sell with vacant possession. Again, this provision will not operate in the case of a landlord dying before section 66 was brought into force[88a]; or

(d) the dwelling is subject to a mortgage by deed granted before the tenancy, and the mortgagee is entitled to sell under a contractual or statutory power, needing possession to dispose of the property with vacant possession; or

(e) the dwelling is not reasonably suitable to the landlord's needs in relation to his place of work, and he requires possession in order to sell with vacant possession, using the proceeds to acquire a more suitable property.

If the court is satisfied that it is just and equitable to do so, it may dispense with the need for either or both of the requirements as to service of the notice.[89]

Despite the use of the phrase "owner-occupier" in the Case, the emphasis is in fact on "occupation" and ownership plays a subsidiary part. In *Tilling* v. *Whiteman*[90] two joint owners of a house (who had both at some time in the past occupied the house) claimed possession on this ground by establishing that it was now required as a residence for one of them only. The House of Lords held that it was not necessary for the house to be required for the residence of both co-owners. The strict application of the doctrine of joint ownership was not intended by the legislature when creating this Case as a ground for possession. For this reason the Case would seem to contemplate claims by owners of subordinate interests as well as freeholders. If the landlords are married co-owners, and the marriage breaks up during the continuance of the tenancy, it will still be possible, relying on *Tilling* v. *Whiteman*, for one co-owner to recover possession on this ground.

In practice this exemption is frequently resorted to by landlords whose job takes them abroad for a short period. If the property is subject to a building society mortgage, the terms of the mortgage will require the mortgagee's consent to the letting. If the building society formally consent, the tenancy will be binding on it but, as a result of the amendments made by the Housing Act 1980, a mortgagee can

[88a] *Ibid.*
[89] But not when a temporary letting was never intended, *Bradshaw* v. *Baldwin-Wiseman* (1985) 49 P. & C.R. 382, *cf. Fernandes* v. *Parvardin* (1982) 264 E.G. 49, and see *Minay* v. *Sentongo* (1983) 45 P. & C.R. 190.
[90] [1980] A.C. 1.

recover possession.[91] Paragraph (e) *supra* also helps in those cases where the owner-occupier returns to work in another part of the country, and needs to sell the tenanted house with vacant possession so that he can buy a more suitable house.

B. Landlord's Retirement Home[92]

The court must grant the landlord possession if he can show that he intends to occupy the house as his residence at such time as he might retire from regular employment, and that he let it on a regulated tenancy before he retired, and:

(i)   not later than the commencement of the tenancy[93] he gave the tenant notice, in writing, that possession might be recovered on this ground; and

(ii) the house has not, since August 14, 1974, been let by him on a protected tenancy without the notice being served; and

(iii) the court is satisfied that: (a) the owner has retired from regular employment and needs the house as his residence, or that the owner has died and the house is required for a member of his family residing with him at the time of his death; or
(b) the owner has died and the house is required by a successor in title as his residence or for the purpose of disposing of it with vacant possession; or
(c) the house is subject to a mortgage by deed granted before the tenancy and the mortgagee is entitled to sell under a contractual or statutory power and he requires possession to dispose of it with vacant possession for that purpose.

However, the Court can dispense with conditions (i) and (ii) above if it considers it just and equitable to make the order notwithstanding the landlord's failure to comply with them.

Although the object of this Case is reasonably clear, vital words are left undefined. Does "employment" cover the self-employed? What does "regular employment" mean?[94] What of the employee who is dismissed rather than one who voluntarily leaves employment? The Case also provides the opportunity of avoiding the system of Rent Act protection since there is no requirement that the landlord actually live in the property after he has recovered possession, so long as he can

---

[91] But not if the letting is a shorthold tenancy.
[92] R.A. 1977, Sched. 15, Pt. II Case 12, as amended by Housing Act 1980, s.66 & Sched. 7.
[93] See n. 87, *supra*.
[94] *cf. R.* v. *Deputy Industrial Injuries Commissioner, ex p. Humphreys* [1966] 1 Q.B. 1.

show he intends to do so at the time of the action. In practice, however, easier means of avoidance are now available.[95]

C. Out of Season Lettings[96]

This ground enables a landlord to recover possession from a tenant, following the giving of appropriate notice, when the dwelling-house was previously occupied for holiday purposes. A court must order possession where the dwelling is let under a tenancy not exceeding eight months, and:

(i) not later than the commencement of the tenancy[97] the landlord gave notice in writing to the tenant that possession might be recovered on this ground; and
(ii) the dwelling was, at some time within the period of 12 months ending on the relevant date, occupied under a right to occupy it for a holiday.

This provision offers a corollary to the Rent Act 1977, s.9,[98] enabling a landlord to alternate holiday-lettings with out-of-season lettings without conferring security of tenure on any of his tenants. Because, however, this ground of possession is not specifically related to section 9 at all, presumably holiday occupation by the landlord himself would be sufficient for the purposes of condition (ii) above.

D. Vacation Lettings[99]

This ground enables an institution of further or higher education[1] to let dwellings for a period not exceeding 12 months, and to recover possession without the court being able to exercise any discretion in the tenant's favour, provided the tenant was informed by written notice before or at the time of the letting that possession might be recovered on this ground, and provided also that at some time within the 12 months before the letting, the dwelling was let to a student under the exemption in the Rent Act 1977, s.8(1).[2] Technically this ground of possession is not wholly confined to educational institutions, and may be used for example, where such an institution, which has been letting accommodation to students, sells a dwelling with

[95] See *post*, and *supra*, Chap. 10.
[96] R.A. 1977, Sched. 15, Pt. II, Case 13.
[97] See note 87, *supra*.
[98] *Supra*, Chap. 10.
[99] R.A. 1977, Sched. 15, Pt. II Case 14.
[1] See the discussion of R.A. 1977, s.8(1), in Chap. 10, *supra*.
[2] *Supra*, Chap. 10.

vacant possession to a new landlord, who re-lets the property within 12 months.

E. Letting of Dwellings for Ministers of Religion[3]

This ground enables possession of a dwelling to be recovered where it is held for the purpose of being available for occupation by a minister of religion as a residence from which to perform the duties of his office, and:

(i) not later than the date of commencement of the tenancy[4] the tenant was given written notice that possession might be recovered on this ground, and

(ii) the court is satisfied that the dwelling-house is required for occupation by a minister of religion as a residence.

F. Lettings by Servicemen[5]

Possession of a dwelling-house can be recovered by a person who, both when he acquired the house and when he let it was a member of the armed forces and who:

(a) let the house after the Housing Act 1980, s.67[6] came into force; and

(b) before the tenancy commenced gave the tenant notice in writing that possession might be recovered on this ground; and

(c) since section 67[6] came into force has not let the house on a protected tenancy without complying with condition (b) above; and

(d) he requires the house, or the house is required, for one of the following purposes:
   (i) as a residence for himself;
   (ii) as a residence for a member of his family residing with him at the date of his death, if the landlord died before possession is sought;
   (iii) the owner has died and possession is required by a successor in title to facilitate disposal with vacant possession;
   (iv) the house is subject to a mortgage by deed granted before the tenancy, the mortgagee is entitled to sell under a

[3] R.A. 1977, Sched. 15, Pt. II, Case 15.
[4] See note 84, *supra.*
[5] Housing Act 1980, s.67, introducing R.A. 1977, Sched. 15, Case 20.
[6] November 28, 1980.

contractual or statutory power and he requires possession to dispose of it with vacant possession for that purpose;

(v)   the house is not reasonably suitable to the landlord's needs in relation to his place of work, and he requires possession in order to sell with vacant possession so that he can use the proceeds to acquire another house more suitable to his needs.

The court may dispense with compliance with conditions (b) and (c) above if it is equitable to do so.

IV. Sub-tenants

The position of sub-tenants at common law when their landlord's interest is determined has already been considered.[7] The usual rule is that the branch falls with the tree, although sub-tenants do have an independent right to ask for discretionary relief if the head lease is being forfeited.[8] Some form of protection may be extended to residential sub-tenants within the Rent Acts. To be considered for that protection, either the sub-tenancy itself must have been lawfully created, or the landlord must be estopped from denying its validity.

A. Lawful Creation of Sub-tenancies

The ability of contractual tenants to create sub-tenancies at common law has been considered.[9] Statutory tenants have an inherent right to create sub-tenancies,[10] although the landlord must be given notice of the exercise of a right within 14 days.[11] The statutory tenant/landlord who sub-lets the whole, ceases himself to be a residential tenant, and so moves outside the protection of the Rent Acts.[12] A sub-tenancy of part created since August 14, 1974, is not a protected tenancy if there is a resident landlord.[13] The sub-tenancy in that event may enjoy some protection as a restricted contract.[14]

In most cases, the original contractual tenancy has expressly prohibited assignments or sub-lettings of the whole or part. The tenancy agreement may further require the premises to be used as a

---

[7] See *Ante*, Chap. 8 (VI) D.
[8] L.P.A. 1925, s.146(4).
[9] See *ante*, Chap. 7 (II) B (III) C.
[10] *Roe* v. *Russell* [1928] 2 K.B. 117. But an outright disposition is unlikely to be regarded as a sub-letting, even if called one: *Trustees of Smith's (Henry) Charity* v. *Willson* [1983] Q.B. 316.
[11] R.A. 1977, s.139.
[12] R.A. 1977, s.2, and see *ante*, Chap. 10, (III).
[13] R.A. 1977, s.12.
[14] See *post*, Chap. 14, (I).

single dwelling-house,[15] or restrict occupancy to the original tenant
and the members of his immediate family. It follows that a sub-letting
of part is likely to be a breach of these covenants, making the sub-
tenancy unlawful and in no way binding on the superior landlord.[16]
The superior landlord may be estopped, however, from denying the
lawfulness of the sub-letting.[17] We have already seen how demanding
rent with knowledge of a breach of the covenants can effect a waiver
of the breach at common law.[18] The position is not quite the same
when it comes to decide if the landlord by demanding and accepting
rent has waived his right to object to the somewhat spectral interest in
the property of the person claiming to be a statutory sub-tenant.

> "As at present advised, we think that the fair rule is that a
> landlord who has acquired full knowledge[19] of a non-continuing
> breach of covenant by a statutory tenant entitling him to invoke
> the court's jurisdiction should be entitled thereafter to receive
> rent and should not by reason of such receipt be held to have
> waived the breach, provided he makes it clear to the tenant at the
> time of, or prior to, the receipt that his receipt is without
> prejudice to his right to go to the court and provided he issues his
> summons for possession within such time, as, having regard to all
> the circumstances of the case, the court hearing the summons
> regards as reasonable."[20]

Waiver will operate to make the sub-tenancy lawful only from the date
of the waiver.[21]

B. Statutorily Protected Sub-tenancies

Section 137 of the Rent Act 1977 gives some protection to sub-tenants
only if the premises have been lawfully sub-let[22]. Section 137(1)
counteracts the "branch falling with the tree" rule, by providing that if

---

[15] *Dobbs* v. *Linford* [1953] 1 Q.B. 48.
[16] *Maley* v. *Fearn* [1946] 2 All E.R. 583; *Carter* v. *Green* [1950] 2 K.B. 76.
[17] Whether lawful or not the tenant/landlord who created it will be bound by it, *cf.* Chap. 3, (IV) B(2) *ante*.
[18] See *ante*, Chap. 5(VII)A(1); Chap. 7(II)C(4).
[19] And see *Metropolitan Properties Co.* v. *Cordery* (1979) 251 E.G. 567, where the lessors were regarded as knowing of the breach because of their porters' knowledge who were under a duty to inform them of changes in occupation of the flats.
[20] *Oak Property Co. Ltd.* v. *Chapman* [1947] K.B. 886 at pp. 899, 900, *per* Somervell L.J., and see *Trustees of Smith's (Henry) Charity* v. *Willson* [1983] Q.B. 316 (demand regarded as "equivocal"); and *Swallow Securities* v. *Isenberg* (1985) 274 E.G. 1028 (unlawful sub-tenant spent some £40,000 on refurbishment, unknown to landlord's porter).
[21] *Muspratt* v. *Johnston* [1966] 2 Q.B. 383.
[22] A sub-letting in breach of a term to sub-let only as high class furnished accommodation renders the sub-tenancy unlawful and outside the protection of s.137, *Patoner* v. *Alexandrakis* (1984) 272 E.G. 330; *Patoner* v. *Lowe* (1985) 275 E.G. 540.

a possession order is made of a dwelling-house against a protected or statutory tenant,[23] or a protected occupier or statutory tenant as defined in the Rent (Agriculture) Act 1976,[24] then nothing in the order affects the right of a lawful sub-tenant to retain possession either of the house or the part of it sub-let to him before the commencement of proceedings. He does not automatically become a trespasser by reason of the order. What happens is that he is "deemed to become the tenant of the landlord on the same terms as if the tenant's statutorily protected tenancy had continued."[25]

The precise nature of the protection afforded to lawful sub-tenants has been the subject of some discussion and speculation.[26] It seems, however, that although he statutorily becomes the head landlord's tenant he does so on the basis that the intermediate tenancy continued notwithstanding that in law it has come to an end either by reason of a possession order "or for any other reason."[27] It seems to follow that the disappearance of the intermediate tenancy does not alter the nature and quality of the sub-tenant's rights.[28] If he was a protected sub-tenant, having had a tenancy of an unfurnished part granted to him prior to August 14, 1974, then he will remain a protected tenant. If he has only a restricted contract because his sub-tenancy was created by a resident landlord since that date, then it is suggested that he still only enjoys the limited protection afforded to the holder of a restricted contract,[29] even though there may be no-one else living in the property at all at that time.[30] The benefit of these provisions is extended to lawful sub-tenants of residential tenants holding under long leases at low rents,[31] provided that the sub-tenancy was not created either after notice to terminate it had been given,[32] or during its period of statutory continuance.[33]

The sub-tenant's position is not as secure as if he were holding a statutory tenancy directly from the landlord. The sub-tenant is only deemed to become the tenant of the landlord "subject to this Act," *i.e.*

---

[23] Under R.A. 1977, ss.98 (1), or 99 (2), and see *supra* (II) *et seq.*
[24] Under Rent (Agriculture) Act 1976, Sched. 4, Pt. I see *post*, Chap. 15(II) R.A. 1977, s.137, is extended to cover sub-tenancies within R.A. 1977, s.99, or the 1976 Act, and s.137(3), applies where the superior tenancy is of an agricultural holding.
[25] R.A. 1977, s.137 (2).
[26] See Woodfall, Vol. 3, paras. 3–0207 *et seq.*; Farrand, *The Rent Act 1977*; (1977) 41 Conv. 96 (Jill Martin).
[27] See R.A. 1977, s.137(2). The position on the surrender of a contractual tenancy is expressly covered by L.P.A. 1925, s.139.
[28] R.A. 1977, s.138, enables the head landlord to avoid any terms relative to furniture or services that might have bound the tenant/landlord by serving a notice to that effect on the sub-tenant within six weeks of the ending of the statutorily protected tenancy.
[29] *cf. Stanley* v. *Compton* [1951] 1 All E.R. 859.
[30] *cf.* the position on the death of a resident landlord, R.A. 1977, Sched. 2, Pt. I, as amended H.A. 1980, s.65(2)–(5), and see *ante.*
[31] See *post*, Chap. 15, note 13; R.A.1977, s.137 (5).
[32] *i.e.* under L. & T.A. 1954, s.4 (1).
[33] *i.e.* under L. & T.A. 1954, s.3 (1), and see R.A. 1977, s.137 (6).

the Rent Act 1977.[34] This phrase, in the judgment of the Court of Appeal "merely means that, where the interest of the original tenant has been determined for any reason, any lawful sub-tenant *who is entitled to retain possession under the provisions of the 1977 Act*[35] shall, notwithstanding that the title under which he derived his interest has come to an end, continue to be the tenant on the terms mentioned in the subsection".[36] The consequences are that "the rights of the sub-tenant do not necessarily stand or fall with those of the tenant; he is entitled to have his rights independently considered and ascertained. Nevertheless, even the lawful sub-tenant in our judgment remains vulnerable to possession proceedings in a case where the head landlord can establish as against him the condition set out in section 98(1) of the 1977 Act."[37] It follows that the landlord can recover possession if he can establish that it is reasonable for such an order to be made against both the tenant and the sub-tenant, where, for example, the lawful sub-tenancy was created without his consent.[38]

Where the tenant/landlord's interest in the dwelling-house[39] was not a statutory or protected tenancy,[40] the sub-tenant's interest may still be protected if he was either a protected or statutory tenant of the tenant/landlord. Section 137(3) operates in these cases where part of the whole premises has been sub-let on a protected or statutory tenancy. This sub-section is of assistance, *e.g.* in those cases where a house has been let as a whole unit, and the original tenant/landlord has moved out, sub-letting the different floors, lawfully of course, on protected tenancies. Here, the sub-tenant is regarded as if there had been let to him his separate part of the premises at a rent "equal to the just proportion of the rent under the superior tenancy." This provision may be something of a two-edged sword for the sub-tenant. On the one hand he may argue if he is sub-tenant of one of four floors that his new rent ought to be one-quarter of the old rent of the whole house. On the other hand, that rent may turn out to be less than two-thirds of the rateable value properly apportioned to his floor, and so put him outside the protection of the Rent Act altogether.[41] This will happen when the tenant/landlord had a lease at a low rent that was not a long tenancy.

If the sub-tenancy is unlawful, or the sub-tenancy does not come within the protection of section 137 of the Rent Act 1977, then the

[34] R.A. 1977, s.137(2).
[35] Italics in original.
[36] R.A. 1977, s.137(2).
[37] *Leith Properties Ltd.* v. *Byrne* [1983] Q.B. 433 at p. 441, and see *ante* (II) G.
[38] And so within R.A. 1977, Sched. 15, Case 6.
[39] R.A. 1977, s.137 (3), refers to the sub-let portion forming part of "premises," but this has been narrowly interpreted as meaning "a dwelling-house," or "buildings" see *Maunsell* v. *Olins* [1974] 3 W.L.R. 835.
[40] For these purposes, long leases at low rents are treated as statutorily protected tenancies, R.A. 1977, s.137(5).
[41] *cf.* R.A. 1977, s.5, and *Cadogan (Earl)* v. *Henthorne* [1957] 1 W.L.R. 1.

superior landlord can treat the "sub-tenant" as a trespasser. There are grounds for considering that if the sub-tenancy was not lawfully created so as to bind the superior landlord, then the sub-tenant cannot claim the benefit of section 3 of the Protection from Eviction Act 1977,[42] and so is liable to eviction without the necessity of court proceedings.[43] However, as the use of force or violence constitutes a serious crime,[44] the more sensible and normal course of action is to obtain an order for possession. In this instance the summary High Court procedure can be used.[45]

V. Procedural Matters

A. Jurisdiction

Jurisdiction in respect of questions concerning security of tenure is given to the county court by the Rent Act 1977, s.141(5). Unless the landlord's claim for security concerns one of the mandatory grounds discussed above, the county court has jurisdiction notwithstanding that by "reason of the amount of the claim or otherwise" the case would not, in the normal way, be within the county court's jurisdiction.[46] So, if a landlord is seeking possession from a former statutory tenant who is no longer qualified to retain his tenancy, or on any of the grounds in Schedule 15, Part I, Cases 1–10, or relies on the provision of suitable alternative accommodation, his action should be brought in the county court. If a landlord brings proceedings on any of these grounds in the High Court, he is not entitled to recover his costs.[47] Action on the mandatory grounds contained in Schedule 15, Part II, Cases 11–15 and Case 20, may be brought in the county court or High Court.[48]

B. Orders and Suspended Orders

Proceedings should be taken against both tenants and sub-tenants if the plaintiff requires vacant possession. Once the court has concluded that the landlord is entitled to possession, it may make an order for

---

[42] *Bolton Building Society* v. *Cobb* [1966] 1 W.L.R. 1, but see (1977) 41 Conv. 197 (Peter Smith).
[43] See further Chap. 19, *post.*
[44] Under Criminal Law Act 1977, s.6.
[45] As in *Moore Properties (Ilford) Ltd.* v. *McKeon* [1976] 1 W.L.R. 1278.
[46] R.A. 1977, s.141(3).
[47] *Ibid.* s.141(4); *Smith* v. *Poulter* [1947] K.B. 339; *Tideway Investment & Property Holdings Ltd.* v. *Wellwood* [1952] Ch. 791.
[48] The procedure in the County Court on grounds 11 to 20 is governed by The Rent Act (County Court Proceedings for Possession) Rules 1981 (S.I. 1981 No. 139).

possession forthwith. Alternatively, it may stay or suspend the execution of the order or postpone the date of possession for such period or periods as it thinks fit.[49] This is a very wide discretion and it can include suspension or postponement on conditions. Where the court exercises these various powers it must impose conditions with regard to payment of any arrears of rent, for payment of current rent or mesne profits, or any other conditions it thinks appropriate.[50] If the imposition of conditions would cause the tenant exceptional hardship, or would otherwise be unreasonable, they may be dispensed with. Where possession is sought on one of the mandatory grounds, any postponement of the effect of the order must normally be limited to 14 days.[51] The delay can be longer in the case of exceptional hardship, up to a maximum of six weeks. In suspending or postponing orders, the judge should be asked to safeguard the position of landlords[52] and this is particularly desirable where the effect of postponement or suspension is to sanction a continuing breach of covenant.[53]

C. Enforcement

A tenant who fails to leave when the court has ordered possession may be met by a warrant for possession taken out by the landlord after the expiration of the day on which the tenant is ordered to give up possession[54]. The warrant covers all persons who are found on the premises at the time of execution. The warrant lasts for one year from the date of its issue, subject to extension by the court.[55] The warrant for possession will be executed by the bailiff's office. For the purposes of executing a warrant to give possession, the bailiff's officers will only need to remove those persons on the premises who are refusing to leave. It is not necessary to remove goods or chattels from the premises.[56]

VI. Attempts to Avoid Rent Act Protection

The Rent Acts are designed to provide both some security of tenure

---

[49] R.A.1977, s.100.

[50] R.A. 1977, s.100(3), H.A.1980, s.75(2); see also *Yates* v. *Morris* [1951] 1 K.B. 77; *Central Estates (Belgravia) Ltd.* v. *Woolgar (No. 2)* [1972] 3 All E.R. 610; *cf. Borthwick-Norton* v. *Romney Warwick Estates Ltd.* [1950] 1 All E.R. 798, *per* Goddard C.J. at p. 801.

[51] Housing Act 1980, s.89. *Quaere* an apparent inconsistency with the Protection from Eviction Act 1977, s.4.

[52] *Metrobarn Ltd.* v. *Gehring* [1976] 1 W.L.R. 776, *per* Cairns L.J. at p. 780.

[53] See, *e.g. Bell London and Provincial Properties Ltd.* v. *Reuben* [1947] K.B. 157; *Tideway Investments & Property Holdings Ltd.* v. *Wellwood* [1952] 1 Ch. 791.

[54] C.C.Rules Ord. 26, r. 17.

[55] C.C.Rules Ord. 26, r. 6.

[56] County Courts Act 1984, s.111(2).

and control over rents. Attempts are made to avoid one or other or, in some cases, both these forms of control. Sometimes the landlord's motive is simply exploitive, and he deliberately sets out to evade and to disregard the Rent Acts. In other cases, landlords may only be prepared to let their property if they can be sure of recovering possession. Certainly the shorthold provisions introduced in 1980 are proving popular. How far they result in a reduction of the more blatant attempts to avoid the Acts is a matter of conjecture. The principal means of avoidance, which are in any event more commonly found in "stress areas" are[57]:

A. Disregard of the Registered Rent

The Francis Report[58] drew attention to the results of a survey indicating that up to 25 per cent. of tenants surveyed were paying a rent in excess of the registered rent. Sometimes this is done inadvertently where premises are let by a later owner ignorant of an earlier registered rent, but in many cases the breach is deliberate. There are no criminal sanctions against charging excess rents for regulated tenancies although if the letting is on a weekly tenancy, there is an obligation on the landlord to insert in the rent book the amount of rent payable. Entry of an incorrect figure, or no figure at all, is an offence.[59] It is a crime to charge more than the registered rent in respect of a restricted contract.[60]

One variation of this theme is for a landlord to apply for a certificate of fair rent, or registered rent in respect of one unit only of a block of flats. For the other units he is quite free to charge what the market can stand, subject to the tenant's right to apply for registration. There is, of course, no obligation on the landlord either to charge or increase the rent to the registered level, unless the tenant is of a subsidised registered housing association.[61]

B. Licences

The use of licences as a means of avoiding the creation of regulated tenancies has been considered at length in other parts of this book.[62] Even if agreements are held to be licences they may nevertheless fall

---

[57] See generally, Francis Report (Cmnd. 4609), Chaps. 15, 25; [1979] S.L.T. 249 (P. Myers).
[58] Cmnd. 4609, p. 117.
[59] L. & T.A. 1985, s.4; The Rent Book (Forms of Notice) Regulations 1982 (S.I. 198 No. 1474).
[60] R.A. 1977, s.81(4).
[61] Housing associations often apply to rent assessment committees with a view to reducing the rent officer's figure.
[62] See *ante*, Chap. 2, (II) Chap. 10, (II).

into the restricted contract category.[63] It is obvious that an increasing number of landlords have been attracted by licence arrangements when the property is to be occupied by a small ad hoc group of individuals, whose composition is likely to change over the months. The disadvantages are not always on the occupiers' side. The arrangement enables changes in the group to be made with less formality and greater flexibility, and also relieves both parties of the need to find someone prepared to undertake the obligations contained in a formal tenancy agreement for a fixed period.

C. The Unlawful Sub-tenant or Licensee

An intermediate stage to the direct granting of licences is for the landlord to grant a lease to a limited company. If the tenancy is of residential accommodation it will be within the rent control provisions of the Rent Acts.[64] If the lease prohibits the creation of sub-tenancies and licences, the rights of the individual occupiers will not be protected on the termination of the grant.[65]

D. The "Holiday-Let"

The exploitation of this form of avoidance has been the subject of considerable litigation[66] and adverse comment. Despite a number of suggestions being made for reform in the debates in the House of Lords on the Housing Bill,[67] no legislative steps were taken in the Housing Act 1980, in the form in which it finally obtained the Royal Assent, to curb any of the alleged abuses.

E. "Bed and Breakfast" Lets

It has already been seen that lettings with attendance may fall outside the regulated sector,[68] and lettings with board and attendance outside the restricted sector.[69] Again, it is argued that this has led to exploitation by landlords prepared to provide little more than a

[63] See *post*, Chap. 14, (I) and Chap. 19.
[64] *Feather Supplies, Ltd.* v. *Ingham* [1971] 2 Q.B. 348, and see *Precedents for the Conveyancer*, 5–63.
[65] *cf.* R.A. 1977, s.137; *Metropolitan Properties Co.* v. *Cordery* (1979) 251 E.G. 567 (where the landlords were deemed to know of the existence of the prohibited sub-tenancy because of their porter's knowledge). And see also *Firstcross (formerly Welgelen N.V.)* v. *East/West (Export/Import)* (1980) 41 P. & C.R. 145.
[66] See *ante*, Chap. 10, (II) C(3) where the cases are fully considered.
[67] H.L.Debates, July 3, 1980. And see T. J. Lyons [1984] Conv. 286.
[68] See *ante*, Chap. 10 (II) C(3)(*b*).
[69] See *post*, Chap. 14, (I) B(2).

continental breakfast,[70] and possibly minimal cleaning services to the occupiers of single rooms. As in so many of these cases, the issue will be to determine whether the agreement is a sham with a common intention to deceive or a bona fide agreement providing some, albeit limited, board and attendance.

F. Rental Purchase

In many areas the only way of selling a house blighted by a prospective compulsory purchase order is by payment of a lump sum of up to 50 per cent. of the price and the balance of the price by weekly instalments, to continue until possession is required under the terms of the order. Interest is usually deferred until instalments are in arrears. However, a variation of this arrangement designed to take the agreement outside Rent Act protection is for the premises to be notionally sold, with completion deferred for, say, two years, the "purchaser" in the meantime to pay interest for the privilege of being granted possession at a weekly rate at or in excess of what would be a fair rent. This method of avoidance relies on the fact that the "purchaser" in possession before completion agrees to occupy as a licensee.

To obtain possession, however, court proceedings must be taken. The "purchaser" cannot be summarily evicted. The benefit of the Protection from Eviction Act 1977 has been extended to such a rental-purchaser[71] as if the premises had been let to him under a tenancy which is not statutorily protected and his tenancy had come to an end with the termination of the agreement or with his right to possession under it.[72] In subsequent proceedings for possession, the court has an unfettered discretion to adjourn the proceedings or stay or suspend the possession order, on any terms the court thinks fit.[73]

---

[70] And see *Holiday Flat Co.* v. *Kuczera* [1978] S.L.T. (Sh.Ct.) 47.

[71] A rental-purchase is an agreement where the price is payable in three or more instalments, and completion is deferred until the whole or part of the price is paid, H.A. 1980, s.88 (4). Most purchases are completed with the price being paid in two instalments, deposit and balance; see Hoggett (1972) 36 Conv.(N.S.) 325.

[72] H.A. 1980, Sched. 25, para. 61.

[73] H.A. 1980, s.88(1), (2).

CHAPTER 14

THE FRAMEWORK FOR PARTIAL PROTECTION

I. Restricted Contracts 473
   A. Introduction 473
   B. Restricted Contracts Defined . 474
   C. Principal Contracts within the
      Restricted Sector 476
   D. The Statutory Restrictions .. 477
II. Agricultural Tied Houses 482
   A. Introduction 482
   B. Protected Occupiers covered by
      the 1976 Act 483
   C. Contracts and Premises cov-
      ered by the 1976 Act 484

   D. Landlords covered by the 1976
      Act 485
   E. The Terms of the Statutory
      Tenancy 486
   F. Recovering Possession 487
III. The Protected Shorthold Tenant .. 491
   A. Introduction 491
   B. The Term 492
   C. Formalities, Rent and Terms . 493
   D. Recovering Possession 495
IV. The Assured Tenant 495

I. RESTRICTED CONTRACTS

A. Introduction

For many years the tenants of furnished premises formed a legal category of their own. From 1920 to 1946 they benefited from some degree of rent control. After 1946 they enjoyed limited protection of tenure afforded by the rent tribunals.[1] In the case of periodic furnished tenancies, the rent tribunal could theoretically postpone the effect of a notice to quit if an application was made to it every six months. In practice nine months' security of tenure was and is likely to be the maximum period of security of tenure given by rent tribunals, and often the period would be much reduced.[2] The Protection from Eviction Act 1964 was designed to prevent landlords of furnished accommodation from evicting their tenants, whether they enjoyed fixed or periodic terms, without the benefit of a court order.[3] The Rent Act 1974 converted most furnished tenancies into regulated tenancies,[4] leaving a rump known as "restricted contracts" still receiving rent tribunal protection. Restricted contracts do not enjoy a common factor by which they can be readily identified. Tenancies where there is a resident landlord are the most significant group and it is immaterial whether the premises are furnished. But a large number of residential licences can also fall within the definition of a restricted contract. Now the important watershed is no longer

[1] Furnished Houses (Rent Control) Act 1946.
[2] And see The Francis Committee Report, Cmnd. 4609, pp. 141, 142.
[3] See now Protection from Eviction Act 1977 and Chap. 19, *post.*
[4] And so within the protection contained in Chap. 13, *ante.*

furnished/unfurnished or resident/non-resident landlord, but pre/post Housing Act 1980 contracts. Restricted contracts entered into or, it is submitted, renewed after the commencement of section 69 of the Housing Act 1980[5] enjoy only the rent control provisions and not the limited security afforded by the rent tribunal. Further, although court proceedings will still be necessary before recovery of possession, the order for possession cannot be postponed or suspended for more than three months from its date.[6]

B. Restricted Contracts Defined

The statutory definition of a restricted contract is meagre—"a contract . . . whereby one person grants to another person, in consideration of a rent which includes payment for the use of furniture or for services,[7] the right to occupy a dwelling as a residence."[8] The definition covers not only leases but also licences, provided there is a monetary payment[9] and the right given is to occupy a dwelling as a residence. Although a personal permissive right to occupy accommodation can be protected, it is not always easy in given circumstances to say with confidence that a case for protection is established. The hotel guest, lodger, occupant under a sharing-arrangement[10] all may be able to point to a room they have the use of on a settled basis. Although unlikely, it is not impossible, for a single room to be a dwelling.[11] In many cases, there is a sharing with others of part of the accommodation, *e.g.* bathroom or kitchen. To be able to claim a restricted contract, one must have "exclusive occupation" of at least part.[12] "A person has a right to 'exclusive occupation' of a room when he is entitled to occupy it himself, and no one else is entitled to occupy it."[13] The fact that the landlady has rights of access is irrelevant. She will have had to reserve the right to put someone else in the room, and, it is suggested, be able to prove that she exercises that right, and that it is not a sham provision. In many cases, however, unless the occupant is a lodger[14] these arrangements are likely to be construed as

---

[5] November 28, 1980.
[6] H.A. 1980, s.69(2); R.A. 1977, s.106A.
[7] These are defined by way of inclusion in R.A. 1977, s.19(8). The provision of services by itself does not bring a tenancy within the restricted contract provisions, *Baldock* v. *Murray* (1981) 257 E.G. 281.
[8] R.A. 1977, s.19(2).
[9] *cf. Barnes* v. *Barratt* [1970] 2 Q.B. 657.
[10] *i.e.* someone subject to the common arrangement of being allowed to enjoy the use of a room or rooms, subject to similar rights in favour of another person.
[11] *cf. Thurrock U.D.C.* v. *Shina* (1972) 23 P. & C.R. 205.
[12] R.A. 1977, s.19(6).
[13] *Luganda* v. *Service Hotels Ltd.* [1969] 2 Ch. 209 at p. 219, *per* Lord Denning M.R.
[14] *R.* v. *Battersea, Wandsworth, Mitcham and Wimbledon Rent Tribunal, ex p. Parikh* [1957] 1 W.L.R. 410.

tenancies rather than licences[15] and thus, unless there is a resident landlord, or attendance provided, will be protected tenancies, and not restricted contracts.

Any of three statutory factors may take the contract outside the restricted category.

(1) *Property Exceeding Rateable Value*

A contract relating to a dwelling will not be restricted if the rateable value for the dwelling exceeds a certain figure. The rating limits are not precisely the same as for protected tenancies,[16] but again one is concerned with the rateable value for the dwelling not exceeding a certain figure on the "appropriate day."[17] The limits are £1,500 for properties in Greater London, or £750 for those outside where the appropriate day falls after April 1, 1973. If it falls before April 1, 1973, the contract will not be a restricted one if the values exceeded £400, or £200 on the appropriate day *and* it exceeded £1,500 or £750 on April 1, 1973.[18]

(2) *The Nature of the Agreement*

Regulated tenancies,[19] protected occupancies within the Rent (Agriculture) Act 1976,[20] and contracts to occupy dwellings for holidays[21] are all outside the restricted contract net. So also are contracts where the payment covers board, and payment for that item forms a substantial proportion of the whole rent. Section 7(2) of the Rent Act 1977 takes a contract out of the protected sector if a substantial[22] part of the payment is attributable to attendance.[23] Section 19(5)(*c*) takes the contract out of the restricted sector if a substantial part of the payment is for board. It is value to the tenant rather than cost to the landlord that is important. Also, one has to determine whether a substantial part of the rent could have been attributed to board at the beginning of the contract,[24] rather than later, when the issue is raised.

[15] Following *Street* v. *Mountford* [1985] 2 All E.R. 289, and see Chap. 2, (II) B *ante.*
[16] See *ante*, Chap. 10, (II) B.
[17] See *ante*, Chap. 10, (II) B(1); R.A. 1977, s.25.
[18] R.A. 1977, s.19(4).
[19] R.A. 1977, s.19(5)(*a*).
[20] R.A. 1977, s.19(5)(*d*).
[21] R.A. 1977, s.19(7), and *ante*, Chap. 10, (II) C(3)(*c*).
[22] "Substantial" is considered *ante* Chap. 10, (III) C, (3).
[23] And see *ante*, Chap. 10, (II) C(3)(*b*).
[24] *Artillery Mansions* v. *Macartney* [1949] 1 K.B. 164; *Stagg* v. *Brickett* [1951] K.B. 648.

This exception obviously encourages some landlords to indulge in sham bed and breakfast arrangements.[25]

(3) *The Nature of the Landlord*

Contracts where the Crown[26] is the lessor are outside the restricted contract sector simply because of that fact. Similarly, contracts where the lessor is a local authority[27] are not restricted contracts.[28] The same applies where the lessor is a housing association, housing trust or the Housing Corporation.[29]

C. Principal Contracts within the Restricted Sector

(1) *Resident or Sharing Landlords*

The largest group of agreements within the restricted sector are tenancies where there is a resident landlord.[30] In this instance it is irrelevant that the payment does not include anything for either furniture or services.[31] A contract can still come within this category where the landlord does not reside on the property, if the property is let on the basis that some of the accommodation is used by the landlord, or by the landlord and others.[32] This latter situation could arise where the tenant has accommodation over the landlord's business premises, but the kitchen, for example, is still on the ground floor and the tenant has to share it with the landlord and his employees. This is not a common situation.[33]

(2) *Tenancies with Attendance, and Contracts with Furniture or Services*

The fact that tenancies with attendance are not protected tenancies

---

[25] *Holiday Flat Co.* v. *Kuczera* [1978] S.L.T (Sh. Ct.) 47 (considering the adequacy of a continental breakfast, since the entry of U.K. into EEC).
[26] *i.e.* where the interest belongs to the Queen in right of the Crown (unless it is under the management of the Crown Estate Commissioners), or a Government Department, R.A. 1977, s.19(5)(*b*), as amended, H.A. 1980, s.73(2).
[27] As defined in R.A. 1977, s.14, as amended, and see *Lambeth London Borough Council* v. *Udechuka* (1980) 41 P. & C.R. 200.
[28] R.A. 1977, s.19(5)(*a*); H.A. 1980, Sched. 25, para. 36.
[29] R.A. 1977, s.19(5)(*e*).
[30] See *ante*, Chap. 10, (II) C(2)(*c*), where R.A. 1977, s.12 is discussed.
[31] R.A. 1977, s.20.
[32] R.A. 1977, s.21.
[33] And see *Marsh Ltd.* v. *Cooper* [1969] 1 W.L.R. 803.

has already been considered.[34] Services are statutorily defined[35] to include "attendance,[36] the provision of heating or lighting, the supply of hot water and any other privilege or facility connected with the occupancy of a dwelling, other than a privilege or facility requisite for the purposes of access, cold water supply or sanitary accommodation." Tenancies with attendance, and contractual licences[37] with furniture or services are a very significant group of restricted contracts. It must be remembered that only those licences that grant "exclusive occupation" are in the restricted sector, and there must be a term requiring monetary payment[38] for either furniture or services. Student lettings may well, therefore, come within the restricted sector where they are prevented by section 8 of the Rent Act 1977 from being a protected tenancy. But in many cases educational institutions will grant non-exclusive licences, which take the arrangement outside the ambit of restricted contracts.

D. The Statutory Restrictions

(1) *Rent*

Until a rent has been registered for the premises, the parties are free to agree any rent they like, and also to charge a premium for the grant or assignment of the term or contract.[39] Curiously this freedom also exists where only part of a larger unit for which there is a registered rent, is being let.[40] There are no formalities to be observed when the rent payments are later varied by agreement, and the tenant need not be given any prescribed information setting out his rights to go to the rent tribunal.[41]

Either party[42] to the contract or the local authority can refer the contract to the rent tribunal.[43] A reference by a local authority will be invalid if it can be shown that they have acted in bad faith, frivolously, capriciously or vexatiously. Such a charge may be

---

[34] R.A. 1977, s.7, and Chap. 10 (II), C(3), *ante.*
[35] R.A. 1977, s.19(8).
[36] And see *Palser* v. *Grinling* [1948] A.C. 291; *Marchant* v. *Charters* [1977] 1 W.L.R. 1181 (cleaning and provision of bed-linen).
[37] *Luganda* v. *Service Hotels Ltd.* [1969] 2 Ch. 209; *R.* v. *South Middlesex Rent Tribunal, ex p. Beswick* (1976) 32 P. & C.R. 67 (occupier of furnished room in Y.W.C.A. hostel).
[38] *cf. Warder* v. *Cooper* [1970] 1 Ch. 495 (rent free accommodation). The contract will still be restricted if separate sums are payable for occupation, furniture and services, R.A. 1977, s.85(3). In such cases the hiring of the furniture will be subject to the Consumer Credit Act 1974: see also 15(1), 18(6).
[39] R.A. 1977, s.122.
[40] *Gluchowska* v. *Tottenham Borough Council* [1954] 1 Q.B. 439.
[41] *cf.* R.A. 1977, s.51.
[42] If there are co-tenants, both must join in the reference, *Turley* v. *Panton* (1975) 29 P. & C.R. 397.
[43] R.A. 1977, s.77(1).

established by showing the local authority have made a block reference without any investigation into the facts of the individual cases.[44]

A rent tribunal is what a rent assessment committee is called when it is handling references relating to restricted contracts. In law a rent tribunal is now the same entity as a rent assessment committee.[45] Matters, however, come direct to rent tribunals and not by way of reference from rent officers. Tenants rather than landlords refer contracts to rent tribunals, generally because they are concerned with security rather than rent levels. Rent tribunals can require from the lessor the provision of additional information about terms of the contract, and provision of services and furniture.[46]

Two preliminary issues may arise on any reference to the tribunal. First, it may be alleged that the tribunal has no jurisdiction because the contract is not a restricted contract at all. Questions of jurisdiction can be determined in the county court under the Rent Act 1977, s.141, and the parties may be given an opportunity to test their contentions there. In view of the likely delay and expense involved in such an application, the invitation is not often accepted. In that event the tribunal should "listen to the contentions of the parties and make up its own mind whether it is better for it to proceed with the determination, having first of all decided the preliminary point of jurisdiction."[47] Next it may be alleged that the application has been withdrawn by the applicant, who often, by the time of the hearing, has left the premises. An application can only be withdrawn before the tribunal members have begun to consider the papers.[48] From then on they are committed to proceed with their statutory duties.

The tribunal's duties are contained in section 78(2). The tribunal must give the parties the opportunity to make representations, and must make such inquiries as they think fit, which will involve an inspection, and then the tribunal must:

(i)   approve the rent, or
(ii) reduce or increase it, to such sum as they think reasonable, or
(iii) dismiss the application, if they think this is the right course of action in all the circumstances.[49]

---

[44] *R.* v. *Barnett & Camden Rent Tribunal, ex p. Frey Investments* [1972] 2 Q.B. 342.

[45] H.A. 1980, s.72. Anomalies arise as a result: see the comments of the editor in [1980] Conv., pp. 318 *et seq.*

[46] R.A. 1977, s.77(2); Furnished Houses (Rent Control) Regulations 1946 (S.R. & O. 1946 No. 781).

[47] *R.* v. *Croydon and South West London Rent Tribunal, ex p. Ryzewska* [1977] Q.B. 876 at p. 880, Caulfield J., and see the discussion *ante* Chap. 11, (III) B(3).

[48] R.A. 1977, s.78(1); *R.* v. *Tottenham District Rent Tribunal, ex p. Fryer Bros. (Properties)* [1971] 2 Q.B. 681.

[49] The security consequences of this course of action are considered later.

Tribunals operate in an informal manner,[50] but it will be generally impossible for them to come to a proper decision on rent if they are unable to gain access to the premises to take an inventory of the furniture and verify the services. In that event they may adjourn the application, if there is a possibility that they might obtain entry on a later appointment, or they may dismiss the application.

The criterion which the rent tribunal is required to apply to a rent for a restricted contract is that it must be "reasonable." Registered rents have to be "fair," and the matters to be regarded and disregarded for registered rents are spelt out in some detail by section 70 of the Rent Act 1977.[51] A considerable amount of ingenuity has gone into explaining the differences between these two criteria,[52] although precisely how this should affect valuation is not very easy to explain. However, restricted contracts tend to have a shorter life than protected contracts and this may have two results. First, there may be more evidence of what is the market rent for the property, and there will also be evidence of how often the premises are in fact left empty ("voids") which may justify a higher rent.

Rent tribunals do not have to give reasoned written decisions, unless they are requested at the hearing.[53] The tribunal must notify their decision to the parties.[54] The register contains prescribed particulars of the contract, a specification of the dwelling to which it relates and details of the rent determined, exclusive of any rate element.[55] The effect of its registration is to determine the rent between the parties and between their successors. The registered rent remains the rent for the premises until it is altered by the Tribunal, unless it has been fixed for a particular period only, when it remains the rent until the end of that period.[56] If the landlord charges in excess of the permitted maximum he commits a crime[57] and the excess can be recovered by the tenant.[58] Applications for reconsideration of the rent can be made every two years[59] in any event. It can be made within that period if there has been such a change in the condition of the dwelling, furniture, services, terms of the contract or other circum-

---

[50] On the applicability of the rules of evidence to rent tribunal proceedings see Yates [1980] Conv. 136. Procedure is governed by Rent Assessment Committees (England and Wales) (Rent Tribunal) Regulations 1980 (S.I. 1980 No. 1700) (as amended).

[51] See *ante*, Chap. 11 (III) B(4).

[52] See especially Farrand, *Rent Act 1977*.

[53] Tribunals and Inquiries Act 1971, s.12(1).

[54] R.A. 1977, s.78(2).

[55] R.A. 1977, s.79(3).

[56] R.A. 1977, s.81; *R.* v. *Fulham, Hammersmith and Kensington Rent Tribunal, ex p. Gormly* [1952] 1 K.B. 179.

[57] R.A. 1977, s.81(4).

[58] R.A. 1977, s.81(3), and see *De Jean* v. *Fletcher* [1959] 1 W.L.R. 341.

[59] R.A. 1977, s.80(2), as amended by H.A. 1980, s.70.

stances as to make the registered rent no longer a reasonable rent.[60] Premiums cannot be charged on grant or assignment of a restricted contract while there is an operative registered rent under section 79.[61]

(2) *Security Provisions*

The tenants of restricted contracts are not afforded statutory security of tenure. There are, however, a number of restraints on the landlord attempting to recover possession, which are significantly reduced for contracts entered into after the commencement of section 69 of the Housing Act 1980.

(a) Pre-section 69 contracts—notice after reference to rent tribunal

Section 103 of the Rent Act 1977 provides for the suspension of a notice to quit served either after a contract has been referred to the rent tribunal, or in the six months immediately following a rent tribunal decision. In both cases, the notice is not to take effect until six months after the decision. The tribunal can direct a period of suspension of less than six months. If the reference is withdrawn, then "the period during which the notice to quit is not to take effect shall end on the expiry of 7 days from the withdrawal."[62]

It is the experience of rent tribunals that time and again references are made to them under the Rent Act 1977, s.77, by tenants in anticipation of an imminent notice to quit. The extent to which the relationship of landlord and tenant has broken down in the resident landlord situation is carefully considered by tribunals. But there will be no justification for reducing the six months' period if it is the landlord who has been the prime cause of the disruption. Subsequent applications for continued suspension can be made under the Rent Act 1977, s.104.

(b) Pre-section 69 contracts—reference to rent tribunal after notice

A notice to quit is only needed to end a periodic tenancy. Tenancies for a fixed period expire automatically and are outside the provisions under consideration. Section 104 enables tenants or licensees[63] occupying under restricted contracts who are served with notices to quit to make an application to the rent tribunal for an extension of the period of the notice to quit, so that it does not have effect until the end

---

[60] R.A. 1977, s.80(2). Applications for cancellation of entries on the register can be made if it is two years since the date of the last entry; the dwelling is not subject to a restricted contract; and the application is made by the person who would be the lessor of the contract, H.A. 1980, s.71; R.A. 1977, s.81A.

[61] R.A. 1977, s.122.

[62] R.A. 1977, s.103(2).

[63] *Luganda* v. *Service Hotels Ltd.* [1969] 2 Ch. 209.

of the period the rent tribunal direct. For the section to operate, the notice to quit must have been served and not already expired.[64] The contract must also have been referred to the rent tribunal either under section 77 or section 80 of the Rent Act 1977, and that reference must not have been withdrawn. The tribunal is under a duty to make such enquiries as it thinks fit, and to give the parties an opportunity either of being heard or making written representations.[65] It can direct that the notice shall not have effect until the end of such period not exceeding six months from the date on which the notice would have effect apart from the direction they make. In theory it is open to the tenant to make an infinite number of applications under section 104 provided he does so before the notice takes effect and until the tribunal refuse to give a direction under section 104. If the tribunal refuse to give a direction under section 104 the notice takes effect but not before the expiry of seven days from the determination of the application, and the tenant has no right to repeat an application.[66]

During a period of suspension, the landlord has the right to make a further application to the rent tribunal for reduction of the period of suspension previously ordered. It can do so on the grounds that the tenant has not complied with the terms of the contract; that he has been guilty of nuisance or annoyance to adjoining occupiers; or that he has been convicted of using the premises for immoral or illegal purposes; or that the premises or their furniture have deteriorated because of his acts or neglect.[67] If the tribunal do reduce the period, the tenant cannot go back to them for a further period of suspension.[68]

(c) Post section 69 contracts

The Housing Act 1980 makes a significant change in the limited security of tenure enjoyed by occupiers under restricted contracts. Section 69(3) provides that sections 103 to 106 of the Rent Act 1977 shall not apply to restricted contracts entered into after the commencement[69] of the section. These are the group of sections just discussed enabling reference to be made to the Rent Tribunal, before or after service of a notice to quit. The only remaining rights of security such tenants have are those relating to notice and court proceedings, discussed in the following subsection. The changes do not affect occupiers whose contracts antedate the commencement of the section, but they do affect such tenants if their contracts were renewed after that date.

---

[64] R.A. 1977, s.104(1), and see *R. v. City of London Rent Tribunal, ex p. Honig* [1951] 1 K.B. 641.
[65] R.A. 1977, s.104(3).
[66] R.A. 1977, s.104(4).
[67] R.A. 1977, s.106(2).
[68] R.A. 1977, s.106(3). If the landlord takes possession proceedings, the county court also may direct a reduction in the period of suspension, R.A. 1977, s.106(4).
[69] November 28, 1980.

(d) Notices and court proceedings

Tenants properly so called of periodic restricted tenancies will need the usual four weeks' notice, together with the prescribed information.[70] But tenants and licensees under restricted contracts cannot be evicted without due process of law.[71] Proceedings are taken in the county court and execution can be stayed, or suspended, or the date for possession postponed. In the case of post section 69 contracts, unless exceptional hardship would be caused to the tenant, there must be an order for the payment of arrears of rent and for rent or mesne profits for the occupation until possession is obtained.[72] Furthermore the order for possession cannot be postponed for longer than three months after the date of the making of the order.[73]

II. AGRICULTURAL TIED HOUSES

A. Introduction

The provision of accommodation tied to employments or appointments is widespread. Ministers of State, members of H.M. forces, medical practitioners, academics in the public sector, numerous employees in residential homes or at outlying Public Works sites, employees in the catering industry, porters and caretakers and also clerics all have, as Archbishop Lang once in an unrecognised capacity laconically observed, "house with job." The precise legal rights enjoyed by the occupant obviously differ with the nature of the appointment. In some cases the connection between employment and tenancy may be almost coincidental, with the employee enjoying a protected tenancy. It is more likely that only a licence has been granted and the occupant has at best only a restricted contract, and at worst simply the protection afforded by the Protection from Eviction Act 1977. The provision of accommodation in the agricultural industry is common. Partly it is essential because of the remote locations involved. As a corollary, many agricultural estates also comprise residential accommodation. Moreover the provision of free or subsidised accommodation reduces the need for cash-flow. Like so much else in agriculture, there are specific statutory provisions (1) restricting recovery of possession where the agricultural employee has a protected tenancy; (2) providing a whole code in the Rent (Agriculture) Act 1976 analogous to that appropriate to protected

---

[70] Protection from Eviction Act 1977, s.5; *Crane* v. *Morris* [1965] 1 W.L.R. 1104.
[71] Protection from Eviction Act 1977, s.3. This section is extended to licences created after the commencement of s.69 of the Housing Act 1980.
[72] R.A. 1977, s.106A; Housing Act 1980, s.69(2).
[73] R.A. 1977, s.106A(3).

tenants for agricultural employees of at least 91 weeks' standing occupying tied property who are outside the protected sector; (3) imposing additional restraints on the recovery of possession where the only protection is that given by the Protection from Eviction Act 1977. This section is primarily concerned with occupants falling within the Rent (Agriculture) Act 1976 (referred to as the "1976 Act").

B. Protected Occupiers Covered by the 1976 Act

The 1976 Act contains its own specialised jargon and index thereto.[74] A "protected occupier" either is a "qualifying worker" or has been a "qualifying worker."[75] The two aspects involved are the nature of the employment and the period of employment. The employment must have been in agriculture or forestry.[76] Agriculture is inclusively defined,[77] in a way that ensures that employees covered by the Agricultural Wages Board will also be covered by the 1976 Act. It is clear that gamekeepers raising pheasants for sporting purposes are not protected.[78]

A qualifying worker must have worked not fewer than 91 out of the last 104 weeks whole time in agriculture.[79] Whole time work is working a 35 hour week,[80] but credit is given for time off work caused by a prescribed disease or injury, or an injury caused by an accident at work in agriculture, or proper holidays or absences with consent.[81] The initial qualifying worker who is given a tenancy or licence covered by the Act will so long as the contractual arrangement lasts be known as a "protected occupier in his own right."[82] If he stays on after his contract or licence is ended, he remains, at least for the time being, as a "statutory tenant in his own right."[83] These occupational rights continue "if and so long as he occupies the dwelling-house as his residence."[84] The original contract or licence will usually come to an end following the termination of his employment and the service of a notice to quit. The service of a statutory notice to increase the rent has the same effect.[85] If the protected occupier or statutory tenant is given

[74] 1976 Act, Sched. 1; and see generally [1978] Conv. 259 (L. M. Clements).
[75] 1976 Act, s.2(1); and see *Skinner* v. *Cooper* [1979] 1 W.L.R. 666.
[76] The extension of the Act to forestry workers has been brought into operation. For the position where the Crown is the employer/landlord, see H.A. 1980, s.73, Sched. 8, Pt. II.
[77] 1976 Act, s.1.
[78] *Normanton (Earl)* v. *Giles* [1980] 1 W.L.R. 28, and see *Glendyne (Lord)* v. *Rapley* [1978] 1 W.L.R. 601.
[79] 1976 Act, Sched. 3, para. 1.
[80] 1976 Act, Sched. 3, para. 12.
[81] 1976 Act, Sched. 3, paras. 2, 4.
[82] 1976 Act, s.2(4).
[83] 1976 Act, s.4(1).
[84] *Ibid.*
[85] 1976 Act, s.16.

a new contract either in respect of the same property, or of a different property in exchange, he nevertheless keeps his existing statutory rights.[86] Protection is given even if the agricultural employment connection ended before the 1976 Act was passed.[87]

One of the main objects of the 1976 Act was to afford some form of protection not only for the original occupier when he lost his job, but also for his family when he died. The provisions for succession on death are very similar to those for protected tenants.[88] Resident spouses are preferred to other relations.[89] In their absence other members of the family residing with the occupier at the time of his death and for six months before it may succeed to the rights.[90] In this context succession can occur on one occasion only.[91]

C. Contracts and Premises Covered by the 1976 Act

The 1976 Act protects contracts whether they are licences or tenancies granting occupational rights of dwelling-houses as separate dwellings,[92] where the agreements would have created protected tenancies within Part I of the Rent Act 1977 were that Act to be modified so as to be applicable to the realities of the agricultural situation.[93] Normally, the accommodation is either free, or let at a much reduced rent, its cost being taken into account in the level of wages. In many cases meals or food will be provided as well. It follows that the occupier will hardly ever have a protected tenancy within the Rent Act 1977, as the rent will usually be less than two-thirds of the rateable value. Licences and tenancies are protected under the 1976 Act when they would have been protected tenancies under the Rent Act if the provisions relating to low rents[94] and tenancies of property in agricultural holdings[95] were omitted,[96] and those relating to board or attendance [97] were modified. The provision of meals in the course of the employment does not constitute board. If attendance is provided, the onus is on the landlord to show that it is substantial if the term is to be regarded as bona fide.[98]

As in the Rent Acts, there are detailed provisions governing the

---

[86] 1976 Act, s.2(3).
[87] 1976 Act, Sched. 9, para. 3; *Skinner* v. *Cooper* [1979] 1 W.L.R. 666.
[88] See *ante*, Chap. 12.
[89] 1976 Act, ss.3(2), 4(3), as amended; H.A. 1980, s.76.
[90] 1976 Act, ss.3(3), 4(4). There are provisions for deciding amongst competing relations.
[91] Unlike protected tenancies, where there can be two statutory successions.
[92] See *ante*, Chap. 10 (II) A.
[93] 1976 Act, Sched. 2, paras. 1, 2.
[94] In R.A. 1977, s.5.
[95] In R.A. 1977, s.10.
[96] 1976 Act, Sched. 2.
[97] In R.A. 1977, s.7.
[98] 1976 Act, Sched. 2, para. 3.

sharing of accommodation. Sharing with landlord/employers is not expressly dealt with by the 1976 Act. The only protection occupiers can hope for here is if they can claim to have a restricted contract under the Rent Act 1977,[99] or the meagre benefit of the Protection from Eviction Act 1977.[1] They will not come into either of these categories unless they have at least a licence to the exclusive occupation of part of the property.[2] If they are paying for board they will not have a restricted contract.[3]

The sharing of accommodation with persons other than the landlord/employer is expressly dealt with by the 1976 Act.[4] Normally, such sharing will not detract from the occupier's rights under the 1976 Act. The landlord will not be able to alter the terms of the contract relating to the shared accommodation,[5] or obtain an order for possession of the shared accommodation unless he also obtains an order for the separately occupied accommodation.[6]

Users of hostel accommodation are not protected at all, even where they are given exclusive use of a single room, if at that time there were not less than three other rooms let or available for letting to separate tenants on similar terms as to sharing.[7] Occupiers of rooms in hostels with four or more separate rooms let or available will therefore be outside the 1976 Act.[8]

D. Landlords Covered by the 1976 Act

There must obviously be a connection between the employer and landlord and the occupier if a contract is to benefit from any part of the legislation affecting agricultural employees. Clearly if the landlord owns the premises and it is part of the agreement that his tenant/employee resides in them, then the contract will only fall outside the 1976 Act if the landlord is the Crown, a government department, a local authority,[9] a housing trust or subsidised housing association.[10] In many cases the employer will not own the dwelling-house. It may belong to other members of the family, or a family trust, or to the farmer personally, the business being conducted through a

---

[99] See *ante*, s.1.
[1] Under section 4 of that Act, see *post*.
[2] 1976 Act, Sched. 2, paras. 1, 2.
[3] R.A. 1977, s.19(5)(*c*). Contracts within the 1976 Act cannot at the same time be restricted contracts, R.A. 1977, s.19(5)(*d*).
[4] 1976 Act, s.23.
[5] 1976 Act, s.23(4), (5).
[6] 1976 Act, s.23(7).
[7] 1976 Act, s.23(2).
[8] They presumably have the benefit of the Protection from Eviction Act 1977, ss.3, as amended, 4, 8(2).
[9] Local authority is widely defined, as in R.A. 1977, s.14.
[10] 1976 Act, s.5, as amended; H.A. 1980, s.73(3). The Crown exception is not extended to interests managed by the Crown Estate Commissioners.

company. Provided the employer has made arrangements with the owner of the dwelling-house for it to be used as housing accommodation by his employees, then the contract will qualify for protection.[11]

E. The Terms of the Statutory Tenancy

The statutory tenancy begins when the contractual occupancy comes to an end.[12] The contractual rights may be ended by the landlord serving a notice to quit, a notice ending the employment, a notice of increase of rent or taking proceedings for forfeiture, or by the occupier dying or terminating his employment himself in a somewhat more voluntary manner. The ending of the original contract brings into existence a statutory tenancy. The terms applicable to all statutory tenancies are contained in Schedule 5, no account being taken of those terms of the original contract which depended in some way or other on the occupier's employment in agriculture.[13] Other terms in the original contract continue to apply to both parties.[14]

On the landlord's part there are implied the usual covenants for quiet enjoyment[15] and the statutory obligations to repair contained in the Landlord and Tenant Act 1985, s.11.[16] The landlord cannot prevent reasonable access[17] or discontinue the supply of necessary services if these have in fact been provided during the contractual occupancy and if they are reasonably necessary and cannot reasonably be provided by the tenant himself, *e.g.* where electricity, water and sewage disposal are provided by the landlord's own installations.[18]

On the tenant's part, he has to use the premises in a tenant-like manner[19] and as a private dwelling-house only,[20] and cannot sub-let or assign all or part. He must also allow the landlord access to carry out repairs he is entitled to execute.[21]

The payments the occupier has to make for rent and rates give rise to more difficulty. It is likely that during the contractual occupancy no money has passed at all. The Schedule 5 terms do not themselves impose a liability to pay rent.[22] The parties may in the original agreement provide for the amount of rent to be paid if the contractual occupancy becomes a statutory tenancy. They cannot agree to pay a

---

[11] 1976 Act, Sched. 3, para. 3.
[12] 1976 Act, s.4(1).
[13] 1976 Act, Sched. 5, para. 1.
[14] *Ibid.* para. 2.
[15] *Ibid.* para. 4.
[16] *Ibid.* para. 6.
[17] *Ibid.* para. 9.
[18] *Ibid.* para. 5.
[19] *Ibid.* para. 4.
[20] *Ibid.* para. 7.
[21] *Ibid.* para. 8.
[22] 1976 Act, s.10(2).

rent in excess of the registered rent, if there is one, which is unlikely, or one and a half times the rateable value of the property.[23] The figure produced by that calculation is likely to be significantly lower than the registered fair rent. If there is no registered rent, and the parties do agree to pay a rent which is more than one and a half times the rateable value, then the excess is irrecoverable from the tenant.[24] Before any rent is payable under the statutory tenancy, there must either be an agreement to pay it,[25] or the landlord must serve a notice under section 12 requiring payment of rent based on the rateable value.[26] In most cases, rent will be paid weekly in arrears.[27] If there already is a registered rent, and it is more than the existing payment, then the landlord has to serve a notice increasing the existing rent up to the level of the registered rent,[28] and the increase will generally be phased over two years.[29] Whether or not the landlord wants possession, it is obviously sensible to apply for a registered rent as soon as possible after the statutory tenancy begins. Subject to minor modifications, the usual Rent Act provisions apply to the registration of a fair rent.[30]

The other payment to be considered is for rates. The tenant will have to reimburse his landlord for general rates and water rates during the period of the statutory tenancy and after he has been served with a notice to that effect.[31]

F. Recovering Possession

(1) *From Occupiers or Tenants within the 1976 Act*

A court can make an order for possession on mandatory or discretionary grounds. The mandatory grounds, Cases XI and XII,[32] relate to lettings by owner/occupiers and of retirement homes, which grounds are also found in the Rent Acts.[33] An order can also be obtained if the house is overcrowded within the meaning of the

[23] 1976 Act, ss.11(2), 12(9).
[24] 1976 Act, s.11(5).
[25] *i.e.* under s.11.
[26] 1976 Act, s.10(2).
[27] 1976 Act, s.10(3).
[28] 1976 Act, ss.14(2), 16.
[29] 1976 Act, s.15, Sched. 6, as amended; H.A. 1980, s.60(3).
[30] 1976 Act, s.13, as amended; H.A. 1980, s.60(1).
[31] 1976 Act, Sched. 5, para. 11. *Mutatis mutandis*, there are similar provisions governing requirements to pay rent in advance, and recovering rent paid in excess of the permitted amounts, 1976 Act, ss.20, 21. Rent allowances are also obtainable, 1976 Act, s.32, and there is a restriction on distress, s.8.
[32] 1976 Act, Sched. 4, Pt. II. But there are no provisions corresponding to R.A. 1977, Sched. 16, Pt. V, enacted by H.A. 1980, Sched. 7.
[33] See *ante*, Chap. 13 (III).

Housing Act 1985 in such a way as to render the occupier guilty of an offence.[34]

The discretionary grounds are likely to be more important. As in the Rent Acts, the court can only make an order if it considers it reasonable to do so,[35] and on the limited grounds contained in Part I of Schedule 4. The discretionary grounds have their counterparts in the Rent Act 1977, Sched. 15, and it is only necessary to mention that Case III relates to non-payment of rent, or breach of other lawful obligations; Case IV, nuisance or annoyance, etc., caused by the tenant, his licensees, lodgers or sub-tenants; Case V, deterioration of the condition of the dwelling-house as a result of waste, neglect or default, or (Case VI) of the furniture from ill-treatment; Case VII, failure to vacate following tenant's notice, when the landlord would be prejudiced as he has contracted to sell or re-let; Case IX, enables recovery for occupation by the landlord or members of his family, where the balance of hardship is in their favour; Case VIII where there has been assigning, sub-letting or parting with possession without consent, and Case X where there is sub-letting at an excess rent.

But the most important reason why a farming landlord is likely to press for possession is because he needs to provide accommodation for a replacement employee. The landlord may be able to proceed on the basis that there is alternative accommodation available not provided by the local authority. This ground, Case I, is identical with that found in the Rent Act 1977, Sched. 15, paras. 4, 5.[36] It is far more likely that the landlord will have to look to the local authority to assist him in this respect, and here there are provisions unique to agricultural tenants. The 1976 Act contains machinery enabling the landlord to compel the local authority to use their best endeavours[37] to provide suitable alternative accommodation.[38] The 1976 Act provisions do not impose an absolute duty on the local authority to provide suitable alternative accommodation, but such duty as they are under is enforceable against them by an action for damages.[39]

The landlord can only operate these provisions if he requires possession to house an agricultural employee, and he is unable to provide alternative accommodation for the protected or statutory tenant and the authority "in the interests of efficient agriculture" should do so.[40] The occupant who needs to be re-housed must have a protected occupancy or statutory tenancy within the 1976 Act. But tenants who are agricultural or forestry employees with ordinary protected tenancies within the Rent Act 1977 can also come within

---

[34] 1976 Act, Sched. 4, Case XIII.
[35] 1976 Act, s7(2), and see Chap. 13 (II), *ante.*
[36] See Chap. 13 (II) A, *ante.*
[37] And see *R.* v. *Bristol Corporation, ex p. Hendy* [1974] 1 W.L.R. 498.
[38] 1976 Act, s.28(7).
[39] 1976 Act, s.28(8).
[40] 1976 Act, s.27(1).

these provisions. They are included where they would be regarded as having a protected occupancy or statutory tenancy within the 1976 Act[41] if their tenancy had been at a low rent.[42] The landlord has to apply in writing to the local authority.[43] The local authority can obtain advice from the agriculture dwelling-house advisory committee[44] on whether the application is justified in the interests of efficient agriculture. The landlord must be notified of the authority's decision within three months of making the application,[45] either that they are satisfied that he has made out his case, or if not, why not.[46] Changes in circumstances have to be notified to the local authority,[47] who are in any event under no duty to rehouse if the tenant was, is and will continue to be employed in the same capacity.[48]

If alternative accommodation is offered by the local authority and the tenant accepts and moves, then that is the end of the problem. Difficulties only arise if the tenant remains. In that event, proceedings will have to be taken on the grounds in Case II. This falls into three alternatives. First, there has been an offer of the future availability of suitable local authority accommodation, secondly, the authority have communicated an offer of suitable alternative accommodation from a third party, which has been accepted, or thirdly, the offers that have been made have been refused, and the tenant cannot satisfy the court that the refusal was reasonable.

(2) *From Occupiers or Tenants not Qualifying under the 1976 Act*

Tenants or licensees granted exclusive occupation of dwellings under the terms of their employment[49] who do not qualify[50] under the 1976 Act receive limited protection under the Protection from Eviction Act 1977, s.4. The section applies to occupation by the former tenant, his surviving spouse, or relatives who were residing with him at his death.[51] The court is given an express power to suspend the execution of an order for possession on such terms as it thinks reasonable.[52] If the order is made within six months of the ending of the former tenancy, then there is a mandatory suspension for the rest of that six

---

[41] *i.e.* falling within s.II, paras. (B)–(D), *supra.*
[42] 1976 Act, s.27(2), R.A. 1977, s.99.
[43] 1976 Act, s.28(1).
[44] 1976 Act, s.28(3), 29.
[45] 1976 Act, s.28(6), as amended. If the committee is consulted, then the decision must be notified within two months of the receipt of their advice. There is a ministerial code of practice.
[46] 1976 Act, s.28(6A).
[47] 1976 Act, s.28(11).
[48] 1976 Act, s.28(9).
[49] Protection from Eviction Act 1977, ss.3(1), 4(1), 8(2).
[50] See *supra* (II) B *et seq.*
[51] Protection from Eviction Act 1977, s.4(2).
[52] *Ibid.* s.4(3), (8).

months period unless the court thinks it would be reasonable not to suspend for that period and a case can be made out that possession should be immediately granted on the grounds of suitable alternative accommodation; needs of efficient agricultural management; greater hardship that would be caused by postponing; or damage caused by the occupiers to the property.[53] The landlord can ask for a variation of the terms of the suspension on similar grounds.[54] There is no power to suspend the making of the order, but only its execution.[55] The court can make no order for costs where possession is suspended unless "having regard to the conduct of the owner or of the occupier . . . there are special reasons for making such an order."[56] Special reasons might include the fact that the landlord has already allowed the tenant some considerable time rent free in the property, or that the tenant has acted in some intransigent or unmeritorious way.[57]

(3) *Misrepresentations*

Landlords who obtain possession of dwellings subject to protected tenancies for their own or their families' occupation[58] by misrepresentation or concealment render themselves liable to an action for damages.[59] The same is true if a possession order is not suspended under the powers given by the Protection from Eviction Act 1977.[60] Anyone who knowingly or recklessly makes a false statement to a local authority to induce them to provide accommodation when possession is being sought under the 1976 Act is liable on conviction to a fine.[61] It is also a crime not to inform the local authority of a material change of circumstances.[62]

(4) *Sub-tenants*

The position of sub-tenants under lawfully created sub-tenancies who have either a Rent Act protected or statutory tenancy is dealt with by section 9 of the 1976 Act. If an order for possession is made on any of

---

[53] *Ibid.* s.4(4).
[54] *Ibid.* s.4(7). It may be doubted if the machinery of justice in all areas moves fast enough to enable the first hearing for possession to be dealt with in the six months period, let alone the repeat application for its variation.
[55] And *cf.* Housing Act 1980, s.89, reducing the general right to suspend orders for possession of land. There appears to be a conflict between H.A. 1980, s.89, and the 1977 Act, s.4(3). See also *Crane* v. *Morris* [1965] 1 W.L.R. 1104.
[56] Protection from Eviction Act 1977, s.4(9).
[57] *Wilson* v. *Croft* [1971] 1 Q.B. 241.
[58] *i.e.* under R.A. 1977, Sched. 15, Case 9.
[59] R.A. 1977, s.102.
[60] Protection from Eviction Act 1977, s.4(10).
[61] 1976 Act, s.28(14).
[62] 1976 Act, s.28(11).

the discretionary grounds,[63] then the tenant of a lawfully created sub-tenancy is deemed to be the tenant of the landlord on the same terms as if he had been granted a separate tenancy by the superior landlord.[64] This is very similar to the situation that arises when a regulated tenancy is ended by a possession order.[65]

(5) *Premises once Occupied by Persons in Agriculture*

This present sub-section is not concerned with tied properties. It is concerned with protected tenancies within the Rent Act 1977. In three separate situations a dwelling may be let that either formerly was a "tied cottage" or is at the time of the letting a "redundant farm house."[66] In all three cases the letting has to be to someone who was not the original tied tenant or his widow, and in all cases the premises are required for housing someone to be employed in agriculture. Notice in writing should be given before the letting that possession might be recovered under the relevant case. The cases cannot be used to circumvent the provisions of the 1976 Act considered in this section[67] of the book.

III. THE PROTECTED SHORTHOLD TENANT

A. Introduction

There is a widely held view that a considerable amount of property is lost to the residential letting market because landlords cannot be sure of recovering possession unless they can bring themselves within the mandatory grounds for possession. In practice that means unless they can benefit from Case 11 (letting by owner occupier), Case 12 (retirement homes), and Case 20 (lettings by servicemen).[68] As a result, landlords will tend to sell houses when they become vacant. When vacant houses form part of deceaseds' estates, the new owners will be inclined to leave them empty with a view to sale with vacant possession. Perhaps more importantly, much flat property is left vacant when it is over lock-up business accommodation, as the landlord does not want to find himself in the position where he can dispose of the vacant business premises only subject to an existing residential tenant of the flat above.

---

[63] *i.e.* 1976 Act, Sched. 4, Pt. I, or R.A. 1977, ss.98, 99(2).
[64] 1976 Act, s.9(2).
[65] See R.A. 1977, s.137, and see Chap. 13 (IV) *ante.*
[66] R.A. 1977, Sched. 15, Cases 16, 17 and 18.
[67] R.A. 1977, s.99(3).
[68] R.A. 1977, Sched. 15, Pt. II, as amended; H.A. 1980, s.67, Sched. 7.

In 1980, much interest was aroused by the proposal to legislate for the creation of short term lets free from the normal statutory protection provisions. The scheme for "shortholds" provides for lettings free from the normal security provisions, when the short term has expired, but still subject to the usual "fair" rent regulation. The scheme is widely used, although it is not favoured by mortgagees, as there are no provisions enabling them to recover possession.[69] The Labour Party have on two occasions, on the passing of the legislation, and the making of a subsequent order, indicated that they would repeal the provisions.[70]

B. The Term

The term has to be for not less than one year nor more than five.[71] The landlord must not be able to bring the term to a premature end except under a proviso for re-entry or forfeiture.[72] The tenant has, on the other hand, a right to end the term by one month's notice if the term is for two years or less, or by three months' notice if the term is for longer.[73] Any attempt to discourage the exercise of this right by the tenant by imposing on him any penalty or disability is void,[74] and it is not possible to contract out of this right.[75]

It seems that the tenant will move into the protected sector if he stays on at the end of the term certain and the landlord accepts the situation, the tenant and his rent. Indeed, section 52(5) of the Housing Act 1980 seems to contemplate that the landlord might want to set up this possibility at the outset. The section provides that if the landlord creates an ordinary protected tenancy for a term certain followed either by a further term at the tenant's option, or by a yearly or other periodic tenancy, and observes all the conditions relating to the creation of shortholds, then the tenancy shall be a protected shorthold "until the end of the term certain." The necessary implication is that the ensuing periodic tenancy will be a protected tenancy. However, Case 19, which contains the grounds on which a mandatory order for possession can be obtained of property that was let under a protected shorthold tenancy, clearly contemplates that the tenancy may well be a periodic tenancy at the time notices of intention to recover possession are served.[76] A tenant who holds over at the end of the fixed

[69] *c.f.* R.A. 1977, Sched. 15, Pt. V, para. 2.
[70] *Hansard*, H.C., Committee F, col. 1180; (March 18, 1980); *Hansard*, Vol. 10, cols. 675–693 (October 26, 1981).
[71] H.A. 1980, s.52(1). For an excellent exposition on shortholds, see P. F. Smith [1982] Conv. 29.
[72] H.A. 1980, s.52(1)(*a*).
[73] H.A. 1980, s.53(1).
[74] H.A. 1980, s.53(2).
[75] H.A. 1980, s.53(1).
[76] H.A. 1980, s.55(1): "Case 19(ii)."

term would appear to have the status of statutory tenant. The provisions for succession to statutory tenancies would seem to apply, and the tenant will be subject to proceedings for possession on the grounds contained in the Rent Act 1977, Sched. 15, Pt. I. His landlord will also have the opportunity, once a year, to remove him under Case 19.[77]

It is submitted that if a protected shorthold tenancy is granted to a tenant who has already enjoyed one shorthold protected tenancy and stayed on at the end of it paying rent on a periodic basis, then the second grant cannot be a protected shorthold tenancy. It seems to fall within section 52(2). Furthermore, it would also not seem to be possible to grant a tenancy as an "owner-occupier"[78] to someone holding over as a periodic tenant at the end of the shorthold term.[79] However, and not entirely logically, it is suggested that the landlord can still recover possession from the tenant by relying on Case 19. The landlord can argue, relying on Case 19(*a*) that "the dwelling-house" was let under a protected shorthold tenancy . . . and . . . (there has been a grant of a further tenancy since the end of the protected shorthold tenancy) . . . to a person who immediately before the grant was in possession of the dwelling-house as a protected or statutory tenant." It will be for the courts to determine what is the precise nature of the intervening "protected or statutory" tenancy in this instance. No doubt these provisions will generate much litigation.

C. Formalities, Rent and Terms

Apart from the normal common law formalities attendant on the grant of terms of years certain, prospective landlords before the grant have to serve prescribed notices, indicating the nature of the tenancy being created.[80] There was considerable alarm during the passage of the Bill through Parliament that the shorthold provisions might be used to diminish the rights of existing protected tenants. Shortholds cannot be granted to persons who immediately before the grant were already protected or statutory tenants.[81]

Rents of shorthold tenancies are still governed by the fair rent code. But for tenancies in the London area more stringent provisions apply. In the London area, either there must already be a registered rent for the premises, or if there is not, then the prospective landlord

---

[77] Case 19(*a*), H.A. 1980, s.55(1).
[78] *i.e.* within R.A. 1977, Sched. 15, Case 11, (see para. (b)).
[79] It is suggested that the rent can be increased by agreement, using R.A. 1977, s.51, during the periodic tenancy at the end of the fixed shorthold term.
[80] H.A. 1980, s.52(1)(*b*), (3). And see The Protected Shorthold Tenancies (Notice to Tenant) Regulations 1981 (S.I. 1981 No. 1579).
[81] H.A. 1980, s.52(2).

should apply for and obtain a certificate of fair rent[82] before the grant and make an application for the registration of the rent within 28 days of the grant.[83] A failure to observe the rent and notice provisions can be waived in possession proceedings, if the court thinks it just and equitable to make a possession order.[84]

The lease need not contain any terms prohibiting assignment or sub-letting. Both the shorthold tenancy itself, and also any protected tenancy created in the dwelling-house[85] are expressed to be incapable of being assigned.[86] Presumably, the purported assignment must have some effect between the parties making it, even though it does not bind the landlord. Is the assignor estopped as against the assignee from asserting the invalidity of the assignment? Any such assignments are denied legal effect until either no-one is in possession as a statutory or protected tenant, or a further protected tenancy is granted to someone who was not, at that time, already a protected or statutory tenant.[87] The creation of sub-tenancies is not forbidden, but sub-tenants have no statutory rights to remain in possession under the Rent Act 1977, s.137,[88] if the landlord becomes entitled to possession as against the shorthold tenant.[89]

In practice, it seems that the prudent landlord will insert in the shorthold tenancy agreement the usual absolute restrictions on assignment and sub-letting of either the whole or part. The lease should contain also the usual proviso for forfeiture. This should not embarrass the tenant who has a right to give notice to end the term prematurely in any event.[90] A breach of the covenant not to assign or sub-let would enable the landlord to take forfeiture proceedings.[91]

Finally, it is suggested that the lease should contain provisions for the giving of one month's notice by the landlord. If by accident or design the initial term is continued as an annual periodic tenancy, then half a year's notice will be needed at common law.[92] The confusing provisions of Case 19[93] contain two apparently inconsistent requirements: first that a notice has to be served in the three months before the end of the fixed term, or its anniversary,[94] and secondly, that in the case of a periodic tenancy the notice shall not expire

---

[82] Under R.A. 1977, s.69, and see Chap. 11, s.II, B, *ante*.
[83] H.A. 1980, s.52(1)(*c*). The rest of the country was removed from these provisions by the Protected Shorthold Tenancies (Rent Registration) Order 1981, (S.I. 1981 No. 1578).
[84] H.A. 1980, s.55(2).
[85] This is only likely to be created by the grant of a sub-tenancy of the whole house for a short term.
[86] H.A. 1980, s.54(2). There is an exception in favour of assignments by court order in divorce proceedings.
[87] H.A. 1980, s.54(3).
[88] See *ante*, Chap. 13 (IV).
[89] H.A. 1980, s.54(1).
[90] H.A. 1980, s.53.
[91] See *ante*, Chap. 8 (VI), H.A. 1980, s.52(1)(*a*).
[92] See *ante*, Chap. 8 (V), B(2).
[93] H.A. 1980, s.55.
[94] Case 19(iii).

before that periodic tenancy could be brought to an end by a notice to quit served on the same day.[95] As a yearly tenancy needs half a year's notice, it is not possible to serve it in the last three months of the term. Hence, it is suggested, the need for the landlord to be able to serve a shorter notice.

D. Recovering Possession

Case 19[96] prescribes not only when but also how possession can be recovered. It applies when the premises were let under a protected shorthold. The Case continues to apply unless and until, it seems, there is a grant of a further tenancy after the end of the shorthold to someone who was not immediately before the grant already in possession as a protected or statutory tenant.[97] At least three months' notice of intention to take proceedings must be served.[98] As we have seen[99] if the tenancy is then a periodic tenancy, the notice must not expire earlier than the tenancy could be ended by a notice to quit served on the same day. The notice must also be served in the last three months immediately before the end of the fixed term, or if that has already passed, its anniversary.[1] Proceedings must be started not later than three months after the notice of intention to proceed expires.[2] If the landlord fails to bring proceedings in time he may serve a fresh notice of the appropriate length not earlier than three months after expiry of the stale notice, the fresh notice being given in the period of three months immediately preceding any anniversary of the date on which the protected shorthold tenancy ended.[3]

IV. THE ASSURED TENANT

Concern is frequently expressed about the lack of incentive for persons wanting to invest new money in the provision of residential accommodation for private letting. The lack of incentive, it is argued, arises from the status of irremovability of the protected tenant, coupled with the argument that an investor relying on "fair rents" is unable to obtain the same return on his capital as he could hope to obtain in other markets. The assured tenancy was in 1980 devised to encourage new building. In appearance, it is an ordinary protected or

[95] Case 19(ii).
[96] H.A. 1980, s.55.
[97] Case 19(*a*), but *cf.* s.52(2).
[98] H.A. 1980, s.55(1), Case 19.
[99] *Supra*, C.
[1] Case 19(iii).
[2] Case 19(*b*).
[3] Case 19(*b*)(iii).

housing association tenancy.[4] In practice it is free from the Rent Act security and rent controls, but subject to the regime later discussed at length in Part III relating to business tenancies, contained in Part II of the Landlord and Tenant Act 1954. There is no control over the level of initial rents. The provisions for statutory continuation of the term, formal notices to terminate or request renewal, the right to apply for a new lease, with the court settling both terms and rent, the grounds for opposition to a new term, and the compensation provisions which apply to business tenancies, apply with only minor modifications.[5]

However, before the tenancy can be created, three important conditions must be satisfied.[6] First, since the creation of the tenancy, the landlord's interest must have belonged to an "approved body." Many "approved body" orders have been made, approving builders, pension funds, insurance companies, etc. Next, to ensure that new money is introduced construction work must first have begun after August 8, 1980.

The third condition is that before the tenant first occupied, no part had been let except under an assured tenancy. Unusually, tenants will come into this category if the three conditions are satisfied *unless* they are given a notice that their tenancy will be a protected, or a housing association tenancy, and not an assured tenancy.[7] Normally, notices are served before the beginning of tenancies to inform the tenant that he will be within a particular category, not outside it.[8]

[4] H.A. 1980, s.56(1).
[5] H.A. 1980, Sched. 5.
[6] HA. 1980, s.56(3).
[7] H.A. 1980, s.56(6).
[8] H.A. 1980, s.57, provides for the contingency of a change in the category of approved bodies—the tenancy remains assured—and transitional provisions where the landlord's interest is transferred to someone who is not an approved body.

CHAPTER 15

LONG AND SHARED OWNERSHIP LEASES

I. Protection of Long Leases by Land-
lord and Tenant Act 1954 497
  A. The Legislative Gap 497
  B. Qualifying Tenants 498
  C. Continuation and Termination
    of the Tenancy 500
  D. Repairs 502
II. The Leasehold Reform Act 1967 . . 503
  A. Purpose and Policy 503

  B. Premises within the Act 505
  C. Tenancies within the Act . . . 509
  D. Tenants within the Act 511
  E. Enfranchising 513
  F. Management Schemes 519
III. Shared Ownership Leases 520
  A. The Scope of Provisions 520
  B. Acquiring a Shared Ownership
    Lease 521

I. Protection of Long Leases by Landlord and Tenant Act 1954

A. The Legislative Gap

In the last century a considerable amount of development was carried out by means of the building lease. There are a number of variations of the basic theme, but normally a land owner would agree to release land for development in consideration of the builder accepting a long lease, *e.g.* for 99 years at a ground rent and agreeing to build a house, or houses. The initial occupier would take either an assignment from the builder, or a sub-lease from him, especially if there were numerous properties comprised in the building estate. In some instances he would take a lease from the original land owner, agreeing to pay him a ground rent for the property, and covenanting to build the house and keep it in repair, and paying a capital sum to the builder. So far as the original tenants were concerned, it would make little difference whether they acquired freehold or leasehold interests; both would be equally marketable. The attraction for the lessor was that when the reversion fell in the freeholder would obtain a substantially more valuable asset than the one he let, *i.e.* a developed estate which he would be able to dispose of with vacant possession. The prices paid by subsequent tenants on the assignment to them of the residue of the term of years would reflect, at least in the last 50 or 25 years, the fact that what they were acquiring was a wasting asset.

Initially, the fact that a tenancy was a long one, *e.g.* for more than 21 years, meant that it fell outside the protection of the Rent Acts. Tenants holding at the fag-end of long terms could therefore face both expensive claims for dilapidations to put back into repair old buildings, and the loss of their residential accommodation, as they enjoyed no statutory protection. Part I of the 1954 Act gave

497

protection to occupying tenants by affording them a statutory tenancy within the Rent Acts and placing some restrictions on actions for breach of covenants to repair. The Leasehold Reform Act 1967 goes much further. This gives qualifying tenants who occupy houses on long tenancies at low rents the right to acquire the freehold. But the basis for calculating the price the tenant has to pay is unusual. It is assumed, whatever in fact may be the situation, that the tenant has already paid for the bricks and mortar, and therefore, generally, need pay only for the site value of the property he is acquiring. This sum will often be substantially less than the market value of the landlord's interest in the property, subject to the tenancy.

B. Qualifying Tenants

The mere fact that a tenancy is a long one, *e.g.* for more than 21 years, does not by itself take it outside the normal Rent Act protection. It will be outside Rent Act protection if the rent is "low." It will be a low rent if it is less than two-thirds of the rateable value, but for this purpose payments for maintenance, insurance, repairs, rates and services are left out of account.[1] Conversely, the tenancy will only be within the protection of Part I of the 1954 Act[2] if it is a long tenancy at a low rent, again disregarding sums paid for rates, services, repairs, insurance and maintenance.[3]

To be a qualifying long term, there must initially have been a grant of at least 21 years running from the date of the grant.[4] A succession of periodic tenancies at low rents lasting for longer than 21 years will not qualify. But if the initial long tenancy has been followed by one or more shorter terms at low rents, then it can be regarded as one long tenancy within the statutory protection.[5] It is essential that the long term cannot be cut short by a landlord's notice.[6]

The tenant must satisfy the "qualifying condition" contained in section 2(1) of the 1954 Act. In *Herbert* v. *Byrne*,[7] Lord Denning M.R. lucidly explained the objectives, requirements and practice of this part of the Act, and dealing with the qualifying condition said[8]:

---

[1] See *ante*, Chap. 10 (II) C(3)(a). and R.A. 1977, ss.5, 146.
[2] It is not possible to contract out of the provisions of Part I of the 1954 Act, s.17, and see also *Re Hennessey's Agreement, Hillman* v. *Davison* [1975] 2 W.L.R. 159.
[3] L. & T.A. 1954, s.2(4), (5), (7), as amended. The rateable values are the same as under the Rent Acts, see *ante*, Chap. 10 (II) B.
[4] *Roberts* v. *Church Commissioners for England* [1972] 1 Q.B. 278; *Bradshaw* v. *Pawley* [1979] 3 All E.R. 273.
[5] L. & T.A. 1954, ss.2(4), 19.
[6] L. & T.A. 1954, s.2(7), as amended. Apparently any reduction in the term by notice will take it outside the Act, not only one that reduces it below 21 years.
[7] [1964] 1 W.L.R. 519.
[8] *Ibid.* p. 525.

"You are to look at the position at the end of the lease, and ask yourself whether the leaseholder would have been protected if it had not been a long lease at a low rent, but a short lease at a rack rent. If the leaseholder would have qualified under the old Rent Acts for protection on the expiry of such a short lease, he qualifies now, under the Act of 1954, for protection on the expiry of the long lease. There is, however, this difference—in determining whether he qualifies or not, you do not look at the terms of the old long lease itself as you would look at the terms of a short lease[9] but you look at the state of affairs as it actually existed at the end of the long lease. That is made clear by section 22(3) of the Act of 1954."

In every case, the tenant must have been in personal occupation of the whole or of a part comprising a separate dwelling as his home.[10] But often at issue is the extent of the property covered by the 1954 Act. This was in dispute in two cases. In *Herbert* v. *Byrne*[11] the whole house had originally been let as a single unit in 1863 at a ground rent of £2 a year for 99 years. Later it had been divided into flats. Shortly before the end of the term Mr. Herbert acquired the fag-end of the term, and vacant possession of the ground and first floors, where he was "pigging" it with minimal furniture, even though the rest of his family lived in a tied flat nearby. The tenancy of the whole property was held covered by the Act.[12] Mr. Herbert was paying a single rent for the whole house, and there was no evidence that he did not intend to reside in the whole house at the end of the other tenant's occupation of the basement and second floors. The tenants of the other floors were his sub-tenants.[13]

More recently, in *Regalian Securities Ltd.* v. *Ramsden*,[14] a tenant occupied a self-contained flat, part of a penthouse suite, the whole being let on a long tenancy. The rest of the suite comprised a maisonette which the tenant had never occupied, but intended so to do. He successfully claimed that the whole penthouse was within the protection of the Act.

It follows that if what is let is a mini-block of flats, and at the end of

---

[9] He referred to *Wolfe* v. *Hogan* [1949] 2 K.B. 194; *Welch* v. *Nagy* [1950] 1 K.B. 455; *Whitty* v. *Scott-Russell* [1950] 2 K.B. 32.

[10] See *ante*, Chap. 10 (III) B(3).

[11] [1964] 1 W.L.R. 519.

[12] And see L. & T.A. 1954, s.3(2)(*a*), (3). If only part of the premises qualify for protection, then the protection will be extended to that part, s.3(2)(*b*).

[13] Lawfully created protected or statutory sub-tenancies survive the termination of the long tenancy at a low rent, Rent Act 1977, s.137. If the sub-tenancy has been created since 1974 by a resident landlord, then it may not immediately be a protected or statutory one, but can be only a restricted contract, and see *ante*, Chap. 13 (I). If the sub-tenancy was created either after service of a notice under s.4(1) of the 1954 Act, or when it was statutorily continued under s.3(1), the superior lessor's written consent is necessary for its lawful creation, Rent Act 1977, s.137(6).

[14] [1981] 1 W.L.R. 61; and see also *Haines* v. *Herbert* [1963] 1 W.L.R. 519.

the tenancy, the tenant occupies none of them, then he will be outside the protection of Part I of the 1954 Act, and the same may follow if the tenant occupies one of the flats.[15]

The tenant has to satisfy the "qualifying condition" not only at the time the term would have expired by effluxion of time,[16] but also at the time the landlord serves an effective notice to end it.[17] The notice must either contain the landlord's proposals for a statutory tenancy, or state the grounds on which the landlord intends to apply for possession, if the tenant is unwilling to give up the tenancy.[18] The landlord may serve this notice to coincide with the end of the term, or it may take effect later. It is obviously in the landlord's interest to end the current arrangements as soon as possible so that he does at least receive a fair rent for the property.

It is common to find that the original property was a large single dwelling-house which has been later split into numerous flats. Often the tenant will not be in occupation, having sub-let the whole. There is obviously a risk that if the non-occupying tenant either starts to occupy or, what is more likely, in the dying months of the lease assigns to someone who occupies, the statutory protection will then be invoked. In this case, the landlord can make a pre-emptive strike. He can make an application to the court for a declaration that as the qualifying condition is not satisfied, the tenancy is not protected by the Act. The declaration will be granted if the court is satisfied that the qualifying condition is not satisfied, and is not likely to be satisfied by the end of the term.[19] If it happens that the condition is later satisfied, *e.g.* by an assignment of the residue of the term to one of the sitting sub-tenants, this will not take the tenancy back into the protection of the Act.

C. Continuation and Termination of the Tenancy

There are very complex procedural steps to be taken by the parties either to end the tenancy or to transform it into a statutory tenancy. Although a small cluster of litigation surrounds the question whether the premises are caught at all by Part I of the 1954 Act, there are almost no reported cases on the transmogrification of the long tenancy at a low rent to a statutory tenancy. It is suggested that if the grounds

---

[15] *Horford Investments Ltd.* v. *Lambert* [1976] Ch. 39, although Russell L.J. pointed out that they were not concerned with protection from eviction after a contractual tenancy, but whether the rent registration provisions applied.

[16] L. & T.A. 1954, s.2(1).

[17] L. & T.A. 1954, ss.2(1), 4(1). For a lucid consideration of the problems that arise when the qualifying condition is not satisfied at the expiration of a notice to terminate, see Woodfall, para. 3-0218.

[18] L. & T.A. 1954, s.4(3).

[19] L. & T.A. 1954, s.2(2).

exist for the change the parties are unlikely to take issue that the precise procedural steps have not been meticulously observed. It is proposed, therefore, to deal with the matter briefly.

If the tenant wants to end the tenancy, he need only give one month's notice to his immediate landlord. This may end on the original term date.[20] A notice from the landlord[21] to end the tenancy must be not longer than 12 nor shorter than six months.[22] It must either contain the landlord's proposals for the terms of the statutory tenancy or contain a notice, that if the tenant is not willing to give up possession the landlord proposes to apply to the court for possession on stated grounds.[23] The notice is the first step the landlord has to take if he is to end the statutory prolongation of the contractual position. The tenancy must still be satisfying the qualifying condition when the notice takes effect.[24] The proposals must cover what property is to be comprised in the statutory tenancy, what rent shall be reserved, and who shall carry out specified initial repairs.[25] Strictly, the notice becomes ineffective unless terms are agreed at least two months before the end of the notice, or an application has been made by that time to the court to settle those matters.[26] If the terms are settled either by the parties or by the court, the result is a statutory tenancy within the Rent Acts.[27]

The Court of Appeal[28] has pointed out that there is no statutory clog or restraint on the discretion which the court has to exercise in settling the terms, and no indication of the matters to be considered.[29] In the exercise of the judicial discretion, the court has to do what is fair between the parties, and the state of affairs as they exist at the date of the hearing is of primary importance. One of the obviously material factors is the terms of the old lease. The court has, therefore, upheld the inclusion of an absolute prohibition against assignment, subletting or parting with possession.[30] It has declined to insert either a qualified or unqualified prohibition on sharing the property.[31] Such a restriction was not part of the parties' original agreement and might inhibit hospitality to family and friends.

---

[20] L. & T.A. 1954, s.5.
[21] The landlord for these purposes must own either the freehold or a reversion which will last five years longer than the "long tenancy," L. & T.A. 1954, s.21.
[22] L. & T.A. 1954, s.4(2).
[23] L. & T.A. 1954, s.4(3).
[24] L. & T.A. 1954, ss.2(1), 6(2).
[25] L. & T.A. 1954, s.7. Repairs are considered in the next subsection.
[26] L. & T.A. 1954, s.7(2).
[27] L. & T.A. 1954, s.6(1).
[28] *Etablissement Commercial Kamira* v. *Schiazzano* [1984] 3 W.L.R. 95.
[29] Contrast L. & T.A. 1954, s.35, dealing with the terms for renewed business tenancies, and *post* Chap. 22.
[30] See *ante*, Chap. 7 (II) B, C.
[31] "Sharing" was regarded as an imprecise concept.

The grounds on which the landlord can rely to recover possession at the end of the long tenancy are contained in the Landlord and Tenant Act 1954, Sched. 3, as amended and correspond to those in Cases 1–9 of Schedule 15 of the Rent Act 1977.[32] Briefly they are the tenant's failure to pay rent and observe the terms of the lease relating to insurance and payment of rates; that he or his lodger caused a nuisance or annoyance, or has been convicted of using the premises for an illegal or immoral purpose, or allowed them to be so used; that there has been a failure to comply with the conditions of an "off-licence"; that the landlord, his adult children, parents or parents-in-law reasonably require the premises for their own occupation[33]; or that there is suitable alternative accommodation available to the tenant. Of course, once the statutory tenancy does start, recovery of possession is then wholly governed by the Rent Act 1977.

D. Repairs

One of the major problems arising at the end of long terms is the liability for long outstanding repairs.[34] The landlord cannot obtain an order for forfeiture or damages for breach of terms of the lease in the last seven months of the term,[35] unless the complaints relate to non-payment of rent or rates, or as to the insurance of the premises, or their use for immoral or illegal purposes.[36] If the proceedings are taken earlier, and an order is made, then it must be suspended for 14 days.[37] The tenant is given the opportunity of electing in that 14 days that the term shall be treated as ending within seven months of the order. In that event the only order that can be made is for the payment of costs.[38]

If there are outstanding repairs at the end of the long term, and the 1954 Act does not apply to protect the tenant, then the matter is dealt with in the same way as at the end of any other unprotected tenancy. If the Act does apply, and the tenant stays on, there must be either agreement, or a determination by the county court what initial repairs have to be done as a result of the tenant's failure to comply with his repairing obligations.[39] Unless the tenant agrees to do the repairs, the

---

[32] L. & T.A. 1954, s.12(1). If certain public bodies are the landlord, they can rely on the ground that they intend to demolish or reconstruct, see L. & T.A. 1954, s.12(1)(a), Leasehold Reform Act 1967, ss.28, 38.

[33] The court has to consider balance of hardship in relation to this ground, *cf.* Chap. 13 (II), J, *ante*, and in any event it is not open to a landlord whose interest was created or purchased since February 18, 1966.

[34] The measure of damages for breaches of covenants to repair is considered generally, in Chap. 6, *ante*.

[35] L. & T.A. 1954, s.16(1).

[36] L. & T.A. 1954, s.16(4).

[37] L. & T.A. 1954, s.16(2).

[38] L. & T.A. 1954, s.16(3). If the tenant elects for this course, he cannot later ask for enfranchisement or an extended 50-year lease, Leasehold Reform Act 1967, Sched. 3, para. 4(4).

[39] L. & T.A. 1954, ss.7, 8.

landlord will execute them and look to the tenant for reimbursement, either by instalments or in a lump sum.[40] The repairs situation has to be borne in mind by the court if it has to determine the rent.[41]

Once the statutory tenancy does come into effect then with limited exceptions, the tenant's liability under the terms of the old lease is extinguished. The exceptions relate to covenants to pay rent and rates and to keep insured, and not to use for illegal or immoral purposes.[42] An obligation to reinstate as a single dwelling-house one that had been carved up into separate flats during the long term was therefore held to be unenforceable in *Byrne* v. *Herbert*.[43]

II. THE LEASEHOLD REFORM ACT 1967

A. Purpose and Policy

The objects of the Act are simply expressed in section 1. They are "to confer on a tenant of a leasehold house, occupying the house as his residence, a right to acquire on fair terms the freehold or an extended lease of the house and premises." The details of the Act which transform that policy into reality are complex. The Act operates for the benefit of the occupying residential tenants under long leases at low rents of houses as distinct from flats. The "fair terms' mentioned in the section are drafted on the assumption that the qualifying tenant has already paid for the bricks and mortar.[44] The price of the landlord's interest is broadly taken to be restricted to the capitalised value of the right to receive the ground rent of the site of the property, subject to a number of assumptions.

A considerable amount of heat has been generated because the Act assumes that the tenant or his predecessors have paid for the structure when this is often not the case. On this point, and the approach to the interpretation of the Act, Roskill L.J. has said[45]:

> "I do not think it right to describe the 1967 Act as confiscatory legislation; it is a statute which obliges a landlord to enfranchise the tenant at a price fixed by the statute. Rather, it is in the nature of a compulsory purchase. But where someone is seeking to

[40] L. & T.A. 1954, s.8, and Sched. 1.
[41] L. & T.A. 1954, s.9, Sched. 2, contains provisions for the situation where the landlord fails to carry out the repairs, and see also Leasehold Reform Act 1967, s.39, and Sched. 5, as amended.
[42] L. & T.A. 1967, s.10.
[43] [1966] 2 Q.B. 121, a further "staging post" in the litigation between the parties already met in subs. B above.
[44] See further the White Paper on Leasehold Reform, Cmnd. 2916.
[45] In *Methuen-Campbell* v. *Walters* [1979] 2 W.L.R. 113 at p. 128.

exercise such a right given by statute it seems to me that it is for the person seeking to exercise that right to show that on the facts found that he can properly bring his claim within the language of the statute which confers that right on him."

It is not possible to contract out of the statutory provisions.[46]

Mention has been made that the Act offers tenants two distinct statutory rights: one to ask for enfranchisement, the other to ask for an extended 50 years' term of the existing lease, to run from the end of the existing lease.[47] These rights are, however, mutually complementary. The right to ask for an extended term will be exercised only infrequently. A tenant who does obtain such an extended term cannot after the extended term has begun to run then change his mind and claim to acquire the freehold as of right.[48] He is also unable to extend his lease again either for another 50 years,[49] or under the Landlord and Tenant Act 1954.[50]

The term is extended for 50 years on the basis that the tenant pays a modern ground rent "in the sense that it shall represent the letting value of the site (without including anything for the value of the buildings on the site)."[51] The rent is to be reviewable after the first 25 years. In those cases where the tenant asks for an extension, the landlord is given a valuable right to recover possession. Section 17 of the 1967 Act enables a landlord to apply to the court for an order that he can resume possession on the ground that for purposes of redevelopment he proposes to demolish or reconstruct the whole or a substantial part of the house and premises. The application can be made no earlier than 12 months before the end of the original term date of the tenancy.[52] Compensation is payable to the dispossessed tenant.[53] The compensation is determined by assessing the amount that the sitting tenant could realise for his interest on the assumption that he had an extended 50 years term, but with no other additional rights to retain possession at the end of the term or to acquire the freehold.[54]

The significance of this largely unused right of the tenant to extend the tenancy and of the landlord to recover possession for development purposes on payment of compensation lies in the fact that these

---

[46] L.R.A. 1967, s.23. A surrender by a tenant who had a right to enfranchise can be reopened if the terms were inadequate, s.23(3).
[47] L.R.A. 1967, s.14.
[48] L.R.A. 1967, s.16(1)(*a*). He may still be able to do so by negotiation.
[49] L.R.A. 1967, s.16(1)(*b*).
[50] See *ante*, s.I, and also L.R.A. 1967, s.16(1)(*c*).
[51] L.R.A. 1967, s.15(2)(*a*). One assumes the site will be used for the purposes for which it has as of right been used during the existing tenancy.
[52] L.R.A. 1967, s.17(1).
[53] L.R.A. 1967, s.17(2).
[54] L.R.A. 1967, Sched. 2, para. 5.

matters have to be borne in mind in calculating the price the tenant pays in the normal case where the tenant enfranchises.

In the standard situation, *e.g.* where the rateable value at the time the tenant serves his notice is less than £500, or £1,000 if the property is in Greater London, the price the tenant pays is broadly calculated on the basis of what someone other than the sitting tenant would pay for an asset producing (a) the existing contractual ground rent for the rest of the current term, (b) the right to receive the ground rent under the hypothetical 50 year term, coupled with the equally hypothetical right to recover possession at the end of the current term for redevelopment purposes on payment of compensation.[55]

B. Premises within the Act

(1) *The Leasehold House*

The tenant has to occupy a house.[56] "House" is not defined by the Act, but is to some extent explained.[57] It

> "includes any building designed or adapted for living in and reasonably so called, notwithstanding that the building is not structurally detached, or was or is not solely designed or adapted for living in, or is divided horizontally into flats or maisonettes; and
>
> (a) where a building is divided horizontally, the flats or other units into which it is so divided are not separate 'houses,' though the building as a whole may be; and
> (b) where a building is divided vertically the building as a whole is not a 'house' though any of the units into which it is divided may be."

One of the major problems in this area is that the functions of buildings change. What started as a single dwelling-house 100 years ago may today be an office. What began life as a Victorian warehouse may be converted into a unit comprising modernised flats. The intermediate stages are where the ground floor is used for commercial purposes with the tenant's living accommodation above, or where the whole has always been used residentially, but now each floor is a separate flat, with the tenant of the whole occupying one.

The courts have been reluctant to embroider the statutory definition. Lord Denning M.R. has indicated that although a town block of

---

[55] L.R.A. 1967, s.9(1), and see *post*, subs. E(2), where details of the price to be paid, and valuations are considered.
[56] L.R.A. 1967, s.1(1).
[57] L.R.A. 1967, s.2(1).

flats would not reasonably be called a house, a four-storied building used both residentially and commercially may be.[58]

> "First, if the tenant occupied the building entirely himself using the ground floor for his shop premises, that would plainly be a 'house' reasonably so called. Secondly, if the tenant instead of using the ground floor himself for business purposes, sub-lets it, that does not alter the character of the building. It is still a 'house' reasonably so called."[59]

By a majority, the House of Lords in *Tandon* v. *Trustees of Spurgeon's Homes*[60] held that premises divided by design into a shop on the ground floor with residential accommodation above could reasonably be called a "house." Lord Roskill stated the following propositions of law that:

> "(1) as long as a building of mixed use can reasonably be called a house, it is within the statutory meaning of 'house,' even though it may also reasonably be called something else;
> (2) it is a question of law whether it is reasonable to call a building a 'house';
> (3) if the building is designed or adapted for living in, by which, as is plain from s.1(1) of the 1967 Act, is meant designed or adapted for occupation as a residence, only exceptional circumstances, which I find hard to envisage, would justify a judge in holding that it could not reasonably be called a house. They would have to be such that nobody could reasonably call the building a house."

The issue is not to be treated by the courts as purely one of fact.[61]

The Act by excluding parts of houses divided horizontally takes outside the ambit of the Act altogether the possibility of enfranchising flats on different floors. Difficulties would result if enfranchisement of separate floors were possible. The major difficulty is enforcement of compliance with positive obligations to repair, insure and maintain against successive owners of the freehold. But there is also excluded a house "which is not structurally detached and of which a material part lies above or below a part of the structure not comprised in the

---

[58] *Lake* v. *Bennett* [1970] 1 Q.B. 663 at p. 670.

[59] *Ibid.* p. 671 (ground floor sub-let to bookmakers), and see *Harris* v. *Swick Securities Ltd.* [1969] 1 W.L.R. 1604 (tenant occupying basement flat, three remaining floors sub-let, held he was occupying the house as his residence), and see also *Peck* v. *Anicar Properties Ltd.* [1971] 1 All E.R. 517, where the tenant used the ground floor of the house and the next property for business purposes.

[60] [1982] A.C. 755, esp. p. 767; and see [1982] Conv. 378.

[61] *Lake* v. *Bennett*, *supra*, and *Tandon* v. *Trustees of Spurgeon's Homes*, *supra*.

house."[62] This provision did not exclude where the first and second floors were built over an arched tunnel giving vehicular access to premises at the rear.[63] But it is not uncommon to find in terraced properties that house A has a larger bedroom built over part of the living accommodation of House B, at the front of the property, and the reverse situation applies at the rear. If a material part is involved in the overhanging or interlocking this will take the house outside the Act.[64] If the single building has been divided vertically, then any rights to enfranchise will only exist in relation to the separate vertical parts.

There is often difficulty in deciding what has been let in addition to and with the house, and so forms "the house and premises." No problem arises if a garden of ordinary size is attached to the house. And the Act provides that there will be included "any garage, outhouse, garden, yard, and appurtenances which at the relevant time are let to him with the house and are occupied with and used for the purposes of the house."[65] It seems that the expressions "premises" and "appurtenances" will be interpreted restrictively.[66] In *Methuen-Campbell* v. *Walters*[67] the Court of Appeal held that a paddock included in the original lease and situated at the bottom of the garden could not be regarded as part of the curtilage of the house. It was therefore not part of the "appurtenances" and could not be included in the tenant's claim.

There is a provision enabling separate long leases of separate parts of the house, or house and land, to be regarded as a single long tenancy.[68] But again this seems of limited assistance to tenants claiming that a larger area of land has been "let . . . with" the house, and so can be enfranchised. In *Gaidowski* v. *Gonville and Caius College, Cambridge*[69] the tenant was claiming to include a valuable strip of land that had originally been let separately. Although both house and strip of land had at the time of the tenant's application the same landlord and tenant this was not the case when the tenancies were originally created. The tenant's claim to include the strip of land failed. Ormrod L.J. held that "let with" implies "some reasonably close connection between the transactions of letting the house and letting the strip."[70]

At the time the tenant makes his claim he may not use or occupy all

---

[62] L.R.A. 1967, s.2(2).

[63] *Cresswell* v. *Duke of Westminster* (1985) 275 E.G. 461 (the brick tunnel, roof, and steel and wood joists supporting the bricks above were all comprised in the demise).

[64] And see *Parsons* v. *Gage (Viscount), Trustees of Henry Smith's Charity* [1974] 1 W.L.R. 435; *Gaidowski* v. *Gonville and Caius College Cambridge* [1975] 1 W.L.R. 1066 (where a separate room used in the adjoining house could be ignored).

[65] L.R.A. 1967, s.2(3).

[66] See Lord Denning in *Wolf* v. *Crutchley* [1971] 1 W.L.R. 99 at p. 101.

[67] [1979] 2 W.L.R. 113.

[68] L.R.A. 1967, s.3(6).

[69] [1975] 1 W.L.R. 1066.

[70] *Ibid.* p. 1073.

the property that can be reasonably regarded as the house and premises. Section 2(4) enables the landlord to take steps by serving notice and either obtaining the tenant's agreement or a court order to have included in the enfranchisement these additional portions which would otherwise remain in his ownership inconveniently severed from the remainder. There is also a limited right for the landlord to ask for the exclusion from enfranchisement of parts of the house and premises interlocked with his own remaining property, and which cannot, of course, be material to the tenant's house.[71] Underlying minerals can be similarly excepted, provision being made for the support of the house.[72] The Act does not help a tenant where the house is ancillary to other lands and premises let to him and occupied by him. Neither does the Act help a tenant whose house is part of an agricultural holding.[73]

(2) *Rateable Values*

For the house to be within the statutory net the rateable value for the house and premises must not be more than a specified figure on an ascertainable date. The original "appropriate day" was March 23, 1965.[74] The original maximum figures were £200, or £400 if the property was in Greater London.[74] If the property was not assessed for rating purposes on March 23, 1965, then the date it was first shown in the valuation list is the "appropriate day."[75] A property is most likely to have an appropriate day later than March 23, 1965, when it has been erected since that date.

If the tenant's house and premises form only part of the unit which is shown in the valuation list as a single hereditament, the rateable value has to be apportioned. On the other hand, if the house and premises form a number of separately rated hereditaments, then they have to be aggregated to find out if the house is within the limits.[76]

If the tenant considers that the rateable value is over the limits because of improvements resulting from structural alterations, extensions or additions he or a previous tenant has carried out at his own expense, then he can apply to the county court to determine what reduction should be made to the rateable value as at the appropriate day because of this.[77] A structural alteration or addition means alterations involving the structure or fabric of the house, e.g. the

[71] L.R.A. 1967, s.2(5).
[72] L.R.A. 1967, s.2(6).
[73] L.R.A. 1967, s.1(3).
[74] L.R.A. 1967, s.1(4).
[74] L.R.A. 1967, s.1(1)(*a*).
[75] L.R.A. 1967, s.1(4), and R.A. 1977, s.25(3).
[76] R.A. 1977, s.25(1), (2).
[77] L.R.A. 1967, s.1(4A), Housing Act 1974, Sched. 8, para. 1(2); H.A. 1980, Sched. 21, para. 2.

installation of central heating, as opposed to the mere provision of equipment, e.g. installing fitted cupboards or updating fireplaces.[78] There is a detailed procedural code governing these applications.[79] The time limits[80] governing if a reduction can be made are not mandatory only in the sense that the county court judge can in his unfettered discretion grant an extension. If he refuses, his discretion can be reviewed on appeal.[81]

The original rateable limits have been subsequently and confusingly altered. If the house was caught by the original limits it will still be caught. But in addition it will be caught where the tenancy was created on or before February 18, 1966, and the property was first separately rated before April 1, 1973, if the rateable value did not exceed £750 or £1,500 in Greater London on April 1, 1973.[82] These rateable limits catch nearly all the pre-1966 long tenancies outside London, and the majority within it.

If the tenancy was created after February 18, 1966, but the property was originally shown on the rating list on March 23, 1965, the old rateable limits of £200 and £400 still apply. This catches new tenancies of the older properties. If the tenancy was created after February 18, 1966, and the property was shown for the first time on the valuation list after April 1, 1973, then the limits are £500 and £1,000.[83] This catches new tenancies of the newer properties. The last group seems limited in its application and relates to tenancies created on or before February 18, 1966, but whose rateable value has not appeared on the list until on or after April 1, 1973. Here the limits are £750 and £1,500 respectively.[84]

C. Tenancies within the Act

(1) *Long Tenancies*

The benefits of the 1967 Act are only available where there is a long tenancy. This is defined as a

> "tenancy granted for a term of years certain exceeding 21 years, whether or not the tenancy is (or may become) terminable before

---

[78] *Pearlman* v. *Keepers and Governors of Harrow School* [1979] Q.B. 56.

[79] H.A. 1974, Sched. 8, para. 2.

[80] Effectively, the tenant has a maximum of 12 weeks to make the application from the date of his notice to the landlord to agree a reduction, H.A. 1974, Sched. 8, para. 2.

[81] *Arieli* v. *Duke of Westminster* (1983) 269 E.G. 535; *Johnston* v. *Duke of Devonshire* (1984) 272 E.G. 661, *cf. Pollock* v. *Brook-Shepherd* (1983) 45 P. & C.R. 357; (mandatory four-week time limit on application to valuation officer to determine actual amount of reduction).

[82] L.R.A. 1967, s.1(6), Housing Act 1974, s.118(1).

[83] L.R.A. 1967, s.1(5)(*b*), Housing Act 1974, s.118(1).

[84] L.R.A. 1967, s.1(5)(*a*), Housing Act 1974, s.118(1).

the end of that term by notice given by or to the tenant or by re-entry, forfeiture or otherwise, and includes a tenancy for a term fixed by law under a grant with a covenant or obligation for perpetual renewal unless it is a tenancy by sub-demise from one which is not a long tenancy."

A tenancy subject to a determinable limitation "until this lease shall cease to be vested in a member of a housing association" is a term of years certain.[85] One that can be ended by notice after a death or marriage is not to be treated as a long tenancy either where granted before April 13, 1980, or where the notice has to be given within three months of the death or marriage of the tenant, who is expressly forbidden to assign and sub-let the whole of the premises.[86]

For the tenancy to qualify as a long term "a tenant must at some point of time be, or have been, in a position to say that, subject to options to determine, rights of entry and so forth, he is entitled to remain tenant for the next 21 years, whether at law or in equity."[87] The term will only run from the date of execution and delivery of the lease, and not from any earlier date expressed to mark its beginning.[88] But the tenancy will not cease to be regarded as a "long term" if it is statutorily continued under Parts I and II of the Landlord and Tenant Act 1954.[89] It will also be regarded as continuing where it is followed by the grant of a contractual term irrespective of its terms.[90] If the original long term is followed by a further long term, then both are regarded "as if there had been a single tenancy"[91] starting from the date of the first and ending with the termination of the later term.[92] But if after the end of the long tenancy the tenant stays on as a tenant at will,[93] or a new business lease is granted or the terms of the statutory tenancy are agreed or determined, then that will mark the end of the "long term."[94]

(2) *Low Rents*

A qualifying tenancy has to be at a low rent.[95] This will normally be a

---

[85] *Eton College* v. *Bard* [1983] Ch. 321.
[86] L.R.A. 1967, s.3(1), as amended by H.A. 1980, Sched. 21, para. 3 (not striking at the genuine "tenancies for life," used for providing a named beneficiary with a residence).
[87] *Roberts* v. *Church Commissioners for England* [1972] 1 Q.B. 278, *per* Russell L.J. at p. 284. S.3(4) expressly covers extensions under covenants to renew, without the payment of premiums.
[88] *Roberts* v. *Church Commissioners for England* [1972] 1 Q.B. 278 (where the term ante-dated the grant and there was no right to extend it beyond the initial term).
[89] L.R.A. 1967, s.3(2), (5).
[90] L.R.A. 1967, s.3(2).
[91] L.R.A. 1967, s.3(3).
[92] And see *Bates* v. *Pierrepoint* (1978) 37 P. & C.R. 420 (where there was a surrender of the original long term followed by a re-grant of a further long term).
[93] *Curtin* v. *Greater London Council* (1970) 114 S.J. 932.
[94] L.R.A. 1967, Sched. 3, paras. 1, 2.
[95] L.R.A. 1967, s.1(1)(*b*).

rent not exceeding two-thirds of the rateable value. For these purposes rent does not include payments for repairs, maintenance and insurance.[96] Also disregarded are penal rents, and provisions for suspension of rent which commonly operate following accidental damage to the property.[97] There are also elaborate provisions for apportionments where either there have been different tenancies or tenancies of different parts of the property.

In the majority of cases the tenant claiming enfranchisement has to establish that his rental did not exceed two-thirds of the rateable value at two distinct times. First, the rent must not exceed two-thirds of the rateable value either on March 23, 1965,[98] or the date when the tenancy was created, if that is a later date.[99] Secondly, the tenancy must still be at a low rent when the tenant takes steps to exercise his statutory rights. The rent must therefore not exceed two-thirds of the rateable value in the last three years before the tenant serves his initial notice under the Act.[1]

Rateable values were substantially increased in 1963, and as a result a number of properties let during the beginning of the Second World War at what originally were market rents fell into the category of properties let at low rents. For properties let between the end of August 1939 and the beginning of April 1963 the tenancy is not to be regarded as one at a low rent if the original rent exceeded two-thirds of the letting value of the property at its commencement.[2] The original letting value is a matter of valuation evidence,[3] but if the property was subject to a standard rent under the Rent Acts that may be taken as the letting value.[4] But in calculating the letting value, one also should take into account the decapitalised value of any premium the landlord lawfully obtained.[5]

D. Tenants within the Act

A qualifying tenant has to occupy the house as his only or main residence.[6] Occupation is a question of fact and degree. A tenant who has long absences will not be able to rely on those periods when he had

---

[96] L.R.A. 1967, s.4(1)(*b*).
[97] L.R.A. 1967, s.4(1)(*c*).
[98] Or if the "appropriate day" is later, that date, see *ante*, B(2).
[99] L.R.A. 1967, s.4(1).
[1] L.R.A. 1967, s.1(1)(*b*), as amended. There is an alternative qualifying period of three out of the last 10 years.
[2] L.R.A. 1967, s.4(1). Building leases are excluded from these provisions.
[3] The onus of proving that the rent exceeds two-thirds of the letting value is on the landlord, L.R.A. 1967, s.4(5).
[4] *Gidlow-Jackson* v. *Middlegate Properties* [1974] Q.B. 361; criticised in *Manson* v. *Duke of Westminster* [1981] Q.B. 323.
[5] *Manson* v. *Duke of Westminster, supra,* and see *Duke of Westminster* v. *Johnson* (1985) 275 E.G. 241.
[6] L.R.A. 1967, s.1(2).

no intention of occupying or residing himself, *e.g.* because he has sub-let, or because a mortgagee is in possession.[7] It is irrelevant that he uses it for other purposes as well, *e.g.* for the conduct of his business, or that part of it is sub-let.[8] Although a husband and wife can each have a main residence, each can only have one main residence.[9] The claiming tenant must occupy "in right of the tenancy,"[10] which does not include a person who has attorned tenant to a mortgagee or chargee,[11] or a person occupying by licence from his company, which is the tenant.[12] The tenant to qualify must show that when he gives his notice "he has been tenant of the house under a long tenancy at a low rent, and occupying it as his residence, for the last three years or for periods amounting to three years in the last ten years."[13] A tenant cannot rely on a period of occupation as a regulated tenant to establish his time qualification.[14] Personal qualification is essential. An assignee could not add his two years' occupation to his predecessor's three years' occupation to qualify,[15] when the qualifying period was five years.

There are detailed provisions for treating occupation by beneficiaries under trusts or settlements as qualifying either for the benefit of the beneficiary personally or for the benefit of the trust itself, depending on whether the settlement is continuing or not.[16] There are also provisions enabling certain resident relatives of an occupying tenant who has died to add together their respective periods of qualifying occupation.[17] But after a qualifying tenant has served a notice claiming the rights the Act gives, then it is possible for him to assign the benefit of those accrued rights along with his leasehold interest. Both the rights under the Act and the leasehold estate together form part of his estate on his death.[18] They cannot be separated.

---

[7] *Poland* v. *Cadogan* [1980] 3 All E.R. 544.
[8] L.R.A. 1967, s.1(2). *Lake* v. *Bennett* [1970] 1 Q.B. 663, and see also *Baron* v. *Phillips* (1978) 38 P. & C.R. 91 (tenant relying on Part I of the Landlord and Tenant Act 1954, but her conduct showed an intention not to re-occupy the shop which had been sub-let).
[9] *Fowell* v. *Radford* (1969) 21 P. & C.R. 99.
[10] L.R.A. 1967, s.1(2).
[11] L.R.A. 1967, s.1(2)(*b*). Tenants of mortgagees who hold free of rights of redemption can enfranchise, see L.R.A. 1967, s.37(1)(*f*) and *Re Fairview, Church Street, Bromyard* [1974] 1 W.L.R. 579.
[12] *Duke of Westminster* v. *Oddy* (1984) 270 E.G. 945.
[13] L.R.A. 1967, s.1(1)(*b*), as amended; H.A. 1980, Sched. 21, para. 1.
[14] *Harris* v. *Plentex* (1980) 40 P. & C.R. 483.
[15] For the position of the assignee of a short term regarded as extending the original long term, see *Austin* v. *Dick Richards Properties Ltd.* [1975] 1 W.L.R. 1033.
[16] L.R.A. 1967, s.6.
[17] L.R.A. 1967, s.7.
[18] L.R.A. 1967, s.5.

E. Enfranchising

(1) *Procedure*

It is not proposed to deal in detail with the mechanics of enfranchisement.[19] The tenant starts the process by serving a notice[20] on his landlord[21] stating perhaps a little quaintly "his desire to have the freehold." If the landlord is the freeholder he then has two months to serve a counter-notice stating that he either does or does not admit the claim.[22] If the immediate landlord does not own the freehold reversion, then the immediate landlord must give notice to his landlord and other persons he believes have an interest in the reversion.[23]

The existence of an intermediate landlord is a common complicating factor. It arises for example where the landlord grants a long lease, generally at a ground rent, to a builder of an estate comprising a number of sites. The builder puts up the houses and then disposes of the individual sites again on long terms on underleases at a premium and subject to a small ground rent. The under-tenant in possession serves his notice on his intermediate tenant/landlord, who must in turn serve it on the head landlord. Assuming the head landlord is the freeholder, then he normally[24] conducts the negotiations in relation to the price to be paid for enfranchisement to all the parties, although immediate tenant/landlords do have the right to be separately represented in legal proceedings relating either to their title or their share of the price,[25] and to conduct their separate negotiations.[26] The freeholder can execute the conveyance of his own interest, and he is also empowered to execute an assignment of the interest of the intermediate tenant/landlord.[27] This is necessary if the enfranchising tenant is to get in the outstanding legal estates. The freeholder can receive the purchase money on behalf of himself and the tenant/landlord, and of course he has to account to him for his share of it. The

---

[19] See further *Woodfall*, paras. 3–0995 *et seq.*

[20] L.R.A. 1967, ss.1(1), 5(1), 8(1), Sched. 3, Pt. II, as amended; Leasehold Reform (Notices) Regulations, 1967 (S.I. 1967 No. 1768).

[21] L.R.A. 1967, s.5, Sched. 1, which contains detailed provisions for enfranchisement by sub-tenants.

[22] L.R.A. 1967, Sched. 3, para. 7.

[23] L.R.A. 1967, Sched. 3, para. 8. There are provisions for ensuring that notices are served on mortgagees, whether or not in possession, L.R.A. 1967, Sched. 3, para. 9. And see L.R.A. 1967, s.25.

[24] The other parties have a right to apply for his replacement if he is unwilling or unable to act, L.R.A. 1967, Sched. 1, para. 3.

[25] L.R.A. 1967, Sched. 1, para. 5(1).

[26] L.R.A. 1967, Sched. 1, para. 5(3).

[27] L.R.A. 1967, Sched. 1, para. 4.

tenant/landlord has the right to give notice that he requires the price payable for his interest to be paid to him.[28]

In some instances the freeholder is replaced by an intermediate tenant/landlord as the person designated to conduct the negotiations and execute the documentation. This situation occurs where the intermediate tenant/landlord is likely to have a greater financial interest in the property than the freeholder. This happens where the intermediate tenant/landlord was likely to have been a tenant in possession for at least 30 years after the end of the long tenancy of the enfranchising tenant in possession.[29] But in all these cases where the enfranchising tenant is an under-tenant a separate price has to be paid for each of the various superior interests.[30]

The county court is designated[31] as the forum for resolving disputes about the eligibility of the tenant; the property he can acquire; the contents of the conveyance in relation to easements to be granted or reserved or restrictive covenants to which the property is to be subject[32]; and other matters relating to the performance or discharge of obligations that flow from the service of the tenant's notice. But in most cases the process of enfranchisement will be resolved by negotiation and ultimately agreement. The effect of a good notice by a qualifying tenant is to oblige the landlord "to make to the tenant and the tenant to accept (at the price and on the conditions so provided) a grant of the house and premises for an estate in fee simple absolute, subject to the tenancy and to the tenant's incumbrances, but otherwise free of incumbrances."[33] The rights and obligations pass to successors of the original parties' estates.[34]

There are specialised provisions to accommodate landlords with unusual legal capacities, *e.g.* the Crown,[35] ecclesiastical landlords,[36] local authorities and other public bodies who are landlords,[37] mortgagees in possession[38] and landlords whose estates are being managed for them under the provisions of the Mental Health Acts 1959 and 1983.[39] But landlords of very long leases often at very nominal rents cannot always be found or identified correctly. After

---

[28] L.R.A. 1967, Sched. 1, para. 5(4). The price to be paid for the interest of the intermediate tenant/landlord is considered in subs. (2)(*a*), *post.*

[29] L.R.A. 1967, Sched. 1, para. 2.

[30] L.R.A. 1967, Sched. 1, para. 7(1)(*b*).

[31] L.R.A. 1967, s.20.

[32] L.R.A. 1967, s.10. In the case of certain public landlords there may be included a covenant restricting redevelopment, L.R.A. 1967, s.29 (as amended).

[33] L.R.A. 1967, s.8(1).

[34] L.R.A. 1967, s.5(1), (2), and see *Austin* v. *Dick Richards Properties Ltd.* [1975] 1 W.L.R. 1033.

[35] L.R.A. 1967, s.33.

[36] L.R.A. 1967, s.31.

[37] L.R.A. 1967, ss.28, 29. Tenants of National Trust property which is inalienable because of National Trust Act 1907, s.21, cannot enfranchise, L.R.A. 1967, s.32.

[38] L.R.A. 1967, s.25.

[39] L.R.A. 1967, s.26.

formal steps have been taken to trace them[40] by advertisement or enquiry, the application is dealt with by the court which appoints a surveyor to agree the correct price with the tenant, the tenant then paying the price into court, and the conveyance is executed by a person whom the court designates for that purpose.[41]

(2) *The Price*

(a) Enfranchiseable houses below £1,000 or £500 rateable values

The rateable value for these purposes is taken at the time the tenant serves his notice, after it has been adjusted to take into account tenant's improvements.[42] The broad principles on which the price is calculated in the normal case have already been mentioned.[43] The valuation exercise is affected by a number of variable factors. The most important of these are the length of the existing term, the development potential of the ground site, and the level of site values, either in terms of ground rents or freehold prices prevailing in the area. If the original term has, say, more than 20 years to run, the other factors are not likely to impinge greatly on the calculations. The valuer will approach the problem by calculating what an investor would pay for an investment producing the current ground rent[44] for the rest of the existing term. No increase is to be made because the sitting tenant is in the market.[45]

If the existing lease has only a short time to run, more attention will be directed to ascertaining the likely ground rent for the hypothetical 50 years' term. If there is evidence of modern ground rents in the area, then these can be used as comparables. Failing that one would look at current prices for comparable ground sites. Attempts to approach that figure by taking the value for the ground site as a percentage of the valuation of the property as it stands are not favoured. But in the absence of any evidence of comparable ground sites this may be the only way to solve the problem.[46]

Once a figure has been determined for the value of the site, the theoretical rent for it is then calculated by asking what rent a landlord would expect to receive from a site of that value. This exercise is known as finding the "section 15" rent. It involves decapitalising the current value put on the ground site, by applying to it a percentage that represents the return the landlord would expect to receive for his

---

[40] L.R.A. 1967, s.27(2), advertisement, etc., may not be required.
[41] L.R.A. 1967, s.27, and see also *Re Howell's Application* [1972] Ch. 509.
[42] L.R.A. 1967, s.9(1A), (1B).
[43] See *ante*, (II) A, and L.R.A. 1967, s.9(1).
[44] And see *Gallagher Estates Ltd.* v. *Walker* (1973) 28 P. & C.R. 113, and (1968) 32 Conv. (N.S.) 168 (A. George and A. K. Dowse).
[45] L.R.A. 1967, s.9(1) as amended.
[46] And see *Official Custodian for Charities* v. *Goldridge* (1973) 26 P. & C.R. 191.

capital outlay. The last step is recapitalising[47] that rental figure to find what an investor would pay now for an investment that would produce the section 15 rental, which theoretically begins only after the end of the existing term date. This involves some discounting, as one is calculating a price to be paid now for an investment producing an income which will start in the future. Again, in the normal case one adds together the capitalised and discounted sum for the rent for the rest of the contractual term and the recapitalised figure for the future rent. There are certain additional factors to be taken into account, such as defects in the lessor's title and other liabilities[48] affecting the lessor's title, but they are unlikely to make any significant impact on the price to be paid.

The major problems arise when the existing term has only a short time to run, and there is a realistic possibility that the site can be redeveloped. This is likely to happen in the case of a large Victorian house in substantial grounds in an area that is no longer entirely residential, and part of which may well be used for commercial or flat purposes already. The site may be ripe for redevelopment either for an office block or a small block of flats. If the development value of the site can be established, then, where only a short period of the current original term remains,[49] this is likely to produce the largest single item in the price for enfranchisement.

(b) Enfranchiseable houses above the £1,000 and £500 rateable values

"The relevant time"[50] for looking at the rateable value in these cases is, it seems, the date the tenant serves his notice.[51] If at that time the rateable values are over these limits, then the following provisions apply.

The assumptions to be applied in this case were altered by the Housing Act 1974, s.118(4), and are contained in section 9(1A) of the 1967 Act as amended. The somewhat abstruse assumptions that the tenant has been granted an extended 50-year term do not apply here. So far as price is concerned, the tenant is in much the same position as any other tenant wanting to purchase his landlord's interest. The fact that the purchaser is a sitting tenant can be taken into account,[52] and will serve to increase the price, as the tenant will generally have a greater incentive than an investor to purchase the freehold rever-

---

[47] The same percentages should be used for decapitalising and recapitalising. *Official Custodian for Charities* v. *Goldridge* (1973) 26 P. & C.R. 191.

[48] L.R.A. 1967, s.9(1)(*b*)(*c*).

[49] The compensation payable to the tenant under L.R.A. 1967, Sched. 2, will operate to reduce the value of the site, and see *ante* (II), A.

[50] L.R.A. 1967, s.9(1A).

[51] *Chada* v. *Norton Estates Trustees* (1985) 276 E.G. 312.

[52] If his tenancy has already been extended, the property is valued subject to that, and not the earlier, tenancy, *Hickman* v. *Trustees of the Phillimore Kensington Estate* (1985) 50 P. & C.R. 476.

sion.[53] Obviously the length of the remaining long term and the level of existing rents are likely to be the most significant factors. But the price is calculated on the assumption that at the end of the long term the tenant will remain in possession under the provisions of Part 1 of the Landlord and Tenant Act 1954.[54] For these purposes any repairing liabilities on the tenant's part are ignored, and the price is reduced by reason of improvements effected by the tenant and his predecessors at their own expense. If the reversion is likely to fall in under, say 10, years then the capitalised value of the fair rent payable under the 1954 Act tenancy will form an important part of the calculations. But in these cases, one ignores any increase likely to accrue from a possible realisation of the potential development value.

(c) Other reversionary interests

The right to enfranchise includes the right to acquire other intermediate interests, *e.g.* where there is both a head lease and underlease. The price of these interests has to be separately valued,[55] usually by reference to the rent payable and the term involved.[56] In most cases additional interests will exist because there has been a head lease, followed by an underlease to the tenant in possession. But the intermediate estate may be a concurrent lease created after the date of the interest of the tenant in possession who is enfranchising. It has not been possible since February 15, 1979, to create, alter or transfer interests superior to that of the tenant in possession in a way that will increase the price payable on enfranchisement.[57]

(d) Costs, disputes and withdrawals

An enfranchising tenant will have to pay the landlord's conveyancing costs and surveyor's charges in addition to the price,[58] but not the costs of a reference to the leasehold valuation tribunal. If there is a failure to agree on the price the matter will be referred to the Leasehold Valuation Tribunal,[59] whose members are drawn especially from the panels of members of Rent Assessment Committees.[60] Appeal from the Leasehold Valuation Tribunal lies to the Lands

---

[53] Sometimes known as "the marriage factor."
[54] See *ante* (I).
[55] L.R.A. 1967, Sched. 1, para. 7(1)(*b*).
[56] If the superior tenancy will only survive the enfranchising tenant's interest by less than a month and the net annual profit to the intermediate tenant/landlord is not more than £5 per annum, a formula determines the precise price for the interest, see Housing Act 1980, Sched. 21, para. 6.
[57] Leasehold Reform Act 1979, s.1(1), reversing the effect of *Jones* v. *Wentworth Securities* [1979] 2 W.L.R. 132. A number of these minor superior interests were created to diminish the financial benefits of enfranchisement. The formula for calculating the price to be paid for these interests is contained in L.R.A. 1967, Sched. 1, para. 7A. (inserted by H.A. 1980, Sched. 21).
[58] L.R.A. 1967, s.9(4).
[59] L.R.A. 1967, s.21, Housing Act 1980, s.142.
[60] Housing Act 1980, Sched. 22.

Tribunal. The appeal can be by way of complete rehearing with fresh evidence being adduced.[61]

A tenant may find that he is unable to proceed with the purchase after the price has been determined. He can resile from the prospective purchase by giving a notice to that effect to the landlord.[62] This terminates the tenant's rights under the current notice, and he cannot serve a further notice under the 1967 Act in the next three years. But a simple failure to proceed cannot be taken as a unilateral abandonment. The tenant is not barred from proceeding under a notice he has served until 12 years have expired.[63]

(3) *Statutory Restrictions on the Rights to Enfranchise or Extend*

There are a number of hazards statutorily and randomly scattered across the path of the prospective freeholder. They will not trap or hinder the majority of tenants who want to enfranchise. But when they do apply they may operate either to delay the tenant's aspirations, or to defeat them entirely.

(1) A notice to treat served by a compulsorily acquiring authority renders a tenant's subsequent notice of no effect.[64]

(2) The service of a ministerial certificate that the tenant's land will be required by his landlord, being a specified public body,[65] for relevant development in the next 10 years, renders the tenant's later notice of no effect.[66] If there is no question of ministerial certificates, the public body landlord may require the insertion of the conveyance of covenants restricting the tenant's rights when he is the freeholder to clear and redevelop the site himself.[67]

(3) A landlord whose interest was purchased or created before February 18, 1966, can oppose an application to enfranchise or extend because he requires possession for residential purposes for himself or a limited group of immediate relatives.[68]

---

[61] *R.* v. *London and Winchester Properties* (1983) 45 P. & C.R. 429.

[62] L.R.A. 1967, s.9(3). He may have to pay the landlord compensation, if the landlord can prove damage resulting from his inability in the meantime to deal with his interest, and also his conveyancing expenses.

[63] *Collin* v. *Duke of Westminster* [1985] 1 All E.R. 463.

[64] L.R.A. 1967, s.5(6).

[65] These include local authorities, the Commission for the New Towns, university bodies, regional health authorities, the nationalised industries, certain harbour authorities and statutory water undertakers, L.R.A. 1967, s.28(5).

[66] L.R.A. 1967, s.28(1)(a). If the ministerial certificate is served after the tenant's notice, the authority needs a county court order to recover possession, L.R.A. 1967, s.28(1)(b).

[67] L.R.A. 1967, s.29.

[68] L.R.A. 1967, s.18, Sched. 2, compensation is payable to the tenant, and see *ante* (II) A.

(4) Service of a tenant's notice to quit invalidates subsequent notices to enfranchise or extend.[69]

(5) If the landlord serves a notice under section 4 of the Landlord and Tenant Act 1954[70] ending the statutory continuation of the long term, then the tenant loses his rights to extend or enfranchise if he fails to serve a notice of his desire to do so within two months.[71]

(6) Forfeiture proceedings will not normally defeat a tenant's claim to enfranchise or extend. But the tenant's claims under the 1967 Act must be made in good faith, and not simply to avoid the forfeiture.[72] In any event if the tenant relies on the Landlord and Tenant Act 1954, s.16(2), as giving relief in actions for damages or forfeiture, then he cannot later exercise the rights given by the 1967 Act.[73]

F. Management Schemes

Before the Act was passed there were a number of large leasehold estates managed as coherent units, with the owners pursuing an estate policy with regard to development, rebuilding and appearance. Some of the more modern estates were the garden village developments erected by large manufacturers originally for their employees, *e.g.* the Reckitt's Garden Village Estate in Hull,[74] or the Bournville (Cadbury's) Estate at Selly Oak.[75] The possibility of individual enfranchisement was likely to destroy the estate concept. The Act[76] enabled landlords to apply within time limits that have now expired[77] for the approval by the court of schemes of management. The objects of the schemes are the maintenance of adequate standards of appearance and amenity and the regulation of redevelopment.[78] Obligations relating to interior repair should not, it seems, be included in a scheme.[79] Those relating to external repair obviously can,[80] and so also can insuring liabilities.[81] Most of the negative

---

[69] L.R.A. 1967, Sched. 3, para. 1.
[70] *Ante* (I), C.
[71] L.R.A. 1967, Sched. 3, para. 2.
[72] L.R.A. 1967, Sched. 3, para. 4(1), and see *Central Estates (Belgravia)* v. *Woolgar; Liverpool Corporation* v. *Husan* [1972] 1 Q.B. 48.
[73] L.R.A. 1967, Sched. 3, para. 4(4), and see *ante* (I) D.
[74] The tenanted parts of this estate are let on regulated tenancies within the Rent Acts.
[75] This estate is subject to a management scheme, and see *Cadbury* v. *Woodward* (1972) 23 P. & C.R. 281, and *Cadbury* v. *Woodward (No. 2)* (1972) 24 P. & C.R. 335, and generally see 39 Conv. (N.S.) 398 (M. Vitoria).
[76] L.R.A. 1967, s.19.
[77] L.R.A. 1967, s.19(1),. Housing Act 1974, s.118(2).
[78] L.R.A. 1967, s.19(1).
[79] *Re Sherwood Close (Barnes) Management Co. Ltd.'s Application* [1972] Ch. 208.
[80] L.R.A. 1967, s.19(8).
[81] See *Re Sherwood Close (Barnes) Management Co. Ltd.'s Application* [1972] Ch. 208.

restrictions will be of the more strenuous nature designed to minimise conduct that can be considered to cause a nuisance, and may be the type of restrictions usually found in leases of flats. The positive obligations are designed to maintain the exterior both structurally and visually according to approved standards, and that includes the boundaries and garden. Only the "landlord," *i.e.* the disenfranchised landlord, has the right to enforce the restrictions and obligations, which are made binding on successive owners because they can be registered as local land charges.[82] The scheme may oblige the enfranchising tenants and their successors to be members of the "tenants' association."[83]

III. Shared Ownership Leases

A. The Scope of the Provisions

The provisions considered in the following part of this chapter give secure tenants,[84] generally council tenants and tenants of housing associations,[85] of two years' standing, the right to buy their houses, or take long leases[86] of their flats.[87] Such tenants are entitled to financial assistance either from the local authority, or the Housing Corporation if the landlord is a housing association.[88] There are financial limits on the amount which can be borrowed.[89] Even with the statutory discount,[90] many tenants are still unable to exercise the right to buy. For some time before 1980 a few local authorities and housing associations had voluntarily been granting their tenants long leases with options to purchase tranches of the landlord's interests, otherwise known as shared ownership leases. These leases are expressly excluded from the provisions of the Leasehold Reform Act 1967 considered earlier in this chapter.[91] This prevents tenants from opting for what might be more favourable acquisition terms under the 1967 Act. The statutory right to claim a shared ownership lease was first given by the Housing and Building Control Act 1984.[92]

---

[82] L.R.A. 1967, s.19(10), as amended.
[83] *Re Abbots Park Estate* [1972] 1 W.L.R. 598.
[84] H.A. 1985, ss.79, 81.
[85] H.A. 1985, s.80.
[86] H.A. 1985, s.119.
[87] H.A. 1985, s.118. Only a lease can be acquired if the landlord does not own the freehold, s.118(1)(*b*).
[88] H.A. 1985, s.132.
[89] H.A. 1985, s.133, and Housing (Right to Buy) (Mortgage Limit) Regulations 1980 (S.I. 1980 No. 1423).
[90] H.A. 1985, s.129.
[91] H.A. 1985, s.173.
[92] ss.12–17, now H.A. 1985, ss.143–153.

B. Acquiring a Shared Ownership Lease

The tenant wishing to acquire a shared ownership lease must have taken a number of steps towards exercising the right to buy. He must have claimed and established his right to buy; he must have claimed, but not established his right to a full mortgage; and claimed deferment of completion, and paid a deposit of £100.[93] At that stage he can give notice[94] that he wants to be granted a shared ownership lease,[95] generally with the assistance of a proportionately smaller mortgage.[96] The share the tenant initially has to acquire must be at least 50 per cent.[97] Like the tenant who is exercising the right to buy outright, the shared ownership tenant is entitled to a discount on the price he has to pay.[98]

The terms of the lease are complex. They are a combination of the provisions designed to give effect to the shared ownership terms grafted[99] onto the long lease terms[1] which are already used either where the property is a flat or the landlord does not own the freehold.[2]

The basic length of the term will be 125 years, or five days less than the landlord's own interest if it is a shorter leasehold term.[3] In the case of flats, the landlord has to keep the structure, exterior and common parts in repair.[4] The tenant has to keep the interior in repair.[5] In the case of dwelling-houses, the tenant has to keep all of it in repair, unless there is a contrary agreement.[6] The grant of a shared ownership lease brings the tenant's secure tenancy to an end.[7]

There are special provisions dealing with the right to acquire further shares of the landlord's interest, the rent to be paid, and the tenant's right of disposal. The lease must contain rights to acquire additional shares in multiples of 12·5 per cent.,[8] and the right to have

---

[93] H.A. 1985, s.143, and see also s.142, and see *post.* Chap. 16 (V), B(5).

[94] Notice can be withdrawn, H.A. 1985 s.144(3), and is regarded as having been withdrawn if he then becomes entitled to a full mortgage. In either case he can complete an outright purchase, s.144(5).

[95] H.A. 1985, s.144.

[96] The terms of the mortgage are contained in H.A. 1985, Scheds. 7, 9 and include the right to further advances.

[97] H.A. 1985, s.145(3), The Secretary of State can vary this and the percentage of the subsequent shares, currently 12·5 per cent., s.145(2).

[98] H.A. 1985, s.148, and see also ss.129–131.

[99] H.A. 1985, s.151(1), and Sched. 8.

[1] H.A. 1985, Sched. 6, esp. Pt. III.

[2] H.A. 1985, s.118(1)(*b*).

[3] H.A. 1985, Sched. 6, para. 12. The rights cannot be exercised at all if the landlord's interest is for less than 21 years in the case of a house or 50 years in the case of a flat, H.A. 1985, Sched. 5, para. 4.

[4] H.A. 1985, Sched. 6, para. 14.

[5] H.A. 1985, Sched. 6, para. 16(b).

[6] H.A. 1985, Sched. 6, para. 16(a).

[7] H.A. 1985, s.151(2).

[8] H.A. 1985, Sched. 8, para. 1. An increased mortgage can be obtained, H.A. 1985, s.151, Sched. 9; Housing (Right to a Shared Ownership Lease) (Further Advances Limit) Regs. 1985 (S.I. 1985 No. 758).

the freehold conveyed to him when he has paid for 100 per cent.[9] If the landlord's interest is leasehold, the fully paid-up tenant obviously ends up owning the whole leasehold interest comprised in the term, at a rent of £10 per annum.[10] Additional shares have to be purchased at a price which reflects the value of the property when the option is exercised.[11] The property has, therefore, to be revalued, but the tenant's discount is also likely to have increased unless it already stands at the maximum of 60 per cent.[12] If the landlord's interest is leasehold then, once the annual rent falls to £10,[13] the tenant of a house[14] can acquire the rights given to tenants under the Leasehold Reform Act 1967 either to acquire the freehold or an extended lease.[15] The price of an enfranchisement is to be calculated on the basis that the property fell into the higher rateable values.[16]

The tenant still has to pay rent for that part of the property he is not yet committed to acquiring. Schedule 8, paragraph 4(2) provides that in determining what the rent should be the landlord should particularly take into account rents of any comparable dwelling-houses let on secure tenancies, as well as other matters that seem to be relevant.[17] If the landlord is a housing association, then the rent can be referred to the Rent Officer, and Rent Assessment Committee, for determination. Leases should provide for adjustment to the rent to take into account the tenant's repairing liabilities. The amount of the reduction is 25 per cent. in the case of all houses, and any property where the landlord is a housing association. In the case of local authority flats the amount the tenant pays directly or indirectly for repairs, etc., is reduced by the same percentage as the tenant's interest in the property.[18]

The lease must contain a covenant that until the shared ownership tenant has paid the full 100 per cent. he can neither assign all or part of the lease.[19] A disposal in breach of this covenant is void.[20] The lease must also contain a provision that the full balance is payable on demand if there is either a disposal, or a compulsory purchase.[21] Certain transfers are not caught by these provisions, principally,

[9] H.A. 1985, Sched. 8, para. 2.
[10] H.A. 1985, Sched. 8, para. 5.
[11] H.A. 1985, Sched. 8, paras. 3, 11.
[12] H.A. 1985, s.129, Sched. 8, para. 3.
[13] This is unlikely to occur before he has acquired a 100 per cent interest.
[14] As opposed to a flat, and see H.A. 1985, s.183(2).
[15] H.A. 1985, s.173, unless the landlord is a housing association, and the freehold belongs to a charitable trust, H.A. 1985, s.172(1).
[16] H.A. 1985, s.175, and see *ante* E, 2(b).
[17] *cf.* the statutory formula for ordinary secure tenancies, H.A. 1985, s.24 ("such reasonable charges . . . ").
[18] Housing Act 1985, Sched. 8, para. 4(3); Housing (Right to a Shared Ownership Lease) (Repairs, etc., Adjustment) Order 1984 (S.I. 1984 No. 1280).
[19] H.A. 1985, Sched. 8, para. 9, s.159.
[20] H.A. 1985, Sched. 8, para. 9(2).
[21] H.A. 1985, Sched. 8, para. 6(1).

disposals on death, divorce, or within the immediate, and generally, resident, family.[22] The tenant here is, in practice, in the same position as any other mortgagor, who would normally discharge all outstanding liabilities on a sale. But in this case the tenant may have to refund the benefit of any discount he has received.[23]

[22] *Ibid.* and s.160.
[23] H.A. 1985, Sched. 8, para. 6(3).

CHAPTER 16

COUNCIL HOUSING[1]

I. Introduction 525
II. The Selection of Tenants 526
III. The Terms of the Agreement 527
    A. The Tenant's Obligations ... 529
    B. The Landlord's Obligations .. 542
IV. Security of Tenure 545
    A. Secure Tenancies 545
    B. Unsecure Tenancies 557

V. Management and Disposal of Local
    Authority Houses 560
    A. Management 560
    B. Disposal 562
VI. The Council House as the Family
    Home 577
    A. Unsecure Tenancies 577
    B. Secure Tenancies 578

I. INTRODUCTION

The number of tenants in council houses now far exceeds the number securing accommodation from private landlords. In 1945 there were about 8·5 million rented dwellings in England and Wales, of which 7·1 million were privately owned and 1·3 million were council owned. By 1975 there were 8·1 million rented dwellings, of which 2·9 million were privately owned and 5·2 million were owned by local authorities.[2] By 1984, the number of dwellings rented from local authorities had fallen to five million (explicable largely as a consequence of tenants exercising "the right to buy") and those rented from private landlords had fallen still further to 2·2 million.[3] Local authorities are principally concerned with housing those on their existing lists and rehousing persons displaced by redevelopment or who present themselves as homeless.[4] However, before any of the housing problems which face a local authority can be solved (overcrowding, homelessness, under-occupation, single person households, single parent families, slum clearance) the extent of them must be ascertained. Local authorities are charged with obligations under the Housing Act 1985, s.8(1), to consider the housing conditions in their areas and, as a result, ought to have secured a clear and detailed understanding of the changing housing situation in their districts.[5] In addition, the authority have to inspect and report on overcrowding.[6]

---

[1] See generally Hoath, *Council Housing* (2nd ed.), *passim.*
[2] D. of E. Consultation paper, *The Review of the Rent Acts* (1977), p. 3.
[3] Housing and Construction Statistics, 1974–1984 (H.M.S.O.).
[4] See *post*, Chap. 19.
[5] s.8(2) requires the authority to review any information brought to their notice as a result of inspections and surveys carried out under s.605, which requires a periodical review by local authorities of housing conditions in their areas, with a view to the performance by authorities of their functions in respect of the issue of repair notices, and powers with regard to area improvement, slum clearance and houses in multiple occupation.
[6] H.A. 1985, s.334(1).

Authorities are also required to have regard to the needs of the chronically sick and disabled, so far as the provision of housing is concerned.[7] These statutory duties have been described as outdated and inadequate.[8] They in no way ensure that a local authority have any residential accommodation of their own at all. However, assuming a local authority have a housing stock, how do they go about selecting their tenants?

II. THE SELECTION OF TENANTS

Local authority practices differ from one area to another. Most authorities operate through a sub-committee of the housing committee, which decides on selection of individual families for the houses available at any given time, sometimes after interviewing applicants. Some authorities lay down a policy of selection and delegate to their officers the business of determining the order in which individual applicants are housed. Only exceptional cases which cannot easily be dealt with along pre-determined lines come to the attention of the committee under this system. Usually, even when councillors themselves select tenants, such great emphasis is laid on the principle of impartiality that applicants are dealt with under a code number. Councillors then cannot (usually) know which particular families they are considering. Irrespective of the way in which tenants are selected, a considerable amount of preliminary work by officials is usually necessary in receiving applications, investigating the housing conditions of applicants, assessing "need" (often on the "points system"[9]) and, where there is a procedure for committee selection, preparing shortlists for a final decision.

Subject to the constraints of the Race Relations Act 1976[10] and the Sex Discrimination Act 1975,[11] local authorities have virtually a free hand in the selection of tenants for their houses. They are not obliged to impose any residential qualifications (though most do) and there is no statutory income limit. The Housing Act 1985, s.22, provides that the local authority shall secure that in the selection of their tenants a reasonable preference is given to persons who are occupying insanitary or over-crowded houses, have large families or are living under unsatisfactory conditions, and to persons towards whom they are subject to a duty under sections 65 or 68 of the Housing Act 1985.[12]

---

[7] Chronically Sick and Disabled Persons Act 1970, s.3.
[8] Report of the Housing Management Sub-Committee of the Central Housing Advisory Committee, *Council Housing Purposes, Procedures and Priorities* (H.M.S.O. 1969).
[9] See [1973] L.A.G. Bull. 170 for a discussion of the details of "points systems." See also Cullingworth, *Housing and Local Government*, Chap. 3.
[10] ss.21(1), 78(1).
[11] ss.1(1), 2(1), 30(1), (2), 31.
[12] *Post*, Chap. 19.

While central government offers guidelines from time to time, local authorities are under few duties with regard to allocation.[13] Except in the case of persons displaced as a result of slum clearance and redevelopment,[14] or persons who are homeless,[15] prospective applicants seem only to have a right to have their applications considered fairly,[16] and a right to information about allocation procedures.[17] They cannot demand a tenancy from the local authority or complain if they have not been allocated one, unless there is clear evidence that the published procedures have not been followed, when judicial review may be available or a complaint made to the appropriate Commission for Local Administration.[18] "Housing need" is capable of many interpretations but even if there were stricter controls over the selection of tenants, they could well be made unworkable by the widely divergent housing situations to be found in different areas: a family considered for a house by a local authority in a small rural area might not be placed on the waiting list in a large industrial city. The most the law can do is ensure fair treatment between applicants on the same list[19] and, ideally, compel authorities to have some "clearly established and well-publicised machinery for the reception and investigation of complaints from the public."[20]

III. THE TERMS OF THE AGREEMENT

Many local authorities require their prospective tenants to sign a standard form tenancy agreement[21] before allowing them into possession of a council house. Many more do not make use of a written agreement but simply state the terms and conditions of the letting in the letter sent out from the office of the director of housing. The terms are usually repeated in the rent book. If the tenancy is a "secure"

---

[13] See Lewis (1976) 54 Public Administration, 147; Lewis and Livock (1979) 2 Urban Law and Policy 133.

[14] Land Compensation Act 1973, s.39(1); *R.* v. *Bristol Corporation ex p. Hendy* [1974] 1 W.L.R. 498.

[15] Housing Act 1985, ss.65, 68.

[16] *cf.* Lewis and Birkinshaw, "Taking Complaints Seriously" in *Welfare Law & Policy* (Partington & Jowell ed.) p. 130.

[17] Under H.A. 1985, s.106, an authority must publish its allocation procedures and its rules for transfers and exchanges. These procedures must be embodied in a set of rules, available for inspection without charge at council offices. Copies of the procedures, or a summary of them, must be made available to the public on payment of a reasonable fee. These duties are presumably enforceable, in appropriate cases, by judicial review under the Supreme Court Act 1981, s.31.

[18] See Hoath (1978) 128 New.L.J. 672.

[19] Under H.A. 1985, s.106(5), a council must supply to an applicant on request, at all reasonable times and without charge, details of the particulars which he has given to the authority about himself and his family and which the authority has recorded as being relevant to his application. It is unclear what the applicant can do if he finds the authority have chosen not to record an item of information which he regards as relevant.

[20] Report of Committee on *Conduct in Local Government*, p. 34, Cmnd. 5636 (H.M.S.O. 1974).

[21] *Quaere* the need for stamping, which in practice rarely, if ever, takes place: Stamp Act 1891, s.75(1), Sched. 1, as amended by Finance Act 1972, s.125(3), and Finance Act 1974, s.49(1), Sched. 11.

tenancy (defined below) the council is obliged, by the Housing Act 1985, s.104(2), to supply the tenant with a copy of the information about the terms of its secure tenancies (which it is bound to publish under section 104(1)). This information (which, so far as is reasonably practicable, must be kept up to date[22]), has to be published

"in such a form as [the council] considers best suited to explain in simple terms and so far as it considers appropriate, the effect of:

(a) the express terms of its secure tenancies;
(b) the provisions [of Parts IV and V of the Housing Act 1985]
(c) the provisions of sections 11 to 16 of the Landlord and Tenant Act 1985."[23]

In addition to the obligation to supply each tenant with a copy of this information, the council must also supply each secure tenant with a written statement of the terms of his tenancy, so far as they are neither expressed in the lease or written tenancy agreement, nor implied by law. These copies must be supplied on the grant of the tenancy, or as soon as possible thereafter.[24] No longer, therefore, may councils rely, as terms of their agreements, on letting rules, possibly available in the council's offices but rarely seen by tenants.

If a council wishes to vary the terms of their tenancy agreements, they must follow the procedure laid down in the Housing Act 1985, ss.102 and 103. First, unless the variation can be effected by agreement between the parties,[25] the council must serve on the tenant a preliminary notice, stating the council's intention to serve a notice of variation. This obligation of prior consultation does not apply to a variation of rent, rates or payments for services or facilities provided by the landlord.[26] The preliminary notice must specify the proposed variation and its effect, and invite the tenant's comments within a specified time. Secondly, after considering any comments, the landlord must serve a notice of variation accompanied by information as to its nature and effect.[27] The notice defines the variation and the date it takes effect, which must not be less than four weeks or a rental period of the tenancy, whichever is greater, after the date of service.[28] The tenant who does not wish to continue his tenancy in the face of the variation can prevent it taking effect by giving a valid

---

[22] H.A. 1985, s.104(1).
[23] *Supra*, Chap. 6, (III), c.
[24] H.A. 1985, s.104(2).
[25] H.A. 1985, s.102(1)(*a*).
[26] *Ibid.* s.103(3).
[27] *Ibid.* s.103(5).
[28] *Ibid.* s.103(4).

notice to quit. If, with the council's written agreement, the tenant withdraws his notice to quit, the notice of variation revives.[29]

A. The Tenant's Obligations

(1) *To Pay Rent*

The tenant will undertake to pay the rent weekly or monthly, in advance. Other periodic tenancies are granted, but the weekly are the most common. Fixed-term tenancies are comparatively rare, although they are more common than formerly.[30] The rent is normally payable on a Monday and, in addition to the rent, the tenant usually has to pay the general rate. He is also usually responsible for the water rate. The rent may be assessed on the basis of 48, 50 or 52 weeks per year. Whether a local authority allow any rent-free periods is a matter entirely within their own discretion.[31] Under the Social Security and Housing Benefits Act 1982, local authorities are under a duty to operate rent rebate schemes for their tenants. This topic is discussed in Chapter 18.

(a) Arrears

The problem of rent arrears is a thorny one for most authorities. Many authorities solve the problem by eviction, although current legislation makes this more difficult than it used to be.[32] It is, in any event, an unsatisfactory solution,[33] since it simply creates a new problem which must then be dealt with under the homelessness legislation.[34] Some authorities have recourse to the ancient remedy of distress,[35] and some to the county court rent action,[36] backed up where appropriate by an attachment order under the Attachment of Earnings Act 1971.[36] There are even cases of authorities attempting to "shame" tenants into paying off arrears by publishing lists of defaulters, or publishing lists of cases on arrears heard in the county court. It is doubted whether such practices achieve any useful purpose

---

[29] *Ibid.* s.103(6). See *Greenwich L.B.C.* v. *McGrady* (1982) 6 H.L.R. 36, where the court held that a notice to quit served by only one of two joint tenants was effective for this purpose.
[30] H.A. 1985, s.103(6).
[31] And see *post* (IV) A(2)(b).
[32] This is a misleading term. Annual rents are divided into 48 or 50 weeks, with no payments required, *e.g.* Christmas and Easter. The rent payments are, therefore, slightly higher than would be the case with a 52-week year, so there are, strictly speaking, no "free" periods at all.
[33] *Post* (IV).
[34] See D. of E. Circ. No. 83/72.
[35] *Post*, Chap. 19 (V).
[36] *Supra*, Chap. 5 (VII) B.

and indeed, the former is specifically prohibited by the Administration of Justice Act 1970, s.40.

(b) "Reasonable" rents

The Housing Act 1985, s.24(1), empowers local authorities to "make such reasonable charges for the tenancy or occupation of the houses as they may determine." What restrictions, if any, do these words impose on the local authority?[37] In *Belcher* v. *Reading Corporation*[38] the plaintiff tenants had challenged the rent increases proposed by the local authority landlord as being *ultra vires* and void since, it was contended, they were not "reasonable" within the statute. Romer J. gave judgment for the council. He held that whether or not increased rents were reasonable depended upon whether the local authority had considered the welfare of the tenants on the one hand, and the interests of the ratepayers as a whole on the other. It is the duty of the authority to maintain a balance between these two sections of the community, so far as possible, having regard to the specific requirements of the Housing Act 1985.[39] If a local authority decide to raise rents, this decision may only be challenged on the ground that the proposed rents are not reasonable. It may not be challenged on the ground that it would have been preferable to charge particular items of expenditure against the ratepayers as a whole.

Rents may be assessed on the basis of gross rateable values.[40] They may be based on a comparison with economic rents charged in the private sector.[41] They may be based entirely on the means of the tenant[42] (an unlikely course today given the statutory housing benefit schemes), which may mean a rent which seems more than the economic rent of the particular property, *i.e.* the amount needed to maintain the property and pay the interest charges in respect of the capital investment it represents.[43] Provided that the ultimate rent is not unreasonable from a market point of view, then the authority are acting properly, although "there is no statutory obligation embodied in the concept of 'reasonableness' to charge market rents."[44] It is perfectly proper within the section, for local authorities to fix lower

---

[37] See Yates (1975) 39 Conv. (N.S.) 387; Lee [1982] Conv. 133.
[38] [1950] Ch. 380.
[39] In practice, this means that rent will be influenced, though not fixed, by reference to those matters covered in H.A. 1985, Pt. XIII, *i.e.* the rules governing housing finance and the level of central government's housing subsidy: see Hughes, *Public Sector Housing Law*, esp. pp. 1–53 and Chap. 4, where these issues are perceptively discussed.
[40] *Luby* v. *Newcastle-under-Lyme Corp.* [1965] 1 Q.B. 214.
[41] *Smith* v. *Cardiff Corp.* (No. 2) [1955] Ch. 159; *Mandeville* v. *G.L.C.*, *The Times*, January 28, 1982; *cf. R.* v. *G.L.C. ex p. Royal Borough of Kensington & Chelsea*, *The Times*, April 7, 1982.
[42] *Evans* v. *Collins* [1964] 1 All E.R. 808.
[43] *Summerfield* v. *Hampstead B.C.* [1957] 1 W.L.R. 167.
[44] *Evans* v. *Collins* [1964] 1 All E.R. 808, *per* Widgery J. at p. 812.

rents for properties in respect of which tenants have undertaken additional repairing obligations.[45]

The usual avenue of attack for a tenant who considers the rents which the council are charging to be unreasonable will be a declaration that the determination of the rents is *ultra vires* and void.[46] There is another avenue of attack open to a secure tenant who, having withheld his rent on the ground that the rental demands are unreasonable, is faced with a claim for possession by the council for non-payment of rent. In the possession proceedings the tenant can make a collateral attack on the rent he is being charged by denying his liability for rent (and hence the ground for claiming possession) because the council's determination is *ultra vires* and void.

(c) Rent increases

A local authority must from time to time review rents and make such changes, either to rents generally or to particular rents, as circumstances may require.[47] Such reviews will usually result in rental increases. The local authority may discriminate between the means of particular tenants in fixing the amount of rent to be paid for houses of the same type in the same area.[48]

At one time technical difficulties surrounded the mechanics of increasing council rents. What was the effect of a notice to increase on the existing tenancy? How much notice had to be given? How effective were rent review conditions? Did the old tenancy have to be ended with a notice to quit?[49] In the case of council tenancies which are not secure tenancies, the Housing Act 1985, s.25, permits rent increases by a notice to increase. The notice must be in writing, and be given at least four weeks before the new rental is payable. There is no need for the existing tenancy to be ended before the rent is increased.

The notice must be given at least four weeks before the date when payment is due, *i.e.* either the commencement of the rental period or, if rent is payable in advance of the first day of the period to which it relates, before that payment day.[50] The notice must inform the tenant that he has a right, instead of accepting the increase, to bring the tenancy to an end by a notice to quit, and of what steps he must take.[51] The notice of increase must specify a date by which, if a notice to quit

---

[45] This is so even though the scheme was designed so as to maximise a local authority's Housing Benefit Subsidy from central government: *R. v. Secretary of State for Health and Social Services ex p. Sheffield County Council* (1985) 18 H.L.R. 6.

[46] A representative action, however, would seem to be unwise: *Smith v. Cardiff Corp.* [1954] 2 Q.B. 210.

[47] H.A. 1985, s.24(2).

[48] *Leeds Corp. v. Jenkinson* [1935] 1 K.B. 168; *Smith v. Cardiff Corp.* (No. 2) [1955] Ch. 159; *Luby v. Newcastle-under-Lyme* [1965] 1 Q.B. 214, and see n. 41, *supra*.

[49] See *Bathavon R.D.C. v. Carlile* [1958] 1 Q.B. 461.

[50] H.A. 1985, s.25(3)(*a*).

[51] *Ibid.* s.25(3)(*b*).

is received by the authority, the notice of increase will not take effect.[52] That date must be not less than two weeks after the date of the notice.[53] The notice of increase must also specify the date by which the tenant's notice to quit must bring the tenancy to an end, *i.e.* a termination date for the tenancy, and that date must be not later than the first day on which the tenancy could be terminated by notice to quit given on the last day of the period during which the notice must be served.[54] By way of illustration, suppose that the landlord's notice of increase specifies a period of two weeks by which a notice to quit must be served by the tenant to prevent the notice of increase from operating. The tenant must give at least four weeks' notice to quit,[55] and thus the earliest date for termination of the tenancy under this procedure will be six weeks after service of the notice of increase. If the tenant's notice to quit is to operate to prevent the increase taking effect during the currency of the notice to quit, it must be drawn to take effect, therefore, six weeks exactly after the service of the notice of increase. If it goes beyond this date, it will not operate to prevent the increase, but it will, if otherwise valid, still be effective to terminate the tenancy on the date specified in the notice.

In the case of secure tenancies, variations in rent may be made, where this is provided for in the tenancy agreement itself, in accordance with the rent review procedures in the lease or agreement.[56] In the absence of a rent review or increase clause, the council must serve a notice of variation specifying the rental increase and the date when it takes effect, which must not be shorter than a rental period of the tenancy or four weeks from the date of service, whichever is greater.[57]

(2) *Not to Part with Possession*

It is a term of every "secure tenancy" (see below) that the tenant shall not, without the council's written consent, prior or subsequent, sublet or part with possession of his council house.[58] However, every secure tenancy contains a statutory implied term enabling the tenant to take in lodgers without the need to obtain consent.[59] The landlord's consent to subletting or parting with possession must not be withheld unreasonably.[60] The former provision, contained in the Housing Act

---

[52] *Ibid.* s.25(3)(*c*).
[53] *Ibid.* s.25(4)(*b*).
[54] *Ibid.* s.25(4)(*c*).
[55] Protection from Eviction Act 1977, s.5.
[56] H.A. 1985, s.102(1).
[57] *Ibid.* s.103(1), (3)–(6). The details are discussed, *supra*, (III).
[58] H.A. 1985, s.93(1)(b). A subletting of the whole house generally removes the head tenancy from the category of secure tenancies: H.A. 1985, s.93(2).
[59] H.A. 1985, s.93(1).
[60] *Ibid.* s.94(2).

1957, s.113(5), requiring an authority to be satisfied before giving consent that no more than a reasonable rent would be charged on the subletting, has been repealed.[61] The onus is on the council to show that their consent was withheld reasonably.[62] Among the factors that may be taken into account are overcrowding consequent upon the subletting, and the hindrance to any building works that the landlord intends to do.[63] Where consent is unreasonably withheld, it is treated as given,[64] although it may be given conditionally. If the tenant has applied for consent in writing, the authority are obliged, if permission is refused, to give the tenant written reasons for the refusal.[65] The tenant must assume that consent has been refused if his request elicits no response at all within a reasonable time,[66] although such inaction will, presumably, automatically place the council in breach of their duty to furnish written reasons for a refusal.

The Housing Act 1985, s.91(1) provides that a secure tenancy is incapable of assignment unless[67] it is by way of an exchange under section 92, pursuant to a property transfer order under the Matrimonial Causes Act 1973, s.24,[68] or an assignment to a person who could have succeeded to the tenancy under the statutory succession rights[69] had the tenant died immediately before the assignment.[70] If there is a purported assignment of a tenancy or, in the case of a fixed-term tenancy granted before November 5, 1982, an assignment leading to loss of security,[71] the tenancy cannot subsequently become secure.[72]

There has been ministerial encouragement of lodgers in under-occupied council properties.[73] This may well create problems for a council house tenant since any lodger or sub-tenant will have access to the rent assessment committee sitting as a rent tribunal for a reasonable rent to be fixed for the contract,[74] unless the lodger makes substantial payments for board.[75] Council house lettings are only excluded from the Rent Act 1977, Pt. V, if the lessor is a local authority.[76] In the case of sub-lettings, the lessor is not the local

---

[61] H.A. 1985, s.35(4).
[62] H.A. 1985, s.94(2).
[63] *Ibid.* s.94(3). The county court has jurisdiction to determine any disputes, and to make declarations even though no other relief is sought: H.A. 1985, s.110(1), (2)(*b*).
[64] H.A. 1985, s.94(2).
[65] *Ibid.* s.94(6)(*a*).
[66] *Ibid.* s.94(6)(*b*).
[67] *Ibid.* s.91(3).
[68] *Post* (VI).
[69] H.A. 1985, s.89; *post* (VI) B. *cf. Peabody Donation Fund* v. *Higgins* [1983] 1 W.L.R. 1091.
[70] The provision does not apply to fixed-term secure tenancies granted before November 5, 1982: Housing (Consequential Provisions) Act 1985, Sched. 4, para. 9.
[71] See H.A. 1985, s.91(1).
[72] H.A. 1985, s.91(2).
[73] D. of E. Circ. No. 24/75.
[74] *Supra*, Chap. 14 (I) C.
[75] R.A. 1977, s.77.
[76] *Ibid.* s.19(5), as amended by H.A. 1980, Sched. 25, para. 36, reversing *Lambeth B.C.* v. *Udechuka*, (1980) 41 P. & C.R. 200.

authority but the council's own tenant. The Rent Act 1977, s.14, only excludes *full* protected tenancy status when the *immediate* landlord is, *inter alia*, a local authority.[77] In the case of sub-lettings or lodging contracts the immediate landlord is not the council, but the Rent Act 1977, Pt. III, will not apply, either because the sub-tenant's landlord is resident,[78] or because the lodging contract is not a lease but a licence.[79] However, the Rent Act 1977, Pt. V, clearly would apply in both these situations, and thus all the consequences of rent tribunal jurisdiction, including the provisions governing the form of notices to quit, would operate.[80]

A secure tenant has an absolute right to allow lodgers to live in the premises.[81] There is no statutory definition of a lodger, though there is a great deal of case law, much of which has already been discussed in Chapter 2 above.[82] However, it should be noted that there is a qualified prohibition on subletting contained in section 93(1)(b), and thus the absolute right to take in lodgers must be distinguished from what amounts to a qualified right to sublet part only with consent. This distinction will thus turn, in part, upon whether the secure tenant has himself granted a tenancy by way of subletting, or a licence by way of a lodging contract. These matters have been discussed in detail in Chapter 2 above.

A tenant who ceases to live in the property loses his secure tenant status.[83] If the agreement itself does not prohibit assignment or subletting then, once the tenancy has thus ceased to be secure there is nothing upon which the qualified right to assign in section 91 or the restricted right to sublet in section 93 may operate. Therefore, in such a case, a tenant who assigned or who sublet, while himself losing secure status, might, nevertheless, be able to impose a new tenant, who might become secure, on his landlord. In order to avoid this eventuality, section 95 of the 1985 Act applies the same restrictions on assignment and subletting to unsecure tenancies as operate in the case of those which are secure, to prevent evasion of sections 91 and 93 by means of non-occupation.

When a council house tenant moves he will frequently move from one council house to another. In housing managers' parlance, a distinction is made between "transfers" and "exchanges." A transfer (which is the most difficult move to make, especially between authorities) is the movement of an existing tenant to another vacant house belonging to the same or another authority. An exchange

---

[77] *Supra,* Chap. 10 (II) C, 2.
[78] R.A. 1977, s.12.
[79] *Supra,* Chap. 2 (II) F(2).
[80] *Supra,* Chap. 14 (I) D(2). There will also be some small measure of security for the lodger under R.A. 1977, s.106A.
[81] H.A. 1985, s.93(1)(*a*).
[82] See Chap. 2 (II) F(2).
[83] H.A. 1985, ss.81, 93(2).

involves at least two families, one of whom may be living in a house belonging to another local authority or a private landlord.[84] Under the Housing Act 1985, s.207, the Secretary of State has power to make grants or loans to authorities towards the costs of schemes facilitating secure tenants moving to become secure tenants of different landlords, or on the exchange of accommodation between two or more tenants of whom at least one is a secure tenant. Conditions may be attached to the grant or loan, breach of which may result in repayment being required forthwith.

The Housing Act 1985, s.92, contains provisions permitting tenants to exchange dwellings, by way of assignment, with the written consent of the landlord. The exchange may be with any other secure tenant, not necessarily of the same landlord, who has the written consent of his landlord to assign to *the* other or *another* secure tenant (thus permitting multi-partite exchanges). Every tenant involved must have permission to assign to another secure tenant, who himself has permission to assign to a secure tenant.[85] Consent is not to be withheld, save on the grounds specified in Schedule 3 of the 1985 Act. There are nine of these grounds, though two relate to housing associations only and are thus considered below in Chapter 17.

The landlord may refuse consent if the tenant or proposed assignee has already been ordered by the court to give up possession, or possession proceedings have already been commenced against the tenant or the proposed assignee on Grounds 1–6 of Schedule 2, or a notice of intention to commence such proceedings has already been served under section 83.[86] If the accommodation is substantially more extensive than is reasonably required by the proposed assignee, this is a ground for refusing consent, as is the case where the accommodation is not reasonably suitable to the needs of the proposed assignee and his family. This latter circumstance pertains where the assignee proposes, for example, for reasons of economy, to move by way of exchange to accommodation which is deemed to be too small for him. If the accommodation was let to the tenant in consequence of his employment by one of the public bodies specified in paragraph (b) of Ground 5 of Schedule 3, and it was situated in a cemetery or in a building held by the landlord mainly for purposes other than housing (the obvious example here is a caretaker's flat in what are otherwise non-residential premises) consent to exchange may be refused. It may also be refused if the accommodation has been specially adapted for a

---

[84] These are discussed in detail by Yates, *Local Authorities and Housing: Social Welfare Law* (Pollard ed.), B.576–B.580.

[85] H.A. 1985, s.92(1), (2), Sched. 2, Ground 6 confers on the landlord a ground for recovering possession should a premium be charged in connection with the exercise of this right.

[86] Possession proceedings against a secure tenant begin with a notice of intention to seek possession, which must specify the ground, under Sched. 2, on which possession is sought (H.A. 1985, s.83). Grounds 1 to 6 are grounds on which possession may be ordered if it is reasonable to do so: see *post* (IV) A.

disabled person and, if the assignment went ahead, no such person would then be living in the accommodation. Finally, if the accommodation is sheltered accommodation and is situated near a special or social service facility so that those housed in the sheltered accommodation may have their special needs met then, if the proposed exchange would result in no-one with those special needs occupying the sheltered accommodation, consent may be withheld.[87]

If the landlord withholds consent on any ground other than those specified in Schedule 3, consent is to be treated as having been given.[88] If the landlord fails to reply to a request for consent within 42 days of the application, or fails, on refusing consent within this period, to specify, and furnish particulars of, the ground upon which consent is being withheld, then he is subsequently prevented from relying on any of the grounds specified in Schedule 3.[89] Section 92(5) of the 1985 Act contains another circumstance, apart from the specified grounds of objection, when consent may be withheld. The landlord is entitled to require payment of any rent arrears, or the remedying of any other breach of the tenancy agreement, as a condition of consent, and this right of the landlord is not subject to the 42 days' time limit.[90] This possibility of a conditional consent therefore suggests that a failure by the landlord to reply within 42 days will not be the equivalent of giving consent,[91] and thus, if a landlord fails to reply at all, as opposed to purporting to withhold consent on a ground not specified in Schedule 3,[92] the tenant will need to take legal action[93] to secure a reply. He cannot simply proceed to exchange by way of assignment, since that would, in the case of a secure tenancy, presumably be a nullity under section 91(1).

(3) *Restrictions on User*

The tenancy agreement will contain a prohibition against business user (if the letting is residential) and usually a prohibition against displaying nameplates or advertisements on the property. The latter stipulation is sometimes qualified in that such display may be permitted with the written approval of the local authority. The tenant will further undertake not to use the premises for illegal or immoral

---

[87] Many of Grounds 1 to 9 in Sched. 3 harmonise with the grounds for possession under Sched. 2, so that, should the assignment actually go ahead, a ground of possession under Sched. 2 would be available, *e.g.* Ground 8 of Sched. 3 corresponds with Ground 14 of Sched. 2; Ground 9 of Sched. 3 corresponds with Ground 15 of Sched. 2.

[88] H.A. 1985, s.92(3).

[89] *Ibid.* s.92(4).

[90] No other conditions may be attached, and if they are they are to be disregarded: H.A. 1985, s.92(6).

[91] *cf.* H.A. 1985, s.94(5).

[92] In which case consent is deemed to have been given: H.A. 1985, s.92(3).

[93] *e.g.* for an injunction or declaration in the county court under H.A. 1985, s.110.

purposes or to cause or permit any nuisance. The tenant will have to undertake not to obstruct common accessways, passage, rubbish chutes and so on, and not to cut down or remove trees or shrubs. There may be restrictions on the parking of vehicles, boats, trailers, or caravans within the curtilage of the premises without the authority's consent. In flats there are frequently restrictions on pets.

(4) *Not to Carry Out Improvements*

The tenancy will usually forbid the tenant to make alterations or additions to the premises (which might include the erection of fences, garden trellis-work or television aerials) without consent. It is a term of every secure tenancy that a tenant will not make any improvement without the council's written consent.[94] If the council's consent is unreasonably withheld, it is treated as given.[95] A consent may be given conditionally and, if a reasonable condition is broken by the tenant, he is treated as being in breach of his tenancy,[96] thus permitting the council a ground upon which to recover possession. Provided the tenant has applied in writing for consent, the council must furnish a written statement of reasons if the request is refused.[97] If, within a reasonable time, the council neither gives nor refuses consent, they are deemed to have withheld it.[98] A council which gives consent subject to an unreasonable condition are deemed to have withheld it unreasonably.[99]

The onus is on the council withholding consent to show that its action was reasonable.[1] In determining the reasonableness of with-holding consent, the court must have regard, in particular, to the extent to which the improvement is likely to make the dwelling, or any other premises, less safe for occupiers, cause the council extra expense or reduce the market price or letting value of the house.[2] For the purposes of these statutory provisions there is a wide definition of "improvement." It means[3] any alteration in, or addition to, the house, and includes:

  (i) additions and alterations to the landlord's fixtures and fittings;
  (ii) additions and alterations connected with the provision of services;

[94] H.A. 1985, s.97(1).
[95] *Ibid.* s.97(3).
[96] *Ibid.* s.99(1), (4).
[97] *Ibid.* s.98(4)(*a*).
[98] *Ibid.* s.98(4)(*b*).
[99] *Ibid.* s.99(2).
[1] *Ibid.* s.98(1). The county court has jurisdiction to determine the issue, and may make a declaration even if no other relief is sought: H.A. 1985, s.110(1), (2).
[2] H.A. 1985, s.98(2).
[3] *Ibid.* s.97(2).

(iii) erection of wireless or television aerials;
(iv) external decoration.

A secure tenant who makes an improvement to his house with the council's consent should not suffer any rent increases, nor should any "qualifying successor" to him, as a result of the carrying out of the improvements, to the extent that he has paid for the improvement himself or the cost is covered by a statutory grant.[4] The only exception is that a tenant who pays a rent inclusive of rates will have to pay extra rent to cover any increase in rates as a result of the improvement.[5] The council has a discretion[6] to pay a secure tenant, at the end of his tenancy,[7] for the cost or likely cost of tenant's improvements, less the amount of any statutory grant.[8] The payment cannot be made unless[9]:

(i)   the council gave its consent, in writing, to the improvements, and
(ii) work on the improvements started after October 3, 1980, and
(iii) the improvements have materially added to the market price or rental value of the house.

For the purposes of the provisions prohibiting rental increases, section 101(3) defines those persons who are to be regarded as "qualifying successors" of the improving tenant and who are thus entitled to the protection of the section. Rent may not be increased while anyone who succeeds under the statutory succession provisions of section 89[10] is a secure tenant of the property. Also protected from increases on account of improvements is someone to whom the tenancy is assigned under section 91(3)(c) discussed above, *i.e.* an assignee who would have been qualified to succeed the tenant under the provisions of section 89 had the tenant died immediately before the assignment. Finally, a spouse to whom the tenancy is transferred under either the Matrimonial Causes Act 1973, s.24, or the Matrimonial Homes Act 1983, Schedule 1, paragraph 2,[11] is also a "qualifying successor."

(5) *Maintenance and Repair*

Council tenants are under the same obligations in this regard as other

---

[4] Under H.A. 1985, Pt. XV: See H.A. 1985, s.101(1).
[5] H.A. 1985, s.101(4).
[6] *Ibid.* s.100(1).
[7] Which may be when he purchases the freehold, thus getting the benefit of the improvement twice!
[8] H.A. 1985, s.100(2).
[9] *Ibid.* s.100(1).
[10] *Post,* (VI) B.
[11] *Ibid.*

periodic or fixed-term tenants of residential accommodation. The position has been fully discussed earlier in this book.[12] Most council tenancy agreements contain a provision under which the tenant agrees to allow the council's agents and workmen all reasonable facilities for entering the premises at all reasonable times to carry out repair and maintenance work.

Under the Housing Act 1985, s.96, the Secretary of State may make regulations for a scheme conferring upon secure tenants a "right to repair". The provisions are designed to allow secure tenants to carry out works of repair for which the landlord is responsible, either by way of express covenant or by implied obligation,[13] recouping the cost of such works from the landlord.[14] The regulations may provide for the landlord's obligations to be suspended "for such period and to such extent as may be determined by or under the scheme"[15] and for any questions arising under the scheme to be resolved by the county court.[16] The scheme can, however, only apply to covenants to repair the premises demised and not to the common parts.[17] The statutory provisions are silent as to the standard of repair to be attained, and also on the question of who carries responsibility for safety hazards encountered during or as a consequence of the works.

The current scheme is limited to "qualifying repairs," *i.e.* those repairs for which the landlord is responsible, other than repairs to the structure and exterior of a flat.[18] A tenant wishing to exercise his right to carry out repairs and then recover the cost from his landlord must first serve the landlord with a notice describing the proposed works and explaining why they need to be carried out and with what materials the repairs are to be undertaken. The landlord must respond within 21 days either consenting to or refusing the tenant's claim to repair.[19] There are two sets of circumstances in which consent may be refused.[20] The landlord is obliged to withhold consent in the following circumstances:

(a) the landlord's costs would be less than £20;
(b) the works do not constitute a qualifying repair;
(c) the works, if carried out using the materials specified, would not, in the landlord's opinion, satisfactorily remedy the lack of repair.

---

[12] *Supra*, Chap. 6.
[13] As under the Landlord and Tenant Act 1985, s.11.
[14] H.A. 1985, s.96(1), (5).
[15] *Ibid.* s.96(2)(*b*).
[16] *Ibid.* s.96(2)(*a*).
[17] *Supra*, Chap. 6 (III) C.
[18] Secure Tenancies (Right to Repair Scheme) Regulations 1985, S.I. 1985 No. 1493, reg. 1(2).
[19] *Ibid.* reg. 4.
[20] *Ibid.* Annex B.

In other circumstances, however, the scheme provides that the landlord *may* withhold consent which, in effect, gives the landlord a discretion whether or not to accede to the tenant's claim. The discretionary grounds for refusing consent are:

(a) the landlord's costs would be more than £200;
(b) the landlord intends to carry out the works within 28 days of the claim;
(c) the works are not reasonably necessary for the personal comfort or safety of the tenant and those living with him and the landlord intends to carry them out within one year as part of a planned programme of repair;
(d) the works would infringe the terms of any guarantee (*e.g.* for cavity wall insulation or timber treatment) of which the landlord has the benefit;
(e) the tenant has unreasonably failed to provide the landlord with access to inspect the site for the works.

If the landlord consents to the claim, it must serve a notice in response specifying the following matters: the date by which a claim for reimbursement of costs must be made following completion of the works (this must be a period of at least three months); the costs the landlord would incur if it were to carry out the works itself; the percentage of those costs which the landlord is willing to pay, which must be at least 75 per cent. of the total; and any modifications that must be adopted to the tenant's proposals as to the scope of the works or the materials to be used.[21] If the landlord fails to serve this notice, or if the landlord replies to the effect that it proposes to do the works itself but then fails to do so within the time limit specified, the tenant may, where the estimate for the works is less than £200, serve a default notice on the landlord. The landlord must respond to this default notice within seven days, either approving the tenant's proposed works or refusing consent, specifying the grounds of such refusal.[22]

Between consent and notification by the tenant that the works are completed or withdrawal by the tenant of his application to exercise his right of repair, the landlord's repairing obligations in respect of the particularised defects are suspended. The landlord's notice will inform the tenant of this fact and advise him of the possible liability for damage he may incur during this suspension period. It will also advise the tenant that he should consequently review his insurance position.

As soon as the landlord notifies approval of the proposed works, or

[21] *Ibid.* reg. 8.
[22] *Ibid.* reg. 10.

fails to respond to the tenant's default notice within seven days, the tenant may carry out the works. When the works are completed, the tenant may make a claim for repayment of his approved costs, within the time limit specified in the landlord's notice, where one has been received. The landlord must reply to this claim within 21 days.[23] The landlord is obliged to refuse reimbursement if it is not satisfied with the works, and has a discretion to refuse payment if the authorised materials have not been used, access has unreasonably been refused, conditions have not been complied with or the claim for payment was not made within the time limit specified in the landlord's notice. If the claim for repayment is rejected on the ground that the landlord is dissatisfied with the works, the tenant may carry out further works and make a further claim. The landlord then has a discretion to allow further costs.[24]

A tenant whose claim to exercise his right of repair is rejected by his landlord, or who finds the conditions imposed by the scheme, or by the landlord acting under the scheme, unduly onerous, may always have recourse to the tenant's rights at common law to set off the cost of repairs against rental payments. This right, which is a right of all tenants, not just those that are secure, has been discussed in detail earlier in this book.[25] However, secure tenants should be aware that some council tenancy agreements purport to exclude the tenant's common law right to carry out repairs and recover the cost by means of deductions from rent, and the efficacy of such attempted exclusions has yet to be tested in the courts. Tenants should, therefore, be advised that insistence on common law rights in such cases may be hazardous.

(6) *Forfeiture*

Council tenancy agreements usually contain a provision for forfeiture for non-payment of rent or breach of any other covenant in the tenancy. The operation of such forfeiture clauses, where the tenancy is not a "secure" one,[26] is governed by the general law, and is described elsewhere in this book.[27] Under the Protection from Eviction Act 1977, s.2, it is unlawful to enforce a forfeiture or a right of re-entry other than by an action for possession in the courts, where the premises are let as a dwelling, while any person is lawfully residing in them.

In the case of a forfeiture of a secure tenancy that is a periodic

---

[23] *Ibid.* regs. 12, 13.
[24] *Ibid.* regs. 16, 17.
[25] *Supra*, Chap. 6 (IV) D.
[26] This term is defined, *post.*
[27] *Supra*, Chaps. 5, 6, 8.

tenancy, the tenancy lasts until the court orders the tenant to give up possession.[28] If a fixed term secure tenancy expires because of forfeiture, then a periodic (but not secure) tenancy arises automatically (unless the court otherwise orders).[29] The terms are the same, in so far as they are compatible with a periodic tenancy, but do not include any provision for re-entry or forfeiture. Rent is payable at the same periods as under the fixed-term tenancy.[30] A tenancy might begin as a secure tenancy and then lose that status as a result of the forfeiture order, continuing as an unsecure periodic tenancy,[31] in which case the ordinary procedure discussed below for ending non-secure council tenancies would still apply.

B. The Landlord's Obligations

Many tenancy agreements for council house lettings are curiously silent about the local authority's obligations. In the absence of express undertakings, the obligations implied by the common law or statute apply.[32] In *Liverpool City Council* v. *Irwin*[33] the House of Lords observed that most contracts of letting between councils and tenants were represented by the conditions of tenancy which the tenants had signed, and that these were usually incomplete because mention was usually made only of tenant's obligations. Consequently, the terms of the agreement were apparently of a unilateral nature and it was necessary to read into the other side of the bargain such obligations as were appropriate to give efficacy to the agreement. The court's powers to imply such terms are, however, only such as may be needed to make clear the bilateral nature of the tenancy contract. The court will not introduce into the tenancy agreement terms that can be justified only on grounds of reasonableness or anticipation of legislative recommendation. It should be remembered, however, that although the law does not require every council house tenancy agreement to be in writing, or to set out all the terms of the agreement, as was discussed earlier in this chapter, the Housing Act 1985, s.104, does now require landlords under secure tenancies to produce information, in simple terms, to explain the effects of the express terms of the agreement, the provisions of Parts IV and V of the Act, and the terms implied under the Landlord and Tenant Act 1985, ss.11 to 16. This should avoid some of the more serious consequences of the former practices of local authority landlords, so criticised by their Lordships in *Irwin's* case.

[28] H.A. 1985, s.82(1).
[29] *Ibid.* ss.82(3), 86(1).
[30] *Ibid.* s.86(2).
[31] *Ibid.* s.86(1)(*b*).
[32] *Supra*, Chaps. 4 & 6.
[33] [1977] A.C. 239.

The council gives the usual implied covenants for quiet enjoyment and non-derogation from grant. If the letting is furnished, the common law implies a warranty that the premises shall be reasonably fit for habitation at the date fixed for the commencement of the tenancy.[34] The council does not undertake to keep the premises fit[35] and there is no common law covenant that unfurnished lettings are fit for habitation.[36] In a weekly tenancy the normal understanding is that the landlord is responsible for keeping the structure and exterior in repair.[37] The landlord also impliedly covenants to use reasonable care to keep common parts reasonably safe.[38] The covenant will apply, inter alia, to steps, staircases, passageways, roofs, gutters, lifts and rubbish chutes.[39] In nearly all council house lettings, the council will be under statutorily implied obligations to maintain structure, plumbing and space heating fittings by virtue of the Landlord and Tenant Act 1985, s.11.[40] The remedies available to tenants for breach of repair or maintenance covenants are the same as those applicable to other residential tenancies, discussed in Chapter 6 of this book.

Under the Housing Act 1985 there are certain controls imposed upon the way in which a landlord may bill tenants for heating charges under district or communal heating schemes. Many tenants felt that they received inadequate explanations from their landlords for what were apparently high heating charges payable under district heating schemes. Section 108 of the 1985 Act attempts to meet this difficulty by empowering the Secretary of State to make regulations requiring local authorities supplying heat to tenants under district heating schemes to adopt particular methods for determining heating charges, payable by secure tenants, in order to ensure that each tenant bears no greater proportion of the heating costs than is reasonable. Regulations may also provide for secure tenants to require information to be provided about heating charges and costs, in a prescribed form, and also authorities may be required to provide reasonable facilities to tenants for inspecting accounts, receipts and other documents supporting the information, and for taking copies or extracts from them.

A heating charge is, for this purpose, defined[41] as a payment by a tenant of the authority's own property, to that authority, for heat that is both produced by them and supplied by them, whether or not the

---

[34] *Collins* v. *Hopkins* [1923] 2 K.B. 617.
[35] *Smith* v. *Marrable* (1843) 11 M. & W.5.
[36] *Sleafer* v. *Lambeth B.C.* [1960] 1 Q.B. 43.
[37] *Mint* v. *Good* [1950] 2 All E.R. 1159.
[38] *Dunster* v. *Hollis* [1918] 2 K.B. 795.
[39] See *Liverpool City Council* v. *Irwin* [1977] A.C. 239.
[40] For a detailed discussion of these provisions see Chap. 6, *supra.* The courts have held, however, that local authority landlords owe no higher duties towards their tenants to repair under s.11 than do other landlords: *Wainwright* v. *Leeds City Council* (1984) 270 E.G. 1289; *Quick* v. *Taff-Ely B.C.* [1985] 3 All E.R. 827.
[41] H.A. 1985, s.108(3), (4).

payment is made as a part of the rent. The heating cost is the actual expenditure incurred in the operating of the heating plant at which the heat is produced.[42] At the time of writing the Secretary of State has made no regulations under this provision.

As was described earlier in Chapter 6, local authorities have extensive powers to deal with defective housing under the Housing Act 1985 and Public Health Acts.[41] However, since the instigators of proceedings under these Acts are generally local authorities, the scheme might appear to suffer from a serious practical drawback in the case of council housing. Because of this, council tenants are able to use a special procedure to deal with statutory nuisances arising from the condition of their houses, contained in the Public Health Act 1936, s.99. This allows private individuals to initiate proceedings in the magistrates' courts,[42] and the procedure has been used successfully against local authorities in the case of defective council houses.[43]

The complainant should apply to the magistrates' court by way of information.[44] If the *local authority* is acting under the 1936 Act, it must serve an abatement notice under section 93, requiring the nuisance to be abated and the necessary work done. However, no such notice is necessary where a private individual proceeds by way of information under section 99.[45] If the tenant proves his case (the criminal law standard of proof is imposed in such cases) the court must make a nuisance order, requiring the authority to abate the nuisance within the time specified by the order. The order will frequently also demand that the authority prevent a recurrence of the nuisance,[46] although the court does have a discretion as to the exact terms of the order. If the authority fail to comply with the nuisance order, they become liable to a fine[47] of up to £2,000[48] with an additional £50 for each day during which the nuisance continues thereafter.[49]

Such a procedure does, however, carry a risk for tenants, for a magistrates' court has power to order the closure of the building if the nuisance renders the property unfit for habitation.[50] The tenant

---

[42] *Ibid.* s.108(5), (*d*).
[43] *Ibid.* s.108(5), (*e*).
[41] See also: Control of Pollution Act 1974, s.59: *Joyce* v. *London Borough of Hackney* (1976) L.A.G. Bull. 211; Oliver [1974] L.A.G. Bull. 130; Pettigrew (1977) N.L.J. 130.
[42] See *R.* v. *Epping (Waltham Abbey) Justices, ex p. Burlinson* [1948] 1 K.B. 79.
[43] *e.g. Salford City Council* v. *McNally* [1975] 2 All E.R. 860.
[44] Magistrates' Courts Act 1980, s.50; *R.* v. *Newham Justices, ex p. Hunt* [1976] 1 All E.R. 839. See (1975) L.A.G. Bull. 296–297.
[45] *R.* v. *Oxted Justices, ex p. Franklin* [1976] 1 All E.R. 839.
[46] Public Health Act 1936, s.94(2).
[47] *Nottingham Corporation* v. *Newton* [1974] 2 All E.R. 760.
[48] *i.e.* level 5 on the Standard Scale: see Criminal Justice Act 1982, ss.37, 38(1)(*b*); Criminal Penalties etc. (Increase) Order 1984, s.I. 1984 No. 447, Art. 2(4) and Sched. 4, made under the Magistrates' Courts Act 1980, s.143(1).
[49] *Ibid.* s.95(1), as amended.
[50] *Ibid.* s.94(2).

therefore runs the risk of eviction and the authority would not be under a duty to rehouse under the Land Compensation Act 1973.[51] He may, however, be eligible for legal aid[52] and, in appropriate cases may have his costs awarded from public funds[53] and/or be awarded compensation.[54]

IV. SECURITY OF TENURE

A. Secure Tenancies[55]

The Housing Act 1985 grants security of tenure to a large group of council tenants, known as secure tenants. A tenant can be a secure tenant, even if his tenancy was granted before the commencement of Part I of the Housing Act 1980, the legislation first introducing the concept of the secure tenancy, on October 3, 1980.[56] Even a licensee is entitled to security provided that, had he been in occupation under a tenancy, he would have otherwise qualified.[57] The one exception is a licence granted as a temporary expedient to a squatter, even where a succession of licences is granted, and although those licences may relate to different houses.[58]

In order for a tenancy of a council house to be a secure tenancy, there must be a letting of a dwelling-house, let as a separate dwelling.[59] A dwelling-house may be a house or part of a house.[60] Land let together with the dwelling-house is considered part of it, unless it is agricultural land exceeding two acres.[61] The considerations applicable here are therefore the same as the requirements for protected tenancies under the Rent Act 1977, s.1, and readers should refer to Chapter 10 for a consideration of what these words mean.

The tenant under a secure tenancy must be an individual, or several

---

[51] See ss. 29(7), 39(1)(*b*), (9).
[52] Legal Aid Act 1974, s.2(4).
[53] Costs in Criminal Cases Act 1973.
[54] Powers of Criminal Courts Act 1973, s.35.
[55] Smith [1982] Conv. 218.
[56] H.A. 1980, s.47. A tenancy which has been ended with the tenant remaining in occupation pending court proceedings is not a secure tenancy: see *Harrison* v. *L.B. of Hammersmith & Fulham* [1981] 1 W.L.R. 650. A former tenant can qualify to exercise the right to buy until an order has been made specifying the date for possession: H.A. 1985, ss.118(1), 121(1), 185(1).
[57] H.A. 1985, s.79(3). This means that the licence must be granted, and not merely arise, *e.g.* by way of the prohibition on eviction in the Protection from Eviction Act 1977: *Harrison* v. *L.B. of Hammersmith and Fulham, supra*; see also *Restormel B.C.* v. *Buscombe* (1982) 14 H.L.R. 91—a period between proper determination of a right of occupation, and eviction by a court, does not qualify as a licence; the occupier is a "tolerated trespasser."
[58] *Ibid.* s.79(4).
[59] *Ibid.* s.79(1).
[60] *Ibid.* s.112(1).
[61] *Ibid.* s112(2).

individuals as joint tenants,[62] at least one of whom occupies the dwelling as a principal or only home. This last phrase is not defined but it is similar to the phrase used in both capital gains tax legislation[63] and in the Leasehold Reform Act 1967.[64] By analogy it would, therefore, include a tenant who occupies a part only of the house and sub-lets the remainder.[65] Possession by the tenant's deserted spouse counts as occupation by the tenant.[66]

(1) *Exemption from Secure Tenancy Status*

The Housing Act 1985, Sched. 1, contains a list of tenancies that cannot be secure.

(a) Long tenancies

Tenancies for fixed terms exceeding 21 years cannot be secure tenancies.[67]

(b) Service tenancies

If the tenant is an employee of the landlord or, if not an employee of the landlord, is an employee of another local authority, an urban development corporation, a new town corporation, the Development Board for Rural Wales, or the governors of an aided school, *and* he is required by his contract of employment to occupy the house for the better performance of his duties, the tenancy cannot be secure.[68] The discussion in Chapters 10 and 13 above in regard to the distinctions between service tenants and service occupants for the purposes of the Rent Act 1977 have equal application here. Property occupied as a service tenancy in these circumstances will continue to be unsecure for a period of three years on a grant to a new occupier, following occupation by a non-secure employee tenant. This, in essence, provides the landlord with a period of grace so that employee accommodation is not lost to the "pool" by using it temporarily for a non-employee.[69]

---

[62] *Ibid.* s.81.
[63] Capital Gains Tax Act 1979, s.10(1).
[64] s.1(2).
[65] *Harris* v. *Swick Securities* [1969] 1 W.L.R. 1064: *Poland* v. *Cadogan* (1980) 40 P. & C.R. 321. Security may be lost if the whole premises are sub-let: see *post.*
[66] Matrimonial Homes Act 1983, s.1(6), as amended by Housing (Consequential Provisions) Act 1985, s.4 and Sched. 2, para. 56.
[67] "Long tenancies" for this purpose are defined in H.A. 1985, s.115.
[68] A number of occupiers who are employees of county councils are taken out of security by H.A. 1985, Sched. 1, para. 2(2), (3). They are various police and fire officers.
[69] H.A. 1985, Sched. 1, para. 2(4).

(c) Development land

Where the house is on land acquired for development and is being used by the council as temporary housing accommodation pending development,[70] it cannot be let on a secure tenancy.

(d) Homeless persons

A tenancy or licence granted under the Housing Act 1985, ss.63, 65(3), and 68(1) cannot be secure unless one year has expired from the date when the tenant received the notification of the local authority's decision on the question of homelessness or threatened homelessness under section 64(1), or notification of which authority has the duty to house under section 68(3), as the case may be.[71] The council may, however, at any time before the year is up, notify the tenant that the tenancy is to be regarded as a secure tenancy, from which time it will, of course, be so treated. In *Eastleigh B.C.* v. *Walsh*[72] the local authority, who had granted occupation rights to the appellant in circumstances covered by this exemption, purported to terminate the appellant's occupation rights before the 12 months had expired in order to prevent him becoming a secure tenant. The notice served by the local authority was sufficient to bring a licence to an end, but was insufficient to determine a tenancy. The House of Lords held that where a homeless person had been granted rights of occupation, at a rent, with exclusive occupation, by a document that contained several references to "tenancy," the arrangement should be regarded as a lease and not a licence, even though the occupation rights were granted under the homelessness legislation. Accordingly, the appellant's occupation had not been validly determined within the 12 months' period and he thus became a secure tenant.

(e) Tenancies to persons seeking employment.

This provision is designed to provide people with temporary accommodation while moving jobs. A tenancy will not be secure until one year from the date of grant if the house is in a district or London borough and is granted to a person who was not formerly resident in that district or borough but who has come there in order to work. The tenancy must therefore be granted to meet the tenant's need for temporary accommodation, pending the securing of permanent accommodation, and the tenant must have secured employment, or the offer of it, in the district or borough *before* the grant of the tenancy in question. To fall within the exempt status the council must also have notified the tenant in writing of the provisions of this exception,

---

[70] On the meaning of "development" see Town and Country Planning Act 1971, s.22(1), (2).
[71] *Post,* Chap. 19 (V) A.
[72] [1985] 1 W.L.R. 525.

and of their opinion that the tenancy will fall within it. The council may, before expiry of the year, elect to waive the exclusion.[73]

(f) Short-term arrangements

A house let *to* the council with vacant possession for use as temporary housing accommodation cannot be subject to a secure tenancy if, under the terms of that letting, the landlord may recover possession from the council either on expiry of a specified period or whenever he requires it back. The lessor to the council must not himself be a landlord bound by the security provisions of the 1985 Act and the council's only interest in the property must be as the lessee under the superior tenancy. If these conditions are satisfied, the sub-tenancy from the council will not be secure. The purpose of providing that the lessor to the council must not himself be a landlord bound by the security provisions of the 1985 Act is to prevent collusive arrangements between councils, or councils and housing associations (who can also grant secure tenancies[74]) to defeat the security provisions of the Act.[75]

(g) Temporary accommodation

A tenancy is not a secure tenancy if it was granted for occupation by a tenant, or the tenant's predecessor in title, while works are carried out to premises he previously occupied as a home, and neither he nor the predecessor in title was a secure tenant of that other home. This provision enables authorities to house people while works, repairs, alterations or improvements are carried out, preventing the tenant from acquiring security in his temporary home.[75a]

(h) Agricultural holdings

A tenancy is not a secure tenancy if the house is comprised in an agricultural holding as defined in the Agricultural Holdings Act 1986,[76] and it is occupied by the person responsible for the control, either as tenant or as the agent or employee of the tenant, of the farming of the holding. Such tenancies, although not common in the public housing field, do exist in some parts of the country, particularly in East Anglia and the West of England.

---

[73] The need for accommodation, and the job, may be within the area of the landlord, or adjoining district or London borough. There must, however, be a coincidence between the district or London borough where the dwelling is situated and that where the place of employment is situated: H.A. 1985, Sched. 1, para. 5.
[74] See *post*, Chap. 17.
[75] See Arden, (1977) 127 N.L.J. 667.
[75a] H.A. 1985, Sched. 1, para. 6(*a*).
[76] *Ibid.* para. 8.

(i) Licensed premises

A tenancy is not a secure tenancy if the house consists of or includes premises with an on-licence.

(j) Student lettings

A tenancy is not a secure tenancy until the expiry of six months from the date when the tenant ceases to attend a designated course at an educational establishment as designated in the council's notice to the tenant, if the tenancy has been granted to enable the tenant to attend a designated course at an educational establishment. The council must notify the tenant of the provisions of this exemption, and of their opinion that the tenancy would fall within it, before the tenancy is granted. The notification must specify the educational establishment which the tenant is intending to attend. A designated course is one designated specially for the purposes of this exemption.[77] The expression "educational establishment" means a university or establishment of further education. If the tenant fails to take up a designated course at the specified establishment, the period of exemption expires six months after the grant. The council may waive the exemption within the six months period should they so desire.[78]

(k) Tenancies within the Landlord and Tenant Act 1954, Pt. II

A tenancy is not a secure tenancy if it is one to which the Landlord and Tenant Act 1954, Pt. II, applies, either because it is a business tenancy or because it is an assured tenancy.[79]

(2) *Losing Secure Tenancy Status*

(a) Exercise of right to buy

Any secure tenancy ends when, after the tenant has exercised his right to buy,[80] the freehold of his house or a long lease of his flat is vested in him,[81] or he acquires a shared ownership lease.[82]

---

[77] See Secure Tenancies (Designated Courses) Regulations 1980, S.I. 1980 No. 1407; Housing (Consequential Provisions) Act 1985, s.2.

[78] See: the Secure Tenancies (Designated Courses) Regulations 1980 (S.I. 1980 No. 1407); Housing (Consequential Provisions) Act 1985, s.2.

[79] *Supra*, Chaps. 10 & 14. N.B. It is important that a secure tenant exercising his right to take in lodgers does not become a business tenant: see *Cheryl Investments Ltd.* v. *Saldanha* [1978] 1 W.L.R. 1329; *Royal Life Saving Society* v. *Page, ibid.*; *Pulleng* v. *Curran* (1980) 44 P. & C.R. 58; *Lewis* v. *Weldcrest* [1978] 1 W.L.R. 1107; *Abernethie* v. *Kleiman Ltd.* [1970] 1 Q.B. 10.

[80] *Post.*

[81] H.A. 1985, s.139(2). The rights of any sub-tenant are preserved as if the secure tenancy had been surrendered.

[82] H.A. 1985, s.151(2).

(b) Effluxion of time

If the secure tenancy is a fixed-term tenancy that expires by effluxion of time, and the council do not grant the tenant a new secure tenancy, then this secure tenancy will expire. In its place a periodic tenancy arises automatically between the same parties and on the same terms as the former secure tenancy, for periods equivalent to the rental periods under the first tenancy. The only difference is that it may not be secure.[83] In practice this could provide a local authority with the most obvious means of avoidance of the secure tenancy provisions. A tenant can be granted a fixed-term tenancy of very short duration (say one month), which the local authority will not renew. The fixed-term tenancy will be secure, but once that has determined by effluxion of time, the periodic tenancy that then arises under the Housing Act 1985, s.86(1) (should the authority not renew the fixed-term), is arguably unsecure.[84]

(c) Order of the court

A secure tenancy continues until such time as the court orders that possession must be given up on one of the statutory grounds set out in Schedule 1 to the 1985 Act.[85] In the case of fixed-term secure tenancies subject to a right of forfeiture or a proviso for re-entry, the court may order possession at the same time as the order ending the fixed term,[86] provided one of the grounds for possession under the Act can be made out. However, it is possible for an order enforcing a proviso for re-entry or forfeiture to end the fixed-term secure tenancy, without giving the landlord the right to possession.[87] In such a case a periodic

---

[83] H.A. 1985, s.86(1).
[84] This view of the operation of s.86(1) has been criticised by some commentators, most notably Alder in [1982] Conv. 298 and 304. The authors' arguments in reply may be found in [1982] Conv. 301. Alder argues that the statutory periodic tenancy which arises under s.86(1) must be a secure tenancy, since it fulfils the general requirements of ss.79–81 of the 1985 Act. He also points to s.88(1)(c), which appears to suggest that the periodic tenancy arising under s.86(1) is secure. The consequence of Alder's view, of course, is that where a court orders termination of a fixed-term secure tenancy as a result of the exercise of a re-entry or forfeiture provision under s.82(3), the periodic tenancy that then arises under s.86(1) is secure. The tenant may, in this circumstance, be less well-off with his secure periodic tenancy than he would have been with his secure fixed-term one, but better off than if the periodic tenancy were unsecure. Against this it may be argued that s.86(1) does not actually specify that the automatic statutory periodic tenancy is secure, whereas elsewhere in the Act the draftsman spells out when a tenancy is to be regarded as a secure one: *e.g.* ss.82(1), (3), 86(1), 87, 88(1), 89(1), 90(2). Section 102(4) would seem to be unnecessary, if Alder's argument is correct, and the Act does contain examples of periodic (as opposed to fixed-term) tenancies becoming unsecure automatically by operation of law, so the *concept* itself is not unique to s.86(1): see *e.g.* ss.91(1), 92. It is probably the case that Parliament did not intend this loophole to exist and the intention almost certainly was that the periodic tenancies arising under s.86(1) should be secure. However, that is not what the sub-section actually says and there is, alas, significant evidence elsewhere in the Act that makes such a construction very much more difficult.
[85] *Ibid.* ss.82(1), 84(1).
[86] *Ibid.* s.83(5), provided the landlord has previously served notice of his intention to seek possession: H.A. 1985, s.83(1).
[87] H.A. 1985, s.82(3).

tenancy then automatically arises, on the same terms as the former secure tenancy, and for periods the same as the rental periods under the former fixed-term.[88] In this instance, depending upon the problematic question of whether the tenancy thus arising is secure or unsecure, the ordinary procedure for ending a public sector tenancy by notice to quit and possession proceedings (with no requirement that a ground be made out), may then be applicable should the landlord wish to recover possession.

(d) Sub-letting and assignment

As has already been explained earlier in this chapter, if a tenant sub-lets the whole of the property (even with consent), or part of it where the remainder is sub-let, the tenancy ceases to be secure.[89] Similarly, where a tenancy is assigned it ceases to be secure.[90] This will not, however, be the case where the assignment is ordered by the court as part of a property settlement on divorce under the Matrimonial Causes Act 1973, s.24.[91] Nor will it be the case where the divorce court exercises its power, after making a decree of divorce or nullity, to order that a secure tenancy be transferred to and vested in one of the former spouses.[92] An assignment will not result in a loss of secure status if it is to a person who would or who might have succeeded to the secure tenancy under the provisions (described later in this chapter) relating to statutory succession of secure tenancies. Sub-letting of the whole of the premises for the remainder of a fixed-term constitutes an assignment at common law[93] but sub-letting by a periodic tenant for the same periods as his tenancy does not.[94] Assignment by way of exchange under section 92 will not result in loss of secure tenancy status.

If a secure tenancy forms part of a deceased tenant's estate, it ceases to be secure unless it passes to someone who might have succeeded to it under the statutory provisions. On the death of a secure tenant under a fixed-term, therefore, the tenancy remains a secure tenancy until it is dealt with in the administration of the estate or until it is known that when it is dealt with it will cease to be secure by virtue of the person inheriting it.[95]

A tenancy that has ceased to be secure under these provisions cannot later become one again.[96] If, at a time when the tenancy is

---

[88] *Ibid.* s.86(1).
[89] *Ibid.* s.93(2).
[90] *Ibid.* s.92.
[91] *Ibid.* ss.81, 91(1), 93(2).
[92] Matrimonial Homes Act 1983, s.7 and Sched. 1.
[93] *Milmo* v. *Carrerras* [1946] K.B. 306.
[94] *Curteis* v. *Corcoran* (1947) 150 E.G. 44.
[95] H.A. 1985, s.90(2).
[96] *Ibid.* ss.91(1), (2), 95(1), (2).

not a secure one, the tenant assigns, or sub-lets the whole of the premises, the tenancy does not as a result become secure.

(3) *Taking Proceedings for Possession*

(a) Service of notice

A council wishing to obtain possession of a house or flat let on a secure tenancy, or wanting an order ending the secure tenancy (which may or may not also involve possession[97]) under a proviso for re-entry of forfeiture, must first serve a notice on the tenant, in the prescribed form, giving particulars of the ground on which the landlord will apply to the court.[98] The court has no power to order possession unless this notice is served.[99] In the case of a periodic tenancy, other than one arising on the termination of a fixed-term secure tenancy in respect of which notice was served, the notice must specify a date after which possession proceedings may be commenced.[1] That date cannot be earlier than the landlord could then have brought the tenancy to an end by notice to quit, *i.e.* it must be at least four weeks or one rental period, whichever is the longer, after service of the notice.[2] The notice expires 12 months after the date specified in it, and proceedings can only be validly brought under the notice during that year,[3] after which the council must commence the whole procedure over again.

(b) Grounds for possession

An order for possession of a house let on a secure tenancy can only be granted on one or more of the grounds set out in Schedule 2 of the 1985 Act.[4] Notice of the grounds relied on must have been served on the tenant, although the court may give leave to alter or add to the grounds specified in the notice.[5] The notice must give particulars of the ground in sufficient detail to enable the tenant to know and to meet the case against him.[6]

There are two possible overriding conditions to be satisfied before a possession order can be made, in addition to establishing one or more of the statutory grounds. One or both of these overriding conditions

---

[97] *Ibid.* ss.82(3), 83(5), 86(1).
[98] *Ibid.* s.83(1), (2). See the Secure Tenancies (Notices) Regulations 1980, S.I. 1980 No. 1339; Secure Tenancies (Notices) (Amendment) Regulations 1984, S.I. 1984 No. 1224; Housing (Consequential Provisions) Act 1985, s.2.
[99] *Ibid.* s.83(1), (4).
[1] *Ibid.* s.83(3)(*a*), (5).
[2] *Ibid.* s.83(3).
[3] *Ibid.* s.83(3)(*b*).
[4] *Ibid.* s.84(1).
[5] *Ibid.* s.84(3).
[6] *Torridge District Council* v. *Jones* (1985) 276 E.G. 1253.

will apply.[7] The first is that the court considers it reasonable to make the order and the second is the availability of suitable alternative accommodation for the tenant when the order takes effect.

(c) Reasonableness of the order[8]

The requirement that the court considers it reasonable to make the order is the same as that applicable to section 98(1) and Schedule 15, Part I of the Rent Act 1977. This requirement is fully discussed in that context in Chapter 13 and what is said there has equal application to the similar provision in the 1985 Act.

(d) Suitable alternative accommodation[9]

In order for a council to satisfy the criterion of suitability, it must be established that the alternative accommodation offered provides suitable security of tenure in that it is either another secure tenancy or (less likely in the case of possession claims by local authorities) a protected tenancy under which the landlord cannot recover possession on any of the mandatory grounds.[10] The accommodation offered must also be suitable to the needs of the tenant and his family, bearing in mind the following factors: the nature of the accommodation the landlord generally allocates to those with similar needs; the distance from their places of work or education; the distance from the home of any member of the tenant's family, if proximity is essential for the well-being of either of them; their means and needs in relation to extent of accommodation[11]; the terms of the old and the new tenancies[12]; the provision (and its amount) of furniture, where furniture is provided under the current tenancy.[13] The statutory factors make no specific mention of "character" or environmental factors. The Court of Appeal has pointed out that, in considering the needs of the tenant under this provision, it is necessary to take account of something which is no concern of the tenant at all, namely the nature of the accommodation which it is the practice of the landlord to allocate to persons with similar needs. Hence, particular environmental needs of the tenant may be overridden by other, more

---

[7] H.A. 1985, s.84(2).
[8] *Ibid.* Sched. 2, Pt. I.
[9] *Ibid.* Sched. 2, Pt. II.
[10] *Supra*, Chap. 13.
[11] When the landlord seeks possession on the ground of overcrowding, the fact that the alternative accommodation can legally house fewer than the number of people currently in the house does not, of itself, make it unsuitable: H.A. 1985, Sched. 2, Pt. II, para. 2 *cf.* R.A. 1977, Sched. 15, Pt. III, para. 5; *cf. Redspring Ltd.* v. *Francis* [1973] 1 W.L.R. 134.
[12] In the case of an offer of alternative council accommodation, these are likely to be the same, unless the change is from a house to a flat, or *vice versa.*
[13] These matters are enumerated in H.A. 1985, Sched. 2, Pt. IV, but are not exhaustive: *Enfield L.B.C.* v. *French* (1985) 40 P. & C.R. 223.

general considerations. The Court of Appeal was required to consider the particular need of the tenant for a garden. It concluded that, although a garden could be seen as one of the needs of a tenant, some of a tenant's needs may be more important than others. The weight to be attached to the various needs is a matter of degree in each case. It may well be that, taking account of all the circumstances of a case, accommodation may be regarded as reasonably suitable even if a particular need of the tenant cannot be met.[14]

(e) Grounds for possession where reasonableness is the overriding criterion[15]

A court may (not must) order possession of a house, if the council persuades the court that it is reasonable so to do.[16] Some of these grounds are almost identical in terms with those in the Rent Act 1977, Sched. 15, and reference should therefore be made to Chapter 13 of this book, where the relevant case law is discussed. The grounds are:

(1) Failure to pay rent or breach of any obligation of the tenancy agreement.
(2) Conduct by the tenant, or anyone residing in the house, which causes a nuisance or annoyance to neighbours, or conviction of using the house for immoral or illegal purposes, or of allowing it to be so used.
(3) Neglect, default or acts of waste by the tenant or anyone living in the house, causing deterioration to it or to the common parts. If a lodger or sub-tenant is responsible, the tenant must have failed to take reasonable steps to remove him.
(4) Ill-treatment of any furniture provided by the landlord under the tenancy or in any common parts, causing its deterioration. If a lodger or sub-tenant is responsible, the tenant must have failed to take reasonable steps to remove him before the ground arises.
(5) The making of a false statement, knowingly or recklessly, which induced the council to grant the tenancy to the tenant, either alone or jointly with others.
(6) The tenant has undertaken an exchange by way of assignment pursuant to the Housing Act 1985, s.92 and has either charged a premium on the assignment of the tenancy he transferred by way of exchange or has paid one for his present tenancy. This ground is available against a successor in title of the tenant who

[14] *Enfield L.B.C.* v. *French, supra.*
[15] H.A. 1985, s.84(2)(*a*).
[16] H.A. 1985, Sched. 2, Pt. I.

charged or paid the illegal premium, but only so long as the predecessor is still living in the house.[16a]

(7) The house forms part of, or is within the curtilage of, a building held by the landlord mainly for non-housing purposes and it was let as tied accommodation to a tenant employee, or a predecessor in title employee, by a landlord who is a local authority, a new town corporation, an urban development corporation, the Development Board for Rural Wales or the governors of an aided school, and the tenant or person residing with him has been guilty of conduct such that, having regard to the purpose for which the building is used, it would not be right for him to remain in occupation.

(8) The house which the tenant, or a predecessor in title, occupied as a secure tenant (and which he vacated pending the carrying out of works there) is again available for the remainder of the period for which the current secure tenancy was granted, on completion of the works.

(f) Grounds where alternative accommodation must be offered[17]

The council may obtain possession of a council house let on a secure tenancy on any one or more of the following grounds, provided they can persuade the court that suitable alternative accommodation within the Housing Act 1985, Sched. 2, Pt. II is available or will be available when the order takes effect. The grounds are:

(9) The house is overcrowded in circumstances rendering the occupier guilty of an offence.[18]

(10) The council intends to carry out, within a reasonable time of obtaining possession, demolition, reconstruction or other works on the building comprising the dwelling or on land treated as part of it, and cannot reasonably do so without obtaining possession.[19]

(g) Grounds where both reasonableness and the offer of alternative accommodation must be established

The council may be granted an order for possession (though again, the grounds are not mandatory) if they can convince the court both that it is reasonable to grant the order and that suitable alternative accommodation will be available to the tenant when the order takes effect,[20] and also make out one or more of the following grounds:

[16a] See H.A. 1985, s.92, discussed *supra* (III) A.
[17] H.A. 1985, s.84(2)(*b*).
[18] H.A. 1985, Pt. X.
[19] See the discussion of the Landlord and Tenant Act 1954, Pt. II, s.30(1)(f), Chap. 22, *post*.
[20] H.A. 1985, s.84(2)(*c*).

Ground 12[21]

The landlord reasonably requires the property for someone in its employment, or the employment of one of the other "specified" bodies, or with whom there is a contract of employment conditional on housing being provided. The dwelling must have been let in consequence of employment with the landlord, or one of the other "specified" landlords, and the tenant, or predecessor in title to the tenant, must have ceased to be in that employment. The dwelling must form part of, or be within the curtilage of a building held by the landlord mainly for non-housing purposes, or be situated in a cemetery. The "specified" landlords are a local authority, a new town corporation, an urban development corporation, the Development Board for Rural Wales and the governors of an aided school.

Ground 13

The accommodation has special features making it suitable for occupation by a physically disabled person; no such person is still living there and the council requires it to house such a person, with or without his family.

Ground 15[22]

Where the house forms one of a group which the council lets to people with special needs, fulfilled by the provision in the area of some social service or special facility (such as special medical care or education facilities), and where it is established that there is no longer a person with those special needs residing there, possession may be obtained so that someone with that special need may be accommodated there.

Ground 16

If the council can show that the accommodation is more extensive than is reasonably required by the present tenant, to whom the tenancy was statutorily transmitted under the 1985 Act[23] on the death of the former tenant, they may recover possession from that successor tenant, provided he or she is not the spouse of the deceased tenant.[24]

---

[21] Ground 11 of H.A. 1985, Sched. 2, Pt. II only applies to charitable housing trusts and is discussed *post*, Chap. 17.

[22] Ground 14 of H.A 1985, Sched. 2, Pt. III, is only available to certain housing associations and housing trusts. It is discussed *post*, Chap. 17.

[23] Under s.89. The present tenant must be a successor qualified under H.A. 1985, S.87(*b*), *i.e.* be a member of the deceased former tenant's family other than a spouse.

[24] To succeed on this ground the council must serve the preliminary notice required by H.A. 1985, s.83(1), more than six months but less than 12 months after the previous tenant's death.

(h) Postponing or suspending possession orders

Under the Housing Act 1985, s.85(1), the court has wide powers to adjourn proceedings for possession of a dwelling-house let on a secure tenancy. Under section 85(2) it may also postpone the date of possession, or stay or suspend the execution of the possession order.[25] The only circumstances in which, it appears, the court does not have this discretion is when possession is ordered on one of those grounds which are subject to the overall requirement of the availability of suitable alternative accommodation.[26]

B. Unsecure Tenancies

A council tenancy may be unsecure because it is one of those tenancies exempt from secure status, or it may have been a secure tenancy that has become unsecure through one of the processes described above. In either case the tenant will not enjoy the rights of security enjoyed by secure tenants. Nor can an unsecure tenant be a protected tenant under the Rent Act 1977 where the immediate landlord is a local authority.[27] Further, the Housing Act 1985, s.612, provides that nothing in the Rent Acts is to prevent possession being obtained of any house, possession of which is required for the purpose of enabling a local authority to exercise their powers under any enactment relating to housing. Notwithstanding these obstacles, there are some hints in the cases that even an unsecure council tenant might, in appropriate cases, have a small measure of security, in that a council will always be restrained from acting in an *ultra vires* fashion, or from abusing its power.

(1) *The "Ultra Vires" Defence*

The Housing Act 1985, s.612, qualifies the exempt status of local authorities under the Rent Act 1977 by its requirement that possession must be to enable "a local authority to exercise their powers under any enactment relating to housing." So, local authorities must, in seeking possession, satisfy themselves as to this condition precedent to the exercise of their power.[28] If a tenant can show that the property is not required for housing purposes but, for example, for

---

[25] *cf. Bristol City Council* v. *Rawlins* (1977) 34 P. & C.R. 12. For enforcement procedures see Chap. 13, *supra*.

[26] H.A. 1985, s.85(1), (2). It is unclear whether the county court might still retain some residual discretion even in these cases: see *Bristol City Council* v. *Rawlins* (1977) 34 P. & C.R. 12; C.C.R. Ord. 24, r. 11; Ord. 25, r. 72. See Rowland (1976) L.A.G. Bull. 109.

[27] R.A. 1977, s.14.

[28] *St. Pancras Borough Council* v. *Frey* [1963] 2 All E.R. 124; *cf. Guppys (Bridport) Ltd.* v. *Brookling* (1984) 269 E.G. 846.

road widening, he has a defence to the possession proceedings, not under the Rent Act 1977 or the secure tenancy provisions of the Housing Act 1985, but on the ground that the local authority are acting *ultra vires* their powers under the Housing Act 1985, s.612.[29]

The major difficulty with this defence is that the tenant carries the burden of proof. In the normal case in which it is alleged that a local authority are acting *ultra vires*, it is for the party making such an allegation to prove it and to prove that there is a duty on the courts to interfere.[30] The Court of Appeal has held[31] that it is not enough for the tenant to raise, by way of defence, simply the fact that the local authority do not require the property for the purpose of exercising their powers under any enactment relating to housing, hoping that the authority will shackle themselves by their reply. The tenant must prove, positively, that in seeking possession the authority do not seek to recover for housing purposes, and are thus acting *ultra vires*.

The effect of these decisions on the burden of proof is to make the *ultra vires* defence a forlorn hope in most cases. The problem is exacerbated by the fact that the council is not required to give reasons for its decision to evict an unsecure tenant nor afford the tenant any opportunity to make representations, or heed them, if made.[32] Since the tenant carries the burden of proof, it will be assumed that a local authority are acting *intra vires* unless the tenant can adduce positive evidence that the council require possession for an *ultra vires* purpose. Such evidence will be exceedingly hard to come by.

(2) *The "Abuse of Power" Defence*

The local authority derive their statutory powers of managing and dealing with property, including the power to grant and terminate tenancies and take proceedings for possession, from the Housing Act 1985.[33] While these powers are not trammelled in any way by the Rent Act 1977, nevertheless in exercising their statutory powers local authorities must not abuse them.[34] In *Bristol District Council* v. *Clark*[35] the local authority claimed possession of a dwelling-house following service of a notice to quit on the tenant on the ground of rent arrears. Before the Court of Appeal the tenant argued that when a

---

[29] See also: *Shelley* v. *L.C.C.* [1949] A.C. 56; *Jenkins* v. *Paddington Borough Council* [1954] J.P.L. 510; *Greater London Council* v. *Connolly* [1970] 2 W.L.R. 659, *per* Lord Denning M.R. at p. 664.
[30] *Short* v. *Poole Corporation* [1926] Ch. 66, *per* Pollock M.R. at p. 88.
[31] *Bristol District Council* v. *Clark* [1975] 1 W.L.R. 1443; affirmed on this point in *Cannock Chase District Council* v. *Kelly* [1978] 1 W.L.R. 1; *Cleethorpes Borough Council* v. *Clarkson* (1978) 128 New L.J. 680.
[32] *Sevenoaks District Council* v. *Emmott* (1979) 39 P. & C.R. 404.
[33] ss.21–24.
[34] *Associated Provincial Picture Houses* v. *Wednesbury Corporation* [1948] 1 K.B. 223, *per* Lord Greene M.R. at pp. 233–234.
[35] [1975] 1 W.L.R. 1443. See also *Cannock Chase District Council* v. *Kelly* [1978] 1 W.L.R. 1.

local authority exercised their housing management powers, in particular their power to evict, they were required to take into account certain policy matters enunciated in ministerial circulars. In so far as they did not, they were acting in abuse of their powers.

The argument is that, in rent arrears cases at least, far from exercising their powers under the Housing Act 1985, the local authority are providing bad housing management by seeking to evict the defaulting tenant. The procedure of the rent action can be used and, where appropriate, the tenant's wages attached under the Attachment of Earnings Act 1971. Department of the Environment Circulars,[36] and the Code of Guidance issued under the homelessness legislation in Part III of the Housing Act 1985, make the point that eviction for rent arrears frequently creates a homelessness problem with which the authority will have to deal in any event, and that therefore, eviction is rarely the best management solution to the problem[37]. In *Clark's* case both Lord Denning M.R. and Scarman L.J. appeared to agree with the general proposition that such ministerial advice might be relevant to the authority's decision whether or not to evict. Lawton L.J. seemed more reluctant to assume review powers except in the most blatant case, preferring to put his trust in the somewhat nebulous (and, practically speaking, ineffective) control exercised over local authorities by the electorate through the ballot box.

Lord Denning M.R. would not commit himself as to whether the omission to take the matters raised by the circulars[38] would be fatal to the local authority, although he did suggest that an authority should, perhaps, take them into account in some way. In the present case, however, he did not think that the authority had abused their powers since they had done everything that could be expected of them. They had given the tenant a chance to pay the arrears, consulted the social services department before eviction proceedings were taken, and given him a rent rebate.[39] There could be no reason for the council to seek an attachment of earnings order since, so far as the council knew, the tenant was unemployed. Scarman L.J. also took the view that the tenant's submissions failed on the particular facts of the case, although he was in no doubt that the local authority's housing management powers had to be exercised and considered in the light of the wider social context, particularly in the light of those matters raised by the relevant ministerial circulars.

Again, the benefits of the abuse of power defence are, practically

[36] *e.g.* D. of E. Circs. No. 83/72 and No. 18/74.
[37] *Post*, Chap. 18.
[38] *e.g.* Whether the tenant was in good employment, whether payment of arrears could be secured by attachment, whether arrears had been paid, whether a homelessness problem would be created or, indeed, whether the tenant had been an exemplary one, as in *Cannock Chase District Council* v. *Kelly* [1978] 1 W.L.R. 1; *Newham London Borough* v. *Patel* [1979] J.P.L. 303.
[39] *Post*, Chap. 19.

speaking, slight. The fact that the tenant appears to carry the burden of proof in such a case results in the tenant having to prove that the authority have failed to consider such matters: a difficult enough task in itself and one on which no tenant has yet succeeded in the higher courts. Secondly, there seems little guidance on how much weight, having considered them, the authority should attach to the relevant factors. In other contexts, the Court of Appeal has placed a very low weight indeed on factors contained in ministerial advice.[40]

(3) *Procedural Matters*

Before even an unsecure tenant can be evicted, a court order is required. A local authority is not exempted from the Protection from Eviction Act 1977, s.1(3), (4) and can, therefore, be guilty of an offence of harassment or unlawful eviction of an occupier if they evict without due process or commit any act which unlawfully interferes with the tenant's occupation or enjoyment of his house.[41] Also, in respect of notices to quit, local authority tenants are in exactly the same position as tenants of private landlords. So, for instance, the notice to quit must be properly served, it must be a clear direction to the tenant to leave the whole of the premises, and the day on which the quitting is to take place must be clear from the notice. In a periodic tenancy, the notice must expire at the end of a rental period, be in writing and given not less than four weeks from the date on which it is to take effect.[42]

V. MANAGEMENT AND DISPOSAL OF LOCAL AUTHORITY HOUSES

A. Management

Local authorities vary enormously in the size and scale of their housing activities and it is, therefore, not surprising to find that administrative organisations and procedures vary also. The law interferes rarely in the routine business of housing management. The Housing Act 1985, s.21, places powers of general management, regulation and control of council houses in the local authority. These powers cover a wide area of activity: recovery of possession in order

---

[40] *De Falco* v. *Crawley Borough Council* [1980] 1 All E.R. 913—a case on the Housing (Homeless Persons) Act 1977—see *post*, Chap. 19.
[41] These provisions are discussed in detail *post*, Chap. 19.
[42] Protection from Eviction Act 1977, s.5(1). Local authority lettings can no longer be restricted contracts within Rent Act 1977: R.A. 1977, s.19(5)(*aa*), *cf. Lambeth London Borough Council* v. *Udechuka* (1980) 41 P. & C.R. 200.

to re-let to another tenant[43]; insurance of the goods and chattels of tenants, including collecting premiums from them[44]; paying, with or without conditions, expenses incurred in removals or incidental to the purchase of new accommodation.[45] Houses owned by the local authority must, at all times, be open to inspection by the authority's officers or representatives, and the authority may make byelaws for the management, use and regulation of local authority provided accommodation,[46] although in practice they rarely do as the ordinary management powers are generally sufficient.[47]

By virtue of the Housing Act 1985, s.105(1), councils are obliged to make arrangements for machinery to be established for consultation with their secure tenants about housing management matters. This machinery must operate so as to inform those of its secure tenants who are likely to be substantially affected of the authority's proposals about housing management matters, and to give them an opportunity to express their views.[48] The authority has to take those views into account before reaching a decision. This duty is probably enforceable by injunction, possibly even in the county court under s.110, and, presumably, any secure tenant who is prejudiced by a failure to consult or to establish machinery for consultation could recover his loss by way of a claim for damages.[49]

"Housing management matters" are, for this purpose, relatively closely defined.[50] Any new housing programme or change of policy (for example a change in the cycle of internal or external decoration), likely to affect all or a group of the council's tenants, is included if it relates to management, maintenance, improvement or demolition of dwellings let on secure tenancies, or if it relates to the services or amenities provided in connection with the accommodation by the council, "in its capacity as landlord." This last phrase is somewhat obscure. The provision of public housing by a local authority is as much a question of social service as it is a contractual matter of landlord and tenant. The dividing line between a social service provision and a landlord provision is not always easy to draw. Is, for example, the provision of a resident warden in old people's sheltered accommodation a service or amenity provided by the council in its capacity as landlord or not? It may be that the section is simply referring to those facilities which the council is contractually obliged to provide. If so, the area of discussion is not very great since, as has

---

[43] *Shelley* v. *L.C.C.* [1949] A.C. 56.
[44] *Att.-Gen.* v. *Crayford U.D.C.* [1962] Ch. 575.
[45] H.A. 1985, s.26.
[46] *Ibid.* s.23.
[47] *Ibid.* ss.21, 22, 24–26.
[48] *Ibid.* s.105(1).
[49] Though presumably any remedy must now be sought by way of judicial review and not by way of action for breach of statutory duty: *O'Reilly* v. *Mackman* [1983] A.C. 237; *Cocks* v. *Thanet D.C.* [1983] A.C. 286.
[50] H.A. 1985, s.105(2).

been observed above, most council house tenancy agreements are silent on the landlord's obligations, falling back on the rather crude provision of basic terms by implication under statute or the common law. None of these implied terms would be likely to cover services or amenities. By virtue of section 105(3), a "group" of tenants is regarded as affected by a housing management matter if those affected form a distinct social group,[51] or occupy a distinct class of dwelling-house, whether distinguished by kind[52] or by area.[53] Unfortunately, excluded from the definition of housing management for this purpose are two matters which are likely to be closest to secure tenants' hearts—rent and service charges.[54]

All councils must make public details of their consultation arrangements.[55] A copy of any published document must be made available for inspection, free, to members of the public at the authorities' principal offices at all reasonable hours. Copies must also be available to be taken away by the public on payment of a reasonable fee.[56]

B. Disposal

(1) *The Qualifying Tenant and the Right to Buy*

Certain secure tenants are given the right to buy their houses,[57] or take long leases of their flats[58] when they have been secure tenants for two years.[59] The council must itself be the freeholder or have an interest sufficient to enable it to grant a long lease, when the right is exercised.[60] The Act defines a dwelling as a house "if it ... is a structure reasonably so called."[61] If a building is divided horizontally, the units into which it is divided are not houses but flats,[62] but if the division is vertical (such as a terrace) each unit may be a house.[63] A building that is not structurally detached is not a house if a material part of it lies above or below the remainder of the structure.[64] A

---

[51] Whatever that may be!
[52] *e.g.* all "deck access" flat dwellers.
[53] *e.g.* all the tenants on a particular estate.
[54] H.A. 1985, s.105(2).
[55] *Ibid.* s.105(5)(a).
[56] *Ibid.* s.105(5)(b).
[57] *Ibid.* s.118(1)(a).
[58] *Ibid.* s.118(1)(b).
[59] *Ibid.* s.119(1). The period(s) taken into account in calculating the two years are determined in accordance with Sched. 4.
[60] *Ibid.* Sched. 5, para. 4.
[61] *Ibid.* s.183(2).
[62] *Ibid.* s.183(2)(a).
[63] *Ibid.* s.183(2)(*b*).
[64] *Ibid.* s.183(2)(*c*). *Quaere* the case of a building with two or more flats per floor.

dwelling that is not a house under these criteria is a flat.[65] A qualifying tenant of a flat is entitled, not to the freehold, but to the grant of a long lease for a term, normally, of not less than 125 years at a rent not exceeding £10 per annum.[66]

A tenant must have been a secure tenant of a public sector landlord[67] for at least two years, or for periods together amounting to two years, before he qualifies for the right to buy. Any period during which the secure tenant, or his or her spouse, or his or her deceased spouse was a public sector tenant or the spouse of a public sector tenant, counts for this purpose provided that the time spent by any of the above occupiers as a spouse of a public sector tenant was spent occupying the property as his or her only or principal home. Reliance may, however, only be placed on a period as a public sector tenant by a spouse if the secure tenant and spouse are living together at the time the right to buy is claimed. Similarly, reliance may only be placed on a period by a deceased spouse as a public sector tenant if secure tenant and deceased spouse were living together at the time of death. However, occupation as a joint public sector tenant is treated as occupation as a sole public sector tenant, provided the dwelling in question was occupied as an only or principal home.[68]

A child of a public sector tenant, who became a secure tenant, whether by grant, by lawful assignment or by statutory succession, and whether under the same tenancy or by virtue of a new grant from the landlord, will be able to count time spent in the property, provided such time was occupation there as an only or principal home. Only time from the age of 16 may be taken into account and the time to be reckoned must be immediately before the date when the new tenant took over, or a period ending not more than two years before that date.[69]

These rather complex provisions can be understood once it is appreciated that the qualification period for the right to buy is simply a two years' period as a secure tenant, not a period as tenant of one particular landlord, nor a period of occupation of the same property. Someone who has been a secure tenant of one local authority for 18 months, who then moves house to a property owned by another local authority, has the right to buy from the second council after being in the house for a further six months only.

Also, the two years do not have to be comprised within any particular period before the right arises. A person who has at some

---

[65] *Ibid.* s.183(3).
[66] *Ibid.* s.118(1)(*b*); Sched. 6, Pt. II, paras. 11 and 12. It is doubtful whether any council flat has such a long life.
[67] Defined to include local authorities, housing associations and a range of other public bodies: H.A. 1985, Sched. 4, para. 7.
[68] H.A. 1985, Sched. 4, paras. 2 and 3.
[69] *Ibid.* Sched. 4, para. 4.

time in the past been a secure tenant for at least two years[70] can exercise a right to buy as soon as he becomes a secure tenant again, without having to accumulate first a further qualifying period of two years.[71] When a secure tenancy is vested in joint tenants, all of them jointly have the right to buy.[72] This applies even though the accommodation in question is not the only or principal home of all of them but only of the one or more seeking to exercise the right. Joint tenants can also agree between themselves that one or some of their number only shall exercise the right to buy.

A tenant with the right to buy can ask that up to three members of his family who are not joint tenants share that right with him and be treated as joint tenants.[73] The tenant can always request that his spouse be brought in as a joint purchaser, but in the case of other members of his family it must be shown that they occupy the dwelling as their only or principal home, and have done so for a continuous period of 12 months ending with the date on which the tenant gives his notice exercising the right to buy.[74] If there is no spouse or member of the family who qualifies as of right under this provision, any other member of the family may be joined, but only with the landlord's consent. In this case the landlord has absolute discretion to approve, or refuse consent.[75]

A tenant against whom a possession order has been made in respect of the dwelling-house cannot claim to buy. This applies even if the order is made before the tenant claims to exercise the right to buy, but is to take effect later.[76] Similarly, there is no right to buy if the tenant, or one of the joint tenants, is an undischarged bankrupt or has made a composition with his creditors.[77] The tenant's right may also be temporarily suspended if he falls into arrears with his rent, even though he validly exercises the right to buy.[78] Once the tenant is four weeks in arrears with his rental payments, or any other payment due from him as tenant (such as a service charge) the council are not bound to complete the sale until all outstanding sums have been paid. If the secure tenant ceases to be such before completion of his purchase or the grant of the long lease, *e.g.* by moving out after

---

[70] Periods of occupancy before the Housing Act 1980 (the Act first introducing the "right to buy") came into force if, had the Act been in force during those periods, the tenant would have been regarded as a secure tenant, will count: H.A. 1980, s.27(3).

[71] H.A. 1985, Sched. 4, para. 2(*a*).

[72] *Ibid.* s.118(2).

[73] *Ibid.* s.123(1).

[74] A member of the tenant's family is his spouse, parent, grandparent, child, grandchild, brother, sister, uncle, aunt, nephew or niece: H.A. 1985, s.186. Relatives by marriage are treated as blood relatives, relatives of the half blood as of the whole blood, and an illegitimate child as the legitimate child of his mother and reputed father. A couple who live together as husband and wife are members of each other's family.

[75] H.A. 1985, s.123(2)(*b*).

[76] H.A. 1985, s.121(1).

[77] *Ibid.* s.121(2).

[78] *Ibid.* s.138(2).

starting the procedure under section 122, the right to buy is no longer available.[79]

(2) *Excluded Dwellings*

There are some dwelling-houses the tenants of which, even if secure tenants, have no right to buy. These are[80]:

(i) Dwellings of which the landlord does not own the freehold or does not have a sufficient interest to grant a long lease. Sufficient interest for this purpose, in the case of a house, means an interest sufficient to grant a term exceeding 21 years, and in the case of a flat means an interest sufficient to grant a term of not less than 50 years, the period of the letting in both cases to commence on the date on which the tenant's notice claiming to exercise the right to buy is served on the landlord.

(ii) Dwellings forming part of, or within the curtilage of, a building held by the landlord mainly for non-housing purposes. The building must consist mainly of non-housing accommodation or be situated in a cemetery,[81] and the dwelling must be let to the tenant, or his predecessor in title, in consequence of employment with the landlord or with another specified landlord. The specified landlords are local authorities, new town corporations, the Development Board for Rural Wales, urban development corporations, or the governors of aided schools. This enables each of these landlords to house one another's employees without the tenants acquiring the right to buy.

(iii) Dwellings with special features for the physically disabled. If they are single dwellings, they will be excluded from the right to buy if they were constructed or converted as dwellings with those special features, or if the landlord or predecessor in title carried out one or more specified alterations, *i.e.* additional floor space, additional bathroom or shower-room, or installation of a lift.[82] Alternatively, "sheltered" accommodation will be exempt from the right to buy if the individual unit is one of a group, whether by construction or subsequent alteration, and is close to a social service or special facility, provided for the purpose of assisting the disabled. Also, in this case, it must be the practice of the landlord to let the group of units for occupation by the physically disabled. For this last class there

[79] *Sutton L.B.C.* v. *Swann, The Times*, November 30, 1985.
[80] See H.A. 1985, s.120 and Sched. 5.
[81] See Local Government Act 1972, s.214.
[82] H.A. 1985, Sched. 5, para. 8.

must be a collection or group of dwellings, of which the unit in question is one. In *Freeman* v. *Wansbeck D.C.*[83] the Court of Appeal was required to consider what amounted to "special features for the physically disabled." It was held that the construction of an indoor downstairs lavatory, so that the disabled occupant did not have to go upstairs, was not, in the words of the Act, "a feature substantially different from those of ordinary dwelling houses," even though it was installed by the local authority pursuant to powers under the Chronically Sick and Disabled Persons Act 1970 for the tenant's daughter who suffered from spina bifida. The Court of Appeal considered that the word "designed" connoted some architectural special feature specifically for disabled people, rather than "intended for use" by a disabled person. The fact that other dwellings in the area did not have a downstairs lavatory was by no means the decisive issue. The feature had to be "special" in the sense that ramps, widened doors, lifts and cooking surfaces at special heights were.

(iv) Dwellings forming part of a group which it is the practice of the landlord to let for occupation by persons who are suffering or who have suffered from a mental disorder and social service or special facilities are provided wholly or partly for the purpose of assisting those persons.[84]

(v) Dwellings forming a group of dwelling-houses that are particularly suitable for occupation by the elderly, having regard to location, size, design, heating systems and other features. It must be the practice of the landlord to let the accommodation to the elderly or to the elderly together with the physically handicapped, and finally there must be special facilities, including either a resident warden, or a non-resident warden on call, together with the use of a communal room in close proximity to the group of houses.

(vi) Dwellings certified by the Secretary of State as exempt. To receive exemption under this head the dwelling has to be particularly suitable, having regard to the location, size, design, heating system and other features, for persons of pensionable age, and must have been let to the tenant or a predecessor in title for occupation either by a person of pensionable age or by a physically disabled person. The landlord must apply for the Secretary of State's certificate within either four weeks or eight weeks, depending upon when the landlord must serve on the tenant, within section 124 of the 1985 Act, a notice admitting

---

[83] [1984] 2 All E.R. 746.
[84] *e.g.* "half-way" houses; see Mental Health Act 1983. In the case of this third category of dwellings for the mentally disordered, there must be a social service or special facility provided "wholly or partly" to assist the occupants: H.A. 1985, Sched. 5, para. 9(*b*).

or denying the tenant's right to buy. If the landlord applies to the Secretary of State, he will not be bound by the reply he gives in the notice he serves on the tenant under section 124.[85]

(vii) Dwellings of which the landlord does not own the freehold but whose interest is derived from a lease from the Crown. The exemption does not apply,[86] however, if either, under the terms of the lease the landlord would be entitled to grant the sub-lease claimed by the tenant without Crown permission, or the Crown consents to the grant of the sub-lease.

(3) *The Price*

The tenant will be bound to pay the dwelling's market value less any discount, disregarding tenant's improvements and neglect of internal decoration,[87] the valuation to be made at the time the right is exercised.[88] Section 127(2) and (3) of the 1985 Act contains certain valuation assumptions. These are, on the sale of the freehold:

(i) the council sells for an estate in fee simple with vacant possession; therefore the presence of the sitting tenant (which would normally depress the market value) is ignored;

(ii) neither the tenant nor a member of his family residing with him wants to buy (thus ignoring the inflationary factor of the tenant's bid).

On the grant of a long lease the assumptions are[89]:

(i) the vendor grants a lease for 125 years (or any shorter period actually granted[90]) with vacant possession;

(ii) neither the tenant nor a member of his family residing with him wants to take the lease;

(iii) the ground rent will not exceed £10 a year.

In both cases there is the additional assumption that the conveyance or grant will be subject to the same rights and burdens as are set out in Part V of the 1985 Act.

The value of the dwelling for sale purposes is determined by the council, and is included in the notice of the terms of sale with which

---

[85] H.A. 1985, s.124(3).
[86] Without the benefit of s.179, *post.*
[87] H.A. 1985, s.126(1), 127(1).
[88] *Ibid.* s.122(2).
[89] *Ibid.* s.127(3).
[90] A shorter lease may be granted, for example, if the landlord is granting a lease of a second or subsequent flat in the same building, and it is granted to *expire* at the same time as the *first* lease which was granted for at least 125 years under the right to buy: H.A. 1985, Sched. 6, para. 12.

they provide the tenant under the Housing Act 1985, s.125, in response to the tenant's exercise, by notice served under section 122, of his right to buy. There are provisions permitting the tenant to refer a valuation with which he disagrees to the district valuer for an adjudication.[91]

The tenant is entitled to a discount dependent upon the period of time for which he or, where appropriate, his spouse, parent or fellow joint tenants,[92] were secure tenants.[93] Where the period is less than three years, the discount is 32 per cent. For periods of at least three years, the discount is 32 per cent. plus 1 per cent. for each complete year in excess of two years. The discount may not, however, exceed either 60 per cent. of the value, or the amount determined by the Secretary of State as representing the costs incurred in respect of the dwelling since March 31, 1974. The determination and imposition of this maximum can result in no discount being allowed at all and, in any event, the Secretary of State is given an independent power to fix, arbitrarily, the maximum amount of the discount by order.[94]

In the case of someone who is a second-time purchaser, his discount must be reduced by deducting from it discounts previously allowed on an earlier purchase, where that discount was given to the purchaser or one of the purchasers, or to the spouse of the purchaser or one of the purchasers, or to the deceased spouse of the purchaser or one of the purchasers. A previous discount given to a spouse is not, however, to be deducted unless the purchaser, or one of the purchasers, and the spouse were living together at the date of the notice claiming the right to buy. Similarly, unless the purchaser, or one of the purchasers, and the deceased spouse were living together at the time of death, the deceased spouse's previous discount is not to be deducted. If a previous discount was given to joint purchasers, only one or less than all of whom is or are now the subject of a reduced discount, the previous discount is treated as having been allowed in equal portions.[95] If the previous discount was the subject of repayment under section 155, the terms of which are described below, then the amount deducted is to be reduced by the amount of the repayment.[96] The purpose of these provisions is to ensure that what the second-time purchaser gains and loses reflects the actual financial advantage secured by the previous exercise of the right to buy.

[91] H.A. 1985, s.128.

[92] See (V) B, 1, *supra*.

[93] H.A. 1985, s.129. Secure tenants who were serving members of H.M. forces are credited, for discount and qualification purposes, with periods of occupation by themselves or their spouses, of forces accommodation: Sched. 4, para. 5.

[94] H.A. 1985, s.131. See: Housing (Right to Buy) (Maximum Discount) Order 1980, S.I. 1980 No. 1342; Housing (Consequential Provisions) Act 1985, s.2. The Housing and Planning Bill currently before Parliament proposes raising the discounts in s.129 of the 1985 Act by 10 per cent. in the case of sales of flats under the right to buy.

[95] H.A. 1985, s.130(1)–(3).

[96] *Ibid.* s.130(4).

A tenant who sells within five years of the conveyance or lease to him is prevented from making an unjustified profit at the ratepayers' and his fellow tenants' expense by the requirement that he repays some or all of the discount.[97] A conveyance of the freehold, assignment of the leasehold, and the grant of a lease or sub-lease for over 21 years, other than leases at a rack-rent and mortgage terms, all invoke the refund covenant if the transactions take place within five years of the purchase.[98] The amount repayable under the covenant is the amount by which the market value has been discounted, reduced by 20 per cent. for each complete year after the date of conveyance or grant.[99] So, a tenant selling his freehold, purchased at a discount, three complete years after the conveyance to him of his fee simple, must refund 40 per cent. of the discount.

(4) *The Mortgage*

A secure tenant who has the right to buy his dwelling, also has the right to a mortgage,[1] entitling him to leave outstanding on mortgage the price he pays for the house or flat, plus certain costs of the transaction.[2] The mortgagee will, therefore, be his landlord, the local authority. The mortgage is repayable by equal instalments of principal and interest,[3] spread over a period of up to 25 years. Each prospective purchaser has an individual income limit, although a council may, in appropriate cases, grant a tenant a mortgage of a sum greater than his income would normally warrant.[4] The detailed calculations of the income limits are in accordance with regulations made by the Secretary of State.[5]

(5) *The Tenant's Exercise of His Rights*

A tenant who decides that he wishes to exercise the right to buy must

[97] *Ibid.* s.155. The purchaser gives a covenant to this effect, which is "a charge taking effect" as "a land charge for the purposes of section 59 of the Land Registration Act 1925:" s.156(3). The intention is that on the exercise of the right to buy, the title to the dwelling shall be registered if it is not already registered land, even if it is not in an area of compulsory registration: s.154(1).

[98] H.A. 1985, s.159. Certain involuntary disposals are excluded, *e.g.* under Matrimonial Causes Act 1973, s.24, or the Inheritance (Provision for Family and Dependants) Act 1975, s.2, and the vesting of the dwelling-house in a beneficiary under a will or on an intestacy—a potential trap for unwary personal representatives, who may be tempted to sell the dwelling to pay debts and legacies (thus invoking the repayment covenant) rather than vesting it *in specie* in the beneficiary: s.160(1).

[99] H.A. 1985, s.155(2).

[1] *Ibid.* s.132(1). See s.139(3) and Sched. 7.

[2] *Ibid.* s.133(1).

[3] At rates determined in accordance with H.A. 1985, s.438(1).

[4] H.A. 1985, s.133(4).

[5] See the Housing (Right to Buy) (Mortgage Limit) Regulations 1980 (S.I. 1980 No. 1423): Housing (Consequential Provisions) Act 1985, s.2.

serve a written notice to that effect on his landlord.[6] If the tenant wishes to share the right to buy with members of his family, it is at this point that he must so claim.[7] The council then has four weeks[8] from the date of service to reply, in the form of a written notice, either admitting the tenant's right to buy, or denying it with reasons.[9] If the local authority do not admit the tenant's right to buy, it is for the tenant to establish it, in the county court if necessary.[10]

Once the local authority have admitted the tenant's right to buy, or it has been established in the county court, they must then serve a further notice,[11] stating:

(i) the price, together with details as to how the price was arrived at;

(ii) the discount to which the tenant is entitled, any reduction on account of a previous discount, and any relevant limit on the amount of the discount;

(iii) the provisions that the landlord considers should be in the conveyance or lease[12];

(iv) the fact that the tenant has a right of appeal, as to value, to the district valuer;

(v) the fact that the tenant has a right to a mortgage;

(vi) the procedure by which the tenant may exercise his right to a mortgage, together with the appropriate time limits;

(vii) the fact that the tenant has a right to postpone completion of his purchase;

(viii) an estimate relating to service charges which will be payable, if any, after the right to buy has been exercised, whether in respect of flats or houses.[13]

The landlord must supply the tenant with a form, at the same time as the above notice is sent, on which the tenant can claim his right to a mortgage.

---

[6] *Ibid.* s.122(1). A statutory form can be prescribed for all notices under Part V, see s.176(1); see the Housing (Right to Buy) (Prescribed Forms) Regulations 1984 (S.I. 1984 No. 1175); Housing (Consequential Provisions) Act 1985, s.2.

[7] H.A. 1985, s.123(1).

[8] Unless the two years' qualifying period was partly served with a different landlord, when the period is eight weeks; H.A. 1985, s.124(1).

[9] H.A. 1985, s.124(1).

[10] *Ibid.* s.181(1), (2).

[11] *Ibid.* s.125. The notice must be served "as soon as possible."

[12] The Housing Act 1985 makes provision in two ways about the contents of the conveyance or lease: s.139(1) and Sched. 6. There are some matters on which the contents are statutorily prescribed, and others in which the requirement is simply that the terms be "reasonable" in the circumstances (see Sched. 6). The county court has jurisdiction to determine any dispute about the contents of a conveyance or lease: s.181(1). It is for the local authority to commence the negotiations as to the contents of the relevant deeds by proposing them in their notice of the terms of sale: s.125(3). See *Precedents for the Conveyancer*, Vol. 2, pp. 16–38, for the standard form of conveyance and *ibid.* Vol. 1, 5–73 for the standard lease on sale of a flat.

[13] H.A. 1985, s.125(4). *cf.* s.46 and Sched. 6, para. 18.

A tenant who wishes to exercise his right to a mortgage then does so by serving yet another written notice to that effect on the council.[14] The tenant must normally make his response within three months of receiving the local authority's notice of the terms of sale or, if an appeal has gone to the district valuer, within three months of receipt of the results of his appeal. This period may, however, be extended by the local authority or the county court, where there are reasonable grounds to do so.[15] If there is a change of tenant after the notice to buy has been served (this, in itself, does not defeat the exercise or the right) the time limit is extended. Once a secure tenant has given notice to buy, a new tenant who takes over the tenancy (or who takes a periodic tenancy on the expiry of the former one) is in the same position as if he had himself given the notice exercising the right to buy.[16] This transfer of rights can take place on any number of occasions.[17]

In two circumstances a change of tenant will change the position of the newcomer from that of the former tenant who gave notice. First, if the original tenant gave notice requiring that members of his family share the right to buy, those members' rights will terminate on a change of tenant unless they are also members of the family of the second tenant.[18] Secondly, the new tenant may be able to exercise the right to a mortgage, even though the first tenant did not do so before the expiry of the time limit. If the local authority have already served the first tenant with notice of the terms of sale, it must also serve the new tenant with another form for claiming a mortgage.[19] The new tenant then has three months (a time limit that may be extended either by the council or the county court if there are reasonable grounds so to do), from the date the form is served within which to claim a mortgage.

When the local authority receive notice from a tenant claiming a mortgage, they must reply as soon as practicable with a notice stating[20]:

(i)   the amount of the mortgage to which it considers the tenant is entitled;
(ii) an explanation of how that sum is arrived at;
(iii) the provisions it considers the mortgage deed should contain;
(iv) the right to a shared ownership lease under the Housing Act

---

[14] H.A. 1985, s.134(1).
[15] *Ibid.* s.134(2)–(4).
[16] *Ibid.* s.136(1).
[17] *Ibid.* s.136(7).
[18] *Ibid.* s.136(6).
[19] *Ibid.* s.136(2).
[20] *Ibid.* s.135(1).

1985, sections 143–153,[21] where the amount to which the tenant is entitled is less than the full amount needed to purchase outright[22];

(v) the rights that a tenant, who postpones completion of the mortgage, has to serve a further notice claiming his mortgage during the period of postponement.[23]

The notice must be accompanied by a form for the tenant to use in claiming to defer completion.[24]

A tenant has the right to defer completion of his purchase provided he has claimed the right to a mortgage and the advance to which he is entitled, or which the local authority agree to leave outstanding, is less than the maximum advance permitted under the Act.[25] So, a tenant who is claiming to borrow the entire purchase price plus costs cannot defer completion. The tenant claims deferment by serving the local authority with notice and, within the next three months or such further time as the landlord allows, paying a deposit of £100. The price will then, effectively, be pegged for a period of two years,[26] beginning with the exercise of the right to buy by the tenant, within which he can either complete or (should his circumstances change), serve a new notice to claim a mortgage,[27] which may result in his being able to borrow more. On completion, the £100 is treated as being paid on account of the purchase price.[28] and is repaid (without interest) if the transaction goes off.

If the tenant does not complete an agreement or determination of all matters relating to the conveyance, grant and mortgage, the local authority can serve the tenant with a notice giving him at least 56 days to complete.[29] The authority must allow at least three months to elapse since the notice of the amount of the mortgage was served. If the tenant has not claimed the right to a mortgage, nine months must have elapsed since the last date he could have claimed one (normally nine months from the date of service of the council's notice in response to the tenant's request to buy). Notice to complete cannot be served on a tenant entitled to defer completion until two years after his notice claiming the right to buy, or nine months after service of notice of the amount of the mortgage, whichever is later. A tenant can, therefore, by serving a new request for a mortgage under section

---

[21] Shared ownership leases, and tenants' rights to call for them, are discussed in detail, *supra*, Chap. 15, (III)

[22] H.A. 1985, s.135(3).

[23] *Ibid.* s.135(2). See also s.142(1), (4).

[24] *Ibid.* s.135(2).

[25] S.142(1).

[26] Thus enabling the tenant to find the difference between the mortgage he is entitled to and the full purchase price: H.A. 1985, ss.142(4), 140(3)(c).

[27] H.A. 1985, s.142(4).

[28] *Ibid.* s.142(5)(a).

[29] *Ibid.* s.140(1), (2).

142(4) on the last day of the two-year period, effectively fix the price
and postpone completion of his purchase for a considerable period of
time, even assuming all time limits are adhered to by the council.

If the tenant does not comply with the local authority's first notice
to complete (called the "preliminary" notice) within the time
specified (which must be not less than 56 days) and refuses either to
complete or state what the outstanding matters for resolution are, the
authority may serve a further and final notice, requiring completion,
also in a specified time which is not less than 56 days. This notice
must also warn the tenant of the consequences of non-compliance.[30]
Failure to comply with the final notice to complete results in a deemed
withdrawal of the tenant's notice to buy.[31] There is no impediment to
a tenant, whose notice is deemed to have been withdrawn under this
provision, recommencing the right to buy procedure all over again.
The landlord does, in any event, have the power to extend the time
specified in the final notice to complete at any time before the notice
expires.[32] A tenant who has given notice to buy may withdraw at any
time. To do so he simply serves the local authority with a written
notice intimating his intention to withdraw.[33] He suffers no penalty by
doing this and cannot be required to pay his landlord's costs.

(6) *The Right to Shared Ownership Lease*

A shared ownership lease is a lease granted on payment of a premium
calculated by reference to a percentage of the value of the property or
the cost of its provision, or under the terms of which a tenant may on
departure receive a sum of money calculated by reference to its
value.[34] It is a device for a modified form of "equity sharing", under
which the tenant purchases a portion of a long lease, with the right to
purchase successive portions until the entire lease has been acquired.
Pending acquisition of the whole, the tenant will pay a rent reduced by
an amount calculated by reference to the proportion of the interest
already acquired by him. There will, in addition, be an amount to pay
on the mortgage in respect of the portion acquired. The right to a
shared ownership lease arises under section 143 of the 1985 Act only
where the tenant has claimed the right to buy and the notice remains
in force, *i.e.* has not been the subject of completion procedures
resulting in its deemed withdrawal. Further, the tenant must have
claimed the right to a mortgage and, as a consequence, it has been
determined that he is not entitled to a 100 per cent. mortgage plus

[30] *Ibid.* s.141(1), (2).
[31] *Ibid.* s.141(4).
[32] *Ibid.* s.141(3).
[33] *Ibid.* s.122(3).
[34] *Ibid.* s.622.

costs under section 134. Finally, the tenant must be entitled to defer completion under section 142, which means that the tenant will have paid the £100 deposit under s.142(1)(*c*). The right to a shared ownership lease is, therefore, an alternative to a deferred purchase under s.142. The procedure for claiming a shared ownership lease is laid down in sections 144 to 153 of the Housing Act 1985. The procedure is fully described in the concluding section of the previous chapter of this book.

(7) *The Unwilling Vendor*

The passing of the Housing Act 1980, which first introduced the right to buy, was greeted by objections from local authorities, concerned at the threatened depletion of their irreplaceable housing stocks, ranging from indifference to vociferous outrage. It would, therefore, have been quite likely that, without some default machinery, some intending purchasers would have found their aspirations thwarted by bureaucratic inactivity, if not hostility.

The 1985 Act imposes on local authorities a statutory duty[35] to convey the freehold of a house, or grant a long lease of a flat, to the tenant as soon as all matters relating to the conveyance, grant and mortgage have been agreed or determined.[36] The tenant can enforce his rights on the local authority by mandatory injunction.[37] In addition, the Secretary of State has default powers to ensure that tenants can exercise the right to buy notwithstanding delay or obstruction by landlords.[38]

The main default power essentially amounts to permitting the Secretary of State to intervene and administer the right to buy machinery in relation to the tenants of any landlord bound to sell to its tenants.[39] If it appears to the Secretary of State that tenants generally, or a tenant or tenants of a particular landlord have or may have difficulty in exercising the right to buy effectively or expeditiously then, provided there is some basis for the Secretary of State's belief in the need for his intervention,[40] he may use his default powers. However, because of the financial consequences to the authority's

---

[35] *Ibid.* s.138(1). The right to buy and the duty to sell are couched in terms of statutory rights and duties. They are in no way dependent upon the conclusion of a binding contract of sale, as in normal conveyancing: *cf. Storer* v. *Manchester City Council* [1974] 1 W.L.R. 1403; *Gibson* v. *Manchester City Council* [1979] 1 W.L.R. 294. So, for example, there is no provision for the tenant to serve a notice to complete on the local authority.

[36] H.A. 1985, s.138(1).

[37] *Ibid.* s.138(3). If the purchasing tenant ceases to be secure after exercising his right to buy but before completion, the tenant's ability to seek an injunction is lost: *Sutton L.B.C.* v. *Swann, The Times*, November 30, 1985.

[38] *Ibid.* ss.164–170.

[39] See *R.* v. *Secretary of State for the Environment ex p. Norwich City Council* [1982] Q.B. 808.

[40] *Ibid.* See also *Secretary of State for Education and Science* v. *M.B. of Tameside* [1977] A.C. 1014.

ratepayers, the Secretary of State must comply with the requirements of natural justice and fair administration, before exercising his statutory powers.[41] In addition, the Secretary of State must give the local authority 72 hours' written notice of his intention to invoke the powers.[42] When such a notice has been served, any steps taken by the landlord before the notice was served, or while it is in force, relating to the right to buy or the right to a mortgage, are avoided, save as otherwise specified in the notice.[43] The notice will also permit the Secretary of State to do all that appears to him to be necessary or expedient to enable secure tenants to exercise the right to buy, to a mortgage or to a shared ownership lease, but he will not be bound to take all those steps which a landlord would have been obliged to take to give effect to tenant's rights under Part V of the 1985 Act.[44] So long as the notice remains in force, the Secretary of State will receive any monies due to the landlord as mortgagee, in relation to mortgages arising after the notice has come into effect. The Secretary of State enjoys all the usual powers of a mortgagee and the local authority is prevented from exercising those powers, or receiving monies due under the mortgage, save with the Secretary of State's consent, which may be given subject to conditions.[45] The Secretary of State's notice may be withdrawn at any time.[46]

There are provisions enabling the Secretary of State to make vesting orders conveying the freehold or granting leases, pursuant to his powers under section 164 of the 1985 Act.[47] There is a power conferred on the Secretary of State to issue a direction to landlords, falling short of full intervention under section 164.[48] This permits the Secretary of State to specify covenants or conditions which are not to be included in a conveyance or grant. These directions can have retrospective effect.[49] They are clearly aimed at avoiding onerous rights of pre-emption and similar collateral "advantages" which local authorities might otherwise be tempted to insert in conveyances or leases. Section 169 of the 1985 Act permits the Secretary of State, for the purposes of determining whether his statutory powers of intervention should be exercised, to give notice in writing requiring a local authority to produce documents at a specified time and place, and also copies of documents or information.[50]

Finally, the Secretary of State has a discretion to give assistance, which may take the form of advice, access to lawyers for advice or

[41] *R.* v. *Secretary of State for the Environment ex p. Norwich City Council, supra.*
[42] H.A. 1985, s.164(3).
[43] *Ibid.* s.164(4).
[44] *Ibid.* s.164(5).
[45] *Ibid.* s.164(6).
[46] *Ibid.* s.166.
[47] *Ibid.* s.165.
[48] *Ibid.* s.167.
[49] *Ibid.* s.168.
[50] *Ibid.* s.169.

representation in legal proceedings, or any other form of assistance he considers appropriate, in connection with legal proceedings. The Secretary of State must, however, be satisfied that the case raises a question of principle, or that it is unreasonable to expect the person applying for assistance to deal with the case without this special assistance, having regard to the complexity of the case or any other matter, or that there are other special considerations meriting the assistance.[51]

In *R.* v. *Secretary of State for the Environment, ex p. Norwich City Council*,[52] the only reported decision in which the Secretary of State's default powers have been considered, the Court of Appeal gave the general power to intervene in section 164 a very wide construction. In that case it was argued that the council had failed to discharge their statutory obligations under what is now Part V of the 1985 Act in several particulars: there was delay in issuing offer notices under section 125; there was further delay caused by the authority's insistence that all potential purchasers should attend counselling interviews; the initial valuations were clearly inflated, thus forcing potential buyers to refer all valuations to the district valuer, whose services were earlier refused by the authority at the initial valuation stage; there were difficulties over exchanges of houses, and the authority had a generally poor record of progress on sales and leases as compared with other councils. The Court of Appeal did observe that, since these default powers of the Secretary of State were very extensive, their exercise would need to be scrutinised particularly carefully. Lord Denning M.R. considered that the powers should not be used other than in accordance with the rules of natural justice. Kerr L.J. held that they should be exercised fairly, a view with which May L.J. concurred, adding that the exercise should also be reasonable. Lord Denning M.R. felt that the Secretary of State should only intervene if the authority's default was unreasonable or inexcusable, but Kerr and May L.JJ. held that intervention was permissible whenever it appeared to the Secretary of State that tenants have or may have difficulty in exercising the right to buy effectively or expeditiously, regardless of whether or not the authority's behaviour was reasonable, provided that the Secretary of State's own decision was one at which a reasonable man might arrive, in accordance with normal administrative law principles. In forming this view it was entirely proper, and relevant, for the Secretary of State to take account of the position and progress of the authority in question in relation to that of other authorities.

[51] *Ibid.* s.170.
[52] [1982] Q.B. 808.

VI. THE COUNCIL HOUSE AS THE FAMILY HOME[53]

A. Unsecure Tenants

Unlike secure tenancies and statutory tenancies under the Rent Act 1977, unsecure council tenancies do not pass as of right to surviving spouses or other members of the family. A widow or deserted spouse can continue the tenancy if the authority agree and in practice, most councils permit transfers of this type, at least so far as widows and deserted wives are concerned. However, it is also possible, if a council follow a policy of dealing with "overhousing," that while a new tenancy may well be granted to a widow or a deserted spouse, it will be on terms that she transfers to a smaller house. This will not be so, of course, where there is still a family living at home, but some authorities use opportunities such as this, particularly bereavement, to move occupiers of houses which have become too large for the families housed therein, to more suitable premises. Some authorities even make transfers conditional upon the wife discharging any rent arrears incurred by the husband. Where there is a marital breakdown a local authority sometimes insisted on the wife obtaining a court order against her husband before any transfer of tenancy could be made.[54] Some local authorities even insisted that such an order should contain a non-cohabitation clause. While that may have been a proper order to make if the husband had been guilty of cruelty to the wife and/or the children, it was quite improper in the case of simple desertion[55] and, at the least, caused unnecessary distress and friction. With the introduction of the Domestic Proceedings and Magistrates' Courts Act 1978, s.16, the power of magistrates' courts to make non-cohabitation orders disappeared, and was replaced by powers to make personal protection orders and exclusion orders when there are

---

[53] See Yates (1977) 41 Conv. (N.S.) 309; Blandy (1981) 131 N.L.J. 520.

[54] See *Finer Report* (Cmnd. 5629), paras. 6.80–6.84. See also the Department of the Environment and Welsh Office Joint Circular on Housing for One-Parent Families (D. of E. Circ. No. 78/77; W.O. Circ. No. 123/77) para. 23. In proceedings for nullity or divorce under the Matrimonial Causes Act 1973, s.24, the courts have, in the past, refused to order a transfer of the tenancy unless the council are prepared to consent to the order; see *e.g. Regan* v. *Regan* [1977] 1 W.L.R. 84; *Rodewald* v. *Rodewald* [1977] Fam. 192; *cf. Thompson* v. *Thompson* [1975] 2 All E.R. 208. However, this was because of H.A. 1957, s.113(5), which imposed a term in every council house letting agreement that the written consent of the authority be secured to any assignment. s.113(5) was repealed by H.A. 1980, s.152 and Sched. 25. Its successor, H.A. 1985, s.91, only applies to secure tenancies. There has thus been a change of judicial attitude towards transfer orders under s.24 of the 1973 Act, both in respect of secure tenancies (because assignments pursuant to orders made under s.24 of the Matrimonial Causes Act 1973 are expressly contemplated in the 1985 Act by s.91(3)(*b*)) and in respect of unsecure tenancies in that, if the lease or tenancy agreement is silent on the need for written consent to assignment, the law will no longer imply such a provision.

[55] *Corton* v. *Corton* [1965] P.1; *Jolliffe* v. *Jolliffe* [1965] P.6.

threats of domestic violence. This resulted in a change of attitude by those local authorities that formerly insisted on a deserted wife establishing her claim to a transfer of the tenancy in the magistrates' court. This is a long-overdue change. The former practices clearly constituted a massive waste of public time and money as well as causing distress to the family by unnecessary legal actions.[56]

B. Secure Tenancies

The problems for the spouse deserted by her tenant husband are as great where the tenant is secure as they are when he is unsecure. However, in the case of the tenant's spouse, or members of his family, bereaved by the death of the secure tenant, the position is different. If a fixed-term secure tenant dies, the tenancy passes to his personal representatives and then to the beneficiary or beneficiaries under the will or on intestacy. Both of these events amount to an assignment of the secure tenancy. If, however, the beneficiary, or at least one of them, would or could have qualified as one of the statutory successors described below had the tenancy been a periodic one,[57] the tenancy remains a secure tenancy in the hands of the beneficiary. Otherwise it ceases to be secure,[58] and the beneficiary only enjoys such contractual protection as remains.

On the death of a secure periodic tenant, the tenancy will vest in a person qualified to succeed him, unless the deceased tenant was himself "a successor" as defined in section 88(1) of the 1985 Act.[59] Those qualified to succeed are any of the following who occupied the dwelling as his only or main home at the tenant's death[60]:

(i) the tenant's spouse, who has preference over all other claimants[61];

---

[56] See Cretney, *Principles of Family Law* (4th ed.), pp. 848–849. The need for the court to acquaint itself with local authority practices and attitudes before making transfer orders under the Matrimonial Causes Act 1973, s.24, was emphasised by Cumming-Bruce J. in *Beard* v. *Beard* [1981] 1 W.L.R. 369 at p. 372.

[57] H.A. 1985, s.90(3)(b).

[58] *Ibid.* s.90(3).

[59] *Ibid.* ss.87, 89(2).

[60] *Ibid.* s.87. The one year residential requirement is twice as long as that required in the private sector (see Chap. 12, *supra*): establishing residence is a matter of fact to be decided in each case: *Middleton* v. *Bull* (1951) 2 T.L.R. 1010.

[61] H.A. 1985, s.89(2)(a).

(ii) any other member of the tenant's family[62] who has resided with the tenant throughout the period of 12 months up to the date of the tenant's death.[63] This period of residence does not need to have been taken entirely in the dwelling-house in question, because the deceased tenant may have moved shortly before he died, taking his relative with him. If more than one member of the family qualifies, they may agree between themselves who is to succeed. In default of agreement, the council may select the successor.[64]

There is another group of persons, defined in the Housing Act 1985, s.88(1), as "successors," upon whose death there can be no *statutory* transmission of a secure tenancy. They are:

(i) a tenant who took the tenancy as a spouse or member of the family, on the death of a former secure tenant (thus making it clear that the automatic statutory transmission is limited to one)[65];

(ii) a sole tenant who was previously a joint tenant[66];

(iii) a tenant under a periodic tenancy that arose on the termination of a fixed-term secure tenancy, where the fixed-term tenancy was originally granted solely or jointly to someone else (*i.e.* if the tenant has already succeeded after a death, or by permissible assignment, or has survived a person who was a joint tenant under the fixed-term);

(iv) a tenant who took the secure tenancy by assignment except pursuant to an order under the Matrimonial Causes Act 1973, s.24 (unless the other party to the marriage was a successor), or under section 92 of the Housing Act 1985 (assignment by way of exchange)[67];

---

[62] Membership of a family is statutorily defined so cases decided under the Rent Act 1977 will not have direct application. Under s.113(1), (2), a person is a member of the family if he is a spouse, parent, grandparent, child, grandchild, brother, sister, uncle, aunt, nephew or niece of the deceased tenant. A relationship by marriage is treated as a blood relationship, one of half-blood is as if of the full-blood, a step-child as a child, an adopted child as a child (Childrens Act 1975, s.8) and an illegitimate child as the legitimate child of the mother and reputed father. A person is also a member of another's family if they live together as husband and wife. *N.B.* a person may be a member of another's family even though he or she is married to another: *Watson* v. *Lucas* [1980] 1 W.L.R. 1493. Where a member of the family is a sub-tenant of the deceased tenant, then he cannot be considered to be residing with the tenant as a member of the family. But otherwise despite the fact that the tenant and the member of his family have lived largely separate lives, the would-be successor could still be regarded as fulfilling the residential requirement: *Edmunds* v. *Jones* [1957] 1 W.L.R. 1118; *Collier* v. *Stoneman* [1957] 1 W.L.R. 1108.
[63] H.A. 1985, s.87(*b*).
[64] H.A. 1985, s.89(2)(*b*). *cf.* the private sector, where the matter is one for the county court: R.A. 1977, Sched. 1, para. 7.
[65] *cf.* the private sector where, under R.A. 1977, s.2 and Sched. 1, two transmissions are permitted.
[66] Thus regarding the *ius accrescendi* at common law as equivalent to statutory succession.
[67] H.A. 1985, s,88(2), (3).

    (v) a tenant who succeeded to the secure tenancy under the will or intestacy of a former tenant[68];

  (vi) a tenant under a periodic secure tenancy who, within six months before it began, was a successor under a previous periodic secure tenancy either of the same house or from the same landlord, or both. The second tenancy agreement may provide that this exclusion from statutory succession shall not operate.[69]

It remains to be seen how generously the court interprets these provisions. The only reported case so far appearing on the provision does not augur well for a generous attitude to its construction by the courts. Even though membership of the family is now statutorily defined[70] (presumably in an attempt to avoid the kind of litigation that has arisen in relation to the counterpart provision in the Rent Act 1977) there is still some scope for judicial innovation with regard to the interpretation of the phrase living together "as husband and wife." While certain relationships which might be construed as "family" are clearly excluded by this definition, much of the case law on this point from the Rent Act 1977[71] is clearly relevant. In *Harrogate B.C.* v. *Simpson*[72] the court was required to decide, whether one partner of a lesbian relationship could qualify to succeed to a secure tenancy held by the other partner, who had died. Had the issue arisen under the Rent Act 1977, s.2 and Sched. 1, Part 1, the defendant might have had a slightly greater chance of success since, under that Act, the question would have been whether the defendant was a member of the deceased tenant's family. However, given the restrictive definition of a member of the family in section 113 of the Housing Act 1985, the defendant's only chance of success was to argue that she and her partner were "living together as husband and wife." It is difficult to see how this phrase could ever be apt to include a lesbian or homosexual relationship, since it appears to presuppose parties of different sexes. Watkins L.J. opined that if Parliament intended homosexual relationships to be included in the statutory succession provisions, this would need to be expressly stated. If this is, indeed, the position then it would seem that such relationships are excluded from family membership for the purposes of the statutory succession machinery in the Rent Act 1977 also, since that Act does not expressly mention homosexual or lesbian relationships either. Nevertheless,

---

[68] But see s.90(3)(*b*), discussed, *supra*.
[69] H.A. 1985, s.88(4). See also Sched. 2, ground 16.
[70] *Ibid.* ss.113(1), (2); 186(1), (2).
[71] *Supra*, Chap. 12.
[72] (1985) 25 R.V.R. 10.

those cases decided on the Rent Act provisions will still, in a general way, be of assistance in interpreting section 113 of the Housing Act 1985, and reference should therefore be made to the consideration of this matter in Chapter 12 of this book.[73]

[73] Chap. 12 (III) B.

CHAPTER 17

HOUSING ASSOCIATIONS

I. Definition	583	V. The Rent Limit	588
II. The Requirement to Register	585	VI. Housing Trusts	590
III. Registration and the Rent Act 1977		VII. Security	590
	586	VIII. Housing Societies	593
IV. Rents	587	IX. The Right to Buy	594

I. DEFINITION

A housing association is defined in the Housing Associations Act 1985, s.1(1)[1] as

"a society, body of trustees or company (a) which is established for the purpose of, or amongst whose objects or powers are included those of providing, constructing, improving or managing or facilitating or encouraging the construction or improvement of housing accommodation, and (b) which does not trade for profit[2] or whose constitution or rules prohibit the issue of capital with interest or dividend exceeding such rate as may be prescribed by the Treasury, whether with or without differentiation as between share and loan capital."

Housing associations are frequently charitable bodies, that is organisations set up to carry out a public purpose, established to provide housing in a particular area or for a particular stratum of the community (such as the aged). In some cases they are sponsored by industry to provide housing for employees. The Church of England Pensions Board has the status of a housing association,[3] and many other religious and educational groups establish such associations to provide housing for their adherents or members. From the late 1960s onwards, there was a considerable growth both in the number of housing associations and in the scope of their activities. Philanthropic bodies of various religious, political and social persuasions became aware of the practical help they could give to the homeless by forming housing associations which would augment the efforts of local

---

[1] An identical definition is contained in H.A. 1985, s.5(1).
[2] "Trading for profit" means trading for profit for use and enjoyment as distinct from raising profits which have to be retained or ploughed back into the business of the association. The latter type of profit will not take an association outside the definition: *Goodman* v. *Dolphin Square Trust Ltd.* (1979) 38 P. & C.R. 257.
[3] Church of England Pensions Board (Powers) Measure 1952.

583

authorities. Associations could obtain from the more co-operative local authorities loans covering 90 or even 100 per cent. of their capital costs plus, in some cases, annual rate fund contributions to help them hold their rents down to a reasonable level, if the Government subsidies were insufficient for this purpose.

Local authorities, unable to house families immediately because of their selection rules and procedures, often refer such cases to local housing associations, which are not necessarily subject to the same constraints as local authority housing departments. Many associations adopt a tolerant attitude to prospective tenants with "bad" housing records. Such associations collaborate with local authorities in dealing with "short-life" properties which local authorities feel unable to re-let, but which can be let by an association on a temporary basis to families it can rehouse elsewhere when the time comes for demolition of the property.[4] Local authorities also provide technical advice on acquisition and conversion of properties by associations,[5] and may provide assistance for the supply of furniture to the occupants of housing association properties.[6]

The proliferation of housing associations, and the consequent uneconomic use of scarce resources,[7] led to a call for some overall control to be exercised over associations, as well as some rationalisation, schemes for joint management and staff training programmes. Further, the pleas for greater control were often founded in fears that some associations had been formed by groups of persons with the aim of providing the members with an income from fees, plus possible

[4] This type of property is also sometimes managed by tenants' co-operatives: see Ward, *Tenants Take Over, passim*; Hands, *Housing Co-operatives, passim*. Co-operative ventures can also involve equity sharing. Half the capital cost is financed by a block building society mortgage, around a third by housing association grant and the remainder by the Housing Corporation on second mortgage. Any outgoing co-owner takes out 50 per cent. of any appreciation in the value of the property, provided he has lived there for a sufficient period. Another co-operative scheme consists of homes where the occupier buys an individual lease for a proportion (initially set at 50 per cent.) of the total value of the home and will benefit from its increasing value—if he paid half the initial value he will get half the new value when he decides to leave. A further variant is the Birmingham "half and half" scheme: see Smith, *Guide to Housing* (2nd ed.), p. 239. Secure tenants now have statutory rights to a shared ownership lease under the Housing Act 1985, ss.143–153: see *supra*, Chap. 15, (III) In housing management terminology, a housing co-operative is more generally used to describe an association where the tenants have no individual stake in the equity or have a stake limited to a share, repayable, on leaving, at its par value. This is sometimes called a "non-equity" or "par value" co-operative. It is usual for all tenants to hold a share in the association, on which a dividend may be paid within the limit set for housing associations. All members of the co-operative are ultimately responsible for the estate and elect the management committee. Another type of co-operative is the management co-operative; see R.A. 1977, s.16 (as amended). These are associations which, under approved agreements, discharge housing functions on behalf of a local authority or new town development corporation: H.A. 1985, s.27. With such associations in mind, the H.A. 1985, s.27(2) defines a housing co-operative, for the purposes of the Act, as a society, company or body of trustees, for the time being approved by the Secretary of State.

[5] H.A. 1985, ss.58, 60.

[6] H.A. 1985, s.61(1).

[7] In some cases the founders and administrators of some associations were suspected of having ulterior motives for their involvement.

future benefits from the fact that they acquired a share in the equity and could benefit from the growth in the appreciating value of the association's assets. Registration of associations under the Industrial and Provident Societies Act 1965, or as charities, provided insufficient control and hence what is now the Housing Associations Act 1985, s.3(1) empowered the Housing Corporation to establish a register of housing associations. Housing associations enjoy certain privileges with regard to access to government funds and exclusions from certain provisions of the Rent Act 1977. However, these privileges are only accorded to registered housing associations, which are placed under the firm control, both in terms of accounting and auditing procedures and with reference to management matters, of the Housing Corporation.[8]

II. The Requirement to Register

Under the Housing Associations Act 1985, s.5(1)[9] the Housing Corporation may register any housing association which[10]:

(a) is a registered charity; or
(b) is a society registered under the Industrial and Provident Societies Act 1965 and which fulfils the following conditions[11]:

   (i) it does not trade for profit;
   (ii) it is established for the purpose of, or has among its objects or powers those of providing, constructing, improving or managing:

   — houses to be kept available for letting; or
   — houses for occupation by members of the association, provided the rules of the association restrict membership of the association to persons entitled or prospectively entitled to occupy association houses; or
   — hostels.

If the association has any additional objects or purposes, they must be only those mentioned in section 4(3) of the 1985 Act. These are:

---

[8] H.A. 1985, ss.5–6, 9, 10, 14, 15(3), 16–23, 24(4), 26–32. See Yates, *Local Authorities and Housing*, paras. B.286–B.375 in *Social Welfare Law* (ed. Pollard).
[9] There is a statutory presumption embodied in H.A.A. 1985, s.5(4), that an association registered by the Housing Corporation has been properly registered and has complied with the statutory requirements for registration. Aside from the Housing Corporation's express statutory power to rectify the register (H.A.A. 1985, s.6(2)), the statutory presumption is conclusive: *Goodman* v. *Dolphin Square Trust* (1979) 38 P. & C.R. 257.
[10] H.A.A. 1985, s.4(1).
[11] H.A.A. 1985, s.4(2).

    (a) providing land or buildings for purposes connected with the requirements of the persons occupying the houses or hostels provided or managed by the association;

    (b) providing amenities or services for the benefit of those persons, either exclusively or together with other persons;

    (c) acquiring, or repairing and improving, or creating by the conversion of houses or other property, houses to be disposed of on sale or lease[12];

    (d) building houses to be disposed of on shared ownership leases[13];

    (e) encouraging and giving advice on the formation of other housing associations which would be eligible for registration by the Housing Corporation;

    (f) effecting transactions falling within the Housing Associations Act 1985, s.45(1), which contains provisions to provide grant aid for projects for the acquisition and disposal of houses at a discount to tenants of charitable housing associations.[14]

A registered association that has never received a grant or loan from public funds may ask the Housing Corporation to remove it from the register. The Corporation has a discretion whether to accede to the request.[15] An association which is not registered by the Housing Corporation under the Housing Associations Act 1985, s.5(1), is henceforth referred to as an "unregistered association." Under the Housing Associations Act 1985, s.60(1), no unregistered association can receive grants or loans from the Housing Corporation.

III. REGISTRATION AND THE RENT ACT 1977

Under the Rent Act 1977, s.15(1),[16] registered housing associations are in a privileged position. A registered housing association tenancy is not a protected tenancy[17] within the Rent Act 1977. Formerly, the registered association also had to comply with certain conditions set out in the Rent Act 1977, s.15(4), before it was exempted from protected tenancy status. These conditions were complex[18] and turned, in the main, on whether the association was established or encouraged with local authority funds. These qualifying conditions were removed by the Housing Act 1980, s.74(1). An unregistered

---

[12] This object relates to the right of secure tenants to buy their houses or take long leases of their flats: H.A. 1985, s.118.

[13] *Supra*, Chap. 15, (III).

[14] Discussed *post*, (IX).

[15] H.A.A. 1985, s.6(4).

[16] As amended by H.A. 1980, s.74. See *Clays Lane Housing Co-operative* v. *Patrick* (1985) 49 P. & C.R. 72.

[17] *Supra*, Chap. 10. It may, however, be a "secure" tenancy; see *post*.

[18] See *Bon-Accord Housing Society Ltd.* v. *Clark* [1957] S.L.T. (Sh.Ct) 24; *Dolphin Square Trust Ltd.* v. *Hartman* [1967] 1 W.L.R. 586.

association will not be entitled to exemption from protected tenancy status unless[19]:

(i) it is registered under the Housing Associations Act 1985, or
(ii) it is a co-operative housing association within the meaning of that Act.[20]

Associations whose tenancies become protected tenancies by reason of their non-qualification within the Rent Act 1977, s.15, must give notice to their tenants that they are not excluded from Rent Act protection.[21] If an association fails, "without reasonable excuse," to give such notice within 21 days beginning on the day on which the tenancy becomes protected, the association (and in certain cases its officers) become liable, on summary conviction, to a fine. Also excluded from protected tenancy status are tenancies where the landlord's interest belongs to a housing management co-operative,[22] *i.e.* a co-operative which receives a housing subsidy to perform local authority housing functions.[23]

IV. RENTS

Although registered housing association tenancies are exempt from the definition of protected tenancies under the Rent Act 1977, they are nevertheless brought into rent regulation only, by virtue of the Rent Act 1977, s.86(2). To come within the Rent Act at all, of course, the tenancies must be dwellings within the rateable value limits specified in the Rent Act 1977, s.4,[24] generally £1,500 in Greater London and £750 elsewhere. They must not be tenancies at rents of less than two-thirds of their rateable values.[25] To fall within the exempting conditions and special provisions for housing association rent registrations in the Rent Act 1977, Pt. VI, the association must be registered. Unregistered association tenancies are, and have been since April 1, 1975, ordinary regulated tenancies.

Tenancies within the Rent Act 1977, Pt. VI, are eligible to have their rents registered as "fair" rents under the Rent Act 1977, s.67. Thus there may be either a landlord's or tenant's application for the rent officer or, in anticipation of the letting, the association may apply

[19] R.A. 1977, s.15(3), as amended by the Housing (Consequential Provisions) Act 1985, Sched. 2, para. 35.
[20] See H.A.A. 1985, s.1(2).
[21] R.A. 1977, s.92(1), as amended by H.A. 1980, Sched. 26.
[22] *Supra*, n. 4.
[23] R.A. 1977, s.16.
[24] *Supra*, Chap. 10.
[25] R.A. 1977, s.5.

for a certificate of a fair rent[26] and there may be a reference to the rent assessment committee for the area. The only parts[27] of the fair rent procedure that will apply to housing associations are those contained in the Rent Act 1977, s.67 (application for registration of fair rent), s.69 (certificate of fair rent), s.70 (rules for the determination of the fair rent), s.71[28] (the amount to be registered as rent) and s.72 (date of effect of registered rent). No other part of the procedure for the registration of rents for private lettings, as described in Chapter 11 above, applies to housing association lettings. If a dwelling for which rent has been registered is disposed of to a housing association, the registered rent for the regulated tenancy becomes the registered rent for the purposes of the Rent Act 1977, Pt. VI.[29] The fair rent is effective from the date of registration, in the case of a determination by a rent officer, or the date of decision, in the case of a determination by a rent assessment committee.[30]

The Rent Act 1977, s.88, prescribes the rent limit for registered housing association tenancies. The association may not charge any sum in excess of the "fair" rent[31] and any rent paid in excess of this figure is recoverable by the tenant,[32] if necessary by deduction from the future rental payments.[33] Any person making an entry in a rent book showing the tenant to be in arrears in respect of any sum which is irrecoverable under Part VI commits a criminal offence.[34] Where such an erroneous entry is not removed from the book within seven days of a request being made to the association for its removal, the landlord is liable to a fine unless it proves that, at the time of the refusal, there was a bona fide claim to recover the sum.[35]

V. THE RENT LIMIT

If a rent has been registered for the association tenancy, that is the maximum recoverable rent. If no rent is registered, then the rent limit can be arrived at in one of three ways[36]:

(i) if the tenancy agreement was made *before* January 1, 1973, it is the rent under that agreement, as varied by any agreement reached *before* that date;

---

[26] *Ibid.* s.69.
[27] See R.A. 1977, s.87(2).
[28] Except subs. (3).
[29] R.A. 1977, s.87(6).
[30] *Ibid.* s.87(2)(*a*), as amended by H.A. 1980, s.61(3).
[31] R.A. 1977, s.88(1).
[32] *Ibid.* s.94(1).
[33] *Ibid.* s.94(2).
[34] *Ibid.* s.94(4).
[35] *Ibid.* s.94(5).
[36] *Ibid.* s.88(4).

(ii) if the tenancy agreement was made on or after January 1, 1973, and not more than three years before the tenancy began there was another tenancy[37] of the house or flat, it is the rent under that former tenancy;

(iii) if the tenancy agreement was made on or after January 1, 1973, and there was no previous tenancy within the period of three years, the limit is the rent agreed under the current tenancy.

It will be appreciated that rents fixed in accordance with (i) and (ii) above will now (should any remain) be of some considerable antiquity and have fallen a long way behind current "fair" rent levels. In such cases there is, therefore, a strong incentive on the part of the association to refer the rent to the rent officer.

Where a higher rent is registered than that which the tenant was formerly paying, hardship may be caused to the tenant by requiring him to pay the new registered rent forthwith. Hence, the Rent Act 1977, s.89 (as amended by the Housing Act 1980. Sched. 10), contains provisions for the phasing of rent increases up to the registered rent. For rents registered before the implementation of the Housing Act 1980, Pt. II, on November 28, 1980, the rent limit is increased by £0·75 per week or such lesser amount as will raise it to the registered rent. The phasing ceases if a new tenancy is granted to someone who is not the tenant or a resident member of his family. The progression by stages is not altered by a subsequent registration of a higher or lower rent. For rents registered after the Housing Act 1980, Pt. II, was implemented, the procedure embodied in the Rent Act 1977, Sched. 8, must be used.[38] Phasing must take place over two years. During the first year of phasing, the permitted increase in rent is the whole of the service element[39] plus half the balance of the amount by which the new registered rent exceeds the old one. The remainder is charged in the second year. The Secretary of State has power by order to vary the period of delay for phasing purposes, and to abolish the requirement to phase increases.[40]

The Rent Act 1977, s.93, contains provisions for increasing the rents of housing association dwellings without the need to serve a prior notice to quit. The section is in similar terms to the Housing Act 1985, s.25 described earlier in Chapter 16.[41] However, the procedure is simplified somewhat from the 1968 Act model,[41a] upon which the

---

[37] The reference to "another" tenancy includes, in addition to a housing association tenancy, a regulated tenancy which subsisted at any time after April 1, 1975, and under which, immediately before it came to an end, the interest of the landlord belonged to a housing association: R.A. 1977, s.88(5).

[38] R.A. 1977, s.89(2), as amended by H.A. 1980, s.77 and Sched. 10.

[39] *i.e.* the amount by which the rent attributable to services provided by the landlord is increased.

[40] See H.A. 1980, s.60(5), (7).

[41] Associations wishing to increase rents must follow this procedure, even for secure tenancies, and not the procedure contained in the H.A. 1985, s.102 (which applies to rental increases for local authority secure tenancies only): H.A. 1985, s.102(3)(*b*).

[41a] *i.e.* Prices and Incomes Act 1968, s.12.

1985 Act provisions were based.[42] The association's notice of increase must state the date the increase is to take effect, and it must be served on the tenant at least four weeks before that date. The tenant can stop the increase by giving a valid notice to quit (*i.e.* in accordance with the ordinary rules as to notice) before the date the increase would have been effective. With the landlord's written agreement, the tenant's notice to quit can be withdrawn before the operative date for the increase, in which case the increase will be effective.

In all cases adjustments may be made for changes in rates, borne by the landlord, after the date of registration, but not so as to affect the stages of rent increases or the rent limits, because payments in respect of rates are treated as additional and separate.[43] Local authorities may not refer rents of registered housing association tenancies to rent officers under the Rent Act 1977, s.68.[44] Tenancies of registered housing associations cannot be "restricted contracts" within the Rent Act 1977, Pt. V.[45]

VI. Housing Trusts

Among the landlords whose lettings fall within the definition of housing association tenancies are charitable housing trusts. The statutory definition of such trusts, for this purpose, is to be found in the Housing Act 1985, s.6, and the Housing Associations Act 1985, s.2.[46]

A housing trust is one under which the trustees are required to devote the whole trust fund, including any surplus which may arise from its operation, to the provision of housing accommodation or other incidental purposes. If the trust deed does not so limit the trustees, but merely requires the funds to be devoted to charitable purposes, the trust will still be a housing trust if the trustees in fact devote the fund to the provision of housing and ancillary purposes. As we shall see, this definition has some significance in relation to an association tenant's claims to security of tenure, and a tenancy granted by a housing trust cannot be a protected tenancy.[47]

VII. Security

Until the implementation of the Housing Act 1980, Pt. I, tenants of registered housing associations enjoyed no security of tenure. The

---

[42] H.A. 1980, Sched. 10, para. 5.
[43] R.A. 1977, ss.71, 87(2).
[44] *Ibid.*, s.87(2).
[45] R.A. 1977, s.19(5)(*e*).
[46] The definition is in identical terms in both Acts.
[47] R.A. 1977, s.15(2)(*b*).

Rent Act 1977, s.15, exempts housing association tenancies from the definition of protected tenancies under the 1977 Act and therefore it was not necessary for an association to make out a ground for possession before the court would grant an order. The position of registered housing associations was, therefore, in this respect, identical with that of local authorities,[48] their decisions to evict being impugnable only on grounds of *ultra vires*.[49] The courts had even denied tenants in possession actions the defence that an association had abused its powers.[50]

Since October 3, 1980, qualifying tenants of registered housing associations have been treated as secure tenants,[51] within what is now the Housing Act 1985, Pts. IV and V. The conditions that must be satisfied by a tenant before he qualifies as a secure tenant are the same as those for tenants of local authorities. With the exception of tenants of co-operative housing associations,[52] all the rules governing secure tenancies relating to security, terms, sub-letting and lodgers, transfers, transmission on death, repairs and improvements, variations, consultation and publicity,[53] which were described in Chapter 16 in relation to local authority secure tenancies, have equal application to registered housing association tenancies. A licence granted by an almshouse charity whose rules prevent it from granting tenancies, is not a secure tenancy.[54] To qualify for the exemption, any sum payable by the occupier of an almshouse must not exceed the minimum contribution to the cost of maintenance and services from time to time authorised or approved by the Charity Commissioners.[55]

The Housing Act 1985, s.92 confers upon secure tenants a "right to exchange" their tenancies with other secure tenants, by way of assignments.[56] This provision does not apply in favour of secure tenants of co-operative housing associations.[57] The exchange by way of assignment requires the written consent of the landlord.[58] However, that consent may be withheld, but only on the grounds set out in

---

[48] See Chap. 16, *supra*.
[49] *Goodman* v. *Dolphin Square Trust* (1979) 38 P. & C.R. 257.
[50] *Peabody Housing Association Ltd.* v. *Green* (1978) 122 S.J. 862.
[51] H.A. 1985, ss.79(1), 80(1), (2). Tenants of registered co-operative housing associations are not secure tenants: H.A. 1985, s.80(2)(a). See *Peabody Donation Fund Governors* v. *Grant* (1982) 264 E.G. 925; *Peabody Donation Fund Governors* v. *Higgins* [1983] 3 All E.R. 122; *Clays Lane Housing Co-operative* v. *Patrick* (1985) 49 P. & C.R. 72.
[52] H.A. 1985, ss.109, 114(1). A co-operative housing association is a fully mutual housing association registered under the Industrial and Provident Societies Act 1965. An association is "fully mutual" if its rules restrict membership to tenants or prospective tenants and preclude the granting or assignment of tenancies to non-members: H.A. 1985, s.5(2). See also H.A.A. 1985, s.1(2); *Clays Lane Housing Co-operative* v. *Patrick* (1985) 49 P. & C.R. 72.
[53] H.A. 1985, ss.79–109
[54] This provision was necessitated by the specific inclusion in the category of secure tenants of licensees generally: H.A. 1985, s.79.
[55] H.A. 1985, Sched. 1, para. 12.
[56] *Supra*, Chap. 16, (III) A, 2.
[57] H.A. 1985, s.109. See n. 52, *supra*.
[58] H.A. 1985, s.92(1).

Schedule 3 of the 1985 Act.[59] Most of these grounds have been considered in the preceding chapter.[60] However, two of them relate specifically to housing association tenancies.[60]

If the landlord is a charity, then consent to an exchange by way of assignment may be withheld if the proposed assignee's occupation of the dwelling-house would conflict with the objects of the charity.[61] Thus, if, for example, a charitable housing trust is established to provide homes for the elderly, consent to an exchange with a tenant who does not satisfy the charity's age criterion could be refused. A housing association or housing trust landlord may also refuse consent to an assignment if it lets dwellings only for occupation by persons whose circumstances (other than their financial circumstances)—an example would be an association formed to provide housing for single parent families—make it especially difficult for them to satisfy their need for housing and, if the assignment were made, there would no longer be such a person residing in the dwelling.[62] Should an assignment actually take place in either of these two circumstances, then the landlord would be able to recover possession from the new tenant.[63]

The grounds which must be made out by a housing association, before a court may grant possession of a secure tenancy, are contained in Schedule 2 of the 1985 Act. They are the same as those applicable to secure council tenancies. Two additional grounds must, however, be mentioned. Schedule 2, Part II, ground 11 is available only to charitable housing trusts, defined above. Provided the landlord can show that suitable alternative accommodation will be available when the order takes effect, possession may be granted to a charitable housing trust if it can be shown that the tenant's continued occupation conflicts with the objects of the charity.[64] Schedule 2, Part III, ground 14 is also available only to a housing association or housing trust. The association which lets dwellings only for occupation by people whose circumstances[65] (other than financial circumstances) make it difficult to satisfy their housing needs, may recover possession where it can be shown either that no such person is still resident, or that a local authority has offered the tenant a secure tenancy. The association or trust must also show that it needs possession of the dwelling so that it can be offered to another person who qualifies because of his or her personal circumstances. The court cannot grant possession on this ground unless satisfied both that it is reasonable to do so and that

[59] *Ibid.*, s.92(3).
[60] *Supra*, Chap. 16 (III) A, 2.
[61] H.A. 1985, Sched. 3, ground 6.
[62] *Ibid.*, Sched. 3, ground 8.
[63] *Ibid.*, Sched. 2, grounds 11 and 14.
[64] Presumably the trustees would be bound to seek possession in such cases, but would be relieved of any liability for breach of trust if the court refused or suspended the order.
[65] *e.g.* ex-prisoners, drug addicts, unmarried mothers.

suitable alternative accommodation will be available to the tenant when the order takes effect.[66]

A tenant of an unregistered housing association, whose rent includes a payment for furniture or services, may apply to a rent assessment committee, sitting as a rent tribunal, for a "reasonable" rent to be fixed for the tenancy. Any landlord wishing to evict tenants falling within the rent tribunal's jurisdiction must serve a proper notice to quit in accordance with the Notices to Quit (Prescribed Information) Regulations 1980.[67] By analogy with the *Udechuka Case*,[68] it would seem that, provided the unregistered housing association tenancy was created before the repeal of the rent tribunal's discretionary powers to award periods of security of tenure,[69] such tenants could also, in appropriate circumstances, claim security from the tribunal. Unregistered housing associations cannot claim the benefit of a provision similar to the Housing Act 1985, s.612, which, in the case of local authorities, precludes anything in the Rent Act 1977 from preventing the council obtaining possession of one of its houses, where it does so for housing purposes.[70] Nor can they claim the benefit of section 19(5)(*e*) of the Rent Act 1977.

VIII. Housing Societies

The term "housing association" might appear to be the genus, which can cover bodies whose title includes the word "society." However, in housing management circles the term "association" is used to describe a body which deals wholly or mainly with subsidised housing, and the term "society" is used when referring to one which deals with the provision of "cost-rent" or "co-ownership" schemes. A "cost-rent" society is one that builds or provides houses to rent at cost, without profit to the society or subsidy to the tenant. The main difficulty for cost-rent societies, however, is that as costs rise, the rents required to cover outgoings, even without any profit element, become too high for the tenants, especially in comparison with local authority rents or rents in the private sector. In consequence, the co-ownership society has become the more generally used. Co-ownership societies provide houses or flats to be occupied exclusively by their own members, who own jointly the dwellings they occupy individually. Societies may be set up by the members who wish to occupy the

---

[66] H.A. 1985, s.84(2)(*c*).

[67] S.I. 1980 No. 1624. See R.A. 1977, s.19(2). See also Chap. 14 *supra. cf. Lambeth London Borough Council* v. *Udechuka* (1980) 41 P. & C.R. 200. A court order will still, of course, be required: Protection from Eviction Act 1977, s.3.

[68] *Supra.*

[69] By the introduction by ministerial order, of H.A. 1980, s.69(3), on November 28, 1980.

[70] H.A. 1980, Sched. 25, para. 36, which amends R.A. 1977, s.19(5), to prevent council lettings from being treated as restricted contracts, does not apply to housing association tenancies.

dwellings when they are completed, but more often they are initiated by sponsoring societies, whose members are replaced on completion of each scheme by members who are the occupiers. Each scheme thus forms a separate society and the sponsoring society sometimes continues to act as managing agent. As a legal concept, the term "housing society" is obsolete, the legislation now merely referring to a housing association, housing co-operative, co-operative housing association and housing trust,[71] all of which expressions have been explained earlier in this chapter.

IX. THE RIGHT TO BUY

The controls on sales by housing associations were relaxed by the Housing Act 1980. The principal purpose of this was to allow associations to sell houses to tenants, even in cases where they are not obliged to do so. Before the implementation of the Act's provisions, all sales and leases, other than certain short leases, needed Housing Corporation consent if the association was registered, or if the land had been acquired or developed with a grant.[72] The only exception was for registered charities, where the Charity Commissioners' consent was required, unless the acquisition of the land was not grant-aided.[73] The current provisions are to be found in the Housing Act 1985. The Corporation's consent is no longer required when a secure tenant exercises his right to buy. Nor is particular consent required where the Corporation has given a general consent.[74] Housing Corporation consent is not required for disposals by charitable, unregistered associations, which require the authority of an order of the Charity Commissioners.[75]

With consent, where required, a registered housing association can dispose of any of its land in any way it thinks fit, including disposition at a discount.[76] A charitable association must nevertheless comply with the objects of the charity.[77] Provisions for repayment of any discount, equivalent to those relating to sales to local authority secure tenants and described in Chapter 16, apply unless the Corporation's consent waives them.[78] A successor in title to a housing association is not generally concerned to see or enquire whether the Corporation's

[71] H.A. 1985, ss.5, 6, 26, 80; H.A.A. 1985, ss.1 & 2. See also Housing (Consequential Provisions) Act 1985, Sched. 2, para. 35.
[72] H.A. 1974, s.2(1), (4).
[73] Charities Act 1960, s.29; Housing Act 1974, s.2(2).
[74] That consent may be restricted to particular associations or properties, or to types of association or property, and may be conditional: H.A.A. 1985, s.9(1), (2).
[75] H.A.A. 1985, s.10(1). The Charity Commissioners are required to consult the Housing Corporation before making an order: *ibid.*
[76] H.A.A. 1985, ss.8(1), (2), 11 and Sched. 2.
[77] *Ibid.* s.8(3).
[78] *Ibid.* Sched. 2.

consent was given, and the absence of consent when it should have been given does not normally invalidate any disposition by an association.[79]

Secure tenants of housing associations, in addition to being granted security of tenure, are also granted the right to buy their houses or to take long leases of their flats, in just the same way as secure tenants of local authorities.[80] The rules and procedures described in Chapter 16 have equal application here. The main exception from the right to buy provisions are tenants of housing co-operatives registered both with the Housing Corporation under the Housing Associations Act 1985 and with the registrar of Friendly Societies under the Industrial and Provident Societies Act 1965, since such tenants are not secure tenants at all.[81] Nor are certain licensees of almshouse charities.[82] The other exceptions to the "right to buy" are associations which are registered charities, associations which have never received any grant from public funds, and tenants of co-operative housing associations.[83]

Housing association secure tenants eligible to exercise the "right to buy" have the right to a mortgage,[84] and the right to defer completion[85] in just the same way as secure tenants of local authorities. However, a tenant who buys from a housing association has the right to borrow from the Housing Corporation and not the local authority.[86] The amount of the loan is the same and the only limit on the amount lent is by reference to the tenant's income.[87]

---

[79] *Ibid.* s.9(3).
[80] H.A. 1985, s.118(1).
[81] H.A. 1985, ss.5, 80(1), (2).
[82] *Ibid.* Sched. 1, para. 12.
[83] *Ibid.* Sched. 5, paras. 1–3. It should be noted that basic residual subsidy received under the Housing Finance Act 1972 amounts to "grant" from public funds for this purpose: *Wood* v. *South Western Co-operative Housing Society* (1982) 4 H.L.R. 101.
[84] H.A. 1985, s.132(1).
[85] *Ibid.* s.142(1).
[86] *Ibid.* s.132(1)(b).
[87] See the Housing (Right to Buy) (Mortgage Limit) Regulations 1980 (S.I. 1980 No. 1423).

CHAPTER 18

FINANCIAL ASSISTANCE WITH RENTED HOUSING COSTS

I. Housing Benefit 597
    A Standard Housing Benefit . . . 597
    B Certified Housing Benefit . . . 601
III. Compensation for Disturbance . . . 602

A. Home Loss Payments 602
B. Disturbance Payments 603
C. Removal Expenses 604

I. HOUSING BENEFIT[1]

In 1972 the Housing Finance Act of that year introduced, for the first time, a national, mandatory rent rebate scheme for council tenants and a similar rent allowance scheme for tenants of private landlords. These benefits, together with rate rebate, were consolidated into a unified housing benefit, which came into operation in 1983. The framework of the scheme is to be found in the Social Security and Housing Benefits Act 1982, as supplemented by the Housing Benefits Regulations 1985.[2] The Department of Health and Social Security also produces a *Housing Benefits Guidance Manual*[3] advising local authorities on how to interpret the regulations and on administrative arrangements. In order to achieve consistency of practice in the discretionary areas of the scheme, local authorities tend to rely heavily on the *Manual*.

A. Standard Housing Benefit

Notwithstanding the somewhat misleading presentation of the housing benefit scheme as "unified" when the new legislation was announced in 1982,[4] the benefit is still comprised of three components: rate rebates, which are paid by the local rating authority; rent rebates, which are provided by the local housing authorities to their tenants,[5] and rent allowances, provided by local authorities to private tenants.[6]

A rate rebate is payable to anyone who qualifies under the means

---

[1] For a discussion of the problems encountered in implementing rent allowances see: Hetzel, Yates and Trutko, (1978) 1 *Urban Law & Policy* 229; Yates, [1978–79] J.S.W.L. 195.
[2] S.I. 1985 No. 677, hereafter referred to as "H.B. regs."
[3] D.H.S.S. 1985, H.M.S.O.
[4] See Social Security and Housing Benefits Act 1982, and Consultation Paper: *Assistance with Housing Costs*, D.o.E. 1981.
[5] Tenants in "equity sharing" schemes are eligible for rebate on the rental element of their payments: H.B. regs. 6.
[6] This includes occupiers paying under a "rental-purchase" scheme: H.B. regs. 2(1), 7.

test and who pays general rates on his or her home. This includes owner-occupiers as well as tenants.[7] Rent rebates and allowances may only be claimed by tenants.

In order to calculate a rebate or allowance under the scheme[8] five considerations must be borne in mind. These are:

(i)   an amount allowed under the regulations for the needs of the tenant and of any spouse or dependant child (the "needs allowance")[9];
(ii) the weekly income of the tenant and spouse[10];
(iii) the amount of weekly rent and rates[11];
(iv) the minimum rebate or allowance[12];
(v)   the amounts to be deducted for non-dependants.[13]

The pivots of the scheme are the various needs allowances. These are set out in the regulations and are amended from time to time. The needs allowances are meant to reflect the basic expenditure needs of the household, and they vary in accordance with the household composition. If a tenant's income is equal to the needs allowance appropriate to his circumstances, he pays 40 per cent. of his rent and rates himself, and the balance of 60 per cent. is met by rebate or allowance. For tenants with incomes below their relevant needs allowances, the amount they must contribute towards their rent is reduced. For tenants who are under pensionable age, their rent allowance or rebate will be 60 per cent. of their rent, plus 25 per cent. of the difference between their incomes and their needs allowance. Their rate rebate will, again, be 60 per cent. of their rates, plus 8 per cent. of the difference between income and the relevant needs allowance. For tenants of pensionable age, the rent allowance or rebate will be 60 per cent. of the rent, plus 50 per cent. of the difference between income and the needs allowance. Their rate rebate will be 60 per cent. of the rates, plus 13 per cent. of the difference between their incomes and the needs allowance.

For tenants whose income is more than the needs allowance, the amount of benefit will be reduced. The rent rebate or allowance will be 60 per cent. of the rent *less* 29 per cent. of the difference between income and the needs allowance. In the case of rate rebate, the benefit will be 60 per cent. of the rates, *less* 13 per cent. of the difference between income and the relevant needs allowance. The minimum rate rebate payable is 10p and the minimum rent rebate or allowance is

[7] H.B. regs. 5.
[8] *Ibid.* reg. 22.
[9] *Ibid.* reg. 15.
[10] *Ibid.* reg. 16.
[11] *Ibid.* regs. 2(1), 6(1), 7(1), 18(2), (6), (7).
[12] *Ibid.* reg. 23.
[13] *Ibid.* reg. 20.

20p, unless a claimant's income is more than his needs allowance,[14] in which case the minimum payable is 50p for a rate rebate, rent rebate or rent allowance.[15]

The local authority may make their calculations by reference to the income of someone other than the tenant where the authority consider that a person residing with the tenant has a higher income and that it is reasonable, in the circumstances of the case, so to do.[16] Where a fair rent is registered with the rent officer or a reasonable rent registered with the rent tribunal, benefit will be calculated on the registered rent.[17] If the accommodation is furnished, any charge for furniture will be included in the rent.[18] However, if the applicant is paying what are regarded as "excessive" housing costs,[19] the rebate or allowance will be calculated on a lower sum than the rent and rates actually paid. If part of the property is sub-let, benefit will be calculated on the rent the claimant pays less the occupational element of any rent received from the sub-tenant.[20]

The local authority has the discretion to pay a higher rebate or allowance where the claimant's circumstances are exceptional,[21] and where exceptional hardship is caused to the claimant by payment of benefit at the normal rates. Also, local authorities are permitted to operate schemes of their own which are up to 10 per cent. more generous than the "model" scheme.

A rent rebate is usually paid in the form of a reduced rent. A rate rebate is usually paid by a reduction in rates, although a cash refund is made where a claimant has paid rates in advance. A rent allowance is paid as a cash grant, either two-weekly, four-weekly or monthly, or at longer intervals where the tenant consents.[22] If rent is paid in arrears, then the rent allowance will be paid in arrears. Otherwise, if a tenant is paid two-weekly, benefit is paid in advance; in other cases, it is paid

---

[14] And the claimant is not in receipt of housing benefit supplement. This is an amount payable to persons whose incomes would otherwise be below Supplementary Benefit levels after paying rent and rates. It may not be claimed by anyone who is in full-time work, who has capital exceeding £3,000, who is involved in a trade dispute, or who is one of a couple who would not qualify for Supplementary Benefit under the rules for couples under that scheme: see Supplementary Benefit (Requirements) Regulations 1983, S.I. 1983 No. 1399, reg. 19.

[15] H.B. regs. 23.

[16] *Ibid.* reg. 50. Local authorities have been advised not to make inquiries, in the normal way, about the income of non-dependants, and to use their discretion to assess the income of someone other than the tenant very sparingly: *Housing Benefits Guidance Manual*, 1985, para. 11.22, 11.23.

[17] H.B. regs. 18(7).

[18] *Ibid.* reg. 2(1). Where a service charge is included, this may be included in the rent for benefit purposes unless it relates to heating, hot water, lighting or cooking: H.B. regs. 18(2), Sched. 3, paras. 2, 7 and 9.

[19] *e.g.* the home is larger than is required for the tenant and dependants, or, in privately rented accommodation, the tenant is paying a rent which the local authority consider to be unreasonably high compared with what would be paid for suitable alternative accommodation in the area: H.B. regs. 19. In many cases the local authority will refer the rent to the Rent Officer, and see *ante*, Chap. 11, (III), B.

[20] H.B. regs. 18(2)(d).

[21] *Ibid.* reg. 25.

[22] *Ibid.* reg. 42(1).

two weeks before the end of the period covered by the rent allowance.[23] If the benefit is less than 50p, the local authority may pay up to six months in arrears.[24] A claimant entitled to a weekly benefit exceeding £2.00 may insist on two-weekly payments,[25] and the local authority has the power to pay the allowance weekly, either to avoid overpayment or where it is in the interests of a tenant who is liable under the tenancy agreement to pay rent weekly.[26]

A local authority having good cause to suspect that a tenant is not paying rent regularly may withhold payment of a rent allowance.[27] Should the tenant subsequently pay off the rent arrears, or should the local authority be satisfied that the arrears will be discharged once the rent allowance is paid, any amount withheld must be paid over.[28] Similar principles apply to any rate rebate paid in cash where the tenant does not pay rates direct to the rating authority, but pays a rent inclusive of rates to the landlord.[29] Where arrears of rent are continuing, and there is a likelihood that the tenant will dissipate any housing benefits unless an order is made, it may be possible for a landlord to obtain an interlocutory order to require the tenant to pay his housing benefit towards the rent.[30]

Payment of a rebate or allowance starts on a claimant's "benefit day," *i.e.* a day of the week chosen by the local authority, which can be up to six days before the date of the claim.[31] Where a claimant is ineligible for benefit on application, but becomes eligible later, benefit will be paid from the date of eligibility.[32] Benefit will be granted for a set period, after which a further claim must be lodged. If the tenant is of pensionable age, or is in receipt of invalidity, war or industrial disablement benefit, or is receiving a widow's pension, and is likely to remain unemployed for at least twelve months, then he or she will be granted a rebate or allowance for up to twelve months after notification of entitlement.[33] Other tenants receive housing benefit for a maximum of seven months from the date of notification of entitlement to benefit.[34]

Claimants whose circumstances change during receipt of benefit must notify the paying local authority.[35] Benefit will then be

---

[23] *Ibid.* reg. 42(2).
[24] *Ibid.* reg. 39(1).
[25] *Ibid.* reg. 42(3).
[26] *Ibid.* reg. 42(4).
[27] *Ibid.* reg. 43(1).
[28] *Ibid.* reg. 43(3).
[29] *Ibid.* reg. 43(2).
[30] *Berg* v. *Markhill* (1985) 17 H.L.R. 455.
[31] *Ibid.* reg. 30.
[32] *Ibid.* reg. 28(7).
[33] Unless the claimant was notified of entitlement in October or November, when a maximum of 14 months' entitlement may be granted: H.B. regs. 29(2), (4).
[34] Claimants notified of entitlement in March or April may receive benefit for a maximum of 9 months: H.B. regs. 29(3).
[35] H.B. regs. 33(1).

withdrawn if the claimant is no longer entitled to it by virtue of the change in circumstances, or the amount of benefit will be altered to reflect the change. The alteration will take effect from the week when the change took place, unless it resulted from a change in income, when the local authority has a discretion as to the date when benefit should change.[36] If the alteration in the rebate or allowance is less than 40p, or the change in rate rebate is less than 20p, the local authority may choose to leave the benefit unchanged.[37] The local authority may recover overpayment, whether this was as a result of claimant default[38] or not.[39] Recovery may be either by way of deduction from future benefit payments or by court proceedings.[40]

B. Certified Housing Benefit

A claimant on supplementary benefit (S.B.) who pays rent and/or rates on his or her house will be eligible to receive certificated housing benefit from the local authority.[41] A tenant on S.B. entitled to certificated housing benefit will not need to make a claim. The Department of Health and Social Security (D.H.S.S.) should grant a certificate automatically to the local authority informing them that the claimant is in receipt of S.B.[42] Once the D.H.S.S. has sent the certificate to the local authority, it will normally treat the claimant as eligible for housing benefit from the date specified in the certificate. This will be the date of the first S.B. payment and no further claim for housing benefit need be lodged so long as the tenant remains on S.B.

As in the standard model scheme, housing benefit in some cases will cover only part of the rent and rates. This will be where part of the accommodation is sublet, where there is a non-dependant member of the household, where the accommodation is considered unreasonably large or expensive, or where the rent includes the cost of personal services or energy costs. In the case of long leaseholders, and Crown tenants, provision for housing costs is made in the supplementary benefit scheme and not as housing benefit.[43]

---

[36] *Ibid.* reg. 34(1).
[37] *Ibid.* reg. 38.
[38] *e.g.* a fraudulent claim, or failure to notify a change of circumstances.
[39] H.B. regs. 47(1).
[40] *Ibid.* reg. 47(2), and see *Housing Benefit Guidance Manual*, 1985, para. 21.10.
[41] H.B. regs. 9(1).
[42] *Ibid.* If the claimant is a tenant of a new Town Corporation, the Development Board for Rural Wales or the Scottish Special Housing Association, the certificate will be sent to them, and they will be responsible for paying the claimant's certificate housing benefit.
[43] H.B. regs. 7(2), 8(2).

II. Compensation for Disturbance

One of the important problems of local authority administration of property resources is to strike a balance between the provision of modern amenities for the community as a whole and the need to protect the interests of those individuals whose personal and property rights are injured in the process. There have been attempts to ensure that community development should be planned so as to minimise disturbance and distress, but where this is not possible, legislation has put the costs of community development on the community as a whole by providing monetary and other compensation for persons who have been adversely affected by development.[44]

A. Home Loss Payments

Any resident who has been in occupation for at least five years before the date of his displacement, is entitled to a home loss payment if the displacement is caused by, *inter alia*[45]

(i)   the compulsory acquisition of an interest in the dwelling;
(ii) the making of a demolition, closing or clearance order, or the service of an improvement notice.[46]

The claimant must have been in occupation for the five-year period by virtue of a right or interest in the dwelling, which includes a right to occupy as a statutory tenant, under a "restricted" contract, or under a contract of employment.[47]

The intention of the home loss payments is to recognise the personal upset and distress which people suffer when they are compulsorily displaced from their homes. A person is not to be treated as displaced from a dwelling in consequence of compulsory purchase if he gives up his occupation of the premises before the date on which the acquiring authority were authorised to acquire the property, but it is not necessary for the acquiring authority to have required him actually to give physical possession of the dwelling.[48] The amount of the payment is a sum equal to the rateable value of the dwelling, multiplied by three, subject to a maximum of £1,500 and a

---

[44] Most of the modern compensatory legislation is contained in statutes dealing with compulsory purchase, compensation and planning blight: see *Encyclopaedia of Planning Law and Practice* (ed. Heap) (for planning blight) and *Encyclopaedia of Compulsory Purchase and Compensation* (ed. Brown) for compulsory purchase, compensation and the provisions of the Land Compensation Act 1973 relating to depreciation caused by highways and other public authorities. For an outline discussion of these provisions see *post*, Chap. 23.
[45] Land Compensation Act 1973, s.29 (as amended).
[46] See H.A. 1985, Pts. VII, IX.
[47] Land Compensation Act 1973, s.29(4).
[48] *Ibid.* s.29(3).

minimum of £150.[49] The claimant must claim within six years of the date of displacement and the authority is statutorily obliged to make the payment within three months of the date of the claim or, if those three months end before the date of displacement, on the date of displacement.[50]

B. Disturbance Payments

Where a resident is actually forced to move to new accommodation as a direct result of action by a public authority, the resident may be entitled to receive a disturbance payment from the authority taking the action. This will be so where the resident is forced to move as a result of, *inter alia*[51]

(i) the acquisition of the dwelling by an authority having compulsory purchase powers;

(ii) the making of a demolition, closing or clearance order, or the service of an improvement notice.

A person will be entitled to a disturbance payment only if he is in lawful possession of the land. He will not receive the payment if he had an interest which, were it purchased by compulsory purchase, would entitle him to compensation beyond site value.[52] The amount of a disturbance payment is to be equal to the reasonable expenses of the person entitled to the payment in removing from the land from which he is displaced. If the person was carrying on a trade or business on the land, the payment is increased by the loss he will sustain by reason of the disturbance of the trade or business, consequent upon his obligation to quit the land, but having regard to the period for which the land may have been reasonably available to be occupied by him, and to the availability of other suitable land. Where displacement is from a dwelling in which structural alterations have been made to meet the requirements of a disabled person, the disturbance payment will include the reasonable expenses incurred by the person entitled to the payment in making comparable modifications to the person's new dwelling.[53]

---

[49] *Ibid.* s.30(1). The Secretary of State may, by order, alter these figures.
[50] *Ibid.* s.32(1), (2).
[51] *Ibid.* s.37(1).
[52] *Ibid.* s.37(2); *post*, Chap. 23.
[53] *Ibid* s.38.

C. Removal Expenses[54]

Claimants receiving S.B. are entitled to a grant to cover removal expenses, provided that the move is in one of the following circumstances:

(i) the claimant's former home is insanitary or structurally unsound;

(ii) the claimant's former home is unsuitable in size, structure or is too far away from close relatives, bearing in mind the following factors:

    (a) age of claimant, claimant's partner or children;

    (b) health of claimant, claimant's partner or children;

    (c) whether any member of the household suffers from a physical disability;

    (d) size of claimant's family;

    (e) whether anyone else lives with the claimant.

(iii) the claimant needs to move because of the death of a partner or because the couple have separated;

(iv) the move will significantly improve the claimant's or the partner of the claimant's employment prospects, or will enable the claimant or the claimant's partner to take a job;

(v) the move will allow the claimant to house a close relative who is a pensioner, chronically sick or mentally or physically disabled, at present in hospital or residential accommodation, or in local authority care; it must, however, be reasonable for the claimant to provide accommodation in these circumstances.

(vi) the move will allow the claimant to reduce housing costs to a lower level, in those cases where housing costs are met by the D.H.S.S. or where they are met by housing benefit;

(vii) the claimant has been receiving a weekly addition to S.B. to meet furniture storage charges.

No removal grant will be paid if removal expenses have been met by the local authority under the Land Compensation Act 1973 as part of a disturbance claim.[55] Nor will a grant be paid if the local authority offers the claimant temporary or permanent housing under its duties towards those who are homeless or threatened with homelessness under the Housing Act 1985, Pt. III. This is because local authorities have the power to pay removal expenses under section 70 of that Act.

[54] Supplementary Benefit (Single Payments) Regulations 1981, S.I. 1981 No. 1528, reg. 13.
[55] *Supra.*

This bar to obtaining a removal grant also applies when the claimant moves from temporary council accommodation for the homeless to a permanent council house. No removal grant will be paid if the housing costs of the new home are considered too high, unless the claimant can meet the part the D.H.S.S. will not pay. Finally, a removal grant will not be paid where the costs of the claimant's move have already been met by the Manpower Services Commission.

The Housing Act 1985, gives power to local authorities and new town corporations to pay removal expenses for their tenants, and also to pay expenses incidental to the purchase of a house by the tenant. This latter power can be used only in the case of the purchase of one of the authority's own houses if the house has not previously been let and was built by the authority either to be sold or let.[56]

---

[56] H.A. 1985, s.26. See also Housing Act 1985, s.178, which imposes statutory limits on the costs the tenant can be required to bear on exercising the right to buy under Part V of that Act.

CHAPTER 19

UNLAWFUL EVICTION, HARASSMENT AND HOMELESSNESS

I. Unlawful Deprivation of Occupation 607
II. Harassment 608
III. Unlawful Re-entry and Eviction .. 609
IV. Sanctions and Remedies 609
V. Homelessness 610
  A. Powers and Duties of Housing
    Authorities under the Housing
    (Homeless Persons) Act 1977 . 610

I. Unlawful Deprivation of occupation

The law has viewed with differing degrees of sympathy the tenant who is thrown on the street by his landlord or his agents; whose belongings are put outside the property during his absence; whose life is made a misery by the wilful disruption of basic services, and in extreme cases, whose property is pulled down about his ears. *Per contra*, it is not unknown for tenants and licensees, residential and others, to remain after their contractual rights have ended, in some cases without benefit of statutory protection, deliberately consuming as much gas and electricity as possible. In non-residential cases, self-help is not regarded with any enthusiasm,[1] and in residential cases, its limits are clearly circumscribed and reinforced by criminal sanctions.[2] The statutory provisions considered in this chapter are to be found in Part I of the Protection from Eviction Act 1977, in this chapter referred to as the "1977 Act."

Section 1 of the 1977 Act protects the "residential occupier." He is someone occupying premises[3] as a residence, under a contract, enactment[4] or rule of law giving him the right to remain in occupation or restricting the right of any other person to recover possession of the premises. Unwelcome guests, licensees contractual and otherwise, whose licences have been effectively ended, are not within the protection of section 1,[5] nor are trespassers.[6] An occupier who has been a Rent Act statutorily protected tenant seems to retain that status until a warrant for possession has been executed, or he has voluntarily given up possession.[7]

---

[1] See *ante*, Chap. 8, (IX) and so *Clifton Securities, Ltd.* v. *Huntley* [1948] 2 All E.R. 283.
[2] See Ashworth [1979] Crim.L.R. 76.
[3] The premises may be a single room, *Thurrock U.D.C.* v. *Shina* (1972) 23 P. & C.R. 205.
[4] For these purposes the most relevant enactments are likely to be the Rent Act 1977, Rent (Agriculture) Act 1976, Landlord and Tenant Act 1954, Pts. I and II, the Agricultural Holdings Act 1986, and see also s.4 of the 1977 Act, relating to agricultural employees, see the 1977 Act, s.8(1), and the Matrimonial Homes Act, 1983.
[5] *R.* v. *Blankley* [1979] Crim.L.R. 166.
[6] But if self-help is being considered, so must the Criminal Law Act 1977, s.6, see Chap. 8, (IX) *ante*.
[7] And see *Kyriacou* v. *Pandeli* [1980] C.L.Y. (County Court).

607

Section 1(2) of the 1977 Act makes it a crime unlawfully to deprive or attempt to deprive the residential occupier of any premises or part of them in his occupation unless he proves that he believed, and had reasonable cause to believe, that the residential occupier had ceased to reside in the premises.[8] Questions about the time and existence of the defendant's belief should be left to the jury.[9] The offence is not restricted to landlords or their agents,[10] but may be committed by "any person."

II. Harassment

Section 1(3) is directed at "acts[11] calculated to interfere with the peace or comfort of the residential occupier or members of his household," or where there is a persistent[12] withdrawal or withholding of services "reasonably required for the occupation of the premises as a residence." Cutting off electricity, water and gas, boarding up the lavatory or bathroom, interfering with access, visitors and post are not infrequent complaints. But before an offence is committed, it must be proved that the acts, etc., were done with the intention of causing the residential occupier:

    (a) to give up occupation of the whole or part, or
    (b) not to exercise his rights, or pursue his remedies in respect of all or part of the premises.

Intention is an essential element of the offence. A persistent failure by the landlord either to carry out repairs or pay bills for services is unlikely to result in his appearance in court on a criminal charge,[13] although his conduct may well amount to a breach of the contractual arrangements between the parties.[14]

---

[8] Any unlawful deprivation of occupation has to have the character of an eviction, even though the word "eviction" is not to be found in s.1(2). This does not necessarily mean that the displacement has to be permanent, but it must be more than a short, temporary displacement, such as that caused by locking the tenant out for the night: *R.* v. *Yuthiwattana* (1984) 16 H.L.R. 49.

[9] *R.* v. *Davidson-Acres* [1980] Crim.L.R. 60.

[10] "Acts" in this context can encompass a single act of harassment: *R.* v. *Polycarpou* (1983) 9 H.L.R. 129. In *R.* v. *Yuthiwattana* (*supra*) the Court of Appeal appeared to accept that the single act of failing to replace a lost key could, if it kept the tenant out of the house for long enough, constitute an offence under s.1(3).

[11] And see s.1(6) of the 1977 Act enabling in certain circumstances directors, managers and secretaries of companies to be proceeded against where the offence was committed by a body corporate.

[12] *Westminster City Council* v. *Peart* (1968) 19 P. & C.R. 736; *R.* v. *Abrol* [1972] Crim.L.R. 318. And see generally, The Francis Report (Cmnd. 4609), Chap. 14.

[13] And see *McCall* v. *Abelesz* [1976] Q.B. 585, and [1975] L.A.G.Bull. 15.

[14] See also *R.* v. *Yuthiwattana* (*supra*).

III. Unlawful Re-entry and Eviction

The restrictions on unlawful re-entry and eviction apply where premises are both let as a dwelling,[15] and also where, since the commencement of section 69 of the Housing Act 1980 on November 28th, 1980, a restricted contract has been created by means of a licence. Furthermore, a person "who, under the terms of his employment, had exclusive possession of any premises other than as a tenant shall be deemed to have been a tenant, and the expressions 'let' and 'tenancy' shall be construed accordingly."[16] The restrictions apply so long as any person is lawfully residing in the premises, or was so residing at the end of the tenancy. For so long as that situation continues re-entry and forfeiture can be enforced only by means of court proceedings.[17] Similarly, proceedings are necessary to recover possession of a dwelling which is not statutorily protected after the tenancy has come to an end.[18] These restrictions apply in two main areas. First, where the tenancy never enjoyed any statutory protection,[19] and secondly, where the protection given by statute has ended,[20] *e.g.* because he has moved his home elsewhere and uses the premises only infrequently, or he is still living in the property on the death of the second statutory successor.[21] The county court must be used if the property is within its financial jurisdiction.[22]

IV. Sanctions and Remedies

The primary sanctions are criminal, and sentences of imprisonment have been imposed and orders for compensation made.[23] The Act does not create new civil liabilities or civil remedies for eviction or harassment.[24] But section 1(5) provides that nothing in that section shall be taken to prejudice any liability or remedy to which a person guilty of an offence may be subject in civil proceedings. The conduct complained of may be a breach of the covenants or agreements between the parties, *e.g.* of the express or implied covenant for quiet enjoyment, or give rise to an action for trespass.[25] Aggravated and

[15] 1977 Act, ss.2, 3. For the position of occupiers of mobile homes, see *ante*, Chap. 10, (II)A(1)(*a*).
[16] 1977 Act, s.8(2), and see *Warder* v. *Cooper* [1970] 1 Ch. 495.
[17] 1977 Act, s.2.
[18] 1977 Act, s.3(1).
[19] "Statutorily protected tenancy" is defined in s.8(1), see note 3, above.
[20] An order for possession does not end statutory protection until it is executed.
[21] s.3(3), specifically mentions the case arising on the death of a tenant under a statutory tenancy within the meaning of the Rent Act 1977, or Rent (Agriculture) Act 1976.
[22] 1977 Act, s.9, and see *Peachey Corporation* v. *Robinson* [1967] 2 Q.B. 543; *Borzak* v. *Ahmed* [1965] 2 Q.B. 320, and [1975] L.A.G.Bull. 15.
[23] See *R.* v. *Bokhari* (1974) 59 Cr.App.R. 303.
[24] *McCall* v. *Abelesz* [1976] Q.B. 585.
[25] And see *ante*, Pt. I, Chap. 4, (IV)E(3).

exemplary damages may be payable,[26] though only in an action brought in tort,[27] and in appropriate cases at least an interim injunction obtained so that the evicted tenant can regain access.[28] In the last resort the tenant may have to call in aid the provisions of the Housing (Homeless Persons) Act 1977, although a tenant facing difficulties with his landlord should at the earliest opportunity make contact with the housing department of his local authority, and if he is in receipt of social security benefits, inform the department of his plight.[29]

V. HOMELESSNESS[30]

Since 1948 local authorities have been under certain statutory obligations to the homeless and have been able to exercise certain statutory powers in relation to homelessness within their areas.[31] However, these powers and obligations gave rise to many difficulties, many of them concerned with the plight of persons made homeless as a result of eviction. The obligation to house only arose if the homelessness was "unforeseen," and there were many disputes between local authorities and homeless persons as to whether homelessness through eviction was an "unforeseen" circumstance.[32] There was also the difficulty of which agency to approach first. Department of Environment Circulars[33] emphasised that homelessness was primarily a housing problem and that it should therefore increasingly become the responsibility of housing authorities. Social services departments should phase out their involvement until they provided only essential social work support where necessary. However, housing authorities were given no specific duties to help the homeless and legal responsibility lay with social service authorities. As a result, homeless persons were passed back and forth between social service and housing authorities.

A. Powers and Duties of Housing Authorities under the Housing Act 1985, Part III

The Housing (Homeless Persons) Act 1977 transferred statutory

---

[26] See *Drane* v. *Evangelou* [1978] 1 W.L.R. 455; *Asghar* v. *Ahmed* (1984) 17 H.L.R. 25; *McMillan* v. *Singh* (1984) 17 H.L.R. 120; *Millington* v. *Duffy* (1984) 17 H.L.R. 232.
[27] *Guppys (Bridport)* v. *Brookling* (1984) 269 E.G. 846 and 942.
[28] As in *Warder* v. *Cooper* [1970] 1 Ch. 495, and see further [1976] L.A.G.Bull. 34.
[29] See *infra.*
[30] See Hoath, *Homelessness, passim.*
[31] National Assistance Act 1948, s.21(1).
[32] See, *e.g. Roberts* v. *Dorset County Council, The Times*, August 2, 1976.
[33] *e.g.* D. of E.Circ. 18/74.

responsibility for the majority of homeless people[34] to housing authorities and placed a duty on those authorities to give varying degrees of help to all homeless people.[35] The provisions of the 1977 Act were re-enacted in Part III of the Housing Act 1985, where the present law is to be found. Commenting upon the policy of the homelessness legislation, however, Lord Brightman observed in *Puhlhofer* v. *London Borough of Hillingdon*[36] that the Act was designed "to assist persons who are homeless, not ... to provide them with homes." Given the very limited nature of a local authority's housing stock, the statutory duties to house in the legislation should be regarded as a "lifeline of the last resort" and not as a way of making inroads into the local authority's housing waiting list. The local authority must balance the priority needs of the homeless against the legitimate expectation of those on the waiting list. It is against such a background that the various duties under the Act must be construed.

(1) *Preliminary Duties of Housing Authorities*

Under the Housing Act 1985, s.62(1), housing authorities are under a duty to make "such inquiries as are necessary" when, being in receipt of an application from a person for assistance in obtaining accommodation, they have reason to believe that such a person may be homeless or threatened with homelessness. The inquiries that have to be made are such as are necessary to satisfy the authority as to whether the applicant is indeed homeless or threatened with homelessness and, once satisfied on that matter, they must make such further inquiries as are necessary to satisfy themselves whether he has priority need,[37] and whether his present predicament has been brought about intentionally.[38] The authority may also make inquiries (although there is no duty to do so) to ascertain whether the applicant has a local connection with the area of another housing authority.[39] The *Code of Guidance* (2nd ed.) on the Act, issued by the Department of the Environment, advises authorities on how to conduct these inquiries.[40] Although the authority should take their duty to make

---

[34] There are still residual obligations to certain categories of homeless persons incurred by social service departments under the National Assistance Act 1948, s.21(1)(*a*). Assistance may also be provided under the Children and Young Persons Act 1963, s.1 (to be replaced by the Child Care Act 1980, s.1). See Freeman [1980] J.S.W.L. 84; *R.* v. *Local Commissioner for Administration for the North East Area of England, ex p. Bradford Metropolitan B.C.* [1979] Q.B. 287; see also *Att-Gen, ex rel. Tilley* v. *Wandsworth L.B.C.* [1981] 1 W.L.R. 854.
[35] See the observation of their Lordships in *Din* v. *L.B. of Wandsworth* [1983] 1 A.C. 657.
[36] (1986) 136 N.L.J. 140.
[37] See *post.*
[38] H.A. 1985, s.62(3). For a useful analysis of the nature of the inquiries required see Arden [1980] L.A.G.Bull. 188.
[39] H.A. 1985, s.62(2).
[40] See paras. 2.2–2.4.

inquiries seriously, there is no obligation to conduct what Browne-Wilkinson J. has called "C.I.D.-type inquiries."[41] The burden of making the inquiries nevertheless rests upon the local authority. They cannot simply require the applicant to adduce evidence to support his claim.[42]

Authorities are under a duty to place applicants in accommodation while they make their inquiries, but only when the authority has reason to believe that the applicant has a "priority need."[43] The results of the inquiries alone must govern the nature of the accommodation offered[44] but any accommodation occupied by the applicant pending completion of the inquiries may be occupied by the applicant as a tenant (though not a secure tenant) and not as a licensee.[45] There is always a discretion (which in practice is infrequently exercised) to provide temporary accommodation, pending inquiries, notwithstanding a failure by the authority to believe that the applicant has priority need, but there will be no duty in the matter.[46]

There are difficulties concerning the local authority's duties on a re-application, since it would clearly be inappropriate to require the authority continually to re-perform its duties of inquiry *in extenso* each time an applicant re-applied, no matter how soon that was after the previous application. It seems that a local authority will only be obliged to re-inquire *de novo* when it appears from the application that there has been a material change in circumstances,[47] though an application by a different member of the same household, [48] or from the same person but to a different authority,[49] must be treated as a new application, attracting the full statutory duties of inquiry by the local authority.

(2) *Duties of Housing Authorities to Homeless Persons*[50]

The duties of housing authorities to homeless persons are made

[41] *Lally* v. *Kensington and Chelsea Royal Borough, The Times* March 27, 1980; but see Lord Denning M.R. in *Tickner* v. *Mole Valley D.C.* [1980] L.A.G.Bull. 187; and see also *R.* v. *Thurrock B.C. ex p. Williams* (1982) 1 H.L.R. 128; *Devenport* v. *Salford City Council* (1983) 8 H.L.R. 54; *R.* v. *Swansea City Council, ex p. John* (1982) 9 H.L.R. 56; *R.* v. *Southampton City Council, ex p. Ward* (1984) 14 H.L.R. 114; *R.* v. *Wyre B.C., ex p. Joyce* (1983) 11 H.L.R. 73.
[42] *R.* v. *Woodspring D.C., ex p. Walters* (1984) 16 H.L.R. 75.
[43] This term is explained *post*.
[44] *R.* v. *Ryedale D.C., ex p. Smith* (1983) 16 H.L.R. 66.
[45] *Eastleigh B.C.* v. *Walsh* [1985] 2 All E.R. 112. *cf. Kensington & Chelsea Royal Borough Council* v. *Hayden* (1984) 17 H.L.R. 114.
[46] H.A. 1985, s.63(1).
[47] *Wyness D.C.* v. *Poole* [1979] L.A.G.Bull. 166: *Delahaye* v. *Oswestry B.C., The Times*, July 29, 1980.
[48] *R.* v. *N. Devon D.C., ex p. Lewis* [1981] 1 W.L.R. 328.
[49] *R.* v. *Slough B.C., ex p. Ealing L.B.C.* [1981] Q.B. 801.
[50] These duties are owed to all homeless persons lawfully in this country, and are not limited to those who have a legal connection with the area of a housing authority in Great Britain: *R.* v. *Hillingdon London Borough Council, ex p. Streeting*, [1980] 1 W.L.R. 1430.

dependent upon two criteria: first, whether the applicant has priority need and secondly, whether he has become intentionally homeless. Once they are satisfied, as a result of their preliminary inquiries, that the applicant is homeless or threatened with homelessness, then a duty arises on the authority to deal with the case in one of several ways.[51]

If they are not satisfied on the question of priority need, or are so satisfied but conclude that the homelessness is intentional, the authority's duty is to furnish the applicant with advice and "appropriate assistance." "Appropriate assistance" is defined as "such assistance as a housing authority consider it appropriate in the circumstances to give . . . in any attempts [the applicant] may make to secure that accommodation becomes or does not cease to be available for his occupation."[52] The *Code of Guidance* advises authorities what might constitute "appropriate assistance" for this purpose,[53] and urges on them "a generous interpretation" of their duty to give assistance.[54]

If the authority are satisfied that the applicant is actually homeless (rather than just being under threat of being made such), and they are only subject to a duty to give advice and appropriate assistance because of the finding that the applicant is intentionally homeless, the authority are nevertheless under a duty to make accommodation available for the applicant's occupation for such period as they consider will give him a reasonable opportunity of finding accommodation himself. This duty to provide temporary accommodation ceases once the authority decide that the applicant has had long enough to find housing for himself, whether he has in fact done so or not. In *Lally* v. *Kensington and Chelsea Royal Borough*[55] a period of 14 days was held to be inadequate to allow the applicant time to find his own accommodation. Because the authority's area was in London, where it was notoriously difficult to secure private accommodation of a kind the applicant could afford, a period of three to four months would have been more appropriate.[56]

Where, as a result of their inquiries, the authority are satisfied that the applicant is threatened with homelessness, and that he has priority need, but "are not satisfied that he became threatened with home-

[51] H.A. 1985, ss.65(2)–(4), 66(2), (3), 67(1).
[52] *Ibid.* s.65(3)(*b*).
[53] Paras. 6.2, 6.5; Annex. A.3.1–A.3.4.
[54] Para. 4.1.
[55] *The Times*, March 27, 1980.
[56] Temporary accommodation, though it need not be of the same standard as permanent accommodation, must be capable of being described as accommodation and must certainly, if provided by the authority, be fit for human habitation: *R.* v. *Exeter City Council ex p. Gliddon* [1985] 1 All E.R. 493; *R.* v. *Southampton City Council, ex p. Ward* (1984) 14 H.L.R. 114; *cf. R.* v. *Rydale D.C. ex p. Smith* (1983) 16 H.L.R 66; *R.* v. *Borough of Dinefwr ex p. Marshall* (1984) 17 H.L.R. 310; *Puhlhofer* v. *L.B. of Hillingdon* (1986) 136 N.L.J. 140.

lessness intentionally," their duty is to take "reasonable steps"[57] to secure that accommodation does not cease to be available.[58] This provision does not, however, operate to restrain a local authority from evicting the applicant from his accommodation if he is a council tenant.[59] The use of the phrase "is not satisfied that," rather than "satisfied that he is not," might indicate that any doubt as to whether or not the homelessness is intentional should be resolved in favour of the applicant.

If the authority are satisfied that the applicant is actually homeless and has priority need, and decide he did not become homeless intentionally, their duty is to provide him with accommodation.[60] The *Code of Guidance* describes a number of possible approaches to the fulfilment of this obligation to provide accommodation, including action by authorities to make full use of the housing resources in their area.[61]

An authority can fulfil this obligation either by providing the appropriate accommodation themselves, or by securing that accommodation is made available from some other person (such as another local authority or a private landlord), or by furnishing such advice and assistance as will secure that the applicant obtains accommodation from some other source.[62] In *R. v. Bristol City Council, ex p. Browne*[63] the Divisional Court decided that an authority can discharge this duty by making such arrangements as are necessary, including payments of appropriate travel costs, for the applicant to be housed by another authority, even where that authority is outside the jurisdiction (in this case in Eire) and not within the definition of a relevant housing authority contained in sections 2 and 77 of the 1985 Act. The Court also decided that the authority discharge their duty, even where the foreign authority makes no offer of any specific property for the applicant to occupy, but merely makes general promises about the availability of some accommodation somewhere

---

[57] These are undefined in detail but presumably include at least the forms of assistance referred to in the *Code of Guidance*, paras. 6.2–6.5; A.3.1–A.3.4.
[58] H.A. 1985, s.66(2).
[59] *Ibid.* s.66(4).
[60] *Ibid.* s.65(2). *N.B.* For the purposes of the H.A. 1985, Pt. III, accommodation is to be regarded as available for a person's occupation "if it is available for occupation both by him and by any other person who might reasonably be expected to reside with him," s.75. See *Code of Guidance*, para. 2.8. See *Din* v. *L.B. of Wandsworth* [1983] 1 A.C. 657; *R.* v. *L.B. of Hillingdon, ex p. Islam*, [1983] 1 A.C. 688; *cf. Puhlhofer* v. *L.B. of Hillingdon* (1986) 136 N.L.J. 140.
[61] See paras. A.2.1–A.2.15.
[62] H.A. 1985, s.69(1). A single offer of accommodation which is appropriate is sufficient to discharge the local authority's duty: *R.* v. *Westminster City Council ex p. Chambers* (1983) 81 L.G.R. 401.
[63] [1979] 1 W.L.R. 1437.

in the area.[64] It is important to remember, however, that the local authority's obligation is to provide *appropriate* accommodation. In *R. v. Wyre B.C. ex p. Parr*[65] the Court of Appeal held that a local authority had not properly discharged its duty by arranging that the applicant receive an offer of accommodation in another local authority area, where this was not pursuant to the "local connection" arrangements.[66] In distinguishing the *Browne* case, the Court of Appeal held that the accommodation offered had to be appropriate, not only as to the premises themselves, but also as to the nature of the locality and the employment prospects. While an offer in another area could, as in *Browne* itself, constitute a proper discharge of the statutory duty, it could not do so where it resulted in sending the applicant to an area far distant from that with which he had a local connection. The applicant's wishes in the matter should be taken into account.

(3) *The Local Connection*

The duty to house does not apply if the authority are of the opinion:

(i)   that neither the person who applied to them for accommodation or for assistance in obtaining accommodation nor any person who might reasonably be expected to reside with him has a local connection with their area; and

(ii) that the person who so applied or a person who might reasonably be expected to reside with him has a local connection with another housing authority's area; and

(iii) that neither the person who so applies nor any person who might reasonably be expected to reside with him will run the risk of domestic violence in that other housing authority's area.[67]

These conditions are cumulative, so that each has to be complied with before the authority are relieved of their duty. However, the duty to house will still arise, these conditions notwithstanding, unless the authority also notify the authority with whose area they consider the

---

[64] It is hard to support this decision on principle. The Act contains specific provisions for dealing with applicants who have a connection with an area of another housing authority (s.5). Ss.1,2 clearly defines "housing authority" as an English, Welsh or Scottish housing authority. The court suggested that one could argue "by analogy" (*per* Lloyd J. at p. 350) to areas within foreign jurisdictions. The operative word of s.69(1) is "secure." How can advice and assistance "secure" that accommodation will be obtained "from some other person," when no specific property has been promised the applicant and the "other person" is, in any event, outside the jurisdiction? *cf. R. v. Wyre B.C, ex p. Parr* [1982] C.L.Y. 1461.

[65] [1982] C.L.Y. 1461.

[66] See *post*.

[67] H.A. 1985, s.67(2).

applicant to have a connection.[68] Persons are to be regarded as running the risk of domestic violence if such violence is likely to be perpetrated by anyone with whom those persons might be expected to reside or with whom they formerly resided.[69] Where there is a likelihood that the threats of violence will actually be carried out, then a threat from anyone (*e.g.* a landlord, another tenant in the same block, or vandals) will suffice without the residence requirement.[70]

If an authority are notified of a local connection, then they must house the applicant provided that they are satisfied that he, or someone who might reasonably be expected to reside with him, has a local connection with the area, and that there is no risk of domestic violence.[71] It may be that, either because the notifying authority are in error and there is no local connection between the applicant or his household and the notified authority, or because the notified authority take time to determine whether or not they are, in the circumstances, obliged to house, the applicant has, in the meantime, nowhere to live. If there is no local connection established, the duty to house reverts back to the notifying authority,[72] who are, in any event, obliged to house during the period of investigation.[73] Should the notifying authority form the view that the applicant is homeless and has priority need, and communicates this to the notified authority, this view will then be binding, so that should the notified authority refuse the reference, a duty to house under section 65 of the 1985 Act immediately arises.[74] If there is a finding of intentional homelessness, there can be no referral; if an authority finds intentional homelessness but, in error, refers the application to another authority, the wrongful referral will be disregarded.[75]

For the purposes of the Act, a local connection with an area will be taken to exist when an applicant:

---

[68] *Ibid.* s.67(1).
[69] *Ibid.* s.67(3)(*a*).
[70] *Ibid.* s.67(3)(*b*).
[71] *Ibid.*, ss.67(2), 68(2). This is not a separate duty from that arising under s.65(2). Accordingly, where an authority is placed under a duty by s.68(2), they are entitled to rely on a former discharge under s.65(2) unless there is a new incidence of homelessness: *R.* v. *L.B. of Hammersmith and Fulham, ex p. O'Brian* (1985) 17 H.L.R. 471.
[72] *Ibid.* s.68(2).
[73] *Ibid.* s.68(1). This duty to provide accommodation for the time being arises as soon as the notifying authority form the view that the applicant is homeless and has priority need. It is in no way dependent on the duty imposed on the authority by the H.A. 1885, s.68(3) to notify the applicant of its decision under s.68(2). Accordingly, the authority cannot delay its duties to house under s.68(2) by delaying its notification under s.68(3): *R.* v. *Beverley Borough Council, ex p. McPhee* (1978) 122 S.J. 766.
[74] H.A. 1985, s.68(2): *R.* v. *Beverley Borough Council, ex p. McPhee, supra.* The notified authority will even be bound by decisions of the notifying authority reached when the notified authority has earlier made a finding of intentional homelessness in respect of the applicant: *R.* v. *Slough Borough Council, ex p. Ealing L.B.C.* [1981] Q.B. 801.
[75] *Delahaye* v. *Oswestry Borough Council, The Times,* July 29, 1980.

(i)   is, or was in the past, normally resident in that area by choice; or
(ii) is employed in that area; or
(iii) has a family association with the area; or
(iv) there are any other special circumstances indicating a local connection.[76]

A person is not resident in a district for this purpose if he is a serving member of the armed forces, and residence will not be by choice if it is because the applicant, or a person who might reasonably be expected to reside with him, became resident in the area through being a serving member of the armed services.[77] Also, residence in a district will not be by choice if the applicant, or a member of his family, became resident in a district by virtue of serving a term of imprisonment there.[78]

In *Re Betts*[79] the House of Lords pointed out that the statutory list of factors indicating a local connection will always be subject to the "fundamental" test of whether the applicant has a local connection with the area of the authority. This means more than "normal residence,"[80] or "employment" or "family association" or "other special circumstances." These are merely factors, though they are the *only* factors, upon which to found a local connection. A local connection having some other origin will not suffice, so that the applicant must have no local connection with the notifying authority, *and* a local connection with the notified authority, based on one or more of these four factors. The local connection, therefore cannot, as can normal residence, be formed or changed in a day; it must be built up and established over a period of time. There cannot be a local connection until residence, employment, family association or other special circumstances are of such a duration and permanence as to establish a local connection. Want of local connection with any local authority area (because, for example, the applicant has entered the country from overseas) does not prevent the obligation to house under section 65 of the Act from arising.[81]

---

[76] H.A. 1985, s.61(1).
[77] *Ibid.* s.61(2). See *R.* v. *Vale of the White Horse D.C., ex p. Smith* (1984) 17 H.L.R. 160.
[78] H.A. 1985 s.61(3).
[79] (1983) 10 H.L.R. 97.
[80] Not the same as "ordinary residence": see *R.* v. *Barnett L.B.C., ex p. Shah* [1983] 2 A.C. 309. The test is whether there is a local connection brought about by a sufficient degree of normal residence; an enhanced degree of normal residence is needed in order to achieve a local connection.
[81] *R.* v. *Hillingdon London Borough Council, ex p. Streeting,* [1981] 1 W.L.R. 1430. A local connection abroad is not a local connection for the purposes of the Act: *R.* v. *Bristol City Council, ex p. Browne* [1979] 1 W.L.R. 1437.

(4) *Priority Need*

It will be recalled that the statutory duty to house under the Housing Act 1985, s.65(2), only arises where there is a "priority need." Section 59 of the Act specifies certain categories of priority need. Assuming an applicant for assistance is homeless or threatened with homelessness, he has priority need if he falls within the categories specified by the Secretary of State by order,[82] or by the Act itself.[83] The statutory classes of priority need are:

(i)   persons with dependent children residing with them, or who might reasonably be expected to reside with them;

(ii) persons homeless or threatened with homelessness as a result of any emergency such as flood, fire or any other disaster[84];

(iii) persons who are, or a member of whose household is, vulnerable as a result of old age, mental illness or handicap or physical disability or other special reason[85];

(iv) pregnant women, or persons who might reasonably be expected to live with them.[86]

The Secretary of State has power to extend the statutory list of priority need categories by order, and also to amend or repeal any part of the statutory list. It might be thought that there was no need to make use of the statutory instrument procedure since the Housing Act 1985, s.71(1), provides that "in relation to homeless persons and persons threatened with homelessness, a relevant authority shall have regard in the exercise of their functions to such guidance as may from time to time be given by the Secretary of State." Such guidance is contained in the Department of the Environment's *Code of Guidance* on the Act. However the Court of Appeal has held in *De Falco* v. *Crawley Borough Council*[87] that there is no obligation imposed on an authority by the Act to follow the advice given in the *Code of Guidance*. Were it otherwise it might be possible, of course, for the Secretary of State to modify the priority need categories without statutory instrument, and

---

[82] H.A. 1985, s.59(2).

[83] *Ibid.* s.59(1).

[84] Perhaps the most frequent cause of "emergency" homelessness is sudden eviction. Eviction is not specifically mentioned here, and it could be that the courts will construe the words "or any other disaster" *ejusdem generis* with flood or fire, so that the emergency would need to be brought about by some natural disaster or Act of God, before priority need in this category can be established: see *Noble* v. *S. Herefordshire D.C.* (1984) 17 H.L.R. 80.

[85] In *R.* v. *Waveney D.C., ex p. Bowers* [1983] Q.B. 238, it was held that a 59 years old chronic alcoholic who had sustained brain damage as a result of an injury, was "vulnerable" under this provision. The court also held that "vulnerability" need not be attributable to one only of the statutory grounds or reasons, but could arise from a combination of them. See also *R.* v. *Bath City Council, ex p. Sangermano* (1984) 17 H.L.R. 94. Such persons might be owed a duty to house by social service departments in any event, under the National Assistance Act 1948, s.21(1)(*a*).

[86] H.A. 1985, s.59(1)(*a*): *R.* v. *Preseli; D.C., ex p. Fisher* (1984) 17 H.L.R. 147.

[87] [1980] 1 All E.R. 913.

also to give other directions to local authorities as to how they are to exercise their powers and obligations under the Act. Lord Denning M.R. argued in the *De Falco* case that section 71(1) imposed a duty upon an authority to have regard to, in the sense of consider, the Code of Guidance but, having done so, they could depart from it if they thought fit.[88]

(5) *Homelessness*

By virtue of the Housing Act 1985, s.58(1), a person is homeless within the Act if he is totally without accommodation of any kind in England, Wales or Scotland. This means that he must not only be without any accommodation which he has a right to occupy by virtue of some legal estate or equitable interest (such as a lease or an agreement for one) but also any which he could occupy under a licence (such as parental permission to live at home or with "in-laws").[89] One major problem homeless families frequently encounter is separation as a direct result of homelessness. Although such separation is now officially discouraged, many families do still find themselves forced to resort to it when a husband, for example, finds himself denied access to accommodation where his wife and children have been given shelter. The Act provides in s.58(2), that a person is to be treated as having no accommodation unless his existing accommodation (where he has any) is available both for him and "any other person who normally resides with him as a member of his family or in circumstances in which it is reasonable for that person to reside with him."

It may also happen that some accommodation may be of such a low standard that, even though the applicant may still be living in it, it ought to be ignored in determining whether the applicant is homeless.[90] However, as the House of Lords warned in *Puhlhofer* v. *L.B. of Hillingdon*,[91] the question of whether or not the accommodation the applicant is currently occupying may be ignored cannot be solved by importing the word "appropriate" or "reasonable" into section 58(2) of the Act. Clearly some accommodation may be so cramped, or so unfit that, on any objective standard, it cannot be regarded as accommodation at all, or cannot be regarded as accommodation in which the applicant, together with other persons who might reasonably be expected to reside with him as members of his family, could be expected to live. However, the fact that the

[88] This dictum was treated as part of the *ratio* of the case, and cited with approval, in *Miller* v. *Wandsworth L.B.C.*, *The Times*, March 19, 1980.
[89] H.A. 1985, s.58(2).
[90] *R.* v. *S. Herefordshire D.C.*, *ex p. Miles* (1985) 83 L.G.R. 607; *R.* v. *Preseli D.C.*, *ex p. Fisher* (1984) 17 H.L.R. 147.
[91] (1986) 136 N.L.J. 140.

accommodation currently occupied by the applicant is, in itself, unfit or is overcrowded, will not, as a matter of law, *per se* result in him and his family being regarded as homeless. It must be a question of fact, to be decided upon by the local authority, in every case.[92]

A person cannot argue that he is homeless, however, if he occupies by virtue of some statutory provision or rule of law, or if the right to evict him is restricted by such a provision or rule. This would cover members of the armed forces, persons with tied accommodation or security of tenure under the Rent Act 1977 or the Rent (Agriculture) Act 1976, spouses with statutory rights of occupation under the Matrimonial Homes Act 1983, and so on. The legislation includes in the definition of homelessness an inability to gain entry to property one has a right to occupy, *de facto* homelessness as a result of domestic violence or the threat of it, and an inability to find an appropriate site for a caravan or a mooring for a houseboat.[93] The fact that the applicant occupies some temporary accommodation of a transient kind, such as a women's refuge, will not prevent the applicant being regarded as homeless.[94]

(6) *Persons Threatened With Homelessness*[95]

A person is threatened with homelessness within the Act if "it is likely that he will become homeless within 28 days."[96] The homelessness merely has to be "likely," not certain. The mere fact that homelessness is "on the cards," as it were, should suffice.

(7) *Intentional Homelessness*

As already explained, the duties of housing authorities towards homeless persons are dependent, to some extent, upon whether the homelessness or threatened homelessness is "intentional." Intentional homelessness is defined in the Housing Act 1985, s.60(1). Under that provision (and the corresponding provision in section 60(2) dealing with intentionally inducing a threat of homelessness) persons become homeless or threatened with homelessness intentionally if they "deliberately do or fail to do" anything in consequence of

---

[92] See the rather more liberal construction placed by the House of Lords upon similar words, where the reasonableness of the applicant's conduct is expressly made a relevant factor, in relation to intentional homelessness, under H.A. 1985, ss.60(1) and 75; *R. v. Hillingdon London Borough, ex p. Islam* [1983] 1 A.C. 657.

[93] H.A. 1985, s.58(3).

[94] *R. v. Ealing London Borough Council, ex p. Sidhu* (1982) 80 L.G.R. 534; see also *Din v. L.B. of Wandsworth* [1983] 1 A.C. 657, *per* Lord Lowry at p. 677; *R. v. Waveney D.C., ex p. Bowers* [1983] Q.B. 238.

[95] See *Code of Guidance*, para. 2.11.

[96] H.A. 1985, s.58(4).

which they cease or are likely to cease to occupy accommodation which is available for their occupation[97] *and* which it would have been reasonable for them to go on occupying. In *R.* v. *Slough Borough Council, ex p. L.B. of Ealing*[98] Lord Denning M.R. appeared to suggest that, however reprehensible an applicant's conduct might be in bringing about a loss of former accommodation, that loss could only be regarded as "deliberate" if it involved a clearly directed intention to bring about that end. The Code of Guidance[99] states that "authorities should in such cases [loss of former home through sale or non-payment of rent] be satisfied that the person has taken the action which has led to the loss of accommodation with full knowledge of the likely consequences." It is significant that the relevant words in section 60 refer to actions, or failure to take actions, resulting in accommodation *ceasing* to be available to the applicant. An authority cannot, therefore, escape its obligations to house, on the ground of intentional homelessness, where an offer of accommodation, never occupied by the applicant, has not been taken up.[1] In the case of threatened homelessness, it will be intentional if persons deliberately do or fail to do anything, the likely result of which is that they will be forced to leave such accommodation. An act or omission is not to be regarded as deliberate in this context if it was done (or omitted to be done) "in good faith and on the part of a person who was unaware of any relevant fact."[2] The legislation provides no statutory definition of what constitutes good faith for this purpose, nor what is to be regarded as a relevant fact.[3] When determining the question of whether a continued occupation would have been "reasonable" for this purpose, a housing authority may have regard to whether it would have been reasonable for the applicant to continue to occupy the accommodation in the general circumstances prevailing in relation to housing in the authority's area.[4]

In *R.* v. *L. B. Hillingdon, ex p. Islam*[5] the applicant had been sharing a single bed-sitting room with another man. When, after a wait for

---

[97] If the accommodation left was not actually available for the accommodation of the applicant and those persons who might reasonably be expected to live with the applicant (see s.75), because, for example, it was simply too small, or was shared with other persons, so that it could not accommodate the whole family, then there can be no finding of intentional homelessness: *R.* v. *London Borough of Hillingdon, ex p. Islam* [1983] 1 A.C. 657; *cf.* the interpretation of "accommodation" in s.58 in *Puhlhofer* v. *Hillingdon L.B.* (1986) 136 N.L.J. 140.

[98] [1981] Q.B. 801; *cf. Devenport* v. *Salford City Council* (1983) 8 H.L.R. 54 *per* Waller L.J. at p. 68.

[99] Para. 2.17.

[1] *Wyness* v. *Council of the Borough of Poole* [1979] L.A.G.Bull. 166; *R.* v. *City of Westminster, ex p. Chambers* (1982) 6 H.L.R. 24; see Arden [1980] L.A.G.Bull. 211.

[2] H.A. 1985, s.60(3); and see *R.* v. *Slough B.C., ex p. L.B. of Ealing* [1981] Q.B. 801.

[3] But see *R.* v. *Eastleigh B.C., ex p. Evans* (1984) 17 H.L.R. 515.

[4] H.A. 1985, s.60(4); and see *Miller* v. *Wandsworth B.C., The Times*, March 19, 1980; *Davis* v. *Kingston-upon-Thames R.L.B., The Times*, March 27, 1981; *R.* v. *L.B. of Wandsworth, ex p. Rose* (1983) 11 H.L.R. 105; *R.* v. *Hammersmith & Fulham L.B.C., ex p. Duro-Rama* (1983) 9 H.L.R. 71; *R.* v. *Eastleigh B.C., ex p. Beattie* (1983) 10 H.L.R. 134; *R.* v. *Westminster City Council, ex p. Ali* (1983) 11 H.L.R. 83; *R.* v. *L.B. of Hillingdon, ex p. Wilson* (1983) 12 H.L.R. 60.

[5] [1983] 1 A.C. 688.

entry clearance of six years, the applicant was joined by his wife and four children from Bangladesh, it was no longer possible for the applicant, together with his family,[6] to live in the shared bed-sitting room and he therefore applied for accommodation under the Act as a homeless person. At no time had the applicant ever lived with his wife and children. He had lived and worked in Uxbridge for 16 years, paying five visits home, on the first of which he married; on later visits his wife conceived. His family had lived with his parents while awaiting permission to come to England. The local authority had determined that the applicant was intentionally homeless. The House of Lords disagreed, on the basis that at no time had the applicant ever occupied accommodation which was "available" in the sense in which that term is used in section 60. The shared room in this country was not "available" and there was no evidence of availability in the family home in Bangladesh. Furthermore, their Lordships rejected any notion of the husband, on the basis of five visits home, occupying family accommodation in Bangladesh through the agency of his wife. As Lord Wilberforce observed[7]: "I do not think that rooms in two separate continents can be combined" to produce "available accommodation."[8]

The result of section 60 is that a tenant who finds himself homeless as a result of a possession order may, in many circumstances, be regarded as intentionally homeless. If, as a protected tenant under the Rent Act 1977, possession has been obtained from him on any of the discretionary grounds[9] involving breach of covenant or some other lapse from the letter or spirit of the tenancy agreement, the authority might argue that the homelessness is intentional in that, being avoidable, it was a consequence of the tenant's "acts or omission." It could be argued, on the other hand, that homelessness is only intentional when it is a *direct* consequence of the tenant's act or omission, so that the homelessness arising in such cases is a consequence of the court exercising its discretion and not a result of the tenants' conduct. It will be necessary for the local authority to consider, even in cases where the possession order was granted on the ground of tenant default, whether the court, in making the order, took account of matters for which the tenant had no responsibility.[10]

Where the possession order is not based on the tenant's default, as is the case in relation to the mandatory grounds for possession under the

---

[6] See H.A. 1980, s.75.
[7] At p. 708.
[8] See also *R.* v. *Westminster C.C., ex p. Ali* (1983) 11 H.L.R. 83; *R.* v. *Preseli D.C., ex p. Fisher* (1984) 17 H.L.R. 147.
[9] R.A. 1977, Sched. 15, Pt. I, Cases 1–7 and 10; *supra* Chap. 13 (II).
[10] *Stubbs* v. *Slough B.C.* [1980] L.A.G.Bull. 16; *Afan B.C.* v. *Marchant* [1980] L.A.G.Bull. 15; *R.* v. *Wyre B.C., ex p. Joyce* (1983) 11 H.L.R. 73; *Devenport* v. *Salford City Council* (1983) 8 H.L.R. 54; *R.* v. *Swansea City Council, ex p. John* (1982) 9 H.L.R. 56; *cf. R.* v. *Southampton City Council, ex p. Ward* (1984) 14 H.L.R. 114.

Rent Act 1977,[11] the former service tenant whose premises are required for another employee,[12] and the "greater hardship" ground,[13] then the authority cannot argue that the former tenant has become homeless intentionally. Clearly, however, a tenant who declines suitable alternative accommodation[14] does involve himself in intentional homelessness unless he can persuade the authority that the court's view of what was "suitable accommodation" was not, nevertheless, accommodation in which it was "reasonable" for him to be in occupation within the Housing Act 1985, s.60.

If a tenant declines to defend a possession action, then the authority is entitled to draw its own conclusions as to whether the applicant is intentionally homeless when, having been evicted, he applies to them for accommodation under the Act. The applicant cannot come before the court, when asking for a review of the authority's decision, and argue that, if the court were to investigate the matter, it would come to a different conclusion and therefore find the authority in breach of their duty. If an applicant wishes to establish that he had no alternative but to leave his original accommodation because of his landlord's claim to possession on a mandatory ground, the Court of Appeal has suggested that this should be done by an attempted defence of the possession action in the county court.[15]

As regards tenants with no security of tenure, or limited security such as that granted to some tenants under restricted contracts,[16] it could be argued that such tenants are not intentionally homeless when a possession order is made against them since there is rarely anything that could be done to prevent the order being made.[17] The same applies to licensees, unless by estoppel.[18] Again, however, the authority may argue that the homelessness is intentional, even in these cases, if they form the view that the notice to quit and consequent possession action was brought about because of some tenant default. The *Code of Guidance* urges local authorities to be generous in their assistance in such cases.[19]

It might appear, therefore, that there are dangers for tenants in leaving possession actions undefended, although where the costs of the defence would be prohibitive, or outside the tenant's means, it

[11] R.A. 1977, Sched. 15, Pt. II, Cases 11–18.
[12] *Ibid.* Sched. 15, Pt. I, Case 8.
[13] *Ibid.* Case 9.
[14] *Ibid.* s.98(1).
[15] *R.* v. *Penwith District Council, ex p. Hughes* [1980] L.A.G.Bull. 188; see also *R.* v. *Portsmouth City Council, ex p. Knight* (1983) 10 H.L.R. 115.
[16] *Supra,* Chap. 14.
[17] *R.* v. *Exeter City Council, ex p. Gliddon* [1985] 1 All E.R. 493.
[18] *Ibid.* See also *Hammersmith & Fulham L.B.* v. *Harrison* [1981] 1 W.L.R. 650; *R.* v. *Surrey Heath B.C., ex p. Li* (1984) 16 H.L.R. 83.
[19] Paras. 2.15–2.17; A.1.3. In *R.* v. *Mole Valley D.C., ex p. Minnett* (1983) 12 H.L.R. 48, a departure one day before the date set by the court for leaving the property was held to be a *de minimis* premature departure.

would be hard to argue that a failure to defend was an "omission" resulting in homelessness. The tenant could argue that in such circumstances his omission was "reasonable" or, alternatively, not "deliberate" because it was made "in good faith" and he was "unaware" of a relevant fact at the time (*i.e.* the attitude the local authority would take to his action).[20] Indeed, in every case in which a tenant commits an act or is guilty of an omission, provided it is not actually illegal (such as a breach of covenant or committing a nuisance), he could argue that it was not deliberate because, at the time he acted or failed to act, he was unaware that the authority would form the view that his homelessness was intentional. The authority cannot reach a decision in advance of knowledge of the facts of the particular case,[21] and provided the tenant holds his view "in good faith," he should not, by virtue of section 60(3) of the 1985 Act, be regarded as rendering himself intentionally homeless.

Nevertheless, it is clear that an act or omission which results in loss of accommodation for the purposes of intentional homelessness may not be the act or omission of the applicant, but may instead be that of someone for whom the applicant is responsible, such as a child, whose acts of nuisance or annoyance cause eviction.[22] It may also be that the applicant has been a party to, or has acquiesced in the acts or omission of another, and it was that other's conduct which resulted in the homelessness.[23] A person cannot be said to have become homeless intentionally by choosing to have additional children[24]; an act or omission occurring while abroad, including leaving accommodation abroad, can, however, constitute an act or omission for the purposes of intentional homelessness.[25]

In *Youngs* v. *Thanet District Council*[26] the court observed that homelessness within what is now the 1985 Act "was a matter of fact, not status." If a homeless person, who has been adjudged intentionally homeless by an authority within section 60 of the Act, finds accommodation for himself from which he is subsequently evicted, so that he presents himself to the authority as homeless again, his original homelessness should be regarded as having come to an end when he found accommodation for himself. When subsequently

---

[20] H.A. 1985, s.60(3).
[21] *cf. Att.-Gen. ex rel. Tilley* v. *Wandsworth London Borough Council*, [1981] 1 W.L.R. 854.
[22] As in *Devenport* v. *Salford City Council* (1983) 8 H.L.R. 54.
[23] *R.* v. *Swansea City Council, ex p. John* (1982) 9 H.L.R. 56; *R.* v. *Swansea City Council, ex p. Thomas* (1983) 9 H.L.R. 64; *R.* v. *N. Devon D.C., ex p. Lewis* [1981] 1 W.L.R. 328; *cf. R.* v. *Ealing L.B.C., ex p. Sidhu* (1982) 50 L.G.R. 534; *R.* v. *West Dorset D.C., ex p. Phillips* (1984) 17 H.L.R. 336.
[24] *R.* v. *Eastleigh B.C., ex p. Beattie* (1983) 10 H.L.R. 134.
[25] *De Falco* v. *Crawley B.C.* [1980] Q.B. 460; *Lambert* v. *L.B. of Ealing* [1982] 1 W.L.R. 550; *R.* v. *Hammersmith & Fulham L.B.C., ex p. Duro-Rama* (1983) 9 H.L.R. 81; *R.* v. *L.B. of Wandsworth, ex p. Nimako-Boateng* (1983) 11 H.L.R. 95; *R.* v. *L.B. of Wandsworth, ex p. Rose* (1983) 11 H.L.R. 105; *R.* v. *L.B. of Hillingdon, ex p. Wilson* (1983) 12 H.L.R. 60; *R.* v. *Reigate & Banstead B.C., ex p. Paris* (1984) 17 H.L.R. 103.
[26] (1980) 78 L.G.R. 474; *cf. Delahaye* v. *Oswestry Borough Council, The Times*, July 29, 1980.

evicted, his new homelessness should be treated as an entirely new situation, and not as a continuation of the old one, and hence the authority are then under a duty to consider his case all over again under section 62, and to take appropriate steps under section 65. The finding of intentional homelessness that may well quite properly have been reached in relation to the first period of homelessness would not necessarily and automatically apply to the second.

In *Dyson* v. *Kerrier District Council*[27] a young woman with a child was granted a tenancy of a council flat; shortly afterwards she surrendered that tenancy and took a winter-only tenancy[28] of a flat next door to her sister. At the end of the tenancy a possession order was made against her, and she applied to the authority for accommodation. The authority made due inquiries and concluded that the applicant was homeless and had priority need, but that she was intentionally homeless. The Court of Appeal held that the authority were quite in order in looking beyond the latest address at which the applicant had been living, and that what is now section 60(1) of the 1985 Act compelled a finding of intentional homelessness where surrender of the initial tenancy had, in due course, led to the applicant's present homelessness. The case does, however, leave open the precise fashion in which the causal link between earlier actions and current homelessness should be traced. On the basis of *Dyson*, the decision in *Youngs* was disapproved by the Court of Appeal in *Lambert* v. *L.B. of Ealing*.[29] A French family left accommodation in Lyons, in circumstances which probably amounted to intentional homelessness, and bought a caravan in which they came to England. Subsequently they had two holiday lettings of living accommodation, after which they found themselves homeless. The county court held that their intentional homelessness had come to an end with the termination of the holiday lettings, but the Court of Appeal disagreed, reversing the decision on the ground that the issue of which act caused the homelessness was a question of fact for the local authority, and the authority was quite entitled to find that the present homelessness had been caused by the past act of vacating accommodation in France and coming to England with no accommodation to which to go.[30] The only constraint upon the local authority would appear to be that the authority must act reasonably in attributing the present homelessness to an act of leaving earlier accommodation.[31]

In *Din* v. *L.B. of Wandsworth*[32] a family left accommodation without waiting for the court order which the landlord would have

---

[27] [1980] 1 W.L.R. 1205.
[28] *Supra*, Chap. 13.
[29] [1982] 1 W.L.R. 550.
[30] See also *R.* v. *London Borough of Harrow, ex p. Holland* (1982) 4 H.L.R. 108; *Davis* v. *Kingston-upon-Thames Royal London Borough, The Times*, March 27, 1981.
[31] *Ibid.*
[32] [1983] 1 A.C. 657.

been required by law to obtain in order to recover possession. This was against the advice of the local authority to remain in occupation. There appeared to be no dispute between the parties that, on an application made immediately after departure, the authority could quite properly have found intentional homelessness, since it would have been reasonable for the family to have remained in occupation until the possession order. However, on application later, the authority conceded that the family would, by then, inevitably have become homeless, since they had no defence to the landlord's proposed possession action. During the interim period the family had stayed with relatives, and it was argued that the original cause of the homelessness (leaving voluntarily before the possession order was obtained) was no longer the effective cause of the homelessness, since regardless of when the family had left, they would *now* be homeless unintentionally. The majority in the House of Lords decided that the material date for deciding whether homelessness was unintentional was the date on which the accommodation was left, and hypothetical events which might have occurred from that date were irrelevant. In this case the homelessness was caused by a departure from accommodation at a time when the family had not been obliged to leave, and this was capable of being treated as unintentional homelessness, the chain of causation not having been broken by the short period of emergency accommodation with relatives.[33]

The duty of a local authority to an applicant and his family with priority need and unintentionally homeless, is to provide accommodation.[34] In the case of an applicant and family intentionally homeless, the authority is merely required to furnish appropriate advice and assistance and to secure that accommodation is made available for such period as the authority consider would give the applicant a reasonable opportunity of finding housing himself.[35] In *De Falco* v. *Crawley Borough Council*,[36] Bridge L.J. observed that the period here contemplated by the Act begins when the local authority's adverse decision on intentional homelessness is communicated to the applicant. In *Lally* v. *Kensington and Chelsea Royal Borough*,[37] Browne-Wilkinson J. held that this period must be long enough (and what is "long enough" is a question of fact to be determined in the light of the circumstances of the case) for the applicant to find accommodation for himself. In the instant case it was clear that the authority had resolved, as a matter of policy, to grant no more than 14 days in such cases, in temporary accommodation. This was not long

---

[33] See also *R.* v. *Basingstoke and Deane B.C., ex p. Bassett* (1983) 10 H.L.R. 125; *R.* v. *S. Herefordshire D.C., ex p. Miles* (1985) 83 L.G.R. 607.
[34] H.A. 1985, s.65(2).
[35] *Ibid.* s.65(3).
[36] [1980] 1 All E.R. 913.
[37] *The Times*, March 27, 1980; *cf. Dyson* v. *Kerrier D.C.* [1980] 1 W.L.R. 1205.

enough, especially in London where his Lordship felt something between three and four months would be a reasonable time.

EEC Regulation No. 1612/68, Art. 9.1, provides: "A worker who is a national of a member state and who is employed in the territory of another member state shall enjoy all the rights and benefits accorded to national workers in matters of housing." This regulation means that EEC nationals can, within the terms of the regulations, claim the benefit of the Housing Act 1985, Part III. This would probably be the position even without the regulation, since the Divisional Court has held that there is no need for a homeless applicant to establish a local connection with a particular housing authority in Great Britain before the duty to provide accommodation arises.[38] However, being able to "enforce all the rights and benefits ... in matters of housing" also involves suffering all the burdens as well. Accordingly, if an EEC national comes to this country without having ensured that he has permanent accommodation to live in, and having voluntarily given up accommodation in his own country, he will be regarded as intentionally homeless, and the authority will, at most, only be under a duty to provide temporary accommodation or appropriate advice and assistance, as the case may be. Such was the opinion of the Court of Appeal in *De Falco* v. *Crawley Borough Council*.[39] The particular unfairness in that case lies in the fact that the local authority and the court seemed to assume that the applicant had given up accommodation it was reasonable to go on occupying in Italy in order to come to England. The authority did not instigate those inquiries sufficient to "satisfy itself" that this was the case, nor did the court. The Court of Appeal appears to be suggesting that there is a difference in the operation of section 60 depending upon whether the applicant comes from Great Britain or overseas. In the case of the latter, the assumption is that the applicant in effect carries the burden of disproving intentional homelessness. In *R.* v. *Reigate and Banstead B.C., ex p. Paris*,[40] however, the court appeared ready to accept that a finding of intentional homelessness would be bad unless the authority first asked itself whether the accommodation occupied overseas was available for occupation and whether it was reasonable for the applicant to continue to occupy it. To this end, inquiries would need to be instituted, and it is not enough for the local authority to assume intentionality merely from a finding that the applicants had come to the United Kingdom without first arranging suitable secure accommodation here.[41]

---

[38] *R.* v. *Hillingdon London Borough Council ex p. Streeting* [1980] 1 W.L.R. 1430.
[39] [1980] 1 All E.R. 913.
[40] (1984) 17 H.L.R. 103.
[41] See also *R.* v. *L.B. of Wandsworth, ex p. Nimako-Boeteng* (1983) 11 H.L.R. 95.

(8) *Duties of Notification*

Many homeless people never understand why they are turned away by the local authority. Hence, once the local authority have completed their inquiries under the Housing Act 1985, s.62,[42] they are then under a duty to notify the applicant of their decision on the question of whether he is homeless or threatened with homelessness and if they have decided that he is, whether he has priority need, whether they regard him as intentionally homeless and whether they have notified or intend to notify another housing authority of the application (with a view to suggesting a local connection).[43] If the authority has, on any of these matters, reached a conclusion that they are not under a duty to house, then they are obliged to notify the applicant of their reasons for the decision.[44]

If the authority, as a result of their inquiries, notify another authority that they are of the opinion that there is a local connection with the notified authority, and hence that the duty to house the applicant rests on them, the two authorities must then enter into discussions to determine which of them actually incurs the duty. When a decision on this has been reached, the notifying authority must inform the applicant which authority is under the duty to house and why.[45]

These duties to notify are independent of any duties to house under sections 65 and 66 of the Act. That being so, an authority cannot defer providing accommodation for the time being while they consider the question of intentional homelessness or local connection. It is homelessness which gives rise to the permanent or temporary obligation to house, not notification of the decision.[46]

(9) *Enforcement*

(a) Application for judicial review

Applications for judicial review may now be made under the Supreme Court Act 1981, section 31. The court may award any one or more of the prerogative orders of mandamus, certiorari and prohibition, or a declaration or an injunction, in a single proceeding. This is the normal method of seeking the review of a local authority's action or decisions under the homelessness legislation.[47] Should judicial

---

[42] *Supra.*
[43] H.A. 1985, s.64(1)–(4).
[44] *Ibid.* s.64(4). The courts do not always hold local authorities bound by these "reasons" in subsequent proceedings: see *De Falco* v. *Crawley B.C., supra*; *Dyson* v. *Kerrier D.C.* [1980] 1 W.L.R. 1205.
[45] H.A. 1985, s.68(3).
[46] *R.* v. *Beverley Borough Council, ex p. McPhee* (1978) 122 S.J. 760.
[47] *Cocks* v. *Thanet D.C.* [1983] A.C. 268; *O'Reilly* v. *Mackman* [1983] A.C. 237.

review be sought, it is important to spell out in the application exactly which duty the authority is to be required to perform, e.g. to provide permanent housing to the applicant, or to provide housing pending the completion of inquiries about a local connection with another authority's area. There are so many duties specified under the Act that an applicaton seeking judicial review to compel an authority to perform its duties generally under a section or sections of the legislation will not be granted.[48] Also, as Lord Brightman observed in *Puhlhofer* v. *L.B. of Hillingdon*[49]: "Where the existence or non-existence of a fact is left to the judgment and discretion of a public body and that fact involves a broad spectrum ranging from the obvious to the debatable to the just conceivable, it is the duty of the court to leave the decision of that fact to the public body to whom Parliament has entrusted the decision-making power save in a case where it is obvious that the public body, consciously or unconsciously, is acting perversely." Their Lordships expressed the hope that judicial review will not be used to monitor the actions of local authorities under the homelessness legislation save in the exceptional case.

(b) Breach of statutory duty

A far more flexible, speedy and cheap course of action to enforce the local authority's statutory obligations is to commence proceedings for breach of statutory duty. The Court of Appeal accepted that an action for breach of statutory duty might be brought against an authority who failed to perform its obligations under the Housing Act 1985.[50] Lord Denning M.R. observed in *De Falco* v. *Crawley Borough Council*[51] that since the legislation had been passed for the protection of private persons rather than for the benefit of the public at large, an individual injured by an authority's failure to carry out its statutory duties could, at his option, bring an action for damages for breach of statutory duty or commence proceedings for judicial review and secure a declaration and interim relief. The damages awarded should include compensation for distress or physical discomfort[52] as well as any financial loss, such as the cost of hotel or bed and breakfast accommodation.[53]

In *Cocks v. Thanet D.C.*[54] the use of an action for breach of statutory duty in homelessness cases was approved by the House of Lords, subject to completion by the local authority of all its public law functions under the Act. The House of Lords in the *Cocks* case were

[48] *Ibid.*
[49] (1986) 136 New L.J. 140.
[50] *Thornton* v. *Kirklees Metropolitan Borough Council* [1979] 2 All E.R. 349.
[51] [1980] 1 All E.R. 913.
[52] *Constantine* v. *Imperial Hotels* (1915) 1 K.B. 693.
[53] *Lally* v. *Kensington and Chelsea Royal Borough Council, The Times*, March 27, 1980.
[54] [1983] A.C. 286; see also *Lambert* v. *Ealing L.B.C.* [1982] 1 W.L.R. 550. See also Robson, 1985 S.L.T. 305.

only prepared to allow an action for breach of statutory duty once all the relevant decisions which determine the authority's duties had been made and it could be shown that the authority was still not complying with its obligations. Should an applicant wish to challenge a local authority on the ground that it has not made a proper determination as to priority need or intentional homelessness, this can only be done by way of judicial review. It is only where these public law functions have been completed and it is clear that, as a result, an applicant has an entitlement under the legislation which the authority is failing to meet (such as by providing unfit or inconveniently located accommodation) that an action for breach of statutory duty will lie.

A local authority who simply fails to reach a decision on any of the matters upon which a decision is required by the Housing Act 1985, Pt. III, may only be compelled to act by an order of mandamus after application under R.S.C., Order 53. No action for breach of statutory duty will lie in such a case until the local authority has performed all its "public law" duties.

(c) Mandatory injunction

An alternative or additional claim may be for a mandatory injunction to require the authority to comply with its duties. Although a mandatory injunction will not be granted where to do so would require continuous review to ensure compliance, or would require the defendant to do a continuous act requiring the continuous employment of people,[55] the duties under the 1985 Act[56] do not seem to fall within this objection. Certainly an order to house would not impose a continuous obligation since the order need only require the authority to allow the plaintiff into accommodation. Thereafter his occupation could eventually, be protected under Part IV of the Housing Act 1985 and, in the meantime, under the general doctrine of abuse of power.[57]

(d) Interim relief

It might also be possible, in appropriate urgent cases, to apply for an interim injunction. Although the grant of such relief depends upon the "balance of convenience" and it is unusual for a mandatory injunction to be granted on an interlocutory application,[58] in the case of a family who are genuinely and literally homeless, it is likely that the balance of convenience would ordinarily be in favour of requiring the authority to give them at least temporary accommodation.

---

[55] *Att.-Gen.* v. *Colchester Corp.* [1955] 2 Q.B. 207.
[56] Except for the duty to make "appropriate inquiries."
[57] See *Associated Provincial Picture Houses Ltd.* v. *Wednesbury Corp.* [1948] 1 K.B. 223.
[58] *Donmar Productions Ltd.* v. *Bart* [1967] 1 W.L.R. 740.

In *American Cyanamid Co.* v. *Ethicon Ltd.*[59] the House of Lords held that, in interlocutory proceedings, while it was the duty of the court to be satisfied that the claim was not frivolous or vexatious (in other words, that there was a serious issue to be tried), the court should proceed to consider whether the balance of convenience lies in favour of granting or refusing the interlocutory relief sought, without the need for the plaintiff first to make out a prima facie case. The only exception arises where there is material available to the court at the hearing of the interlocutory matter that makes it plain that the plaintiff has no real prospect of succeeding in his claim for a permanent injunction when the matter comes for trial. In *Budget Rent A Car International Inc.* v. *Mamos (Slough) Ltd.*[60] Geoffrey Lane L.J. observed that the principles laid down in the *American Cyanamid Case* apply even where the life of the injunction may be brief and the decision on the application for an interim injunction may influence future proceedings.

In *De Falco* v. *Crawley Borough Council*[61] Lord Denning M.R. distinguished the *American Cyanamid Case* in an application for interlocutory relief under the Housing (Homeless Persons) Act 1977, the forerunner of Part III of the Housing Act 1985, observing that the *American Cyanamid Case* was not the same as homelessness cases, because an applicant for accommodation could not give any worthwhile undertaking in damages. However, this was not a requirement imposed by the House of Lords in the *American Cyanamid Case*. The question the House maintained *should* be asked was whether, if the plaintiff were to succeed at the trial in establishing his right to a permanent injunction, he would be adequately compensated by an award to damages. If so, he should not secure the interim injunction. This clearly does not apply in the case of a family that are homeless at the time of the application. The only mention of an *ability* to pay damages, as opposed to their adequacy, was in the context of the *defendant's* ability to pay which was, if uncertain, a factor *in favour* of granting the injunction. The *applicant's* ability to pay damages is a totally irrelevant factor unless there is a cross-claim against him by the local authority, which there will rarely be in such cases. This case displays confusion between the usual undertaking in damages required for interim relief, and the "balance of convenience" argument used to resolve the policy question of whether the case is a proper one for the grant of an interlocutory injunction. It is likely, in view of the fact that the applicant, if successful on the interlocutory matter, would still be required to pay rent, that this is one of those rare cases where the usual undertaking could be dispensed with since it is difficult to see exactly what damage the authority would need to

[59] [1975] A.C. 396.
[60] [1977] 121 S.J. 734.
[61] [1980] 1 All E.R. 913.

be safeguarded against, except perhaps legal costs (which would again be an irrelevant consideration where the applicant is legally aided).

Nevertheless, Lord Denning M.R. maintained in the *De Falco case* that no interim injunction should be granted against a local authority in disputes arising under the homelessness legislation unless a prima facie case was made out that the local authority's decision not to house was invalid. Interlocutory relief should not be granted unless it was a case where, on an application for judicial review, certiorari would be granted to quash the decision and a mandamus issued.[62]

(e) Practical difficulties

Several cases decided under the legislation tend to support the view that the courts are not always ready to interfere. As Lord Denning M.R. observed in *De Falco* v. *Crawley Borough Council*,[63] throughout the Act, there are words requiring the authority to be "satisfied" or "not satisfied." This means that, in order to mount a successful challenge to an authority's decision it has to be shown that no reasonable authority could possibly have reached the decision it did without misdirecting themselves on the facts or in law in some material respect, or that the authority had acted in bad faith. In *R.* v. *Bristol City Council, ex p. Browne*[64] Lord Widgery C.J. said that the actual language used in the Act in describing an authority's duties and powers meant that:

> "to attack a local authority's exercise of discretion one must normally show that the authority erred in principle, which means either that it took into account a consideration which it should have left out, or left out a consideration of which it should have taken account. Once one can be satisfied that the local authority avoided those dangers, then it is not open to the court to interfere."

The danger of relying on the common law remedies is that the courts may decide, for reasons of policy, to limit the scope of remedies which would normally be available. There is some evidence, although not wholly one-sided, that this is now happening.[65] In *Puhlhofer* v. *Hillingdon London Borough*[66] Lord Brightman urged that "great restraint" should be exercised in questioning decisions of local

---

[62] This somewhat unsound reasoning was followed at first instance by Walton J. in *Miller* v. *Wandsworth London Borough Council, The Times*, March 19, 1980.

[63] [1980] 1 All E.R. 913.

[64] [1979] 3 All E.R. 344 at p. 352. *cf. Lally* v. *Kensington and Chelsea Royal Borough, The Times*, March 27, 1980.

[65] Note the obligation to rehouse under the Land Compensation Act 1973, s.39, and the limits placed upon that obligation by the courts: *R.* v. *Bristol Corp., ex p. Hendy* [1974] 1 W.L.R. 498; see Arden [1980] L.A.G.Bull. 91.

[66] (1986) 136 N.L.J. 140.

authorities in those areas where Parliament had entrusted the decision-making power to a public body.

(f) Maladministration

A failure to perform duties under the 1977 Act, or any other acts of the authority, may amount to maladministration. This can be investigated by the Commission for Local Administration.[67]

---

[67] Hoath (1978) 128 N.L.J. 872.

PART III

BUSINESS TENANCIES

In this Part the following abbreviations are used:

Legislation

A.H.A.	Agricultural Holdings Act
H.A.	Housing Act
L. & T.A.	Landlord and Tenant Act
L.P.A.	Law of Property Act
R.A.	Rent Act
T. & C.P.A.	Town and Country Planning Act

Books

Hill & Redman: *Hill & Redman's Landlord and Tenant* (17th ed.), by M. Barnes, L. Dennis, G. Lockhart-Mummery & J. Gaunt.
Woodfall: *William Woodfall's Landlord and Tenant* (28th ed.), by V. G. Wellings and G. N. Huskinson

CHAPTER 20

THE CONTEXT OF THE BUSINESS TENANCY CODE

I. History and Objectives of Business
    Tenancy Protection 637
II. Tenancies Covered by the Act 640
    A. Tenancy 641
    B. Occupation 642
    C. Business 646
    D. Unlawful Business User 648
III. Exclusions 648
    A. Agricultural Holdings 648
    B. Mining Leases 649

    C. Part-Residential Use 649
    D. Licensed Premises 649
    E. Service Tenancies 650
    F. Tenancies Limited in the Public
       Interest 650
    G. "National Security" Provisions 651
    H. Extended Leases 652
    I. Short Leases 652
    J. Commercial Licences 652
IV. Contracting Out 655

I. History and Objectives of Business Tenancy Protection

Most people are at least aware of, if not familiar with, the code discussed earlier in this book, now contained in the Rent Act 1977, the Protection from Eviction Act 1977, and the Housing Act 1985. That legislation provides a substantial measure of protection to tenants of residential accommodation. Such protection has been on the statute book, in one form or another, since 1915.[1] However, the tenant of a lock-up shop, department store or suite of offices will not be helped by these provisions, even though it is just as important for business tenants to know whether they will be able to continue trading at the same premises as it is for residential tenants to know that their rights of occupation are protected.

Before 1927, which saw the enactment of the first major piece of legislation aimed specifically at business premises, most of the law of landlord and tenant affecting leases of such property was regulated by the common law. Statutory modifications, mainly in the interests of the tenant, had been introduced from time to time. In 1925 the Law of Property Act introduced controls on a landlord's powers to forfeit a lease on account of his tenant's breach of covenant, and also gave the court a discretion to relieve a tenant, who was in breach of his agreement with his landlord, from forfeiture.[2] The Act also permits the court to relieve him from some or all of his obligations to carry out decorative repairs,[3] and these provisions apply to business tenants as to any other. It was, however, the Landlord and Tenant Act 1927, Pt. I, that really marked the first significant statutory intervention in the letting of business premises.

---

[1] Increase of Rent and Mortgage (War Restrictions) Act 1915.
[2] L.P.A. 1925, s.146. See Chap. 6, *supra*.
[3] *Ibid.* s.147. See Chap. 6, *supra*.

The legislation was the result of the deliberations of a Select Committee on Business Premises, which reported at the end of 1920. The Committee felt that tenants of business property were frequently forced to submit to unconscionable increases in rent in order to retain possession. Further, business tenants were often forced to quit at the end of the lease, without any option of retention on fair terms. This hardship and frequently forced change of accommodation, resulting in substantial loss of business goodwill, called for legislative intervention. This did not in fact come for a further seven years.

The Landlord and Tenant Act 1927, Pt. I, enabled tenants, who were required to leave their business premises on the expiration of their leases, to obtain compensation from their landlords for certain improvements they had carried out on the property during their occupancy,[4] provided that the tenant had served notice on his landlord of his intention to make the improvement, and had fulfilled certain other conditions.[5] There were also provisions for limited compensation for loss of goodwill, provided that the tenant proved, to the satisfaction of a tribunal, that either he or his predecessors in title had carried on a trade or business at the premises for a period of not less than five years, whereby goodwill had become attached to the premises, which enabled them to be let at a higher rent.[6]

A business tenant might also claim a new lease if he could prove that he would be entitled to compensation for loss of his goodwill, and that the sum which could be awarded to him as compensation would not be sufficient for the loss of goodwill occasioned by being forced to move to, and carry on business in, other premises.[7] Except in regard to improvements, a tenant carrying on a profession on the premises could not avail himself of the protection of the Act[8] and a landlord might defeat a claim for compensation by offering to renew the tenancy on terms agreed or fixed by the tribunal.[9] A claim for a new lease, or for compensation for loss of goodwill, could also be defeated by the landlord's offer of suitable alternative accommodation.[10] A landlord could oppose a new lease by proving that he required the premises for himself or for a son or daughter over 18, or that he intended to demolish or remodel the premises, or that he intended to re-develop and consequently required vacant possession, or finally that the grant of a new lease would not be consistent with "good estate management."[11] The tribunal was normally the county court judge, with certain powers to remove the proceedings to the High Court.

[4] Landlord and Tenant Act 1927, s.1.
[5] *Ibid.* ss.2, 3.
[6] *Ibid.* s.4.
[7] *Ibid.* s.5.
[8] *Ibid.* s.17.
[9] *Ibid.* ss.2(1), 4(1) proviso (*b*).
[10] *Ibid.* s.6.
[11] *Ibid.* s.5(3).

Provision was made for reference of the proceedings, for the purposes of inquiry and report, to a referee selected from a panel of referees appointed by a Reference Committee consisting of the Lord Chief Justice, the Master of the Rolls, the President of the Law Society and the President of the Institute of Surveyors.[12]

The protection given to business tenants by the 1927 Act was thus somewhat limited. Tenants of less than five years' standing, and professional men occupying office premises, could claim neither compensation for loss of goodwill nor a new lease. Protection took the form, essentially, of compensation rather than protection against eviction, and renewal was available only in special cases. If renewal was obtained, the rent payable by the successful tenant was, in principle, determined by what the landlord could expect to get in the open market. Before any claim for renewal could arise, the tenant had to prove what was called "adherent goodwill." The difficulties of such proof meant that, in practice, business tenants enjoyed little protection, outside the terms of their tenancies, in respect either of security of tenure or rent.

In 1948 the government set up a committee to investigate, *inter alia*, the problems of business tenants. It published two reports[13] which examined, at some length, the deficiencies of the existing statutory scheme, and also made extensive recommendations for reform. This led, in turn, to the Leasehold Property (Temporary Provisions) Act 1951, a purely stop-gap measure having a short life of barely three years—and finally to a government White Paper, published in January 1953.[14] The White Paper introduced proposals for permanent legislation based on the Leasehold Committee's Reports.

As far as business premises were concerned, the White Paper accepted the general proposition of the Leasehold Committee that improved security of tenure should be made available to business tenants, including tenants of premises used for professional purposes. It also endorsed the Committee's view that no attempt should be made to control the rents charged on first lettings of business premises (in sharp contrast to the position with regard to residential tenancies). However, the Committee's recommendations as to the detailed provisions of the new legislation did not receive whole-hearted government support in the White Paper.

The White Paper proposals were based on the view that the landlord of business premises, when an existing tenancy came to an end, should have the right to resume possession himself if he needed the premises for his own business, or for redevelopment. If, however,

[12] *Ibid.* s.21.
[13] Reports of the Leasehold Committee (Uthwatt Committee): Interim Report, Cmd. 7706, 1949; Final Report, Cmd. 7982 (1950).
[14] *Government Policy on Leasehold Property in England and Wales,* Cmd. 8713, 1953.

he did not require the premises for one of those purposes, he was entitled, as landlord, to a fair, current market rent. If the sitting tenant was willing and able to pay that rent, and to enter into other reasonable terms for his continued occupation, then he had a greater right than any alternative tenant to the tenancy on those terms. Unless, therefore, he had been in serious breach of his agreement with his landlord, or was in other ways an unsatisfactory tenant, or had declined an offer of suitable alternative accommodation, or had failed to exercise any reasonable right to renew conferred on him by his existing lease, the sitting tenant ought to be allowed to obtain a new tenancy of the business premises without having to prove "adherent goodwill." In cases of dispute, he should be able to apply, it was proposed, to a tribunal, who would be empowered to fix a reasonable rent on a statutory formula, and also settle the other contentious terms of the tenancy. The proposal was that the tribunal should be the county court, cases being heard by the judge, assisted as necessary by assessors. Cases involving large amounts would be heard in the High Court. The White Paper also contained proposals on compensation provisions.

The Landlord and Tenant Act 1954, based on the White Paper, was a permanent measure which contains, in Pt. II, provisions for renewal by business tenants of tenancies which are about to expire, or which might be terminated by notice to quit; Pt. III contains the statutory controls relating to compensation for improvements and these two Parts remained the main statutory business tenancy code until 1969, when the Law of Property Act, based, in part, upon the work of the Law Commission,[15] enacted some amendments to Part II. The Landlord and Tenant Act 1954, Pts. II and III, as amended, are, therefore, the main sources of reference for the current law specifically relating to leases of business premises, although some of the compensation provisions of the Landlord and Tenant Act 1927, Pt. I, remain in force.[16]

II. Tenancies Covered by the Act

The protection afforded by the statutory measures, it can thus be seen, falls neatly into two main classes—that dealing with security of tenure and that dealing with compensation for displacement. The security of tenure provisions in the Landlord and Tenant Act 1954, Pt. II, apply to business tenants but, although "business" is widely defined, many persons who might ordinarily be regarded as business occupiers cannot benefit from the Act. A tenancy is within the Act if the whole

[15] Law Com. No. 17.
[16] See *post.* Chap. 21.

or part of the premises subject to the tenancy is occupied by the tenant for the purposes of his business or for those and other purposes.[17] There are three essential conditions embodied in this statement. First, there must be a tenancy; secondly, the tenant must occupy at least part of the premises and thirdly, the occupation must be for business purposes.

A. Tenancy

The statement that there must be a tenancy is designed to exclude from the statutory protection arrangements for occupation which are not, technically, leases at all, but simply licence agreements. The differences between leases and licences have been discussed earlier in this book,[18] and the matter is considered further later in this chapter.[19] The Act of 1954 applies to tenancies only and does not cover mere licences.[20] Tenancies at will are also excluded from the legislation.[21] This is so whether the tenancy at will has been created expressly, or by implication, as in the case of the tenant who remains in occupation of the premises after his lease has expired, with the consent of his landlord but paying no rent on a periodic basis. Lord Denning M.R. has explained the exclusion of such tenancies from protection on the ground that they are clearly beyond the contemplation of the legislation.[22] Since contracting out is expressly permitted[23] Lord Denning M.R. assumed that there was no reason of policy why alternative devices of avoidance should not be permitted. This is, perhaps, a false assumption. Under section 38(4) of the 1954 Act the requirement of the court's sanction to make the contracting out effective is the tenant's safeguard against exploitation and is a virtual guarantee of fair treatment. Where avoidance is by the device of a genuine licence, the tenant has no protection at all.

Under-leases and sub-leases are included within the Act, as is an equitable interest under an agreement for a lease.[24] Particular difficulties are created for landlords who wish to exercise control over their premises by forbidding sub-letting. In *D'Silva* v. *Lister House Developments Ltd.*[25] Buckley J. held that even a sub-tenant was protected in circumstances in which the head landlord had refused his

---

[17] L. & T.A. 1954, s.23(1).
[18] *Supra*, Chap. 2. See also Dawson & Pearce, *Licences Relating to the Occupation or Use of Land, passim.*
[19] *Post*, (II) J.
[20] *Shell-Mex and B.P. Ltd.* v. *Manchester Garages Ltd.* [1971] 1 W.L.R. 612.
[21] *Wheeler* v. *Mercer* [1957] A.C. 416; *Manfield & Sons Ltd.* v. *Botchin* [1970] 1 Q.B. 612; *Hagee (London) Ltd.* v. *A.B. Erikson & Larson* [1976] Q.B. 209; *supra*, Chap. 2.
[22] *Hagee (London) Ltd.* v. *A.B. Erikson and Larson* [1976] Q.B. 209 at p. 213.
[23] By s.38 of the 1954 Act, as amended.
[24] L. & T.A. 1954, s.69(1).
[25] [1971] Ch. 17. See also (1956) 20 *Conv.* (N.S.) 99.

licence for sub-letting, as required under the terms of the headlease. The provisions of section 23(4), which prevent the Act from applying where the tenant is in breach of a covenant in the lease as to user,[26] unless the landlord has consented to or acquiesced in it, were held not to cover the point. The sub-tenant is not a party to the lease, containing the restriction on sub-letting and thus is not deprived of protection under the Act by the absence of the appropriate licence from the head landlord.

B. Occupation

The tenant must occupy premises, which may include land with no buildings upon it, such as a field used for car-parking.[27] In *Jones* v. *Christy*[28] Lord Denning M.R. suggested, *obiter*, that tenancies of incorporeal hereditaments were not included. He has since been proved correct by the decision of the Court of Appeal in *Land Reclamation Co. Ltd.* v. *Basildon District Council.*[29] The plaintiffs were landowners granted a lease by the defendant council. Under this lease the plaintiffs were entitled to a right of way over a roadway which formed the sole means of access to their business premises. Before expiry of the term they applied under the 1954 Act for a new tenancy of the right of way. At first instance, Brightman J. held that the right of way was not capable of occupation within the meaning of section 23(1). The Court of Appeal affirmed Brightman J. adding that enjoyment of a right of way did not involve occupation of *premises*, a necessary requirement for the operation of section 23(1). Where corporeal premises are included in the tenancy along with an incorporeal hereditament, such as a right of way, Part II of the 1954 Act will apply.[30]

The occupation by the tenant must be real and genuine and not a mere sham.[31] Occupation through a manager acting on behalf of the tenant is sufficient.[32] Representative occupation is essential where the tenant is a limited liability company. In *Lee-Verhulst (Investments) Ltd.* v. *Harwood Trust*[33] the tenant company had a tenancy of premises comprising a number of fully furnished apartments, each

[26] See *Real & Leasehold Estates Investment Society Ltd.* v. *Medina Shipping Ltd.* (1968) 112 S.J. 862; *Bell* v. *Alfred Franks & Bartlett Co. Ltd.* [1980] 1 All E.R. 356.
[27] See *Bracey* v. *Read* [1963] Ch. 88.
[28] (1963) 107 S.J. 374.
[29] [1979] 2 All E.R. 993.
[30] *Nevil Long & Co. (Boards)* v. *Firmenich & Co.* (1984) 47 P. & C.R. 59.
[31] *Teasdale* v. *Walker* [1958] 1 W.L.R. 1076.
[32] *Cafeteria (Keighley) Ltd.* v. *Harrison* (1956) 168 E.G. 668. Occupation by the employees of a district health authority was treated as occupation by the Secretary of State for Social Services for the purposes of s.23(1) in *Linden* v. *Secretary of State for Social Services*, [1986] 1 All E.R. 69.
[33] [1972] 1 Q.B. 204; *cf. Lewis* v. *Weldcrest Ltd.* [1978] 1 W.L.R. 1107.

separately occupied. The tenants' employees and agents had access to all parts of the building to provide services. The Court of Appeal held that on the facts, including degree of control and extent of services provided, the tenant company occupied the entire premises for the purposes of its business, even though each resident had exclusive occupation of his apartment as a residence for the purposes of the Rent Acts.

This decision was followed in *William Boyer & Sons Ltd.* v. *Adams.*[34] The tenant of business premises occupied part as his residence and sublet the remainder for business use. He personally provided various services (including repair of the central and water heating services) for the sub-tenants. In view of the degree of control and extent of the services provided, the court held that the tenant occupied the premises for the purposes of a business. Templeman J. observed[35] that "the activities of the defendant are sufficient to show that he is not so much acting as a landlord passively receiving rent[36] but as the manager of a business actively earning profits by providing accommodation, facilities and services by devoting time for this purpose."

However, the degree of control or management is crucial in such cases. In *Ross Auto Wash* v. *Herbert*[37] the plaintiff tenant, a company, applied for a new tenancy of a shopping precinct. The landlord contended that the business was carried on by an associated company of the tenant. The plaintiff claimed that the associated company merely managed the premises while the tenant retained possession and control of them and carried on the business of granting licences to stall-holders and providing a variety of services to them. Fox J. held that the tenant did occupy the premises for the purposes of a business carried on by it within the meaning of section 23(1) and was entitled to a new tenancy. It would have been otherwise if the real task of dealing with the stall-holders had been carried out by the associated company.

Occasionally the court will treat someone other than the tenant named in the lease as the occupying tenant, where it is clear that the lease was taken in a representative capacity. In *Town Investments Ltd.* v. *Department of the Environment*[38] premises were let to a Minister "for and on behalf of Her Majesty." The premises were occupied as offices by various government departments, though not by those

---

[34] (1975) 32 P. & C.R. 89.
[35] *Ibid.* p. 93.
[36] Which will not amount to occupation for the purposes of business: *Bagettes* v. *G.P. Estates* [1956] Ch. 290.
[37] (1974) 250 E.G. 971. See also *Christina* v. *Seear* (1985) 275 E.G. 898, where the Court of Appeal held that occupation by a company, in which the tenant had a controlling interest, could not be regarded as occupation for business purposes by the tenant; *cf. Tunstall* v. *Steigman* [1962] 2 Q.B. 593, reversed, so far as occupation by landlords only is concerned, by L.P.A. 1969, s.6; *cf.* L. & T.A. 1954, s.42(1).
[38] [1977] 1 All E.R. 813.

employed in the department of the Minister named in the case. One function of the Minister was to provide accommodation for other Ministries. The question arose, *inter alia*, whether the premises were occupied by the tenant within the terms of legislation identical to the wording of section 23 of the 1954 Act.[39] As a matter of public law the lessee was here the Crown and not the Minister named in the lease and the use of the premises by government servants for government purposes thus constituted occupation of the premises by the Crown.

Where such phrases as "for and on behalf of" are found in leases to tenants other than the Crown, the matter ceases to be one of public law and becomes one of agency or trust.[40] If the legal tenancy is vested in trustees and the persons having the beneficial interest are (and are *entitled* to be[41]) in occupation, then the beneficiaries' occupation and business activities are treated as those of the tenant.[42] Where the tenancy is held jointly by two or more persons, some of whom carry on a business either alone or in partnership with others and some of whom do not, there might be a difficulty in application by all the joint tenants for a new tenancy, since not all the applicants could satisfy the requirements of section 23,[43] and not all might be prepared to co-operate. The Law of Property Act 1969 amended the 1954 Act by inserting a new provision, section 41A, to deal with this eventuality. The section provides that the tenant or joint tenants involved in the business can alone request a new tenancy, can alone be served with notices by the landlord, and recover any compensation payable. The court can order a new tenancy to be granted to the business tenants, or to them jointly with their partners in the business.

Modifications are made by the 1954 Act when the tenants' interest is held by one company within a group of companies. Companies are within the same group when one is a subsidiary of the other or both are subsidiaries of a third.[44] There is a third situation, in which a company will be regarded as being a subsidiary of another, and that is where that other company is itself a subsidiary of the parent company. So, if company A controls company B, which in turn controls company C, company C is a subsidiary of company A. Where one company in the group is the tenant, and another company in the same group occupies or carries on business, the occupation and business are

---

[39] Counter-Inflation (Business Rents) Orders 1972 and 1973. Had the question been whether the tenancy was one to which Part II of the Landlord and Tenant Act 1954 applied there could have been no argument, since s.56(3) of the Act expressly applies Pt. II to such tenancies.

[40] *Town Investments Ltd.* v. *Dept. of the Environment* [1977] 1 All E.R. 813.

[41] *Frish Ltd.* v. *Barclays Bank Ltd.* [1955] 2 Q.B. 541.

[42] L. & T.A. 1954, s.41(1); see *Carshalton Beeches Bowling Club* v. *Cameron* (1979) 249 E.G. 1279.

[43] *Jacobs* v. *Chaudhuri* [1968] 2 Q.B. 470.

[44] For a company to be a subsidiary, the parent company must hold more than half the subsidiary's nominal share capital, or be a shareholder of the subsidiary controlling the composition of its board of directors: Companies Act 1985, s.736.

taken to be that of the tenant for the purposes of the Landlord and Tenant Act 1954, s.23.[45]

When the time comes for the security provisions to operate, the tenant must still be occupying for business purposes some part of the premises originally let.[46] Although sub-letting business premises may itself be business and may not deprive the tenant of his "occupation" for the purposes of the Act,[47] if this results in the tenant sub-letting the *whole* premises, he enjoys no statutory protection, although his sub-tenant may be protected.[48] It is only those parts of the demised premises which the tenant occupies that can be the subject of a new tenancy under the 1954 Act. Thus, if a part of the premises is sub-let, the tenant cannot insist on a new tenancy of that part. A tenant may occupy a part of the demised premises for business purposes, so bringing the tenancy as a whole within the Act, and occupy the remainder residentially. In that case the whole of the premises can be the subject of a new tenancy, even though part is not in business use, since there is no part not occupied by the tenant.[49] In this context, "occupation" imports an element of control and use and thus, in its normal popular meaning, involves the notion of physical occupation.[50]

Although it is necessary for the tenant to occupy premises for the purposes of a business carried on by him, the business does not have to be carried on at the premises. It is sufficient that the tenant occupies for the purposes of a business. There is little authority on the situation where premises are occupied for purposes ancillary to a business, but no actual business activity goes on there, *e.g.* a garage let in which to keep a delivery van. The commonly held view[51] is that such a letting would be within the Act, although some doubt has been thrown on this proposition by the decision of the Court of Appeal in *Chapman* v. *Freeman*.[52] The owner of a small hotel had taken a tenancy of a neighbouring cottage and used it to house hotel staff. When the owner of the cottage died, her administrator served notice to quit on the hotel owner. The tenant claimed that he was a business tenant and was thus entitled to the protection of Part II of the 1954 Act. The landlord conceded that the tenant occupied the cottage through his staff who lived there, but the real question was whether he occupied it for the purpose of the hotel business. The Court of Appeal held that the test in such a case was whether it was necessary for the staff to live there to be able to carry out their duties in relation to the

---

[45] L. & T.A. 1954, s.42(1).
[46] *Ibid.* s.23(1).
[47] *Lee Verhulst (Investments) Ltd.* v. *Harwood Trust* [1972] 1 Q.B. 204.
[48] *D'Silva* v. *Lister House Developments Ltd.* [1971] Ch. 17.
[49] L. & T.A. 1954, s.23(3).
[50] *Hancock & Willis* v. *G.M.S. Syndicate Ltd.*.(1983) 265 E.G. 473.
[51] See, *e.g.* Hill and Redman, p. 711.
[52] [1978] 1 W.L.R. 1298; see also *Bell* v. *Frank & Bartlett Co.* [1980] 1 W.L.R. 340.

business. While it was admittedly convenient for the staff to live in the cottage, it was not necessary, and the court, therefore, was not persuaded that the tenancy was a business tenancy within the Act. It would seem that where premises are occupied for a purpose ancillary to a business, it is essential for the tenant to show, not only that their occupation is convenient for the business, but also necessary for it.[53]

In *Royal Life Saving Society* v. *Page*,[54] Lord Denning M.R. considered this problem in the context of the business tenant who uses his home for business purposes. Clearly the mere fact that a tenant takes office work home in the evenings or at weekends does not turn, through merely incidental business use, a residential letting into a business tenancy. On the other hand, where the business use is part residential, part business, as is the case with a doctor who has his consulting room in his rented house, or a businessman who has his office at home, the business use cannot be considered incidental, and there is a genuine "mixed" business and residential user. The legislation then provides for the letting to be governed by the Landlord and Tenant Act 1954, Part II.[55] It should also be remembered that tenants do not cease to occupy premises for business purposes merely because they are temporarily absent, so that if, for example, the premises are damaged by fire and are unfit for business use, the tenants' business occupation will continue if they intend it to do so.[56] Finally, if the lease restricts user to business purposes and the tenant's business user ceases, the tenancy will not be covered either by the 1954 Act nor (if an unlawful residential user is commenced) the Rent Act 1977.[57] A business tenant using part for residential purposes who then ceases the business use would seem to be outside the protection of both the business and residential codes.[58] If, in a residential tenancy, the tenant commences a substantial business use, Part II of the 1954 Act may then apply.[59]

C. Business

Business is defined to include a trade, profession or employment, and as including any activity carried on by a body of persons, whether corporate or unincorporate.[60] A distinction appears to exist between tenants who are individuals and tenants who are bodies of persons so that, in the latter case an activity carried on by the tenants may be a

---

[53] See also *Hillil Property & Investment Co.* v. *Naraine Pharmacy* (1979) 39 P. & C.R. 67.
[54] [1979] 1 All E.R. 5 at p. 9.
[55] L. & T.A. 1954, s.43(1)(*d*); R.A. 1977, s.24(3).
[56] *Morrison Holdings* v. *Manders Property (Wolverhampton)* [1976] 2 All E.R. 205.
[57] *Pulleng* v. *Curran* (1980) 44 P. & C.R. 58.
[58] See Martin, [1983] Conv. 380.
[59] *Cheryl Investments Ltd.* v. *Saldhana* [1979] 1 All E.R. 5.
[60] L. & T.A. 1954, s.23(2).

business even though it is not a trade, profession or employment. The activities of the governors of a hospital in administering the hospital premises have been held to be a business,[61] as has the activity of a members' tennis club.[62] However, in *Hillil Property and Investment* v. *Naraine Pharmacy*[63] the Court of Appeal suggested that to be an "activity" for this purpose it must be something in some way similar to a trade, profession or employment. It thus excluded, in the instant case, use by the tenant of the premises, at the expiration of the tenancy, for dumping waste materials from other premises which he was reconstructing. However, where the activity is carried on by a single individual, then it must be shown that the activity is a "trade, profession or employment" since, in this context, those three categories are exhaustive.[64] Where the activity may be carried on by the tenant in both a private capacity and as a trade, such as taking in lodgers, it is a question of degree in the light of all the circumstances (*e.g.* the number of lodgers, the size of the establishment, the sort of sums and services involved, etc.) whether the activity amounts to a business within the Act.[65]

The definition of business is widely drawn to include all forms of commercial activity. Lindley L.J. defined a business as embracing "almost anything which is an occupation, as distinguished from a pleasure—anything which is an occupation or a duty which requires attention is a business. . . . "[66] Continuous day to day trading is not essential to occupation for business purposes providing the thread of business user is not broken,[67] although sporadic spare time activity may not amount to business.[68]

[61] *HIlls (Patents) Ltd.* v. *University College Hospital Board of Governors* [1956] 1 Q.B. 90. A flat used by a medical school to house its students has been held to be occupied by the school for the purposes of a business: *Groveside Properties* v. *Westminster Medical School* (1984) 47 P. & C.R. 507.

[62] *Addiscombe Garden Estates Ltd.* v. *Crabbe* [1958] 1 Q.B. 513.

[63] (1979) 39 P. & C.R. 67.

[64] *Lewis* v. *Weldcrest Ltd.* [1978] 3 All E.R. 1226.

[65] *Ibid.*, and see *Cheryl Investments* v. *Saldhana*; *Royal Life Saving Society* v. *Page* [1978] W.L.R. 1329, *supra.*.

[66] *Rolls* v. *Miller* (1884) 27 Ch.D. 71 at p. 88. This definition was given in the context of a covenant in a lease against the carrying on of any trade or business in the demised premises. However, the Court of Appeal disapproved of attributing to the word "business" in the 1954 Act the technical meanings afforded it in the context of covenants against business user. Notwithstanding these reservations, such an approach has found favour with the House of Lords. Lord Diplock cited Lindley L.J.'s words with approval in *Town Investments Ltd.* v. *Department of the Environment* [1977] 1 All E.R. 813. Although the issue in this case was whether premises were occupied for the purposes of a business within the meaning of the Counter-Inflation (Business Rents) Orders 1972 and 1973, the definition of "business" in those Orders was in all respects the same as that in L. & T.A. 1954, s.23(2).

[67] *I. & H. Caplan Ltd.* v. *Caplan (No. 2)* [1963] 2 All E.R. 930.

[68] *Abernethie* v. *Kleinman Ltd.* [1970] 1 Q.B. 10; *Cheryl Investments Ltd.* v. *Saldhana* [1978] 1 W.L.R. 1329.

D. Unlawful Business User

A business carried on in breach of a prohibition in general terms, applying to the whole of the premises let, against use for business, trade, any profession or employment, does not qualify. A business carried on in breach of a stipulation for or against particular trades, businesses, professions or employments does qualify under the Act, as does a business carried on in breach of a general prohibition where there has been either consent or acquiescence on the part of the immediate landlord.[69] "Acquiescence" in this context probably means such a course of conduct by the landlord that his consent to the breach must be inferred.[70] A landlord cannot consent to a business user of premises let for residence when the necessary planning permission for change of use had not been obtained.[71] Acquiescence in a prohibited business user must be that of the tenant's *immediate* landlord, and not that of a predecessor in title of that landlord, before section 23(4) of the 1954 Act will operate.[72]

III. EXCLUSIONS

A. Agricultural Holdings

The 1954 Act does not apply to an agricultural holding,[73] defined as "the aggregate of the agricultural land comprised in a contract of tenancy, not being a contract under which the land is let to the tenant during his continuance in any office, appointment or employment held under the landlord."[74] If there is a tenancy of agricultural land which is not within the protection of the Agricultural Holdings Act 1986 because it is a grazing or mowing letting for less than a year, it also falls outside the protection of the 1954 Act. Similarly a tenancy of less than from year to year approved by the Minister under the Agricultural Holdings Act 1986, s.2(1) (which is outside the security of tenure provisions of that Act) is not protected by the 1954 Act either. A tenancy for a period exceeding one year but less than two years is outside the protection of the 1954 Act because it is a tenancy of an agricultural holding and it is excluded from most of the protection of the 1986 Act because it does not take effect as a tenancy

---

[69] L. & T.A. 1954, s.23(4).
[70] *Real & Leasehold Estates Investment Society Ltd.* v. *Medina Shipping Ltd.* (1968) 112 S.J. 862; *Biggs* v. *Trustees of J.R.S.S.T. Charitable Trust* (1965) 109 S.J. 273.
[71] *Daimar Investment Ltd.* v. *Jones* (1962) 112 L.J. 424.
[72] *Bell* v. *Alfred Frank & Bartlett Co. Ltd.* [1980] 1 All E.R. 356.
[73] L. & T.A. 1954, s.43(1)(a), as amended by A.H.A. 1986, Sched. 14, para. 21.
[74] *Ibid.* s.69(1); Agricultural Holdings Act 1986, s.1; see *post*, Chap. 25.

from year to year under section 2(2) of that Act.[75] However, in one case a term of 18 months was granted as from an anterior date, but the period between the date of the grant and the expiration of the term was less than a year. The tenancy was regarded as converted into a tenancy from year to year.[76]

B. Mining Leases

Tenancies created by mining leases do not carry the right to renew under the Landlord and Tenant Act 1954.[77] A mining lease is one granted for mining or a connected purpose. This is defined by the Landlord and Tenant Act 1927, s.25 as "sinking and searching for, winning, working, getting, making merchantable, smelting or otherwise converting or working for the purposes of any manufacture, carrying away and disposing of mines and material, in or under land, and the erection of buildings, and the execution of engineering and other works suitable for those purposes." A lease for the working of sand and gravel is therefore outside the Act.[78]

C. Part-Residential Use

The provisions in Part II of the 1954 Act can apply to tenancies of premises let for joint business and residential use. This provision affects, in the main, small retail shops with living accommodation over the shop. If a mixed business and residential letting would otherwise qualify as a regulated tenancy,[79] the Rent Act 1977 does not apply to it, but the 1954 Act does.[80] Assured tenancies within the Housing Act 1980, s.56, will, if let for joint business and residential use, fall within Part II of the 1954 Act, subject to certain modifications and exceptions set out in Schedule 5 to the 1980 Act.

D. Licensed Premises

Tenancies of premises with on-licences for the sale of intoxicants are, with certain exceptions, outside the business tenancy code.[81] Premises with only an off-licence are protected. However, tenancies of certain

---

[75] *Gladstone* v. *Bower* [1960] 1 Q.B. 170. See *post*, Chap. 25.
[76] By virtue of A.H.A. 1986, s.2; *Keen* v. *Holland* [1984] 1 W.L.R. 251.
[77] s.43(1)(*b*). This has the same meaning as in L. & T.A. 1954, s.46.
[78] *O'Callaghan* v. *Elliott* [1966] 1 Q.B. 601; *Earl of Lonsdale* v. *Att.-Gen.* (1982) 45 P. & C.R. 1 (oil and gas not minerals).
[79] For a discussion of the meaning of this term see *supra*, Chap. 10, (II)C, (2), f.
[80] Rent Act 1977, s.24(3).
[81] L. & T.A. 1954, s.43(1)(*d*).

on-licensed premises fall within Part II of the 1954 Act where they are both structurally adapted and bona fide used for certain stated purposes. These are: hotels, inns and restaurants[82]; theatres, places of public or private entertainment, public gardens or picture galleries, places for exhibitions and those used for judicial or public administration purposes. In these cases the holding of the licence must be ancillary to the purpose for which the premises are used. Finally within the 1954 Act are railway station refreshment rooms.

E. Service Tenancies

If a tenancy is granted to the tenant as the holder of an office, appointment or employment, which ends or becomes liable to termination when the tenant's service or employment terminates, then that tenancy has no protection under the 1954 Act.[83] This exclusion applies to a tenancy granted after October 1, 1954, only if it is in writing expressing the purpose of the tenancy. In appropriate circumstances the court will institute enquiries to ascertain whether an alleged service agreement of this kind is a sham.[84]

F. Tenancies Limited in the Public Interest

The Landlord and Tenant Act 1954, s.57, provides that the rights of tenants under Part II to new tenancies shall be curtailed in some instances when the landlord's interest or the interest of a superior landlord belongs to certain public bodies. These bodies include government departments, local authorities, development corporations, statutory undertakers and some authorities concerned with the administration of the health service. The Minister of the appropriate government department[85] may certify that it is requisite for the purposes of the body in question that the use or occupation of the whole or part of the property shall be changed by a specified date[86]. The tenant must be notified that the issue of such a certificate is under consideration, and he has 21 days to make written representations, which the Minister must consider before deciding whether to give the certificate.

The general effect of the certificate is that the tenant cannot be granted a new tenancy, under the 1954 Act, to endure beyond the date

---

[82] Provided that the sale of alcohol is not the main aspect of the business: see *Grant* v. *Gresham* (1979) 252 E.G. 66. The matter is one of fact and degree.

[83] *Ibid.* s.43(2).

[84] *Teasdale* v. *Walker* [1958] 1 W.L.R. 1076.

[85] Trade, Environment, Health and Social Security, Agriculture, etc., as the case may be.

[86] For the meaning of this expression see: *R.* v. *Secretary of State for the Environment and Buckinghamshire C.C., ex p. A. G. Powis* [1981] 1 All E.R. 788.

specified in it. The landlord will serve a notice on the tenant terminating the tenancy, and if the date of termination is the same or later than the date specified in the certificate, the tenant cannot apply to the court for a new tenancy. If the date of termination is earlier than the date specified in the certificate, the tenant can apply for a new tenancy, but any tenancy ordered by the court to be granted under the 1954 Act must expire not later than the date given in the certificate. Occasionally a specific statutory provision will exclude security of tenure in the case of premises used for certain business purposes.[87] Since these cases appear to arise in connection with the privatisation or putting out to tender of services or facilities formerly owned or operated by central or local government, the justification for such exemption would appear to be that it lies within the larger public interest.[88]

G. "National Security" Provisions

A tenant of a government department or a statutory undertaker may be occupying premises required for some government use or activity. To allow him to enjoy unfettered security of tenure of those premises under the business code might result in subordination of the public or national interest to the interests of an individual private tenant. Therefore the Landlord and Tenant Act 1954, s.58, contains provisions whereby the rights of tenants under the Act may be limited where the landlord's interest is held by a government department. The Minister in charge of the department may certify that, for reasons of national security, it is necessary that the use and occupation of the property should be discontinued or changed. The landlord can then prevent the tenant from obtaining a new tenancy under the Act.

Subject to certain exceptions which are discussed in the following pages, contracting out of the 1954 Act is not permitted. However, where the landlord's interest is held by a government department, the parties may agree that, on the giving of the Minister's certificate, the landlord may end the tenancy by a notice to quit without the tenant having any security of tenure under the Act.[89] Where the landlord's interest is held by statutory undertakers such as the Gas Corporation or a water authority, an agreement in the same terms as those just mentioned may be validly concluded. In this case the Minister's certificate, which permits the landlord to serve a notice to quit, must state that possession of the whole or a part of the premises is urgently

---

[87] *e.g.* Transport Act 1982, s.14(1).
[88] See *Hansard* H.C. Deb. Vol. 24, cols. 657, 745, 797.
[89] L. & T.A. 1954, s.58(2).

needed for carrying out repairs (on that property or elsewhere) to enable the undertaker to fulfil its statutory responsibilities.[90]

Where the court grants a new tenancy under the 1954 Act, a Minister may certify that the public interest requires the tenancy to include an agreement entitling the landlord to serve a notice to quit (thus taking the tenancy outside the Act) on receipt of a ministerial certificate to the effect that the interests of national security demand the use or occupation of the property be discontinued or changed. If the landlord's interest is held by a government department or by statutory undertakers, the court must, on the landlord's application, order that such an agreement be embodied in the new tenancy.[91]

H. Extended Leases

There is no right to renew an extended tenancy granted under the Leasehold Reform Act 1967, s.16(1).[92] Nor, after the 50-year term granted by that Act expires, can there be renewal under the 1954 Act of any sub-tenancy directly or indirectly derived out of it.

I. Short Leases

There are many cases where a landlord would be willing to let on a temporary basis, and a tenant would be willing to accept such a tenancy, for example, when the landlord has obtained possession and intends to sell, demolish or reconstruct the property, but is not ready to do so immediately. He would, however, be reluctant to grant a temporary letting if he thereby risked having to oppose a tenant's claim for a new tenancy when the time came. He might, therefore, prefer to leave the premises unoccupied—a clear waste of resources. The Landlord and Tenant Act 1954, s.43(3), therefore allows landlords to grant short, temporary tenancies by providing that grants of terms not exceeding six months are outside Part II. To fall within this provision the tenancy must not contain any term allowing for renewal or extension beyond the initial six months' period, nor must the tenant have been in occupation for more than 12 months (counting any period of occupation by a predecessor in the business).

J. Commercial Licences

As stated earlier in this chapter, the 1954 Act applies only to leases

---

[90] *Ibid.* s.58(3).
[91] *Ibid.* s.58(4).
[92] *Supra*, Chap. 15. See Leasehold Reform Act 1967, s.16(1)(c), (d).

and not to licences. For landlords wishing to avoid the protective provisions of the legislation, therefore, the licence is the obvious device. Sometimes, indeed, the very nature of the premises, or the tenant's business, would make it extremely inconvenient were it not possible for the landowner to grant occupation rights outside the protection of the business tenancy code. A person occupying a kiosk in an hotel foyer, or a charity occupying a shop in the high street "between tenants," may well have been unable to secure premises at all if the landlord were only able to grant business leases within the 1954 Act. Owners of property used for hypermarkets housing different trading units may often find it convenient to create licences in favour of different commercial organisations occupying the trading floor, giving them limited trading rights in defined areas but no security of tenure.

The decision of the House of Lords in *Street* v. *Mountford*[93] has created considerable uncertainty in this area of the law. This decision has been discussed in detail earlier in Chapter 2, but it will be recalled that the House of Lords decided that, save in exceptional "special category" cases, such as service tenancies, lodging contracts, certain vendor and purchaser relationships or relationships based on friendship or charity, the grant of exclusive possession for a fixed or periodic term in consideration of periodic payments will create a tenancy. No exception was made by Lord Templeman, who delivered the only reasoned speech, for occupation arrangements for the purposes of business. Indeed, some of the authorities cited by his lordship in formulating his general proposition were cases on business licences.[94] It would seem, therefore, that notwithstanding the fact that *Street* v. *Mountford*[95] was a Rent Act case, the general nature of the House of Lords' discussion of the relevant principles does not, as things stand at present, appear to admit of any exception based upon the fact that the premises in question are for the purposes of business rather than residence. The only relevant enquiry, therefore, is whether the parties intended by contract to grant and accept exclusive possession for a term at a rent (whether or not so described). If exclusive possession is, in fact, enjoyed by the occupier under the arrangement, the law will determine the nature of the interest created, and the parties' expression of intention as to the interest they wished to create would seem to be entirely irrelevant, however unambiguously that intention is expressed.[96] Indeed, Lord Templeman, in considering *Shell-Mex & B.P. Ltd.* v. *Manchester Garages*[97] expresses

---

[93] [1985] 2 All E.R. 289.
[94] *Glenwood Lumber Co.* v. *Phillips* [1904] A.C. 405; *Addiscombe Garden Estates* v. *Crabbe* [1958] 1 Q.B. 513; *Isaac* v. *Hotel de Paris Ltd.* [1960] 1 W.L.R. 239; *Shell-Mex & B.P. Ltd.* v. *Manchester Garages Ltd.* [1971] 1 W.L.R. 612.
[95] *Supra.*
[96] [1985] 2 All E.R. 289 at pp. 294–295.
[97] [1971] 1 W.L.R. 612.

the view[98] that the agreement in that case was only a licence creating a personal privilege "if [it] did not confer the right to exclusive possession of the filling station. No other test for distinguishing between a contractual tenancy and a contractual licence appears to be understandable or workable." It would seem, therefore, that all those other factors so carefully enunciated by the Court of Appeal as relevant to the lease/licence distinction in the *Shell-Mex* case, such as the personal nature of the solus agreement promoting the plaintiffs' products, the control given by the agreement to the plaintiffs to organise the defendants' forecourt displays etc., are now of no significance.

In view of the current uncertainty in the law relating to business licences, it is probably now unwise for an owner of business premises to rely upon a commercial licence in an endeavour to avoid the Act. Clearly some arrangements will survive as licences, simply because the occupier does not obtain, in fact or law, exclusive possession. Lord Templeman, in *Street* v. *Mountford*,[99] was clearly of the view that this was the case in *Shell-Mex & B.P. Ltd.* v. *Manchester Garages*,[1] and it would also probably be so in the case of a kiosk in an hotel foyer, a stall in a hypermarket, a "shop within a shop" such as is now common in large department stores, and similar arrangements. However, where exclusive possession is given, in fact or law, of any premises, it would seem, until further consideration is given to the matter by the courts in a business rather than a residential context, that the arrangement will be construed, regardless of the parties' intentions, as a lease not a licence and thus, assuming all other conditions are satisfied, will fall within the Landlord and Tenant Act 1954, Part II. Indeed, in the only reported case subsequent to *Street* v. *Mountford*[2] in which the principles of that case have been considered in a business context, Leonard J. held that the determining feature in what purported to be "licences" granted by the plaintiffs to the defendants to use racehorse gallops over an area which included scrubland of use neither to the plaintiffs' farming activities nor to the defendants' horse training business, was whether or not the defendants had exclusive possession of the gallops and scrubland. The learned judge decided that exclusive possession was enjoyed and thus the arrangement created a tenancy.[3]

If the granting landowner is a limited liability company lacking the legal capacity to grant leases, the chances of a business occupation agreement being construed as a licence rather than a lease are that much stronger. This can be achieved by incorporating a clause in the

---

[98] [1985] 2 All E.R. 289 at p. 298.
[99] *Ibid.*
[1] *Supra.*
[2] *Supra.*
[3] *University of Reading* v. *Johnson-Houghton* (1985) 276 E.G. 1353; *cf. Bracey* v. *Read* [1963] Ch. 88.

company's memorandum of association (which clause is also recited in the licence agreement itself to avoid the difficulties created by the Companies Act 1985, s.35), expressly restricting its powers over land (save for its power of sale) to creation of licences and sub-licences over land. The ramifications of such a device are discussed in detail earlier in this book.[4]

IV. CONTRACTING OUT

Any agreement relating to a tenancy to which Part II of the 1954 Act applies (unless the court sanctions it under subsection (4)) is void under the Landlord and Tenant Act 1954, s.38(1), in so far as it precludes the tenant from making an application or request for a new tenancy. This is so whether that "contracting out" agreement is contained in the lease itself or in some other document. Any attempt to get round this provision by imposing some penalty or disability on the tenant if he makes such an application or request, or by providing for the termination or surrender of the tenancy if he does so, is also void. This prohibition is absolute and applies to every tenancy which comes within Part II. The court may, however, sanction such agreements to exclude the Act's protection, under section 38(4), provided that the application for the court's authorisation is made jointly by landlord and tenant. If the contracting-out takes the form of an exclusion of the protective provisions of the 1954 Act, then the court's approval is required before the lease takes effect. If the contracting-out takes the form of an agreement by the tenant to surrender his tenancy at some future date,[5] then approval must be given before the surrender takes effect.[6] For the contracting-out provision to be effective, even with the court's approval, it must either be contained in or indorsed on the instrument creating the tenancy or such other instrument as the court may specify.

Section 38(1) clearly renders void any agreement between the landlord and tenant whereby the tenant undertakes to perform a future act, such as surrender the tenancy,[7] whether the undertaking is enforceable at law or in equity,[8] or to pay the landlord's expenses on an application for a new tenancy,[9] which has the effect of disqualifying him from applying for a new lease. Section 38(1) has also been

---

[4] *Supra*, Chap. 2, *cf.* Pettit [1980] Conv. 112.

[5] A tenancy terminated by surrender is not entitled to protection under the 1954 Act: see *post*, Chap. 22.

[6] This must be the effect of the use of the future tense in L. & T.A. 1954, s.38(4)(*a*)—"on the joint application of the persons *who will be the landlord and the tenant* . . . "—as opposed to the present tense in L.T.A. 1954, s.38(4)(*b*)—"on the joint application of the persons *who are the landlord and the tenant* . . . "

[7] *Joseph* v. *Joseph* [1967] Ch. 78.

[8] *Tarjomani* v. *Panther Securities Ltd.* (1983) 46 P. & C.R. 32.

[9] *Stevenson & Rush (Holdings) Ltd.* v. *Langdon* (1979) 38 P. & C.R. 208.

held to vitiate an acceptance of an offer to surrender back the lease of business premises in an assignment clause. In *Allnatt London Properties* v. *Newton*[10] the Court of Appeal held that part of a covenant against assignment requiring the tenant to make an offer to surrender the lease as a condition precedent to obtaining the right to assign was void under s.38(1). However, there might be some difficulty in the case of an agreement under which a prospective tenant undertook to give the landlord a notice, under section 27 of the Act,[11] indicating that he did not wish to apply for a new tenancy. If this notice was given to the landlord in blank, *before the tenancy was granted*, then it might not necessarily be invalid under section 38(1) because the relationship of landlord and tenant cannot come into existence before the tenancy comes into effect. To avoid this difficulty it is provided that such notices given by tenants or prospective tenants are ineffective if given before they have been in occupation under the tenancy for one month.[12] This raises the wider question of what might be called inducements to the tenant to give up possession before the tenancy would have been validly terminated, for instance by means of punitive rent escalation clauses. The line between agreements of this nature and genuine agreements to fix periodic rent increases is difficult to draw and for that reason resort is sometimes had to devices[13] which, in effect, create short lettings of less than six months' duration which are, as has already been explained, outside Part II of the 1954 Act. It would seem to be no longer necessary for landlords to resort to such involved, untested and possibly unreliable devices now that the courts' approval can be sought to a straightforward contracting-out.[14] Lord Denning M.R. has intimated that, provided both landlord and tenant are in receipt of proper legal advice, a court would hardly ever refuse to grant the necessary authorisation sought on a joint application under section 38(4).[15]

---

[10] (1983) 45 P. & C.R. 94. Megarry V.-C., at first instance, had held that the tenant was not entitled to a declaration that he could assign without making such an offer: (1980) 41 P. & C.R. 11.
[11] *Post*, Chap. 22.
[12] L. & T.A. 1954, ss.24(1), 27.
[13] See Woodfall (27th ed.), Vol. 2, para. 2544; Aldridge, *Letting Business Premises* (4th ed.), p. 74.
[14] L. & T.A. 1954, s.38(4) was inserted by L.P.A. 1969, s.5.
[15] *Hagee (London) Ltd.* v. *A. B. Erikson & Larson* [1976] Q.B. 209 at p. 212.

CHAPTER 21

CREATION AND MANAGEMENT OF THE BUSINESS TENANCY

I. Creation 657
  A. Terms as to User 658

II. Management 659
  A. Assigning and Sub-letting . . . 660
  B. Improvements 662

I. CREATION

The same problems arise in relation to the creation of a business tenancy as those in relation to the creation of any other tenancy. They are discussed in detail in Chapter 3 and it is not proposed to go over the same ground again here. Both prospective landlord and prospective tenant will need to be satisfied that the terms as to rent and rent reviews properly reflect their agreement,[1] that the terms as to repairs are fair and reasonable in the light of the rent payable,[2] that any limitations on the tenant's ability to assign or sub-let are not unduly restrictive in the light of his business requirements[3] (and the landlord will wish to ensure that any tenant or sub-tenant likely to use the premises will be able to meet his rental payments and, in other respects, be a "satisfactory" tenant), that any premiums payable on the grant or assignment of the tenancy are reasonable in relation to the rent and will not involve any onerous tax liability,[4] and that the premises are, in all other respects, suitable for the business to be carried on there by the tenant. In addition to normal legal advice, therefore, that the parties always seek before entering into the relationship of landlord and tenant, they are quite likely to consult a surveyor. The parties will be interested in his views on the rent, the amount of any premium, the likely amount of a rent increase brought about by any future rent review, and the state and general condition of the premises. The surveyor will draw up a schedule of dilapidations, agreed by both parties, before the lease commences. This will avoid the need, given a suitably worded covenant for repair, for the tenant to carry out repairs not attributable to his period of occupation.[5] Certain aspects of the transaction, however, will require special consideration by virtue of the fact that the premises are to be put to business use.

[1] *Supra*, Chap. 5.
[2] *Supra*, Chap. 6.
[3] *Supra*, Chap. 7.
[4] *Supra*, Chap. 5.
[5] *Supra*, Chap. 6.

657

A. Terms as to User[6]

It is usual for leases of business premises to contain terms restricting the use to which the premises are put. If there is no restriction, the tenant may make whatever use of the premises he chooses, so long as he complies with the provisions of the law, such as obtaining the necessary planning consents, licences and so on.[7] Restrictions as to user in business leases normally take one of four forms: limitation of the use of the premises to one or more specific uses[8]; restrictions against carrying on specified businesses, leaving the tenant free to choose between the remainder[9]; prohibitions against certain classes of trade, defined in such terms as "offensive, noxious and dangerous"[10]; prohibitions in general terms of any action on the property causing a nuisance or annoyance, which could, of course, involve the prohibition of certain businesses of a noisy or malodorous kind.[11]

The tenant will also be affected by some restrictions which are not necessarily mentioned in the lease. He will be bound by any enforceable restrictive covenants affecting the freehold of which he has, or is deemed to have notice[12]; and he is also bound by covenants in any head lease which extend to use by a sub-tenant, even though he does not know of them.[13] He will also be bound by the general provisions of the law affecting user, including the prohibition on immoral user and the Town and Country Planning Acts.

In addition to the frequent need to obtain the landlord's consent to a change of user,[14] planning permission is required for the making of any material change in the use of buildings or land,[15] and to abandon an authorised use and do nothing with the property is a material change of use.[16] Since planning controls are enforced against the occupier of premises, they are clearly the concern of tenants as well as landlords. Many leases contain a tenant's covenant to comply with the planning legislation,[17] so adding to the statutory enforcement proce-

---

[6] For a more detailed consideration of this topic see *supra*, Chap. 4.

[7] *Yelloly* v. *Morley* (1910) 27 T.L.R. 20.

[8] *e.g.* "not to use the premises otherwise than for . . . " This negative form of words may create a positive obligation to carry on that particular business: *Wadham* v. *Postmaster-General* (1871) L.R. 6 Q.B. 644. The covenant in this form is not, in itself, a warranty by the landlord that the tenant is entitled to carry out the particular business specified: *Hill* v. *Harris* [1965] 2 Q.B. 601.

[9] These are often inserted to restrict competition: see Chap. 24, *post*, and *Rother* v. *Colchester Corporation* [1969] 1 W.L.R. 720.

[10] See, *e.g. Nussey* v. *Provincial Bill Posting Co. and Eddison* [1909] 1 Ch. 734, *per* Cozens-Hardy M.R. at p. 739.

[11] *e.g.* fish frying: *Duke of Devonshire* v. *Brookshaw* (1899) 81 L.T. 83; music from a restaurant: *Hampstead & Suburban Properties Ltd.* v. *Diomedous* [1969] 1 Ch. 248.

[12] See *Cleveland Petroleum Co. Ltd.* v. *Dartstone Ltd.* [1969] 1 W.L.R. 116.

[13] *Hill* v. *Harris* [1965] 2 Q.B. 601.

[14] *Supra*, Chap. 4, and see *Guardian Assurance Co. Ltd.* v. *Gants Hill Holdings Ltd.* (1983) 267 E.G. 678; *Anglia Building Society* v. *Sheffield City Council* (1983) 266 E.G. 311.

[15] T. & C.P.A. 1971, s.22(1).

[16] *Hartley* v. *Minister of Housing and Local Government* [1969] 2 Q.B. 46.

[17] *Supra*, Chap. 4.

dures the sanction of forfeiture of the lease.[18] There may also be a covenant not to carry out any development. This offers the landlord the additional advantage of being able to prevent the premises from losing an authorised use he considers valuable, even though the tenant obtains planning permission for a change of use. Another safeguard landlords may want is an indemnity against expenditure required by a planning consent obtained by the tenant, but which is not incurred until after the lease is terminated. For example, a tenant with a seven-year term of a grocery shop may obtain permission to change the use to enable him to sell fresh meat, and carry out ancillary works of opening up the shop front, for the period of 10 years, subject to the condition that the premises are reinstated at the end of that period. Without some financial safeguard, this would give the tenant the right to carry out his chosen use, leaving the landlord with the obligation to reinstate.

Many trades and businesses require a licence,[19] or registration of the premises,[20] before the appropriate activity can be carried on. This is normally the tenant's concern, but in some cases, where the licence or registration is transferable (as opposed to those cases where each new tenant must make a separate application), the tenant must ensure that the appropriate licence, or the benefit of any registration, is transferred to him. The landlord may also have an interest in ensuring compliance with any statutory licensing requirements. If the premises are structurally adapted for, or planning consent is restricted to, use for a particular trade or business, the loss of the licence authorising the business activity to be carried on there could depreciate the value of the landlord's interest in the property. Hence, leases of such premises frequently contain a tenant's covenant to obtain, maintain and renew as necessary the licence or registration, and to do nothing to prejudice its continuance, transfer or future grant to any other person.

II. MANAGEMENT

The day to day management of the premises is, largely, a matter for the tenant. However, two matters deserve special mention.

---

[18] *Supra*, Chap. 6.
[19] *e.g.* premises used for the storage and sale of petrol, intoxicants, game, gunpowder and upholstery materials. For a complete list see Aldridge, *Letting Business Premises* (4th ed.), pp. 20–24.
[20] *e.g.* late night refreshment houses, premises used for the selling of ice cream, sausages and prepared foods, premises used for the dealing in scrap metal: see Aldridge, *op. cit.*

A. Assignment and Sub-letting

The general law governing the assignment and sub-letting of leasehold property has been discussed earlier in this book in Chapter 7. Unless otherwise provided in the lease, a tenant may assign or sub-let. A covenant is, therefore, frequently inserted in leases of business premises, prohibiting assignment or sub-letting, to prevent the lease coming into the hands of an undesirable tenant. Such covenants are of two types. First, the covenant might be absolute, in which case the tenant cannot assign or sub-let unless the landlord waives the benefit of the covenant. This he may refuse to do and his decision, however unreasonable, is in this case binding on the tenant.[21] However, the covenant may be of the second type, in that it is qualified, providing that assignment and sub-letting are forbidden only when carried out without the landlord's consent. Such covenants are, except in the case of agricultural holdings,[22] subject by statute, despite any agreement to the contrary, to the proviso that the landlord's consent is not to be unreasonably withheld.[23] The result is that, if a landlord unreasonably refuses consent, the tenant commits no breach of covenant if he assigns or sub-lets. If, however, he does so without first *asking* for consent, then he commits a breach, no matter how unreasonable it would have been for the landlord to refuse.[24]

The onus is always on the tenant, when challenged by the landlord, to show that withholding of consent was unreasonable. In most cases no objection will be reasonable unless based on the person of the assignee or sub-tenant (*e.g.* his lack of credit worthiness) or the proposed use of the premises.[25] It is unreasonable for the landlord to refuse consent for a collateral purpose wholly unconnected with the lease, such as that he wishes to obtain a surrender or a merger of the tenant's lease for reasons of good estate management of other parts of the property together with that part let to the tenant seeking to assign. The reason for refusal of consent, therefore, must be confined to the proper management of the part of the property leased to the tenant actually requesting consent.[26] Moreover, statute provides that it is unlawful, and thus clearly makes it unreasonable, to withhold consent

---

[21] Assignment necessarily involves parting with possession, so that if the covenant prohibits parting with possession but does not mention assignment, it will, nevertheless be taken as impliedly prohibiting assignments: *Marks* v. *Warren* [1979] 1 All E.R. 29.

[22] *Post*, Chap. 29.

[23] L. & T.A. 1927, s.19. See *Adler* v. *Upper Grosvenor Street Investments Ltd.* [1975] 1 All E.R. 229; *Bocardo S.A.* v. *S. & M. Hotels Ltd.* [1980] 1 W.L.R. 17; see also Adams (1979) 252 E.G. 897.

[24] *Eastern Telegraph Co.* v. *Dent* [1899] 1 Q.B. 835.

[25] For a detailed consideration of the circumstances when consent will be regarded as unreasonably withheld by the landlord see *supra*, Chap. 7(II)C.

[26] *Bromley Park Garden Estates Ltd.* v. *Moss* [1982] 1 W.L.R. 1019; see Wilkinson (1982) 132 N.L.J. 658; *International Drilling Fluids Ltd.* v. *Louisville Investments (Uxbridge) Ltd.* [1986] 1 All E.R. 321.

on the grounds of race[27] or sex.[28] Unless the lease provides for it, in most cases the landlord may not require the payment of a premium or other valuable consideration for giving his consent.[29]

There is no legal requirement that the landlord's consent be in writing, although leases nearly always provide for this.[30] Frequently, leases of business premises impose on the assignor a requirement that he secure that the proposed assignee, and sometimes the proposed sub-tenant, join in a deed of licence to covenant directly with the landlord, or head landlord, to observe the terms of the lease. These covenants will extend to the whole of the unexpired term of the lease, so that the assignee cannot escape liability subsequently by a further assignment which would terminate his privity of estate with the landlord. This device serves the landlord as additional security for the performance of the tenant's covenants.[31]

It is by no means clear that such a device would always be upheld. The courts have decided that insistence upon it by a landlord in the case of a sub-letting, at least where the sub-letting is at a loss which can be justified by the mesne landlord, amounts to the unreasonable refusal of consent.[32] In the case of an assignment it has been argued, unsuccessfully, that such an assignee's covenant constitutes an unlawful premium, contrary to the proviso implied by the Law of Property Act 1925, s.144.[33] Whether it is reasonable, in the case of an assignment, to demand a direct covenant from the assignee must, therefore, be regarded as still open to debate.[34] Licences to assign commonly state expressly that they relate only to the one occasion to which they refer, and that the prohibition in the lease remains otherwise in full force and effect.[35]

It is for the assignor or sub-lessor to obtain any licence that the lease requires for the contemplated dealing,[36] although he is not bound to institute proceedings to obtain it.[37] In a contract subject to the Law Society's Conditions of Sale (1984 revision) the assignor is required forthwith, at his own cost, to apply for and endeavour to obtain the licence, when necessary.[38] The assignee must supply such information and references as may reasonably be required by the landlord. If no licence is granted at least five working days before the contractual

[27] Race Relations Act 1976, s.24.
[28] Sex Discrimination Act 1975, s.31.
[29] L.P.A. 1925, s.144.
[30] A landlord who is aware of a breach of this covenant will be taken to have waived the requirement if he does not object. Knowledge through an agent or employee is enough: *Metropolitan Properties Co. Ltd.* v. *Cordery* (1979) 251 E.G. 567.
[31] See also the observations *supra*, Chap. 5(III)C.
[32] *Balfour* v. *Kensington Gardens Mansions Ltd.* (1932) 49 T.L.R. 29.
[33] *Waite* v. *Jennings* [1906] 2 K.B. 11.
[34] *Balfour* v. *Kensington Gardens Mansions Ltd.* (1932) 49 T.L.R. 29, *per* Macnaughten J. at p. 31.
[35] This seems to be unnecessary: see L.P.A. 1925, s.143.
[36] *Davis* v. *Nisbet* (1861) 10 C.B.(N.S.) 752.
[37] *Lehmann* v. *McArthur* (1868) L.R. 3, Ch.App. 496.
[38] Condition 8(4).

completion date, or is subject to conditions to which the assignee reasonably objects, either party may rescind the contract. In that case, the assignor must repay the deposit and any money paid on account of the purchase price.[39] A contract to which the National Conditions of Sale (20th ed.) apply also requires the assignor to use his best endeavours to obtain the licence and pay the fee for it.[40] The assignee agrees to supply any information and references reasonably required of him. The assignment is subject to the licence being obtained, and if it cannot be, the assignor can terminate.[41] The deposit is then repayable, but without interest, costs or other compensation or payment.[42] The assignor is under no obligation to allow the assignee to approach a reluctant landlord directly.[43]

B. Improvements

Leases of business premises usually contain a covenant by the tenant not to make alterations to the premises, which is an absolute prohibition, or not to make alterations without the landlord's consent, which is a qualified prohibition. In the absence of such a restriction, and subject to any other relevant term in the lease, *e.g.* a repairing covenant,[44] the tenant is free to do what he pleases to the premises, subject only to the law of waste.[45] If the covenant is qualified, the landlord is not entitled unreasonably to withhold his consent to improvements.[46] Improvements must be distinguished from alterations. The complex body of law governing the distinction between repairs, improvements and renewal has been discussed earlier in this book.[47] It will be recalled that improvements are considered from the tenant's point of view, not the landlord's, in considering whether consent has been unreasonably withheld.[48] The improvements need not increase the value of the premises and, indeed, they may even have the reverse effect.[49] However, the works must, if they constitute alteration to the premises, be such as to confer a positive benefit to the tenant as occupier.[50]

Unlike the similar case of consent to assignment or sub-letting, the

---

[39] Condition 16(2), which also deals with interest.
[40] Condition 11(5).
[41] Under the terms of the lease: *Bickel* v. *Courtenay Investments (Nominees) Ltd.* [1984] 1 All E.R. 657.
[42] Conditions 11(5), 10(2).
[43] *Lipmans Wallpaper Ltd.* v. *Mason & Hodghton Ltd.* [1969] 1 Ch. 20.
[44] *Supra*, Chap. 6.
[45] *Ibid.*
[46] L. & T.A. 1927, s.19(1).
[47] *Supra*, Chap. 6.
[48] *Lambert* v. *Woolworth & Co. (No. 2)* [1938] Ch. 883; *supra*, Chap. 4.
[49] *Ibid.*
[50] *Woolworth & Co.* v. *Lambert* [1937] Ch. 37.

landlord is entitled to impose certain conditions on giving consent. He may require payment of a reasonable sum in respect of damage to or diminution of the value of the premises leased or any neighbouring premises owned by him. If an improvement would not add to the letting value of the premises, he may impose a condition that they be reinstated, where that would be reasonable. He may also require payment of legal and other expenses in connection with the grant of his consent.[51] The statutory proviso that consent shall not be unreasonably withheld cannot be excluded by agreement.[52]

The Landlord and Tenant Act 1927 contains provisions enabling a tenant of business premises to claim compensation for improvements, and these provisions also allow the tenant to apply to the court for authority to carry out the work, even where the lease contains an absolute prohibition. This machinery is discussed below.

(1) *Compensation for Improvements*

A tenant who is forced to leave his business premises because his tenancy has come to an end, may well have carried out, with his landlord's consent, certain improvements to the property which have enhanced its letting value. It would be quite unfair if the value of these improvements enured solely for the benefit of the landlord, and hence statutory provisions allow a tenant, on quitting the holding, the right to be paid compensation in respect of any permitted improvement (including the construction of any building) carried out on the holding, either by him or by his predecessors in title. There are, however, certain conditions that the tenant must fulfil, and he cannot recover compensation in respect of trade or other fixtures which, by law, he is entitled to remove.[53] The relevant statutory provisions are to be found in the Landlord and Tenant Act 1927, Pt. I, as modified by the Landlord and Tenant Act 1954, Pt. III.

(2) *Tenancies Within the Compensation Provisions*

Part I of the 1927 Act applies to holdings as defined *in that* Act (*not* the 1954 Act) and it is a tenant of a holding to which Part I applies who is entitled to the compensation. These holdings are defined in the Landlord and Tenant Act 1927, s.17, as any premises held under a lease and used wholly or partly for carrying on upon them any trade or business. Trade or business is not defined in the 1927 Act. The expression embraces a very wide range of activities. "Business"

[51] L & T.A. 1927, s.19(2).
[52] *Ibid.*
[53] *Supra*, Chap. 4.

carries with it a connotation of commercial activity with a view to gain or profit,[53a] trade does not necessarily carry that implication.[54] In the case of a trade, it is not necessary that a profit should be made or desired. Where a company was carrying on a college, the income and property of which were to be held and applied solely for its object, and no profits were to be distributed, it was held that though the college was a charity it was carrying on a trade or business,[54a] and even a guest home, run on non profit-making lines, for elderly ladies, has been treated as a trade.[55] It is expressly provided that premises regularly used for carrying on a profession are deemed to be premises used for carrying on a trade or business, for the purposes of the compensation provisions only.[55a]

While in general terms it can be said that both Part I of the 1927 Act and Part II of the 1954 Act apply to business tenancies, there is in the language of the Acts a difference between the holdings to which Part I of the 1927 Act applies and the tenancies to which Part II of the 1954 Act applies. The essential requirements for the application of the 1927 Act's provisions are first, that there must be a letting of the premises (which includes a sub-letting or an agreement for a letting[56]) and, secondly, that a trade, business or profession must be carried on at the whole or a part of the premises let. Where the premises are used partly for other purposes, the right to compensation is limited to improvements in relation to the trade or business.[57]

The difference in language between the two Acts creates some problems. It will be recalled that tenants of certain on-licensed premises are not entitled to new tenancies under the 1954 Act,[58] yet they are able to claim compensation for improvements under the 1927 Act. On the one hand, there are some exclusions from the compensation provisions of the 1927 legislation. Premises let under a mining lease are excluded, as are agricultural holdings.[59] Nor do the provisions for compensation apply to a holding let to a tenant as the holder of any office, appointment or employment from the landlord, which continues for as long as the tenant holds that position. In the case of tenancies created after March 24, 1928 (the commencement date of the 1927 Act), this last exclusion applies only if the tenancy is in writing and expresses the purpose for which it was created.[60] It is

---

[53a] *Smith* v. *Anderson* (1880) 15 Ch.D. 247.
[54] *Re Incorporated Council of Law Reporting for England and Wales* (1888) 22 Q.B.D. 279.
[54a] *Brighton College* v. *Marriott* [1925] 1 K.B. 312; [1926] A.C. 192.
[55] *Ireland* v. *Taylor* [1949] 1 K.B. 300.
[55a] L. & T.A. 1927, s.17(3). As to the meaning of "profession" see *Currie* v. *I.R.C.* [1921] 2 K.B. 332, *per* Scrutton L.J. at p. 341; *I.R.C.* v. *Maxse* [1919] 1 K.B. 647; *Carr* v. *I.R.C.* [1944] 2 All E.R. 163, *per* du Parcq L.J. at pp. 166, 167; *Stuchberry* v. *General Accident Assurance Corp.* [1949] 2 K.B. 256.
[56] L. & T.A. 1927, s.25(1).
[57] *Ibid.* s.17(4).
[58] L. & T.A. 1954, s.43(1)(d).
[59] L. & T.A. 1927, s.17(1).
[60] *Ibid.* s.17(2).

likely to be an extremely loyal (and long-lived) employee who would be thus debarred from claiming compensation in respect of a tenancy created before the Act came into force!

(3) *The Right to Compensation*

The basic principle is that a tenant of a holding to which Part I of the 1927 Act applies is entitled, on leaving at the end of the tenancy, to compensation from his landlord for any improvement (including the erection of any building) on the holding made by him or his predecessors in title.[61] His predecessors in title will include any person through whom he has obtained the tenancy by assignment, will, intestacy or operation of law.[62] In order to attract compensation the improvements must add to the letting value of the holding at the end of the tenancy, and it must not be a trade or other fixture which the tenant is, by law, entitled to remove.[63]

A tenant of business premises, during or at the end of his term, has the right to remove trade fixtures. They must not, however, be removed *after* possession has been given up[63a]. Trade fixtures include display cabinets, machinery, boilers, pipework, shop and office fittings, petrol pumps, light fittings, partitions and so on. A tenant can remove these even though to do so causes substantial damage to the decorative state (although a tenant removing fixtures should also bear in mind any covenant he may have given to leave the premises in a good state of repair or in decorative repair). Any fixture installed by the tenant with a view and intent to make it a permanent improvement cannot be removed, although in the case of trade fixtures the courts are more ready to infer an intention ultimately to remove them at the end of the tenancy, thus negating any intention of permanent improvement.[64]

Improvements made before March 25, 1928, do not qualify for compensation,[65] nor do improvements made pursuant to any contract for valuable consideration whenever made,[66] regardless of whether the agreement was made between a tenant and the landlord or a sub-tenant and the landlord.[67] But improvements made pursuant to any statutory requirements, *e.g.* to conform to planning controls or fire regulations, also qualify for compensation, provided they were begun

---

[61] *Ibid.* s.1(1).
[62] *Ibid.* s.25(1).
[63] *Ibid.* s.1(1). This will include a sub-tenant who assigns his sub-tenancy to an assignee who then claims the right to compensation: *Pelosi* v. *Newcastle Arms Brewery (Nottingham) Ltd.* (1981) 43 P. & C.R. 18.
[63a] *New Zealand Government Property Corp.* v. *H.M. & S. Ltd.* [1982] Q.B. 1145.
[64] *Supra*, Chap. 3.
[65] L. & T.A. 1927, s.2(1).
[66] *Ibid.*
[67] *Owen Owen Estate Ltd.* v. *Livett* [1955] 2 All E.R. 513.

after October 1, 1954.[68] The 1954 Act[69] renders void any agreement purporting to contract out of the compensation provisions of the 1927 Act, unless made before December 10, 1953, for valuable consideration.[70]

Where there is only a freeholder, and a tenant who is in occupation, *i.e.* there are no sub-tenancies, the freeholder will secure the benefit of the improvements on the termination of the tenancy, and it is thus he who must pay the compensation. Where there is a chain of sub-tenancies, the immediate landlord of the tenant who carried out the improvement gets the immediate benefit of it at the end of the sub-tenancy, and he must therefore pay the compensation. However, at the end of his tenancy the benefit accrues to his landlord and so that landlord must then pay compensation to his immediate tenant, and so on up the chain.[71]

(4) *The Qualifying Conditions*

Before the tenant can qualify for the right to claim compensation on leaving at the termination of the tenancy (for a tenant who leaves in mid-term, *e.g.* by assignment or surrender, is not entitled to any compensation), he must satisfy certain conditions laid down in section 3 of the 1927 Act. Simply carrying out an improvement will not, automatically, entitle the tenant to his compensation. The improvement must have been authorised in accordance with the statutory procedure. This procedure requires the landlord to be notified of the proposed improvement and either have consented, or had his objection overruled by the court.

The tenant must serve on his landlord written notice of his intention to carry out the improvement.[72] There is no statutorily prescribed form for this notice, but it must carry with it a specification and plan of what is proposed, showing those parts of the premises that will be affected by the works.[73] The landlord then has three months in which to serve a notice of objection. No notice of objection can be served in relation to an improvement made in pursuance of a statutory obligation. If no notice of objection is served, the improvement is treated as authorised and prima facie qualifies for compensation.[74] If the landlord serves notice of objection, the tenant can then

---

[68] *i.e.* the commencement date for the 1954 Act: L. & T.A. 1954, s.48(1).
[69] s.49.
[70] See L. & T.A. 1927, s.9.
[71] *Ibid.* s.8.
[72] *Ibid.* s.3(1).
[73] *Ibid.* See *Deerfield Travel Services Ltd.* v. *Wardens etc. of the Leathersellers of the City of London* (1982) 46 P. & C.R. 132, where an outline specification only was treated as insufficient for this purpose.
[74] L. & T.A. 1927, s.3(1).

apply to the court for a certificate that the improvement is a proper improvement. The court must so certify if satisfied on three matters.[75]

First, it must be satisfied that the improvement is of such a nature as to be calculated to add to the letting value of the holding at the end of the tenancy. Secondly, it must be satisfied that the improvement is reasonable and suitable to the character of the holding. In considering this question the court must have regard to evidence adduced by the landlord or any superior landlord (but *not* by any other person) that the improvement is calculated to injure the amenity or convenience of the neighbourhood.[76] Thirdly, the court must be satisfied that the improvement will not diminish the value of any other property belonging to the landlord or to any superior landlord. Assuming the tenant is able to persuade the court on these three matters, it must issue the certificate, although in so doing it may make modifications in the specification or plan or impose conditions.[77] The landlord can resist the issue of the certificate by offering to execute the proposed improvement himself, in consideration of an increase in rent and, in that event, no certificate will be given unless it is subsequently proved that the landlord has not fulfilled his undertaking.[78] Once the court has issued the certificate, the improvement becomes authorised.[79]

The tenant may now carry out the improvement, complying with any conditions imposed by the court and completing the work within a time agreed with the landlord or fixed by the court.[80] He, or his successor in title, will then be entitled to compensation at the termination of the tenancy, upon quitting the holding. The tenant can require the landlord to give him a certificate that the improvement has been duly executed.[81] Notices of intended improvements have to be served on superior landlords, who have a right to be heard before the court.[82] A landlord, who has to pay compensation, has the right to claim compensation from a superior landlord in due course only if he has served on him copies of all documents and claims received.

This procedure for approval of improvements has two purposes. First, it is an essential step towards entitlement to compensation. Secondly, and quite apart from any question of compensation, it affords a method whereby a tenant may lawfully carry out the improvement even though there is a prohibition against it in his lease. It is provided in section 3(4) of the 1927 Act that, having received no objection from the landlord, or having obtained a certificate from the

[75] *Ibid.*
[76] *Ibid.* s.3(2).
[77] *Ibid.* s.3(1).
[78] *Ibid.*
[79] *Ibid.* s.3(1), (4).
[80] *Ibid.* s.3(5).
[81] *Ibid.* s.3(6).
[82] *Ibid.* s.8.

court, the tenant may carry out the improvement "anything in any lease of the premises to the contrary notwithstanding."

Power is conferred on the landlord by section 10 of the 1927 Act, and on any person authorised by him, to enter the holding at all reasonable times for the purposes of executing any improvement he has undertaken to carry out. It also contains a power to make any inspection reasonably required for the purposes of Part I of the 1927 Act.

(5) *The Procedure of the Claim*

A tenant who has satisfied the qualifying conditions in respect of his claim for compensation for improvements must, in accordance with section 1(1) of the 1927 Act, make his claim in the prescribed form,[83] in writing, and either sign it personally or through his agent. The notice of claim must specify the holding and the business, and state the nature of the claim, the cost and other particulars of the improvement, the date when it was carried out and the amount claimed. The claim must be served on the landlord in accordance with section 2(3) of the 1927 Act, within the strict time limits imposed by section 47 of the 1954 Act.[84] These are:

1. Within three months of the giving of a notice to quit or a notice to terminate (or if the tenancy is terminated under section 26 of the 1954 Act, within three months of the landlord's counter-notice); or
2. If the tenancy is one that will expire by simple effluxion of time, not more than six but not less than three months before the termination of the tenancy; or
3. Within three months of the effective date of an order for possession in forfeiture proceedings, or within three months of re-entry without an order for possession.

The practical significance of these compensation provisions in the 1927 Act has been much reduced since 1954 because, as we have seen, the right to compensation arises only if the tenant quits the holding on the termination of the tenancy. Normally he will not quit, but be entitled to a new tenancy under Part II of the 1954 Act.[85] Nevertheless, as a general rule tenants should always try to satisfy the qualifying conditions in respect of improvements which they propose to make. Not only will it be too late to remedy the defect later should the unexpected happen and the tenant be forced to quit, but it may

[83] See R.S.C., Ord. 97: C.C.R., Ord. 43.
[84] *Donegal Tweed Co. Ltd.* v. *Stephenson* (1929) 98 L.J.K.B. 657.
[85] *Ibid.*

also be necessary for a tenant to have the added value of any improvement disregarded in fixing the rent under section 34 of the 1954 Act in respect of any new tenancy granted under Part II within the next 21 years.[86]

(6) *Effect on Rent*

A tenant who improves the premises will generally avoid the penalty of having his new rent assessed on the value of the improvement when he subsequently exercises his right to renew his lease under the Landlord and Tenant Act 1954, unless he was under *an obligation* to his immediate landlord to do the work concerned.[87] For the purposes of rental increases the improvement is ignored if it was carried out at any time during the term of the lease which falls to be renewed.[88] It is also ignored if it was effected during the 21 years preceding the application for a new tenancy, and ever since the time it was carried out the premises, or any part of them affected by the improvement, have been subject to a tenancy to which Part II of the 1954 Act did or would have applied, and the then tenant did not quit at the end of any of those tenancies.[89] An applicant for a new tenancy obtains the benefit of improvements satisfying these conditions even if carried out by one of his predecessors in title as tenant.

This provision is clearly fair where the tenant made the improvements at his own expense, and the rental terms had not taken this into consideration, as they would have done if the lease had imposed an obligation to do the work.[90] The statutory words of section 34(2) are, however, "any improvement carried out by a person who at the time it was carried out was the tenant." It is arguable that this includes improvements carried out by or at the direction of the tenant, pursuant to some statutory obligation, in circumstances where he was able to persuade the court to order that some or all of the cost should be paid by the landlord.[91] Although it is unlikely to have been the Act's intention, the obligation to ignore the improvements, imposed on the court assessing the new rent, is mandatory, even though the landlord may have been compelled to meet part of their cost. On the other

---

[86] *Ibid.*

[87] L. & T.A. 1954, s.34: L.P.A. 1969, s.1. If carried out under licence, disregard is a question of construction: *Godbold* v. *Martin's Newsagents Ltd.* (1983) 268 E.G. 1202.

[88] This does not include an improvement carried out when the tenant had a mere licence which preceded his tenancy: *Euston Centre Properties Ltd.* v. *H. & J. Wilson Ltd.* (1981) 262 E.G. 1079.

[89] L. & T.A. 1954, s.34(2); *cf. East Coast Amusement Co. Ltd.* v. *British Transport Board* [1965] A.C. 58.

[90] *cf. Ponsford* v. *H.M.S. Aerosols* [1978] 2 W.L.R. 241; *Grea Real Property Investments* v. *Williams* (1979) 250 E.G. 651; *Estates Projects* v. *Greenwich Borough Council* (1979) 251 E.G. 851.

[91] *e.g.* Under the Office, Shops and Railway Premises Act 1963, s.73(2); the Food Act 1984, s.13(4), (5); London Building Acts (Amendment) Act 1939, s.107; Clean Air Act 1956, s.28; Docks and Harbours Act 1966, s.34.

hand, the various Acts which give the court power to apportion the expense of carrying out works to comply with statutory requirements all confer a discretion. A landlord who could show that he would probably be deprived of all benefit of those improvements because the tenant, in claiming a new lease, could prevent the reversion falling into possession and prevent future rentals from properly reflecting the value of the improvements, might escape any liability to contribute.

(7) *The Amount of the Compensation*

In the absence of agreement between the parties, section 1(1) of the 1927 Act provides that the sum to be paid as compensation for any improvement shall not exceed the net addition to the value of the holding as a whole, which may be determined to be the direct result of the improvement, or the reasonable cost of carrying out the improvement, at the end of the tenancy. The reference to "net addition" was explained by Morton J. in this way[92]: "With regard to these words, it would appear that the Act is dealing with net additions to the value and is contemplating that the works to be carried out might in some respects be detrimental and in other respects beneficial to the holding."

If, at the end of the tenancy, the improvement is out of repair, there has to be deducted from the compensation, which has been estimated by reference to reasonable cost, an amount equal to the cost of putting it into a reasonable state of repair. However, no such deduction should be made in respect of repairs which the tenant is obliged to carry out under any covenant in the lease or other agreement, which thus becomes the subject of an entirely separate claim by a landlord who wishes to pursue it.[93] In arriving at the amount of the net addition to the value of the holding, the court must consider the purposes for which it is intended to use the premises after the end of the tenancy. If it is shown that the landlord intends to demolish or to make structural alterations to the premises, or any part of them, or to use the premises for a different purpose, regard must be had to the effect of such demolition, alteration or change of use on the additional value which has been attributed to the improvements. Regard must also be had to the length of time likely to elapse between the termination of the tenancy and the demolition, alteration or change of use.[94] It may be that the improvement will not add anything to the value of the holding when these additional matters are considered, and no compensation will then be payable. If the court holds that no compensation, or reduced compensation, is payable because of such

---

[92] *National Electric Theatres Ltd.* v. *Hudgell* [1939] Ch. 553 at p. 561.
[93] L. & T.A. 1927, s.1(1)(*b*).
[94] *Ibid.* s.1(2).

matters, it may authorise a further application to be made by the tenant if the proposed works or change of use are not carried out within such time as it fixes.[95]

In fixing the amount of compensation, a reduction must be made for any benefit received by the tenant from the landlord in consideration of the improvement.[96] It will only be in very limited circumstances that such a reduction would be made since, if the consideration has been offered by the landlord in return for the tenant's offer to do the work, then there will be a contract between the parties obliging the tenant to carry out the improvement, and in this circumstance, it will be recalled, no compensation is payable at all.[97] Section 11 of the 1927 Act contains mutual rights of deduction between landlord and tenant. The landlord can deduct out of the compensation due, any sum owing to him from the tenant under or in respect of the tenancy (*e.g.* arrears of rent, the amount of any damages awarded for breach of a repairing covenant and so on). The tenant can deduct out of such sum due from him any compensation payable to him by the landlord.

(8) *Improvements Taxed as Premiums*

Where a short lease (*i.e.* for a term not exceeding 50 years) obliges the tenant to improve the premises, the landlord is normally liable to pay income tax under Schedule A or corporation tax as if a premium had been paid on the grant of the lease equal to the amount by which the landlord's interest in the property was thereby increased in value immediately after the lease commenced.[98] The sum so charged to tax may be substantially different from the amount spent on the improvement by the tenant.

The amount charged to tax is the increase in value, less one-fiftieth of that sum for every year by which the term of the lease exceeds one year. The full sum is therefore subject to tax when the lease is for one year only, and it is reduced proportionately with increases in the length of the term. The tax is normally payable in one sum in the year in which the lease is granted, but is subject to "top-slicing" relief for higher rate tax payers.[99] Premiums payable by instalments can be taxed as rent as the instalments are received (with no reduction for the term of the lease) and it is possible that provisions requiring a tenant to carry out successive improvements in different years could be so treated.

---

[95] *Ibid.* s.1(3).
[96] *Ibid.* s.2(3).
[97] *Ibid.* s.2(1)(*b*).
[98] Income and Corporation Taxes Act 1970, s.80; *supra*, Chap. 5.
[99] See Chap. 5, *supra.*

To avoid such a charge to tax, leases containing covenants on the part of the tenant to effect improvements (*e.g.* to instal air conditioning or a new shop front) may include a covenant to remove the improvement before the end of the term. As tenants are naturally reluctant to increase their liabilities by assuming the burden of reinstating the premises, such clauses are frequently made subject to the proviso that the obligation to remove the improvement shall apply only if the landlord so requires, which most tenants (but not, it seems, the Inland Revenue) assume he will not do.

A tenant paying a premium by way of effecting improvements, which is taxable in the hands of his landlord under these provisions, may deduct it from the taxable profits of his trade, business or profession in the same way as he deducts the rent for his business premises.[1] Where a sub-lease is granted, and a tenant is taxed on a premium received under it, before arriving at the taxable figure, any premium he paid to the head landlord may be deducted.[2]

---

[1] Income and Corporation Taxes Act 1970, s.134.
[2] *Ibid.* s.83.

CHAPTER 22

TERMINATIONS AND RENEWALS

I. The Statutory Protection 673
II. The Continuation Tenancy 676
    A. Nature 676
    B. Terms 677
III. The New Tenancy 682
    A. Taking the Initiative—Land-
        lord or Tenant? 682
    B. Termination of the Tenancy by
        the Landlord 682
    C. Receipt of the Notice—Action
        by the Tenant 687
    D. Request for a New Tenancy by
        the Tenant 689
    E. Receipt of the Notice—Action
        by the Landlord 692
    F. Agreement 692
IV. The Statutory Grounds of Opposition 693
    A. Breach of Repairing Obliga-
        tions: s. 30(1)(a) 694
    B. Persistent Delay in Paying
        Rent: s. 30(1)(b) 694

    C. Other Substantial Breaches of
        Obligations: s. 30(1)(c) 694
    D. Availability of Suitable Alter-
        native   Accommodation:
        s. 30(1)(d) 695
    E. Possession Required for Letting
        or Disposing of the Property as
        a whole in the Case of a Sub-
        tenancy: s. 30(1)(e) 696
    F. The   Landlord   Intends   to
        Demolish   or   Reconstruct:
        s. 30(1)(f) 697
    G. The Landlord's Intention to
        Occupy the Premises Himself:
        s. 30(1)(g) 701
    H. The Landlord's Intention ... 704
V. The New Tenancy 706
    A. The Court 706
    B. The Terms of the New Tenancy 708
    C. Carrying Out the Order 717
    D. Renewing Sub-tenancies 717

I. THE STATUTORY PROTECTION

The basic protection given by the Landlord and Tenant Act 1954, Pt. II, is to provide for the tenancy to continue irrespective of whether the term granted by the lease has come to an end by effluxion of time or notice to quit. Section 24(1) of the Act grants security of tenure by providing that a tenancy within Part II "shall not come to an end unless terminated in accordance with the provisions of this part of this Act." So, an ordinary notice to quit served by a landlord will be totally ineffective, and a tenancy for a fixed term will continue under the Act after the expiration of the term. The tenant will be able to remain in possession under a "continuation tenancy."

The Act prescribes various methods for terminating the tenancy. These are a landlord's notice under section 25(2), a tenant's request for a new tenancy under section 26(3), and a tenant's notice under section 27(2). These are all discussed in detail later in this chapter. Section 24(2) does, however, preserve certain common law methods of terminating a business tenancy that do not result in the statutory continuation of the tenancy thus ended. Forfeiture of the lease by the landlord pursuant to a clause entitling him to enter and forfeit for non-payment of rent or some other breach of covenant will, subject to the court's discretion to grant relief, terminate a tenancy within Part II of the 1954 Act. No statutory security of tenure will then be given.[1]

Another circumstance in which a termination of the tenancy will not involve any statutory continuation of it arises when the tenant buys out his landlord's interest. A tenant holding under a long lease granted before or just after the last war, when long leases of business premises were rather more common, and rent review clauses rarer, than they are today, will be in possession of a most valuable asset. His profit rental (the difference between the rent payable under the lease and the current market rent) will be high, and if the landlord attempts to sell the property he will receive substantially less than he would have received had he been able to sell with vacant possession or with a rent review imminent. As a result the sitting tenant will often be able to purchase the landlord's interest in the premises at a favourable price. The landlord's reversionary interest in the premises is, as we have seen earlier in this book, greater than that of the tenant. One would expect that the results of such a transaction would be to submerge the tenant's interest as tenant in the larger interest just acquired from the landlord. However, the interest of the tenant, as tenant, will not merge or disappear in the larger interest unless that is what he intended.[2] It is therefore important for a tenant purchaser who wishes to extinguish his lease and merge it with the newly-acquired reversion to state clearly and in writing that he regards his two interests in the property as having merged.[3]

The Landlord and Tenant Act 1954, s.24(2), also provides that a tenant who terminates by notice to quit or by surrender is not entitled to the protection of section 24(1). This raises a difficulty already mentioned in an earlier chapter.[4] It is not possible to sidestep the protection given by the Act by persuading the tenant to give a notice to quit or execute a deed of surrender before he has taken up occupation. He must have been in occupation for at least one month before he can take those steps.[5] A surrender in these circumstances will deprive the tenant of the statutory right to a new tenancy conferred by sections 24 and 29 of the 1954 Act. Both a completed surrender, and an agreement to surrender, will be effective for this

[1] Although a tenancy in respect of which there has been a judgment for forfeiture, coupled with a subsisting application for relief against forfeiture, will not be treated as at an end by reason of forfeiture, provided there was no undue delay in seeking relief. Accordingly a tenant can apply for a new tenancy under the 1954 Act notwithstanding judgment for forfeiture: *Meadows* v. *Clerical, Medical and General Life Assurance Society* [1980] 1 All E.R. 454; *Associated Deliveries Ltd.* v. *Harrison* (1984) 272 E.G. 321 at p. 325. Similarly, s.24(2) does not prevent s.24(1) applying where a vesting order could have been granted under L.P.A. 1925, s.146(4): *Cadogan* v. *Dimovic* [1984] 1 W.L.R. 609.
[2] L.P.A. 1925, s.185.
[3] *Supra*, Chap. 7. It seems that merger does not involve "an instrument of surrender" within the meaning of L. & T.A. 1954, s.24(2)(*b*), even though it is a means of determining the tenancy permitted by s.24(2): *Watney* v. *Boardley* [1975] 1 W.L.R. 857.
[4] *Supra*, Chap. 20.
[5] L. & T.A. 1954, s.24(2).

purpose if authorised by the court.[5a] A tenant wishing to determine by notice to quit where the tenancy is for a fixed term must give three months' notice in writing, to expire at the end of the term, or on any quarter day thereafter.[6] No special form is necessary. Once validly given, the tenant will lose any further rights under the Act, and the current tenancy will be terminated on the date specified in the notice. By way of example, suppose that from November 1, 1986, T takes a lease of business premises from L for a period of one year. Should he wish to quit those premises at the end of this term, *i.e.* October 31, 1987, he must serve a notice at any time between December 1, 1986 and July 31, 1987. If, on the other hand, he wishes to stay in possession under the tenancy continued by virtue of section 24(1) of the 1954 Act, until December 1, 1987, he must service his notice at any time between December 1, 1986, and September 24, 1986 to expire on December 25, 1987, (*i.e.* the first quarter day after the date desired, albeit later than the desired date).

Business leases sometimes contain "break clauses," entitling the landlord to terminate the tenancy, usually on giving a specified period of notice to the tenant. The service of a notice operating a break clause will be effective to stop the rights under the original lease but it will not operate to terminate the lease for the purposes of Part II of the 1954 Act unless a statutory notice in accordance with section 25(2) is also served by the landlord.[7] This point is neatly illustrated by a decision which also, coincidentally, provides cogent evidence for the continuing need for statutory protection of business tenants. In *Morrison Holdings Ltd.* v. *Manders Property (Wolverhampton) Ltd.*[8] shop premises had been seriously damaged by fire so that the tenants were obliged to vacate. The landlords operated a break clause in the lease. The tenants applied to the court for a new tenancy under the 1954 Act. Throughout they maintained their intention of returning to the premises as soon as they had been made fit again for occupation. They left certain fixtures and fittings in the premises and retained the keys. The court held that the application for a new tenancy had been validly made. In order to apply for a new tenancy the tenant must show either that he is continuing in occupation of the premises for the purposes of a business carried on by him,[9] or if events over which he has no control have led him to vacate the premises, that he is continuing to exert and claim his right to occupancy. The tenants in this case satisfied the second of the alternatives. However, a further complication arose in that about a month after the fire the landlords

---

[5a] L. & T.A. 1954, s.38(1); see also *Allnatt London Properties* v. *Newton* (1983) 45 P. & C.R. 94; *Tarjomani* v. *Panther Securities* (1982) 46 P. & C.R. 32, discussed *supra*, Chap. 20.
[6] *Ibid.* s.27.
[7] *Weinberg's Weatherproof Ltd.* v. *Radcliffe Paper Mill Co. Ltd.* [1958] Ch. 437; *Scholl Manufacturing Co. Ltd.* v. *Clifton (Slim Line) Ltd.* [1967] Ch. 41.
[8] [1976] 1 W.L.R. 533.
[9] *(I. & H.) Caplan, Ltd.* v. *Caplan* [1963] 2 All E.R. 930.

demolished the premises and started to rebuild on the site. These actions were unlawful. The Court of Appeal held that the landlords could not defeat the tenant's claim to a new tenancy of the premises by their own unlawful actions in destroying those premises before the matter could be heard.

Where a landlord serves a notice to terminate the tenancy in accordance with s.25, the tenant is required by s.25(5), within two months, to notify the landlord whether or not, at the date of termination, he will be willing to give up possession of the premises. If he fails to comply strictly with this provision, the court is precluded by s.29(2) from considering any application for a new tenancy that he may make. He will, therefore, have lost all further rights under Part II of the 1954 Act, and the s.25 notice to terminate will operate on the date specified in it.[10] It is therefore vital that a tenant wanting to stay who has been served with a notice to quit notifies his landlord in writing in unequivocal terms that he does not intend to give up possession, *and* that he notifies him within the time limit. He should either ask for and obtain an acknowledgement of his letter, or send it by recorded delivery. If a tenant loses his rights under the Act, he may also have lost all the goodwill he may have earned or paid for.[11]

II. THE CONTINUATION TENANCY

A. Nature

The termination of the current tenancy *under the 1954 Act* results in an automatic right in the tenant to apply for a new tenancy. The termination of the *contractual* tenancy at common law by notice to quit or effluxion of time automatically invokes section 24(1) of the Landlord and Tenant Act 1954. This section does not create any new form of interest in the tenant,[12] but simply prolongs the tenant's estate, subject to a statutory variation as to the mode of determination.[13] A right in the tenant or sub-tenant to remove tenant's fixtures will be enforceable during the continuation tenancy,[14] as will rights of way enjoyed under the contractual tenancy,[15] but not, in the absence

---

[10] See *Lewington* v.*Trustees of the Society for the Protection of Ancient Buildings* (1983) 45 P. & C.R. 336; *Stile Hall Properties* v. *Gooch* [1979] 3 All E.R. 848; *Polyviou* v. *Seeley* [1980] 1 W.L.R. 55.

[11] See *post* (III)C.

[12] Unlike the statutory tenancy created by the Rent Act 1977.

[13] *Bolton (H.L.) Engineering) Co. Ltd.* v. *T. J. Graham & Sons Ltd.* [1957] 1 Q.B. 159, *per* Denning L.J. at p.168. See also *G.M.S. Syndicate* v. *Gary Elliott* (1980) 41 P. & C.R. 124 (covenants running with the land enforceable during statutory continuation).

[14] *New Zealand Government Property Corp.* v. *H.M. & S. Ltd.* [1982] Q.B. 1145.

[15] *Nevill Long & Co. (Boards) Ltd.* v. *Firmenich & Co.* (1983) 47 P. & C.R. 59.

of clear words, a guarantor's possible liability in respect of rent.[16] Since the duration of the estate itself in the land is prolonged, it follows that the tenant still has an interest which, subject to restrictions imposed by the terms of the tenancy, is assignable and, in the event of a breach of a condition of the tenancy, liable to forfeiture. Similarly, the landlord's reversion is also assignable and any assignment by the landlord of his interest will not affect the rights of the tenant under the Act.[17]

A continuation tenancy under section 24 is one of uncertain duration and thus, were it not created by statute,[18] would be void at common law.[19] A landlord's notice to terminate a continuation tenancy can be given for any date he chooses not more than 12 nor less than six months ahead,[20] but section 24(2) expressly contemplates the alternative of the continuation tenancy being brought to an end by a notice to quit given by the tenant. A tenant is not, therefore, obliged to submit to a continuation of his tenancy under section 24(1). By section 27(1) he is able to serve on his immediate landlord, not less than three months before the expiry date of the contracted term, a notice in writing that he does not want the tenancy to be continued, in which case section 24 will not apply to the tenancy. In the case of a periodic tenancy, or a tenancy for a fixed term subject to a clause permitting the tenant to break the term, he can, by serving on his immediate landlord a notice to quit in accordance with the terms of the tenancy, bring it to an end, in which case section 24 will not operate. Where a tenancy originally granted for a fixed term has been continued under section 24(1), the tenant can bring the continuation to an end by serving on his immediate landlord not less than three months' notice in writing given for any quarter day.[21] These notices deprive the tenant of the new tenancy rights[22] given by the Act, but none of these notices may be served after the tenant has made a request for a new tenancy under section 26,[23] or before the tenant has been in occupation under the tenancy for one month.[24]

B. Terms

All the terms and conditions of the contractual tenancy, save those

---

[16] *Junction Estates Ltd.* v. *Cope* (1974) 27 P. & C.R. 482; *A. Plesser & Co. Ltd.* v. *Davis* (1983) 267 E.G. 1039. These cases are discussed in B, *post.*

[17] Although it may affect the ability of the landlord to oppose the tenant's application for a new tenancy: L. & T.A. 1954, s.30(2): see *post.*

[18] *Castle Laundry (London)* v. *Read* [1955] 1 Q.B. 586, *per* Sellers J. at p. 592.

[19] *Lace* v. *Chantler* [1944] K.B. 368.

[20] L. & T.A. 1954, s.25.

[21] *Ibid.* s.27(2).

[22] Conferred by ss.24 and 29.

[23] L. & T.A. 1954, s.26(4).

[24] *Ibid.* ss.24(2), 27.

relating to the termination by the landlord of the contractual relationship, will govern the continuation tenancy under the Act. The tenant is entitled to the same premises as were comprised in the original tenancy during its statutory continuation,[25] unless there was a right to remove some part of the premises, such as a fixture, during the original contract period.[26] However, in *Junction Estates* v. *Cope*[27] a guarantor covenanted that the tenant would pay the rent reserved in the manner provided in the lease. The question arose as to whether the guarantor's liability under this covenant survived the expiration of the fixed term granted by the lease, notwithstanding that the tenancy had thereafter continued by virtue of Part II of the 1954 Act. The court held, as a matter of construction, that it did not and that if such an indefinite liability was to be imposed on the guarantor, clear words should have been used.

Since a tenancy within the Act has this potential continuation beyond its term date, a sub-tenancy created out of it to endure beyond the term date does not operate as an assignment, as would be the case if there were no continuation by statute.[28] It seems that the tenancy must have been within the Act at its contractual term date for the statutory continuation to apply.[29] The fact that the tenancy ceases to be one to which Part II of the Act applies *after* the continuation tenancy comes into existence,[30] does not of itself bring the continuation tenancy to an end. Such a tenancy can, however, be terminated by not less than three nor more than six months' notice in writing given by the landlord to the tenant.[31]

During the period of continuance the tenant owes rent to the common law landlord.[32] For one reason or another it is perfectly possible for the continuation tenancy to last for some considerable time before the matter of the new tenancy is resolved. The question may then arise as to what, in the meantime, should be the rent the tenant can be required to pay. Until the tenant's application for a new tenancy was determined by the court, the 1954 Act, as originally drafted, preserved the existing rental obligations by continuing the current tenancy at the same rent until a new rent was determined along with all the other provisions of the new tenancy. If proceedings were commenced under the Act, this new tenancy (and hence the higher rent), would not operate until three months after the proceedings were concluded.[33] There were (and still are), various

[25] *Poster* v. *Slough Estates Ltd.* [1969] 1 Ch. 495.
[26] *Ibid.*
[27] (1974) 27 P. & C.R. 482; see also *A. Plesser & Co.* v. *Davis* (1983) 267 E.G. 1039.
[28] *William Skelton & Son Ltd.* v. *Harrison & Pinder Ltd.* [1975] Q.B. 361.
[29] L. & T.A. 1954, s.24(3)(*b*); see *Orman Bros.* v. *Greenbaum* [1954] 3 All E.R. 731; [1955] 1 All E.R. 610.
[30] *e.g.* by the tenant discontinuing the business.
[31] L. & T.A. 1954, s.24(3)(*a*).
[32] Not to the "competent landlord" if he is a different person. This term is explained *post.*
[33] L. & T.A. 1954, s.64.

methods of causing delay available to tenants wishing to postpone a final court order, and it would clearly be worth a tenant's while to resort to whatever delaying tactics were at his disposal where the original rent had fallen below the current market rent for those premises.[34] To prevent this the Law of Property Act 1969 added the new section 24A to the 1954 Act, enabling a landlord to apply to the court (either where he has given notice to determine the tenancy in accordance with the Act, or where the tenant has made a statutory application for a new tenancy[35]) for an "interim rent" to be determined, *i.e.* a rent that is a reasonable one for the tenant to pay while the old tenancy is statutorily continued. The court is given a discretion under section 24A(1) whether or not to determine an interim rent. It is not bound to do so, and may decline, although such a refusal is rare.[36] Withdrawal by the tenant of his application for the grant of a new tenancy has no effect on the landlord's application for an interim rent, since the latter is in the nature of a counter-claim.[37] The court can determine an interim rent notwithstanding that the landlord at the time of the determination is not the landlord who originated the application.[38]

An interim rent determined in proceedings under section 24A is deemed to be the rent payable under the tenancy from the date on which proceedings for an interim rent to be fixed were commenced, the date specified by the tenant in his notice requesting a new tenancy or the date specified by the landlord in his notice terminating the old tenancy, whichever is latest.[39]

The interim rent is an open market rental fixed in accordance with the same principles that have to be applied in fixing the rent under the new tenancy granted under the Act,[40] but with two qualifications. First, the rent is to be fixed on the assumption of an annual tenancy. Secondly, the court is obliged to have regard to the rent payable under the current tenancy.[41] However, the general assumption might be that the interim rent should be lower than the final rent fixed for the new tenancy ordered by the court because a tenant under the annual tenancy, which has to be assumed, might pay less than he would under the new tenancy which carries with it a secure period of tenure. Also, a

---

[34] Re *88 High Road, Kilburn* [1959] 1 W.L.R. 279.

[35] The landlord's application to fix an interim rent need not be the subject of an originating application, but may be contained in his answer to the tenant's application to the court for a new tenancy: *Thomas* v. *Hammond-Lawrence,* [1986] 2 All E.R. 214.

[36] See *English Exporters (London) Ltd.* v. *Eldonwall Ltd.* [1973] Ch. 415.

[37] *Michael Kramer & Co.* v. *Airways Pension Fund Trustees* (1976) 246 E.G. 911; *Texaco* v. *Benton & Bowles (Holdings)* (1983) 267 E.G. 355; *Artoc Bank Trust* v. *Prudential Assurance Co.* [1984] 1 W.L.R. 1181.

[38] *Bloomfield* v. *Ashwright* (1983) 47 P. & C.R. 78.

[39] *Stream Properties* v. *Davies* [1972] 1 W.L.R. 645; *Secretary of State for Social Services* v. *Rossetti Lodge Investment Co. Ltd.* (1975) 119 S.J. 339; *Victor Blake (Menswear) Ltd.* v. *Westminster City Council* (1979) 38 P. & C.R. 448.

[40] L. & T.A. 1954, s.34(1), (2); see *post.*

[41] *Ibid.* s.24A(3).

tenant under an annual tenancy might be expected to pay less because he would not get that safeguard against inflation and increasing rent levels which is obtained by a tenant under a longer term at a fixed rent, even with rent reviews.

In *Regis Property Co. Ltd.* v. *Lewis & Peat Ltd.*[42] the interim rent was determined as that under the new lease to be granted, discounted by 33 and one-third per cent. to take account of the annual tenancy assumption. The demised premises in that case were office accommodation in the City of London at a time of escalating rents. The percentage deduction was made on valuation principles determined by the particular facts pertaining at a particular time in a particular place, and no general principle can be deduced from it. In *English Exporters (London) Ltd.* v. *Eldonwall Ltd.*[43] the existing rent was £7,655 per annum and valuers' evidence established the market rent at about £15,000 per annum. On the basis that the court should apply values existing when the interim period began to run, but "for reasons which defied detailed analysis," Megarry J. fixed the interim rent at £14,000 per annum.

The purpose of the interim rent procedure is to prevent the injustice to landlords which arose from continuance of the old out of date rent while negotiations or court proceedings went on. If the interim rent can be substantially lower than the new rent, that injustice is mitigated rather than removed, and tenants still have a financial interest in delay. In *Regis Property Co. Ltd.* v. *Lewis & Peat Ltd.*[44] Stamp J. felt that, notwithstanding the fact that section 24A(3) of the 1954 Act requires the court to "have regard to the rent payable under the terms of the tenancy," the determination of the interim rent involved only one operation. That was the assessment of the rent as a matter of market value, on the basis of a yearly tenancy. One could have regard to the rent under the existing tenancy only if it had evidential value for the purposes of ascertaining market value. Once the valuation exercise has been performed the matter is at an end, and the figure arrived at cannot be modified either by the reference in section 24A(1) to the fact that the rent fixed be one that "it would be reasonable for the tenant to pay," or by the direction in subsection (3) to have regard to the rent payable under the terms of the tenancy. In the view of Stamp J. therefore, it is incorrect to ascertain the open market rent on an annual tenancy, then the existing rent, and finally to determine the interim rent as somewhere between these two figures according, not to any formula, but on whim. Stamp J. therefore,

[42] [1970] Ch. 695.
[43] [1973] Ch. 415, see also *Janes (Gowns)* v. *Harlow Department Corp.* (1979) 253 E.G. 799 (interim rents fixed by negotiation generally ten *per cent* less than agreed current market rent) but *N.B. Ratners (Jewellers) Ltd.* v. *Lemnoll Ltd.* (1980) 255 E.G. 987, where deduction was fifteen *per cent*, and *O'May* v. *City of London Real Property Co. Ltd.* [1983] 2 A.C. 726, where interim rent had been agreed at figure lower than current rent.
[44] [1970] 1 Ch. 695.

tacitly took the view that there should not, necessarily, be any financial incentive to the tenant to delay.

This decision was not followed in *English Exporters (London) Ltd. v. Eldonwall Ltd.*[45] There Megarry J. held that the effect of the requirement in section 24A, that the court should have regard to the rent payable under the existing tenancy, was to enable the court to fix an interim rent less than the market rent when it was reasonable to do so, bearing in mind the level of the existing rent. He considered Stamp J. to be wrong in thinking that, unless his construction were adopted, one could not refer to the existing rent, even in the examples given by him where it would have evidentiary value. Both judges, therefore, agreed, though for different reasons, that the court, and the valuers appearing to give expert testimony, may, and should where it has evidentiary value, have regard to the existing rent, but the difference between them lies in Stamp J.'s view that, apart from this circumstance, existing rent is irrelevant. Megarry J.'s view, on the other hand, is that it has, in any event, to be considered in order to determine whether adoption of the valuation without modification is reasonable. This principle, of allowing the rent valuation of a hypothetical yearly tenancy, to be "tempered" by the old rent, was relied upon by Dillon J. to effect a twenty per cent. deduction from the market rent valuation in assessing an interim rent in *Ratners (Jewellers) Ltd. v. Lemnoll.*[46]

This judicial difference of opinion has been considered by the Court of Appeal in *Fawke v. Viscount Chelsea.*[47] Although both parties in that case conceded that Megarry J.'s decision was correct, Goff L.J. (in whose judgment Brandon and Stephenson L.JJ. concurred on the point) hazarded that he preferred the view of Megarry J. and that Stamp J.

> "fell into error, because he overlooked the fact that there are two tenancies and two rents involved, not one. The rent to which the court is directed to have regard under subsection (3) is the rent payable under the contractual tenancy, which is continuing by virtue of the 1954 Act, but when one applies section 34 to the determination of an interim rent, as directed by section 24A(3), one is considering a new hypothetical yearly tenancy, and one can no more consider the rent appropriate to such a tenancy when determining that rent, than one can consider the rent under a new tenancy when determining that rent.[48]

The values to be applied are those existing when the interim period

---

[45] [1973] Ch. 415.
[46] (1980) 255 E.G. 987.
[47] [1979] 3 All E.R. 568. See also *U.D.S. Tailoring* v. *B.L. Holdings* (1982) 261 E.G. 49.
[48] *Ibid.* at p. 573.

begins to run, which is not necessarily the same date as that on which the contractual tenancy expires.[49]

The Court of Appeal further held that the valuation should be made on the basis of all that is known at the date of the hearing as to the condition the premises were actually in at the commencement of the interim period. The court rejected the tenant's contention that valuation of the interim rent should be based on what knowledge of the state of the premises at the commencement of the interim period a reasonable prospective tenant properly advised, and having such survey, if any, as might be reasonable, would or should have obtained, since that basis imported a large measure of uncertainty. Nor should the valuation be based on the actual knowledge of the parties themselves, since that is subjective, whereas the test ought to be objective. Accordingly, the court could order a differential interim rent varying with the state of repair of the premises, with a provision for the rent to increase once the repairs had been carried out.

III. The New Tenancy

A. Taking the Initiative—Landlord or Tenant?

Most landlords will want to bring the continuation tenancy to an end as soon as possible. Either the landlord will want to obtain a higher rent for the property[50] or he will want to deal with it in some other, more profitable manner. Landlords can always set in motion the process that may lead to the grant or refusal of a new tenancy, provided the period of the contractual term has expired or been terminated, or a break clause can be operated in the lease. A tenant, however, can take the initiative only if his tenancy was granted for longer than a year.[51] Inability to take the initiative is unlikely to worry the tenant unduly, for in the meantime he will remain in possession under the continuation tenancy, paying the old rent unless a new interim rent has been awarded.[51a]

B. Termination of the Tenancy by the Landlord

The only methods available to a landlord to terminate a tenancy to which Part II of the 1954 Act applies, other than by forfeiture, are by agreement or by giving the tenant a notice to terminate in accordance with the terms of section 25 of the Act. Where the landlord and tenant

[49] Having regard to L. & T.A. 1954, s.24A(2).
[50] As we have seen, the interim rent may be lower than the market rent under the new tenancy.
[51] L. & T.A. 1954, s.26(1).
[51a] See *Thomas* v. *Hammond-Lawrence* [1986] 2 All E.R. 214.

agree for the grant to the tenant of a future tenancy of the holding, or of the holding with other land, from a specified date, the continuation tenancy will come to an end on that date. Once such an agreement for a new tenancy is made the tenant cannot change his mind and claim instead a new tenancy under the Act.[52] In the absence of such an agreement, however, the first step to be taken by a landlord who wishes to terminate the continuation tenancy is for the landlord to serve a statutory notice to terminate.

(1) *The "Competent" Landlord*

The landlord who has to serve the notice is not necessarily the tenant's immediate landlord, but someone who is known as the "competent" landlord. He will be the first landlord in the chain who either owns the freehold or has a tenancy, superior to the one in issue, that will not expire within the next 14 months.[53] So, suppose Albert, the freeholder, lets premises to Basil for a term of years expiring on March 31, 1987. Basil sub-lets to Charles, whose sub-tenancy is now continuing by virtue of section 24 of the 1954 Act. On June 30, 1986, Charles's tenancy can be terminated by a notice under section 25, expiring not earlier than December 31, 1986, and not later than June 30, 1987. If Basil, to whom the freeholder has let, were the competent landlord for the purposes of section 25, it would mean that he could serve a notice, bringing Charles's tenancy to an end, on a date at which he, Basil, would have ceased to have any interest in the premises. Since, however, Basil's tenancy will then have less than 14 months to run, Albert is the competent landlord for the purposes of serving a section 25 notice.

According to the definition in the Landlord and Tenant Act 1954, s.44(1), there can, in any particular chain of title, be only one competent landlord and the purpose of the definition is to find the first landlord in the chain who has more than a merely nominal reversion. The competent landlord may not be the same person throughout.[54] As respects the various stages of action under the Act, each steps into the shoes of his predecessor, and the person for the time being answering the description of "the landlord" is a necessary party to any proceedings under the Act.[55] The material time at which the definition in section 44(1) must be applied therefore varies, according to circumstances. Where a landlord wishes to serve a section 25 notice, the material time is the date of service of the notice but if, during

---

[52] *Ibid.* s.28.
[53] *Ibid.* s.44(1).
[54] *X.L. Fisheries* v. *Leeds Corporation* [1955] 2 Q.B. 636.
[55] *Piper* v. *Muggleton* [1956] 2 Q.B. 569; *Beardmore Motors* v. *Birch Bros. (Properties)* [1959] Ch. 298.

proceedings on the tenant's application, there is a relevant change affecting interests in reversion, the material date will be the date of such change. Thus, where a tenant requests a new tenancy, the material time is the time of the hearing and the person who qualifies as the competent landlord at that time must be a party to the tenant's application.[56] The 14 months' period begins to run from the material time.[57]

(2) *Form of Notice*

To be effective to determine a tenancy to which Part II of the 1954 Act applies, the section 25 notice must be in writing, in the form prescribed by the Landlord and Tenant Act 1954 Part II (Notices) Regulations 1983,[58] or in a form "substantially to the like effect." So, minor deviations from the statutory form will be overlooked. In *Falcon Pipes Ltd.* v. *Stanhope Gate Property Co. Ltd.*[59] an otherwise correct notice in which the space for the date and signature was left blank was held to be "substantially to the like effect," the date being immaterial. In *Tegerdine* v. *Brooks*[60] the omission of certain marginal notes from the statutory notice was held not to be prejudicial to the validity of the landlord's notice. Where two premises are demised to a tenant under one tenancy, a section 25 notice must refer to both premises.[61] A section 25 notice which relates to part only of the holding is bad.[62]

(3) *Date of Termination*

The section 25 notice must state the date on which the current tenancy must come to an end. The date given in the notice must not be earlier than[63]:

    (a) the date on which, in the case of a fixed-term tenancy, it would have expired by effluxion of time,[64] or

---

[56] *René Claro (Haute Coiffure)* v. *Hallé Concerts Society* [1969] 1 W.L.R. 909.
[57] *Diploma Laundry* v. *Surrey Timber Co. Ltd.* [1955] 2 Q.B. 604.
[58] S.I. 1983 No. 133, Form 1. The forms now include warnings in bold print stating the effect of the notice and notifying the tenant of the consequences of his failing to act within the statutory time limit. It is unwise to use out-of-date forms.
[59] (1967) 117 New L.J. 1345. See also *British Railways Board* v. *A. J. A. Smith Transport Ltd.* (1981) 259 E.G. 766 (notice incorrectly stating rateable value limits of county court's jurisdiction held valid).
[60] (1978) 36 P. & C.R. 261.
[61] *Dodson Bull Carpet Co.* v. *City of London Corporation* [1975] 1 W.L.R. 781; *Nevill Long & Co. (Boards)* v. *Firmenich & Co.* (1984) 47 P. & C.R. 59.
[62] *Southport Old Links* v. *Naylor* (1985) 273 E.G. 767.
[63] L. & T.A. 1954, s.25(3),(4).
[64] See *Westbury Property & Investment Co. Ltd.* v. *Carpenter* [1961] 1 All E.R. 481.

(b) the earliest date on which, in the case of a periodic tenancy or the exercise of a break clause, the current tenancy could otherwise have been brought to an end by a notice to quit given by the landlord.

The notice need not specify as its date of determination the precise day on which a notice to quit at common law could end the tenancy, but must specify a date not earlier than that precise date.[65] In one case, however, the court is prepared to relax the formalities even further. A section 25 notice will be valid, even if a wrong date is inserted, provided that it can be clearly established that, in the circumstances, no reasonable tenant would have been misled.[66]

(4) *Time of Giving Notice*

The notice must be given by the landlord not less than six months, nor more than 12 months, before the termination date specified in that notice.[67] The requirement is not for a "clear" six months, so that a notice served on April 2, purporting to terminate the tenancy on October 2 is valid.[68] Where, however, the tenancy agreement requires a period of notice longer than six months in order to terminate it, then the 12 months period is extended to a period equal to the period of notice required under the tenancy, plus six months.[69]

(5) *The Landlord's Opposition*

If the landlord does not want the tenant to have a further tenancy, the notice must say so, and state which of the statutory grounds of objection will be relied on.[70] The statutory grounds of objection are the *only* grounds that may be maintained, and they are to be found in paragraphs (*a*) to (*g*) of section 30(1). The statutory grounds are discussed more fully below, but they broadly fall either into the category of breach by the tenant of his obligations, or of a need for the premises for specified purposes other than letting to this particular tenant. The landlord should, at this stage, state every possible ground on which he may wish to rely since he may, in later proceedings, find himself bound by the statements in his section 25 notice. He may rely on as many of the grounds as he can sustain and, if he can substantiate

---

[65] *Ibid.*
[66] *Germax Securities* v. *Spiegal* (1979) 37 P. & C.R. 204; *Safeway Foodstores* v. *Morris* (1980) 254 E.G. 1091.
[67] L. & T.A. 1954, s.25(2).
[68] *Hogg Bullimore & Co.* v. *Co-operative Insurance Society* (1985) 50 P. & C.R. 105.
[69] L. & T.A. 1954, s.25(3)(b).
[70] L. & T.A. 1954, s.25(6).

any of the grounds in section 30(1)(*a*) to (*d*), which are essentially grounds based on tenant default, the tenant will not be able to claim compensation.[71] While the landlord does not need, at this stage, to set out his full case in respect of the paragraphs relied on, he must, in some way, identify them, either by reference to the paragraph letter (*e.g.* "under paragraph (*a*) of section 31(1) of the Landlord and Tenant Act 1954") or by language clear enough to indicate the particular paragraph intended (*e.g.* "tenants in breach of covenants to repair"). The paragraphs, once stated, cannot subsequently be changed,[72] although provided the notice makes clear an intention to rely on any particular paragraph of section 30(1), the landlord can rely on any facts falling within that paragraph or any portion of it, notwithstanding that the words actually used in the notice were more limited.[73]

(6) *Effect of Notice*

A section 25 notice ends the *contractual* tenancy if it has not already ended. There is no need to serve a separate notice to quit.[74] A notice given under the Act may itself be sufficient to operate a break clause in the lease.[75] The notice must, of course, comply with the contractual provisions as to the time for, and the form of, notice as well as the statutory requirements. If a notice is given which is sufficient to operate a break clause but does not comply with the Act, the tenancy will not end but will continue under section 24.[76] The common law principle that a notice to quit must apply to the whole of the premises let applies to a notice under section 25. Therefore, where a tenant held separate properties under a single tenancy, and subsequently the reversion is severed between the two properties, the landlord of one only of those properties cannot serve a section 25 notice to terminate the tenancy of that property. The right to give notice under section 25 covers the right to serve a notice to quit in respect of the whole of the premises originally let, and it is not a right that can be apportioned on a severance of the reversion.[77]

---

[71] *Post*, Chap. 24.
[72] See *Betty's Cafés Ltd.* v. *Phillips Furnishing Stores Ltd.* [1957] Ch. 67.
[73] *Biles* v. *Caesar* [1957] 1 W.L.R. 156; *Lewis* v. *M.T.C. (Cars)* [1975] 1 W.L.R. 457; *Philipson-Stow* v. *Trevor Square* (1981) 257 E.G. 1262.
[74] *Scholl Manufacturing Co. Ltd.* v. *Clifton (Slim-Line) Ltd.* [1967] Ch. 41.
[75] *René Claro (Haute Coiffure) Ltd.* v. *Hallé Concerts Society* [1967] 2 All E.R. 842.
[76] *Weinbergs Weatherproofs* v. *Radcliffe Paper Mill Co.* [1958] Ch. 437; *Castle Laundry (London) Ltd.* v. *Read* [1955] 1 Q.B. 586. It is sometimes argued that such a notice determines the contract but not the tenancy—see Hill & Redman, p. 718—and, in case this view is correct, two notices may be served, one under the break clause and one under the Act.
[77] *Dodson Bull Carpet Co. Ltd.* v. *City of London Corporation* [1975] 1 W.L.R. 781. It is difficult to see how, in this case, a proper section 25 notice could have been served. One solution may have been for the landlords of the two separate parts to have joined together to serve one notice in order to determine the tenancy. See also *Nevill Long & Co. (Boards)* v. *Firmenich & Co.* (1984) 47 P. & C.R. 59; *Southport Old Links* v. *Naylor* (1985) 273 E.G. 767.

The date of termination specified in a section 25 notice is not always the date when the current tenancy comes to an end. Under section 64 of the 1954 Act, if the service of a section 25 notice results in the tenant making an application to the court for a new tenancy, and the effect of the notice would be to terminate the tenancy before the expiration of three months from the date on which the application is finally disposed of, the tenancy is continued until that three months' period has expired. An application is not, for this purpose, finally disposed of until the issue has been decided and any time for appealing has expired, or the application is withdrawn or any appeal abandoned.[78]

C. Receipt of the Notice—Action by the Tenant

What does a tenant do when he receives a section 25 notice? Not all tenants wish to renew their leases. They may have other, cheaper premises to which they may move. They may want to wind up their businesses and these may not be of a kind that can be sold. If the tenant does nothing in response, the tenancy will end on the date specified in the landlord's notice. Alternatively, the tenant can give notice to his landlord, at least three months before the termination of a fixed term letting, that he does not wish to renew. The tenancy will not then continue under the Act but will, by virtue of section 27(1) of the 1954 Act, simply end by effluxion of time. There is no statutory form of tenant's notice for this purpose.[79] An informal notice which makes plain the tenant's intentions as to giving up possession at the date of termination is sufficient.[80] However, in *Mehmet* v. *Dawson*[81] the Court of Appeal held that a letter from the tenant seeking to negotiate a purchase of the landlord's freehold did not suffice for this purpose. If the contractual expiry date has passed, and the tenancy is continuing by virtue of section 24 of the Act, the tenant may end the tenancy under section 28(2) by a written notice to his landlord which must have a minimum period between service and expiry of three months, and which must expire on a quarter day. In many cases, however, the tenant will want a new tenancy. In this case he must reply to the landlord's section 25 notice by serving a counter-notice on the landlord that unequivocally expresses the tenant's refusal to give up possession.[82] This counter-notice is vital if the tenant is to preserve his right to apply for a new tenancy from the court. Failure to serve

---

[78] L. & T.A. 1954, s.69(2).
[79] For a suitable precedent see *Woodfall*, Vol. 2, App. C3, No. 10.
[80] *Smale* v. *Meakers* (1957) 169 E.G. 287; *Lewington* v. *Trustees of the Society for the Protection of Ancient Buildings* (1983) 45 P. & C.R. 336.
[81] (1983) 270 E.G. 139.
[82] L. & T.A. 1954, s.29(2); *Chiswell* v. *Griffon Land and Estates Ltd.* [1975] 1 W.L.R. 1181.

the counter-notice on the landlord within two months results in a loss of the right to apply.

If, on the other hand, the tenant does serve the counter-notice, then this has the same effect as if he had himself initiated the procedure by requesting a new tenancy under section 26,[83] that is, it entitles him to apply to the court under section 24(1) of the 1954 Act for a new tenancy if the parties cannot reach agreement themselves. The parties may be able to agree quickly on the terms of the new lease. In this case, the current tenancy will end on the date from which the parties have agreed that the new lease shall run.[84] If the parties cannot agree on terms, then the tenant will have to apply to the court for a new tenancy. He gives the landlord notice within two months that he is not yielding up possession.[85] In addition to serving this counter-notice, however, a tenant wishing to apply to the court for a new tenancy must also preserve that right by filing an application to the county court or High Court not less than two, nor more than four months after the landlord's section 25 notice is given.[86] In computing the four months' period, the "corresponding date" rule is applied, *i.e.* the day of service of the s.25 notice[87] is ignored and the application to the court must be made not later than the day corresponding to the day of service four calendar months thereafter, whether or not the day of service is after the 27th day of months with fewer than 31 days.[88] Thus, where notice under section 25 was served on September 30, 1978, the last day for making an application to the court was January 30, 1979 and the tenant's application made on January 31, 1979 was invalid.[89] Similar principles apply to the ascertainment of the two months' period. Hence, where a section 25 notice was given on March 23, 1983 and the tenant's application to the court was made on May 23, 1983, the application was held by the Court of Appeal to have been made not less than two months after March 23, 1983. It was, therefore, not premature and was upheld as a valid application.[90] The Court of Appeal has held that a failure by the tenant to apply to the court for a new tenancy within the time limit specified is fatal to his claim for a new tenancy, even though he has notified the landlord within the appropriate period that a new tenancy is being sought.[91] The reason for this was explained by the Court of Appeal[92] as being

---

[83] This procedure is discussed below.
[84] L. & T.A. 1954, s.28; see the discussion by Pearson J. of the distinction between an agreement for a future tenancy under this section and a reversionary tenancy in *Green* v. *Bowes-Lyon* [1960] 1 All E.R. 301.
[85] L. & T.A. 1954, s.29(2).
[86] *Ibid.* s.29(3).
[87] Or the s.26 request.
[88] *Dodds* v. *Walker* [1981] 1 W.L.R. 1027.
[89] *Ibid.*
[90] *E. J. Riley Investments* v. *Eurostile Holdings* [1985] 3 All E.R. 181.
[91] *Polyviou* v. *Seeley* [1979] 3 All E.R. 853.
[92] *Stile Hall Properties Ltd.* v. *Gooch* [1979] 3 All E.R. 848.

the prevention of tenants' attempts to frustrate the scheme of the 1954 Act by making successive requests for new tenancies, thus prolonging the original tenancies under section 24, without ever appearing before a court and giving landlords the opportunity to contest the renewal.

D. Request for a New Tenancy by the Tenant

The primary right of a tenant of business premises is to apply for and obtain the grant of a new tenancy to follow the determination of the current tenancy. There is, as we have seen, no reason why the parties should not agree to the grant of a new tenancy without recourse to the statutory procedures. If they do so agree, the current tenancy continues until the date fixed for the new tenancy and, in the meantime, is not a tenancy within the 1954 Act.[93]

In the absence of agreement, the tenant obtains his new tenancy by applying for it to the court.[94] He can make an application in two circumstances only. The first arises when the landlord has terminated the current tenancy by a notice served under section 25 of the Act.[95] The second occurs when the tenant has himself terminated the current tenancy by a request for a new tenancy under section 26.

Whereas *any* tenant served by his landlord with a section 25 notice is, by virtue of serving the requisite counter-notice under section 29(2), entitled to apply for a new tenancy, only tenants under a tenancy originally granted for a term exceeding one year are entitled to request a new tenancy under section 26 upon the expiry of their original tenancy, or during its continuance under section 24.[96] A tenant cannot make a section 26 request if the landlord has given a section 25 notice (the tenant must then serve a counter-notice under section 29(2)), or if the tenant has indicated he does not wish to continue pursuant to section 27, or has given his landlord notice to quit. A tenant cannot give notice that he does not wish to continue with the tenancy under section 27 when he has already requested a new tenancy under section 26. The procedures are mutually exclusive.[97]

A tenant may decide to take the initiative under section 26 because he wants a greater measure of security for his business than he obtains by merely holding over on his continuation tenancy under section 24. However, tenants under short-term fixed and periodic tenancies may not, as we have seen, initiate the section 26 procedure; they have the right to apply for a new tenancy only when the landlord serves a

[93] L. & T.A. 1954, s.28.
[94] *Ibid.* ss.24(1), 29(1).
[95] *Ibid.* s.29(2).
[96] *Ibid.* s.26(1).
[97] *Ibid.* s.26(4).

section 25 notice. If it were otherwise a weekly tenant, for example, would have the right, from the first week of his tenancy, to request a fixed term tenancy for up to 14 years. It will be recalled that tenancies granted for a *fixed term* of six months or less are, in any event, outside the protection of Part II of the 1954 Act altogether.[98]

(1) *The Competent Landlord*

The notice must be served by the tenant on the competent landlord. He is defined in the same terms as those appropriate for the service of section 25 notices, described earlier in this chapter.

(2) *Form*

The tenants' notice must be in writing, in the form prescribed by the regulations,[99] or in a form "substantially to the like effect.[1] This is the only case in the 1954 business code in which the tenant is required to use a prescribed form, the other forms prescribed for the purposes of the 1954 Act being required to be served by the landlord on the tenant.

(3) *Time*

The notice must indicate the date on which the new tenancy is to commence, which must not be earlier than the date on which the current tenancy would otherwise have expired. The date on which the new tenancy is to commence must be at least six but not more than 12 months after the request for the new tenancy has been made to the landlord.[2] So, the date specified in the notice as the commencement of the new tenancy automatically puts an end to the old tenancy on that date. The date for commencement can therefore be the date on which the contractual tenancy is due to end or *any* date thereafter, provided it is within the seventh to twelfth month after the section 26 notice has been served.

However, a failure by the tenant to comply with these time limits is capable of being waived. In *Bristol Cars* v. *R.K.H. (Hotels) (In Liquidation)*[3] the tenants gave the landlords a section 26 notice requesting a new tenancy. The notice was dated February 4 and

---

[98] *Ibid.* s.43(3).
[99] Landlord and Tenant Act 1954 Part II (Notices) Regulations 1983, Form 8, S.I. 1983 No. 133.
[1] L. & T.A. 1954, s.26(3).
[2] *Ibid.* s.26(2).
[3] (1979) 33 P. & C.R. 411. See also *British Railways Board* v. *A. J. A. Smith Transport* (1981) 259 E.G. 966; *Watkins* v. *Emslie* (1982) 261 E.G. 1192.

requested a tenancy commencing on February 16. Under section 26(2) of the 1954 Act the date should have been at least six months ahead and not earlier than the date when the tenancy should have come to an end, which would have been October 31. Neither the landlords nor the tenants noticed the mistake, and the landlords indicated that they would not oppose the new tenancy but applied to the court for an interim rent. The landlords then sold the reversion to assignees who, at first, continued the negotiations for an interim rent but later asserted that the tenants' request was bad, and served a notice purporting to terminate the tenancy. They then applied for the tenants' application for a new tenancy to be struck out on the ground of the defective request. The Court of Appeal held that the landlords, having led the tenants to expect that the application would not be opposed, were estopped from denying the validity of the tenants' request. Alternatively, the landlords' application for an interim rent amounted to a waiver of any defect in the tenants' notice.[4]

(4) *Proposed Terms of the Tenancy Requested*

The tenant is required, as part of his notice, to suggest terms for the new tenancy.[5] These proposals fall into four groups:

(a) the tenant must state the property to be comprised in the new tenancy, which may not necessarily include all of the premises held under the current tenancy;

(b) the length of the new tenancy; the courts have held that the same length as under the current tenancy may be implied in the notice, as the term proposed, in those cases where the notice fails to mention the duration expressly, but does mention that the renewal should be on the same terms as the current tenancy[6];

(c) the rent to be payable under the new tenancy;

(d) the other terms of the new tenancy; this will usually be satisfied

---

[4] The court has adopted a similar approach to the time limits imposed on tenants by s.29(3), *viz*: an application to the courts for a new tenancy must be made not earlier than two months and not later than four months after the making of the s.26 request. Since the limits are laid down by statute, the court has no jurisdiction to extend the time: *Hodgson* v. *Armstrong* [1967] 2 Q.B. 299. However, the time limits are procedural requirements and may be waived by the landlord: *Kammins Ballrooms Co. Ltd.* v. *Zenith Instruments (Torquay) Ltd.* [1971] A.C. 850. In *Meah* v. *Sector Properties Ltd.* [1974] 1 All E.R. 1074 an application made after the four months' period, and so late that the tenancy had ended in accordance with the tenant's request, was ordered to be struck out. By the time of the purported application the applicant had ceased to be a tenant at all within the meaning of section 24(1). A tenant cannot withdraw a previous notice and serve a new one with a view to applying to the court within the prescribed time under the new notice: *Stile Hall Properties Ltd.* v. *Gooch* [1979] 3 All E.R. 848; *Polyviou* v. *Seeley* [1979] 3 All E.R. 853.
[5] L. & T.A. 1954, s.26(3).
[6] *Sidney Bolsom Investment Trust* v. *E. Karmios & Co. (London) Ltd.* [1956] 1 Q.B. 529.

by a statement to the effect that in all other respects the renewal should be on the same terms as the current tenancy.

E. Receipt of the Notice—Action by the Landlord

If the tenant requests a new tenancy under section 26, he is not, unlike the landlord serving a section 25 notice, obliged to include in his notice a request to the landlord to make a reply. A landlord who does not reply with a counter-notice to the tenant's section 26 notice, loses any right he may have to oppose the tenant's application. A landlord wishing to oppose his tenant's application for a new tenancy *must* so state in his counter-notice, at the same time basing the grounds of his opposition on the Landlord and Tenant Act 1954, s.30(1), paras. (*a*)—(*g*).[7]

There is no form prescribed for the landlord's counter-notice.[8] The landlord should exercise considerable care in stating whether he will oppose the tenant's application and the grounds on which he will do so, since both he and his successors as landlords will be bound by his decision and will be limited to the grounds specified. The same considerations apply to the statement of grounds of opposition in a counter-notice under s.26(6) as apply to the corresponding statement of grounds in a landlord's notice under s.25(6).

F. Agreement

Landlord and tenant may find themselves in agreement that a new tenancy shall or shall not be granted; they may agree, in the event of a new grant, all the terms of the new tenancy, or they may only be able to agree some of them. Where the parties are agreed in principle on the grant of a new tenancy but are not agreed on all the terms, an application to the court by the tenant is necessary to enable the outstanding terms to be settled. Where they are agreed on all terms, no application to the court need be made. Where the competent landlord and tenant agree for the grant to the tenant of a future tenancy of the holding, or of the holding with other land, on terms and from a date specified in the agreement, the current tenancy continues until that date, and is not a tenancy to which Part II applies.[9] If such an agreement is reached after the tenant has applied to the court and the application is not withdrawn, then the application is automatically invalidated by virtue of the fact that the current tenancy ceases, before

---

[7] L. & T.A. 1954, s.26(6).
[8] For a precedent see *Woodfall*, Vol. 2, App. C3, No. 11.
[9] L. & T.A. 1954, s.28.

the hearing, to qualify under Part II of the 1954 Act.[10] This situation must, however, be distinguished from that in which the parties reach agreement on terms which the court is then asked to incorporate in an order for a new tenancy. In this case the continuation tenancy remains subject to Part II.

Where, after the tenant has applied to the court for a new tenancy, the parties reach agreement as to all the terms of a proposed new tenancy, the agreement can be embodied in an order of the court, although the simpler and cheaper course is for the tenant to withdraw the application on the terms agreed. If the parties wish to settle the matter on the basis that the tenant shall abandon his claim for a new tenancy, this can be done through admission, on the tenant's part, of the facts constituting the landlord's ground of opposition under s.30(1), whereupon the court, by consent, will dismiss the application. Another possibility is for the tenant to withdraw the application. The tenant may withdraw on the basis of a new agreement, for example, that the tenant shall be granted a lease of the whole or part of the reconstructed premises, where the landlord's ground of opposition to a new tenancy had been based on section 30(1)(f) of the 1954 Act.[11] The court is likely to take a fairly liberal view in such a case as to whether an agreement has been reached.[12] In the High Court leave is required for withdrawal,[13] but is usually given, provided the landlord will suffer no injustice.[14] In granting leave, the court will not put the tenant on terms not to claim compensation under s.37 of the Act,[15] and the landlord's statutory obligation to pay compensation is not regarded as, of itself, evidence of injustice or prejudice occasioned by the withdrawal.[16] The advantage to the landlord of a withdrawal is that there can be no appeal and the current tenancy will come to an end on a known date *i.e.* the end of the period of three months beginning with the date of withdrawal.[17]

IV. THE STATUTORY GROUNDS OF OPPOSITION

In resisting the tenant's demands for a new tenancy the landlord can rely on seven statutory grounds of opposition. These grounds are set

[10] *cf. I. & H. Caplan* v. *Caplan (No. 2)* [1963] 1 W.L.R. 1247; *Hancock & Willis* v. *G.M.S. Syndicate* (1983) 265 E.G. 473.
[11] See below.
[12] *Trustees of National Deposit Friendly Society* v. *Beatties of London* (1985) 275 E.G. 54.
[13] R.S.C., Ord. 21, r. 3(1).
[14] *Covell Matthews & Partners* v. *French Wools* [1977] 1 W.L.R. 876; *Young, Austen & Young* v. *B.M.A.* [1977] 1 W.L.R. 881.
[15] *Ove Arup Inc.* v. *Howland Property Investment Co.* (1981) 42 P. & C.R. 37; *Fribourg & Treyer* v. *Northdall Investments* (1982) 44 P. & C.R. 284.
[16] Because of the provision for payment of compensation if the landlord had served a counter-notice under the Act: *Lloyds Bank* v. *London City Corporation* [1983] Ch. 192.
[17] See *Woodfall*, paras. 2–0689—2–0690.

out in the Landlord and Tenant Act 1954, s.30(1), paras. (*a*)—(*g*). Under paragraphs (*a*)—(*c*) and paragraph (*e*), the court has a discretion to order the grant of a new tenancy even when the landlord has made out his ground. In the other cases the court is obliged to refuse the application for a new tenancy if the ground of opposition is made out by the landlord to its satisfaction.

A. Breach of Repairing Obligations: s.30(1)(*a*)

This ground requires the landlord to prove that the tenant ought not to be granted a new tenancy in view of the state of repair of the premises resulting from the tenant's failure to observe repairing obligations under the current tenancy. It is not sufficient for the landlord to prove simply that the tenant is in breach of his repairing covenants: he must satisfy the court that the breach is so serious that the tenant ought not to be granted a new tenancy. The court, therefore, has a discretion and consequently in exercising its discretion, would take into account an undertaking by the tenant to remedy the breach.[18]

B. Persistent Delay in Paying Rent: s.30(1)(*b*)

A landlord may object that the tenant ought not to be granted a new tenancy in view of his persistent delay in paying rent due under the current tenancy. The requirement of "persistent delay" means that there must have been more than one occasion, or a very long delay, in paying rent. It indicates a course of conduct over a period,[19] and the court will have to take into account the number of times there has been a delay, the length of the delay, the steps which the landlord was obliged to take to secure payment,[20] the reason, if any given for the delay, and whether the landlord can be adequately safeguarded against future delays by inserting in the new tenancy a suitable proviso for re-entry and by requiring security for prompt payment to be given.[21]

C. Other Substantial Breaches of Obligations: s.30(1)(*c*)

The landlord may object that the tenant ought not to be granted a new tenancy in view of other substantial breaches of obligations under the

---

[18] See *Lyons* v. *Central Commercial Properties London* [1958] 1 W.L.R. 869.
[19] *Horrowitz* v. *Ferrand* [1956] 5 C.L. 207.
[20] *Ibid.*
[21] *Hopcutt* v. *Carver* (1969) 209 E.G. 1069.

current tenancy, or for any other reason connected with the tenant's use or management of the holding. Any breach of any obligation under the current tenancy can be relied upon by the landlord but in exercising its discretion the court will consider the seriousness of the breach, proposals for its remedy, and whether the landlord has acquiesced in it.[22] This particular ground of objection goes beyond just breaches of obligation and embraces also "any other reason connected with the tenant's use or management of the holding." It is by no means clear what this means. Does it, for example, go so far as to allow the landlord to object to the tenant on personal grounds? In *Turner & Bell* v. *Searles (Stanford-le-Hope)*[23] the court refused a new tenancy on the ground that the tenant intended to use the premises in breach of an enforcement notice. Thus, "any other reason" can relate to future, as well as to past conduct of the tenant.

D. Availability of Suitable Alternative Accommodation: s.30(1)(*d*)

A landlord is entitled to object to the tenant's request for a new tenancy on the ground that he has offered, and is willing to provide, suitable alternative accommodation for the tenant on terms which are, in all the circumstances, reasonable. The offer must be on terms which are reasonable having regard to the terms of the current tenancy and to all other relevant circumstances. These will include whether or not the goodwill attaching to the business will be preserved, the nature and character of the tenant's business, and the situation, size and other facilities of the premises under the current tenancy. The alternative accommodation may consist of part of the accommodation already occupied by the tenant under the current tenancy.[24]

If the court is satisfied that suitable alternative accommodation has been offered on reasonable terms, it has no discretion[25] to order a new tenancy and must refuse the application. From the wording of section 30(1)(*d*) it would appear that a tenant who is refused a new tenancy under this paragraph can elect forthwith to accept the offer of alternative accommodation. However, the Act contains no provision for the landlord's offer to be kept open for a time sufficient to enable the tenant to accept should his application for a new tenancy be

---

[22] *Eichner* v. *Midland Bank Executor and Trustee Co.* [1970] 1 W.L.R. 1120; *Hutchinson* v. *Lamberth* (1983) 270 E.G. 545.

[23] (1977) 33 P. & C.R. 208.

[24] *Thompson* v. *Rolls* [1926] 2 K.B. 426; *Parmee* v. *Mitchell* [1950] 2 K.B. 199; *Mykolyshyn* v. *Noah* [1970] 1 W.L.R. 1217. The court has, however, warned against arguing, by analogy, with cases decided under the Rent Act 1977, s.98 and Sched. 15, Pt. IV: see *post*. Principles applicable to retention by tenants of places which are required as a home have little bearing on the position of a tenant who requires a place in which to conduct his business: *Singh* v. *Malayan Theatres* [1953] A.C. 632. This will not be the case with "assured" tenancies which are, by virtue of H.A. 1980, s.56, within L. & T.A. 1954, Pt. II.

[25] *Betty's Cafés* v. *Phillips Furnishing Stores* [1957] Ch. 67, *per* Birkett L.J. at p. 84.

unsuccessful. Hence, once the landlord has withdrawn his offer, the tenant would appear to have no redress unless the circumstances of the withdrawal are such as to indicate that the landlord misrepresented his intentions to the court, (thereby inducing the court to refuse the grant of a new tenancy), in which case the tenant may be able to claim damages from the landlord under section 55 of the 1954 Act.[26]

E. Possession Required for Letting or Disposing of the Property as a Whole in the Case of a Sub-tenancy: s.30(1)(e)

The landlord may object that the tenant ought not to be granted a new tenancy in view of the fact that the current tenancy was created by a sub-letting of only a part of the premises let under a superior tenancy by the landlord, that he might reasonably expect to re-let more advantageously as a whole, and that consequently he requires possession for the purpose of re-letting, or otherwise disposing of the whole property as a single unit. This ground will, of course, only be relevant where the interest of the tenant's *immediate* landlord is shortly to end. It is only in such a circumstance that the superior landlord will be the "competent" landlord for the purposes of serving the section 25 notice or receiving the section 26 notice.[27] Therefore, because there will be an intermediate tenant between the "competent" landlord, who is claiming possession, and the sub-tenant, who is disputing the claim, the "competent" landlord will have some difficulty establishing that he requires possession in order to dispose of the property as a whole. Unless the intermediate interest would end at about the same time as the applicant sub-tenant's interest would end if the landlord was successful, resisting the claim for a new tenancy would not, of itself, make the disposal of the property as a whole any easier. In practice therefore, this ground does not often arise.

This ground is again discretionary, and in exercising its discretion the court takes into account the fact that the landlord had consented to the sub-letting, for instance, as required under a term of the tenancy out of which the sub-tenancy was derived. The landlord will need to show that the rental income from the property as a whole would be substantially higher (one assumes in net terms, although the subsection is not specific on the point), if it were re-let as a whole than if it were re-let in parts. This reason for requiring possession is not, however, limited to re-letting, for a landlord may rely on the ground if, on the termination of the current tenancy, he intends to sell with vacant possession.

[26] *Post* Chap. 24.
[27] L. & T.A. 1954, s.44(1); see *supra*.

F. The Landlord Intends to Demolish or Reconstruct: s.30(1)(*f*)

The landlord can maintain that on the termination of the current tenancy he intends to demolish the whole or a substantial part of the premises, or to carry out substantial work of construction upon them, and that he could not reasonably do so without obtaining possession of the premises. If the landlord is able to prove this ground to the satisfaction of the court, it must refuse the application for a new tenancy and grant him possession.

The landlord must, therefore, establish the relevant intention and also his need for possession. With regard to the issue of intention, since an appropriate intention must also be established to maintain the ground contained in section 30(1)(*g*), and since also the issues involved there are similar to those in paragraph (*f*), consideration of what amounts to the requisite intention will be deferred until paragraph (*g*) has been discussed.

The intention of the landlord to demolish or reconstruct has to be established as at the date on which the application is heard by the court,[28] not at the time of service of the notice. As we shall see presently, the continuation tenancy does not come to an end immediately the landlord secures his order for possession from the court, but there is a further period of grace allowed to the tenant by the 1954 Act to enable him to find other premises. During this period the continuation tenancy is further extended. So, the date of termination of the current tenancy cannot always be accurately assessed at the hearing. Aside from the possibility of an appeal, (a delaying tactic frequently resorted to by tenants, even where there are no meritorious grounds besides the desire to secure more time), the continuation tenancy will normally end, in practice, approximately four and a half months after the court's decision. It follows that the landlord has to show an intention to start the work on which he relies at or shortly after a date which is four and a half months from the hearing. If he cannot establish his intention to start at that date, but can do so in relation to a date within the next year, he may still succeed, ultimately, in securing possession, though not until the date upon which he intends to commence the work.[29] Plans to start work within three months of termination were held, in *Livestock Underwriting Agency* v. *Corbett & Newton*,[30] to be sufficient.

The landlord must show his intention to demolish or reconstruct an existing structure. If the holding subject to dispute is largely unbuilt upon, then the premises that are capable of demolition or reconstruction for this purpose are such structures as do exist.[31] The courts have

---

[28] *Betty's Cafés* v. *Phillips Furnishing Stores* [1959] A.C. 20.
[29] L. & T.A. 1954, s.30(2); see *post*.
[30] (1955) 165 E.G. 469.
[31] *Houseleys Ltd.* v. *Bloomer-Holt Ltd.* [1966] 2 All E.R. 966.

held that reconstruction means rebuilding[32] and clearly implies the demolition of at least part so that reconstruction, as against construction or building on a vacant site, can take place.[33] Reconstruction therefore involves some substantial interference with the existing structure and this has led to difficult decisions of fact as to the degree of work required. The words "demolition or reconstruction" are construed conjunctively. In *Joel* v. *Swaddle*[34] an intention to change the character or identity of the premises from a small shop with two storage rooms, into part of a large hall intended to become an amusement arcade, was held to be within paragraph (*f*). In *Percy E. Cadle & Co. Ltd.* v. *Jacmarch Properties Ltd.*[35] an intention to change a building by turning three floors, which had been occupied separately, into a self-contained unit with internal staircases, was found not to be within the ground of opposition, although had there been in this case an intention also to change the nature of the premises, *e.g.* from retail premises to office accommodation, the landlords might have succeeded. In *Atkinson* v. *Bettison*[36] the installation of a new shop front was held not to be a sufficient act of reconstruction. Matters such as the making of a service road, the laying of concrete and pipes, cables and drains, may be works of reconstruction, depending upon the amount and intensity of the operation.[37] The landscaping of a field, without any building construction or reconstruction, has been held by the Court of Appeal not to amount to "reconstruction" within paragraph (*f*).[38] The proper approach to the question seems to be whether what is intended will or will not amount to reconstruction of a substantial part of the holding, having regard to the position as a whole and comparing the effect on the premises of carrying out the proposed work with the condition and state of the premises before the work is done.[39]

The landlord is also required to show that he has need for possession of the premises. Before 1969 a landlord could defeat a tenant's application on the ground that he required possession, even though, in fact, he needed possession of only part of the holding, or needed possession for a short time only.[40] There was no provision enabling the tenant either to accept a new tenancy of those parts of the premises not required by the landlord, or to vacate the premises temporarily while the work was being done. The Law of Property Act 1969 therefore added a new section to the 1954 Act.[41] Section 31A(1)

[32] *e.g. Percy E. Cadle & Co. Ltd.* v. *Jacmarch Properties Ltd.* [1957] 1 Q.B. 323.
[33] *Cook* v. *Mott* (1961) 178 E.G. 637.
[34] [1957] 1 W.L.R. 1094.
[35] [1957] 1 Q.B. 323.
[36] [1955] 3 All E.R. 340.
[37] See *Cook* v. *Mott* (1961) 178 E.G. 637; *Houseleys Ltd.* v. *Bloomer-Holt Ltd.* [1966] 2 All E.R. 966.
[38] *Botterill* v. *Bedfordshire County Council* (1985) 273 E.G. 1217.
[39] *Bewlay (Tobacconists) Ltd.* v. *Bata Shoe Co. Ltd.* [1958] 3 All E.R. 652.
[40] *Fernandez* v. *Walding* [1968] 2 Q.B. 606.
[41] L.P.A. 1969, s.7(1).

of the 1954 Act now provides that the landlord cannot establish his need for possession under paragraph (*f*) if:

(i)   the tenant is willing to have included in the terms of the new tenancy a reservation giving the landlord access and other facilities reasonably necessary and sufficient for carrying out the proposed work, without interfering to a substantial extent or for a substantial time with the tenant's business on the premises; *or*

(ii) the tenant is willing to accept a new tenancy of an economically separable part of the holding, provided that the landlord can reasonably carry out the works by having possession of the remainder (if necessary with rights reserved, as in (i) above, over the parts retained by the tenant). For the purposes of this provision, whether the part is an economically separable part is judged from the landlords point of view. The test[42] is whether, after the landlord has carried out the work intended, the aggregate rent of the part and the remainder of the premises affected by the work will not be substantially less than the rent then obtainable on a letting of the premises as a whole.

As far as (i) above is concerned, it will clearly only be relevant in those cases in which the tenant's lease does not already contain a term permitting the landlord entry for the carrying out of works. If the lease does contain such a term, it is unlikely that the landlord would be able to oppose the grant of a new tenancy on the ground contained in paragraph (*f*) anyway, because he could not show that he needed the court to grant him possession in opposition to the tenants claim.[43]

Whether the tenant's business will be interfered with to a substantial extent or for a substantial time, is very much a matter of fact and degree. It probably marks the difference between the situation where the work can go ahead with only temporary and minor inconvenience to the tenant's business, from which it will soon recover again, and the situation when the business is totally disrupted and has to close down for a time.

It might be thought that, in so far as the requirement that the works be not too disruptive of the tenant's business is solely for the tenant's benefit, he might, if desperate to retain his tenancy, waive this

---

[42] See s.31A(2).

[43] See *Little Park Service Station Ltd.* v. *Regent Oil Co. Ltd.* [1967] 2 Q.B. 655, *per* Russell L.J. at p. 661. It is not clear that the learned judge is correct in his observation. It is not possession under the original tenancy, (to which the landlord may have had a right by virtue of a right of entry to do the works), which is in issue, but whether he could be given a right of entry and possession in the new tenancy consistent with the tenant's enjoyment of the property. *cf.* The discussion of *Heath* v. *Drown* [1973] A.C. 498, *post.*

provision. However, this is not so, as *Redfern* v. *Reeves*[44] illustrates.
The tenant occupied business premises under a lease which allowed
the landlord to enter the premises to carry out structural repairs. The
tenant applied for a new lease under the 1954 Act and was opposed by
the landlord on the ground, *inter alia*, that he intended to reconstruct
and could not reasonably do so without securing possession. The
tenant argued that, pursuant to section 31A(1), she would give the
landlord access to carry out the work, regardless of the interference of the
her business. It was found that, in order to do the work, the tenant
would have to be completely out of occupation for some four months.
The Court of Appeal held that, for section 31A(1) to apply, it had to
be shown that the landlord could carry out the work without
interfering with the tenant's use of the building for the purpose of her
business. The test was not solely whether the work could be done
without substantial interference to the tenant's business or goodwill,
nor did the section confer upon the tenant an option to disregard any
matter of disruption or inconvenience if she so wished.

However, the usual result of section 31A(1) is undoubtedly to
reduce the significance of the landlord establishing his need for
possession of a substantial part of the premises to carry out his works.
It is now more difficult than it was for a landlord to recover possession
on the ground in paragraph (*f*). Aside from cases involving complete
demolition or reconstruction, which are not really affected by section
31A, the main issues are whether or not the proposed work could
reasonably be carried out with the tenant remaining in occupation,
and whether or not the landlord could reasonably make do with
possession of only part of the premises.

The word "possession" in paragraph (*f*) means legal possession
rather than physical possession,[45] so that the fact that the landlord
could not carry out the intended work without obtaining physical
possession of the holding does not conclude the matter in the
landlord's favour. In *Heath* v. *Drown*[46] the current tenancy reserved to
the landlord the right, upon notice, to enter the demised premises to
carry out any necessary repairs. In answer to the tenant's application
for a new tenancy the landlord relied on paragraph (*f*). The deputy
county court judge held that the landlord needed exclusive physical
possession of the premises for the execution of the repairs and that,
given access and facilities by the tenant, the landlord could not
reasonably carry out the work without interfering substantially with
the tenant's right of enjoyment. Accordingly, he held that section
31A(1) was inapplicable and that, as the landlord could not reasonably carry out the works without obtaining physical possession of the
holding, the landlord succeeded. The Court of Appeal affirmed this

[44] (1978) 37 P. & C.R. 364; *cf. Heath* v. *Drown* [1973] A.C. 498.
[45] *Heath* v. *Drown* [1973] A.C. 497.
[46] *Ibid.*

decision. However, the House of Lords, by a majority, held that the word "possession" in section 30(1)(*f*) meant the legal right to possession and that "obtaining possession of the holding" meant putting an end to such rights of possession of the holding as were vested in the tenant under the terms of his current tenancy. Therefore, in this case, section 31A was irrelevant because the reservation to the landlord of the right to do the repairs would inevitably be imported into the new tenancy and, because of this, it was not reasonably necessary for the landlord to obtain possession of the holding. Since possession is largely a question of fact, it could be argued that the term "legal possession" (unless used in contrast to adverse possession, which it is not here) is meaningless, and misled the courts.

If the right of access granted by the lease is extensive enough to permit the landlord to complete the work, such as a right to carry out improvements, alterations and additions, and these are the only works the landlord intends to undertake, s.31A(1)(*a*) precludes reliance on paragraph (*f*).[47] Paragraph (*f*) may, however, be utilised if the works in contemplation go outside the ambit of the right of access so as to render the tenant's permitted user thereafter impossible, such as a total rebuilding.[48]

G. The Landlord's Intention to Occupy the Premises Himself: s.30(1)(g)

A landlord may object to the tenant's application for a new tenancy on the ground that, on the termination of the current tenancy, he, the landlord, intends to occupy the premises for the purposes of his own business to be carried on there, or for his own residence, provided that his interest in the holding was not purchased or created within the previous five years. For this purpose, the landlord's intentions to carry on business on the premises in partnership with someone else suffices.[49] Also, the landlord is within the ground if his intention is to occupy through a manager of the business.[50] As in the case of the ground established by paragraph (*f*), the landlord's intention has to be proved, and must exist, at the date of the hearing, and the landlord can be successful if he shows that the occupation of a substantial part of the property is intended to take place within a reasonable time after the end of the tenancy.[51] Paragraph (*g*) cannot be utilised by a landlord who intends to *demolish* on a site consisting solely of existing buildings and put new buildings on the site in their place, since he

---

[47] *Price* v. *Esso Petroleum Ltd.* (1980) 255 E.G. 243.
[48] *Leathwoods Ltd.* v. *Total Oil (Great Britain) Ltd.* (1984) 270 E.G. 1083; *Mularczyk* v. *Azralnove Investments* (1985) 276 E.G. 1064.
[49] *Re Crowhurst Park, Sims-Hilditch* v. *Simmons* [1974] 1 W.L.R. 583.
[50] *Hills (Patents) Ltd.* v. *Board of Governors of University College Hospital* [1956] 1 Q.B. 90.
[51] *Method Developments Ltd.* v. *Jones* [1971] 1 W.L.R. 168.

does not then intend to occupy "the property comprised in the holding."[52] Different considerations, however, apply where the site is vacant. Section 30(1)(*g*) may then be used by a landlord seeking possession in order to erect buildings on that site for use in his own business.[53] It is not necessary to show an intention to occupy the whole immediately. The factors relevant to the establishment of the landlord's intention are the same as those affecting paragraph (*f*) and are therefore discussed generally below. The landlord must intend to occupy the whole of the premises,[54] though he need only use them partly for his business. This allows for "mixed" use. Alternatively the landlord may require the whole of the premises as his residence and still maintain the ground. The landlord cannot, however, rely on paragraph (*g*) if he wishes to occupy the premises for the purposes of reletting parts of the premises as residential flats,[55] and this disability is not circumvented if the landlord intends to occupy the premises himself for his own residence during a short period while conversion and redecoration works are carried out.[56]

The question of *who* is to occupy may create problems, in that it may not, strictly, be the same person as the "competent" landlord. As we have seen earlier,[57] there are a number of ways in which the question whether the occupation is for the *landlord's* own business is answered in a somewhat lenient fashion. The Landlord and Tenant Act 1954, s.41(2), provides that where the landlords are trustees, holding the reversionary interest on trust for the beneficiaries, the intention of any beneficiary under the trust to occupy for his business is sufficient to establish the ground.[58] The landlord's notice stating the ground of opposition to the tenant's obtaining a new tenancy can be validly given by the trustees.[59] Where premises are owned by a landlord as trustee, both he and the beneficiaries may oppose the grant of a new tenancy under paragraph (*g*),[60] provided that, as far as any beneficiary is concerned, the beneficial interest has not been created within the five years immediately preceding the determination of the tenancy.[61] In so far as the landlord is concerned, it is irrelevant to his reliance on paragraph (*g*) whether his interest has been held

---

[52] See L. & T.A. 1954, s.23(3): *Nursey* v. *P. Currie (Dartford) Ltd.* [1959] 1 W.L.R. 273; *cf. McKenna* v. *Porter Motors* [1956] A.C. 688, on a similar question arising on the New Zealand Tenancy Act 1948, and *Houseleys* v. *Bloomer-Holt* [1966] 1 W.L.R. 1244 on L. & T.A. 1954, s.30(1)(*f*).

[53] *Cam Gears Ltd.* v. *Cunningham* [1981] 1 W.L.R. 1011. Similarly, where the site consists partly of buildings and partly of vacant site, para. (g) may be relied upon by a landlord intending to demolish the buildings and construct others: *Leathwoods Ltd.* v. *Total Oil (Great Britain) Ltd.* (1984) 270 E.G. 1083.

[54] See *Lightcliffe & District Cricket and Lawn Tennis Club* v. *Walton* (1977) 245 E.G. 393.

[55] *Jones* v. *Jenkins, The Times,* December 14, 1985.

[56] *Ibid.*

[57] *Supra,* Chap. 20.

[58] *Carshalton Beeches Bowling Club* v. *Cameron* (1979) 249 E.G. 1279.

[59] *Sevenarts Ltd.* v. *Busvine* [1968] 1 W.L.R. 1929.

[60] L. & T.A. 1954, s.41(2).

[61] *Morar* v. *Chauhan* [1985] 3 All E.R. 493.

beneficially or as trustee.[62] By virtue of section 42(3) of the 1954 Act, where a landlord is a company, and that company is a member of a group of companies, occupation for its own use by any member of the group suffices to sustain the landlord's opposition to renewal. Companies are regarded as in the same group for this purpose if one is a subsidiary of the other or both are subsidiaries of a third.[63]

Where a company is controlled not by another company but by an individual, that individual can, as landlord, obtain possession, so that the company can carry on its business in the premises.[64] The landlord will be regarded as having a controlling interest either where he holds more than half of the company's equity share capital (disregarding nominee and fiduciary holdings) or he is a shareholder and can alone appoint or remove the holders of at least a majority of the directorships. It is the landlord who must be the individual in this situation. If a family company owns the reversion and its majority shareholders wish to carry on a business personally there, the company cannot oppose a renewal on the ground set out in paragraph (*g*).[65]

A landlord cannot successfully oppose a new tenancy on the ground contained in paragraph (*g*) if the circumstances set out in section 30(2) pertain, *i.e.* if:

(i)   the landlord's interest in the property was purchased by him, or created (where the landlord himself is only a leaseholder) within the five years preceding the termination date specified in the original notice served under section 25, or the request made under section 26; *and*

(ii) throughout that five year period, there has been a tenancy or succession of tenancies of the holding, to all of which Part II of the 1954 Act applied or applies.

So, if the landlord has acquired the freehold, or a tenancy of the premises, whether by purchase or (in the case of a head lease) by grant or assignment, within the five years period, he cannot rely on paragraph (*g*) unless there was a time during that period when there was no business tenancy of the holding in being within Part II of the 1954 Act. For example, suppose A had bought the freehold on January 1, 1976, subject to a six years' business tenancy granted to B in 1968, which has been renewed; A could oppose under paragraph (*g*) in 1986, but not in 1980, because of the five years rule. However, if B's tenancy had first come up for renewal *after* A had bought the freehold,

---

[62] *Ibid.*
[63] L. & T.A. 1954, s.42(1).
[64] *Ibid.* s.30(3); *Harvey Textiles Ltd.* v. *Hillel* (1978) 249 E.G. 1063.
[65] These provisions probably do not extend to assist partnerships who wish to secure a new tenancy from a landlord who is one of the partners, nor will they assist partners who are shareholders in the landlord company if the premises are required for the partnership business.

and B had renewed it, A would then be B's landlord by grant and not by purchase, and he might then oppose B's subsequent application for statutory renewal on the ground in paragraph (*g*), even though five years may not have elapsed since A became the owner of the freehold. It is tentatively suggested that the five years limitation may have no application if the landlord himself granted the tenancy in question.[66] For the purposes of the five years rule, the landlord's interest in the property dates from its first purchase or creation, and can include a succession of tenancies granted to that landlord.[67] So, if A takes a lease by assignment on January 1, 1976, and had been granted a new head lease on January 1, 1977, he would be entitled to rely on paragraph (*g*) from January 2, 1981.

Even though the five years rule may preclude the court from denying the tenant a new tenancy, it may still be in the landlord's interest to plead and prove the other facts that need to be established to sustain paragraph (*g*), since these may well influence the judge in reducing the length of the term granted on renewal.[68] Another tactical advantage may be secured if the landlord gives an undertaking to the court that he will occupy the premises. Notwithstanding its apparently self-validating character, judges sometimes accept that such undertakings materially add to the evidence tending to prove a genuine intention to occupy.[69] The question whether the landlord's interest was acquired by "purchase" within the preceding five years requires the word "purchase" to be given its ordinary meaning of buying for money.[70] It does not cover the landlord who has become so by virtue of a surrender (*i.e.* merger) of an intermediate tenancy, without payment of consideration, for his interest has not then been "purchased" or "created."[71]

H. The Landlord's Intention

Both paragraph (*f*) and paragraph (*g*) require proof of the requisite intention, either of demolition and reconstruction, or own occupation, as the case may be, on the part of the landlord. Satisfactory proof of intention often gives rise to difficulties. In *Cunliffe* v. *Goodman*[72] Asquith L.J. indicated[73] that the project must have "moved out of the

---

[66] *cf. Northcote Laundry Ltd.* v. *Frederick Donnelly Ltd.* [1968] 1 W.L.R. 562; see pp. 692–693, *supra.*
[67] *Artemiou* v. *Procopiou* [1966] 1 Q.B. 878.
[68] *Upsons Ltd.* v. *E. Robins Ltd.* [1956] 1 Q.B. 131.
[69] *Espresso Coffee Machine Co. Ltd.* v. *Guardian Assurance Co. Ltd.* [1959] 1 W.L.R. 250. See also *Chez Gerard Ltd.* v. *Greene Ltd.* (1983) 268 E.G. 575.
[70] *H. L. Bolton (Engineering) Co. Ltd.* v. *T. J. Graham & Sons Ltd.* [1957] 1 Q.B. 159.
[71] *Lawrence (Frederick) Ltd.* v. *Freeman, Hardy and Willis* [1957] Ch. 731.
[72] [1950] 2 K.B. 237.
[73] *Ibid.* pp. 253, 254. Refusal of planning consent is clearly relevant to proof of the relevant intention, unless the tenant is the local planning authority: *Westminster City Council* v. *British Waterways Board* [1984] 3 All E.R. 737.

zone of contemplation—out of the sphere of the tentative the provisional and the exploratory—into the valley of decision."[74] Oft quoted and eloquent though these words may be, they do not advance us very far and seem, rather, to be merely another way of stating the problem. It is clear that the landlord must have taken some active steps that would enable him to implement his intention. For example, if planning permission is likely to be necessary, he should either have taken steps to obtain permission, or have ascertained that it is unnecessary.[75] The onus of proof is on the landlord. He must produce evidence that would cause a reasonable man to think that he had a reasonable prospect of giving effect to his intention but if the tenant's delaying tactics are the only obstacle to the landlord's intention possession will generally be ordered.[76] The test is an objective one.[77] The question of intention can be tried as a separate, preliminary issue before questions about the terms of the new tenancy are considered.[78]

Evidence of intention can be given by showing, for example, that plans have been drawn up, that tenders have been sought for building work, that the requisite finance will be available, that decisions had been recorded in the landlord company's board minutes and that quotations for work had been received,[79] and so on. It will be recalled that the decision in *Betty's Cafés* v. *Phillips Furnishing Stores*[80] requires the landlord's intention to be proved at the time of the hearing. If, therefore, the landlord subsequently changes his mind when he has gained possession, the tenant has no remedy,[81] unless the landlord has practised deliberate deception.[82] Intention to reconstruct need not be the primary purpose of seeking possession under paragraph (*f*). Paragraph (*f*) may make it possible for a landlord to recover possession, even though his primary intention, which he is precluded from asserting because of the five years' rule, is to carry on his own business on the premises.[83] The fact that a landlord has until the hearing to get his evidence of the appropriate intention in order, is a factor a tenant should bear in mind in deciding whether to oppose the landlord.

---

[74] These words were approved by the Court of Appeal in *DAF Motoring Centre (Gosport)* v. *Hutfield & Wheeler* (1982) 263 E.G. 976.
[75] *Gregson* v. *Cyril Lord Ltd.* [1963] 1 W.L.R. 41.
[76] *A. J. A. Smith Transport Ltd.* v. *British Railways Board* (1980) 257 E.G. 1257.
[77] *Poppett's (Caterers) Ltd.* v. *Maidenhead Borough Council* [1971] 1 W.L.R. 69.
[78] *Dutch Oven Ltd.* v. *Egham Estate & Investment Co. Ltd.* [1968] 1 W.L.R. 1483.
[79] *Europark (Midlands)* v. *Town Centre Securities* (1985) 271 E.G. 289.
[80] [1959] A.C. 20, *supra.*
[81] *Reohorn* v. *Barry Corp.* [1956] 1 W.L.R. 845.
[81] L. & T.A. 1954, s.55; *post*, Chap. 24.
[82] *Betty's Cafés Ltd.* v. *Phillips Furnishing Stores Ltd.* [1959] A.C. 20.
[83] An application for a new tenancy will not be out of time merely because it is erroneously made to a county court outside the district in which the premises are situated and consequently is not received by the proper court until after the time limit has expired: *Sharma* v. *Knight* (1986) 136 N.L.J. 332.

V. THE NEW TENANCY

A. The Court

The application for a new tenancy can be made either to the High Court or the County Court. The rateable value of the premises will determine to which court the tenant applies. Where the rateable value of the property subject to the new tenancy does not exceed £5,000, the application is made to the County Court in whose district the premises lie.[83a] In all other cases it is made to the High Court. Whether the application is made to the County Court or High Court, there are detailed procedures and very strict time limits to be observed.[84] These have been discussed earlier in this chapter and are rarely waived.[85]

In many cases the issues between the landlord and tenant will be settled, eventually, by agreement. However, where an agreement is reached between the parties in an effort to avoid going to court, but that agreement is made "subject to contract and without prejudice" to the tenant's rights under the Landlord and Tenant Act 1954 (as it will usually be pending the formal execution of the new lease by both parties), it is still open to either party, at any time before the new lease is executed, to change his mind and press on through the courts.[86]

A compromise is generally reached on the rent to be paid somewhere between the figure settled on by the landlord's surveyor and that put forward by the tenant's surveyor. In the meantime there is the possibility that the tenant will continue in occupation under the old rent while negotiations are proceeding. As we have already seen, there is machinery for a landlord to apply for an interim rent increase which will run from the date when proceedings were commenced, or the proposed date of the new tenancy in the section 25 or section 26 notices, whichever is latest.[87] A separate application merely for an interim rent is unlikely to be a financially attractive proposition in terms of costs and is, therefore, in practice, normally only resorted to by a landlord who is seeking to put as much "pressure" as possible on his tenant. It is most likely that the interim rent will be disposed of at the same time as the tenant's application. This may mean that he then has to pay a substantial amount in arrears of rent.

[83a] *Ibid.*

[84] See generally, C.C.R., Ord. 43; R.S.C., Ord. 97; L. & T.A. 1954, s.63. *N.B.* C.C.R., Ord. 7, r. 20, permitting the county court to allow extended time: *Ali* v. *Knight* (1984) 272 E.G. 1165.

[85] *Kammins Ballrooms Co. Ltd.* v. *Zenith Investments (Torquay) Ltd.* [1971] A.C. 850; *Lewis & Weksler* v. *Wolking Properties* [1978] 1 W.L.R. 403.

[86] *Derby & Co. Ltd.* v. *I.T.C. Pensions Trusts Ltd.* [1977] 2 All E.R. 890; *cf. Trustees of National Deposit Friendly Society* v. *Beatties of London* (1985) 275, E.G. 55.

[87] L. & T.A. 1954, s.24A.

Procedure in the High Court is by originating summons in the Chancery Division. The normal course is for each side to file its evidence by affidavit as directed by the Master and for the summons then to be adjourned to the judge. In the County Court the procedure is by originating application and answer. The proceedings in either court fall into two parts, the first being the determination of the question whether the tenant is entitled to an order for the grant of a new tenancy, and the second being the determination of the exact terms of the new tenancy. A single application may validly be made so as to request two new tenancies in adjoining premises.[88]

Where the landlord's opposition succeeds, the court cannot make an order for a new tenancy.[89] There is a compromise position in certain cases[90]. Where the landlord's opposition is on the grounds of an offer of alternative accommodation (s.30(1)(d)), uneconomic subletting (s.30(1)(e)) or demolition and reconstruction (s.30(1)(f)) and the court would have been satisfied on the grounds of opposition had the date for the termination of the tenancy been up to a year later than the date specified in the section 25 or section 26 notices, it must make a declaration to that effect without an order for a new tenancy. Within 14 days the tenant can then require the court to make an order that the later date be substituted in the landlord's notice or the tenant's request, which takes effect accordingly. If the tenant takes no action, the current tenancy terminates on the date originally specified. An example of the operation of this provision is where the court is satisfied that a necessary planning permission will be obtained, but not until after a certain delay.[91] The landlord's intention to carry out the works must, however, be proved just as clearly as if this provision did not apply. It is not the date on which the intention must be proved but the date upon which the intention is to be implemented, that changes.

Unless one of the statutory grounds for refusal of the application for a new tenancy is established, the court will make an order for the grant of a new tenancy.[92] The tenant then has a chance to reconsider his position. He may, within 14 days of the order, apply to the court for its revocation.[93] The court must accede to such an application and revoke the order. The result, of course, is that no new tenancy is then granted. The purpose of this provision is to give the tenant the chance to reject a tenancy granted on terms which he finds onerous or otherwise unacceptable. The revocation does not, of itself, affect any order for costs already made, and the court can, in the light of the tenant's subsequent actions in respect of revocation, make an order

[88] *Curtis* v. *Calgarry Investments Ltd.* (1983) 47 P. & C.R. 13.
[89] L. & T.A. 1954, s.31(1).
[90] *Ibid.* s.31(2).
[91] *Accountancy Personnel Ltd.* v. *Worshipful Company of Salters* (1972) 116 S.J. 240.
[92] L. & T.A. 1954, s.29(1).
[93] *Ibid.* s.36(2).

for costs if none has been made.[94] When an order for a new tenancy is revoked, the current tenancy continues for any period which the parties may agree or the court determine to be necessary to give the landlord a reasonable opportunity to re-let or dispose of the premises.[95] Revocation of the order for the grant of a new tenancy will not affect any order made in respect of an interim rent.

It may well be the case that by the date fixed by the section 25 notice or the section 26 request for the termination of the current tenancy, the application for the new tenancy has not been disposed of. There cannot conveniently be a gap between the end of the current tenancy and the start of the new one and consequently the Act contains a provision for interim continuation of the current tenancy.[96] Where there has been an application to the court for a new tenancy, the current tenancy continues for the period of three months from the final disposal of the application. The final disposal of the application means the date by which the proceedings are determined *and* any time for lodging an appeal or further appeal has expired.[97] Thus, if there is no appeal to the Court of Appeal, the interim continuation of the current tenancy is three months and six weeks from the date of the decision of the court of first instance, that is the six week time limit for lodging an appeal together with the three months' period from the final disposal. The interim continuation applies equally whether the court does or does not order the grant of a new tenancy. If a new tenancy is ordered, it cannot commence until the termination of the current tenancy so that, unless there is an appeal, the new tenancy will normally commence 18 weeks after the decision of the court ordering it. The new tenancy, therefore, the duration of which is fixed by the court,[98] must commence from the date when the current tenancy comes to an end, taking into account any interim continuance under section 64.[99] If the parties agree the duration of the new tenancy themselves, as they may do under section 33, it is possible that they may agree some other date of commencement.[1]

B. The Terms of the New Tenancy

The Act lays down relatively broad principles to be observed when the court orders a new tenancy. The term cannot be for more than 14

---

[94] *Ibid.* s.36(3).
[95] *Ibid.* s.36(2).
[96] *Ibid.* s.64(1).
[97] *Ibid.* s.64(2).
[98] See below.
[99] *Re No. 88 High Road, Kilburn* [1959] 1 W.L.R. 279. To prevent long delays through appeals prolonging the original term, the court may well order that the term should start from the final disposal of the application and end on a specified date: *Chipperfield* v. *Shell U.K. Ltd.* (1980) 42 P. & C.R. 136; *Turone* v. *Howard de Walden Estates* (1982) 263 E.G. 1189.
[1] The argument is discussed in Woodfall, para. 2.–0739.

years. The premises to be let can consist only of "the holding." The "holding" does not include any of the property that was formerly let to, but not occupied by, the tenant or his employees. The rent has to be the open market rent for the property, and so on. It is now proposed to examine these principles in detail.

(1) *The Term*

In the absence of a written agreement between landlord and tenant on the length of the term of the new tenancy, the court may grant such a term, up to a maximum of 14 years, as it considers reasonable in all the circumstances.[2] The court's discretion in fixing the length of the new tenancy is very wide, but case-law has established certain guidance as to how this discretion will be exercised. The duration of the old lease is a relevant factor,[3] and the courts will rarely grant, by way of renewal, a longer term than the original lease. In *Betty's Cafés Ltd.* v. *Phillips Furnishing Stores Ltd.*[4] a 14 years' term ordered by the trial judge was reduced to five years by the Court of Appeal on this principle. The length of time over which the tenant has held over under the old rent is also relevant.[5] In *Re Sunlight House, Quay Street, Manchester*[6] a tenant asked for a very short tenancy but the court ordered a rather longer period than requested in order to give the landlords a fair opportunity to re-let the premises.

The question of comparative hardship between the parties may also be relevant, so that where the landlord owns only one shop, but the tenant is a large company with many premises, a comparatively short term may be appropriate.[7] The wide discretion vested in the court in this matter can sometimes be used to remedy hardship caused to the landlord by section 30(1). A landlord may be unable to rely on his intention to occupy the premises under section 30(1)(*g*) because he acquired the premises by purchase within the previous five years. In such a case the court may, for example, order a new tenancy of only limited duration.[8] Again, a landlord may be unable to prove his intention to redevelop with the degree of certainty and precision required to satisfy section 30(1)(*f*), but if the court is satisfied that redevelopment is likely soon, it can order a short tenancy so as not to frustrate the prospects of development.

---

[2] L. & T.A. 1954, s.33.
[3] *London & Provincial Millinery Stores* v. *Barclays Bank Ltd.* [1962] 1 W.L.R. 510.
[4] [1957] Ch. 67.
[5] *London & Provincial Millinery Stores Ltd.* v. *Barclays Bank Ltd.* [1962] 1 W.L.R. 510.
[6] *The Times,* February 4, 1959. *cf. C.B.S. (U.K.)* v. *London Scottish Properties* (1985) E.G. 718, where a tenancy of one year sought by tenant was granted even though landlord proposed 14-years term.
[7] *Upsons Ltd.* v. *E. Robins Ltd.* [1956] 1 Q.B. 131.
[8] *Ibid.*

This last approach has, however, come in for some criticism from the Court of Appeal, who observed that the 1954 Act was not intended to give security of tenure, for however short a period, at the expense of preventing redevelopment. In *Adams* v. *Green*[9] the landlord owned a row of 12 shops, on one of which the tenant had a lease, which had expired. The tenant applied for a new tenancy under the 1954 Act and the landlord asked that it be for 14 years subject to the right of the landlord for the time being to determine at any time on two years notice if he wished to rebuild or reconstruct the premises. Seven of the 11 other shops had similar clauses in their leases. The landlord himself was not able to redevelop, but wished to be free to sell to a prospective developer. The County Court judge refused to include the break clause, holding that the terms of the new lease must depend on its facts. He granted a seven years' lease with no break clause. On appeal the Court of Appeal held that the tenant be given the full 14 years' term, but with the break clause requested by the landlord. The landlord would only be able to use the break clause if he were actually going to redevelop and the tenant would still be protected if the landlord's notice was not bona fide and would be entitled to the compensation provided in the Act. The adoption of this solution was far more likely to achieve justice between the parties than the more arbitrary one of simply granting the tenant a shorter term.[10]

(2) *The Property*

Normally the property included in the new tenancy is that part of the property included in the current tenancy which is occupied by the applicant tenant or by a person employed by him for the purposes of the business which brings the tenancy within the 1954 Act.[11] The whole of the property currently let may be included but, if it is not, the extent of what is to be in the new tenancy may be agreed in writing between the landlord and tenant.[12] In default, the court will decide the extent of the property to be included by reference to the circumstances prevailing at the date of the order.[13] The tenant cannot, however, be forced to accept the landlord's offer of a tenancy of part only of the premises. If the tenant cannot obtain a new tenancy of the whole of the premises he may apply for, and should be granted, unconditional leave to withdraw his application.[14] The landlord may require the

[9] (1978) 247 E.G. 49; *McCombie* v. *Grand Junction Co. Ltd.* [1962] 1 W.L.R. 581; *Amika Motor Ltd.* v. *Colebrook Holdings Ltd.* (1981) 259 E.G. 243; *J. H. Edwards & Sons* v. *Central London Commercial Estates* (1984) 271 E.G. 697. *cf. Reohorn* v. *Barry Corporation* [1956] 1 W.L.R. 845.
[10] But see *C.B.S.(U.K.)* v. *London Scottish Properties* (1985) 275 E.G. 718.
[11] L. & T.A. 1954, s.32(1).
[12] *Ibid.*
[13] *Ibid.*
[14] *Fribourg & Treyer Ltd.* v. *Northdale Investments Ltd.* (1982) 44 P. & C.R. 284.

whole of the property comprised in the current tenancy to be included in the new one, notwithstanding that some of it is sub-let. He cannot, however, insist that some sub-let portions are included while others are not.

Where the tenant agrees to accept a new tenancy of part only of the property comprised in the current tenancy, so that the landlord can carry out works on the remainder, the new tenancy is confined to the part he accepts.[15] Appurtenant rights included in the current tenancy, such as rights of access, to use lifts, of drainage, light and so on, are included in the new one, unless excluded by written agreement between the parties or by the court.[16] The court, cannot, however, grant rights to the tenant under the new tenancy not hitherto enjoyed by him,[17] nor create a new saleable asset for the tenant by adding new rights.[18]

(3) *The Rent*

Where the parties are not able to agree the amount of rent payable under the new tenancy, the court must determine what the new rent must be. Such a rent is one at which, having regard to the terms of the tenancy (other than those relating to rent) the premises comprised in the holding might reasonably be expected to be let in the open market by a willing lessor disregarding certain matters.[19] The requirement that the court is to have regard to the terms of the new tenancy results, where there is a dispute between the parties not only as to the amount of the rent but also as to some of the other terms, in the court, in determining the rent, first settling the other disputed terms before moving to the issue of rent, at least in those cases where these other terms are likely to affect the amount of the rent at which the holding might reasonably be expected to be let.[20] The matters to be disregarded in setting the rent are set out in section 34(1)(*a*)—(*d*). These are:

(a) The fact that the premises have been occupied by the tenant or his predecessors in title, so that the rent may not be increased, or decreased, simply because of the presence of a sitting tenant[21];

---

[15] L. & T.A. 1954, s.32(1A).
[16] *Ibid.* s.32(3).
[17] *G. Orlick (Meat Products) Ltd.* v. *Hastings & Thanet Building Society* (1974) 29 P. & C.R. 126.
[18] *Kirkwood* v. *Johnson* (1979) 38 P. & C.R. 392.
[19] L. & T.A. 1954, s.34(1).
[20] *O'May* v. *City of London Real Property Co.* [1982] 1 All E.R. 660 *per* Lord Hailsham L.C. at p. 665.
[21] *Harewood Hotels Ltd.* v. *Harris* [1958] 1 W.L.R. 108; *O'May* v. *City of London Real Property Co.*, *supra.*

(b) Any goodwill attached to the premises by reason of the carrying on there of the tenant's business, whether by him or by any predecessor in that business. So, the *court* must ascertain whether there is, objectively, any difference between the open market rental of the holding with or without the attached goodwill. If there is, the court must disregard it. The *tenant* must show that by reason of the carrying on of the business, whether by himself or by a predecessor, there has been an enhancement of the letting value for the purpose of the disregard. Whether a tenant has succeeded to the business of his predecessor is a question of fact. Regard must be had to the questions whether he continued to trade under the same name and whether he purchased his predecessor's stock-in-trade.

(c) Any relevant improvement. The object of this provision as originally enacted, was to give the tenant the benefit of improvements which he or his predecessor in title had carried out. In Re *"Wonderland," Cleethorpes*[22] the House of Lords held that this disregard applied only to improvements carried out by the tenant or his predecessors in title during the current tenancy, and not to improvements carried out during earlier tenancies. The improvements carried out by the tenant during his first tenancy would not, of themselves, cause his rent to be increased in respect of the second tenancy, but would result in an increase of rent payable under a third or subsequent tenancy if they had added to the letting value. Accordingly, in 1969 this decision was reversed by section 1(1) of the Law of Property Act, which inserted a new subsection (2) into section 34 of the 1954 Act. Any increase in the letting value resulting from improvements carried out by the then tenant (otherwise than in pursuance of an obligation owed to his immediate landlord) have to be disregarded if they were effected *either* during the current tenancy *or* if the conditions in section 34(2) are satisfied. These are:

(i) the improvement was completed not more than 21 years before the application for a new tenancy. A period of 21 years is stipulated because, with the passage of time, it becomes increasingly difficult to calculate what effect, if any, improvements have on the letting value. It is irrelevant whether there has been a change of business use subsequent to the time at which the improvements were completed. If an improvement made for the purposes of one kind of business does not increase the letting value of the premises for a different kind of business carried on at the time of the

[22] [1965] A.C. 58.

application, there is then no beneficial improvement to consider. If, however, improvements so carried out increase the letting value of the premises when they are used for other business purposes, the increased rental value must be disregarded;

(ii) the premises (or at least the part affected by the improvement) must at all times since the improvement was made, have been let on business tenancies[23];

(iii) the then tenant must have remained in possession at the end of each of those tenancies referred in (ii) above.

(d) Any value attributable to a licence to sell intoxicating liquor where the benefit of the licence belongs to the tenant must also be disregarded.

The state of repair of the premises is also relevant. It may be held that, as a result of the landlord's failure to repair, the proper market rent is less than it would be were the repairs carried out. In *Fawke* v. *Viscount Chelsea*[24] the Court of Appeal decided that it had the power, within section 34 of the 1954 Act, to determine a differential rent for property that was out of repair, since this was subsumed in the notion of a market rent. However, both Brandon and Stephenson L.JJ. expressed the strong view[25] that cases in which the evidence would support a differential rent on the basis of the state of repair are likely to be limited to those in which the state of disrepair at the commencement of the new tenancy is of a very serious character.

The factors the court takes into account in arriving at the new rent will depend largely on the evidence presented. The open market rent may, for instance, be affected by the profitability of the tenant's business, evidence of which can, therefore, be given.[26] Examples of such businesses would be hotels, petrol-filling stations and race-courses. However, evidence of profitability may not always be relevant. In the case of an ordinary shop, for example, with no special features, and where there are ample comparable rents which may be called in evidence, profitability is likely to be irrelevant.[27] If the premises could be used for a more profitable purpose, the more valuable use must be considered, provided that user is not forbidden under the terms proposed for the new lease.[28] So the fact that club premises could be used more valuably as offices will clearly affect the

---

[23] See *Euston Centre Properties* v. *H. & J. Wilson* (1982) 262 E.G. 1079 (when the improvement was carried out by the tenant when he was a mere licensee prior to the grant of his tenancy).

[24] [1979] 3 All E.R. 568; *supra.*

[25] *Ibid.* at pp. 578 and 579 respectively.

[26] *Harewood Hotels Ltd.* v. *Harris* [1958] 1 W.L.R. 108.

[27] *W. J. Barton* v. *Long Acre Securities* (1982) 1 W.L.R. 398.

[28] *Ibid.*

market value of a new rent,[29] although the rent under the new tenancy must be fixed on the basis of any clause in the tenancy agreement restricting user of the premises, even though the landlord could put the premises to more profitable use at a later date.[30] In *Charles Clements (London)* v. *Rank City Wall*[31] Golding J. held that the court should not use its powers[32] to modify covenants restrictive of user when granting the new tenancy, unless there were very special circumstances that required it. It was not a sufficient circumstance that, if the user covenants were modified, the tenant could be required to pay a higher market rent. The existence of a protected residential sub-tenancy of part of the premises may reduce their open market value.[33]

Where the parties are in disagreement about the new rent level it will be unusual if their evidence does not consist of or include that of a surveyor with knowledge of and experience in the valuation of business premises, particularly in the locality, or in respect of similar property. Evidence of rents of recent lettings of comparable properties may be persuasive. In any event, valuers giving testimony will be bound by the rules of evidence, in particular the hearsay rule. In *English Exporters (London) Ltd.* v. *Eldonwall Ltd.*[34] Megarry J. held that a valuer giving expert evidence, even in chief, (*i.e.* not in cross examination), may express his opinion as to values, even though substantial contribution towards the formation of that opinion has been made by matters of which he has no first-hand knowledge. He may also give evidence as to the details of any transactions within his personal knowledge, in order to prove matters of fact. Finally, he may express his opinion as to the significance of any transactions which are, or will be, proved by other admissible evidence, (not necessarily given by him), in relation to the valuation with which he is concerned. A valuer may not, however, give hearsay evidence stating the details of any transaction not within his personal knowledge in order to establish them as matters of fact. If there are no comparable rents, general rent increases in the area may be applied,[35] although ultimately the matter will be at the general discretion of the judge.[36]

In most cases the expert evidence will be a valuation on a square foot basis supported, where available, by current values for comparable property. Nevertheless, a judge having before him rental values advocated both by landlord and tenant witnesses will not necessarily act wrongly if he accepts the evidence of the experts on one side

[29] *Aldwych Club Ltd.* v. *Copthall Property Co.* (1962) 185 E.G. 219.
[30] *Gorleston Golf Club Ltd.* v. *Links Estate (Gorleston)* (1959) 109 L.J. 140.
[31] (1978) 246 E.G. 739.
[32] Under L. & T.A. 1954, s.35.
[33] *Oscroft* v. *Benabo* [1967] 1 W.L.R. 1087.
[34] [1974] Ch. 415.
[35] *National Car Parks* v. *Colebrook Estates Ltd.* (1982) 266 E.G. 810.
[36] *Turone* v. *Howard de Walden Estates Ltd.* (1982) 263 E.G. 1189.

completely, and rejects that of the other. There is no compulsion to split the difference in cases of conflict of expert testimony as to market value.[37] Section 34(3) of the 1954 Act specifically empowers the court to include a rent review clause, in appropriate cases, in the terms of a new tenancy granted by order of the court.[38]

The amount of the rent is the final matter to be determined by the court. It may well be that other terms fixed upon (for example, the amount of any service charge or responsibility for repairs) will have an effect on the rent level. For this reason, the court cannot settle on an appropriate figure for rent until the other terms of the new tenancy have been fixed.[39] In any event, the court has to decide whether the fixed rent, the insurance rent and the service rent are part of the rent payable under the tenancy, or whether they are additional charges. If the former, then they fall to be determined under section 34. If the latter, they are matters for section 35 (discussed below).[40] In particular, section 35 and not section 34 has been held by the House of Lords to be the section applicable to service charges.[41]

(4) *The Other Terms*

The remaining terms of the new lease will either be as agreed by the parties or, in the absence of agreement, as determined by the court.[42] The court must have regard, in settling these new terms, to the terms of the old tenancy and all relevant circumstances. The new lease will generally (though not always in every particular) follow the old one and, in practice, a party wanting a variation must adduce cogent reasons, such as the need to permit subsequent redevelopment of the property.[43] One purpose of the Act is to protect the tenant in his business and a variation in the terms which prejudice his business will have to be very clearly justified by the landlord. In *Gold* v. *Brighton Corporation*[44] it was held to be wrong to introduce a clause controlling the use to which the premises could be put in the new lease which prevented the tenant from carrying on the business of a dealer in second-hand clothes. In *Cardshops Ltd.* v. *Davies*[45] the current lease contained a prohibition on assignment without the landlord's consent. It was held to be wrong to add into the new lease a requirement

---

[37] *Leizer* v. *Ostim Properties Ltd.* (1965) 109 S.J. 456. As to the inappropriateness of using rateable values as a basis of valuations, see *supra*, Chap. 5.
[38] *Meakers Ltd.* v. *D.A.W. Consolidated Properties Ltd.* [1959] 1 All E.R. 527.
[39] *O'May* v. *City of London Real Property Co. Ltd.* [1982] 1 All E.R. 660 *per* Lord Hailsham L.C. at p. 665.
[40] *Ibid.*, in the Court of Appeal, *per* Brightman L.J., [1981] Ch. 216.
[41] *O'May* v. *City of London Real Property Co. Ltd.* [1982] 1 All E.R. 660.

[42] L. & T.A. 1954, s.35.

[43] *Adams* v. *Green* (1978) 247 E.G. 49.
[44] [1956] 1 W.L.R. 1291.
[45] [1971] 1 W.L.R. 591.

that the tenant must offer a surrender of the lease to the landlord without assigning. Without powerful reasons, new terms which are much harsher on the tenant than the old ones cannot be introduced.

The courts will be reluctant to impose, without good reason, terms that were not present in the former lease, and the party seeking to urge such terms on the court must justify a change as fair, reasonable and adequately compensated for.[46] In particular, the court will be wary of settling new terms which give the tenant a more valuable asset than he formerly had, especially if there is a real likelihood of the tenant then assigning the new tenancy.[47]

In *O'May* v. *City of London Real Property Co. Ltd.*[48] the House of Lords was required to consider whether section 35 permitted the insertion of a service charge into a proposed three-year term as a corollary to the assumption by the landlords of responsibility for all repairs and the provision of services. The landlords were endeavouring to render certain and quantifiable that which, without the service charge, would clearly be an open-ended commitment. The tenants argued that the introduction of the term as to service charges in the new tenancy imposed upon them risks and burdens which, hitherto, had been borne by the landlords. Since section 35 generally prohibited the imposition of new, more onerous, terms in the new lease than were contained in the old, the tenants contended that the proposed new term be omitted. The Court of Appeal[49] upheld the tenants' argument and their decision was affirmed by the House of Lords. It was not possible to compensate the tenants for their additional financial risk, were the term to be imposed, by the simple expedient of reducing the rent, since any rent reduction might, in the future, prove wholly inadequate. The landlords were, in effect, attempting to make their liabilities more certain at the expense of the tenant, and this is not a proper matter for the terms settled under section 35. If the risk is disadvantageous and unacceptable to the landlord at a commensurable rent, it is equally unacceptable and disadvantageous to the tenants at a reduced rent, and the change from the terms of the original lease should not, therefore, be permitted. A landlord, whose interest, generally, lasts for longer than that of a tenant, can spread the risk of deterioration, dilapidation and depreciation over a longer period, and possibly over several properties. Tenants have neither the opportunity nor the interest to do so. A risk which is normally acceptable to a landlord as an incident of his ownership might be oppressive and intolerable to a tenant, whose interest in the premises is co-extensive with his tenure. The Court of Appeal has, however, recently held that the court does have power under section 35 to impose a term that the

---

[46] *O'May* v. *City of London Real Property Co. Ltd.* [1982] 1 All E.R. 660.
[47] *Kirkwood* v. *Johnson* (1979) 38 P. & C.R. 392.
[48] [1982] 1 All E.R. 660.
[49] [1981] Ch. 216.

tenant provide guarantors of his performance of the terms of the new lease, at least where such a guarantee requirement was contained in the original lease. However, in this case the original lease was for one year, whereas the new tenancy was for ten years,[50] arguably a much more onerous guarantee than was contemplated by the original lease.

C. Carrying out the Order

Once the court has granted the order for a new tenancy, the landlord must execute a lease embodying the terms as agreed or determined by the court. The tenant must accept the lease and, if required so to do by the landlord, must himself execute a counterpart.[51] The Act contains no sanctions in the event of either party failing to comply with his obligations, although presumably a decree of specific performance would be available against the unwilling party.

If the landlord and tenant agree on the terms of the new tenancy to be ordered by the court, there is no reason why they should not also agree on how the legal costs should be borne. However, any agreement as to the costs of preparing such documents that involves one party paying part or all of the other party's costs, will not be enforceable unless in writing.[52] It should also be noted that such a term as to payment of the other party's drafting costs will not be incorporated as a term in the new tenancy by court order.[53]

D. Renewing Sub-Tenancies

The Landlord and Tenant Act 1954, Sched. VI, contains special provisions for dealing with sub-tenancies to cover the fact that enforcement of the tenant's renewal rights may affect the rights of more than one of those with interests superior to his, and to take account of the effect of a change in superior landlords. Where the new tenancy is longer than the reversion enjoyed by the immediate landlord (and even by any superior landlord with a leasehold reversion), the court can order the grant of one or more reversionary tenancies necessary to make up the full period.[54]

The "competent" landlord has power to bind any mesne landlord. This applies to any notice he gives to terminate the tenancy in possession, and any agreement he makes with the tenant as to the grant, duration or terms of a new tenancy. He has power to give effect

[50] *Cairnplace Ltd.* v. *C.B.L. (Property Investment) Ltd.* [1984] 1 W.L.R. 696.
[51] L. & T.A. 1954, s.36(1).
[52] Costs of Leases Act 1958, s.1.
[53] *Regis Property Co. Ltd.* v. *Lewis & Peat Ltd.* [1970] 1 Ch. 695; *Cairnplace Ltd.* v. *C.B.L. (Property Insurance) Co. Ltd., supra.*
[54] L. & T.A. 1954, Sched. 6, para. 2.

to such an agreement. A document executed in exercise of this power takes effect as if the mesne landlord had been a party thereto.[55] If, however, the competent landlord acts without the mesne landlord's consent, he is liable to pay compensation for any loss arising as a consequence of what he does. The mesne landlord's consent shall not be unreasonably withheld, but it may be conditional. The court will decide whether consent has been unreasonably withheld or conditions unreasonably imposed.[56] The tenant does not need to inquire whether the mesne landlord's consent has been given, as its absence does not invalidate his agreement with the competent landlord.

On the other hand, the competent landlord has no power to bind anyone with an interest superior to his, whether leaseholder or freeholder. If the new tenancy will last longer than the remainder of the competent landlord's own lease, then every superior landlord who will, in due course, become the tenant's immediate landlord at any time during the period concerned, must give his consent to the acts of the competent landlord, and be a party before any agreement the competent landlord may make is binding on them. In this case the tenant does need to inquire as to the length of the interests of all persons who might be involved, to ensure that all necessary parties have been joined in the agreement.[57]

If the competent landlord's interest is one that will or could be brought to an end (*e.g.* through the operation of a break clause) within 16 months of the date when he gives notice to terminate the tenancy or receives a tenant's request for a new tenancy, he must forthwith send a copy of the notice or request to his immediate landlord, and the copies must be passed all the way up the chain of landlords.[58] If the competent landlord changes within two months of the giving of a notice to terminate a tenancy, the new competent landlord can withdraw the notice within two months by serving a notice, in the statutory form, on the tenant.[59]

[55] *Ibid.* para. 3.
[56] *Ibid.* para. 4.
[57] *Ibid.* para. 5.
[58] *Ibid.* para. 7.
[59] *Ibid.* para. 6.

CHAPTER 23

TERMINATION ON COMPULSORY PURCHASE

I. Powers as to Compulsory Purchase . 719
II. Effect on Tenancies of Compulsory
  Purchase Orders 720
  A. Conveyancing: Normal Proce-
    dure 720
  B. Conveyancing: Quick Proce-
    dure 723
  C. Compulsory Purchase of Lease-
    holds 724
  D. Dispensing with the Notices . 726
  E. Tenants Protected under the
    Landlord and Tenant Act 1954,
    Pt. II 728

III. Compensation for Compulsory
  Purchase 730
  A. The "Market Value" Basis of
    Compensation 730
  B. Severance and Injurious Affec-
    tion 732
  C. Disturbance 733
  D. Compensation for Loss of Pro-
    fits and Goodwill 736
  E. Compensation under the Land-
    lord and Tenant Act 1954 . . . 738

I. POWERS AS TO COMPULSORY PURCHASE

Business and commercial men will be only too aware that roads have to be widened, corner shops acquired to provide better sight lines, houses and shops bought and demolished to provide car parks, business and commercial properties reorganised and sometimes demolished to make way for new city centre shopping precincts and developments, decaying warehouses and factories pulled down, and new industrial units laid out. In many of these schemes for comprehensive development the business tenant is as likely to fall victim to the planner as the freeholder. To put their plans into operation, the local authority will require control of the land, and this they are unlikely to obtain on a voluntary basis. Various statutes therefore provide extensive powers to buy land compulsorily and within these compulsory purchase powers, procedures and compensation provisions tenants, and in particular business tenants, receive special consideration.

Compulsory purchase of land normally brings into play four main sets of statutory provisions. First, there is the Act authorising the public body, local authority or minister to exercise compulsory purchase powers for some specified purpose or function.[1] The empowering legislation will specify which bodies are granted the compulsory purchase powers and for what purposes. It will also deal with such matters as whether the authorised bodies may obtain the land necessary for carrying out their statutory functions by compulsory purchase order specifying the land required and, if so, what

---

[1] *e.g.* Local Government Act 1972, s.121; Town and Country Planning Act 1971, ss.112, 113.

719

procedure is to be followed when making the compulsory purchase order.

The Acquisition of Land Act 1981, lays down a standardised procedure for the making of compulsory purchase orders.[2] Most acquisitions are made under that Act, and this constitutes the second set of statutory provisions governing the compulsory purchase process. Third is the Compulsory Purchase Act 1965, which governs the actual procedure for acquisition once the order has been made, and fourth is the Land Compensation Act 1973, which contains particular provisions for assessing the compensation paid to business tenants who find themselves "on the receiving end" of a compulsory purchase order.[3]

II. EFFECT ON TENANCIES OF COMPULSORY PURCHASE ORDERS

A. Conveyancing: Normal Procedure

The mechanics of acquisition of property subject to a compulsory purchase order are governed by the Compulsory Purchase Act 1965. The acquiring authority will, at the end of the day, need to acquire the legal estate in the land, normally unencumbered and with vacant possession, from a frequently unwilling vendor, who must be compensated for his loss. The C.P.O. will lapse, in relation to any of the land comprised in it, unless it is acted on within three years.[4]

When the acquiring authority wish to act on the order, they must serve a notice, known as a "notice to treat", on the persons with interests in the land to be acquired.[5] The notice must relate to a particular transaction with a particular estate owner. It must specify the land to which it relates, demand details of the recipients' rights in the land and require them to submit their claims for compensation. The notice will express the authority's willingness "to treat for the purchase of the land," but is not a contract for the sale of the recipients' interests in the land until a compensation figure is agreed or assessed.[6] When the compensation is settled, it and the notice together amount to an enforceable contract for the sale of the land.

---

[2] Though alternative procedures are occasionally specified instead by legislation; *e.g.* the slum clearance powers under the Housing Act 1985, sched. 22.

[3] For a detailed consideration of the compulsory purchase procedure see Davies, *Law of Compulsory Purchase and Compensation* (4th ed.), Pt. I.

[4] Compulsory Purchase Act 1965, s.4. The courts have held that undue delay, in any event, results in the order being treated as abandoned, or at least rendered unenforceable through the equitable doctrine of laches: *Grice* v. *Dudley Corporation* [1958] Ch. 329.

[5] Compulsory Purchase Act 1965, s.5.

[6] *West Midland Baptist (Trust) Association (Incorporated)* v. *Birmingham Corp.* [1968] 1 All E.R. 205, *per* Salmon L.J. at p. 216. See also *Simpson's Motor Sales (London) Ltd.* v. *Hendon Corp.* [1964] A.C. 1088.

This is then subject to completion by the execution of a conveyance, assignment or transfer in the same way as a private land transaction. The notice to treat must, however, be enforced within a reasonable time, and the courts will only permit enforcement beyond that period if the delay can be satisfactorily explained and enforcement remains equitable in all the circumstances of the case.[7] Indeed, the circumstances surrounding the delay may evince an intention to abandon, by the authority, the rights conferred by the notice to treat.[8]

The Compulsory Purchase Act 1965, s.6, provides that, if the recipient of a notice to treat does not, within 21 days of service, submit his claim for compensation to the authority or open negotiations on compensation with them, or if both sides cannot agree on the amount of compensation, the matter must be referred to the Lands Tribunal. Either the authority or the person whose interest is to be acquired, can invoke the Lands Tribunal's jurisdiction unilaterally by giving notice to the registrar of the Tribunal.[9] So, once a notice to treat has been served, the acquiring authority can be compelled to proceed[10] without the need to apply to the Court for a *mandamus*.[11] If compensation is assessed by the Tribunal and the authority delays further, the owner can sue for specific performance of the order which, by virtue of the fixing of compensation, has become a contract of sale.

The notice to treat fixes the interests to be acquired by the authority, and this has a particular significance in relation to tenanted property. Thus, in *Re Marylebone (Stingo Lane) Improvement Act, ex p. Edwards*[12] a landlord received a notice to treat and subsequently granted a lease for three years to his tenant, who had hitherto held under a weekly tenancy. It was held that the interest to be acquired by the authority was fixed on the service of the notice to treat and, therefore, the new three years' lease was not compensatable, although it was, presumably, still acquired on execution of the notice. Existing leases can, however, be dealt with after the notice to treat has been served. In *Cardiff Corporation* v. *Cook*[13] a leasehold interest was the subject of the notice. The tenant claimed a low compensation figure, claiming nothing for the lease itself and a mere £550 for disturbance. Before the authority agreed this figure the lease was assigned. The

---

[7] *Grice* v. *Dudley Corporation* [1958] Ch. 329.

[8] *Ibid. cf. Simpson's Motor Sales (London) Ltd.* v. *Hendon Corp.* [1964] A.C. 1088.

[9] Lands Tribunal Rules 1975, r. 17.

[10] Unless the empowering Act permits the acquiring authority to withdraw: *e.g.* Land Compensation Act 1961, s.31. The authority may also be permitted to withdraw, by virtue of the Compulsory Purchase Act 1965, s.8(1), under which a notice to treat in respect of part of a property can be met by a statement that the recipient is "willing and able to sell the whole." An authority unwilling to take the whole, and not empowered by s.8(1) to take part, may, by implication, perhaps be able to withdraw altogether: see *King* v. *Wycombe Railway Co.* (1860) 28 Beav. 104; *Thompson* v. *Tottenham & Forest Gate Railway Co.* (1892) 67 L.T. 416.

[11] *cf. R.* v. *Hungerford Market Co., ex p. Davies* (1832) 4 B. & Ad. 327.

[12] (1871) L.R. 12 Eq. 389.

[13] [1923] 2 Ch. 115.

assignee submitted a revised claim comprising £3,375 for the lease. The authority refused to consider this as a proper claim for compensation, since the assignment had taken place after the service of the notice to treat. The court held that, since the dealing was with an existing interest in the land, and did not involve the creation of a new one, the assignment and submission of a revised claim were both perfectly permissible, and that the assignor's own claim for a disturbance payment remained valid also. Presumably, if the authority had agreed the original compensation figure submitted to the assignor before the assignment had taken place, then no new claims for compensation need have been entertained, for by then an enforceable contract of assignment between the tenant and the authority would have been created.

To some extent these decisions may have been modified by the Acquisition of Land Act 1985. Section 4(2) requires the Lands Tribunal to ignore any interest in land, or any enhancement in the value of land which is attributable to works or activities carried out on the land being acquired or on other land with which the claimant was concerned, if the creation of that new interest or the carrying out of those activities "was not reasonably necessary and was undertaken with a view to obtaining... increased compensation."[14] It is important to note, however, that before this principle can operate to defeat payment of increased compensation on a dealing subsequent to the service of the notice to treat, it must be proved that the dealing was not reasonably necessary *and* was carried through with the intention of increasing the compensation payable.

The final stage is the transfer of the vendor's interest in the land being acquired to the acquiring authority. This will be effected by conveyance, transfer or assignment as in private conveyancing. The Compulsory Purchase Act 1965, s.23, provides that "the costs of all conveyances of the land subject to compulsory purchase shall be borne by the acquiring authority,"[15] and that conveyances may be in the form prescribed by Schedule 5 of the Act, or in similar form, "or by deed in any other form which the acquiring authority may think fit." Section 9 of the 1965 Act provides that if the owner of any land being compulsorily purchased fails or refuses to make title or convey the property or otherwise complete the transaction, the acquiring authority may pay the compensation into court, giving all reasonably available details of the recalcitrants and their interests. The authority may then vest the legal title to the land in themselves, unilaterally, by deed poll "containing a description of the land in respect of which the payment into court was made, and declaring the circumstances under

---

[14] *cf. Banham v. London Borough of Hackney* (1971) 22 P. & C.R. 922.
[15] See *Re West Ferry Road, Poplar* [1955] 1 W.L.R. 751.

which, and the names of the parties to whose credit, the payment into court was made."

It may be that an acquiring authority take possession of land in ignorance of some estate or interest, such as a lease, which they should have expropriated. If so, section 22 of the 1965 Act protects them from an action for trespass[16] provided that within six months they make good this default, paying not only the capital value of the interest but also mesne profits where appropriate.[17] The assessment may well take longer than six months, but it is presumably sufficient time within which to make an offer and, if necessary, refer the matter to the Lands Tribunal. No notice to treat is needed, but the appropriate conveyance will have to be executed.

B. Conveyancing: Quick Procedure

The Compulsory Purchase (Vesting Declarations) Act 1981, s.4(1) empowers any Minister or local or other public authority authorised to acquire land by means of a compulsory purchase order to telescope the two separate stages of notice to treat and conveyance into one, called a general vesting declaration, in the case of compulsory acquisition. The main advantage of this procedure is speed, but there are still cases in which the slower notice to treat procedure is more advantageous to the acquiring authority. In particular, notices to treat rather than general vesting declarations are appropriate where acquiring bodies wish to acquire leaseholds but not freeholds.

Any of the specified acquiring authorities can use the procedure of a general vesting declaration, set out in sections 3 to 11 of the 1981 Act, provided a compulsory purchase order has been made. The notice that the authority is obliged to serve communicating the confirmation of the compulsory purchase order, must also explain the procedure for general vesting declarations, in a prescribed form,[18] and must invite every owner of land covered by the order "to give information with respect to his name and address and the land in question." It must also specify the earliest date when the general vesting declaration can be executed, which will be two months or more ahead. An earlier date can be chosen if all the occupiers of the land concerned agree in writing.[19] After executing the declaration the authority must serve a notice, in set form, on every occupier of the land in question,[20] and on anyone else who has given information as invited, stating that the land will vest in the authority at the end of a period of 28 days or more

---

[16] See *London & South Western Railway Co.* v. *Gomm* (1882) 20 Ch.D. 562.
[17] *Supra*, Chap. 5.
[18] See the Compulsory Purchase of Land Regulations 1982.
[19] Compulsory Purchase (Vesting Declarations) Act 1981, s.5(2).
[20] Apart from land subject to certain excluded tenancies: see *post*.

specified in that notice.[21] The notice in which the intention of making the general vesting declaration is disclosed must be registered in the local land charges registry.[22] In practice the quick conveyancing procedure is rarely used by acquiring authorities who wish to acquire leaseholds.

C. Compulsory Purchase of Leaseholds

The Compulsory Purchase Act 1965, s.20(1), regulates the acquisition of fixed term or periodic tenancies for a year or less.[23] Where land is let to tenants there will clearly be complications absent from those cases where owner-occupied land is acquired. Leaseholds of which the term is a year or less are normally excluded from compulsory purchase, so that the acquiring body need only acquire the landlord's reversion and (since, as we shall see, statutory security of tenure does not prevail against compulsory purchase) wait until the tenancies end by notice to quit or effluxion of time. This is normally the most convenient course for an acquiring authority in any event, since they will not wish to go through all the procedural stages of expropriation merely to acquire an interest which will come to an end anyway before they are likely to want to go into physical possession. This is the practice envisaged by the 1965 Act, since section 20 of that Act proceeds on the assumption that tenancies for a year or less will not, in the normal case, be compulsorily purchased at all.

Section 20 provides:

> "If any of the land subject to compulsory purchase is in the possession of a person having no greater interest in the land than as a tenant for a year, or from year to year, and if that person is required to give up possession of any land so occupied by him before the expiration of his term or interest in the land, he shall be entitled to compensation for the value of his unexpired term or interest in the land, and for any just allowance which ought to be made to him by an incoming tenant, and for any loss or injury he may sustain."

In order to understand the implications of this provision, it is necessary to understand the means whereby an acquiring authority take possession of land subject to a compulsory purchase order. Possession cannot normally be taken by the acquiring authority until completion, which will not normally occur until the compensation has

---

[21] Compulsory Purchase (Vesting Declarations) Act 1981, s.6(1).
[22] *Ibid.* s.3(4).
[23] See *Runcorn Association Football Club* v. *Warrington & Runcorn Development Corp.* (1983) 45 P. & C.R. 183.

been settled and is to be paid. Payment, conveyance and entry into possession should all coincide, although again, in practice, the matter of compensation may be deferred, by agreement, for a long time. The Compulsory Purchase Act 1965, s.11(1), which does not apply when a general vesting declaration is used, empowers an acquiring authority to serve on the relevant owner, occupier or lessee 14 days' "notice of entry," by virtue of which they can enter into possession of any land in advance of payment of compensation, provided that they have already served a notice to treat. If they do this, any compensation payable for the land carries interest at the rate prescribed by the regulations made under the Land Compensation Act 1961, s.32, from the time of entry until the compensation is paid, either to the owner or into court. A similar right to serve 14 days' notice of entry at any time after service of a notice to treat exists in relation to leasehold interests excluded from the scope of a general vesting declaration.

Under a general vesting declaration the legal title passes at the date when the declaration is specified to take effect, and the right to take possession coincides with the vesting. However, excluded from the operation of general vesting declarations are what are called "minor tenancies,"[24] *i.e.* leaseholds for a term of a year or less, whether fixed-term or periodic. A general vesting declaration, therefore, will vest the legal estate in the acquiring authority, giving them the right to take physical possession but subject to the rights of tenants who are not being bought out.[25] These exclusions will cover "minor tenancies" and long tenancies about to expire.[26] This latter group consists of tenancies granted for periods greater than minor tenancies, but having, at the date of the declaration, a period still to run which, while exceeding one year, does not exceed such period as may be specified in the vesting declaration itself.

The object of this apparently confusing provision is to give the acquiring authority some flexibility. Where they wish to acquire land subject to a tenancy they can either acquire the tenancy as well as the reversion, in which case they get possession of the land (assuming there is no sub-tenancy) at the price of paying compensation, or they can avoid paying compensation by not buying out the tenancy, in which case they must wait until the tenancy comes to an end. If the notice to treat procedure is being used, the authority will either serve or refrain from serving a notice to treat on the tenant, depending upon whether they wish to wait, or to acquire possession forthwith. Where a general vesting declaration is used, the authority will acquire, and must pay compensation for, all freehold and leasehold interests greater than minor tenancies, unless they specify leaseholds with stated periods, longer than a year to run, which will then be excluded

[24] Compulsory Purchase (Vesting Declarations) Act 1981, s.2(1).
[25] *Ibid.* s.7(1)(ii).
[26] *Ibid.* s.2(2).

from the declaration. This they are likely to do if they do not require physical possession for some time. They will not buy out these leaseholds, and possession will be delayed so long as that lease lasts, thus saving on compensation.

Should circumstances change after the authority have made their tactical decision, they can still serve a notice to treat in respect of any tenancy excluded from the general vesting declaration, and gain possession that way. This they may do not only in the case of long leaseholds about to expire, but also in the case of minor tenancies as well. Having served a notice to treat they can then go on to obtain possession by serving a notice of entry. However, if the land is let to a tenant on a minor tenancy, the notice to treat need only be served on the landlord. The notice of entry, on the other hand, will be served on both the landlord and the tenant and, in the tenant's case, this is the only formal warning which he need receive that the acquisition is in fact going ahead. In strict law, however, it may be possible to argue that in the case of these "minor tenancies" neither a notice to treat nor a notice of entry need be served on the tenant.

D. Dispensing with the Notices

Compulsory purchase consists of forcing an unwilling freeholder or tenant to sell his interest to the acquiring authority. It is, therefore, an act of expropriation. It may not necessarily, however, involve dispossession. If the person whose interest is being acquired is a freeholder or an occupying tenant, compulsory purchase will involve both expropriation and dispossession. As a tenant, however, the "victim" of compulsory purchase can be dispossessed without being expropriated. This will occur if the authority acquire his landlord's interest and are then able to terminate his tenancy, or prevent its renewal. A short-term or periodic tenant who has sub-let may well lose his interest without being either expropriated or dispossessed.

If notice of entry is served on an owner-occupier, it is clear that he is being both expropriated and dispossessed of his land. Notice of entry served on an occupying tenant who could otherwise have been evicted at common law, will not merely dispossess him, but have the effect of expropriating his interest as well, especially where he would otherwise have enjoyed statutory security of tenure, even though he may not have been the recipient of any notice to treat. In this case (where the acquiring authority serve notice to treat on a landlord but not on his tenant occupying under a periodic tenancy), the implication from the Compulsory Purchase Act 1965, s.11(1),[27] is that, provided compensation has already been assessed and paid to the landlord, even the

---

[27] Discussed *infra*.

notice of entry to the tenant can be dispensed with. If the authority are impatient for physical possession and wish to enter before the tenancy can be terminated at common law by notice to quit or effluxion of time, the Compulsory Purchase Act 1965, s.20, (quoted above) would seem to permit them to do so by enabling them to require a yearly or lesser tenant to give up possession at any time.

By section 20 the authority's obligation to pay compensation to tenants having terms not exceeding one year arises, not on the service of any notice to treat or notice of entry, but on the date when the authority require to go into physical possession. If this date falls before a tenancy for a year or less can determine at common law, the section requires compensation to be paid. The implication from this is that, subject to the payment of compensation, such a tenant can be required to give up possession at any time even though his interest has not been subject to any general vesting declaration, notice to treat or notice of entry. It follows that a notice to treat can be served in respect of a lease of over a year, that no action need be taken until the lease has less than a year to run, and that the acquiring authority can then serve a notice of entry and take possession, paying compensation under section 2, which they could not have done before.[28] If the compensation for the reversionary interest of the landlord has already been assessed and paid, then, as has already been observed, section 11(1) of the 1965 Act would seem to imply that not even a notice of entry is required to be served on a tenant. In *Greenwoods Tyre Services Ltd.* v. *Manchester Corporation*[29] it was held that in such a case there is no need to serve a notice to quit upon the periodic tenant, (even though this would have been essential to terminate his interest at common law), because entry (*not* notice of entry) impliedly has the effect of a notice to quit, so that the "unexpired term or interest in the land," for the purposes of section 20 of the 1965 Act, is valued as continuing until the date on which a valid notice to quit, if served when entry actually occurred, would have taken effect. The logic of this decision is not free from doubt. If, as has been argued, the act of entry itself can lawfully give the acquiring authority the right to immediate possession, then it is hard to see how the tenancy is deemed to continue for some further period, fixed by reference to some notional (but unserved) notice to quit, for the purposes of compensation.

While, in theory, it seems possible to dispense with the notices, in practice they are often used in order to give advance warning of the authority's intentions and to obtain details of claims.[30] So, for example, if a general vesting declaration is executed in respect of a piece of land the authority wish to acquire, this will vest the legal title

[28] *R.* v. *Kennedy* [1893] 1 Q.B. 533.
[29] (1971) 23 P. & C.R. 246.
[30] *Newham London Borough Council* v. *Benjamin* [1968] 1 W.L.R. 694.

in the acquiring authority automatically, except for tenancies for a year or less and longer leases which are specified by the authority in the declaration. The longer procedures can then be used in respect of these, should the authority so wish, starting with a notice to treat, however short the tenancy. Alternatively the authority can wait until those tenancies determine, or they can go into immediate possession paying compensation under section 20 of the 1965 Act. If they adopt this last course, however, they must still serve a notice of entry on the tenant, unless this can also be dispensed with because the compensation has already been assessed and agreed.[31]

E. Tenants Protected under the Landlord and Tenant Act 1954, Pt. II

Statutory protection of tenants will not prevail against compulsory purchase, whether the acquiring authority expropriate the tenants direct or displace their landlords. The Landlord and Tenant Act 1954, s.39(3), specifically provides, in addition, that nothing in section 24 of the 1954 Act is to affect the operation of section 121 of the Lands Clauses Consolidation Act 1845,[32] which relates to the payment of compensation and the obtaining of possession by an acquiring authority in the case of tenancies from year to year or lesser interests. The Land Compensation Act 1973, s.47, provides that a business tenant is, however, to have the benefit of his statutory protection taken into account when compulsory purchase compensation is assessed. Conversely, the landlord's compensation must be assessed on the basis that he holds the reversion on a protected and not an unprotected tenancy.

If the landlord's reversion only is expropriated, and not the interest of the tenant, the acquiring authority will be in the same position as that landlord, *vis-à-vis* the tenant. Were this a transfer of the landlord's reversion by private treaty rather than compulsory purchase, the authority would have been able to defeat the tenant's claim for a new tenancy under section 30(1)(*f*) of the 1954 Act, since the purpose of their acquisition will invariably involve redevelopment.[33] This is not a ground that the original (expropriated) landlord could normally have been able to rely on unless, fortuitously, he also was planning to redevelop. Section 47 of the 1973 Act requires it to be assumed, for the purposes of compensation, that neither the acquiring authority, nor any other body with compulsory purchase powers, are acquiring the property. Therefore, normally no ground is left for dispossessing the tenant under the 1954 Act, and this must be

---

[31] Compulsory Purchase Act 1965, s.11(1).
[32] The reference to s.121 of the Act of 1845 includes a reference to s.20 of the Compulsory Purchase Act 1965 (Act of 1965, s.39 and Sched. 7).
[33] *Supra*, Chap. 22.

reflected in the amount of any compensation paid, since the market value of the landlord's reversion will thus be low.

If, however, the landlord already had independent grounds for opposing the grant of a new tenancy under section 30(1) of the 1954 Act, before the expropriation of his own interest supervened, then, in principle, the market value of his reversion would be higher and this would be reflected in the compensation. If, however, the expiration of the current tenancy is, aside from the compulsory purchase, some time in the future, and the tenant has a contractual term with some time still to run, there would be little prospect of the landlord actually being able to recover possession (unless he were able to forfeit the lease for some breach of covenant, and even here there is the possibility of relief to consider). An authority exercising their powers of compulsory purchase over the landlord's interest, therefore, but not that of the tenant, need only pay for his reversion a market value price which recognises the tenant's relatively secure position. They will pay comparatively little compensation, but will not get immediate possession.

If, on the other hand, the authority compulsorily purchase the interest of the business tenant, or take possession of the property under one of the procedures described in (iii) and (iv) above, they must compensate him accordingly. Compensation for the tenant's interest, like the landlord's, proceeds on the basis that no compulsory purchase powers are being exercised, in accordance with the Land Compensation Act, 1973, s.47. The threat of compulsory purchase, involving, as it must normally do, redevelopment, must be disregarded as a ground enabling the landlord to refuse a request for a new tenancy under the 1954 Act. Unless the existing landlord has an independent ground for recovering possession, the tenant must be compensated on the assumption that he is fully protected and entitled to a new tenancy on the termination of his current one.

One might expect that section 47 of the 1973 Act would push the tenant's compensation up and reduce the landlord's compensation by the same factor. However, the effect is actually to assess the compensation on the basis of the market cost of an assignment of the landlord's or the tenant's interest, as the case may be, to the acquiring authority by private treaty, thus preserving the tenant's security of tenure. The capital value of the landlord's reversion will be lower on the open market if he has a fully protected business tenant in possession. There is no necessary reason why this low capital value of the reversion should yield a corresponding increase in the capital value of the tenancy. Most modern business leases contain frequent rent reviews so that, even in times of high inflation, the fact that most business tenants pay market rents will depress the capital value of the tenancy, regardless of the capital value of the reversion. An assignee of the tenancy is unlikely to be prepared to pay a substantial premium to the assigning tenant on top of a market rent and there is, therefore, no reason why an acquiring authority should pay the tenant substantial sums by way of compensation on compulsory purchase, other than by way of disturbance compensation.[34] It is only when a leasehold has been granted for what has become appreciably less than a market rent, so that the tenant has a substantial "profit rental," that it constitutes an asset commanding any market value compensation for its loss commensurate with the loss of a freehold property. The result is that section 47 substantially benefits acquiring bodies at the expense of landlords. It is for this reason that landlords and tenants frequently agree, when compulsory purchase threatens, to a surrender or merger for an appropriate consideration so that, when the acquisition takes place, it will be owner-occupied. The compulsory acquisition of owner-occupied commercial property costs the acquiring authority significantly more by way of compensation than does the acquisition of such property let to tenants protected by the Landlord and Tenant Act 1954, Pt. II.

III. Compensation for Compulsory Purchase

A. The "Market Value" Basis of Compensation

The acquiring authority must compensate the expropriated landlord and/or tenant for the interest taken, by way of purchase price, and for any depreciation of the property retained by him, as well as for "all damage directly consequent on the taking."[35] The basis of compensation for the expropriation or depreciation is "market value." "Market value" means "the amount which the land, if sold in the open market by a willing seller might be expected to realize."[36] "Special suitability or adaptability" of the land which depends solely on "a purpose to which it could be applied only in pursuance of statutory powers, or for which there is no market apart from the special needs of a particular purchaser or the requirements of any authority possessing compulsory purchase powers," must be disregarded.[37] There is, therefore, for the purposes of compensation, no effective market for the land if demand for it is evinced only by a particular purchaser's "special needs," or by a project which cannot be achieved except by a public body with compulsory powers under an authorising Act, such as a large waterworks scheme.

---

[34] See *post.*
[35] *Harvey* v. *Crawley Development Corp.* [1957] 1 Q.B. 485, *per* Denning L.J. at p. 492.
[36] Land Compensation Act 1961, s.5. See *Wilkinson* v. *Middlesborough B.C.* (1983) 45 P. & C.R. 142.
[37] *Ibid.*

A similar problem may arise where there is industrial or commercial land which is likely to have more attraction for a neighbouring owner, to enable him to expand his business, than for a newcomer in the same line of activity. The statutory limitation on enhancing the market value by reference to the "needs of a particular purchaser" would seem to prevent the compensation being increased in this regard, although if there is more than one interested neighbour then one might be able to argue that the enhancement of value is due essentially to its position rather than the needs of any one particular purchaser, and thus be allowable. Particular illustrations of this problem arise in the case of sitting tenants. In *Lambe* v. *Secretary of State for War*[38] the factor that, it was argued, inflated the market value of the landlord's reversion was the sitting tenant. A sitting tenant would pay more for the reversion than any other purchaser, who would only be obtaining the right to receive the rents. The landlord therefore maintained that the "market value" of his reversion was the higher amount he could obtain from a sitting tenant. This argument, like the similar one based on special attraction for neighbouring owners, may be open to attack on the ground that the prospect is not sufficiently generalised to amount to a "market." The sitting tenant may not, in fact, be sufficiently interested or prosperous to purchase the reversion were it offered to him. Even as a factor enhancing market value, therefore, it is quite hypothetical, unless the means and wishes of the sitting tenant are actually known. Despite these cogent arguments, however, it seems to be generally accepted that a sitting tenant does enhance market value.

The Court of Appeal accepted the argument for the higher amount in *Lambe's* case and rejected the acquiring authority's claim that it was excluded by the "special suitability or adaptability" rule. Parker L.J. said[39]:

> "The expression 'special suitability or adaptability of the land' . . . is . . . clearly referring to the quality of the land . . . . The fact that the sitting tenant may be prepared to pay more than an investor in order not to be turned out does not clothe the land with special suitability . . . the value of which is to be ignored."

While it may be justified for a valuer, in advising a landlord, to claim the higher figure, even if it turns out afterwards that the special purchaser was not forthcoming, the acquiring body in *Lambe's* case were themselves the sitting tenant. Had they not been sitting tenants but merely an outside acquiring authority purchasing the reversion on the same basis as an investor, the result might not have been the same.

[38] [1955] 2 Q.B. 612.
[39] *Ibid.* p. 619.

The difference between what has actually happened and what is potential, and therefore only might happen, must be taken into account, but it is not finally settled how much weight is attached to these alternatives.[40]

In assessing compensation there must be no addition to nor deduction from market value purely on the ground that the purchase is compulsory, nor any addition specifically on account of the project to be carried out by the acquiring authority.[41] An increase in the value of adjoining land of the owner not taken by the authority, if it results from the compulsory acquisition, must be "set-off" against compensation.[42]

B. Severance and Injurious Affection

In addition to purchase price compensation there is compensation for depreciation in the value of any land retained as a result of the compulsory purchase. If, for example, a landlord owns the reversion on a parade of shops and a compulsory purchase order is made in respect of part of that parade only, leaving only a few shops to carry on business, both the landlord and the various tenants are likely to suffer loss by the depreciation of the parade as an attractive shopping area with a variety of retail units. This depreciation is usually called "severance" if it relates to the *pro rata* reduction in value of the land retained over and above its reduction in size.[43] It is termed "injurious affection" if it results in depreciation caused by what is done on the land taken.[44] Land "retained" by an owner may be considered for severance or injurious affection compensation even if not immediately contiguous with the land taken,[45] and even if enjoyed under a

---

[40] *Bwllfa and Merthyr Dare Steam Collieries (1891) Ltd.* v. *Pontypridd Waterworks Co.* [1903] A.C. 426; *L.C.C.* v. *Tobin* [1959] 1 All E.R. 649; *Pointe Gourde Quarrying and Transport Co.* v. *Sub-Intendent of Crown Lands* [1947] A.C. 565.

[41] Land Compensation Act 1961, ss.5, 9; *Pointe Gourde Quarrying and Transport Co. Ltd.* v. *Sub-Intendent of Crown Lands* [1947] A.C. 565; *Wilson* v. *Liverpool Corp.* [1971] 1 W.L.R. 302; *Jelson Ltd.* v. *Blaby D.C.* [1977] 1 W.L.R. 1020; *Birmingham D.C.* v. *Morris & Jacombs Ltd.* (1976) 33 P. & C.R. 27; *Melwood Units Pty. Ltd.* v. *Commissioner for Main Roads* [1979] A.C. 426. It has been cogently argued that the so-called "*Pointe Gourde* rule" cannot always be reconciled with the "willing seller rule," and can cause injustice: see Davies, *Law of Compulsory Purchase and Compensation*, (3rd. ed.) Chap. 7.

[42] Land Compensation Act 1961, s.7. There must be no purely notional additions to or reductions from the price of the land taken, on the assumption that it might *not* have been taken, which are attributable to the authority's development to be carried out on the rest of the land taken, if that is unlikely to have been carried out in circumstances other than those of the acquisition itself; *ibid.* s.6. Special situations are catered for, *e.g.* the payment of site value if the property comprises dwellings unfit for human habitation: Housing Act 1985, s.585(1).

[43] See *Holt* v. *Gas Light & Coke Co.* (1872) L.R. 7 Q.B. 728; *Palmer & Harvey Ltd.* v. *Ipswich Corporation* (1953) 4 P. & C.R. 5.

[44] The depreciation need not be caused *entirely* by what is done on the land taken as distinct from other land, provided that it is at least *partly* so caused: Land Compensation Act 1973, s.44.

[45] *Cowper Essex* v. *Acton Local Board* (1889) 14 App.Cas. 153.

different interest, such as a lease or an option.[46] If, however, what is done on the land by the acquiring authority goes beyond what it is authorised by statutory powers to do, then it will be unlawful and, if compensatable at all, will be so in tort and not as injurious affection.[47]

It may also be possible to obtain compensation for "injurious affection" when no land has been acquired from the claimant. This might be the case with those tenants who remained in their shops in the example given above. To qualify the claimant must prove four things. First, he must show that the loss is caused by acts authorised by statute. Secondly, the loss must be actionable at common law if it were not so authorised. Thirdly, the claim must be limited strictly to any depreciation in the value of the claimant's interest in the land, and finally the loss must arise from the carrying out of works on the compulsorily acquired land and not from its subsequent use.[48] Depreciation caused by the *use* of public works, such as highways, airports and the like, is in many cases compensatable under Part I of the Land Compensation Act 1973, if attributable to physical factors such as noise, vibration, smell, fumes, smoke, artificial lighting or discharge of solids or liquids. The claim period is one to three years after the use begins,[49] but only owner-occupiers are eligible

C. Disturbance

Disturbance is a head of compensation which falls into two distinct divisions. First there is compensation for disturbance that arises on the acquisition of a freehold, or leasehold interest greater than that of a year or from year to year. Then there are the special statutory provisions granting compensation for disturbance arising from the Compulsory Purchase Act 1965, s.20.[50] Disturbance compensation is not strictly land value but "must ... refer to the fact of having to vacate premises."[51] Thus it may include the loss of business goodwill and profits, removal expenses and the cost of acquiring new premises.[52] The additional capital cost of buying dearer property or premises however, is not compensatable. Compensation for disturbance is not the same as equivalent reinstatement.[53] To claim for disturbance an owner must forego prospective development value in his purchase price compensation. So, his true loss will be whichever is

---

[46] *Oppenheimer* v. *Minister of Transport* [1942] 1 K.B. 242.
[47] *Lagan Navigation Co.* v. *Lambeg Bleaching Co.* [1927] A.C. 226.
[48] *Metropolitan Board of Works* v. *McCarthy* (1874) L.R. 7 H.L. 243; *Argyle Motors (Birkenhead) Ltd.* v. *Birkenhead Corp.* [1975] A.C. 99.
[49] See *Hickmott* v. *Dorset C.C.* (1977) 35 P. & C.R. 195.
[50] *Supra.*
[51] *Lee* v. *Minister of Transport* [1966] 1 Q.B. 111, *per* Davies L.J. at p. 122. A dispossessed licensee, as such, will get nothing: *Woolfson* v. *Strathclyde Regional Council* (1978) 38 P. & C.R. 521.
[52] *Harvey* v. *Crawley Development Corporation* [1957] 1 Q.B. 485.
[53] *Ibid.*

the higher: existing use plus prospective development or existing use plus disturbance.[54] In a private sale to a developer a vendor would expect to sacrifice all the profits arising from the existing use in order to secure the additional value which the prospect of development would put on to the market price of the land. But even a vendor selling purely at existing use value would not expect to get his removal expenses paid by the purchaser. To this extent, disturbance compensation may be a bonus.

Since disturbance compensation is supposed to be integral with, even if not strictly a part of, land value, it is not payable where the acquiring body, having expropriated the landlord's interest, displace a short-term tenant by notice to quit or by effluxion of time. In such cases, the Land Compensation Act 1973[55] provides for "disturbance payments" (removal expenses, business losses) by the acquiring body to the tenant.[56]

The rule that if the claimant is only able to find alternative premises at a higher price than that which he receives in compensation he cannot claim the difference,[57] may be subject to an exception in the case of relocation of a business. If the rent demanded for the only alternative premises reasonably available exceeds that previously paid, compensation may be payable in respect of that excess which reflects no advantage to the business, *e.g.* extra space which cannot be put to productive use or a more salubrious neighbourhood which is of no commercial advantage to the business in question.[58] On the other hand, where structural additions and improvements to the new premises are carried out so that these premises are an improvement on the old, and the cost of such alterations represents value for the extra money spent rather than replacement of facilities lost, the costs will be disallowed.[59] Similarly, even where the improvements to the new premises are carried out under an express covenant in the lease, they still represent value for money and will not be allowed.[60] The same applies to other improvements that add to the value of the lease and will give rise to a claim against the lessor upon its expiration.[61]

Expenses incurred before the notice to treat has been served are, in general, not allowable. Losses incurred can only be the subject of compensation for disturbance if they are the natural and reasonable

[54] *Horn* v. *Sunderland Corporation* [1941] 2 K.B. 26.
[55] ss.37–8.
[56] *n.b.* a business tenant may have compensation rights against his landlord for loss of a new tenancy.
[57] Since he is presumed to have got value for his money, *i.e.* better premises than those given up, for which he is also presumed to have given full market value.
[58] *Eastern* v. *Islington Corporation* (1952) 3 P. & C.R. 145; *Greenberg* v. *Grimsby Corporation* (1961) 12 P. & C.R. 212.
[59] *Smith* v. *Birmingham Corporation* (1974) 29 P. & C.R. 265.
[60] *Bresgall & Sons Ltd.* v. *London Borough of Hackney* (1976) 32 P. & C.R. 442.
[61] *i.e.* under the Landlord and Tenant Act 1927, Pt. I.

consequence of dispossession.[62] This rule can, however, cause hardship and anomaly. It is likely, in many cases, to take much longer to find and equip alternative business premises than is available between notice to treat and the date on which the acquiring authority require possession. In such cases the claimant will be in a dilemma. If he awaits notice to treat he increases the risk either of being forced to close down his business altogether or of incurring a delay between vacating the premises being acquired and his ability to reopen elsewhere, thereby suffering loss of profit and increasing the compensation payable. Moreover, to incur expenses before notice to treat, and even more so before confirmation of any relevant compulsory purchase order is in any event to take the risk that the property may not ultimately be acquired and the expenditure prove abortive. But if the property is in fact ultimately required and compulsorily purchased, and if relocation mitigates the loss and therefore the compensation payable, it seems unjust that the claimant should be penalised by inability to recover items of costs which are undoubtedly allowable after notice to treat.

Curiously in this context, in many cases where the property comprises business premises, the "owner-occupier" can serve a blight notice as soon as a compulsory purchase order covering the property is made.[63] If the acquiring authority does not object to such a notice within two months, it is then deemed to have served a notice to treat. It seems more than a little anomalous and administratively cumbersome for it to be necessary for persons affected by a compulsory purchase order to serve a blight notice, if qualified to do so, in order to protect their right to such costs of relocation as may be incurred before the acquiring authority would otherwise in fact have served notice to treat.

Losses upon the forced sale of business stock and equipment are claimable. In *Somers & Somers* v. *Doncaster Corporation*[64] articles of equipment, retained by the claimant on giving up the business, were valued on the basis of their value to a purchaser of the business as a going concern at £240, but only at £50 on the basis of the price they would be likely to fetch if separately auctioned. The claimant was held to be entitled to the £190 difference as disturbance compensation. On the same principle, damages resulting from disturbance include the cost of replacing fixtures.[65]

---

[62] *Webb* v. *Stockport Corporation* (1962) 13 P. & C.R. 339; *Bostock, Chater & Sons Ltd.* v. *Chelmsford Corporation* (1973) 26 P. & C.R. 321.
[63] Land Compensation Act 1973, s.70.
[64] (1965) 16 P. & C.R. 323.
[65] *Gibson* v. *Hammersmith and City Railway Co.* (1863) 32 L.J. Ch. 337.

D. Compensation for Loss of Profits and Goodwill

Claims for loss of profits arise where, as a result of dispossession the business has to be wholly closed down or where, despite relocation, the move involves a curtailment of business which may be temporary or permanent. For example, it may have proved impossible for the new premises to be got ready for the resumption of business before the original premises have to be vacated; there may, therefore, either be a complete break or, if business can be immediately transferred at a reduced level pending completion of necessary alterations or installation of plant and equipment, only a partial break. Alternatively, there may be partial extinguishment as, for example, where an engineering works comprising several production lines cannot be reinstated *in toto* in the new premises. In such circumstances compensation may be payable on the basis of the total extinguishment of part of the business that has to be abandoned. Moreover, where a business is totally or partially extinguished it is not to be assumed, when assessing compensation for loss of profits, that the business will in any event be extinguished on the termination of the lease. This is because, as we have seen, account has to be taken of any expectation of renewal of the lease under the Landlord and Tenant Act 1954, Pt. II.[66]

Goodwill may be defined as the value of that element of the profitability that arises from specific business connections related to the location of the premises acquired or the personality of the proprietor. It is more fully defined and discussed in the next chapter. As far as compensation for loss of goodwill is concerned, it is not the market value of the claimant's local connection that has to be ascertained, but the quantum of loss suffered by him in having to sacrifice potential business arising from an established business or practice.[67] So, although it is unlawful to sell the goodwill of a national health medical practice,[68] the fact that such goodwill has no market value does not prevent a valid claim for compensation for loss of the goodwill of a medical practice if, as a result of the acquisition, the practice cannot be continued in the locality or is entirely extinguished.[69]

For the purposes of compensation, loss of profits as such and loss of goodwill are both normally calculated on the basis of the average profit over the previous three years multiplied by a multiplier expressed as so many "years' purchase." There is, however, no hard and fast rule as to the appropriate number of years' purchase and even an average of three years' profits may in certain circumstances be inappropriate as a starting point. For example, profits during the

[66] Land Compensation Act 1973, s.47.
[67] *Remnant* v. *L.C.C.* (1952) 3 P. & C.R. 185.
[68] National Health Service Act 1977, s.54(1), Sched. 10, para. 1(1).
[69] *Roy* v. *Westminster City Council* (1975) 31 P. & C.R. 458.

previous three years may have been affected by special circumstances and require adjustment either directly[70] or indirectly by altering the multiplier. In so far as special circumstances have depreciated profits, they themselves are likely to be the reasonable result of the dispossession. Conversely, where the profits have been increasing over the previous three or more years, and but for the dispossession would have been expected to continue to do so, this too can be taken into account by taking the last year's profit only as the basis of the calculation, by increasing the number of years' purchase, or by a combination of the two.

Where a claim for loss of profits arises from a forced removal of a business, account may be taken of defects associated with the new premises which are likely adversely to affect the level of profits as compared with those earned at the original premises. So, increases in the cost of transport of men and materials,[71] and adaptation of new premises, may be allowed, as also may the cost of running two sets of premises during the transition period.[72]

In assessing the number of years' purchase to be applied in the valuation of goodwill the Lands Tribunal tend to give the most weight to evidence derived from private sales of similar businesses in the open market, the multiplier being readily calculable where details of both profits and the premises, as well as the purchase price, are available.[73] In the absence of such information as to the behaviour of the market, reliance will be placed upon settlements of compensation reached between the District Valuer and owners of similar businesses compulsorily acquired.

In calculating profits for the purpose of disturbance compensation, certain deductions are made from net profits deduced from the ordinary profit and loss account. So, a deduction is made in respect of the interest on the capital employed in the business, *i.e.* capital sunk in plant, vehicles, stock and debtors (less creditors). Also, since the rental value of the premises is reflected in the capital value, and therefore the compensation payable in respect of the land, a corresponding deduction has to be made from the profits. In the case of tenants a further deduction is made equivalent to any profit rental, for the same reason. Sometimes deductions are also made in respect of the notional wages earned by the proprietor,[74] though not in the case of a "one-man business."[75]

---

[70] By, for instance, taking an average of five years: *Drake & Underwood* v. *L.C.C.* (1960) 11 P. & C.R. 427.
[71] *W. Rought Ltd.* v. *West Suffolk County Council* [1955] 2 Q.B. 338.
[72] *W.J. Mogridge (Bristol 1937) Ltd.* v. *Bristol Corporation* (1956) 8 P. & C.R. 78.
[73] *Zarraga* v. *Newcastle upon Tyne Corporation* (1968) 19 P. & C.R. 609.
[74] *Matthews* v. *Bristol Corporation* (1954) 4 P. & C.R. 401.
[75] *Perezic* v. *Bristol Corporation* (1955) 5 P. & C.R. 237.

E. Compensation under the Landlord and Tenant Act 1954

The problems created by disturbance arising from the acquisition of short tenancies are the same as those arising for compensation generally in respect of such tenancies, and they were discussed earlier in this chapter when the Land Compensation Act 1973, s.47, was considered. In this context, however, it is important to consider the compensation which would be available under the Landlord and Tenant Act 1954 if the tenancy had been allowed to run its course. The circumstances in which such compensation is available under the 1954 Act, should the court refuse to grant a new tenancy, are discussed in the next chapter. But, it is important to note here that, should the compensation payable under the 1954 Act be greater than that payable under the Compulsory Purchase Act 1965, the claimant is entitled to the larger sum.[76] The same principle operates in respect of disturbance payments.[77]

[76] Land Compensation Act 1965, s.20.
[77] *Ibid.*

CHAPTER 24

TRANSFER AND PROTECTION OF BUSINESS GOODWILL

I. Definition	739	A. History of Compensation for Loss of Goodwill	747
II. Disposal	740	B. When is Compensation Payable	748
III. Protection	742	C. The Amount of Compensation Payable	750
A. No Protection Covenant	742		
B. Protection Covenant	743	D. Compensation for Misrepresentation	751
IV. Compensation	747		

I. DEFINITION

The goodwill of a business is the benefit which arises from its having been carried on for some time in particular premises, or by a particular person or firm, or from the use of a particular trade-mark or name. Its value consists in the probability that the old customers will continue to be customers notwithstanding a change in the firm or place of business.[1] Goodwill, therefore, represents the value of the attraction to customers which the name and reputation possesses. It is the advantage or benefit which is acquired by a business, beyond the mere value of the capital, stock, premises or lease, in consequence of the general public patronage and encouragement which it receives from constant or habitual customers.[2]

There is a distinction between personal goodwill, which is merely the advantage of the recommendation of the owner of a business and the use of his name, and local goodwill, which is attached to premises and must be taken into account in calculating the value of such premises. There may be a goodwill attached to a business which is dependent upon the personal relationship between the person who carries it on and his clients or customers, such as the business of a stockbroker, doctor, dentist or even perhaps a hairdresser. Even though a successor may not, in such a case, use the old name, it may be an advantage of appreciable value merely to be a successor, though in some cases such goodwill may be so personal as to be unsaleable and worthless.

Some cases have characterised personal goodwill as being dependent upon the personal character, that is the personal skill or reputation, of the person who carries on the business. In the case of certain businesses the goodwill is not personal in this sense, because it merely consists in the habit which the customers have of resorting to

[1] *Cruttwell* v. *Lye* (1810) 17 Ves. Jr. 335.
[2] *Trego* v. *Hunt* [1896] A.C. 7.

the business premises. Therefore, if the owner of such a business mortgages the property without mentioning the goodwill, and the mortgagee, on the mortgagor's default, realises his security and sells the business as a going concern, thus obtaining the financial benefit of the goodwill, the mortgagor is not allowed to reclaim that part of the purchase money which represents the value of the goodwill, since it is not personal to him.[3]

Goodwill is therefore personal property,[4] but it is property of a peculiar kind. A person selling his goodwill along with his business merely undertakes with the purchaser that he will not solicit the purchaser's customers. Thus, he gives the purchaser of that goodwill an opportunity to keep old customers, but if the purchaser adopts a trading policy which does not please the old customers, they will leave him, and the goodwill thereby evaporates. However, being property, certain consequences flow from this status of goodwill: first, it can be assigned; secondly, it can be protected against interference and thirdly, if it is the forced surrender of a trader's rented business premises that causes its dissipation, it can, in an indirect way and in certain circumstances, be compensated for.

II. Disposal

Goodwill, whether it is attached to premises or to a particular trade-mark or name, being property, should be treated as part of the assets of the business,[5] and as such may be sold or otherwise disposed of by its owner to another individual or company. One consequence of this is that goodwill will pass to the purchaser, as part of and incident to the business, when it is sold as a business (as against a bare assignment of the lease of business premises), or when sold "with stock-in-trade and premises." Goodwill cannot be sold apart from the business,[6] but premises may be retained and the goodwill sold separately.[7] Goodwill cannot be split up into parts, so that, for instance, a seller of a business that has a general goodwill, together with a particular goodwill attached to a special trade-mark, cannot split the goodwill up so that part only follows the special mark and is sold with it while the rest is retained.[8]

An assignment of goodwill implies a recommendation of the assignee by the assignor to his customers, and an agreement by him to abstain from solicitation of the assignee's customers. So, if Smith carries on a business under a firm name which is wholly or partially

[3] *Ex p. Punnett, Re Kitchin* (1881) 16 Ch.D. 226.
[4] See *Potter* v. *I.R.C.* (1854) 10 Ex. 147.
[5] *Wedderburn* v. *Wedderburn* (No. 4) (1856) 22 Beav.84.
[6] *Smale* v. *Graves* (1850) 3 De G. & Sm. 706.
[7] *Morris* v. *Moss* (1855) 25 L.J. Ch. 194.
[8] *Re Dobie & Son Ltd.* Trade Mark (1935) 52 R.P.C. 333.

artificial (such as "Smith and Jones" or "Smith & Co.") and assigns the goodwill of his business to Brown, then Brown becomes entitled to the exclusive use of the firm name as against Smith and as against all the world, so that Smith can neither complain of Brown's use of the name nor use any name himself that so resembles it that it could be taken as calculated to represent to the world that he (Smith) is carrying on the business which he has assigned to Brown.[9] In this context it should be noted that the Business Names Act 1985 imposes certain obligations to disclose the names and addresses of individuals, partners and companies trading under business names other than their own.

An assignment of goodwill in the form of a registered trade-mark or service mark must be made in accordance with the Trade Marks Act 1938.[10] Unregistered common law trade-marks pass, by implication, on an assignment of the goodwill of the business, unless there is a clear intention expressed to reserve the marks. The right to protect the goodwill of a business against the use of deceptive imitations, by means of the action in tort for "passing off,"[11] will pass to an assignee of the goodwill.

The assignment will normally be by deed and, in the case of a tenant selling his business along with the assignment of his lease, the goodwill will frequently be assigned by means of an additional clause in the deed of assignment of the lease executed by the tenant in favour of the purchaser.[12] A payment made for goodwill is not a payment made in respect of the grant or assignment of a tenancy and is not, therefore, a premium,[13] and cannot be taxed as such although it can, presumably, in appropriate circumstances, be subject to capital gains tax or corporation tax.[14] Sometimes the assignor may not wish to dispose of his goodwill for a lump sum but may wish to secure annual payments, or an annuity, in return for the assignment. In such a case the annuity is usually calculated as a percentage of the assignee's turnover.

---

[9] *Churton* v. *Douglas* (1859) Johns. 174.
[10] As amended by the Trade Marks (Amendment) Act 1984. See also Blanco White and Jacob, *Kerley's Law of Trade Marks and Trade Names* (11th ed.), Chap. 13.
[11] See *Reddaway* v. *Banham* [1896] A.C. 199; *Parker-Knoll* v. *Knoll International* [1962] R.P.C. 265; *Short's Ltd.* v. *Short* (1914) 31 R.P.C. 294; *Bollinger* v. *Costa Brava* [1960] Ch. 262; *Vine Products* v. *Mackenzie* (No. 2) [1969] R.P.C. 1; *Walker* v. *Ost* [1970] 2 All E.R. 106; *Evern Warninck* v. *Townend* [1979] A.C. 731; *White Hudson* v. *Asian Organisation* [1964] 1 W.L.R. 1466. See also Trade Marks Act 1938, s.2; *Borthwick* v. *Evening Post* (1888) 37 Ch.D. 449; *Walter* v. *Ashton* [1902] 2 Ch. 282; *Street* v. *Union Bank* (1885) 30 Ch.D. 156; *Day* v. *Brownrigg* (1878) 10 Ch.D. 294; cf. *McCulloch* v. *May* [1947] 2 All E.R. 845; *Wombles* v. *Wombles Skips* [1975] F.S.R. 488.
[12] For a suitable precedent see Melville, *Precedents on Intellectual Property and International Licensing* (2nd ed.), para. 4–35.
[13] *R.* v. *Barnet etc. Rent Tribunal, ex p. Millman* [1950] 2 K.B. 506.
[14] Capital Gains Tax Act 1979, s.191; Income and Corporation Taxes Act 1970, ss.265, 386(3).

III. Protection

A. No Protection Covenant

Goodwill would be a worthless business asset were it not possible to protect it. This is particularly so in the case of assignees of goodwill for, were the assignor permitted, having sold the goodwill of a business, to set out to solicit the return of his old customers or clients, then any goodwill that was sold to the assignee would soon revert back to the business of the assignor. However, the vendor of the goodwill of a business is not prevented from setting himself up in competition to the purchaser. Only when he has expressly covenanted not to compete, or he has by his fraudulent conduct led others to believe that he will not compete, will the law restrain his business activity.[15] In the leading case of *Trego* v. *Hunt*[16] Lord Macnaghten said:

> "How far may [the vendor of a business] go? He may do everything that a stranger to the business, in ordinary course, would be in a position to do. He may set up where he will. He may push his wares as much as he pleases. He may thus interfere with the custom of his neighbour as a stranger and an outsider might do; but he must not, I think, avail himself of his special knowledge of the old customers to regain, without consideration, that which he has parted with for value. He must not make his approaches from the vantage-ground of his former position, moving under cover of a connexion which is no longer his. He may not sell the custom and steal away the customers in that fashion."

So, what can he do? In the absence of contrary agreement he can advertise himself as having been a partner, manager of, or in other ways associated with, the business,[17] but he cannot represent himself as a successor to, or associate of, the business,[18] nor may he use any trade-mark of the business.[19] He cannot solicit his former customers by direct means,[20] though he may advertise his new business to the public at large[21] and trade with ex-customers who come to him unsolicited.[22] Presumably ex-customers may be solicited once they

---

[15] *Shackle* v. *Baker* (1808) 14 Ves.Jr. 468.
[16] [1896] A.C. 7 at p. 25.
[17] *Hookham* v. *Pottage* (1872) 8 Ch.App. 91.
[18] *Hudson* v. *Osborne* (1869) 39 L.J. Ch. 79.
[19] *Rodgers* v. *Nowill* (1853) 3 De G.M. & G. 614.
[20] *Trego* v. *Hunt* [1896] A.C. 7.
[21] *Labouchere* v. *Dawson* (1872) L.R. 13 Eq. 322.
[22] *Trego* v. *Hunt* [1896] A.C. 7.

have expressed their dislike of the purchaser's business or in some other way been alienated from him.

Lord Macnaghten explained, in somewhat laboured fashion, the basis of these rules in this way[23]:

> "A man may not derogate from his own grant; the vendor is not at liberty to destroy or depreciate the thing which he has sold; there is an implied covenant, on the sale of goodwill, that the vendor does not solicit the custom which he has parted with: it would be a fraud on the contract to do so. . . . It is not right to profess and to purport to sell that which you do not mean the purchaser to have; it is not an honest thing to pocket the price and then to recapture the subject of sale, to decoy it away or call it back before the purchaser has had time to attach it to himself and make it his very own."

So, competition is allowed, solicitation is not. The buyer of a business has the right, in the absence of the vendor's express covenant, to restrain the seller from representing that he still owns the same business, and to restrain him from soliciting his old customers. He can also prevent the seller from disclosing confidential information. If the purchaser of goodwill wants more protection than this, he should bargain for it, *e.g.* by negotiating a covenant to prevent the seller from competing. Negotiations on this matter often occur on the assignment of a business and lease of the business premises, and their outcome will obviously affect the price.

B. Protection Covenant

The purchaser of the goodwill of a business is entitled to protect his purchase by taking from the vendor a reasonable covenant to restrain competition. This most usually takes the form of protecting the customer connection. Thus the covenant will be aimed at preventing or reducing the seller's opportunity to attract as customers those persons who would otherwise be regarded as customers, or potential customers of the purchaser. Similarly a covenant may attempt to protect trade secrets, since the value of the business bought will obviously be diminished if the seller uses for his own subsequent advantage the secrets that made it profitable in the first place. In both these cases, provided that the purchaser is indeed able to prove ownership of these interests needing protection,[24] the law will permit him to enforce reasonable covenants taken for the protection of such

---

[23] *Ibid.* p. 25.
[24] See *Vancouver Malt and Sake Brewing Co. Ltd.* v. *Vancouver Breweries Ltd.* [1934] A.C. 181.

interests. In construing covenants for the protection of goodwill, courts seem to take a liberal view, construing them in the light of the business carried on by the seller.[25]

In deciding whether to enforce a covenant taken from the vendor of a business in order to protect the goodwill sold to the purchaser, the courts tend to ask themselves four questions. First, is the trade restrained unduly wide? Secondly, is the area or scope of the restraint unduly wide? Thirdly, is the duration of the restraint unduly long? Fourthly, is the covenant in the public interest? The answers to these four questions will, when taken together, determine whether or not the covenant is reasonable.

(1) *The Trade Restrained*

The rules on this matter were stated in very clear form in the leading case of *British Reinforced Concrete Engineering Co. Ltd.* v. *Schelff.*[26] In that case the purchasers, who were a large firm manufacturing and selling steel reinforcements for roads and whose business extended throughout the United Kingdom, bought from the seller a small business which dealt in, but did not manufacture, a certain kind of reinforcement in one small part of the country. On the sale the vendor agreed not to carry on, or "act as servant of any person concerned . . . in the business of the manufacture or sale of road reinforcements in any part of the United Kingdom." The court took the view that the true test was what was necessary to protect *the business sold*, not to protect other businesses run by the purchasers. The covenant taken was, therefore, too wide in numerous respects. The "servant clause" would prevent the vendor from becoming the employee of a company holding shares in a road reinforcement manufacturing or marketing company. It was too wide in area, since the vendor's business did not extend to anything like the entire United Kingdom. It was too wide also in that it restrained the vendor from becoming concerned in the manufacture, as opposed to the sale, of reinforcements, bearing in mind that the vendor had never engaged in manufacture in his former business. Sitting as an additional judge in the Chancery Division, Younger L.J. said[27] that the law was clear:

> "It is the business sold which is the legitimate subject of protection, and it is for its protection in the hands of the purchaser, and for its protection only, that the vendor's restrictive covenant can be legitimately exacted. A restrictive covenant

---

[25] *e.g. Avery* v. *Langford* (1854) Kay 663; *William Cory & Son Ltd.* v. *Harrison* [1906] A.C. 274; See also *A. Schroeder Music Publishing Co. Ltd.* v. *Macaulay* [1974] 1 W.L.R. 1308.
[26] [1921] 2 Ch. 563.
[27] *Ibid.* pp. 574–575.

by a grocer on the sale of his business in a country town, if it would be unreasonable and void when the purchaser was acquiring it as his sole business, does not become valid if the purchasers are, say, Messrs. Lipton, with branches everywhere."

With perhaps the substitution of "Tesco" for "Lipton," the tenor of this opinion is clear and as applicable today as in 1921. A covenant restraining trade in too wide a fashion than is necessary to protect the business sold will not be enforced.

(2) *Area and Scope*

The rule is that the area of scope of the covenant must not be more extensive than that of the business sold. In *Connors Bros. Ltd.* v. *Connors*[28] Viscount Maugham said of a covenant, taken on the sale of a sardine canning business, not to engage in any sardine business in Canada:

"It has never yet been supposed that it is necessary in relation to the trade of a large manufacturer or merchant to prove to the satisfaction of the court that the business which the covenant is designed to protect has been carried on in every part of the area mentioned in the covenant. In the cases in which the area has been the whole of England, or a substantial part of it, such as 100 miles or 150 miles from a named town, it has never been held that the covenantee was under an obligation to prove that the business has been carried on in all the towns and villages within the area. In the *Nordenfelt* case[29] no attempt was made to prove that all the governments of the world, or even all the civilized world, had ordered goods from the company, though the greater number had no doubt done so. A great deal no doubt depends on the nature of the business and of the area in question. In a country of vast spaces, like the Dominion of Canada, it will always be possible, until the population of the country reaches a point now scarcely contemplated, to point to areas where there are only few settlers or inhabitants and where, accordingly, few, if any, of the goods sold by the manufacturer have penetrated.... However, the goodwill of a business such as is now under consideration would not adequately be protected if the restrictive covenant had to be limited to the town and villages where actual sales could be proved, while leaving the vendor free to establish a business,

[28] [1940] 4 All E.R. 179 at p. 194.
[29] *Nordenfelt* v. *Maxim Nordenfelt Guns and Ammunition Co. Ltd.* [1894] A.C. 535, a case concerned with a world-wide restraint, held to be valid by the House of Lords.

which would almost certainly be competitive, in all the adjoining
places."

On the facts of that case, sufficient dealings by the business sold were
proved to justify a countrywide restraint. A covenant will not be void
if its surplus area consists of more or less vacant country, in which the
covenantor could find no opportunities for earning a living at his
trade.

The chances of really wide restraints being upheld are greatest when
the nature of the business is a specialist one and the market rather
limited, but even in this case there must be sales throughout the bulk
of the area in question to justify the covenant. The inclusion of
important areas of population wherein the seller never traded is likely
to make the covenant bad. One important factor in validating
geographically wide covenants is the issue of whether the business is
carried on by personal contact or, instead, by correspondence and
through local agencies. The latter type of business appears to justify
wider covenants,[30] although the courts will normally take the view that
restrictions extending only to the town in which the business is
situated, or the same small area round it, are adequate to protect small
trading businesses.[31]

In addition, therefore, to an area covenant, a non-solicitation
covenant may also conveniently be used.[32] It has a greater chance of
being held valid than an area covenant, because it is related precisely
to the interest to be protected—goodwill, consisting in the main of the
likelihood that customers will return. However, such a covenant will
not always be so useful because first, it provides no protection at all
against solicitation of *potential* customers, and second, it is more
difficult to prove breach of a non-solicitation covenant than that of an
area covenant.

(3) *Time*

The test for duration of a covenant ought, perhaps, to depend upon
how long it will take for the seller's connection with his customers to
fade away. In fact the courts have tended to lean in favour of
purchasers in this area and, if the restriction is not held to be too wide,
it is rare that it will be declared unreasonable because no time limit
was set for its duration. There are cases in which long restraints on the
vendors of small businesses have been struck down because they were

---

[30] *Whittaker* v. *Howe* (1941) 3 Beav. 383.
[31] *Nordenfelt* v. *Maxim Nordenfelt Guns and Ammunition Co. Ltd.* [1894] A.C. 535; *Leather Cloth Co.* v. *Lorsont* (1869) L.R. 9 Eq 345.
[32] See *Rannie* v. *Irvine* (1844) 7 Man & G. 969; *Home Counties Dairies* v. *Skilton* [1970] 1 W.L.R. 526; *Gledhow Autoparts Ltd.* v. *Delaney* [1965] 1 W.L.R. 1366; *Spafax* v. *Harrison* [1980] I.R.L.R. 442.

capable of enduring too long,[33] but they are uncommon. A seller of a business who was able to show real hardship and oppression because the covenant he had given was of too long a duration might, however, be able to get it declared void.

(4) *The Public Interest*

The courts are, in theory, required to uphold the covenant as reasonable, not only as being in the interests of the parties, but also as being in the public interest,[34] although in practice the courts are unlikely to strike down as unreasonable in the public interest a covenant which they have held reasonable between the parties. They will usually find that the loss of the vendor to trade, and thus to the public good, is unimportant because many competitors will step in, who are not so trammelled by covenants, to perform his services to the public.[35]

IV. COMPENSATION

A. History of Compensation for Loss of Goodwill

Under the Landlord and Tenant Act 1927, s.4, a tenant was formerly entitled to compensation from his landlord on quitting the premises if he could show that because he and his predecessors had carried on a trade or business there for not less than five years, goodwill had become attached to those premises, so that the landlord could obtain a higher rent than he would otherwise have got. In the alternative, if the tenant considered that the compensation would be insufficient to compensate him for the loss that he would suffer by leaving the premises he could, under section 5 of the Act, serve a notice on the landlord requiring a new lease. These provisions were, however, repealed by the Landlord and Tenant Act 1954, which abolishes the right of a tenant to compensation for loss of goodwill as such, and gives security of tenure irrespective of the existence of goodwill.

The inability of a tenant to obtain the renewal of a business tenancy can prove very expensive for him. Any enforced removal to new premises is likely to lead, initially at least, to the loss of some business which is, of course, why the 1954 Act contains elaborate provisions for security of tenure.[36] However, the tenant can lose possession on

---

[33] *e.g. Pellow* v. *Ivey* (1933) 49 T.L.R. 422.
[34] *Toby* v. *Major* (1899) 43 S.J. 778.
[35] *Nordenfelt* v. *Maxim Nordenfelt Guns and Ammunition Co. Ltd.* [1894] A.C. 535.
[36] *Supra*, Chap. 22.

the grounds set out in the Landlord and Tenant Act 1954, s.30(1)(*e*), (*f*) and (*g*)[37] through no fault of his own. These are the cases where re-letting the building as a whole unit would be more economic, or where the landlord intends to redevelop, or to occupy himself. In these cases a tenant who is unable to renew his tenancy can obtain a measure of compensation for the expense of disturbance.[38] The goodwill basis of compensation, set up by the 1927 Act, was not adopted by the 1954 Act, largely because of the difficulties which had been encountered in its assessment in the past.[39] Instead the Act adopted what the then Solicitor-General termed "compensation for loss of the contingent right of renewal."[40] The 1954 Act does not mention goodwill at all but the compensation provisions are clearly based upon an assumption that a business forced to move to new premises is inevitably going to lose something of value, which might act as a windfall to the landlord, and for which the tenant ought to be compensated. The major difference between the 1927 Act and its successor is that a loss of valuable goodwill is now assumed, and that rather than the tenant who is forced to leave having to prove the lost value of adherent goodwill, he is compensated on the basis of a simple, arbitrary formula. There is, however, no reason to doubt that the present system is, nevertheless, an indirect and somewhat crude method for compensating dispossessed business tenants for the loss of their business goodwill.

B. When is Compensation Payable

The principle which underlines compensation under the 1954 Act is that a tenant is entitled to be paid a sum, amounting to the rateable value of the holding or, in certain circumstances twice that sum, multiplied by what is called "the appropriate multiplier."[41] The appropriate multiplier is at present fixed at 3.[42] Compensation may be payable when the tenant is precluded from obtaining a new tenancy because of the landlord's opposition on grounds (*e*), (*f*) or (*g*) of section 30(1). The precise circumstances in which the entitlement to compensation arises are twofold.[43] The first is where there is an application to the court for a new tenancy and the court is precluded from ordering the grant of a new tenancy on the above-mentioned

[37] *Ibid.*
[38] L. & T.A. 1954, s.37(1).
[39] See White Paper: *Government Policy on Leasehold Property in England and Wales* (Cmd. 8713), paras. 39–52.
[40] H.C. Official Report, S.C.D., April 13, 1954, col. 533.
[41] *i.e.* such multiplier as the Secretary of State prescribes: Local Government, Planning and Land Act 1980, s.193 and Sched. 33, para. 4(2).
[42] Landlord and Tenant Act 1954 (Appropriate Multiplier) Order 1984, S.I. 1984 No. 1932.
[43] L. & T.A. 1954, s.37(1).

grounds contained in section 30(1). The second is where the landlord's notice under section 25[43a] or the landlord's notice of opposition to a new tenancy under section 26(6)[44] relies on those grounds and no others, and the tenant either does not apply for a new tenancy[45] or applies and then withdraws his application. The compensation is payable to the tenant on quitting the holding. It is because the Act permits compensation in these limited circumstances only that the tenant is entitled to require the court to certify the reason why his application for a new tenancy failed.[46]

A tenant who applies for a new tenancy and is met by landlord opposition on one of the three grounds for which compensation is allowable may, at a later date, seek leave to withdraw his application because, for instance, he has in the meantime found suitable alternative premises. The court originally held that in such circumstances leave will only be granted to withdraw the application provided that the tenant gave an undertaking not to pursue his claim for compensation.[47] The reason for this was that if the tenant did not give such an undertaking, he would have been in a better position by withdrawing his application than he would have been by pursuing it. If leave to withdraw were not given, the tenant would be required to proceed with the application. In that case the tenant would not be able to obtain compensation since his application for a new tenancy would not be dismissed *only* on the grounds of landlord opposition within section 30(1)(*e*), (*f*) or (*g*), but also on the ground that the tenant no longer sought a renewal of the lease, having found new premises (which is not a ground for compensation). The 1954 Act does, however, provide, in section 37(1), that a tenant may be entitled to compensation even though his application for a new tenancy is withdrawn.

The Court of Appeal, however, disapproving *Young, Austen and Young* v. *British Medical Association*[48], has recently held in *Lloyds Bank* v. *London City Corporation*[49] that a discontinuance of the tenant's claim for a new tenancy should be permitted if the landlord will not be prejudiced, and the fact that the landlord may thereby be under an obligation to pay compensation should not be regarded as prejudice in this context. Further, in *Ove Arup Inc.* v. *Howland Property Investment Co.*[50] it was said that the court would not, in granting leave to withdraw, put the tenant on terms not to claim compensation, and finally, in *Fribourg & Treyer* v. *Northdall Invest-*

[43a] *Supra*, Chap. 22.
[44] *Ibid.*
[45] *cf. Re 14 Grafton Street, W.1.* [1971] Ch. 935.
[46] L. & T.A. 1954, s.37(4).
[47] *Young, Austen and Young Ltd.* v. *British Medical Association* [1977] 1 W.L.R. 881.
[48] *Ibid.*
[49] [1983] Ch. 192.
[50] (1981) 42 P. & C.R. 284.

ments[51-52] a tenant was permitted to discontinue his action for a new tenancy without any requirement that he refrain from seeking compensation. It must, therefore, now be the case that the earlier reservations expressed by the court, preventing the tenant from withdrawing without an undertaking not to pursue compensation, no longer represent the law.

In certain cases the right to compensation can be excluded by written agreement between landlord and tenant.[53] Agreements excluding or restricting the right to compensation for disturbance are valid in cases where the period of business occupation will have been less than five years by the date on which the tenant leaves the holding. This comparatively simple idea is, however, legislated for in a characteristically complex way. The Act provides that contracting out of the compensation provision is permitted where the premises the tenant occupies have not been occupied by *someone* carrying on a business there for the whole of the five years ending with the date on which the tenant is obliged to quit. Even if there has been a continuous occupation for five years, however, the right to compensation can still be excluded by agreement if there was a change of occupier during that five year period, unless each occupier was *successor* to the business (not just to the lease) of his predecessor. A provision excluding compensation will frequently be found in leases of business premises for terms longer than five years. These are inserted by landlords in the hope that circumstances may change (*e.g.* the lease may permit premature termination, or there may be a late change both in the tenant and in the nature of the business carried on in the property) rendering the exclusion effective.

C. The Amount of Compensation Payable

If the occupier has carried on that business in the premises for 14 years before the end of the tenancy, he will be entitled to twice the rateable value of the holding, times the appropriate multiplier, should he qualify for compensation.[54] Compensation will still be payable at this rate if the successor to the tenancy has also been the successor of the business that was carried on there.[55] If the business has changed in that time, or the tenant's occupation does not qualify by reference to its duration, then the compensation is reduced to the simple rateable value of the holding, again times the appropriate multiplier.[56] If a tenant thinks that his landlord is likely to succeed on one of the

---

[51-52] (1982) 44 P. & C.R. 284.
[53] L. & T.A. 1954, s.37(2), (3).
[54] *Ibid.* s.37(2)(*a*), 3(*a*). See also *Edicron* v. *William Whiteley* [1984] 1 W.L.R. 59.
[55] *Ibid.* s.37(2)(*a*), 3(*b*).
[56] *Ibid.* s.37(2)(*b*).

qualifying grounds of opposition in section 30(1), there is no need for the tenant to be put to the inconvenience of applying for a new tenancy merely to obtain compensation[57] (although it may be worth his while doing so in order simply to delay eviction, thus giving him a longer period in occupation). An application can be made solely for the purpose of obtaining compensation directly.[58] The relevant date for assessing compensation is generally the date upon which the tenant quits the holding.[59]

The rateable value is that shown in the valuation list in force on the date of the landlord's notice terminating the tenancy, or his notice in reply to the tenant's request for a new tenancy.[60] If there is no separate rateable value, a proper apportionment or aggregation must be made. Any dispute is to be referred to the Commissioners of Inland Revenue for decision by a valuation officer, with the possibility of an appeal to the Lands Tribunal.

D. Compensation for Misrepresentation

When there is a misrepresentation or concealment of material facts, it will generally be in respect of the landlord's intention to redevelop or the landlord's intention to occupy the premises himself, that is the grounds of opposition specified in paras (*f*) and (*g*) of section 30(1) of the Act. In cases where one or both of these grounds are relied upon the facts will, of course, be particularly within the province of the landlord. There is nothing to stop the landlord genuinely changing his mind between the date of the hearing and a subsequent date. A misrepresentation made in evidence at the trial may well amount to the crime of perjury. The tenant may also be able to sue for damages in the tort of deceit.

The Landlord and Tenant Act 1954, s.55, empowers the court to award the tenant compensation if he fails to have his tenancy renewed because of misrepresentation or concealment of a material fact before the court. Where this is shown to have occurred, the court may order the landlord to pay to the tenant the sum which appears to the court to be sufficient compensation for damage or loss sustained by him as a result of the refusal to renew.[61] The compensation is also available in cases where the refusal to renew has already resulted in payment to

---

[57] *Ibid.* s.37(1) as amended by L.P.A. 1969, s.11.
[58] *Ibid.* Capital gains tax is not payable on the compensation: *Drummond* v. *Brown* [1984] 2 All E.R. 699.
[59] *Cardshops Ltd.* v. *John Lewis Properties Ltd.* [1983] Q.B. 161; *Sperry Ltd.* v. *Hambro Life Assurance Ltd.* (1982) 265 E.G. 223; *International Military Services* v. *Capital and Counties plc.* [1982] 1 W.L.R. 575.
[60] L. & T.A. 1954 s.37(5)–(7).
[61] See *Clark* v. *Kirby-Smith* [1964] Ch. 506. Loss of anticipated profits and removal expenses may constitute a further head of loss.

the tenant of compensation calculated on the rateable value, although that compensation would be taken into account in deciding on the sum to be awarded under section 55.

The standard of conduct required of the landlord with regard to disclosure of material facts is one of utmost good faith.[62] The cause of action afforded by section 55 is additional to and not in substitution for common law remedies such as an action for deceit. Innocent misrepresentation will be sufficient for the purposes of the section.[63] However, section 55 compensation can be awarded only where there has been a refusal of a new tenancy by the court. Further, an action will lie only if it can be established that the court was induced by misrepresentation or concealment of material facts to refuse the grant of a new tenancy. Therefore where it is *the tenant* who is induced, by misrepresentation or concealment, either to *consent* to the court's refusal of a new tenancy or to fail to apply for one at all, then a section 55 action would not be maintainable, since the necessary inducement to the court could not be established. However, common law remedies might remain to the tenant.

---

[62] *Thorne* v. *Smith* [1947] K.B. 307.
[63] Though not, of course, for the common law crime of perjury or the tort of deceit.

PART IV

AGRICULTURAL TENANCIES

In this Part the follow abbreviations are used:

Legislation

A.H.A. 1986	Agricultural Holdings Act 1 1986
The Tribunal	The Agricultural Land Tribunal

CHAPTER 25

THE STATUTORY UMBRELLA

I. Introduction 755
II. The Function Carried On 757
   A. Trade or Business 757
   B. Agriculture 757
   C. Trade need not be Agricultural 757
   D. Part of Land Used for Private
      Purposes 758
   E. Change of Use 759
III. The Nature of the Interest Protected 760
   A. Common Yearly Tenancy . . . 760
   B. Protection Extended to Certain
      Licences 761
   C. The Capacity of the Grantor . 762
   D. Sub-tenancies 763

IV. Tenancies Outside the Statutory Um-
   brella 764
   A. Generally 764
   B. Tenancies to Office Holders . 764
   C. Tenancies Granted with Minis-
      try Approval 765
   D. Lettings for Mowing or Grazing 765
   E. Lettings for Fixed Periods be-
      tween 12 and 24 Months . . . 766
   F. Permitted Contracting-Out . . 766
   G. Death during a Fixed Term
      Contract 767

I. INTRODUCTION

The problems of agricultural tenancies have for long pre-occupied Parliament, even when that pre-occupation has not always resulted in legislation. In the last century the bulk of agricultural land was held in settlements. The tenant for life holding the legal estate for the time being would have only a limited power of sale or none at all and often would only be able to create tenancies co-terminous with his own interest. When he died the agricultural tenancy would be unlikely to bind his successors, and even while he was alive the farming tenancy could be ended by giving half a year's notice.

Farming is a continuous activity and a tenant who could not reap where he had sown would be seriously out of pocket on the ending of his tenancy, and in any event would be unwilling to incur expenditure that would enure for the medium and long term benefit of the holding. General statutory leasing powers were granted to certain settlements in 1833,[1] and are now enjoyed by all settlements.[2] A complex set of archaic rules entitled the departing agricultural tenant to emble-ments,[3] which was the right to harvest crops growing on his land at the end of the tenancy, and in certain districts the tenant would be entitled by custom of the country at common law to additional compensation. Over the years, the right to remove fixtures was also extended.[4]

The statutory protection of farming tenants has been broadened

[1] Fines and Recoveries Act 1833, s.41.
[2] See Pt. (I) Chap. 3, *ante*.
[3] See further *Woodfall*, 2–0064.
[4] See Pt. (I) Chap. 3, *ante*.

755

and strengthened as a matter of deliberate public policy, and not simply to redress injustices that might otherwise afflict individual private tenants. Lord Hailsham L.C. has recently[5] summarised the history and policy of the Acts: "At least since the 1880s successive Parliaments have considered the fertility of the land and soil of England and the proper farming of it as something more than a private interest. Fertility is not something built up as the result of a mere six months' activity on the part of the cultivator, which was all the period of notice given by the common law to the individual farming tenant, by whom in the main the land was cultivated then, as now, mainly under a yearly tenancy. It takes years (sometimes generations) of patient and self-abnegating toil and investment to put heart into soil, to develop and gain the advantage of suitable rotations of crops, and to provide proper drains, hedges and ditches. Even to build up a herd of dairy cattle, between whose conception and first lactation at least three years must elapse, takes time and planning, whilst to disperse the work of a lifetime of careful breeding is but the task of an afternoon by a qualified auctioneer. Even within the space of a single year the interval between seed time and harvest, between expenditure and return, with all the divers dangers and chances of weather, pest or benignity of climate is sufficient to put an impecunious but honest cultivator at risk without adding to his problems any uncertainty as to his next year's tenure. At first Parliament was concerned simply with compensation for cultivation, manuring and improvement. But it never regarded these as matters simply for private contract, or something wholly unconnected with any public interest. From the first, Parliament was concerned with the management of the soil, the land of England which had grown gradually into its present fertility by the toil of centuries of husbandmen and estate owners. By the 1920s Parliament similarly concerned itself with the length of notice to which the yearly tenant was entitled. Such provisions are now to be found in ss.23 and 24 of the 1948 Act. But they date from this time. In 1947 a new and momentous step was taken. The landlord's notice to quit, save in certain specified instances, was at the option of the tenant to be subject to consent, at first of the Minister, but latterly of a quasi-judicial tribunal, the agricultural land tribunal. Even the consent of the agricultural land tribunal is carefully regulated by s.25 of the 1948 Act (consolidating and amending the 1947 provisions). The circumstances in which its consent may be accorded are thus defined and limited by objective and justiciable criteria. These are not simply matters of private contracts. . . . It is a public interest introduced for the sake of the soil and husbandry of which both landlord and tenant are in a moral, though not of course a legal sense, the trustees for posterity."

[5] *Johnson* v. *Moreton* [1978] 3 W.L.R. 538, at pp. 551, 552. And see N. D. M. Parry [1980] Conv. 117.

Until 1986, the parties position was governed principally by the Agricultural Holdings Act 1948 (the 1948 Act) overlaid with what had been charitably described as a "morass"[6] of other Acts, regulations and statutory instruments, in which substantive law and procedural requirements were intermixed. The confusion has been reduced by the consolidation of the Acts and the introduction of some additional material into the Agricultural Holdings Act 1986 (the 1986 Act).

II. THE FUNCTION CARRIED ON

A. Trade or Business

The Act affords protection only where the activity conducted on the land was carried on "for the purposes of trade or business."[7] There is no need to establish that the trade was successful.[8] But the renting of a separate paddock for the benefit of the tenant's hunters or as his practice jumping ring would not qualify as this involves using the premises for private purposes.

B. Agriculture

In addition to the tenant's renting for trade purposes, he also has to use the land for agriculture, if it is to qualify as agricultural land. Agriculture is defined by section 96(1) of the 1986 Act as including: "horticulture, fruit growing, seed growing, dairy farming and live-stock breeding and keeping, the use of land as grazing land, meadow land, osier land,[9] market gardens and nursery grounds, and the use of land for woodlands where that use is ancillary to the farming of land for other agricultural purposes." And "livestock" includes "any creature kept for the production of food, wool, skins or fur or for the purpose of its use in the farming of land or the carrying on in relation to land of any agricultural activity."[10]

C. Trade Need Not be Agricultural

Although the activity carried on upon the land has to be agricultural, it does not follow that the trade with which it is associated has to be

---

[6] By H. A. C. Densham in Scammell and Densham's *Law of Agricultural Holdings* (7th ed.), referred to in this Part as Scammell & Densham.
[7] A.H.A. 1986, s.1(4)(*a*); *Hickson and Welch* v. *Cann (Note)* (1977) 40 P. & C.R. 218 (discontinued casual horsetrading, breeding and pig fattening insufficient).
[8] *cf.* Income and Corporation Taxes Act 1970, s.180.
[9] *i.e.* reeds, an activity which it is understood is now only carried on in very limited areas.
[10] A.H.A. 1986, s.96(1).

agricultural. It has therefore been held[11] that the letting of five acres to graze horses used in a riding school was the letting of an agricultural holding, although the running of a riding school is not agriculture. The use of land to breed horses in a stud,[12] or for training them to race[13] or jump,[13a] or as a riding school,[14] or to house kennels to breed and train dogs, or breed racing pigeons, or as a site for a permanent clay pigeon shoot, or the letting of land for a game shoot, even if pheasant poults are put down and reared, will not involve an agricultural use of the land. But all may not be lost for such a tenant whose landlord serves him with a notice to quit. Even though he may not be the tenant of an agricultural holding, he may nevertheless be carrying on a "business" or "activity," and so, as a business tenant, be protected by Part II of the Landlord and Tenant Act 1954.[15] And in that respect he does not have to show that the activity is connected with a venture that purports to make a profit.

D. Part of Land Used for Private Purposes

The fact that part of the property is used for non-agricultural purposes will not cause that part to fall outside "the agricultural holding." That expression "means the aggregate of the land (whether agricultural land or not) comprised in a contract of tenancy which is a contract for an agricultural tenancy . . . "[16] "The literal construction of the word 'used' in [s.1(4)(a)] as requiring actual use of every inch of the holding for agriculture or for the purposes of an agricultural trade or business at any given time would make the Act wholly unworkable."[17] The use of part of a holding for private purposes does not result in loss of protection for those parts. But if the land taken as a whole is not in substance used for agriculture, but, *e.g.* for retail trading, then it will not be a tenancy of an agricultural holding.[18]

---

[11] *Rutherford* v. *Maurer* [1962] 1 Q.B. 16.

[12] *McClinton* v. *McFall* (1974) 232 E.G. 707; [1975] C.L.Y. 38.

[13] *Bracey* v. *Read* [1963] Ch. 88 (where the letting of training gallops was covered by L. & T.A. 1954, Pt. II).

[13a] *Wetherall* v. *Smith* [1980] 2 All E.R. 530.

[14] *Rutherford* v. *Maurer* [1962] 1 Q.B. 16, and see *Deith* v. *Brown* [1956] J.P.L. 736; [1956] C.L.Y. 127.

[15] See *ante* Pt. (III) Chap. 20 (III)A.

[16] A.H.A. 1986, s.1(1). This was held in *Blackmore* v. *Butler* [1954] 2 Q.B. 171 to mean a single contract of tenancy. But the cottage there separately let from the agricultural land was itself "agricultural land" when it was let for housing a worker on the adjoining agricultural land, the question being one of fact and degree.

[17] *Howkins* v. *Jardine* [1951] 1 K.B. 614 at p. 629, *per* Jenkins L.J. (sub-lettings of three cottages to persons not engaged in agriculture did not take the tenancy of the cottages part of a seven acre holding outside the 1948 Act); and see *McClinton.* v. *McFall* (1974) 232 E.G. 707.

[18] *Monson (Lord)* v. *Bound* [1954] 1 W.L.R. 1321, where the land produced only 10 per cent. of the turnover of the premises selling horticultural products by retail. And see *Wetherall* v. *Smith* [1980] 2 All E.R. 530.

E. Change of Use

Protection is afforded where there is an "agricultural holding."[19] As has been seen,[20] this refers to "agricultural land," meaning "land used for agriculture[21] which is so used for the purposes of a trade or business."[22] Two questions arise. First, when agricultural land in an agricultural tenancy ceases to be used for those purposes, is agricultural protection lost? Second, when non-agricultural land is later put to agricultural use, is agricultural protection acquired? Initially, one only has an agricultural tenancy if substantially the whole land is let for use as agricultural land.[23] To determine that one looks to the terms of the tenancy, the actual or contemplated use when the contract was made,[24] and other relevant circumstances.[25] If the land ceases to be used "as a matter of substance"[26] for agricultural purposes, it will cease to enjoy protection as an agricultural tenancy. This will be so whether or not the landlord has consented to the abandonment. The relevant period to look at is the time leading up to the service of the notice. Strong evidence will be needed to show that agricultural user has been abandoned.[27] If there is a cessation of agricultural and business activity without the landlord's consent, the tenant may also find himself outside the Rent Act protection.[28]

Effective changes of use that would take a non-agricultural letting into the agricultural sector are inhibited by statute, *e.g.* a change from use for horse jumping to grazing. If the change involves a breach of the terms of the tenancy agreement then it is to be disregarded, unless the landlord has given his permission for or acquiesced in the change.[29] Landlords letting rural land for business purposes, *e.g.* golf courses, sports grounds, agricultural showgrounds, etc., should expressly prohibit agricultural use. If such use occurs, they should be vigilant to oppose it, or they may be regarded as having acquiesced in the change.

---

[19] A.H.A. 1986, s.25(1).
[20] *Ante* D.
[21] *Ante* B.
[22] *Ante* D.
[23] A.H.A. 1986, s.1(2).
[24] The section refers to the "time of the conclusion of the contract"—an expression not free from ambiguity.
[25] A.H.A. 1986, s.1(2)(*c*).
[26] *Howkins* v. *Jardine* [1951] 1 K.B. 614 at p. 628, Jenkins L.J.; *Wetherall* v. *Smith* [1980] 2 All E.R. 530 at p. 537, Sir David Cairns.
[27] *Wetherall* v. *Smith, supra,* and see also *Hickson and Welch* v. *Cann (Note)* (1977) 40 P. & C.R. 218.
[28] *Russell* v. *Booker* (1982) 263 E.G. 513.
[29] A.H.A. 1986, s.1(3).

III. THE NATURE OF THE INTEREST PROTECTED

A. Common Yearly Tenancy

The basic protection given by the Act is to continue the tenant's rights of occupation until they are ended in accordance with very complicated statutory provisions, generally following the service of a 12 months' notice to quit.[30] It will be recollected from Part 1, Chapter 8, that a yearly tenant needs only half a year's notice, that shorter periodic tenants have to be served with notices equivalent to the short period of their tenancy, and that tenants for fixed terms of years do not need any notice at common law to end their estate in the land. The 1986 Act destroys the common law right of the landlord of an agricultural holding to end the term on short notice, or to regard it as ended at the expiration of a fixed number of years.

If the tenancy is granted "for an interest less than a tenancy from year to year,"[31] it takes effect "as if it were an agreement for the letting of the land for a tenancy from year to year."[32] One has to look at what, as a matter of law, is the tenant's interest in the land. Where an agreement for 13 months was backdated in an attempt to make it run for some 12 months before it was signed, the backdating period was ignored. This left, in law, a tenancy for less than a year, which was protected.[33] A short periodic tenancy of agricultural land or a letting of such land for a fixed period for a year[34] or less is therefore converted statutorily into a yearly tenancy. Tenancies for a fixed period of two years or more, *e.g.* 7, 14, or 21 years, continue at the end of the term as tenancies from year to year. To end such tenancies requires service of a notice not less than one year nor more than two years before the date fixed for the expiration of the term.[35] If the tenancies continue because of the statutory protection after the end of the fixed term, they will usually need the standard 12 months' minimum notice. A very limited amount of contracting out is permitted,[36] but usually it is prohibited.[37] Further, a tenant cannot be estopped[38] from relying on his statutory rights.

---

[30] A.H.A. 1986, s.25(1).
[31] A.H.A. 1986, s.2(2)(*a*).
[32] A.H.A. 1986, s.2(1).
[33] *Keen* v. *Holland* [1984] 1 All E.R. 75.
[34] *Bernays* v. *Prosser* [1963] 2 Q.B. 592.
[35] A.H.A. 1986, s.3(1).
[36] A.H.A. 1986, s.5.
[37] A.H.A. 1986, s.5(1).
[38] *Keen* v. *Holland* [1984] 1 All E.R. 75.

B. Protection Extended to Certain Licences

The Act therefore protects what may be regarded as the normal common form yearly tenancy of property let for farming purposes. But it will also be recollected[39] that considerable legal ingenuity is often devoted to granting interests in land that are less than terms of years absolute, usually licences, with a view to excluding the occupier from the statutory protection afforded both to residential and business tenants. The Agricultural Holdings Act 1986 seeks to obviate many of the problems caused in other areas of owner and occupier relationships by treating the licensee as a tenant where he is granted "a licence to occupy land for use as agricultural land, and the circumstances are such that if his interest were a tenancy from year to year he would in respect of that land be the tenant of an agricultural holding."[40]

A licence, to enjoy protection under these provisions, must be analogous to the grant of a tenancy. It must be granted for valuable consideration, and not be merely voluntary.[41] The parties must have intended to create legal relationships.[42] It must grant the licensee an exclusive right of occupation for agricultural purposes during its currency as against the licensor or any other person authorised by the licensor.[43] The licence must also grant the licensee sole occupational rights. A genuine partnership agreement between a landowner and a farm manager, both liable to share losses and enjoy profits, will not give the partner who does not initially have an estate in the land any right to claim that his licence to occupy the land to be farmed has been converted, by the Act, into a tenancy from year to year at no rent.[44] It may be otherwise if the partnership agreement is just a dressed up *de facto* tenancy, *e.g.* if the land owning "partner" is merely a salaried partner with the benefit of an indemnity against losses. But the fact that the licence agreement does not provide for payments analogous to rent will not prevent its conversion by section 2(2) into a tenancy from year to year at no rent.[45] There still may be some other consideration supporting the licence and following conversion the landlord can apply for a proper rent to be determined.[46] Any dispute

---

[39] See Pt. I, Chap. 2, and Pt. III, Chap. 20.
[40] A.H.A. 1986, s.2(2).
[41] *Goldsack* v. *Shore* [1950] 1 K.B. 708; *Avon County Council* v. *Clothier* (1977) 75 L.G.R. 344 (voluntary licence to stable ponies). And see *Mitton* v. *Farrow* (1980) 255 E.G. 449 (agreement to occupy, in consideration of clearing derelict land).
[42] *Collier* v. *Hollinshead* (1984) 272 E.G. 941.
[43] *Bahamas International Trust Co. Ltd.* v. *Threadgold* [1974] 1 W.L.R. 1514. There is a difference between exclusive occupation and exclusive possession. The decision in *Street* v. *Mountford* [1985] 2 All E.R. has created great uncertainty in this area of the law, and it may now be much more difficult for landowners to create genuine licences of agricultural property: see Chap. 2, *supra*, (II) A–H.
[44] *Harrison-Broadley* v. *Smith* [1964] 1 W.L.R. 456.
[45] *Verrall* v. *Farnes* [1966] 1 W.L.R. 1254 (where the licensee was on trial as a prospective tenant).
[46] See *post*, Chap. 26, and A.H.A. 1986, s.8.

about the operation of section 2 in relation to any agreement has to be determined by arbitration under the Act.[47]

C. The Capacity of the Grantor

The extent of the interest of the grantor of a tenancy or licence can have the effect of depriving the grantee of statutory protection. There has been a suggestion that if the grantor is in law incapable of granting or creating a legal estate, then the tenant will not obtain any statutory protection.[48] It is difficult to understand how this argument can be sustained at least as regards the relationship between the original tenant and landlord. Both of them, in accordance with normal principles, must be estopped from denying the nature of the relationship *inter se*, although whether the contractual rights they have created will bind either the land, or their respective successors in title is a different matter.[49] An agreement to permit occupation at a substantial consideration by one or two executors can bind the estate.[49,49a]

But the issue of estoppel aside, there is a curious provision in the 1986 Act, s.21, under the section heading "Extension of tenancies in lieu of claims to emblements." Subsection (1) provides: "Where the tenancy of an agricultural holding held by a tenant at a rack rent determines by the death or cesser of the estate of any landlord entitled for his life, or for any other uncertain interest, instead of claims to emblements the tenant shall continue to hold and occupy the holding until the occupation is determined by a 12 months' notice to quit expiring at the end of a year of the tenancy, and shall then quit upon the terms of his tenancy in the same manner as if the tenancy were then determined by effluxion of time or other lawful means during the continuance of his landlord's estate."

This section would seem to apply quite clearly to tenancies created by persons who are in an analogous situation to tenants for life. Vicars, or rectors enjoying glebe land, which may consist of substantial market garden holdings, or the more usual arable land, attached to the living, would seem to qualify as landlords within this section,[50] although additional complicated provisions should properly be observed if they are to create tenancies binding on their successors to the corporation sole. Similarly, other corporations sole also would seem to qualify as relevant landlords. Tenancies created by persons who are tenants for life within the meaning of the Settled Land Act 1925 are also caught when the statutory provisions governing the

---

[47] A.H.A. 1986, s.2(4).
[48] See *Finbow* v. *Air Ministry* [1963] 1 W.L.R. 697; *cf.* P. H. Pettitt [1980] Conv. 112.
[49] See *ante* Pt. I, Chap. 3(IV)B, on the creation of tenancies by estoppel.
[49a] *Collier* v. *Hollinshead* (1984) 272 E.G. 941.
[50] *cf. Stephens* v. *Balls* (1957) 107 L.J. 764; [1957] C.L.Y. 1154, a county court decision.

creation of such tenancies have not been strictly observed,[51] although in this instance all the tenant has to show to qualify for protection is simply that he is paying a rack-rent, and not that he is paying the "best rent," or even, seemingly, that he has acted in good faith.[52]

It is not uncommon for a farmer to give all his estate by will to his executors upon trust for sale and direct them to pay the income to a specified beneficiary for life. The trustees are often permitted to allow the beneficiary to reside and run the farm for his own benefit for as long as he wants. Such a beneficiary can request the trustees to delegate to him by writing their leasing powers,[53] and if that is done, he can create agricultural and other tenancies in their name. It is not unusual to find after such a life beneficiary's death that the necessary formalities have never been observed, but that what appear to be agricultural tenancies have been created. It is submitted that these tenancies, if at a rack-rent, do receive the protection of the 1986 Act. They are granted by someone with an interest in the land,[54] even though he is only technically entitled to an interest issuing out of the proceeds of sale. He is furthermore a "landlord" within the definition of the 1986 Act, s.96.[55] Indeed, it would seem consonant with the whole policy of the Act to extend protection to such tenancies.

D. Sub-tenancies

If the tenancy which has been created is a sub-tenancy, and would otherwise qualify as an agricultural tenancy, then it will normally enjoy the protection of the Act. There are two qualifications to this general statement, the first being one of considerably greater importance than the latter. Although normally the sub-tenant will enjoy the protection *vis-à-vis* his own mesne landlord, he will not necessarily be able to enforce his statutory rights of protection against the landlord of the reversionary interest. In this respect the treatment of agricultural tenancies is markedly different from the treatment of business tenants,[56] where an extended meaning is given to the expression "relevant landlord."[57] If therefore the head tenancy is ended, then

[51] S.L.A. 1925, s.42, and see *ante* Pt. I, Chap. 3(II)B.
[52] And so within S.L.A. 1925, s.110, or the limited protection given by L.P.A. 1925, s.152, to save leases that would otherwise be invalid because they are not granted in compliance with the terms of the relevant powers.
[53] L.P.A. 1925, ss.28, 29, and see also s.30 where there is a refusal to delegate.
[54] See L.P.A. 1925, s.205(1)(x).
[55] *i.e.* "any person for the time being entitled to receive the rents and profits of any land," but see *Schalit* v. *Nadler (Joseph) Ltd.* [1933] 2 K.B. 79. If such a tenancy does bind the testator's estate, it renders otiose in this respect, L.P.A. 1925, s.29 (formalities relating to the delegation of leasing powers). Furthermore, it may not be correct to regard the granting beneficiary's interest in the land as being subject to "cesser," when it can be brought to an end by the trustees selling the land, thereby overreaching the beneficiary's interest.
[56] See *ante* Pt. III, Chap. 20(II)A.
[57] L. & T.A. 1954, s.44.

subject to the usual rights of a sub-tenant to ask for relief against forfeiture,[58] the sub-tenancy will fall with it.[59] This does not apply where the immediate tenancy is surrendered voluntarily.[60] Furthermore, a collusive or sham arrangement between the head tenant and the intermediate landlord/tenant designed to frustrate the object of the Act might not survive critical judicial scrutiny.[61] Nevertheless, the interposition of an intermediate non-agricultural tenancy is a device which is suggested as a possible means of mitigating the effects on the landlord of the 1986 Act.

The second occasion when an otherwise qualifying agricultural sub-tenancy does not enjoy statutory protection is when it is granted "by a person whose interest in the land is less than a tenancy from year to year. . . . "[62] This provision, it is suggested, could operate where fields are, *e.g.* let to a circus, or to a camping organisation for a fixed period in the summer and they purport to grant an agricultural sub-tenancy. Such a sub-tenant could not claim the protection of the Act.

IV. TENANCIES OUTSIDE THE STATUTORY UMBRELLA

A. Generally

Obviously falling outside the statutory umbrella are the various interests mentioned in the last sections, *e.g.* tenancies where the land is not used for agriculture, or in connection with a trade, where it is held under a voluntary licence, or a "joint" licence with the landowner[63] or where a sub-tenancy is created by a landlord whose own interest is insufficient to support the grant of a yearly tenancy. But in addition to these matters, there are a number of important tenancies outside the general protection of the Act.[64]

B. Tenancies to Office Holders

Section 1(1) excludes "a contract under which the . . . land is let to the tenant during his continuance in any office, appointment or employment held under the landlord" from being an agricultural holding.

---

[58] See *ante* Pt. I, Chap. 8(VI)D, and L.P.A. 1925, s.146(4).
[59] The extent of the sub-tenant's rights against the head landlord are considered, in Chap. 27, s.III, B, *post.*
[60] L.P.A. 1925, s.139 will apply, and see *Brown* v. *Wilson* discussed (1949) 93 S.J. 640, and *Woodfall*, Vol. 2–0054.
[61] *cf. Megaw* L.J. in *Johnson* v. *Moreton* (1977) 35 P. & C.R. 378, at pp. 384, 385 affd. [1980] A.C. 37. (H.L.).
[62] A.H.A. 1986, s.2(3).
[63] But see *post*, Chap. 27(I), on the ability of the actual tenant to serve an effective counter-notice.
[64] And see generally A. M. Prichard [1978] Conv. 188.

The normal appointment of a farm manager will not give rise to an agricultural tenancy, although it may be different if what in fact is a tenancy is dressed up as a managership.

C. Tenancies Granted with Ministry Approval

Landlords are sometimes reluctant to let property because they foresee a situation where they will need to recover possession for their own purposes. This may particularly be the situation of local authorities who own agricultural property. If ministerial consent is obtained before the tenancy agreement is entered into[65] or renewed[66] for a short term letting, then it will not automatically be regarded as a tenancy from year to year. Consent need only be to the letting, not its precise terms.[67]

D. Lettings for Mowing or Grazing

Often a landowner, whether he is a farmer or not, has no immediate use for grassland, and would not be prepared to sterilise his future freedom of action by risking the possibility of creating an agricultural tenancy. However, if there is a letting or licence to occupy "in contemplation of the use of the land only for grazing or mowing during some specified period of the year,[68] then the tenancy will not be regarded as a yearly one. It is not necessary for the letting to restrict the use expressly: what matters is the intention of the parties.[69] But "contemplation" means more than uncommunicated expectation,[70] both in relation to the use to which the land can be put and the ultimate duration of the tenancy. There must be no express or implied agreement that the tenancy will be renewed,[71] and each individual letting can be for no longer than 364 days.[72] A letting for "6 months' periods" will therefore fall within the protection of the Act,[73] as this contemplates a letting for at least one year. It must be clear that the grazing should be for less than a year,[74] but it is not necessary for the

[65] A.H.A. 1986, s.2(1).
[66] And see *Bedfordshire County Council* v. *Clarke* (1974) 230 E.G. 1587, where there was a failure to obtain consent before the renewal of a "364" day licence.
[67] *Epsom and Ewell Borough Council* v. *Bell (C.) Tadworth* [1983] 1 W.L.R. 379.
[68] A.H.A. 1986, s.2(3).
[69] *cf. Lory* v. *Brent London Borough Council* [1971] 1 W.L.R. 823, where the licence envisaged ploughing and crop rotation and was held to take effect as if it was a tenancy from year to year.
[70] And see *Short Bros. (Plant)* v. *Edwards* (1978) 249 E.G. 539.
[71] *Scene Estate* v. *Amos* [1957] 2 Q.B. 205 where a three months' grazing letting of a former golf course had been renewed 21 times was held to be within the proviso and not a yearly letting. And see *Chaloner* v. *Bower* (1984) 269 E.G. 725.
[72] *Reid* v. *Dawson* [1955] 1 Q.B. 214.
[73] *Rutherford* v. *Maurer* [1962] 1 Q.B. 16.
[74] *Lampard* v. *Barker* (1984) 272 E.G. 783.

agreement to specify dates.[75] One has to be careful not to create a protected tenancy either inadvertently or by estoppel.[76] Whether or not a letting is within the mowing or grazing exception has to be determined by arbitration under the Act.[77]

E. Lettings for Fixed Periods Between 12 and 24 Months

Lettings for fixed periods of less than one year are dealt with expressly by section 2, and subject to the matters discussed earlier in this chapter, take effect as tenancies from year to year. This applies to a lease for 12 months exactly.[78] But following the decision in *Gladstone* v. *Bower*[79] a tenancy for a fixed period of more than 12 months but for less than 2 years falls outside the security of tenure provisions of the Act. However, although this seems to be a surprising gap which has never been rectified in later legislation, it does not follow that one often counters fixed 18 month tenancies. Faced with the offer of such a tenancy a tenant should be advised to take it only if it made farming sense to him at that time on the basis that he would not get security of tenure. This might well stultify his proposed use of the land in the latter part of the tenancy. And acting for a landlord, it would have to be pointed out that if in fact the arrangement was renewed there might be real difficulty in persuading the court that the provisions were outside the ambit of section 3 which is concerned with tenancies of two years or more.[80]

F. Permitted Contracting-Out

Limited contracting out has been permitted for post-12 September, 1984 tenancies. The provisions only apply to tenancies of not less than two or more than five years' duration. Both parties must agree that the security provisions will not apply to the tenancy. They must make a joint application to the Minister, whose approval is necessary. The written tenancy agreement must either contain or have endorsed on it a statement that the security provisions do not apply to the tenancy.[81] One important consequence is that the tenant cannot make a claim for disturbance at the end of his tenancy. He can, however,

---

[75] *Stone* v. *Whitcombe* (1980) 40 P. & C.R. 296 (during the grazing season—from about April to October), and see also *Luton* v. *Tinsey* (1978) 249 E.G. 239 on the use of "grass keeps."
[76] *South West Water Authority* v. *Palmer* (1983) 268 E.G. 357, 443.
[77] A.H.A. 1986, s.2(4).
[78] *Bernays* v. *Prosser* [1963] 2 Q.B. 592.
[79] [1960] 2 Q.B. 384.
[80] And see further Scammell & Densham, pp. 25, 26.
[81] A.H.A. 1986, s.5.

claim for his improvements and tenant-right matters.[82] Unlike similar provisions in relation to residential tenancies,[83] there is nothing to prevent such agreements from being made with existing tenants on new grants. Also there are no provisions restricting the grant of a series of repeated limited tenancies. The proposals are intended, presumably, to provide a more attractive alternative to the present convoluted arrangements[84] which are often entered into, designed to avoid statutory security.

G. Death During a Fixed Term Contract

It will be seen that the death of the sole surviving tenant under a protected periodic tenancy enables the landlord to serve a notice to quit.[85] For post-12 September, 1984 tenancies the death of the *original*[86] tenant has the automatic effect of removing the security provisions in the case of tenancies granted for two years or more.[87] If the original tenant[88] dies in the last year of the fixed term, then the tenancy continues for a further 12 months, on the same terms. It ends on the first anniversary of what should have been the end of the fixed term.[89] If the original tenant dies earlier than in the last year, then the tenancy will automatically end with the expiration of the fixed term,[90] and will not be statutorily continued.[91] The tenancy is deemed to have come to an end as if it had been terminated by a landlord's notice.[92] This fiction preserves the tenant's right to claim compensation for disturbance.

---

[82] See *post*, Chap. 28.

[83] See, for example, the restrictions on granting shorthold tenancies to existing regulated tenants, *ante* Chap. 14(III)C. A landlord might well consider providing some inducement to persuade his existing tenants to take a new unprotected tenancy.

[84] *e.g.* "sham" partnerships, with the landlord, coupled with licences, or contracting arrangements. The arrangements are not always successful in avoiding security.

[85] A.H.A. 1986, Sched. 3, Case G, and *post* Chap. 27(II)G.

[86] Emphasis supplied. It is not the death of the current tenant under the contract that is relevant here, a matter to be considered in the unlikely event of consent being given to assign a fixed term of years.

[87] *i.e.* tenancies within A.H.A. 1986, s.3(1).

[88] Or the survivor of the persons granted the tenancy.

[89] A.H.A. 1986, s.4(2). These provisions do not apply if an effective notice ending the tenancy has already been given.

[90] A.H.A. 1986, s.4(2).

[91] *e.g.* under A.H.A. 1986, s.3(1).

[92] A.H.A. 1986, s.5(3), and see *post* Chap. 28. A landlord's notice or deemed notice is an essential pre-condition to claiming compensation for disturbance, *cf.* the position under A.H.A. 1986, s.5, *supra*.

CHAPTER 26

OBLIGATIONS IMPOSED DURING THE TENANCY

I. Terms of the Tenancy 769
   A. Written Terms 769
   B. Manner of Farming and Man-
      agement 770

C. Repair 772
D. Rent 774

I. Terms of the Tenancy

A. Written Terms

Like business tenancies, the majority of tenancy agreements for at least the larger farms are the subject of detailed and lengthy written agreements setting out the obligations of both parties. This can be particularly important for inheritance tax purposes if it becomes necessary to establish the value of the holding subject to the tenancy, where the tenancy is between the owner on the one hand and his family farming company on the other. And where the parties are in no way related, a detailed written agreement will obviously help to reduce the points of conflict between landlord and tenant. Section 6 of the 1986 Act enables either party to ask for a written agreement, or for their existing agreement to make provision for the matters specified in the First Schedule. In the absence of agreement, the matter can be referred to an arbitrator. The topics to be covered by the agreement[1] should include the parties' names, particulars of the holding, the length of term on which the whole or different parts are let, details of the rent and liability for rates and a covenant by the landlord to insure and reinstate buildings following fire damage, and by the tenant not to assign, sub-let or part with the possession of the whole or any part of the holding without the landlord's written consent.[2] The agreement should also contain a covenant by the tenant that in the event of fire destroying harvested crops he will return to the holding their full equivalent manurial value so far as good husbandry requires its return, and that he will insure such crops and dead stock[3] against damage by fire. Finally, the agreement should enable the landlord to re-enter the holding in the event of the tenant's failure to perform his

---

[1] *i.e.* the matters mentioned in A.H.A. 1986, Sched. 1.
[2] The statutorily implied proviso that such consent cannot be unreasonably withheld does not apply to agricultural tenancies, see Landlord and Tenant Act 1927, s.19(4) and Pt. I, Chap. 7, *ante*.
[3] Certain tenants (The Crown, Government Departments, etc.) are exempt from insurance liability, as they will carry their own "insurance."

769

obligations under the agreement. If there is a landlord's request to the tenant to enter into an agreement containing the matters which should be included,[4] especially the covenant restricting assignment without consent, the tenant cannot take avoiding action by assigning or subletting without written consent while the terms are being settled. Such an attempted assignment is void.[5] The terms do not need to contain any express provisions relating to repair, etc., as this point is dealt with by the deemed inclusion of "model clauses" under section 7.[6]

B. Manner of Farming and Management

The broad principles of good estate management and good husbandry were contained in the Agricultural Act 1947. An owner manages his holding in accordance with the principles of good estate management if it is done in such a way as "to enable an occupier of the land reasonably skilled in husbandry to maintain efficient production"[7] of quantity, quality and type of produce. One of the relevant factors to be considered is the extent to which the landlord is providing,[8] maintaining and improving fixed equipment, unless this obligation is thrown on the other party.

The occupier farms in accordance with good husbandry if he is maintaining a reasonable standard of efficient production.[9] In particular permanent pasture has to be kept properly mown or grazed, arable land clean, and both kept in a good state for cultivation, fertility and condition; livestock must be efficiently managed, and livestock and crops kept free from disease, insects and pests; crops must be properly preserved after lifting or harvesting, and all necessary maintenance carried out. These statutory guidelines are not elevated into the status of implied covenants entitling either party to take proceedings for breach of covenant. But, as will be seen,[10] whether the proper standards have been observed is often important when the landlord takes steps to end the tenancy. In formal written tenancies the parties often covenant to farm and manage respectively in accordance with the rules provided by these sections.

It is obviously important at the beginning of a tenancy to agree the state of cultivation of the different parts of the holding and the

---

[4] The request cannot be made if the parties' agreement already contains express provisions consistent, or more importantly, inconsistent with the First Schedule terms, A.H.A. 1986, s.6(2).
[5] A.H.A. 1986, s.6(5).
[6] See *post* (I)C.
[7] s.10 of the 1947 Act.
[8] A.H.A. 1986, s.11 contains machinery designed to enable tenants to require their landlords to provide fixed equipment. These provisions cannot be used to obtain equipment for a new agricultural activity which would be a substantial alteration to the tenant's type of farming, s.11(2).
[9] s.11 of the 1947 Act.
[10] See *post*, Chap. 27. Compensation for dilapidations is considered in Chap. 28.

condition of those parts. Section 22 of the 1986 Act entitles either party to require the making of a record of condition of the farm, and its buildings, gates, fences, roads, drains and ditches. In addition the tenant can ask for a record to be kept of improvements carried out by him with the landlord's written consent, and in respect of which he may be entitled to compensation as an outgoing tenant, and also in respect of buildings and fixtures which he may be entitled to remove.[11]

But so far as the state of the farmland is concerned a considerable amount of the older law was devoted to the detailed rights of a landlord to compel his tenant to keep permanent pasture as a permanent pasture.[12] And a covenant to that effect is still likely to be inserted "but without prejudice to the provisions of section 14" of the 1986 Act. If the tenant wants to put some of the permanent pasture under plough he will initially ask for his landlord's consent. If it is not given then under section 14[13] the matter can be submitted to arbitration to decide "whether it is expedient to secure the full and efficient farming of the holding that the amount of land required to be maintained as permanent pasture should be reduced." The arbitrator can modify the area to be kept as permanent pasture, and may make consequential directions requiring the tenant on quitting to leave a specified area either of permanent or temporary pasture.

The tenant is statutorily[14] entitled to practise any system of cropping on the arable land that he chooses, and until the last year of his tenancy has full right to dispose as he may wish of all the produce of the arable land, except manure. Good husbandry, and section 15(4) of the 1986 Act require him to make suitable provisions for returning to the holding the equivalent manurial value of crops sold off or removed. This does not enable the tenant to grow, for example, white straw crops, and nothing else. Section 15(5) entitles the landlord to take proceedings for an injunction to restrain the tenant if he exercises his rights in such a way as will injure the holding,[15] and if the tenant has done so, to claim damages from the tenant, on his quitting but not before.[16]

There is a more stringent restriction on the sale or removal of manure, compost, hay, straw or roots grown in the last year, after a notice to quit has been given either by the landlord or the tenant. The

[11] See *ante* Pt. I, Chap. 3 (I)E, 6 for the rights to remove agricultural fixtures.
[12] And see *Woodfall*, para. 2–0006.
[13] Either party may demand a reference, s.14(2).
[14] A.H.A. 1986, s.15(1).
[15] The issue of whether the tenant's cropping and disposal of produce has injured the holding is determined by an arbitrator, A.H.A. 1986, s.15(6).
[16] The landlord may be able to sue for a breach of covenant during the tenancy, *Kent* v. *Conniff* [1953] 1 Q.B. 361.

tenant needs his landlord's consent if he wants to sell or remove such produce.[17]

C. Repair

It is easier to consider the question of repairs in relation to agricultural leases on the assumption that the parties have reached no agreement on the matter. In that case, the code contained in the Schedule to the Agriculture (Maintenance, Repair and Insurance of Fixed Equipment) Regulations 1973 is deemed to be incorporated in the agreement. The code is comprehensive and detailed.

The landlord is under a liability to execute all repairs to the main and exterior walls, roofs, chimneys, eaves-gutterings and downpipes of the farmhouse, cottages and farm buildings. This liability extends to walls and fences of open and covered yards and consequential repairs to decoration where this has been made necessary by structural defects. He is also obliged to repair the underground water supply pipes, wells, bore-holes, sewage disposal systems and septic tanks. He is under a liability to insure the same buildings against damage by fire and thereafter to reinstate or replace them, laying out the insurance money for that purpose. The landlord has to decorate externally every five years, and this liability extends to the interior structural steelwork of open sided farm buildings, and except for the farmhouse and cottages, the inside wood and ironwork of all external outward opening doors and windows. There are also a number of "half-cost" items, where the landlord is under a duty to effect the repair, but can recover half the cost from the tenant. These items include repairs and replacements of floorboards, interior staircases, doors, windows and skylights and gutters and drainpipes. The painting of doors, windows, gutters and down-pipes is also paid for on a "half-cost" basis.

The tenant has to repair,[18] keep and leave clean and in good tenantable repair and condition the farmhouse, cottages, and farm buildings, except so far as these matters are specifically allocated to the landlord. He is under a duty to decorate the interior of these buildings every seven years, and if this work is not done in the last year of the tenancy he will be charged with dilapidations, the measure of his liability being either the cost of decorations or one-seventh of the cost of the work for each year going back to the date the premises were last decorated, whichever is less. He is under a duty to repair and

---

[17] A.H.A. 1986, s.15(3). The restriction applies to items which have been grown in the last year, even before a notice to quit has been served, a situation that can only arise where a shorter notice than usual can be served, and see *Eldon (Earl)* v. *Hedley Bros.* [1935] 2 K.B. 1.

[18] And see Sir R. Evershed M.R. in *Evans* v. *Jones* [1955] 2 Q.B. 58 at p. 66. The tenant's duty is not limited by reference to the condition of the premises when he went in. *cf.* liability under a covenant to repair.

leave clean the fixtures and fittings in the buildings, and in particular the drains, sewers, gulleys, grease-traps and manholes, the electrical supply systems and fittings, the water supply systems so far as they are above ground, and the fences, hedges, walls, gates and posts, bridges and culverts, watercourses, ditches, roads and yards. Watercourses and ditches have to be dug out where necessary and field drains and their outlets kept free from obstruction. A reasonable proportion of the hedges have to be trimmed, cut or laid each year. The tenant has to keep the guttering and sewage systems clean, and replace broken or slipped tiles up to a maximum cost of £25 in any one year, a figure which looks remarkably dated. More importantly, the tenant has to repair and replace all items of fixed equipment,[19] and other items that may have worn out as a result of the tenant's failure to repair.

Disputes about the parties' respective liabilities to repair are to be referred to arbitration and, subject to that, the landlord can effect repairs following the tenant's failure to begin within two months or complete the work within three months of receiving a written notice from the landlord. The tenant can also carry out repairs which are the landlord's responsibility if the landlord fails to do them within three months of receiving a notice from the tenant. The tenant can recover from the landlord the reasonable cost of the repairs to a limit of £500 or the amount of the yearly rent,[20] whichever is the smaller.

It is possible to contract out of this statutorily imposed code.[21] This can be done either by varying the incidence of the scheduled liabilities or by providing that neither party shall be under any duty to attend to certain items, *e.g.* hedges.[22] But if the written agreement substantially modifies or varies the scheduled liabilities, then either party can ask the other that it should be varied to bring it in line with the regulations. In the absence of agreement, the contractual terms relating to the maintenance, repair and insurance of fixed equipment can be referred to arbitration.[23] The arbitrator has a wide discretion to vary the terms, but in coming to his decision he must ignore the rent payable for the holding.[24] After he has made his decision, he can then consider whether the rent needs varying in the light of the altered

---

[19] A.H.A. 1986, s.96(1) defines fixed equipment.

[20] See *ante*, Pt. 1, Chap. 6, for the tenant's rights in respect of the cost of the landlord's repairs borne by the tenant.

[21] A.H.A. 1986, s.7(3).

[22] *cf. Burden* v. *Hannaford* [1956] 1 Q.B. 142 (holding that a conflict between the contractual terms and the schedule liabilities had to be resolved in favour of the contractual terms).

[23] A.H.A. 1986, s.8(2). Applications for these arbitrations cannot be made more often than once in three years, s.8(6).

[24] A.H.A. 1986, s.8(3).

liabilities.[25] The alterations vary the old agreement, but do not operate to create a new agreement.[26]

Obviously if the tenant is persistently and seriously failing in his duty to farm competently or keep the premises in repair, then the landlord will begin to take steps in his own financial interest to bring the tenancy to an end. In the meantime, he has a right to enter to view, and carry out his own obligations.[26a] But his right to sue for damages for breach of the tenant's obligations is limited to the actual damage suffered. He cannot call on the tenant to pay under covenants for penal rents or even for liquidated damages.[27]

D. Rent

(1) *Mechanics of Review*

The amount of the rent is one of the matters to be specified in the agreement.[28] Both parties to the tenancy have the right to refer the question of rent to arbitration at no greater frequency than once in every three years,[29] and a revised rent cannot take effect within the first three years of the tenancy. But a variation in the rent by the arbitrator in the last three years following an alteration of the repairing liabilities,[30] the reduction in the size of the holding after a notice to quit,[31] or the installation of certain improvements by the landlord,[32] does not start the three year period running all over again.[33]

At least 12 months' notice has to be given by either party to the other requiring the revision of the rent from the date on which the tenancy could be ended by a notice to quit given on the date demanding the reference.[33a] Unless a fixed term lease contains a rent review clause, the rent cannot be reviewed to take effect before the end of the term. But in every case, either the parties must have appointed the arbitrator by agreement, or applied to the President of

---

[25] A.H.A. 1986, s.8(4). Applications under s.6(2) (arbitration to specify terms of agreement) can also give rise to an application to vary the rent, s.6(3). A transfer of liability to repair fixed equipment can give rise to an application for compensation if there has been a previous failure to repair, etc., s.9.

[26] A.H.A. 1986, s.8(5).

[26a] A.H.A. 1986, s.23, and see Agriculture (Maintenance, Repair, etc.) Regulations 1973, Sched., Pt. 1, para. 4(2), enabling the landlord to enter to carry out the tenant's obligations.

[27] A.H.A. 1986, s.24.

[28] A.H.A. 1986, Sched. 1.

[29] A.H.A. 1986, Sched. 2, para. 4.

[30] *Ibid.* and A.H.A. 1986, s.8(4).

[31] A.H.A. 1986, s.33.

[32] A.H.A. 1986, s.13.

[33] A.H.A. 1986, Sched. 2, para. 4(2).

[33a] A.H.A. 1986, s.12(1), (4).

the Royal Institution of Chartered Surveyors[34] for appointment by him, before the date[35] on which the tenancy could have ended.[36] The date is the earliest date on which the new rent can take effect, although it has to be determined as on the date the matter was referred to him.[37]

(2) *Criteria for determining the rent*

In the last edition, it was suggested that logically rent for farmland should bear some relation to its potential profitability. It was observed that the application of logic to farm rents and prices was not always apparent. The statutory criteria used in determining rents have been recast. The Act moves away from the open-market concept. Profitability is now an important factor to be considered. It has been doubted if the statutory change will make significant practical difference, as rents in the past were not necessarily fixed in accordance with the strict interpretation of the law.[38]

The arbitrator can either increase or decrease the rent, or leave it unchanged, when he is asked to determine the rent properly payable.[39] He has to find the rent at which a prudent and willing landlord would let to a prudent and willing tenant. This formula enables one to value out excessively high bids that might be made by persons over-enthusiastic to become tenants, either generally, or of that particular holding. Neighbours may be prepared to bid over market rates because they can conveniently add the holding to their existing farm without significantly increasing their overheads.[40] The arbitrator has to pay attention to a number of "regards," some of which are fairly obvious—all relevant factors, the terms of the tenancy, the character and situation of the holding.[41] But the remaining "regards" are novel in this area. The first two are related. They are the productive capacity[42] of the holding and its related earning capacity. This directs attention to the profits a reasonably competent tenant could make from the farm.[43] The last "regard" has echoes of rent determinations in the residential sector. The arbitrator is directed to consider the

---

[34] A.H.A. 1986, s.12(3).
[35] The appointment cannot be made more than four months before this date, A.H.A. 1986, Sched. 11, para. 1(3).
[36] A notice requesting arbitration which is not acted on lapses after 12 months, and, unlike a notice to quit, can be withdrawn, *Personal Representatives of the Estate of the late Dr. Cotton* v. *Gardiner* [1980] C.L.Y. 24.
[37] A.H.A. 1986, s.12(2).
[38] [1984] Law Society's Gazette, November 14, 3165, Richard Law, and see also Muir Watt, *Agricultural Holdings Act 1984*, Current Law Statutes Annotated, commentary on ss.8, 8A.
[39] A.H.A. 1986, s.12(2).
[40] Commonly known as the "marriage factor."
[41] A.H.A. 1986, Sched. 2, para. 1.
[42] A.H.A. 1986, Sched. 2, para. 2(*a*). One takes into account existing fixed equipment, and other available facilities and assumes a competent tenant following a suitable system of farming.
[43] A.H.A. 1986, Sched. 2, para. 2(*b*).

current rent levels of comparable holdings, let on similar terms. In evaluating these comparable rents, he has to disregard any appreciable scarcity[44] and the possible existence of a "marriage factor,"[45] both of which may have increased the rent. He also has to consider if the rent payable has been reduced because a premium has been charged.[46] It is curious that the arbitrator is only asked to disregard scarcity when looking at comparable rents and not expressly directed to disregard this item when considering what a prudent and willing tenant might offer.

The "disregards" are:

(a) that the tenant is in occupation as a sitting tenant;
(b) that the tenant has voluntarily effected improvements,[47] unless he has received an allowance for them from the landlord;
(c) that the landlord has effected grant-aided improvements;
(d) that the tenant has permitted the land or buildings to deteriorate.[48]

(3) *Increases Following Landlord's Improvements*

The landlord can obtain an increase in rent following improvements he has carried out. These will either be improvements carried out at the tenant's request, or with his consent, or to comply with various statutory directions or notices, or to improve sanitary facilities. The landlord's application must be made within six months of completion of the improvement.[49] The increase is the amount by which the rental value has been increased as a result of the improvement. If the improvement was "grant-aided," the rent increase is reduced proportionately.[50]

(4) *Decrease Following Notice to Quit of Part*

Most well-drawn agricultural tenancies contain a provision enabling the landlord to resume possession either of the whole[51] or a limited part of the property for specified purposes. Obviously this right will be

[44] A.H.A. 1986, Sched. 2, para. 1(3)(*a*), and *cf.* Chap. 11(III)B(4), *ante.*
[45] A.H.A. 1986, Sched. 2, para. 1(3)(*b*), and see fn. 40, *supra.*
[46] A.H.A. 1986, Sched. 2, para. 1(3)(*c*).
[47] A.H.A. 1986, Sched. 2, para. 2(1). And see *Tummon* v. *Barclays Bank* (1979) 39 P. & C.R. 300 (tenant used part of holding as caravan site after making substantial improvements, only *potential* of land as caravan site could be taken into account).
[48] A.H.A. 1986, Sched. 2, para. 3.
[49] A.H.A. 1986, s.13(1).
[50] A.H.A. 1986, s.13(4).
[51] An artificial severance of the reversion will be ignored for these purposes, *Persey* v. *Bazley* (1983) 47 P. & C.R. 37.

reserved if the land has development potential. But even if it has not, the prudent landlord will still reserve such a right.[52] The tenant is entitled under section 33 of the 1986 Act to require the amount of the rent reduction to be settled by arbitration, unless the parties agree a reduction after the landlord has resumed possession. When the arbitrator calculates the reduction in rent he does not simply reduce it by the amount per hectare multiplied by the number of hectares given up. He has to take into account the depreciation of the rest of the holding caused by loss of the part given up and the use to which the landlord intends to put the severed part.[53] Obviously some parts of the holding are of greater agricultural value than other parts. Development might well have an inhibiting effect on the way the immediately adjoining land is farmed, *e.g.* residential occupiers might well consider that the deposit of slurry or certain intensive farming methods would constitute an actionable nuisance and take steps to restrain it. A rent reduction under these provisions does not start the three year rent review period running again.[54]

---

[52] The statutory security provisions considered in the next chapter still apply when the landlord serves notice to quit a part.

[53] A.H.A. 1986, s.33(1).

[54] A.H.A. 1986, Sched. 2, para. 4(2)(*c*).

CHAPTER 27

SECURITY OF TENURE

I. Introduction 779
II. The Statutory Grounds 782
  A. Post-Notice Consent 782
  B. Case B—Alternative Use of the
    Land 784
  C. Case C—Certificate of Bad
    Husbandry 784
  D. Case D—Failure to Comply
    with Notice to Pay Rent or
    Remedy Breach 785
  E. Case E—Irremediable Breaches 790
  F. Case F—Insolvency 790

  G. Case G—Death and Succession
    on Death 791
  H. Case H—Ministerial Certifi-
    cates 796
III. Lifetime successions 797
IV. Additional and Consequential Mat-
  ters 798
  A. Compensation 798
  B. The Existence of Sub-tenancies 799
  C. Notices to Quit Part of the
    Holding 800

I. Introduction

Security of tenure is assured to the majority of tenants by providing that their interests in the land are to be treated as yearly tenancies[1] to continue until ended by a 12 months'[2] notice to quit.[3] The tenancy may be ended by an ordinary 12 months' notice[4] that does not rely on any of the statutory grounds for recovering possession. If the notice fails to make it plain whether it is an ordinary 12 months' notice or one relying on a statutory ground, then it will fail for ambiguity.[5] The tenant may decide because of finance, health or age that the time has come to give up farming. He may be able to operate the provisions for nominating a successor on retirement.[6] If the tenant wants to stay he must give written counter-notice requiring that section 26(1) of the 1986 Act shall apply. The counter-notice does not have to be in a prescribed form. An angry letter to the landlord, objecting to the notice, will not be sufficient to invoke the tenant's statutory rights. "But if the meaning is so plain that the landlord cannot reasonably mistake what is meant, then effect should be given to the notice."[7] The

---

[1] A.H.A. 1986, ss.1–3 and see Chap. 25 ante.
[2] A.H.A. 1986, s.25(1).
[3] A shorter notice may be given by the landlord on four limited grounds set out in A.H.A. 1986, s.25(2), see post, or by agreement, Elsden v. Pick [1980] 1 W.L.R. 899. After an arbitrator has determined a rent increase, the tenant can give notice of at least six months to end with the year of the tenancy, A.H.A. 1986, s.25(3).
[4] There is no prescribed form. But a landlord who serves a simple 12 months' notice may find himself paying four years' additional rent as compensation for disturbance to the outgoing tenant, under A.H.A. 1986, s.60(4).
[5] Mills v. Edwards [1971] 1 Q.B. 379.
[6] See post (III).
[7] Per Romer L.J. in Mountford v. Hodkinson [1956] 1 W.L.R. 422, at p. 427.

written counter-notice must be served on the landlord not later than one month from the giving of the notice to quit.[8] The counter-notice prevents the notice to quit from having any effect unless the Agricultural Land Tribunal consents to its operation. As will be seen, there are only limited grounds on which the Tribunal can grant its consent.[9]

In the same way that landlords of residential and business accommodation can recover possession by proving specified statutory grounds, so landlords of agricultural holdings can recover possession by giving notices expressly relying on specified statutory grounds, and, of course, proving them.[10] The principal grounds on which a landlord can recover possession are[11]:

Case A: It is a tenancy of a smallholding, let by a smallholdings authority after September 12, 1984, expressly subject to this Case, entitling recovery of possession when the tenant is over 65, and suitable alternative living accommodation is available[12];

Case B: The land is required for a use, other than for agriculture, usually after planning permission has been obtained;

Case C: The landlord has obtained a certificate with six months of giving the notice to quit that the tenant has failed to farm in accordance with the rules of good husbandry;

Case D (i): The tenant was in arrears with his rent even after receiving a notice to pay within two months;

(ii): The tenant has been served with a notice to remedy remediable breaches of terms of his tenancy, and failed to comply with it;

Case E: The tenant has committed irremediable breaches to the material prejudice of the landlord;

Case F: The tenant has become insolvent, and this is stated in the notice;

Case G: The notice to quit was served within three months of the landlord being given notice of the death of the sole or last surviving tenant;

Case H: The Minister of Agriculture as landlord has served the notice because he wants to amalgamate or re-shape the holding, having reserved a right to do so.

There is no uniform procedure applying to all these cases. But a substantial part of the policy behind the Acts is to remove disputes

---

[8] A.H.A. 1986, s.26(1).
[9] A.H.A. 1986, s.27.
[10] The landlord may serve an ordinary 12 months' notice and a notice relying on one or more of the statutory grounds. In that event, the time within which the tenant has to serve his counter-notice to the ordinary 12 months' notice may be extended by Agricultural Holdings (Arbitration on Notices) Order 1978, Art. 10, to one month after the end of a relevant arbitration relating to the statutory grounds.
[11] A.H.A. 1986, Sched. 3, Pt. I.
[12] The criteria are contained in Sched. 3, Pt. II.

from the ambit of the courts and have them settled in the majority of cases by arbitration and in a smaller number of cases by the Tribunal. The country is divided into eight areas[13] for the purposes of the Tribunal and the Tribunal obviously is differently constituted in each area. The principal thrust of their jurisdiction lies in the fields of consents to notices to quit in various forms,[14] and the determination of questions of succession to tenancies on death.[15]

Numerous other matters, as seen from the last two chapters, are reserved for arbitration. In the context of terminations, questions are referred to arbitration under Cases B, D and E.[16] Matters can only be taken from the Tribunal to the High Court by stating a case,[17] and from an arbitrator by way of case stated to the county court.[18] An application can be made by way of certiorari to quash the Tribunal's decision. This may be done where the Tribunal has admitted inadmissible evidence,[19] and that error appears on the face of the record.[19a] The arbitrator has to give his reasons.[20] The county court can set aside an arbitrator's award if there is an error on its face[21] or if the arbitrator has misconducted himself, or if the award has been improperly procured. However, there is an intermediate step. The county court, instead of setting aside, can remit the award for reconsideration to the arbitrator[22] or can vary the award itself.[23] These limited situations apart, the tenant's remedies lie almost exclusively within the express procedural framework. The time limits for giving counter-notices to refer questions either to arbitration or the Tribunal must be complied with strictly. All this has the result that there are not competing jurisdictions deciding the same issue, and further that questions about the validity of notices to quit are determined at the beginning rather than at the end of the period of notice to quit.[24] It is open to the court to determine whether or not a notice has been validly served on the tenant.[25]

[13] Agricultural Land Tribunals (Areas) Order 1982, S.I. 1982, No. 97.
[14] See generally The Agricultural Land Tribunals (Rules) Order 1978, S.I. 1978, No. 259, as amended by S.I. 1984 No. 301.
[15] The Agricultural Land Tribunals (Succession to Agricultural Tenancies) Order 1984, S.I. 1984, No. 1301, discussed *post.* (II), G. 2.
[16] See generally A.H.A. 1986, Sched. 11 and in particular the Agricultural Holdings (Arbitration on Notices) Order 1978, S.I. 1978, No. 257, as amended by S.I. 1984, No. 1300.
[17] Agriculture (Miscellaneous Provisions) Act 1954, s.6.
[18] A.H.A. 1986, Sched. 11, para. 26.
[19] See *R.* v. *Agricultural Land Tribunal for the South Eastern Area, ex p. Parslow* (1979) 251 E.G. 667.
[19a] See *R.* v. *Agricultural Land Tribunal for the South Eastern Area, ex p. Bracey* [1960] 1 W.L.R. 911 (where no remedy could be given as the error did not appear on the face of the record).
[20] A.H.A. 1986, Sched. 11, para. 21.
[21] A.H.A. 1986, Sched. 11, para. 27. And see *Re Allen and Mathews' Arbitration* [1971] 2 Q.B.
[22] A.H.A. 1986, Sched. 11, para. 28(1).
[23] A.H.A. 1986, Sched. 11, para. 28(2). 518.
[24] *Attorney-General of the Duchy of Lancaster* v. *Simcock* [1966] Ch. 1; *Magdalen College, Oxford* v. *Heritage* [1974] 1 W.L.R. 441.
[25] *Magdalen College, Oxford* v. *Heritage* [1974] 1 W.L.R. 441, at p. 446, *per* Megaw L.J., and see *Datnow* v. *Jones* (1985) 275 E.G. 145.

II. The Statutory Grounds

A. Post-Notice Consent

The landlord may serve an ordinary common law notice, not relying on any of the grounds in Cases A–H. The tenant has one month within which to serve a counter-notice. This has the effect of requiring the Tribunal's consent to the operation of the notice.[26] The counter-notice should be signed by all the tenants,[27] but this requirement may be waived,[28] or an unco-operative tenant compelled to join in.[29] If the notice is to have any effect, the landlord has to bring himself within one of five grounds. Even then the consent of the Tribunal is not automatic for additionally the Tribunal has to withhold its consent if it considers that "a fair and reasonable landlord would not insist on possession."[30]

The five grounds are:

(a) That the termination of the tenancy is desirable in the interests of good husbandry to facilitate a purpose proposed by the landlord. For these purposes the tenanted property has to be treated as a separate unit.[31] It seems as if the landlord must show under this head that his proposals would lead to the more efficient farming of the tenanted unit, which does not necessarily involve establishing that the unit is being farmed badly. "This provision . . . involves a comparison between what I may call the present regime under the existing tenant and the proposed regime, which will appertain in future if the tenancy is terminated. . . . It seems to me that a landlord must give some evidence of the proposed user and the tribunal can then and must proceed to make a comparison."[32]

(b) That the termination of the tenancy is desirable in the interests of sound management, again to facilitate a purpose proposed by the landlord.[33] Here the Tribunal can take into account the landlord's proposals both in relation to the tenanted property and other parts of his estate that he may want to manage in the

---

[26] A.H.A. 1986, s.26(1).

[27] *Newman* v. *Keedwell* (1978) 35 P. & C.R. 393.

[28] *Featherstone* v. *Staples* (1984) 49 P. & C.R. 273 (unwilling tenant was lessor's nominee company).

[29] As in *Sykes* v. *Land* (1984) 271 E.G. 1264 (existing contract to purchase unwilling tenant's share).

[30] A.H.A. 1986, s.27(1), (2). *cf.* the requirements of Rent Act 1977, s.98(1) that the court must consider it reasonable to make an order for possession of residential property, in addition to the establishing of one of the Cases in Pt. I, Sched. 15, Rent Act 1977. And see also *Evans* v. *Roper* [1960] 1 W.L.R. 814.

[31] A.H.A. 1986, s.27(3)(*a*).

[32] *Davies* v. *Price* [1958] 1 W.L.R. 434, *per* Parker L.J. dealing with the earlier provision in A.H.A. 1948, s.25(1)(*a*).

[33] A.H.A. 1986, s.27(3)(*b*).

future as a single unit.[34] But the purpose must relate to the way the land is managed, and not simply to the landlord's personal financial interest in isolation, unless this impinges on the standard of management.[35]

(c) That the termination is desirable for the purposes of agricultural research, education experiment or demonstration, or for the purposes of the enactments relating to smallholdings or allotments.[36]

(d) That greater hardship would be caused by withholding than by giving consent.[37] This gives rise to a very anxious jurisdiction. The Tribunal can consider the hardship which a refusal to grant consent would cause not only to the landlord, but also to his widow, where, *e.g.* a sale with vacant possession is necessary to prevent insolvency to the landlord's estate.[38] Similarly, the financial effect on the tenant can be considered either on an application on this ground, or in any case on the overriding issue of whether a fair and reasonable landlord would want possession.[39]

(e) That the landlord proposes to use the land for a non-agricultural purpose outside those covered by Case B.[40]

If the landlord brings himself within one of the five cases, and generally it will be (a), (b) or (d), and survives the "fair and reasonable" hurdle, it is still open to the Tribunal to make consequential orders. First, and pertinent to this particular ground, the Tribunal can impose conditions designed to ensure that the landlord carries out his proposals.[41] Secondly, where the Tribunal has consented to the operation of a notice, it can, either on its own motion or on the application of the tenant, postpone the termination of the tenancy for not more than 12 months.[42] A landlord is not estopped

---

[34] *Evans* v. *Roper* [1960] 1 W.L.R. 814.
[35] *National Coal Board* v. *Naylor* [1972] 1 W.L.R. 908 (where the agreement provided for the supply of cheap electricity, and the landlord wanted to re-let on more favourable terms).
[36] A.H.A. 1986, s.27(3)(c)(d).
[37] A.H.A. 1986, s.27(3)(e), cf. Rent Act 1977, Sched. 15, Pt. III, para. 1 (balance of hardship where landlord requires possession for himself, etc.).
[38] *Purser* v. *Bailey* [1967] 2 Q.B. 500.
[39] cf. *Evans* v. *Roper* [1960] 1 W.L.R. 814.
[40] A.H.A. 1986, s.27(3)(f), and see the next section for Case B. This ground does not seem to be of great significance, and see *Ministry of Agriculture, Fisheries and Food* v. *Jenkins* [1963] 2 Q.B. 317.
[41] A.H.A. 1986, s.27(4). s.27(5), enables application to be made for variation and revocation of the conditions. The landlord may forfeit up to two years' rent to the Crown if he fails to comply with the conditions, s.27(6)(b). The tenant cannot take advantage from a breach of condition, *Martin-Smith* v. *Smale* [1954] 1 W.L.R. 247.
[42] Agricultural Holdings (Arbitration on Notices) Order 1978, art. 12; Agricultural Land Tribunals (Rules) Order 1978, r. 3.

from serving repeat notices relying on the same grounds, at least if he can adduce evidence of changed circumstances.[43]

B. Case B—Alternative Use of the Land

There are certain similarities between this ground for recovering possession and that contained in the Landlord and Tenant Act 1954, s.30(1)(*f*), where a landlord of business premises proposes to demolish and reconstruct. Here the landlord has to establish that he requires the land for a purpose other than agriculture, for which planning permission has been obtained[43a] or is unnecessary by reason of provisions outside the Town and Country Planning code.[43b] It seems that he must require substantially the whole land[44] for re-development and that his requirement must be a present and continuing one.

A landlord relying on this case will serve a 12 months'[45] notice that must state that it is served on this ground. The tenant can contest the reason by serving a counter-notice within one month after the service of the notice to quit, requiring the matter to be submitted to arbitration.[46] This is the tenant's only method of challenge, and again if it fails, the arbitrator can extend the operation of the notice to quit.[47] An artificial transfer of part of the land to trustees for himself will not enable a notice to be served under this Case, alleging a separate tenancy of the severed part the landlord wants to develop.[48]

C. Case C—Certificate of Bad Husbandry

This is not a conspicuously overworked ground for recovering possession, partly because there are difficulties in proving that a

---

[43] *Wickington* v. *Bonney* (1984) 47 P. & C.R. 655. Agricultural Holdings (Arbitration on Notices) Order 1978, art. 12; Agricultural Land Tribunals (Rules) Order 1978, r. 3.

[43a] See *Paddock Investments* v. *Lory* (1975) 236 E.G. 803, where the express provisions of the lease were more stringent than the section, and only applied if the landlord "obtained" permission. Permissions granted to the N.C.B. for open-cast mining subject to restoration (which permissions enure for the land) are not to be taken into account, A.H.A. 1986, Sched. 3, Pt. II, para. 8.

[43b] A.H.A. 1986, Sched. 3, Pt. I, Case B. This enabling provision is of benefit to the Crown or statutory bodies authorised to develop without obtaining planning permission under the planning Acts. It does not cover development permitted by General Development Orders or Use Classes Orders.

[44] *cf. Public Trustee* v. *Randag* [1966] Ch. 649.

[45] A shorter notice may be served if a right to do so has been duly reserved in the agreement, and see A.H.A. 1986, s.25(2)(*b*). The terms of such a reservation are strictly construed against the landlord, see *Coates* v. *Diment* [1951] 1 All E.R. 890.

[46] Agricultural Holdings (Arbitration on Notices) Order 1978, art. 9.

[47] *Ibid*, art. 12.

[48] *Persey* v. *Bazley* (1983) 267 E.G. 519.

tenant is "not fulfilling his responsibilities to farm in accordance with the rules of good husbandry,"[49] if he is fulfilling all the other terms of his agreement.[50] In fact, a failing farmer is far more likely to be committing remediable breaches and therefore be more vulnerable under Case D. A landlord who nevertheless proceeds under Case C must apply to the Tribunal for a certificate, and issue his notice to quit within six months of his application. The landlord can also ask the Tribunal to specify a shorter period of notice instead of the usual 12 months. Not less than two months can be specified, but it can end at any time during the year.[51] There is no defence to such a notice, once a certificate has been obtained and notice served in time.

D. Case D—Failure to Comply with Notice to Pay Rent or Remedy Breach

This is the most important case, and covers two distinct situations: (i) the consequences of a failure to pay rent,[52] and (ii) the results of committing remediable breaches of the terms or conditions of the tenancy.[53] There are prescribed forms of notice to pay rent or to remedy which *must* be used.[54]

(1) *Form 1, Non-compliance with Notice to Pay Rent*

The operation of the statutory provisions relating to recovery of possession following non-payment of rent by the tenant resemble very much proceedings for forfeiture of leases in the last century for breaches in respect of which there was no available statutory or equitable relief. Irrespective of any merits, if the landlord can bring himself within the letter of the statutory provisions he will be entitled to possession. The statutory provisions, at least in this respect, supersede any express provisions relating to forfeiture for non-payment of rent.[55]

The first step the landlord has to take is to serve the tenant with the prescribed form of notice[56] requiring payment to him of rent which is

---

[49] A.H.A. 1986, Sched. 3, Pt. I, Case C; The Agricultural Land Tribunals (Rules) Order 1978, r. 4, and Agriculture Act 1947, s.11.

[50] Farming practices adopted with the landlord's agreement in the interests of conservation are disregarded, A.H.A. 1986, Sched. 3, Pt. II, para. 9(2), both here and when dealing with notices under Cases D and E, *post*.

[51] A.H.A. 1986, s.25(4).

[52] A.H.A. 1986, Sched. 3, Pt. I, Case D(*a*).

[53] *Ibid.* Case D(*b*).

[54] A.H.A. 1986, Sched.3, Pt. II, para. 10.

[55] *Beevers* v. *Mason* (1978) 37 P. & C.R. 452.

[56] Agricultural Holdings (Forms of Notice to Pay Rent or to Remedy) Regulations 1984 (S.I. 1984 No. 1308), Form 1.

then in arrears within two months from the service of the notice. If the notice is served by someone who is not at that time the landlord,[57] or there are no arrears at the time the notice is served,[58] or the arrears are incorrectly stated[59] or it does not specify payment within two months, it is defective.[60]

If the arrears of rent are not paid within the strict time limits of the notice, the landlord can serve a 12 months' notice to quit expressly relying on this ground. Payment even a short time later, or by the time the notice to quit is served, will not save the tenant's position.[61] But payment on the last day of the two months by cheque sent by post to the landlord, and not his agent as was usual and requested, can be regarded as a payment in time.[62]

The only step[63] open to a tenant served with a notice on this ground is to serve a counter-notice within one month requesting that the matter be submitted to arbitration.[64] The tenant may want to allege that the notice was not correctly served, or did not specify the time limit, that no arrears were then due,[65] or that the rent has been paid within the time limit. If a point of law arises, which is likely on this ground, the arbitrator may well refer it to the county court under the case stated procedure.[66] But a failure to request that the matter be the subject of an arbitration makes the notice indefeasible irrespective of the rent position at that time.[67]

(2) *Non-compliance with Notice to Remedy Breach*

It is at this point that procedure and substantive law become difficult to separate. An immediate distinction has to be made between those cases where the tenant is required to do some work to remedy the breach, and the other remaining remediable breaches, *e.g.* where there has been a failure to insure, or the tenant is allowing part of the property to be used as a caravan park or for motor sports, or in some other way amounting to a nuisance.

---

[57] *Pickard* v. *Bishop* (1975) 31 P. & C.R. 108 (devolution of landlord's interest on the settlement trustees, but notice requiring payment to original landlord).
[58] *cf. French* v. *Elliott* [1960] 1 W.L.R. 40.
[59] *Dickinson* v. *Boucher* (1983) 269 E.G. 1159.
[60] *cf. Magdalen College, Oxford* v. *Heritage* [1974] 1 W.L.R. 441.
[61] There is no prescribed form for this notice, telling the tenant of the necessity to request arbitration, and see *Harding* v. *Marshall* (1983) 267 E.G. 161.
[62] *Stoneman* v. *Brown* [1973] 1 W.L.R. 459.
[63] *Magdalen College, Oxford* v. *Heritage* [1974] 1 W.L.R. 441.
[64] Under Agricultural Holdings (Arbitration on Notices) Order 1978, art. 9.
[65] The tenant may want to claim he has paid for repairs which are the landlord's liability, and so should be set-off against the rent *cf. British Anzani (Felixstowe) Ltd.* v. *International Marine Management (U.K.) Ltd.* [1979] 2 All E.R. 1063.
[66] Under A.H.A. 1986, Sched. 11, para. 26.
[67] And see *Parrish* v. *Kinsey* (1983) 268 E.G. 1113, and *Harding* v. *Marshall, supra.*

(3) *Form 2, Notices to do Works of Repair, Maintenance or Replacement*

If the tenant is failing to repair, keep hedges and ditches in order, cultivate in accordance with the rules of good husbandry, or to weed, or manure, or any of these matters, then the landlord should take steps to have served on the tenant a Form 2 Notice under the Agricultural Holdings (Forms of Notice to pay Rent or Remedy) Regulations 1984.[68] This is a prescribed form and the notes to the form are an integral part of it. The notice will generally be prepared by the landlord's land agent. It must specify the terms that have been broken and the defects of repair, maintenance and lack of replacement needing remedial work by the tenant. The notice must also specify a reasonable period, which cannot be less than six months, for doing the work.[69]

If the tenant wishes to challenge the notice on the grounds (a) that he is under no liability under his tenancy agreement to do the specified work, or (b) that the item of work should be deleted because it is unjustified or unnecessary, *e.g.* painting a building only recently painted, or digging out a ditch below a reasonable level, or (c) that a different method or material should be substituted for the material specified by the notice, he has one month in which to give a counter-notice requiring the issue to be dealt with by arbitration.[70] This is the tenant's only opportunity to challenge the notice on those three grounds. If he wishes any of those three matters to be referred to arbitration, he must also refer to arbitration any other questions he wants to raise on the validity of the notice.[71] The most common additional issue will be that the time specified in the notice is unreasonably short. If the tenant does not want to raise matters covered by grounds (a), (b) or (c) above, but has other matters for argument in respect of the notice, he has an option to refer them to arbitration either then, or later on if he receives a notice to quit.[72]

The arbitrator may decide that the tenant is under no liability to do the work, and he has wide powers to delete items he considers are unnecessary or unjustified, bearing in mind the principles of good husbandry and estate management, and he can order substitute materials to be used, where those specified by the landlord would be unduly expensive or difficult to obtain.[73] If the tenant is raising the question of validity or of inadequacy of time, then the time for doing the work is extended in any event until the end of the arbitration and can be further extended by the arbitrator as he thinks fit.[74] However, if

---

[68] S.I. 1984 No. 1308.
[69] A.H.A. 1986, Sched. 3, Pt. II, para. 10(1)(*c*).
[70] Agricultural Holdings (Arbitration on Notices) Order 1978, art. 3(1).
[71] *Ibid.* art. 4(1).
[72] *Ibid.* art. 4(2).
[73] *Ibid.* art. 5.
[74] *Ibid.* art. 6.

the tenant obtains an extension of time in which to do the work the arbitrator[75] can nevertheless specify the date on which the tenancy can be ended by notice if the tenant fails to do the work in time. That date cannot be earlier than six months after the extended time for doing the work, or the date the tenancy could have been ended by a 12 months' notice served at the end of the period originally given to the tenant to do the work.[76] This may mean that although the tenant is given longer to do the work, if he fails to do the work in time he may end up with a notice to quit that is for less than 12 months, or one that ends at some time other than the anniversary of the tenancy.[77]

Obviously if the tenant does the work there are no further problems. The landlord cannot serve a second Form 2 notice within 12 months of the first, unless with the tenant's written agreement[78] the first was withdrawn. If the landlord thinks that the tenant has failed to comply with the Form 2 notice he can serve a Case D notice to quit expressly relying on the tenant's failure to do the work.

The tenant has one month after service of the notice to quit to have the matter referred to arbitration.[79] It is too late for him to argue that he was under no liability to do the work; that the work was unnecessary or that different materials should have been specified. But he may want to argue that he has complied with the notice, or that in the circumstances the time specified proved to be unreasonable.[80] It is not sufficient for the tenant to show that he "substantially complied" with the requirements of the notice to remedy unless the matters left undone can be regarded as insignificant.[81] So far as time is concerned, the tenant may be able to show the time allowed was unreasonable even as at the time the notice was served. In that case the whole notice is invalid. Here the totality of the work required to be done must be considered.[82] It is not open to the landlord to argue that the length of time was sufficient for some defects, if not for all of them. However, if the notice was valid as to time when it was served, but supervening circumstances have prevented the tenant from complying with part of it, that fact will not excuse the tenant for his failure to comply with the rest which could have been dealt with in time.[83]

The tenant still has one more string to his bow. Either instead of his

---

[75] The arbitrator can extend either *ex proprio motu*, or on the landlord's application, *ibid.* art. 7(1).
[76] *Ibid.* art. 7(2).
[77] *Ibid.* art. 7(4).
[78] A.H.A. 1986, Sched. 3, Pt. II, para. 10(1)(*a*); and see *Mercantile and General Re-insurance Co.* v. *Groves* [1974] Q.B. 43.
[79] Agricultural Holdings (Arbitration on Notices) Order 1978, art. 9.
[80] *e.g.* because he could not obtain the necessary supplies of materials, *Shepherd* v. *Lomas* [1963] 1 W.L.R. 962.
[81] *Price* v. *Romilly* [1960] 1 W.L.R. 1360. Substantial compliance may be a relevant matter for the Tribunal to consider if the matter is later referred to them, see (74) *infra*.
[82] *Wykes* v. *Davis* [1975] Q.B. 843.
[83] *Shepherd* v. *Lomas* [1963] 1 W.L.R. 962. The arbitrator can extend time for compliance. Agricultural Holdings (Arbitration of Notices) Order 1978, art. 13.

application for arbitration,[84] or in addition to it if it was unsuccessful,[85] the tenant can serve on the landlord a counter-notice with the result that the notice to quit has no effect unless the Tribunal consents to its operation. The landlord then has to apply to the Tribunal for its consent to the notice to quit. Consent will be granted unless it appears to the Tribunal in having regard to the extent and consequences of the failure to do the work, and the circumstances surrounding the failure "that a fair and reasonable landlord would not insist on possession."[86] A discretionary element is introduced here, but only in this one case arising out of a failure to comply with a work notice. At this point the Tribunal can take into account questions of substantial compliance and the merits of the case, *e.g.* whether the landlord seems to be acting in an unreasonably oppressive manner, or whether the tenant is intentionally defaulting and adopting every tactical ploy open to him. Less cynically, the fact that the tenant had complied with the notice by the time the matter comes before the Tribunal might well be relevant.

(4) *Form 3, Notice to Remedy not Involving Work*

Situations giving rise to the service of such a notice have been mentioned, *e.g.* failing to attend to insurances or payments of interest or permitting the land to be used in a way that causes a nuisance or failing to reside personally on the land.[87] The characteristics of these breaches are that they can be remedied, but that the remedy does not involve work. A Form 3 notice in the prescribed form has to be served,[88] but in this case the tenant has no right to serve a notice asking for arbitration unless and until a subsequent notice to quit is served for his failure to remedy the breach within the specified period, which in this instance may be less than six months. If a notice to quit is served, the tenant can by counter-notice require the matter to be submitted to arbitration.[89] But he cannot then go to the Tribunal as he can following a notice to quit for failure to comply with a notice to do work. Obviously the arbitration has the effect of suspending the notice to quit until the proceedings are ended.[90]

---

[84] A.H.A. 1986, s.28(1), (2).
[85] A.H.A. 1986, s.28(4).
[86] A.H.A. 1986, s.28(5).
[87] See *Sumnall* v. *Statt* (1985) 49 P. & C.R. 367 (four-year term of imprisonment, three months' notice to remedy).
[88] Agricultural Holdings (Forms of Notice to Pay Rent or to Remedy) Regulations 1984, Form 3.
[89] Agriculture Holdings (Arbitration on Notices) Order 1978, art. 9, and see *Sumnall* v. *Statt, supra.*
[90] *Ibid.* art. 11, and see also art. 13.

E. Case E—Irremediable Breaches

Irremediable breaches are met in connection with notices under the Law of Property Act 1925, s.146, and in those cases the landlord does not have to specify how he wants the matter putting right because that is not possible. The most obvious example is an assignment without consent. But in addition to the breach being irremediable the landlord may also have to show that he has been materially prejudiced by it, and that the term broken was not inconsistent with the rules of good husbandry.[91] The notice must state the grounds on which it is served. The tenant's only recourse is service of a counter-notice within one month requiring reference to arbitration.[92]

There was an interesting but unsuccessful attempt to rely on this ground in *Johnson* v. *Moreton*.[93] The lease was for 10 years and contained an agreement to give up possession at the expiration of the term and not to serve a counter-notice under the security provisions of the 1948 Act or take any steps to claim the benefit of those provisions. The tenant did precisely that, and the landlord issued a further notice claiming that this was an irremediable breach. The House of Lords, upholding the Court of Appeal, dismissed the landlord's contentions on public policy grounds, ruling that it was undesirable to permit contracting out of the statutory security provisions.

F. Case F—Insolvency

The assistance given by the law to landlords of insolvent tenants is more vigorous in relation to agricultural holdings than other kinds of tenancies. If, at the date of the notice to quit, the tenant has become bankrupt or entered into a composition with his creditors for the payment of his debts or had a receiving order made against him, a notice to quit can be served relying on that ground,[94] if he is insolvent the notice need not be for the full 12 months.[95] It will be recollected that in relation to other tenancies there are a number of provisions suspending the effects of forfeiture on bankruptcy in the Law of Property Act 1925, s.146(10), but even those limited rights of suspension do not apply to tenancies of agricultural or pastoral land.[96] There is no counter-notice machinery in this case.

The statutory provisions are extended to bodies corporate where winding up orders are made, or resolutions are passed, unless they are

---

[91] A.H.A. 1986, Sched. 3, Pt. I, Case C.
[92] Agricultural Holdings (Arbitration on Notices) Order 1978, art. 9.
[93] [1980] A.C. 37.
[94] A.H.A. 1986, Sched. 3, Pt. I, Case F.
[95] A.H.A. 1986, s.25(2)(a).
[96] L.P.A. 1925, s.146(9).

made or passed for the purposes of amalgamation or reconstruction.[97] Usually the tenancy agreement contains a forfeiture clause operative on non-payment of rent, breach of the tenant's obligations, bankruptcy and compulsory or voluntary liquidation except for the purposes of amalgamation or reconstruction. There are difficulties about whether landlords can generally rely on the common law forfeiture provisions.[98] If they can do so, then much of the elaborate statutory protection considered in this chapter could be sidestepped. It seems however to be clear that the written notification of the landlord's intention to take steps to forfeit must in any event give the tenant sufficient time for service of a notice claiming compensation under the Agricultural Holdings Act 1986, s.60 (for disturbance generally), or section 70 (for additional compensation for having continuously adopted a special system of farming). Such notices must be served on the landlord not less than one month before the termination of the tenancy.[99] Arrangements between the parties designed to restrict the tenant's right to claim compensation will probably be held invalid.[1] In *Parry* v. *Million Pigs*[2] a forfeiture clause which provided for re-entry without notice was held to be void. Furthermore, since *Johnson* v. *Moreton*[3] it seems that the court will take a severe line with clauses designed to diminish the tenant's statutory protection. It is therefore suggested that where the grounds for recovering possession on which the landlord is relying are covered by statutory provisions, he must rely on those provisions exclusively.

G. Case G—Death and Succession on Death

(1) *Notice*

For many years, until the passing of the Agricultural Holdings (Notices to Quit) Act 1977, the landlord could serve a notice to quit within three months of the death of the original tenant. There was no defence to the notice. It operated to end the estate of the original tenant when he was still in possession as tenant. It also operated to end the estate of any assignee of the original tenant, which subsisted

---

[97] A.H.A. 1986, s.96(2).
[98] See *ante*, Pt. 1, Chap. 8, and see *Scammell & Densham*, pp. 132, 133, *Hill & Redman* (16th ed.), p. 1825; *Encylopaedia of Forms and Precedents* (4th ed.), Vol. 1, pp. 433, 434; Muir Watts, *Agricultural Holdings* (12th ed.), p. 142, and see *Kent* v. *Conniff* [1953] 1 Q.B. 361.
[99] A.H.A. 1986, ss.60(2), 70(2).
[1] *cf. Re Disraeli Agreement, Cleasby* v. *Park Estate (Hughenden)* [1939] Ch. 382; *Coates* v. *Diment* [1951] 1 All E.R. 890, and see A.H.A. 1986, s.78.
[2] (1981) 260 E.G. 281.
[3] [1980] A.C. 37.

as a species of interest lasting for so long as the original tenant lived.[4] If the landlord failed to serve a notice within three months of the original tenant's death, *e.g.* because he did not know of it, the personal representatives of the deceased tenant would continue as tenants, or the assignee's estate would continue. Notice could not be served on the deaths of the original tenant's personal representatives,[5] or on the death of the assignee as the case might be. Tenancy agreements frequently imposed an obligation on the tenant to give notice of death within one month thereafter. Obviously the tenant could not give notice, but a failure by the personal representative might amount to an irremediable breach.

The two defects in the law were that notice was essentially connected to the death of the original tenant, and that there was no provision for statutory succession for the benefit of members of the tenant's family. The Agricultural Holdings (Notices to Quit) Act 1977 dealt with the first defect.[6] Part II of the Agriculture (Miscellaneous Provisions) Act 1976 provided some machinery for statutory succession, but the provisions now only benefit tenancies created before July 12, 1984,[7] unless they resulted from the application of the statutory succession machinery.[8]

Notice can be given under Case G[9] following the death of the person who was the sole or last surviving tenant[10] under a contract of tenancy, and within three months of the landlord being given written notice of the death either by the personal representatives, or others as a result of the use of the statutory succession machinery.[11] The notice must state that it is given because of the tenant's death. Service can be effected on the President of the Family Division of the High Court of Justice, the personal representatives if they have obtained a grant, or under the Agricultural Holdings Act 1986, s.93(3), on "the agent or servant . . . responsible for the control of the . . . farming . . . of the agricultural holding." In many cases the last group will comprise the deceased tenant's family who are continuing to run the farm. The "belt and braces" principle urges service on everybody because at least one of them must be right, and time cannot be extended for mistakes, honest or otherwise.

Notices to quit served following the tenant's death have only a qualified effect. They become absolute if no application is made to the

---

[4] *Clarke* v. *Hall* [1961] 2 Q.B. 331. Where a tenancy comes within L.P.A. 1925, s.149(6), having been granted for a life or lives, etc., notice shorter than 12 months can be given, A.H.A. 1986, s.25(2)(*c*). Such a tenancy is outside the normal security provisions, A.H.A. 1986, s.3(3).

[5] *Costagliola* v. *Bunting* [1958] 1 W.L.R. 580.

[6] But see A. W. Brown (1977) 41 Conv. 273.

[7] A.H.A. 1986, s.34(1)(*a*).

[8] A.H.A. 1986, s.34(1)(*b*), and see C. P. Rodgers [1984] Conv. 207, [1985] Conv. 111.

[9] A.H.A. 1986, Sched. 3, Pt. I, Case G.

[10] *Ibid.*

[11] A.H.A. 1986, Sched. 3, Pt. II, para. 12. The effect of death on a fixed term tenancy has been considered, *ante* Chap. 25(IV)G.

agricultural land tribunal to succeed to the tenancy within three months of the tenant's death.[12] The notice still has a qualified effect if a proper application is made and even if someone is designated as suitable to take over the tenancy.[13] In that event, the landlord is given a statutory last gasp to save his notice to quit by being allowed to apply to the Tribunal for their consent to its operation, in the same way as if he had served a notice not relying on any of the grounds in Cases A–H and the tenant had served a counter-notice under section 26(1) of the 1986 Act.[14] If the tribunal consent to the operation of the notice to quit, they can, with the tenant's consent, postpone its operation for up to a maximum of three months.[15] Obviously, if the Tribunal had not been able to designate anyone as suitable to take over the tenancy, the notice becomes absolute.[16]

(2) *Succession*

For succession on death to residential tenancies, provision is made in the Rent Acts. But the provisions relating to agricultural tenancies are far more elaborate and require the claimants to satisfy the Tribunal that to be eligible they fulfil three qualifications. The eligible candidates then have to satisfy the Tribunal who is more or most suitable. Although the provisions were probably designed with a view to affording widows some continuity of tenure, they have had to be extensively modified to achieve this objective.

(a) Disqualifying circumstances

The succession machinery cannot be operated at all if at the date of death the tenant was already under notice and had exhausted all his effective grounds of opposition.[17] It cannot be operated if the original tenancy was for too long,[18] *i.e.* a fixed term of years with more than 27 months left to run, or if it is a *Gladstone* v. *Bower*[19] type of tenancy, *i.e.* granted for a fixed period of more than one but less than two years. And like the loss of protection on the death of the second statutory

---

[12] A.H.A. 1986, ss.43(1), 39(1); The Agricultural Land Tribunals (Succession to Agricultural Tenancies) Order 1984 (S.I. 1984 No. 1301), r. 3. A failure to serve the landlord (as opposed to making an application to the tribunal) may not be fatal, *Kellett* v. *Alexander, Kellett* v. *Cady* (1981) 257 E.G. 495.
[13] A.H.A. 1986, s.43(1).
[14] A.H.A. 1986, s.44(1); Agricultural Land Tribunals (Succession to Agricultural Tenancies) Order 1984, r. 4. If the tenant agrees, consent may be given to the notice to quit in respect of part of the land, A.H.A. 1986, ss.39(10), 44(5).
[15] A.H.A. 1986, s.44(6)(7).
[16] A.H.A. 1986, s.43(1)(*b*)(i).
[17] A.H.A. 1986, s.38(1).
[18] A.H.A. 1986, s.36(2).
[19] [1960] 2 Q.B. 384, and see *ante*, Chap. 25, (IV) E, and A.H.A. 1986, s.36(2)(*b*).

successor to a protected residential tenancy[20] the agricultural succession provisions can be operated on two occasions only.[21] The provisions are regarded as having operated where the tenant has agreed in his lifetime to the holding being let or assigned to someone who could have claimed to succeed had the tenant kept on farming until his death,[22] *e.g.* where the landlord agrees to let the farm to the son on his father's retirement.[23]

(b) "Eligible persons"

People who think they are eligible have to make their applications within three months of the death,[24] and it is for the Tribunal to decide if they were eligible at the death, and are still eligible.[25] The eligible person has to satisfy two positive conditions, one of relationship and one of income, and not be caught by a third negative condition relating to his occupation of other farming land. Husbands, wives, brothers, sisters, children of the deceased, and those treated as children of the family[26] qualify as eligible relations.

The income condition is that in the seven years ending with the tenant's death the claimant's "only or principal source of livelihood throughout a continuous period of not less than 5 years, or two or more discontinuous periods together amounting to not less than 5 years, derived from his agricultural work on the holding or on an agricultural unit of which the holding forms part."[27] The provisions are designed to assist the full-time working farmer,[28] and not the part-time or hobby farmer, and this requirement requires disclosure of all sources of income.[29] Undrawn profits cannot be taken into account, and investment income weakens the claimant's case.[30] A wife can rely on her own or her late husband's agricultural work, or on their joint efforts.[31] This will help where she has not been paid a wage or was not a partner, and so cannot point to specific income she derived from the farm. Brothers and sons who worked either as partners with the

[20] See *ante*, Pt. II.

[21] A.H.A. 1986, s.37.

[22] A.H.A. 1986, s.37(2).

[23] The specific provisions for retirement are considered *post* in s.III. The succession provisions have no application to tenancies of smallholdings granted by smallholdings authorities within Part III of the Agriculture Act 1970, or to tenancies granted by charitable trustees whose principal objective is the settlement in farming of ex-servicemen, see A.H.A. 1986, s.38(4)(5).

[24] A.H.A. 1986, s.39(1); Agricultural Land Tribunals (Succession to Agricultural Tenancies) Order 1984, rr. 2(3), 3(3).

[25] A.H.A. 1986, s.39(2).

[26] An expression common in Family Law.

[27] A.H.A. 1986, s.36(3).

[28] Up to three years spent in full-time tertiary study can be treated as a period when his principal income derived from his agricultural work on the holding, A.H.A. 1986, Sched. 6, para. 2.

[29] Agricultural Land Tribunals (Succession to Agricultural Tenancies) Order 1984, Appendix, Form 1.

[30] *Trinity College, Cambridge* v. *Caines* (1984) 272 E.G. 1287.

[31] A.H.A. 1986, s.36(4). This provision does not help unwaged sisters, or siblings who worked on the farm.

deceased or as his employees are likely to be able to qualify. The applicant may derive some help from section 41 of the 1986 Act, which enables the Tribunal to treat a person as eligible on income grounds if it considers that would be fair and reasonable where the applicant has for some part of the seven years ending with the death done agricultural work full-time or part-time on the holding. The Tribunal has to be "satisfied to a material extent"[32] that the claimant's principal source of livelihood came from her agricultural work. It has been held that the condition must be fulfilled substantially in terms of time and value,[33] or that the holding has provided more than 51 per cent. of the claimant's livelihood.[34] The section expressly adverts to the possibility that the applicant might not have been able to look to the holding for his principal source of livelihood because it was too small.[35]

The disqualifying condition[36] to be avoided is that the applicant is already the occupier of a commercial unit of agriculture.[37] This seemingly simple expression has given rise to immense difficulty. The object of the provision is to eliminate as an eligible applicant someone who already occupies a viable agricultural unit. Prospective applicants who do occupy other units might try to dispose of their interest, at least in the short term to make themselves eligible. The concept of occupation is therefore elaborated in Schedule 6 of the 1986 Act. In deciding if the applicant is occupying another unit there is taken into account land occupied by him jointly, or through a controlled company, or where he and his spouse has granted a close relative a short term—generally an unprotected, tenancy or licence.[38] However, one disregards occupation by the applicant of land similarly held by means of an unprotected lease or licence, or held in a representative capacity.[39]

There is a complex procedure to be followed to decide if any parcel of land is a commercial unit of agriculture. Land falls within this category if it is regarded as capable of producing a total of two full-time male agricultural workers' annual wages.[40]

The disqualification condition operates most frequently where the deceased and his sons in partnership farm other land in conjunction with the tenanted land. It is too late for the family to rearrange matters after the tenant's death to avoid this condition, *e.g.* by the

---

[32] A.H.A. 1986, s.41(1)(*b*).
[33] *Littlewood* v. *Rolfe* (1982) 43 P. & C.R. 262.
[34] *Wilson* v. *Earl Spencer's Settlement Trustees* (1985) 274 E.G. 1254.
[35] A.H.A. 1986, s.41(6).
[36] A.H.A. 1986, s.36(3)(b).
[37] Defined in A.H.A. 1986, Sched. 6, para. 3, 4.
[38] A.H.A. 1986, Sched. 6, paras. 6–10
[39] A.H.A. 1986, Sched. 6, para. 6.
[40] A.H.A. 1986, Sched. 6, paras. 3, 4.

applicant's withdrawal from the partnership. The condition must be satisfied at the date of death.[41]

(c) "Suitable person"

Having established himself as a member of the class of eligible candidates, the applicant then has to get into the class of "suitable" applicants. These are applicants whom the Tribunal consider suitable persons to become tenants of the holding. His farming, training, experience, age, health and financial position and the landlord's views are all relevant.[42] The impact of the likely rental increase is a relevant consideration.[43] In selecting the suitable person to be given the tenancy, the Tribunal must first see if the deceased either bequeathed his tenancy to an eligible person or effectively nominated him in his will.[44] If that designated person is "suitable" the Tribunal need go no further. But if that does not apply, then the Tribunal must select the most suitable eligible person, or they can select up to four persons to be joint tenants.[45] But before a direction is given entitling the applicant to the tenancy, the Tribunal must give the landlord an opportunity to apply for their consent to the operation of Notice to Quit if he has served one under Case G.[46] If the landlord does not want to pursue that application, or it is unsuccessful, then the Tribunal will proceed to direct who is entitled to the tenancy.[47]

(d) The terms of the new tenancy

Although frequent reference is made to succeeding to the agricultural tenancy, in fact an entirely new tenancy with its own starting date[48] is created. There are detailed provisions for the determination of the terms of the new tenancy, and its rent,[49] designed to enable the parties to update the old tenancy arrangements. Questions of compensation can also be referred to arbitration.[50]

H. Case H—Ministerial Certificates

The final statutory case does not seem to be overworked. The Minister of Agriculture has statutory power to acquire land for the purposes of effecting amalgamations of agricultural land and reshaping agricultu-

[41] A.H.A. 1986, s.39(2).
[42] A.H.A. 1986, s.39(7).
[43] *Dagg* v. *Lovett* (1980) 256 E.G. 491.
[44] A.H.A. 1986, ss.39(4), 40(1)(2).
[45] A.H.A. 1986, s.39(9).
[46] A.H.A. 1986, s.44(1).
[47] A.H.A. 1986, s.39(5)(6).
[48] A.H.A. 1986, s.45(1).
[49] A.H.A. 1986, ss.47, 48.
[50] A.H.A. 1986, s.48(5)(8).

ral units.[51] Tenancies created by him in the course of his statutory duties should contain an acknowledgement signed by the tenant that they are granted subject to the statutory provisions enabling the Minister to amalgamate and reshape. It follows that a notice expressly given by the Minister for that purpose cannot be opposed by the tenant.[52]

III. LIFETIME SUCCESSIONS

Most tenant farmers are anxious to pass their tenancies on to their heirs. Straightforward assignments of agricultural tenancies are, of course, generally prohibited.[53] The succession provisions just considered accentuate the tendency of tenant farmers to cling to their tenancies until they die with their boots on. The Agricultural Holdings Act 1984 introduced some very sensible, although detailed, provisions designed to alleviate the problems caused by the reluctance of farmers to retire.

The provisions apply to tenancies from year to year granted before July 12, 1984.[54] The provisions and terminology are largely based on the succession on death provisions.[55] Notice must be given to the landlord by the tenant[56] that he wishes a specified close relative,[57] who is an eligible person,[58] to succeed him as tenant from a date not less than one year nor more than two years ahead, on which the tenancy could be ended by a notice to quit. The tenant can only give the notice if he is over 65 or permanently unfit and unable to continue work.[59] The named successor makes the application to the Tribunal for a direction entitling him to the tenancy.[60]

The tenant cannot operate these provisions if his tenancy is already doomed by an effective notice to quit.[61] If a landlord has already served a notice under Cases B, D or E[62] but it is not yet possible to say that it will be effective because the statutory procedures have not been

---

[51] Agriculture Act 1967, s.29(1).
[52] A.H.A. 1986, Sched. 3, Pt. I, Case H.
[53] A.H.A. 1986, Sched. 1, para. 9.
[54] A.H.A. 1986, ss.49(1), 34(1). The provisions do not apply to tenancies granted by smallholdings authorities or by specified charitable trusts for the resettlement of ex-members of the forces, A.H.A. 1986, s.38(4)(5), Sched. 6, para. 14.
[55] *Supra.*
[56] A.H.A. 1986, s.49(1)(*b*).
[57] A.H.A. 1986, s.49(3).
[58] Defined *ibid.* There is the same income from the holding qualification, and occupation of another agricultural unit disqualification as in the succession on death provisions, above.
[59] The notice can be given in anticipation of reaching 65 or of permanent unfitness, but the Tribunal must be satisfied either that the tenant has reached 65 by the date specified in the notice or that by that date the physical infirmity exists or will exist at that date, A.H.A. 1986, ss.51(3), 53(3).
[60] A.H.A. 1986, ss.50(1), 53. The procedure is governed by Agricultural Land Tribunals (Succession to Agricultural Tenancies) Order 1984, Sched. Pt. III (S.I. 1984 No. 1301).
[61] A.H.A. 1986, s.51(1).
[62] *Supra.*

exhausted, then the application is suspended until those matters are resolved.[63] The same situation applies if, after the retirement notice is served but before the application is heard, the landlord serves a notice on Cases B or D.[64] If the landlord serves a notice under Case C (Certificate of Bad Husbandry) or Case F (Insolvency) before the application is heard, the retirement notice has no effect at all.[65] Apart from that the landlord cannot impede the application for a transfer by serving a notice to quit.[66] The provisions cannot be operated if the retiring tenant dies before the application has been finally disposed of.[67] If, however, a direction for a succession has been given, but the time for it to be implemented has not arrived, then the direction still takes effect.[68]

In addition to deciding that a successor is an eligible and suitable person at the time of the hearing,[69] the tribunal can also entertain an application from the landlord that no direction entitling the applicant to the tenancy should be given because greater hardship would be caused by granting it than refusing it.[70]

If a direction is made, the specified relative is entitled to a new tenancy on the same terms as that enjoyed by the retiring tenant,[71] with the usual consequential provisions for the terms of the new tenancy to be settled by arbitration.[72] A tenancy granted under these provisions counts as one of the two successions permitted under the succession on death provisions.[73]

If the tribunal decline to make a direction, the unsuccessful applicant cannot apply under the succession on death provisions on the death of the tenant who had hoped to retire.[74]

IV. ADDITIONAL AND CONSEQUENTIAL MATTERS

A. Compensation

At the end of a tenancy there is obviously the possibility of complex cross-claims by both parties. Formerly the subject of detailed

---

[63] A.H.A. 1986, s.51 (4–6).
[64] A.H.A. 1986, s.51(1)(2).
[65] *Ibid.* and see s.38(2).
[66] A.H.A. 1986, s.54(1)(2).
[67] A.H.A. 1986, s.57. An application can, however, be made under the succession on death provisions.
[68] A.H.A. 1986, s.57(3).
[69] A.H.A. 1986, s.53(5).
[70] A.H.A. 1986, s.53(6)(8).
[71] A.H.A. 1986, ss.53(7), 55.
[72] A.H.A. 1986, ss.56(3), 48(3) to (12). A covenant against assignment is implied, s.56(2). The rights to a new tenancy conferred by the tribunal's direction cannot be assigned, s.55(6).
[73] A.H.A. 1986, s.37(6).
[74] A.H.A. 1986, s.57(4). Other persons can apply, however.

common law and well established local custom, the question of compensation is now substantially dependent on statutory provisions and orders considered in the following chapter.

B. The Existence of Sub-tenancies

The law is inconsistent in the protection afforded to sub-tenants. The ordinary common law provisions have been considered and apply, in relation to agricultural tenancies, where the tenant/landlord either surrenders[75] his estate or is subject to forfeiture proceedings.[76] Lawfully created sub-tenancies protected under the Rent Act generally retain their statutory protection,[77] and there are detailed provisions relating to business sub-tenancies.[78] Generally, agricultural sub-tenants enjoy the protection of the Agricultural Holdings Act 1986 *vis-à-vis* their own immediate tenant/landlord. They cannot normally inflict their statutory rights on superior landlords.[79] It therefore follows that the statutory provisions considered in Part IV of this book govern the relationship between the sub-tenant and his immediate tenant/landlord. The acute problems arise where a superior landlord gives a tenant/landlord notice to quit his holding all or part of which may have been sub-let. Where the tenant/landlord serves a counter-notice which operates to bring the matter to the Tribunal, then the sub-tenant is automatically a party to those proceedings, and can, of course, be heard in them.[80] Apparently no correlative provision is made where arbitration follows service of the superior landlord's notice. If the tenant/landlord does not serve a counter-notice and so the matter does not go to the Tribunal, the sub-tenant is not heard at all. If the tenant/landlord is served with notice to quit then he should serve notice to quit on his sub-tenant. If he does, and the notice to the sub-tenant states that it is served because of the service of the notice to quit on the tenant/landlord, then the sub-tenant is automatically deprived of any rights he might otherwise have under section 26(1) of the 1986 Act to oppose or delay the effect of the notice.[81] To make matters worse, the notice on the sub-tenant can be shorter than the normal 12 months.[82]

---

[75] See *ante*, Pt. I, Chap. 8, (III) A, 1.
[76] See *ante*, Pt. 1, Chap. 8, (VI) D.
[77] See *ante*, Pt. II.
[78] See *ante*, Pt. III, Chap. 22.
[79] There is an unused statutory power enabling the Lord Chancellor to fill this hiatus by Order, see A.H.A. 1986, s.29, Sched. 4, para. 7.
[80] The Agricultural Land Tribunals (Rules) Order 1978, r. 13(1).
[81] Agricultural Holdings (Arbitration on Notices) Order 1978, art. 15(1). The notice to the sub-tenant takes effect only if the notice to the tenant/landlord takes effect, *ibid*, art. 15(2). And see *Sherwood* v. *Moody* [1952] 1 All E.R. 389.
[82] A.H.A. 1986, s.25(2)(c).

C. Notices to Quit Part of the Holding

A landlord cannot, of course, simply terminate a tenancy of part of the property let,[83] and the same is true of the tenancy of an agricultural holding.[84] But far more than other landlords a landlord of an agricultural holding is likely to want to end the tenancy of part of the property. The most obvious reason is that he wants to use part of the land for building. Or he may be in the business of recovering minerals or gravel, which may have been his motive for acquiring the holding initially.[85] In most cases the landlord reserves a right to give notice for part of the holding, generally for specified purposes. This is one of the occasions when the notice can be for less than the usual 12 months.[86] But even when the notice is served under an express power in the agreement, the tenant can still serve a counter-notice relying on his statutory security outlined earlier in this chapter. It is, however, likely that the landlord will be able to recover possession relying on Case B.[87]

In the absence of an express power to recover possession of part there is a statutory right to give notice if the recovery is required for certain limited purposes, specified in section 31 of the 1986 Act. The statutory grounds do not assist the landlord who has obtained a normal planning permission for building development of part of the holding. A landlord can recover possession of part if he wants the land for cottages, houses or gardens for farm labourers, or if he requires it for a wide range of mining and quarrying purposes.[88] But in the relatively unlikely event of a landlord proceeding under section 31, his tenant can serve a notice within 28 days[89] that he accepts the notice as notice to quit the whole holding.[90] A prudent landlord will endeavour to negotiate a surrender of the relevant part with his tenant, rather than take the mildly hostile step of serving a notice to quit and attempting to rely on express or statutory provisions.

---

[83] *Re Bebington's Tenancy, Bebington* v. *Wildman* [1921] 1 Ch. 559.
[84] *Woodward* v. *Dudley (Earl of)* [1954] Ch. 283.
[85] Minerals can be acquired separately from the surface of the land, and see L.P.A. 1925, s.205(1)(ix).
[86] A.H.A. 1986, s.25(2)(*b*).
[87] A.H.A. 1986, Sched. 3, Pt. I, Case B. Alternatively he may obtain the Tribunal's consent under s.27(3)(*f*). In either case the rent may be adjusted as a result of the reduction in the holding let, see Chap. 26(I)D, *ante.*
[88] There are another five practically useless grounds, A.H.A. 1986, s.31(2) Notice can also be given for the purpose of adjusting boundaries and amalgamating agricultural units or parts of units, s.31(1).
[89] Either of the notice, or exhausting his procedural rights under the 1986 Act, s.32(2).
[90] A.H.A. 1986, s.32(2).

CHAPTER 28

COMPENSATION

I. Introduction 801
II. Tenant-Right Matters 802
   A. When Can the Claim be Made? 802
   B. What Can be Claimed? 803
   C. How is the Claim Made? ... 803
III. Short Term Improvements 804
   A. When and How Can the Claim be Made? 804
   B. What Can be Claimed? 805
IV. Long Term Improvements 805
   A. When and How Can the Claim be Made? 805
   B. What Can be Claimed? 807

V. Disturbance 808
   A. When Can the Claim be Made? 808
   B. What Can be Claimed? ... 809
   C. How Can the Claim be Made? 810
VI. Short Notice 811
VII. High Farming 811
VIII. Compensation for Market Gardens 812
IX. Landlord's Claim for Dilapidations 813
   A. During the Tenancy 813
   B. At the End of the Tenancy . 814

I. INTRODUCTION

The continuing nature of farming makes it desirable that farming activities are carried on until the end of the tenancy. It follows that in his last year the outgoing tenant may not benefit from his ploughing, sowing and manuring. For many years local custom, "the custom of the country," gave rights which were, in some circumstances, a partial solution of this problem by permitting the incoming tenant to do certain work on the land before the end of the term, and the outgoing tenant to reap the benefit of his work even after the tenancy had ended.[1] But since 1948 the basic compensation for what is known as "tenant right" matters is dealt with on a statutory valuation basis between outgoing tenant and landlord. There are no analogous provisions for business tenancies, where the outgoing tenant can only look to a purchaser of his business for the payment of work in hand or stock in trade at a valuation.

Further, the tenant may be able to raise statutory claims for disturbance to compensate for the cost of either removing or terminating his business, which compensation can be increased if he does it on short notice or can prove additional loss. He may also claim for certain improvements to the holding made by him, and have a limited right to remove his trade fixtures.[2]

On his part, the landlord may claim that the tenant's failure to attend to his contractual and statutory responsibilities to repair and farm competently have resulted in loss which either reduces the tenant's claim or wipes it out altogether, leaving the tenant owing him

[1] See further *Woodfall*, Vol. 2, paras. 2–0066 *et seq.*
[2] See *ante*, Chap. 3(I)E, 6.

money. These claims are now almost entirely statutory. The timing of
the claims, the mode of making them and their quantification are
matters governed by the Agricultural Holdings Act 1986 and the
statutory regulations. The common form procedure requires the
giving of notice within strict time limits, which is followed by
attempts by the parties, or more usually their valuers, to agree figures,
and in default of agreement the matter has to be referred to
arbitration, again within a strict time limit.

II. TENANT-RIGHT MATTERS

A. When Can the Claim be Made?

The tenant can claim compensation for "tenant-right" matters and for
what are called "new improvements"[3] only "on termination of the
tenancy, on quitting the holding."[4] Both these conditions have to be
fulfilled. "Termination" is defined for these purposes as the "cesser of
the contract of tenancy by effluxion of time or from any other cause."[5]
The conditions are most obviously satisfied when the tenant leaves at
the end of a fixed term of years absolute, or, more usually, following a
notice given either by or to the landlord. Abandonment of possession
by the tenant does not terminate the contract of tenancy. But the
tenant can claim compensation where the tenancy is brought to an
end by forfeiture proceedings.[6] If forfeiture proceedings are taken the
tenant must be given sufficient time to serve some statutory notices
for additional compensation for disturbance.[7] The tenant cannot
contract out of his rights to compensation,[8] or claim to be entitled to
compensation based on custom.[9] This does not prevent the parties
agreeing that the tenant should have more extensive rights of
compensation than those laid down by statute,[10] or agreeing the
quantum of the claim when it is made. Sub-tenants can claim
compensation where their interests end, following the service of
notices or counter-notices between the head landlord and their
tenant/landlord.[11]

---

[3] These are improvements begun on or after March 1, 1948, A.H.A. 1986, s.64(1). There are detailed
provisions for "old improvements" but because of their rarity they are not dealt with in this book,
see A.H.A. 1986, s.64(4), and Sched. 9, and see Woodfall, Vol. 2, para. 2–0096, *et seq.*
[4] A.H.A. 1986, s.65(1).
[5] A.H.A. 1986, s.96(1).
[6] And see *Parry* v. *Million Pigs* (1981) 260 E.G. 281.
[7] *e.g.* under A.H.A. 1986, s.60(6), and *Coates* v. *Diment* [1951] 1 All E.R. 890. Disturbance is
considered later.
[8] A.H.A. 1986, s.78(1).
[9] A.H.A. 1986, s.77(1).
[10] A.H.A. 1986, s.78(1).
[11] A.H.A. 1986, s.63(1).

B. What Can be Claimed?

The actual items for which compensation can be claimed are contained in Part II of Schedule 8 to the 1986 Act. And the approach valuers have to adopt is spelt out in Part II of the Agriculture (Calculation of Value for Compensation) Regulations 1978,[12] Sched. 1, Pt II. The rules are detailed and enable the tenant to recover the value of growing crops or harvested crops and produce grown in the last year of his tenancy and which he has no right to sell or remove. The property in these goods passes to the landlord on the termination of the tenancy. In their place the tenant is given the statutory right to claim compensation.[13] He can recover the reasonable cost of his acts of husbandry, *e.g.* ploughing, seeding, cultivating[14] and leaving fallow, and there are special provisions for pastures. In some areas tenant farmers leave hill sheep on quitting because it is an inherent asset of the flock that it can both survive on the particular hill and stay on it. A claim for up to £8 per sheep plus 10 per cent. of its value can be made for this added value. And in certain areas additional compensation can be claimed where the temporary grass land has been put down to seed and there is an accumulating agricultural value locked up in the unploughed temporary grass or ley.

C. How Is the Claim Made?

The first step in the proceedings is for the tenant to give his landlord[15] a written notice of his claim. The notice must specify the nature of the claim, but need not state any figure. Service[16] of the notice must be within two months of the termination of the tenancy.[17] This procedure has to be followed for each type of claim for compensation by either landlord or tenant, and whether or not additional notices are required by other parts of the 1986 Act.[18] The date of termination is not always the same as the date the tenant quits, but the last date for serving a notice claiming compensation is tied to the termination date. The tenant may quit different parts quite lawfully on different dates. In that case the two months' periods for making claims for compensation

---

[12] S.I. 1978 No. 809 as amended by S.I. 1980 No. 751, S.I. 1981 No. 822, S.I. 1983 No. 1475.
[13] *Thomas* v. *National Farmers Union Mutual Insurance Society* [1961] 1 W.L.R. 386.
[14] Assuming these activities are not contrary to the terms of his tenancy agreement, unless the tenant can show that the terms themselves are inconsistent with his duty to farm according to the rules of good husbandry, A.H.A. 1986, s.65(2), and see the 1978 Regs. (*supra*), reg. 4(3).
[15] And see A.H.A. 1986, ss.93(5), 96, and *Frankland* v. *Capstick* [1959] 1 W.L.R. 205.
[16] Service by a certain date means the notice must be received by that date, *Lady Hallinan* v. *Jones and Jones* [1985] C.L.Y. 38.
[17] A.H.A. 1986, s.83(2). The nature of the claim must be specified, s.83(3).
[18] A.H.A. 1986, s.83(2).

for the different parts is tied to the different dates occupation ended of the separate parts.[19]

The parties can then try and settle their claims in writing within eight months.[20] Failing agreement the issues must be determined by arbitration under the Act.[21]

Arbitration is the only way of settling compensation disputes at the end of a tenancy[22] and the provisions common to all arbitrations under the 1986 Act are found in Schedule 11 and the regulations made by the Lord Chancellor under section 84. For current purposes, it is sufficient to note that each party must deliver a written statement of his claim within 35 days from the appointment. He cannot amend his claim after 35 days without the arbitrator's consent, and he is confined to his statement and particulars.[23] The object of this prohibition is to cut down wearisome pleadings, amendment of pleadings, answers and replies. There is provision for an oral hearing with both parties and their witnesses giving evidence.[24] The award should be made and signed within 56 days of appointment, although an application can be made to the Minister to extend that time.[25]

Compensation should be paid within 14 days of an award. In default it can be enforced, if the county court so orders, as if it was a sum ordered by a county court to be recoverable.[26] If that remedy is unsuccessful, an unpaid tenant may be able to obtain a charging order on the land itself.[27]

III. Short Term Improvements

A. When and How Can the Claim be Made?

This claim is made at the same time, and in the same way as the last claim discussed, *i.e.* on termination, on quitting,[28] and following notice given within two months of the termination.[29] If agreement is not reached within the same time limits, then the matter proceeds to arbitration.

[19] A.H.A. 1986, s.83(6).
[20] A.H.A. 1986, s.83(4).
[21] A.H.A. 1986, s.83(5).
[22] A.H.A. 1986, s.84.
[23] A.H.A. 1986, Sched. 11, para. 7. But see *E. D. & A. D. Cooke Bourne (Farms)* v. *Mellows* [1982] 3 W.L.R. 793 (arbitrator should have allowed substantial amendment fundamentally changing claim where no injustice would be caused).
[24] A.H.A. 1986, Sched. 11, para. 8. An oath may be administered, para. 9.
[25] *Ibid.* para. 14.
[26] A.H.A. 1986, s.85(1).
[27] A.H.A. 1986, s.85(2). s.85(3) relieves a trustee/landlord who holds in a representative capacity from personal liability, but entitles an unpaid tenant to an order charging the holding.
[28] A.H.A. 1986, s.64(1).
[29] A.H.A. 1986, s.83(2).

B. What Can be Claimed?

The short term improvements are contained in Part I of Schedule 8 of the 1986 Act and are designed to ensure the return to the outgoing tenant of expenditure he has undertaken which has done something to put or keep the land in good heart, the benefit of which will enure to his successor. The specified items are:

1. Mole drainage and works carried out to secure the efficient working of the drains.[30]
2. Chalking and liming of the land and clay burning.
3. Application of natural and artificial manure and fertilisers including the consumption by farm animals and poultry of corn wherever grown and cake and other foodstuffs produced off the holding.
4. The protection of fruit trees against animals.

There are pages of tables in the Agriculture (Calculation of Value for Compensation) Regulations 1978 (as amended) setting out how the values are calculated, the underlying principle being their value to an incoming tenant.[31] The value of most of these improvements reduces to nil after three years.[32] Compensation can be reduced if the work done was grant-aided[33] or where it has been done badly.[34] The calculation of compensation requires the services of a skilled agricultural valuer and detailed records.

IV. LONG TERM IMPROVEMENTS

A. When and How Can the Claim be Made?

The time for making this claim, and the mechanics for making it are the same as for those claims already discussed.[35] The improvements under this head are described as "long-term new improvements." They are improvements specified in the Agricultural Holdings Act 1986 Act, Sched. 7 which were begun on or after March 1, 1948. The Schedule is in two parts. Part I comprises some fairly obscure

---

[30] The tenant must give the landlord notice before he starts this improvement if he wants to claim compensation. The landlord cannot object, and see A.H.A. 1986, s.68(1).

[31] A.H.A. 1986, s.66(2).

[32] The value of the mole drainage reduces to nil after six years, see Sched. 1, Pt. I, para. 1 of the 1978 Regs. *supra.*

[33] A.H.A. 1986, s.66(5).

[34] Agriculture (Calculation of Value for Compensation) Regs. 1978, reg. 4.

[35] See *ante* (II) A, C; (III) A.

improvements.[36] But if the tenant wants to claim compensation for carrying them out he must first have obtained his landlord's written consent.[37] The Part II improvements are more important and are:

1. Erection, alteration or enlargement of buildings, and making or improvement of permanent yards, and the construction of loading platforms, ramps and hard standing.
2. Construction of silos.
3. Claying of land.
4. Marling of land.
5. Making or improvement of roads or bridges.
6. Making or improvements of water courses, culverts, ponds, wells or reservoirs, or of works for the application of water power for agricultural or domestic purposes or for the supply of water for such purposes.
7. Making or removal of permanent fences.
8. Reclaiming waste land.
9. Making or improvement of embankments or sluices.
10. Erection of wirework for hop gardens.
11. Provision of permanent sheep-dipping accommodation.
12. Removal of bracken, tree roots, boulders or other like obstructions to cultivation.
13. Land drainage (other than mole drainage and works carried out to secure the efficient functioning thereof).
14. Provision or laying-on of electric light or power.
15. Provision of facilities for the storage or disposal of sewage or farm waste.
16. Repairs of fixed equipment, being equipment reasonably required for the proper farming of the holding, other than repairs which the tenant is under an obligation to carry out.
17. Grubbing up orchards and fruit trees.
18. Planting trees otherwise than as an orchard and bushes other than fruit bushes.
19. Carrying out works in compliance with improvement notices under Part VII of the Housing Act 1985 and Part VIII of the Housing Act 1974.

If the tenant wants to be in the position to claim compensation for these improvements, again he needs his landlord's prior consent.[38] If it is refused or granted only on terms the tenant considers unreasonable, he can seek the consent of the Tribunal.[39] Either the landlord or the

---

[36] Included are making water meadows, watercress beds, osier beds, gardens and the provision of underground tanks, planting hops, orchards and fruit bushes, and warping and weiring of land (an unusual form of controlled tidal flooding to secure a precipitation of mud held in suspension).
[37] A.H.A. 1986, s.67.
[38] A.H.A. 1986, s.67(1).
[39] A.H.A. 1986, s.67(3).

Tribunal can grant its consent conditionally[40] which may relate to reduced compensation being payable at the end of the tenancy. One of the major problems relating to compensation for long term improvements is that the tenant may be able to run off the cost of the improvements against his taxable income. When he looks to the landlord for compensation, the landlord may not be in a position to produce a lump sum equivalent to the compensation claimed. He may therefore be happy for the improvement to be carried out, provided he does not have to pay for it in the end. A similar situation arises in relation to improvements proposed to be executed by business tenants.[41] In that case the landlord will often not object to the improvement, but will not give his formal consent which effectively prevents the tenant from claiming compensation.[42] In an agricultural tenancy there is a strong argument for recourse to the Tribunal by the tenant faced with a refusing landlord. If the Tribunal approve the tenant's proposal, the landlord may elect to carry out the improvement himself,[43] and then put in a claim for increased rent.[44]

B. What Can be Claimed?

The measure of compensation is different in this instance, and is "an amount equal to the increase attributable to the improvement in value of the agricultural holding as a holding, having regard to the character and situation of the holding and the average requirements of tenants reasonably skilled in husbandry."[45] The tenant does not, therefore, necessarily recover the cost to himself of the improvement, or its current capital value or replacement cost. But these factors will be taken into account in working out what a tenant would pay if he had to rent the improvements, which sum is then likely to be capitalised to find the amount of compensation payable. Grants the tenant may have received from central or local government funds, including improvement grants for living accommodation, have to be taken into account and will reduce the amount of compensation.[46]

The tenant can claim compensation for improvements made during earlier tenancies.[47] These are more usually his own earlier tenancies, which were renewed, so that the question of compensation would not have arisen as there was no "quitting." Less usually, the tenant as an incoming tenant may have paid his predecessor or the landlord for

[40] A.H.A. 1986, s.67(2)(4).
[41] See *ante*, Pt. III and L. & T.A. 1927, Pt. I.
[42] A business tenant has a right to go to court for consent, L. & T.A. 1927, ss.3, 21.
[43] A.H.A. 1986, s.67(5).
[44] A.H.A. 1986, s.13.
[45] A.H.A. 1986, s.66(1).
[46] A.H.A. 1986, s.66(5).
[47] A.H.A. 1984, s.69.

post-1948 improvements made by the outgoing tenant, or paid for by the landlord. The later tenant can claim for the improvements he himself has paid for in this way,[47a] if the payment was made with the landlord's written consent.

V. DISTURBANCE

A. When Can the Claim be Made?

The remaining additional claims for compensation are open only to restricted classes of tenants, and are subject to further conditions and procedural requirements. The common form of claim for disturbance is granted by the Agricultural Holdings Act 1986, s.60. Compensation can be claimed only when the tenant quits the holding "in consequence" of a notice to quit served by his landlord.[48] However, a sub-tenant can claim for disturbance if he loses his sub-tenancy as a result of a notice given by the head landlord to his tenant/landlord, or as a result of a counter-notice given by his tenant/landlord to the head landlord.[49] Unlike the claim for compensation for tenant-right matters or improvements, it does not apply when the tenant initiates the steps to end the tenancy. But a tenant can claim for disturbance where he is given a notice to quit part[50] and serves a counter-notice under section 32, requiring the notice to be treated as a notice to quit the whole. He can also claim where he quits only part of the holding, either following notice, or under the terms of the tenancy.[51]

Whether or not the tenant has quitted "in consequence" of the notice or because of some other extraneous factor is a question of fact.[52] Certainly it seems to be irrelevant that the notice was technically bad, provided that the tenant acted on it.[53] The compensation is not subject to capital gains tax.[54]

Tenants cannot claim disturbance where they are precluded from serving a counter-notice under section 26(1) of the 1986 Act because they have been served notices under Case C (certificate of bad

---

[47a] A.H.A. 1986, s.69(2)(3).
[48] This seems to include a notice under L.P.A. 1925, s.146, initiating forfeiture proceedings, as it is not possible to contract out of the compensation provisions, A.H.A. 1986, s.78(1), and see *Re Disraeli Agreement, Cleasby* v. *Park Estates (Hughenden) Ltd.* [1939] Ch. 382.
[49] A.H.A. 1986, s.63(1).
[50] A.H.A. 1986, s.60(1)(*b*). Not every notice to quit part is sufficient, but only those rendered valid by s.31 (specifying reasons for serving notices of part), or where they have been served by the landlord of an already severed part of the reversionary estate.
[51] A.H.A. 1986, s.74.
[52] *Preston* v. *Norfolk County Council* [1947] K.B. 775; *Gulliver* v. *Catt* [1952] 2 Q.B. 308 (tenants leaving following court orders held to do so in consequence of notices to quit).
[53] *Westlake* v. *Page* [1926] 1 K.B. 298; *Kestell* v. *Langmaid* [1950] 1 K.B. 233.
[54] *Davis* v. *Powell* [1977] 1 W.L.R. 258.

husbandry), Case D (failure to comply with notice to pay rent, or remedy breaches), Case E (irremediable breaches), Case F (insolvency) or Case G (death).[55] Tenants who can claim compensation for disturbance may have the right to make additional cumulative claims, and the circumstances when this can be done are considered in the next subsection.

B. What Can be Claimed?

(1) *One Year's Rent*

The standard compensation is one year's rent at the rate paid at the time the tenancy was ended. There is no need to prove any loss resulting from disturbance.[56] Even tenant/landlords out of occupation can claim this compensation if they are themselves liable to pay compensation for disturbance to their own sub-tenants.[57] The amount of compensation can be restricted where the tenancy ends after the serving of a counter-notice by the tenant under section 32 of the 1986 Act.[58] If the part affected by the original notice was less than one-quarter of the original holding and what was left could be reasonably farmed on its own, then the compensation is limited proportionately to the part covered by the original notice.[59]

(2) *Costs of Disturbance up to Two Years' Rent*

Proof of claims for compensation for disturbance is commonplace in relation to the compulsory purchase of premises occupied by businesses, where the claim may be made either on termination of the business or its removal. Similarly a farming tenant who qualifies for the standard disturbance compensation may be able to prove additional loss from disturbance. The loss must be "unavoidably incurred" and "directly attributable" to quitting the holding.[60] The section expressly refers to loss from sale or removal of household goods, farm implements, fixtures, produce and stock, and the reasonable costs of preparing the claim. If he sells all these farming items, as opposed to household items, he can claim additional compensation only if he gives his landlord a reasonable opportunity

---

[55] A.H.A. 1986, s.61(1).
[56] A.H.A. 1986, s.60(2),(3).
[57] A.H.A. 1986, s.63(2).
[58] See *supra*, para. A.
[59] A.H.A. 1986, s.63(3).
[60] A.H.A. 1986, s.60(5).

of making a valuation of them.[61] In any event this claim is limited to a further year's rent, making two years' rent[62] the maximum that can be claimed under section 60(6) of the 1986 Act.

(3) *Four Years' Rent*

Tenants who qualify for the basic section 60 compensation may be eligible to claim a further four years' rent as compensation for disturbance without any proof of loss under section 60(4) of the 1986 Act. The provisions of the section weed out a number of likely claimants. The tenant will not qualify for this additional compensation if the notice to quit states that the landlord is serving it because he wants to end the tenancy in the interests of good husbandry, sound estate management, agricultural research or because he will suffer hardship, and the Tribunal in consenting to the operation of the notice relies on one of these reasons for their decision.[63] But if the Tribunal find at the same time that one of the reasons why the landlord wants possession is for a use of the land for certain non-agricultural purposes, then the tenant will still qualify for this additional compensation.[64] The most common situations when this additional compensation is recovered are when the landlord serves an ordinary 12 months' notice and does not specifically rely on any ground or give any reason at all and the tenant accepts it, or where the landlord serves a case B notice,[65] *e.g.* where he wants the land back for development purposes.

C. How Can the Claim be Made?

As in all these cases, the normal standard notice of claim has to be given within two months from the termination of the tenancy specifying the various heads of claim[66] and the strict time limits must be observed thereafter. But if the tenant wants to make the additional disturbance claim under the Agricultural Holdings Act 1986, s.60(5), of the amount of his actual loss up to two years' rent, he has to give notice of claim in writing not less than one month before the termination of his tenancy.[67] A landlord cannot contract out of these

---

[61] A.H.A. 1986, s.60(6).
[62] A.H.A. 1986, s.60(3)(*b*).
[63] A.H.A. 1986, s.61(3). The same applies when the Minister serves a Case H notice with a view to boundary changes or amalgamations, s.61(2), or when a smallholder is given a Case A notice (over 65 and suitable alternative living accommodation available), *ibid.*
[64] A.H.A. 1986, s.61(4).
[65] See *ante* Chap. 27(II)B.
[66] A.H.A. 1986, s.83(2), (3).
[67] A.H.A. 1986, s.60(6)(*a*).

compensation provisions,[68] and therefore notices to end the tenancy have to allow the tenant sufficient time to serve a notice under section 60(6) of the 1986 Act.

VI. SHORT NOTICE

The landlord who foresees the possibility that part of the land might be used for development purposes generally reserves an express right to serve a notice to quit part of the land for specified purposes. A landlord will generally reserve the right to serve notice to quit ending at some time other than the anniversary of the tenancy, and also provide for less than 12 months' notice. The landlord serving such a notice will usually be relying on Case B.[69] Where he re-acquires either the entire holding or part of it for a specified non-agricultural purpose, then the tenant can claim additional compensation under section 62 of the 1986 Act. There are no formalities additional to those already mentioned, although the tenant's notice under section 83 of the 1986 Act should specify that he is making this particular claim. If the tenant can prove that he has suffered additional loss by giving up possession of the whole or part of the holding following the short notice, rather than at the end of a 12 months' notice ending with the anniversary of the tenancy, then he can claim from his landlord for this loss which will include anticipated profit.

VII. HIGH FARMING

A tenant who has increased the value of the holding by adopting a continuous system of farming more beneficial to the holding than the one required by his agreement or practised normally has a claim to recover that enhanced value. This ground of claim has not, hitherto, been of much importance. This was partly because of the evidential difficulty of establishing it. However, this difficulty might now be alleviated as a result of the right to ask for a record of the condition of the fixed equipment and general condition of the holding.[70] That right must be exercised if a high farming claim is to be made.[71]

---

[68] A.H.A. 1986, s.78(1).
[69] A.H.A. 1986, Sched. 3, Pt. I, Case B, and see *ante* Chap. 27(II)B.
[70] Under A.H.A. 1986, s.22.
[71] A.H.A. 1986, s.70(2). Compensation for improvements are deducted from this claim, and notice of intention to make the claim has to be given not less than one month before the end of the tenancy.

VIII. COMPENSATION FOR MARKET GARDENS

Market gardens come under the normal provisions for agricultural holdings, but there are specific provisions affecting compensation on termination. Tenancies do not come within the scope of these provisions at all unless the landlord,[72] or the Tribunal, agree[73] that the holding or part of it shall be treated as a "market garden." A market garden is likely to be a particularly capital intensive unit, which could result in a heavy claim for compensation against the landlord. The landlord or the Tribunal can agree the terms on which the whole or part of the holding is to be treated as a market garden, and these terms can relate to compensation. The parties can also validly agree the amount of compensation for improvements when they are made,[74] and can also agree that an entirely different basis of compensation known as the "Evesham Custom" shall apply.[75]

A market gardener has more extensive rights at the end of his tenancy than a normal agricultural tenant. His right to remove fixtures[76] extends to every fixture he has made or building he has put up or acquired for his trade purposes as a market gardener.[77] Alternatively, he can leave the buildings and claim compensation.[78] He can claim compensation for improvements he has paid for as an incoming tenant, even though the landlord may not have given his written consent to the purchase,[79] and he can remove all fruit trees and bushes he has planted which are not permanently set out.[80] He has to remove them before the end of the tenancy, and cannot claim compensation for them if he does not, or go back and dig them up.

Obviously a market gardener is likely to want to make more specialised improvements. The improvements which he can carry out as a market gardener without consent, and for which he can claim compensation are:

(a) Planting of standard or other fruit trees, or fruit bushes permanently set out.
(b) Planting of strawberry plants.
(c) Planting of asparagus, rhubarb and other vegetable crops which continue productive for two or more years.
(d) Erection, alteration, enlargement of buildings for his trade or business purposes as a market gardener.[81]

---

[72] A.H.A. 1986, s.79(1), and see *Saunders-Jacob* v. *Yates* 1933 2 K.B. 240.
[73] A.H.A. 1986, s.80(1), (2).
[74] A.H.A. 1986, s.81(1).
[75] A.H.A. 1986, s.81(2).
[76] A.H.A. 1986, s.10, and see *ante* Pt. I Chap. 3(I)E.
[77] A.H.A. 1986, s.79(3).
[78] *Ibid.*
[79] A.H.A. 1986, s.79(5).
[80] A.H.A. 1986, s.79(4).
[81] See A.H.A. 1986, Sched. 10.

For compensation purposes, these items are treated in the same way as if they were short term improvements.[82] Apart from these matters, he is entitled to make all the other claims for compensation previously considered for agricultural tenants.

Mention has been made of the "Evesham Custom." This is likely to apply in two cases. The parties may agree at the outset that the "custom" is to apply to certain improvements when the property is originally let as a market garden, or when the landlord agrees to treat it as such.[83] Alternatively, the Tribunal may consent to treatment of the unit or part of it as a market garden on the basis that the "Evesham Custom" applies.[84] This has the effect of reducing the tenant's claim for compensation from his landlord in respect of all or some of the specialised improvements mentioned in the last paragraph if the tenancy comes to an end either on the tenant's own notice or his insolvency. If that happens then initially no compensation is payable by the landlord for the specialised improvements. It is open to the tenant within one month of his notice or insolvency to produce a suitable prospective successor to his tenancy, who is prepared to take it on the same terms, and pay the outgoing tenant all the compensation due to him under the 1986 Act. The offer has to remain open for three months.[85] If it is accepted the incoming tenant pays the outgoing tenant all the compensation due to him under the 1986 Act less any sums due to the landlord for breaches of the agreement or dilapidations, which have to be paid to the landlord.[86] If the landlord does not accept the prospective new tenant, he is responsible to pay all the compensation.[87] If the outgoing tenant cannot produce a new one, then the landlord just remains liable to pay the standard compensation payable to an agricultural tenant,[88] but nothing in respect of the specialised items covered by the "Evesham Custom."

IX. Landlord's Claim for Dilapidations

A. During the Tenancy

If the landlord is faced with a tenant who is failing to carry out his statutory or contractual repairing and farming obligations he will generally be able to enter and carry out the work himself under either

---

[82] A.H.A. 1986, s.79(2), *i.e.* as if they were within A.H.A. 1986, Sched. 8, Pt. I.
[83] A.H.A. 1986, s.81(2).
[84] A.H.A. 1986, s.80.
[85] A.H.A. 1986, s.80(4).
[86] A.H.A. 1986, s.80(5).
[87] A.H.A. 1986, s.80(3).
[88] For the accessible example of how the different heads of tenant's compensation are collated, and taxed see *Davis* v. *Powell* [1977] 1 W.L.R. 258.

the terms of the lease itself, or the Agriculture (Maintenance, Repair and Insurance of Fixed Equipment) Regulations 1973,[89] Sched., Pt. I, para. 4(2). The landlord can also consider serving a notice to remedy, and if that is not complied with, then he can serve a Case D notice to quit.[90]

However, it is open to the landlord to take proceedings for damages for breach of a covenant to repair during the tenancy.[91] These actions are uncommon, both in agricultural and non-agricultural tenancies. But in any event damages cannot exceed the amount by which the value of the reversion has diminished as a result of the breach.[92]

B. At the End of the Tenancy

(1) *Cost of Making Good*

When the landlord is concerned with dilapidations and disrepair at the end of the tenancy, he has a statutory right to claim the cost of making good the dilapidation, deterioration or damage to the holding.[93] But the damages he recovers cannot exceed the amount by which his interest has gone down as a result of the dilapidation, etc.[94] He cannot claim for all the disrepair to the property but only that "caused by non-fulfilment by the tenant of his responsibilities to farm in accordance with the rules of goods husbandry."[95] For this purpose, the tenant's liabilities are found by amalgamating his contractual duties with those contained in the Agriculture (Maintenance, Repair and Insurance of Fixed Equipment) Regulations 1973. The arbitrator is bound to have regard to the contractual terms under which the property is held, as these may well vary the tenant's statutory liabilities,[96] either diminishing them or increasing them.

(2) *Claim Under the Contract*

The landlord has an option either to elect for recovering the cost of making good, or pursuing a claim solely under the terms of the written contract, under section 71(3) of the 1986 Act. He can give notice that

---

[89] S.I. 1973, No. 1473, see *ante*, Chap. 26(I)C.
[90] See *ante*, Chap. 27(II)D, 2.
[91] *Kent* v. *Conniff* [1953] 2 W.L.R. 41.
[92] See *ante*, Pt. I, Chap. 6 (VI) B.
[93] A.H.A. 1986, s.71(2); *Evans* v. *Jones* [1955] 2 Q.B. 58.
[94] A.H.A. 1986, s.71(5).
[95] A.H.A. 1986, s.71(1).
[96] *Barrow Green Estate Co.* v. *Walker's Executors* [1954] 1 W.L.R. 231, and see *Burden* v. *Hannaford* [1956] 1 Q.B. 142.

he intends to make both claims, but must elect between them at latest by the time of arbitration.[97] The reason for giving the landlord this option is "to cover the possibility of a contract of tenancy which imposes on the tenant a liability greater than that which the Act imposes on him. It was, no doubt, considered wrong to deprive the landlord of a right to proceed under such a contract."[98] He cannot claim in respect of some items under section 71(1) and under section 71(3) for the rest. But again, the maximum amount of damages he can claim under the contract is the diminution in value of his reversion due to the dilapidations, deterioration or damage.[99]

(3) *Claim for General Deterioration*

In many ways this is the reverse of the tenant's claim for compensation for "high farming." If the landlord can show that the value of the holding has generally been reduced either by reason of the tenant's failure to repair and farm properly, or because of his wrongful acts, then he can claim compensation from the tenant of an amount equal to the decrease in the value of the holding. The measure of damages will be the difference between the value of the holding if the tenant had left the land clean, in good heart and the buildings in good repair and all the other appurtenances properly cared for, and its value in the actual condition in which the tenant left it. The landlord cannot make a double claim, and so has to give credit for what he has recovered under section 71(1) and 71(3).[1]

(4) *Making the Claims*

The procedure for making the claim under section 71 is straightforward. The same procedure is used as in the making of normal tenant's claims. Within two months[2] of the termination, notice has to be given of the landlord's intention to make the claim, and he must specify what claims he is making. At this stage he can make a claim on both section 71(1) (cost of making good) and section 71(3) (damages in accordance with the contract). The landlord's valuer will produce a detailed schedule of dilapidations. It is at this stage that both parties are helped if a schedule of dilapidations or record of repair of the holding was prepared at the beginning of the tenancy. If the parties cannot agree figures, then the matter goes to arbitration within the same time limits and follows the same procedure as for the

---

[97] *Boyd* v. *Wilton* [1957] 2 Q.B. 277.
[98] *Barrow Green Estate Co.* v. *Walker's Executors* [1954] 1 W.L.R. 231 at p. 235, *per* Somervell L.J.
[99] A.H.A. 1986, s.71(5).
[1] A.H.A. 1986, s.72.
[2] *i.e.* under A.H.A. 1986, s.83.

tenant's claims. The landlord has to elect by the time he goes to arbitration whether he is pursuing a section 71(1) or (3) claim.[3] The landlord can claim under section 71 on the termination of the tenancy and only on the tenant's quitting the holding. He cannot make claims under section 71 during the tenancy. And he can only claim compensation by using the arbitration procedure at the end of it. He cannot at that stage bring an action for damages.[4] He can, however, include in his claim compensation for matters that occurred in earlier preceding tenancies enjoyed by the tenant.[5]

If the landlord is proposing to make a section 72 claim for general depreciation he must give notice of his intention one month before termination of the tenancy.[6]

[3] *Boyd* v. *Wilton* [1957] 2 Q.B. 277.
[4] A.H.A. 1986, s.83(1).
[5] A.H.A. 1986, s.73.
[6] A.H.A. 1986, s.72(4).

INDEX

Agent,
  lease, creation of. *See* Lease, creation.
Agreement,
  agricultural tenancy, of, 769–770
  characteristics, of, 15–17, 32–36
  sham, 10, 20–24
Agricultural Holdings Act 1986,
  s. 1 definition, 648–649, 757, 758, 759, 764
  s. 2 tenancies of less than a year and from
    year to year, 648, 760, 761–762, 764,
    765, 766
  s. 3 leases for two years and more—
    expiration, 341–342, 760, 766
  s. 4 death of tenant during tenancy, 767
  s. 5 contracting out, 766–767
  s. 6 written agreement, right to, 769–770
  s. 7 model clauses, 770, 773
  s. 12 and Sched. 2, arbitration of rent,
    774–777
  s. 15 produce and cropping, disposal of,
    771–772
  s. 21 succession on death of landlord for
    life, 762
  s. 22 farm, record of condition of, 771
  s. 25 notice to quit, 760, 779
  s. 33 rent reduction, arbitration for,
    776–777
  s. 44 lands tribunal consent to notice, 793
  s. 60 compensation, for disturbance, 791,
    808, 810
  s. 71 (3) dilapidations, claims under
    contract for, 814–815
  Sched. 3 grounds for possession, 780,
    782–797
  Sched. 7 pre-March 1948 items assessable
    for compensation, 805
  Sched. 8 Pt. II "tenant right" items,
    compensation for, 803
  Sched. 11 compensation dispute,
    arbitration for, 803–804
Agriculture (Maintenance, Repair and
  Insurance of Fixed Equipment)
  Regulations 1973, 772–774
Agricultural Land Tribunal, 780–781,
  782–784
Agricultural Tenancies. *See also*
  Agricultural Tied Houses.
  agricultural holdings occupied by farmer,
    393, 648–649
  compensation, 798–799, 801–816
    disturbance, for, 808–811

Agricultural Tenancies—*cont.*
  compensation—*cont.*
    high farming, for, 811
    improvements, long-term, 805–808
    improvements, short-term, 804–805
    market gardens, for, 812–813
    short notice, for, 811
    "tenant right" matters, for, 802–804
  dilapidations, landlord's claim for,
    813–816
  function carried on, the, 757–760
    agricultural, trade need not be,
      757–758
    agriculture, 757
    private purpose, part used for, 758
    trade or business, 757
    use, change of, 759
  interest protected, nature of, 760–764
    grantor, capacity of, 762–763
    licences, 761–762
    sub-tenancies, 763–764
    tenancy, common yearly, 760
  rent, 774–777
    determination of, 775–776
    improvements, landlords increase,
      following, 776
    notice to quit part, decrease, following,
      776–777
    review, mechanics of, 774–775
  secure tenancy, agricultural holdings,
    and, 548
  security of tenure, 779–800
    additional matters, 798–800
    part of holding, notice to quit, 800
  possession, grounds for, 782–797
    Agricultural Land Tribunal, post
      notice consent, 780, 782–784
    bad husbandry, certificate of—case C,
      780, 784–785
    breaches, irremediable—case E, 780,
      790
    death and succession—case G, 780,
      791–796
    Insolvency, case F, 780, 790–791
    lifetime succession, 797–798
    ministerial certificates—case H, 586
    notice to pay rent or remedy breach,
      non-compliance with—case D,
      780, 785–789
    use of land, alternative—case B, 780,
      784

Agricultural Tenancies—*cont.*
  sub-tenancies, existence of, 799
    tenancies outside 1986 Act, 764–767
    contracting out, permitted, 766–767
    fixed term, death during, 767
    fixed periods between 12 and 24
      months, 766
    generally, 764
    ministry approval, those with, 765
    mowing or grazing, lettings for,
      765–766
    officeholders, to, 764
  terms, 769–777
    farming and management, method of,
      770–772
    rent, 774–777
    repair, 772–774
    written, 769
    use, 759
Agricultural Tied Houses, 482–491
  contracts and premises, 484–485
  landlords, 485–486
  protected occupiers, 483–484
  Rent (Agriculture) Act 1976, 483–491
  statutory tenancy, terms of, 486–487. *See
    also* Agricultural Tenancies,
    Possession, 487–491.
  misrepresentation, by 490
  occupier and tenants
    outside statute, 489–490
  occupier and tenants within statute,
    487–489
  premises once occupied by persons in
    agriculture, 491
  sub-tenants, 490–491
"Appropriate Day," The, 388–389
  April 1, 1973, on or after, 390
  deeming provisions, 391
  March 22, 1973, before, 389–390
  March 22, 1973, on or after, 390
  leasehold enfranchisement, for, 508–509
Assignment. *See also* Transfer; Premium.
  assignee, 302–303
  assignment, on,
    covenants binding and enforceable by,
      317–319
    meaning of, 319–321
  bankruptcy and, 300, 329–331
  business tenancies, of, 660–662
  consent to, 306–313
    limit, attempts to, 307–308
    refusal of, 307
    statutory provisions, avoiding, 307–308
    unreasonable refusal of, 308–312
    waiver of, 312–313
    without, 453–454

Assignment—*cont.*
  contract, the, 313–314
  covenants binding assignee, 298–299,
    317–319
  covenants enforceable by assignee,
    317–319
  death and, 326–329, 433–434
    assignee tenant, of, 328
    estate, devolution of, 326–327
    estate, distribution of, 328–329
    tenant's assignee, personal
      representative as, 327
  divorce and, 332
  effecting, 313–314
  inter-vivos, 433–434
  position after, 315–332
    original guarantor, 315–315
    landlord and assignee, 316–321
    original landlord and tenant, 315
    original lessors and their transferees,
      324–326
    original tenant and assignee, 321–322
    sub–lessors, sub–lessees and their
      assigns, 322–324
  premiums on. *See* Premium.
  prohibition of, 297–298
    absolute, 297
    conditional, 219, 306, 312–313
  right to assign, the, 301–302
    restrictions on, 302–306
  secure tenancy and, 551–552
  shorthold tenancy incapable of, 494
  sub-letting, distinguished from, 303–305
Assured Tenant, The, 495–496
  part-business, part-residential, 649

Bankruptcy,
  agricultural tenant, of, 790–791
  non-payment of rent, on, 202–205
Beneficiaries,
  agricultural estate, of, 762–763
  lease and, creation of. *See* Lease,
    creation of.
Breach,
  contract, of, 10, 194
  covenant, of, 111–112, 694, 785–786,
    790
  irremediable, 353. *See also* Notice,
    s. 146
Break Clause, 60. *See* Lease, contents;
    Rent, review clauses.
Building Act 1984,
  s. 76 prejudicial to health, premises in,
    264
  s. 77 dangerous structures, 272–273

Business. *See* Agricultural Tenancies, function carried on; Business Tenancies, tenancies covered; Trade.
Business Tenancies,
  compulsory purchase and. *See* Compulsory Purchase, tenancies, effect on; Compulsory Purchase, compensation for.
  contracting out, 655–656
  creation, 657–659
    user, terms as to, 658–659
  exclusions, 648–655
    agricultural holdings, 648–649
    lease, extended, 652
    lease, short, 652
    licences, commercial, 652–655
    licensed premises, 649–650
    mining leases, 649
    "national security" provisions, 651–652
    part-residential use, 649
    public interest, tenancies limited in, 650–651
    service tenancies, 650
  goodwill, protection of. *See also* Goodwill.
  improvements, compensation and, 663–671
    amount of, 670–671
    claims procedure, 668–669
    qualifying conditions, 666–668
    rent, effect on, 669–670
    right to, the, 665–666
    statutory provisions, 663
    tenancies covered, 663–665
  improvements taxed as premiums, 671–672
  management, 659–672
    assignment and sub-letting, 660–662
    hybrid premises, 664
    improvements, 662–672. *See also* Business Tenancies, improvements, compensation and.
  misrepresentation *re* renewal, 751–752
  new tenancy, the, 682–693, 706–718
    agreement, 692–693
    court, the, 706–708
    initiative, landlord's or tenant's? 682
    order for carrying out the, 717
    request by tenant for, 689–692
      action by landlord, 692
      competent landlord, 690
      form, 690
      terms, proposed, 691–692
      time, 690–691

Business Tenancies—*cont.*
  new tenancy, the—*cont.*
    sub-tenancies, renewing, 717–718
    termination by landlord, 682–687
      action by tenant, 687–689
      competent landlord, the, 683–684
      date of, 684–685
      notice, effect of, 686–687
      notice, form of, 684
      notice, time of giving, 685
      opposition, landlord's, 685–686
    terms, 692–693, 708–717
      agreement, 692–693
      other, 715–717
      property, the, 710–711
      rent, 711–715
      term, the, 709–710
      valuation, 711–715
  opposition to grounds for, 693–706
    alternative accommodation, availability of suitable, 695–696
    demolish or reconstruct, landlord's intention to, 697–701
    intention, landlord's, 704–705
    letting or disposing of property as whole, 696
    obligations, other breaches of, 694–695
    occupy, landlord's intention to, 701–704
    paying rent, persistent delay in, 694
    repairing obligations, breach of, 694
  protection, history and objectives of, 637–640
  residential regulated tenancies mixed with, 392–393
  tenancies covered by Landlord and Tenant Act 1927, 640–648
    "business," meaning of, 646–647
    management, degree of control by, 643
    occupation, need for, 642–646
    "tenancy," meaning of, 641–642
    unlawful business user, 648
  terminations and renewals, 673–718. *See also* Business Tenancies, new tenancy, the, continuation tenancy the.
    nature, 676–677
    rent, interim, 679–682
    terms, 677–682
      statutory protection, 673–676

Capital Gains Tax,
  premiums taxed as. *See* Premium, taxation.

Charity,
  commissioners, 591, 592, 594
  trustees, lettings by, 66–67
Club,
  tenant, competency as, 71–72
Company,
  capacity, Companies Act 1985, s. 35,
    under, 14
  landlord of business premises, as, 703
  lease, as grantor of, 69–70
  rent, bankruptcy and liquidation
    affecting, 202–205
Compensation. *See* Agricultural Tenancy,
  compensation; Business Tenancy,
  improvement, compensation for;
  Goodwill, compensation for loss;
  Housing Financial Assistance,
  disturbance, compensation for;
  Compulsory Purchase, compensation.
Compulsory Purchase, 719–738
  compensation, 730–738
    disturbance, for, 733–735
    Landlord and Tenant Act 1954, under,
      738
    "market value" basis of, 730–732
    profits and goodwill, for loss of,
      736–737
  Compulsory Purchase Act 1965,
    s. 6 notice to treat, procedure after,
      720–721
    s. 9 acquiring authority, unilateral
      vesting by, 722
    s. 11 (1) notice of entry, 725, 726–727
    s. 20 fixed or periodic tenancies,
      acquisition of, 724, 727, 728, 733
    s. 22 action for trespass, protection
      from, 723
    s. 23 conveyances, costs of, 722
    Sched. 5 conveyances, form of, 572
  powers of, 719–720
  tenancies, effect on, 720–730
    conveyancing: normal procedure,
      720–723
    conveyancing: quick procedure,
      723–724
    leaseholds, on, 724–726
    notices, dispensing with, 726–728
    protected tenants under the Landlord
      and Tenant Act 1954, Pt. II,
      728–730
Compulsory Purchase Act 1965. *See*
  Compulsory Purchase.
Compulsory Purchase (Vesting
  Declarations) Act 1981, s. 4 (1), 723
  general vesting declaration, procedure,
    723

Continuation Tenancy. *See* Business
  Tenancy.
Contract,
  assign, to, 437
  breach of, 10, 194–195
  complete, failure to, 92–99
    agreement, entry before, 93
    agreement or void lease, entry
      following, 93–94
    damages for, 94–95
    specific performance, action for. *See*
      Contract, specific performance.
  lease, for a, 86–87
    joinder and signature, 84–86
    part-performance, evidenced by,
      86–87
    requirements, 81–82
    variation and waiver, 84
    writing, evidenced in, 83–84
  Rent (Agriculture) Act 1976, covered by,
    484–485
  restricted. *See* Restricted Contracts sale,
    for—agricultural tenancies and, 799.
  specific performance of, 93, 96–99
    damages and, 97
    failure to complete, for, 96–99
    parties, conduct of, 96–97
    surrounding circumstances, 96
    terms of lease, settlement of, 97–99
Controlled Tenancies. *See* Statutory
  Tenancies, controlled.
Conveyance. *See* Compulsory Purchase,
  tenancies, effect on.
Co-ownership, 593–594
Council Housing, 525–581
  agreement, terms of, 527
  alternative accommodation, certificate
    of, 450
  disposal, 562–577
    excluded dwellings, 565–567
    mortgage, the, 569
    price, the, 567–569
    rights, tenant's exercise of, 569–573
    right to buy, qualifying tenant and,
      562–565
    vendor, the unwilling, 574
  family home, the, 577–581
    tenants, secure, 578–581
    tenants, unsecure, 577–578
  landlord's obligations, 542–545
  leases, creation of, 49
  management, 560–562
  possession. *See* Council Housing,
    security of tenure; Council Housing,
    tenancies, unsecure; Secure
    Tenancy, The, possession.

Council Housing—*cont.*
    rent rebates and. *See* Housing Financial
      Assistance, rent rebates and
      allowances.
    security of tenure, 545–557
      secure tenancies. *See* Secure Tenancy.
      unsecure tenancies. *See* Council
        Housing, tenancies, unsecure.
    sub-lettings, 532–536
    tenant's obligations, 529–542
    forfeiture and, 541–542
      improvements, not to carry out,
        537–538
      maintenance and repair, 538–541
      rent, to pay, 529
      user, restrictions on, 536–537
    tenants, selection of, 526–527
    unsecure tenancies, 557–560. *See also*
      Council Housing, family home, the.
      "abuse of power" defence, 558–560
      possession, procedure for, 560
      ultra vires defence, 557–558
Courts. *See also* Remedies, Security of
    Tenure, procedure.
    business tenancy, improvements and,
      667–668
    forfeiture. *See* Forfeiture, High Court;
      Forfeiture, County Court.
    new business tenancy, application for,
      706–708
    penal rent clause, construction of, 170
    possession. *See* Possession; Security of
      Tenure, possession.
    rent arrears, action for, 196–199
    rent review clauses and, 178–184
    restricted contract proceedings, 482
    secure tenancy, order for possession of,
      550–551
    security of tenure, and. *See* Security of
      Tenure.
Covenant,
    agricultural tenancies of. *See* Agricultural
      Tenancy, terms of assignee, burden
      and benefit on, 317–319, 321–322
    alter, not to, 111, 120–122
      consent to, withholding unreasonably,
        121
    assignment, against, 297–301, 522
    benefit of, 317–320, 324–325
    breach of. *See* Remedies.
      acts causing 130–132
      damages for, 132–133
    burden of, 317–320, 324–326
    business goodwill, protecting, 743–747
    business tenancy, of, 658–659, 692–693
    council tenancies, and, 529–545

Covenant—*cont.*
    dilapidations and inventory, for, 55
    enforcement of, 126–127
    fitness for purpose, licence implied term
      in, 10
    flats' management schemes, in 133–134
    implied, 110, 217–218, 238–250, 280–283
    indemnities, 322–323
    insure, to, 117–120
    land, running with the, 317–320, 324–326
    no-derogation from grant, implied term
      for, 9
    paint, to. *See* Repair, express covenants.
    parting with possession, against,
      305–306, 532–536
    personal representative and, 327–329
    quiet enjoyment, for, 9, 128–133
      breach of, acts causing, 130–132
      contractual licence, on, 9
      damages for breach of, 132–133
      nature of, 128–130
    rates and taxes, to pay, 112–115, 164
      assessment, 115–117
    rent, to pay, 112
    repair and maintain, etc., to. *See* Repair.
    restrictive. *See* Restrictive Covenants.
    s. 146 notice and. *See* Notice, s. 146.
    service charges, 134–136, 171–172
      shared ownership leases, and, 521–523
      rent, as, 399–400
    sub-letting, against, 303–305
    sub-tenant, burden and benefit on,
      322–324
    title, *re*, 321
    trade, in restraint of. *See* Covenant,
      business goodwill, protecting.
    trustee in bankruptcy and, 329–331
    user, *re*, 122–126
      enforcement of, 126–127
      variation, 127–128
    variation of, 127
Crown, The, 358, 395, 476

Damages. *See* Remedies,
    repudiation, on others, 97
    dangerous structure. *See* Structure.
Death,
    succession on, 438–442, 578–581
      agricultural tenancies and, 791–796
      Rent Act protected tenancy and,
        438–447
      secure tenancy and, 551, 578–581
      transfer on. *See* Transfer, death, on.
Deed,
    formal parts of a lease by, 101–102

Defective Premises Act 1972, 257
  s. 1 person working on dwelling, duty of
    care of, 371
  s. 4 disrepair, notice of, 244
  s. 4 (1) duty of reasonable care,
    landlord's, 236, 244, 249, 367
  s. 6 (2) duty of care, landlord's, 248–250
Dilapidations,
  agricultural, landlord's, claim for,
    813–816
    during tenancy, 813–814
    end of tenancy, at, 814–816
  repair and, 224–226. *See also* Repair,
    generally.
  survey and inventory on grant of lease, 78
Distress,
  rent, for. *See* Remedies, distress.
Duty. *See* Landlord, duties; Tenant, duties.
Dwelling-house. *See* Protected Tenancies,
  dwelling-house.

Easement,
  grant of, 106–107
  lease of, 51–52
  reservation of, 106–107
  rent, and, 153
Employee, Occupation as. *See* Service
  Tenancy.
Equity,
  estoppel, waiver and, 176–177
  licences, protection of, 9–13
Estate in Land, 1–8
  agricultural, 755
  compulsory purchase, transfer on, 725
  creation of. *See* Lease, creation.
  devolution of, after death, 326–327
  distribution of, after death, 328–329
  leasehold, characteristics of, 13–47
  merger of, 340–341
  termination of. *See* Termination,
    generally.
  types of, 1
Estate Management,
  leasehold estates and Leasehold Reform
    Act 1967 and, 519–520
Estoppel,
  equitable, 176–177
  grant, derogation from and, 762
  licence, by, 4
  payment of rent, by, 165–166
  proprietary, 12, 13
  rent, waiver of and, 176–177
  tenancy by, 11, 12, 79–80
Eviction. *See also* Security of Tenure.
  harassment and, 608

Eviction—*cont.*
  harassment and—*cont.*
    sanctions and remedies, 609–610
  homelessness and, 610, 619–620
  Protection from Eviction Act 1977,
    s. 1 residential occupier, protection of,
      560, 607–609
    s. 2 re-entry or forfeiture, enforcing,
      194, 361, 448, 541–542, 609
    s. 3 residential occupier, possession
      and, 448
    s. 5 notice, formal requirements of, 448
  unlawful, 607–608
    occupation, deprivation of, 607–608
    re-entry and, 609
Executors. *See also* Personal
  Representatives.
  agricultural estate of, 762–763
  estate, devolution of, on, 326–327
  estate, distribution of, 328–329

Fee Simple,
  absolute in possession, 2
Fixtures and Fittings, 55–61
  damage on removal, 61
  definition of, 55, 56–57
  first letting, installed at, 55–56
  freehold, attachment to, 57
    mode of, 58
  landlord, intended for, 58
  old tenant, left by, 61
  removal, 59
  repair, remedies in respect of, 148–150,
    295
  trade fixtures, exception, 60
Forfeiture,
  agricultural tenancies. *See* Agricultural
    Tenancies, security of tenure.
  assignment and, 298–300
  clause, need for, 351
  council housing and. *See* Council
    Housing, tenant's obligations.
  County Court, in, 198–199
  covenants outside s. 146 of the Law of
    Property Act 1925 and, 356
  disrepair, in respect of. *See* Repair,
    tenant's obligations, enforcement.
  forestalling, assistance in, 199–200
  formalities, 351–353
    irremediable breaches and, 353
    s. 146 notice, contents of, 352
  High Court, in, 196–198
  lease of, 194–196
  relief against, 196
    avoidance of, 357

Forfeiture—*cont.*
  s. 146 notice, service and effect of, and, 353–354
  sub-tenant, effect on, 354–356
Freehold, 2–3
  lease of, right to grant, 62
Furnished Tenancies, 450. *See also* Security of Tenure, generally; Restricted Contracts.

Goodwill, 739–752
  compensation for loss, of, 747–757
    amount payable, 750–751
    history of, 747–748
    misrepresentation for, 751–752
    when payable, 748–750
  compulsory purchase and, 736–737
  definition of, 739–740
  disposal of, 740–742
  protection of, 742–747
    covenant for, 743–747
      area and scope of, 745–746
      public interest and, 747
      time and, 746–747
      trade restrained and, 744–745
    no protection covenant and, 742–743
  transfer, 739–740
Grant,
  fixed term for. *See* Lease, contents fixed then periodic term for; Lease, contents.
  grantor's capacity *re* agricultural tenancies and, 762–763
  new, rent limits on, 414–415
  periodic term, for. *See* Lease contents.
  premium permitted on, 430
  premium prohibited on, 428
  profits à prendre, of, 51, 52
  right of way, of, 52
    commercial not "for purposes of business," 51
  rights, of, 102
Grantee. *See* Tenant.
Grantor. *See* Landlord.

Harassment. *See* Eviction, harassment and.
Holiday Lettings,
  out-of-season and vacation. *See* Security of Tenure, possession, mandatory Rent Act protection, as attempt to avoid, and Taxation, rental income of, 470.
  s. 9 of the Rent Act 1977, exempt from, 402–404

Homelessness and, 610–633. *See* Housing Act 1985, Pt. III.
  definition of, 619–620
  EEC nationals and, 627
  eviction and, 609–610, 620
  housing authority, powers and duties, 610–633
    enforcement of, 628–633
    homeless persons, duties to, 612–615
    intentional homelessness and, 620–627
    local connection, the, 615–617
    notification, duties of, 628
    persons threatened with homelessness, towards, 620
    preliminary duties, 611–612
    priority need and, 618–619
Housing Act 1980,
  s. 52, shorthold, protected tenancy plus further term may be, 492–493
  s. 55 (1) Rent Act Case 19 shorthold tenancy, possession of, 492–493
  s. 60 registered rent increases, two year phasing, 424
  s. 69 restricted contracts, notice and rent tribunals, 480–482
  s. 74 (1) housing associations exempted from protected tenancy status, 586
Housing Act 1985,
  s. 6, "Housing Trust", definition of, 590
  s. 8 (1) housing conditions, local authorities to consider, 525–526
  s. 21 management, general powers of, 560
  s. 22 unsanitary or overcrowded houses, local authority preference for families in, 526–527
  s. 24 (1) "reasonable" rent, 530–531
  s. 25 notice of increase of rent, 531
  Pt. III, homelessness,
  s. 58 (4) threatened with, 620
  s. 59 poverty need, categories of, 618–619
  s. 62 (1) duty to make enquiries, 611–628
  s. 60 intentional homelessness, definition of, 620–627
  s. 64 (4) notification, duty of, 628
  s. 65 obligation to rehouse, 617, 618–619
  s. 67 (2) local connection, 615
  s. 88 succession, secure tenancies and, 578–581
  s. 91 (1) assignment, 533
  s. 92 and Sched. 3 exchange, 533, 535, 551, 554
  s. 93 not to sub-let, 532
  s. 95 unsecure tenancy, assignment or sub-letting of, 534
  s. 96 right to repair, 539–541

Housing Act 1985—*cont.*
s. 97 (1) not to make improvements, 537–538
s. 101 (3) qualifying successors, 538
ss. 102, 103 variation of agreement, procedure, 528
s. 105 consultation with secure tenants *re* management, 561
s. 108 heating charges, 543
s. 115 long tenancies, definition of, 546
s. 118 right to buy, 562–565
s. 120 and Sched. 5 right to buy, excluded dwellings, 565–567
s. 122 notice claiming right to buy, 570
s. 127 valuation, 567–569
ss. 132–134 mortgage, right to a, 569, 571–2
ss. 144–153 shared ownership lease, procedure for claiming, 521–523, 574
s. 151 (2) shared ownership lease, 549
s. 158 exercise of power by local authorities, 593
s. 164 Secretary of State, powers of, 574–576
s. 183 house or flat, definition of, 561
s. 189 (1) houses repairable at reasonable expense, local authority and, 265–268
s. 190 (1) houses in disrepair, local authority and, 270–271
s. 190 (1) (3) repair notice service, local authority, by, 270
s. 207 secure tenants moving, Secretary of State powers to make grants or loans, 535
s. 210 (1) "provisional notice," local authority, service by, 275
s. 212 (1) occupying tenant's request for action, local authority to, 278–279
s. 264 (1) houses not repairable at reasonable expense, local authority and, 265–268
s. 300 (2) decision to purchase, local authority, by, 268–269
s. 612 possession needed by local authority, 557–558
Pt. III, 610–611
s. 58 homelessness, definition of, 619–620
Pts. IV and V housing association tenants, security for, 590–593
Pt. VII compulsory improvement, housing, of, 275–280
Pts. VIII and IX housing action areas, 274–275
Pt. X overcrowding, 394–395

Housing Act 1985—*cont.*
Sched. 2 statutory grounds for possession, 550, 552, 555–557, 592
Housing Associations Act 1985,
s. 1 "housing association," definition of, 583
s. 3 Housing Corporation, register of housing associations, 585
s. 4 (3) additional objects or purposes, 585–586
s. 5 housing associations, register of, 585–586, 587
s. 45 (1) grant aid, 586
Housing Associations, 583–595
definition, 583–585
Housing Corporation and, 476, 585, 586
Housing Societies and, 593–594
register, requirement to, 585–586
additional objects or purposes, 585
registration, Rent Act 1977 and, 586–587
rent, 587–588
increases, and, 588–590. *See* Rent, increases.
limit, 588–590
right to buy, the, 594–595
security of tenure, 590–593
trusts, housing, 476, 590
Housing Benefit,
standard, 597
"needs allowances," 598–599
"benefit day," 600
certificated, 601
supplementary benefit and, 601
Housing Benefits Act 1982,
rent rebate, duty to operate scheme, 529, 597
Housing Corporation, The, 476, 585–586, 594, 595
register of housing associations and, 585–586
Housing Financial Assistance, 597–605
disturbance, compensation for, 602–605
home loss payments, 602–603
payments for, 603
removal expenses and, 604–605
Homeless Persons. *See* Housing Act 1985, Pt. III.
Housing Society. *See* Housing Association; housing societies and.

Improvement,
agricultural tenancy, to, 804–808
business tenancy, to, 662–672
compulsory, 275–279
course, choice of, 279–280

Improvement—*cont.*
  compulsory—*cont.*
    local authority action, 275–278
    occupying tenant action, 278–279
  council housing, to, 537–538
  renewal, repair and, 226–233. *See also*
    Repair, generally.
Insurance,
  agricultural tenancy, of, 769
  covenant in respect of, 117–120
Intention. *See* Tenancy.
Interests,
  agricultural, nature of, 760–764
  creation of, 49
  occupier's, 9–13
  transfer of, 301–313

Joint Tenants,
  licences, as opposed to, 22

Land Compensation Act 1973, 728–730,
    733, 734, 738
Landlord,
  agricultural. *See* Agricultural Tenancies,
    generally.
  "approved body" in creation of assured
    tenancies, 496
  assignee, relationship with, 316–321
  company, as, business tenancies and,
    703–704
  competent, the, 683–684, 690,
    717–718
  duties of. *See also* Repairs, landlord's
    express covenants; Repairs,
    landlord's obligations.
    care. *See* Third Parties, landlord's
      liability to.
    Defective Premises Act 1972, under,
      367
    fair rent certificate, under, 493–494
    Occupier's Liability Act 1957, under,
      366–367
    repair. *See* Repair.
    third parties, to. *See* Third Parties,
      landlord's liability to.
    trespasser, to, 367
  exclusion of, 15–17
  generally, 1–3, 13–14
  mesne, 525, 661
  non-payment of rent, remedies for,
    194–205
  opposition to business tenancy, intention
    in, 704–705
  restricted contracts and, 476

Landlord—*cont.*
  retirement home under the Rent Act
    1977, and, 460–461
  rights of. *See also* Covenants, generally;
    Repair, tenant's obligations.
    entry to repair, 283–286
    forfeiture and, 351
    third parties, against, 369–370
  tenant and, 1–5
  title, capacity to grant, 62–63
  trespasser, as, 370
  trustee, as, business tenancies and,
    702–703
Landlord and Tenant Acts, The,
  Landlord and Tenant Act 1927, the,
    s. 1 (1) improvement to business
      tenancy, assessing compensation,
      668–669
    s. 2 (3) compensation for
      improvements, service of claim
      for, 668
    s. 10 inspection of improvements,
      landlord's entry for, 668
    s. 17 "business" premises entitled to
      compensation, 663
    s. 18 (1) breach of repairing covenant,
      damages for, 286–289
    s. 19 assignment with consent of
      landlord, 300
    s. 25 mining lease, definition of, 649
    Pt. I business premises, etc., 637–640,
      663, 664, 667, 668
  Landlord and Tenant Act 1954, the,
    s. 2 "qualifying conditions" for long
      tenancies, 498–500
    s. 23 "occupation" of "business"
      tenancy, meaning of, 642–646
    s. 24 security for business tenancies,
      673, 674, 675, 676, 677, 679–682,
      687
    s. 25 landlord's notice to business
      tenant, 673, 675, 676, 682–685,
      686, 687, 692, 707–708, 749
    s. 26 new business tenancy, tenant's
      request for, 673, 687–689,
      690–691, 692, 708, 749
    s. 27 business tenant's notice, 673, 677,
      687, 689
    s. 28 ending continuation tenancy,
      tenant's notice, 688
    s. 30 (1) (*a*)–(*g*) business tenancy,
      grounds of opposition to, 685–686,
      692, 694–704, 728, 748–749, 751

Landlord and Tenant Acts, The—*cont.*
Landlord and Tenant Act 1954, the—
    cont.
    s. 31A (Law of Property Act 1969,
        amendment by) demolition or
        reconstruction, landlord's access
        for, 698–701
    s. 34 rent, determination of, 711–715
    s. 34 (1) (*a*)–(*d*) determination of
        rent, matters to disregard in,
        711–713
    s. 34 (2) improvements to business
        tenancy at tenant's expense, 669
    s. 37 (1) loss of business goodwill,
        compensation for, 749
    s. 38 business tenancies, anti-
        avoidance provisions *re*, 641–642,
        655–656
    s. 39 compulsory purchase, 728–730
    s. 41 (2) trustee, landlord as, 702
    s. 42 (3) company as landlord, 703
    s. 43 short, temporary business
        tenancies, 652
    s. 44 (1) competent landlord,
        definition of, 683–684
    s. 47 claim for improvements against
        landlord, time limits for, 668
    s. 55 misrepresentation, compensation
        for, 751–752
    s. 57 rights of some business tenancies,
        limitation of, 650–651
    Pt. I long leaseholders, 497–512
    Pt. II business tenancies and assured
        tenancies, 495–496, 640, 649, 650,
        655, 664, 668, 673
    Pt. III business tenancies,
        compensation for improvements
        to, 663–671
    Sched. 3 long leaseholder, cases for
        possession against, 502
    Sched. 6 sub-tenancies, provisions in
        respect of, 717–718
    licence, to avoid security under, 5
Landlord and Tenant Act 1985,
    s. 8 (1) fitness for habitation, generally,
        221, 239–241
    s. 10 unfitness for habitation, matters
        to which regard must be had,
        241–243
    s. 11 (1) structure and essential
        services, landlord's implied
        obligations, 134, 236, 243–248,
        285, 486, 528, 543
        landlord, right to re-entry, 285
    s. 17 specific performance, *re* repair
        covenants, 253

Lands Tribunal, The, 720
Law of Property Act 1925, The,
    s. 62 rights included in a grant, 104–105
    s. 79 (1) successors in title, covenants
        binding, 299
    s. 141 benefit of covenant, annexation of,
        324–325
    s. 142 burden of covenant, annexation of,
        324–325
    s. 146 breach of covenant, notice in
        respect of, 289–293, 637, 790–791.
        See also Notice, s. 146.
    s. 196 notice to quit, service of, 349
Lease,
    agreement for, 13–20
    agricultural tenancy of. *See* Agricultural
        Tenancy, terms of.
    assignment of, 301, 302–303
    break clause, on, 6, 41
    characteristics of, 13–47
        agreement, terms of, 20–24
        creation, mode of, 13–15. *See also*
            Lease, creation of.
        duration. *See* Lease, duration.
        intention, 20–26
        occupation, exclusive, 4, 15–17
    compulsory purchase and, 724–726
    concurrent, 39, 53–54
    contents, 101–150, 657–659, 677–682,
        708–717, 769–777
        agricultural tenancy, of, 769–777
        arbitration clauses, 147
        break clauses, 109–110, 138–139
        business goodwill, covenant
            protecting, 743–747
        business tenancies, of, 657–659,
            677–682
        costs, *re*, 147–148
        covenants. *See* covenant.
        exceptions and reservations, 105
        first refusal, 144
        fixed term, grant of, 107–108
        fixed then periodic terms, grant for,
            109–110
        habendum, the, 101, 107–110
        new business tenancy of, 708–717
        options, 101
        parcels, the, 102–105
        periodic terms, grants of, 108–109
        pre–emption, rights of, 144, 300
        premises, the, 101, 102–107
        prohibition against assignment. *See*
            Assignment, prohibition of.
        protection of, 145–146
        purchase, option to, 142–143

Lease—*cont.*
  contents—*cont.*
    reddendum, the, 101, 110. *See also*
      Rent.
    rent review and, 184
    renew, option to, 136, 139–142
    shorthold tenancies, *re*, 493–495
    suspension of rent, proviso for, 137
  contract for. *See* Contract, lease, for.
  costs of, 89–90
  creation, 11–47, 49–99
    agents and attorneys, by, 71
    business tenancies, of. *See* Business
      Tenancies, creation.
    charity trustees, by, 66–67
    companies, trading, by, 69–70
    complete, failure to. *See* Contract,
      complete, failure to; Contract,
      specific performance.
    concurrent and in reversion. *See* Lease,
      concurrent; Lease, reversion, in.
    counterpart, of, 88
    dilapidations survey and inventory. *See*
      Dilapidations, survey and
      inventory.
    estoppel, tenancy by, 14, 79–80. *See*
      also Estoppel, payment of rent,
      by.
    execution, 88–89
      in "escrow", 89
    fixtures and fittings. *See* Fixtures and
      Fittings.
    formalities, 87–89
    intermittent use, lettings involving,
      50–51
    local authorities, by, 70
    mode of, 11–47
    mortgagor and mortgagee, by, 67–69
    orally, 87–88
    personal representatives, by, 64–65
    planning and, 73–74
    premiums and Capital Gains Tax,
      90–92. *See also* Premiums,
      assignment, on; Taxation,
      premiums, of.
    property, identity of, 50, 83
    restrictive covenants and, 73–78. *See*
      also Restrictive Covenants.
    reversion, in, 53–55
    rights only, grant of, 51–52
    sole owner, by, 62
    tenant, competency of, and, 71
    title, landlord's capacity to grant, 62
    trustees and beneficiaries and, 64–66
  deed, need for, 55, 71, 87–89
  duration of, 36–38

Lease—*cont.*
  duration of—*cont.*
    certainty of, 38–40
    death or marriage, until, 41
    fixed term of years, for, 38–42, 108–109
    periodic tenancies, 109–110. *See*
      Tenancy, periodic.
    perpetuity rule applied to, 38
    renewable perpetually, 38, 46, 47
    sufferance, tenancies at. *See* Tenancy,
      sufferance, at.
    war, for, 40
    will, tenancies at. *See* Tenancy, will, at.
  enfranchisement of. *See* Leasehold
    Reform Act 1967.
  extension of. *See* Leasehold Reform Act
    1967; Business Tenancies,
    exclusions, leases, extended.
  legal estate, as, 3, 5, 9, 38
  licence and, 9–47
    orally, 87–88
    special circumstances, 16
  long. *See* Long Leaseholder, The.
  merger of. *See* Termination, merger.
  mining. *See* Business Tenancies,
    exclusions, mining leases.
  notices, service of, 146–147
  operation of, 151–214
    rent. *See* Rent.
  oral, 49, 87–88
  perpetually renewable, 46–47
  property,
    identity of, 50
    tenant's purpose, fitness for, 72–78
  remedies in respect of the, 148–150
  renewal of,
    option in respect of, 139–142
    perpetuity, in, 45–47
  reversion, in, 54, 55
    deed, need for, 55
  service charges. *See* Covenant.
  shared ownership, 520–523. *See also*
    Council Tenancy.
    acquisition of, 521–523
    buying landlords interest, 521
    covenants, against assignment, 522
    discount, 522
    length of lease, 521
    rent, 522
    terms of, 521
  sham transaction, 20–24
  short—business premises of, 652
  sub-lease, repair and, 289
  termination of. *See* Termination terms;
    Covenant; Lease, contents,
    variation and waiver of, 84

Lease—*cont.*
  written, 49, 83, 84
Leasehold Reform Act 1967, The, 503–520
  enfranchising and, 513–519
    price of, the, 515–519
    procedure of, 513–515
    statutory restrictions on, 518–519
  estate management schemes and,
      519–520
  premises within, 505–509
    leasehold house, the, 505–508
    rateable values of, 508–509
  purpose and policy of, 503–505
  tenancies within, 509–511
    long tenancies, 509–510
    low rents and, 510–511
  tenants within, 511–512
Leasehold Property (Repairs) Act 1938
  generally, 289–291
  tenants relief, 284
Lessee. *See* Tenant.
Licence,
  agreement, so called, 5
  Agricultural Holdings Act 1986, covered
      by, 761–762, 764
  assignment, 10
  bare, 3
  bed-sitters, 5
  characteristics of, 3, 13,–36
    agreement, terms of, 20–24
    duration, 36, 37
    intention, 17–26
    landlord, exclusion of, 15–17
  commercial, 652–655
  equity and, 11
  estoppel, by, 11, 12
  exclusive possession and, 15–17
  family arrangements, 31
  intention. *See* Licence, characteristics.
  irrevocable, 11, 13
  lease and, 19–47, 483
  lodgings, and, 28–31
  Rent Act protection, avoiding, 468–471
  secure tenancy and, 545
  service occupancy and, 27–28
  sub-letting, 10
  tenancy at will, and, 45
Licensee,
  death of,
    occupation rights, transmission of, 11
    termination, 11
  position of, 9–13
  unlawful, Rent Act 1977 and, 470
Local Authorities,
  abuse of power by. *See* Remedies, abuse
      of power, defence of.

Local Authorities—*cont.*
  compulsory purchase and. *See*
      Compulsory Purchase, generally.
  housing and. *See* Council Housing.
  Landlord, as. *See* Council Housing,
      generally; Secure Tenancy,
      generally.
  Landlord's repairing obligations and,
      259–279
    area action and, 273–275
    compulsory improvement and,
        275–279
    human habitation, fitness for, 264–270
    statutory nuisance and, 259–264
  lease, creation of, by. *See* Lease, creation
      of.
  lettings by. *See* Council Housing,
      generally; Lease, creation of.
  possession by. *See* Council Housing,
      security of tenure; Secure Tenancy,
      The, possession.
  remedies against. *See* Remedies,
      homelessness, in respect of;
      Remedies, abuse of power, defence
      of; Remedies, *ultra vires*, defence of.
  rent increases and. *See* Rent, increases.
  rent of council houses. *See* Council
      Housing, tenant's obligations.
  rent rebates and. *See* Housing Financial
      Assistance, rent rebates and
      allowances and.
  rent tribunal, reference to, 477–479
  secure tenancies and. *See* Secure
      Tenancy, The.
  statutory nuisance, causing, 264
  tenants, selection of and. *See* Council
      Housing, tenants, selection of.
  ultra vires, acting. *See* Remedies, *ultra
      vires*, defence of.
Long Leaseholder, The, 497–523
  Landlord and Tenant Act 1954,
      protection under, 497–503
    continuation and termination of the
        tenancy, 500–502
    qualifying tenants and, 498–500
    repairs, 502–503
  Leasehold Reform Act 1967 and. *See*
      Leasehold Reform Act 1967,
  secure tenancy status, exempt from, 546

Maintenance. *See* Repair.
Market Gardens, 812–813
Matrimonial Causes Act 1973. *See*
    Spouse, Matrimonial Causes Act
    1973.

Matrimonial Homes Act 1983, 442–445. *See also* Spouse.
Merger of Lease. *See* Termination, merger.
Misrepresentation, 490
  business tenancy and, compensation for, 751–752
Mortgage, right to, 569
Mortgagee/Mortgagor,
  lease, creation of, by, 67–69
Mowing or Grazing, Lettings for, 705–706

Negligence, 1, 37. *See* Defective Premises Act 1972; Landlord, duties of; Third Parties, landlord's liability to; Third Parties, tenant's liability to.
Notice,
  blight, 735
  breach of agricultural tenancy, to remedy, 786–789
  enfranchisement, of, 513
  entry under compulsory purchase, procedure, of, 725, 726–728
  intention, of,
    business tenancy, improving, 666
    shorthold, to possess, 494–495
  lease, service on. *See* Lease, notice, service of.
  quit, to, 341–351
    agricultural holding, and, 573, 776–777. *See also* Agricultural Holdings (Notices to Quit) Act 1977.
    authority, authenticity and service of, 348–350
    effect of, 350
    legal requirements of, 342–350
    length of, 343–346
    operational date of, 346–348
    restrictive contracts, of, 482
    shorthold tenancy and, 494–495
    tenant's. *See* Security of Tenure.
  rent of agricultural tenancy, to pay, 785–786
  short, 811
  s. 25 of the Landlord and Tenant Act 1954, under. *See* Business Tenancies, termination by landlord.
  s. 26 of the Landlord and Tenant Act 1954, under. *See* Business Tenancies, new tenancy, tenant's request for.
  s. 146 of the Law of Property Act 1925, under, 351–357
    avoid, attempts to, 357
    contents of, 352

Notice—*cont.*
  s. 146 of the Law of Property Act 1925, under—*cont.*
    covenants outside, 356
    irremediable breaches and, 353
    service and effect of, 353–354
    sub-tenants, effect on, 354–356
  treat in compulsory purchase proceedings, to, 720–722
  works of repair to agricultural tenancy, to do, 786–789
Nuisance. *See also* Third Parties, generally.
  landlord, by 367–369
  possession under Rent Act 1977, case for. *See* Security of Tenure, possession.
  statutory, 269–274. *See also* Public Health Act 1936.
  tenant, by, 369
  third parties, by, 370

Occupation. *See also* Possession.
  business tenancy, of, 642–646
  employer's work, for the purposes of performing, 4
  exclusive, 4, 15–17
    agricultural holding and, 761
    restricted contract and, 474
  intermittent, 50–51
  "non-exclusive agreements", 21–22
  rent. *See* Rent, payment of.
  rights of, 4–6
Occupiers Liability Act 1957,
  duty of care of legal occupier, 248–250
  visitors, to, 366–367
Option,
  purchase, to. *See* Lease, contents.
  renew, to. *See* Lease, contents.
Owner,
  compulsory purchase and. *See* Compulsory Purchase, generally.
Owner-Occupier,
  compulsory purchase and, 724
  possession and, 458–460

Parties,
  intention of,
  relationship between, 17–24
  third. *See* Third Parties.
Partners,
  lettings, by, 71
Part-Performance,
  contracts evidenced by, 86–87
Personal Representatives,
  assignee, liability as, 327–328

Personal Representatives—*cont.*
  assignee-tenant, on death of, 328
  covenants and. *See* Covenants, personal
    representatives and.
  estate, devolution of, 326–327
  estate, distribution of, 328–329
  lease, creation of, and. *See* Lease,
    creation of.
  tenant, on death of, 327
Planning. *See also* Town and Country
    Planning Acts, The.
  agricultural holding, permission to
    develop part of, 800
  business user and, 658–659
  compulsory purchase and, 719, 723–724
  lease and, creation of. *See* Lease,
    creation of.
Possession,
  adverse,
    squatters, by, 337
    wrongful receipt of rent, by, 173
  agricultural tenancies, of. *See*
    Agricultural Tenancies, security of
    tenure.
  agricultural tied houses, of. *See*
    Agricultural Tied Houses,
    possession
  business tenancy, of. *See* Business
    Tenancies, termination and
    renewals.
  compulsory purchase, by. *See*
    Compulsory Purchase, generally.
  council houses, of. *See* Council Housing,
    security of tenure; Secure Tenancy.
  County Court proceedings, 361–362
  exclusive, 15–17
    tenancy presumption, 17
  grounds for under Rent Acts. *See*
    Security of Tenure, possession.
  High Court proceedings, 362–363
  long tenancy at low rent, of, 502
  "not to part with," 305–306, 532–536
  recovery of. *See* Termination, possession
    and.
  restricted contract and, 482
  secure tenancy, of. *See* Secure Tenancy,
    possession.
  security of tenure and. *See* Security of
    Tenure.
  self-help and, 360
  shortholds, of. *See* Shorthold Tenancy,
    possession and.
  sub-tenant, against a, 463–467, 490–491
Powers of Attorney, 71
Premises. *See* Lease, contents.
  unoccupied, 272

Premium,
  assignment, on, 429, 434–436
    furniture, payments for, 428, 438
    lawful payments, and, 436
    meaning of, 434–435
    prohibition of, 428, 435–436
    restricted contracts and, 438
    statutory tenancies and, 438
    tenancy, effect on of illegal premiums,
      437
  business tenancy improvements as,
    671–672
  definition of, 428, 435
  permitted,
    assignment on, 430–431
  prohibited, 428
    assignment, payments on. *See*
      Premium, assignment, on.
    furniture, excessive price for, 428–429
    grants, on, 428
    other payments and, 430
    rent, pre-payments of, 429
  rent, distinguished from, 173
  taxation of. *See* Taxation, premiums, of.
Protected Occupiers. *See* Agricultural Tied
    Houses, protected occupiers.
Protected Shorthold Tenancy, The. *See*
    Shorthold Tenancy.
Protected Tenancies, 378–404
  assured tenancies, and, 398–399
  business premises of. *See* Business
    Tenancies.
  caravans, etc., and, 380
  dwelling-house let as a separate dwelling,
    378–388
    deeming provisions, 391–404
    "dwelling," meaning of, 386–388
    house or part of house must be,
      379–380
    letting, purpose of the, 380–382
    rateable value on particular dates,
      388–391. *See also* "Appropriate
      Day," The.
    separate dwelling, let as, 380–388
    shared premises and, 382–386
  exemptions, 391–404
    agricultural holdings, 393
    assured tenancies, 398–399
    board or attendance provided, 400–402
    Crown property, 395
    educational institutions, lettings by,
      398
    exempt bodies and, 395
    holiday homes, 402–404
    houses let with substantial quantity of
      land, 392

Protected Tenancies—*cont.*
  exemptions—*cont.*
    low rent, tenancies at, 399–400
    ministerial order, by, 404
    mixed business and residential
      regulated tenancies, 392–393
    overcrowded or insanitary dwellings,
      394
    parsonage houses, 393
    public houses, 393
    resident landlord and, 395–397
    sharing with landlord, 398
  repairs, 211, 218. *See also* Repair,
    tenant's obligations.
  rent, variation of, 416–418
  security of tenure. *See* Security of
    Tenure.
  shorthold tenancy. *See* Shorthold
    Tenancy.
Protection from Eviction Act 1977. *See*
  Eviction.
Provisions. *See* Covenant; Lease, contents.
Proviso. *See* Lease, contents.
Public Health Act 1936,
  s. 92 (1) nuisance, statutory, 259–264,
    279–280
  s. 99 statutory nuisance, action of person
    aggrieved by, 264, 544

Quiet Enjoyment. *See* Covenant.

Regulated Tenancies, 411, 447–449. *See
  also* Statutory Tenancy.
Remedies,
  abuse of power, defence of, 558–560
  breach of covenant, for, 126–127,
    130–133, 148–156
  damages, 94–98, 111–112
  forfeiture. *See* Forfeiture.
  homelessness and, 628–633. *See also*
    Homelessness, enforcement and.
    injunction, mandatory, 630
    interim relief, 630–632
    maladministration, complaint of, 633
  judicial review, application for, 628–629
  limitation, common law, by, 632–633
    statutory duty, for breach of, 629–630
  local authority, complaint to, 259–280
    abatement notices, 263
    area action, 273–275
    closing order, 279
    compensation, order for, 263
    compulsory improvement, 275, 278
    condensation, and, 260–261

Remedies—*cont.*
  local authority, complaint to—*cont.*
    dangerous structures, 272–273
    demolition order, 279
    fine, 263
    occupying tenant, actions and, 278–279
    prejudicial to health, 264
    "provisional notice," 275–278
    unoccupied premises, 273
  penal rent, 170–172
    liquidated damages or penalty as, 172
  possession. *See* Possession.
  rent, for non-payment of, 194–206
    arrears, action for, 202, 529–530
    bankruptcy and liquidation, on,
      202–205
    distress for, 200–202
    forfeiture. *See* Forfeiture.
    possession, 451–452, 785–786
  repairs, in respect of landlord's, 250–280
    damages, 250–253
    declaration, 253–254
    local authority, complaint to, 259–280
    negligence action, 257
    receiver, appointment of, 258
    specific performance, 253
    settlement and undertaking, 257
    set-off, 254–257
  repairs, in respect of tenant's, 283–295
    damages, 286–291
    entry, right of, exercise of, 283–286
    fixtures, of. *See* Fixtures and Fittings,
      repair.
    forfeiture, 291–293
    long leaseholder, against, 502–503
    specific performance, 293
    waste, 293–294
  specific performance, 96–99, 253, 293
  ultra vires, defence of, 557–558
Rent,
  agricultural tenancy, of. *See* Agricultural
    Tenancies, terms of, rent.
  arrears. *See* Remedies, non-payment of
    rent, for.
  ascertainability, need for, 155–156
  book, provision of, 431–432
  business tenancy, of. *See* Business
    Tenancies, improvements,
    compensation for, rent, effect on;
    Business Tenancies, terms, rent.
  control. *See* Rent Control.
  council house, of, 529–532
  different kinds and other payments,
    166–173
    best, 170
    charge, 166

Rent—*cont.*
  different kinds and other payments—
      cont.
    dead, 170
    "equity," 167
    ground, 170
    insurance, 169
    net, 169
    penal, 170–172
    peppercorn, 166
    premium and, 173, 428, 429. *See also*
        Premium, generally.
    progressive, 167
    rack, 167
    seck, 166
    service, 166
    service charge and, 171–172
    sliding scale, 168
  distress for. *See* Remedies, non-payment
      of rent, for.
  fair. *See* Rent Control, fair rents.
  free, 44
  frustration of contract, and, 153
  gold clauses and, 191–192
  housing association tenancy, of. *See*
      Housing Association, rent.
  index linked clauses, 191–192
  interim, 679–682
  increases, 177–178, 531–532
  levels, determination of, 185–191
  limits. *See* Rent Control, limits on new
      grants.
  low, tenancy at a, 399–400, 510–511
  nature of, 151–157
  non-payment of,
    effect of, 173
    landlord's remedies for, 194–205
    reduction and, 174–176
    suspension of, and, 174
    waiver, 176–177
  payment of, 159–173
    apportionment of, 165
    deductions and, 164
    estoppel by, 165–166
    manner of, 160–161
    receipts for, 163
    recipient of, 162–163
    time of, 159–160
    whom, by, 161–162
  payment in lieu for occupation at
      expiration of lease, 192–193
  premiums and. *See* Rent, different kinds
      and other payments.
  quarter days and, usual, 159–160
  "reasonable," 530–531
  reddendum, 151

Rent—*cont.*
  registration of, 413–414, 418–427,
      477–480, 587–588
    fair rent, determination of, 424–427
    first registration, 418–419
    procedure, 419–424
    re-registration, 419
  rental income and, taxation of. *See*
      Taxation, rental income, of.
  reservation of, 106–107, 151
  restricted contracts and, 477–480
  review clauses, 156, 178–184
    agreement or arbitration and,
        178–179, 182–183
    automatic, 179
    back-dating and, 183–184
    break clauses and, 180–181
    time of the essence and, the question
        of, 179–180, 181–184
    void for uncertainty, 178
  service, 151–152
  services or goods in lieu of, 157–158
  suspension of, proviso for. *See* Lease,
      contents.
  variation of, 416–427
    agreement, by, 416–418
    obtaining registered rent, by, 418–427
Rent Act 1977, The,
  s. 1 "house let as a dwelling," meaning of,
      379–380, 380–382, 386–388
  s. 2 statutory tenancy, the, 407–410, 443
  s. 3 terms and conditions *re* statutory
      tenant, 410, 448
  s. 4 "appropriate day," the, 388–391,
      587
  s. 5 service charges and rent levels,
      399–400
  s. 6 dwelling-house let with land on
      another site, 392
  s. 7 board or attendance provided,
      400–402
  s. 8 educational establishments. lettings
      by, 398
  s. 9 holiday homes, 402–404
  s. 12 resident landlords, 395–397
  s. 13 Crown property, 395
  ss. 14–16 exempt bodies, 395, 586-587,
      591
  s. 18 regulated tenancies, 411
  s. 19 restricted contracts, 474, 475, 476,
      477, 593
  s. 21 sharing with landlord, 398
  s. 22 sharing with others, 383–386
  s. 26 land let with house, 392
  s. 44 rent, maximum recoverable, 414,
      418

Rent Act 1977, The—*cont.*

ss. 45, 46, 47 rent of statutory tenancies, varying, 417

s. 49 Rent (Forms, etc.) Regulations 1978, 424

s. 51 rent increase agreements, 414, 416

s. 52 (as amended) controlled tenancies, rent increases and, 417–418

s. 67 (as amended) re-registration of rent, 417, 588

s. 68 fair rent, application to register, 418, 590

s. 69 fair rent, certificate of, 415, 588

s. 70 fair rent assessment, matters to disregard in, 424–425, 588

s. 71 determined registered rent, composition of, 423, 588

s. 73 registered rent, cancellation of, 417

s. 77 rent tribunals, references by tenants, 477–478

s. 78 rent tribunal's duties, 478

s. 79 rent register, the, 479

s. 80 restricted contract rent, cancellation and reconsideration of, 479–480

s. 81 restricted contracts, excess rent of, 479

s. 86 housing association tenancy, rent regulation of, 398–399, 587

s. 88 registered housing association tenancies, rent limit for, 588

s. 89 (as amended) increases of registered rent, phasing of, 589

s. 93 housing association rents, increasing, 589–590

s. 98 possession, grounds for, 447–449, 458, 553

s. 101 overcrowding, 394–395

s. 103 notice to quit of restricted contract, suspension of, 480–481

s. 104 suspension of notice to quit, continued, 481

s. 106 possession and restricted contracts, 481

s. 119 illegal premiums, 428, 436

s. 120 premiums on assignment of protected tenancy, 429, 431, 435, 436, 438

s. 122 grant or assignment of restricted contract, premiums on, 438

s. 123 furniture, 428, 438

s. 125 illegal premiums, effect of, 428

s. 126 pre-payments of rent, prohibition of, 429–430

s. 127 permitted premiums, 430, 431

s. 128 premiums defined, 430, 435

s. 137 sub-tenants, protection of, 466

Rent Act 1977, The—*cont.*

s. 141 jurisdiction, 478

s. 143 ministerial exemptions, 404

s. 148 entry to repair, landlord's right, 218

Pt. V sharing with landlord, 383, 590

Pt. VI housing associations, rent registration and, 588

Sched. 1 succession and transfer, 433, 438–442

Sched. 1 para. 12 illegal premiums, 410

Sched. 8 (as amended) registered rent increases, phasing of, 424, 589

Sched. 10 rent assessment committees, 421

Sched. 11 rent registration procedure, 420–421

Sched. 15 possession, cases for, 397, 553

case 1 alternative accommodation suitable, 450–451; non-payment of rent and other breaches, 451–452

case 2 nuisance, immoral or illegal user, 452

case 3 dwelling-house, deterioration of, 453

case 4 furniture, deterioration of, 453

case 5 notice to quit, tenant's, 453

case 6 assignment or sub-letting without consent, 453–454

case 8 employee, premises required for, 454–455

case 9 landlord or family, premises required for, 455–457

case 10 sub-tenants, over-charging, 457

case 11 (as amended) owner-occupier, dwelling-house let by, 369, 458–460,

case 12 (as amended) retirement home, landlord's, 460–461

case 13 out-of-season lettings, 461

case 14 vacation lettings, 461–462

case 15 ministers of religion, lettings of dwellings for, 393, 462

case 19 (introduced by Housing Act 1980) shorthold tenancy, possession of, 492–494

case 20 (introduced by Housing Act 1980) servicemen, lettings by, 462–463

Sched. 18 Pt. I lawful premiums, 436

Rent (Agriculture) Act 1976. *See* Agricultural Tied Houses.

Rent Assessment Committee. *See* Rent Control, variation and.

Rent Control, 413–432

anti-avoidance provisions, 428–432

Rent Control—*cont.*
  anti-avoidance provisions—*cont.*
    Accommodation Agencies Act 1953, 432
    associated payments, prohibition of, 428–430
    furniture, excessive price for, 428–429
    premiums, permitted, 430–431
    premiums, prohibited, 429
    rent books and, 431–432
  assured tenant and, 495–495
  fair rent and, 424–427, 493–494, 587–588
  housing association tenancies, of, 587–590
  limits on new grants and, 414–415
    previous registered rent and, 414–415
    registered rent, no previous, 414
  rent assessment committee and, 419–424
  rent officer and, 418–419
  restricted contracts and, 477–480
  suspension, proviso for, 137
  variation and, 416–428
    agreement, by, 416–418
    obtaining registered rent, by, 418–428
Rent Officer. *See* Rent Control, variation and.
Rent Tribunal, 477–480, 593. *See also* Restricted Contracts.
Repair and Maintenance,
  agricultural, 772–774, 813–816
  council housing, of, 538–541
  Defective Premises Act 1972 and. *See* Defective Premises Act 1972.
  dilapidations survey and inventory, 57
  express provisions in respect of, 217–250
    buildings erected during the term and, 224
    fair wear and tear excepted and, 224–226
    fire, liability in the case of, 233–234
    good, habitable or tenantable repair, 220–223
    improvement renewal and, 226–233
    keep in repair, to, 219
    leave in repair, to, 219
    paint, to, 223
    put in repair, to, 220
  fixtures, remedies in respect of, 148–150
  houses, in, 270–272
  landlord's express covenants, 234–238
    notice, requirement of, 235–236
    structural repairs and, 236–237
  landlord's implied obligations and, 238–250
    habitation, fitness for, 239–243
    housing stock, condition of, 238–239

Repair and Maintenance—*cont.*
  landlord's implied obligations and—*cont.*
    "right to repair," 539–541
    safe premises, duty of care to ensure, 248–250
    secure tenancies and, 542–545
    structure, in respect of, 243–248
  landlord's obligations and, enforcement of, 250–280
    breach, damages for, 250–253
    declaration, 253–254
    local authority, complaint to, 259–280
    negligence action, 257
    nuisance, statutory, 259–264
    receiver, appointment of, 258
    set-off, rent, against, 254–257
    settlement and undertaking, 257
    specific performance, 253
  Leasehold Property (Repairs) Act 1938, 289–291
  long lease, under. *See* Long Leaseholder, The, repairs.
  Occupiers' Liability Act 1957 and. *See* Occupiers' Liability Act 1957.
  tenant's implied obligations, 280–283
    user, tenant-like, 282–283
    waste, 280–282
  tenant's obligations, enforcement of, 283–295
    damages, action for, 286
    entry, right of, 283
    forfeiture and, 291–293
    former tenants, liability of, 294–295
    sub-leases, 289
    specific performance, 293
    waste and, 280–282
Residential Tenancies,
  protected tenancies. *See* Protected Tenancies.
  statutory tenancies. *See* Statutory Tenancy.
Restricted Contracts, 473–482
  definition of, 474–476
    agreement, nature of, 475–476
    landlord, nature of, 476
    rateable value, property exceeding, 475
  premiums and, 438
  principal types, 476–478
    attendance, furniture or services and, 476–477
    resident or sharing landlords, 476
  restrictions, the statutory, 477–482
    rent and, 477–480
    security and, 480–482

Restricted Contracts—*cont.*
  s. 69 of the Housing Act 1980 and
    480–482, 609
  termination, notice, 482
Restrictive Covenants,
  freeholder, on grant by, 74–76
  leaseholder, on grant by, 76–77
Reversion, 54–55

Sale,
  compulsory purchase compensation
    valuation and, 730–737
  council houses, of. *See* Council Housing,
    disposal
Secure Tenancy, The, 545–557. *See also*
  Council Housing.
  creation of leases, 70
  death and succession and, 551, 578–581
  exemptions from, 546–549
    agricultural holdings, 548
    development land, 547
    homeless persons and, 547
    Landlord and Tenant Act 1954, Pt. II,
      tenancies within, 549
    licensed premises, 549
    long tenancies, 546
    persons seeking employment,
      tenancies to, 547–548
    service tenancies, 546
    short-term arrangements, 548
    student lettings, 549
    temporary accommodation, 548
  expiration of, 550
  forfeiture, court order and, 292, 541–542.
    See also Law of Property Act 1925,
    s. 146.
  housing association of, 591–593
  possession, proceedings for, 552–557
    accommodation, suitable alternative
      and, 553–554
    ground: alternative accommodation,
      mandatory offer of, 555
    ground: reasonableness and offer of
      alternative accommodation,
      mandatory, 555–556
    ground: reasonableness is overriding
      criterion, 554–555
    notice, service of, 552
    order, reasonableness of, 553
    orders, postponing or suspending, 557
  repair. *See* Repair, tenant's obligations.
  status of, losing, 549–552
    court order, by, 550–551
    right to buy, by exercise of, 549
    sub-letting and assignment and, 551

Secure Tenancy, The—*cont.*
  status of, losing—*cont.*
    time, by effluxion of, 550
Security of Tenure,
  agricultural tenants. *See* Agricultural
    Tenancies, security of tenure.
  assured tenant, of the, 495–496
  business tenancy, of. *See* Business
    Tenancies, termination and
    renewals, statutory protection.
  council housing and. *See* Council
    Housing security of tenure; Secure
    Tenancy, The.
  forfeiture, enforcing. *See* Forfeiture,
    lease of
  housing association tenancy, of. *See*
    Housing Associations, security of
    tenure.
  long leaseholder, of. *See* Long
    Leaseholder, continuation and
    termination of the tenancy.
  possession, discretionary grounds for,
    449–458
    accommodation, suitable alternative,
      450–451
    assignment/sub-letting whole without
      consent, 453–454
    dwelling-house, deterioration of, 453
    employee, premises required for,
      454–455
    furniture, deterioration of, 453
    notice to quit, tenant's, 453
    nuisance, immoral or illegal user, 452
    rent, non-payment of and other
      breaches, 451–452
    residence for landlord or family,
      premises required for, 455–457
    sub-tenants, overcharging, 457
  possession, mandatory grounds for,
    458–463
    landlord's retirement home, 460–461
    ministers of religion, dwellings let for,
      462
    out-of-season lettings, 461
    owner-occupier, dwelling-house let by,
      458–460
    servicemen, lettings by, 462–463
    vacation lettings, 461–462
  procedure, 467–468
    enforcement, 468
    jurisdiction, 467
    orders and suspended orders, 467–468
  Rent Act protection, attempts to avoid,
    468–471
    "bed and breakfast" lets, 470–471
    "holiday let", the, 470

Security of Tenure—*cont.*
  Rent Act protection, attempts to
      avoid—*cont.*
    licences, 469
    registered rent, disregard of, 469
    rental purchase, 471
    sub-tenant or licensee, unlawful, 470
  secure tenancy and, 545–546
  shorthold tenancies and, 493–495
  sub-tenants and, 463–467
    statutory protection of, 464–467
    sub-tenancies, lawful creation of,
        463–464
  terminating the tenancy, 447–449. *See
      also* Termination
Service Charge. *See* Covenant.
Service Tenancy, The,
  business tenancy and, 650
  occupancy and, 27–28, 483–484
  possession of, 454–455, 484–485
  secure tenancy status and, 546
Servicemen, Lettings by, 462–463
Sharing of Accommodation,
  landlord, with, 398, 476
  protected tenancies and, 382–386
Shorthold Tenancy, The, 491–495
  formalities, rent and terms of, 493–495
  possession of, recovering, 495
  term, the, 492–493
Spouse,
  family home and, council house as. *See*
      Council Housing, family home, the.
  homelessness and, 619–620
  lease, as joint trustee of, 62–63
  Matrimonial Causes Act 1973 and secure
      tenancy, assignment of, 551–552
  matrimonial home and, transfer of, 332,
      442–445, 551–552
  secure tenancy, court order of transfer to,
      551
Statutory Tenancy, The, 404–411
  agricultural. *See* Agricultural Tenancies.
  assignment of. *See* Transfer, statutory
      tenancy, of.
  commencement, 406–410
    contractual tenancy, determination of,
        407–408
    contractual tenancy, holding over
        from, 406–407
    tenant continuing to occupy, 408–410
  determination, 5, 410–411
  long leaseholder and, 500–502
  nature, 404–406
  occupation, ceasing, 5
  possession of. *See* Security of Tenure,
      possession.

Statutory Tenancy, The—*cont.*
  rent, variation of, 416–417
  sub-tenants and, 463–467
  succession and, 438–442
  terms and conditions of, 410
  termination of, 447–449. *See also* Security
      of Tenure, possession.
  transfer and. *See* Transfer, statutory
      tenancies, of.
  transmission on death, 5
Structures. *See also* Covenants, and
      Building Act 1984,
  dangerous, 272–273
Sub-Letting. *See also* Sub-tenant.
  agricultural tenancy, of, 763–764, 799
  agricultural tied house, of, 491
  assignment, distinguished from, 303–305
  bankruptcy and, 329–331
  business premises, of, 645, 660–662, 711,
      717–718
  consent to, 306–313
    reasonably refused, 308–312
    refusal, 307
    waiver of, 312–313
    without, 453–454
  council housing, of. *See* Council Housing,
      sub-letting.
  death and, 326–329
  divorce and, 332
  effecting, 313–314, 315
  forfeiture, effect of, 354–356
  licensee, by, 10
  long leases and, 499–500
  position after, 315–332
    guarantor's, 315–316
    original landlord and tenant, of,
        315–316
    sub-lessors, sub-lessees and their
        assigns of, 322–324
  secure tenancy and, 551–552
  shorthold tenants and, 494
  statutorily protected, 464–467
  statutory tenant, by, 463–464
  surrender of head lease, effect of,
      336–337
  unlawful, Rent Act 1977 and, 470
Sub-Tenancy. *See* Sub-Letting, Sub-
      Tenant.
Sub-Tenant,
  agricultural, 763–764, 799
  breach of repairing covenant, damages
      and, 289
  business premises, renewal and, 717–718
  capacity to create, 62
  covenants and, burden and benefit of,
      322–324

Sub-Tenant—*cont.*
  creation of,
      common law, at, 303–305, 315
      statutory tenant, by, 463–464
  forfeiture—effect on, 354–356
  long lease, and, 499–500
  rent of superior tenancy and, 164
  shorthold tenancy, under 373
  statutorily protected, 464–467
  surrender—effect on, 336–337
  taxation of premiums, relief from. *See*
      Taxation, premiums of.
  unlawful, Rent Act 1977 and, 470
Succession. *See* Death, succession and;
      Covenant, benefit and burden of.
Supreme Court Act 1981,
  s. 37 (1) receiver, appointment, power of,
      258
Surrender. *See* Termination, surrender.

Taxation,
  leases, of, 90–92, 114–115
  premiums, of, 90–92, 212–216
      assignment at undervalue and,
          215–216
      charge on, the, 214–215
      duration of term and, 213–214
      improvements to business tenancies
          taxed as, 671–672
      nature, 212–213
      sale with right of re-conveyance, on,
          216
      sub-lessor's relief and, 215
  rental income, of, 205–216
      assessment and collection of, 212
      charge to tax, Schedule A, under,
          205–206
      deductions and expenses of, 208–209
      expenses, pooling of, 209–210
      furnished lettings, rent from, 206
      holiday lettings, furnished, 206–208
      management expenses and, 210–211
      premiums as. *See* Taxation, premiums
          of.
      sale and leaseback and, 211
Tenancy,
  agricultural. *See* Agricultural Tenancies.
  assured. *See* Assured Tenant, The.
  attendance with. *See* Restricted
      Contracts, principal types.
  automatic, 43
  business. *See* Business Tenancies.
  common, yearly, agricultural, 760
  compulsory purchase affecting,
      720–730

Tenancy—*cont.*
  continuation, the. *See* Business
      Tenancies, continuation tenancy,
      the.
  contractual. *See* Lease; Contract;
      Termination, contractual tenancy,
      of.
  controlled. *See* Statutory Tenancy,
      controlled, the.
  council. *See* Council Housing; Secure
      Tenancy, The.
  determination of. *See* Termination.
  duration of. *See* Lease, duration of.
  exclusive enjoyment, 17
  estoppel, by. *See* Estoppel, tenancy, by.
  fixed, 107–108
      compulsory purchase and, 724–726
  housing association type. *See* Housing
      Associations.
  illegal premium affecting, 437
  implication, by, 42
  intention of parties,
      evasion, legislation of, 19
      grantor, 17
      licence, and, 16
  Leasehold Reform Act 1967, with the.
      See Leasehold Reform Act 1967,
      tenancies within the Act.
  licensed premises, of, 649–650
  long, 509–511. *See also* Long
      Leaseholder, The.
  low rent, at a, 399–400, 510–511
  part business-part residential, 649
  periodic, 42–43, 281–283, 448
      automatic by statute, 42
      compulsory purchase and, 724–726
  protected. *See* Protected Tenancies.
  public interest, limited in, 650–651
  secure. *See* Secure Tenancy, The.
  service. *See* Service Tenancy.
  short, temporary, business, 652
  shorthold. *See* Shorthold Tenancy, The.
  statutory. *See* Statutory Tenancy, The.
  sufferance, at, 45–46, 281
  unsecure. *See* Council Housing, unsecure
      tenancies.
  will, at, 43–45, 281
Tenant. *See also* Tenancy.
  agricultural. *See* Agricultural Tenancies.
  assured. *See* Assured Tenant, The.
  business. *See* Business Tenancies
  buy as council tenant, right to. *See*
      Council Housing, disposal.
  competent, 71
  controlled. *See* Statutory Tenancy,
      controlled.

Tenant—*cont.*
  council. *See* Council Housing, tenant,
    selection of; Council Housing,
    tenant's obligations; Secure
    Tenancy, The.
  duties of. *See also* Covenants.
    care, 369
    third parties, *re. See* Third Parties,
      tenant's liabilities to.
  employee, as. *See* Service Tenancy.
  former tenant, liability for repair, 294
  landlord and, 1–5
  Leasehold Reform Act 1967, within. *See*
    Leasehold Reform Act 1967,
    tenancies within.
  licensed premises, of, 649–650
  life, for, 63–64
  long leaseholder, qualifying as, 498–500
  part business-part residential, 649
  protected. *See* Protected Tenancies rent
    and. *See* Rent periodic. *See*
    Tenancy, periodic.
  "right," compensation and, 802–804
  rights of. *See also* Covenants.
    assign, to, 301–302
    limited by statute, 650–652
    repairs. *See* Repair and Maintenance,
      landlord's obligations.
    sub-tenancy, to create, 62, 297–300,
      315
    third parties, *re. See* Third Parties,
      tenant's rights against.
  secure. *See* Secure Tenancy, the.
  security of tenure and. *See* Security of
    Tenure.
  service. *See* Service Tenancy.
  shorthold. *See* Shorthold Tenancy, The.
  statutory. *See* Statutory Tenancy.
  sufferance, at, 45, 281
  temporary, business, 652
  unsecure. *See* Council Housing, unsecure
    tenancies.
  will, at, 45, 281
Termination. *See also* Forfeiture; Notice to
    quit, to; Possession.
  agricultural tenancy, of. *See* Agricultural
    Tenancies, security of tenure.
  business tenancy, of. *See* Business
    Tenancies, termination and
    renewals.
  compulsory purchase, on, 719–738
  contractual licences, of, 357–360
  contractual tenancy, of, 447–449
  disclaimer and, 357
  expiration of term, by, 334–335
  forfeiture, by, 351–357

Termination—*cont.*
  forfeiture, by—*cont.*
    clause, need for, 351
    formalities, 351–353
    relief provisions, avoidance of, 357
    s. 146 notice, contents, 352
    service and effect of, 353–354
    sub-tenant, effect on, 354–356
  long-lease, of. *See* Long Leaseholder,
    continuation and termination of the
    tenancy.
  merger, by, 340–341
  notice to quit and, 341–351
    effect of, 350
    formal requirements of, 342–350
    tenancies necessitating, 341–342
  possession and, 360–363
    agricultural tied house, of, 487–491
    County Court proceedings, of, 361–362
    High Court proceedings, of, 362–363
    restricted contract and, 480–482
    self-help, 360–361
    shorthold, of, 495
    sub-tenant, against a, 369, 463–467
  secure tenancy, of. *See* Secure Tenancy,
    The, possession.
  security of tenure and. *See* Security of
    Tenure.
  statutory tenancy, of, 410–411
  surrender, by, 339–340
    capacity *re,* 337–338
    effecting, 338–340
    express, 338
    future, provisions against, 655–656
    nature and effect of, 335–336
    operation of law, by, 338–340
    squatters, effect on, 337
Term of Years, 1–3
  expiration of, 334–335
  fixed, leases for, 38–40
  new business tenancy, of, 708–710
Terms. *See also* Lease, contents; Covenant.
  agricultural tenancy, 769–777
  assured tenancy, of, 495–496
  business tenancy, of, 691–692, 708–717
  council tenancy, of, 527–545
  covenants. *See* Covenant.
  lease, of. *See* Lease, contents.
  option to renew, 54
  statutory tenancy, of, 410
  tenancy, of. *See* Lease, contents;
    Covenant.
Third Parties, 365–372
  distress and, 200
  landlord's liability to, 365–369
    negligence, for, 365–367

Third Parties—*cont.*
  landlord's liability to—*cont.*
    nuisance, for, 367–369
    landlord's rights against, 369–370
    tenant's liability to, 369
    tenant's rights against, 370–372
Tied Houses. *See* Agricultural Tied Houses.
Title,
  compulsory purchase and, 725, 727
  covenants in respect of, 321
  "good root", 78
  landlord's capacity to grant, 78–79
Town and Country Planning Acts, The. *See also* Planning.
  Town and Country Planning Act 1971, s. 52 developer, restrictions on, 74
Trade, 742–747, 757
Transfer, 297–332, 433–445. *See also* Assignment.
  assignment. *See* Assignment.
  bankruptcy, on, 329–331
  compulsory purchase, on, 720–725
  covenants and, 315–331
  death, on, 326, 329, 433
    assignee tenant, of, 328
    estate, devolution of, 326–327
    estate, distribution of, 328–329
    original tenant, of, 327
  disposal,
    attempts to limit, 307–308
    consent to, 306–313
    refusal of consent, 307
      reasonable, 308–312
    restrictions on right of, 302–306
    statutory provisions, avoidance of, 307–308
    waiver of consent to, 312–313
  divorce, following, 332
  effecting, 313–315

Transfer—*cont.*
  effecting—*cont.*
    assignment, the, 314–315
    contract, the, 313–314
    sub-leases, 315
  goodwill, of, 739–752
  inter vivos, 433–434
  matrimonial home and, 442–445
  possession "not to part with," 305–306
  secure tenancy of, 551–552, 578–581
  statutory tenancies and, 433–445
    inter vivos and on death, 433–434
    involuntary, 438–445
    premiums on assignment, 434–438
  sub-lettings. *See* Sub-Letting.
Trespass,
  landlord, by, 10. *See also* Contract, breach of.
  licensee, and, 9
Trust. *See also* Trustee.
  housing, 476, 590. *See also* Housing Associations.
  sale, for, 62–64
Trustee,
  bankruptcy, in, 329–331
  charity, letting by, 66–67
  lease, created by, 62–67
  sale, for, 64

Use,
  business tenancies and, 658–659
  change of, lease and, 73, 74, 480
  council house, restrictions on, 536–537
  covenant in respect of, 122–128
  illegal or immoral, 452
  intermittent, 50–51
  part residential-part business, 649
  unlawful business, 648